15-

BARBARA ASHFIELL
Interior Design & Decoration
980 David Road, Suite C
Burlingame CA 94010

INTERIOR GRAPHIC AND DESIGN STANDARDS

S. C. REZNIKOFF

INTERIOR GRAPHIC AND DESIGN STANDARDS

WHITNEY LIBRARY OF DESIGN
an imprint of Watson-Guptill Publications, New York

DISCLAIMER

The information selected for inclusion in *Interior Graphic and Design Standards* includes product sizes and dimensions recognized by numerous industry standards. The information and data herein are believed to be reliable but are not to be construed as a warranty or representation for which the author or publisher assume legal responsibility. Users should undertake verification and testing to determine suitability for their own particular purpose of any information or product presented herein. No warranty of fitness for a particular purpose is made.

The appearance of an item in *Interior Graphic and Design Standards* is not a representation that owners of patents or copyrights have granted any release to users of this volume.

First published in 1986 in New York by Whitney Library of Design
an imprint of Watson-Guptill Publications
a division of Billboard Publications, Inc.
1515 Broadway, New York, NY 10036

Library of Congress Cataloging-in-Publication Data

Reznikoff, S. C.,
 Interior graphic and design standards.

 Includes index.
 1. Architectural drawing—Standards. 2. Architectural
drawing—Techniques. 3. Interior architecture—Standards.
4. Interior architecture—Designs and plans. 5. Perspective.
6. Visual rendering. 7. Architectural rendering.
I. Title.
NA2708.R49 1986   720′.28′4   86-18965
ISBN 0-8230-7298-3

Published in Great Britain by The Architectural Press Ltd.
9 Queen Anne's Gate, London SW1H 9BY

Manufactured in U.S.A.

First Printing, 1986

13 14 15 16/98 97

Senior Editor: Julia Moore
Editor: Susan Davis
Associate Editor: Victoria Craven-Cohn
Designers: Harry Chester & Associates and Jay Anning
Production Manager: Ellen Greene

For Gulnar K. Bosch
friend, mentor, and teacher par excellence

CONTENTS

Acknowledgments

Interior Graphic and Design Standards could not have been produced without the assistance of outstanding senior interior design students in the Department of Design, College of Architecture and Environmental Design, Arizona State University. For each of the five years of the book's development, the senior drafter carefully selected and trained an outstanding junior to take over after graduation. Large portions of this book were drawn by Vito Dascoli, Chris Connelley, and John McKelvey. Mark Parry worked weekends and evenings while heading up the drafting team during the final two years. Another indispensable member of the development team was Joy Tormey, ASID, who for the first two years performed outstandingly as my research assistant.

Special thanks also to my faculty colleagues in the Department of Design, to Department Chair, Professor Robert Wolf, and to Arizona State University Vice President, Gerald McSheffrey, for moral support and encouragement.

The following designers and design firms contributed important projects and casework details: Eric Bron Associates; Don Henning, IBD; Beams-Boshara Ltd.; Clyde Hueppelsheuser, AIA; Fred Messner, IBD; Phoenix Design One; Colby Construction Company; Arizona Booth and Fixture Manufacturers; Model Display and Fixtures Company; Dr. Robert Hirschberger, AIA; John Peterson, AIA; Dr. Michael Kroelinger, IBD, IDEC; and Professor Hildergarde Streufert, HFL. Many product manufacturers provided examples of recognized industry standards. They are listed in the Data Sources section on pages 603–605.

I am especially indebted to Walter Geisinger, Administrator of Technical and Educational Programs of the Construction Specifications Institute (CSI) for his advice and cooperation in adapting CSI's Masterformat classification system to interior design applications. Dick Parrell, FCSI, also assisted in locating data resources.

In addition, the following associations were especially generous in providing material: American Plywood Association (APA); Architectural Woodwork Institute of California (AWI); Associated Landscape Contractors of America (ALCA); Brick Institute of America (BIA); Ceramic Tile Institute (CTI); Gypsum Association (GA); Illuminating Engineering Society of North America (IESNA); National Fire Protection Association (NFPA); National Terrazzo and Mosaic Association (NTMA); and Woodwork Institute of California (WIC).

Since this book was first begun, two senior editors at the Whitney Library of Design have contributed expertise to the book's development. Former executive editor Steve Kliment, FAIA, provided thoughtful guidance during the first two years of production. The author deeply appreciates senior editor Julia Moore's outstanding editorial abilities during the final year. She meticulously fine-tuned the content and calmly steered the project to completion. Associate editor Victoria Craven-Cohn performed skilled editorial review and patient production coordination. Special accolades go to Harry Chester and his staff for typesetting and pasting up every page and locating each dimension line and to production manager Ellen Greene for exceptionally capable production management.

This book would not have happened without the encouragement and support of Susan Davis. She worked with me on shaping the manuscript from the early layout stage through editing the final, hand-typed tissue overlays. Her tireless drive for consistency and quality has been inspiring.

INTRODUCTION

Originally envisioned as a companion volume to my book *Specifications for Commercial Interiors* (Whitney Library of Design, 1979), *Interior Graphic and Design Standards* has taken on a life of its own. It has become a self-contained, comprehensive data source that both reflects and supports the many complex areas of expertise encompassed, first, by contemporary interior design practice and, second, in a curriculum that supports a fully professional education for interior design. While this book does satisfy my original intention that it complement *Specifications for Commercial Interiors*, it also far exceeds that intention.

Designed to facilitate rapid retrieval of acknowledged industry standards, *Interior Graphic and Design Standards* is divided into three parts. Part One, Standard Dimensions of Manufactured Interior Components, is a compendium of information basic to interiors work. It is based on the Construction Specifications Institute (CSI) Masterformat organization of Broadscope headings and standard referencing system and is used with permission of CSI. In Part One, there is necessarily extensive information on basic construction elements, such as non-load bearing walls, doors, windows, skylights, and ceiling details. Interior finish materials, decorative design elements, and casework detailing are covered. Vertical exits—stairs, ramps, and escalators—as well as lighting design, lighting control, and lighting plan details are included. Manufactured interior equipment and furnishing specialities that serve multi-function occupancies purposely are placed in Part One. For example, such diverse components as window blinds, wall safes, table lamps, mattresses, and reproductions of period-style furnishings, all of which may be used in either residential or commercial installations, are assigned to this part of the book instead of to Part Two or Part Three.

Part Two, Residential Graphic and Design Standards, contains minimum size and space requirements for single-family and multi-family housing. From single-room accommodations for the elderly to a large home with much custom casework, plans and detailing are emphasized in Part Two. Special design criteria for kitchens and bathrooms include accessible barrier-free needs, as well as minimum federal requirements for linear counter frontage and surface dimensions and cabinet storage.

Part Three, Commercial Graphic and Design Standards, places a heavy emphasis on custom casework detailing and carefully cross-references it with floor plans and layouts showing installation locations. Extensive data is presented for public washrooms, commercial offices, banks, retail spaces, beauty salons and health studios, restaurants and bars, commercial kitchens, hotels and motels, medical offices, surgical suites and treatment facilities, libraries, and religious spaces. Products in Part Three that are specifically designed for commercial spaces are grouped by function rather than by material composition. For example, library equipment in Chapter 22 includes not only library furnishings of wood, steel, and plastics, but also dimensioned floor plans, calculations of shelf capacity, and other data useful in preliminary library design.

To promote rapid locating of information and to prevent possible oversights, three areas of concern have been addressed by placing information in sections that treat the appropriate space or design component. These areas of concern are (1) accessible barrier-free requirements; (2) flammability and life safety factors; and (3) historic restoration or rehabilitation needs. For example, accessible barrier-free requirements for drinking fountains are placed on the same page with drinking fountain dimensions.

Other time-saving and easy-access features include the extensive keyword index, which is linked to CSI Masterformat classification numbers; a summary of chapter contents on the opening page of each chapter; and a complete, alphabetical listing of resources, by chapter, in the Data Sources section at the back of the book.

STANDARD DIMENSIONS OF MANUFACTURED INTERIOR COMPONENTS

Chapter 1

BASIC GRAPHIC AND DESIGN ELEMENTS

PROFESSIONAL INSTITUTES & SOCIETIES

AIA   American Institute of Architects
1735 New York Ave. N.W.
Washington, D.C. 20006

ANSI   American National Standards Institute
1430 Broadway
New York, NY 10018

ASHRAE   American Society of Heating, Refrigerating, and Air Conditioning Engineers
United Engineering Center
345 E. 47th St.
New York, NY 10017

ASID   American Society of Interior Designers
1430 Broadway
New York, NY 10018

ASTM   American Society for Testing and Materials
1916 Race St.
Philadelphia, PA 19103

CSI   Construction Specifications Institute
1150 17th St. N.W.
Washington, D.C. 20036

IBD   Institute of Business Designers
1155 Merchandise Mart
Chicago, IL 60654

IESNA   Illuminating Engineering Society of North America
c/o United Engineering Center
345 East 47th St.
New York, NY 10017

NIBS   National Institute of Building Sciences
1015 15th St. N.W.
Suite 700
Washington, D.C. 20005

SPE   Society of Plastics Engineers
Division of Plastics in Building
14 Fairfield Dr.
Brookfield Center, CT 06805

U.S. GOVERNMENT AGENCIES

CPSC   Consumer Product Safety Commission
1111 18th St. N.W.
Washington, D.C. 20207

DOE   U.S. Department of Energy
1000 Independence Ave.
Washington, D.C. 20585

FHA   Federal Housing Administration
Department of Housing and Urban Development
451 7th St. S.W.
Washington, D.C. 20410

GSA   General Services Administration
18th and F Streets N.W.
Washington, D.C. 20405

NBS   National Bureau of Standards
U.S. Department of Commerce
Standards Development Services Section
Washington, D.C. 20234

NTIS   National Technical Information Service
U.S. Department of Commerce
5285 Port Royal Rd.
Springfield, VA 22161

USGPO   U.S. Government Printing Office
Superintendent of Documents
Washington, D.C. 20402

U.S. REGULATORY AGENCIES

BOCA   Building Officials and Code Administrators International, Inc.
17926 S. Halsted St.
Homewood, IL 60430

CPSC   Consumer Product Safety Commission
1111 18th St. N.W.
Washington, D.C. 20207

NBC   National Building Code
c/o American Insurance Association
85 John St.
New York, NY 10038

NFPA   National Fire Protection Association
Batterymarch Park
Quincy, MA 02269

SBCC   Southern Building Code Congress International
900 Monclair Rd.
Birmingham, AL 35213

UBC (ICBO)   Uniform Building Code
c/o International Conference of Building Officials (ICBO)
5360 South Workman Mill Rd.
Whittier, CA 90601

UL   Underwriters Laboratories, Inc.
333 Pfingsten Rd.
Northbrook, IL 60062

CANADIAN GOVERNMENT AGENCIES

CGSB   Canadian Government Specifications Board
Technical Services Branch
Department of Supply and Services
88 Metcalfe St.
Ottawa, Ontario

NRCC   National Research Council of Canada
Division of Building Research
Ottawa, Ontario

cm	in.	cm	in.	cm	in.
1	3/8	61	24	121	47 5/8
2	3/4	62	24 3/8	122	48
3	1 1/8	63	24 3/4	123	48 3/8
4	1 5/8	64	25 1/4	124	48 7/8
5	2	65	25 5/8	125	49 1/4
6	2 3/8	66	26	126	49 5/8
7	2 3/4	67	26 3/8	127	50
8	3 1/8	68	26 3/4	128	50 3/8
9	3 1/2	69	27 1/8	129	50 3/4
10	4	70	27 1/2	130	51 1/8
11	4 3/8	71	28	131	51 5/8
12	4 3/4	72	28 3/8	132	52
13	5 1/8	73	28 3/4	133	52 3/8
14	5 1/2	74	29 1/8	134	52 3/4
15	5 7/8	75	29 1/2	135	53 1/8
16	6 1/4	76	29 7/8	136	53 1/2
17	6 3/4	77	30 1/4	137	53 7/8
18	7 1/8	78	30 3/4	138	54 3/8
19	7 1/2	79	31 1/8	139	54 3/4
20	7 7/8	80	31 1/2	140	55 1/8
21	8 1/8	81	31 7/8	141	55 1/2
22	8 5/8	82	32 1/4	142	55 7/8
23	9	83	32 5/8	143	56 1/2
24	9 1/2	84	33	144	56 3/4
25	9 7/8	85	33 1/2	145	57
26	10 1/4	86	33 7/8	146	57 1/2
27	10 5/8	87	34 1/4	147	57 7/8
28	11	88	34 5/8	148	58 1/4
29	11 3/8	89	35	149	58 5/8
30	11 7/8	90	35 1/2	150	59
31	12 1/4	91	35 7/8	206.5	81 1/4
32	12 5/8	92	36 1/4	207	81 1/2
33	13	93	36 5/8	208.5	82 1/8
34	13 3/8	94	37	229	90 1/8
35	13 3/4	95	37 3/8	231	91
36	14 1/8	96	37 3/4	244	96
37	14 5/8	97	38 1/4	246	96 5/8
38	15	98	38 5/8		
39	15 3/8	99	39		
40	15 3/4	100	39 3/8		
41	16 1/8	101	39 3/4		
42	16 1/2	102	40 1/8		
43	16 7/8	103	40 1/2		
44	17 1/4	104	41		
45	17 3/4	105	41 3/8		
46	18 1/8	106	41 3/4		
47	18 1/2	107	42 1/8		
48	18 7/8	108	42 1/2		
49	19 1/4	109	42 7/8		
50	19 5/8	110	43 1/4		
51	20	111	43 3/4		
52	20 1/2	112	44 1/8		
53	20 7/8	113	44 1/2		
54	21 1/4	114	44 7/8		
55	21 5/8	115	45 1/4		
56	22	116	45 5/8		
57	22 1/2	117	46		
58	22 7/8	118	46 1/2		
59	23 1/4	119	46 7/8		
60	23 5/8	120	47 1/4		

in.	cm	in.	cm	in.	cm
1/16	0.16	41	104.14	91	231.14
1/8	0.32	42	106.68	92	233.68
3/16	0.48	43	109.22	93	236.22
1/4	0.64	44	111.76	94	238.76
5/16	0.79	45	114.30	95	241.30
3/8	0.95	46	116.84	96	243.84
7/16	1.11	47	119.38	97	246.38
1/2	1.27	48	121.92	98	248.92
		49	124.46	99	251.46
9/16	1.43	50	127.00	100	254.00
5/8	1.59				
11/16	1.75	51	129.54	101	256.54
3/4	1.91	52	132.08	102	259.08
13/16	2.06	53	134.62	103	261.62
7/8	2.22	54	137.16	104	264.16
15/16	2.38	55	139.70	105	266.70
		56	142.24	106	269.24
1	2.54	57	144.78	107	271.78
2	5.08	58	147.32	108	274.32
3	7.62	59	149.86	109	276.86
4	10.16	60	152.40	110	279.40
5	12.70				
6	15.24	61	154.94	111	281.94
7	17.78	62	157.48	112	284.48
8	20.32	63	160.02	113	287.02
9	22.86	64	162.56	114	289.56
10	25.40	65	165.10	115	292.10
		66	167.64	116	294.64
11	27.94	67	170.18	117	297.18
12	30.48	68	172.72	118	299.72
13	33.02	69	175.26	119	302.26
14	35.56	70	177.80	120	304.80
15	38.10				
16	40.64	71	180.34		
17	43.18	72	182.88		
18	45.72	73	185.42		
19	48.26	74	187.96		
20	50.80	75	190.50		
		76	193.04		
21	53.34	77	195.58		
22	55.88	78	198.12		
23	58.42	79	200.66		
24	60.96	80	203.20		
25	63.50				
26	66.04	81	205.74		
27	68.58	82	208.28		
28	71.12	83	210.82		
29	73.66	84	213.36		
30	76.20	85	215.90		
		86	218.44		
31	78.74	87	220.98		
32	81.28	88	223.52		
33	83.82	89	226.06		
34	86.36	90	228.60		
35	88.90				
36	91.44				
37	93.98				
38	96.52				
39	99.06				
40	101.60				

METRIC EQUIVALENTS

LINEAR MEASURE

10 millimeters (mm)	= 1 centimeter (cm)
10 centimeters	= 1 decimeter
10 decimeters	= 1 meter (m)
10 meters	= 1 decameter
10 decameters	= 1 hectometer
10 hectometers	= 1 kilometer

1 inch (in.)	=	= 2.54 centimeters
1 foot (ft)	= 12 in.	= 0.3048 meter
1 yard (yd)	= 3 ft	= 0.9144 meter
1 rod	= 5½ yd or 16½ ft	= 5.029 meters
1 furlong	= 40 rods	= 201.17 meters
1 mile (statute)	= 5280 ft or 1760 yd	= 1609.3 meters
1 league (land)	= 3 miles	= 4.83 kilometers

SQUARE MEASURE

100 sq millimeters	= 1 sq centimeter
100 sq centimeters	= 1 sq decimeter
100 sq decimeters	= 1 sq meter
100 sq meters	= 1 sq decameter
100 sq decameters	= 1 sq hectometer
100 sq hectometers	= 1 sq kilometer

1 sq inch	=	= 6.452 sq centimeters
1 sq foot	= 144 sq in.	= 929 sq centimeters
1 sq yard	= 9 sq ft	= 0.8361 sq meter
1 sq rod	= 30¼ sq yd	= 25.29 sq meters
1 acre	= 43,560 sq ft or 160 sq yd	= 0.4047 hectare
1 sq mile	= 640 acres	= 259 hectares or 2.59 sq kilometers

CUBIC MEASURE

1000 cu millimeters	= 1 cu centimeter
1000 cu centimeters	= 1 cu decimeter
1000 cu decimeters	= 1 cu meter

1 cu inch	=	= 16.387 cu centimeters
1 cu foot	= 1728 cu in.	= 0.0283 cu meter
1 cu yard	= 27 cu ft	= 0.7646 cu meter

HOW TO COMPUTE CONVERSIONS*

When you know		You can find	Multiply by
Liquid volume	ounces	milliliters	30
	pints	liters	0.47
	quarts	liters	0.95
	gallons	liters	3.80
	milliliters	ounces	0.034
	liters	pints	2.10
	liters	quarts	1.06
	liters	gallons	0.26
Mass	ounces	grams	28
	pounds	kilograms	0.45
	short tons	megagrams	0.90
	grams	ounces	0.035
	kilograms	pounds	2.20
	megagrams	short tons	1.10

When you know		You can find	Multiply by
Length	inches	millimeters	25.40
	feet	centimeters	30.48
	yards	meters	0.90
	miles	kilometers	1.60
	millimeters	inches	0.04
	centimeters	inches	0.40
	meters	yards	1.10
	kilometers	miles	0.60
Area	square inches	square centimeters	6.50
	square feet	square meters	0.09
	square yards	square meters	0.80
	square miles	square kilometers	2.60
	acres	square hectometers	80.40
	square centimeters	square inches	0.16
	square meters	square yards	1.20
	square kilometers	square miles	0.40
	square hectometers	acres	2.50

*Examples: To convert 615.72 cm to inches, multiply by 0.4 = 246.3″. To convert 151⅜″ (151.375″) to centimeters, multiply by 2.54 = 384.5 cm.

WOOD/LUMBER

Finished

Rough

Interrupted

As noted

PLYWOOD

Large scale

ROCK/STONE

Gravel

Slate, flagging, soapstone

Marble

Rough cut marble

Rubble

Terrazzo

TERRA COTTA

TILE

Structural clay

Ceramic

CONCRETE

Block

Cast stone

Cast in place

Lightweight

PLASTER

Cement, grout, sand, mortar

Gypsum wall-board

BRICK

Common/face

Fire brick

Glazed

EARTH

GLASS

Structural

Block

INSULATION

Batt, loose filled, blanket

Rigid

Sheathing

ACOUSTIC TILE

METAL

Aluminum

Brass, bronze, steel

Large scale

Small scale

Metal lath

PLASTIC

Fiberglass (clear)

Reinforced glass

Laminate

GYPSUM BLOCK

TEMPERED HARDBOARD

RESILIENT FLOOR TILE

RUBBER FLOOR

Pastilles

WOOD FLOOR
(impregnated)

CARPETING

With foam pad

With rippled pad

With hair jute pad

Direct glue

VERTICAL BLINDS

DRAPERY
One way

Two way

TAMBOUR WALL

POLY FOAM

Acoustic	ACST	Marble	MAR
Above finished floor	AFF	Masonry	MAS
Aluminum	AL or ALUM	Masonry opening	MO
Architect, architectural	ARCH	Material	MTL
Average	AVG	Maximum	MAX
Beam	BM	Mechanical	MECH
Board	BD	Meter	M
Brass	BR	Minimum	MIN
Bronze	BRZ	Miscellaneous	MISC
Building	BLDG	Mullion	MULL
Built-in	BLT-IN	Natural	NAT
Cabinet	CAB	Nominal	NOM
Ceiling	CLG	Not in contract	NIC
Center line	CL or ℄	Not to scale	NTS
Centimeter	CM	Number	NO
Ceramic	CER	On center	OC
Clear	CLR	Opening	OPG
Cold water	CW	Opposite	OPP
Column	COL	Partition	PTN
Concrete	CONC	Plaster	PL
Concrete masonry unit	CMU	Plastic laminate	PL LAM
Construction	CONST	Plumbing	PLBG
Continuous	CONT	Plywood	PLY
Contractor	CONTR	Quantity	QTY
Demolition	DEMO	Quarry tile	QT
Detail	DET	Radius	R
Diameter	DIA	Reference	REF
Dimension	DIM	Reinforce	REINF
Door	DR	Remove	RMV
Down	DN	Required	REQD
Drawing	DWG	Revision	REV
Drinking fountain	DF	Riser	R
Each	EA	Room	RM
Electric	ELEC	Rough opening	RGH OPNG
Electric water cooler	EWC	Schedule	SCH
Equal	EQL	Section	SECT
Equipment	EQUIP	Sheet	SH
Estimate	EST	Similar	SIM
Existing	EXIST	Solid core	SC
Exterior	EXT	Specifications	SPECS
Fabricate	FAB	Square feet	SQ FT
Feet	' or FT	Square inches	SQ IN.
Finish	FIN	Stainless steel	S ST
Finished all over	FAO	Standard	STD
Fireproof	FP	Steel	ST
Floor	FL	Structural	STRL
Fluorescent	FLUOR	Suspended	SUSP
Full size	FS	System	SYS
Furnish	FURN	Telephone	TEL
Gauge	GA	Temperature	TEMP
General	GEN'L	Tongue & groove	T&G
Glass	GL	Tread	TR
Gypsum board	GYP BD	Typical	TYP
Hardware	HDW	Unfinished	UNF
Hardwood	HDWD	Urinal	UR
Height	HT or HGT	Vent through roof	VTR
Hollow core	HC	Verify in the field	VIF
Horizontal	HOR or HORIZ	Vertical	VERT
Hot water	HW	Vinyl tile	V TILE
Inch	" or IN.	Wainscot	WCT
Insulation	INSUL	Water closet	WC
Interior	INT	Waterproof	WP or WTRPRF
Junction box	J-BOX or JB	Weight	WT
Lavatory	LAV	Width	W
Light	LT	With	W/
Lighting	LTG	Without	W/O
Linear	LIN	Wood	WD
Linoleum	LINO	Wrought iron	WI
Manufacture	MFR	Yard	YD
Manufactured	MFD		

NETWORK PATTERNS

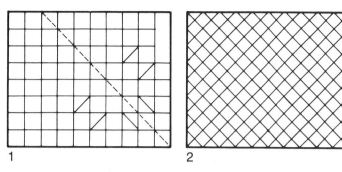

1

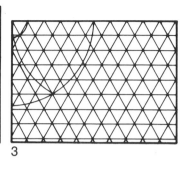

2

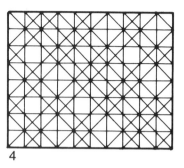

4

Network patterns create the system of subsidiary lines required in geometric design work. (1) The most common network pattern is quadrangular, with equal divisions set off in one direction and parallels drawn through points of division at 45° angles; (2) oblique quadrangle; (3) triangular net; (4) combination network.

Diaper patterns represent repeated ornament, extending on all sides without interruption. They may be either biaxial or polyaxial.

Biaxial diaper patterns expand in an upward direction and move left and right by repetition of the pattern or by turning the pattern over symmetrically. A pattern with a downward or oblique upward direction is an exception to this rule. Biaxial diapers are often used on medallions or large single panels. Polyaxial patterns expand on all sides and are based on circle, square, and triangular networks.

DIAPER PATTERNS

BIAXIAL DIAPERS

POLYAXIAL DIAPERS

Circle diaper

Circle diaper

Square diaper

Square diaper

SQUARE

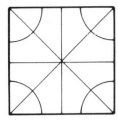 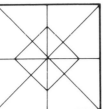 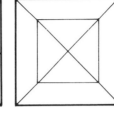 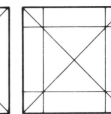 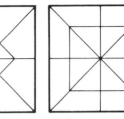 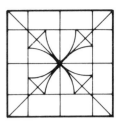

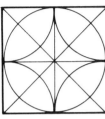 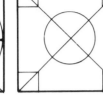 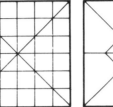 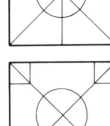 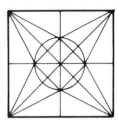

Square is a regular four-sided figure that is frequently divided into compartments by diagonals connecting at angles and by lines connecting the center to each side.

Oblong is a right-angled plane with unequal pairs of sides, which is found in many popular motifs for doors, wainscoting, ceilings, rugs, and panel inserts.

Rhombus (lower right corner) is an equilateral four-sided figure that has pairs of unequal angles. Diagonals used to divide the space create oblong or hexagonal panels in the center (1).

Trapezium (lower right corner) can be either parallel or symmetrical. The parallel trapezium has two parallel sides that are unequal and two equal sides that are not parallel (2-5). The symmetrical trapezium has two pairs of adjacent equal sides (6-7).

OBLONG

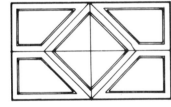 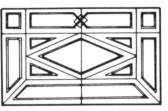 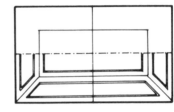 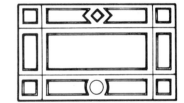

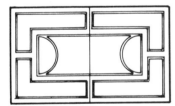 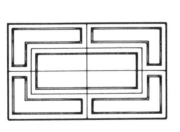 

OCTAGON

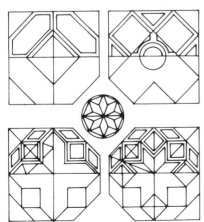

TRIANGLE & HEXAGON

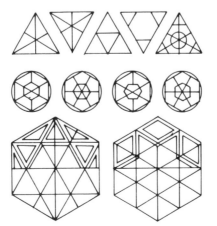

RHOMBUS & TRAPEZIUM

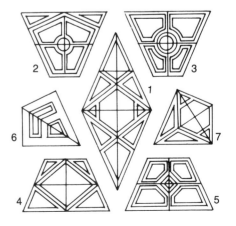

CIRCLES

A common form of ornament created by division of curved lines and arcs. Any ornament in a circular shape that radiates from a center is called a "rosette."

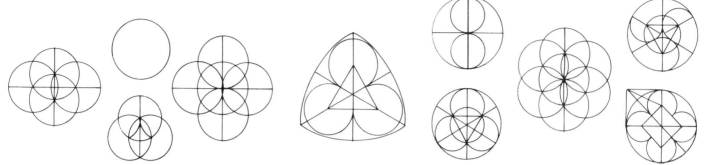

SECTOR, POLYGON, & STAR

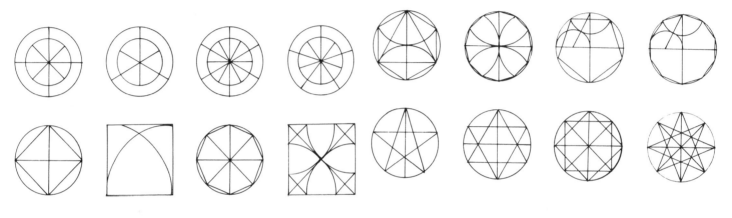

ELLIPSE

An ornament pattern based on continually changing curves.

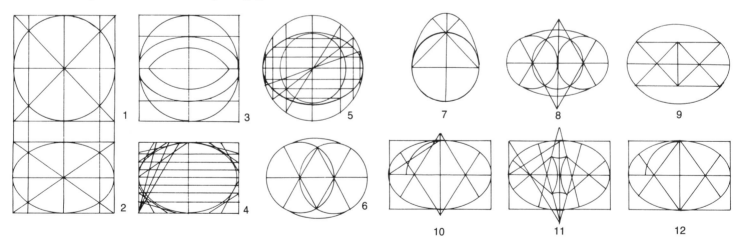

1–2 Constructed by means of eight points. When the square with its diagonals and transversals is projected as an oblong, the circle becomes an ellipse.

3 Constructed by dividing the transverse axis into two unequal parts and using the foci as centers of curves. The points of intersection are four points of the ellipses.

4 Constructed from an oblong that contains an axis.

5 Constructed by means of two circles.

6–9 Examples of ellipsoids, in which every plane surface is an ellipse or a circle.

10–12 Ellipse construction based on rectangles and oblongs.

BANDS & MOLDING

Geometric and stylized plant forms are used to construct bands. This ancient
method of bordering, framing, and connecting constitutes an endless horizontal
design element.

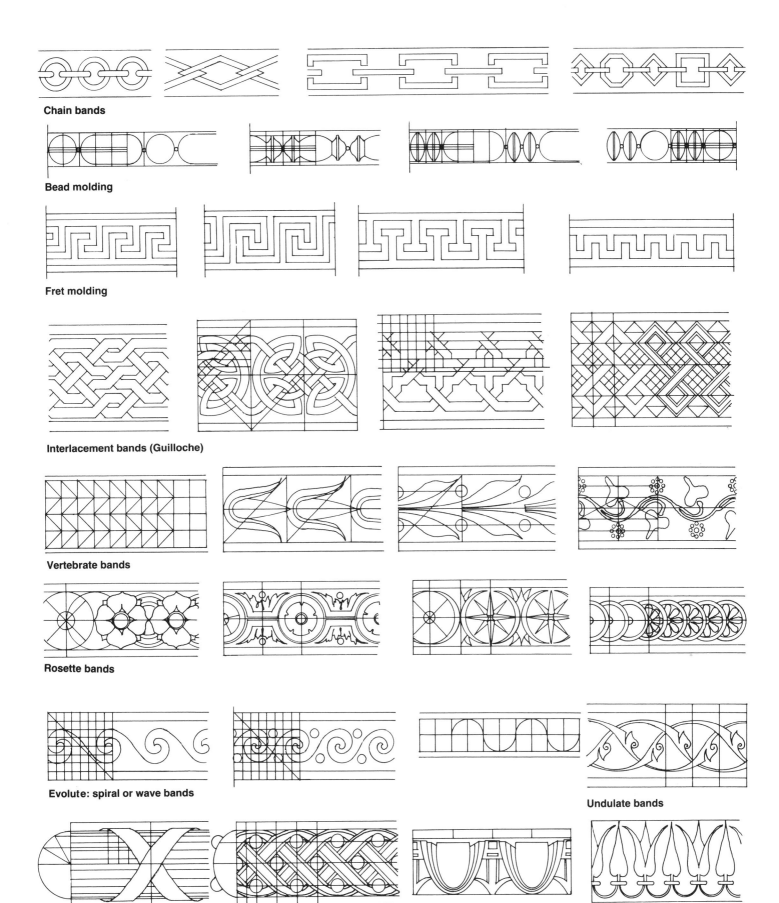

Chain bands

Bead molding

Fret molding

Interlacement bands (Guilloche)

Vertebrate bands

Rosette bands

Evolute: spiral or wave bands

Undulate bands

Torus molding

Cyma & ovolo bands

DORIC STYLE COLUMNS

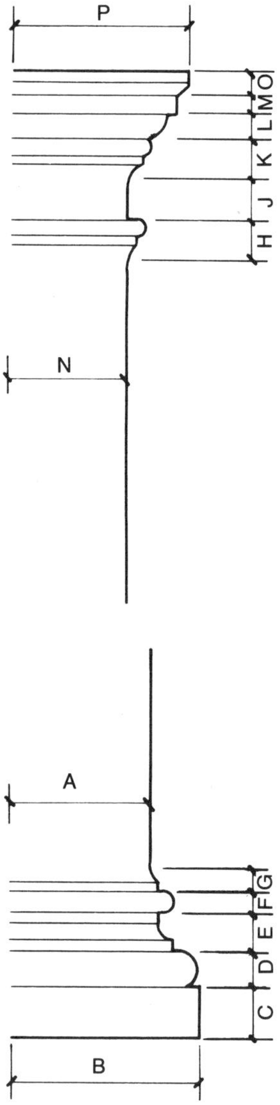

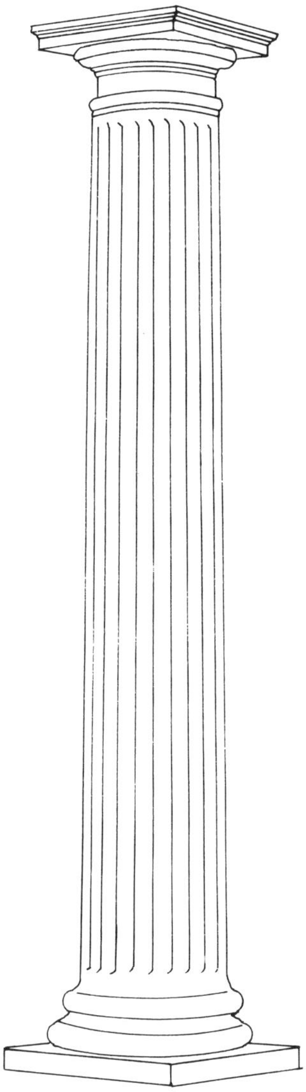

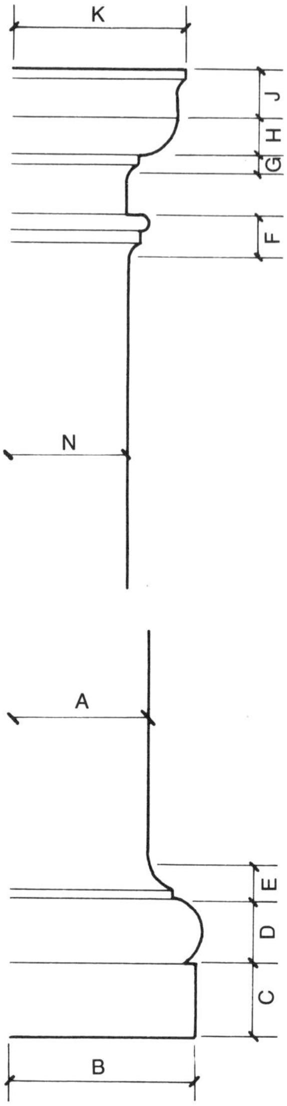

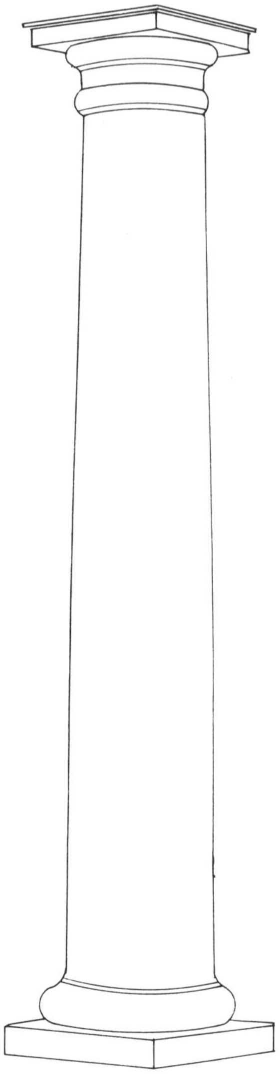

Dia.	Square		Round								Square	Dia.	Square	
A	B	C	D	E	F	G	H	J	K	L	M	N	O	P
6	8	1	¾	¾	½	½	⅞	⅞	¾	⅝	⅜	5	½	7½
8	11	1½	1⅛	1⅛	⅝	½	⅞	1¼	⅞	¾	¾	6	½	9¼
10	13½	1¾	1⅜	1⅜	¾	1	1⅛	1⅝	1⅛	⅞	⅞	8	⅞	12
12	16	2¼	1⅜	1⅜	⅞	⅞	1⅛	2⅛	1⅛	1¼	1	10	¾	15
14	18½	2¼	1¾	1¾	⅞	⅞	1⅛	2¼	1⅛	1⅜	1½	12	¾	17½
16	21	2½	1⅞	1⅞	1¼	1⅛	1¾	2⅝	1¾	1⅝	1¾	13½	1	20
18	24	3	2¼	2¼	1⅜	1¼	1¾	3¼	1¾	1⅞	1⅞	15	1⅛	22½
20	26½	3¼	2⅜	2⅜	1⅜	1½	1¾	3⅜	1¾	1⅞	1⅞	16½	1⅛	23½
22	29	3½	2¾	2¾	1¾	1⅞	2¼	3½	2¼	2¼	2¼	18	1⅜	27
24	32	4½	2¾	2¾	1¾	1¾	2⅜	4⅛	2⅜	2⅜	2⅜	20	1¾	30
26	34½	4¼	3¼	3¼	2⅛	2	2½	4½	2½	2½	2½	21½	1½	32
28	37	4½	3½	3½	2¼	2¼	2¾	4⅝	3	2¾	2¾	23¼	1⅞	34¾
30	40	5	3¾	3¾	2½	2⅜	3¼	4¾	3¼	2⅞	2⅞	25	1⅞	37½

Dia.	Square		Round					Square		Dia.
A	B	C	D	E	F	G	H	J	K	M
6	8	1½	1¼	¾	⅞	½	¾	1	7½	5
8	11	2	1½	¾	⅞	½	1	1⅜	9¼	6
10	13½	2⅜	1⅞	1	1⅛	⅝	1¼	1¾	12	8
12	16	3	2⅜	1⅜	1⅜	⅞	1⅜	1¾	15	10
14	18½	3½	2¾	1⅜	1⅜	⅞	1¾	2¼	17½	12
16	21	4	3¼	1¾	1¾	⅞	1⅞	2¾	20	13½
18	24	4½	3¾	1¾	1¾	1⅜	2¼	2⅞	22½	15
20	26¼	5	3¾	1⅞	1¾	1⅜	2⅜	3¼	24½	16½
22	29	5½	4½	2¼	2¼	1¾	2¾	3¾	25½	18
24	32	6	5	2½	2½	1¾	3	4	30	20
26	34½	6½	5¼	2⅝	2⅝	1¾	3¼	4⅜	32⅛	21⅝
28	37	7	6	2¾	2⅞	1¾	3½	4¾	35	23½
30	40	7½	6¼	2⅞	3⅛	2½	3¾	5	37½	25

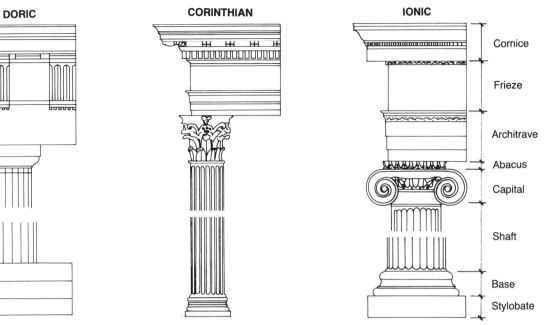

DORIC   **CORINTHIAN**   **IONIC**

Cornice
Frieze
Architrave
Abacus
Capital
Shaft
Base
Stylobate

Note: Columns not to scale.

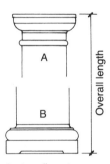

A = top diameter

B = bottom diameter

TYPICAL SIZES

Stock sizes dia. (in.)	Heights* (ft)						Bottom dia. (in.)	Top dia. (in.)
6	8	9					5⅝	4⅝
8	8	9	10	12			7⅝	6¼
10	8	9	10	12	14		9⅝	8¼
12	8	9	10	12	14	16	11⅝	9¾
14	10	12	14	16	18		13⅝	11⅜
16	10	12	14	16	18	20	15⅝	13
18	12	14	16	18	20		17⅝	14⅝
20	14	16	18	20			19⅝	16⅜

*Heights are overall dimensions and include column base, shaft, and capital.

GREEK IONIC COLUMNS

Column dia. (in.)	Capital height (in.)	Abacus* (in.)
5	3⅜	6 x 6
6	3¾	7½ x 7½
8	5⅛	10¹¹⁄₁₆ x 10¹¹⁄₁₆
8½	5⅝	11 x 11
9	6	12½ x 12½
10	6½	14½ x 14½
11	6¾	15 x 15
12	6⅞	15¼ x 15¼
14	9	17½ x 17½
15	10¼	21½ x 21½
16	10¼	22 x 22
18	11	26 x 26
20	13	30¾ x 30¾
22	13	32 x 32
24	14¾	33 x 33

*Square block that supports entablature.

ROMAN CORINTHIAN COLUMNS

Column dia. (in.)	Capital height (in.)	Abacus* (in.)
4	5¾	9½ x 9½
4½	7	9½ x 9½
5	7	9½ x 9½
6	8½	11½ x 11½
6	12	11½ x 11½
7	10	14 x 14
7½	10¾	14½ x 14½
8	11½	15 x 15
8½	12½	15½ x 15½
9½	13¾	18 x 18
10	14½	19 x 19
11	15½	19½ x 19½
12	17	22½ x 22½
14	19¾	28 x 28
16	22½	31 x 31
18	25¼	37½ x 37½
20	28	40 x 40

Chapter 2

ARCHITECTURAL MILLWORK, INTERIOR TRIM, HARDWARE, AND LAMINATES

24

FASTENERS — INTERIOR USE

INTERIOR USE	Lightweight						Medium- to heavyweight									Notes
	Finishing nails	Casing nails	Common nails	Brads	Wood screws	Sheet metal screws	Wood screws	Sheet metal screws	Molly bolts	Expansion shield ¼″ (0.64 cm) bolt	Lag anchor	Lead anchor with wood screw	Toggle bolt ½″ (1.27 cm) dia.	Plastic anchor	Wooden dowels	
Hanging furnishings on																Weights: light = 0-5 lb, medium = 10-50 lb, heavy = 50+ lb. X = fastener type recommended.
Brick walls						X				X		X		X		Nails: Use nail 3 times longer than material thickness. Thin nails should be used with hardwoods.
Concrete block (hollow)			4d							X		X	X			
Gypsum wallboard		8d							X				X	X		
Stone wall										X		X		X		
Wood stud/wallboard	4d		6d		X		X				X					
Metal stud/wallboard						X		X								Wood screws: Select size so that half of length will enter material. Fine threads should be used on hard woods.
Thick plaster [2″ (5.08 cm)]	4d							X		X		X		X		
Mortar joints*	4d					X		X			X			X		
Interior construction																
Paneling	X				X											
Doors	X				X										X	Molly bolts must equal wall thickness.
Molding	X			X												
Casework																
Bookcases	X		X	X	X										X	
Cabinets	X	X	X		X										X	
Drawers	X			X	X										X	
Plywood construction (thickness)																
¾″ (1.90 cm)	6d				8											
⅝″ (1.59 cm)	6d				8											
½″ (1.27 cm)	4d				6											
⅜″ (0.95 cm)	3d				6											
¼″ (0.64 cm)				X	4											

*Joints crumble; not recommended for hanging furnishings.

HOLLOW WALL FASTENERS

When objects are attached to a hollow wall there can be several types of loading conditions:
1. Static or dead loads.
2. Tensile load/direct axial or ceiling load.
3. Shear load: pulls at right angle against installed anchor.

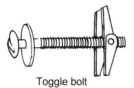

Toggle bolt

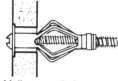

Toggle bolt closed before installation

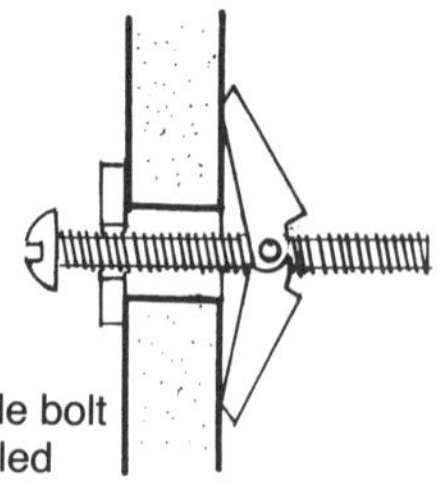

Toggle bolt installed

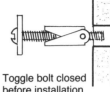

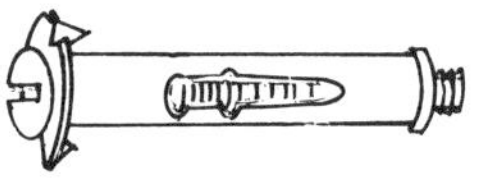

Expansion bolt (Molly)

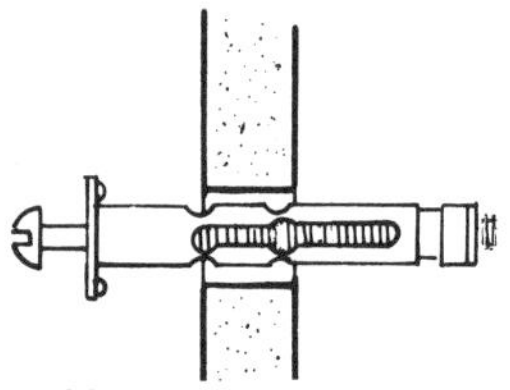

Molly inserted into hollow wall

Molly expanded

Molly reinserted through object to be supported

Lag screw shield closed and expanded

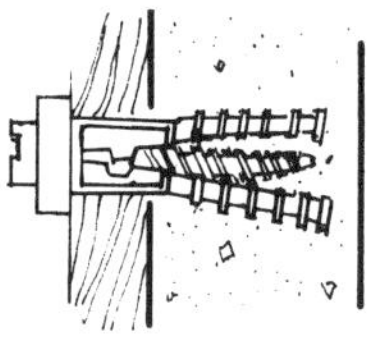

Lag screw

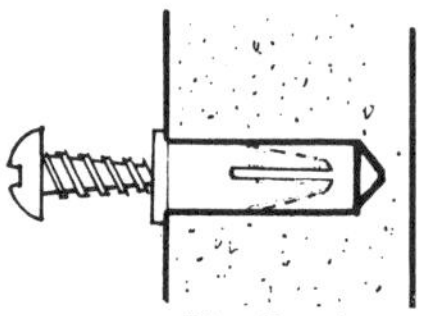

Plastic plug

Tee nut

Tee nut with grip prongs

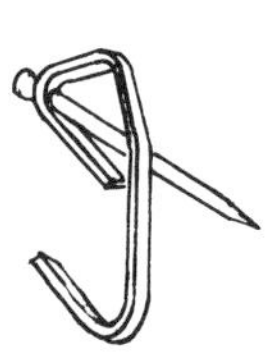

Picture-hanging hook (Consult manufacturer for weight requirements)

Note: Lag anchors (not shown) are excellent for use in hollow wall construction. Brick walls: combine with 2″ or 3″ (5.08 or 7.62 cm) screws. Concrete block: combine with 6″ (15.24 cm) screw for hanging extra heavy items (over 50 lb).

WOOD SCREWS

Not to scale

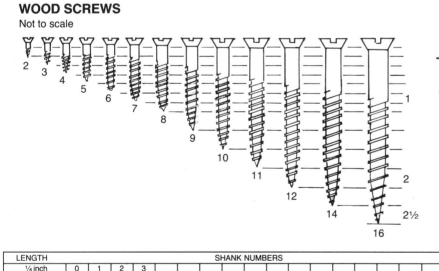

SCREW HEADS

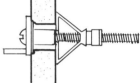
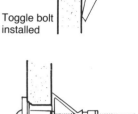

Flat   Round   Oval   Phillips   Flat countersunk

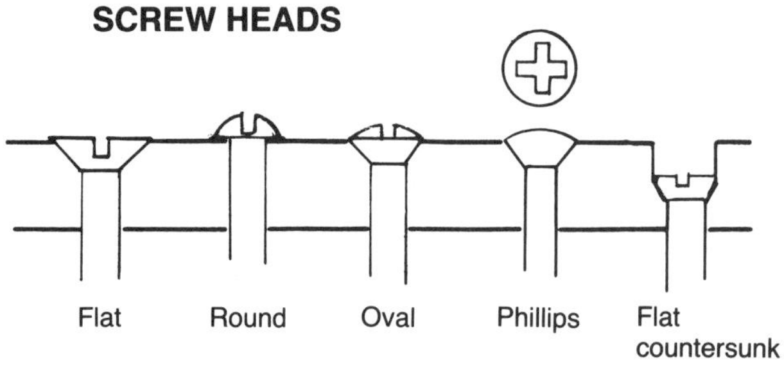

BOLTS & OTHER ATTACHMENT HARDWARE

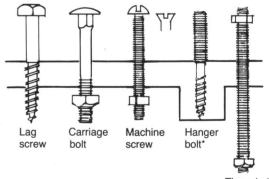

Lag screw   Carriage bolt   Machine screw   Hanger bolt*   Threaded rod

*Hanger bolt has wood threads at the bottom and metal threads at the top. It is used to attach parts of furniture, for example, a leg to a chair base. The top is fitted into a tee nut.

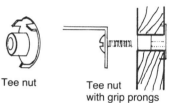

LENGTH	SHANK NUMBERS																
	0	1	2	3	4	5	6	7	8	9	10	11	12	14	16	18	20
¼ inch	0	1	2	3													
⅜ inch			2	3	4	5	6	7									
½ inch			2	3	4	5	6	7	8								
⅝ inch				3	4	5	6	7	8	9	10						
¾ inch					4	5	6	7	8	9	10	11					
⅞ inch							6	7	8	9	10	11	12				
1 inch							6	7	8	9	10	11	12	14			
1¼ inch								7	8	9	10	11	12	14	16		
1½ inch							6	7	8	9	10	11	12	14	16	18	20
1¾ inch									8	9	10	11	12	14	16	18	20
2 inch									8	9	10	11	12	14	16	18	20
2¼ inch										9	10	11	12	14	16	18	20
2½ inch										9	10	11	12	14	16	18	20
2¾ inch														14	16	18	20
3 inch															16	18	20
3½ inch																18	20
4 inch																18	20
0 to 24 DIAMETER DIMENSIONS IN INCHES AT BODY	.060	.073	.088	.099	.112	.125	.138	.151	.164	.177	.190	.203	.216	.242	.268	.294	.320

PENNY SIZES OF NAILS* (d = penny)
Not to scale

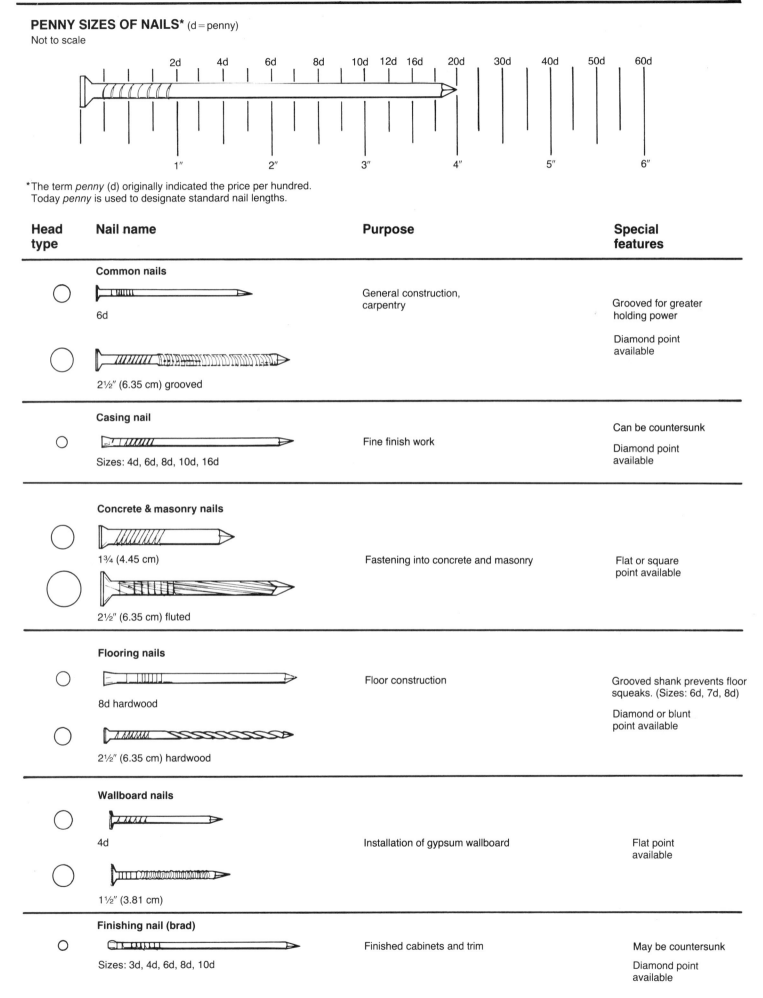

*The term *penny* (d) originally indicated the price per hundred.
Today *penny* is used to designate standard nail lengths.

Head type	Nail name	Purpose	Special features
◯	**Common nails** 6d	General construction, carpentry	Grooved for greater holding power
◯	2½″ (6.35 cm) grooved		Diamond point available
◯	**Casing nail** Sizes: 4d, 6d, 8d, 10d, 16d	Fine finish work	Can be countersunk Diamond point available
◯	**Concrete & masonry nails** 1¾ (4.45 cm)	Fastening into concrete and masonry	Flat or square point available
◯	2½″ (6.35 cm) fluted		
◯	**Flooring nails** 8d hardwood	Floor construction	Grooved shank prevents floor squeaks. (Sizes: 6d, 7d, 8d) Diamond or blunt point available
◯	2½″ (6.35 cm) hardwood		
◯	**Wallboard nails** 4d	Installation of gypsum wallboard	Flat point available
◯	1½″ (3.81 cm)		
◯	**Finishing nail (brad)** Sizes: 3d, 4d, 6d, 8d, 10d	Finished cabinets and trim	May be countersunk Diamond point available

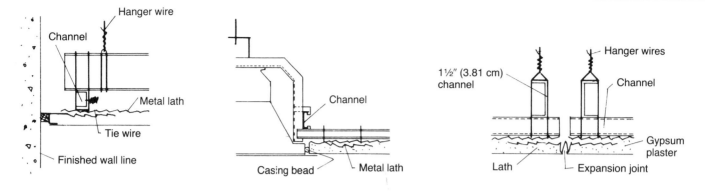

LIGHTING TROFFERS

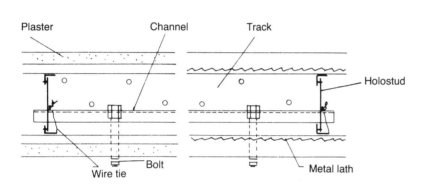

HEAVY FIXTURE FASTENING

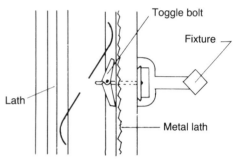

LIGHTWEIGHT FIXTURE ATTACHMENT

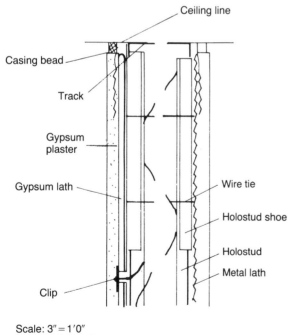

Scale: 3″ = 1′0″
(7.62 = 30.48 cm)

PARTITION SECTION

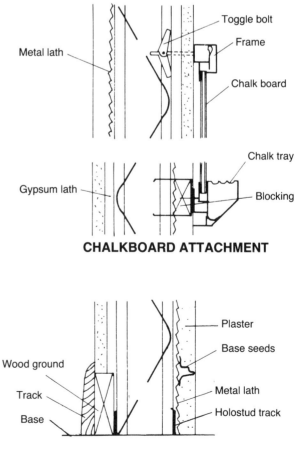

CHALKBOARD ATTACHMENT

FLOOR ATTACHMENT

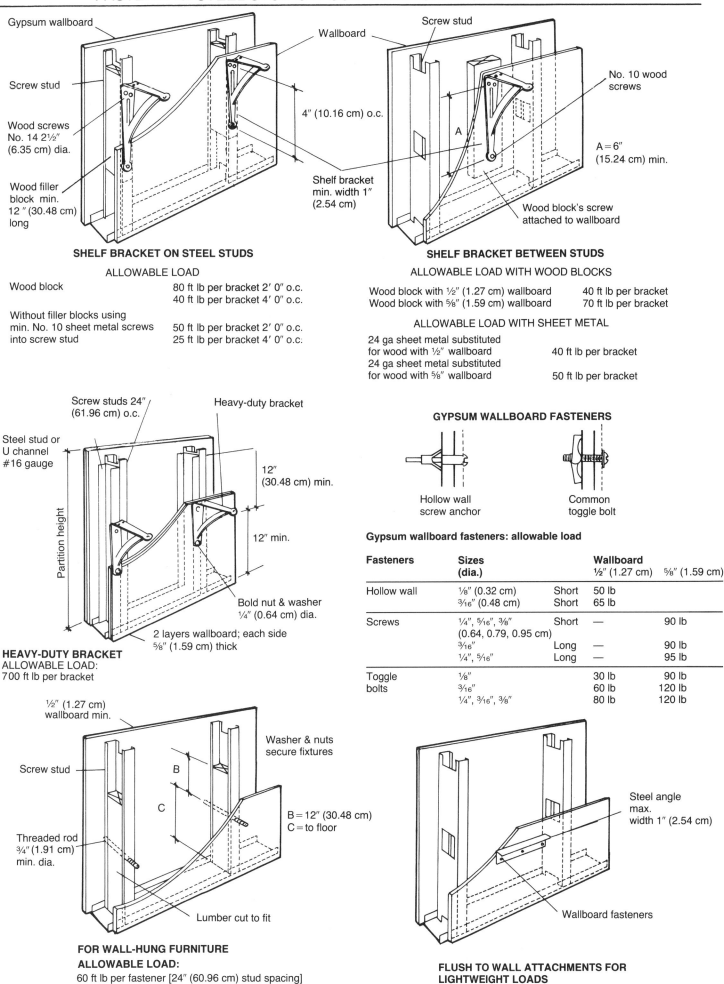

Gypsum wallboard

Screw stud

Wood screws
No. 14 2½″
(6.35 cm) dia.

Wood filler
block min.
12 ″ (30.48 cm)
long

Wallboard

4″ (10.16 cm) o.c.

Shelf bracket
min. width 1″
(2.54 cm)

SHELF BRACKET ON STEEL STUDS

ALLOWABLE LOAD

Wood block   80 ft lb per bracket 2′ 0″ o.c.
                                    40 ft lb per bracket 4′ 0″ o.c.

Without filler blocks using
min. No. 10 sheet metal screws   50 ft lb per bracket 2′ 0″ o.c.
into screw stud   25 ft lb per bracket 4′ 0″ o.c.

Screw studs 24″
(61.96 cm) o.c.

Heavy-duty bracket

Steel stud or
U channel
#16 gauge

Partition height

12″
(30.48 cm) min.

12″ min.

Bold nut & washer
¼″ (0.64 cm) dia.

2 layers wallboard; each side
⅝″ (1.59 cm) thick

HEAVY-DUTY BRACKET
ALLOWABLE LOAD:
700 ft lb per bracket

½″ (1.27 cm)
wallboard min.

Screw stud

Threaded rod
¾″ (1.91 cm)
min. dia.

Washer & nuts
secure fixtures

B

C

B = 12″ (30.48 cm)
C = to floor

Lumber cut to fit

FOR WALL-HUNG FURNITURE
ALLOWABLE LOAD:
60 ft lb per fastener [24″ (60.96 cm) stud spacing]

Screw stud

No. 10 wood
screws

A

A = 6″
(15.24 cm) min.

Wood block's screw
attached to wallboard

SHELF BRACKET BETWEEN STUDS

ALLOWABLE LOAD WITH WOOD BLOCKS

Wood block with ½″ (1.27 cm) wallboard   40 ft lb per bracket
Wood block with ⅝″ (1.59 cm) wallboard   70 ft lb per bracket

ALLOWABLE LOAD WITH SHEET METAL

24 ga sheet metal substituted
for wood with ½″ wallboard   40 ft lb per bracket
24 ga sheet metal substituted
for wood with ⅝″ wallboard   50 ft lb per bracket

GYPSUM WALLBOARD FASTENERS

Hollow wall
screw anchor

Common
toggle bolt

Gypsum wallboard fasteners: allowable load

Fasteners	Sizes (dia.)		Wallboard ½″ (1.27 cm)	⅝″ (1.59 cm)
Hollow wall	⅛″ (0.32 cm)	Short	50 lb	
	³⁄₁₆″ (0.48 cm)	Short	65 lb	
Screws	¼″, ⁵⁄₁₆″, ⅜″ (0.64, 0.79, 0.95 cm)	Short	—	90 lb
	³⁄₁₆″	Long	—	90 lb
	¼″, ⁵⁄₁₆″	Long	—	95 lb
Toggle bolts	⅛″		30 lb	90 lb
	³⁄₁₆″		60 lb	120 lb
	¼″, ³⁄₁₆″, ⅜″		80 lb	120 lb

Steel angle
max.
width 1″ (2.54 cm)

Wallboard fasteners

FLUSH TO WALL ATTACHMENTS FOR
LIGHTWEIGHT LOADS

COMPARATIVE TABLE OF WOOD SPECIES

Species	Botanical Name	Principal Uses	Appearance: Color	Appearance: Figure	Grain	Relative Costs A.: Lumber	Relative Costs A.: Plywood	Practical size limitations: Max. Prac. Tickness Without Lam.	Practical size limitations: Max. Prac. Width	Practical size limitations: Max. Prac. Length	Availability of matching plywood B.	Hardness	Dimensional Stability C.	Finishing: Paint	Finishing: Transparent	Remarks
ASH, White	Fraxinus americana	Trim & cabinetry	Creamy white to light brown	High	Open	100	175	1½"	7½"	12'	3	Hard	10/64"	Not normally used	Excellent	Excellent strength; bold grain
BASSWOOD	Tilia. americana	Decorative moldings & carvings	Creamy white	No figure	Closed	85		1½"	7½"	10'	4	Soft	10/64"	Excellent	Excellent	Good for moldings; uniform grain
BEECH	Fagus grandifolia	Semi-exposed cabinet parts	White to reddish brown	Medium	Closed	80		1½"	7½"	12'	4	Hard	14/64"	Excellent	Good	Good utility hardwood
BIRCH, Yellow—"Natural"	Betula alleghaniensis	Trim, paneling & cabinetry	White to dark red	Medium	Closed	100	100	1½"	7½"	12'	1	Hard	12/64"	Excellent	Good	Excellent architectural wood—plentiful supply
BIRCH, Yellow—"select red" (heartwood)	Betula alleghaniensis	Trim, paneling & cabinetry	Dark red	Medium	Closed	150	150	1½"	5½"	11'	2	Hard	12/64"	Not normally used	Excellent	Rich color
BIRCH, Yellow—"select white" (sapwood)	Betula alleghaniensis	Trim, paneling & cabinetry	Creamy white	Medium	Closed	130	120	1½"	5"	11'	2	Hard	12/64"	Not normally used	Excellent	Uniform appearance
BUTTERNUT	Juglans cinerea	Trim, paneling & cabinetry	Pale brown	High	Open	300	500	1½"	5½"	8'	3	Medium	8/64"	Not normally used	Excellent	Beautiful wood
CEDAR, Western Red	Thuja plicata	Trim, paneling exterior & interior	Reddish brown nearly wt sapwd.	Medium	Closed	100	100	3¼"	11"	16'	1&3	Soft	10/64"	Not normally used	Good	Decay resistant; rough texture
CHERRY, American Black	Prunus serotina	Trim, paneling & cabinetry	Reddish brown	High	Closed	160	200	1½"	5½"	7'	2	Hard	9/64"	Not normally used	Excellent	Beautiful wood
CHESTNUT—Wormy	Castanea dentata	Paneling & trim	Grayish brown	High	Open with worm holes	150		¾"	7½"	10'	4	Medium	9/64"	Not normally used	Excellent	Very limited supply
CYPRESS, Yellow	Taxodium distichum	Trim, frames & special siding	Yellowish brown	High	Closed	75		2½"	9½"	16'	4	Medium	8/64"	Good	Good	Subject to regional availability
FIR, Douglas—flat grain	Pseudotsuga taxifolia	Trim, frames & paneling	Reddish tan	High	Closed	100	80	3¼"	11"	16'	1	Medium	10/64"	Fair	Fair	Good supply
FIR, Douglas—vertical grain	Pseudotsuga taxifolia	Trim, frames & paneling	Reddish tan	Low	Closed	100		1½"	11"	16'	4	Medium	6/64"	Good	Good	Very limited supply
MAHOGANY, African—plain sawn	Khaya ivorensis	Trim, frames, paneling & cabinetry	Reddish brown	Medium	Open	250	250	2½"	11"	15'	3	Medium	7/64"	Good	Excellent	Fine hardwood
MAHOGANY, African—quarter sawn	Khaya ivorensis	Trim, frames, paneling & cabinetry	Reddish brown	Low	Open	350	350	2½"	7½"	15'	3	Medium	5/64"	Not normally used	Excellent	Limited supply
MAHOGANY, Tropical American—"Honduras"	Sweitenia macrophylia	Trim, frames, paneling & cabinetry	Rich golden brown	Medium	Open	200	300	2½"	11"	15'	3	Medium	6/64"	Not normally used	Excellent	One of the world's finest cabinet woods
MAPLE, Hard—natural	Acer saccharum	Trim, paneling & cabinetry	White to reddish brown	Medium	Closed	75	150	3½"	9½"	12'	3	Very hard	12/64"	Excellent	Good	Plentiful supply; excellent properties
MAPLE, Hard—select white (sapwood)	Acer saccharum	Trim, paneling & cabinetry	White	Medium	Closed	90	150	2½"	9½"	12'	3	Very hard	12/64"	Not normally used	Excellent	Uniform appearance
MAPLE, Soft—natural	Acer saccharum	Trim, semi exposed cabinet parts	White to reddish brown	Low	Closed	75		3¼"	9½"	12'	4	Medium	9/64"	Excellent	Not normally used	Good utility hardwood
OAK, English brown	Quercus robur	Veneered paneling & cabinetry	Leathery brown	High	Open	500	780	1½"	5½"	8'	3	Hard		Not normally used	Excellent	Distinctive appearance; high cost
OAK, Red—plain sawn	Quercus rubra	Trim, paneling & cabinetry	Reddish tan to brown	High	Open	90	130	1½"	7¼"	12'	1	Hard	11/64"	Not normally used	Excellent	Excellent architectural wood; plentiful supply
OAK, Red—rift sawn	Quercus rubra	Trim, paneling & cabinetry	Reddish tan to brown	Low	Open	200	250	1⅛"	5½"	10'	3	Hard	7/64"	Not normally used	Excellent	Closer grain pattern; limited supply
OAK, Red—Quarter sawn	Quercus rubra	Trim, paneling & cabinetry	Reddish tan to brown	Low	Open	200	250	1 1/16"	5½"	8'	3	Hard	7/64"	Not normally used	Excellent	Shows flakes; limited supply
OAK, White—plain sawn	Quercus alba	Trim, paneling & cabinetry	Grayish tan	High	Open	100	165	1 1/16"	5½"	10'	2	Hard	11/64"	Not normally used	Excellent	Excellent architectural wood; moderate supply
OAK, White—rift sawn	Quercus alba	Trim, paneling & cabinetry	Grayish tan	Low	Open	200	250	¾"	4½"	10'	3	Hard	7/64"	Not normally used	Excellent	Closer grain pattern; limited supply
OAK, White—quarter sawn	Quercus alba	Trim, paneling & cabinetry	Grayish tan	Low figure accented w/flakes	Open	200	250	¾"	4½"	10'	3	Hard	7/64"	Not normally used	Excellent	Shows flakes; limited supply
PECAN	Carya species	Trim, paneling & cabinetry	Reddish brown w/ dk brown stripes	Medium	Open	100	200	1½"	5½"	12'	3	Hard	11/64"	Not normally used	Good	Subject to regional availability; attractive
PINE, Eastern or Northern White	Pinus strobus	Trim, frames, paneling & cabinetry	Creamy white to pink	Medium	Closed	100		1½"	9½"	14'	3	Soft	8/64"	Good	Good	True white pine, wide range of applications for general usage
PINE, Idaho	Pinus monticola	Trim, frames, paneling & cabinetry	Creamy white	Low	Closed	100		1½"	9½"	14'	4	Soft	8/64"	Good	Good	True white pine, wide range of applications for general usage
PINE, Ponderosa	Pinus ponderosa	Trim, frames, paneling & cabinetry	White to pale yellow	Medium	Closed	100	125	1½"	9½"	16'	3	Soft	8/64"	Good	Good	Most widely used pine, wide range of aplications for general usage
PINE, Sugar	Pinus lambertiana	Trim, frames, paneling & cabinetry	Creamy white	Low	Closed	110		3¼"	11"	16'	4	Soft	7/64"	Good	Good	True white pine, wide range of applications for general usage
PINE, Southern Yellow—shortleaf	Pinus echinata	Trim, frames, paneling & cabinetry	White to pale yellow	High	Closed	65		1½"	7½"	16'	3	Medium	10/64"	Fair	Good	Wide range of application for general usage
POPLAR, Yellow	Liriodendron tulipfera	Trim, paneling & cabinetry	White to brown with green cast	Medium	Closed	85		2½"	7½"	12'	3	Medium	9/64"	Excellent	Good	Good utility hardwood; excellent paintability
REDWOOD—flat grain (heartwood)	Sequoia sempervirens	Trim, frames & paneling	Deep red	High	Closed	110		2½"	11"	16'	1 & 3	Soft	6/64"	Good	Good	Superior exterior wood; high natural decay resistance
REDWOOD—vertical grain (heartwood)	Sequoia sempervirens	Trim, frames & paneling	Deep red	Low	Closed	120		2½"	11"	16'	3	Soft	3/64"	Excellent	Excellent	Superior exterior wood; high natural decay resistance
ROSEWOOD, Brazilian	Dalbergia nigra	Veneered paneling & cabinetry	Mixed reds, brns, and bks	High	Open	Not gen. avail.	780				3	Very hard		Not normally used	Excellent	Exotic figure; high cost
ROSEWOOD, Honduras	Dalbergia stevensonii	Solid trim incidental to Brazilian rosewood	Lighter in color than Brazilian	High	Open	1000		1½"	5"	8'	4	Very hard	7/64"	Not normally used	Excellent	Limited availability
SPRUCE, Sitka	Picea sitchensis	Trim, frames	Light yellowish tan	High	Closed	100		3¼"	9½"	16'	4	Soft	10/64"	Fair	Fair	Limited general availability
TEAK	Tectona grandis	Trim, paneling & cabinetry	Tawny yellow to dark brown	High	Open	400	400	1½"	7½"	10'	2	Hard	6/64"	Not normally used	Excellent	Outstanding wood for decorative applications; high cost
WALNUT, American black	Juglans	Trim, paneling & cabinetry	Chocolate brown	High	Open	300	300	1½"	4½"	6'	1	Hard	10/64"	Not normally used	Excellent	Fine domestic hardwood, extremely limited width and lengths; more readily available in veneer; high cost
WALNUT, Nogal	Juglans nigra neotropica	Trim, paneling & cabinetry	Chocolate brown	High	Open	200		¾"	9½"	9'	4	Medium	12/64"	Not normally used	Good	Substitute for juglans nigra where better widths and lengths required
ZEBRAWOOD, African—quarter sawn	Brachystegea fleuryana	Trim, paneling & cabinetry	Lt gold clr/strks & dk brn to blk	High	Closed	400	450	1½"	9"	16'	3	Hard	7/64"	Not normally used	Excellent	Highly decorative

Note: Regional distribution may affect availability and cost.

A. Relative cost with Natural Birch as 100.

B. Rated from 1 to 4 as follows:
1. In warehouse stock in good quantities and fair assortment of thicknesses and lengths.
2. In warehouse stock in fair quantity but not in thicknesses other than ¼" and ¾", or sizes other than 4'0" × 8'0".
3. Produced on a special order only.
4. Not generally available.

C. These figures represent possible width change in a 12' (30.48 cm) board when moisture content is reduced from 10% to 5%. Figures are for plain sawn unless indicated otherwise in species column.

Used with permission of the Architectural Woodwork Institute.

LUMBER SIZING CHART

Lumber is sold by the "nominal" size, which is not the actual size of individual boards. Example: A 2" X 4" (5.08 X 10.16 cm) is actually 1½" X 3½"(3.81 X 8.89 cm) when fully seasoned and dry.

Dry lumber is defined as having 19 percent or less moisture content. Lumber containing more than 19 percent moisture is said to be "unseasoned."

Nominal size (in.)	Actual size (in.)	Board feet per foot of length	Linear feet per 1,000 board feet
1 X 2	¾ X 1½	⅙	6,000
1 X 3	¾ X 2½	¼	4,000
1 X 4	¾ X 3½	⅓	3,000
1 X 6	¾ X 5½	½	2,000
1 X 8	¾ X 7¼	⅔	1,500
1 X 10	¾ X 9¼	⅚	1,200
1 X 12	¾ X 11¼	1	1,000
2 X 2	1½ X 1½	⅓	3,000
2 X 3	1½ X 2½	½	2,000
2 X 4	1½ X 3½	⅔	1,500
2 X 6	1½ X 5½	1	1,000
2 X 8	1½ X 7¼	1⅓	750
2 X 10	1½ X 9¼	1⅔	600
2 X 12	1½ X 11¼	2	500

Note: This table applies to softwood and ordinary framing lumber. Special lumber for decking or hardwood for furni- ture may be available in actual or nominal sizes. Particle board and plywood are listed by the actual size.

BOARD FEET MEASUREMENTS (BFM)

"Lumber" is the general term given to wood used for carpentry work. Boards are pieces of lumber 1" (2.54 cm) thick and 2" to 12" (5.08 to 30.48 cm) wide. Lumber is sold by the board foot, which is the equivalent of a piece of lumber 1" thick, 12" wide, and 12" long. Example: To calculate the board feet for one book shelf 1" thick X 10" wide X 10' long: $\frac{1 \times 10 \times 10}{12} = 8⅓$ or 9 BFM

LUMBER GRADES

Yard lumber is classified according to the number and type of knots:

1. Select grade
   A. Excellent; almost totally free from defects.
   B. Devoid of all but minute blemishes.
   C. Small, tight knots. Suitable for paint finish.
   D. Slight imperfections. Use for surfaces that will be painted.

2. Common grade lumber
   No. 1 Tight knots, little waste.
   No. 2 Larger knots, but tight grain (paneling, flooring).
   No. 3 Loose knots. Can use for painted shelving.
   No. 4 Crating.
   No. 5 Lowest grade. Not suitable for interior use.

LUMBER SPECIFICATION CHECKLIST
(For more terms, see Glossary on page 60)

1. Use standard lumber terms.
2. Make specifications as complete as possible:
   a. Grade*.
   b. Species: such as red oak, white pine.
   c. Quantity: board feet.
   d. Thickness: List nominal size such as 2" or 1" (5.08 or 2.54 cm).
   e. Width and length: nominal width and actual length, such as 8" (2.44 m) long.
   f. Surface: "dressed" lumber refers to lumber surfaces that have been planed smooth and brought to uniform size. Options:
      S1S = dressed one side
      S2S = dressed two sides
      S1E = dressed one edge
      S4S = dressed four sides
   g. Condition of seasoning: AD = air dried; KD = kiln dried.

*Hardwood grades: FAS = best grades; RW & L = random widths and lengths.

TYPES OF VENEER CUTS

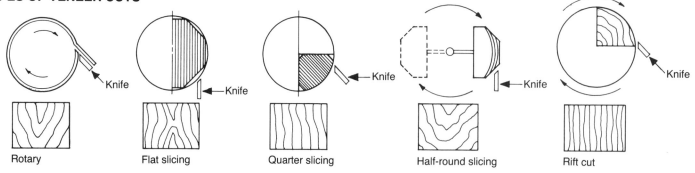

Rotary   Flat slicing   Quarter slicing   Half-round slicing   Rift cut

VENEER MATCHES & PATTERNS

Book match for color
and grain at joints

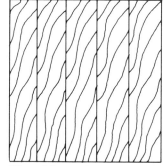

Slip match repeats
flitch marks from piece
to piece; no joint match

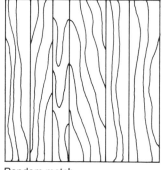

Random match

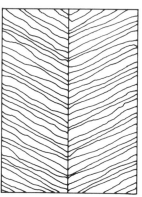

Chevron match

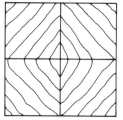

Diamond pattern

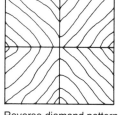

Reverse diamond pattern

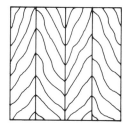

Herringbone pattern

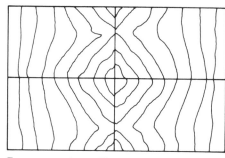

Four-way center and butt pattern

MATCHING FACES WITHIN A PANEL

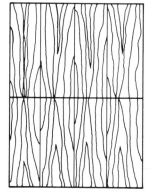

Vertical butt and
horizontal book match

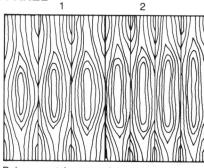

Balance match means that each individual
panel (1 and 2) is made of an odd or even
number of veneer pieces that are needed
to balance the grain in each panel.

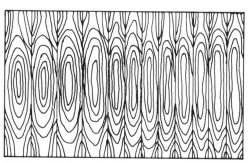

Center match is made with an even number of
equal width veneer sheets to produce symmetrical
panel matches. Grain continuity may change as
shown from left to right.

METHODS OF MATCHING VENEER WALL PANELS

Sequence-matched panel sets: These are usually man-ufactured for a specific installation with uniform panel width and height. If more than one flitch or set is needed to produce the required match, similar flitches may be used. This type of match works best where there are walls with-out doors or windows and where the majority of panels are nearly equal in width. Doors are not matched and corners may or may not match.

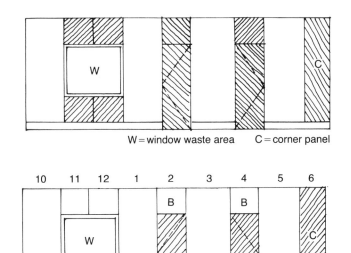

W = window waste area   C = corner panel

Warehouse matched sets: These are premanufactured and numbered sequence sets usually 48″ (121.92 cm) wide x 96″ or 120″ (243.84 or 304.80 cm) high. They may be part of one flitch or part of several flitches. The panel set may vary from 6 to 12 panels. If more than one set is required, no matching can be expected. Doors cannot be matched. These panels are best used in full widths with necessary adjustments made at the corner panel.

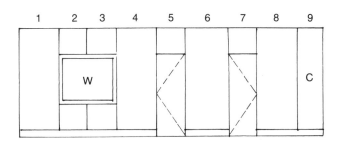

B = balance of panel is waste

Blueprint matching: These panels are custom matched from flitches that provide perfect match of both grain and color for various size-panels. Doors match everything in the room. The designer submits scaled drawings of the room so the mill can match all areas.

VENEER WALL PANEL DETAILS

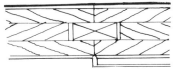

Flush joint

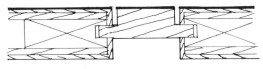

Typical reveal joint that allows slight panel movement

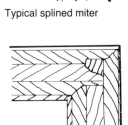

Typical splined miter

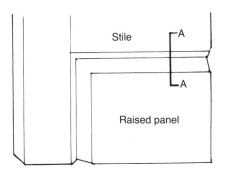

Stile

A

A

Raised panel

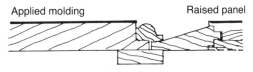

Applied molding   Raised panel

A = typical panel-stile details

Stile or rail mold

Flat panel

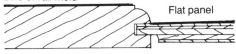

Information the mill needs from the designer:

1. Scale elevations of walls showing panel layout.
2. Are panels to be raised or flat?

3. Instructions about whether the panel mold is to be applied or constructed as a profiled portion of the stile and rail.

Typical lock miter

Exterior corners: Should be mitered as shown above and glued and braced. In custom grade, this is done on site.

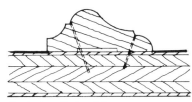

Typical applied molding

Fastening of exposed members to panels is accomplished by spot gluing and finish nailing. Nails must be spaced as required by the molding and counter sunk for filling. Custom grade does not require spot gluing.

PANEL PLACEMENT & INSTALLATION FOR ACOUSTIC CONTROL

Floating panels

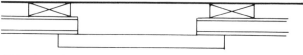

Raised panels

BATTEN MOLDINGS

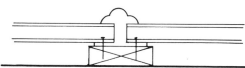

Metal moldings available in many shapes

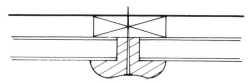

Wood moldings attached with nails or screws

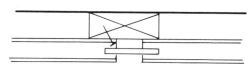

Spline application

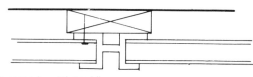

Recessed metal moulding

MECHANICAL FASTENERS

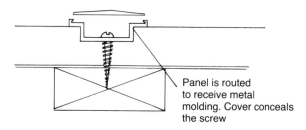

Panel is routed to receive metal molding. Cover conceals the screw

NAILED OR MECHANICAL APPLICATIONS

Z metal clips stabilize center of panel

Slip panel in place   Corner panel nailed

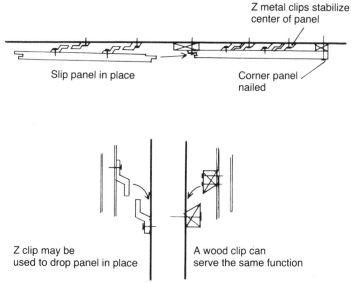

Z clip may be used to drop panel in place

A wood clip can serve the same function

ACOUSTICAL TREATMENT

The acoustic quality of hardwood plywood paneling can be increased by (1) modifying the panel construction or (2) selecting an appropriate method of installation.

Designers may specify panel modification in the following manner:

1. Require that face veneers be laid up in random 4″ (10.16 cm) wide strips with a ⅛″ x ⅛″ (3.17 x 3.17 mm) routed grove 4″ o.c. Edges should be shiplapped and groves either accented or colored to blend with the face veneer.

2. Require that panels be perforated with holes of varying dimensions, spaced as specified [³⁄₁₆″ (4.76 mm) holes spaced ½″ (12.70 mm) o.c.]. These perforations, if kept to a minimum size, will absorb high-frequency sound and not disturb the overall grain or surface effect.

3. Placement of recessed or protruding battens between panels provides good sound diffusers.

4. Alternation of floating panels is also very effective. Panel cores can be altered to meet special project requirements. There are core materials or combination of materials that can be used to achieve special properties. For example:

Treatment desired	Material
Acoustics	Lead sheet
	Asbestos sheet
	Manufacturer's standard
	Acoustical panel
	Particle board panel
Fire resistance	Chemically impregnated core
	Mineral core
	Asbestos sheet
Light weight	Aluminum honeycomb
	Kraft paper honeycomb
	Wood coils and grids

UNSANDED GRADE MARKING

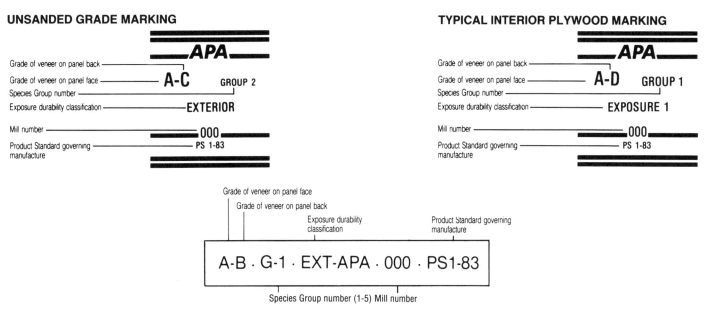

Grade of veneer on panel back
Grade of veneer on panel face — **A-C** GROUP 2
Species Group number
Exposure durability classification — **EXTERIOR**
Mill number — **000**
Product Standard governing manufacture — **PS 1-83**

TYPICAL INTERIOR PLYWOOD MARKING

Grade of veneer on panel back
Grade of veneer on panel face — **A-D** GROUP 1
Species Group number
Exposure durability classification — **EXPOSURE 1**
Mill number — **000**
Product Standard governing manufacture — **PS 1-83**

Grade of veneer on panel face
Grade of veneer on panel back
Exposure durability classification
Product Standard governing manufacture

A-B · G-1 · EXT-APA · 000 · PS1-83

Species Group number (1-5) Mill number

CLASSIFICATION OF SOFTWOOD SPECIES

Group 1	Group 2		Group 3	Group 4	Group 5
Apitong[a][b] Beech, American Birch 　Sweet 　Yellow Douglas Fir 1[c] Kapur[a] Keruing[a][b] Larch, Western Maple, Sugar Pine 　Caribbean 　Ocote Pine, Southern 　Loblolly 　Longleaf 　Shortleaf 　Slash Tan oak	Cedar, Port Orford Cypress Douglas Fir 2[c] Fir 　Balsam 　California Red 　Grand 　Noble 　Pacific Silver 　White Hemlock, Western Lauan 　Almon 　Bagtikan 　Mayapis 　Red Lauan 　Tangile 　White Lauan	Maple, Black Mengkulang[a] Meranti, Red[a][d] Mersawa[a] Pine 　Pond 　Red 　Virginia 　Western White Spruce 　Black 　Red 　Sitka Sweetgum Tamarack Yellow Poplar	Alder, Red Birch, Paper Cedar, Alaska Fir, Subalpine Hemlock, Eastern Maple, Bigleaf Pine 　Jack 　Lodgepole 　Ponderosa 　Spruce Redwood Spruce 　Engelmann 　White	Aspen 　Bigtooth 　Quaking Cativo Cedar 　Incense 　Western Red Cottonwood 　Eastern 　Black (Western Poplar) Pine 　Eastern White 　Sugar	Basswood Poplar, Balsam

(a) Each of these names represents a trade group of woods consisting of a number of closely related species.

(b) Species from the genus Dipterocarpus are marketed collectively: Apitong if originating in the Philippines; Keruing if originating in Malaysia or Indonesia.

(c) Douglas fir from trees grown in the states of Washington, Oregon, California, Idaho, Montana, Wyoming, and the Canadian Provinces of Alberta and British Columbia shall be classed as Douglas fir No. 1. Douglas fir from trees grown in the states of Nevada, Utah, Colorado, Arizona and New Mexico shall be classed as Douglas fir No. 2.

(d) Red Meranti shall be limited to species having a specific gravity of 0.41 or more based on green volume and oven dry weight.

APPPEARANCE GRADES OF SOFTWOOD PLYWOOD

N Special order "natural finish" veneer. Select all heartwood or all sapwood. Free of open defects. Allows some repairs.

A Smooth and paintable. Neatly made repairs permissible. Also used for natural finish in less demanding applications.

B Solid surface veneer. Circular repair plugs and tight knots permitted.

C Knotholes to 1″ (2.54 cm). Occasional knotholes ½″ (1.27 cm) larger permitted providing total width of all knots and knotholes within a specified section does not exceed certain limits. Limited splits permitted. Minimum veneer permitted in exterior-type plywood.

C Improved C veneer with splits limited to ⅛″ (0.32 cm) in width and knotholes
Plgd and borer holes limited to ¼″ x ½″ (0.64 x 1.27 cm).

D Permits knots and knotholes to 2½″ (6.35 cm) in width and ½″ larger under certain specified limits. Limited splits permitted.

PLYWOOD FABRICATION

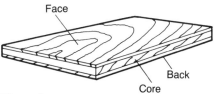

Face
Back
Core

Three-ply veneer core

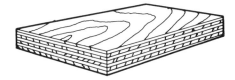

Multiple veneer core

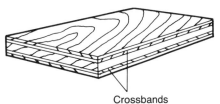

Crossbands

Five-ply veneer core

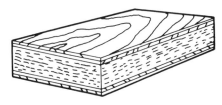

Five-ply particle board core

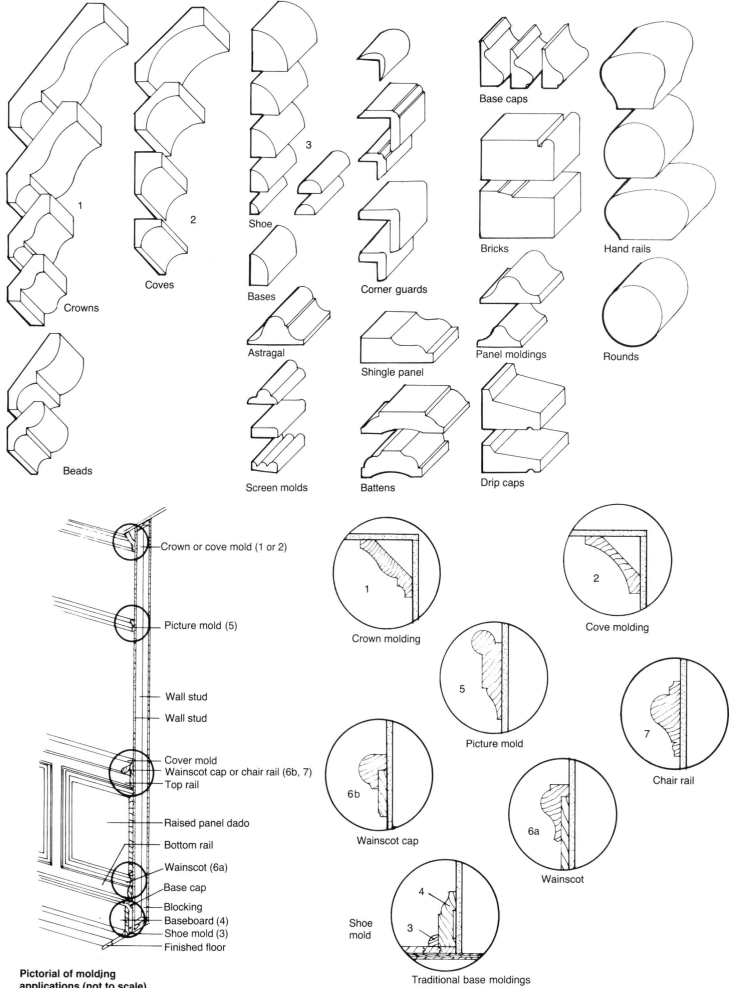

Crowns

1

2

Coves

Beads

Shoe

3

Bases

Astragal

Screen molds

Corner guards

Shingle panel

Battens

Base caps

Bricks

Panel moldings

Drip caps

Hand rails

Rounds

Crown or cove mold (1 or 2)

Picture mold (5)

Wall stud

Wall stud

Cover mold
Wainscot cap or chair rail (6b, 7)
Top rail

Raised panel dado

Bottom rail

Wainscot (6a)

Base cap

Blocking
Baseboard (4)
Shoe mold (3)
Finished floor

**Pictorial of molding
applications (not to scale)**

1

Crown molding

2

Cove molding

5

Picture mold

6b

Wainscot cap

7

Chair rail

6a

Wainscot

Shoe
mold

4

3

Traditional base moldings

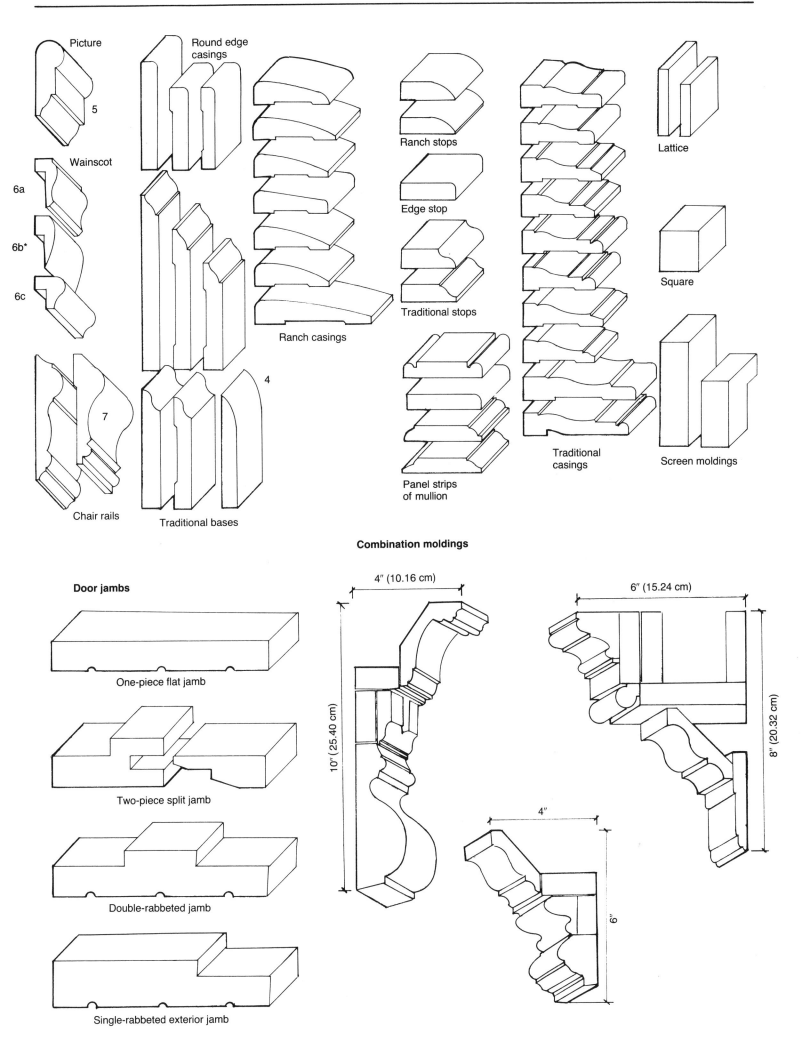

Picture

5

Wainscot

6a

6b*

6c

7

Chair rails

Round edge casings

Traditional bases

4

Ranch casings

Ranch stops

Edge stop

Traditional stops

Panel strips of mullion

Combination moldings

Traditional casings

Lattice

Square

Screen moldings

Door jambs

One-piece flat jamb

Two-piece split jamb

Double-rabbeted jamb

Single-rabbeted exterior jamb

4″ (10.16 cm)

10″ (25.40 cm)

6″ (15.24 cm)

8″ (20.32 cm)

4″

6″

TYPES OF MILLWORK/CASEWORK

Millwork is defined as ready-made products that are manufactured at a wood mill or woodworking plant.

Interior trim refers to wood used for baseboards, railings, chair rails, picture and corner molding, and door and window trim.

Architectural millwork or **custom millwork** is ready-made millwork that has been produced to meet custom specifications for a particular job. It is not produced from standard items.

Casework or **cabinet work** makes use of joinery of fine quality. It is used in the construction of built-in cabinets and shelves.

Modular casework includes laminated plastic-covered wood modular casework that is factory finished. Examples: sink cabinets, wall cabinets, boots, built-up shelving, shelves installed on adjustable wall-mounted standards, chalkboards or tackboards that are a part of the cabinet.

Conventional casework is all-wood casework and cabinets, which includes or excludes the following:
Typical inclusions: Altars, assembled railings, bars and back bars, bookcases, built-up wood bulletin boards, counters, display cases, lecterns, pews, pullman cases, pulpits, sink cases, storage cabinets, shelving built up or machined and knocked down, wall cabinets, wardrobes. Cabinet doors and cabinet sash.
Tops of hardboard, particle board, plywood, or wood, which are to be covered by other trades with cork, linoleum, metal, vinyl, or resilient coverings. Cutting of holes for sinks and other appliances is included.
Plastic laminate tops, facings, and covering; hardboard tops, facings, and coverings; special purpose tops, such as cement asbestos board, chemical-resistant plastic, stone, or composition stone, and polyester fiberglass.
Furnishing and installing hardware that is necessary to the fabrication of the case. Unless otherwise specified, the following items will be included: metal shelf standards and rests for adjustable wood or glass shelves in cabinets; track with corresponding sheaves, slides, or hangers for mill-made sliding doors; top fasteners; casters; metal grilles; metal drawer slides; file drawer rods and followers; metal poles and hangers; nonremovable coat hangers; extension garment carriers.
Prefinishing and/or job-site installation may be included by specification or agreement. The furnishing and/or installation of cabinet hardware may be included by specification or agreement.
Excluded: Any cutting of holes for job-applied vents, weeps, or grilles; any cutting for job-applied hardware.
Any linoleum, cork, leather, vinyl, metal, or resilient covering or lining.
Any hinges, pulls, catches, locks, coat and hat hooks, and track assemblies for frameless glass doors.
Any metal angles or brackets for attaching cabinets to the walls or floor.
Any glass or glazing, unless specified to be furnished by the mill.

SPECIFICATION INFORMATION REQUIRED FOR CASEWORK

1. Grade of construction: Architectural Woodwork Institute (AWI) or Woodwork Institute of California (WIC).
2. Grade of materials to be used on exposed, semi-exposed, and concealed portions.
3. Species of materials.
4. Whether intended for opaque or transparent finish.
5. Face-frame construction or flush overlay type of construction. Recommended that flush type of construction have door hinges installed by manufacturer and be specified with wood grain run and matched vertically.
6. Whether lipped or flush drawers and doors are to be used and thickness of doors.
7. Species and grade of wood for doors if they are to be installed at the site.
8. Type of plastic laminate desired for counter tops or other areas.
9. Required joinery tolerances and allowable warp and clearance for casework doors.
10. Method of casework joinery on body, doors, and drawers.
11. Type of glue.

INFORMATION NEEDED FOR FLOOR PLANS & ELEVATIONS

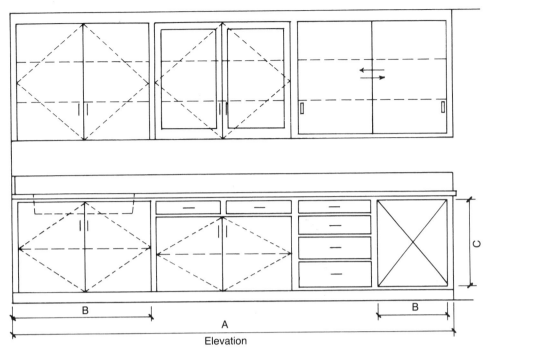

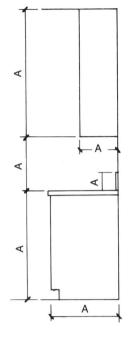

Elevation

The following information should be included on floor plans or elevations for casework:

1. A = indicates basic overall dimensions.
2. B = indicates dimensions of those portions that are required to conform to a set size.
3. C = indicates dimensions required for installation of items of equipment.
4. Indicate whether face frame construction or flush overlay type construction.
5. Indicate either lipped or flush installation of doors and drawers if face frame construction.
6. Indicate either sliding or hinged doors, including swing if hinged.
7. Indicate thickness of cabinet doors if other than ¾″ (1.91 cm) is required.
8. Show details that involve installation of unusual equipment in the casework.
9. Note if and where locks are required.
10. Indicate shelves, either fixed or adjustable. Indicate shelf thickness.
11. Indicate top surfacing.

DEFINITIONS

1. **Exposed portions:** This includes all surfaces visible when doors and drawers are closed. The underside of cabinets over 48″ (121.92 cm) above the floor is considered exposed. Visible edges only of shelves and divisions in open cabinets or behind glass are considered exposed. In flush overlay construction the visible front edges of web framing, bottoms, ends, divisions, tops, and hanging stiles are considered exposed. Sloping tops of cabinets are considered exposed.

2. **Semi-exposed portions:** This includes shelves; divisions; drawer sides, backs, and bottoms; interior faces of doors, ends, backs, and other similar members. Flat tops of cabinets 69″ (175.26 cm) or more above the floor are considered semi-exposed. The underside of bottoms of cabinets between 24″ and 48″ (60.96 and 121.92 cm) from the floor are considered semi-exposed.

3. **Concealed portions:** This includes sleepers, web frames, security panels, and other surfaces not normally visible. The underside of bottoms of cabinets less than 24″ (60.96 cm) from the floor is considered concealed.

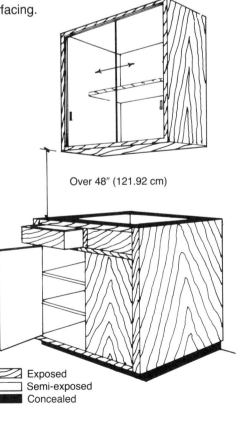

Over 48″ (121.92 cm)

Exposed
Semi-exposed
Concealed

CLAD REVEAL OVERLAY CABINETS

DOORS

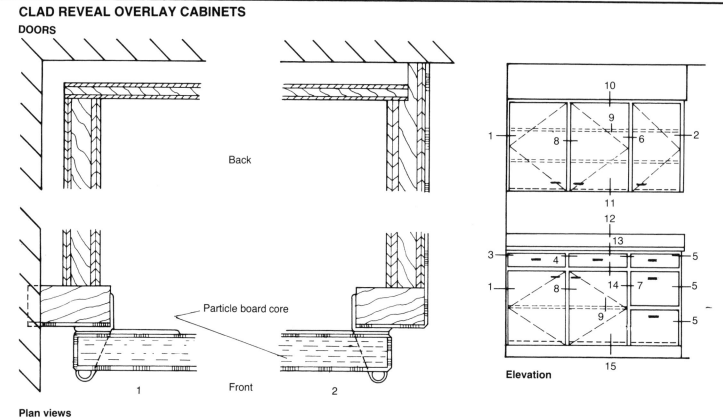

Back

Particle board core

Front

1

2

10

9

1   8   6   2

11

12

13

3   4   5

1   8   14   7   5

9

5

15

Elevation

Plan views

DRAWERS

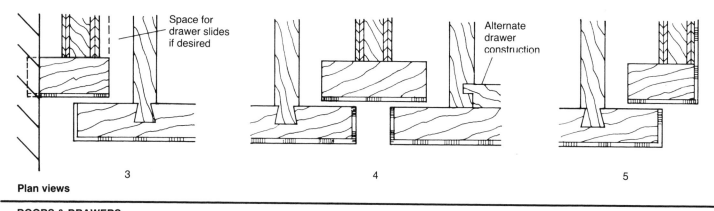

Space for drawer slides if desired

Alternate drawer construction

3

4

5

Plan views

DOORS & DRAWERS

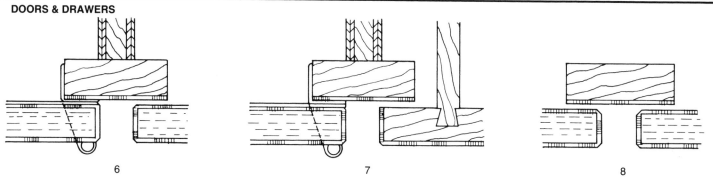

6

7

8

Plan views

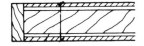

9   **Shelf section**

Note: If projecting or unsupported areas of laminate-faced cabinet body components exceed AWI minimum requirements, backing sheets must be provided.

Example: 1″ (2.54 cm) if adjustable and length exceeds 36″ (91.44 cm)

Note: The use of laminate or cabinet liner and/or drawer interiors is optional and if required must be specified or indicated on drawing details.

These drawings are based on Architectural Woodworking Institute (AWI) Standards.

CLAD REVEAL OVERLAY CABINETS

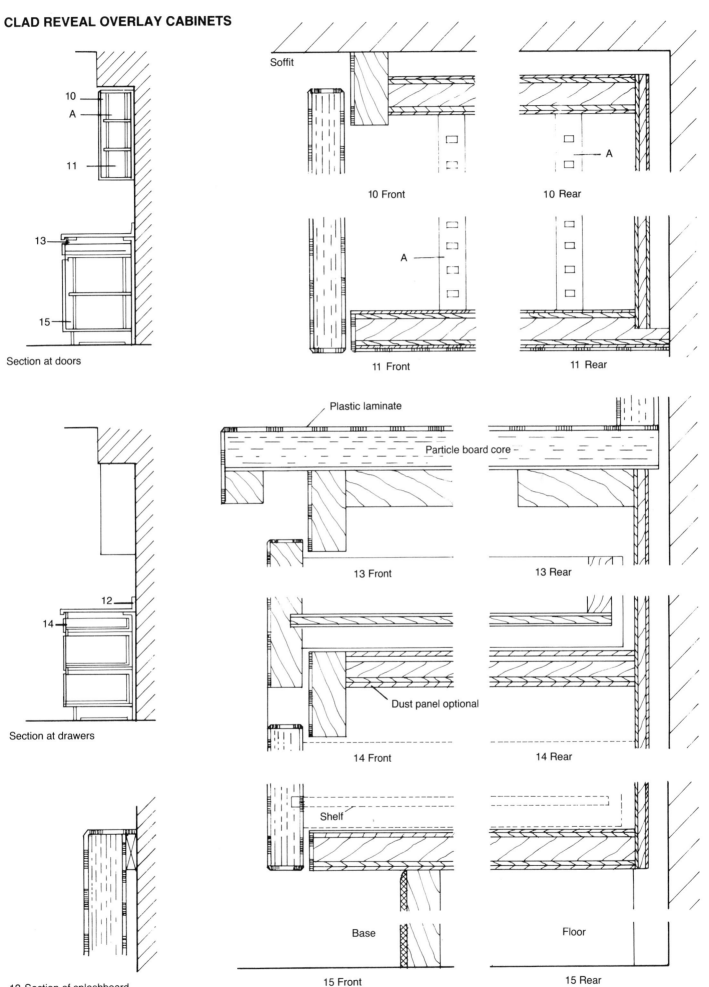

Section at doors

Section at drawers

12 Section of splashboard

Scale: ⅜″ = 1′0″

Soffit

10 Front

10 Rear

11 Front

11 Rear

Plastic laminate

Particle board core

13 Front

13 Rear

Dust panel optional

14 Front

14 Rear

Shelf

Base

Floor

15 Front

15 Rear

Sections

CORE CONSTRUCTION & EDGE FINISH OF PREMIUM GRADE CABINET DOORS

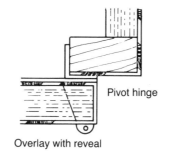

Pivot hinge

Overlay with reveal

Overlay

½" (1.27 cm) wood edge

Flush front frame

Legend to types of cores

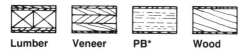

Lumber   Veneer   PB*   Wood

Dimensions:
A = 1" to 1½" (2.54 to 3.18 cm)
B = ¾" (1.91 cm)
*Particle board

Match and attachment of edge bands. Bands shown are typical. Any band configuration can be used if all the all-grade requirements are met.

PREMIUM GRADE

For case doors of ¾" (B) thickness, the maximum size should be 26" (66.04 cm) wide and 48" (121.92 cm) high. The cores should be particle board, banded with pressure-glued lumber of species that match the door face.

Size A case doors should be the maximum size of 36" (91.44 cm) wide and 66" (167.64 cm) high. The cores may be of particle board or lumber stave core with matching edges.

Banding is required on all edges if the edge is visible on the face of the door. If not visible, built-in bands are used; horizontal edges more than 72" (182.88 cm) or less than 18" (45.72 cm) from the floor may be omitted. Banding that shows more than ⅛" (0.32 cm) on the face of the door must be mitered at the corners.

CUSTOM GRADE

For flush-type doors of size A thickness, the maximum size should be 36" (91.44 cm) wide and 72" (182.88 cm) high. Cores should conform with requirements for premium grade, except that the banding species is optional. Thin sliding doors should be ¼" (0.64 cm) thick, made of tempered hardboard not exceeding 6 sq ft (0.56 m²). Banding is required on all edges if visible on the face of the door. If invisible built-in bands are used, horizontal edges more than 72" (182.88 cm) or less than 18" (45.72 cm) from the floor may be omitted.

Doors of type B thickness should have a maximum size of 26" (66.04 cm) wide and 54" (137.16 cm) high.

ECONOMY GRADE

Doors of type B thickness should have a maximum size of 26" (66.04 cm) wide and 60" (152.40 cm) wide. No banding is required. Thin sliding doors should be ¼" (0.64 cm) thick hardboard, not to exceed maximum size of 6 sq ft (0.56 m²).

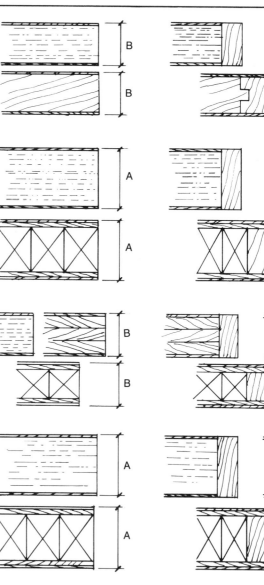

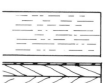

Built-in or plowed edge bands

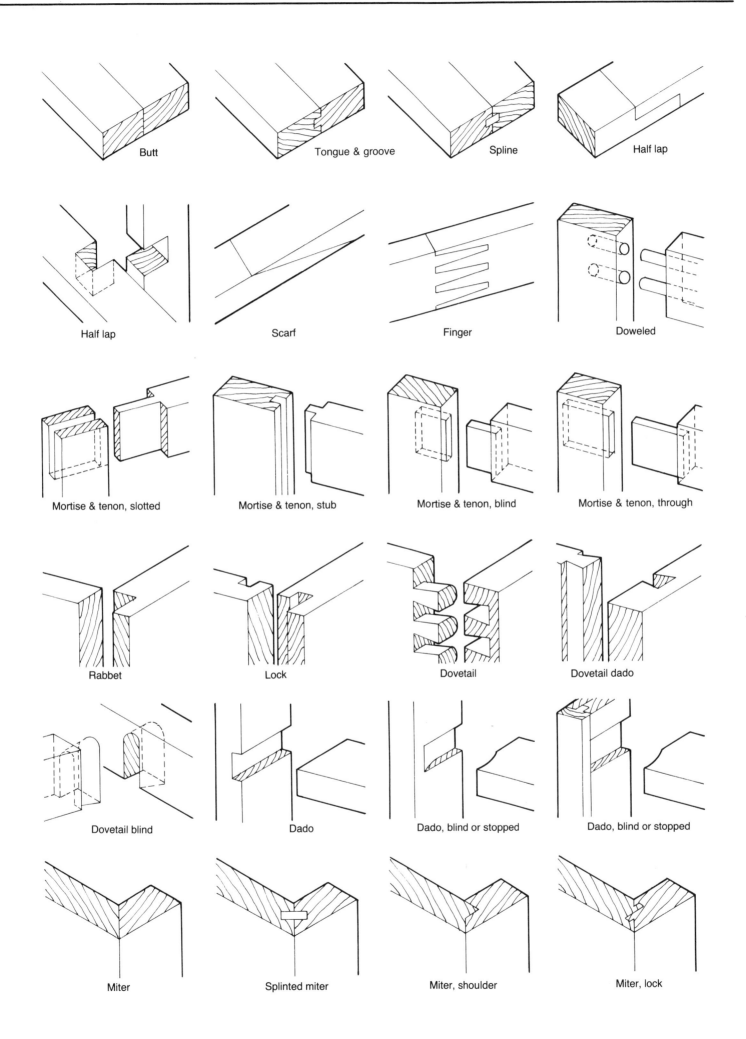

Butt

Tongue & groove

Spline

Half lap

Half lap

Scarf

Finger

Doweled

Mortise & tenon, slotted

Mortise & tenon, stub

Mortise & tenon, blind

Mortise & tenon, through

Rabbet

Lock

Dovetail

Dovetail dado

Dovetail blind

Dado

Dado, blind or stopped

Dado, blind or stopped

Miter

Splinted miter

Miter, shoulder

Miter, lock

CABINET & TABLE HINGES

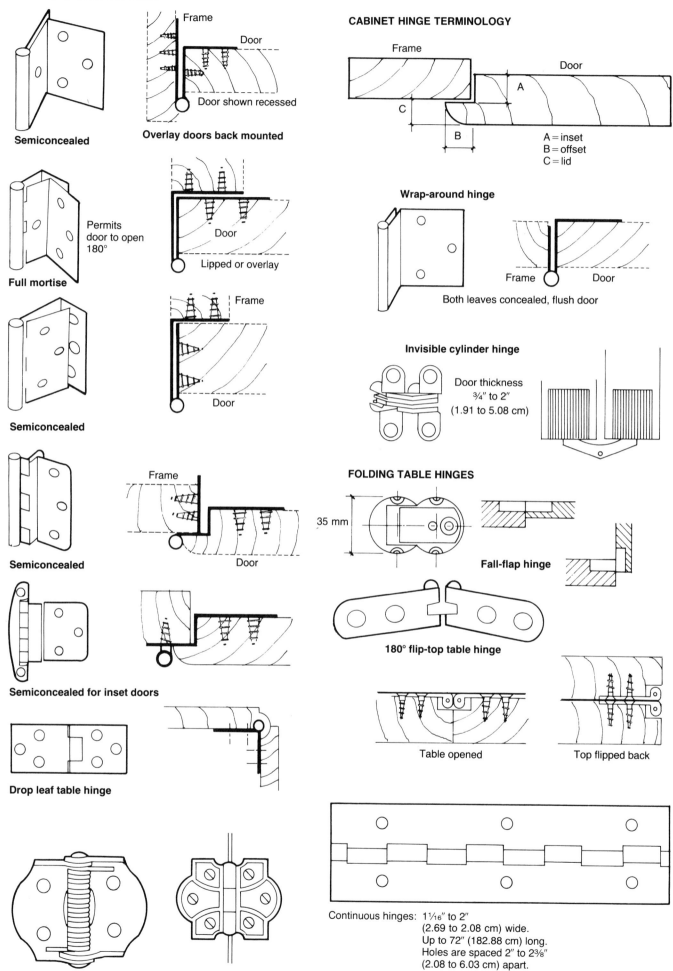

Semiconcealed

Frame

Door

Door shown recessed

Overlay doors back mounted

Full mortise

Permits
door to open
180°

Door

Lipped or overlay

Semiconcealed

Frame

Door

Semiconcealed

Frame

Door

Semiconcealed for inset doors

Drop leaf table hinge

Spring hinges

CABINET HINGE TERMINOLOGY

Frame

Door

A

C

B

A = inset
B = offset
C = lid

Wrap-around hinge

Frame   Door

Both leaves concealed, flush door

Invisible cylinder hinge

Door thickness
¾" to 2"
(1.91 to 5.08 cm)

FOLDING TABLE HINGES

35 mm

Fall-flap hinge

180° flip-top table hinge

Table opened

Top flipped back

Continuous hinges: 1¹⁄₁₆" to 2"
(2.69 to 2.08 cm) wide.
Up to 72" (182.88 cm) long.
Holes are spaced 2" to 2³⁄₈"
(2.08 to 6.03 cm) apart.

ADJUSTMENT HINGES FOR CABINETS

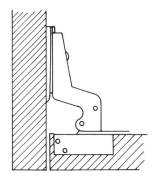

Inset adjustable   **Overlay adjustable**

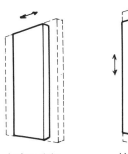

Left to right   Up-down   In-out

Adjustable hinges allow perfect fitting
on project site

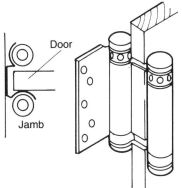

Door

Jamb

Double-acting hinge for door

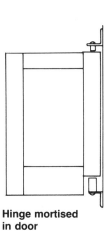

**Hinge mortised
in door**

RECOMMENDED CABINET DOOR HINGES

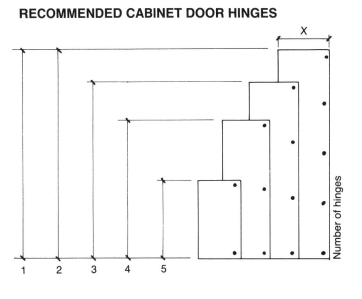

Dimensions:
1 = door height
2 = up to 96" (243.84 cm)
3 = up to 84" (213.36 cm)
4 = up to 60" (152.40 cm)
5 = up to 36" (91.44 cm)
X = 24" (60.96 cm)

The number of recommended hinges is also
based on the door weight. A typical
24" (60.96 cm) wide door:

Up to 20 lb (9.72 kg) = 2 hinges
20 to 40 lb (18.14 kg) = 3 hinges
40 to 60 lb (27.21 kg) = 4 hinges

Note: Small swinging cafe doors installed
with double-acting hinges should not
exceed 30" (76.20 cm) in width or maximum
weight of 50 lb (22.68 kg). Recommended:
flat 1¼" (3.18 cm) jamb brackets.

HIDDEN AUTOMATIC CLOSURE HINGES

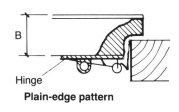

Hinge

Plain-edge pattern

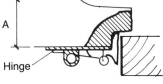

Hinge

Diamond-edge pattern

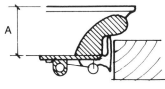

Reverse-cover pattern

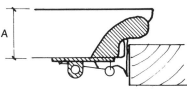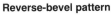

Reverse-bevel pattern

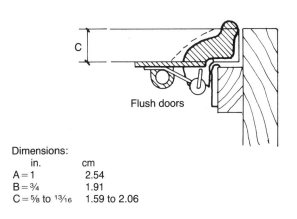

Flush doors

Dimensions:
	in.	cm
A =	1	2.54
B =	¾	1.91
C =	⅝ to ¹³/₁₆	1.59 to 2.06

PIVOT HINGES

Pivot hinge for horizontal stile

Pivot hinge for vertical stile

Hinges for jamb-to-ceiling mounting

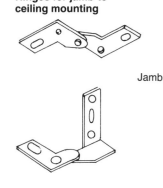

Ceiling with header or wood top jamb

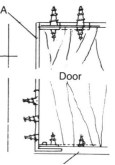

A

Jamb

Door

Wardrobe or room floor

Note: A = ³⁄₁₆″ (0.48 cm) clearance between jamb and door

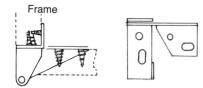

HINGES FOR FRAMELESS GLASS DOORS

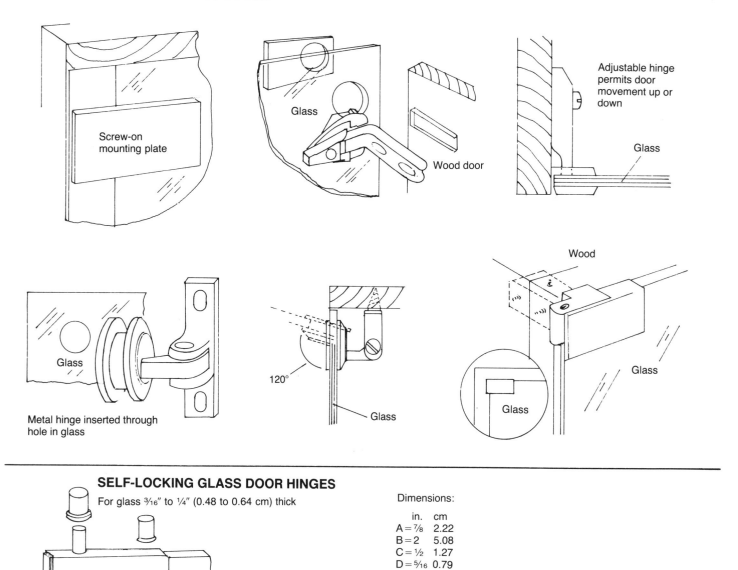

Screw-on mounting plate

Glass

Wood door

Adjustable hinge permits door movement up or down

Glass

Glass

Metal hinge inserted through hole in glass

120°

Glass

Wood

Glass

Glass

SELF-LOCKING GLASS DOOR HINGES

For glass ³⁄₁₆″ to ¹⁄₄″ (0.48 to 0.64 cm) thick

Metal

Glass

Dimensions:

	in.	cm
A =	⁷⁄₈	2.22
B =	2	5.08
C =	¹⁄₂	1.27
D =	⁵⁄₁₆	0.79

A

B

C

Glass

D

ROLLER CATCHES IN DIFFERENT INSTALLATIONS

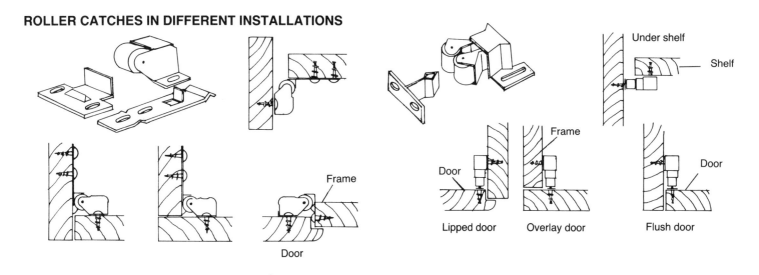

Frame

Door

Lipped door | Overlay door | Flush door

Under shelf

Shelf

Frame

Door

Door

MAGNETIC CATCHES IN VARIOUS APPLICATIONS

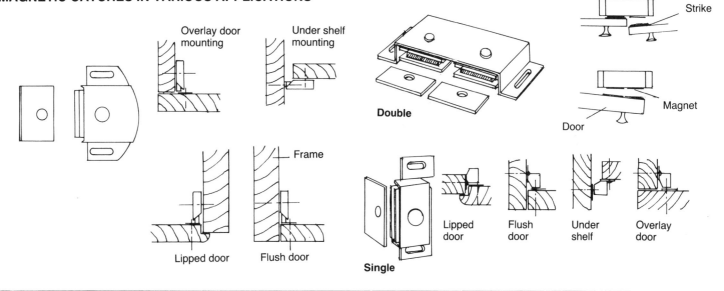

Overlay door mounting

Under shelf mounting

Double

Strike

Magnet

Door

Frame

Lipped door | Flush door

Single

Lipped door | Flush door | Under shelf | Overlay door

FRICTION CATCHES

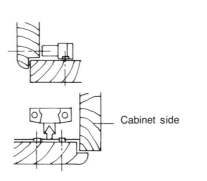

Cabinet side

KEYED LOCKS

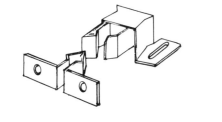

Sliding cabinet doors

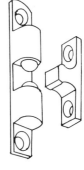

Cabinet lock

PREMIUM GRADE

Vertical section through front and back

Horizontal section through drawer sides

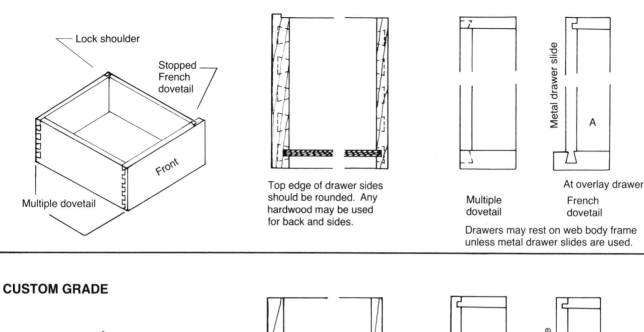

Lock shoulder

Stopped French dovetail

Front

Multiple dovetail

Top edge of drawer sides should be rounded. Any hardwood may be used for back and sides.

Metal drawer slide

A

Metal drawer slide

A

At overlay drawer

Multiple dovetail

French dovetail

Multiple

Drawers may rest on web body frame unless metal drawer slides are used.

CUSTOM GRADE

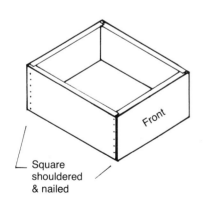

Front

Lock shouldered, glued, & nailed

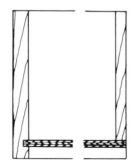

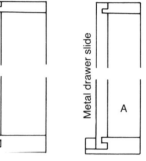

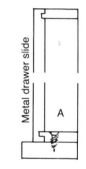

Metal drawer slide

A

Metal drawer slide

A

Two softwood guides and one tilt strip or hardwood center guide may be used. Sides and back may be of any softwood.

Lock shoulder joint

Drawers may rest on web body frame unless metal drawer slides are used.

ECONOMY GRADE

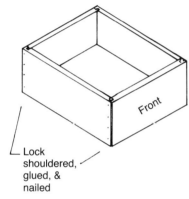

Front

Square shouldered & nailed

No web frame required as side guides may form same. One softwood tilt strip is required.

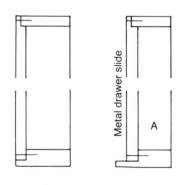

Metal drawer slide

A

Square shoulder joints

Notes: Drawers marked A were designed to take metal drawer slides on the side.

Wood thickness for drawer construction: front usually ¾″ (1.91 cm) lumber core plywood. Sides ½″, ⅜″, or ¾″ (1.27, 0.95, or 1.91 cm) if using side guide hardware. Back ½″ (1.27 cm).

Bottom usually ¼″ (0.64 cm) plywood or hardboard.

DRAWER CONSTRUCTION: PREMIUM & CUSTOM GRADES

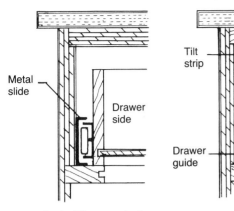

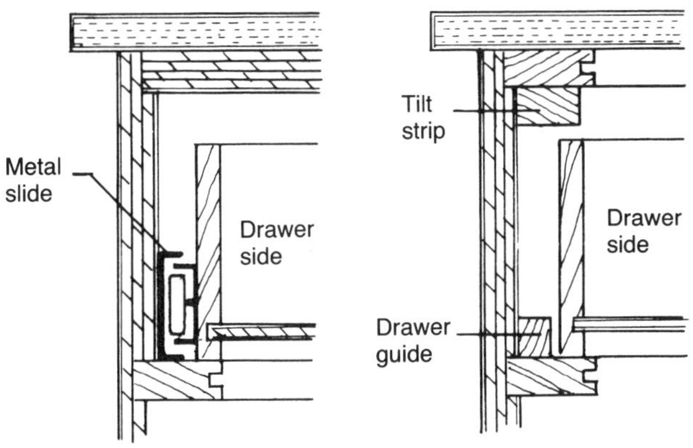

Metal slide

Tilt strip

Drawer side

Drawer side

Drawer guide

Grade differences in drawer construction shown on page 48

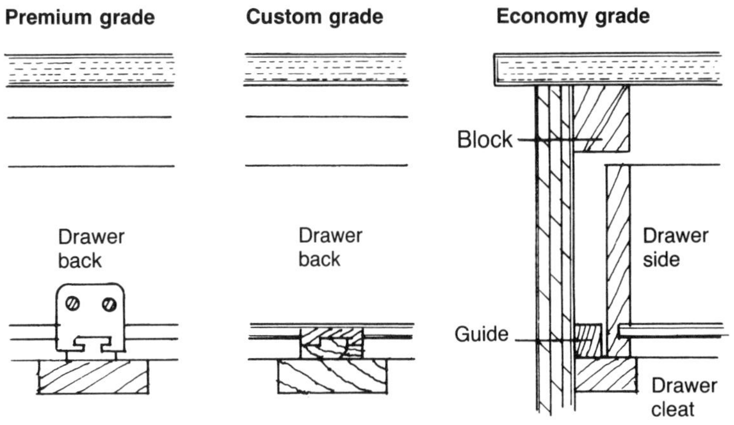

Detail of side-mounted hardware

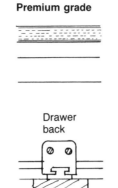

Premium grade	Custom grade	Economy grade

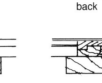
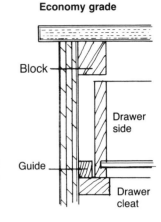

Drawer back

Drawer back

Block

Drawer side

Guide

Drawer cleat

Metal or plastic guide and track

TYPICAL CENTER GUIDES

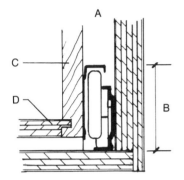

A
C
D
B

Side elevation

E
Drawer
G
F

Dado on drawer side is ³⁄₈″ (0.95 cm) from drawer side bottom

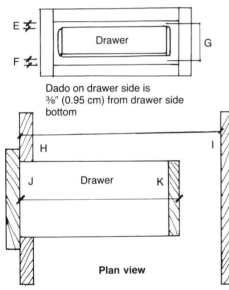

H
J   Drawer   K
I

Plan view

Opened drawer showing side-mounted hardware

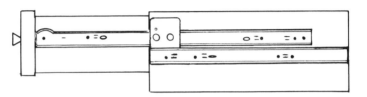

Notes and dimensions:
A = space for side-mounted drawer hardware ½″ (1.27 cm)
B = side of casing, height of drawer hardware
C = drawer side
D = drawer bottom
E = ¼″ (0.64 cm)
F = ¾₁₆″ (2.06 cm)
G = vertical difference totals ⁷⁄₁₆″ (1.11 cm)
H = outside face of cabinet
I = inside mounting surface
J = inside face of drawer
K = outer edge of drawer

Hardware sizes of typical center guides

Slide length in.	Fits drawer length (C-D) in.	Fits cabinet depth (A-B) in.	Drawer extension in.
12	7¼-10¾	12-12½	6
14	9¼-12¾	14-14½	8½
16	11¼-14¾	16-16½	10
18	13¼-16¾	18-18½	11
20	15¼-18¾	20-20½	13
22	17¼-20¾	22-22½	14½
23	18¼-21¾	23-23½	15½
24	19¼-22¾	24-24½	16

SPECIFICATION GUIDELINES FOR DRAWER HARDWARE

Use	50 lb, light*	75 lb, medium	100-50 lb, heavy	250 lb, extra heavy
Kitchen	X			
Desks	X			
Vanities	X			
Store fixtures		X		
Wardrobes		X		
Lab equipment		X	X	X
File cabinets			X	X
Pull-out shelf for TV/stereo			X	X

*Most lightweight drawer slides do not allow for full extension of drawer. Slides are usually available in 2″ (5.08 cm) increments from 12″ to 30″ (30.48 to 76.20 cm) lengths.

CYLINDER CAM FURNITURE LOCKS

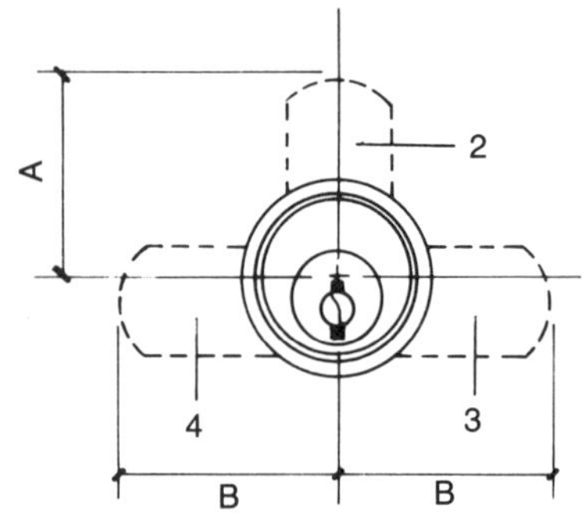

Pin tumbler cylinder cam

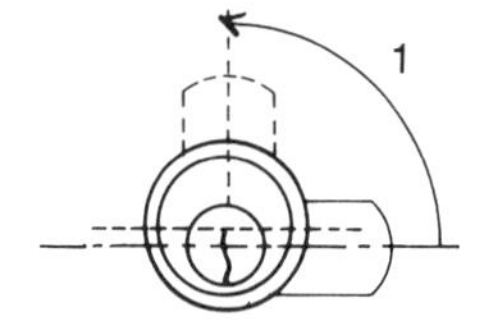

Left-hand door, front view

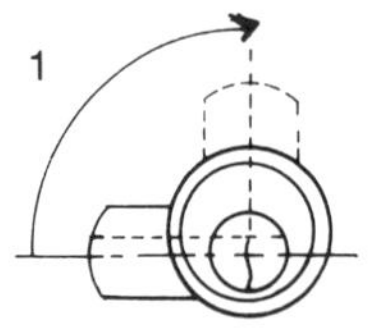

Right-hand door, front view

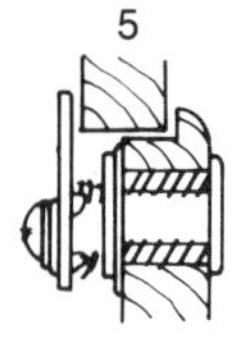

Lipped

Dimensions:

in.	cm
A = 1⅛	2.86
B = 1¼	3.18
C = 1½	3.81

Notes: (1) 90° clockwise; (2) drawer; (3) left door; (4) right door; (5) 90° pin tumbler cam can only be used with lipped construction on drawers and cabinet doors. Pin tumbers allow key to be removed in the locked and unlocked position.

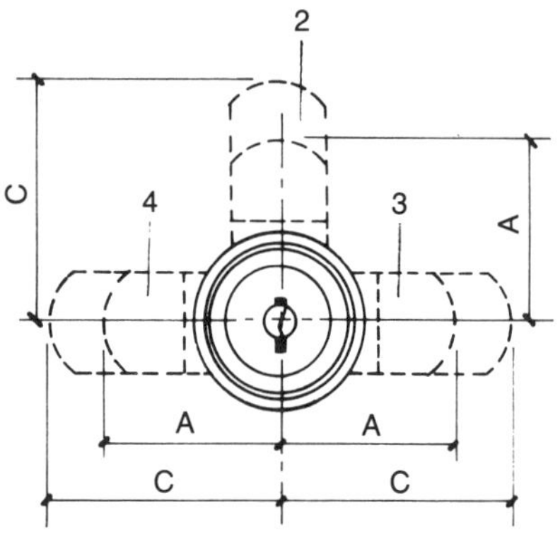

Disk tumbler cylinder cam

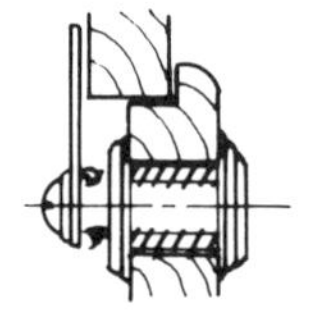

Lipped disk tumbler

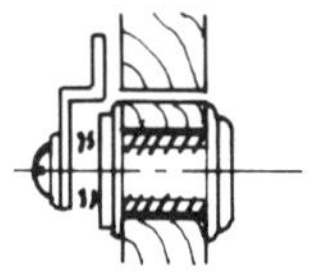

Flush

Typical sizes of disc tumbler

Cylinder length in.	cm	Maximum material thickness in.	cm
7/16	1.11	7/64	0.11
5/8	1.59	15/64	0.23
1 3/16	3.02	7/8	2.22
1 1/16	2.69	3/4	1.91

FURNITURE DEAD BOLT DISC LOCKS, TUMBLERS, & GANG LOCK

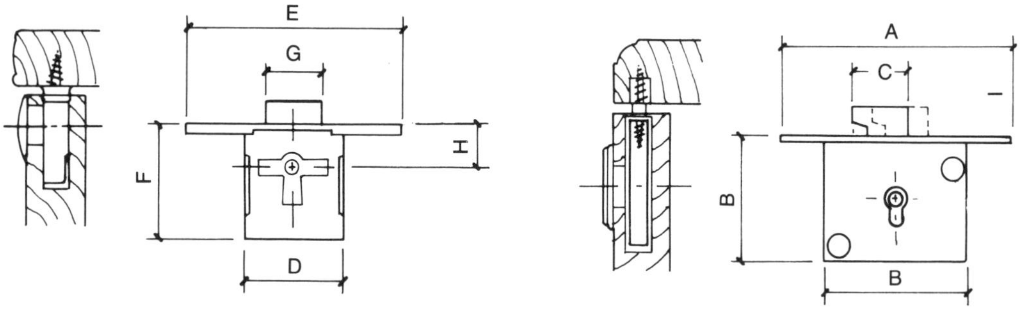

Dead bolt disc locks

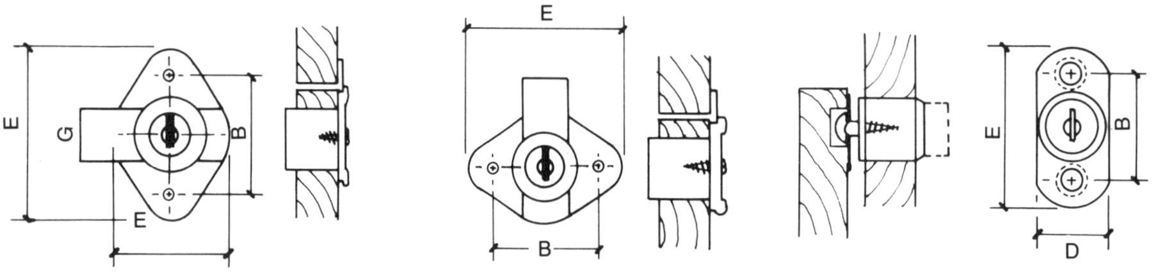

Tumblers

Dimensions

in.	cm	in.	cm
A = 3	7.62	F = 1⅛	2.86
B = 1⅝	4.13	G = ½	1.27
C = ¼	0.64	H = ⅜	0.95
D = 1	2.54	I = 13/16	2.06
E = 2	5.08		

Dead bolt cylinder length 13/16″ (2.06 cm); bolt travel 11/32″ (0.87 cm).

Gang locks for drawers in desk pedestals or filing cabinets require ⅞″ (2.22 cm) diameter hole. Special dado may be required.

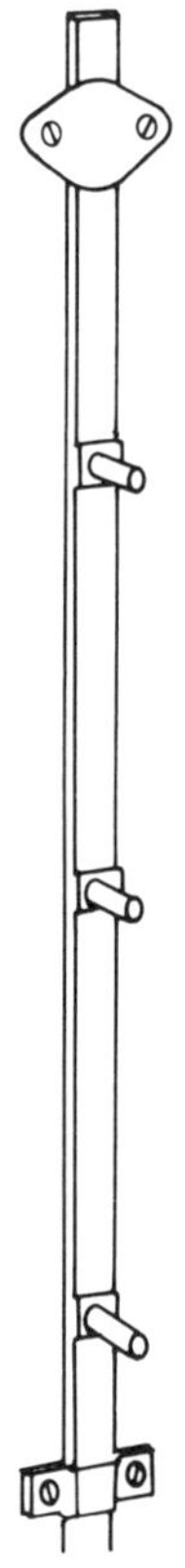

Gang lock

BACK-FASTENED METAL DRAWER PULLS

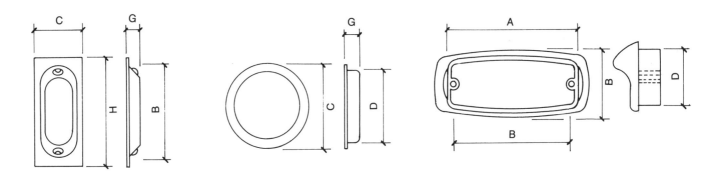

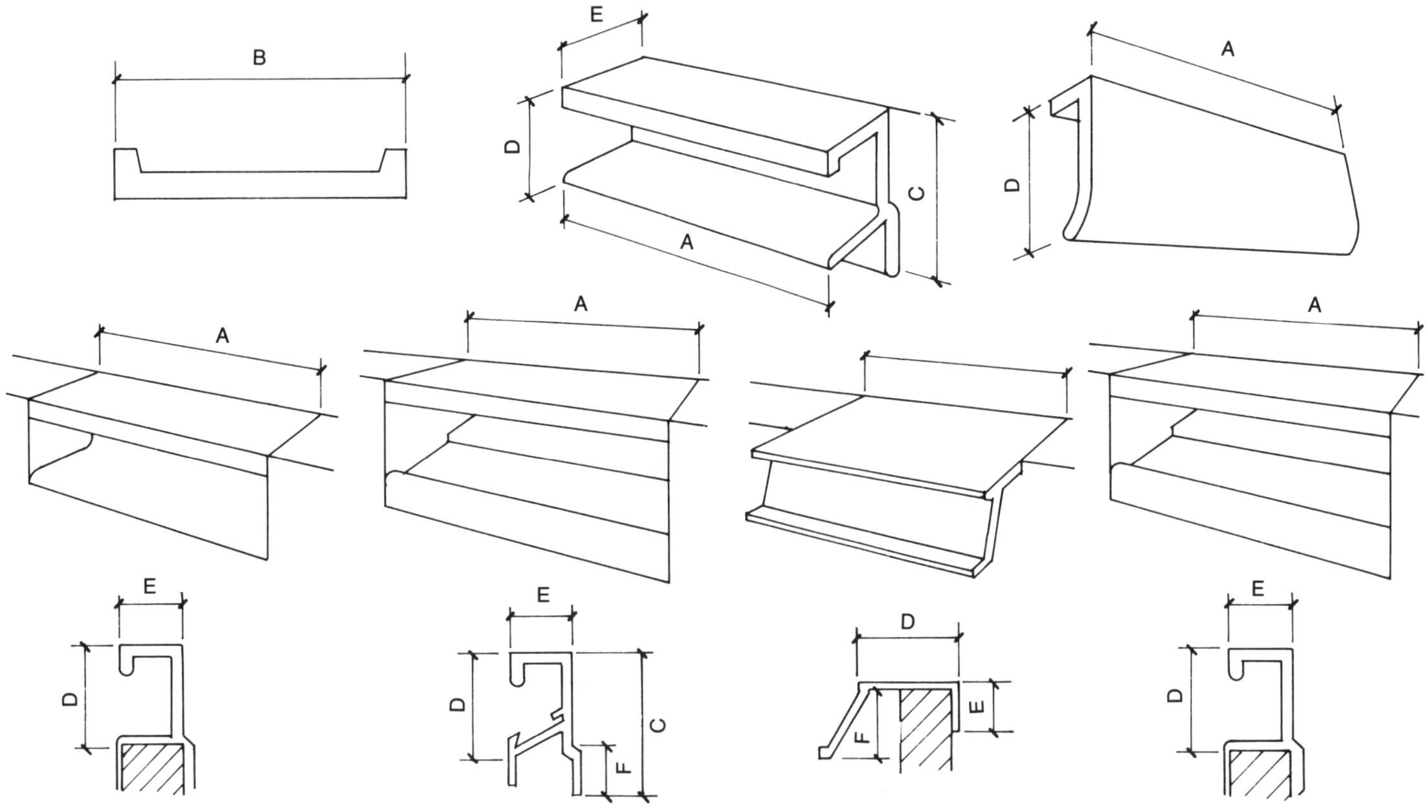

FLUSH PULLS FOR SLIDING CABINET DOORS

DRAWER PULLS

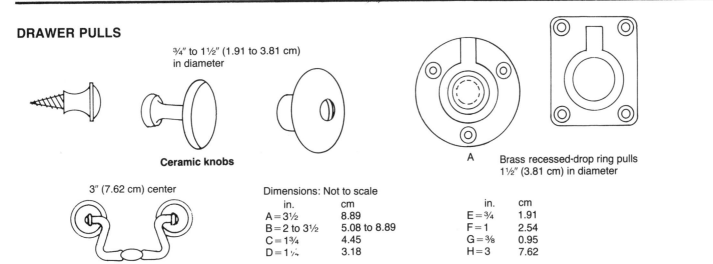

¾″ to 1½″ (1.91 to 3.81 cm) in diameter

Ceramic knobs

A   Brass recessed-drop ring pulls
     1½″ (3.81 cm) in diameter

3″ (7.62 cm) center

Bail pull

Dimensions: Not to scale

	in.	cm		in.	cm
A =	3½	8.89	E =	¾	1.91
B =	2 to 3½	5.08 to 8.89	F =	1	2.54
C =	1¾	4.45	G =	⅜	0.95
D =	1¼	3.18	H =	3	7.62

SHELF STANDARDS, RESTS, & BRACKETS

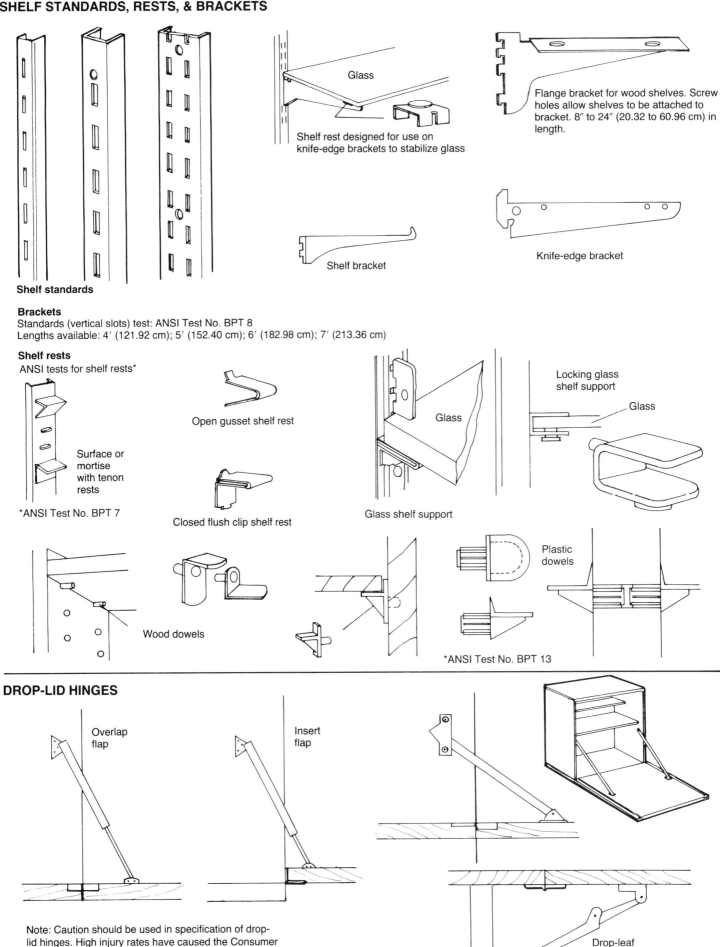

Glass

Shelf rest designed for use on knife-edge brackets to stabilize glass

Flange bracket for wood shelves. Screw holes allow shelves to be attached to bracket. 8″ to 24″ (20.32 to 60.96 cm) in length.

Shelf bracket

Knife-edge bracket

Shelf standards

Brackets
Standards (vertical slots) test: ANSI Test No. BPT 8
Lengths available: 4′ (121.92 cm); 5′ (152.40 cm); 6′ (182.98 cm); 7′ (213.36 cm)

Shelf rests
ANSI tests for shelf rests*

Open gusset shelf rest

Surface or mortise with tenon rests

*ANSI Test No. BPT 7

Closed flush clip shelf rest

Glass

Locking glass shelf support

Glass

Glass shelf support

Wood dowels

Plastic dowels

*ANSI Test No. BPT 13

DROP-LID HINGES

Overlap flap

Insert flap

Drop-leaf table support

Note: Caution should be used in specification of drop-lid hinges. High injury rates have caused the Consumer Product Safety Commission (CPSC) to publish warnings on some types of hinges. Consult CPSC, ANSI, and the Door and Hardware Institute for current testing standards.

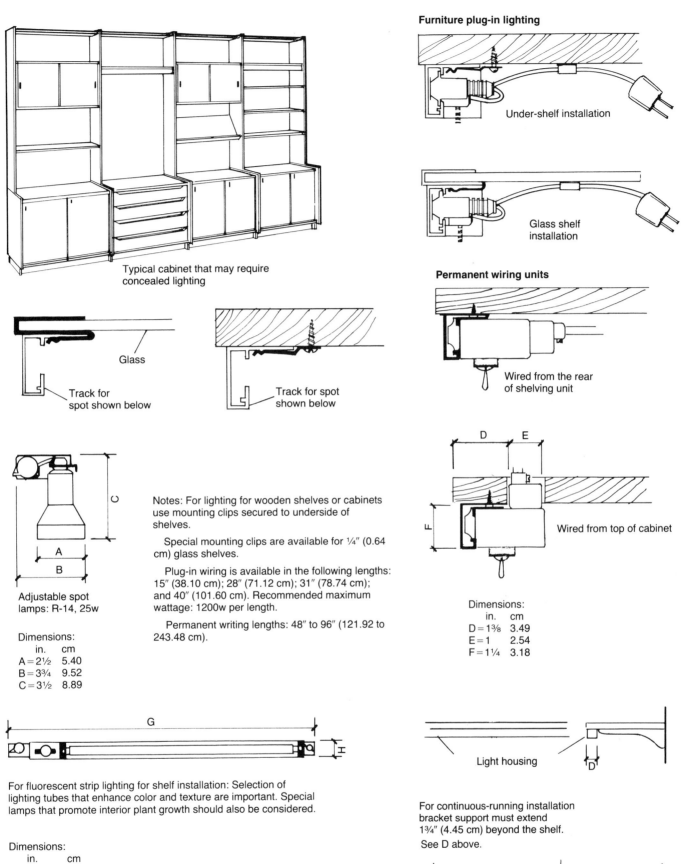

Typical cabinet that may require concealed lighting

Furniture plug-in lighting

Under-shelf installation

Glass shelf installation

Glass

Track for spot shown below

Track for spot shown below

Permanent wiring units

Wired from the rear of shelving unit

Adjustable spot lamps: R-14, 25w

Dimensions:
	in.	cm
A =	2½	5.40
B =	3¾	9.52
C =	3½	8.89

Notes: For lighting for wooden shelves or cabinets use mounting clips secured to underside of shelves.

Special mounting clips are available for ¼″ (0.64 cm) glass shelves.

Plug-in wiring is available in the following lengths: 15″ (38.10 cm); 28″ (71.12 cm); 31″ (78.74 cm); and 40″ (101.60 cm). Recommended maximum wattage: 1200w per length.

Permanent writing lengths: 48″ to 96″ (121.92 to 243.48 cm).

Wired from top of cabinet

Dimensions:
	in.	cm
D =	1⅜	3.49
E =	1	2.54
F =	1¼	3.18

G

For fluorescent strip lighting for shelf installation: Selection of lighting tubes that enhance color and texture are important. Special lamps that promote interior plant growth should also be considered.

Dimensions:
	in.	cm
G =	22½	57.15
H =	1½	3.81
I =	16 o.c.*	40.64

*On-center distance between fasteners

Light housing

For continuous-running installation bracket support must extend 1¾″ (4.45 cm) beyond the shelf. See D above.

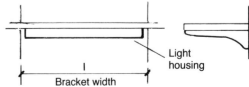

Light housing

Bracket width

RECEPTION ROOM DESK DESIGNED AROUND PREEXISTING COLUMNS

Not to scale

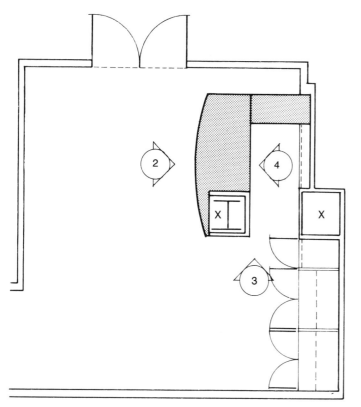

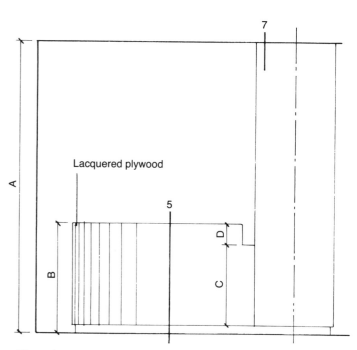

Elevation 2

Plan
In a reception office of a New York firm, a desk is designed to be built around the existing columns (X) shown above.

Dimensions:

	in.	cm
A =	63	160.02
B =	30	76.20
C =	29	73.66
D =	7	17.78
E =	27	68.58
F =	26	66.04

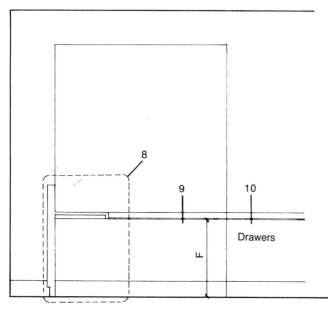

Elevation 3

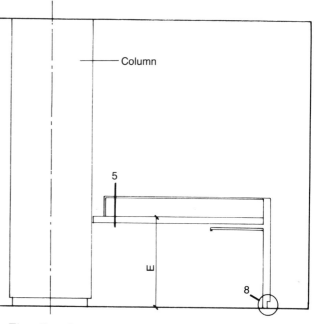

Elevation 4

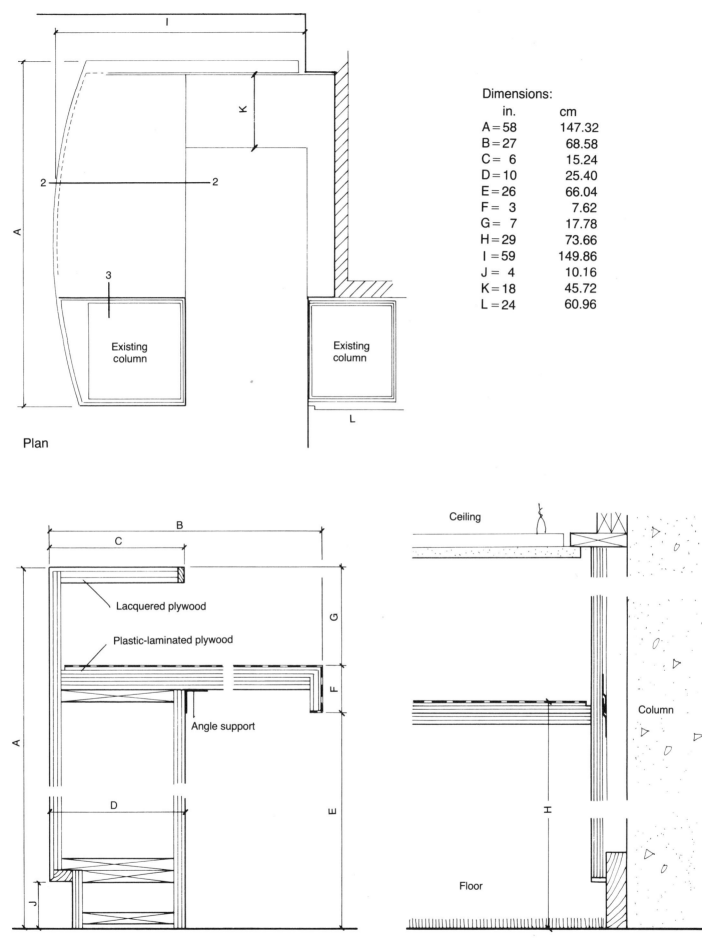

Plan

Dimensions:

	in.	cm
A =	58	147.32
B =	27	68.58
C =	6	15.24
D =	10	25.40
E =	26	66.04
F =	3	7.62
G =	7	17.78
H =	29	73.66
I =	59	149.86
J =	4	10.16
K =	18	45.72
L =	24	60.96

Existing column

Existing column

Lacquered plywood

Plastic-laminated plywood

Angle support

Section 2

Ceiling

Column

Floor

Section 3

RECEPTION ROOM DESK DETAILS

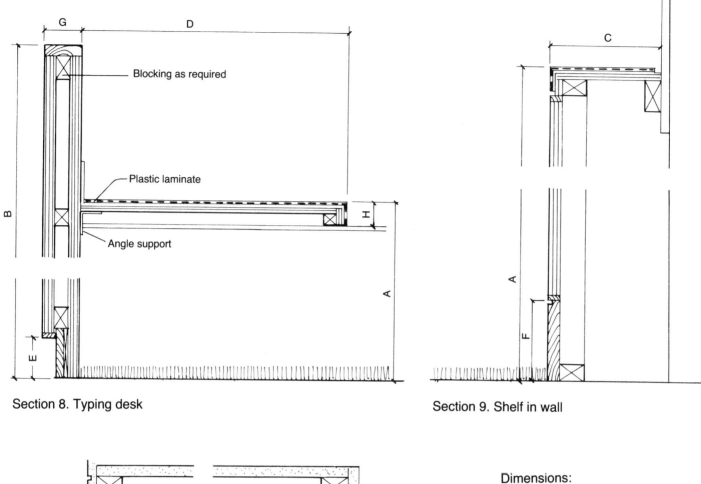

Blocking as required

Plastic laminate

Angle support

Section 8. Typing desk

Section 9. Shelf in wall

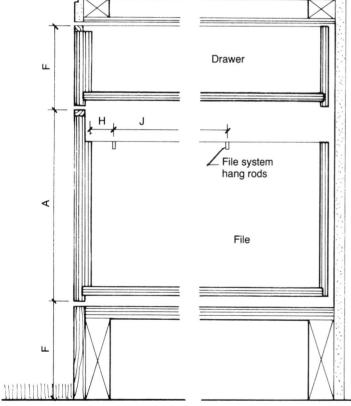

Drawer

File system
hang rods

File

Section 10. Drawers in wall

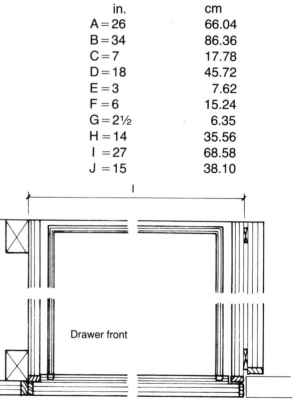

Drawer front

Detail of drawer plan

Dimensions:

	in.	cm
A =	26	66.04
B =	34	86.36
C =	7	17.78
D =	18	45.72
E =	3	7.62
F =	6	15.24
G =	2½	6.35
H =	14	35.56
I =	27	68.58
J =	15	38.10

CUSTOM-DESIGNED, WALL-HUNG TELEPHONE SHELF FOR RESTAURANT

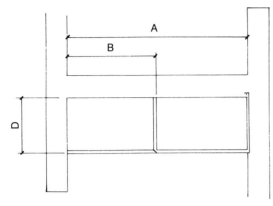

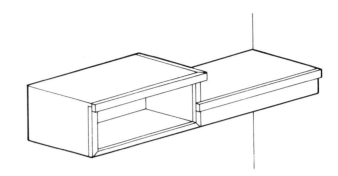

Plan view

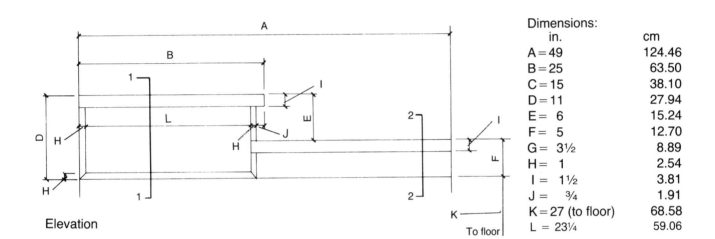

Elevation

Dimensions:		
	in.	cm
A =	49	124.46
B =	25	63.50
C =	15	38.10
D =	11	27.94
E =	6	15.24
F =	5	12.70
G =	3½	8.89
H =	1	2.54
I =	1½	3.81
J =	¾	1.91
K =	27 (to floor)	68.58
L =	23¼	59.06

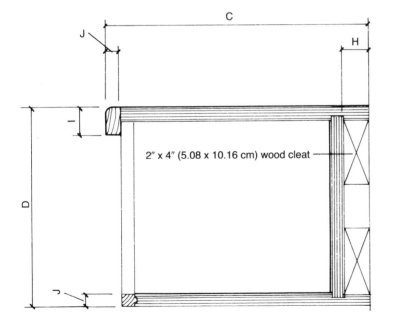

2″ x 4″ (5.08 x 10.16 cm) wood cleat

Section 1

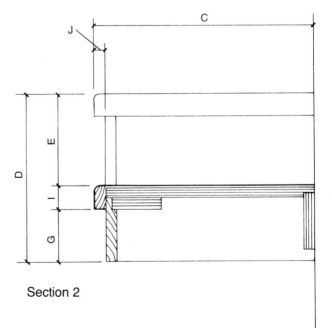

Section 2

COCKTAIL TABLE

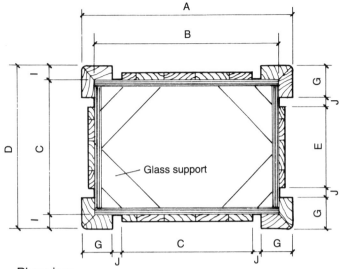

Glass support

Plan view

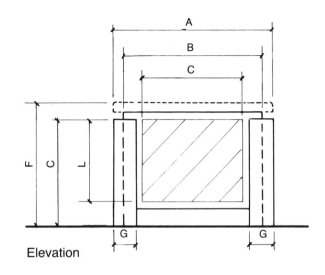

Elevation

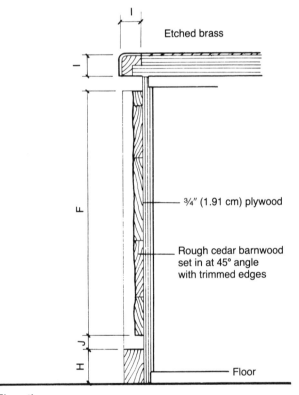

Etched brass

¾″ (1.91 cm) plywood

Rough cedar barnwood
set in at 45° angle
with trimmed edges

Floor

Elevation

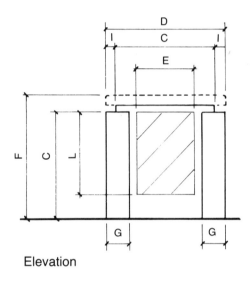

Elevation

In custom millwork for restaurants or cocktail
lounges, tables may be constructed in various
heights. Top may be glass inset or etched brass
coated with fiberglass resin.

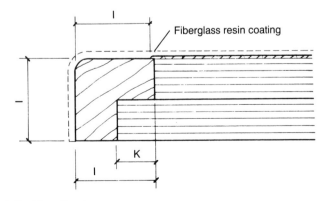

Fiberglass resin coating

Detail of top & edge

Dimensions: Not to scale

	in.	cm
A =	24	60.96
B =	21	53.34
C =	15	38.10
D =	18	45.72
E =	9	22.86
F =	as per table design	
G =	3½	8.89
H =	2½	6.35
I =	1½	3.81
J =	1	2.54
K =	¾	1.91
L =	12	30.48

LAMINATED TABLETOPS & EDGES

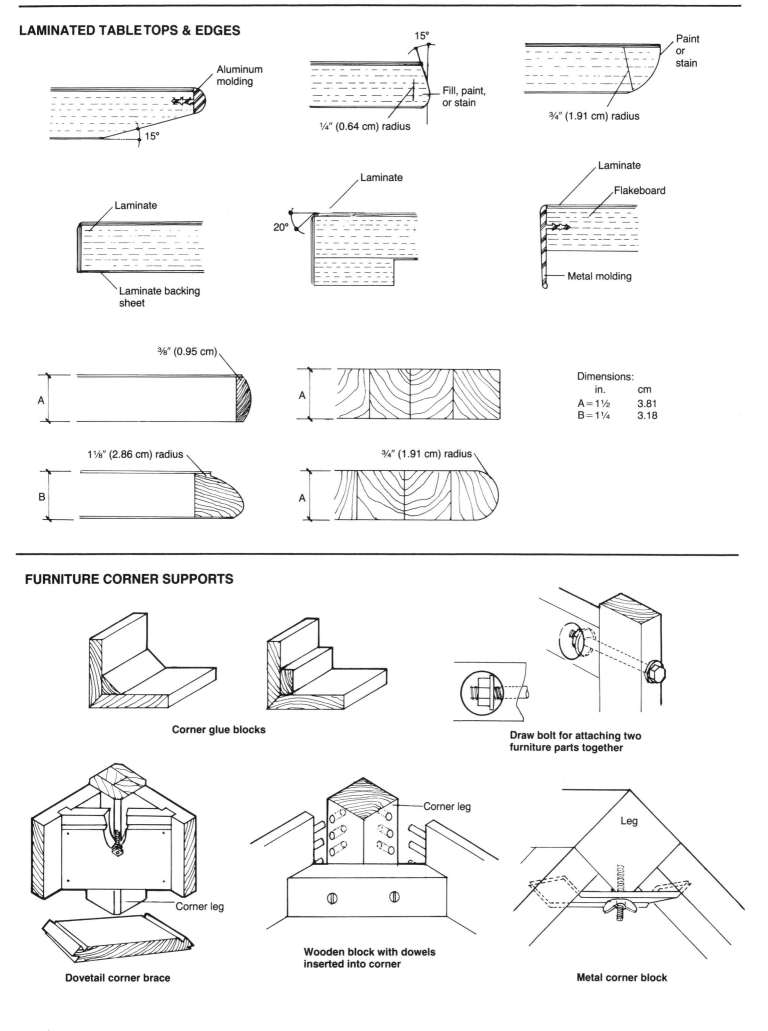

15°

Aluminum molding

15°

Fill, paint, or stain

¼″ (0.64 cm) radius

Paint or stain

¾″ (1.91 cm) radius

Laminate

Laminate backing sheet

Laminate

20°

Laminate

Flakeboard

Metal molding

⅜″ (0.95 cm)

A

A

Dimensions:
	in.	cm
A =	1½	3.81
B =	1¼	3.18

1⅛″ (2.86 cm) radius

B

¾″ (1.91 cm) radius

A

FURNITURE CORNER SUPPORTS

Corner glue blocks

Draw bolt for attaching two furniture parts together

Corner leg

Dovetail corner brace

Corner leg

Wooden block with dowels inserted into corner

Leg

Metal corner block

Back putty
After the glass has been face-puttied, it is turned over and putty is run into any voids that may exist between the glass and the wood parts.

Backing out
Wide, shallow groove machined in back surface of members.

Balancing species
A species, of similar density, to achieve balance by equalizing the rate of moisture absorption or emission.

Bedding in putty
Glazing whereby a thin layer of putty or bedding compound is placed in the glass rabbet and the glass is inserted and pressed onto this bed.

Birdseye
A small central spot with wood fibers arranged around it so as to give the appearance of an eye.

Board
A piece of lumber before gluing for width or thickness.

Bow
A deviation from a straight line drawn from end to end of an otherwise flat piece. It is measured at the point of greatest distance from the straight line.

Burl
In softwoods, a distortion of the grain due to injury of the tree. In hardwoods, a swirl or twist of the grain near a knot but not containing a knot. It must have a sound center. The measurement of the burl is the average of the maximum and minimum dimensions of the burl.
1. Very small burl does not exceed ½″ (1.27 cm) in diameter.
2. Small burl does not exceed ¾″ (1.91 cm) in diameter.
3. Medium burl does not exceed 1″ (2.54 cm) in diameter.

Casework
All the parts that constitute a finished case or cabinet, inclusive of doors, drawers, and shelves.

Compatible for color and grain
For purposes of this book, this phrase means that members shall be selected so that lighter than average color members will not be adjacent to darker than average color members, and there will be no sharp contrast in color between the adjacent members. Two adjacent members shall not be widely dissimilar in grain, character, and figure.

Coped
To cut the end of one member to match the profile of another molded member.

Crook
A deviation from a straight line drawn from end to end of the edge of a piece. It is measured at the point of greatest distance from the straight line.

Crossbanding
In the construction of flush doors, the veneer that is placed between the core and face veneers with the direction of the grain at right angles to that of the face veneer.

Cup
A deviation in the face of a piece from a straight line drawn from edge to edge. It is measured at the point of greatest distance from the straight line.

Decay
Disintegration of wood due to the action of wood-destroying fungi. "Doze," "rot," and "unsound wood" mean the same as decay.

Defect
Fault that detracts from the quality, appearance, or utility of the piece. Handling marks and/or grain raising due to moisture shall not be considered a defect.

Delamination
The separation of layers in an assembly because of failure of the adhesive, either in the adhesive itself or at the interface between the adhesive and the lamination.

For plywood, if separation between the plys is greater than 2″ (5.08 cm) in continuous length, over ¼″ (0.64 cm) in depth at any part, and .003″ in width, it shall be considered delamination.

For solid stock, if the separation between the members is greater than ¼″ deep and more than .005″ in width and the total length of all such delamination is more than 5 percent of the total length of the glue line, it shall be considered delaminated.

If more than one delamination occurs in a single glue line, the total length of all such delamination shall determine whether or not it is considered to be delaminated.

Dowel
Wood peg or a metal screw used to strengthen a wood joint.

Eased edge
Slightly rounded edge not to exceed ¹⁄₁₆″ (0.16 cm) radius; recommended to eliminate sharp corners.

Edge band, concealed
Not more than ¹⁄₁₆″ of the edge band shall show on the face of the plywood or particle board.

Exposed surfaces
Surfaces visible after installation, except for exposed portions of casework.

Glue block
A wood block, usually triangular in cross section, securely glued to an angular joint between two members to ensure greater glue bond area.

Glued, securely
The bonding of two members with an adhesive forming a tight joint and no visible delamination at the lines of application.

Grain
The fibers in wood and their direction, size, arrangement, appearance, or quality. When severed, the annual growth rings become quite pronounced and the effect is referred to as "grain."

Flat grain (FG) or **slash grain (SG)** lumber or veneer is a piece sawn or sliced approximately parallel to the annual growth rings so that some or all of the rings form an angle of less than 45° with the surface of the piece.

Mixed grain (MG) is any combination of vertical or flat grain in the same member.

Vertical grain (VG) lumber or veneer is a piece sawn or sliced at approximately right angles to the annual growth rings so that the rings form an angle of 45° or more with the surface of the piece.

Reprinted with permission of the Woodwork Institute of California.

Quartered grain is a method of sawing or slicing to bring out certain pattern produced by the medullary or pith rays, which are especially conspicuous in oak. The log is flitched in several different ways to allow cutting the veneer in a radial direction.

Rift or comb grain lumber or veneer that is obtained by cutting at an angle of about 15° off of the quartered position. Twenty-five percent of the exposed surface area of each piece of veneer may contain medullary ray flake.

Grain character
A varying pattern produced by cutting through growth rings, exposing various layers. It is most pronounced in veneer cut tangentially or in a rotary cut.

Grain figure
The pattern produced in a wood surface by annual growth rings, rays, knots, or deviations from natural grain, such as interlocked and wavy grain, and irregular coloration.

Groove
Rectangular slot of three surfaces cut parallel with the grain of the wood.

Hardboard
A generic term for a panel manufactured primarily from interfelted lignocellulose fibers consolidated under heat and pressure in a hot press and conforming to the requirements of PS 58-74.

Hardwood
General term used to designate lumber or veneer produced from broadleaved or deciduous trees in contrast with softwood, which is produced from evergreen or coniferous trees.

Heartwood
The wood extending from the pith or the center of the tree to the sapwood, usually darker in color than sapwood.

Heat resistance test
A sample of the laminated plastic approximately 12″ X 12″ (30.48 X 30.48 cm) glued to substrate for a minimum of 21 days shall be used for this test. A hot air gun rated at 14 amperes, 120 volts, with a nozzle temperature of 500°F or 274°C shall be directed at the surface of the test panel. A thermometer set at the panel surface shall register 356°F or 180°C for an exposure time of 5 minutes. The formation of a blister or void between the overlay and substrate shall constitute a failure of the adhesive. A metal straight edge shall be used to determine if a blister has occurred. This determination shall be made within 30 seconds of removal of the heat.

High-pressure laminated plastic
Laminated thermosetting decorative sheets intended for decorative purposes. The sheets consist essentially of layers of a fibrous sheet material, such as paper, impregnated with a thermosetting condensation resin and consolidated under heat and pressure. The top layers have a decorative color or a printed design. The resultant product has an attractive exposed surface that is durable and resistant to damage from abrasion and mild alkalies, acids, and solvents, meeting the requirements of the National Electrical Manufacturers Association (NEMA) LD 3-80, or latest revision thereof.

Hole
Applies to holes from any cause. A pin hole is approximately $\frac{1}{16}″$ in diameter.

Joints, tight
Distance between members shall not exceed those set forth in the following table:

Interior use exposed:
Premium grade	0.007″	Not to exceed 15% of the length of the joint
Custom grade	0.010″	Not to exceed 15% of the length of the joint
Economy grade	0.030″	Not to exceed 15% of the length of the joint

Interior use semi-exposed:
Premium grade	0.030″	Not to exceed 30% of the length of the joint
Custom grade	0.040″	Not to exceed 30% of the length of the joint
Economy grade	0.060″	Not to exceed 30% of the length of the joint

Exterior use exposed:
Premium grade	0.015″	Not to exceed 30% of the length of the joint
Custom grade	0.025″	Not to exceed 30% of the length of the joint
Economy grade	0.040″	Not to exceed 30% of the length of the joint

Kiln dried
Lumber dried in a closed chamber in which the removal of moisture is controlled by artificial heat and usually by controlled relative humidity.

Knocked down
Unassembled, as contrasted with assembled or built-up.

Knot, sound tight
A portion of a branch or a limb whose growth rings are partially or completely intertwined on the face with the growth rings of the surrounding wood. It shall not contain any decay and shall be so fixed by growth shape that it will retain its place in the piece. The average of the maximum and minimum dimensions of the knot on the exposed surface shall be used in measuring the size.

For plywood:
A pin knot does not exceed $\frac{1}{4}″$ in diameter.

For solid stock:
1. A small pin knot does not exceed $\frac{1}{4}″$ in diameter.
2. A pin knot does not exceed $\frac{1}{2}″$ in diameter.
3. A small knot is larger than $\frac{1}{2}″$ but does not exceed $\frac{3}{4}″$.

Laminated
Layer construction of lumber. May be either horizontal or vertical layers securely glued together.

Loose and long
Run to pattern only. Not assembled, nor machined for assembly, nor cut to length. The terms "material only" and "mill run" mean the same as "loose and long."

Low-pressure decorative polyester overlay
The overlays are comprised of polyester resin-saturated cellulosic sheets thermo-bonded to the particle board, hardboard, or plywood core. The face overlay shall contain a decorative color or printed design. The other side may have a suitable balance sheet bonded in the same manner. The resultant product has an attractive exposed surface that is durable and resistant to damage from abrasion and mild alkalies, acids, and solvents and shall meet the requirements of the following standards:
National Electrical Manufacturers Association LQ 1-77, General Purpose
Woodwork Institute of California Standards for Particle Board

Low-pressure laminated melamine

This material shall be melamine-saturated sheets thermal-fused to the particle board core that meets the WIC requirements. The material shall also meet the requirements of NEMA LQ 1-77, General Purpose.

Low-pressure polyester overlay cabinet liner

The overlays are comprised of polyester resin-saturated cellulosic sheets thermo-bonded to the particle board, hardboard, or plywood core. The resultant product has a solid color exposed surface that is durable and resistant to damage from abrasion and mild alkalies, acids, and solvents, and shall meet the requirements of the following standards:

National Electrical Manufacturers Association LQ 1-77 Light Duty

Woodwork Institute of California Standards for Particle Board

Machine run

Not sanded after machining.

Machined and knocked down

All pieces fully machined, ready for assembly.

Machined, smoothly

Free of defective manufacturing, with a minimum of 16 knife marks to the inch. Torn grain is not permitted. Handling marks and/or grain raising due to moisture shall not be considered a defect.

Material only

Run to pattern only. Not assembled, nor machined for assembly, nor cut to length. The terms "loose and long" and "mill run" mean the same as "material only."

Medium-density fiberboard

A dry-formed panel product manufactured from lignocellulosic fibers combined with a synthetic resin or other suitable binder. The panels are compressed to a density of 31 pounds per cubic foot to 50 pounds per cubic foot in a hot press by a process in which substantially the entire interfiber bond is created by the added binder. Other materials may have been added during manufacture to improve certain properties. The product shall meet the standards of National Particleboard Association NPA 4-73.

Member

An individual piece of solid stock or plywood that forms an item of millwork.

Mill run

Run to pattern only. Not assembled, nor machined for assembly, nor cut to length. The terms "material only" and "loose and long" mean the same as "mill-run."

Millwork

Architectural woodwork and related items as defined in Scope of Millwork.

Mineral streak

An olive greenish-black or brown discoloration of undetermined cause in hardwoods.

Moisture content

The weight of the water in the wood expressed in percentage of the weight of the oven-dry wood.

Molded edge

Edge of piece machined to any profile other than square or eased edge.

Nailed

Members secured together with nails, including power driven nails or staples. On exposed surfaces, staples shall run parallel to the grain.

Opaque finish

A paint or pigmented stain finish that hides the natural characteristics and color of the grain of the wood surface and is not transparent.

Particle board

A mat-formed flat panel consisting of particles of wood bonded together with a synthetic resin or other suitable binder. The particles are classified by size and dried to a uniform moisture content, after which they are mixed with a binder, mat-formed into a panel, compressed to proper density, and then cured under heat and pressure.

Patch

A repair made by inserting and securely gluing a sound piece of wood of the same species in place of a defect that has been removed. The edges shall be cut clean and sharp and fit tight with no voids. "Boat" patches are oval shaped with sides tapering in each direction to a point or to a small rounded end; "router" patches have parallel sides and rounded ends; "sled" patches are rectangular with feathered ends.

Pitch

An accumulation of resin that occurs in separations in the wood or in the wood cells themselves.

Pitch pocket

A well-defined opening between the annual growth rings, which contains pitch.

1. A very small pocket is a maximum of $1/16''$ in width X $3''$ (7.62 cm) in length, or $1/8''$ (0.32 cm) X $2''$ (5.08 cm) in length.

2. A small pocket is a maximum of $1/16''$ in width X $6''$ (15.24 cm) in length, or $1/8''$ in width X $4''$ (10.16 cm) in length.

3. A medium pocket is a maximum of $1/16''$ in width X $12''$ (30.40 cm) in length, or $1/8''$ in width by $8''$ (20.32 cm) in length.

Pitch streak

A well-defined accumulation of pitch in the wood cells in a more or less regular streak.

1. A very small pitch streak is a maximum of $1/16''$ in width X $12''$ in length, or $1/8''$ in width X $6''$ in length.

2. A small streak is a maximum of $1/8''$ in width X $12''$ in length, or $1/4''$ in width X $6''$ in length.

3. A medium streak is a maximum of $1/4''$ in width X $16''$ (40.64 cm) in length, or $3/8''$ (0.95 cm) in width X $12''$ in length.

Pith

A small, soft core occurring in the center of the log.

Plastic backing sheet

A thin sheet, usually phenolic, applied under pressure to the back of a laminated plastic panel to achieve balance by equalizing the rate of moisture absorption or emission.

Plow

A rectangular groove or slot of three surfaces cut parallel

with the grain of a wood member, in contrast to a dado, which is cut across the grain.

Plywood
A panel composed of a cross-banded assembly of layers or plies of veneer, or veneers in combination with a lumber core or particle board core, that are joined with an adhesive. Except for special constructions, the grain of alternate plies is always approximately at right angles, and the thickness and species on either side of the core are identical for balanced effect. An odd number of plies is always used.

Polyester decorative paper edging
A 2-or-more-ply, cured, polyester-saturated decorative paper a minimum of 12 mils in thickness. A high-viscosity hot-melt adhesive may be preapplied to the edging. The edging shall be applied to the panel with 375° to 450° heat and pressure. The surface shall withstand 500° temperature without blistering. The surface shall meet the requirements of NEMA LD 3-80. The adhesive, whether preapplied or not, shall be a pigment-extended, resin-modified, ethylene-vinyl acetate co-polymer base, hot-melted adhesive. Physical properties of this glue are

Viscosity a 200°	75M to 100 CPS
Ring and ball melting point	97° to 101°C
Penetrameter, 150 grs at 25°C	6.0 to 8.0

Polyvinyl edging
Application: Vinyl (PVC) edging on seamless rolls to be applied on single/double side edge banding machines using hot-melt adhesives. Specifications: Product to be calendered, of wood design, grained or smooth material solid color. Product to be chip proof, flame resistant, and impervious to moisture. Thickness of 0.45 mm (0.0177″), 0.40 mm (0.0157″), 0.60 mm (0.0256″) with tolerance of ±0.001″ and tear strength of approximately 1800 lb per sq in. Product to be antistatic and equipped with an adhesive agent for bonding.

Preservative
Noun: A treating solution that prevents decay in wood. Adjective: Having the ability to preserve wood by inhibiting the growth of decay fungi.

Rabbet
Rectangular cut, consisting of two surfaces cut on the edge of a member. A "rabbet" has two surfaces and a "plow" has three.

Raised grain
Roughened condition on surface of dressed lumber on which hard summerwood is raised above the softer springwood, but is not torn loose from it.

Ring, annual growth
The growth layer put on in a growth year.

Sanded, cross
Sanded across, rather than parallel to, the grain of a wood surface.

Sanded, machine
Sanded by drum or equivalent sander to remove knife or machine marks. Handling marks and/or grain raising due to moisture shall not be considered a defect.

Sanded, smoothly
Sanded sufficiently smooth so that sander marks will be concealed by painter's applied finish work. Handling marks and/or grain raising due to moisture shall not be considered a defect.

Sapwood
Wood occurring between the bark and the heart of the tree.

Sash
A single assembly of stiles and rails into a frame for holding glass, with or without dividing bars, to fill a given opening. It may be either open or glazed.

Scribe
To mark and cut an item of millwork so it will abut an uneven wall, floor, or other adjoining surface without any gaps.

Securely attached
Attached by nails or screws or by a groove or plow joint securely glued, forming a rigid assembly.

Self-edge
Application to the edge of plywood or particle board of a plastic laminate of the same pattern as the face surface.

Shake
A separation of the wood, normally between growth rings.

Solid stock
Solid, sound lumber (as opposed to plywood), which may be more than one piece of the same species, securely glued for width or thickness.

Solid stuck
A mold that is worked on the article itself, as opposed to an applied mold.

Sound
Absence of decay.

Species
A distinct kind of wood.

Specific gravity
A ratio of the weight of the body to the weight of an equal volume of water at some standard temperature.

Split
A separation of the wood due to the tearing apart of the wood cells.

1. A very short split is approximately as long as one-half the width of the piece.
2. A short split is approximately as long as the width of the piece.

Stain
A variation (normally blue or brown) from the natural color of the wood. It should not be confused with natural red heart.

1. Slight stain is a light color that is barely perceptible.
2. Medium stain is a pronounced discoloration.
3. Heavy stain is the darkest color that develops in lumber.

Surface check
The separation of a wood, normally occurring across the rings of annual growth, usually as a result of seasoning, and occuring only on one surface of the piece.

1. A fine surface check is not longer than 4″ (10.16 cm).
2. A small surface check is over 4″ and not longer than 6″.
3. A medium surface check is over 6″ but not longer than 8″.

Tenon
Projecting a tonguelike part of a wood member to be inserted into a slot (mortise) of another member to form a mortise and tenon joint.

Tongue
Projection on the edge or end of a wood member that is inserted into the groove or plow of a similar size to form a joint.

Top flat surface
The flat surface that can be sanded with a drum sander.

Torn grain
A roughened area caused by machine work in processing.

Transparent finish
A stain or a clear finish that allows the natural characteristics and color of the grain of the wood surface to show through the finish.

Twist
A distortion caused by the turning or winding of the edges of the surface so that the four corners of any face are no longer in the same plane.

Veneer
A thin sheet or layer of wood, usually rotary cut, sliced or sawn from a log or flitch. Thickness may vary from $\frac{1}{100}''$ to $\frac{1}{4}''$.

Veneer, quartered
Veneer in which a log is sliced or sawed to bring out certain figure produced by the medullary or pith rays, which are especially conspicuous in oak. The log is flitched in several different ways to allow the cutting of the veneer in a radial direction.

Veneer, rift cut
Veneer in which the rift or comb grain effect is obtained by cutting at an angle of about 15° off of the quartered position. Twenty-five percent of the exposed surface area of each piece of veneer may contain medullary ray flake.

Veneer, rotary cut
Veneer in which the entire log is centered in a lathe and is turned against a broad cutting knife that is set into the log at a slight angle.

Veneer, sliced
Veneer in which a log or sawn flitch is held securely in a slicing machine and is thrust downward into a large knife that shears off the veneer in sheets.

Vinyl
Heavy vinyl film a minimum of 4 mils in thickness. Opaque or reversed printed types have the following average property requirements:

Property	Value	Test procedure
Widths	50″ & 62″ (127.00 & 157.48 cm)	Measuring tape
Mil thickness	4, 6, 7, 8 mils	Caliper gauge
Light stability	300 hr no change	Fadeometer ASTM-E-42-64
Flame retardance	(Free film) Self-extinguishing	ASTM E-82-67
Gloss level	10–45	Gardner glossmeter
Flame spread	21–23 (laminated to asbestos board) 25 (laminated to treated FB)	ASTM E-84 tunnel test
Abrasion resistance	Reverse prints 30–45 Sandwich type 45–60 Opaques 25–60	MG Loss/1000 cycles on CS 10 wheel
	Reverse prints 6000–1100 Sandwich types 4000–8000	Cycles to print failure CS 17 wheel

Surface appearance is not affected when exposed to the following agents:

Water	Coffee	Olive oil
Alcohol	Mustard	Shoe polish
Washable inks	Crayon	Household detergents and soaps
Mercurochrome	Tea	Beet juice
		Vinegar

AHA	American Hardboard Association 887-B Wilmette Road Palatine, IL 60067
AHM	Appalachian Hardwood Manufacturers, Inc. P.O. Box 427 High Point, NC 27261
AITC	American Institute of Timber Construction 333 West Hampden Ave. Englewood, CO 80110
APA	American Plywood Association P.O. Box 11700 Tacoma, WA 98411
AWI	Architectural Woodwork Institute 2310 S. Walter Reed Dr. Arlington, VA 22206
AWPA	American Wood Preservers' Association 7735 Old Georgetown Rd. Suite 4444 Bethesda, MD 20014
AWPB	American Wood Preservers Bureau P.O. Box 6085 2772 South Randolph St. Arlington, VA 22206
AWPI	American Wood Preservers Institute 1651 Old Meadow Rd. McLean, VA 22101
CRA	California Redwood Association One Leonard Street San Francisco, CA 94111
HPMA	Hardwood Plywood Manufacturers Association P.O. Box 2789 Reston. VA 22090
MFMA	Maple Flooring Manufacturers Association 2400 E. Devon Des Plaines, IL 60018
NFPA	National Forest Products Association 1619 Massachusetts Ave. N.W. Washington, D.C. 20036
NHPMA	Northern Hardwood and Pine Manufacturers Association Northern Building Suite 501 Green Bay, WI 54301
NKCA	National Kitchen Cabinet Association 136 St. Matthews Ave. Louisville, KY 40207
NLMA	Northeastern Lumber Manufacturers Association Four Fundy Road Falmouth, ME 04105
NWMA	National Woodwork Manufacturers Association 205 W. Touhy Avenue Park Ridge, IL 60068
SFI	Southern Forest Institute 3395 Northeast Freeway Suite 380 Atlanta, GA 30341
SFPA	Southern Forest Products Association P.O. Box 52468 New Orleans, LA 70152
SHLMA	Southern Hardwood Lumber Manufacturers Association 805 Sterick Building Memphis, TN 38103
WIC	Woodwork Institute of California 1833 Broadway P.O. Box 11428 Fresno, CA 93773
WWPA	Western Wood Products Association Yeon Bldg. Portland, OR 97204

Chapter 3

WALLS, PARTITIONS, AND DOORS

BALLOON FRAMING

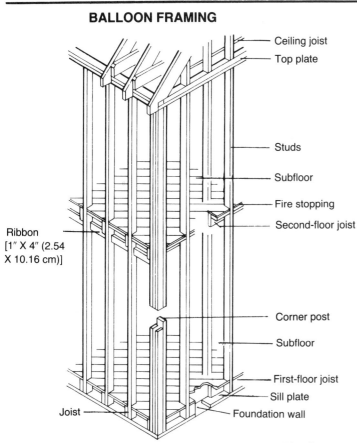

- Ceiling joist
- Top plate
- Studs
- Subfloor
- Fire stopping
- Second-floor joist

Ribbon
[1″ X 4″ (2.54 X 10.16 cm)]

- Corner post
- Subfloor
- First-floor joist
- Sill plate

Joist
- Foundation wall

The major difference between these two types of framing methods is evident where the first and second floors join. Note that in platform framing each floor is framed separately.

WESTERN PLATFORM FRAMING

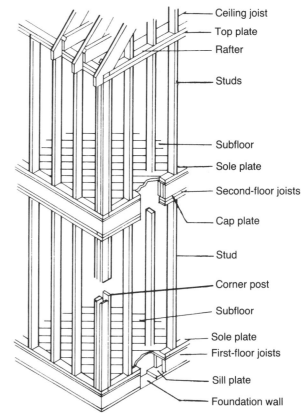

- Ceiling joist
- Top plate
- Rafter
- Studs
- Subfloor
- Sole plate
- Second-floor joists
- Cap plate
- Stud
- Corner post
- Subfloor
- Sole plate
- First-floor joists
- Sill plate
- Foundation wall

This construction method provides greater fire safety because each floor becomes a "fire stop." Balloon framing is seldom used in current building practices.

WALL STUD CONSTRUCTION

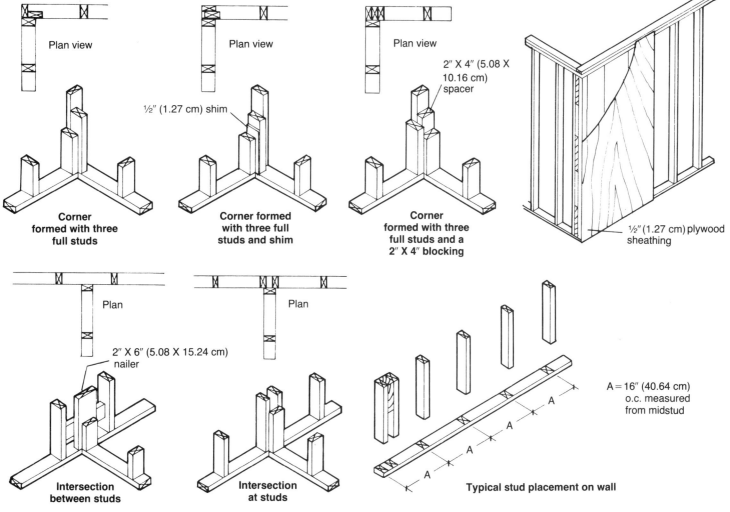

Plan view

Corner formed with three full studs

Plan view

½″ (1.27 cm) shim

Corner formed with three full studs and shim

Plan view

2″ X 4″ (5.08 X 10.16 cm) spacer

Corner formed with three full studs and a 2″ X 4″ blocking

½″ (1.27 cm) plywood sheathing

Plan

2″ X 6″ (5.08 X 15.24 cm) nailer

Intersection between studs

Plan

Intersection at studs

A = 16″ (40.64 cm) o.c. measured from midstud

Typical stud placement on wall

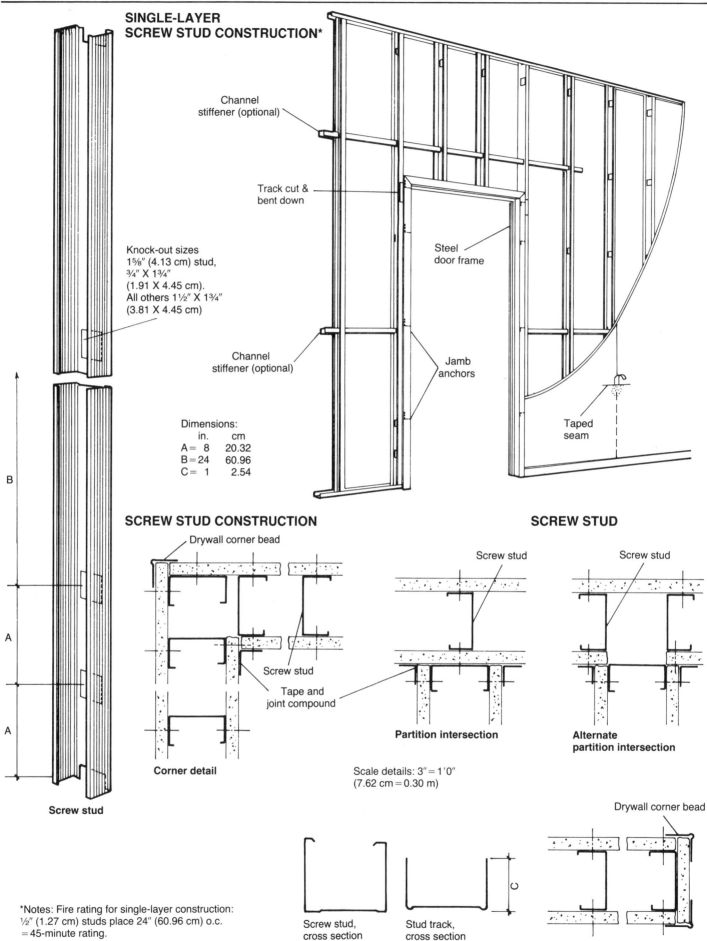

SINGLE-LAYER SCREW STUD CONSTRUCTION*

Channel stiffener (optional)

Track cut & bent down

Steel door frame

Jamb anchors

Taped seam

Channel stiffener (optional)

Knock-out sizes 1⅝″ (4.13 cm) stud, ¾″ X 1¾″ (1.91 X 4.45 cm). All others 1½″ X 1¾″ (3.81 X 4.45 cm)

Dimensions:
	in.	cm
A =	8	20.32
B =	24	60.96
C =	1	2.54

B

A

A

Screw stud

SCREW STUD CONSTRUCTION

Drywall corner bead

Screw stud

Tape and joint compound

Corner detail

SCREW STUD

Screw stud

Screw stud

Partition intersection

Alternate partition intersection

Scale details: 3″ = 1′0″ (7.62 cm = 0.30 m)

Screw stud, cross section

Stud track, cross section

C

Drywall corner bead

Partition end detail

*Notes: Fire rating for single-layer construction: ½″ (1.27 cm) studs place 24″ (60.96 cm) o.c. = 45-minute rating.

Fiberglass-filled cavity: ⅝″ (1.59 cm) studs = 1-hour rating.

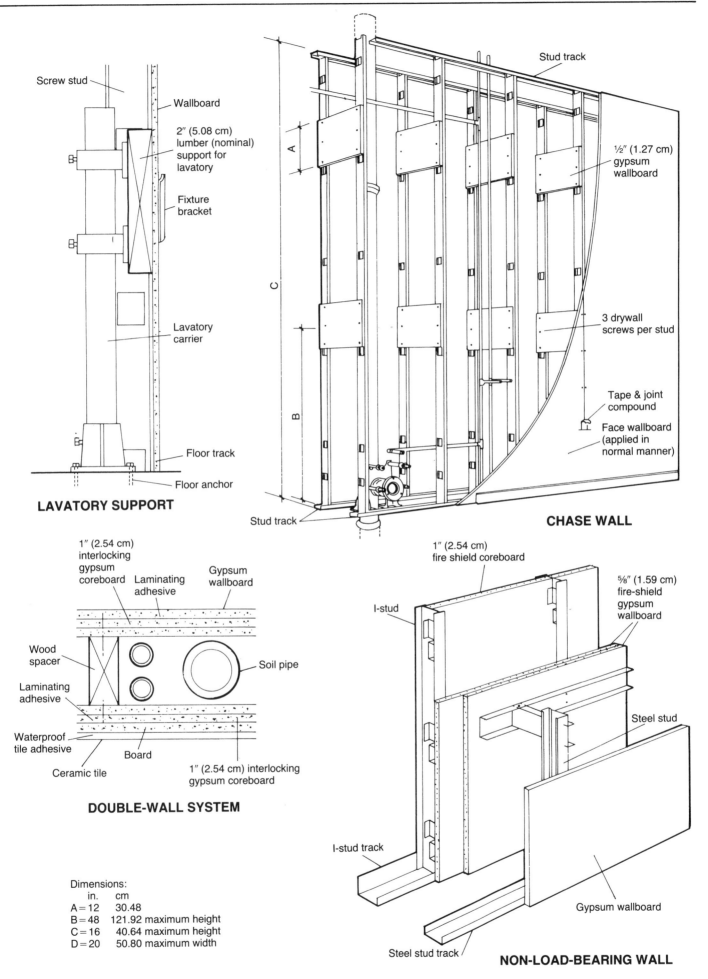

LAVATORY SUPPORT

Screw stud
Wallboard
2″ (5.08 cm) lumber (nominal) support for lavatory
Fixture bracket
Lavatory carrier
Floor track
Floor anchor

CHASE WALL

Stud track
½″ (1.27 cm) gypsum wallboard
3 drywall screws per stud
Tape & joint compound
Face wallboard (applied in normal manner)
Stud track

DOUBLE-WALL SYSTEM

1″ (2.54 cm) interlocking gypsum coreboard
Laminating adhesive
Gypsum wallboard
Wood spacer
Laminating adhesive
Waterproof tile adhesive
Ceramic tile
Board
Soil pipe
1″ (2.54 cm) interlocking gypsum coreboard

NON-LOAD-BEARING WALL

1″ (2.54 cm) fire shield coreboard
I-stud
5/8″ (1.59 cm) fire-shield gypsum wallboard
Steel stud
I-stud track
Gypsum wallboard
Steel stud track

Dimensions:
	in.	cm	
A =	12	30.48	
B =	48	121.92	maximum height
C =	16	40.64	maximum height
D =	20	50.80	maximum width

CEILING DETAILS

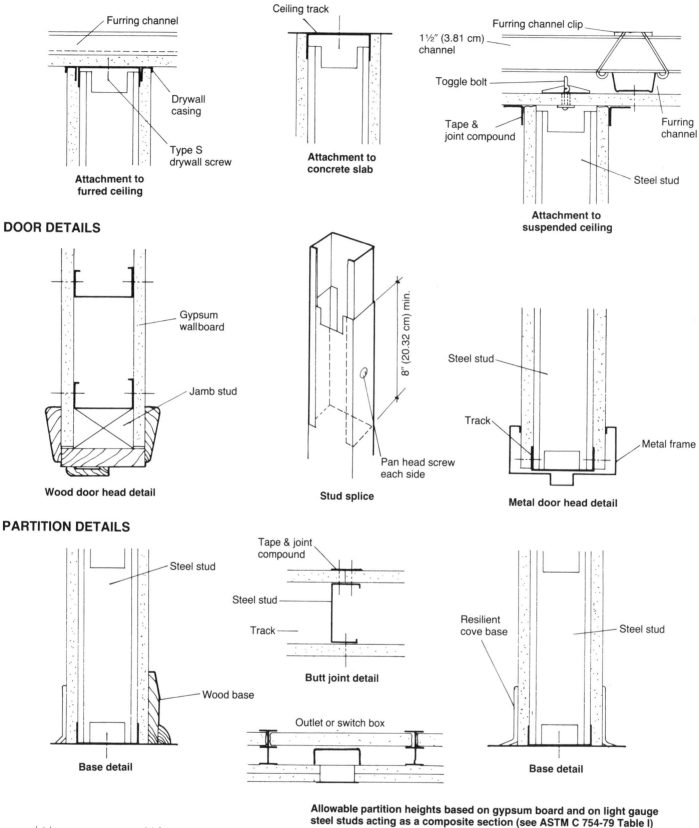

Furring channel

Drywall casing

Type S drywall screw

Attachment to furred ceiling

Ceiling track

Attachment to concrete slab

Furring channel clip

1½″ (3.81 cm) channel

Toggle bolt

Tape & joint compound

Furring channel

Steel stud

Attachment to suspended ceiling

DOOR DETAILS

Gypsum wallboard

Jamb stud

Wood door head detail

8″ (20.32 cm) min.

Pan head screw each side

Stud splice

Steel stud

Track

Metal frame

Metal door head detail

PARTITION DETAILS

Steel stud

Wood base

Base detail

Tape & joint compound

Steel stud

Track

Butt joint detail

Outlet or switch box

Resilient cove base

Steel stud

Base detail

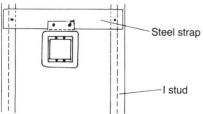

Steel strap

I stud

Electrical outlet support

Allowable partition heights based on gypsum board and on light gauge steel studs acting as a composite section (see ASTM C 754-79 Table I)

Stud spacing (in.)	Facing on each side (in.)	Stud depth (in.)			
		1⅝	2½	3⅝	4
		Height*			
16	½ one ply	11′0″	14′8″	19′5″	20′8″
24	½ one ply	10′0″	13′5″	17′3″	18′5″
24	½ two ply	12′4″	15′10″	19′5″	20′8″

*Heights may be varied by using deeper studs, closer spacing, or heavier gypsum board.

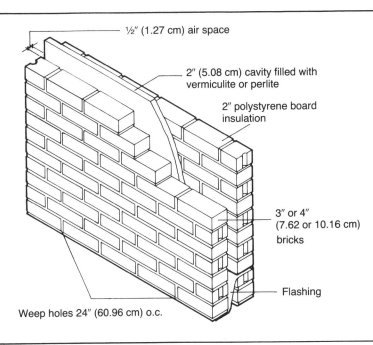

½" (1.27 cm) air space

2" (5.08 cm) cavity filled with vermiculite or perlite

2" polystyrene board insulation

3" or 4" (7.62 or 10.16 cm) bricks

Flashing

Weep holes 24" (60.96 cm) o.c.

CAVITY WALL

Common Residential Use: Single-family homes, townhouses, and garden apartments.

Principal Properties: Excellent resistance to rain penetration. Provides excellent thermal properties when the cavity is filled with waterproof insulation. High degree of sound resistance obtained with this wall. Check wall construction specifications for fire ratings.

Construction Advantages: Interior surfaces may be left exposed, eliminating the need for additional interior surfacing unless desired.

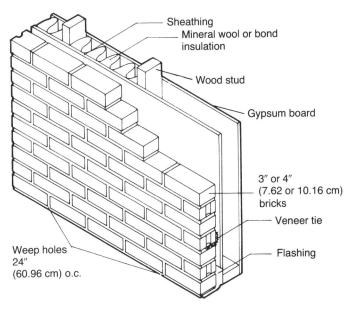

Sheathing

Mineral wool or bond insulation

Wood stud

Gypsum board

3" or 4" (7.62 or 10.16 cm) bricks

Veneer tie

Flashing

Weep holes 24" (60.96 cm) o.c.

BRICK VENEER WALL

Common Residential Use: Single-family homes, townhouses, and garden apartments.

Principal Properties: Brick veneer on frame provides an excellent combination of low maintenance and energy conservation. Excellent fire resistance achieved by the addition of brick veneer.

Construction Advantages: Brick veneer can be added to an existing building. The application can be accomplished in a relatively short time.

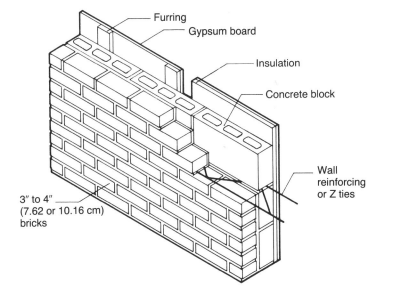

Furring

Gypsum board

Insulation

Concrete block

Wall reinforcing or Z ties

3" to 4" (7.62 or 10.16 cm) bricks

COMPOSITE BRICK & BLOCK WALL

Common Residential Use: Single-family homes, townhouses, and apartments. Usually used in a load-bearing capacity. May also be used as in-fill walls in mid- to highrise construction.

Principal Properties: Offers excellent fire resistance and sound insulation. Good resistance to rain penetration. Resists heat gain and loss.

Construction Advantages: This form of construction is less expensive than precast concrete or metal panels of similar quality.

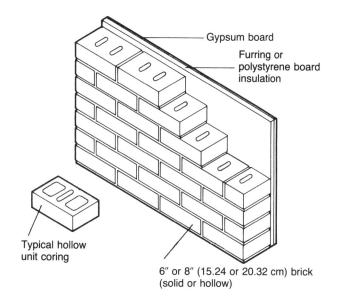

Gypsum board

Furring or polystyrene board insulation

Typical hollow unit coring

6″ or 8″ (15.24 or 20.32 cm) brick (solid or hollow)

SINGLE WYTHE WALL

Common Residential Use: Becoming popular as structural system for highrise apartments and condominiums. Can also be used for party walls in townhouses and other high-density developments.

Principal Properties: High compressive strength enables apartment construction of over 20 stories. Excellent fire resistance [4 hours for 8″ (20.32 cm) solid wall]. Excellent sound insulation Hollow units offer opportunity for extra insulation in cells.

Construction Advantages: Larger units increase mason productivity. Load-bearing apartment construction less expensive than concrete frame or steel frame construction. Construction time can be reduced since the shell of the building is constructed at the same time as the structural frame. Interior walls left exposed reduce maintenance costs.

ESTIMATING TABLES

Except for the nonmodular "standard" brick [3¾″ x 2¼″ x 8″ (9.53 x 5.72 x 20.32 cm)] and some oversize brick [3¾″ x 2¾″ x 8″ (9.53 x 6.99 x 20.32 cm)], virtually 100 percent of the brick produced and used in the United States is sized to fit the modular system. Even the standard brick is available also in modular size [(nominal dimensions 4″ X 2⅔″ X 8″ (10.16 X 7.49 X 20.32 cm)].

Because of its simplicity and accuracy, the most widely used estimating procedure is the "wall area" method. It consists simply of multiplying known quantities of material required per square foot by the net wall area (gross areas less areas of all openings).

Estimating material quantities is greatly simplified under the modular system. For a given nominal size, the number of modular masonry units per square foot of wall will be the same regardless of mortar joint thickness—assuming, of course, that the units are to be laid with the thickness of joint for which they are designed. There are only three standard modular joint thicknesses: ¼″, ⅜″, and ½″ (0.64, 0.95, 1.27 cm).

In the estimating procedure, determine the net quantities of *all* material before adding any allowances for waste. Allowances for waste and breakage vary, but, as a general rule, at least 5 percent should be added to the net brick quantities and 10 to 25 percent to the net mortar quantities. Particular job conditions or experience may dictate different factors.

The table below gives net quantities of brick and mortar required to construct walls one wythe in thickness with various modular brick sizes and the two most common joint thicknesses (⅜″ and ½″). Mortar quantities are for full bed and head joints.

Modular brick and mortar required for single wythe walls in running bond (no allowances for breakage or waste)

Nominal size of brick (in.)			Number of brick per 100 sq ft	Cubic feet of mortar			
				Per 100 sq ft		Per 1000 brick	
t	h	l		⅜″ joints	½″ joints	⅜″ joints	½″ joints
4 x 2⅔ x	8		675	5.5	7.0	8.1	10.3
4 x 3⅕ x	8		563	4.8	6.1	8.6	10.9
4 x 4 x	8		450	4.2	5.3	9.2	11.7
4 x 5⅓ x	8		338	3.5	4.4	10.2	12.9
4 x 2 x	12		600	6.5	8.2	10.8	13.7
4 x 2⅔ x	12		450	5.1	6.5	11.3	14.4
4 x 3⅕ x	12		375	4.4	5.6	11.7	14.9
4 x 4 x	12		300	3.7	4.8	12.3	15.7
4 x 5⅓ x	12		225	3.0	3.9	13.4	17.1
6 x 2⅔ x	12		450	7.9	10.2	17.5	22.6
6 x 3⅕ x	12		375	6.8	8.8	18.1	23.4
6 x 4 x	12		300	5.6	7.4	19.1	24.7

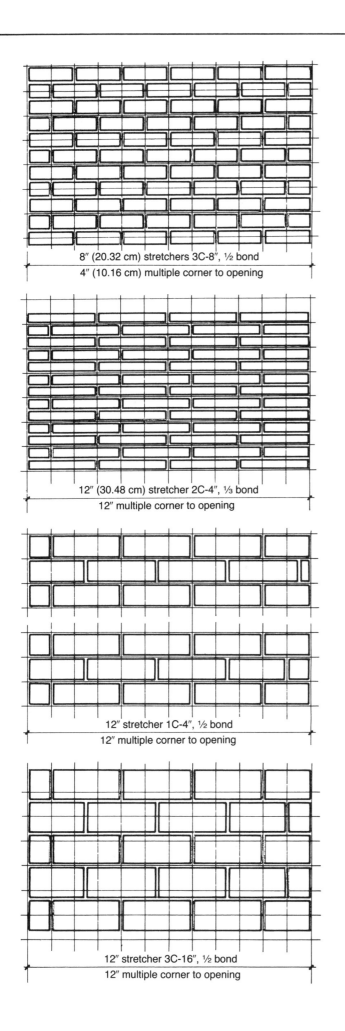

8" (20.32 cm) stretchers 3C-8", ½ bond
4" (10.16 cm) multiple corner to opening

12" (30.48 cm) stretcher 2C-4", ⅓ bond
12" multiple corner to opening

12" stretcher 1C-4", ½ bond
12" multiple corner to opening

12" stretcher 3C-16", ½ bond
12" multiple corner to opening

GRID LOCATION OF MASONRY WALLS

The drawings on the left show the grid locations of mortar joints in walls constructed with various modular units when walls are centered between grid lines. Note that all grid lines coincide with horizontal mortar joints for only 2" (5.08 cm) and 4" (10.16 cm) nominal heights, thus providing 4" flexibility.

The fact that alternate grid lines coincide with the mortar joints when the 2⅔" (7.49 cm) high brick is used provides a simple rule for determining the location of a grid line with respect to the masonry at any point above or below a given reference grid line. Any grid line that is an even multiple of 4" from the reference line will have the same relative position with respect to the masonry coursing, while any grid line that is an odd multiple of 4" will have the alternate position. This simple rule greatly simplifies the checking of course heights, particularly for lintels, where it is usually essential that the head of the opening coincide with a horizontal mortar joint.

A symmetrical grid location for walls is usually preferred to an unsymmetrical position. The correct symmetrical location (centered between grid lines or centered on a grid line) will often be influenced by the length of the masonry units to be used.

MORTAR JOINTS

Compression of the mortar makes the concave, V, and grapevine joints the most weather tight and acceptable for exterior use. The remaining six joint types are not recommended for exterior use. Joints should be tooled when the mortar is "thumbprint" hard.

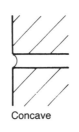

Concave

V

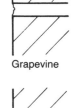

Grapevine

Weathered

Beaded

Struck

Flush

Raked

Extruded

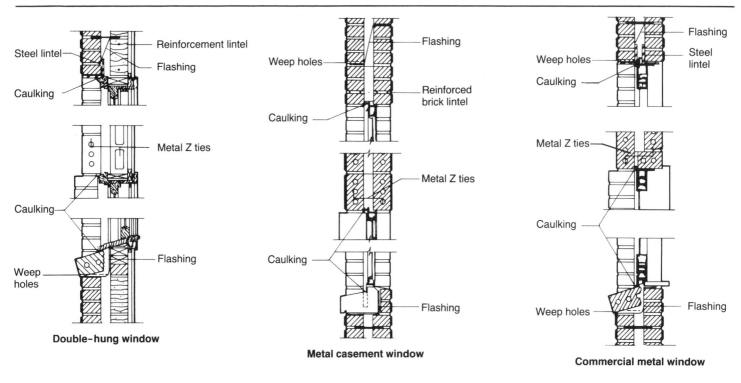

Double-hung window

Metal casement window

Commercial metal window

WINDOW & DOOR DETAILS

Stock sizes of windows and door frames are used in cavity walls, although sometimes additional blocking is needed for anchorage. Avoid solid masonry jambs at windows and doors in cavity walls. However, in steel windows the jamb must be partially solid to accept most standard jamb anchors. Wood or steel surrounds must be used to adapt nonmodular steel casement windows to modular cavity walls. Cavity wall ties spaced at 3′ (0.91 m) or less should be placed around all openings.

PERFORMANCE OF BRICK VENEER WALLS

This depends on six major factors: (1) an adequate foundation; (2) a sufficiently strong, rigid, well-balanced back-up system; (3) proper attachment of the veneer to the back-up system; (4) proper detailing; (5) the use of proper materials; and (6) good workmanship in the construction phase. The strength of brick veneer depends on the height of the veneer. In addition to its own weight, the only other weight a brick veneer should carry is a proportionate share of the lateral load. Brick veneer walls allow for drainage. It is essential that a 1″ (2.54 cm) clear space be maintained between the brick and back-up space.

ANCHORAGE OF WOOD ROOF FRAMING TO BRICK CAVITY WALLS

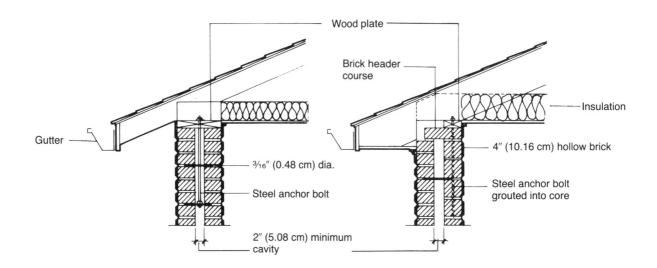

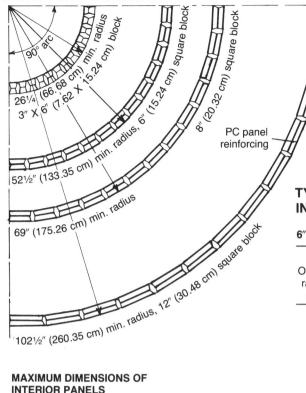

26¼" (66.68 cm) min. radius

3" X 6" (7.62 X 15.24 cm) block

52½" (133.35 cm) min. radius, 6" (15.24 cm) square block

69" (175.26 cm) min. radius

8" (20.32 cm) square block

PC panel reinforcing

90° arc

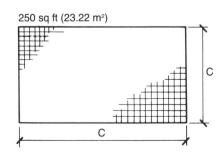

102½" (260.35 cm) min. radius, 12" (30.48 cm) square block

Glass block construction

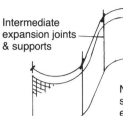

Intermediate expansion joints & supports

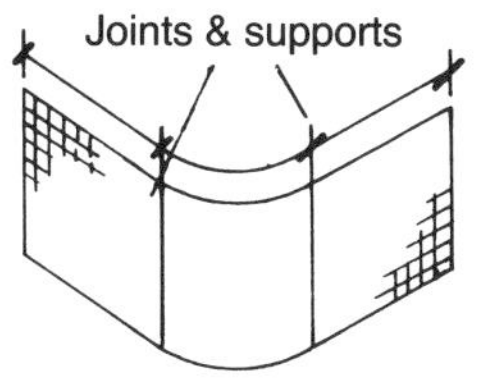

Joints & supports

Note: It is suggested that curved areas be separated from the flat areas by intermediate expansion joints and supports as indicated in the diagrams above.

TYPICAL CURVED INSTALLATIONS

6″ square

Outside radius (in.)	Number of blocks in 90° arc	Joint thickness (in.) Inside	Outside
52½	13	⅛	⅝
56¼	14	⅛	9/16
56¾	14	3/16	⅝
60	15	⅛	9/16
61	15	3/16	⅝
63¾	16	⅛	½
65	16	¼	⅝
67½	17	⅛	½
69	17	¼	⅝
71¼	18	⅛	7/16
73	18	5/16	⅝

No maximum limitations.
*Half the radius may be achieved with 3″ X 6″ rectangular block.

8″ square*

Outside radius (in.)	Number of blocks in 90° arc	Joint thickness (in.) Inside	Outside
69	13	⅛	⅝
74	14	⅛	9/16
74¾	14	3/16	⅝
79	15	⅛	⅝
80	15	¼	⅝
84	16	⅛	½
85¼	16	¼	⅝

No maximum limitations.
*Half the radius may be achieved with 4″ X 8″ and 4″ X 12″ rectangular blocks.

12″ square

Outside radius (in.)	Number of blocks in 90° arc	Joint thickness (in.) Inside	Outside
102	13	⅛	⅝

No maximum limitations.
*Radius given to closest ¼″. Joint thickness to closest 1/16″.

MAXIMUM DIMENSIONS OF INTERIOR PANELS

All interior panels should have a maximum height of 25′ (7.62 m). Panels over 144 sq ft (13.37 m²) must be properly braced to limit movement and settlement. Local building codes should be checked for possible limits on panel sizes and details.

DETAIL SECTIONS

RECOMMENDED SIZES FOR MAXIMUM AREA

100 sq ft (9.29 m²)

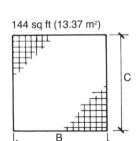

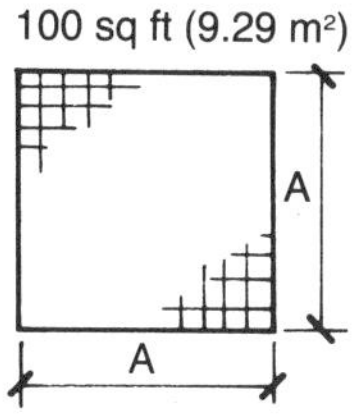

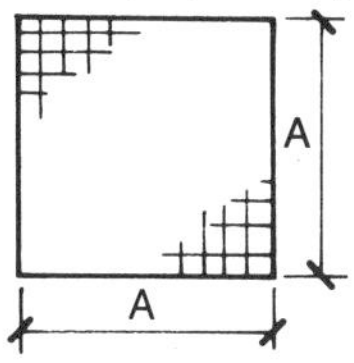

A
A

Dimensions:
A = 10′ (3.05 m) maximum
B = 15′ (4.57 m) maximum
C = 25′ (7.62 m) maximum

144 sq ft (13.37 m²)

C
B

250 sq ft (23.22 m²)

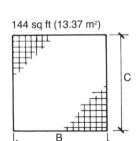

C
C

Metal channel
Plaster

Heads

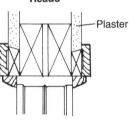

Plaster

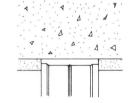

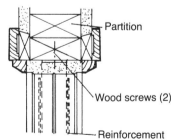

Anchors

Jambs

Partition

Wood screws (2)

Reinforcement

Masonry partition

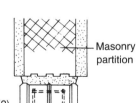

Sills

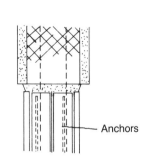

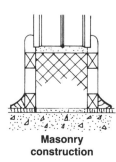

Masonry construction

Wood stud construction

Masonry construction

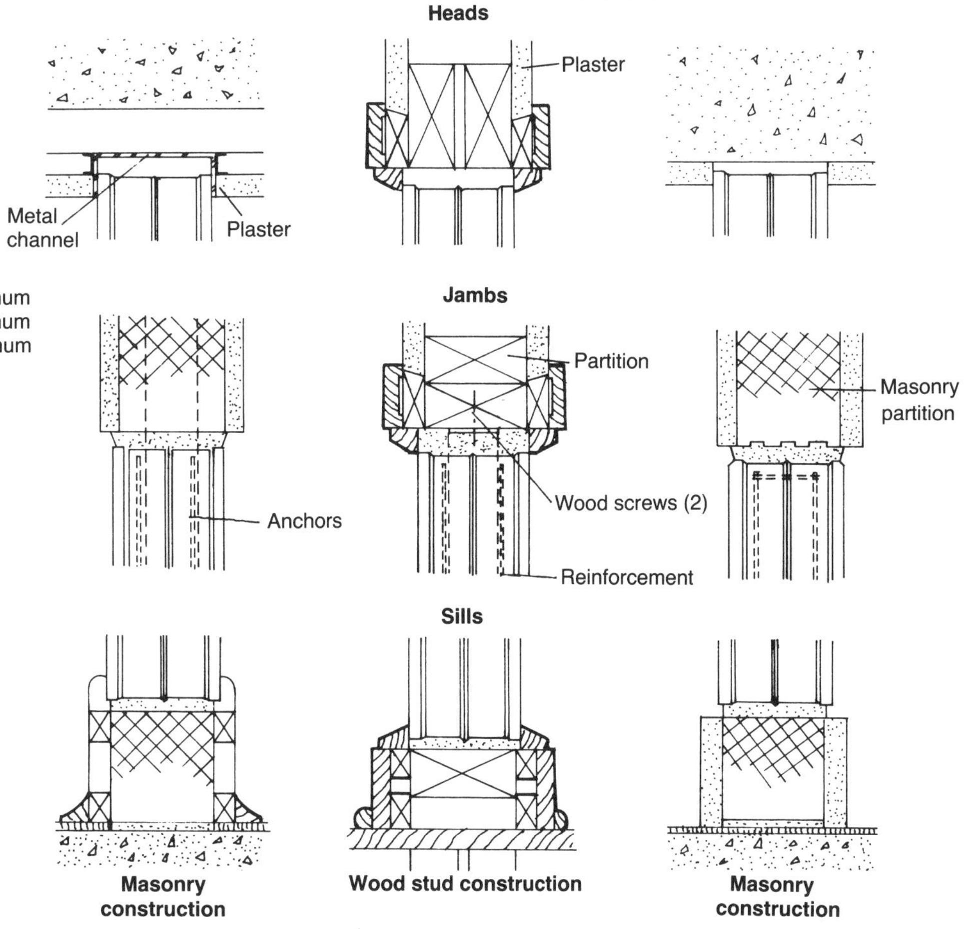

OPERABLE PARTITIONS

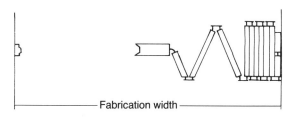

Single, fixed-jamb door partition;
attached permanently to either jamb

Joining pair;
fixed to jambs on both sides

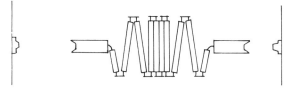

Double-end post partition;
stacks & latches at either jamb

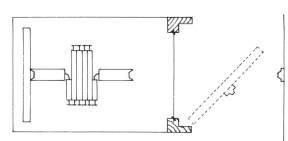

Partition concealed in pocket

Notes: Fire codes usually require that a solid wall or smoke partition be provided at maximum intervals of 300' (91.44 m).
    Partitions in flexible-plan schools may be rearranged periodically if the authority with jurisdiction approves plan revisions.

X TYPE OF FOLDING PARTITIONS

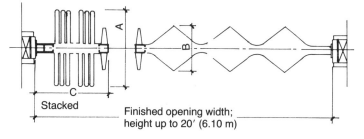

Stacked

Finished opening width;
height up to 20' (6.10 m)

Double-jamb partition

Dimensions:

	in.	cm
A =	9 to 13	22.86 to 33.02
B =	7 to 10	17.78 to 25.40
C =	1¾ to 2⅛ per foot	4.45 to 5.40 cm per 30.48 cm of partition

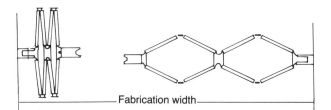

Fabrication width

Single, fixed-jamb partition;
stacks permanently at either jamb

Floating posts

  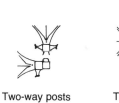   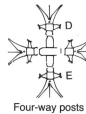

Two-way posts   Three-way posts   Four-way posts

Note: Floating posts can stack
in either D or E position

Ceiling mounting

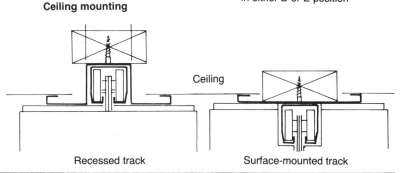

Ceiling

Recessed track   Surface-mounted track

COILING PARTITION

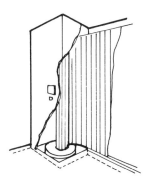

Typical coil box

Extruded
aluminum jamb

Foam-filled
nose molding

Wood slats

Detail

Ceiling-hung, coil partitions are constructed of tongue-and-groove wood slats and/or aluminum rods. May be operated manually or mechanically. Extended lengths depend on method of operation. Coil box sizes range from 4' to 6' (1.21 to 1.82 m) in diameter.

TYPICAL INSTALLATIONS

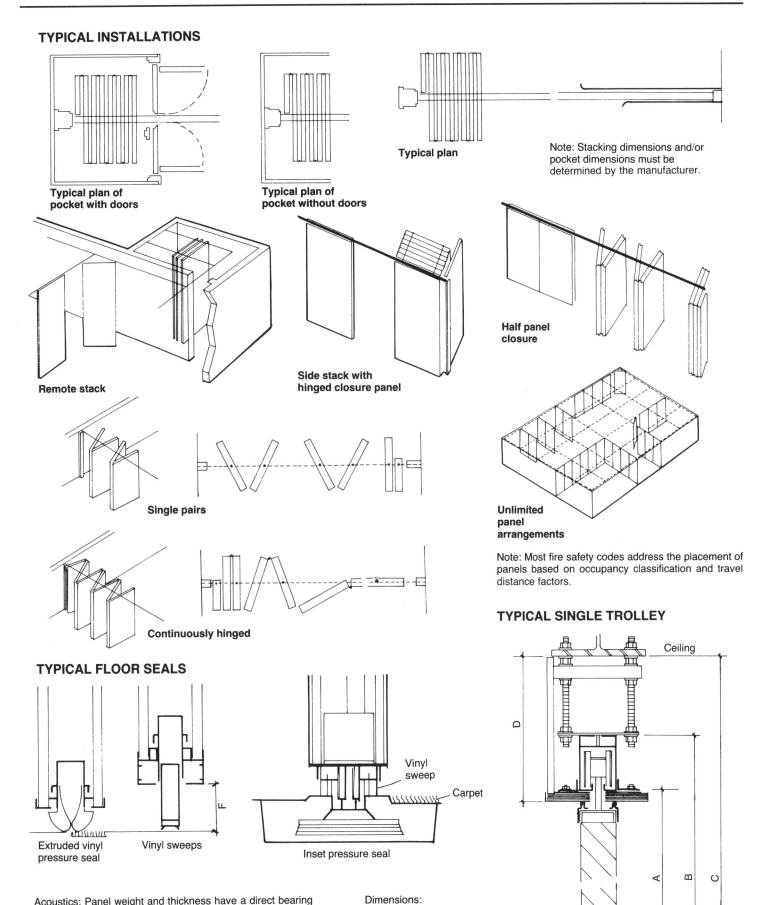

Typical plan of pocket with doors

Typical plan of pocket without doors

Typical plan

Note: Stacking dimensions and/or pocket dimensions must be determined by the manufacturer.

Remote stack

Side stack with hinged closure panel

Half panel closure

Single pairs

Continuously hinged

Unlimited panel arrangements

Note: Most fire safety codes address the placement of panels based on occupancy classification and travel distance factors.

TYPICAL FLOOR SEALS

Extruded vinyl pressure seal

Vinyl sweeps

Inset pressure seal

Vinyl sweep

Carpet

TYPICAL SINGLE TROLLEY

Ceiling

Floor

Acoustics: Panel weight and thickness have a direct bearing on the Sound Transmission Class (STC) and the Noise Reduction Coefficient (NRC) rating. Average single-trolley STC rating: 23 to 54. Designer should specify NRC for either one or both sides of panel. Tests: ASTM E90-70 (STC) and ASTM C423-66 (NRC).

Dimensions:
A = ceiling height
B = fabrication height
C = suspension height
D = 11¼″ (28.58 cm) min.
E = 3″ (7.62 cm)
F = 2½″ (6.35 cm)

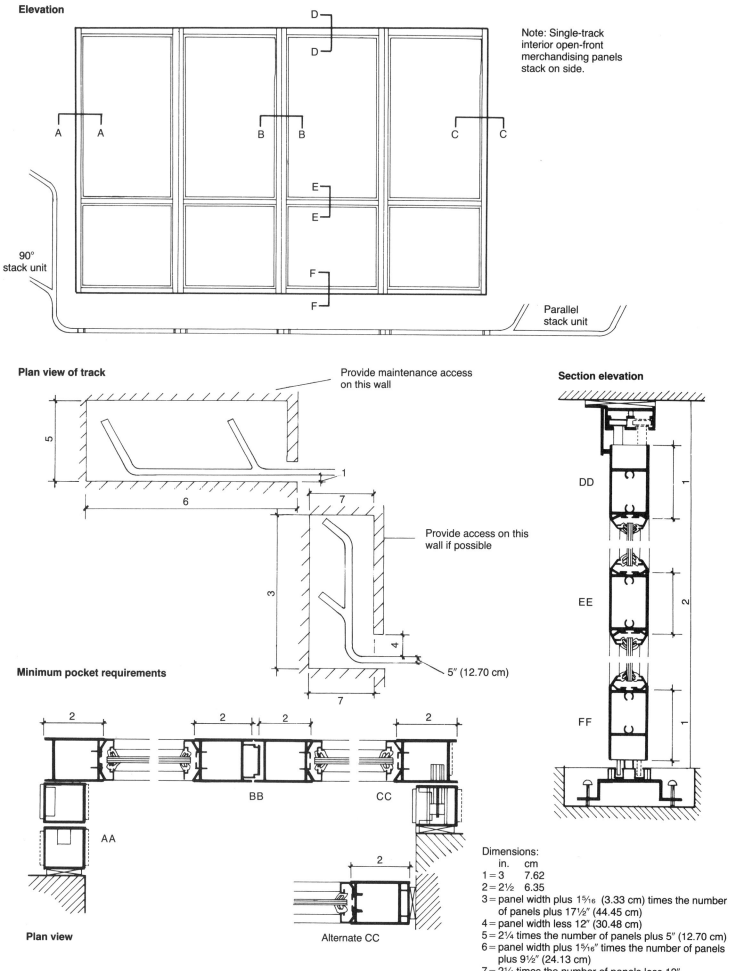

Elevation

D
D

Note: Single-track interior open-front merchandising panels stack on side.

A   A

B   B

C   C

E
E

90°
stack unit

F
F

Parallel stack unit

Plan view of track

Provide maintenance access on this wall

5

1

6

7

3

Provide access on this wall if possible

4

5″ (12.70 cm)

7

Section elevation

DD

1

EE

2

FF

1

Minimum pocket requirements

2

2   2

2

BB

CC

AA

2

Alternate CC

Plan view

Dimensions:
in.   cm
1 = 3   7.62
2 = 2½   6.35
3 = panel width plus 1⁵⁄₁₆ (3.33 cm) times the number of panels plus 17½″ (44.45 cm)
4 = panel width less 12″ (30.48 cm)
5 = 2¼ times the number of panels plus 5″ (12.70 cm)
6 = panel width plus 1⁵⁄₁₆″ times the number of panels plus 9½″ (24.13 cm)
7 = 2¼ times the number of panels less 12″

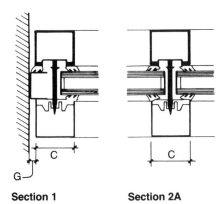

Section 1   **Section 2A**

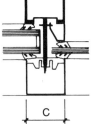

Section 2B

INSULATED STORE FRONT SYSTEMS

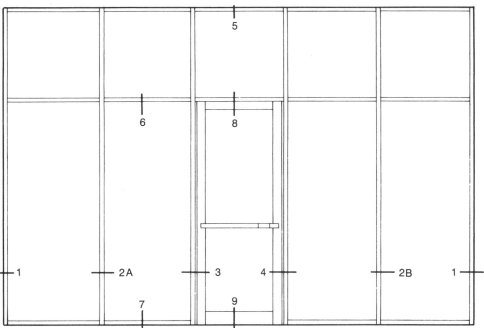

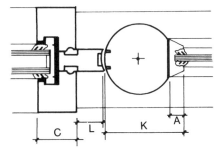

Section 3

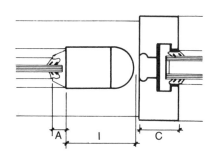

Section 4

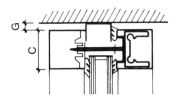

Section 5

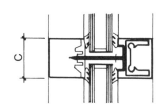

Section 6

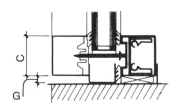

Section 7

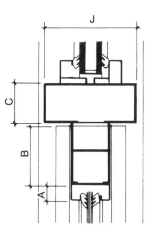

Section 8

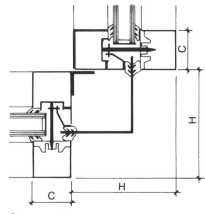

Section 9

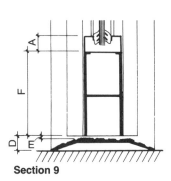

Corner post

Dimensions:

	in.	cm		in.	cm
A =	⅝	1.59	G =	¼	0.64
B =	2½	6.35	H =	4½	11.43
C =	1¾	4.45	I =	3	7.62
D =	½	1.27	J =	4	10.16
E =	3⁄16	0.48	K =	2¾	6.99
F =	3½	8.89	L =	1	2.54

Notes: Glazing is 1″ (2.54 cm) thick.
Door sizes:
Height: 84″   (213.36 cm)
Widths: 36″   (91.44 cm) or 42″ (106.68 cm) for single door
Widths: 72″   (182.88 cm) or 84″ (213.36 cm) for double doors

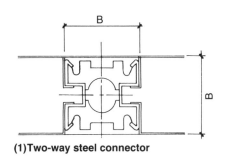

(1)Two-way steel connector

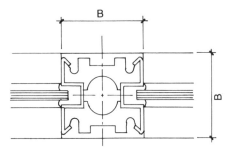

(2)Two-way glass connection

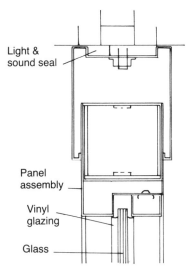

Light & sound seal

Panel assembly

Vinyl glazing

Glass

(3)Glass at ceiling

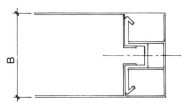

(4)Finished wall end

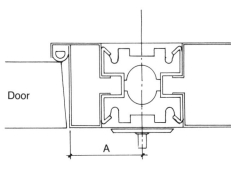

Door

(5)Two-way connector at door jamb

Elevation

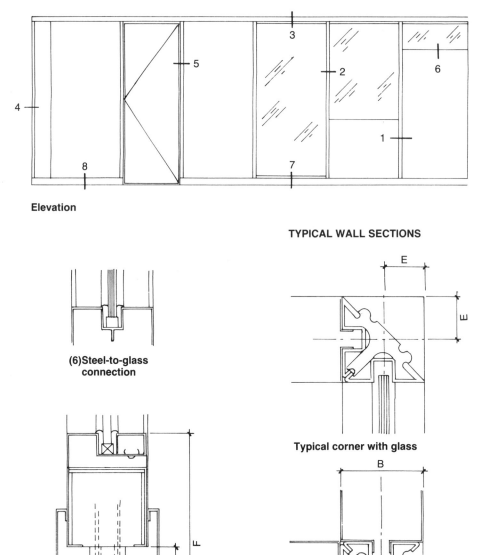

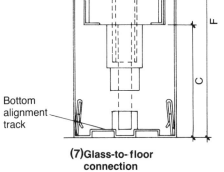

(6)Steel-to-glass connection

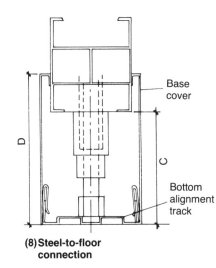

Bottom alignment track

(7)Glass-to-floor connection

Base cover

Bottom alignment track

(8)Steel-to-floor connection

TYPICAL WALL SECTIONS

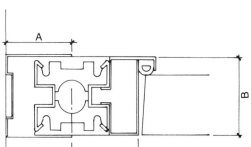

Typical corner with glass

Typical three-way steel wall connection

Typical wall end at door jamb

Dimensions:

	in.	cm		in.	cm
A =	2	5.08	D =	4	10.16
B =	2¼	5.72	E =	1⅛	2.86
C =	3	7.62	F =	6	15.24

Vertical sections

Elevation

Plan sections

Vertical section

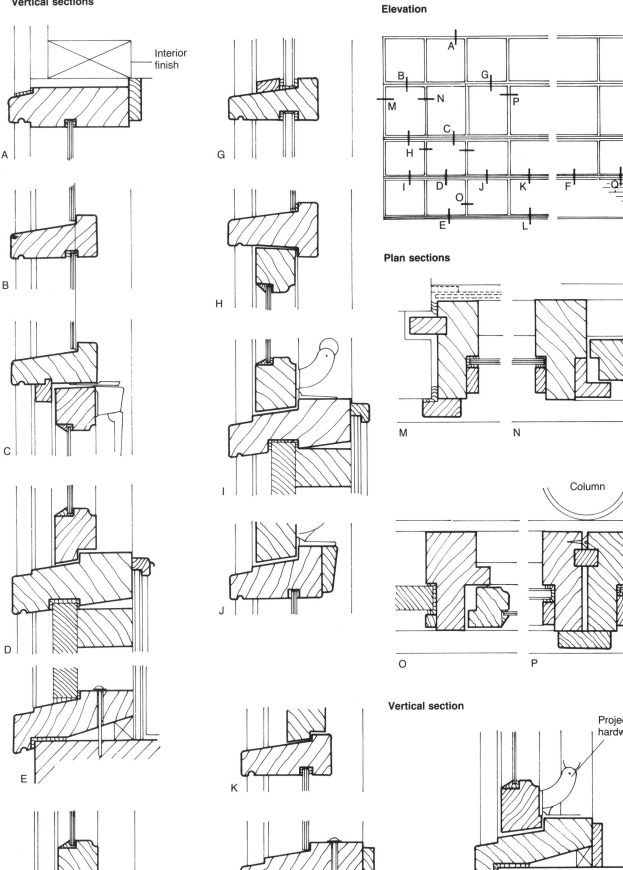

Interior finish

A

B

C

D

E

F

G

H

I

J

K

L

M

N

Column

O

P

Projecting hardware

Q

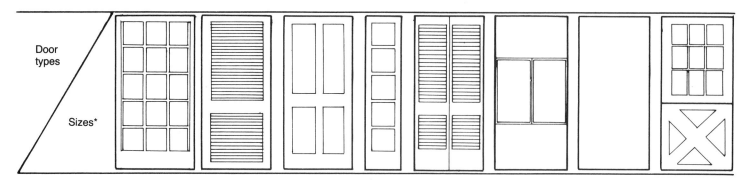

ft	Width in.	cm	Sash (French)	Louver	Panel	Side-lights	Bifold	Cafe	Flush exterior	Dutch
1	0	30.48				X	X			
1	2	35.56				X	X			
1	4	40.64				X	X			
1	6	45.72		X	X	X	X			
1	8	50.80		X	X		X			
1	10	55.88		X			X			
2	0	60.96		X	X					
2	4	71.12		X	X		X			
2	6	76.20	X	X	X			X	X	X
2	8	81.28	X	X	X			X	X	X
3	0	91.44	X	X	X			X	X	X

*Standard door heights range from 96″ to 120″ (243.84 to 304.80 cm).

INSTALLATION CHECKLIST

1. Hang door
   a. Butts, hinges, pivots, or floor closers
   b. Floor closers & butt hinges (should be listed after butts or pivots)
   c. Threshold
   d. Track & hangers
2. Lock the door (pairs of doors only)
   Inactive leaf
   a. Flush (automatic or manual) or surface bolts, indicate if a dustproof strike is required
   b. Exit device or two-point lock
   c. Cremone bolts (locking devices for French doors)
   Active leaf
   d. Lockset
   e. Exit device or 3-point lock
   f. Threshold (when furnished by exit device manufacturer)
   g. Dead lock
3. Operating trim
   a. Door pulls
   b. Push plates
   c. Push & pull bars
4. Exit device accessories (pairs of doors only)
   a. Mullion
   b. Coordinator times carry bar
   c. Astragal (molding strip cover)

5. Closing devices
   a. Surface or concealed overhead closers
   b. Mounting brackets, as required
6. Door controls
   a. Overhead door holders
   b. Electromagnetic holders
   c. Smoke detectors
7. Protective plates & trim
   a. Kick or armor plates
   b. Mop plates
   c. Stretcher plates
   d. Door edges
8. Stops & holders
   a. Floor & base stops
   b. Wall bumpers
9. Special accessories
   a. Thresholds (when not cut or fitted for floor closers or exit devices)
   b. Weather stripping
10. Miscellaneous
    a. Door silencers
    b. Room number
    c. Door knockers
    d. Card holders
    e. Letter box plates
    f. Key control cabinets
    g. Electromechanical hardware (not listed elsewhere)

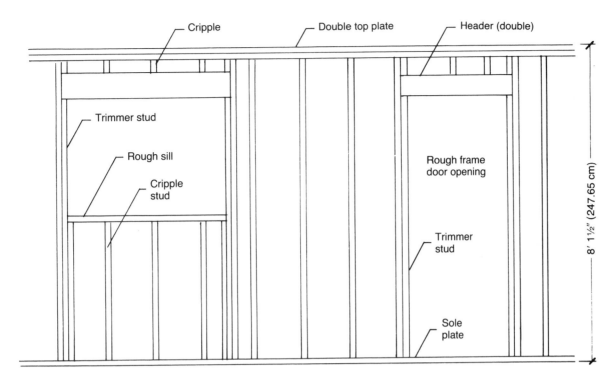

Platform framing with studs 16″ (40.64 cm) o.c.

Specifications for entrance construction should include the following measurements:

1. Rough opening of the width: In wood frame construction, measure between the entrance opening double studs. For masonry walls, measure from the header or lintel for the extreme edge, nose, or lip of the door sill.

2. For overall width, measure between the outside casing or pilaster edges. For overall height, measure between the upper edges of the entrance head.
3. Height and width of sidelights.

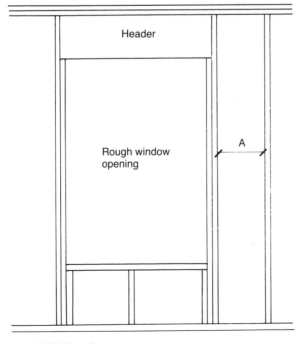

A = 14″ (35.56 cm)

Trussed headers increase support strength & span

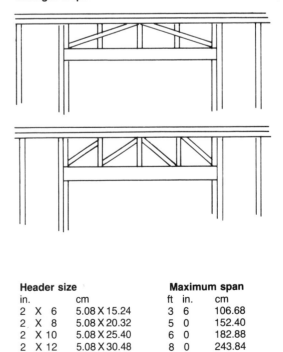

Header size		Maximum span		
in.	cm	ft	in.	cm
2 X 6	5.08 X 15.24	3	6	106.68
2 X 8	5.08 X 20.32	5	0	152.40
2 X 10	5.08 X 25.40	6	0	182.88
2 X 12	5.08 X 30.48	8	0	243.84

SOLID CORE DOORS

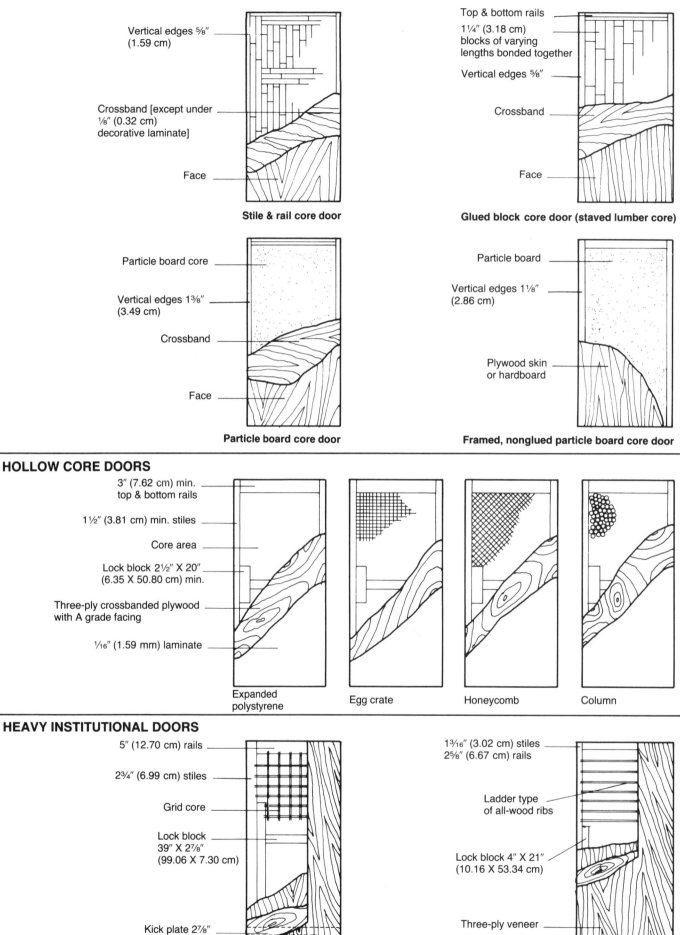

Vertical edges ⅝″ (1.59 cm)

Crossband [except under ⅛″ (0.32 cm) decorative laminate]

Face

Stile & rail core door

Top & bottom rails 1¼″ (3.18 cm) blocks of varying lengths bonded together

Vertical edges ⅝″

Crossband

Face

Glued block core door (staved lumber core)

Particle board core

Vertical edges 1⅜″ (3.49 cm)

Crossband

Face

Particle board core door

Particle board

Vertical edges 1⅛″ (2.86 cm)

Plywood skin or hardboard

Framed, nonglued particle board core door

HOLLOW CORE DOORS

3″ (7.62 cm) min. top & bottom rails

1½″ (3.81 cm) min. stiles

Core area

Lock block 2½″ X 20″ (6.35 X 50.80 cm) min.

Three-ply crossbanded plywood with A grade facing

1/16″ (1.59 mm) laminate

Expanded polystyrene

Egg crate

Honeycomb

Column

HEAVY INSTITUTIONAL DOORS

5″ (12.70 cm) rails

2¾″ (6.99 cm) stiles

Grid core

Lock block 39″ X 2⅞″ (99.06 X 7.30 cm)

Kick plate 2⅞″

1³/₁₆″ (3.02 cm) stiles
2⅝″ (6.67 cm) rails

Ladder type of all-wood ribs

Lock block 4″ X 21″ (10.16 X 53.34 cm)

Three-ply veneer

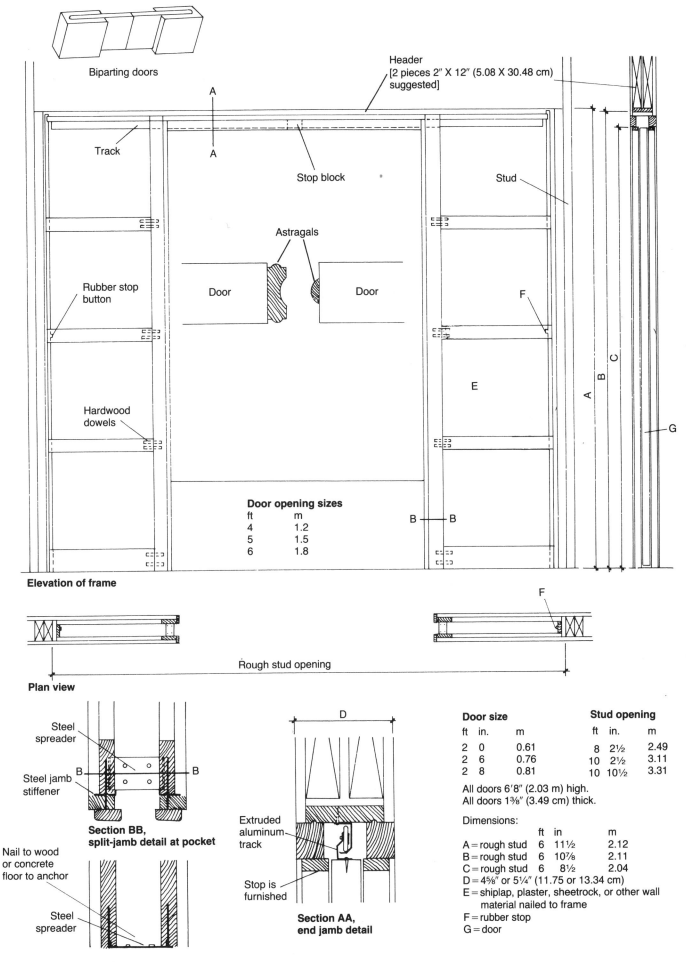

Biparting doors

Header
[2 pieces 2″ X 12″ (5.08 X 30.48 cm)
suggested]

Track

Stop block

Stud

Astragals

Door

Door

Rubber stop
button

F

Hardwood
dowels

E

A

B

C

G

Door opening sizes
ft	m
4	1.2
5	1.5
6	1.8

B — B

Elevation of frame

F

Rough stud opening

Plan view

Steel
spreader

Steel jamb
stiffener

B — B

**Section BB,
split-jamb detail at pocket**

Nail to wood
or concrete
floor to anchor

Steel
spreader

Jamb detail at floor line

D

Extruded
aluminum
track

Stop is
furnished

**Section AA,
end jamb detail**

Door size			Stud opening		
ft	in.	m	ft	in.	m
2	0	0.61	8	2½	2.49
2	6	0.76	10	2½	3.11
2	8	0.81	10	10½	3.31

All doors 6′8″ (2.03 m) high.
All doors 1⅜″ (3.49 cm) thick.

Dimensions:

		ft	in	m
A =	rough stud	6	11½	2.12
B =	rough stud	6	10⅞	2.11
C =	rough stud	6	8½	2.04

D = 4⅝″ or 5¼″ (11.75 or 13.34 cm)
E = shiplap, plaster, sheetrock, or other wall
    material nailed to frame
F = rubber stop
G = door

HISTORIC ENTRANCE MOTIFS, WITH DIMENSIONS

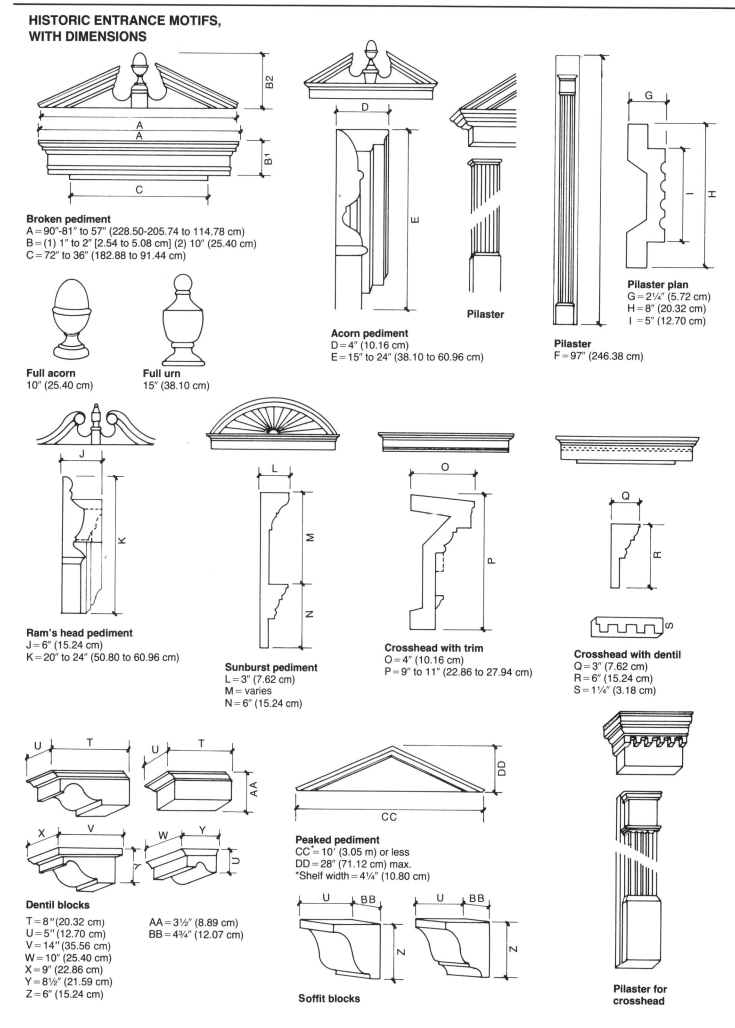

Broken pediment
A = 90″-81″ to 57″ (228.50-205.74 to 114.78 cm)
B = (1) 1″ to 2″ [2.54 to 5.08 cm] (2) 10″ (25.40 cm)
C = 72″ to 36″ (182.88 to 91.44 cm)

Full acorn
10″ (25.40 cm)

Full urn
15″ (38.10 cm)

Pilaster

Acorn pediment
D = 4″ (10.16 cm)
E = 15″ to 24″ (38.10 to 60.96 cm)

Pilaster plan
G = 2¼″ (5.72 cm)
H = 8″ (20.32 cm)
I = 5″ (12.70 cm)

Pilaster
F = 97″ (246.38 cm)

Ram's head pediment
J = 6″ (15.24 cm)
K = 20″ to 24″ (50.80 to 60.96 cm)

Sunburst pediment
L = 3″ (7.62 cm)
M = varies
N = 6″ (15.24 cm)

Crosshead with trim
O = 4″ (10.16 cm)
P = 9″ to 11″ (22.86 to 27.94 cm)

Crosshead with dentil
Q = 3″ (7.62 cm)
R = 6″ (15.24 cm)
S = 1¼″ (3.18 cm)

Dentil blocks

T = 8″ (20.32 cm)
U = 5″ (12.70 cm)
V = 14″ (35.56 cm)
W = 10″ (25.40 cm)
X = 9″ (22.86 cm)
Y = 8½″ (21.59 cm)
Z = 6″ (15.24 cm)

AA = 3½″ (8.89 cm)
BB = 4¾″ (12.07 cm)

Peaked pediment
CC* = 10′ (3.05 m) or less
DD = 28″ (71.12 cm) max.
*Shelf width = 4¼″ (10.80 cm)

Soffit blocks

Pilaster for crosshead

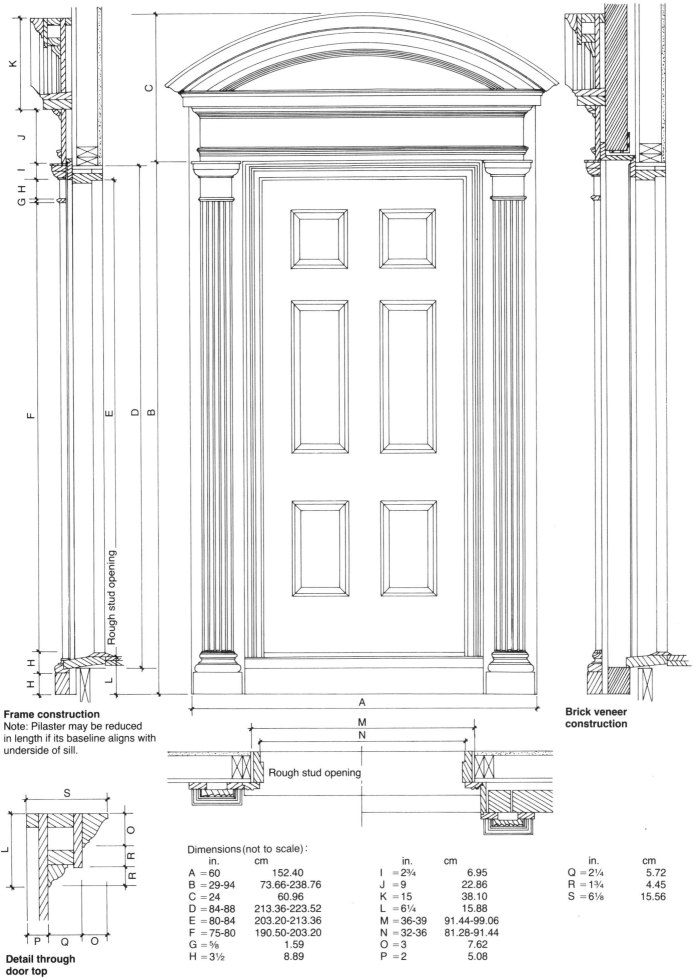

Frame construction
Note: Pilaster may be reduced
in length if its baseline aligns with
underside of sill.

**Brick veneer
construction**

**Detail through
door top**

Rough stud opening

Rough stud opening

Dimensions (not to scale):

	in.	cm		in.	cm		in.	cm
A =	60	152.40	I =	2¾	6.95	Q =	2¼	5.72
B =	29-94	73.66-238.76	J =	9	22.86	R =	1¾	4.45
C =	24	60.96	K =	15	38.10	S =	6⅛	15.56
D =	84-88	213.36-223.52	L =	6¼	15.88			
E =	80-84	203.20-213.36	M =	36-39	91.44-99.06			
F =	75-80	190.50-203.20	N =	32-36	81.28-91.44			
G =	⅝	1.59	O =	3	7.62			
H =	3½	8.89	P =	2	5.08			

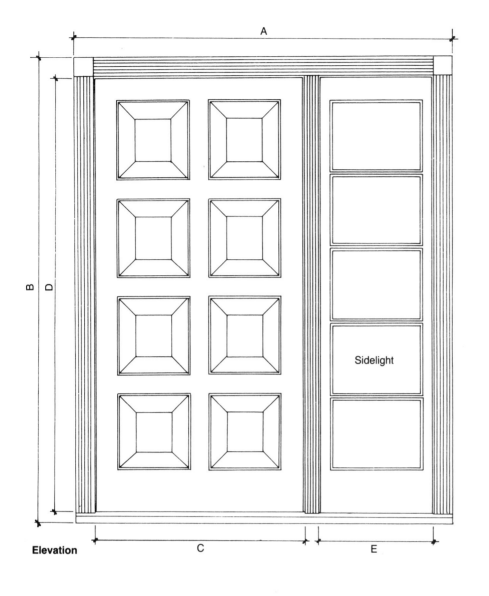

Sidelight

Elevation

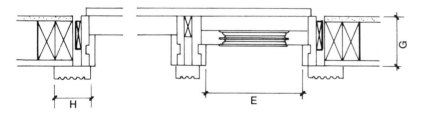

Plan

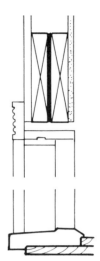

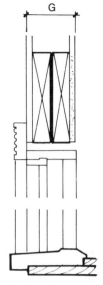

Section through head & sill at door

Section through head & sill at sidelight

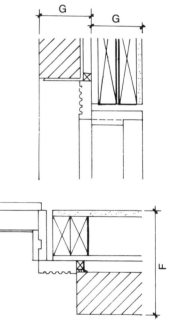

Plan details
When door is installed with brick or masonry, it should be set flush with plaster line on the inside

Specifications for exterior sidelights

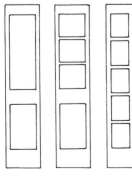

1⅜ sidelights

	in.	cm
Stiles (minimum)	1⅔	4.23
Top rail	4½	11.43
Lock rail	7½	19.05
Bottom rail	9¾	24.77
Panels, raised	½	1.27

Dimensions:

		in.	cm
A	=	72	182.88
B	=	84	213.36
C	=	40	101.60
D	=	80	203.20
E	=	22	55.88
F	=	10	25.40
G	=	4	10.16
H	=	3½	8.89

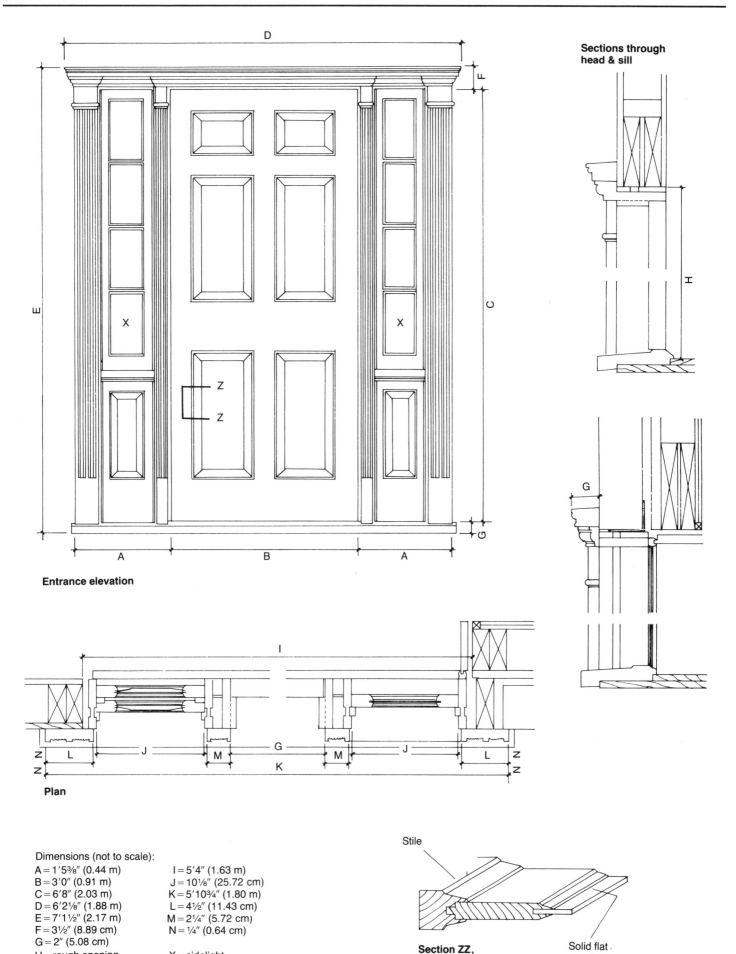

Sections through head & sill

Entrance elevation

Plan

Dimensions (not to scale):
A = 1′5⅜″ (0.44 m)   I = 5′4″ (1.63 m)
B = 3′0″ (0.91 m)   J = 10⅛″ (25.72 cm)
C = 6′8″ (2.03 m)   K = 5′10¾″ (1.80 m)
D = 6′2⅛″ (1.88 m)   L = 4½″ (11.43 cm)
E = 7′1½″ (2.17 m)   M = 2¼″ (5.72 cm)
F = 3½″ (8.89 cm)   N = ¼″ (0.64 cm)
G = 2″ (5.08 cm)
H = rough opening   X = sidelight
     6′11″ (2.11 m)

Stile

Solid flat panel

Section ZZ, Inner frame

DOOR CONSTRUCTION DETAILS

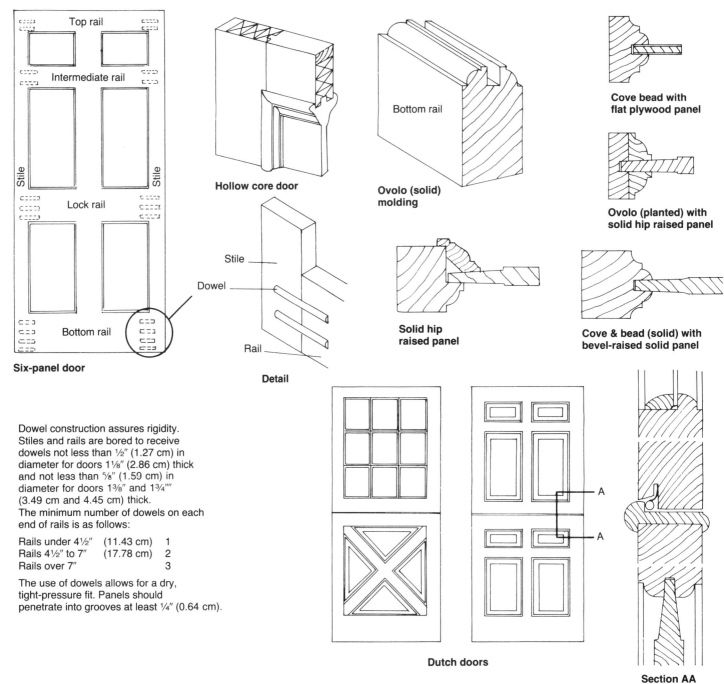

Six-panel door

Hollow core door

Detail

Ovolo (solid) molding

Solid hip raised panel

Cove bead with flat plywood panel

Ovolo (planted) with solid hip raised panel

Cove & bead (solid) with bevel-raised solid panel

Dutch doors

Section AA

Dowel construction assures rigidity. Stiles and rails are bored to receive dowels not less than ½″ (1.27 cm) in diameter for doors 1⅛″ (2.86 cm) thick and not less than ⅝″ (1.59 cm) in diameter for doors 1⅜″ and 1¾″″ (3.49 cm and 4.45 cm) thick. The minimum number of dowels on each end of rails is as follows:

Rails under 4½″   (11.43 cm)   1
Rails 4½″ to 7″   (17.78 cm)   2
Rails over 7″   3

The use of dowels allows for a dry, tight-pressure fit. Panels should penetrate into grooves at least ¼″ (0.64 cm).

STANDARD LOUVER CONSTRUCTION

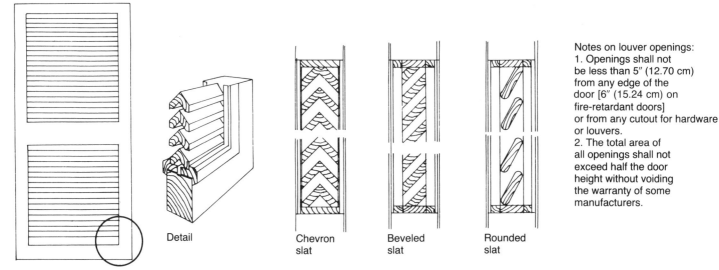

Detail

Chevron slat

Beveled slat

Rounded slat

Notes on louver openings:
1. Openings shall not be less than 5″ (12.70 cm) from any edge of the door [6″ (15.24 cm) on fire-retardant doors] or from any cutout for hardware or louvers.
2. The total area of all openings shall not exceed half the door height without voiding the warranty of some manufacturers.

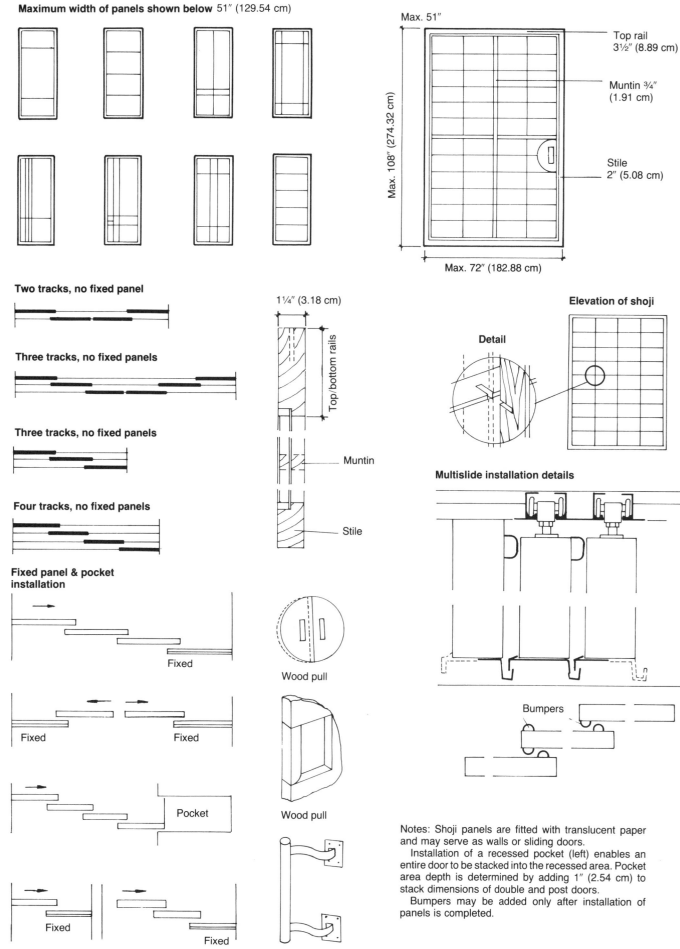

Maximum width of panels shown below 51" (129.54 cm)

Max. 51"

Max. 108" (274.32 cm)

Max. 72" (182.88 cm)

Top rail 3½" (8.89 cm)

Muntin ¾" (1.91 cm)

Stile 2" (5.08 cm)

Two tracks, no fixed panel

Three tracks, no fixed panels

Three tracks, no fixed panels

Four tracks, no fixed panels

Fixed panel & pocket installation

Fixed

Fixed

Fixed

Fixed

Pocket

Fixed

Fixed

1¼" (3.18 cm)

Top/bottom rails

Muntin

Stile

Wood pull

Wood pull

Metal handle

Elevation of shoji

Detail

Multislide installation details

Bumpers

Notes: Shoji panels are fitted with translucent paper and may serve as walls or sliding doors.

Installation of a recessed pocket (left) enables an entire door to be stacked into the recessed area. Pocket area depth is determined by adding 1" (2.54 cm) to stack dimensions of double and post doors.

Bumpers may be added only after installation of panels is completed.

ACCORDION DOOR INSTALLATION

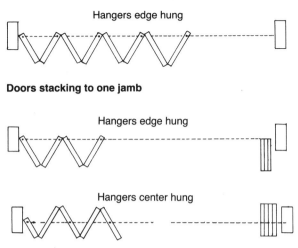

Hangers edge hung

Doors stacking to one jamb

Hangers edge hung

Hangers center hung

Doors stacking to both jambs

Note: Because hanger guides are placed on every other door, only an even number of same width doors may be installed.

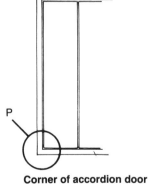

Note: To trim doors:
A = small amount; cut pivot edge.
B = major amount; cut hinge edge.
To trim height, cut from top of doors.

Note: A door height equals B opening height.
To obtain proper finish width:
Two-door unit = add ½″ (1.27 cm) to total width of two doors
Four-door unit = add ¾″ (1.91 cm) to total width of four doors
To obtain proper finish of opening height:
Two- or four-door unit = add 1⅞″ (4.76 cm) to total height of doors plus additional for carpet thickness

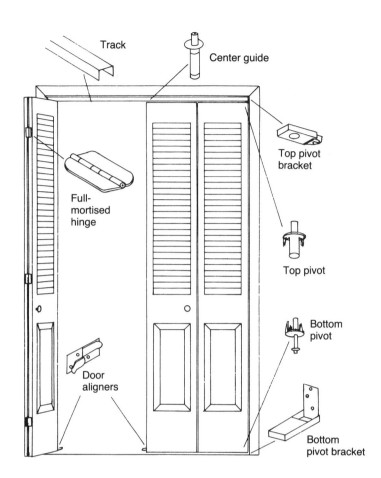

Track
Center guide
Full-mortised hinge
Top pivot bracket
Top pivot
Door aligners
Bottom pivot
Bottom pivot bracket

How to estimate number of doors needed

Opening size (in.)	(cm)	Number of doors
24	60.96	2
30	76.20	2
36	91.44	2
48	121.92	4
60	152.40	4
72	182.88	4

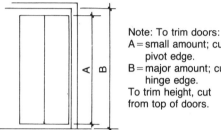

Corner of accordion door

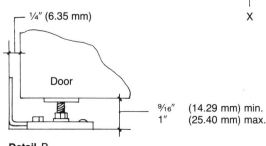

¼″ (6.35 mm)

Door

9/16″ (14.29 mm) min.
1″ (25.40 mm) max.

Detail P

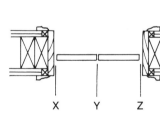

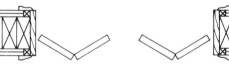

Two bifolding doors

Four bifolding doors

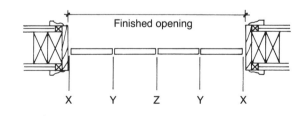

Finished opening

X Y Z

X Y Z Y X

To estimate finished opening widths, addition spaces must be left at points X, Y, and Z.
X = ¼″ (6.35 mm); Y = 1/32″ (0.79 mm); Z = 3/16″ (4.76 mm)

SOLID GLASS DOORS

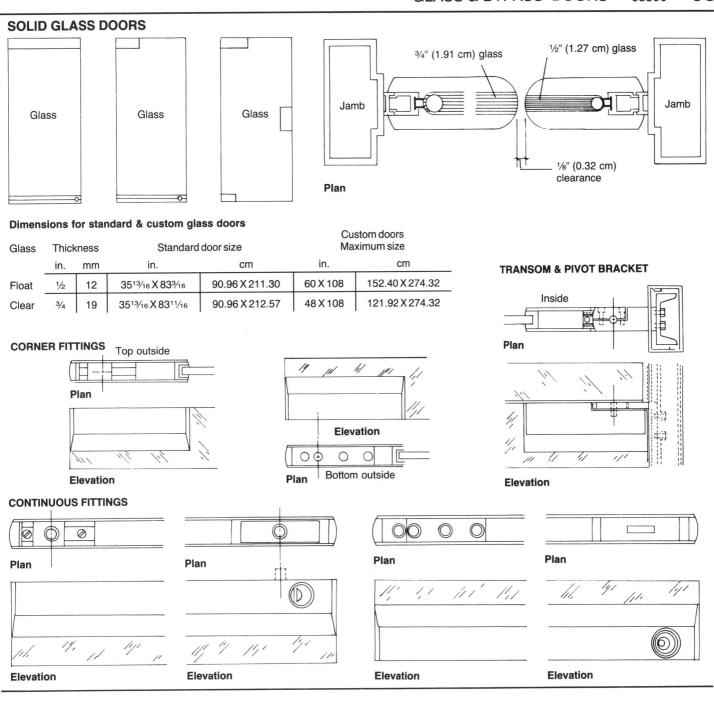

Glass

Glass

Glass

Jamb

¾″ (1.91 cm) glass

½″ (1.27 cm) glass

Jamb

⅛″ (0.32 cm) clearance

Plan

Dimensions for standard & custom glass doors

Glass	Thickness		Standard door size		Custom doors Maximum size	
	in.	mm	in.	cm	in.	cm
Float	½	12	35¹³⁄₁₆ X 83³⁄₁₆	90.96 X 211.30	60 X 108	152.40 X 274.32
Clear	¾	19	35¹³⁄₁₆ X 83¹¹⁄₁₆	90.96 X 212.57	48 X 108	121.92 X 274.32

TRANSOM & PIVOT BRACKET

Inside

Plan

Elevation

CORNER FITTINGS

Top outside

Plan

Elevation

Elevation

Plan   Bottom outside

CONTINUOUS FITTINGS

Plan   **Plan**   **Plan**   **Plan**

Elevation   **Elevation**   **Elevation**   **Elevation**

BYPASS WOOD DOORS

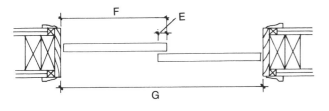

F   E

G

Note: Standard door thicknesses range from ¾″ to 1⅜″ (1.91 to 3.49 cm)

Dimensions:

	in.	cm	
A =	¾	1.91	
B =	1⅜	3.49	
C =	2⅛	5.40	
D =	⅝	1.59	
E =	1	2.54	overlap

F = width is half finish opening plus ½″ (1.27 cm)
G = finished opening 2 X door width minus 1″

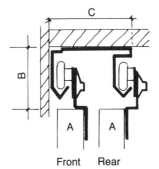

C

B

A   A

Front   Rear

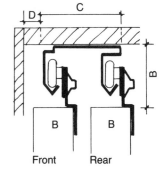

D   C

B

B   B

Front   Rear

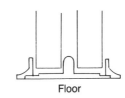

Floor

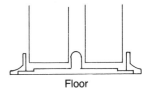

Floor

SPECIFICATIONS FOR FEDERAL ENTRANCES

All general entrances to federal buildings are required to be accessible. A service entrance is not to be used as the only accessible entrance unless it is the only entrance to the building. Accessible routes shall be provided from an accessible entrance to the building's elevators.

Gates, including ticket gates, shall comply with accessible regulations.

Double-leaf doorways shall have at least one active leaf that meets accessible requirements. Double-leaf automatic doors are generally excepted from the one-leaf provision if both leaves are automatic.

Revolving doors or turnstiles are not considered accessible doors and are not to be considered as the sole means of egress. Accessible doors shall be provided immediately adjacent to the turnstile or revolving door.

Width clearance

Doors shall provide clear openings of 2'8" (81.28 cm), measured with the door open 90° between the face of the door and the latch side stop. Openings deeper than 2'0" (60.96 cm) shall be a minimum of 3'0" (91.44 cm) wide. Exception: If a space and the elements within that space comply with the requirements and the user does not require full passage into that space, then the opening into that space may be 1'8" (50.80 cm) wide.

Maneuvering space for front approach

Clearance for front approach only (on the latch side) is 1'6" (45.22 cm), but 2'0" (60.96 cm) is recommended where space is available. Exception: Front approach entry doors to places like hospital patient rooms shall be exempt from the 1'6" requirement if the door is at least 3'8" (111.76 cm) wide.

Thresholds

Raised thresholds shall be beveled with a slope not to exceed 1:2 and with heights not to exceed the following:
Exterior sliding doors: ¾" (1.91 cm) maximum.
Other doors: Maximum ½" (1.27 cm) with bevels not required on thresholds less than ¼" (0.64 cm)

Based on ANSI, A117.1 (1980).

General maneuvering space

Floors shall be clear and have a slope in any direction no greater than 1:48 (¼" per foot).

Doors in series

When doors are placed in a series, the designer shall provide a minimum of 4'0" (121.92 cm) plus the width of any door swinging into the space. Opposing doors shall not swing toward each other into the intervening space.

Hardware

Handles, pulls, latches, locks, and other operating hardware shall be easy to grasp with one hand and shall not require twisting of the wrist or tight pinching to operate. Accessible designs may include, but not be limited to, lever-operated hardware, push-type hardware, and U-shaped handles.

Operating hardware shall be exposed (visible) from both sides of sliding glass doors when they are open.

No hardware shall be mounted higher than 4'0" (121.92 cm) above the floor. Exception: Mortise and surface-mounted bolts used to secure the inactive leaf of a double-leaf door without center mullion may be mounted at any height.

Hazardous areas

Doors opening to such areas shall be provided with textured surfaces on the door handles, knobs, and pulls to alert the blind to possible hazards.

Dimensions (min.):

	in.	cm
A =	12	30.48
B =	18	45.72
C =	48	121.92
D =	60	152.40
E =	24	60.96

*Provide Z additional space if the door is equipped with both a latch and an automatic closer.

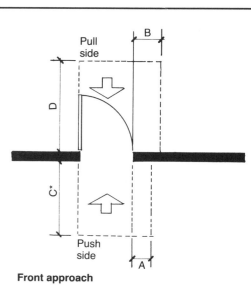

Front approach

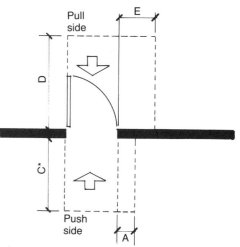

Front approach

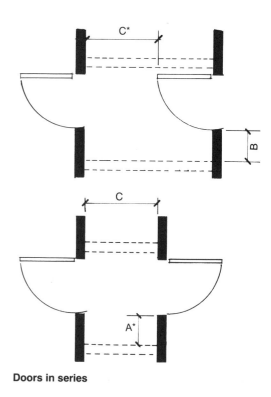

Doors in series

AUTOMATIC ACTUATION DEVICES

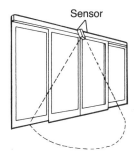

Radar equipment
A self-contained radar detects movement by means of microwaves. The sensor is located in a central position above the door and provides a semicircular detection area in front of the door.

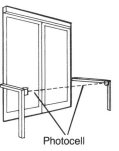

Photocell
This system is supplied in a flush- or surface-mount installation. The photocell does not respond to abnormal light conditions. Its maximum range is 20' (6.10 m).

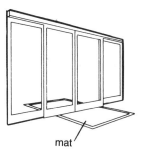

Contact mat
The mat is surface or recessed mounted in several standard sizes. When pressure is exerted on the mat the door receives an impulse instructing it to open. The mat is not affected by dampness or wet conditions.

S = safety mat
A = active mat
1 = 30" X 60" (76.20 X 152.40 cm)
2 = 30" X 30" (76.20 X 76.20 cm)

Specifications for contact mats:
Safety mats are recommended for the swing side of double doors. The safety mat length should always exceed the door panel width by 5" (12.70 cm). All swing door mats should fit within the door frame width.

Recommended mat lengths:
Moderate to light nonpublic traffic: 48" (121.92 cm).
Moderate to fast public traffic: 48" to 60" (121.92 to 152.40 cm)
Fast public traffic with wide door: 60".

Perspective & plan views

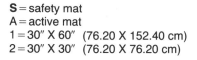

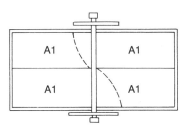

Typical 2-way traffic

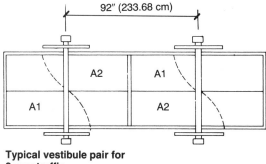

Typical vestibule pair for 2-way traffic

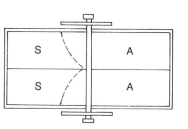

One-way traffic

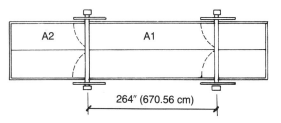

Typical vestibule pair for 1-way traffic

Door guard rail

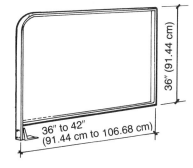

MANUAL ACTUATION DEVICES

Foot switch
The switch for this pneumatic, explosive-proof actuation devise is installed approximately 5" (12.70 cm) above the floor and a maximum distance of 20' (6.10 m) from the control box.

Elbow switch
This is available as an inset- or surface-mounted actuator press button and should be installed 43" (109.22 cm) above the floor.

Push button
This is available in both inset- or surface-mounted fittings.

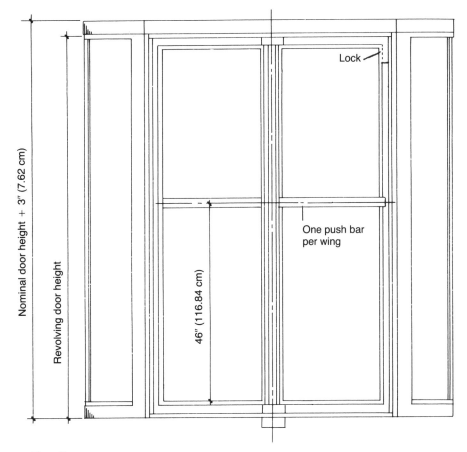

Elevation

Life safety factors
Major fire codes do not recognize revolving doors as means of egress.

1. If revolving doors are used at the level of discharge, they shall not be used at the foot or the top of stairs.
2. If revolving doors are allowed in a particular type of occupancy, each revolving door may receive credit for one-half unit of exit width.
3. The number of revolving doors used shall not exceed the number of swinging doors used as exits within 20′ (6.10 m). Exception: Revolving doors may serve as exits without adjacent swing doors for street-floor elevator lobbies if no stairways or doors from other parts of the building discharge through the lobby.
4. These doors must be equipped with means to prevent their rotation at too rapid a rate.

Handicapped access
Revolving doors shall not be the only means of egress at any accessible entrance or route.

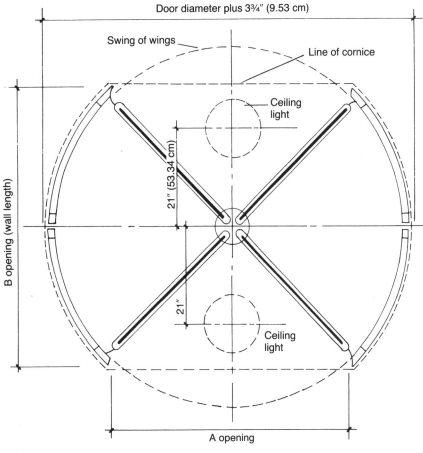

Plan

Door diameters
The most popular dimensions are the diameter 6′6″ X 7′0″ (1.98 X 2.13 m).

Standard sizes:

Diameter			A			B		
ft	in.	m	ft	in.	m	ft	in.	m
6	6	1.98	4	5¼	1.35	5	0	1.52
6	8	2.03	4	6	1.37	5	1	1.42
6	10	2.08	4	8	1.42	5	2½	1.58
7	0	2.13	4	9½	1.44	5	3	1.62
7	2	2.18	4	10	1.50	5	5	1.65
7	4	2.24	5	0	1.52	5	6¾	1.70
7	6	2.29	5	1¾	1.58	5	8⅛	1.73

DETAILS OF SINGLE-EGRESS FRAME

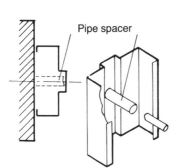

Pipe spacer

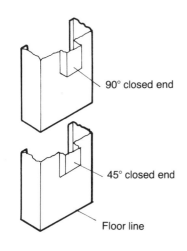

Mold optional

Rough buck
14 ga. min.

Cabinet jamb,
field assembled

Split jamb,
preassembled

Anchorage of frames in prepared openings

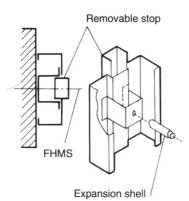

Removable stop

FHMS

FHMS

Expansion shell

FHMS = flathead machine screws

Frames with rough buck

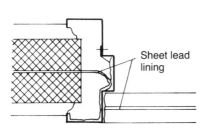

Sheet lead
lining

Lead-lined frame

Lead lining in frame provides barrier to
x rays, which travel in straight line in
gap between lead-lined wall and door

90° closed end

45° closed end

Floor line

Cutoff (sanitary) stops

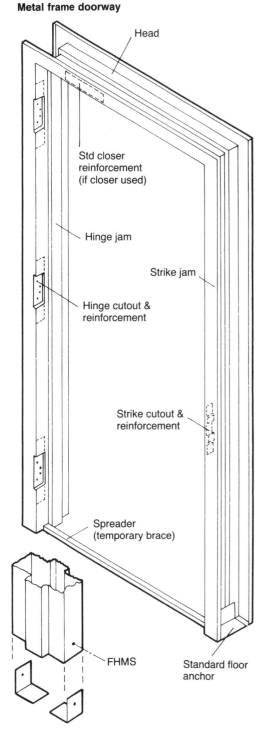

Metal frame doorway

Head

Std closer
reinforcement
(if closer used)

Hinge jam

Strike jam

Hinge cutout &
reinforcement

Strike cutout &
reinforcement

Spreader
(temporary brace)

Standard floor
anchor

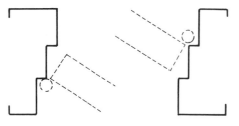

FHMS

Fixed mullion anchor

DETAILS OF DOUBLE-EGRESS FRAME

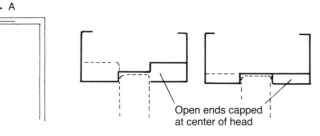

A

Open ends capped
at center of head

Key elevation

Alternate head sections A

Jamb sections

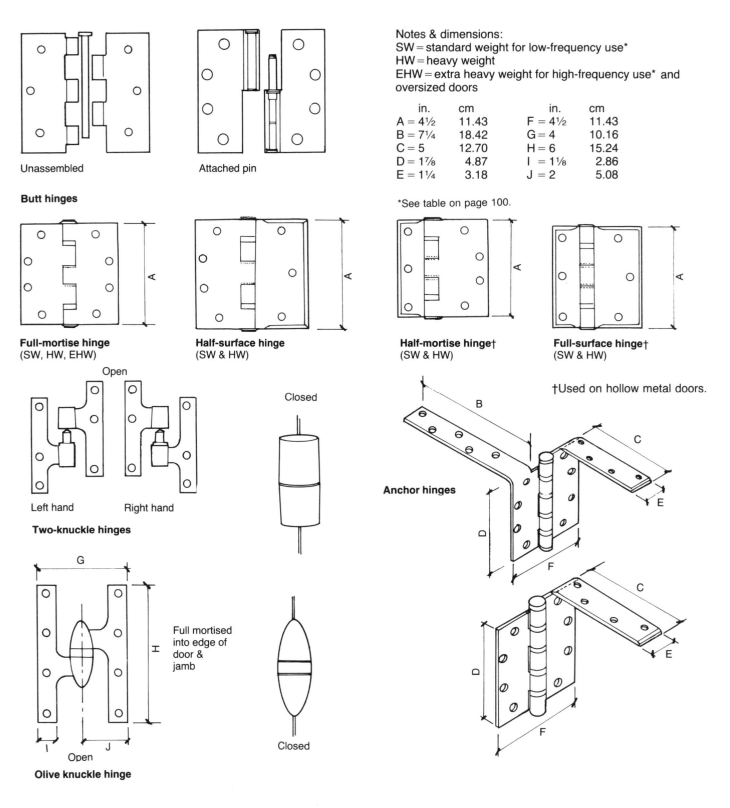

Unassembled   Attached pin

Butt hinges

Notes & dimensions:
SW = standard weight for low-frequency use*
HW = heavy weight
EHW = extra heavy weight for high-frequency use* and oversized doors

	in.	cm		in.	cm
A =	4½	11.43	F =	4½	11.43
B =	7¼	18.42	G =	4	10.16
C =	5	12.70	H =	6	15.24
D =	1⅞	4.87	I =	1⅛	2.86
E =	1¼	3.18	J =	2	5.08

*See table on page 100.

Full-mortise hinge
(SW, HW, EHW)

Half-surface hinge
(SW & HW)

Half-mortise hinge†
(SW & HW)

Full-surface hinge†
(SW & HW)

†Used on hollow metal doors.

Open   Closed

Left hand   Right hand

Two-knuckle hinges

Anchor hinges

Full mortised into edge of door & jamb

Closed

Open

Olive knuckle hinge

Hinges for Class A hollow metal doors
Only extra-heavy steel hinges with a minimum .180 gauge thickness and 4½″ (11.43 cm) minimum height are approved. If hinges are exposed to corrosive atmosphere, the finish must be rust resistive.

Hinges for Class B, C, D, and E type of hollow metal and composition core doors
Steel hinges for these openings must have a minimum of .134 gauge thickness and a minimum height of 4½″ (11.43 cm). Exception: Doors not exceeding 5′ (152.40 cm) in height and 3′ in width (91.44 cm) may be hung on hinges with a minimum of .130 gauge thickness and a minimum height of 4″ (10.16 cm). All doors over 8′ (244 m) must have hinges with minimum 0.180 gauge thickness and 4½″ height.

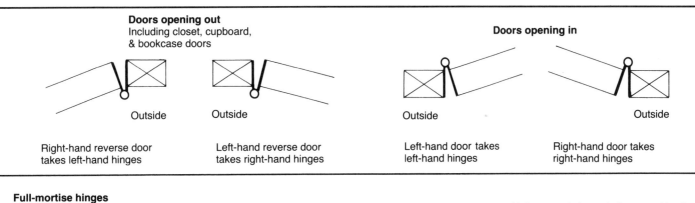

Doors opening out
Including closet, cupboard,
& bookcase doors

Doors opening in

Outside   Outside   Outside   Outside

Right-hand reverse door
takes left-hand hinges

Left-hand reverse door
takes right-hand hinges

Left-hand door takes
left-hand hinges

Right-hand door takes
right-hand hinges

Full-mortise hinges
Wood doors, wood jamb

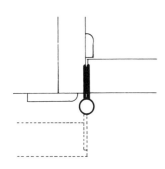

Wood doors, hollow metal jamb

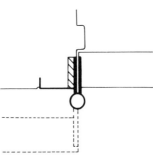

Hollow metal doors, hollow metal jamb

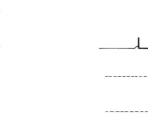

Half-mortise hinge
Hollow metal doors, channel iron
jamb

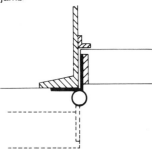

Half-surface hinges
Wood doors, wood jamb

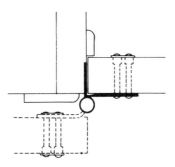

Mineral core doors, hollow metal jamb

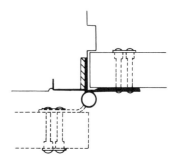

Full-surface hinges
Mineral core doors, channel iron
jamb

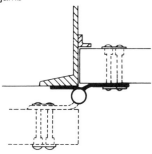

Hollow metal doors, channel iron
jamb

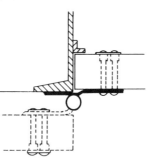

Swing-clear, full-surface hinge
Wood doors, hollow metal jamb

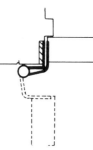

Swing-clear, half-mortise hinge
Wood doors, channel iron jamb

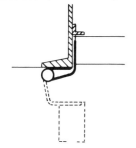

Swing-clear, half-surface hinge
Mineral core doors, hollow metal jamb

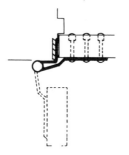

Swing-clear, full-surface hinge
Mineral core doors, channel iron jamb

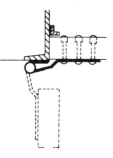

HINGE SPECIFICATION GUIDE

Factors determining selection of proper hinge:

1. Material of door and frame
2. Size, thickness, and weight of door with all hardware accessories
3. Clearance required
4. Use: exterior or interior, frequency
5. Exposure: sea air, dust, corrosive atmosphere
6. Quality desired
7. Special application or use (such as in schools)
8. Door accessories (overhead holders, closers, stops, kick plates, and so on) that affect hinge performance
9. Hinge edge of door beveled or square

Weight of doors

Door material	Skin	Core	Lb/sq ft 1¾"	1⅜"
Wood	Hardwood	Hollow	2.5	2.2
Wood	Hardwood	Mineral	4.0	3.5
Wood	Hardwood	Lumber	4.5	4.0
Wood	Hardwood	Particle	5.0	4.0
Wood	Plastic	Particle	5.5	4.5
Metal	16 ga.	Hollow	5.8	5.7
Metal	16 ga.	Mineral	6.2	6.1

Frequency of door operation

Type of building and door	Estimated frequency Daily	Yearly		Hinge type
Large dept. store entr.	5,000	1,500,000	High frequency	Heavy weight
Large office bldg entr.	4,000	1,200,000		
School entrance	1,250	225,000		
School toilet door	1,250	225,000		
Store or bank entr.	500	150,000		
Office bldg toilet door	400	118,000		
School corridor door	80	15,000	Av. frequency	Standard weight
Office bldg corridor door	75	22,000		
Store toilet door	60	18,000		
Dwelling entrance	40	15,000		
Dwelling toilet door	25	9,000	Low frequency	Plain bearing hinges may be used on light doors
Dwelling corridor door	10	3,600		
Dwelling closet door	6	2,200		

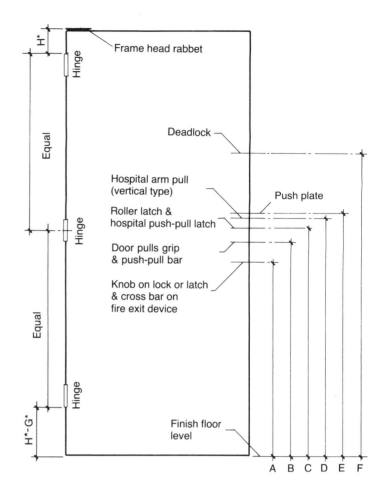

Dimensions:

	in.	cm		in.	cm
A	= 38	96.52	E	= 48	121.92
B	= 42	106.68	F	= 60	152.40
C	= 45	114.30	G	= *10	25.40
D	= 47	119.38	H	= *5	12.70

*Some Western states require that hinges be located 7" (17.78 cm) from the top and 11" (27.94 cm) from the bottom.

Note: Three hinges are usually required on doors up to and including 7⅕' (2.29 m), with one additional hinge for each additional 2½' (0.76 m) or fraction thereof.

Hinge height: determined by width & thickness of door

Thickness (in.)	Width of doors (in.)	Height of hinges (in.)
¾ to 1⅛ cabinet	to 24	2½
⅞ and 1⅛ screen or combination	to 36	3
1⅜	{ to 32	3½-4
	over 32	4-4½
1¾	{ to 36	4½†
	over 36 to 48	5†
	over 48	6†
2, 2¼, 2½	{ to 42	5†
	over 42	6

†Heavy-weight hinge required.

TYPES OF FINISH HARDWARE FOR DOORS

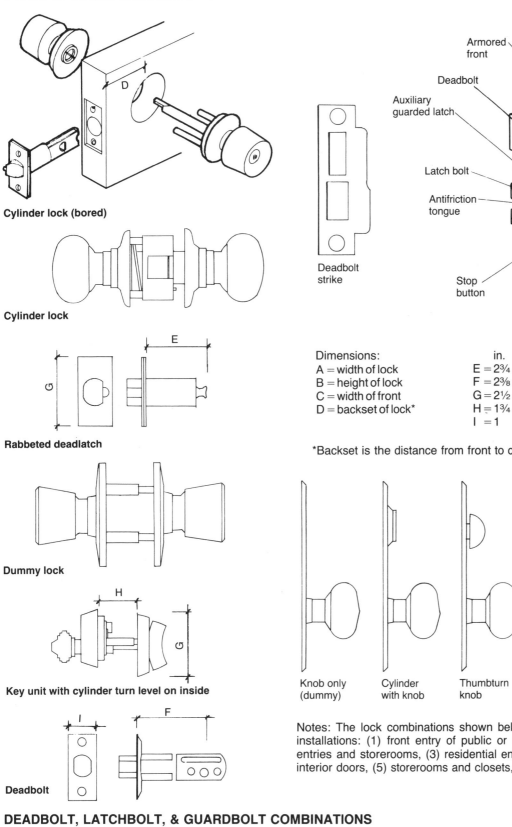

Cylinder lock (bored)

Cylinder lock

Rabbeted deadlatch

Dummy lock

Key unit with cylinder turn level on inside

Deadbolt

MORTISED LOCK SET

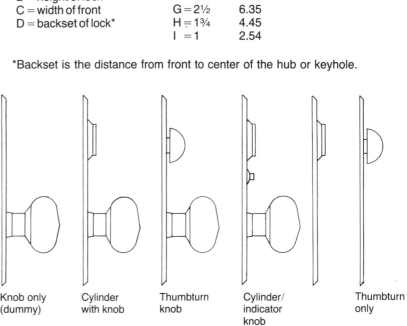

Armored front

Deadbolt

Auxiliary guarded latch

Latch bolt

Antifriction tongue

Case mortised into door

Stop button

Deadbolt strike

Dimensions:		in.	cm
A = width of lock			
B = height of lock	E = $2\frac{3}{4}$	6.99
C = width of front	F = $2\frac{3}{8}$	6.03
D = backset of lock*	G = $2\frac{1}{2}$	6.35
	H = $1\frac{3}{4}$	4.45
	I = 1	2.54

*Backset is the distance from front to center of the hub or keyhole.

Knob only (dummy)

Cylinder with knob

Thumbturn knob

Cylinder/ indicator knob

Thumbturn only

Notes: The lock combinations shown below are suggested for the following installations: (1) front entry of public or residential buildings, (2) residential entries and storerooms, (3) residential entry, (4) entrances to apartment and interior doors, (5) storerooms and closets, (6) office and corridor doors.

DEADBOLT, LATCHBOLT, & GUARDBOLT COMBINATIONS

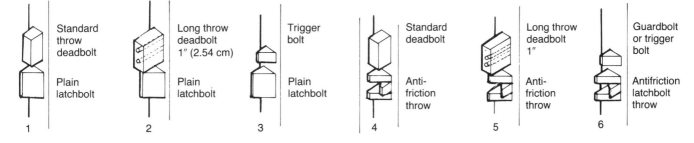

1	2	3	4	5	6
Standard throw deadbolt / Plain latchbolt	Long throw deadbolt 1″ (2.54 cm) / Plain latchbolt	Trigger bolt / Plain latchbolt	Standard deadbolt / Antifriction throw	Long throw deadbolt 1″ / Antifriction throw	Guardbolt or trigger bolt / Antifriction latchbolt throw

Keying Chart

Keys and terms	Traditional abbreviations	Definition
Change key		Individual lock key.
Keyed differently	KD	Each lock is set to a different key combination.
Keyed alike	KA	Two or more locks set to the same key combination, for example, KA2, KA3, KA4.
Master key	MKD	Operates any given quantity of cylinders with different key changes.
Grand master key	GMKD	Operates all individual locks already operated by two or more master keys.
Great grand master key	GGMKD	Operates all locks under the various master keys and grand master keys already established.
Emergency key	EMKD	Operates hotel locks having shut-out feature that blocks entry by all other keys.
Construction key	CKD	Operates all cylinders designated for a temporary period during construction.

RELATIONSHIP OF DOOR FUNCTION TO FINISH HARDWARE

Keyed Locks

Office lock
By key from outside when outer knob is locked by inside push button.

Entrance lock
By key from outside when outer knob is locked by turn button in inner knob.

Vestibule lock
By key from outside when outer knob is locked by key in inner knob. Inner knob always free.

All-purpose lock
By key from outside when outer knob is locked by universal button in inner knob. Outer knob may be fixed by rotating universal button.

Utility closet lock
Outer knob fixed. Entrance by key only. Inside thumb turn always free.

Closet lock
Locked or unlocked by key from outside. Inside thumb turn always free.

Communicating lock
Key in either knob only unlocks its own knob.

Dormitory and motel lock
Locked or unlocked by key from outside knob. Push-button locking from inside. Automatic latch prevents lockout.

Hotel lock
Key in outer knob locks and unlocks own knob. Push button in inner knob locks outer knob and throws indicator, shutting out all keys except emergency master key.

Communicating suite lock
By key from outside when outer knob locked by push button. Key in outer knob locks or unlocks both knobs simultaneously.

Apartment house lock
Outer knob fixed. Entrance by key only. Push button in inner knob throws out visual occupancy indicator, locking out all keys except emergency master key.

Classroom lock
Outer knob locked or unlocked by key from outside. Inner knob always free.

Service station lock
By key from outside when outer knob is locked by universal button in inner knob. Closing door releases button. Outer knob may be fixed by rotating universal button.

Store lock
Key in either knob locks both knobs.

Storeroom lock
Outer knob fixed. Entrance by key only. Inner knob always free.

Institutional lock
Both knobs fixed. Entrance by key in either knob.

Nonkeyed Locks

Passage latch
Both knobs are always free.

Exit lock
By knob from inside only. Outer knob always fixed.

Closet latch
Outer knob and inside thumb turn are always free.

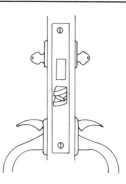

Public entrance door

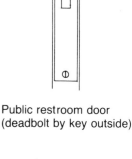

Public restroom door (deadbolt by key outside)

Exit lock (Specify door thickness)
Blank plate outside. Inner knob always free.

Patio lock
Push-button locking. Automatic latch prevents locking out.

Exit lock
Outer knob locked or unlocked by turn button in inner knob.

Privacy lock
Push button locking. Can be opened from outside by emergency key, screwdriver, or similar tool.

Communicating lock
Turn button in either knob locks opposite knob.

Hospital privacy lock
Push button locking. Emergency turn button in outer knob releases push button unlocking outer knob.

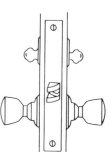

Institutional door

Dummy Trim

Single-dummy trim
For one side of door. Pull only.

Pair-dummy trim
For both sides of door. Pulls only.

Single-working trim
For one side of door. Knob free.

Pair-working trim
For both sides of door. Knobs free.

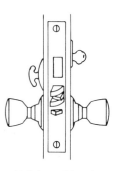

Hotel corridor door

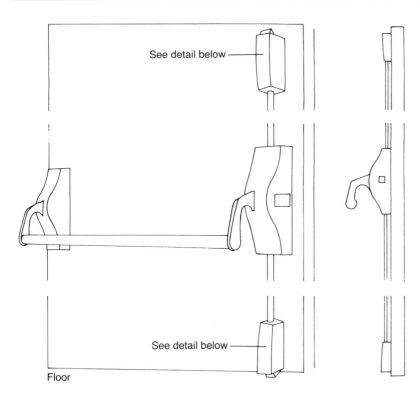

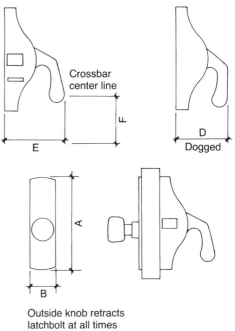

Case dimensions

Crossbar center line

Dogged

Outside knob retracts latchbolt at all times

See detail below

See detail below

Floor

PANIC HARDWARE

This consists of a door-latching assembly incorporating a device that releases the latch upon the application of force in the direction of exit. Most codes require that panic hardware not be equipped with any locking or dogging device, set screws, or other arrangement that can be used to prevent release of the latch when pressure is applied to the bar. The force required to fully open any door used for means of egress shall not exceed 50 lb (222 N) applied to the latch stile.

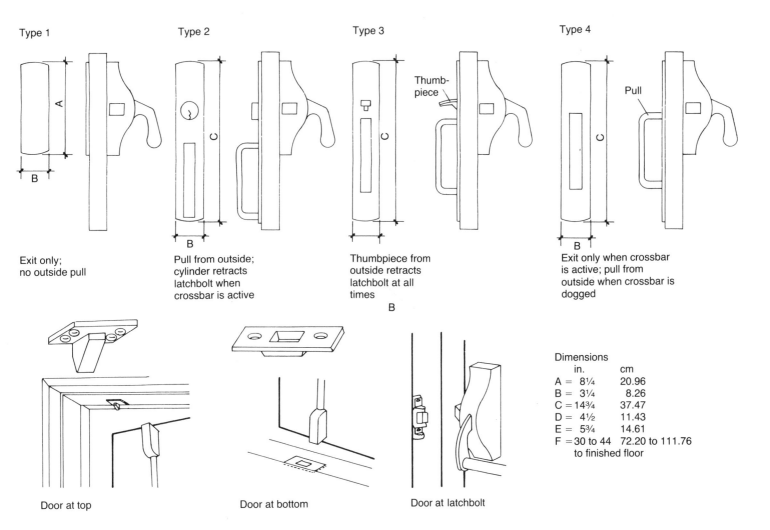

Type 1

Exit only;
no outside pull

Type 2

Pull from outside;
cylinder retracts
latchbolt when
crossbar is active

Type 3

Thumb-
piece

Thumbpiece from
outside retracts
latchbolt at all
times

Type 4

Pull

Exit only when crossbar
is active; pull from
outside when crossbar is
dogged

Door at top

Door at bottom

Door at latchbolt

Dimensions		
	in.	cm
A =	8¼	20.96
B =	3¼	8.26
C =	14¾	37.47
D =	4½	11.43
E =	5¾	14.61
F =	30 to 44	72.20 to 111.76
	to finished floor	

CLASSIFICATION OF FIRE DOORS

Label	Hour rating	Use in building	Maximum glass area	Max. size of wood veneer (1¾" thick)	
A	3	Openings in fire walls and division walls between building with a rating of 3 hours	No glass permitted	**3′ X 7′, 4′ X 8′, 4′ X 10′**	
B	1½	Openings in vertical shafts with a rating of 1½ hours	100 sq in. per leaf	Single Pair (each leaf)	4′ X 10′ 4′ X 8′
C	¾	Openings in corridors and room partitions with a rating of ¾ hour	1,296 sq in. per lite; neither dimension to exceed 54″	Single Pair (each leaf)	4′ X 10′ 4′ X 8′
E	¾	Openings to exterior fire escapes with a rating of ¾ hour	1,296 sq in. per lite; neither dimension to exceed 54″	2′8″ X 7′, 3′ X 5′	
D	1½	Openings in exterior walls with a rating of 1½ hours.	No glass permitted	3′ X 7′, 4′ X 10′	

GLAZING

Glass installed within fire doors must be ¼″ (0.64 cm) wired glass labeled for installation in a fire door. In general, the Model Codes limit the amount of wired glass that can be installed within a given fire door as shown in the table on the right. Doors must be prepared under label service to receive wired glass lites since field modifications are not permitted for window openings within fire door assemblies. Wired glass can only be installed in steel frames that comply with the label requirements of the door assembly with a minumum ½″ (1.27-cm) frame/glass overlap for lites up to 100 sq in. (645.16 sq cm) and a minimum of ¾″ (1.9-cm) frame/glass overlap for light over 100 sq in. in order to assure their integrity during the fire exposure period and the subsequent hose stream application. It should be noted that there now exists a 20-minute label glazing bead for installation of wired glass in 20-minute doors without steel frames.

Wired glass installed in fire doors has been exempted from the Consumer Product Safety Commission requirement for safety glazing (CPSC Standard 16-CF, Part 1201) and must only comply with ANSI Standard Z97.1: *Performance Specifications and Methods of Test for Safety Glazing Materials Used in Buildings.*

DOOR FRAME SPECIFICATIONS

Up to 3′0″ X 8′0″ (0.91 X 2.44 m) allowed with soft maple frame (or any species of greater density) with a 20-minute fire door with *untreated* stiles and rails.

Up to 4′0″ X 8′0″ (4.22 X 2.44 m) allowed with soft maple frame (or any species of greater density) with a 20-minute fire door with *treated* stiles and rails.

Underwriters Laboratories has established two specific label codes to indicate specific coverage for wood type door frames in their use with UL classified or listed doors for a comprehensive 20-minute rating.

UL Label Code No. 63-11: This label applies to wood door frames for use with UL Classified Wood or Plastic Composite or Wood Core Fire Doors up to and including 3′ (width) X 8′ (height) doors, with treated or untreated stiles and rails.

UL Label Code No. 63-12: This label applies to wood door frames for use with UL Classified Wood or Plastic Covered Composite or Wood Core Fire Doors up to and including 4′ (width) X 8′ (height) doors, with *treated* stiles and rails.

Limiting size of wired glass lites

Fire door rating (hours) & opening class	Max. area per lite (sq in.)	Max. height (in.)	Max. width (in.)	Total max. area of all lites (sq in.)
3 (A)	0	0	0	0
1½ (B)	100	33*	10[1,2]*†	100
1 (B)	100	33*	10[1,2]*†	100
¾ (C)	1,296	54	54	Tested size‡
½	1,296	54	54	Tested size‡
⅓	1,296	54	54	Tested size‡
1½ (D)	0	0	0	0
¾ (E)	1,296	54	54	1,296

*The UBC requires a minimum dimension of 4″.
†The SBC allows a maximum width of 12″.
‡Number of lites is not limited, only the total area. The tested size indicates that the only limit is based on what manufacturers have successfully tested. To date the maximum tested sizes for wood and composite wood doors are:

¾ (C)	1,200[a]	40	30	1,200[a]
½	None			
⅓	1,296[b]	40	30	1,200[b]

[a]Paired doors only 100 sq in. per leaf.
[b]Double-egress doors 720 sq in. per leaf.

Average density of various species (lb/cu ft)

Soft maple	32.0	Walnut	36.9	Imbuya	43.7
Aromatic cedar	32.0	Honduras mahogany	37.8	Oriental wood	44.1
Tigerwood	32.5	Padouk	38.8	Benge	44.6
Avodire	33.0	Teak	38.8	English brown oak	45.0
Korina	33.0	Holly	38.8	Paldao	45.6
Sycamore	33.0	Zebrawood	39.3	Pecan	46.0
Red gum	33.0	Andiroba	40.7	Hickory	46.0
Brown ash	33.0	White ash	40.7	White oak	46.6
Elm	34.0	African cherry	41.2	Pear	46.6
Cherry	34.0	Birch	41.7	Blackbean	48.0
Tupelo gum	34.0	Bella rosa	42.7	Brazilian rosewood	50.0
Phil. mahogany	34.9	Red oak	42.7	East Indian satinwood	51.1
Lacewood	35.9	Hard maple	42.7	East Indian rosewood	51.4
Circassian walnut	36.4	Beech	43.7	East Indian laurel	53.0-56.0
Queensland maple	36.9	Sapele	43.7	Olive	55.8
				Sucupira	60.1

Note: Wood fire door frames constructed of any species with a minimum density of 32 lb/ft[3] must meet requirements for UL Label Code Numbers 63-11 and 63-12.

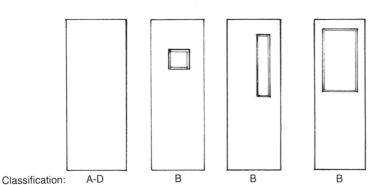

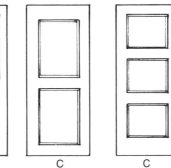

| Classification: | A-D | B | B | B | C | C |

FIRE DOOR DOS & DON'TS

Dos

Do study the applicable codes carefully before selecting material. Be sure there are no conflicts.

Do specify the door and frame so that the design will meet the traffic and code requirements.

Do select hardware acceptable to the authorities having jurisdiction in the area.

Do make the door self-closing and self-latching so that during a fire it will close and latch automatically.

Do mark fire exits clearly.

Do purchase doors and frames from a nationally known reputable manufacturer.

Do use correct size and number of doors and frames.

Do use wired glass in doors where glass is allowed.

Do make sure fire doors and frames receive proper maintenance.

Don'ts

Don't substitute doors of a lower rating than those required.

Don't make substitutions on hardware without checking to see if they meet the requirements.

Don't use nonlabel frames with label doors or nonlabel doors with label frames.

Don't place obstructions in the area of the fire exit.

Don't wedge or tie label doors open.

Don't lock or chain label doors closed.

Don't swing the door against traffic flow.

Don't alter label doors or frames.

Don't remove or alter labels.

Recommended hinge sizes

Door size max. (in.)	Door label	Hinge size Height (in.)	Thickness (in.)
36 X 90 X 1¾	Any	4½	0.134*
41 X 90 X 1¾	Any	4½	0.180
48 X 120 X 1¾	Any	5	0.190
36 X 84 X 1⅜	Any	3½	0.123

*If doors are in critical or high frequency of use locations, increase leaf thickness to 0.180 (extra heavy).

Note: All hinges or pivots, except spring hinges, must be of the ball bearing type. Steel hinges of the olive knuckle type may be used on labeled doors when permitted in the door manufacturer's procedure.

Hinge spacing

Doors up to 60″ (152.40 cm) in height shall be provided with two hinges and an additional hinge for each additional 30″ (76.20 cm) of height or fraction thereof

Door height (in.)	Hinges required
To 60	2
61 to 90	3
91 to 120	4

Transom width (in.)	Hinges required
To 48	2
49 to 84	3

Access door & transoms

Access doors and transoms not exceeding 3′ in height and 2′ (91.44 X 60.96 cm) in width shall have hinges of 0.092 gauge minimum thickness and 3″ (7.62 cm) minimum height.

STANDARD ARM APPLICATION

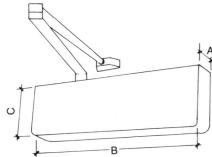

Handling of doors: Always specify hand from outside

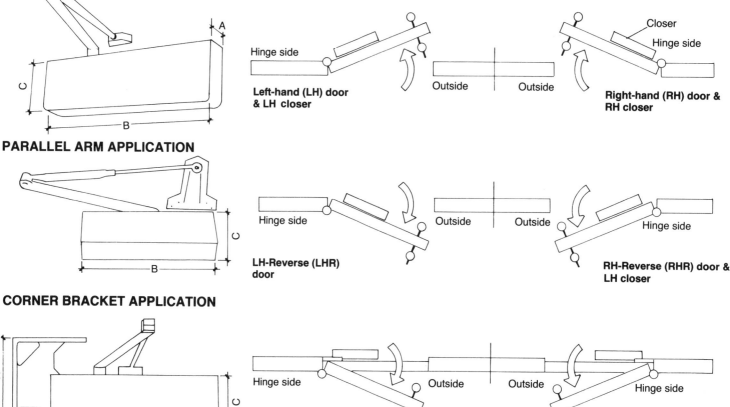

Hinge side

Left-hand (LH) door & LH closer

Outside   Outside

Closer

Hinge side

Right-hand (RH) door & RH closer

PARALLEL ARM APPLICATION

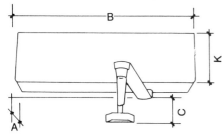

Hinge side

LH-Reverse (LHR) door

Outside   Outside

Hinge side

RH-Reverse (RHR) door & LH closer

CORNER BRACKET APPLICATION

Hinge side

LHR door & LH closer

Outside   Outside

Hinge side

RHR door & RH closer

TOP JAMB APPLICATION

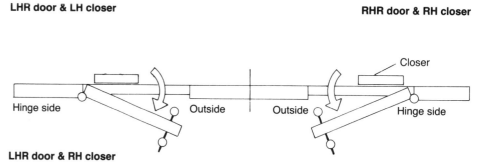

Closer

Hinge side

LHR door & RH closer

Outside   Outside

Hinge side

RHR door & LH closer

SMOKE-ACTIVATED CLOSERS

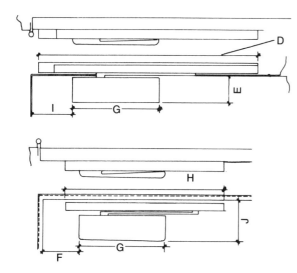

Door closer/holder has adjustable, single-point, hold-open and built-in detector that automatically closes fire and smoke barrier doors.* Built-in, dual-volume ionization detector reacts to visible and invisible particles of combustion.
*Consult with manufacturer for wiring requirements.

Dimensions:

	in.	cm		in.	cm
A =	1¾	4.45	G =	12¼	31.12
B =	9¹/₁₆	23.01	H =	22¾	57.79
C =	2⅞	7.30	I =	3⅞	9.84
D =	31	78.74	J =	5¾	14.61
E =	3⅝	9.21	K =	6	15.24
F =	3¾	9.53			

Note: Right-hand-reverse (RHR) door is the same as left-hand door. Left-hand-reverse (LHR) door is the same as right-hand door.

TYPES OF ACCESSIBLE DOORS

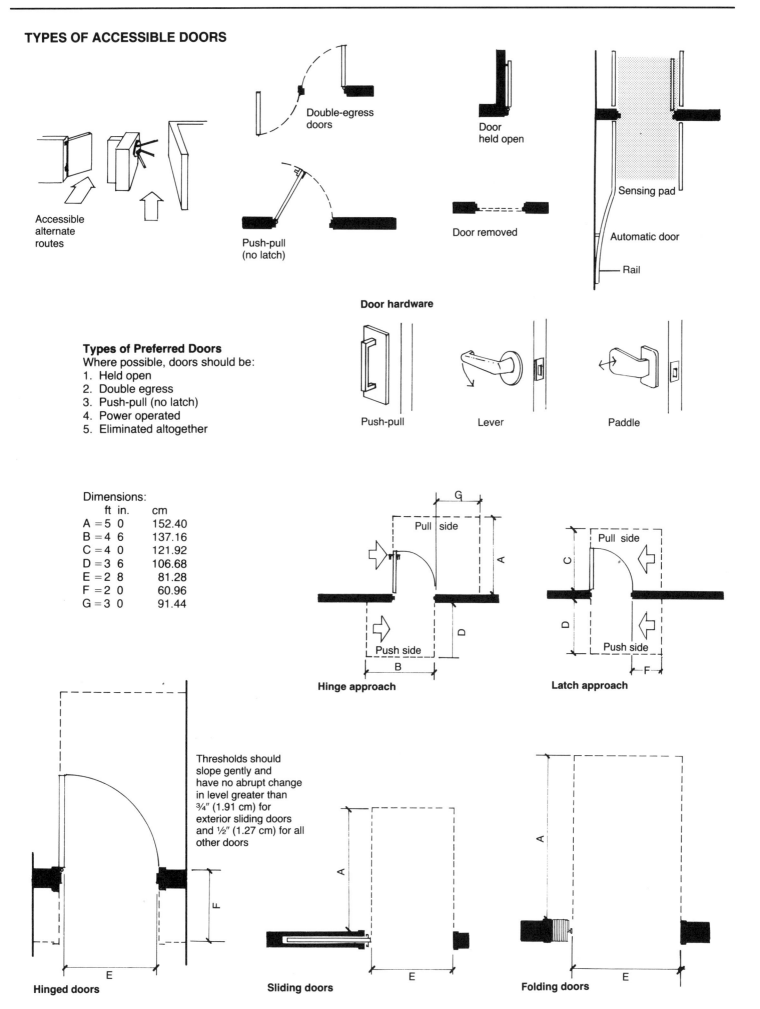

Accessible alternate routes

Double-egress doors

Push-pull (no latch)

Door held open

Door removed

Sensing pad

Automatic door

Rail

Door hardware

Push-pull

Lever

Paddle

Types of Preferred Doors
Where possible, doors should be:
1. Held open
2. Double egress
3. Push-pull (no latch)
4. Power operated
5. Eliminated altogether

Dimensions:

	ft	in.	cm
A =	5	0	152.40
B =	4	6	137.16
C =	4	0	121.92
D =	3	6	106.68
E =	2	8	81.28
F =	2	0	60.96
G =	3	0	91.44

Pull side

Push side

Hinge approach

Pull side

Push side

Latch approach

Thresholds should slope gently and have no abrupt change in level greater than ¾″ (1.91 cm) for exterior sliding doors and ½″ (1.27 cm) for all other doors

Hinged doors

Sliding doors

Folding doors

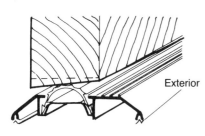

(B) Door may be beveled when installed on this type of threshold

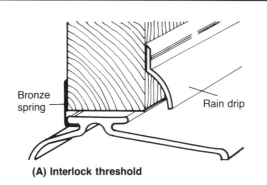

Bronze spring

Rain drip

(A) Interlock threshold

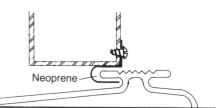

Exterior

(A) Threshold with weepholes; door swings inward; note door mortised to fit

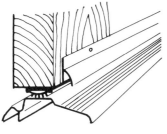

(B) 1″ (1.27 cm) door clearance above threshold, neoprene compression seal

DETAILS OF WEATHER STRIPS

Type A
Composed of a metal seal and special type of saddle. Long wearing and good in heavy-traffic areas.

Type B
Compression seal used for lightweight doors and medium traffic. May be surface mounted or inset vinyl or neoprene.

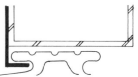

Neoprene

(A) Door swings outward

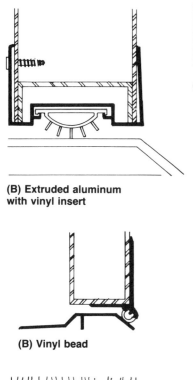

(B) Extruded aluminum with vinyl insert

(A) Flexible hook

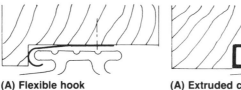

(A) Extruded concealed hook

(A) Extruded angle hook

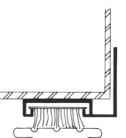

(B) Adjustable Neoprene seal

(B) Adjustable poly pile seal

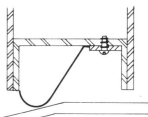

(B) Spring bronze clip for hollow metal doors

(B) Vinyl bead

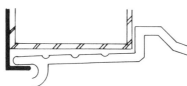

(A) Rabbeted saddles for metal door

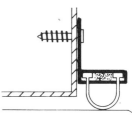

(B) Extruded aluminum with neoprene insert; mounted outside door

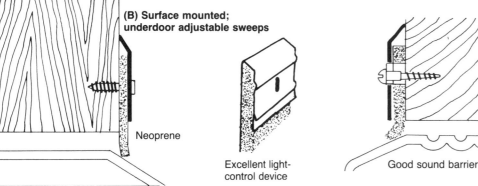

(B) Surface mounted; underdoor adjustable sweeps

Neoprene

Excellent light-control device

Good sound barrier

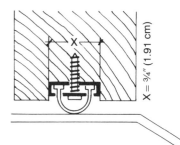

X = ¾″ (1.91 cm)

(B) Extruded aluminum with neoprene insert; mounted in center of door

DETAILS OF DOOR JAMBS

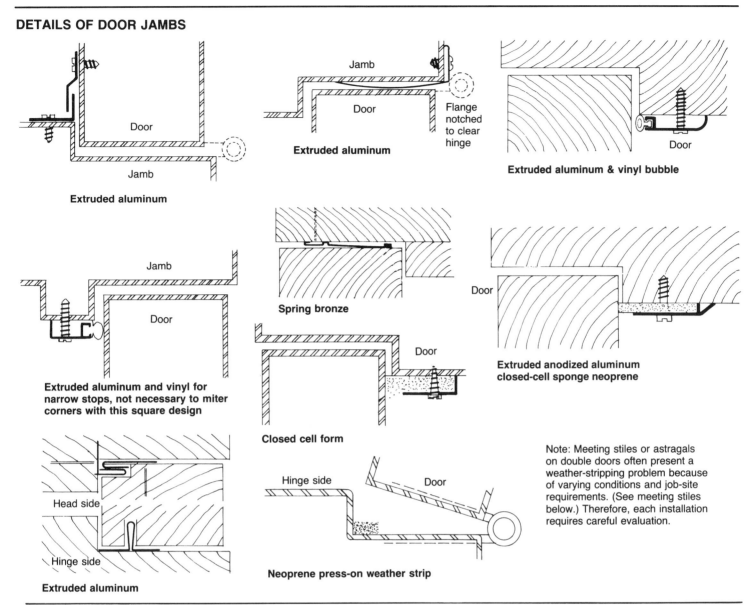

Extruded aluminum

Extruded aluminum

Flange notched to clear hinge

Extruded aluminum & vinyl bubble

Extruded aluminum and vinyl for narrow stops, not necessary to miter corners with this square design

Spring bronze

Closed cell form

Extruded anodized aluminum closed-cell sponge neoprene

Extruded aluminum

Neoprene press-on weather strip

Note: Meeting stiles or astragals on double doors often present a weather-stripping problem because of varying conditions and job-site requirements. (See meeting stiles below.) Therefore, each installation requires careful evaluation.

MEETING STILES

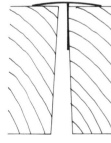

Extruded aluminum for light residential installations

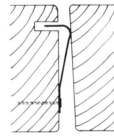

Spring bronze

Bronze or stainless steel

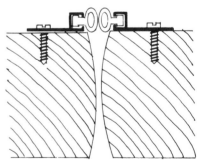

Extruded aluminum slotted with vinyl insert

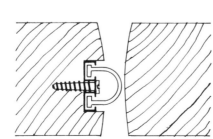

Extruded neoprene for use with metal hollow door

Extruded neoprene for use with wood door

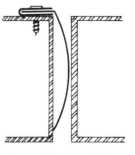

Spring bronze retainer

DETAILS OF SLIDING DOORS

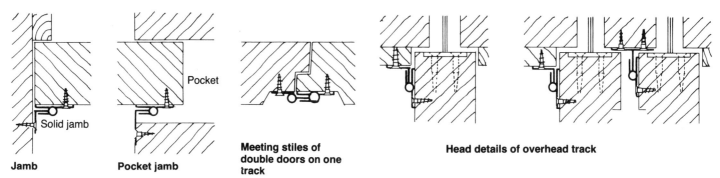

Jamb — Solid jamb

Pocket jamb — Pocket

Meeting stiles of double doors on one track

Head details of overhead track

DETAILS OF AUTOMATIC DOOR INSULATION

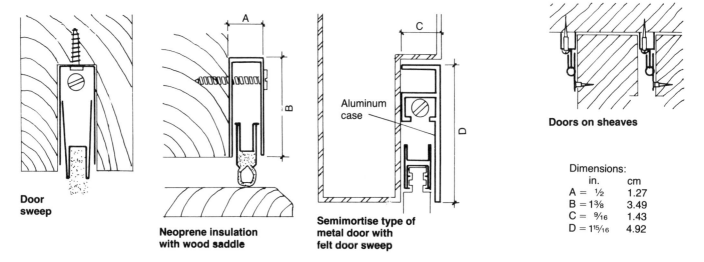

Door sweep

Neoprene insulation with wood saddle

Aluminum case

Semimortise type of metal door with felt door sweep

Doors on sheaves

Dimensions:

	in.	cm
A =	½	1.27
B =	1⅜	3.49
C =	9/16	1.43
D =	1¹⁵/₁₆	4.92

METAL OR RUBBER DOOR SADDLES

Note: When specifying door saddles, consider the needs of the disabled. Check local codes on requirements.

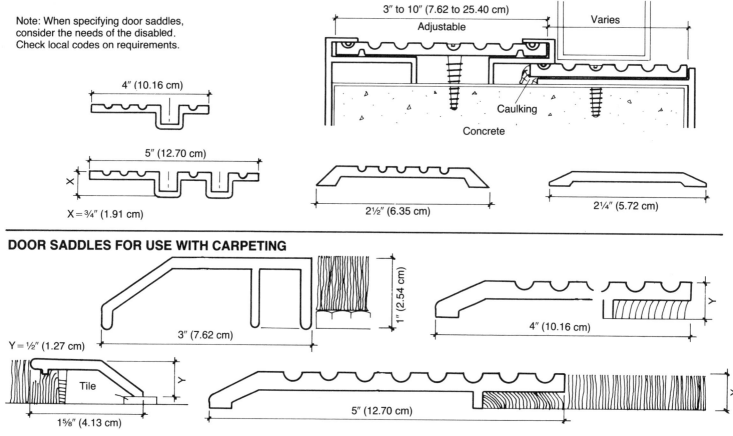

4″ (10.16 cm)

5″ (12.70 cm)

X = ¾″ (1.91 cm)

3″ to 10″ (7.62 to 25.40 cm)

Adjustable

Varies

Caulking

Concrete

2½″ (6.35 cm)

2¼″ (5.72 cm)

DOOR SADDLES FOR USE WITH CARPETING

1″ (2.54 cm)

3″ (7.62 cm)

4″ (10.16 cm)

Y = ½″ (1.27 cm)

Tile

1⅝″ (4.13 cm)

5″ (12.70 cm)

AA	Aluminum Association 818 Connecticut Ave. N.W. Washington, D.C. 20006
AAMA	Architectural Aluminum Manufacturers Association 35 E. Wacker Dr. Chicago, IL 60601
ASC	Adhesive and Sealant Council 1600 Wilson Blvd. Suite 910 Arlington, VA 22209 (formerly: Rubber and Plastics Adhesive and Sealant Manufacturers Council)
AWI	Architectural Woodwork Institute 2310 S. Walter Reed Rd. Arlington, VA 22206
BHMA	Builders' Hardware Manufacturers Association c/o Trade Group Associates, Mgrs. 60 E. 42nd St. Room 1807 New York, NY 10017
CDA	Copper Development Association 405 Lexington Ave. 57th Floor New York, NY 10174
DHI	The Door and Hardware Institute 1815 N. Fort Meyer Dr. Suite 412 Arlington, VA 22209
FGMA	Flat Glass Marketing Association White Lakes Professional Bldg. 3310 Harrison St. Topeka, KS 66611
GA	Gypsum Association 1603 Orrington Ave. Evanston, IL 60201
GTA	Glass Tempering Association White Lakes Professional Bldg. 3310 Harrison St. Topeka, KS 66611

IMI	International Masonry Institute 823 15th St., N.W. Suite 1001 Washington, D.C. 20005
ML/SFA	Metal Lath/Steel Framing Association 221 N. LaSalle Chicago, IL 60601
NAAMM	National Association of Architectural Metal Manufacturers 221 N. LaSalle Chicago, IL 60601
NSDJA	National Sash & Door Jobbers Association 20 N. Wacker Dr. Chicago, IL 60606
NWMA	National Woodwork Manufacturers Association 205 W. Touhy Ave. Park Ridge, IL 60068
PIA	Plastics Institute of America Stevens Institute of Technology Castle Point Station Hoboken, NJ 07030
PICC	Plastics in Construction Council Society of the Plastics Industry 355 Lexington Ave. New York, NY 10017
SDI	Steel Door Institute c/o A. P. Wherry & Assoc., Inc. 712 Lakewood Center N. Cleveland, OH 44107
SIGMA	Sealed Insulating Glass Manufacturers Association 111 E. Wacker Dr. Chicago, IL 60601
SMA	Screen Manufacturers Association 410 North Michigan Ave. Chicago, IL 60611

GENERAL

AAMA	Architectural Aluminum Manufacturers Association
402	Voluntary Specifications for Aluminum Sliding Glass Doors
906	Voluntary Specifications for Aluminum Sliding Glass Door Roller Assemblies
1303	Voluntary Specifications for Forced-Entry Resistant Aluminum Sliding Glass Doors
AWI	Architectural Woodwork Institute Architectural Woodwork Quality Standards, Guide Specifications and Quality Certification Program Section 1300-Architectural Flush doors
DHI	(The) Door & Hardware Institute Hardware Reinforcements on Steel Doors and Frames
FS RR-D-575B	Federal Specifications Door, Metal, Sliding and Swinging: Door Frame Metal (Flush and Semi-flush)
NAAMM	National Association of Architectural Metal Manufacturers • Hollow Metal Technical & Design Manual • Fire-Rated Custom Doors & Frames, 1974 • The Entrance Manual • Custom Hollow Metal Doors and Frames
NFPA	National Fire Protection Association
NFPA 80-81	Standard for Fire Doors and Windows (ANSI A2.7-73)
NFPA 252	Standard Methods of Fire Tests of Door Assemblies
NWMA	National Woodwork Manufacturers Association
1.S.3-70	Wood Sliding Patio Doors
NWMA1.S.1-80	Wood Flush Doors
NWMA/ANSI 1.S.5-73	Ponderosa Pine Doors Standard

ASSEMBLIES

ANSI	American National Standards Institute
A134.2-1972	Aluminum Sliding Glass Doors (AAMA 402.9-1977)
A151.1-1980	Performance Test for Standard Steel Doors, Frames, Anchors, Hinge Reinforcings, and Exit Device Reinforcings
A123.1-1974	Nomenclature for Steel Doors and Steel Door Frames
A117.1 (1980)	Specifications for Making Building and Facilities Accessible to and Usable by Physically Handicapped People
A115.1- A115.17 Series	Covers the Preparation of Doors and Frames for Bolts, Closers, Latches, Locks, Pivots, and Strikes
A123.1-74	Nomenclature for Steel Doors and Steel Door Frames
UL	Underwriters Laboratories, Inc.
UL 63	Safety Standard for Fire Doors and Frames (ANSI 155.1-70)
UL 10A	Fire Test of Door Assemblies
UL 325	Door, Drapery, Gate, Louver, and Window Operators and Systems • Fire Protection Equipment List • Building Materials Directory

DHI	Door & Hardware Institute Society of Architectural Hardware Consultants • Tech Talk Bulletins SP-1 through SP-4: Specifications • Tech Talk Bulletin EH-1: Electronic Hardware • Tech Talk Bulletin HH-1: Hospital Hardware Problems • Tech Talk Bulletin HTL-1: Hotel Keying • Tech Talk Bulletin HTL-2: Hotel/Motel Hardware • Architectural Hardware Schedule Sequence and Scheduling Format, January 1974 • Recommended Procedure for Processing Hardware Schedules and Templates, December 1974 • Keying Procedure and Nomenclature, February 1975 • Door Butts and Hinges, March 1951 • Doors and Hardware, a monthly magazine
FGMA	Flat Glass Marketing Association Flat Glass Glazing Manual
NAAMM	National Association of Architectural Metal Manufacturers Metal Finishes Manual, 1976 Hollow Metal Technical Design Manual, 1977

HARDWARE & WEATHER STRIPPING

ANSI	American National Standards Institute
A 117.1-1980	Making Buildings and Facilities Accessible to, and Usable by, the Physically Handicapped
A156.3-1978	Exit Devices (BHMA701)
A156.4-1980	Door Controls-Closers (BHAM301)
A156.6-1979	Architectural Door Trim (BHMA1001)
A156.1-1976	Butts and Hinges (BHMA)
BHMA	Building Hardware Manufacturer's Association
BHMA-1601	Power Operated Pedestrian Door Standard
BHM301	• Door Controls (Closers) (ANSI A156.4-1980) • Product Standards and Performance Specifications • Hardware for Labeled Fire Doors • Hardware for Hospitals and Nursing Homes, Revised January 1959 • Hardware for Schools, December 1957 • ". . . or equal" Handbook • Standardization for Terms and Nomenclature of Keying • Materials and Finishes Standard • Sliding and Folding Door Hardware • Locks and Lock Trim
FS	Federal Specifications
FF-H-106C/Gen	Hardware, Builders'; Locks and Door Trim: General Specification for
FF-H-106/1	Hardware, Builders'; Locks and Door Trim: Cylinder Entrance Door Type 121A and 122A
FF-H-106/2	Hardware, Builders'; Locks and Door Trim: Cylinder Entrance Door Type 123A and 123B
FF-H-106/3	Hardware, Builders'; Locks and Door Trim: Letter Box Plates
FF-H-00116D	Hinges, Hardware, Builders'
FF-H-121D	Hardware, Builders'; Door Closers
FF-H-1819	Hardware, Builders'; Auxiliary Devices
FF-H-1820	Hardware, Builders'; Exit Devices
AA-C-30D	Cabinet, Key (Boxes and Racks, Metal, and Identification Systems)
FF-H-111C	Hardware, Builders'; Shelf and Miscellaneous
OSHA	Standards for Wood Products: Means of Egress

Chapter 4

WINDOWS, SKYLIGHTS, AND GLAZING

Window types, X = characteristics

	Double hung	Double hung reversed	Casement, out	Casement, in	Awning, with canopy	Pivoted, vertical	Pivoted, horizontal	Top hinged, out	Bottom hinged, in	Fixed sash	Jalousie	Monitor, continuous	Projected	Horizontal sliding			
Advantages																	
Does not sag	X	X			X	X	X	X	X	X		X		X			
Screen easy to install	X	X		X	X			X						X			
Provides 100% vent opening			X	X	X	X	X	X	X		X	X					
Easy to wash		X		X		X	X		X								
Deflects drafts			X	X	X	X	X				X	X					
Deflects rain when partly open					X		X	X	X		X	X	X				
Directs incoming air upward					X		X		X		X	X	X				
Odd sizes available											X			X			
Large sizes practical										X				X			
Disadvantages																	
Only 50% of area can be opened	X	X												X			
No rain protection when open	X	X	X			X								X			
Vent projects into path				X	X	X	X	X	X			X	X				
Requires weather stripping	X	X	X	X		X	X	X	X					X			
Horizontals prevent view	X	X			X		X				X	X	X				
Verticals prevent view			X	X										X			
Structural weakness: sagging			X	X													
Glass soils when vent open					X		X	X	X		X	X	X				
Air cannot be directed down	X	X	X		X	X		X	X		X		X	X			
Excessive air leakage											X						
Hard to wash											X						
Interferes with drapery				X		X	X		X								
Screens difficult to use						X	X										
Sash must be removed to wash	X							X		X		X		X			

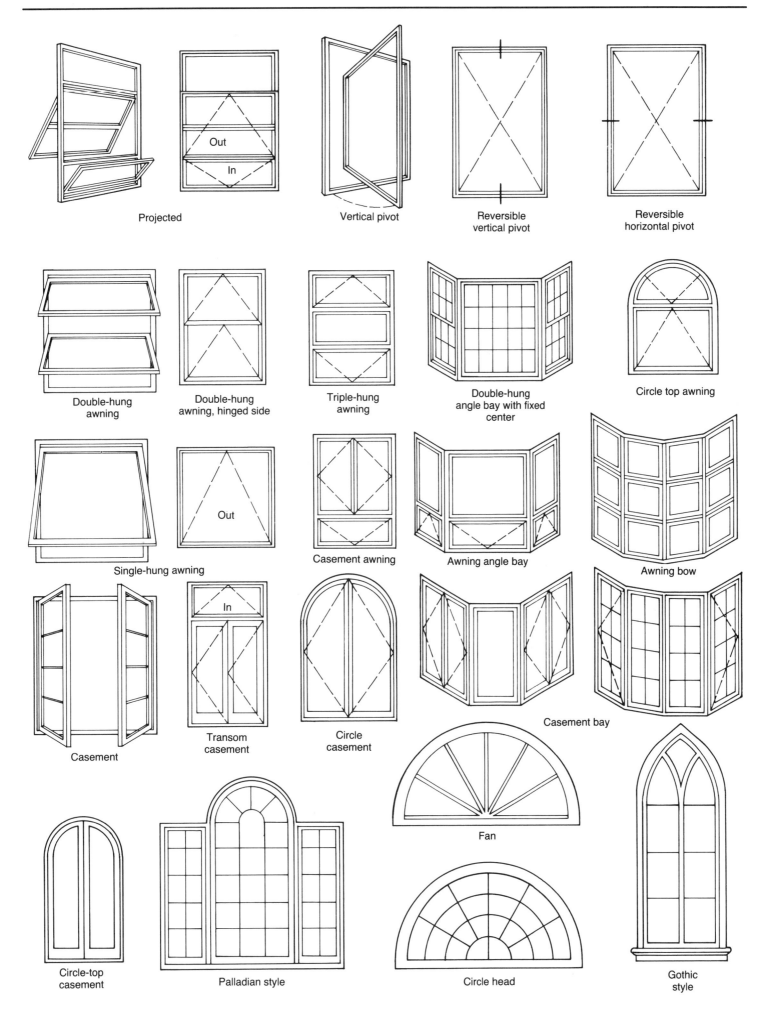

Projected

Vertical pivot

Reversible vertical pivot

Reversible horizontal pivot

Double-hung awning

Double-hung awning, hinged side

Triple-hung awning

Double-hung angle bay with fixed center

Circle top awning

Single-hung awning

Casement awning

Awning angle bay

Awning bow

Casement

Transom casement

Circle casement

Casement bay

Circle-top casement

Palladian style

Fan

Circle head

Gothic style

WOOD DOUBLE-HUNG WINDOW

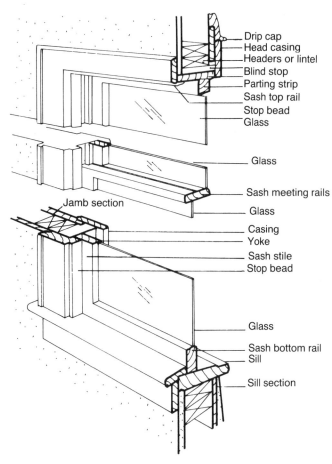

Drip cap
Head casing
Headers or lintel
Blind stop
Parting strip
Sash top rail
Stop bead
Glass

Glass

Sash meeting rails

Glass

Jamb section

Casing
Yoke
Sash stile
Stop bead

Glass

Sash bottom rail
Sill

Sill section

ALUMINUM DOUBLE-HUNG WINDOW

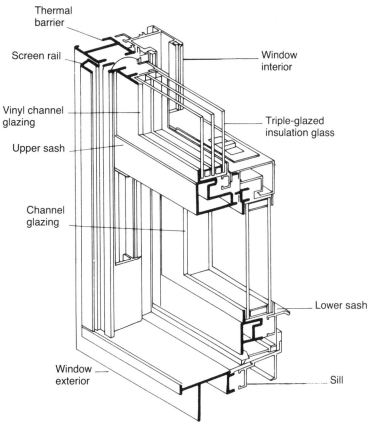

Thermal barrier
Screen rail
Vinyl channel glazing
Upper sash
Channel glazing
Window exterior

Window interior
Triple-glazed insulation glass

Lower sash

Sill

DETAILS OF DOUBLE-HUNG WINDOWS

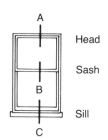

Head
Sash
Sill

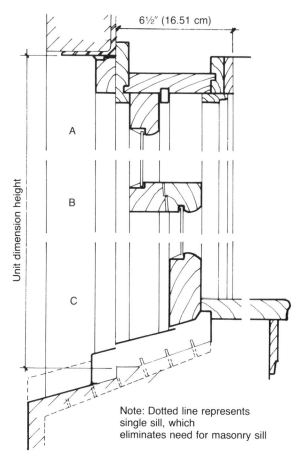

6½" (16.51 cm)

Unit dimension height

A

B

C

Note: Dotted line represents single sill, which eliminates need for masonry sill

Section

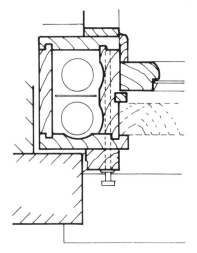

Plan of interior finish of window frame

CASEMENT WINDOW OPTIONS

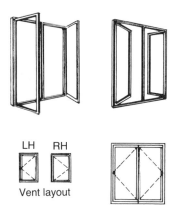

LH   RH

Vent layout

A = 36″ to 42″
    (91.44 to 1065.68 cm)
B = 60″ to 75″
    (152.40 to 190.50 cm)
C = 48″ to 72″
    (121.92 to 182.88 cm)

Note: Hinging of sash shown is standard.
Single sash indicates hinging left, right, or stationary.
Specify left or right as *viewed from the outside.*

TYPICAL WOOD FRAME

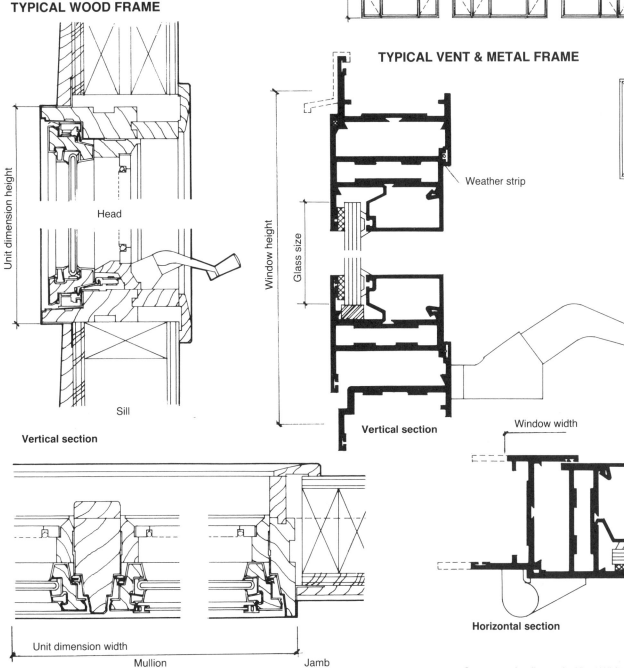

Unit dimension height

Head

Sill

Vertical section

Unit dimension width

Mullion   Jamb

Horizontal section

Basic sizes

| 2′0″ (60.96 cm) | 2′5″ (73.66 cm) | 3′5″ (104.14 cm) | 4′0″ (121.92 cm) | 4′9″ (144.78 cm) | 6′0″ (182.88 cm) |

A

B

Typical combinations

| 8′ (243.84 cm) | 10′ (304.80 cm) | 12′ (365.76 cm) |

C

TYPICAL VENT & METAL FRAME

Weather strip

Window height

Glass size

Vertical section

Window width

Horizontal section

Casement details: scale 3″ = 1′0″ (7.62 cm = 0.3048 m)

AWNING WINDOWS

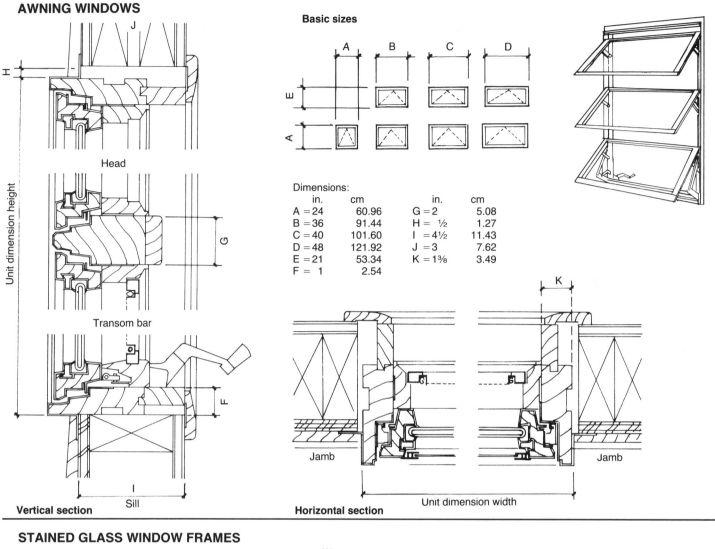

Basic sizes

Dimensions:

	in.	cm		in.	cm
A =	24	60.96	G =	2	5.08
B =	36	91.44	H =	½	1.27
C =	40	101.60	I =	4½	11.43
D =	48	121.92	J =	3	7.62
E =	21	53.34	K =	1⅜	3.49
F =	1	2.54			

Head

Transom bar

Sill

Vertical section

Jamb　　　Jamb

Unit dimension width

Horizontal section

STAINED GLASS WINDOW FRAMES

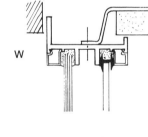

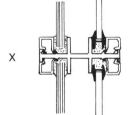

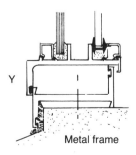

W

X

Y

Metal frame

Sections

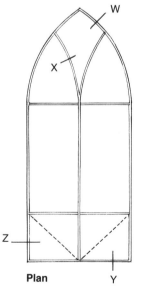

Plan

Z　　　Y

Z

Horizontal section

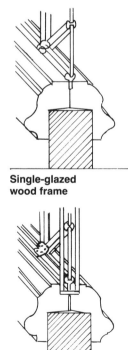

Single-glazed wood frame

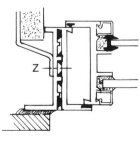

Triple-glazed wood frame

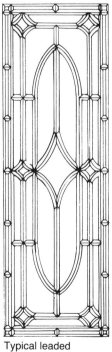

Typical leaded pattern for stained glass

45° ANGLE BAY CASEMENT WINDOW

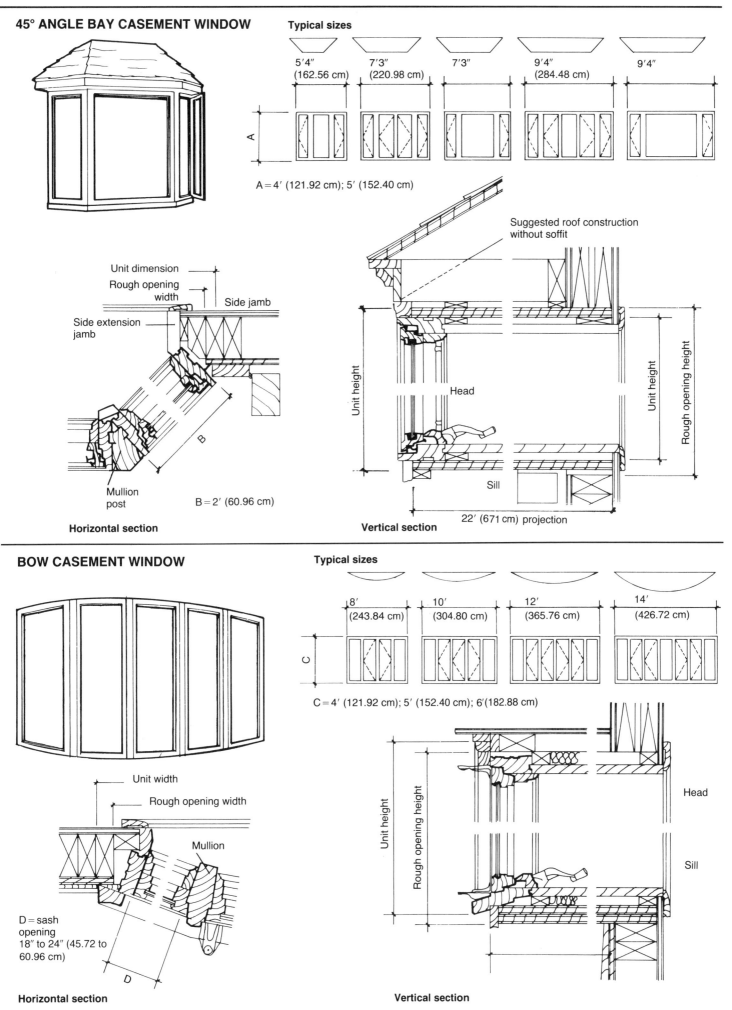

Typical sizes

5'4" (162.56 cm)   7'3" (220.98 cm)   7'3"   9'4" (284.48 cm)   9'4"

A = 4' (121.92 cm); 5' (152.40 cm)

Horizontal section

Unit dimension
Rough opening width
Side jamb
Side extension jamb
Mullion post
B = 2' (60.96 cm)

Suggested roof construction without soffit

Unit height
Head
Sill
Unit height
Rough opening height
22' (671 cm) projection

Vertical section

BOW CASEMENT WINDOW

Typical sizes

8' (243.84 cm)   10' (304.80 cm)   12' (365.76 cm)   14' (426.72 cm)

C = 4' (121.92 cm); 5' (152.40 cm); 6' (182.88 cm)

Horizontal section

Unit width
Rough opening width
Mullion
D = sash opening 18" to 24" (45.72 to 60.96 cm)
D

Unit height
Rough opening height
Head
Sill

Vertical section

WOOD SLIDING GLASS WINDOW DETAILS

Door frame with drywall

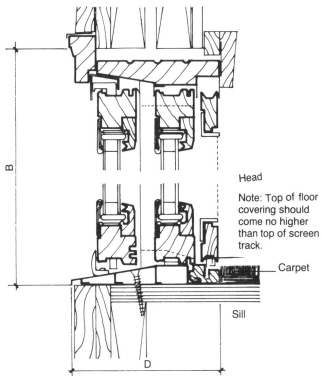

Head

Note: Top of floor covering should come no higher than top of screen track.

Carpet

Sill

Horizontal section

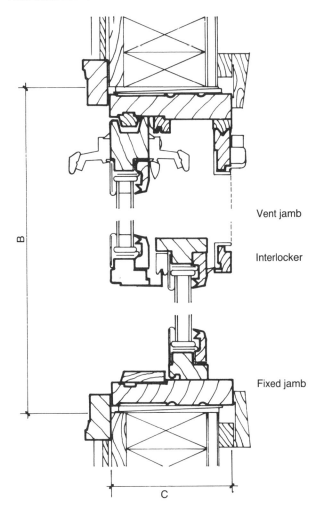

Vent jamb

Interlocker

Fixed jamb

Brick veneer with drywall

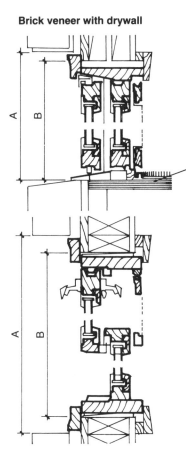

Carpet

Residential stationary glass panel

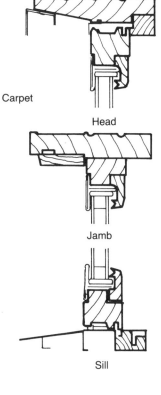

Head

Jamb

Sill

8″ (20.32 cm) masonry with drywall

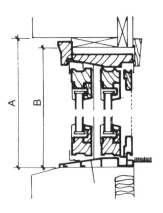

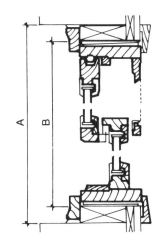

Dimensions:
A = masonry opening height   C = 5¼″ (13.34 cm)
B = rough opening height   D = 6⅜″ (16.19 cm)

Notes: To determine the rough opening width for multiple wood door groupings, add ½″ (1.27 cm) to the combined frame widths. Add 3⅛″ (7.94 cm) to the combined widths to determine the masonry opening width.

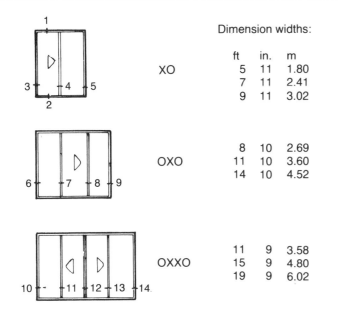

Dimension widths:

		ft	in.	m
XO		5	11	1.80
		7	11	2.41
		9	11	3.02
OXO		8	10	2.69
		11	10	3.60
		14	10	4.52
OXXO		11	9	3.58
		15	9	4.80
		19	9	6.02

Notes:
X = sliding panel
O = stationary panel
when viewed from outside.

Unit widths are 6' to 20' (1.83 to 6.10 m); always indicate widths first. Standard height is 6'10" (2.08 m). For rough opening, add ½" (1.27 cm) to combined frame widths and heights. Frames, with either single or double glazing, are 3⅝" to 5½" (9.21 or 13.97 cm). Surrounding wall conditions as shown do not necessarily comply with regional construction conditions.

Horizontal section of type XO

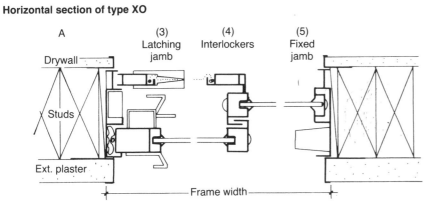

Horizontal section of type OXO

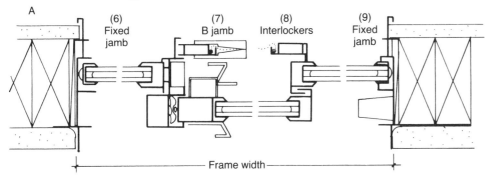

Horizontal section of type OXXO

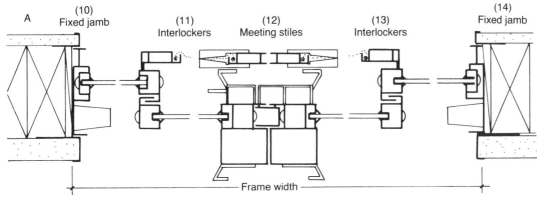

Vertical section of type XO

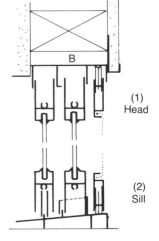

Vertical section of type OXO

A = ¼" (0.64 cm) shim space
B = ½" (1.27 cm) space

WOOD CONSTRUCTION

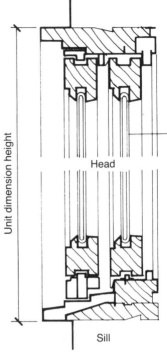

Heights (A) = 1 ft (30.48 cm)
increments
from 2′ to 6′
(60.96 to 182.88 cm)

Glass

Head

Unit dimension height

Sill

Typical sizes

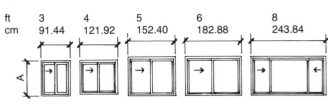

ft	3	4	5	6	8
cm	91.44	121.92	152.40	182.88	243.84

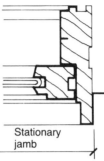
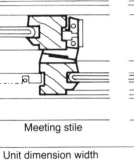

A

Multiple-opening wood residential window

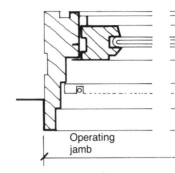

Operating jamb   Meeting stile   Stationary jamb

Unit dimension width

ALUMINUM CONSTRUCTION

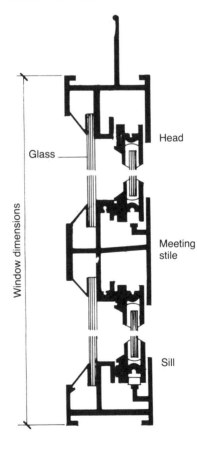

Glass

Head

Meeting stile

Sill

Window dimensions

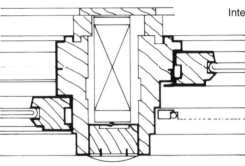

Interior trim

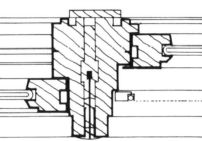

Support mullion
Overall unit dimension width: The
sum of individual unit dimension
widths plus 2″ (5.08 cm) for each
support mullion used.

Overall rough opening width: The
overall unit dimension width plus
½″ (1.27 cm) for both narrow and
support mullions.

Narrow mullion
Overall dimension width:
The sum of individual unit widths
plus ⅜″ (0.95 cm) for each
narrow mullion used.

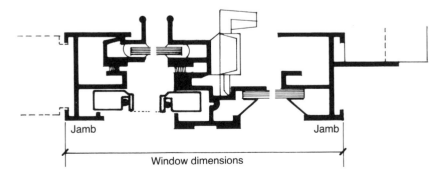

Jamb   Jamb

Window dimensions

Horizontal section

SINGLE-GLASS SLIDE

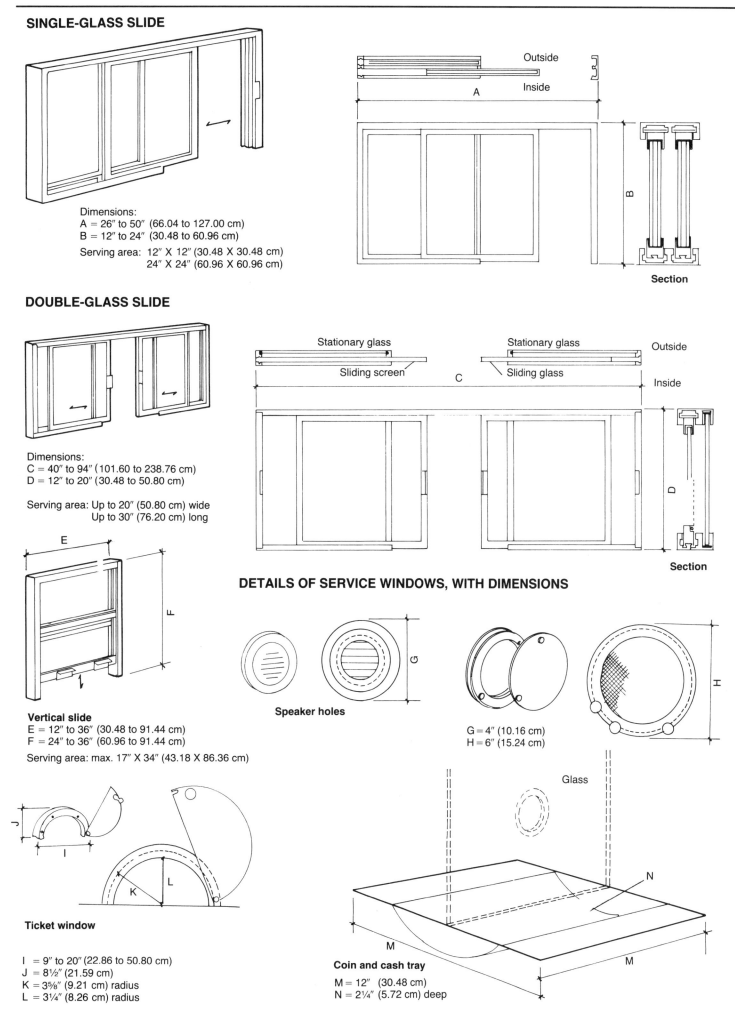

Dimensions:
A = 26″ to 50″ (66.04 to 127.00 cm)
B = 12″ to 24″ (30.48 to 60.96 cm)

Serving area: 12″ X 12″ (30.48 X 30.48 cm)
24″ X 24″ (60.96 X 60.96 cm)

Section

DOUBLE-GLASS SLIDE

Dimensions:
C = 40″ to 94″ (101.60 to 238.76 cm)
D = 12″ to 20″ (30.48 to 50.80 cm)

Serving area: Up to 20″ (50.80 cm) wide
Up to 30″ (76.20 cm) long

Stationary glass   Stationary glass   Outside
Sliding screen   Sliding glass   Inside

Section

Vertical slide
E = 12″ to 36″ (30.48 to 91.44 cm)
F = 24″ to 36″ (60.96 to 91.44 cm)

Serving area: max. 17″ X 34″ (43.18 X 86.36 cm)

DETAILS OF SERVICE WINDOWS, WITH DIMENSIONS

Speaker holes

G = 4″ (10.16 cm)
H = 6″ (15.24 cm)

Glass

Ticket window

I = 9″ to 20″ (22.86 to 50.80 cm)
J = 8½″ (21.59 cm)
K = 3⅝″ (9.21 cm) radius
L = 3¼″ (8.26 cm) radius

Coin and cash tray

M = 12″   (30.48 cm)
N = 2¼″ (5.72 cm) deep

PIVOT WINDOWS

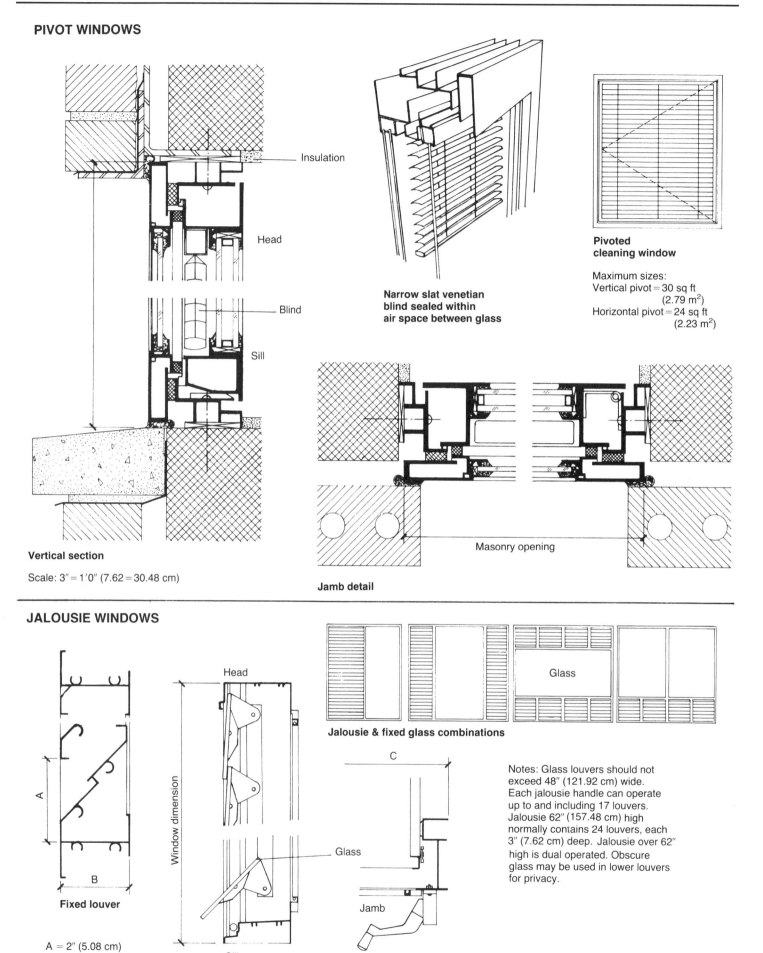

Insulation

Head

Blind

Sill

Vertical section

Scale: 3″ = 1′0″ (7.62 = 30.48 cm)

Narrow slat venetian blind sealed within air space between glass

Pivoted cleaning window

Maximum sizes:
Vertical pivot = 30 sq ft
(2.79 m²)
Horizontal pivot = 24 sq ft
(2.23 m²)

Masonry opening

Jamb detail

JALOUSIE WINDOWS

A

B

Fixed louver

A = 2″ (5.08 cm)
between fixed
louvers
B = 1¾″
(4.45 cm)

Head

Window dimension

Glass

Sill

Movable louver

Jalousie & fixed glass combinations

Glass

C

Glass

Jamb

Detail of movable louver

C = width of glass
louver

Notes: Glass louvers should not
exceed 48″ (121.92 cm) wide.
Each jalousie handle can operate
up to and including 17 louvers.
Jalousie 62″ (157.48 cm) high
normally contains 24 louvers, each
3″ (7.62 cm) deep. Jalousie over 62″
high is dual operated. Obscure
glass may be used in lower louvers
for privacy.

WINDOW REPLACEMENT FIELD MEASUREMENT GUIDE*

You will need to provide measurements for all dimension areas shown here (A-R).

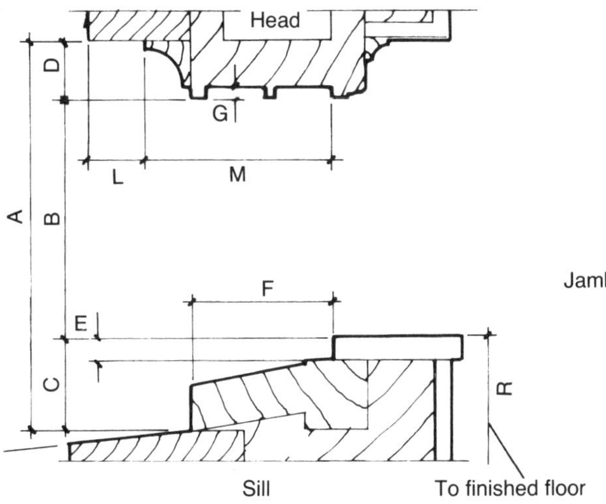

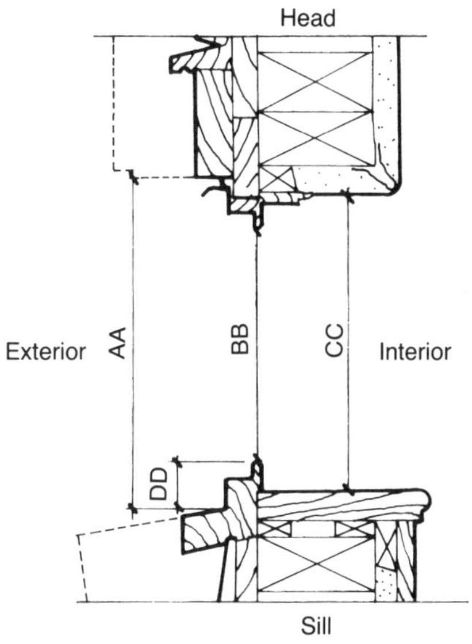

Vertical section

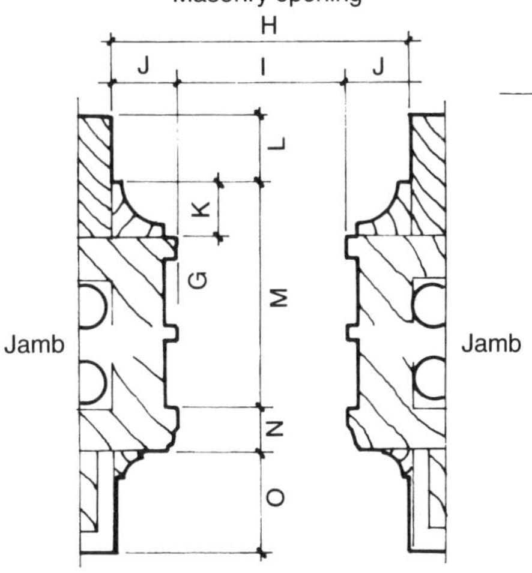

Horizontal section

Masonry opening

Head

Jamb

Sill

To finished floor

Jamb

Horizontal section

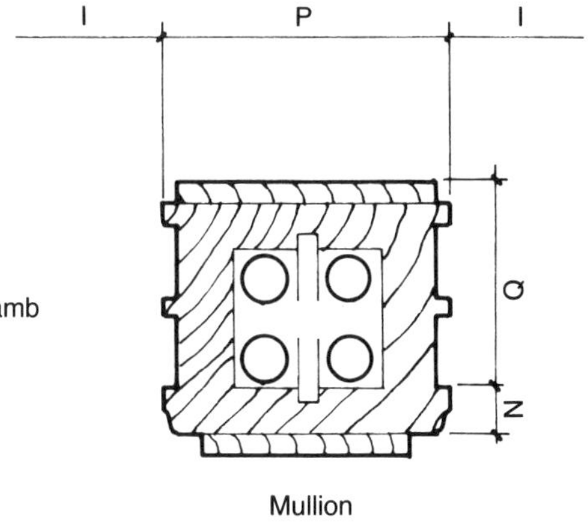

Mullion

Designers should provide the following information when replacing a window:

_____ Building height
_____ Floors or stories
_____ Ceiling height
_____ Are existing blinds mounted on stops?

_____ Clad color
_____ Standard glazing
_____ Double glazing
_____ Slim shades
_____ Diameter of regular muntins

*If sill, head, or jamb conditions are different than shown, draw and dimension their particular profile.

RESIDENTIAL WINDOW REPLACEMENT DETAILS

You will need to provide measurements for all dimension areas shown here (AA-GG).

Steel or aluminum units
in wood frame or brick veneer

Submit the following information:

Existing exterior:
_____ Good
_____ New siding to be installed
_____ New siding recently installed
_____ Brick veneer

Existing interior:
_____ Good, not to be disturbed
_____ To be remodeled

Dashed line = brick veneer

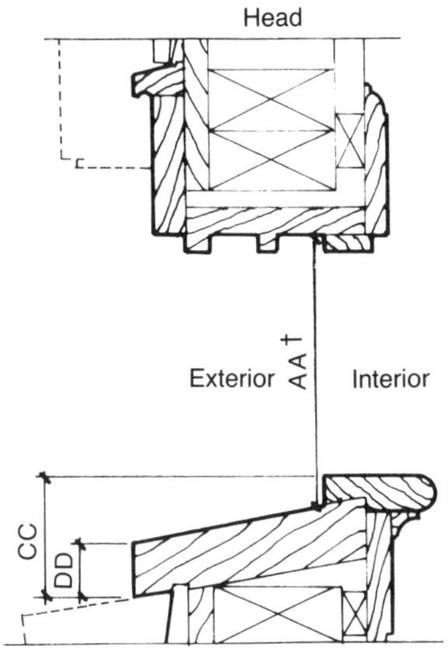

Head

Exterior   Interior

Vertical section

Head

Exterior   Interior

Sill

Vertical section

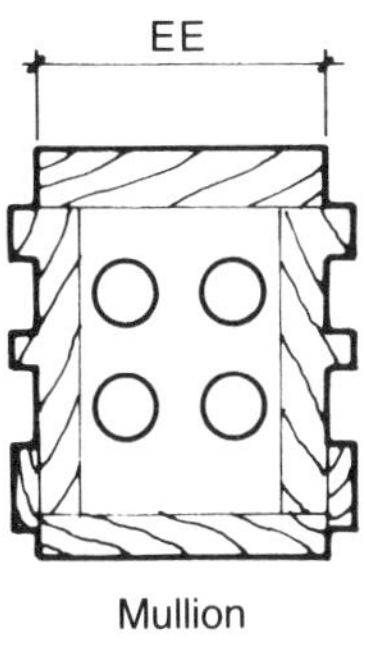

Mullion

Horizontal section

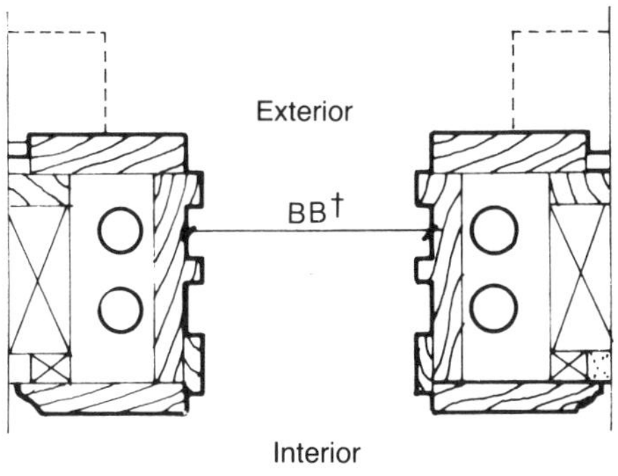

Exterior

Interior

Horizontal section

Exterior

Interior

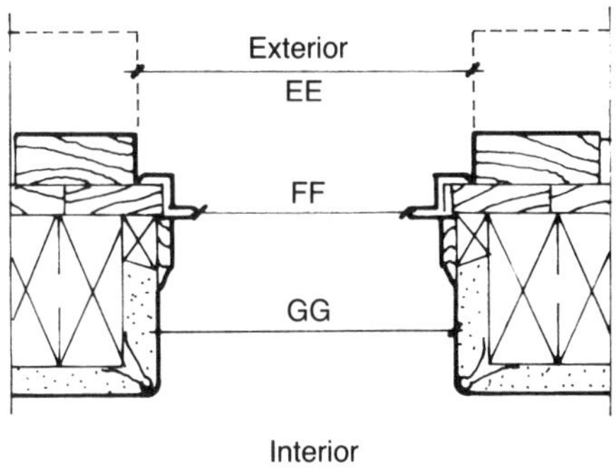

Horizontal section

†Measure width
or height indicated.

Typical sizes

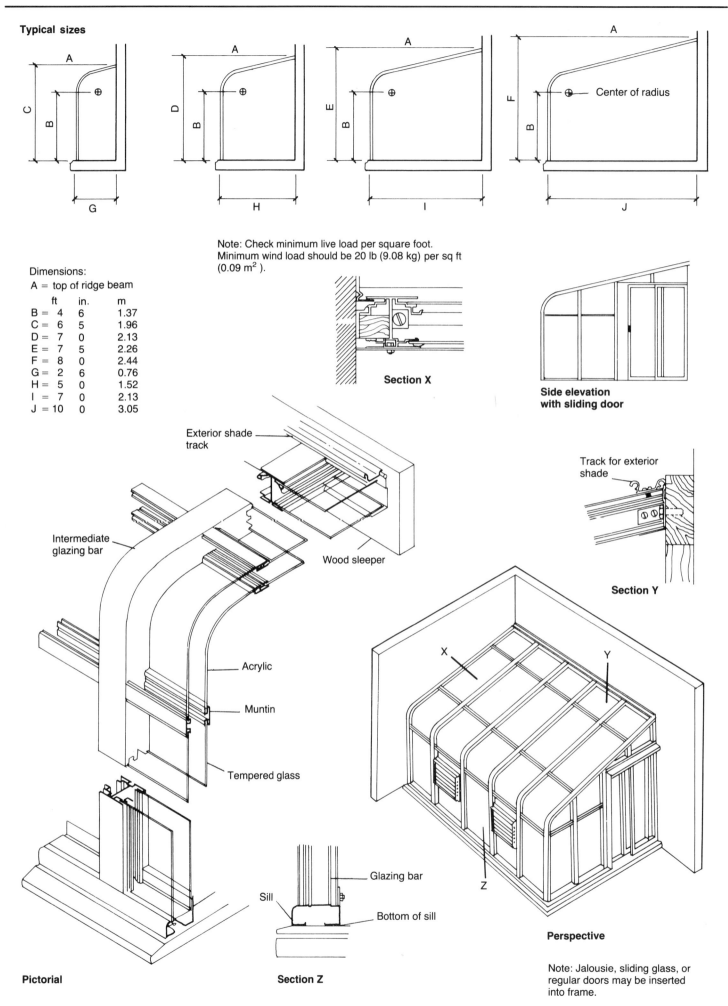

Note: Check minimum live load per square foot. Minimum wind load should be 20 lb (9.08 kg) per sq ft (0.09 m²).

Dimensions:

A = top of ridge beam

	ft	in.	m
B =	4	6	1.37
C =	6	5	1.96
D =	7	0	2.13
E =	7	5	2.26
F =	8	0	2.44
G =	2	6	0.76
H =	5	0	1.52
I =	7	0	2.13
J =	10	0	3.05

Section X

Side elevation with sliding door

Exterior shade track

Intermediate glazing bar

Wood sleeper

Track for exterior shade

Section Y

Acrylic

Muntin

Tempered glass

Glazing bar

Sill

Bottom of sill

Pictorial

Section Z

Perspective

Note: Jalousie, sliding glass, or regular doors may be inserted into frame.

FIVE BASIC TYPES

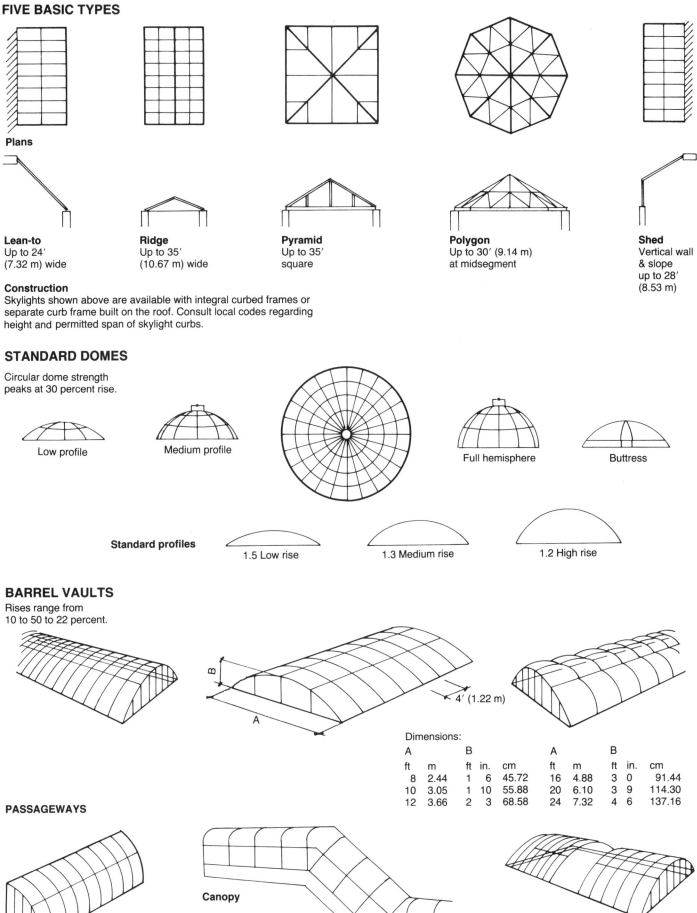

Plans

Lean-to
Up to 24'
(7.32 m) wide

Ridge
Up to 35'
(10.67 m) wide

Pyramid
Up to 35'
square

Polygon
Up to 30' (9.14 m)
at midsegment

Shed
Vertical wall
& slope
up to 28'
(8.53 m)

Construction
Skylights shown above are available with integral curbed frames or separate curb frame built on the roof. Consult local codes regarding height and permitted span of skylight curbs.

STANDARD DOMES

Circular dome strength peaks at 30 percent rise.

Low profile

Medium profile

Full hemisphere

Buttress

Standard profiles

1.5 Low rise

1.3 Medium rise

1.2 High rise

BARREL VAULTS

Rises range from 10 to 50 to 22 percent.

4' (1.22 m)

Dimensions:

A		B			A		B		
ft	m	ft	in.	cm	ft	m	ft	in.	cm
8	2.44	1	6	45.72	16	4.88	3	0	91.44
10	3.05	1	10	55.88	20	6.10	3	9	114.30
12	3.66	2	3	68.58	24	7.32	4	6	137.16

PASSAGEWAYS

Quarter vault

Canopy

Walkway canopy rises range from 10 to 65 percent. Canopy glazed with acrylics.

Movable barrel vault

Straight shafts

Splayed shafts

Tilted shafts

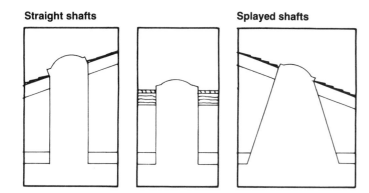

STRAIGHT SHAFT CONSTRUCTION

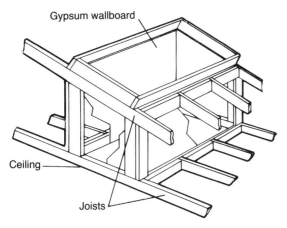

Gypsum wallboard

Ceiling

Joists

SPLAYED SHAFT CONSTRUCTION

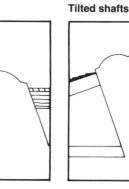
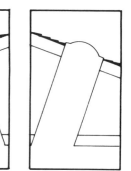

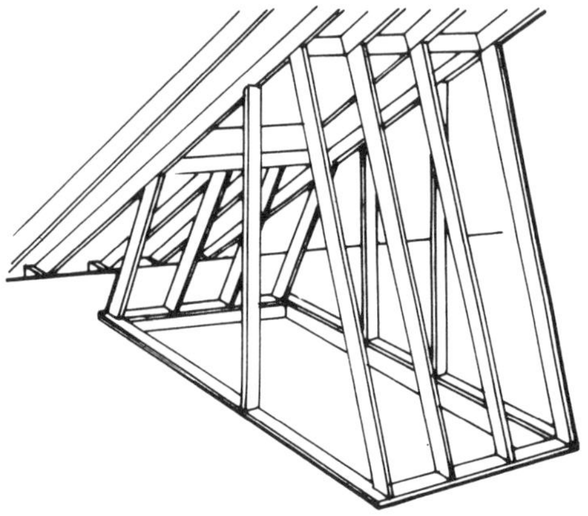

When the area to be lighted is directly under the ridge, locate the skylight as close to the ridge as possible. The shaft can then be built on an angle to the ceiling opening. This may also help to avoid pipes and ductwork in the attic.

On a flat or pitched roof, it is possible to make openings in the ceiling larger than the roof opening so that more light is permitted to enter. Even though the sides may be vertical, the bottom and top are splayed. A 45½" X 30" (115.57 X 76.20 cm) roof opening can become 45½" X 72" (182.88 cm) in the room ceiling.

Note: Glazing shall have an exterior load-carrying element made from 100 percent cast acrylic sheet of a minimum thickness, all as specified in AAMA Std. 1601.1-1976 "Voluntary Thickness Specifications for Acrylic Plastic Domes." The edges of the glazing shall be encased and supported with noncombustible aluminum retainers. Skylights must meet minimum overall thermal performance test criteria including an applied heat loss due to air infiltration or exfiltration that does not exceed 0.05 BTU/hr/ft of periphery in an annual average 7½ mph wind and a heat loss that is less than 6 BTUs/hr/F° [for standard 30¼" X 30¼" (76.84 X 76.84 cm) test unit]. Tests must be conducted in a commercial laboratory certified by the Architectural Aluminum Manufacturers Association.

Vertical section

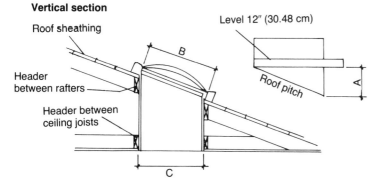

Roof sheathing

Header between rafters

Header between ceiling joists

B

C

Level 12" (30.48 cm)

Roof pitch

A

Recommended skylight sizes in proportion to room size

Inside of curb dimension*	Suitable for room areas
22½ X 22½	up to 80 sq ft
22½ X 30½	up to 100 sq ft
30½ X 30½	up to 140 sq ft
22½ X 46½	up to 160 sq ft
46½ X 30½	up to 225 sq ft
46½ X 46½	up to 340 sq ft

A	Roof pitch*	12/12			6/12			4/12			3/12		
B	Roof dimension*	46½	30½	22½	46½	30½	22½	46½	30½	22½	46½	30½	22½
C	Ceiling dimension*	32¾	21½	15¾	41¼	27	20	44	28¾	21¼	44¾	29¼	21½

*Dimensions in inches.

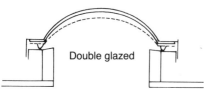

Double glazed

Low-profile skylight (self-flashing or curbed)

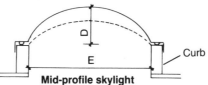

D

E

Curb

Mid-profile skylight
D = dome rise dimension
E = curb-to-curb dimension

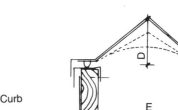

D

E

High-profile skylight

TYPICAL STANDARD DOME

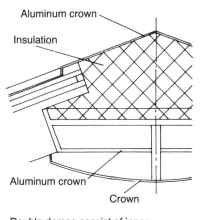

- Aluminum crown
- Insulation
- Aluminum crown
- Crown

Double domes consist of inner and outer domes separated by an insulating air space. This conserves energy plus reduces condensation. Double domes should always be used over heated spaces in northern climates. Single domes should be used in southern climates and over unheated spaces.

DOUBLE DOME SKYLIGHT

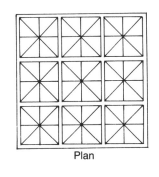

- Double glazing
- Sealant
- Cross rafter
- Curb

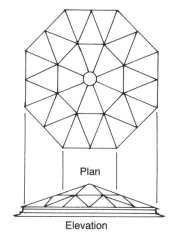

Plan

Elevation

Standard domes are available in diameters (flat-to-flat dimensions) of 12', 15', 18', and 22' (3.66, 4.57, 5.49, 6.71 m) in two bar patterns.

PYRAMID SKYLIGHT

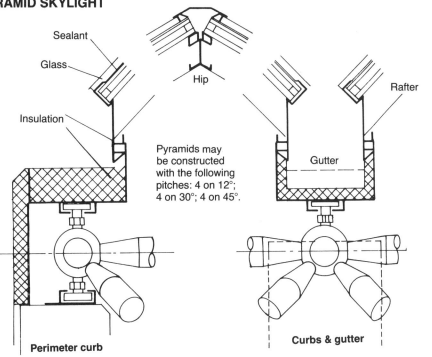

- Sealant
- Glass
- Insulation
- Hip
- Rafter
- Gutter

Pyramids may be constructed with the following pitches: 4 on 12°; 4 on 30°; 4 on 45°.

Perimeter curb

Curbs & gutter

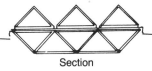

Plan

Section

Pyramid skylights may be constructed in any number of modules, but it is recommended that they be limited to between 8' and 12' (2.44 to 3.66 m). For economy, modules should be kept square.

BARREL VAULT SKYLIGHT

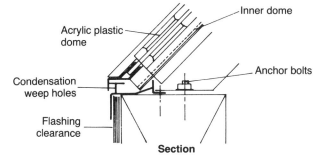

- Acrylic plastic dome
- Inner dome
- Condensation weep holes
- Anchor bolts
- Flashing clearance

Section

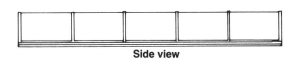

Side view

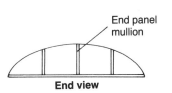

- End panel mullion

End view

AA	Aluminum Association 818 Connecticut Ave., NW Washington, D.C. 20006
AAMA	Architectural Aluminum Manufacturers' Association 35 E. Wacker Dr. Chicago, IL 60601
AHMA	American Hardware Manufacturers' Association 117 E. Palatine Rd. Palatine, IL 60067
AIA	American Insurance Association 85 John St. New York, NY 10038
ASC	Adhesive and Sealant Council 1600 Wilson Blvd., Suite 910 Arlington, VA 22209 (formerly: Rubber and Plastics Adhesive and Sealant Manufacturers' Council)
AWI	Architectural Woodwork Institute 2310 S. Walter Reed Dr. Arlington, VA 22206
BHMA	Builders Hardware Manufacturers' Association c/o Trade Group Associates, Mgrs. 60 East 42nd St. Room 1807 New York, NY 10017
FGMA	Flat Glass Marketing Association White Lakes Professional Bldg. 3310 Harrison St. Topeka, KS 66611
GTA	Glass Tempering Association 3310 Harrison St. Topeka, KS 66611
NAAMM	National Association of Architectural Metal Manufacturers 221 N. LaSalle Chicago, IL 60601
NGDA	National Glass Dealers Association 1000 Connecticut Ave., NW Suite 802 Washington, D.C. 20036
NWMA	National Woodwork Manufacturers' Association 205 W. Touhy Ave. Park Ridge, IL 60068
PIA	Plastics Institute of America Stevens Institute of Technology Castle Point Station Hoboken, NJ 07030
PICC	Plastics in Construction Council Society of the Plastics Industry 355 Lexington Ave. New York, NY 10017
SGAA	Stained Glass Association of America 1125 Wilmington Ave. St. Louis, MO 63111
SIGMA	Sealed Insulating Glass Manufacturers Association 111 E. Wacker Dr. Chicago, IL 60601
SMA	Screen Manufacturers' Association 410 North Michigan Ave. Chicago, IL 60611
SWI	Steel Window Institute c/o Thomas Associates, Inc. 1230 Keith Building Cleveland, OH 44115

GENERAL

AAMA	Architectural Aluminum Manufacturers Association
	Metal Curtain Wall, Windows, Store Front and Entrance Guide Specifications Manual, 1977
T1R-A1-1975	Sound Control for Aluminum Curtain Walls and Windows
302.9-1977	Specifications for Aluminum Windows (ANSI A134.1-1972)
1502.6-1978	Voluntary Standards and Tests of Thermal Performance of Residential Insulating Windows and Sliding Glass Doors
	Voluntary Thickness Specification for Acrylic Plastic Skylight Domes
ANSI	American National Standards Institute
A39.1-1969	Safety Requirements for Window Cleaning
A134.1-1972	Specifications for Aluminum Windows (AAMA 302.9-1977)
ANSI/UL 972	(November 1972) Safety Standard for Burglary—Resisting Glazing Material
Z97.1-1975	Performance Specifications and Methods of Test for Safety Glazing Material Used in Buildings
A-STM STP-552	Window & Wall Testing
B-117-73	Salt Spray (Fog) Testing
E-119-80	Fire Tests of Building Construction and Materials
E-163-80	Fire Test of Window Assemblies
E 331-70 (1975)	Test for Water Penetration of Exterior Windows, Curtain Walls and Doors by Uniform Static Air Pressure Difference
E 413-73	Determination of Sound Transmission Class (for Windows)
CSI 08520	Aluminum Windows, May 1973
	Federal Government
08520	Corps of Engineers—Guide Specifications: Aluminum Windows, November 1980
GSH-8.6a	Department of Defense—Guide Specifications for Military Family Housing: Aluminum Windows and Jalousies, July 1970
TS-08520	Department of Navy, Naval Facilities Engineering Command—(NAVFAC) Type Specifications: Aluminum Windows, November 1971

08-1	Federal Construction Guide Specifications: Windows, November 1971
NFPA	National Fire Protection Association
	• Bulletin #68 Explosion and Venting
	• Bulletin #101 Life Safety Code
	• Bulletin #204 Guide to Heat and Smoke Venting
NWMA	National Woodwork Manufacturers Association
	• Advantages of Wood Windows
	• Care & Finishing of Wood Windows
NWMA/ANSI A200.1	Wood Window Units Standard
NWMA/ANSI A200.4	Wood Sliding Patio Door Standard
NWMA 1.5.4-81	Water-Repellent Preservative Non-Pressure Treatment for Millwork
8WI	Recommended Specifications for Steel Windows, 1975

GLASS & GLAZING

ANSI	American National Standards Institute
ANSI Z97.1-1975	American National Standard Performance Specifications and Methods of Test for Safety Glazing Material Used in Buildings
ANSI/UL 972	Safety Standard for Burglary-Resisting Glazing Material
ANSI/NFPA 80	Standard for Fire Doors and Windows
ANSI/NWMA I.S.5-73	Standard for Ponderosa Pine Doors
ANSI/NWMA I.S.3-70	Standard for Wood Sliding Patio Doors
ANSI/NWMA I.S.2-80	Standard for Wood Window Units
ANSI/AAMA 302.9	Specifications for Aluminum Windows
ANSI/AAMA 402.9	Specifications for Aluminum Sliding Glass Doors
	Federal Government
16 CFR 1201	Safety Standard for Architectural Glazing Materials, Consumer Product Safety Commission
DD-G-451D	Specifications for Flat Glass for Glazing, Mirrors, and Other Uses
DD-G-001403B(1)	Specifications for Plate, Float, Sheet, Patterned and Spandrel Glass—Heat Strengthened and Tempered

INTERIOR FINISHES

METAL LATH

Most plaster bases are supported by metal lath. Lath is used where it is necessary to span open spaces, between either metal or wooden studs. Center-to-center spacing between supports varies from 16″ to 24″ (40.64 to 60.96 cm) depending on the lath used and manufacturer recommendations. Consult local codes when specifying partitions over 10′ (3.05 m) high.

Lath is manufactured in cold-rolled sheets of steel. The sheets are 24″ to 27″ (60.96 to 68.58 cm) wide and 96″ (243.84 cm) long. Some sheets are prepared with water vapor-resistant paper backing.

Metal lath plan symbols

Small diamond mesh

⅛″ (0.32 cm) rib lath

⅜″ (0.95 cm) rib lath

DETAILS OF CORNERS & JOINTS

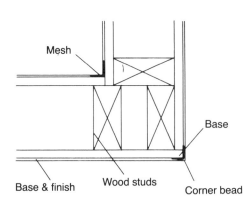

Corner: wood studs

Mesh · Base · Base & finish · Wood studs · Corner bead

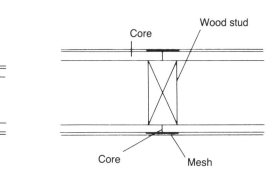

Corner: steel studs

Track · Mesh · Metal stud · Core · Base · Corner bead

Expansion joint

Fiberglass · Steel stud · Track · Expansion joint

Joint

Core · Wood stud · Core · Mesh

Specifications for plaster terminology with metal lath

1. Concrete plaster is used where fire or water resistance is required.

2. Gypsum plaster is used on gypsum block or plasterboards.

3. Lime plaster is a basecoat of hydrated lime and an aggregate.

4. Scratch coat is a first coat in a three-coat job and is composed of lime, sand, and hair. It is scratched with a tool to provide texture to hold subsequent coats.

5. Brown coat is the second coat of plaster in a three-coat job. In a two-coat job, it is the basecoat.

6. Float is another term for a second coat. The thickest coat, it is made of lime and sand.

7. Final coat is composed of lime and plaster of paris. Usually ⅛″ (0.32 cm) thick, it becomes the surface for painting or application of pliant wall coverings.

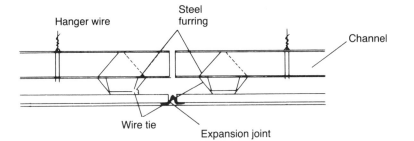

Hanger wire · Steel furring · Channel · Wire tie · Expansion joint

Ceiling control joint

Note: In estimating all plasterwork, measure by the square yard on flat surfaces and by the linear foot for molding and corners. Some estimators deduct for openings (doors and windows) over 21 sq ft (1.95 m²).

Gypsum board is the generic name for a family of panel products consisting of a noncombustible core, primarily of gypsum, with a paper surface covering its face, back, and long edges.

Gypsum board is often called "drywall" or "plasterboard" and differs from products such as plywood, hardboard, and fiber board because of its noncombustible core. It provides a monolithic surface when installed with joint treatment compound.

The various thicknesses of gypsum wallboard available in regular, type X, and predecorated board are as follows:

1/4" (6.35 mm): A lightweight, low-cost board used as a base in a multilayer application to improve sound control or cover existing walls and ceilings when remodeling.

5/16" (7.94 mm): A lightweight gypsum board developed for use in such manufactured construction as mobile homes.

3/8" (9.51 mm): A lightweight board principally applied in a double-layer system over wood framing and as a face layer in repair or remodeling.

1/2" (12.70 mm): Generally used as a single-layer wall and ceiling construction in residential work and in double-layer systems for greater sound and fire ratings.

5/8" (15.88 mm): Used in quality single- and double-layer wall systems. The greater thickness provides additional fire resistance, higher rigidity, and better impact resistance.

1" (25.40 mm): Either a single 1" board or two 1/2" factory-laminated boards used as a liner or as a coreboard in shaft walls, semisolid, or solid gypsum board partitions.

Standard gypsum boards are 4' (1.22 m) wide and 8', 10', 12', or 14' (2.44, 3.05, 3.66, 4.27 m) long. The width is compatible with the standard framing of studs or joists spaced 16" and 24" o.c. (Other lengths and widths are available from the manufacturer on special order.)

The standard edges are tapered, square edge, beveled, rounded, tongue and grooved, and featured joint edge.

Regular gypsum board is used as a surface layer on walls and ceilings (ASTM C 36).

Type X gypsum board is available in 1/2" and 5/8" thicknesses and has improved fire resistance made possible through the use of special core additives. It is also available with a predecorated finish. Type X gypsum board is used in most fire-rated assemblies (ASTM C630).

Gypsum board substrate for floor or roof assemblies has a type X core 1/2" thick and is available in 24" or 48" (121.92 cm) widths. It is used under combustible roof coverings to protect the structure from fires originating on the roof. It can also serve as an underlayment when applied to the top surfaces of floor joists and under subflooring. It may also be used as a base for built-up roofing applied over steel decks.

Gypsum base for veneer plaster is used as a base for thin coats of hard, high-strength gypsum veneer plaster.

Gypsum lath is a board product used as a base to receive hand- or machined-applied plaster. It is available in a 3/8" or 1/2" thickness, 16" or 24" nominal widths, and normally 48" lengths. Other lengths are available on special order.

Predecorated gypsum board has a decorative surface that does not require further treatment. The surfaces may be coated or printed or have a vinyl film. Other predecorated finishes include factory-painted and various textured patterns.

Water-resistant gypsum board has a water-resistant gypsum core and water-repellent paper. It serves as a base for application of ceramic or plastic wall tile or plastic finish panels in bath, shower, kitchen, and laundry areas. It is available with a regular or type X core and in 1/2" and 5/8" thicknesses.

Gypsum backing board is designed to be used as a base layer or backing material in multilayer systems. It is available with aluminum foil backing and with regular and type X cores (ASTM C442).

Commonly used metric conversions

Gypsum board thickness		Framing spacing		Fastener spacing		°F	°C	K•M^2/W
in.	mm	in.	cm	in.	cm			
1/4	6.35	16	40.64	2	5.08	50	10	
5/16	7.94	24	60.96	2 1/2	6.35	125	52	0.056
3/8	9.51			7	17.78			0.079
1/2	12.70			8	20.32			0.099
5/8	15.88			12	30.48			0.150
1	25.40			16	40.64			
				24	60.96			

GYPSUM OVER MASONRY

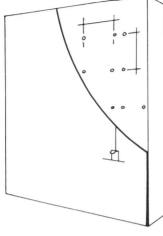

Daub method using
joint compound

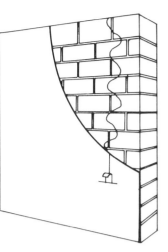

Bead method using
joint compound

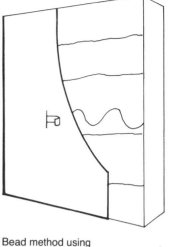

Bead method using
adhesive or wallboard

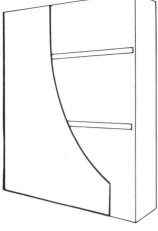

Wood furring

GYPSUM OVER FOAM-INSULATED MASONRY

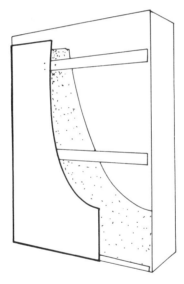

Horizontal
foam furring channels

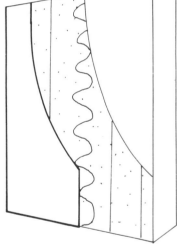

Vertical installation
with joint compound

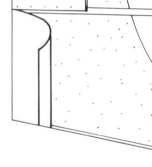

Horizontal installation
with wallboard panel
adhesive

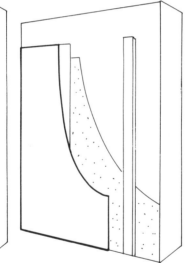

Vertical installed
foam furring channels

Notes
1. Power-driven fasteners should be used to secure furring only to monolithic concrete. Regular concrete nails should be used for fastening to unit masonry. If concrete block is old, test nailing is recommended.
2. When adhesive is applied during cold weather, maintain room temperature between 55° and 70°F.
3. In all wallboard installations, mechanical fasteners should be long enough so they do not penetrate completely to the masonry or concrete.
4. In single-layer applications, all joints between gypsum boards should be reinforced with tape and finished with joint compound.

Rigid plastic foam insulation
Gypsum board may be applied over rigid foam insulation on the interior side of masonry and concrete walls to provide a finished wall and protect the insulation from early exposure to fire originating in the interior space.

Most fire codes require minimum fire protection for rigid foam by application of ½" (1.27 cm) type X gypsum board. Wallboard must cover the entire insulated wall surface including enclosed, unoccupied spaces and the surface above ceilings. Vertical furring should be designed to minimize thermal transfer through the member. Spacing should be 24" (60.96 cm) o.c.

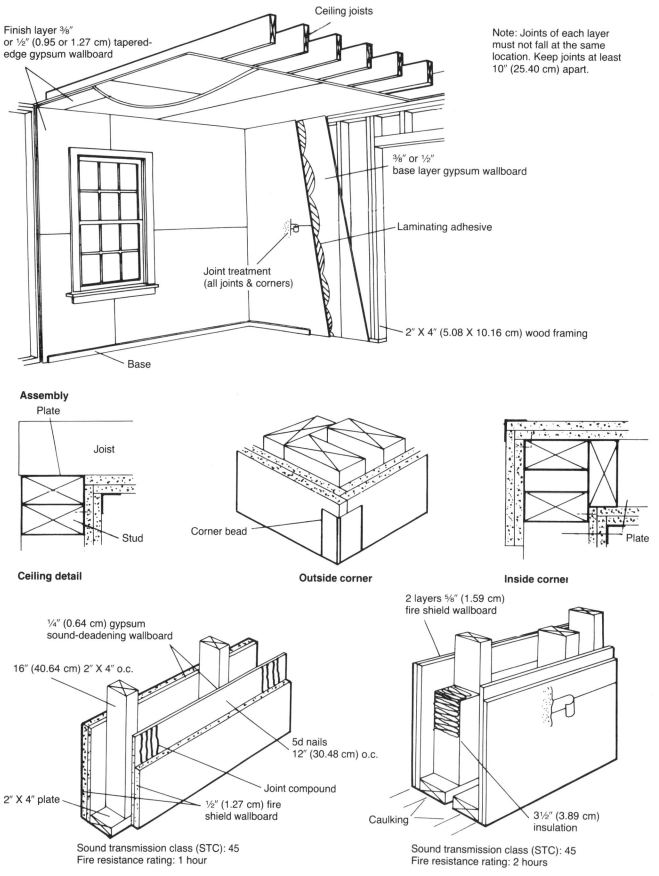

Finish layer ³⁄₈″ or ½″ (0.95 or 1.27 cm) tapered-edge gypsum wallboard

Ceiling joists

Note: Joints of each layer must not fall at the same location. Keep joints at least 10″ (25.40 cm) apart.

³⁄₈″ or ½″ base layer gypsum wallboard

Laminating adhesive

Joint treatment (all joints & corners)

2″ X 4″ (5.08 X 10.16 cm) wood framing

Base

Assembly

Plate

Joist

Stud

Ceiling detail

Corner bead

Outside corner

Plate

Inside corner

2 layers ⁵⁄₈″ (1.59 cm) fire shield wallboard

¼″ (0.64 cm) gypsum sound-deadening wallboard

16″ (40.64 cm) 2″ X 4″ o.c.

5d nails 12″ (30.48 cm) o.c.

2″ X 4″ plate

Joint compound

½″ (1.27 cm) fire shield wallboard

Sound transmission class (STC): 45
Fire resistance rating: 1 hour

Caulking

3½″ (3.89 cm) insulation

Sound transmission class (STC): 45
Fire resistance rating: 2 hours

Typical construction for sound insulation & fire protection*

Notes: Base layer gypsum board should be applied to ceilings first and then to sidewalls. The material is secured with 1¼″ (3.18 cm) screws placed 12″ (30.48 cm) o.c. The finished layer of wallboard is temporarily nailed or braced until the adhesive dries.

*For additional examples, see pages 138-145.

Double-wall construction is recommended in areas where increased fire protection and better sound insulation are desired between rooms.

PERPENDICULAR CEILING APPLICATION

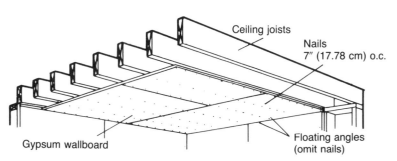

Ceiling joists

Nails
7″ (17.78 cm) o.c.

Gypsum wallboard

Floating angles
(omit nails)

Note: Floating-angle construction helps prevent nail popping and corner cracking. Fasteners at the intersections of walls or ceilings are omitted.

Pictorial detail

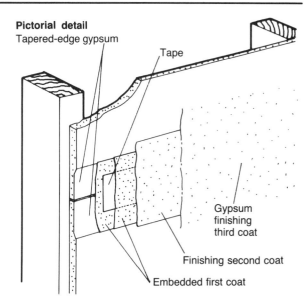

Tapered-edge gypsum

Tape

Gypsum
finishing
third coat

Finishing second coat

Embedded first coat

SINGLE NAILING

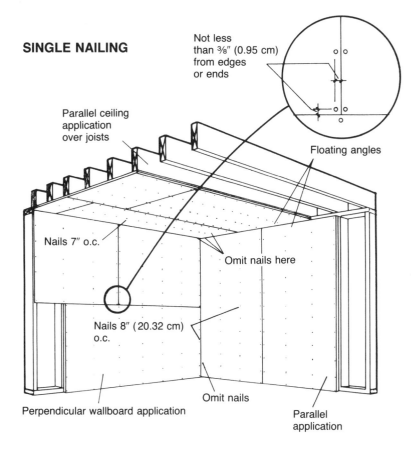

Not less
than ⅜″ (0.95 cm)
from edges
or ends

Floating angles

Parallel ceiling
application
over joists

Nails 7″ o.c.

Omit nails here

Nails 8″ (20.32 cm)
o.c.

Perpendicular wallboard application

Omit nails

Parallel
application

Maximum spacing of framing

Single-ply gypsum board (thickness)		Maximum o.c., spacing of framing	
in.	cm	in.	cm
⅝*	1.59	16	40.64
½*	1.27	24	60.96

*Only ⅝″ thick gypsum board should be used for the face layer, applied perpendicular (horizontally) on ceilings to receive a spray-applied, water-based texture finish. Gypsum board ⅜″ should be increased to ½″ thickness and applied perpendicular to 16″ o.c. framing.

Note: For two-layer sidewall application, with no adhesive between plies, ⅜″, ½″, or ⅝″ thick gypsum board may be applied perpendicularly (horizontally) or parallel (vertically) on framing spaced a maximum of 24″ o.c. Maximum spacing should be 16″ o.c. when ⅜″ thick board is used as the face layer.

DOUBLE NAILING

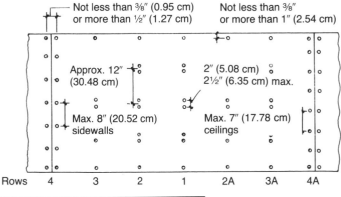

Not less than ⅜″ (0.95 cm)
or more than ½″ (1.27 cm)

Not less than ⅜″
or more than 1″ (2.54 cm)

Approx. 12″
(30.48 cm)

2″ (5.08 cm)
2½″ (6.35 cm) max.

Max. 8″ (20.52 cm)
sidewalls

Max. 7″ (17.78 cm)
ceilings

Rows   4   3   2   1   2A   3A   4A

Base-ply fastener spacing [1]

Location	Nail spacing		Screw spacing		Staple spacing	
	Laminated face ply	Nailed face ply[2]	Laminated face ply[3]	Screwed face ply[2]	Laminated face ply	Nailed or screwed face ply[2]
Walls	8″ (20.32 cm) o.c.	16″ (40.64 cm) o.c.	16″ o.c.	24″ (60.96 cm) o.c.	7″ o.c.	16″ o.c.
Ceilings	7″ (17.78 cm) o.c.	16″ o.c.	16″ o.c.	24″ o.c.	7″ o.c.	16″ o.c.

[1]Fastener size and spacing for applying sound-deadening boards vary for different fire- and sound-rated constructions. The manufacturer's recommendations should be followed.

[2]Fastener spacing for face ply shall be the same as for single-layer application.

[3]Apply 12″ o.c. for both ceilings and walls when supports are spaced 24″ o.c.

Note: The term "on center" (o.c.) refer to the measurement between the center of like objects.

Fire rating (hr)	Sound rating (STC)	Width (in.)	Detailed description	Sketch & design data	
				Fire	Sound
1	40 to 49	3½	**Construction type: gypsum wallboard, mineral fiber, metal studs** One layer ½″ (1.27 cm) type X gypsum wallboard or veneer base applied parallel to each side of 2½″ (6.35 cm) metal studs 24″ (60.96 cm) o.c. with 1″ (2.54 cm) type S drywall screws 8″ (20.32 cm) o.c. to edges and 12″ (30.48 cm) o.c. to intermediate studs; 2″ (5.08 cm) mineral fiber 2.5 pcf friction fit in stud space. Also fire tested with 1½″ (3.81 cm) mineral fiber 3.0 pcf stapled to board in stud spaces. Stagger joints 24″ o.c. each side. (NLB)	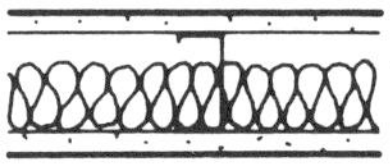	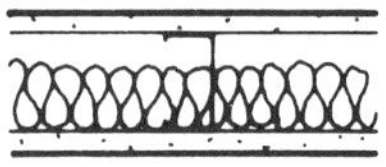
		4½	**Construction type: gypsum wallboard, metal studs** One layer ⅝″ (1.59 cm) type X gypsum wallboard or veneer base applied at right angles or parallel to each side of 3⅝″ (9.21 cm) metal studs 24″ o.c. with 1″-type S drywall screws 8″ o.c. to vertical edges and top and bottom runners and 12″ o.c. to intermediate studs. Stagger all vertical and horizontal joints 24″ o.c. each side. (NLB)	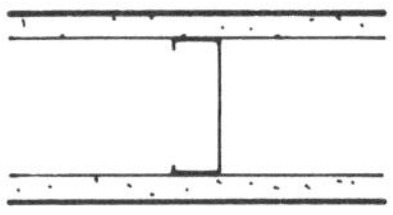	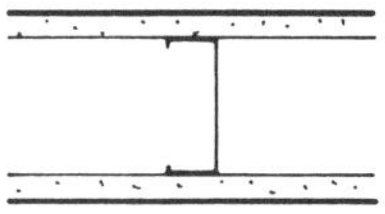
		5½	**Construction type: gypsum wallboard, metal studs** One layer ⅝″-type X gypsum wallboard or veneer base applied parallel to each side of 3⅝″ metal studs 24″ o.c. with 1″-type S drywall screws 8″ o.c. to edges and vertical joints and 12″ o.c. to intermediate studs. Face layer ⅝″ type X gypsum wallboard or veneer base applied on one side parallel to studs with 1⅝″ (4.13 cm) type S drywall screws 8″ o.c. to edges and sides and 12″ o.c. to intermediate studs. Apply ½″ beads of laminating compound 2″ o.c. to full field of face layer. Stagger joints 24″ o.c. each layer and side. Sound tested using 3½″ (8.89 cm) glass fiber in stud space. (NLB)	Fireside 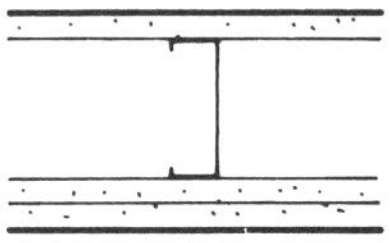 Fireside	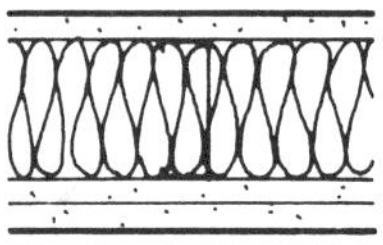
	50 to 54	4	**Construction type: gypsum wallboard, metal studs** One layer ½″ type-X gypsum wallboard applied parallel to one side of 2½″ metal studs 24″ o.c. with 1″ type S drywall screws 8″ o.c. to vertical edges and ⅜″ (0.95 cm) adhesive beads to intermediate studs. Opposite side base layer ½″ type X gypsum wallboard applied parallel to studs with 1″ type S drywall screws 8″ o.c. to vertical edges and 12″ o.c. to intermediate studs. Face layer ½″ type X gypsum wallboard applied parallel to studs with 1⅝″ type S drywall screws 8″ o.c. to vertical edges and with adhesive beads over joints at intermediate studs. Stagger joints 24″ o.c. each layer and face. Face layer may be predecorated. Sound tested using 3″ (7.62 cm) glass fiber friction fit in stud space and all layers screw attached without adhesive. (NLB)	Fireside 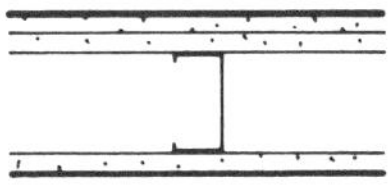 Fireside	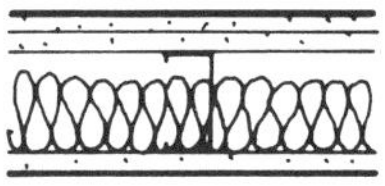
2	50 to 54	3⅝	**Construction type: gypsum wallboard, metal studs** Base layer ½″ type X gypsum wallboard or veneer base applied parallel to each side of 1⅝″ metal studs 24″ o.c. with 1″ type S drywall screws 12″ o.c. Face layer ½″ type X gypsum wallboard or veneer base applied on each side parallel to studs with 1⅝″ type S drywall screws 12″ o.c. Stagger joints 24″ o.c. each layer and side. Sound tested using 1½″ mineral fiber in stud space. (NLB)	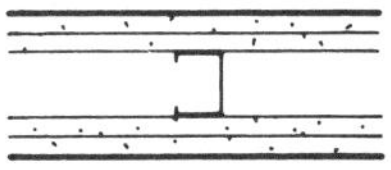	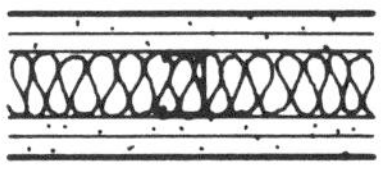
		5	**Construction type: gypsum wallboard, metal studs** Base layer ⅝″ type X gypsum wallboard or veneer base applied at right angles to each side of 2½″ metal studs 24″ o.c. with 1″ type S drywall screws 24″ o.c. Screws spaced ½″ from vertical end joints and ¾″ (1.91 cm) from horizontal edge joints. Face layer ⅝″ type X gypsum wallboard or veneer base applied at right angles to each side with 1⅝″ type S drywall screws 12″ o.c. Screws spaced ½″ from vertical end joints and 1″ from horizontal edge joints. Stagger joints 24″ each layer and side. Sound tested with 2½″ glass fiber in stud space. (NLB)	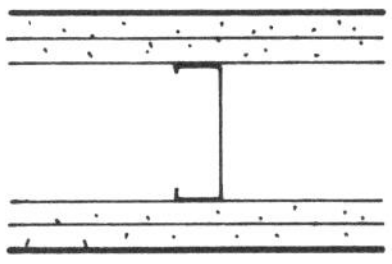	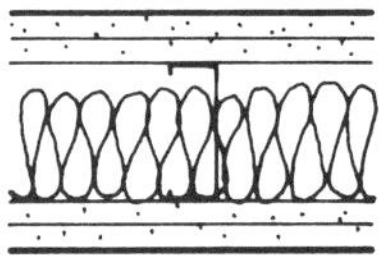

FIRE-RESISTANCE WALL TESTS

All the gypsum walls and partitions officially tested and classified must be at least 100 sq ft (9.29 m²), with no side dimensions less than 9′ (2.74 m). The walls are exposed in a furnace that reaches temperatures designated by the test standard. Many of the walls shown here and on pages 139–143 are tested according to procedures outlined in ASTM Standard E119, "Fire Test Building Construction and Materials." The fire side is the side exposed to the fire during the test.

The time failure is the time in which there is excessive heat transmission, passage of flame, or structural failure. The wall assemblies must sustain a load for which the assembly was designed throughout the test and not allow either flame or hot gases to penetrate. The unexposed surface temperature must not rise more than an average of 250°F above its initial temperature. Unsymmetrical assemblies often require two tests, one for each side. Test results are rated by the amount of time the assembly will withstand the test-regulated temperatures.

LB = load-bearing wall

NLB = non-load-bearing wall

Fire rating (hr)	Sound rating (STC)	Width (in.)	Detailed descriptions	Sketch & design data: Fire	Sketch & design data: Sound
	30 to 39	4 7/8	**Construction type: gypsum wallboard, wood studs** One layer 5/8″ (1.59 cm) type X gypsum wallboard or veneer base applied parallel with or at right angles to each side of 2″ X 4″ (5.08 X 10.16 cm) wood studs spaced 24″ (60.96 cm) o.c. with 6d coated nails 1 7/8″ (4.76 cm) long, 0.0915″ shank, 1/4″ (0.64 cm) heads, 7″ (17.78 cm) o.c. Wallboard nailed to top and bottom plates at 7″ o.c. Stagger joints 24″ o.c. each side. (LB)	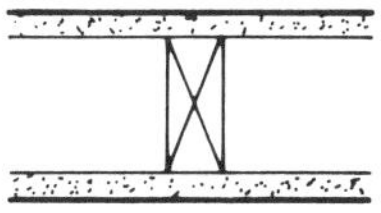	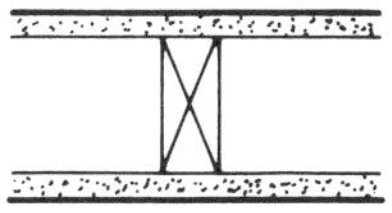
		5 3/8	**Construction type: gypsum lath, gypsum plaster, wood studs** 1/2″ (1.27 cm) 1:2 gypsum-perlite or vermiculite plaster over 3/8″ (0.95 cm) perforated gypsum lath applied at right angles to each side of 2″ X 4″ wood studs 16″ (40.64 cm) o.c. with four No. 13 gauge, 1 1/8″ (2.86 cm) long, 9/32″ (0.71 cm) heads, blue lath nails per lath per stud. (LB)	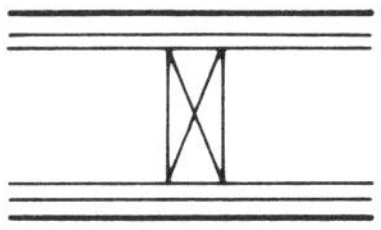	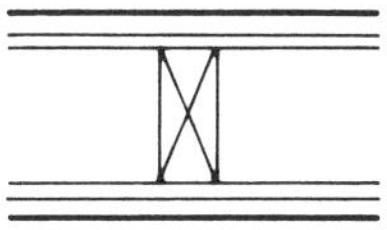
		5 1/8	**Construction type: gypsum wallboard, wood studs** Base layer 3/8″ gypsum wallboard or veneer base applied parallel to each side of 2″ X 4″ wood studs 16″ o.c. with 4d coated nails, 1 3/8″ (3.49 cm) long, 0.080″ shank, 7/32″ (0.56 cm) heads, 8″ (20.32 cm) o.c. Face layer 3/8″ gypsum wallboard or veneer base applied at right angles to each side of studs with laminating compound combed over the entire contact surface and nailed to studs with 5d coated nails 1 5/8″ (4.13 cm) long, 0.086″ shank, 15/64″ (0.60 cm) heads, 8″ o.c. Stagger joints 16″ o.c. each layer and side. (LB)	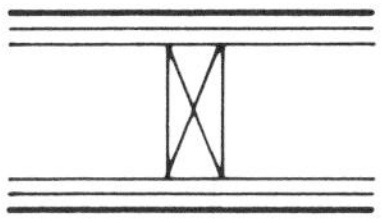	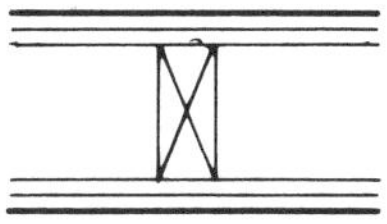
		5 7/8	**Construction type: gypsum lath, gypsum plaster, wood studs** 1/2″ 1:2-1:3 gypsum-sand plaster applied over 3/8″ type X gypsum lath attached at right angles to resilient channels with 3/4″ (1.91 cm) type S drywall screws three across each lath at each strip. Lath attached at top of wall with 5d coated nails, 1 5/8″ long, 0.072″ shank, 7/32″ heads, 3 per lath. Resilient channels attached 16″ o.c. at right angles to each side of 2″ X 4″ wood studs 16″ o.c. with 5d nails as described above. 1/2″ X 3″ (1.27 X 7.62 cm) strips of gypsum wallboard nailed to upper stud plate at ceiling and at mid-height of studs on each side of wall with 5d nails as described above 16″ o.c. Stagger horizontal joints 16″ o.c. and vertical joints 6″ (15.24 cm) o.c. (LB)	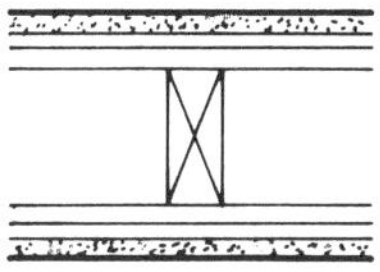	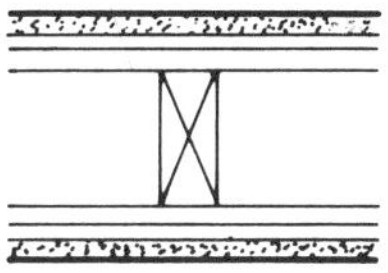
1	40 to 44	5 3/8	**Construction type: gypsum lath, gypsum plaster, wood studs** 1/2″ 1:2 gypsum-sand plaster over 3/8″ plain or perforated gypsum lath applied at right angles to 2″ X 4″ wood studs 16″ o.c. and nailed with 13 gauge, 1 1/8″ long, 0.0915″ shank, 19/16″ (0.75 cm) heads, blue lath nails 4″ o.c. (LB)	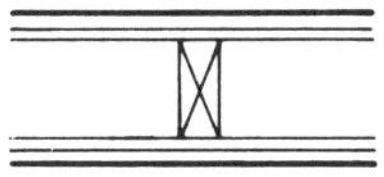	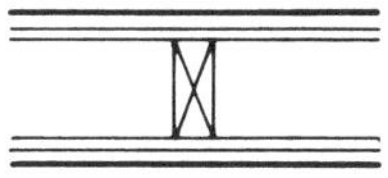
	50 to 59	5 3/8	**Construction type: gypsum wallboard, mineral fiber, wood studs** Base layer 1/4″ proprietary gypsum wallboard applied parallel to each side of 2″ X 4″ wood studs 16″ o.c. with 4d coated nails 1 1/2″ (3.81 cm) long, 0.099″ shank, 1/4″ heads, 12″ (30.48 cm) o.c.; 1 1/2″ mineral fiber 0.8 pcf in stud space. Face layer 5/8″ type X gypsum wallboard or veneer base applied parallel to studs and attached with 6″ wide strips of laminating compound each edge and center and 6d coated nails 1 7/8″ long, 0.0915″ shank, 1/4″ heads, 16″ o.c. to plates. Stagger joints 16″ o.c. each layer and side. (LB)	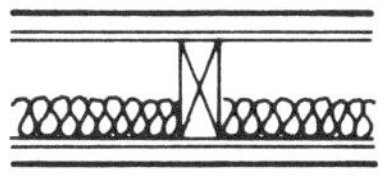	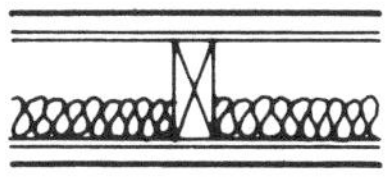
		6 3/4	**Construction type: gypsum wallboard, mineral fiber wood studs** Base layer 5/8″ type X gypsum wallboard or veneer base applied at right angles with 1″ type S drywall screws 12″ o.c. to resilient channels 24″ o.c. attached at right angles to one side of 2″ X 4″ wood studs 16″ o.c. with 1″ (2.54 cm) type S drywall screws. Face layer 5/8″ type X gypsum wallboard veneer base applied on same side parallel with studs and spot laminated with 3/4″ daubs at adhesive 12″ o.c. each way. Opposite side base layer 5/8″ type X gypsum wallboard or veneer base applied parallel to studs with 5d coated nails 1 5/8″ long, 0.086″ shank, 15/64″ heads, 32″ (81.28 cm) o.c. Center layer 1/2″ type X gypsum wallboard or veneer base applied parallel to studs with 8d coated nails 2 3/8″ (6.03 cm) long, 0.113″ shank, 9/32″ heads, 12″ o.c. Face layer 1/4″ regular gypsum wallboard applied parallel with studs and spot laminated to center layer with 3/4″ daubs of adhesive 12″ o.c. each way. Staple 2″ glass fiber 0.90 pcf to three-layer side in stud space. Stagger joints 16″ o.c. each layer and side. (LB)	Fireside 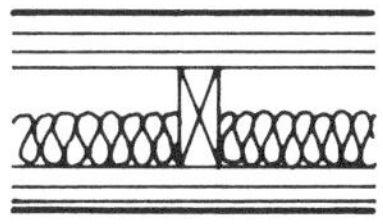	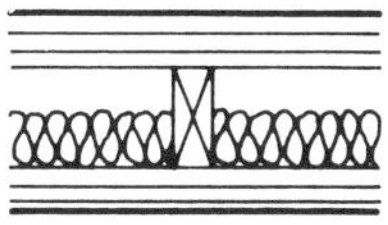
	60 to 64	6 7/8	**Construction type: gypsum wallboard, mineral fiber, wood studs** Base layer 5/8″ type X gypsum wallboard or veneer base applied at right angles with 1″ type S drywall screws 12″ o.c. to resilient channels 24″ o.c. attached at right angles to one side of 2″ X 4″ wood studs 16″ o.c. with 1″ type S drywall screws. Face layer 5/8″ type X gypsum wallboard or veneer base applied on same side parallel with studs and spot laminated with 3/4″ daubs of adhesive 12″ o.c. each way. Opposite side base layer 5/8″ type X gypsum wallboard or veneer base applied parallel to studs with 5d coated nails 1 5/8″ long, 0.086″ shank, 15/64″ heads, 32″ o.c. Center layer 1/2″ type X gypsum wallboard or veneer base applied parallel to studs with 8d coated nails 2 3/8″ long, 0.113″ shank, 9/32″ heads, 12″ o.c. Face layer 3/8″ regular gypsum wallboard applied parallel with studs and spot laminated to center layer with 3/4″ daubs of adhesive 12″ o.c. each way. Staple 2″ glass fiber 0.90 pcf to three-layer side in stud space. Stagger joints 16″ o.c. each layer and side. (LB)	Fireside 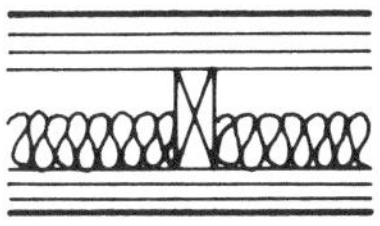	

Fire rating (hr)	Sound rating (STC)	Width (in.)	Detailed descriptions	Sketch & design data	
				Fire	Sound
2	40 to 44	6⅛″	**NONCOMBUSTIBLE GYPSUM WALLS** **Construction type: gypsum wallboard, wood studs** Base layer ⅝″ (1.58 cm) type X gypsum wallboard or veneer base applied at right angles to each side of 2″ X 4″ (5.08 X 10.16 cm) wood studs 24″ (60.96 cm) o.c. with 6d coated nails, 1⅞″ (4.76 cm) long, 0.085″ shank, ¼″ (0.64 cm) heads, 24″ o.c. Face layer ⅝″ type X gypsum wallboard or veneer base applied at right angles to studs over base layer with 8d coated nails, 2⅜″ (6.03 cm) long, 0.10″ shank ¼″ heads, 8″ (20.32 cm) o.c. Stagger joints 24″ o.c. each layer and side. Sound tested with studs 16″ (40.64 cm) o.c. and with nails for base layer spaced 6″ (15.24 cm) o.c. (LB)	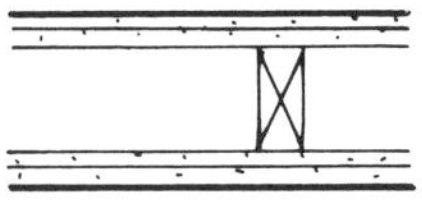	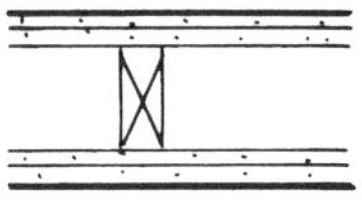
	50 to 54	8	**Construction type: gypsum wallboard, wood studs** Base layer ⅝″ type X gypsum wallboard or veneer base applied at right angles to each side of 2″ X 4″ wood studs 16″ o.c. staggered, 8″ o.c. on 2″ X 6″ wood plates with 6d coated nails 1⅞″ long, 0.085″ shank, ¼″ heads, 24″ o.c. Face layer ⅝″ type X gypsum wallboard or veneer base applied on each side at right angles to studs with 8d coated nails 2⅜″ long, 0.113″ shank, 9/32″ (0.71 cm) heads, 8″ o.c. Stagger vertical joints 16″ o.c. each layer and side. Sound tested with nails for base layer spaced 6″ o.c. Could be load bearing. (LB)	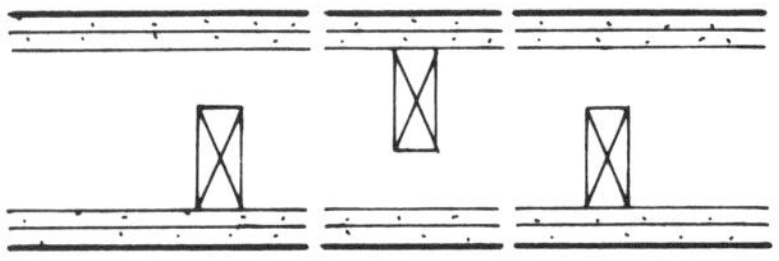	
1	35 to 39	3¾	**MOVABLE & OFFICE PARTITIONS** **Construction type: gypsum wallboard, metal studs** One layer ⅝″ type X predecorated gypsum wallboard applied parallel to each side of 2½″ (6.35 cm) metal studs 24″ o.c. with ⅞″ wide, No. 25 gauge galvanized steel tracks fastened over each stud with 1⅛″ type S drywall screws 9″ (22.86 cm) o.c. Aluminum battens snapped over steel track and 2½″ aluminum base applied along bottom edge on steel base clips screw applied with 1¼″ (3.18 cm) type S drywall screws 24″ o.c. Stagger joints 24″ o.c. each side. (NLB)	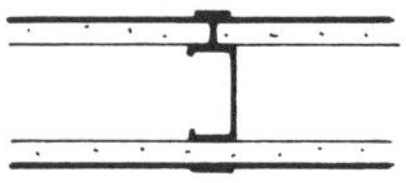	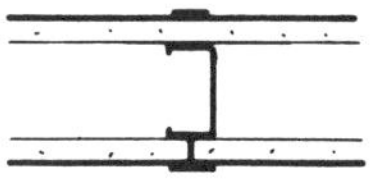
	45 to 49	3½	**Construction type: gypsum wallboard, mineral fiber, metal studs** One layer ½″ type X gypsum wallboard applied parallel to each side of 2½″ metal studs 24″ o.c. with 1″ (2.54 cm) type S drywall screws 12″ (30.48 cm) o.c. Aluminum battens applied over joints with 1″ type S drywall screws 12″ o.c. Boards held to intermediate studs with adhesive. 2″ mineral fiber 3.8 pcf in stud space. Stagger joints 24″ o.c. each side, 3½″ (8.89 cm) aluminum base applied along bottom edge on steel base clips, screw applied with 1¼″ type S drywall screws 24″ o.c. (NLB)	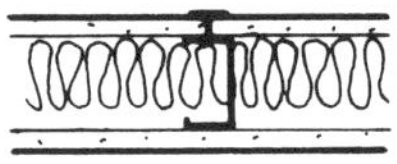	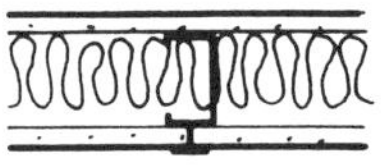
		3⅜	**Construction type: gypsum panels, metal studs** 24″ or 30″ (76.20 cm) wide ¾″ (1.91 cm) kerfed, beveled-edge proprietary gypsum panels installed vertically with 2 9/16″ (6.51 cm) wide H-studs in the kerfed panel edges. Panels fastened to top and bottom 1⅞″ wide metal runners with 1″ type S drywall screws, 2 per panel at top and 1 per panel at bottom runner. Aluminum trim strips screw attached 12″ o.c. through panel into top runner. An aluminum one-piece combination runner and trim may be used in lieu of the steel top runner and aluminum trim strips. Aluminum base trim may be used each side of base with clips screw attached through panel into each stud. Sound tested with 24″ wide panels, one-piece top runner and trim, and 1″ mineral fiber in partition cavity. (NLB)	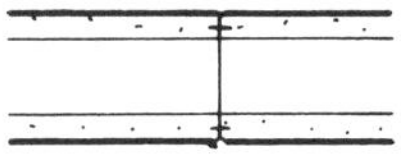	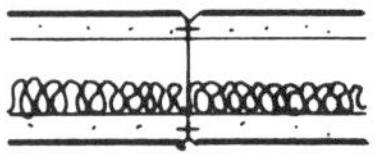
		3¾	**Construction type: gypsum wallboard, metal studs** One layer ⅝″ type X predecorated or plain gypsum wallboard 30″ wide applied parallel to each side of 2½″ metal studs 30″ o.c. with 1¼″ type S drywall screws 30″ o.c. Steel batten retainer strips attached vertically at each stud with 1¼″ Type S drywall screws 9″ (22.86 cm) o.c. and covered with snap-on aluminum batten strips. Aluminum battens fastened horizontally at ceiling over steel batten retainer strips attached with 1¼″ type S drywall screws 9″ o.c. and at floor over steel screw clips 24″ o.c. Sound tested using 2″ glass fiber in stud space. (NLB)	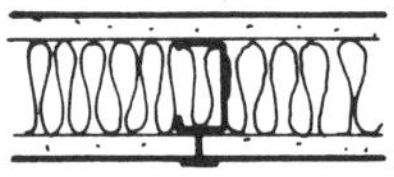	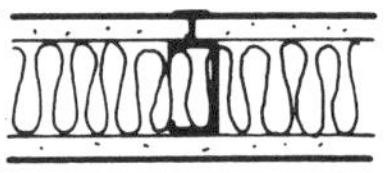
2	50 to 54	4½	**Construction type: gypsum panels, mineral fiber, metal studs** 24″ wide, ¾″ kerfed, beveled-edge proprietary gypsum panels installed vertically each side of 1⅞″ wide top and bottom runners with two 1¼″ type S drywall screws per panel; 2⅝″ (6.67 cm) wide H-studs in kerfed panel edges. On one face only, apply 24″ wide ¾″ kerfed, beveled-edge proprietary gypsum panels vertically with ⅜″ X 2″ (0.95 X 5.08 cm) wide gypsum board spacer strips behind the panels and along the partition top and bottom and ¾″ Z-splines in the kerfed panel edges. Spacer strips fastened into runners with 1⅝″ (4.12 cm) type S drywall screws 24″ o.c. Gypsum panels secured with two 2⅜″ type S drywall screws per panel through spacers into runners. Z-splines secured with screw-attached metal clips 24″ o.c.; 1¼″ wide metal trim strips screw-attached both faces at top; 1¼″ thick mineral fiber batts in stud space. (NLB)	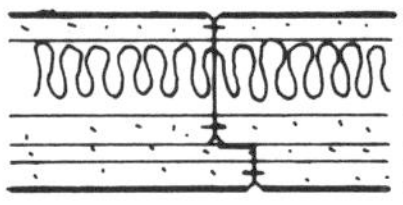	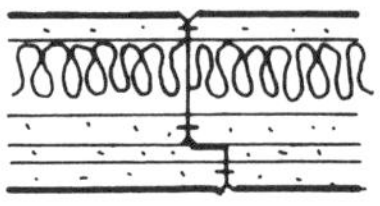
		5¼ to 6¾	**Construction type: gypsum panels, mineral fiber, metal studs** Double row of proprietary hollow core tongue and groove gypsum panels set 3″ (7.62 cm) apart. Panels made of two layers of ⅝″ type X gypsum wallboard or veneer base laminated to ⅝″ type X gypsum wallboard ribs. Panels attached to floor and ceiling runners with 2¼″ (5.72 cm) type S drywall screws 18″ (45.72 cm) o.c. Joints reinforced with 1½″ (3.81 cm) type G drywall screws at quarter points. Sound tested using 2″ mineral fiber in stud space. (NLB)	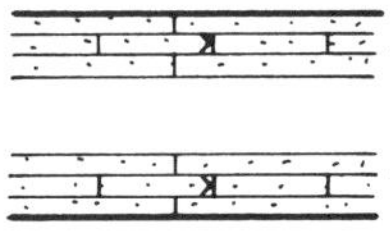	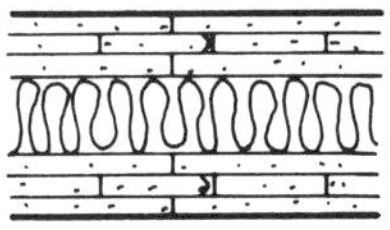

Fire rating (hr)	Sound rating (STC)	Width (in.)	Detailed descriptions	Sketch and design data	
				Fire	Sound
1	50 to 59	10¾	**MOVABLE & OFFICE PARTITIONS** **Construction type: gypsum wallboard, metal studs** ⅝″ (1.58 cm) type X gypsum wallboard or veneer base applied parallel to a double row of 1⅝″ (4.13 cm) metal studs 24″ (60.96 cm) o.c. and 6¼″ (15.88 cm) apart with 1″ (2.54 cm) type S drywall screws 8″ (20.32 cm) o.c. at edges and top and bottom runners, 12″ (30.48 cm) o.c. in field. Stagger joints 24″ each side, No. 25 gauge X 9½″ (24.13 cm) long runner pieces located at ⅓ points used as cross braces and attached with two No. 8 X ½″ (1.27 cm) self-drilling steel screws at each end. Optionally ⅝″ gypsum board pieces 12″ wide X 9½″ long may be used as cross braces fastened to stud pairs with three 1″ type S drywall screws at each end of brace. Sound tested using 3½″ (8.89 cm) glass fiber stapled to one side in cavity. (NLB)	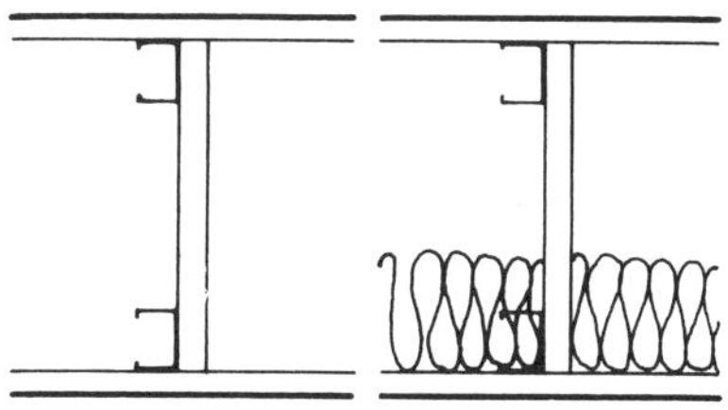 Height limit: 16′0″ (4.88 m)	
		10¼	**Construction type: gypsum wallboard, wood studs** Base layer ¼″ (0.64 cm) gypsum wallboard applied parallel to each side of double row of 2″ X 4″ (5.08 X 10.16 cm) wood studs 16″ (40.64 cm) o.c. and 1½″ (3.81 cm) apart with 4d coated nails 1½″ long, 0.099″ shank, ¼″ heads, 12″ o.c. Face layer ½″ type X gypsum wallboard, veneer base or vinyl faced gypsum board laminated to base layers parallel to studs with ⅜″ (0.95 cm) ribbons of adhesive 16″ o.c. and 5d coated nails 1¾″ (4.45 cm) long, 0.099″ shank, ¼″ heads, 16″ o.c. to top and bottom plates and 4d finish nails 1½″ long, 0.072″ shank, 0.1055″ heads, at 45° angle 16″ o.c. horizontally, 24″ o.c. vertically; 1½″ mineral fiber in stud space. Stagger base layer joints 16″ o.c. and face layer joints 24″ o.c. each layer and side. (LB)		
2	55 to 59	12	**Construction type: gypsum wallboard, metal studs** Base layer ⅝″ type X gypsum wallboard or veneer base applied parallel to a double row of 1⅝″ metal studs 24″ o.c. and 6¼″ apart with 1″ type S drywall screws 8″ o.c. at edges, 12″ o.c. in field; No. 25 gauge X 9½″ long runner pieces located at ⅓ points used as cross braces and attached with two No. 8 X ½″ self-drilling steel screws at each end. Optionally ⅝″ gypsum board pieces 12″ wide X 9½″ long may be used as cross braces fastened to stud pairs with three 1″ type S drywall screws at each end of brace. Face layers ⅝″ type X gypsum wallboard or veneer base applied parallel to studs with 1⅝″ type S drywall screws 8″ o.c. at joints and top and bottom runners, 12″ o.c. in field. Stagger joints each layer and side. Sound tested using 3½″ glass fiber stapled to one side in cavity. (NLB)	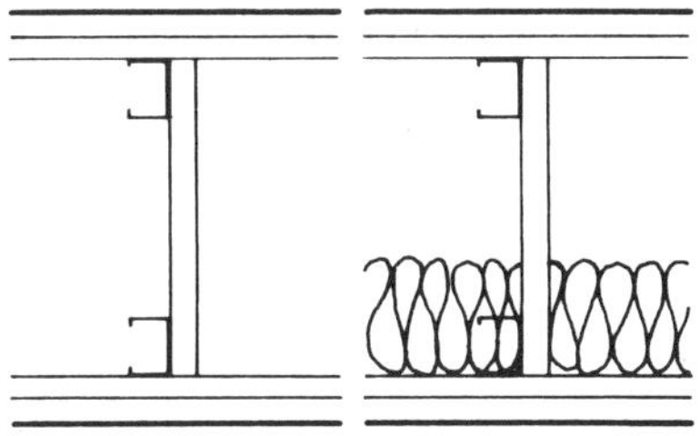 Height limit: 16′0″	
		4	**Construction type: double solid gypsum wallboard** One layer ½″ gypsum wallboard or veneer base applied with ⅜″ beads of laminating compound 2″ o.c. to exterior side only of 1″ gypsum coreboards placed on each side of 1″ air space. Coreboard fastened with No. 6 X 1⅝″ type S screws three per board, into floor and ceiling runners. Sound tested with 3″ (7.62 cm) air space and 1½″ mineral fiber stapled on one side in cavity. (NLB)	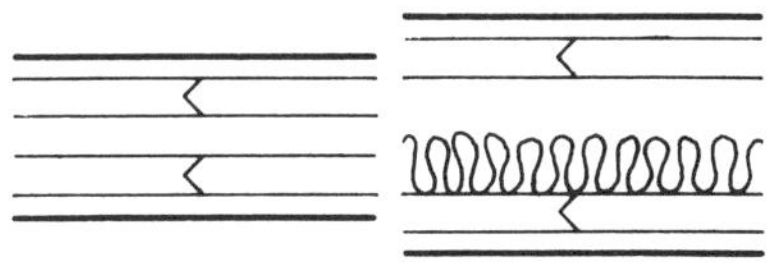 Height limit: 8′6″ (2.59 m)	
		4⅝	**Construction type: double solid gypsum wallboard** One layer ½″ gypsum wallboard or veneer base applied with ⅜″ beads of laminating compound 2″ o.c. to exterior side only of 1″ gypsum coreboards placed on each side of 1⅝″ air space. Coreboard fastened with No. 6 X 1⅝″ type screws, 2 per board, into ceiling runners. Sound tested with 3″ air space and 1½″ mineral fiber stapled on one side in cavity. (NLB)	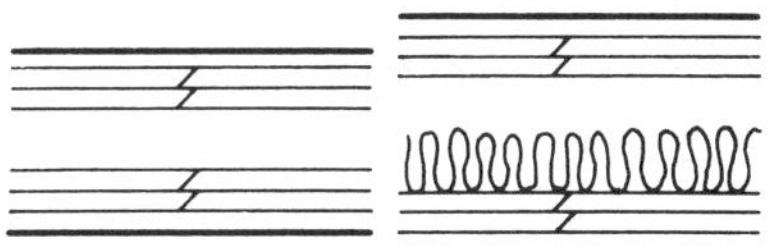 Height limit: 8′6″	
1	35 to 39	3⅛	**SHAFT WALLS** **Construction type: gypsum wallboard, metal C-H studs** 1″ X 24″ proprietary type X gypsum panels inserted between 2½″ (6.35 cm) floor and ceiling J runners with 2½″ proprietary vented C-H studs between panels. One layer ⅝″ proprietary type X gypsum wallboard or veneer base applied parallel to studs on side opposite proprietary gypsum panels with 1″ type S drywall screws spaced 12″ o.c. in studs and runners. STC estimate based on 1″ mineral fiber in cavity. (NLB)	Fireside 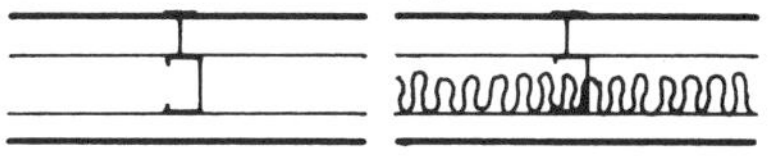 Fireside	
2	45 to 49	3½	**Construction type: gypsum wallboard, metal I studs** 1″ X 24″ type X proprietary gypsum panels inserted between 2½″ floor and ceiling track with tab-flange section of 2½″ metal I studs between proprietary gypsum panels. Resilient channels screw attached, top leg only at right angles to I studs 24″ o.c. maximum with ⅜″ type S screws. Two layers of ⅝″ type X gypsum wallboard or veneer base over resilient channels with base layer applied parallel to resilient channels with 1″ type S drywall screws 24″ o.c. and face layer applied at right angles to base layer with 1⅝″ type S drywall screws 12″ o.c. Sound tested using 1½″ glass fiber friction fit in stud space. (NLB)	Fireside 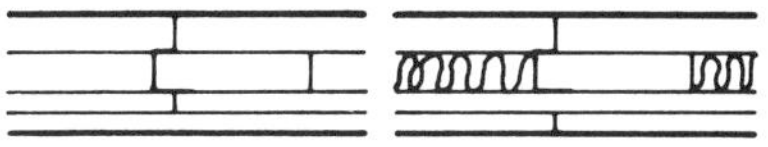 	

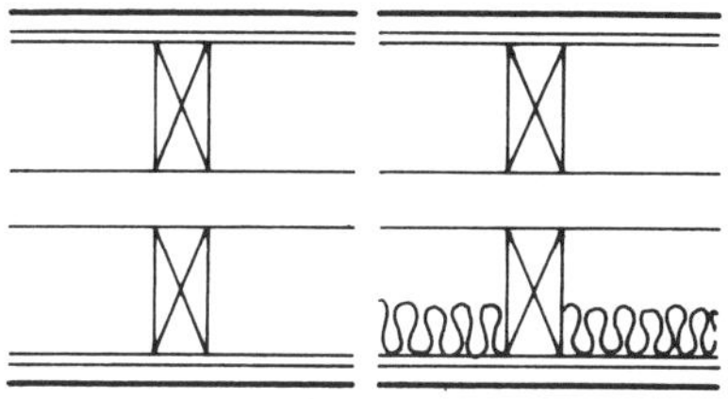

Fire rating (hr)	Sound rating (STC)	Width (in.)	Detailed descriptions	Sketch & design data	
				Fire	Sound
2	50 to 54	3¼	**SHAFT WALLS** **Construction type: gypsum wallboard, metal C-H studs** 1″ X 24″ (2.54 X 60.96 cm) proprietary type X gypsum panels inserted between 2½″ (6.35 cm) floor and ceiling J runners with 2½″ proprietary vented C-H studs between panels. Two layers ½″ (1.27 cm) proprietary type X gypsum wallboard or veneer base applied parallel to studs on side opposite gypsum panels with 1″ type S drywall screws 24″ o.c. in the base layer and 1⅝″ (4.13 cm) type S screws 12″ (30.48 cm) o.c. in studs and runners for the face layer. Face layer joints offset 24″ o.c. from base layer. Sound tested with 1″ mineral fiber in cavity. (NLB)	 Weight: 8 psf	
		4¼	**Construction type: gypsum wallboard, metal I studs** 1″ X 24″ type X proprietary gypsum panels inserted between 2½″ floor and ceiling track with tab-flange section of 2½″ metal I studs between proprietary gypsum panels. Resilient channels screw attached, top leg only at right angles to I studs 24″ o.c. maximum with ⅜″ (0.95 cm) type S screws. Two layers of ⅝″ (1.58 cm) type X gypsum wallboard or veneer base over resilient channels 1″ type S drywall screws 24″o.c. and face layer applied at right angles to base layer with 1⅝″ type S drywall screws 12″ o.c. Sound tested using 1½″ (3.81 cm) glass fiber friction fit in stud space. (NLB)	 Weight: 9 psf	
3	50 to 54	5¾	**Construction type: gypsum board, slotted metal I studs** ¾″ X 24″ (1.91 X 60.96 cm) type X proprietary gypsum panels inserted between 2¼″ (5.72 cm) floor and ceiling tracks and fitted to 2¼″ slotted metal I studs with tab-flange. First layer ⅝″ type X gypsum board applied at right angles to studs with 1″ type S drywall screws, 24″ o.c. Second layer ⅝″ type X gypsum board applied parallel to studs with 1⅝″ type S drywall screws, 42″ (106.68 cm) o.c. starting 12″ from bottom. Third layer ⅝″ type X gypsum board applied parallel to studs with 2¼″ type S drywall screws, 24″ o.c. Resilient channels applied 24″ o.c. at right angles to studs with 2¼″ type S drywall screws. Fourth layer ⅝″ type X gypsum board applied at right angles to resilient channels with 1″ type S drywall screws, 12″ o.c. Sound tested with 1″ glass fiber friction fit in stud space and with ½″ regular gypsum board applied parallel or perpendicular to studs on gypsum panel side with 1″ type S drywall screws, 12″ o.c. (NLB)		
3	45 to 49	5¼	**Construction type: gypsum board, slotted metal I studs** ¾″ X 24″ proprietary type X gypsum panels inserted between 2¼″ floor and ceiling tracks and fitted to 2¼″ slotted metal I studs with tab-flange. First layer ⅝″ type X gypsum board applied at right angles to studs with 1″ type S drywall screws 24″ o.c. Second layer ⅝″ type X gypsum board applied parallel to studs with 1⅝″ type S drywall screws 42″ o.c. starting 12″ from bottom. Third layer ⅝″ type X gypsum board applied parallel to studs with 2¼″ type S drywall screws, 24″ o.c. Resilient channels applied 24″ o.c. at right angles to studs with 2¼″ type S drywall screws. Fourth layer ⅝″ type X gypsum board applied at right angles to resilient channels with 1″ type S drywall screws, 12″ o.c. Sound tested with 1″ glass fiber friction fit in stud space. (NLB)		
1	45 to 49	Weight 4 psf	**NONCOMBUSTIBLE FLOOR-CEILING ASSEMBLIES** **Construction type: steel joists, concrete slab, metal lath, gypsum plaster** ⅝″ 1:2-1:3 gypsum-sand plaster applied over ⅜″ rib metal lath wire tied with No. 18 gauge steel wire 5″ (12.70 cm) o.c. to open web steel joists 24″ o.c. supporting ⅜″ rib metal lath and 2″ (5.08 cm) concrete slab. (Passed 90-minute fire test.)		
2	40 to 44	2 psf	**Construction type: steel joists, concrete slab, metal lath, gypsum tiles** Nominal 24″ X 24″ X ½″ proprietary type X gypsum wallboard lay-in panels supported by steel framing members suspended from steel open web joists supporting ⅜″ rib metal lath and 2½″ concrete slab. (Two-hour restrained and unrestrained.)		
		3 psf	**Construction type: concrete slab, pan joists, gypsum wallboard** ⅝″ type X gypsum wallboard or veneer base screw attached at right angles to rigid furring channels with 1″ type S drywall screws 8″ (20.32 cm) o.c. Furring channels 24″ o.c. suspended from 2½″ precase reinforced concrete joists 35″ (88.90 cm) o.c. with 21 gauge galvanized steel hanger straps fastened to sides of joists. Joist leg depth, 10″ (25.40 cm). End joints on continuous channel with additional channels on each side midway between continuous channels.		

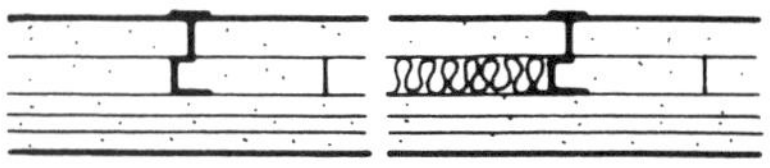

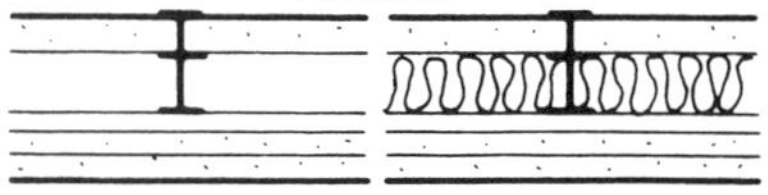

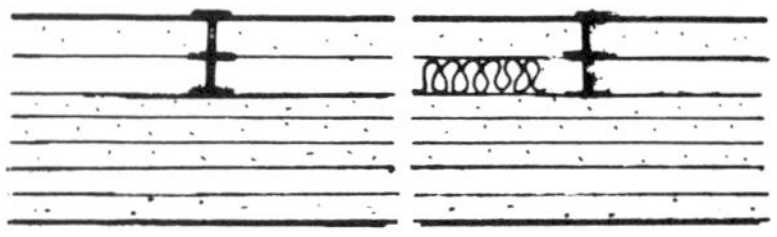

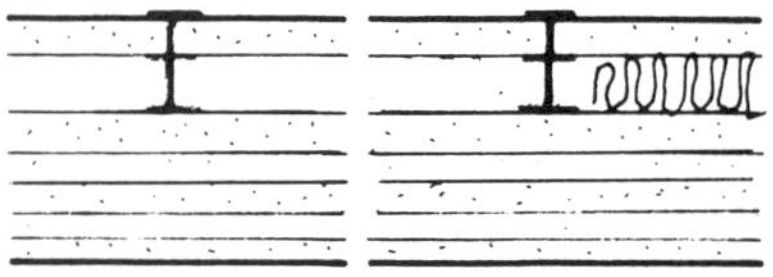

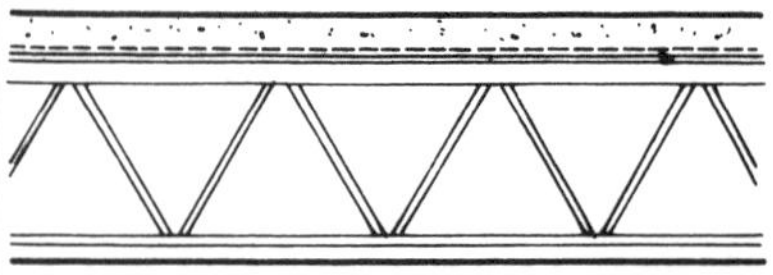

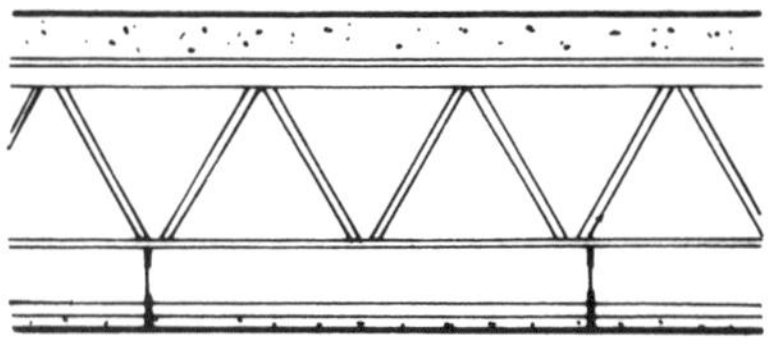

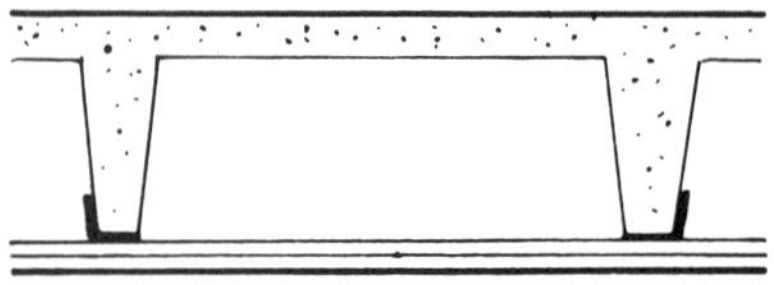

Fire rating (hr)	Fire test	Detailed description	Sketch & design data	
			Fire	Sound
1	UL R1319-133	**NONCOMBUSTIBLE FLOOR-CEILING ASSEMBLIES** **Construction type: steel frame, gypsum wallboard** Two layers ½" (1.27 cm) proprietary type X gypsum wallboard attached to beam cage with type S-12 drywall screws, 1" (2.54 cm) long for base layer and 1⅝" (4.13 cm) for face layer, spaced 12" (30.48 cm) o.c. Base and face joints staggered. Beam cage fabricated from No. 24 gauge ⅞" X 1⅜" (2.22 X 3.49 cm) steel angle screws attached to steel joists and No. 25 gauge 2½" (6.35 cm) steel runner track supporting 1⅝" steel studs 24" (60.96 cm) o.c. below beam lower flange. (One-hour unrestrained beam.)	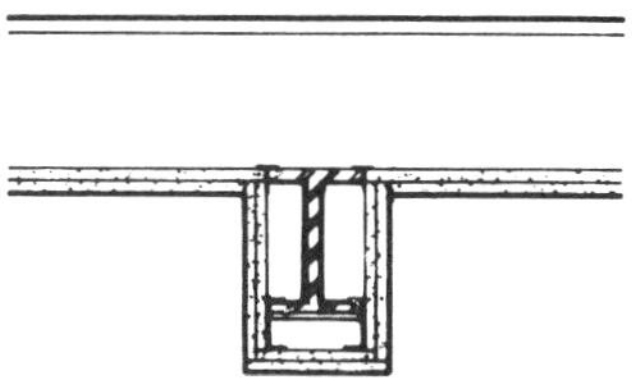	
2	UL R4024-5	**Construction type: steel frame, gypsum wallboard** Two layers of ⅝" (1.58 cm) type X gypsum wallboard or veneer base around beam. Base layer attached with 1¼" type S drywall screws 16" (40.64 cm) o.c., face layer attached with 1¾" (3.18 cm) type S drywall screws 8" (20.32 cm) o.c. to frame of 25 gauge runner and corner angles suspended from 25 gauge channel brackets 24" o.c. Runners attached to steel deck units with fasteners 12" o.c.; ½" space provided between beam and angle edges all around. Outside corners protected by 20 gauge corner bead crimped or nailed. (Two-hour restrained and unrestrained beam.)		
3	UL R4024-5	**Construction type: steel frame, gypsum wallboard** Three layers of ⅝" type X gypsum wallboard or veneer base applied to U-shaped brackets spaced 24" o.c. No. 25 gauge 1⅝" X 1" galvanized metal channels installed parallel to and on each side of the top beam flange to provide a 2⅛" (5.40 cm) clearance between the inner layer of gypsum board and the sides and bottom of the beam, respectively. A 1" X 2" X 24 gauge angle frame attached to lower corners of U brackets with drill screws. U brackets are formed from same material as runner channels or corner angles. First layer of gypsum board attached with 1" type S drywall screws 16" o.c. Second layer attached with 1⅝" type S drywall screws 12" o.c. Apply one layer No. 20 gauge 1" hexagonal galvanized wire mesh under soffit to middle layer and up sides approximately 2" (5.08 cm) with 1⅝" type S drywall screws 12" o.c. Face layer applied with 2¼" type S drywall screws 8" o.c. and one screw at middepth of bracket in each layer. Reinforce bottom corners with 1" metal corner beads nailed with 4d coated nails. 1½" (3.81 cm) long. 0.099" shank, ¼" (0.64 cm) heads; 12" o.c. both legs of bead. (Three-hour restrained beam. Two-hour unrestrained beam.)		
	UL R4197-1	**Construction type: ceiling membrane fireproofing, metal channels, gypsum wallboard** ⅝" proprietary type X gypsum wallboard or veneer base screw attached with 1" type S drywall screws 12" o.c. to rigid furring channels 24" o.c. tied with 18 gauge wire to bottom chord of steel joist spaced 24" o.c. supporting 2½" of concrete. Two furring channels at end joints with ⅝" X 2¾" (1.58 X 6.99 cm) gypsum board strips over joints. (Three-hour unrestrained beam.)		
1	NBS 303,7-3-52	**COLUMNS** **Construction type: gypsum wallboard** Base layer ½" gypsum wallboard or veneer base tied to column with 18 gauge wire 15" (38.10 cm) o.c. Face layer ½" gypsum wallboard or veneer base applied with laminating compound over entire contact surface.		
2	UL R1319-33	**Construction type: gypsum wallboard** Three layers of ⅝" type X gypsum wallboard or veneer base around column with first and second layers nailed with 1⅜" (3.49 cm) long ring shank nails as required for support; ½" X 0.015" metal strapping 30" (76.20 cm) o.c. around second layer beginning 18" (45.72 cm) from each end of column. Face layer attached to 1¼" X 1¼" 25 gauge steel angles held on corners by metal strapping. Drywall corner bead applied each corner with 1" type S drywall screws spaced 12" o.c. at each corner.		
3	UL R2717-31	**Construction type: metal studs, gypsum wallboard** Three layers of ⅝" type X gypsum wallboard or veneer base screw attached to 1⅝" metal studs located at each corner of column. Base layer attached with 1" type S drywall screws 24" o.c. second layer with 1⅝" type S drywall screws 12" o.c. and 18 gauge wire tied 24" o.c. Face layer attached with 2¼" (5.72 cm) type S drywall screws 12" o.c. and 1¼" corner bead at each corner nailed with 6d coated nails, 1⅞" (4.76 cm) long, 0.0915" shank, ¼" heads, 12" o.c.		

NORMAL CONSTRUCTION

Arrows show flanking paths.

SELECT CONSTRUCTION

Caulk relief detail at perimeter
of partition to prevent sound leakage.

PREDESIGN CONSTRUCTION

Simulate laboratory conditions.

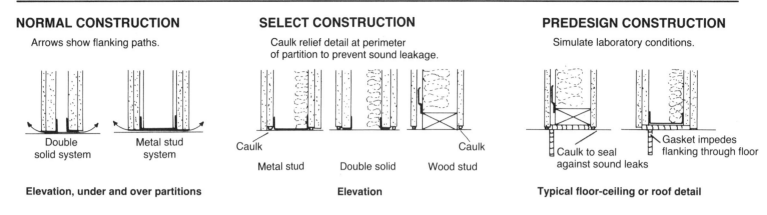

Double solid system

Metal stud system

Elevation, under and over partitions

Caulk

Metal stud   Double solid   Wood stud

Caulk

Elevation

Caulk to seal
against sound leaks

Gasket impedes
flanking through floor

Typical floor-ceiling or roof detail

SOUND LEAKAGE THROUGH ELECTRICAL OUTLET BOXES

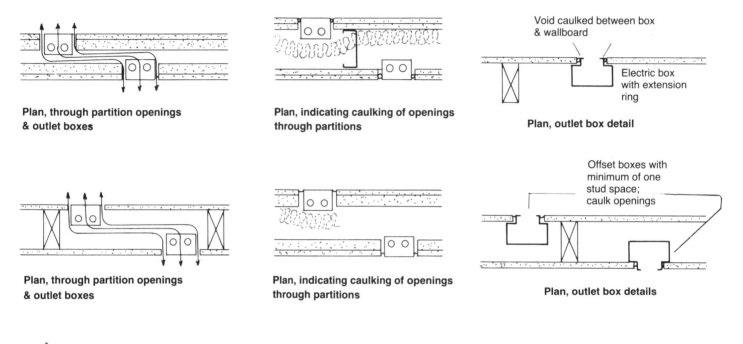

**Plan, through partition openings
& outlet boxes**

**Plan, indicating caulking of openings
through partitions**

Void caulked between box
& wallboard

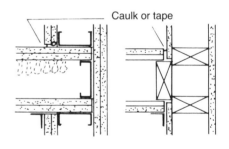

Electric box
with extension
ring

Plan, outlet box detail

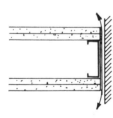

**Plan, through partition openings
& outlet boxes**

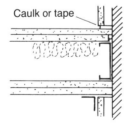

**Plan, indicating caulking of openings
through partitions**

Offset boxes with
minimum of one
stud space;
caulk openings

Plan, outlet box details

SOUND LEAKAGE AT PARTITION ENDS & AT INTERSECTIONS

**Plan, metal stud around flanking
partition ends**

Caulk or tape

Plan, intersection with interior wall

Caulk or tape

Plan, typical partition intersections

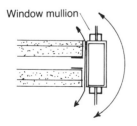

Window mullion

**Plan, double solid, around flanking
partition ends**

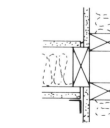

Plan, typical partition-mullion intersection

Plan, intersection with exterior wall

SOUND ABSORPTION COEFFICIENTS OF GENERAL BUILDING MATERIALS & FURNISHINGS

Complete tables of coefficients of the various materials that normally constitute the interior finish of rooms may be found in various books on architectural acoustics. The following short list of materials gives approximate values that will be useful in making simple calculations of reverberation in rooms.

Materials/Frequencies	125 Hz	250 Hz	500 Hz	1000 Hz	2000 Hz	4000 Hz
Brick, unglazed	.03	.03	.03	.04	.05	.07
Brick, unglazed, painted	.01	.01	.02	.02	.02	.03
Carpet						
⅛″ (0.32 cm) pile height	.05	.05	.10	.20	.30	.40
¼″ (0.64 cm) pile height	.05	.10	.15	.30	.50	.55
3⁄16″ (0.48 cm) combined pile & foam	.05	.10	.10	.30	.40	.50
5⁄16″ (0.79 cm) pile & foam	.05	.15	.30	.40	.50	.60
Concrete block, painted	.10	.05	.06	.70	.09	.08
Fabrics						
Light velour, 10 oz per sq yd, hung straight, in contact with wall	.03	.04	.11	.17	.24	.35
Medium velour, 14 oz per sq yd, draped to half area	.07	.31	.49	.75	.70	.60
Heavy velour, 18 oz per sq yd, draped to half area	.14	.35	.55	.72	.70	.65
Floors						
Concrete or terrazzo	.01	.01	.01	.02	.02	.02
Linoleum, asphalt, rubber, or cork tile on concrete	.02	.03	.03	.03	.03	.02
Wood	.15	.11	.10	.07	.06	.07
Wood parquet in asphalt on concrete	.04	.04	.07	.06	.06	.07
Glass						
¼″, sealed large panes	.05	.03	.02	.02	.03	.02
24 oz, operable windows (in closed condition)	.10	.05	.04	.03	.03	.03
Gypsum board, ½″ (1.27 cm) nailed to 2″ X 4″ (5.08 X 10.16 cm) 16″ (40.64 cm) o.c., painted	.10	.08	.05	.03	.03	.03
Marble or glazed tile	.01	.01	.01	.01	.02	.02
Plaster, gypsum or lime, rough finish or lath	.02	.03	.04	.05	.04	.03
Same, with smooth finish	.02	.02	.03	.04	.04	.03
Hardwood plywood paneling— ¼″ thick, wood frame	.58	.22	.07	.04	.03	.07
Water surface, as in a swimming pool	.01	.01	.01	.01	.02	.03
Wood roof decking, tongue-and-groove cedar	.24	.19	.14	.08	.13	.10
Air, sabins per 1000 cu ft @ 50% RH				.9	2.3	7.2

Absorption of seats & audience*
Values are given in sabins per person or unit of seating at the indicated frequency

	125 Hz	250 Hz	500 Hz	1000 Hz	2000 Hz	4000 Hz
Audience, seated, depending on spacing and upholstery of seats	2.5–4.0	3.5–5.0	4.0–5.5	4.5–6.5	5.0–7.0	4.5–7.0
Seats, heavily upholstered with fabric	1.5–3.5	3.5–4.5	4.0–5.0	4.0–5.5	3.5–5.5	3.5–4.5
Seats, heavily upholstered with leather, plastic, etc.	2.5–3.5	3.0–4.5	3.0–4.5	2.0–4.0	1.5–3.5	1.0–3.0
Seats, lightly upholstered with leather, plastic, etc.			1.5–2.0			
Seats, wood veneer, no upholstery	.15	.20	.25	.30	.50	.50
Wood pews, no cushions, per 18″ (45.72 cm) length			.40			
Wood pews, cushioned, per 18″ length			1.8–2.3			

*Multiply coefficients by 100 for absorption percentage.

Note: Refer to acoustical manufacturers' catalogs for acoustical materials data.

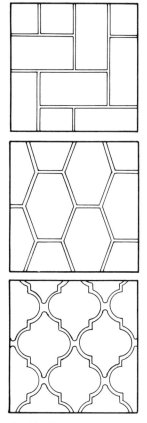
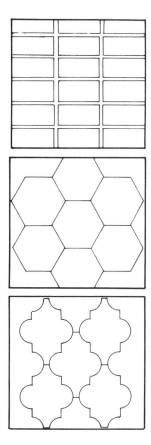
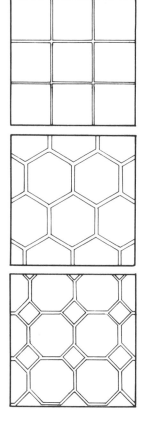
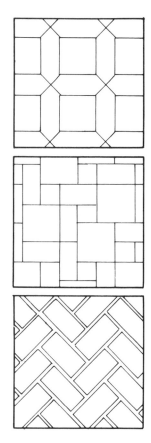

Quality Assurance

Reference standards
1. **American National Standards Institute (ANSI)**
   a. A108.1-1976 Installation of Glazed Wall Tile, Ceramic Mosaic Tile, Quarry Tile, and Paver Tile with Portland Cement Mortar.
   b. A108.5-1976 Installation of Ceramic Tile with Dry-Set Portland Cement Mortar or Latex-Portland Cement Mortar.
   c. A118.1-1976 Dry-Set Portland Cement Mortar.
2. Tile Council of America, Inc. (TCA)
   a. TCA 127-1-1976 Recommended Specifications for Ceramic Tile.
   b. TCA "1979 Handbook for Ceramic Tile Installation."

Inspection
1. Examine surfaces to receive ceramic tile, setting beds, and accessories before tile installation begins for the following:
   a. Defects or conditions adversely affecting quality and execution of tile installation.

b. Deviations beyond allowable tolerances of surfaces to receive tile.
   (1) Portland cement mortar method:
      (a) Maximum variation in subfloor surface: ¼" in 10' (6.35 mm in 3.05 m).
      (b) Maximum variation in vertical and ceiling surfaces: ¼" in 8' (2.44 m).
   (2) Dry-set, latex-portland, and cement mortar methods:
      (a) Maximum variation in subfloor surface: ⅛" in 10' (3.18 mm in 3.05 m).
      (b) Maximum variation in vertical surfaces: ⅛" in 8'.
2. Do not proceed with installation work until unsatisfactory conditions are corrected.

Conditions of surfaces to receive tile
1. Surfaces to be firm, dry, clean, and free of oily or waxy films.
2. Grounds, anchors, plugs, hangers, bucks, electrical and mechanical work in or behind tile to be installed prior to proceeding with tile work.

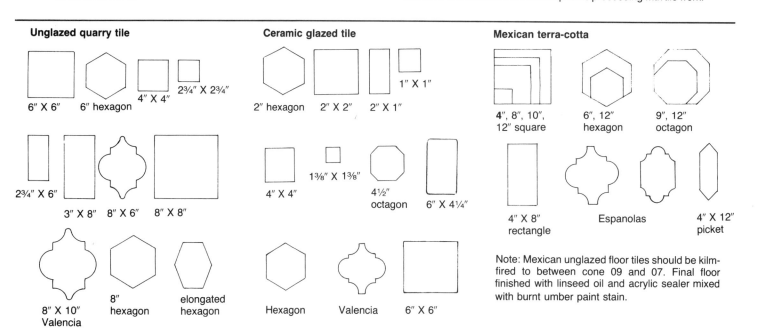

Unglazed quarry tile

6" X 6"   6" hexagon   4" X 4"   2¾" X 2¾"

2¾" X 6"   3" X 8"   8" X 6"   8" X 8"

8" X 10" Valencia   8" hexagon   elongated hexagon

Thickness from ½" to 1½" (1.27 to 3.81 cm)

Ceramic glazed tile

2" hexagon   2" X 2"   2" X 1"   1" X 1"

4" X 4"   1⅜" X 1⅜"   4½" octagon   6" X 4¼"

Hexagon   Valencia   6" X 6"

Thickness from ¼" to ½" (0.64 to 1.27 cm)

Mexican terra-cotta

4", 8", 10", 12" square   6", 12" hexagon   9", 12" octagon

4" X 8" rectangle   Espanolas   4" X 12" picket

Note: Mexican unglazed floor tiles should be kiln-fired to between cone 09 and 07. Final floor finished with linseed oil and acrylic sealer mixed with burnt umber paint stain.

Installation performance levels of ceramic tile floors

Use this guide to find the performance level required, then consult the selection tables and choose an installation that meets or exceeds that performance level. For example, Method F113, rated heavy, can also be used in any area requiring a lower performance level.

General area descriptions		Recommended performance-level rating
Office space, commercial, reception areas	General	Light
Public space in restaurants & stores, corridors, shopping malls	General	Moderate
Kitchens	Residential	Residential or light
	Commercial	Heavy
	Institutional	Extra heavy
Toilets, bathrooms	Residential	Residential
	Commercial	Light or moderate
	Institutional	Moderate or heavy
Hospitals	General	Moderate
	Kitchens	Extra heavy
	Operating rooms	Heavy (use Method F122)
Food plants, bottling plants, breweries, dairies	General	Extra heavy
Exterior decks	Roof decks	Extra heavy (use Method F153)
	Walkways & decks on grade	Heavy, extra heavy (use Method F151 or F152)
Light work areas, laboratories, light receiving & shipping, etc.	General	Moderate or heavy

ANSI installation specifications

A108.1-1976	Glazed Wall Tile, Ceramic Mosaic Tile, Quarry Tile and Paver Tile Installed with Portland Cement Mortar
A108.4-1976	Ceramic Tile Installed with Water-Resistant Organic Adhesives
A108.5-1976	Ceramic Tile Installed with Dry-Set Portland cement Mortar or Latex-Portland Cement Mortar
A108.6-1976	Ceramic Tile Installed with Chemical-Resistant, Water Cleanable Tile-Setting and Grouting Epoxy
A108.7-1967 (R1976)	Electrically Conductive Ceramic Tile Installed with Conductive Dry-Set Portland Cement Mortar
A118.1-1976	Dry-Set Portland Cement Mortar
A118.2-1967 (R1976)	Conductive Dry-Set Portland Cement Mortar
A118.3-1976	Chemical-Resistant, Water-Cleanable Tile-Setting and Grouting Epoxy
A118.4-1973 (R1976)	Latex-Portland Cement Mortar
A136.1-1967 (R1972)	Organic Adhesives for Installation of Ceramic Tile
A137.1-1980	Ceramic Tile

ASTM material specifications

C-36-76a	Gypsum Wallboard
C-144-81	Aggregate for Masonry Mortar
C-150-81	Portland Cement
C-206-79	Special Finishing Hydrated Lime (1968)
C-207-79	Hydrated Lime for Masonry Purposes (1968)
C-627-76	Evaluating Ceramic Floor Tile Installation Systems
C-630-76	Water-Resistant Gypsum Backing Board
C-645-76	Light-Gage Steel Studs, Runners, and Rigid Furring Channels
E-90-75	Laboratory Measurement of Airborne Sound Transmission Loss of Building Partitions
E-413-73	Determination of Sound Transmission Class, Classification

Grout specifications guide		Grout Type							
		Commercial portland cement		Sand-portland cement	Dry-set	Latex portland cement[1]	Mastic[1]	Epoxy[2,3]	Furan[2,3]	Silicon or urethane[4]
A rubber-faced trowel should be used when grouting glazed tile with sanded grout		Wall use	Floor use	Wall-floor use	Wall-floor use					
Tile type	Glazed wall tile (more than 7% absorption)	●			●	●	●			●
	Ceramic mosaics	●	●	●	●	●		●		●
	Quarry, paver & packing house tile	●	●	●		●		●	●	
Areas of use	Dry and intermittently wet areas	●	●	●	●	●	●	●	●	●
	Areas subject to prolonged wetting	●	●	●	●	●		●	●	●
	Exteriors	●	●	●	●	●[5]		●[5]	●[5]	
Performance	Stain resistance[6]	D	C	E	D	B	A	A	A	A
	Crack resistance[6]	D	D	E	D	C	C	B	C	A Flexible
	Colorability[6]	B	B	C	B	B	A	B	Black only	Restricted

[1]Special cleaning procedures and materials recommended.
[2]Mainly used for chemical-resistant properties.
[3]Epoxies are recommended for prolonged temperatures up to 140°F, furans up to 350°F.
[4]Special tools needed for proper application. Silicone, urethane, and modified polyvinylchloride used in pregrouted ceramic tile sheets. Silicone grout should not be used on kitchen countertops or other food-preparation surfaces FDA Regulation No. 21-CFE 177.2600.
[5]Follow manufacturer's directions.
[6]Five performance ratings: best to minimal (A, B, C, D, E).

CEMENT SUBFLOOR WITH CLEAVAGE MEMBRANE

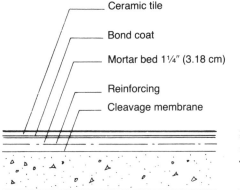

- Ceramic tile
- Bond coat
- Mortar bed 1¼" (3.18 cm)
- Reinforcing
- Cleavage membrane

F111-84

CEMENT MORTAR & BOND

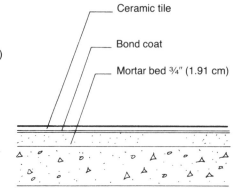

- Ceramic tile
- Bond coat
- Mortar bed ¾" (1.91 cm)

F112-84

DRY-SET MORTAR OR LATEX-PORTLAND CEMENT MORTAR

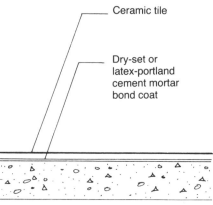

- Ceramic tile
- Dry-set or latex-portland cement mortar bond coat

F113-82

RECOMMENDED USES

Over structural floors subject to bending and deflection.

Requirements
Reinforcing mesh mandatory.
Mortar bed thickness to be uniform.
Nominal 1¼" (3.18 cm) thick.

Materials
Portland cement: ASTM C-150 Type 1.
Sand: ASTM C-144.
Water: potable.
Mortar: 1 part portland cement, 6 parts damp sand by volume.
Reinforcing: 2" X 2" X 16/16 gauge (5.08 X 5.08 cm) welded wire mesh or equivalent.
Cleavage membrane: 15-lb (6.81 kg) roofing felt or 4-mil polyethylene film. (May be omitted over waterproof membranes and pans, by other trades. See Method F121.)
Bond coat: portland cement paste on a plastic bed or dry-set mortar or latex-portland cement mortar on a cured bed.
Expansion joints.
Grout: specify type.

Preparation by other trades
Slab depression to be accurate with float finish.
Slope, when required, to be in subfloor.
Maximum variation in the slab shall not exceed ¼" (0.64 cm) in 10'0" (3.05 m) from the required plane.

Expansion joint (designer must specify expansion joints and show location and details on drawings)
Where tile work abuts restraining surfaces such as perimeter walls, curbs, columns, pipes, etc.
Directly over joints in structural floors including construction joints or cold joints.
In large areas 24' to 36' (7.32 to 10.97 m) each way.
Expansion joints mandatory with quarry tile, recommended with other tile.

Installation specifications
ANSI A108.1.

RECOMMENDED USES

On slab-on-grade construction where no bending stresses occur.
On properly cured structural slabs of limited area.

Limitations
On precast concrete floor systems use cleavage membrane, follow Method F111.

Requirements
Mortar bed thickness to be uniform.
Nominal 1¼" thick.

Materials
Portland cement: ASTM C-150 Type 1.
Sand: ASTM C-144.
Water: potable.
Mortar: 1 part portland cement, 6 parts damp sand by volume.
Bond coat: portland cement paste on a plastic bed or dry-set mortar or latex-portland cement mortar on a cured bed.
Expansion joints.
Grout: Specify type.

Preparation by other trades
Slab depression to be accurate with screed finish and free of cracks, waxy or oily films, and curing compounds.
Slope when required, to be in subfloor.
Maximum variation in the slab shall not exceed ¼" in 10'0" from the required plane.

Expansion joint (designer must specify expansion joints and show location and details on drawings)
Where tile work abuts restraining surfaces such as perimeter walls, curbs, columns, pipes, etc.
Directly over joints in structural floor including construction joints or cold joints.
Expansion joints mandatory in accordance with Method EJ711.

Installation specifications
ANSI A108.1.

RECOMMENDED USES

On plane, clean concrete.
On slab-on-grade construction where no bending stresses occur.
On properly cured structural slabs where limited bending stresses occur and expansion joints are installed in accordance with Method EJ711.

Limitations
Use Method F111 over precast concrete floor systems.

Requirements
Slab to be well cured, dimensionally stable, and free of cracks, waxy or oily films, and curing compounds.
Mortar bond coat ³⁄₃₂" (0.24 cm) minimum.

Materials
Dry-set mortar: conform with ANSI A118.1.
Latex-portland cement mortar: Conform with ANSI A118.4.
Water: potable.
Expansion joints.
Grout: specify type.

Preparation by other trades
Slab to have steel trowel and fine broom finish with no curing compounds used.
Slope, when required, to be in subfloor.
Maximum variation in the slab shall not exceed ⅛" (0.32 cm) in 10'0" from the required plane.

Expansion joint (designer must specify expansion joints and show location and details on drawings)
Where tile work abuts restraining surfaces such as perimeter walls, curbs, columns, pipes, etc.
Directly over joints in structural floor including construction joints or cold joints.
Expansion joints mandatory in accordance with Method EJ711.

Installation specifications
ANSI A108.5.
Note: For tile bonded directly to waterproofing membrane, follow membrane manufacturer's directions.

CEMENT MORTAR WITH EPOXY OR FURAN GROUT

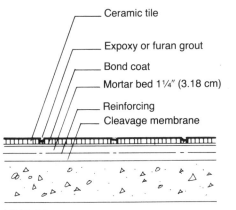

- Ceramic tile
- Expoxy or furan grout
- Bond coat
- Mortar bed 1¼″ (3.18 cm)
- Reinforcing
- Cleavage membrane

F114-84

DRY-SET MORTAR WITH EPOXY OR FURAN GROUT

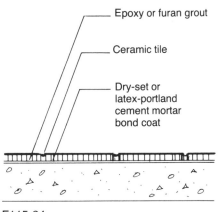

- Epoxy or furan grout
- Ceramic tile
- Dry-set or latex-portland cement mortar bond coat

F115-84

ORGANIC ADHESIVE

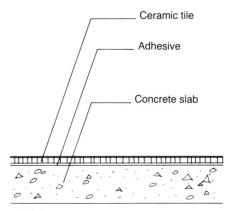

- Ceramic tile
- Adhesive
- Concrete slab

F116-84

RECOMMENDED USES

With tile set by Method F111 requiring good stain resistance and resistance to erosion caused by occasional contact with mild chemicals such as found in commercial dining areas, photographic dark rooms, public toilets, public foyers, etc.
For use with quarry tile and paver tile.

Requirements
Tile surface must be waxed before grouting with furan resin.

Materials
Epoxy grout: ANSI A118.3.
Furan resins: certified by manufacturer as suitable for intended use.

Published specifications
Tile installation: ANSI A108.1.
Epoxy grout: ANSI A108.6.
Furan grout: See manufacturer's literature.

Tile installation
Follow Method F111.

Note: Joints must be clean and completely filled with epoxy or furan. Partial filling with sand or mortar is unacceptable.

RECOMMENDED USES

With tile set by Method F112 or Method F113 requiring good stain resistance and resistance to erosion caused by occasional contact with mild chemicals such as those found in commercial dining areas, photographic dark rooms, public toilets, public foyers, etc.
For use with quarry tile and paver tile.

Requirement
Tile surface must be waxed before grouting with furan resin.

Materials
Epoxy grout: ANSI A118.3.
Furan resins: certified by manufacturer as suitable for intended use.

Published specifications
Tile installation: ANSI A108.5.
Epoxy grout: ANSI A108.6.
Furan grout: See manufacturer's literature.

Tile installation
Follow Method F112 or F113.

RECOMMENDED USES

For use over concrete floors in residential construction only. For heavier service select method F113.

Limitations
Will not withstand high impact or wheel loads.
Consult adhesive manufacturer for installation over floors with radiant heating.
Organic adhesives are not recommended in areas exposed to temperatures exceeding 140°F.

Requirements
Slab to be well cured, dimensionally stable, and free of cracks, waxy or oily films, and curing compounds.

Materials
Organic adhesive: floor type conforming to ANSI A136.1.
Grout: Specify type.

Preparation by other trades
Slab to have steel trowel finish, with no curing compounds used.
Maximum variation in the slab shall not exceed ¹⁄₁₆″ (0.16 cm) in 3′0″ (91.44 cm) from the required plane.

Expansion joint (designer must specify expansion joints and show location and details on drawings)
Optional except in large areas.
Directly over joints in structural floor including construction joints or cold joints.
Expansion joints mandatory with quarry tile abutting rigid surfaces.

Installation specifications
ANSI A108.4.

CONDUCTIVE FLOOR: WATERPROOFING MEMBRANE

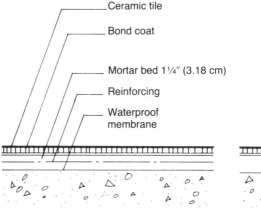

F121-84

RECOMMENDED USES

Wherever a positively waterproof interior floor is required in conjunction with ceramic tile.

Limitations

Not recommended for severe chemical exposure.

Requirements

Waterproofing membrane must be installed in accordance with manufacturer's directions.
Depressed subfloor is mandatory when required to maintain floor elevation.

Preparation by other trades

Maximum variation in the slab shall not exceed ¼" (0.64 cm) in 10'0" (3.05 m) from the required plane.
Slope subfloor to drain.

Preparation by tile trade

Maximum variation in the mortar bed shall not exceed ⅛" (0.32 cm) in 10'0" from the required plane.

Specifications

Waterproofing membrane is installed by other trades and is separate from tile work. Specify type of waterproofing, i.e., built-up roofing, lead pan, synthetic rubber, or other proprietary type.

Expansion joints

None in subfloor beneath membrane unless special installation method is designed to accommodate them.

CONCRETE SUBFLOOR: CEMENT MORTAR BED

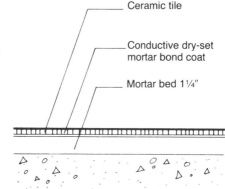

F122-84

RECOMMENDED USES

Preferred method of installing conductive tile in new construction.
In hospital operating rooms, certain laboratories, etc.
Where leveling of subfloor is required.

Limitations

Perimeter expansion joints recommended.

Materials

Portland cement: ASTM C-150 Type 1.
Sand: ASTM C-144.
Water: potable.
Mortar: 1 part portland cement, 4 to 5 parts damp sand by volume.
Conductive dry-set mortar: ANSI A118.2.
Expansion joints.
Grout: specify type. Conductive mortar shall not be used as grout.

Preparation by other trades

Slab depression to be accurate with screed finish.
Maximum variation in the slab shall not exceed ¼" in 10'0" from the required plane. plane.

Preparation by the tile trade

Mortar bed to be installed and damp-cured for three days under vaporproof membrane and then allowed to dry for at least four additional days before installing tile.
Maximum variation in the mortar bed shall not exceed ⅛" in 10'0" from the required plane.

Expansion joint (designer must specify expansion joints and show location and details on drawings)

Where tile work abuts restraining surfaces such as perimeter walls, curbs, columns, pipes, etc.
Directly over joints in structural floor including construction joints or cold joints.
In large areas 24' to 36' (7.32 to 10.97 m) each way.

Installation specifications

ANSI A108.7.
NFPA NO. 56A.

Note: Thin-bed method directly on concrete slab suitable only over sound, smooth, well-cured subfloors of existing concrete, existing ceramic tile, or terrazzo.

CHEMICAL RESISTANT: EPOXY GROUT & MORTAR

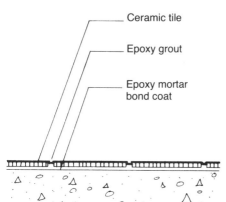

F131-84

RECOMMENDED USES

For setting and grouting ceramic mosaics, quarry tile, and paver tile.
Where moderate chemical exposure and severe cleaning methods are used, such as in commercial kitchens, dairies, breweries, food processing plants, etc.

Limitations

For severe chemical exposures and where complete protection is needed, refer to Method F134.

Requirements

Structurally sound subfloor, carefully finished to proper elevation and slope.
Surfaces to receive epoxy mortar must be free of sealers, curing compounds, oil, dirt, and dust; must be dry.

Materials

Epoxy mortar and grout: ANSI A118.3.

Preparation by other trades

Slab to have steel trowel and fine broom finish.
Slope, when required, to be in subfloor.
Maximum variation in the slab shall not exceed ⅛" in 10'0" from the required plane.

Expansion joints

Directly over joints in structural floors including construction joints or cold joints.

Installation specifications

ANSI A108.6.

Note: Extreme heat or improper steam-cleaning will soften epoxy grouts and wash them out of joints. Architect should consult resin manufacturer for special precautions when chemical exposure is severe or at high temperature.

EPOXY GROUT & MORTAR

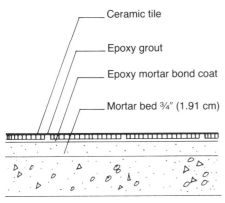

- Ceramic tile
- Epoxy grout
- Epoxy mortar bond coat
- Mortar bed ¾″ (1.91 cm)

F132-84

FURAN RESIN GROUT & MORTAR

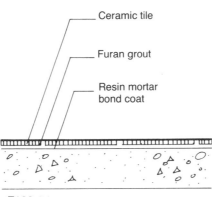

- Ceramic tile
- Furan grout
- Resin mortar bond coat

F133-84

EPOXY GROUT & MORTAR OR FURAN RESIN

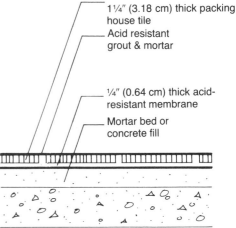

- 1¼″ (3.18 cm) thick packing house tile
- Acid resistant grout & mortar
- ¼″ (0.64 cm) thick acid-resistant membrane
- Mortar bed or concrete fill

F134-84

RECOMMENDED USES

Where leveling of subfloor is required.
For setting and grouting ceramic mosaics, quarry tile, and paver tile.
Were moderate chemical exposure and severe cleaning methods are used, such as in commercial kitchens, dairies, breweries, food processing plants, etc.

Limitations

For severe chemical exposures and where complete protection is needed, refer to Method F134.

Requirements

Surfaces to receive epoxy mortar must be free of sealers, curing compounds, coatings, oil, dirt, and dust; must be dry.
Over structural floors subject to bending and deflection use cleavage membrane under mortar bed; see Method F111.

Materials

Epoxy mortar and grout: ANSI A118.3.

Preparation by tile trade

Follow Method F112 for mortar bed over slab on grade where no bending stresses occur.
Follow Method F111 for mortar bed over structural floors subject to bending and deflection.

Installation specifications

Tile installation: ANSI A108.6.

Notes: Extreme heat or improper steam cleaning will soften epoxy grouts and wash them out of joints. Architect should consult resin manufacturer for special precautions when chemical exposure is severe, or at high temperature.
Joints must be completely filled with epoxy. Partial filling with sand or mortar is unacceptable.

RECOMMENDED USES

For setting and grouting quarry tile and paver tile.
In kitchens, chemical plants, etc.

Limitations

For severe chemical exposures and where complete protection is needed, refer to Method F134.

Requirements

Structurally sound subfloor, carefully finished to proper elevation.
Tile surface shall be waxed before installation.

Materials

Furan resins: certified by manufacturer as suitable for intended use.
Resin mortar bed as recommended by grout manufacturer.

Preparation by other trades

Slab to have steel trowel and fine broom finish.
Slope, when required, to be in subfloor.
Maximum permissible variation in slab ¼″ (0.64 cm) in 10′0″ (3.05 m) from required plane.

Expansion joint (designer must specify expansion joints and show location and details on drawings)

Where tile work abuts restraining surfaces such as perimeter walls, curbs, columns, pipes, etc.
Directly over joints in structural floor including construction or cold joints.
16′ to 24′ (7.32 to 10.97 m) each way in large areas or as recommended by resin manufacturer.

Installation specifications

Consult manufacturer's literature.

RECOMMENDED USES

For setting 1¼″ (3.18 cm) thick packing house tile in areas of continuous or severe chemical exposure where special protection against leakage or damage to concrete subfloor is required.

Requirements

Requires acid-resistant membrane.
Structurally sound subfloor, carefully finished to proper elevation and slope.
For epoxy installation, follow Method F131.
For furan installation, follow Method F133.

Preparation by other trades

Maximum variation in the concrete fill or mortar bed shall not exceed ⅛″ (0.32 cm) in 10′0″ from the required plane.
Acid-resistant membrane may be installed by other trades separate from tile work.

Expansion joint

None in subfloor beneath continuous membrane unless special installation method is designed to accommodate them.

Specifications

Acid-resistant membrane: See manufacturer's literature.

Note: The entire floor system is usually installed by a specialty ceramic tile flooring contractor and should be so specified.

CEMENT MORTAR

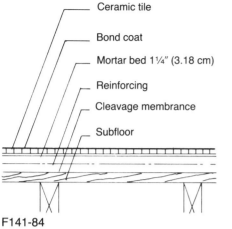

Ceramic tile
Bond coat
Mortar bed 1¼" (3.18 cm)
Reinforcing
Cleavage membrance
Subfloor

F141-84

ORGANIC ADHESIVE

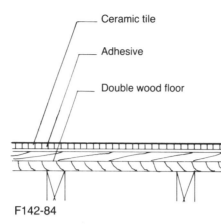

Ceramic tile
Adhesive
Double wood floor

F142-84

EPOXY MORTAR & GROUT

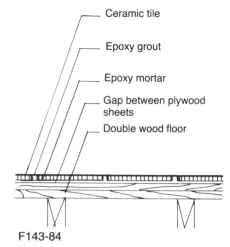

Ceramic tile
Epoxy grout
Epoxy mortar
Gap between plywood sheets
Double wood floor

F143-84

RECOMMENDED USES

Over all wood floors that are structurally sound.

Requirements
Cleavage membrance required.
Reinforcing mandatory.
Deflection not to exceed 1/360 of span, including live and dead load.

Materials
Portland cement: ASTM C-150 Type 1.
Sand: ASTM C-144.
Water: potable.
Mortar: 1 part portland cement, 6 parts damp sand by volume.
Bond coat: portland cement paste on a plastic bed or dry-set mortar or latex-portland cement mortar on a cured bed.
Reinforcing: 2" X 2" X ¹⁶⁄₁₆ gauge (5.08 X 5.08 cm) welded wire mesh or equivalent. Metal lath or other acceptable wire reinforcing nailed to the floor may be used in small residential bathrooms. Do not use ribbed lath.
Cleavage membrane: 15 lb (6.81 kg) roofing felt or 4-mil polyethylene film (may be omitted over waterproof membranes and pans).
Expansion joints.
Grout: specify type.

Preparation by other trades
Subfloor: ⅝" (1.59 cm) plywood or 1" (2.54 cm) nominal boards when on joists 16" (40.64 cm) o.c.
Depressing floor between joists on ledger strips permissible in residential use.

Expansion joint (designer must specify expansion joints and show location and details on drawings)
Optional except in large areas.
Expansion joints mandatory with quarry tile abutting rigid surfaces.

Installation specifications
ANSI A108.1.

RECOMMENDED USES

Over wood floors exposed to residential traffic only. For heavier service select Methods F141 or F143.

Limitations
Will not withstand high impact or wheel loads.
Not recommended in wet areas.

Requirements
Deflection not to exceed 1/360 of span, including live and dead load.
Double wood floor required.
Special grout required.

Materials
Organic adhesive: floor type conforming to ANSI A136.1.
Expansion joints.
Grout: specify latex-portland cement or epoxy.

Preparation by other trades
Subfloor: ⅝" plywood or 1" nominal boards when on joists 16" o.c.
Overlay: ⅜" (0.95 cm) minimum exterior plywood with ⅛" (0.32 cm) gap between sheets.
Maximum variation in the plywood surface shall not exceed ¹⁄₁₆" (0.16 cm) in 3'0" (91.44 cm) from the required plane. Adjacent edges of plywood sheets shall not be more than ¹⁄₃₂" (0.79 mm) above or below each other.

Expansion joint (designer must specify expansion joints and show location and details on drawings)
Optional except in large areas.
Expansion joints mandatory with quarry tile abutting rigid surfaces.

Installation specifications
ANSI A108.4.

RECOMMENDED USES

Over wood floors where resistance to foot traffic in better residential, normal commercial, and light institutional use is desired with thin-bed construction.
Where water, chemical, and stain resistance is desired.

Requirements
Deflection not to exceed ¹⁄₃₆₀ of span, including live and dead load.
Double wood floor required except in some residential uses.
Gap in top layer of exterior grade plywood required.
Gap between exterior grde plywood sheets to be filled with epoxy when it is spread for setting tile.
With single floors in residential use, solid blocking required under all end joints of plywood.

Materials
Epoxy mortar: ANSI A118.3.
Epoxy grout: ANSI A118.3.
Modified epoxy emulsion mortar: certified by manufacturer as suitable for intended use.

Preparation by other trades
Subfloor: ⅝" plywood or 1" nominal boards when on joists 16" o.c.
Overlay: ⅝" exterior grade plywood with gap of ¼" (0.64 cm) between sheets.
Residential use: overlay of ½" (1.27 cm) exterior grade plywood or single layer of ⅝" exterior grade plywood permissible. Maintain ¼" gap between sheets and provide solid blocking under single floor.
Maximum variation in the plywood surface shall not exceed ⅛" in 10' 0" (3.05 m) from the required plane. Adjacent edges of plywood sheets shall not be more than ¹⁄₃₂" (0.79 mm) above or below each other.

Expansion joint (designer must specify expansion joints and show location and details on drawings)
Required over structural joints.

Installation specifications
ANSI A108.6.

DESIGN OF EXPANSION JOINTS

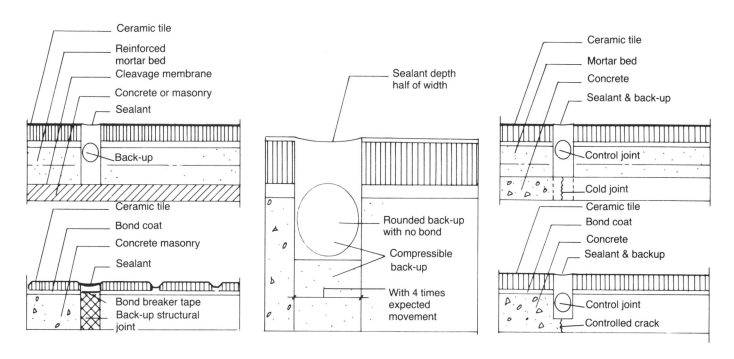

EXPANSION JOINT WIDTHS: VERTICAL & HORIZONTAL

Exterior (all tile): minimum ⅜″ (0.95 cm) for joints 12′ (3.66 m) o.c., minimum ½″ (1.27 cm) for joints 16′ (4.88 m) o.c. Minimum widths must be increased ¹⁄₁₆″ for each 15°F of the actual temperature range greater than 100°F between summer high and winter low. [Decks exposed to the sky in northern U.S.A. usually require ¾″ (1.91 cm) wide joints on 12′ centers.]

Interior for quarry tile and paver tile: same as grout joint, but not less than ¼″(0.64cm).

Interior for ceramic mosaic tile and glazed wall tile: preferred not less than ¼″, but never less than ⅛″ (0.32 cm).

Joints through tile and mortar directly over any structural joints in the backing must never be narrower than the structural joint.

Preparation

Tile edges to which the sealant will bond must be clean and dry. Sanding or grinding of these edges is recommended to obtain optimum sealant bond.

Primer on these tile edges is mandatory when recommended by the sealant manufacturer. Care must be taken to keep primer off tile faces.

Installation

Set compressible back-up strip when mortar is placed, or utilize removable wood strip to provide space for back-up after mortar has cured.

Install sealant after tile work and grout are dry. Follow sealant manufacturer's recommendations.

Refer to sealant section in ANSI tile installation specification.

Materials

Single-component sealant (for nontrafficked areas) shall be a nonsag type complying with Federal Specification TT-S-001543 or TT-S-00230c.

Two-component sealant shall comply with Federal Specification TT-S-00227e; use Type II (nonsag) for joints in vertical surfaces and Type I (self-leveling) for joints in horizontal surfaces. Trafficked areas of floors: Shore A hardness greater than 35.

Back-up strip shall be a flexible and compressible type of closed-cell foam polyethylene or butyl rubber, rounded at surface to contact sealant, as shown above, and as recommended by sealant manufacturers. It must fit neatly into the joint without compacting and to such a height to allow a sealant depth of half the width of the joint. Sealant must not bond to the back-up material.

Notes: In very small rooms (less than 12′ wide) and also along the sides of narrow corridors (less than 12′) expansion joints are not needed.

The performance requirements of certain special locations, such as exterior swimming pools, dairies, food plants, etc., may exceed the minimum requirements of the sealant specifications given above. Therefore, follow recommendations of experienced manufacturers as to specific sealants suitable in the job environment. In some severe environments a program for regular maintenance of sealant in joints may be required.

COLD JOINTS

Cold joints are formed primarily between slab pours where the size of a concrete slab may be too large to be poured at one time. The remainder of the slab would be poured at a later time, forming a cold joint between the two sections. Such joints are often shown on drawings as "CJ" or cold joints. A cold joint becomes a weakened joint that upon movement would crack, permitting leakage or buckling and cracking of a tile floor set over the slab.

Some large slabs on grade are poured monolithically and then later saw-cut at intervals providing control joints to allow for cracking at these weakened points.

Installation

Expansion joints in tile should be located over all cold joints and saw-cut control joints.

Joints in tile and setting materials shall never be less than the width of the saw-cut control joint.

Width, preparation, and installation shall be as required for expansion joints.

RESIDENTIAL & LIGHT CONSTRUCTION FOR WET AREAS: TUB ENCLOSURES & SHOWERS

BONDED CEMENT MORTAR

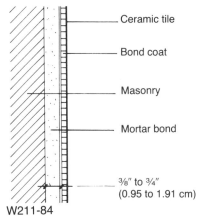

- Ceramic tile
- Bond coat
- Masonry
- Mortar bond
- ⅜" to ¾" (0.95 to 1.91 cm)

W211-84

DRY-SET MORTAR OR LATEX-PORTLAND CEMENT

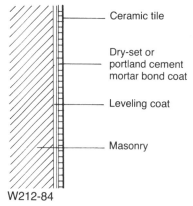

- Ceramic tile
- Dry-set or portland cement mortar bond coat
- Leveling coat
- Masonry

W212-84

DRY-SET MORTAR OR LATEX-PORTLAND CEMENT MORTAR

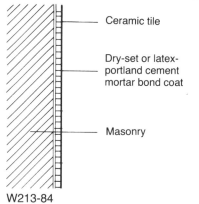

- Ceramic tile
- Dry-set or latex-portland cement mortar bond coat
- Masonry

W213-84

RECOMMENDED USES

Over clean, sound, dimensionally stable masonry or concrete.

Limitations
Do not use over cracked or coated surfaces. Select Method W221 or W222 for such surfaces.

Requirements
Require a scratch coat over smooth concrete or if surface is irregular or if thickness of mortar bed would exceed ¾" (1.91 cm).

Materials
Portland cement: ASTM C-150 Type 1.
Lime: ASTM C-206 Type S or ASTM C-207 Type S.
Sand: ASTM C-144.   Water: potable.
Scratch coat (for use where thickness of mortar bed exceed ¾": 1 part portland cement, ½ part lime, and 4 parts dry sand or 5 parts damp sand; or 1 part portland cement, 3 parts dry sand, or 4 parts damp sand.
Mortar bed: 1 part portland cement, ½ part lime, and 5 parts damp sand up to 1 part portland cement, 1 part lime, and 7 parts damp sand, by volume.
Bond coat: portland cement paste. Dry-set or latex-portland cement mortar permissible with wall tile. (For dry-set or latex portland cement mortar on a mortar bed cured for a minimum of 20 hr at 70°F or above, follow Method W213.)
Expansion joints.   Grout: Specify type.

Preparation by other trades
Surface must be free of coatings, oil, wax.
All concrete should be bush-hammered or heavily sand-blasted.
Maximum variation in the masonry surface shall not exceed ¼" (0.64 cm) in 8'0" (2.44 m) from the required plane.

Preparation by tile trade
Maximum variation in the scratch coat shall not exceed ¼" in 8'0" from the required plane.

RECOMMENDED USES

Over clean, sound, dimensionally stable masonry, concrete, or cured portland cement mortar when variation in surface exceeds ⅛" (0.32 cm) in 8'0".

Limitations
Do not use over cracked or coated surfaces. Select Method W221 or W222 for such surfaces.

Requirements
Maximum variation in the surface of leveling coat shall not exceed ⅛" in 8'0" from the required plane.
Provide expansion joints directly over expansion or control joints in backing.
Leveling coat shall be cured at least 24 hr before tile is applied.

Materials
Leveling coats or spot patching ¼" thick or less: dry-set mortar that is suitable for use with vitreous tile or latex-portland cement mortar; or dry-set mortar to which an equal volume of a mixture of 1 part portland cement and 1½ parts sand has been added.
Leveling coats thicker than ¼": a minimum of ½" thick mortar bed or 1 part portland cement, ½ part lime, and 5 parts damp sand up to 1 part portland cement, 1 part lime, and 7 parts damp sand, by volume.

Preparation by other trades
Surface must be free of coatings, oil, wax.
All concrete should be bush-hammered or heavily sand-blasted.

Tile installation
Follow Method W213.

Expansion joint (designer must specify expansion joints and show location and details on drawings)
Directly over all masonry control joints, changes in materials, and 24' to 36' (7.32 X 10.98 m) elsewhere.

Installation specifications
ANSI A108.1

RECOMMENDED USES

Over clean, sound, dimensionally stable masonry or concrete.

Limitations
Do not use over cracked or coated surfaces. Select Method W221 or W222 for such surfaces.

Materials
Dry-set mortar: Conform with ANSI A118.1.
Latex-portland cement mortar: Conform with ANSI A118.4.
Mortar bed minimum thickness 3/32" (0.24 cm).
Expansion joints.
Grout: Specify type.

Preparation by other trades
Surface must be free of coatings, oil, wax.
All concrete should be bush-hammered or heavily sand-blasted.
Maximum variation in the masonry surface shall not exceed ⅛" in 8'0" from the required plane.

Expansion joint (designer must specify expansion joints and show location and details on drawings)
Directly over all masonry control joints and changes in back-up materials.

Installation specifications
ANSI A108.5.

KITCHENS & TOILET ROOMS

CEMENT MORTAR

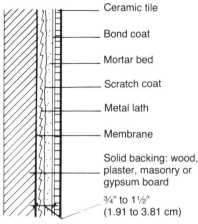

- Ceramic tile
- Bond coat
- Mortar bed
- Scratch coat
- Metal lath
- Membrane
- Solid backing: wood, plaster, masonry or gypsum board

¾″ to 1½″ (1.91 to 3.81 cm)

W221-84

RECOMMENDED USES

Over masonry, plaster, or other solid backing that provides firm anchorage for metal lath.
Ideal for remodeling or on surfaces that present bonding problems.

Requirements

Require a leveling coat if variation in scratch coat exceed ¼″ (0.64 cm) in 8′0″ (2.44 m) from the required plane or if thickness of mortar bed would exceed ¾″ (1.91 cm).
Apply membrane, metal lath (self-furring lath preferred), and scratch coat.
Cut lath at all expansion joints.

Materials

Membrane: 15 lb (6.81 kg) roofing felt or 4 mil polyethylene film.
Portland cement: ASTM C-150 Type 1.
Lime: ASTM C-206 Type S or ASTM C-207 Type S.
Sand: ASTM C-144.
Water: potable.
Scratch coat: 1 part portland cement, ½ part lime, and 4 parts dry sand to 5 parts damp sand or 1 part portland cement, 3 parts dry sand to 4 parts damp sand.
Mortar bed: 1 part portland cement, ½ part lime, and 5 parts damp sand up to 1 part portland cement, 1 part lime, and 7 parts damp sand, by volume.
Bond coat: portland cement paste. dry-set or latex-portland cement mortar permissible with wall tile. (For dry-set or latex-portland cement mortar on a mortar bed cured for a minimum of 20 hr at 70°F or above, follow Method W213.)
Expansion joints.
Grout: Specify type.

Expansion joint (designer must specify expansion joints and show location and details on drawings)

Directly over control joints and 24′ to 36′ elsewhere.

Installation specifications

ANSI A108.1

ONE-COAT METHOD

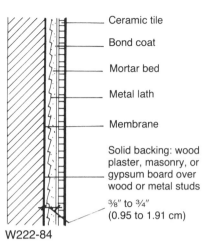

- Ceramic tile
- Bond coat
- Mortar bed
- Metal lath
- Membrane
- Solid backing: wood plaster, masonry, or gypsum board over wood or metal studs

⅜″ to ¾″ (0.95 to 1.91 cm)

W222-84

RECOMMENDED USES

Over masonry, plaster, or other solid backing that provides firm anchorage for metal lath.
Ideal for remodeling or on surfaces that present bonding problems.
Ideal for remodeling where space limitations exist.
Preferred method of applying tile over gypsum plaster or gypsum board in showers and tub enclosures.

Requirements

Maximum variation in the backing surface shall ot exceed ¼″ in 8′0″ from the required plane.
Apply membrane and metal lath.
Cut lath at all expansion joints.

Materials

Membrane: 15 lb roofing felt or 4 mil polyethylene film.
Metal lath: galvanized or painted expanded metal lath or other approved wire reinforcing.
Portland cement: ASTM C-150 Type 1.
Lime: ASTM C-206 Type S or ASTM C-207 Type S.
Sand: ASTM C-144.
Water: potable.
Mortar bed: 1 part portland cement, ½ part lime, and 5 parts damp sand up to 1 part portland cement, 1 part lime, and 7 parts damp sand, by volume.
Bond coat: portland cement paste. Dry-set or latex-portland cement mortar permissible with wall tile. (For dry-set or latex-portland cement mortar on a mortar bed cured for a minimum of 20 hr at 70°F or above, follow Method W213.)
Expansion joints.
Grout: Specify type.

Expansion (designer must specify expansion joints and show location and details on drawings)

Directly over control joints and 24′ to 36′ elsewhere.

Installation specifications

ANSI A108.1.

ORGANIC ADHESIVE

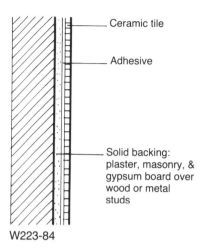

- Ceramic tile
- Adhesive
- Solid backing: plaster, masonry, & gypsum board over wood or metal studs

W223-84

RECOMMENDED USES

Interiors over gypsum board, plaster, or other smooth surfaces.

Limitations

Organic adhesives are not recommended in areas exposed to temperatures exceeding 140°F. Some backing materials may require lower temperatures.

Materials

Organic adhesive: ANSI A136.1. Type I organic adhesive is recommended for tub and shower surrounds and Type II for intermittent water resistance.
Water-resistant gypsum backing board ASTM C630. (Required in wet areas.)
Gypsum board: ASTM C36 (suitable for dry areas only).
Expansion joints.
Grout: Specify type.

Preparation by other trades

Seal surface of taped joints in water-resistant gypsum backing board installations to prevent water damage.
Prime surface before applying adhesive when recommended by adhesive manufacturer.
Allow minimum of 24 hr after tile is set for solvent evaporation before grouting.

Installation specifications

ANSI 108.4.

WOOD STUDS OR FURRING WITH CEMENT MORTAR

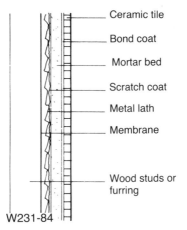

Ceramic tile
Bond coat
Mortar bed
Scratch coat
Metal lath
Membrane
Wood studs or furring

W231-84

RECOMMENDED USES

Over dry, well-braced wood studs or furring. Preferred method of installation over wood studs in showers and tub enclosures.

Requirements

Wood studs for furring must be protected from moisture by building felt or polyethylene film.
Apply membrane, metal lath, and scratch coat.
Require a leveling coat if variation in scratch coat exceeds ¼" (0.64 cm) in 8'0" (2.44 m) from the required plane or if thickness of mortar bed would exceed ¾" (1.91 cm).

Materials

Membrane: 15-lb (6.81 kg) roofing felt or 4-mil polyethylene film.
Portland cement: ASTM C-150 Type 1.
Lime: ASTM C-206 Type S or ASTM C-207 Type S.
Sand: ASTM C-144.
Water: potable.
Scratch coat: 1 part portland cement, ½ part lime, and 4 parts dry sand to 5 parts damp sand or 1 part portland cement, 3 parts dry sand to 4 parts damp sand.
Mortar bed: 1 part portland cement, ½ part lime, and 5 parts damp sand up to 1 part portland cement, 1 part lime, and 7 parts damp sand, by volume.
Bond coat: portland cement paste. Dry-set or latex-portland cement mortar permissible with wall tile. (For dry-set or latex-portland cement mortar on a mortar bed cured for a minimum of 20 hr at 70°F or above, follow Method W213.)
Grout: Specify type.

Installation specifications

ANSI A108.1.

METAL STUDS WITH CEMENT MORTAR

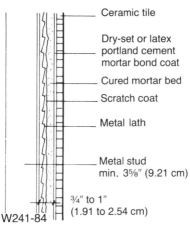

Ceramic tile
Dry-set or latex portland cement mortar bond coat
Cured mortar bed
Scratch coat
Metal lath
Metal stud min. 3⅝" (9.21 cm)
¾" to 1" (1.91 to 2.54 cm)

W241-84

RECOMMENDED USES

Over metal studs.

Requirements

Set tile in dry-set or latex-portland cement mortar on a mortar bed cured for a minimum of 20 hr at 70°F or above.
Scratch coat and mortar bed must not be richer than specified below.
Do not exceed 1" (2.54 cm) total thickness of mortar and scratch coat.
Stud spacing not to exceed 16" (40.64 cm) o.c.
Minimum recommended stud with is 3⅝" (9.21 cm).
Studs shall be 20 gauge or heavier.

Materials

Membrane; 15 lb roofing felt or 4-mil polyethylene film (required in wet areas).
Portland cement: ASTM C-150 Type 1.
Lime: ASTM C-206 type S or ASTM C-207 Type S.
Sand: ASTM C-144.
Water: Potable.
Scratch coat: 1 part portland cement, ½ part lime, and 4 parts dry sand to 5 parts damp sand or 1 part portland cement, 3 parts dry sand to 4 parts damps sand.
Mortar bed: 1 part portland cement, ½ part lime, and 5 parts damp sand up to 1 part portland cement, 1 part lime, and 7 parts damp sand, by volume.
Dry-set mortar: Conform with ANSI A118.1.
Latex-portland cement mortar: Conform with ANSI A118.4.
Metal lath: galvanized or painted expanded metal lath 3.4 lb/sq yd or sheet lath 4.5 lb/sq yd. Do not use rib lath.
Metal studs: ASTM C-645.
Expansion joints.
Grout: Specify type.

Preparation

Apply metal lath and scratch coat.

Expansion joint (designer must specify expansion joints and show location and details on drawings)

Refer to ANSI installation specification.

Installation specifications

Cured mortar bed: ANSI A108.1.
Tile: ANSI A108.5.

GYPSUM BOARD WITH ORGANIC ADHESIVE

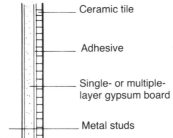

Ceramic tile
Adhesive
Single- or multiple-layer gypsum board
Metal studs

W242-84

RECOMMENDED USES

Over gypsum board screwed to metal studs, single or double layer installed in accordance with GA-216.
Where a gypsum board, non-load bearing partition is desired with durable, low-maintenance finish.
For fire-resistant, sound-insulated, ceramic tiled walls. (Fire-resistance and sound-insulation ratings calculated on partitions before tiling.)
For dry areas in schools, institutions, and commercial buildings.

Limitations

See method W223.

Requirements

Maximum spacing for 2½" (6.35 cm) wide studs is 16" o.c.
Studs shall be 25 gauge or heavier.
In tub enclosures and shower stalls use water-resistant gypsum backing board with all openings carefully sealed, or use Method W222 or W231.
Minimum recommended single layer gypsum board thickness is ½" (1.27 cm).

Materials

Organic adhesive: ANSI A136.1. Type I organic adhesive is recommended for tub and shower surrounds and Type II for intermittent water resistance.
Metal studs: ASTM C-645.
Water-resistant gypsum backing board ASTM C-630.
Gypsum board: ASTM C-36 (suitable for dry areas only).
Expansion joints: none required, except over discontinuity in backing.
Grout: Specify latex-portland cement grout or mastic grout (ACRI-FIL).

Preparation by other trades

Maximum variation in the gypsum board surface shall not exceed ⅛" (0.32 cm) in 8'0" (2.44 m) from the required plane nor more than 1⁄16" (0.16 cm) per foot. Corners, door jambs, etc., must be plumb with ⅛" in 8'0".
All gypsum board face layer joints shall be taped and filled with one 4" (10.16 cm) wide coat of joint compound. Nail heads one coat only.

Preparation by tile trade

Seal surface of taped joints in water-resistant gypsum-backing board installations to prevent water damage.
Prime surface before applying adhesive as directed by adhesive manufacturer.
Allow minimum of 24 hr after tile is set for solvent evaporation before grouting.

Installation specifications

Tile: ANSI A108.4.
Gypsum board: GA-216.

Geologic categories	Treads	Flags	Paving slabs	Saddle	Sills	Furniture tops	Wall veneer		Honed	Sawed	Polished	Rubbed	Textured	Tooled	Sand blasted	Split-faced	Sanded	Standards
Sedimental origin																		
Sandstone		X								X				X		X		ASTM C 616
Quartzite	X	X					X			X		X				X		
Limestone																		ASTM C 568
Standard	X	X			X		X		X	X		X	X	X	X	X		
Dolomitic	X	X		X	X		X		X	X		X	X	X	X	X		
Travertine	X	X	X	X	X	X	X		X		X	X						
Metamorphic																		
Marble									X		X	X					X	ASTM C 503
Grade A	X		X	X	X	X	X		X		X	X				X	X	
Grade B	X		X	X	X	X	X		X		X	X				X	X	
Serpentine						X	X		X	X	X					X	X	
Onyx						X	X		X		X	X				X	X	
Slate	X	X	X				X		X							X	X	ASTM C 629
Igneous origin																		
Granite	X	X	X	X	X				X	X	X	X	X	X	X			ASTM C 615
Veneer						X	X		X	X	X	X	X	X	X			

The information on marble that appears on pages 158 through 161 is reprinted with permission from *Dimensional Stone— Volume III,* Section 3. Permission granted by the Marble Institute of America, Inc., 33505 State Street, Farmington, MI 48024. Purchase price of the volume available on request. © 1985, Marble Institute of America.

3. PRODUCT DESCRIPTION

3.1 GEOLOGICAL CLASSIFICATION

The rock forming the earth's crust falls into three generic groups: igneous, sedimentary and metamorphic.

Heat, pressure, and chemical reactions may change either igneous or sedimentary rock into metamorphic rock, meaning "changed in form," usually into a more compact and crystalline condition, and even metamorphic rocks may be further altered to higher ranks of metomorphism.

Rocks may become plastic under great pressure and high temperature and by earth movement. They may be folded into complex forms with a banded or schistose structure. Many constituent minerals may be dissolved, transported and reprecipitated by thermal waters. Heat and pressure may cause recrystalization.

In this way, new rocks are formed, differing widely from the igneous or sedimentary types, and usually much harder than either. Thus, shales and related rocks may be altered into slate, and limestones into marbles.

Marble is, therefore, metamorphic rock resulting from the recrystallization of limestone. Commercially, however, all calcareous rocks produced by nature and capable of taking a polish are called marbles, as are some dolomitic and serpentine rocks.

.2 COLOR AND VEINING

The color, veinings, clouds, mottlings, and shadings in marble are caused by substances included in minor amounts during formation. Iron oxides make the pinks, yellows, browns and reds. Most grays, blue-grays and blacks are of bituminous origin. Greens are caused by micas, chlorite, and silicates.

.3 TEXTURE

The term "texture," as applied to marble, means size, degree of uniformity, and arrangement of constituent minerals. Grains of calcite, the chief constituent of most marbles, are crystalline and have definite cleavage which show bright reflecting faces on a broken surface. In most marbles, however, the grains are elongated in one direction by the folding and plication of the beds.

.4 SOUNDNESS

As a result of knowledge gained in extensive practical experience of its Members, marbles have been classified into four groups. The basis of this classification is the characteristics encountered in fabricating and has no reference whatsoever to comparative merit or value. The classifications merely indicate what method of fabrication is considered necessary and acceptable in each instance, as based on standard trade practice. Classification of marble is done by MIA producer and finisher Members. A written warranty should be obtained from them prior to installation.

The groupings—A, B, C, and D—should be taken into account when specifying marble, for all marbles are not suitable for all building applications. This is particularly true of the comparatively fragile marbles classified under groups C and D which may require additional fabrication before or during installation.

These four groups are:

GROUP "A"   Sound Marbles and Stones, with uniform and favorable working qualities.

GROUP "B"   Marbles and Stones similar in character to the preceding group, but working qualities somewhat less favorable; may have natural faults; a limited amount of waxing and sticking necessary.

GROUP "C"   Marbles and Stones with some variations in working qualities; geological flaws, voids, veins, and lines of separation are common; it is standard practice to repair these variations by sticking, waxing, and filling; liners and other forms of reinforcements employed when necessary.

GROUP "D"   Marbles and Stones similar to the preceding group, but containing a larger proportion of natural faults, and a maximum variation in working qualities, requiring more of the same methods of finishing. This group comprises many of the highly colored marbles prized for their decorative qualities.

.5 FABRICATION

The MIA Member is capable and ready to advise on the fabrication, installation and the best marbles to use for a specific project. Even though this Manual gives details on construction, our Member should be consulted during all phases of planning, design and construction to identify problems in advance, and to advise on the best way to prepare for the installation.

MIA Members use both domestic and foreign marbles. They may either import blocks, rough sawn slabs, or polished slabs. Members may fabricate in their own shop or have products fabricated by others.

MIA Members can advise as to source and fabrication requirements. Depending on the scope and complexity of the job, it may be advantageous to have the Member fabricate in his own shop. This is particularly true for the small quantities required in remodeling and residential work.

Regardless of who fabricates, the MIA Member can make the adjustments necessary for a good fit at the time of installation.

.6 FINISHES

Marble's surface may be finished in a number of ways. In general, smooth finishes tend to emphasize color and veining, whereas rough finishes tend to subdue the veining or markings.

Typical finishes for marble are:

POLISHED FINISH	A glossy surface which brings out the full color and character of the marble. It is not generally recommended for exterior use, or commercial floors.
HONED FINISH	A satin smooth surface with little or no gloss, recommended for commercial floors.
SAND-BLASTED	A matte textured surface with no gloss; recommended for exterior use.
ABRASIVE FINISH	A flat non-reflective surface, usually recommended for exterior use.

The type of finish desired bears some small relationship to final cost, as the smoother, more highly reflective surfaces require more finishing, and consequently more time. The most economical finish for exterior use is the abrasive finish.

Other finishes such as axed, bush-hammered, rock-faced, rough sawn, or tooled are also available.

.7 THICKNESS

Standard thicknesses for marble veneer are ¾ inch (cm 2), ⅞ inch (cm 2.5), 1¼ inch (cm 3), 1½ inch (cm 4) and 2 inches (cm 5). When a marble thinner than ¾ inch (cm 2) is specified, the ratio between thickness and overall size and the use of reinforcing backup materials must be considered. Marble thicker than 2 inches (cm 5) is usually regarded as cubic stock.

Metric thicknesses are based on full centimeter measurements. However, cutting can be made to the English system through conversion to metric equivalents.

.8 SIZES

Marble is a product of nature of which hundreds of varieties are available, each possessing varying characteristics. Little can be done to alter the condition in which nature presents these varieties to us. Therefore, size may become a limiting factor to consider in the selection of marble.

Most blocks of marble are generally produced so as to make fabricated sizes shown in the following table. These should be regarded as the standard maximum fabricated sizes. In special cases, larger sizes may be available.

Classification	Maximum Fabricated Sizes	
Group "A"	5'-0" Wide x 7'-0" Long	cm 150 × 210
Group "B"	2'-6" to 4'-0" Wide,	cm 75/120
	4'-0" to 7'-0" Long	cm 120/210
Group "C"	2'-6" to 4'-0" Wide,	cm 75/120
	4'-0" to 7'-0" Long	cm 120/210
	(Reinforcement employed when necessary) (Maximum 20 square feet [2 square meters] per piece recommended)	
Group "D"	2'-6" to 4'-0" Wide,	cm 75/120
	4'-0" to 7'-0" Long	cm 120/210
	(Reinforcement employed when necessary) (Maximum 20 square feet [2 square meters] per piece recommended)	

NOTE: Selection and delivery can be greatly facilitated by a jointing scheme which permits the use of smaller sizes. A final jointing scheme should be agreed upon after the Marble has been selected and the Marble Contractor has been consulted.

.9 TOLERANCES

All sizes are subject to the following gauged fabrication tolerances:

Thickness	Finished both faces	Finished one face
Thin Stock (¾ inch-2 inch) (cm2/5)	+ 0 -1/16 inch + 0 -2 mm	+ 1/8 -1/16 inch ±3 mm
Cubic Stock (over 2 inch) (over cm5)	±1/16 inch ±2 mm	+3/16 -1/8 inch + 5 -3 mm
Marble Tile		±1/32 inch ±1 mm
Sizes and Squareness		
Thin Stock	±1/16 inch ±2 mm	±1/16 inch ±2 mm
Cubic Stock		±1/16 inch ±2 mm

.10 VENEER CUTTING

Quarry blocks are reduced to slabs by a gang saw. The gang saw consists of a series of steel blades set parallel in a frame that moves forward and backward. Today the most productive and precision gang saws use diamond tipped blades with individual hydraulic blade tensioners. Others are fed a cutting abrasive in a stream of water.

Marble blocks can be sawn either parallel or perpendicular to the bedding plane. The perpendicular cut is referred to as an across-the-bed or Vein cut. The parallel cut is with-the-bed or Fleuri cut. Some marbles produce a pleasing surface when sawed in either direction, and are available as either Vein or Fleuri. Other marbles produce a pleasing surface only when sawed in one direction and are generally available only in that variety.

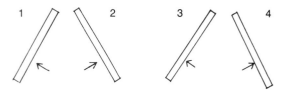

Arrows denote sides to be finished

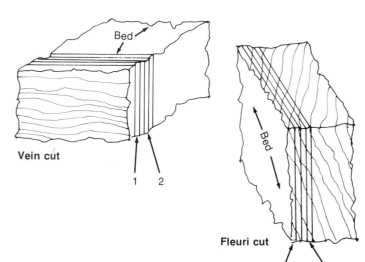

.11 VENEER PATTERNS

Only certain marbles lend themselves to specific pattern arrangement, such as, Side Slip Pattern and End Slip Pattern. This is because a constant natural marking trend throughout the marble block is required. Formal patterns require selectivity which usually increases the installed cost of the marble veneer. Usually, material sawed for a vein cut can be matched; Fleuri cuts can only be blended.

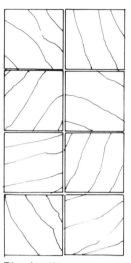

Blend pattern

Panels of the same variety but not necessarily from the same block arranged at random. This scheme is followed when no other pattern is specified.

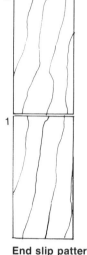

Side slip pattern

Panels are placed side by side to give a repetitive pattern and blended color in the horizontal.

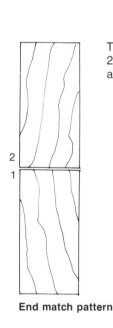

End slip pattern

Panels from the same block are placed end to end in sequence to give a repetitive pattern and blended color in the vertical.

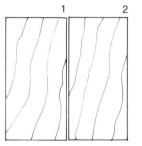

Book match pattern

The adjacent faces of panels 1 & 2 are finished. Panel 2 is placed next to panel 1 as the pages of a book are opened.

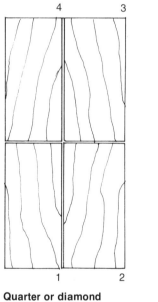

Quarter or diamond match pattern

Panels 1 & 2 are book matched. Panels 3 & 4 are book matched and then inverted over the top of panels 1 & 2.

End match pattern

The adjacent faces of panels 1 & 2 are finished. Panel 2 is inverted above panel 1.

Note: Although these six arrangements of matched panels indicate an almost perfect match of the veining lines, it is impossible to achieve this perfection due to that portion of the marble block lost during the sawing process and due to the shifting of the veining. Ideally, jointing should be planned for grouping of four panels of equal size.

.13   FILLING OF TRAVERTINE

Travertine may be obtained from a producer with its normal voids unfilled or filled. Travertine may be filled by a finisher in his shop under controlled conditions, with particular attention paid to temperature. Least desirable is filling at the job site.

Common materials used for filling are natural (gray-colored) or tinted portland cement, and clear or colored epoxy or polyester resins. Unless otherwise specified, natural portland cement is used as a filler.

Thru-holes and holes larger than a U.S. 25¢ piece in size (25mm) should be filled and raked.

.14   AGGLOMERATE MARBLE AND GRANITE TILES

These products are recent introductions to the industry. Typical composition is 90–95% natural marble or granite contained in either a cementitious or resinous binder. Technical details can be obtained from the manufacturers.

.15   PRODUCT SAMPLING

You must always remember marble and other stones are formed by nature. It is the variations in veining and the differences in tonal qualities that make marble unique, valuable and highly desirable. For these reasons, selection should never be made on the basis of one sample alone. Ask your supplier to provide several samples so that a more complete approximation of the available ranges may be seen.

Recommended sample sizes are 12″ x 12″.

MARBLE FLOORING†

Marble flooring can be installed by several methods. Consideration should be given to the various features of each method in making a selection for a specific installation.

Setting marble flooring over a wood sub-floor should only be attempted after sub-floor has been reinforced to insure against deflection.

Final design should always be based on specific values for the marble to be used. If several varieties of marble are used together in an alternating pattern, care should be taken to insure that the abrasive hardness (Ha) of the marbles selected are similar. These values may be available from the marble supplier. Abrasive Hardness (Ha) is determined by testing in accordance with ASTM C241—Standard Test Method for Abrasion Resistance of Stone Subjected to Foot Traffic. (Note: "Abrasion Resistance" does not measure values for "coefficient of friction" or "slip resistance.")

Since marble tiles are installed in the same manner as ceramic tiles, reference current Tile Council of America "Handbook" for specific details. Attention should be given to placement of control and isolation joints as presented in the "Handbook." [See also pages 148–156, this volume.]

"Lippage is a condition which occurs when tiles are installed by a thin-bed method over an even subsurface. Tiles may "Lip," one edge higher than their neighbors, giving the finished surface a ragged appearance. In some conditions, a certain amount of lippage is unavoidable. As a general rule, the recommended maximum variation of the finished surface should be no more than 3/16-inch (5 mm) cumulative over a 10′-0″ (3 meters) lineal measurement, with no more than 1/32-inch (1 mm) variation between individual tiles. (See Secion 3.9 Tolerances, [page 159.])

Avoid the use of curing compounds on concrete slabs. They prevent proper bonding. Marble dust must be washed off the tile prior to installation.

Joint width should always be specified. 1/16-inch to 1/8-inch is considered "standard."

Where marble abuts softer flooring materials, terrazzo divider strips may be used. They will help prevent edge chipping.

†From Supplemental Information, *Dimensional Stone—Volume III.* © 1985, Marble Institute of America.

SOUNDNESS RATING OF MARBLE

The Letter A, B, C or D preceding or following the name of each marble refers to its Group Classification for Soundness. Detailed information is in Part I General Information, Section 3.4 Product Description, [on page 158, this volume].

BEFORE COMPLETING SPECIFICATIONS, ALWAYS OBTAIN CURRENT AVAILABILITY INFORMATION FROM THE SUPPLIER OF THE DESIRED VARIETY OR FROM A MARBLE INSTITUTE OF AMERICA MEMBER.

The names used to identify marbles are generally chosen by the producer. At times these names contain clues as to the source of the marble; the name of the owner of the quarry from which it was quarried, or the area, state or province where the quarry is located. But equally as often, the name is chosen merely to be descriptive of the color or marking of the marble. "Belgian Black," for example, is a black marble from Belgium, but only seldom are the names so descriptive and straightforward. Occasionally the names are fanciful or commemorative. Names often become confused through translation from one language to another. "Coral Pink," for example, is the anglicized version of "Rosa Corallo," an Italian name for a rose colored marble.

The names on the following list are those by which certain marbles are best known. The list is by no means complete, but it does contain the names of the better known, currently available marbles. For proper identification of marbles whose names do not appear on the list, contact a member of the Marble Institute of America.

AVAILABLE MARBLE VARIETIES, BY COLOR RANGE

BLACK (Blk)
(D) Belgian Black . . . . .Belgium
(D) Black and Gold (all types) . . . . .Italy
(A) Champlain Black . . . . .Vermont
(C) Doppio Nero . . . . .China
(B) Formosa Black . . . . .Taiwan, R.O.C.
(B) Gris Antique . . . . .Belgium
(B) Imperial Black . . . . .Tennessee
(C) Mino Nero Antique . . . . .Mexico
(C) Negro Marquina . . . . .Spain
(C) Negro V.I.P. or Florido . . . . .Spain
(C) Nero Caracolese . . . . .Puerto Rico
(A) Noir Cihigue . . . . .France
(A) Noir Fleuri . . . . .France
(B) Petit Granit (not a granite) . . . . .Belgium
(C) St. Anne African Vein . . . . .Morocco
(D) St. Laurent
    (Pyrenees Black & Gold) . . . . France

BLUE—GRAY (Bl/Gy)
(A) Minnesota Skyrose Fleuri . . . .Minnesota
(B) Minnesota Skyrose Vein . . . . .Minnesota
(D) Onyx Cabrino . . . . .Peru
(A) Regal Blue . . . . .No. Carolina

BRECCIATED—BLACK & WHITE (Brc-Blk-W)
(C) Breche Ronceveaux . . . . .France
(C) Breche Noire (Roman Breche) . .France
(B) Veined Black B . . . . .Taiwan, R.O.C.
(C) Veined Black C . . . . . . .Taiwan, R.O.C.

BROWN (Brw)
(C) African Rose Light . . . . .Morocco
(C) Agata Malaga Onyx . . . . .Spain
(A) Baker Dark Cedar . . . . .Tennessee
(C) Breche Nouvelle . . . . .France
(A) Brown Terra . . . . .Venezuela
(B) Brown Terra . . . . .Venezuela
(C) Continental Cedar . . . . .Tennessee
(C) Crema Nuevo . . . . .Spain
(C) Emperador Medium & Dark . . . . . .Spain
(C) Imperial Emperador Brown . . . . . .Spain
(A) Jura . . . . .Germany
(C) Paradiso "D" . . . . .Italy

BUFF—BROWN—YELLOWISH (Bf-Brw-Y)
(B) Arabesco .Spain
(A) Bethlehem Buff . . . . .Minnesota
(A) Buxy Ambré . . . . .France
(A) Chassagne Beige . . . . .France
(B) Chanteuil . . . . .France
(A) Chocolate Brun Amazone . . . . . . .Brazil
(C) Cliffdale "A" Dark . . . . .Missouri
(C) Cliffdale "B" Light . . . . .Missouri

(A) Comblanchien (all types) . . . . .France
(A) Cream Kasota . . . . .Minnesota
(A) Cream Mankato . . . . .Minnesota
(A) Cream Mansota . . . . .Minnesota
(A) Ka-Kato Cream Fleuri . . . . . . .Minnesota
(A) Kasota Buff . . . . .Minnesota
(C) Lioz Creme . . . . .Portugal
(A) Mankato Golden Buff . . . . . . .Minnesota
(A) Minnesota Golden Buff . . . . . .Minnesota
(A) Minnesota Tavernelle . . . . . . .Minnesota
(B) Mocha Creme . . . . .Portugal
(A) Northern Cream . . . . .Minnesota
(B) Northern Tan . . . . .Minnesota
(A) Pouillenay . . . . .France
(B) Sierra Madre . . . . .Philippines

BUFF—CREAM OR LIGHT (Bf-C/L)
(C) Alagao Beige . . . . .Philippines
(C) Beige Serpentina . . . . .Spain
(C) Botticino Classico . . . . .Italy
(C) Botticino Classico . . . . .Puerto Rico
(C) Botticino Fiorito . . . . .Italy
(C) Botticino Standard . . . . .Italy
(C) Caliza Capri . . . . .Spain
(C) Capistrano . . . . .Philippines
(A) Combe Brune . . . . .France
(B) Comblanchien . . . . .France
(C) Crema Levante . . . . .Spain
(C) Crema Marfil (Light & Dark) . . . . . .Spain
(A) Cream Wombeyan . . . . .Australia
(A) Estremoz Creme . . . . .Portugal
(B) Hauteville . . . . .France
(B) Larrys .France
(B) Light Beige . . . . .Philippines
(A) Loupinnes . . . . .France
(B) Marblehaus Beige . . . . Philippines
(C) Notre Dame . . . . .France
(C) Onyx Honey . . . . .Spain
(C) Perlato Sicilia . . . . .Italy
(B) Saint Corneille . . . . .France
(B) Selje Cream . . . . .Yugoslavia
(C) Tavernelle Chiampo Mandorlato . . .Italy

BUFF—DARK (Bf-Dk)
(B) Brown Beige . . . . .Philippines
(C) Napoleon Tigre . . . . .France
(C) Napoleon Grand-Melange . . . . . . .France
(C) Rubanne . . . . .France

GRAY (Gy)
(B) Aurisina (all types) . . . . .Italy
(A) Gray St. Anne Alpha . . . . .France
(A) Gray St. Anne Basque . . . . .France
(B) Gray/White Wombeyan . . . . . . .Australia
(B) Gris Duquesa . . . . .Spain

(A) Gris Macael . . . . .Spain
(A) Guatemala Gray . . . . .Guatemala
(A) Guatemala Veined Gray . . . . .Guatemala
(A) Highland Danby . . . . .Vermont
(A) Mankato Gray . . . . .Minnesota
(A) Mezzotint . . . . .Georgia
(A) Minnesota Pearl Gray . . . . . .Minnesota
(A) Minnesota Silver Gray Fleuri .Minnesota
(A) Northern Gray . . . . .Minnesota
(A) Ozark .Missouri
(A) Ruivina Escuro . . . . .Portugal
(A) Solar Gray . . . . .Georgia
(A) Sterling . . . . .No. Carolina
(A) Trigaxes Claro . . . . .Portugal
(A) Trigaxes Escuro . . . . .Portugal

GRAY—BLUISH (Gy-Bl)
(B) Aqua Beige . . . . .Philippines
(C) Bardigliotto (all types) . . . . .Italy
(A) Buxy Bleu . . . . .France
(B) Chanteuil Bleu . . . . .France
(B) Marmara Vein . . . . .Turkey
(A) Nuvolato .Italy
(C) Payolle Jumbo . . . . .France

GREEN (Gr)
(C) Campan Rose Vert . . . . .France
(B) Cipollino Verde Apuano . . . . .Italy
(C) Connemara Dark Green . . . . .Ireland
(C) Forest Green (all types) . . . . .Italy
(C) Guatemala Antique Green . . .Guatemala
(B) Guatemala Emerald Green . .Guatemala
(A) Nana Jade . . . . .Alaska
(D) Pakistan Onyx . . . . .Pakistan
(C) Payolle Irise . . . . .France
(C) Serpentine (all types) . . . . .Italy
(C) Sirocco Green . . . . .Italy
(D) Verde Acceglio . . . . .Italy
(C) Verde Alpi .Italy
(C) Verde Antique . . . . .Vermont
(C) Verde Antonio . . . . .Italy
(C) Verde Aver . . . . .Italy
(A) Verde Cristal . . . . .Portugal
(C) Verde Bosco "P" . . . . .Italy
(C) Verde Gonari . . . . .Italy
(C) Verde Gressoney . . . . .Italy
(C) Verde Imperial . . . . .Italy
(C) Verde Irisado (Anasol) . . . . .Spain
(C) Verde Issorie . . . . .Italy
(B) Verde Pastor . . . . .Spain
(C) Verde Pirineos . . . . .Spain
(C) Verde Polcevera . . . . .Italy
(C) Verde St. Nicholaus . . . . .Italy
(C) Verde Tinos . . . . .Greece
(A) Verde Viana . . . . .Portugal

(C) Vert d'Estours ....France
(C) Vert Floran........................Italy
(C) Vert Luceto ....Italy
(C) Vert Racega ....Italy
(C) Vert Ste. Anna ....Italy
(C) Vert Jade ....Italy

PINK (P)
(C) Chassagne Rose or Violine .....France
(A) Craig Pink ....Tennessee
(A) Continental Birch ....Tennessee
(A) Continental Mahogany ......Tennessee
(A) Continental Maple ....Tennessee
(A) Continental Oak ....Tennessee
(A) Edward Pink ....Tennessee
(A) Etowah Fleuri ....Georgia
(B) Kingstone Cherry Pink ..Taiwan, R.O.C.
(B) Light Rosso Marblehaus ....Philippines
(C) Mariposa ....Philippines
(A) Marmor.....................Tennessee
(A) Northern Pink Buff ....Minnesota
(C) Pink Alagao ....Philippines
(A) Pink Aurora ....Alabama
(A) Pink Buff Kasota ....Minnesota
(A) Pink Buff Mankato ....Minnesota
(A) Pink Buff Mansota ....Minnesota
(A) Pink Caroline ....Minnesota
(C) Rose Liseron ....France
(C) Salmon Pink ....Spain
(B) Valencia Rose ....Spain
(B) Venezuelan Pink ....Venezuela

ORANGE (O)
(A) Rosa de Monte ....Portugal

RED (R)
(C) Belgian Red Light ....Belgium
(C) Breche Isabella ....Italy
(C) Breche Rouge Antique ....Italy
(D) Collemandina ....Italy
(C) Crocidolite ....Italy
(C) Dark Rosso Marblehaus ....Philippines
(C) Languedoc Turquin ....France
(C) Ramello Rosso ....Italy
(D) Red Levanto (all types) ....Italy
(C) Red Verona ....Italy
(C) Rojo Alicante ....Spain
(C) Rojo Andalucia ....Spain
(C) Rojo Bilbao ....Spain
(C) Rojo Coralito ....Spain
(C) Rosso Alberato ....Italy
(C) Rosso Magnaboschi ....Italy
(A) Rosso Venato ....Puerto Rico
(C) Rosso Verona Broccato ....Italy
(B) Rouge Daniel ....Spain
(C) Rouge de Neuville ....Belgium
(C) Rouge Fleuri ....Rumania
(C) Rouge Incarnat ....France
(C) Rouge Languedoc ....France
(C) Rouge Royal (all types) ....Belgium
(C) Trani ....Italy

RED—REDDISH BROWN (R-RBrw)
(C) Breccia...................New Mexico
(C) Brech D'Aleps ....France
(A) Cedar Tavernelle ....Tennessee
(B) Kingstone Coral Corona. Taiwan, R.O.C.
(C) Romarin ....France
(C) Royal Fleuri ....Tennessee

ROSE (Rs)
(C) Almiscado ....Portugal
(C) Brazilian Rose ....Brazil
(C) Brechardo Espanol ....Spain
(D) Cassino Rose ....Italy
(C) Corati Rose ....Italy
(C) Chiampo Porfirico ....Italy
(D) Fiorito Adige ....Italy
(B) Jaune Rose ....Norway
(A) Kasota Antique Rose ....Minnesota
(D) Loredo Rosato ....Italy
(B) Norwegian Rose ....Norway
(A) Pardais ....Portugal
(A) Rose Aurora ....Portugal
(A) Rosa de Borba ....Portugal
(C) Rosa Duquesa ....Spain
(A) Rosa Vergado ....Portugal
(C) Rosalit ....Yugoslavia
(C) Rose Agate ....Missouri
(C) Rose Alhambra ....Spain
(C) Rose Turquesa ....Spain
(B) Rose Pholeen ....France
(D) Rosora (Tuscan Rose) ....Italy
(C) St. Florient Rose ....Portugal

VEINED, BRECCIATED (BLUISH OR GRAY BACKGROUND (V, Brc[Bl-Gy])
(C) Bois Jourdan ....France
(D) Fior di Pesco (all types) ....Italy
(B) Classic Blue ....Philippines
(D) Grigio Carnico ....Italy
(B) Gris Lilas ....Morocco
(C) Gris Perle (all types) ....Morocco
(C) Monte Azul ....Spain
(C) Platina Gris ....Morocco
(C) Platina Rose ....Morocco
(C) Repocevo ....Yugoslavia
(B) St. Anne (all types) ....France

VEINED, BRECCIATED (CREAM OR WHITE BACKGROUND (V,Brc[Cr-W])
(B) Arabescato (all types) ....Italy
(A) Bettogli Vein ....Italy
(B) Breccia Fantasia ....Italy
(D) Breche Violeta ....Italy
(C) Calacata (all types) ....Italy
(C) Crema Delicato..................Italy
(A) Cumulus.....................Alabama
(A) Gioia Vein ....Alabama
(B) Hualien White B ....Taiwan, R.O.C.
(C) Hualien White C ....Taiwan, R.O.C.
(A) Mariposa Danby Veined ....Vermont
(C) Mexican Onyx (all types) ....Mexico
(D) Paonazzo (all types) ....Italy
(A) Pavonazzo ....Vermont
(C) Piastraccia ....Italy
(B) Statuary Vein (all types) ....Italy
(C) Verde Fantastico ....Italy

VEINED, BRECCIATED (TAN OR YELLOWISH BACKGROUND) (V,Brc[T-Y])
(D) Breccia Pernice ....Italy
(C) Breche Aurora ....Italy
(B) Caramela ....Philippines
(B) Imperial Brown ....Philippines
(D) Loredo Chiaro (all types) ....Italy
(C) Loredo Zani (all types) ....Italy
(D) Macciavecchia.............Switzerland
(C) Ondagata ....Italy

(C) Rosato ....Italy
(C) Serpeggiante ....Italy
(C) Thassos ....Greece

WHITE (W)
(B) Aegean Crystal ....Greece
(B) Bianco di Nieve ....Yugoslavia
(A) Bianco "P" (all types) ....Italy
(A) Blanco Macael ....Spain
(A) Blanco Macael del Rio ....Spain
(A) Blanco Macael Heavy Veined ....Spain
(A) Brazilian White (Cintilante) ....Brazil
(A) Carrara White/Bianco (all types) ...Italy
(A) Creme d'Ivoire ....Alabama
(A) Estremoz Blanco ....Portugal
(A) Estremoz Vergado ....Portugal
(A) Estremoz Vergado Escuro .....Portugal
(A) Formosa White ....Taiwan, R.O.C.
(A) Glacier ....Alabama
(A) Guatemala Extra White .....Guatemala
(A) Guatemala Standard White ..Guatemala
(A) Imperial Danby ....Vermont
(A) Naxos ....Greece
(A) Royal White ....Philippines
(A) Sivec ....Yugoslavia
(A) White Alabama ....Alabama
(A) White Cherokee ....Georgia
(A) White Georgia Golden Vein ....Georgia

WHITE—BLUISH (W-Bl)
(B) Adair Marble ....Canada
(A) Creole ....Georgia
(A) Royal Danby ....Vermont

WHITE—BROWNISH (W-Brw)
(A) Eureka Danby ....Vermont

WHITE—CREAMY (W-Cr)
(C) Calacata (gold vein) ....Italy
(A) Caribe Cream ....Venezuela
(A) Cream D'Or (gold vein) ....Alabama
(D) Italian Cremo ....Italy
(B) Kingstone Noble Ivory ..Taiwan, R.O.C.
(A) Regal White Danby ....Vermont
(A) Select White Alabama ....Alabama

WHITE—GOLDISH (W-Go)
(A) Gold Mist ....Philippines

WHITE—GRAYISH (W-Gy)
(B) Gray Mist ....Philippines
(A) Ruivina Raiado ....Portugal

WHITE—GREENISH (W-Gr)
(B) Green Mist ....Philippines
(A) Mariposa Danby Clouded .....Vermont
(A) Montclair Danby ....Vermont
(A) Plateau Danby ....Vermont
(A) Suez Vert Argent ....Brazil

YELLOW OR GOLD (Y/G)
(C) Brocatelle ....France
(C) Bronceado (bronze) ....Spain
(C) Crema Espanol (all types) ....Spain
(A) Guatemala Gold ....Guatemala
(D) Jaune Mireille ....France
(B) Kingstone Golden Yellow. Taiwan, R.O.C.
(D) Yellow Siena (all types) ....Italy
(C) Yellow Verona (all types) ....Italy

TRAVERTINE MARBLES

ALPHABETICAL

KEY:
BROWN	Brw
BUFF—BROWN—YELLOWISH	Bf-Brw-Y
BUFF—CREAM or LIGHT	Bf-C/L
BUFF—DARK	Bf-Dk
PINK	P
RED—REDDISH BROWN	R-RBrw
VEINED, BRECCIATED (Tan or Yellowish Background)	V,Brc(T/Y)
YELLOW OR GOLD	Y/G

Almond . . . . (C) Bf-C/L
Continental Buff . . . . (C) Bf-C/L
Cream "A" . . . . (C) Bf-C/L
Desert Gold . . . . (C) Y/G
Etruscan (all types) . . . . (C) V,Brc(T/Y)
Geneva Light . . . . (C) Bf-C/L
Golden (light or dark) . . . . (C) Y/G
Golden Ribbon . . . . (C) Y/G
Iberico Dark . . . . (C) Bf-Brw-Y
Iberico Light . . . . (C) Bf-C/L
Imperial (all types) (Italian) . . . . . . (D) Bf-C/L
Imperial (Spain) . . . . (C) Y/G
Minnesota Pink . . . . (A) P
Onciato . . . . (C) Brw
Palm . . . . (C) Bf-C/L
Peruvian Golden . . . . (C) Y/G
Pueblo . . . . (D) Bf-C/L
Rojo Travertine . . . . (C) R-RBrw

Roman . . . . (C) Bf-C/L
Roman Cream Select . . . . (C) Bf-C/L
Roman Light . . . . (C) Bf-C/L
St. Peter . . . . (C) Brw
Scheherazade . . . .(C) P
Spanish Gold . . . . (C) Bf-Brw-Y
Temple Creme . . . . (C) Bf-C/L
Travertine "N" . . . . (C) Bf-C/L
Tuscan Light
 (see Geneva Light) . . . . (C) Bf-C/L
Walnut . . . . (C) Brw
Winona . . . . (B) Bf-C/L
Wood Grain . . . .(C) Bf-Dk

BY COLOR RANGE

BROWN (Brw)
(C) Travertine Oniciato . . . . .Italy
(C) Travertine St. Peter . . . . .Italy
(C) Travertine Walnut . . . . .Italy

BUFF—BROWN—YELLOWISH (Bf-Brw-Y)
(C) Travertine Iberico Dark . . . . .Spain
(C) Travertine Spanish Gold . . . . .Spain

BUFF—CREAM OR LIGHT (Bf-C/L)
(C) Cream "A" Travertine . . . . .Italy
(C) Continental Buff Travertine . . . . . . .Idaho
(C) Roman Cream Select . . . . .Italy
(C) Roman Light "P" Travertine . . . . Italy
(C) Temple Cream . . . . .New Mexico

(C) Travertine Almond . . . . .Italy
(C) Travertine General Light
 (Tuscan Light) . . . . .Italy
(C) Travertine Iberico Light . . . . .Spain
(D) Travertine Imperial (all types) . . . . . .Italy
(C) Travertine "N" . . . . .Italy
(C) Travertine Palm . . . . .Italy
(C) Travertine Roman . . . . .Italy
(C) Travertine Roman Light . . . . .Italy
(D) Travertine Roman Light . . . . .Mexico
(B) Winona Travertine . . . . .Minnesota

BUFF—DARK (Bf-Dk)
(C) Travertine Wood Grain . . . . .Spain

PINK (P)
(A) Minnesota Pink . . . . .Minnesota
(C) Scheherazade· . . . . .New Mexico

RED—REDDISH BROWN (R-RBrw)
(C) Rojo Travertine . . . . .Spain

VEINED, BRECCIATED (TAN OR YELLOWISH BACKGROUND) (V,Brc[T/Y])
(C) Travertine Etruscan (all types) . . . . . Italy

YELLOW OR GOLD (Y/G)
(C) Desert Gold . . . . .New Mexico
(C) Golden Ribbon Travertine . . . . .Italy
(C) Imperial Travertine . . . . .Spain
(C) Travertine Golden (light or dark) . . .Italy
(C) Travertine Peruvian Golden . . . . . . .Peru

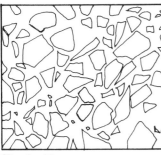

Standard terrazzo
Composed of #1 and #2 chips.

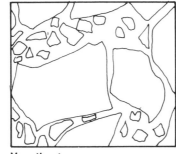

Venetian terrazzo
Makes use of larger #3-#8 chips.

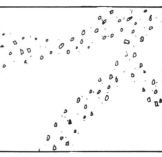

Palladiana terrazzo
Composed of thin, random, fractured slabs of 3/8" (0.95 cm) thick marble.

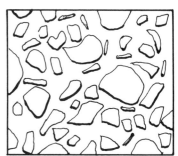

Rustic terrazzo
A uniformly textured mixture in which the matrix is depressed to expose the chips.

SPECIFICATION GUIDELINES FOR TERRAZZO

Terrazzo is a composite material poured in place or precast that is used for floor and wall treatments. It consists of marble, quartz, granite, or other suitable chips, sprinkled or unsprinkled, with a binder or matrix that is cementitious, chemical, or a combination of both. Terrazzo is poured, cured, ground and polished, or otherwise finished to produce a uniformly textured surface.

Cost factors
The following factors affect the price of terrazzo installations. However, it is recommended that a reliable local contractor be consulted for exact figures.
1. Factors causing slight moderate increases in costs:
   a. Use of chips larger than #1 and #2 chips.
   b. Palladiana.
   c. Intricate or complex divider strip layout.
   d. Use of overly complicated formula.
   e. Use of large proportions of relatively rare and therefore expensive marble chips.
   f. Use of extremely hard chips such as granite and quartz. (Added grinding costs.)
   g. Use of chips not locally available. (Added freight costs.)
   h. Use of color pigments in matrix. (Usually only a slight cost increase.)
2. Factors causing slightly decreased costs:
   a. Use of gray cement rather than white.
   b. Use of locally available chips.
   c. Use of #1 and #2 chips only.
   d. Uncomplicated divider strip layout with relatively large panels [4' X 4' (1.22 X 1.22 m)].
   e. Use of white metal or plastic divider strips rather than brass.

Samples
All samples should be at least 6" X 6" (15.24 X 15.25 cm) and should contain only those materials locally available or which the terrazzo contractor intends using.

Custom designs
Special effects are often created in terrazzo by designers who wish to custom design a specific feature or pattern. Floor maps, seals, logos, and even unsual shapes and contours can be custom designed for either precasting or on-site application.

Matrix data
The matrix is that ingredient in a terrazzo floor which acts as a binder to hold the chips in position. There are three basic types of matrix: cementitious, modified cementitious, and resinous.

Precast terrazzo
It is sometimes advisable to precast custom terrazzo items such as treads and risers window sills, bases, thresholds, and outdoor furniture. This is because of their intricate shape or the design elements of the building. Precast terrazzo items are poured in molds, after which they are moisture-cured, ground and polished, or otherwise finished. Some shapes are standard, but it is possible to accurately cast custom designs.

Chip size chart

Number	Passes screen (in.)	Retained on screen (in.)
0	1/8	1/16
1	1/4	1/8
2	3/8	1/4
3	1/2	3/8
4	5/8	1/2
5	3/4	5/8
6	7/8	3/4
7	1	7/8
8	1 1/8	1

Note: Quarries normally produce #0, #1, and #2 as separate sizes, sizes are frequently grouped as follows: #3 and #4 mixed, #5 and #6 mixed, #7 and #8 mixed, and #4 through #7 mixed.

Thickness & weight allowance
This chart indicates the cross-sectional and weight allowances that should be observed in using the various types of terrazzo. For further information and architectural details, see NTMA's Technical Data Book.

Type of installation	Allowance for finish (in.)	Weight per sq ft (lb)
Sand cushion	2 1/2	27
Bonded	1 3/4	18
Monolithic	1/2	7
Exterior & frame	2 1/2	28
Venetian	2 3/4	28
Epoxy	1/4	3
Polyester	1/4	3
Polyacrylate	3/8	4 1/2
Latex matrix	3/8-1/2	4 1/2-6

INSTALLATION DETAILS

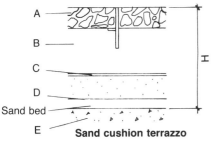

A
B
C
D
Sand bed
E   **Sand cushion terrazzo**

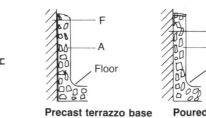

F
A
Floor
Precast terrazzo base

F
A
Floor
Poured terrazzo base

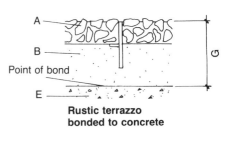

A
B
Point of bond
E
Rustic terrazzo bonded to concrete

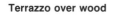

Divider strip
A
B
C
D
Terrazzo over wood

A
B
E
Terrazzo bonded to concrete

Notes & dimensions:
A = terrazzo
B = underbed
C = wire mesh
D = isolation membrane
E = concrete slab
F = block wall
G = 1 3/4" (4.45 cm)
H = 2 1/2" (6.35 cm)

CHART OF GRANITE COLORS & TYPES

Color & variegation		Grain	Name of granite	Quarry location
White	All white	Medium	Plymouth White	Plymouth, VT
		Medium	Chelmsford White	West Chelmsford, MA
		Fine	North Jay White	North Jay, ME
		Medium	Mount Airy White	Mount Airy, NC
		Fine	Sierra White	Raymond, CA
		Fine	Woodbury	Woodbury, VT
		Coarse	Rockville White	Rockville, MN
Gray	Dark to purple gray	Coarse	Dark Pearl	Cold Spring, MN
	Light to medium gray	Coarse	Rockville	Rockville, MN
	Light gray (with waves)	Medium	Iridian	Isle, MN
	Dark to greenish gray	Medium	Mason	Mason, NH
	Light gray	Fine	Chelmsford Gray	West Chelmsford, MA
	Light gray	Fine	Swenson Light Woodbury	Woodbury, VT
	Light to medium gray	Fine to medium	Swenson Gray	Concord, NH
	Very light gray	Medium	Mount Airy	Mount Airy, NC
Buff	Gray buff with black	Coarse	Texas Pearl	Marble Falls, TX
	Reddish buff	Fine	Lac Du Bonnet	Lac Du Bonnet, Man.
	Greenish gray and variegated brown	Medium	Bears Den Quarry	Mason, NH
	Brown with dark spots	Medium to coarse	Milford Buff	Milford, MA
Beige	Beige	Medium	Sunset Beige	Marble Falls, TX
Pink	Variegated pink and black	Fine	Rainbow	Morton, MN
	Gray pink with black	Medium to coarse	Diamond Pink	Cold Spring, MN
	Pink with dark spots	Medium to coarse	Milford Pink	Milford, MA
	Reddish pink mottled with large gray and medium black spots	Coarse	Conway Pink	Redstone, NH
	Pink	Medium to coarse	New Hampshire Pink	Madison, NH
Red	Variegated brownish red	Medium	Agate	Ortonville, MN
	Brownish red	Medium	Carnelian	Milbank, SD
	Bright red	Fine	Bright Red	Wausau, WI
	Pinkish red	Coarse	Sunset Red	Marble Falls, TX
	Light red	Medium to coarse	New Hampshire Pink	Madison, NH
	Red	Medium to coarse	Jonesboro Red	Jonesboro, ME
Blue	Grayish blue	Medium	Lake Placid Blue	Jay, NY
Green	Dark with brown and black	Coarse	Opalescent	Cold Spring, MN
	Green	Medium	Cold Spring Green	Jay, NY
	Dark yellowish green gray with black spottings	Coarse	Conway Green	Redstone, NH
Black	Dark gray	Fine	Charcoal Black	Cold Spring, MN
	Dark gray	Fine	Academy Black	Clovis, CA

GRANITE STANDARDS

ASTM	C97	Absorption by weight	0.4% max.		ASTM	C170	Compressive strength	per cu ft min. 19,000 psi min.
ASTM	C97	Density	160 lb (72.64 kg)		ASTM	C99	Modulus of rupture	1,500 psi min.

GRANITE
A natural igneous rock of visibly crystalline texture. Consists mainly of quartz, orthocase, feldspar, or micra. Very hard and durable.

FINISHES

Polished
Mirror gloss, with sharp reflections.

Honed
Dull sheen, without reflections.

Rubbed
Plane surface with occasional slight "trails" or scratches.

Fine rubbed
Smooth and free from scratches; no sheen.

Shot ground
Plane surface with pronounced circular markings or trails having no regular pattern.

Thermal
Plane surface with flame finish applied by mechanically controlled means to ensure uniformity. Surface coarseness varies, depending upon grain structure of granite.

Sand blasted, coarse stippled
Coarse plane surface produced by blasting with an abrasive; coarseness varies with type of preparatory finish and grain structure of the granite.

Sand blasted, fine stippled
Plane surface, slightly pebbled, with occasional slight trails or scratches.

Sawn
Relatively plane surface with texture ranging from wire sawn, a close approximation of rubbed finish, to shot sawn, with scoring $\frac{3}{32}''$ (0.24 cm) in depth. Gang saws produce parallel scorings; rotary or circular saws make circular scorings. Shot-sawn surfaces are sandblasted to remove all rust stains and iron particles.

Stained
Materials especially likely to cause staining of granite are oak (when wet), knots in soft wood, oil- and asphalt-based compounds.

INSTALLATION

Mortar
Mortar for setting and pointing shall be 1 part portland cement and 1 part plastic lime hydrate to 3 parts of clean, nonstaining sand.

Anchors, cramps, and dowels
All anchors, cramps, dowels, and other anchoring devices shall be type 304 stainless steel or suitable nonferrous metal of the types and sizes shown on approved shop drawings.

Flatness tolerances
Variation from true plane, or flat surfaces, shall be determined by use of a 4' (1.22m) long straightedge, applied in any direction on the surface.

TERMINOLOGY

Arris
The sharp edge or exterior corner formed by the meeting of two surfaces, whether plane or curved.

Bed
(a) The top or bottom horizontal surface of a piece, which is covered when the piece is set in place.
(b) A filled or open space extending horizontally between adjacent pieces set in place.

Cramp
An anchoring device in the form of a metal bar bent at both ends in the shape of a flat U.

Joint
(a) The end or side surface of a piece, which is covered when the piece is set in place.
(b) A filled or open space extending vertically between adjacent pieces set in place.
(c) Minimum recommended bed and joint width is $\frac{1}{4}''$ (0.64 cm). The use of greater width decreases the cost of the work.

Scabbled
Roughly shaped or dressed to approximate shape and size.

Seam
A crack or fissure in a rough quarry block.

Start
The beginning of a crack, caused by quarrying, fabrication, or handling.

DIMENSIONS
Maximum variation in the dimensions of any piece shall be $\frac{1}{4}''$ of the specified bed and joint width.

Minimum thickness for exterior veneer in either bush-hammered or pointed finish should be 4" (10.16 cm). All other finishes may be 2" (5.08 cm).

Whenever ashlar or veneer is used as a facing, a setting space of at least 1" (2.54 cm) measured from the nominal thickness of the piece is required.

SHOP DRAWINGS
The granite supplier should submit several copies of all necessary shop drawings to the designer for approval. The drawings should show all bedding, bonding, jointing, and anchoring details.

The dimensions and setting number of each piece of granite should be included. No final sizing or finishing should be done until the shop drawings have been approved.

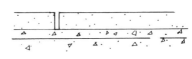

Pavers with open joint

Veneer over concrete

Granite attached with cramp

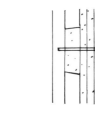

Veneer on wallboard

Mortar bed methods:
slate flooring over concrete slab

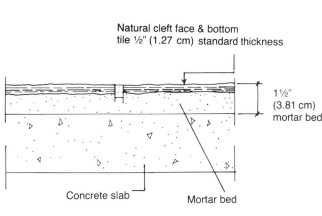

Natural cleft face & bottom
tile ½″ (1.27 cm) standard thickness

1½″
(3.81 cm)
mortar bed

Concrete slab   Mortar bed

Natural cleft-face slate
¼″ (0.64 cm) thick installed with thin-set
mastic

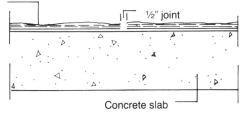

½″ joint

Concrete slab

Thin-set mastic method: over
plywood subfloors†

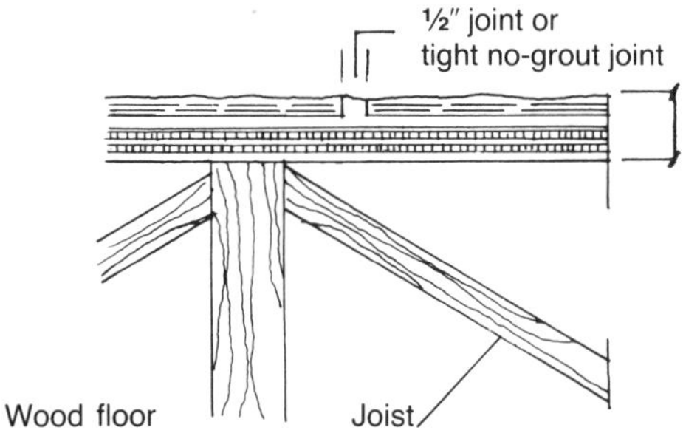

½″ joint or
tight no-grout joint

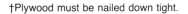

Wood floor   Joist

†Plywood must be nailed down tight.

Plan showing pavers

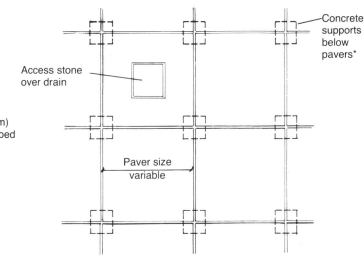

Concrete
supports
below
pavers*

Access stone
over drain

Paver size
variable

*The size of the support varies with the size and thickness of pavers. The average size supports for 42″ (106.68 cm) square pavers are about 10″ (25.40 cm) square.

Sizes of slate used in flooring

Slate flooring is supplied in a variety of sizes. Larger pieces are thicker and therefore cost more. Pieces are usually supplied with sawed parallel edges unless otherwise specified. Irregular flagging is available in a natural sculptured shape with two parallel sides (sizes in inches).

	Length (max.)	Width (max.)	Thickness		
			Light foot traffic	Moderate foot traffic	Heavy foot traffic
Flagging	18	22	¾	¾	1
Treads	60	18	1¼	1¼-1½	1½
Thresholds	48	6	¾-⅞	⅞-1	1-1¼

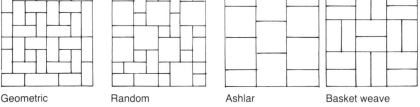

Geometric   Random   Ashlar   Basket weave

Performance criteria

Slate flooring shall have sufficient tensile and compressive strength to withstand pedestrian and equipment weight to which it will be subjected during normal use.

Slate flooring shall be fabricated to facilitate uniform installation to provide an even and true solid plane.

Slate flooring shall require only minimal maintenance to keep it clean by hosing, mopping, or swabbing.

Slate flooring shall be fireproof and impervious to moisture to permit such cleaning.

Slate flooring shall be resistant to staining by materials dropped upon it.

Slate flooring shall be fireproof and neither ignite nor support combustion. It shall not be marked nor marred by lighted cigarettes dropped on it.

Slate flooring shall be resistant to the constant abrasion of foot traffic including resistance to grit, sand, and other abrasives tracked onto its surface. An accelerated wear test such as ASTM C241 is suggested for determining relative degrees of resistance to foot traffic.

Slate flooring shall have a proven service life consistent with its intended use. Unless waived, the service life shall be for the life of the building in which it is installed and for a minimum of 25 years when installed on the exterior, depending on the extent of foot traffic and environmental conditions.

The surface of slate flooring shall provide safety underfoot. The finish shall not be so smooth as to induce slipping when wet.

Slate flooring shall conform to an acceptable standard such as ASTM C629 for Structural Slate.

Cleaning during and after installation

Exposed surfaces of the slate should be sponged down during installation to prevent mortar stains from forming. Wash water should be clear and kept clear by frequent changing. One trade practice is to rub sawdust over mortar stains to help soak up the mix. Rubbing with burlap also can be helpful, particularly at the joints. All mortar stains should be sponged from the slate within 24 hours of its installation. After slate has been set for at least 14 days, it should be scrubbed with an approved detergent or cleaning agent followed by thorough rinsing with clean water and drying with soft toweling or chamois.

Popular sizes of brick pavers

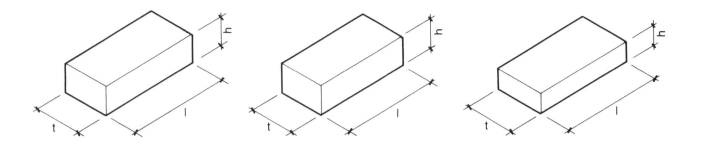

ESTIMATING PAVING MATERIALS

Brick paving units are manufactured in many sizes. Ranges of the most available sizes are listed in Tables A and B along with estimating information. It should be noted that not all sizes listed are suitable for interior brick flooring. It is advisable to check with local manufacturers or brick dealers before making a selection. Tables A and B should be used as design and estimating guides for either mortared or mortarless jobs. Table C provides information on types of mortar used in setting beds. Note that the varying proportions of portland cement and hydrated lime directly affect the material weight per cubic foot.

Estimating Table A
Brick paver units for mortarless paving*

Face dimensions (actual size, in.) t X l		Paver face area (sq in.)	Paver units (psf)
4	8	32.0	4.5
3¾	8	30.0	4.8
3⅝	7⅝	27.6	5.2
3⅞	8¼	32.0	4.5
3⅞	7¾	30.0	4.8
3¾	7½	28.2	5.1
3¾	7¾	29.1	5.0
3⅝	11⅝	42.1	3.4
3⅝	8	29.0	5.0
3⅝	11¾	42.6	3.4
3⁹⁄₁₆	8	28.5	5.1
3½	7¾	27.1	5.3
3½	7½	26.3	5.5
3⅜	7½	25.3	5.7
4	4	16.0	9.0
6	6	36.0	4.0
7⅝	7⅝	58.1	2.5
7¾	7¾	60.1	2.4
8	8	64.0	2.3
8	16	128.0	1.1
12	12	144.0	1.0
16	16	256.0	0.6
6	6 hexagon	31.2	4.6
8	8 hexagon	55.4	2.6
12	12 hexagon	124.7	1.2

*Table is based on BIA survey conducted in 1973. According to the survey approximately 38 sizes are currently manufactured.
†This table does not include provisions for waste. Allow at least 5 percent for waste and breakage.

Estimating Table B
Brick paver units for mortared paving*

Brick paver units (t X h X l)	Paver units (psf)	Cubic feet of mortar joints per 1,000 units	
		⅜″ joint	½″ joint
3⅝ X 2¼ X 8†	4.3	5.86	
3⅝ X 2¼ X 7⅝	4.5	5.68	
3¾ X 2¼ X 8	4.0		8
3⅝ X 1¼ X 7⅝	4.5	3.15	
3¾ X 1⅛ X 8	4.0		4

*The table does not include provisions for waste. Allow at least 5 percent for brick and 10 to 25 percent for mortar.
†Running bond pattern only.

Estimating Table C
Material quantities for ½″ mortar setting beds*

Mortar type & material	Cubic feet† per 100 sq ft	Material weight per cu ft in lb
Type N (1:1:6):	4.17	
portland cement		15.67
hydrated lime		6.67
sand		80.00
Type S (1:½:4½):	4.17	
portland cement		20.89
hydrated lime		4.44
sand		80.00
Type M (1:¼:3):	4.17	
portland cement		31.33
hydrated lime		3.33
sand		80.00

*These quantities are only for setting bed. For mortar joint quantities see Table B.
†The table does not include provisions for waste. Allow 10 to 25 percent for waste.

NONMODULAR BRICK (ACTUAL DIMENSIONS)

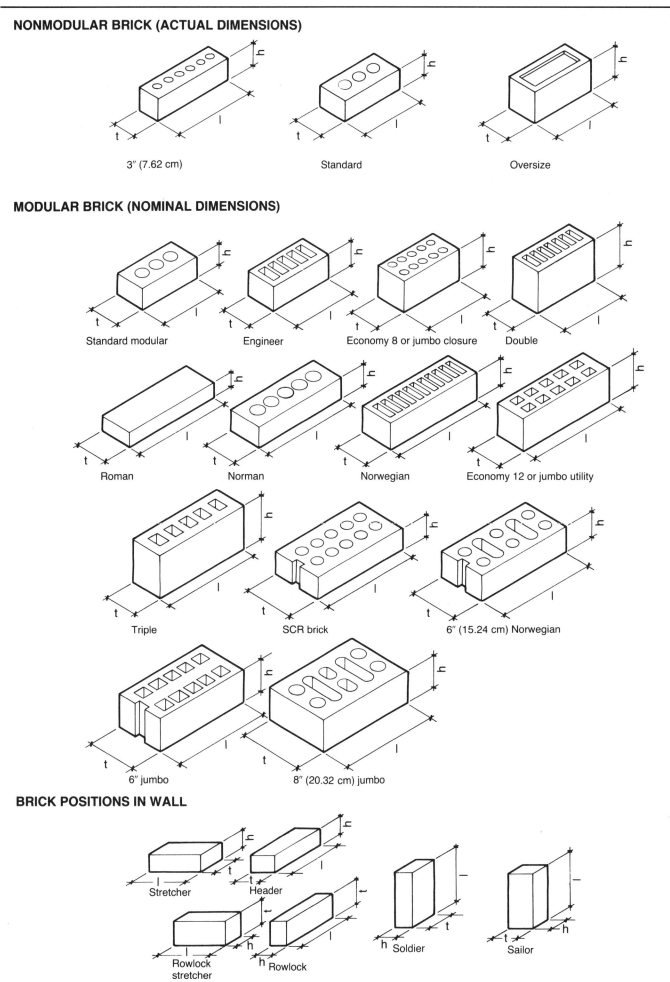

3″ (7.62 cm)   Standard   Oversize

MODULAR BRICK (NOMINAL DIMENSIONS)

Standard modular   Engineer   Economy 8 or jumbo closure   Double

Roman   Norman   Norwegian   Economy 12 or jumbo utility

Triple   SCR brick   6″ (15.24 cm) Norwegian

6″ jumbo   8″ (20.32 cm) jumbo

BRICK POSITIONS IN WALL

Stretcher   Header

Rowlock stretcher   Rowlock   Soldier   Sailor

CHART OF MODULAR BRICK SIZES*

Unit designation	Nominal dimensions (in.)			Joint thickness (in.)	Manufactured dimensions (in.)			Modular coursing (in.)
	t	h	l		t	h	l	
Standard modular	4	2⅔	8	⅜	3⅝	2¼	7⅝	3C = 8
				½	3½	2¼	7½	
Engineer	4	3⅕	8	⅜	3⅝	2¹³⁄₁₆	7⅝	5C = 16
				½	3½	2¹¹⁄₁₆	7½	
Economy 8 or jumbo closure	4	4	8	⅜	3⅝	3⅝	7⅝	1C = 4
				½	3½	3½	7½	
Double	4	5⅓	8	⅜	3⅝	4¹⁵⁄₁₆	7⅝	3C = 16
				½	3½	4¹³⁄₁₆	7½	
Roman	4	2	12	⅜	3⅝	1⅝	11⅝	2C = 4
				½	3½	1½	11½	
Norman	4	2⅔	12	⅜	3⅝	2¼	11⅝	3C = 8
				½	3½	2¼	11½	
Norwegian	4	3⅕	12	⅜	3⅝	2¹³⁄₁₆	11⅝	5C = 16
				½	3½	2¹¹⁄₁₆	11½	
Economy 12 or jumbo utility	4	4	12	⅜	3⅝	3⅝	11⅝	1C = 4
				½	3½	3½	11½	
Triple	4	5⅓	12	⅜	3⅝	4¹⁵⁄₁₆	11⅝	3C = 16
				½	3½	4¹³⁄₁₆	11½	
SCR brick†	6	2⅔	12	⅜	5⅝	2¼	11⅝	3C = 8
				½	5½	2¼	11½	
6″ (15.24 cm) Norwegian	6	3⅕	12	⅜	5⅝	2¹³⁄₁₆	11⅝	5C = 16
				½	5½	2¹¹⁄₁₆	11½	
6″ jumbo	6	4	12	⅜	5⅝	3⅝	11⅝	1C = 4
				½	5½	3½	11½	
8″ (20.32 cm) jumbo	8	4	12	⅜	7⅝	3⅝	11⅝	1C = 4
				½	7½	3½	11½	

*Available as solid units conforming to ASTM C 216- or ASTM C 62- or, in a number of cases, as hollow brick conforming to ASTM C 652-.
†Reg. U.S. Pat. Off., SCPI.

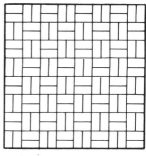

Basket weave

Variations of basket weave

Variations of basket weave

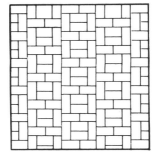

Herringbone

Running bond

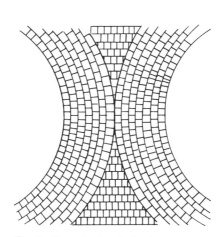

Circular & running bond mixed

Stack bond

¼ running bond

Running & stack bond mixed

BRICK PAVING OVER WOOD JOISTS

BRICK PAVING OVER CONCRETE SLAB

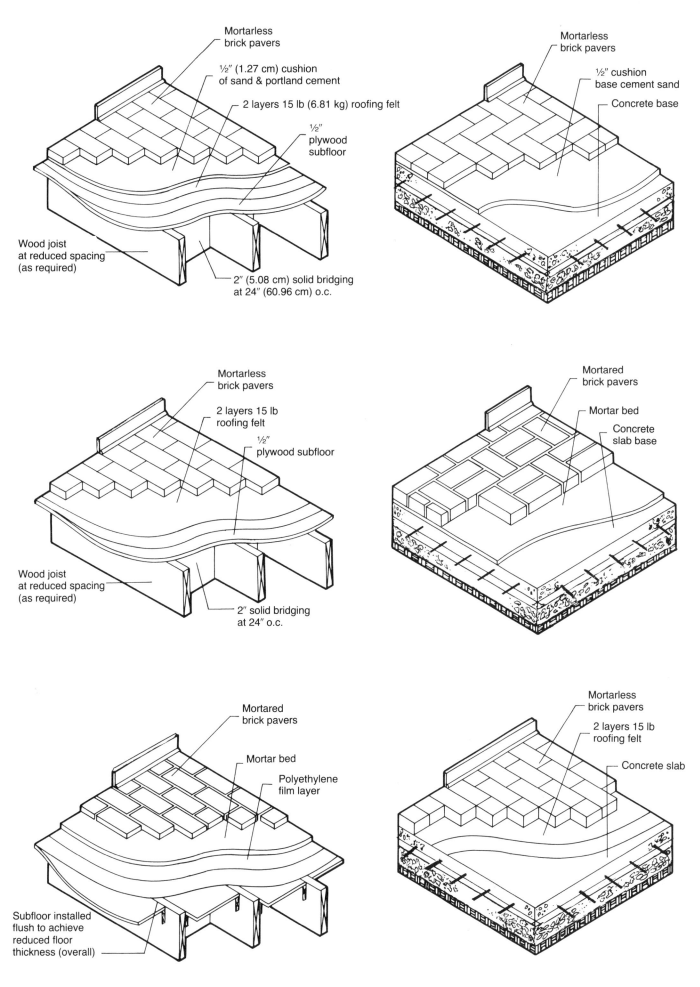

Mortarless brick pavers

½" (1.27 cm) cushion of sand & portland cement

2 layers 15 lb (6.81 kg) roofing felt

½" plywood subfloor

Wood joist at reduced spacing (as required)

2" (5.08 cm) solid bridging at 24" (60.96 cm) o.c.

Mortarless brick pavers

½" cushion base cement sand

Concrete base

Mortarless brick pavers

2 layers 15 lb roofing felt

½" plywood subfloor

Wood joist at reduced spacing (as required)

2" solid bridging at 24" o.c.

Mortared brick pavers

Mortar bed

Concrete slab base

Mortared brick pavers

Mortar bed

Polyethylene film layer

Subfloor installed flush to achieve reduced floor thickness (overall)

Mortarless brick pavers

2 layers 15 lb roofing felt

Concrete slab

Product Pattern and Description	Dimensions	Grade	Species
CANTERBURY Paper Faced 4 equal squares with alternating diagonal center slats	5/16" x 13-1/4" x 13-1/4"	Par & Better	Angelique Teak Red Oak White Oak Black Walnut
CHAUCER Paper Faced 4 alternating squares on diagonal framed by pickets	5/16" x 13-7/16" x 13-7/16"	Par & Better	Angelique Teak Red Oak White Oak Black Walnut
DOMINO Paper Faced 400 equal sized pieces butt-joined	5/16" x 18" x 18"	Par & Better	Angelique Teak Red Oak White Oak
HADDON HALL Paper Faced 4 equal squares	5/16" x 14-1/4" x 14-1/4"	Par & Better	Angelique Teak Red Oak White Oak Black Walnut Ash
HERRINGBONE Paper Faced	5/16" x 14-1/8" x 18-1/8" Slat Length 4-3/4" _____ 5/16" x 16-1/4" x 18-1/8" Slat Length 5-1/2"	Par & Better	Angelique Teak Red Oak White Oak Black Walnut Ash
MONTICELLO Paper Faced 4 equal alternating squares with pickets	5/16" x 13-1/4" x 13-1/4"	Par & Better	Angelique Teak Red Oak White Oak Black Walnut
PARALLEL Paper Faced _____ WebBac All slats run in one direction	5/16" x 19" x 19" _____ 5/16" x 11" x 11"	Par & Better	Angelique Teak Red Oak White Oak Black Walnut _____ Red Oak White Oak
RHOMBS Paper Faced 12 rhombs of 4 slats each	5/16" x 15-1/8" x 15-1/8"	Par & Better	Angelique Teak Red Oak White Oak Black Walnut
SAXONY Paper Faced 4 squares on diagonal and 8 half-squares	5/16" x 19" x 19"	Par & Better	Angelique Teak Red Oak White Oak Black Walnut
STANDARD Paper Faced 16 alternating squares	5/16" x 19" x 19"	Par & Better	Angelique Teak • Ash Red Oak • White Oak Black Walnut • Maple
		Par (Select)	Walnut
		Rustic	Angelique Teak • Ash Black Walnut • Maple Mixed Red Oak and White Oak
STANDARD WebBac 4 alternating squares	5/16" x 11" x 11"	Par & Better _____ Rustic	Red Oak White Oak Maple Ash
STANDARD WebBac 4 alternating squares *For commercial use*	11/16" x 11" x 11"	Par & Better _____ Rustic	Red Oak White Oak Maple
TIMES SQUARE Paper Faced	5/16" x 11" x 16-1/2"	Par & Better	Red Oak White Oak Angelique Teak Ash

Carpet: square feet to square meters conversion table

Ft²	Yd²	M²	Ft²	Yd²	M²	Ft²	Yd²	M²
50	5.6	4.5	310	34.4	27.9	570	63.3	51.3
60	6.7	5.4	320	35.6	28.8	580	64.4	52.2
70	7.8	6.3	330	36.7	29.7	590	65.6	53.1
80	8.9	7.2	340	37.8	30.6	600	66.7	54.0
90	10.0	8.1	350	38.9	31.5	700	77.8	63.0
100	11.1	9.0	360	40.0	32.4	800	88.9	72.0
110	12.2	9.9	370	41.1	33.3	900	100.0	81.0
120	13.3	10.8	380	42.2	34.2	1,000	111.1	90.0
130	14.4	11.7	390	43.3	35.1	2,000	222.2	180.0
140	15.6	12.6	400	44.4	36.0	3,000	333.3	270.0
150	16.7	13.5	410	45.6	36.9	4,000	444.4	360.0
160	17.8	14.4	420	46.7	37.8	5,000	555.5	450.0
170	18.9	15.3	430	47.8	38.7	6,000	666.7	540.0
180	20.0	16.2	440	48.9	39.6	7,000	777.8	630.0
190	21.1	17.1	450	50.0	40.5	8,000	888.9	720.0
200	22.2	18.0	460	51.1	41.4	9,000	1,000.0	810.0
210	23.3	18.9	470	52.2	42.3	10,000	1,111.1	900.0
220	24.4	19.8	480	53.3	43.2	20,000	2,222.2	1,800.0
230	25.6	20.7	490	54.4	44.1	30,000	3,333.3	2,700.0
240	26.7	21.6	500	55.6	45.0	40,000	4,444.4	3,600.0
250	27.8	22.5	510	56.7	45.9	50,000	5,555.5	4,500.0
260	28.9	23.4	520	57.8	46.8	60,000	6,666.7	5,400.0
270	30.0	24.3	530	58.9	47.7	70,000	7,777.8	6,300.0
280	31.1	25.2	540	60.0	48.6	80,000	8,888.9	7,200.0
290	32.2	26.1	550	61.1	49.5	90,000	10,000.0	8,100.0
300	33.3	27.0	560	62.2	50.4	100,000	11,111.1	9,000.0

Examples of carpet conversion

Ft²	Yd²	M²
5,000	555.5	450.0
600	66.7	54.0
50	5.6	4.5
5,650	627.8	508.5

Number of square yards of walls & ceiling in rooms with 8′0″ ceiling height

Room size	3	4	5	6	7	8	9	10	11	12	13	14	15	16	17	18	19	20	21	22
3	11.6	13.7	15.8	18.0	20.1	22.2	24.3	26.4	28.5	30.6	32.7	34.8	37.0	39.1	41.2	43.3	45.4	47.5	49.6	51.7
4	13.7	16.0	18.2	20.4	22.6	24.8	27.1	29.3	31.5	33.7	36.0	38.2	40.4	42.6	44.8	47.1	49.3	51.5	53.7	56.0
5	15.8	18.2	20.5	22.8	25.2	27.5	29.8	32.2	34.5	36.8	39.2	41.5	43.8	46.2	48.5	50.8	53.2	55.5	57.8	60.2
6	18.0	20.4	22.8	25.3	27.7	30.2	32.6	35.1	37.5	40.0	42.4	44.8	47.3	49.7	52.2	54.6	57.1	59.5	62.0	64.4
7	20.1	22.6	25.2	27.7	30.3	32.8	35.4	38.0	40.5	43.1	45.6	48.2	50.7	53.3	55.8	58.4	61.0	63.5	66.1	68.9
8	22.2	24.8	27.5	30.2	32.8	35.5	38.2	40.8	43.5	46.2	48.8	51.5	54.2	56.8	59.5	62.2	64.8	67.5	70.2	72.8
9	24.3	27.1	29.8	32.6	35.4	38.2	41.0	43.7	46.5	49.3	52.1	54.8	57.6	60.4	63.2	66.0	68.7	71.5	74.3	77.1
10	26.4	29.3	32.2	35.1	38.0	40.8	43.7	46.6	49.5	52.4	55.3	58.2	61.1	64.0	66.8	69.7	72.6	75.5	78.4	81.3
11	28.5	31.5	34.5	37.5	40.5	43.5	46.5	49.5	52.5	55.5	58.5	61.5	64.5	67.5	70.5	73.5	76.5	79.5	82.5	85.5
12	30.6	33.7	36.8	40.0	43.1	46.2	49.3	52.4	55.5	58.6	61.7	64.8	68.0	71.1	74.2	77.3	80.4	83.5	86.6	89.7
13	32.7	36.0	39.2	42.4	45.6	48.8	52.1	55.3	58.5	61.7	65.0	68.2	71.4	73.6	77.8	81.1	84.3	87.5	90.7	94.0
14	34.8	38.2	41.5	44.8	48.2	51.5	54.8	58.2	61.5	64.8	68.2	71.5	74.6	78.2	81.5	84.8	88.2	91.5	94.8	98.2
15	37.0	40.4	43.8	47.3	50.7	54.2	57.6	61.1	64.5	68.0	71.4	74.8	78.3	81.7	85.2	88.6	92.1	95.5	99.0	102.4
16	39.1	42.6	46.2	49.7	53.3	56.8	60.4	64.0	67.5	71.1	74.6	78.2	81.7	85.3	88.8	92.4	96.0	99.5	103.1	106.6
17	41.2	44.8	48.5	52.5	55.8	59.5	63.2	66.8	70.5	74.2	77.8	81.5	85.2	88.8	92.5	96.2	99.8	103.5	107.2	110.8
18	43.3	47.1	50.8	54.6	58.4	62.2	66.0	69.7	73.5	77.3	81.1	84.8	88.6	92.4	96.2	100.0	103.7	107.5	111.3	115.1
19	45.4	49.3	53.2	57.1	61.0	64.8	68.7	72.6	76.5	80.4	84.3	88.2	92.1	96.0	99.8	103.7	107.6	111.5	115.4	119.3
20	47.5	51.5	55.5	59.5	63.5	67.5	71.5	75.5	79.5	83.5	87.5	91.5	95.5	99.5	103.5	107.5	111.5	115.5	119.5	123.5
21	49.6	53.7	57.8	62.0	66.1	70.2	74.3	78.4	82.5	86.6	90.7	94.8	99.0	103.1	107.2	111.3	115.4	119.5	123.6	127.7
22	51.7	56.0	60.2	64.6	68.8	72.8	77.1	81.3	85.5	89.7	94.0	98.2	102.4	106.6	110.8	115.1	119.3	123.5	127.7	132.0
23	53.8	58.2	62.5	66.8	71.2	75.5	79.8	84.2	88.5	92.8	97.2	101.5	105.8	110.2	114.5	118.8	123.2	127.5	131.8	136.2
24	56.0	60.4	64.8	69.3	73.7	78.2	82.6	87.1	91.5	96.0	100.4	104.8	109.3	113.7	118.2	122.6	127.1	131.5	136.0	140.4

Summary of tested carpet performance attributes

Attribute	Tests	Minimal federal performance requirements*
1. Flammability		
a. Flame spread	ASTM E 84	Flame spread $\leq$ 75 unsprinklered
	NFPA 255	Flame spread $\leq$ 200 sprinklered
	UL 992	Flame spread 4.0 unsprinklered
		Flame spread 8.0 sprinklered
b. Surface flamma-bility ignition	DCC-FF1-70	Charred portion not to exceed
	DDD-C-95 (Rev)	within 2.54 cm (1″) of frame
	ASTM 2859-70T	edge
	DOC-FF 2-70	
c. Flooring radiant panel test	ASTM E-162-67	Commericial: 0.22 w/cm^2 (unsp)
	NBS IR-75-950	FF-1 70 (w/sp)
	NFPA 253	Health care: 0.45 w/cm^2 (unsp)
		022 w/cm (w/sp)
d. Smoke	NBS 708	Specific op density = 450/critical
	NFPA A 258/1976	16 @ 90 sec
2. Acoustics		
a. Airborne sound	ASTM C 423	SPP $\geq$ 60 in OPP/SPP $\geq$ 70 in RM
	PBS C.1	NIC′ + (NC 40) $\geq$ 60 in OPP
		NIC″ + (NC $\leq$ 35) $\geq$ 70 in RM
b. Impact sound	ASTM C 423-66	Mask vertical footfall with NC $\leq$
	PBS C.2	40
3. Colorfastness		
a. To light	AATCC 16E-1971	Rating of 4.0
b. To gas	AATCC 23-1972	Rating of 4.0
c. To ozone	AATCC 109-1972	Rating of 3.0
d. Crocking (W/D)	AATCC 8-1972	Rating of 4.0
e. Shampooing	AATCC 138-1972	Rating of 4.0
4. Electrostatics	AATCC 134-1975	Static level 3KV
5. Light reflectance	ASTM E 97	No more than 5%
	IES Transaction 33. P .378-1938	Not to exceed 15%
6. Azotic control	AATCC 112/30/90 100/103	High antibacterial level
7. Physical strength		
a. Tuft bind	ASTM D 1335-67 DD C 0095A	7 lb
b. Delamination	FTMS 191-5100†	Withstand wheel load of 1500 lb (681.00 kg)
c. Breaking	FTMS 191-5100	Withstand at least 100 lb (45.40 kg)
d. Shrinkage	DOC C 0095 A	Not to exceed 5% in any direction
8. Appearance		
a. Pilling/fuzz	Dupont TRL 609	4.0
b. Stain resistant	PBS-F.2	No noticeable stain
c. Crush resistant	FTMS 501A/3231	85% recovery
d. Abrasion	ASTM D 1175 641 (Taber)	6000-8000 cycles

*Required by majority of federal agencies.
†FTMS=Federal Test Method Standard.

Type	Class	Characteristics	Class 1‡	Class 2§	Test method
1. Felt	a. Uncoated animal hair	Weight, oz/sq yd, min.	40.0 −5%	50.0 −5%	FTMS 191, Method 5040 or 5041
		Thickness, in., min.	0.25	0.375	FTMS 191, Method 5030
		Compression set, %, max.	15	15	FTMS 601, Method 12131
		CLD, 25% defl., psi, min.	30	30	FTMS 191, Method 5100
		Flammability*	Pass	Pass	DOC FF 1-70
			75 or less	75 or less	ASTM E-84
	b. Rubberized animal hair/jute	Weight, oz/sq yd, min.	40.0 −5%	50.0 −5%	FTMS 191, Method 5040 or 5041
		Thickness, in., min.	0.27	0.375	FTMS 191, Method 5030
		Compression set, %, max.	15	15	FTMS 601, Method 12131
		CLD, 25% defl., psi, min.	30	30	FTMS 191, Method 5100
		Flammability*	Pass	Pass	DOC FF 1-70
			75 or less	75 or less	ASTM E-84
2. Cellular rubber	a. Rippled	Weight, oz/sq yd, min.	48.0 −5%	64.0 −5%	FTMS 191, Method 5040 or 5041
		Thickness, in., min.	0.30	0.40	FTMS 601, Method 12031
		CLD, 25%, defl., psi, min	0.615	0.875	FTMS 601, Method 12151
		Compression set, %, max. @ 50% deflection	15	15	FTMS 601, Method 12131
		Tensile strength, psi, min.	8	8	FTMS 191, Method 5100
		Flammability*	Pass	Pass	DOC FF 1-70
			75 or less	75 or less	ASTM E-84
	b. Flat sponge	Weight, oz/sq yd, min.	56.0 −5%	64.0 −5%	FTMS 191, Method 5040 or 5041
		Thickness, in., min.	0.250	0.250	FTMS 601, Method 12031
		CLD, 25% defl., psi, min.	0.75	1.5	FTMS 601, Method 12131
		Compression set, %, max. @ 50% deflection	10	10	FTMS 601, Method 12131
		Tensile strength, psi, min.	8	8	FTMS 191, Method 5100
		Flammability*	Pass	Pass	DOC FF 1-70
			75 or less	75 or less	ASTM E-84
	c. Latex foam	Weight, oz/sq yd, min.	38.0 −5%	46.0 −5%	FTMS 191, Method 5040 or 5041
		Thickness, in., min.	0.25	0.25	FTMS 601, Method 12031
		CLD, 25% defl., psi, min.	1.0	2.0	ASTM D 1564
		Compression set, %, max. @ 50% deflection	15	15	FTMS 601, Method 12131
		Tensile strength, psi, min.	8	8	FTMS 191, Method 5100
		Flammability*	Pass	Pass	DOC FF 1-70
			75 or less	75 or less	ASTM E-84
3. Urethane foam	a. Prime	Density, lb/ft^3, min.†	2.2 −5%	3.0 −5%	ASTM D 3574
		Thickness, in., min.	0.375	0.375	ASTM D 3574
		CLD, 65% defl., psi, min.	0.7	1.0	ASTM D 3574
		Compression set, %, max. @ 50% deflection	15	15	ASTM D 3574
		Tensile strength, psi, min.	10	10	ASTM D 3574
		Fatigue height loss, max.	5.0	5.0	ASTM 1564
		Load deflection loss & max.	25.0	25.0	ASTM 1564
		Elongation, %, min.	100	100	ASTM D 3574
		Flammability*	Pass	Pass	DOC F 1-70
			75 or less	75 or less	ASTM E-84
	b. Densified	Density, lb/ft^3, min.†	2.2 −5%	3.0 −5%	ASTM D 3574
		Thickness, in., min.	0.313	0.25	ASTM D 3574
		CLD, 65% defl., psi, min.	0.85	1.30	ASTM D 3574
		Compression set, %, max. @ 50% deflection	10	10	ASTM D 3574
		Tensile strength, psi, min.	17	20	ASTM D 3574
		Elongation, %, min.	100	100	ASTM D 3574
		Flammability*	Pass	Pass	DOC F 1-70
			75 or less	75 or less	ASTM E-84
	c. Grafted & modified	Density, lb/ft^3, min.†	2.2 −5%	2.7 −5%	ASTM D 3574
		Thickness, in., min.	0.375	0.25	ASTM D 3574
		CLD, 65% defl., psi, min.	0.85	1.30	ASTM D 3574
		Compression set, %, max. @ 50% deflection	15	15	ASTM D 3574
		Tensile strength, psi, min.	12	17	ASTM D 3574
		Elongation, %, min.	100	100	ASTM D 3574
		Flammability*	Pass	Pass	DOC FF 1-70
			75 or less	75 or less	ASTM E-84
	d. Bonded	Density, lb/ft^3, min.†	5.0 −5%	6.5 −5%	L-C-001369
		Thickness, in., min.	0.375	0.375	L-C-001369
		CLD, 65% defl., psi, min.	4.0	5.0	L-C-001369
		Compression set, %, max. @ 50% deflection	15	15	L-C-001369
		Tensile strength, psi, min.	5	7	L-C-001369
		Elongation, %, min.	45	45	L-C-001369
		Particle size, in., max.	0.50	0.50	L-C-001369
		Debris	1%	1%	See Section 4, Type III d
		Flammability*	Pass	Pass	DOC FF 1-70
			75 or less	75 or less	ASTM E-84

*Either test may be used for compliance; in DOC FF 1-70 the laundering requirement does not apply.

†Apparent density will be corrected to urethane polymer density by performing the following test: Ash content, %, as determined in ASTM D 297, subtracted from 100%, and multiplied by apparent density, shall equal the minimum values listed in the above table.

‡Medium-light traffic.

§Heavy traffic.

Source: HUD Standard for Detached Carpet Padding UM 72-1979.

General physical characteristics of resilient flooring

Material	Size	Gauges in.	Federal specification	Load limit (psi)	Construction & recommended use
Vinyl asbestos	9"X 9" 12" X 12"	1/16	SS-T-312 Type IV	25	Vinyl resins, asbestos fibers, plasticizors, color pigments, and fillers. Semiflexibility. Resistant to chemicals and moisture. Install all grades. Poor resilient quality.
Rubber tile	9" X 19" 12" X 12"	1/8 (0.125)	SS-T-312 Type II	200	Rubber compounds of synthetic butadiene-styrene type. Similar to vinyls in quality, but less durable and less resistant to grease and alkalis.
Vinyl sheet	6' wide 90'	.090	L-F-00460 A L-F-475a Type II	100	Vinyl resin surface with a backing of asbestos-flex felt or resin-saturated rag fiber. Install all grades. Use only in light or moderate traffic. Low resistance to cigarette burns. Very resilient.
Vinyl tile	9" X 9" 12" X 12"	.080 1/16 1/8	L-F-475 a Type II SS-T-312 Type I	200	Blended composition of thermoplastic binders, fillers, and pigments. Binders are polyvinyl chloride. Expensive in translucent type. Very resilient, but low resistance to cigarette burns.
Cork tile	6" X 6" 9" X 9" 12" X 12"	1/8 3/16 5/16		75	Pure cork particles bonded by baking process and thermosetting binders. May be finished or unfinished. Light to moderate traffic. Install on grade or suspended grade.
Vinyl cork tile	9" X 12"	1/8 (0.125)		150	Same as above, but may have thermoplastic binders and plastic film finishes.

Slipperiness

This is a health and safety factor that has been the subject of research by private industry, shoe manufacturers, insurance companies, and the National Bureau of Standards. National safety statistics have shown that falls in the home kill as many as 12,000 people and injure 6 million a year in the United States. Although the precise causes of the falls are not recorded, slippery floors are listed as a large contributor to these casualty rates. Several laboratory tests have been developed to determine the factors that contribute to slipperiness, that is, skid resistance or coefficient of friction between flooring and other materials such as sole and heel materials of footwear.

The coefficient of friction between two surfaces is defined as the ratio of the force required to move on surface over the other to the total force pressing the two surfaces together. Thus:

$$\text{Coefficient of friction} = \frac{\text{horizontal force}}{\text{vertical force}}$$

The two types of friction that are considered in these test methods are static and dynamic (kinetic). *Static* friction is the amount of friction between two surfaces at the moment that one begins to move across the other. *Dynamic* friction occurs between two surfaces when movement is in progress without interruption. Laboratory equipment is designed to test flooring materials in a horizontal position, with the application of static friction or the use of dynamic friction in the form of a swinging pendulum. The test results are recorded as an "index of slipperiness" or a "skid resistance index." The specification of flooring that may result in falls is especially critical in lobby or vestibule areas. The GSA specification for office buildings requires that resilient flooring be tested according to the ASTM D-2047 and have a slip-resistance coefficient of greater than or equal to 0.5.

Flammability

Resilient flooring is tested for flame spread and smoke obscuration in the following test procedures:

ASTM E-84
NFPA Standard 258
UL 992
NBS Smoke Chamber

Most federal specifications require a flame spread of 75 in unsprinkled areas and a 200 flame spread in sprinkled areas.

Protection against indentation

Floor protectors are necessary to retain the beauty of resilient flooring. The concentrated weight of furniture legs can be more evenly distributed over the surface by using flat composite cups under the legs. Furniture that is frequently moved should be equiped with casters 2" (5.08 cm) in diameter with soft rubber treads at least 3/4" (1.91 cm) wide. Glides should have a smooth, flat base with rounded edges and a flexible shank. These should be 1 1/4" to 24" (3.16 to 6.35 cm) in diameter. The Resilient Tile Institute recommends a maximum loading of 75 lb psi for vinyl asbestos tile and 40 lb psi for asphalt tile. To prevent scratch-producing dirt build-up, protectors should be cleaned each time the flooring is washed.

Light reflectance

This affects the brightness and quality of light in an interior. Too much reflectance can be a source of glare and discomfort in areas where critical work is taking place, such as offices and schools. A person seated at a desk looking downward toward the task will view the floor as a secondary background. Research has established that the task surface (book or papers) should not exceed a reflectance factor of 30 to 50 percent, and the floor should not exceed a 50 percent reflectance level.

Pliant wallcoverings

Covering	Use	Advantages	Disadvantages
Paper	Decorative	Many different patterns and colors. Moderate cost.	Subject to soiling, abrasion, and fading. No flammability criteria.
Vinyl	Light, medium, or heavy	Can be cleaned, resistant to fading, abrasion, and tested for flammability. Many textures available.	No major disadvantages. Installation cost varies according to surface preparation.
Foil	Decorative	Add high-reflectance levels, unusual decorative effects.	May create glare in certain areas. Conductor of electricity. Surface subject to abrasion and scratches; expensive installation costs.
Fabric	Decorative	Available in wide sizes and unlimited lengths. Can be installed over wide range of surfaces. Moderate cost.	Must be treated for soil resistance, may require extra backing.
Felt	Decorative, acoustic	Large widths available. Good for acoustic control.	Must be backed with paper. Tends to fade and difficult to spot clean.
Wood veneer	Moderate, heavy	Fire resistant, may be finished on site to desired finish, easy maintenance.	Expensive, special installation requirements.

Wallcovering installation procedures

Covering	Sizes	Adhesives	Seams	Surface preparation & installation
Paper	18″-27″(45.72-68.58cm)wide Single or double roll 30-36 sq ft (2.79-3.34 m²) per roll	Wheat paste or cellulose paste; apply to paper back	Butted or wired	Clean and smooth surface. Wash to prevent bacteria growth after paper application. Apply with soft, wide brush working from center of panel outward. Matching patterns should be cut from alternating rolls.
Vinyl	54″ (137.16 cm) wide by 30 yd (27.43 m) in length 405 sq ft (37.63 m²) per bolt.	Apply paste to fabric back	Overlap and double cut	Prime and seal all surfaces. Apply panels in exact order as cut from roll, using rolls in consecutive order. Use stiff bristle brush or flexible broad knife to eliminate air pockets. Wrap covering 6″ (15.24 cm) beyond outside corners and 3″ (7.62 cm) at inside corners.
Foil	18″-27″ wide Double and triple rolls	Premixed vinyls with low water content; apply to wall	Butted smooth with oval seam roller	Wall surfaces must be painted with oil-base enamel undercoat or wall primer. Prewash walls to remove bacteria. Surface must be very smooth. Apply with soft brush. Work from center out to edges. Puncture air bubbles and press down immediately. Wash finished panels with warm, clean water and soft cloth to avoid scratching. Avoid contact with electrical sources. When matching random patterns, reverse every other strip.
Fabric	36″-54″ (91.44-137.16 cm) any length Sold by yard	Wheat or cellulose; apply paste to wall	Butted or wired	Clean and smooth surface. Apply antibacteria primer. Staple fabric along top as hanging to handle weight of wet fabric. Staples may be removed later. If not paper backed, do not stretch too tightly or pull out of shape. Use same corner installation as vinyl.
Felt	54″-72″ (137.16-182.88 cm) wide Sold by yard	Wheat paste applied to wall	Butted or wired	Felt should be paper-backed for later removal. Wall should be clean and smooth and washed with antibacteria solution. Apply nap in same direction. Do not overstretch when applying.
Cork	Up to 36″ wide 36′-45′ (10.97-13.72 m) lengths	Wheat or vinyl	Butted	Clean and smooth surface. May require lining paper. Cork does not require matching. Follow manufacturers' installation recommendations.
Wood veneer	10″-24″ (25.40-60.96 cm) wide, up to 12′ (3.66 m) long	Recommended by material supplier	Butted	Follow manufacturers' recommendations. Wood may be prefinished or finished on site. Temperature control usually necessary prior to and during installation.

Estimation

The formula for estimating the quantity of wallcovering material needed for a given project is based on the number of square feet on the roll. Many wallcoverings are packaged in single rolls of 36 sq ft (3.44 m²) or double rolls of 72 sq ft (6.69 m²).

Measurements of the interior space are made in feet, noting the number of windows, doors, and other major architectural features, such as bookcases. For example, in estimating the wallcovering needed for a 12′ X 12′ (3.66 x 3.66 m) room with 8′ (2.44 m) ceilings, two windows, and a door, proceed in this manner:

1. Measure the length of each wall and total
   12′ + 12′ + 12′ + 12′ = 48′
2. Multiply the distance around the room by the ceiling height to determine the total number of square feet.
   48′ X 8′ = 384 sq ft
3. Allow a 20 percent margin for waste
   384 sq ft + 20% = 460.8 sq ft
4. Calculate the actual areas for doors, windows, and other architectural features. Allow 15 sq ft as an average size per door and for every two windows.
   2 × 15 sq ft = 30 sq ft
5. Subtract the areas for doors, windows, and other architectural features.
   460.8 sq ft − 30 sq ft = 430.8 sq ft

This last figure represents the total number of square feet of wallcovering that is required to complete the space, and from it the number of rolls of wallcovering that will be needed can be determined.

If the selected wallcovering is packaged in standard rolls containing 36 sq ft:
430.8 ÷ 36 sq ft/roll = 11.97, or 12 single rolls
The amount needed would be 12 single rolls, or 6 double rolls. In the event that the wallcovering is packaged in rolls containing 30 sq ft (2.79 m²), the project would require more wallcovering.
430.8 ÷ 30 sq ft/roll = 14.4, or 15 single rolls
In this case the project would require 15 single rolls, or 7 double rolls plus 1 single roll.

Classification of interior primers

Primer	Description	Frequent use
Wall primers		
Latex	Quick drying, offers excellent alkali resistance. Provides for ease of equipment cleaning.	Drywall, brick, metal.
Alkyd	Made from odorless alkyd, somewhat slow drying.	May be applied over partially cured plaster and metal.
Alkali	Alkali-resistant content based on butadine-styrene copolymer or chlorinated rubber.	Masonry, but do not use on below-grade.
Wood primers		
Enamel undercoat	Provides a low gloss and hard film that prevents penetration of the enamel paints that may be applied as top coats.	Excellent on surfaces that require a smooth finish.
Paste wood fillers	Made from transparent and coarse pigment held together with a binder.	Used on open-grain woods. Provides added color and smoothness.
Clear wood sealer	Transparent pigment often added to reduce penetration and improve sealing.	Often used under clear wood finishes.
Masonry primers		
Cement grout	A thin mortar applied with a brush or trowel.	Used to provide a smooth surface to rough masonry.
Block fillers	Composed of either latex or a solvent-thinned epoxy-ester. Relatively thick and applied with a brush or roller.	May be applied to damp surfaces. Provides resistance to alkali.

Classification of interior finish coatings

Finishes	Description	Frequent use
Gloss enamels		
Enamels	Usually alkyd enamels that are very resistant to yellowing and alkaline cleaners.	Brick, wood, particle board, metal plywood
Floor enamels	Alkyd enamels that are abrasion resistant, but will blister and peel if wet. Alkali-resistant enamels that are abrasion resistant, but provide poor resistance to solvents. Epoxy or urethane enamels are abrasion resistant. Not affected by water or solvents. Latex floor paint provides good abrasion resistance.	Masonry, wooden floors
Dry fallout spray gloss	Similar to gloss enamels, but dries very rapidly.	Walls
Semigloss		
Semigloss enamel	Alkyd-based product with good gloss retention, also grease and alkali resistance.	
Semigloss latex	Has moderate hiding power, ease of application and clean-up, rapid cleaning, low odor.	Drywall, plaster, wood, plywood
Dry fallout spray semi-gloss	Provides a moderate gloss level.	Walls, ceilings
Flat finishes		
Alkyd flat	Superior to latex paints in hiding power and washability. Odorless, but should be used in well-ventilated areas.	Drywall, brick, wood, metal, plywood
Latex flat	Good hiding power, spreadability, odorless. Requires special primers prior to application on porous surfaces. Do not apply during temperature extremes.	Plaster, drywall, brick, masonry

Labor hours required for brushwork application

Paint	Sq ft per hour per coat
Calcimining (ceilings)	200-250
Enameling	100-150
Flat painting	120-180
Shellacking	120-180
Staining	120-180
Varnishing	120-180
Trim: filling, spackling (given in linear ft)	50-75
Floors, filling, putting	120-180
Floor staining	150-200
Floor shellacking	150-200
Floor varnishing	140-200
Floor waxing	140-200
Floor polishing	100-150
Machine sanding	100-200

Pigment-hiding power

Pigment	Hiding power	Coats	
		Semigloss	Flat
Gold	Fair	2	2
Yellow	Poor	3	3+
Green	Fair	2	2
Blue	Fair	2	2
Pink	Poor	3	3+
Off-white	Fair	2	2

Classification of transparent finishes

Finishes	Description	Frequent use
Varnishes Flat or satin	Flatting agent added that makes it less glossy in finish than glossy varnishes. Mar resistance is inferior to gloss varnish.	All types of wood surfaces
Counter or bar varnish	Dries very hard and is resistant to alcohols. Made from polyurethanes and polyesters.	Bar tops
Penetrating sealers	Very thin varnishes that are applied and removed while the surface is still wet. Fair resistance to marring.	All types of open-grained woods
Conversion varnish	Produced with alkyd and urea formaldehyde resins. Has good resistance to abrasion and allows a higher gloss build-up because of its solid content.	
Shellac	Often terms a "wash" coat on wood surfaces before final sanding. Fast drying, light colored, but has a poor resistance to abrasion, water, or alcohols.	Wood, plaster, drywall, brick, plywood
Lacquers Standard	A coating material with high nitrocellulose content that is modified with resins and plasticizers. Good durability, but little resistance to chemicals. Dries quickly and is easy to repair. Increases flammability of surfaces.	Wood furniture and paneling
Catalyzed	Superior to standard lacquer in resistance to chemicals.	Wood furniture and paneling
Vinyls Catalyzed	This is a clear converting catalyst vinyl coating. Fast drying and highly resistant to abrasion.	Wood furniture and paneling

Average coat requirements for interior surfaces

Surfaces	Finishes	Coats
Woodwork	Oil gloss paint	2-3
	Semigloss paint	2-3
Plaster	Alkyd flat	2-3
Drywall	Alkyd flat	3
	Vinyl latex	3
Masonry	Vinyl latex	3
Wood floor	Enamel	3

Volume solids

Paints having 100 percent volume solids (no thinners) will cover more surface and provide a thicker film. This film (when dry) is referred to as the "dry film thickness" (DFT) and the measurement is expressed in mils (1/1000"). When reference is made to the dry film thickness, the measurement always refers to the total coating system, not the thickness of one coat.

Because federal and industrial specifications frequently require a dry-film-thickness measurement (usually 5 mils), designers should be familiar with the terminology involved. Manufacturers usually list the amount of volume solids contained in each gallon and provide information on the number of DFT mils that can be obtained from the particular coating system. The mils, however, can vary depending on the amount of square feet that will be covered by the paint. For example, if the paint is 100 percent volume solid, the DFT mils may be listed in this manner:

Coverage per gallon

1,200 sq ft = 1 mil DFT

600 sq ft = 2 mils DFT

300 sq ft = 4 mils DFT

If the paint is 50 percent volume solid (thinned 50 percent), the mils of dry film thickness will be considerably altered:

Coverage per gallon

600 sq ft = 1 mil DFT

300 sq ft = 2 mils DFT

In the event that a designer wishes to specify the dry film thickness, the required mils should be specified as the total thickness. For example, if the surface requires a primer, two coats of paint, and a dry film thickness of 5 mils, do not specify 2½ mils per coat. The specification should state "5 mils dry film thickness applied in two coats."

AHA	American Hardboard Association 887-B Wilmette Rd. Palatine, IL 60067	MIA	Marble Institute of America 33505 State St. Farmington, MI 48024
APA	American Plywood Association P.O. Box 11700 Tacoma, WA 98411	ML/SFA	Metal Lath/Steel Framing Association 221 N. LaSalle St. Chicago, IL 60601
AWI	Architectural Woodwork Institute 2310 S. Walter Reed Dr. Arlington, VA 22206	NAAMM	National Association of Architectural Metal Manufacturers 221 N. LaSalle St. Chicago, IL 60601
BIA	Brick Institute of America 1750 Old Meadow Rd. McLean, VA 22102	NCMA	National Concrete Masonry Association P.O. Box 781 Herndon, VA 22070
BSI	Building Stone Institute 420 Lexington Ave. New York, NY 10017	NFMA	National Forest Products Association 1619 Massachusetts Ave. N.W. Washington, D.C. 20036
CDA	Cooper Development Association 405 Lexington Ave. 57th Floor New York, NY 10174	NOFMA	National Oak Flooring Manufacturers Association 804 Sterick Building Memphis, TN 38103
CFFA	Chemical Fabrics and Film Association c/o Thomas Associates 1230 Keith Building Cleveland, OH 44115	NPA	National Particleboard Association 2306 Perkins Pl. Silver Spring, MD 20910
CRA	California Redwood Association One Lombard St. San Francisco, CA 94111	NTMA	National Terrazzo & Mosaic Association, Inc. 3166 Des Plaines Ave. Suite 15 Des Plaines, IL 60018
CRI	Carpet & Rug Institute P.O. Box 2048 Dalton, GA 30720	PCA	Portland Cement Association 5420 Old Orchard Rd. Skokie, IL 60077
FTI	Facing Tile Institute c/o Box 8880 Canton, OH 44711	RFCI	Resilient Floor Covering Institute 1030 15th St. N.W. Suite 350 Washington, D.C. 20005
GA	Gypsum Association 1603 Orrington Ave. Evanston, IL 60201	SFI	Southern Forest Institute 3395 Northeast Freeway Suite 380 Atlanta, GA 30341
HPMA	Hardwood Plywood Manufacturers Association P.O. Box 2789 Reston, VA 22090	SFPA	Southern Forest Products Association Box 52468 New Orleans, LA 70152
ILI	Indiana Limestone Institute Stone City Bank Building Suite 400 Bedford, IN 47421	TCA	Tile Council of America, Inc. P.O. Box 326 Princeton, NJ 08540
IMI	International Masonry Institute Suite 1001 823 15th St. N.W. Washington, D.C. 20005	UISPI	Urethane Institute Division of the Society of the Plastics Industry 355 Lexington Ave. New York, NY 10017
JCBC	Jute Carpet Backing Council 30 Rockefeller Plaza New York, NY 10020	WB	Wool Bureau 360 Lexington Ave. New York, NY 10017
MBCMA	Metal Building Component Manufacturers Association 1326 Freeport Rd. Pittsburgh, PA 15238	WSFI	Wood & Synthetic Flooring Institute 2400 E. Devon Des Plaines, IL 60018
MFMA	Maple Flooring Manufacturers Association 2400 E. Devon Des Plaines, IL 60018	WWPA	Western Wood Products Association Yeon Building Portland, OR 97204

ANSI	**American National Standards Institute**
A41.1-53 (R1970)	Building Code Requirements for Masonry
ANSI/TCA	**American National Standards Institute/ Tile Council of America Standard Specifications**
	Specification Manual—Standard Specifications and Official Grading Rules for Beech, Birch and Hard Maple Flooring.
ASTM	**American Society for Testing and Materials. Test Methods for:**
C241	Abrasion Resistance of Stone Subjected to Foot Traffic.
C482	Bond Strength of Ceramic Tile to Portland Cement.
C483	Electrical Resistance of Conductive Ceramic Tile.
C484	Thermal Shock Resistance of Glazed Ceramic Tile.
C499	Facial Dimensions and Thickness of Flat, Rectangular Ceramic Wall and Floor Tile.
C501	Relative Resistance to Wear of Unglazed Ceramic Tile by the Taber Abraser.
C502	Wedging of Flat, Rectangular Ceramic Wall and Floor Tile.
C609	Measurement of Small Color Differences Between Ceramic Wall or Floor Tile.
C627	Evaluating Ceramic Floor Tile Installation Systems.
C648	Breaking Strength of Ceramic Tile.
C650	Resistance of Ceramic Tile to Chemical Substances.
D418	Woven and Tufted Pile Floor Covering.
D543	Resistance of Plastics to Chemical Reagents.
D638	Tensile Properties of Plastics.
D968	Test Abrasion Resistance of Coatings of Paint, Varnish, Lacquer and Related Products by the Falling Sand Method.
D1335	Tuft Bind of Pile Floor Coverings.
D1546	Performance Tests of Clear Floor Sealers.
D1776	Conditioning Textiles for Testing.
D1777	Measuring Thickness of Textile Materials.
D1894	Static and Kinetic Coefficients of Friction of Plastic Film and Sheeting.
D2261	Tearing Strength of Woven Fabrics.
D2394	Simulated Service Testing of Wood & Wood-Base Finish Flooring.
D2401	Service Change of Appearance of Pile Floor Coverings.
D2646	Backing Fabrics.
D2843	Density of Smoke from the Burning or Decomposition of Plastics.
D2859	Flammability of Finished Textile Floor Covering Materials.
E84	Surface Burning Characteristics of Building Materials.
E648	Critical Radiant Flux of Floor Covering Systems Using a Radiant Heat Energy Source.
F137	Flexibility of Resilient Flooring Materials with Cylindrical Mandrel Apparatus.
F142	Indentation of Resilient Floor Coverings.
F150	Test Electrical Resistance of Conductive Resilient Flooring.
F373	Embossed Depth of Resilient Floor Coverings.
F386	Thickness of Resilient Flooring Materials Having Flat Surfaces.

BOCA	**Building Officials and Code Administrators International**
	Basic Building Code 1975, Sixth Edition Section 813.0 Natural Stone Section 835.0 Bonding of Walls Section 863-0 Thin Stone and Tile Veneers
BSI	**BSI Building Stone Institute** Stone Information Manual
CRI	**Carpet & Rug Institute** Carpet Specifiers Handbook, Second Edition
ICBO	**International Conference of Building Officials** Uniform Building Code, 1976 Edition Chapter 24 Masonry Chapter 30 Veneer Chapter 42 Interior Wall and Ceiling Finishes
NOFMA	**National Oak Flooring Manufacturers' Association** • Architect's Specifications Manual. • Official Flooring Grading Rules for Oak, Beech, Birch, Pecan and Hard Maple Flooring. • Oak Flooring Guide. • How to Keep Oak Floors Beautiful. • How to Install Hardwood Strip Floors.
NTMA	**National Terrazzo & Mosaic Association, Inc.** Terrazzo Design Data, Division 9.
RFC	**Resilient Floor Covering Institute**
A118.4	Latex-Portland Cement Mortar.
A137.1	Recommended Standard Specification for Ceramic Tile.
A108.4	Ceramic Tile Installed with Water-Resistant Organic Adhesives.
A108.7	Electrically Conductive Ceramic Tile Installed with Conductive Dry-Set Portland Cement Mortar.
	• Recommended Installation Specification for Vinyl Asbestos and Asphalt Tile Flooring.
WFSI	**Wood and Synthetic Flooring Institute** • Specifications for Cushioned Subfloor Construction with Laminated Subflooring and Finish Flooring. • Specifications for Herringbone Flooring Set in Mastic. • How to Control Cupping of Wood Floors. • Specifications for Mastic Cushioned Construction with Nailers, Subflooring and Finish Flooring. • Specifications for Mastic-Nailed Construction with Mastic-Set Subflooring and Nailed Finish Flooring. • Specifications for Mosaic Wood Parquet Flooring Set in Adhesive. • Specifications for Rubber Cushion-Sleeper Construction with Nailers and Finish Flooring. • Specifications for Steel Splined Continuous Strip Mastic—Set Maple Flooring.
WSFI	**Wood & Synthetic Flooring Institute** The Care and Preservation of Your Wood Floors.

INTERIOR SPECIALTIES

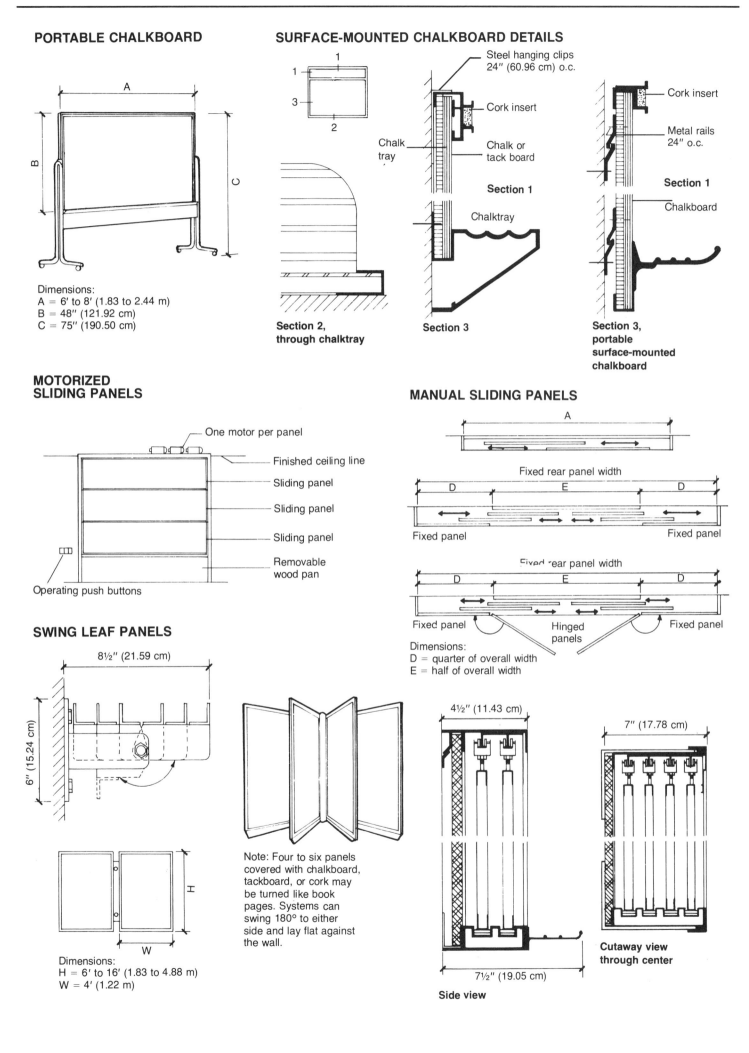

PORTABLE CHALKBOARD

Dimensions:
A = 6' to 8' (1.83 to 2.44 m)
B = 48" (121.92 cm)
C = 75" (190.50 cm)

SURFACE-MOUNTED CHALKBOARD DETAILS

Steel hanging clips
24" (60.96 cm) o.c.

Cork insert

Chalk tray

Chalk or tack board

Section 1

Section 2, through chalktray

Chalktray

Section 3

Cork insert

Metal rails
24" o.c.

Section 1

Chalkboard

Section 3, portable surface-mounted chalkboard

MOTORIZED SLIDING PANELS

One motor per panel

Finished ceiling line

Sliding panel

Sliding panel

Sliding panel

Removable wood pan

Operating push buttons

MANUAL SLIDING PANELS

A

Fixed rear panel width

D   E   D

Fixed panel   Fixed panel

Fixed rear panel width

D   E   D

Fixed panel   Hinged panels   Fixed panel

Dimensions:
D = quarter of overall width
E = half of overall width

SWING LEAF PANELS

8½" (21.59 cm)

6" (15.24 cm)

Note: Four to six panels covered with chalkboard, tackboard, or cork may be turned like book pages. Systems can swing 180° to either side and lay flat against the wall.

Dimensions:
H = 6' to 16' (1.83 to 4.88 m)
W = 4' (1.22 m)

4½" (11.43 cm)

7½" (19.05 cm)

Side view

7" (17.78 cm)

Cutaway view through center

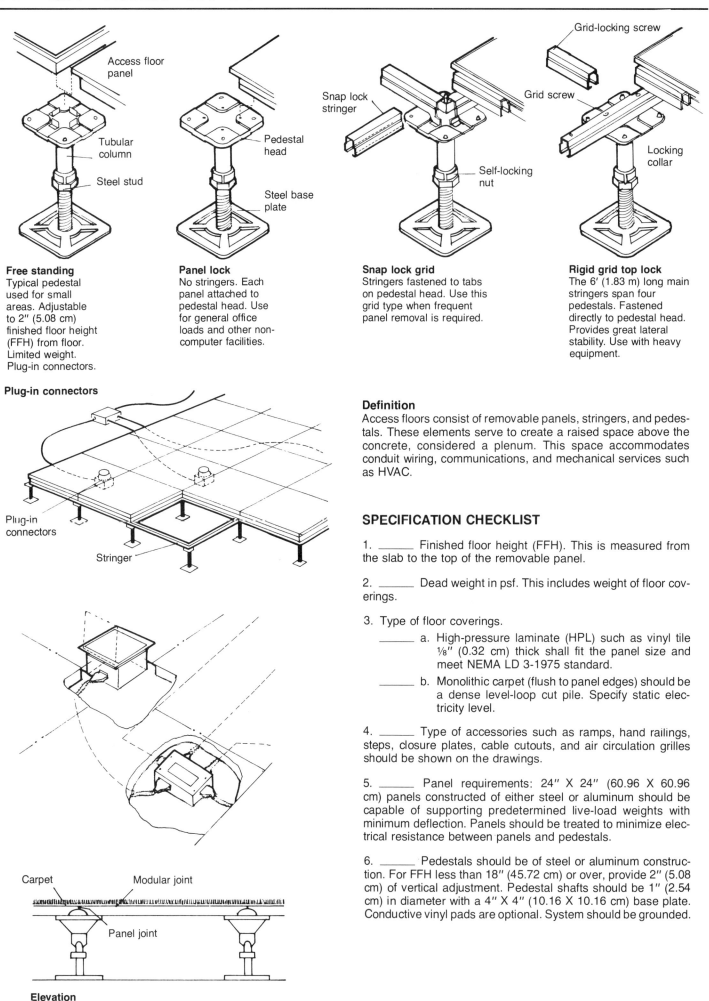

Free standing
Typical pedestal used for small areas. Adjustable to 2″ (5.08 cm) finished floor height (FFH) from floor. Limited weight. Plug-in connectors.

Panel lock
No stringers. Each panel attached to pedestal head. Use for general office loads and other non-computer facilities.

Snap lock grid
Stringers fastened to tabs on pedestal head. Use this grid type when frequent panel removal is required.

Rigid grid top lock
The 6′ (1.83 m) long main stringers span four pedestals. Fastened directly to pedestal head. Provides great lateral stability. Use with heavy equipment.

Plug-in connectors

Elevation

Definition

Access floors consist of removable panels, stringers, and pedestals. These elements serve to create a raised space above the concrete, considered a plenum. This space accommodates conduit wiring, communications, and mechanical services such as HVAC.

SPECIFICATION CHECKLIST

1. _____ Finished floor height (FFH). This is measured from the slab to the top of the removable panel.

2. _____ Dead weight in psf. This includes weight of floor coverings.

3. Type of floor coverings.

   _____ a. High-pressure laminate (HPL) such as vinyl tile ⅛″ (0.32 cm) thick shall fit the panel size and meet NEMA LD 3-1975 standard.

   _____ b. Monolithic carpet (flush to panel edges) should be a dense level-loop cut pile. Specify static electricity level.

4. _____ Type of accessories such as ramps, hand railings, steps, closure plates, cable cutouts, and air circulation grilles should be shown on the drawings.

5. _____ Panel requirements: 24″ X 24″ (60.96 X 60.96 cm) panels constructed of either steel or aluminum should be capable of supporting predetermined live-load weights with minimum deflection. Panels should be treated to minimize electrical resistance between panels and pedestals.

6. _____ Pedestals should be of steel or aluminum construction. For FFH less than 18″ (45.72 cm) or over, provide 2″ (5.08 cm) of vertical adjustment. Pedestal shafts should be 1″ (2.54 cm) in diameter with a 4″ X 4″ (10.16 X 10.16 cm) base plate. Conductive vinyl pads are optional. System should be grounded.

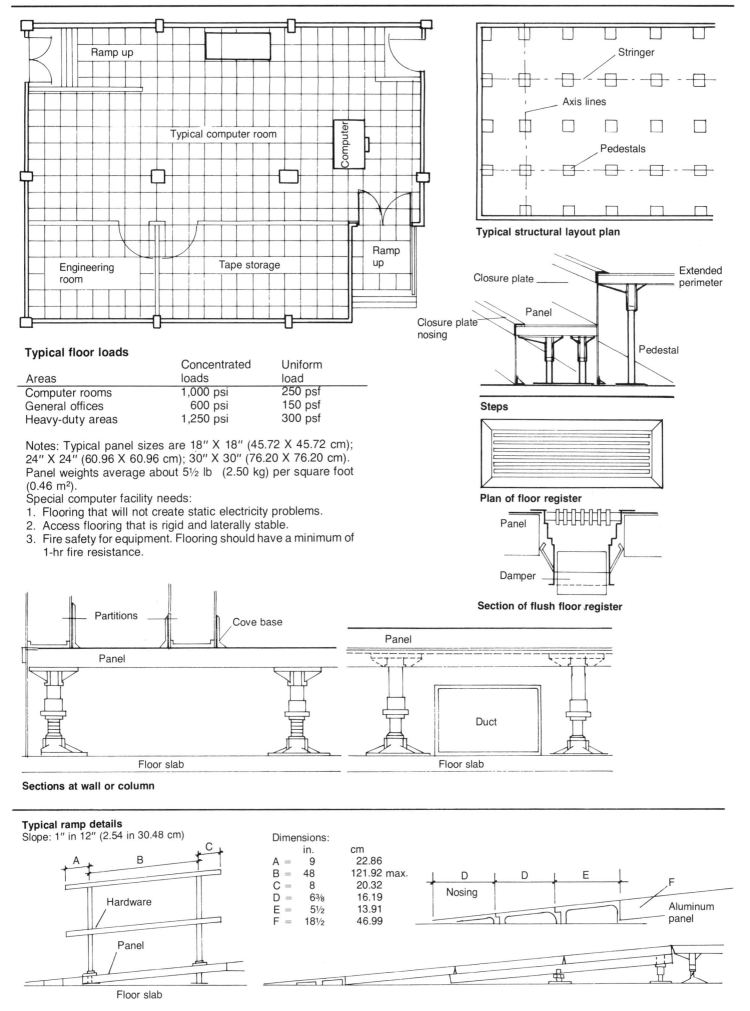

Typical structural layout plan

Closure plate — Extended perimeter
Panel
Closure plate nosing
Pedestal

Steps

Plan of floor register

Panel
Damper

Section of flush floor register

Typical floor loads

Areas	Concentrated loads	Uniform load
Computer rooms	1,000 psi	250 psf
General offices	600 psi	150 psf
Heavy-duty areas	1,250 psi	300 psf

Notes: Typical panel sizes are 18" X 18" (45.72 X 45.72 cm); 24" X 24" (60.96 X 60.96 cm); 30" X 30" (76.20 X 76.20 cm). Panel weights average about 5½ lb (2.50 kg) per square foot (0.46 m²).
Special computer facility needs:
1. Flooring that will not create static electricity problems.
2. Access flooring that is rigid and laterally stable.
3. Fire safety for equipment. Flooring should have a minimum of 1-hr fire resistance.

Sections at wall or column

Typical ramp details
Slope: 1" in 12" (2.54 in 30.48 cm)

Dimensions:

	in.	cm
A =	9	22.86
B =	48	121.92 max.
C =	8	20.32
D =	6⅜	16.19
E =	5½	13.91
F =	18½	46.99

FLOOR MATS

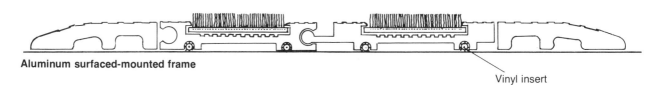

Aluminum-recessed frame with carpet tread inserts

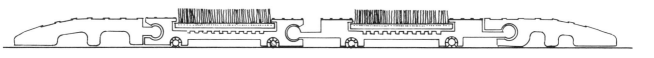

Aluminum surfaced-mounted frame

Vinyl insert

Flexible vinyl frame with carpet tread inserts

FOOT GRATINGS

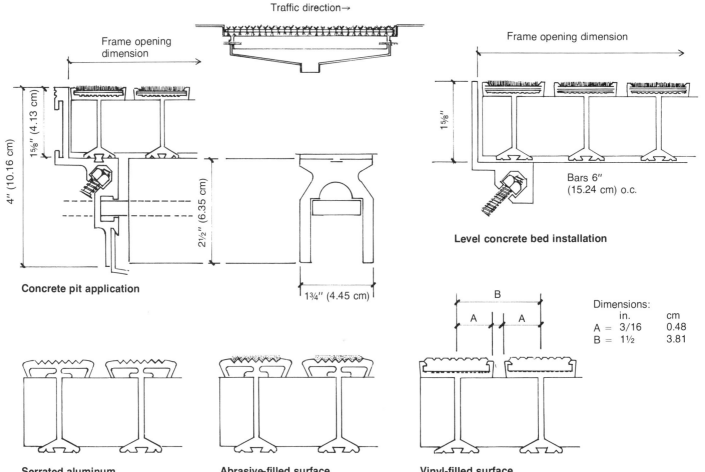

Concrete pit application

Level concrete bed installation

Bars 6″ (15.24 cm) o.c.

Serrated aluminum surface

Abrasive-filled surface

Vinyl-filled surface

Dimensions:
	in.	cm
A =	3/16	0.48
B =	1½	3.81

CORNER GUARDS

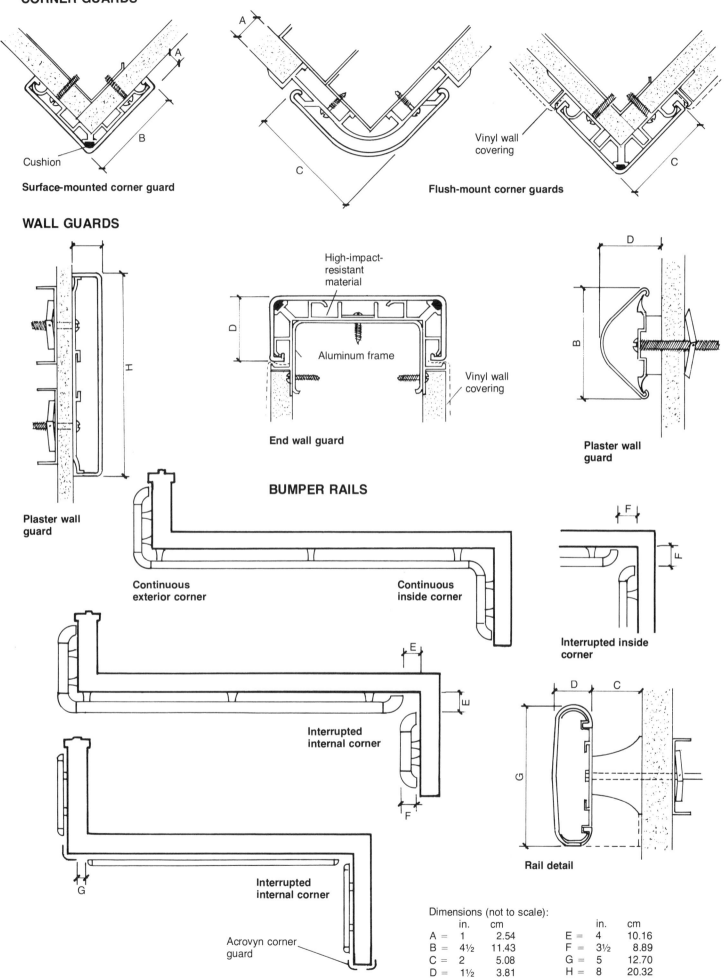

Cushion

Surface-mounted corner guard

Vinyl wall covering

Flush-mount corner guards

WALL GUARDS

High-impact-resistant material

Aluminum frame

Vinyl wall covering

End wall guard

Plaster wall guard

Plaster wall guard

BUMPER RAILS

Continuous exterior corner

Continuous inside corner

Interrupted inside corner

Interrupted internal corner

Interrupted internal corner

Acrovyn corner guard

Rail detail

Dimensions (not to scale):

	in.	cm			in.	cm
A =	1	2.54		E =	4	10.16
B =	4½	11.43		F =	3½	8.89
C =	2	5.08		G =	5	12.70
D =	1½	3.81		H =	8	20.32

Scale: ¾″ = 1′0″ (1.91 cm = 30.48 cm)

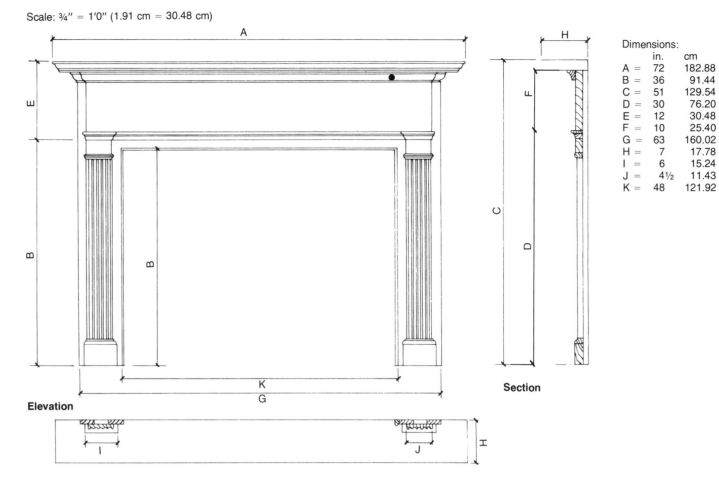

Elevation

Section

Plan

Dimensions:

	in.	cm
A =	72	182.88
B =	36	91.44
C =	51	129.54
D =	30	76.20
E =	12	30.48
F =	10	25.40
G =	63	160.02
H =	7	17.78
I =	6	15.24
J =	4½	11.43
K =	48	121.92

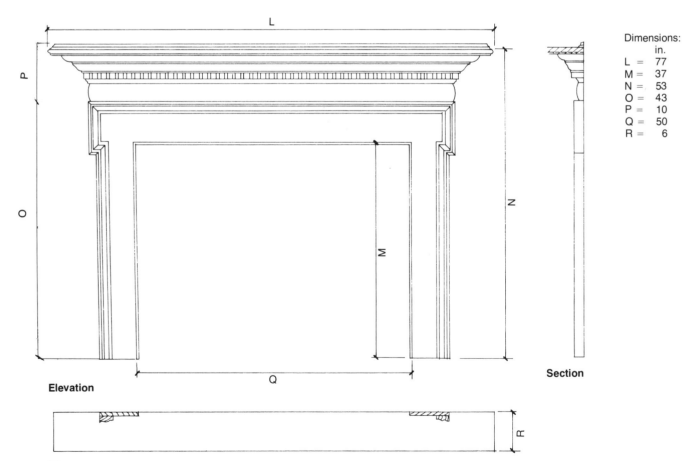

Elevation

Section

Plan

Dimensions:

	in.	cm
L =	77	195.58
M =	37	93.98
N =	53	134.62
O =	43	109.22
P =	10	25.40
Q =	50	127.00
R =	6	15.24

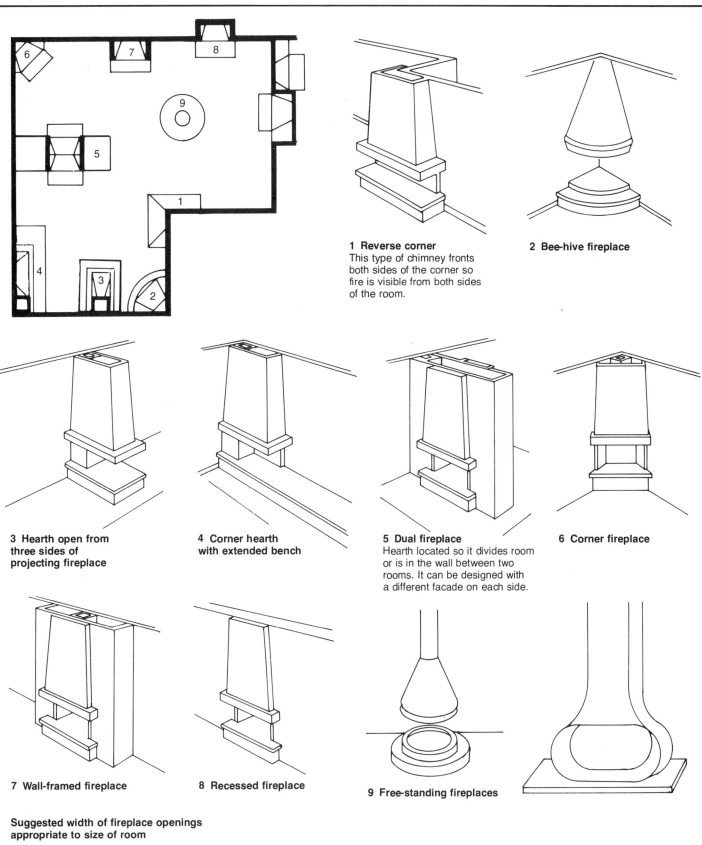

1 Reverse corner
This type of chimney fronts both sides of the corner so fire is visible from both sides of the room.

2 Bee-hive fireplace

3 Hearth open from three sides of projecting fireplace

4 Corner hearth with extended bench

5 Dual fireplace
Hearth located so it divides room or is in the wall between two rooms. It can be designed with a different facade on each side.

6 Corner fireplace

7 Wall-framed fireplace

8 Recessed fireplace

9 Free-standing fireplaces

Suggested width of fireplace openings appropriate to size of room

Size of room (ft)	Width of fireplace opening (in.)	
	In short wall	In long wall
10 X 14	24	24 to 32
12 X 16	28 to 36	32 to 36
12 X 20	32 to 36	36 to 40
12 X 24	32 to 36	36 to 48
14 X 28	32 to 40	40 to 48
16 X 30	36 to 40	48 to 60
20 X 36	40 to 48	48 to 72

Notes: Fireplaces create a strong focus of attention anywhere they are placed. Therefore, fireplace arrangement within a room should take into consideration future placement of furniture. For instance, a corner fireplace may create problems if large seating pieces are placed near the hearth.

FIREPLACE COMPONENTS

Chimney flue
Smoke and combustion gases from the burning wood pass up the chimney inside a flue, which is usually a large-diameter terra-cotta pipe.

Smoke chamber
The smoke chamber acts as a funnel, compressing the smoke and gases rising from the fire so they squeeze into the chimney flue above.

Smoke shelf
A smoke shelf bounces stray downdrafts up the chimney before they can neutralize the updraft and blow smoke into the room.

Damper
The damper is a steel or cast iron door that opens or closes the throat opening. Used to check and regulate draft, it prevents loss of heat up the chimney.

Throat
The throat is a slotlike opening above the firebox, where flame, smoke, and combustion gases pass into the smoke chamber. It is usually fitted with a damper.

Lintel
The lintel is a heavy steel brace that supports the masonry above the fireplace opening. Sometimes, it is incorporated in the damper assembly.

Firebox
The chamber where the fire is built is made of fire-resistant brick. Walls and back are slanted slightly to radiate heat out into the room.

Hearth
Inner hearth of fire-resistant brick holds the burning fuel: outer hearth of tile or brick protects house flooring from heat, sparks. Supported by subhearth.

Ash pit
Ashes are dumped through an opening in the hearth into the fireproof storage compartment below. Many fireplaces today are built without ash pits.

Foundation
The fireplace and chimney structure has its own foundation. The concentrated weight of the masonry is usually carried by a reinforced concrete slab.

Face
The masonry surrounding the fireplace opening is known as the fireplace "face." It may be built of various materials: brick, stone, concrete, tile, wood.

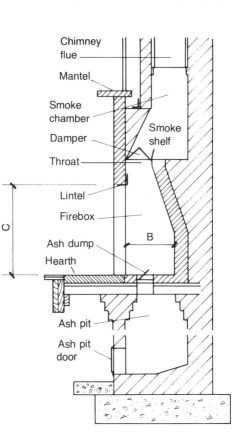

FIREPLACE DETAILS

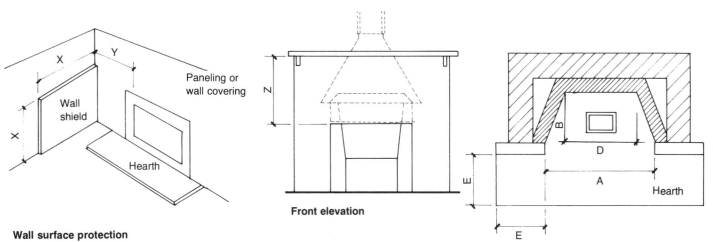

Wall surface protection

Dimensions:
X = 40" (101.60 cm)
Y = less than 18" (45.72 cm)
Z = 8" (20.32 cm) min.

To relate fireplace size to room size:
A 12' X 25' (3.66 X 7.62 m) living room [300 sq ft (27.87 m²)] is well served by a fireplace with an opening 30" to 36" (76.20 to 91.44 cm) wide. For larger rooms the width may be increased. However, the opening should not be too high—rarely more than 32" (81.28 cm) above the hearth for most standard width openings. All dimensions may be varied slightly to fit regular brick courses and joints.

Front elevation

Brick fireplace dimensions

Finished opening dimensions:

| A | | B | | C | | D | |
| Width | | Depth | | Height | | Back | |
in.	cm	in.	cm	in.	cm	in.	cm
24	60.46	16	40.64	24	60.96	11	27.94
30	76.20	16	40.64	29	73.66	17	43.18
36	91.44	16	40.64	29	73.66	23	58.42
48	121.92	18	45.72	32	81.28	33	83.82
60	152.40	22	55.88	37	93.98	42	106.68

E = 12" (30.48 cm) hearth extension

FREESTANDING STOVES

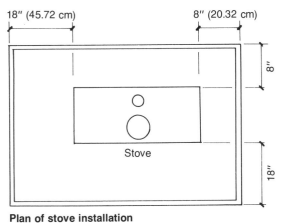

18" (45.72 cm)   8" (20.32 cm)

8"

18"

Stove

Plan of stove installation

Required clearance from stove (in.)

Heat source	Top	Front	Back	Sides
Radiant stove	36	36	36	36
Circulating stove	36	24	12	12
Cookstove (unlined firebox)	30	*	36	36 (firing side) 18 (opposite side)
Cookstove (lined firebox)	30	*	24	24 (firing side) 18 (opposite side)
Single-wall stovepipe	18	18	18	18

*Clearance of the front of a cookstove should be sufficient to permit normal use for cooking, servicing, and cleaning.

FREESTANDING FIREPLACES

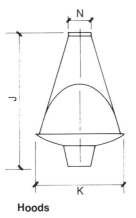

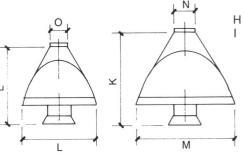

Hoods

Minimum dimensions:

	in.	cm		in.	cm
J =	52	132.08	O =	7	17.78
K =	36	91.44	P =	28	71.12
L =	30	76.20	Q =	24	60.96
M =	40	101.60	R =	69	175.26
N =	9	22.86			

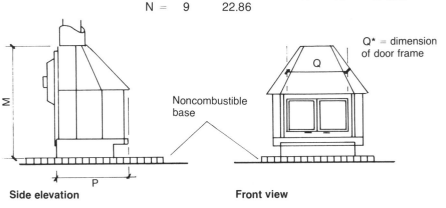

Q* = dimension of door frame

Noncombustible base

Side elevation   **Front view**

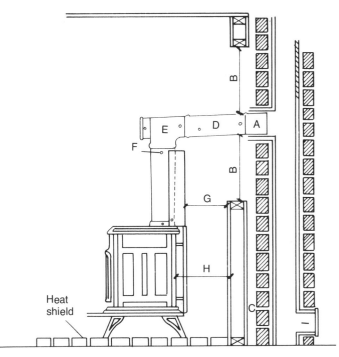

Top-exit stove installed in thimble through combustible wall

Notes:
A = stovepipe must not extend into chimney liner
B = 18" (45.72 cm) between pipe and unprotected combustible materials
C = 2" (5.08 cm) between chimney and combustible materials
D = ¼" (0.64 cm) per foot of horizontal run
E = clean-air tee
F = all pipe joints secured with three sheet metal screws
G = stovepipe heat shield allows 10" (25.40 cm) clearance to combustible material
H = stove heat shield 10" to combustible material
I = clean-out, access-tight door

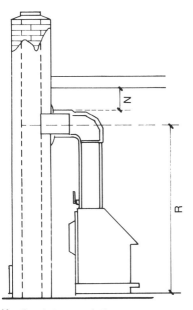

Venting into an existing chimney

FURRING BAR SYSTEM

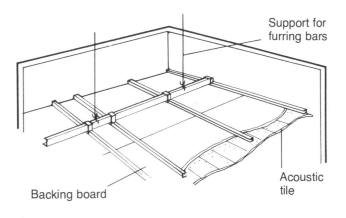

Support for furring bars

Acoustic tile

Backing board

DIRECT HUNG SYSTEM

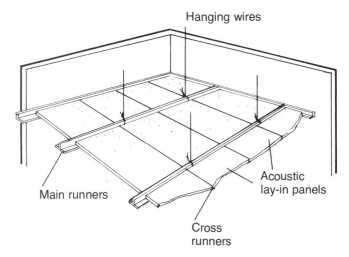

Hanging wires

Main runners

Cross runners

Acoustic lay-in panels

CONCEALED SPLINE SYSTEM

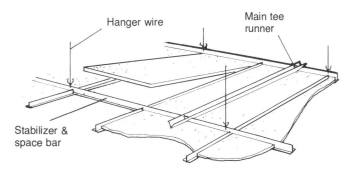

Hanger wire

Main tee runner

Stabilizer & space bar

INDIRECT HUNG SYSTEM

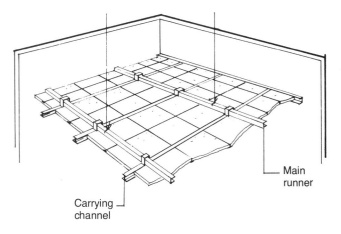

Carrying channel

Main runner

CONCEALED ACCESSIBLE SYSTEMS

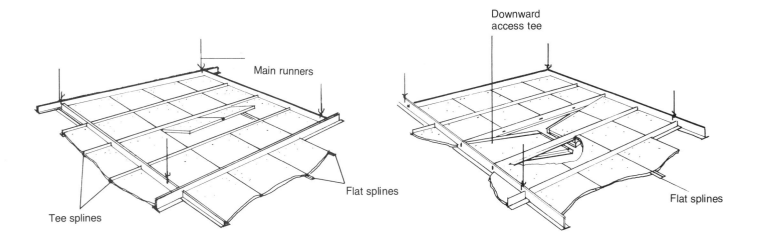

Main runners

Flat splines

Tee splines

Downward access tee

Flat splines

Upward access

Downward access

Pictograph

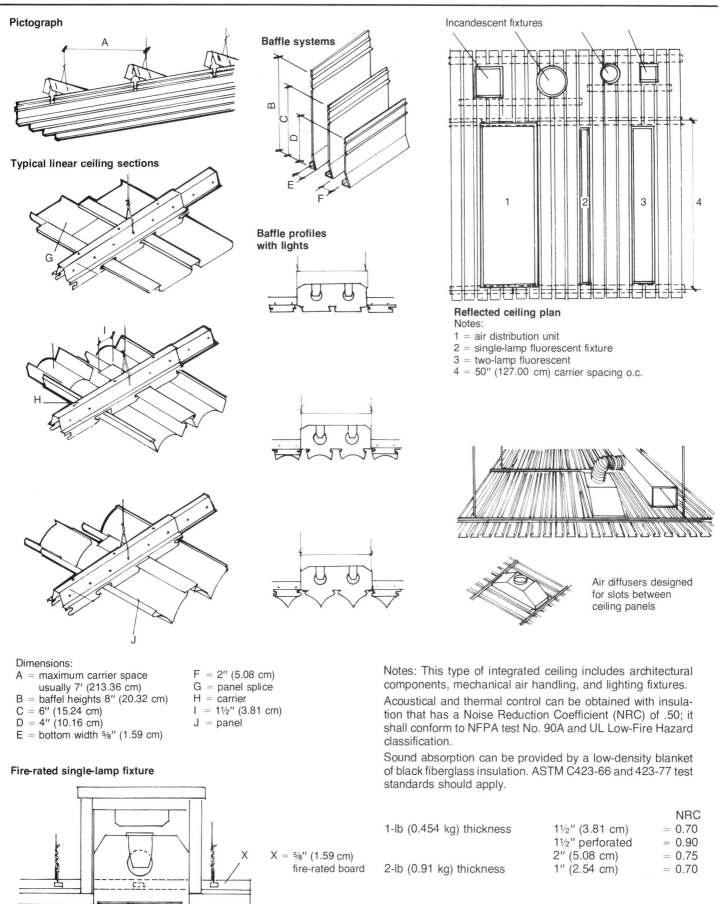

Typical linear ceiling sections

Baffle systems

Baffle profiles with lights

Incandescent fixtures

Reflected ceiling plan
Notes:
1 = air distribution unit
2 = single-lamp fluorescent fixture
3 = two-lamp fluorescent
4 = 50" (127.00 cm) carrier spacing o.c.

Air diffusers designed for slots between ceiling panels

Dimensions:
A = maximum carrier space
     usually 7' (213.36 cm)
B = baffel heights 8" (20.32 cm)
C = 6" (15.24 cm)
D = 4" (10.16 cm)
E = bottom width ⅝" (1.59 cm)

F = 2" (5.08 cm)
G = panel splice
H = carrier
I = 1½" (3.81 cm)
J = panel

Notes: This type of integrated ceiling includes architectural components, mechanical air handling, and lighting fixtures.

Acoustical and thermal control can be obtained with insulation that has a Noise Reduction Coefficient (NRC) of .50; it shall conform to NFPA test No. 90A and UL Low-Fire Hazard classification.

Sound absorption can be provided by a low-density blanket of black fiberglass insulation. ASTM C423-66 and 423-77 test standards should apply.

		NRC
1-lb (0.454 kg) thickness	1½" (3.81 cm)	= 0.70
	1½" perforated	= 0.90
	2" (5.08 cm)	= 0.75
2-lb (0.91 kg) thickness	1" (2.54 cm)	= 0.70

Fire-rated single-lamp fixture

X = ⅝" (1.59 cm)
     fire-rated board

Ceiling pan

Acrylic-plastic diffuser lens

SUSPENDED SYSTEM

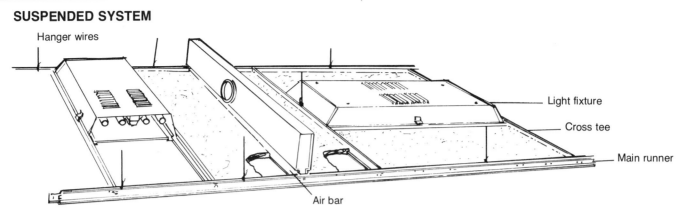

Hanger wires

Light fixture

Cross tee

Main runner

Air bar

Typical system incorporating heating, air conditioning, & lighting

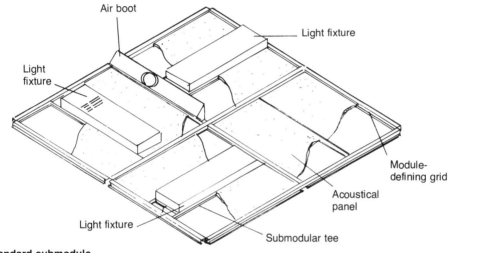

Air boot

Light fixture

Light fixture

Module-defining grid

Acoustical panel

Light fixture

Submodular tee

Standard submodule

Reflected ceiling plan of light fixtures in standard submodules

---

COFFERED SYSTEM

12" to 30" (30.48 to 76.20 cm)   12" to 30"

Acoustical side panel

Elevation

Return air fixture

Air

Air

Return air pattern

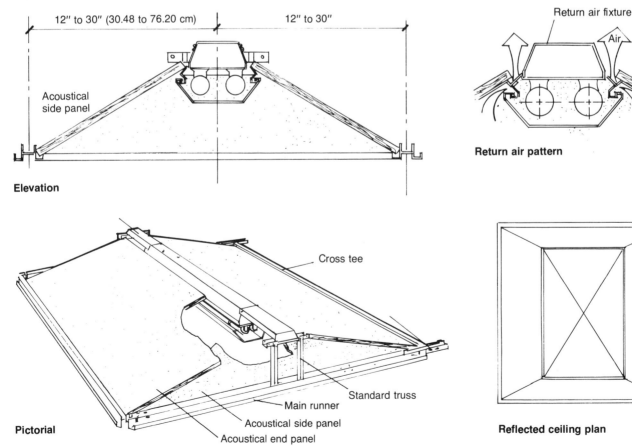

Cross tee

Standard truss

Main runner

Acoustical side panel

Acoustical end panel

Pictorial

Reflected ceiling plan

**Restrained/unrestrained assembly:
1-hour rating**

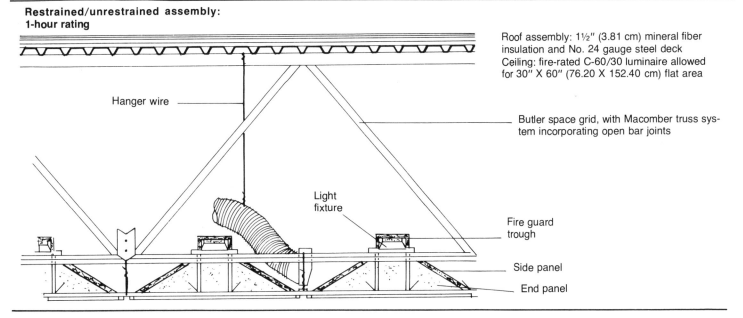

Hanger wire

Light fixture

Fire guard trough

Side panel

End panel

Roof assembly: 1½" (3.81 cm) mineral fiber insulation and No. 24 gauge steel deck
Ceiling: fire-rated C-60/30 luminaire allowed for 30" X 60" (76.20 X 152.40 cm) flat area

Butler space grid, with Macomber truss system incorporating open bar joints

Restrained assembly: 1-hour rating; unrestrained assembly: ¾-hour rating

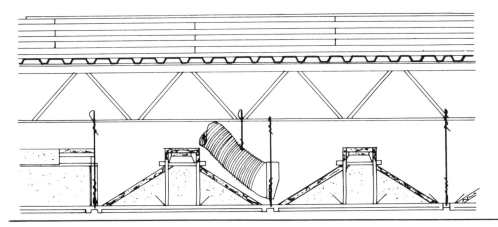

Roof deck: mineral fiber insulation over one-layer ⅝" (1.59 cm) gypsum board placed directly on steel roof deck
Ceiling: fire-rated C-60/30 luminaire, 0-100% vaulted modules (C-60 fixture); fire-rated C-60/60 luminaire, 0-100% vaulted modules [flooring fixtures: 24" X 24" (60.96 X 60.96 cm) G, 30" X 30" (76.20 X 76.20 cm) G, 36" X 36" (91.44 X 91.44 cm) G, AW 3600 G, AW 1400 F, 12" X 48" (30.48 X 121.92 cm), AW 2400 F, and 24" X 48" G]

Restrained 2-hour rating assembly; unrestrained beam assembly: 1½-hour rating

Floor

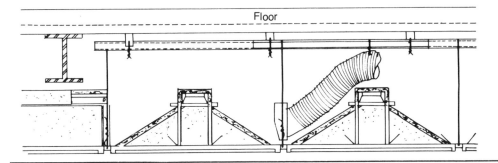

Ceiling: fire-rated C-60/60 luminaire (30" X 60" flat areas allowed); fire-rated C-60/60 luminaire (24" X 24"; 30" X 30"; 36" X 36"; 12" X 48"; 24" X 48" fixtures)
Floor: 2½" (16.13 cm) concrete on flat cellular steel deck with beam

Restrained 2-hour rating assembly; unrestrained beam assembly: 3-hour rating

Floor

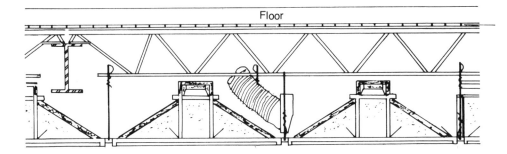

Concrete floor: 3" (7.62 cm) on joist & metal lath
Ceiling: ventilating ceilings approved for 30" X 60" flat areas; fire-rated C-60/60 luminaire with same size fixtures as described in floor-ceiling assembly above

Human scale from age 2 to adult (composite of men & women)

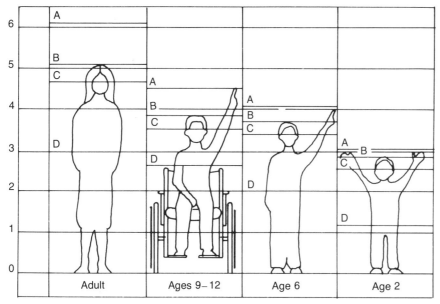

Note: The height and length of the junior-size wheelchair are almost identical to that of an adult chair. Only the width is noticeably smaller by 3″ to 6½″ (7.62 to 16.5 cm).

Dimensions:
A = easy high reach
B = height
C = eye level
D = low counter height

Note: It is recommended that the lowest clothes bar in a child's closet be equipped with an adjustable rod.

Recommended heights of casework for various school grade levels:

	in.	cm
Kindergarten & Grade 1	24	60.96
Grades 2 and 3	27	68.58
Grades 4, 5, and 6	30	76.20
Grades 7, 8, and 9	33	83.82
Grades 10 and above	36	91.44

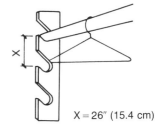

X = 26″ (15.4 cm)

Comparison of wheelchair sizes for children & adults

	Junior size		Adult size	
	in.	cm	in.	cm
Average seat height	16½-18½	41.91- 46.99	19	48.26
Average width	20½-24	52.07- 60.96	27	68.58
Average length	42-46	106.68-116.84	42-46	106.68-116.84

Comparison of basic barrier-free standards for children & adults

If facilities are intended for use specifically for students, which may include disabled users under 12 years of age, the following criteria shall be used:	Criteria for adults from ANSI Standard A117.1 (1980)
Toilet grab bar size	1¼″ (3.18 cm) with 1½″ (3.81 cm space between grab bar and wall	1¼ -1½″ space between grab bar and wall
Toilet grab bar height	Mounted 10″ (25.40 cm) above the seat	2′9″ to 3′0″ (35.82 to 91.44 cm) from floor surface
Toilet grab bar length alongside the water closet	3′0″ (91.44 cm) with 1′6″ (45.72 cm) length extending beyond the front edge of the water closet	3′6″ (106.68) minimum length
Grab bar must be capable of supporting a 150-lbf load applied anywhere along the length. Connections must also be capable of supporting a 150-lbf load		Support 250-lbf load
Toilet height	1′3″ (38.10 cm) to top of seat from floor surface	1′5″ to 1′7″ (43.18 to 48.26 cm) to top of seat from floor surface
Lavatory height	2′5″ (73.66 cm) below apron to floor surface	2′5″ minimum below apron to surface
Maximum height of controls, receptacles, and dispensers	3′4″ (101.60 cm) from center of operable part to the floor	4′0″ (121.92 cm) from center of operable part to floor
Height of handrails	2′0″ (60.96 cm) to the center of the bar from the floor surface	2′6″ to 2′10″ (76.20 to 86.30 cm) to the center of the bar from the floor surface
Height of water fountain spigot	2′6″ (76.20 cm) from the floor surface	3′0″ minimum from the floor surface
Height of telephone to highest operable mechanism	3′8″ (111.76 cm) from the floor surface	4′0″ from the floor surface

CLOTHING STORAGE

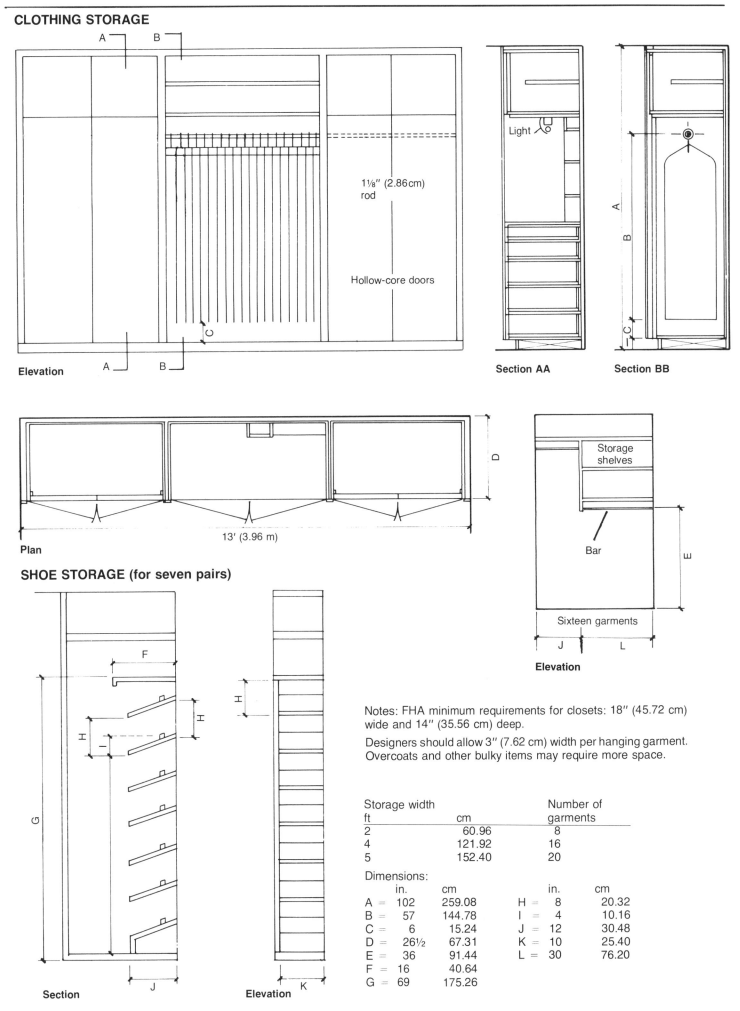

Elevation

Section AA

Section BB

1⅛″ (2.86 cm) rod

Hollow-core doors

Light

Plan

13′ (3.96 m)

Storage shelves

Bar

Sixteen garments

Elevation

SHOE STORAGE (for seven pairs)

Section

Elevation

Notes: FHA minimum requirements for closets: 18″ (45.72 cm) wide and 14″ (35.56 cm) deep.

Designers should allow 3″ (7.62 cm) width per hanging garment. Overcoats and other bulky items may require more space.

Storage width		Number of
ft	cm	garments
2	60.96	8
4	121.92	16
5	152.40	20

Dimensions:

	in.	cm			in.	cm
A =	102	259.08		H =	8	20.32
B =	57	144.78		I =	4	10.16
C =	6	15.24		J =	12	30.48
D =	26½	67.31		K =	10	25.40
E =	36	91.44		L =	30	76.20
F =	16	40.64				
G =	69	175.26				

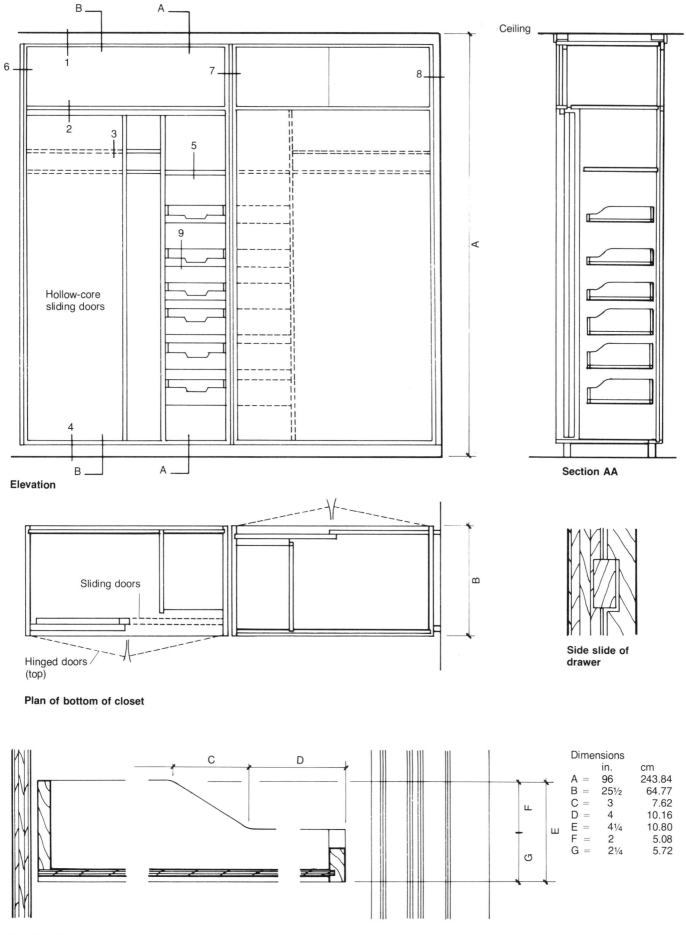

Elevation

Hollow-core
sliding doors

Section AA

Ceiling

Plan of bottom of closet

Sliding doors

Hinged doors
(top)

Side slide of drawer

Detail 9. Drawer

Dimensions

	in.	cm
A =	96	243.84
B =	25½	64.77
C =	3	7.62
D =	4	10.16
E =	4¼	10.80
F =	2	5.08
G =	2¼	5.72

* Details on page 201.

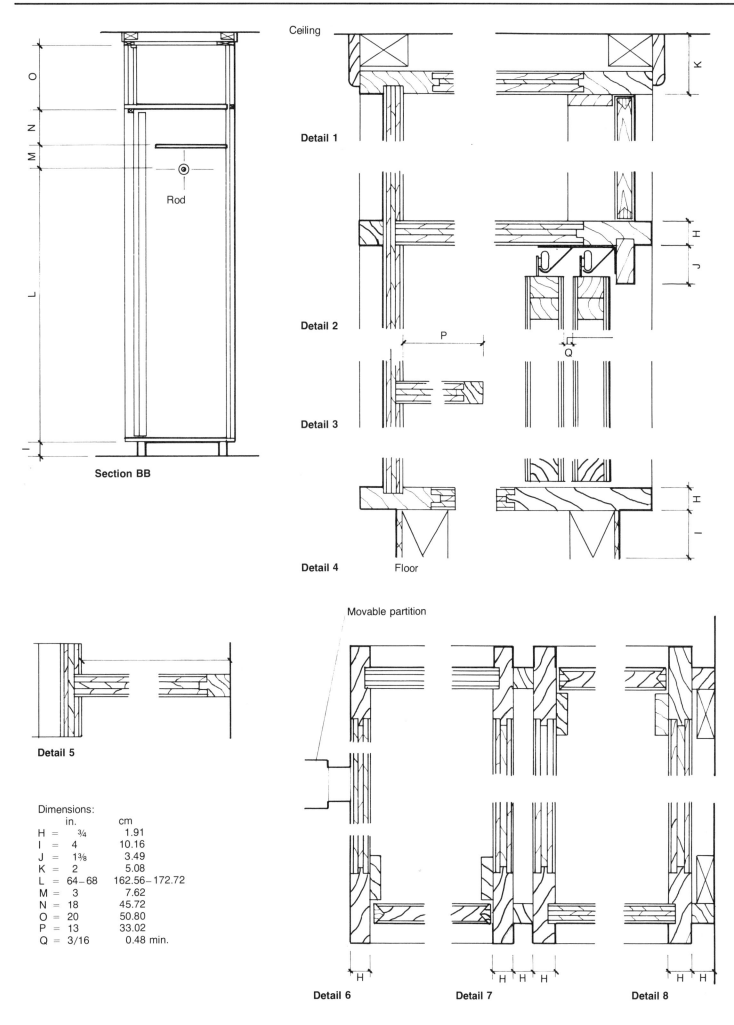

Section BB

Ceiling

Detail 1

Detail 2

Detail 3

Detail 4   Floor

Rod

Detail 5

Movable partition

Detail 6   Detail 7   Detail 8

Dimensions:
		in.	cm
H	=	¾	1.91
I	=	4	10.16
J	=	1⅜	3.49
K	=	2	5.08
L	=	64–68	162.56–172.72
M	=	3	7.62
N	=	18	45.72
O	=	20	50.80
P	=	13	33.02
Q	=	3/16	0.48 min.

VINYL-COATED STEEL ROD SHELVING

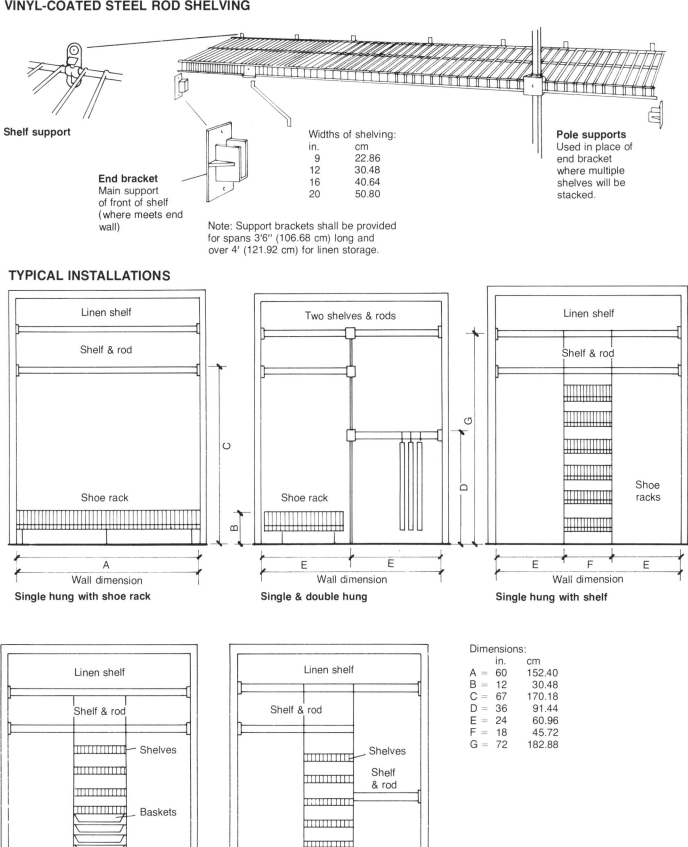

Shelf support

End bracket
Main support
of front of shelf
(where meets end
wall)

Widths of shelving:

in.	cm
9	22.86
12	30.48
16	40.64
20	50.80

Note: Support brackets shall be provided
for spans 3'6" (106.68 cm) long and
over 4' (121.92 cm) for linen storage.

Pole supports
Used in place of
end bracket
where multiple
shelves will be
stacked.

TYPICAL INSTALLATIONS

Linen shelf
Shelf & rod
Shoe rack
A
Wall dimension
Single hung with shoe rack

Two shelves & rods
Shoe rack
E   E
Wall dimension
Single & double hung

Linen shelf
Shelf & rod
Shoe racks
E   F   E
Wall dimension
Single hung with shelf

Linen shelf
Shelf & rod
Shelves
Baskets
Shoe rack
E   Wall dimension   E
F
Double hung with baskets

Linen shelf
Shelf & rod
Shelves
Shelf & rod
Single & double hung with shelves

Dimensions:

	in.	cm
A =	60	152.40
B =	12	30.48
C =	67	170.18
D =	36	91.44
E =	24	60.96
F =	18	45.72
G =	72	182.88

SEMICONCEALED WARDROBES

EXAMPLES OF OPEN STORAGE

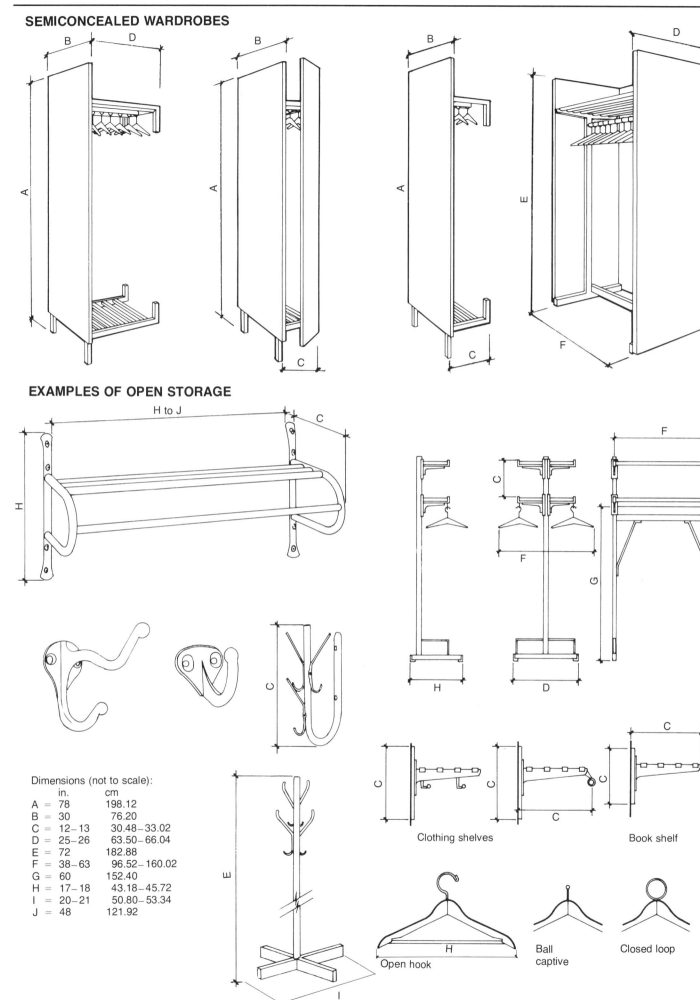

Dimensions (not to scale):

	in.	cm
A =	78	198.12
B =	30	76.20
C =	12–13	30.48–33.02
D =	25–26	63.50–66.04
E =	72	182.88
F =	38–63	96.52–160.02
G =	60	152.40
H =	17–18	43.18–45.72
I =	20–21	50.80–53.34
J =	48	121.92

Clothing shelves

Book shelf

Open hook

Ball captive

Closed loop

SPECIFICATION INFORMATION FOR COMPARTMENTS:

One tier
Width: 9″ to 24″ (22.86 to 60.96 cm) [in 3″ (7.62cm increments]
Depth: 12″ to 24″ (30.48 cm) [in 3″ increments]

Two tier
Width: 9″, 12″, 15″ (38.10 cm)
Height: 12″, 15″, 18″ (45.72 cm)

Three tier
Width: 9″ to 12″
Height: 12″, 15″, 18″, 21″ (53.34 cm), 24″

Four tier
Width: 9″, 12″, 15″, 18″
Height: 12″, 15″, 18″

Five tier
Width: 12″, 15″
Height: 12″, 15″, 18″

Six tier
Width: 12″, 15″
Height: 12″, 15″, 18″

Notes: Three tier used for gym uniforms and often used in combination with 1-tier units.
Multitiered lockers often used for security of such personal items as books and purses.

Locker base may be closed or open. Each compartment should be well ventilated.

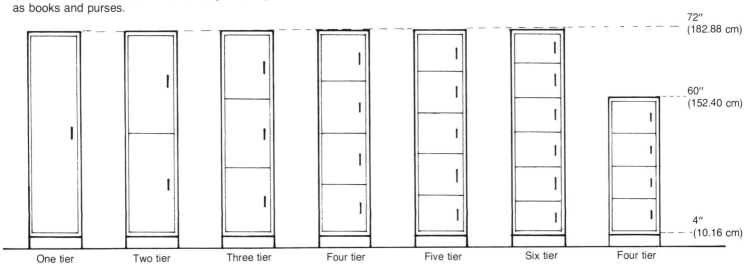

One tier   Two tier   Three tier   Four tier   Five tier   Six tier   Four tier

72″ (182.88 cm)
60″ (152.40 cm)
4″ (10.16 cm)

RECESSED LOCKERS

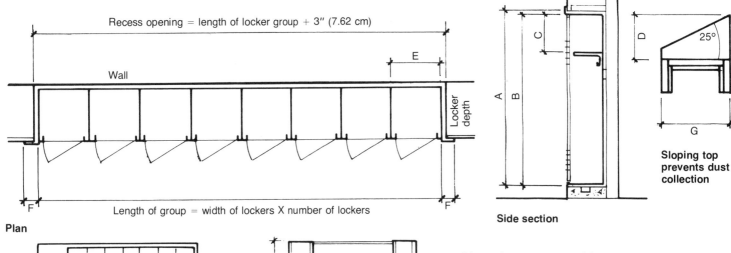

Recess opening = length of locker group + 3″ (7.62 cm)

Wall

E

Locker depth

Length of group = width of lockers X number of lockers

F   F

Plan

A
B
C
25°
D
G

Side section

Sloping top prevents dust collection

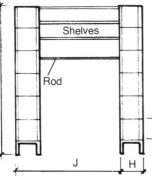

Plan of flat-top lockers with detail of corner filler

Shelves
Rod

J   H
H

Plan of locker racks for 12 people in 15″ (38.10 cm) space

Dimensions (not to scale):
A = height of recess = height of locker + 1″ (2.54 cm)
B = height of locker
C = 9″ (22.85 cm)
D = 8″ to 11″ (20.20 to 27.94 cm)
E = locker width + 1/32″ (0.08 cm)
F = 3″ (7.62 cm)
G = 12″, 16″, or 22″ (30.48, 40.64, or 55.88 cm)
H = 12″ (30.48 cm)
I = 79½″ (201.93 cm)
J = 60″ (152.40 cm)

LIGHT-CONTROL REVOLVING DOOR

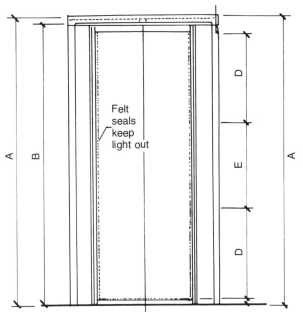

Felt seals keep light out

Elevation

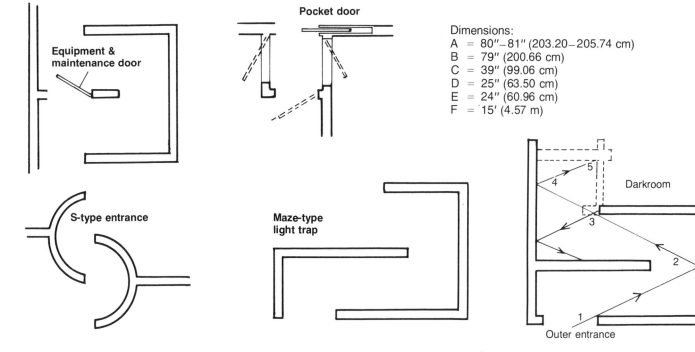

Sink

Print darkroom

Film dark-room

X

Print pass-through

Finishing area

Workbench

X = 4-way revolving light-control door

Plan

OTHER MEANS OF LIGHT CONTROL

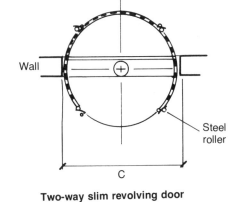

Wall

Steel roller

C

Two-way slim revolving door

Fire safety

Panic-type exits are available in 4-way revolving light-control doors. They are equipped with two continuous hinges on one side and two coaster-roller hinges on the other.

Pop-out door mechanisms should be specified so doors can be totally removed when moving furniture and equipment

Notes: A 4-way revolving light-control door is 48" (121.92 cm) in diameter and allows entry to three or four connected rooms.

Two-way revolving doors connecting two rooms range in width from 17"–22" to 40" (43.18–55.88 to 101.60 cm); 17" doors revolve at 360° and 22" doors revolve at 270°.

Equipment & maintenance door

Pocket door

Dimensions:
A = 80"–81" (203.20–205.74 cm)
B = 79" (200.66 cm)
C = 39" (99.06 cm)
D = 25" (63.50 cm)
E = 24" (60.96 cm)
F = 15' (4.57 m)

S-type entrance

Maze-type light trap

Darkroom

Outer entrance

Light deflection in maze

CODE CONSIDERATIONS

Most codes require that turnstiles which restrict travel to one direction so that fares can be collected or tickets sold should not be placed to obstruct any required means of egress. Turnstiles that regulate access to required exits should be designed to provide 22″ (55.88 cm) clear width as they rotate. (See drawing below.)

Turnstiles and revolving doors are often rated with similar standards. Turnstiles not over 3′ (91.44 cm) high that move freely in the direction of exit travel are permitted by most codes that allow revolving doors in the same circumstances. Multiple-bar turnstiles that prevent people from crawling under are objectionable in the event of a fire. When these are used, most codes require that alternate exit gates be provided.

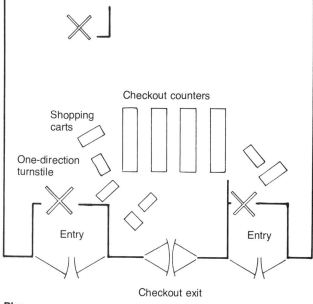

Plan

Note: In an effort to prevent theft, many stores obstruct means of egress. For example, turnstiles are frequently designed to bar leaving the store. The center exit is blocked with carts, while checkout counters also form a barrier.

TYPICAL INSTALLATIONS

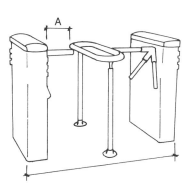

Railing assembly

Dimensions (not to scale):

	in.	cm
A =	22	55.88
B =	26	66.04
C =	37	93.98
D =	29	73.66
E =	11	27.94
F =	8	20.32
G =	optional	

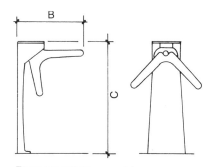

Standard weight: 65 lb (29.51 kg)

Standard weight: 45 lbs (20.43 kg)

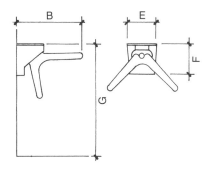

Wall-mounted assembly

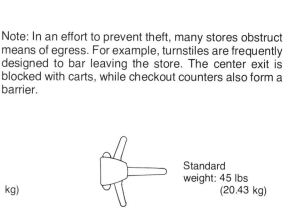

Portable assembly

Floor-mounted assembly

PORTABLE POSTS & ROPES USED AS RESTRICTIVE DIVIDERS

Note: When specifying, indicate tight measurement of area (X) and how measurement was taken, that is, from post to post or wall to post. Manufacturer will allow for slack if requested.

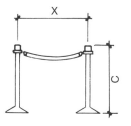

Post to post

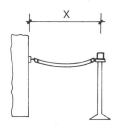

Wall to post

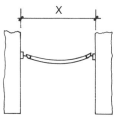

Wall to wall

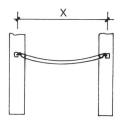

Eye to eye

STAIR RAILS

Typical joint combinations

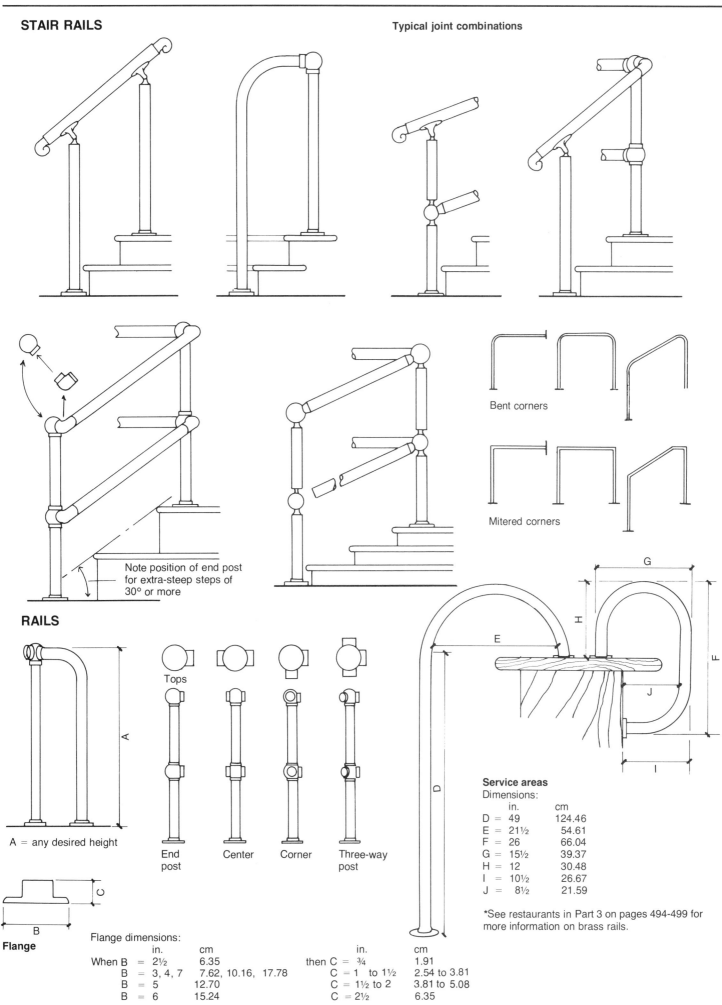

Note position of end post for extra-steep steps of 30° or more

Bent corners

Mitered corners

RAILS

Tops

A = any desired height

End post

Center

Corner

Three-way post

Flange

Service areas
Dimensions:

	in.	cm
D =	49	124.46
E =	21½	54.61
F =	26	66.04
G =	15½	39.37
H =	12	30.48
I =	10½	26.67
J =	8½	21.59

*See restaurants in Part 3 on pages 494-499 for more information on brass rails.

Flange dimensions:

		in.	cm			in.	cm
When B	=	2½	6.35	then C =	¾	1.91
B	=	3, 4, 7	7.62, 10.16, 17.78	C	= 1 to 1½	2.54 to 3.81
B	=	5	12.70	C	= 1½ to 2	3.81 to 5.08
B	=	6	15.24	C	= 2½	6.35

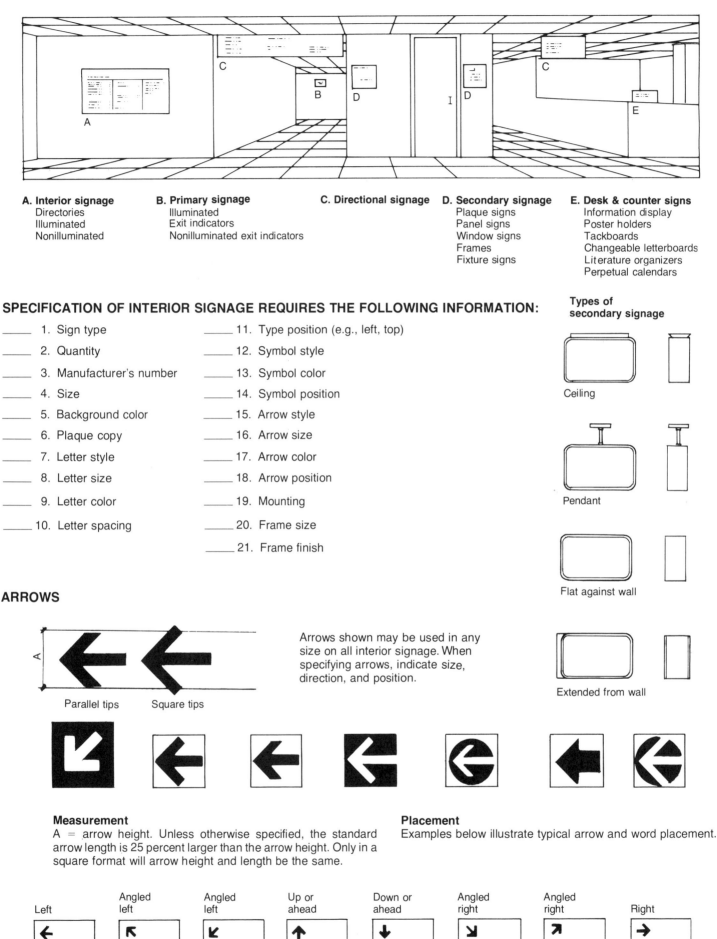

A. Interior signage
Directories
Illuminated
Nonilluminated

B. Primary signage
Illuminated
Exit indicators
Nonilluminated exit indicators

C. Directional signage

D. Secondary signage
Plaque signs
Panel signs
Window signs
Frames
Fixture signs

E. Desk & counter signs
Information display
Poster holders
Tackboards
Changeable letterboards
Literature organizers
Perpetual calendars

SPECIFICATION OF INTERIOR SIGNAGE REQUIRES THE FOLLOWING INFORMATION:

_____ 1. Sign type

_____ 2. Quantity

_____ 3. Manufacturer's number

_____ 4. Size

_____ 5. Background color

_____ 6. Plaque copy

_____ 7. Letter style

_____ 8. Letter size

_____ 9. Letter color

_____ 10. Letter spacing

_____ 11. Type position (e.g., left, top)

_____ 12. Symbol style

_____ 13. Symbol color

_____ 14. Symbol position

_____ 15. Arrow style

_____ 16. Arrow size

_____ 17. Arrow color

_____ 18. Arrow position

_____ 19. Mounting

_____ 20. Frame size

_____ 21. Frame finish

Types of secondary signage

Ceiling

Pendant

Flat against wall

Extended from wall

ARROWS

Parallel tips   Square tips

Arrows shown may be used in any size on all interior signage. When specifying arrows, indicate size, direction, and position.

Measurement
A = arrow height. Unless otherwise specified, the standard arrow length is 25 percent larger than the arrow height. Only in a square format will arrow height and length be the same.

Placement
Examples below illustrate typical arrow and word placement.

Left	Angled left	Angled left	Up or ahead	Down or ahead	Angled right	Angled right	Right

BUILDING DIRECTORIES

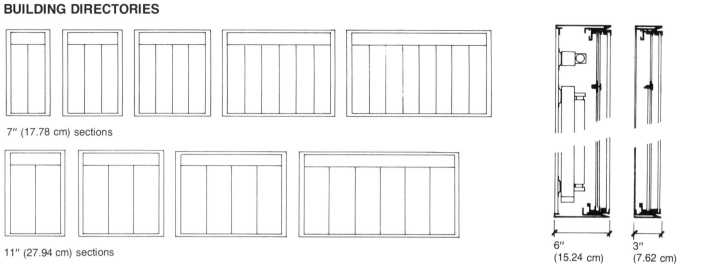

7" (17.78 cm) sections

11" (27.94 cm) sections

6"
(15.24 cm)

3"
(7.62 cm)

Sections of directories

Front elevations: no scale

Sizes & name capacities of directories

No. of sections	Suggested name capacity	Overall widths 7" section (in.)	11" section (in.)
2	80	19	26¼
3	120	26¼	37¼
4	160	33⅝	48¼
6	240	48¾	70¼
8	320	63⅛	
10	400	78¼	

Note: Overall heights: 36" (91.44 cm); 70 actual name plates per column.

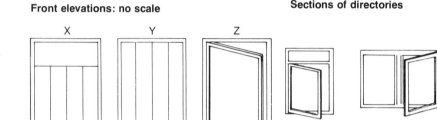

X

Y

Z

Heading over door

Double-door signs

X = integral header with dividers for ½" X 7" (1.27 x 17.78 cm)
Y = with dividers for ½" X 7" standard magnetic namestrips
Z = without dividers
Note: To determine directory size, allow one name strip per 400 sq ft (37.16 m²) of usable building space.

INFORMATION DISPLAYS

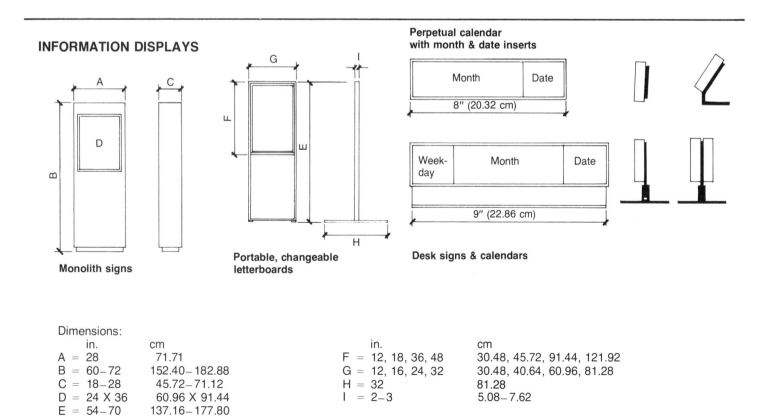

Perpetual calendar with month & date inserts

Month	Date

8" (20.32 cm)

Week-day	Month	Date

9" (22.86 cm)

Monolith signs

Portable, changeable letterboards

Desk signs & calendars

Dimensions:

	in.	cm
A =	28	71.71
B =	60–72	152.40–182.88
C =	18–28	45.72–71.12
D =	24 X 36	60.96 X 91.44
E =	54–70	137.16–177.80

	in.	cm
F =	12, 18, 36, 48	30.48, 45.72, 91.44, 121.92
G =	12, 16, 24, 32	30.48, 40.64, 60.96, 81.28
H =	32	81.28
I =	2–3	5.08–7.62

FIXED CONSTRUCTION

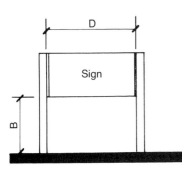

Plan

Note: Free-standing objects or signs on posts or pylons should not overhang passage areas more than 12″ (30.48 cm) when placed from 27″ to 80″ (68.58 to 203.20 cm) above finished floor (ANSI 4.4.1).

Elevation

Dimensions (not to scale):
A = 36″ (91.44 cm)
B = 27″ (68.58 cm)
C = 6′8″ (203.20 cm)
D = 12″ (30.48 cm)

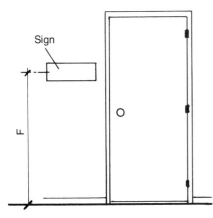

Signage mounting height at doors

CLEAR WIDTH

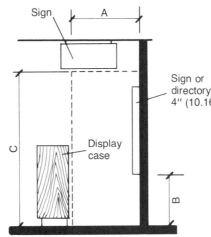

Elevation

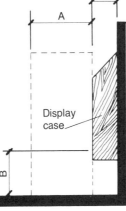

Elevation

E = any amount*
F = 60″ (152.40 cm)
G = ⅝″ (1.59 cm) min.
H = 1/32″ (0.32 cm) min.

*As long as object does not obstruct required clear passage.

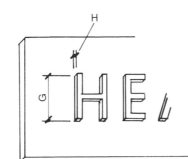

Raised letters for visually impaired

CODE CONSIDERATIONS FOR TACTILE WARNINGS

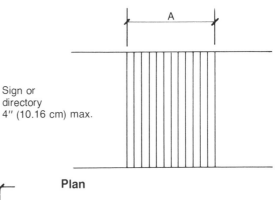

Plan

Tactile warnings within a building, facility, or site shall be standardized. Those used on ground and floor surfaces shall:

1. Have contrasting textures with surrounding surfaces.

2. Comply with drawing shown above. Use a minimum 3′0″ (91.44 cm) width of raised strips or recessed grooves.

3. Not have grooves that are recessed below adjoining surfaces on exterior surfaces.

4. Have surfaces, raised strips, or grooves that are made of exposed concrete, rubber, or plastic-cushioned materials.

5. Warn users of hazardous areas if a walk crosses or adjoins a frequently used vehicular way if there are no curbs, railings, planted areas, or similar boundary elements to separate the areas [ANSI A117.1 (1980)].

Note: See information on signage requirements for elevators on pages 298–299 in Chapter 9.

INCANDESCENT & FLUORESCENT EXIT SIGNS

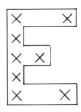  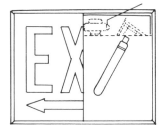 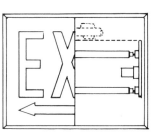 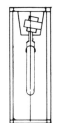

Legibility

Two foot lamberts* (6.85 lx) in total darkness are required for legibility from a distance of 100' (30.48 m) by a 65-year-old adult with 20/20 vision. The average luminance may be computed by measuring the luminance of ¾" (1.91cm) diameter circular areas at the positions indicated in the above diagram by Xs.

Arrows

Horizontal arrows are standard on exit signs. Most codes avoid requiring any specific colors, assuming that either red or green will be used. These colors provide good contrast against a matte white background; a glossy background should be avoided. Signs should have self-contained power sources. However, batteries do not qualify as a power source.

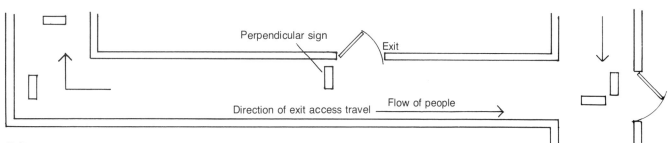

Exit access

Exits shall be marked with an approved sign readily visible from any direction of exit access. Arrows should point in the direction of travel. Any door or passage that is neither an exit nor a way of exit shall be marked with the words "NOT AN EXIT."

Reprinted with permission of **NFPA 101-1985, Life Safety Code**. Copyright © 1985, National Fire Protection Association, Quincy, MA 02269. This reprinted material is not the complete and official position of the NFPA on the referenced subject which is represented only by the standard in its entirety.

Copyright © 1985, *Life Safety Code® Handbook.*

     Exit light on emergency circuit, surface or pendant mounted

Surface- or wall-mounted exit light with directional arrows

 Exit light on emergency circuit, wall mounted

Ceiling or wall outlet with incandescent lighting connected to emergency circuit (emergency white light)

Design

Exit signs are designed to be distinctive in color and size and specifically located so that they will be readily visible and provide contrast with decorations, interior finish, or other signs.

Codes do not permit exit signs to be obscured by plants, drapery, furnishings, or brightly lit art objects. No decorative item should be placed in or near the line of vision of the required exit sign.

Some exit signs may be designed to flash on and off upon activation of the fire alarm system. Flashing signs offer assistance to people with hearing impairments.

Exit sign sizes

Letters shall be not less than 6" (15.24 cm) high, with the principal strokes of the letters not less than ¾" wide. Approved existing signs may be granted an exception to this requirement.

New exit lighting concerns

In view of major hotel fires in the United States and the large number of deaths from dense smoke encountered in hallways, many code agencies are reviewing the size and location of exit signage. The following suggestions are under consideration:

1. Signage at door-knob height.
2. Signage at baseboard level.
3. Signage equipped with verbal directional messages.
4. Signage with three-dimensional directional elements placed along hallway walls.

RECESSED CASES

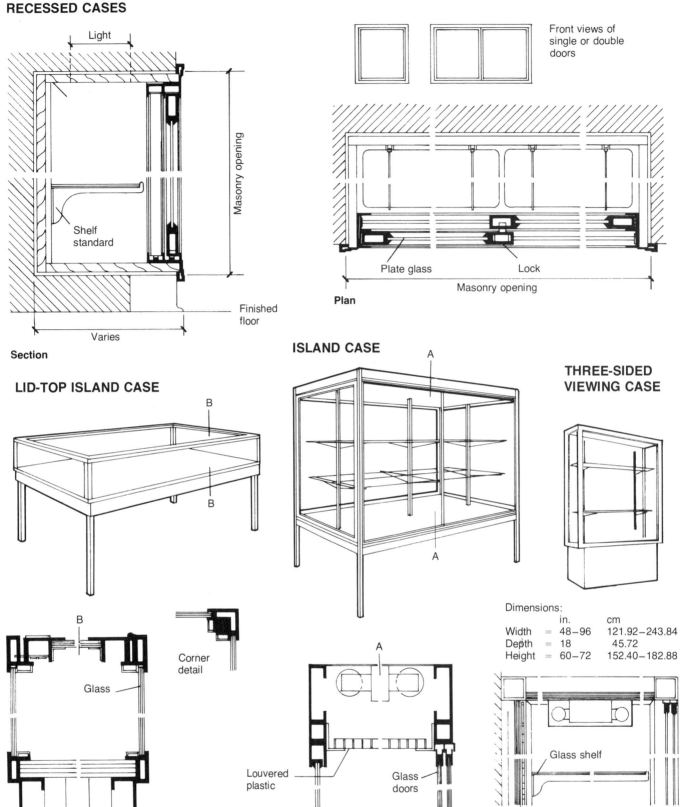

Light

Masonry opening

Shelf standard

Finished floor

Varies

Section

Front views of single or double doors

Plate glass

Lock

Masonry opening

Plan

ISLAND CASE

A

A

THREE-SIDED VIEWING CASE

LID-TOP ISLAND CASE

B

B

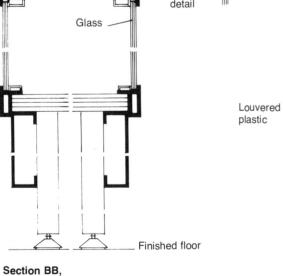

B

Corner detail

Glass

Finished floor

Section BB, head & sill of lid-top case

A

Louvered plastic

Glass doors

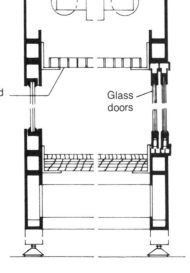

Section AA, head & sill of island case
Doors may be placed on side or ends

Dimensions:
	in.	cm
Width	= 48–96	121.92–243.84
Depth	= 18	45.72
Height	= 60–72	152.40–182.88

Glass shelf

Floor

Section of three-sided viewing case

Front view

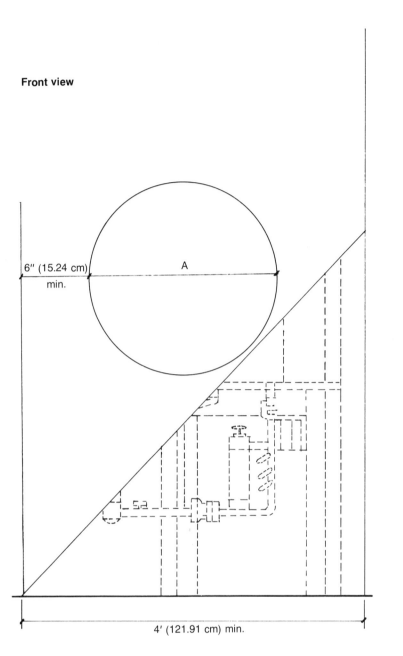

6″ (15.24 cm) min.

A

4′ (121.91 cm) min.

Side view

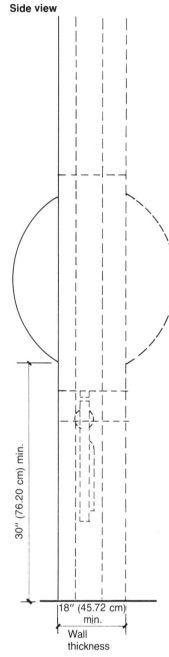

30″ (76.20 cm) min.

18″ (45.72 cm) min.

Wall thickness

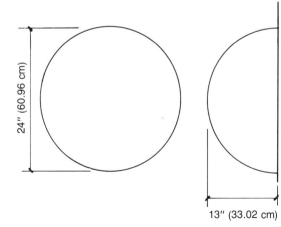

24″ (60.96 cm)

13″ (33.02 cm)

Globes of 24″ are available in full or half sizes shown above.

Notes: Globes to display fish come in A sizes: 20″ (50.80 cm), 24″, 30″, 36″ (91.44 cm), 40″ (101.60 cm), 46″ (116.84 cm). Globes may be installed through a wall for viewing from both sides of the wall.

Designers must consult with manufacturers for information on the weight factors, plumbing, and structural and code requirements.

VERTICAL LETTERBOXES

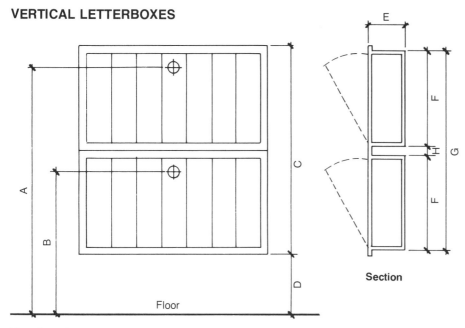

Elevation of double row

Section

Dimensions:

	in.	cm
A =	58	147.32 max.
B =	30	76.20 min.
C =	38½	97.79
D =	14½	36.83
E =	6	15.24
F =	17	43.18
G =	37	93.98
H =	2¼	5.72

SUMMARY OF U.S. POSTAL SERVICE REGULATIONS FOR VERTICAL LETTER-BOXES EFFECTIVE MAY 1, 1975

Arrangement
Receptacles must be placed so master lock is no more than 58" (147.32 cm) from finished floor. No more than two tiers of boxes may be installed. Master lock in lower tier to be no less than 30" (76.20 cm) from finished floor. Maximum number of boxes that may be installed under one Post Office lock is seven. Minimum number is three.

Receptacle
Minimum inside dimension of letterbox must be 5" (12.70 cm) wide, 15" (38.10 cm) high, and 6" (15.24 cm) deep.

Number and name cards
Boxes may be numbered or lettered in sequence from left to right.

Directories
In mailbox installations serving 15 or more tenants, a directory of tenants receiving mail must be maintained.

Locks
Doors to be equipped with five-pin cylinder lock, with minimum of 1,000 key changes. All locks keyed differently. Master keying is not permitted.

LETTER CHUTES

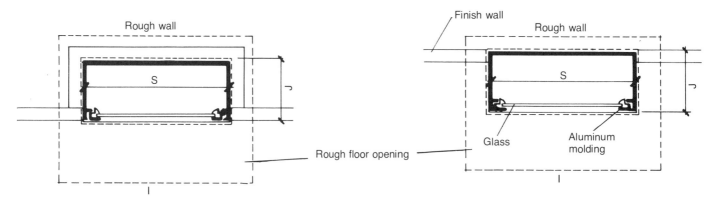

Recessed mounting guide

Surface-mounted guide

LETTER SLOT

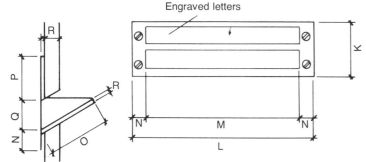

Dimensions (not to scale):

		in.	cm
I	=	12 X 18	30.48 X 45.72
		rough floor opening	
J	=	3½	8.89
K	=	3	7.62
L	=	10½	26.67
M	=	9	22.86
N	=	¾	1.91
O	=	2	5.08
P	=	1¼	3.18
Q	=	1	2.54
R	=	⅛	0.32
S	=	8¾	22.23

Engraved letters

FRONT-LOADING HORIZONTAL LETTERBOXES

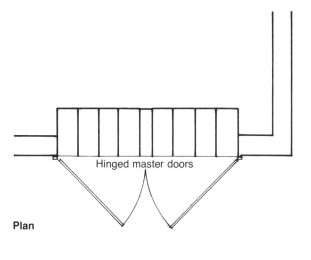

Hinged master doors

Plan

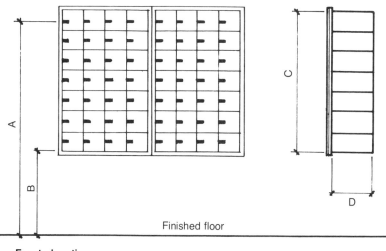

Finished floor

Front elevation

REAR-LOADING HORIZONTAL LETTERBOXES

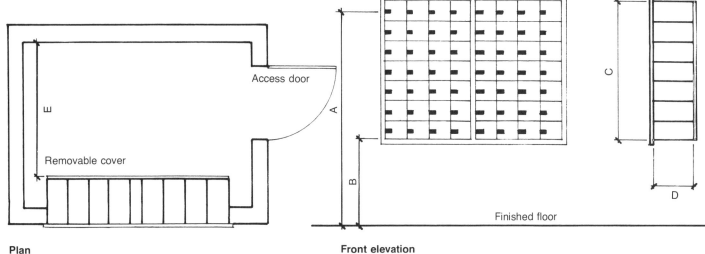

Access door

Removable cover

Plan

Finished floor

Front elevation

SUMMARY OF U.S. POSTAL SERVICE REGULATIONS* FOR HORIZONTAL LETTERBOXES† EFFECTIVE MAY 1, 1975

Arrangement
Maximum height from finished floor to tenant lock on top tier of boxes is 67″ (110.18 cm). Minimum height from finished floor to lowest tier is 28″ (71.12 cm).

Receptacles
Minimum interior dimension of letterbox must be 6″ (15.24 cm) wide, 5″ (12.70 cm) high, and 15″ (38.10 cm) deep.

Doors
Each receptacle must be equipped with full-length door. Vision panels or slots are prohibited.

Cabinets
Rear-loading cabinets must have rear panels securely attached on loading side (rear) of nest. Front-loading cabinets must be equipped with master door no wider than 34″ (86.36 cm).

Identification
Doors must be numbered or lettered in sequence from top to bottom.

Dimensions:

	in.	cm
A =	67	170.18 max.
B =	28	71.12 max.
C =	unit height	
D =	15	38.10
E =	36	91.44

*Due to periodic revisions of postal regulations by the Postal Service, mailbox size and capacity are subject to change to comply with such regulations.

†For mail boxes serviced by the Postal Service, maximum height is the equivalent of seven standard-size compartments.

Note: To determine space requirements for multi-unit installations, use the following formula:
Total wall opening width = sum of mailbox widths + ¼″ (0.64 cm)

Decking details

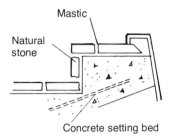

Stone decking

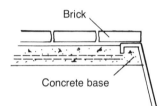

Brick decking

Wooden decking

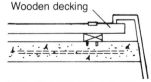

Note: The spa lip is not designed for structural support. Do not hang spa by lip.

Chord decking

Warning

1. Spa water should not be heated above 102° F (38.88° C).
2. Elderly persons and those having heart disease, diabetes, high or low blood pressure should not enter the spa.
3. Do not use while under the influence of alcohol, antico-agulants, antihistamines, vasoconstrictors, vasodilators, stimulants, hypnotics, narcotics, or tranquilizers.
4. Do not use while alone. Unsupervised use by children should not be allowed.
5. Observe a reasonable time limit. Long exposures may result in nausea, dizziness, or fainting.

Below grade

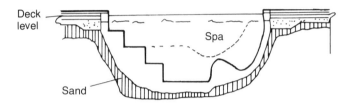

Partial excavation

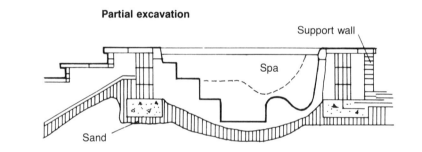

Note: Excavation area should be calculated to accommodate each spa. An additional 9″ (22.86 cm) should be excavated on all sides to allow for plumbing and thermal insulation.

Above ground

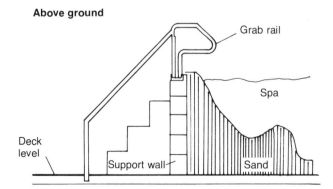

Note: Before specification or installation, consult local building and health codes.

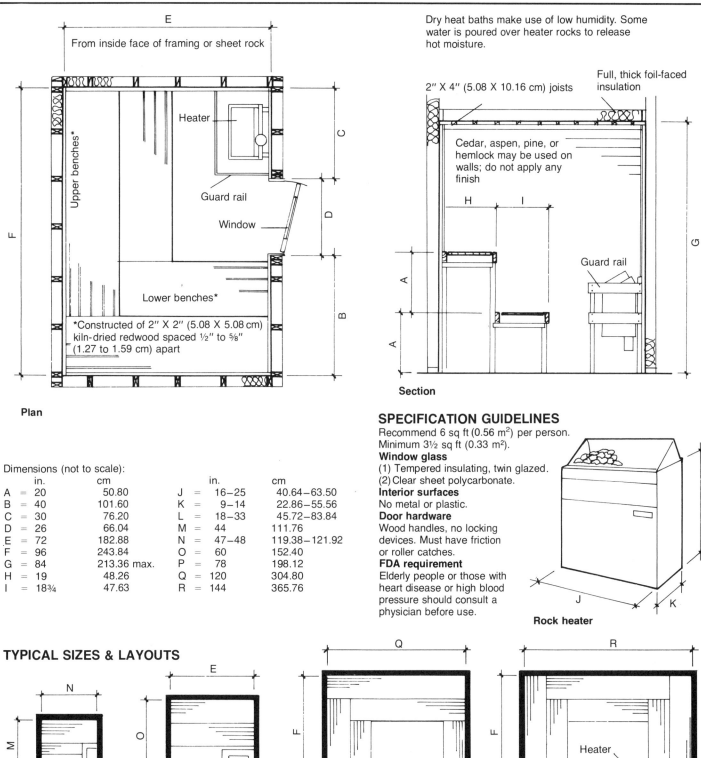

E

From inside face of framing or sheet rock

Heater

Upper benches*

Guard rail

Window

F

C

D

B

Lower benches*

*Constructed of 2″ X 2″ (5.08 X 5.08 cm) kiln-dried redwood spaced ½″ to ⅝″ (1.27 to 1.59 cm) apart

Plan

Dry heat baths make use of low humidity. Some water is poured over heater rocks to release hot moisture.

2″ X 4″ (5.08 X 10.16 cm) joists

Full, thick foil-faced insulation

Cedar, aspen, pine, or hemlock may be used on walls; do not apply any finish

H   I

A

A

Guard rail

G

Section

Dimensions (not to scale):

	in.	cm		in.	cm
A =	20	50.80	J =	16–25	40.64–63.50
B =	40	101.60	K =	9–14	22.86–55.56
C =	30	76.20	L =	18–33	45.72–83.84
D =	26	66.04	M =	44	111.76
E =	72	182.88	N =	47–48	119.38–121.92
F =	96	243.84	O =	60	152.40
G =	84	213.36 max.	P =	78	198.12
H =	19	48.26	Q =	120	304.80
I =	18¾	47.63	R =	144	365.76

SPECIFICATION GUIDELINES

Recommend 6 sq ft (0.56 m²) per person. Minimum 3½ sq ft (0.33 m²).
Window glass
(1) Tempered insulating, twin glazed.
(2) Clear sheet polycarbonate.
Interior surfaces
No metal or plastic.
Door hardware
Wood handles, no locking devices. Must have friction or roller catches.
FDA requirement
Elderly people or those with heart disease or high blood pressure should consult a physician before use.

L

J   K

Rock heater

TYPICAL SIZES & LAYOUTS

N

M

D   H

E

O

D   C

Q

F

N   D   N

R

F

Heater

B   D   P

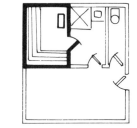

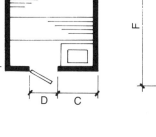

Note: Try to locate saunas adjacent to shower areas. Heater controls are placed inside the sauna for safety. No electrical receptacles are allowed in the sauna.

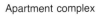

Apartment complex   Office building   Poolside cabana

ASTM	**American Society for Testing and Materials**
	Test Methods for:
C367	Strength Properties of Prefabricated Architectural Acoustical Materials
C384	Impedance and Absorption and Acoustical Materials by the Impedance Tube Method
C423	Sound Absorption and Sound Absorption Coefficient by the Reverberation Room Method
C518	Steady State Thermal Transmission Properties by Means of the Heat Flow Meter
C522	Airflow Resistance of Accoustical Materials
C523	Light Reflectance of Acoustical Materials by the Integrating Sphere Reflectometer
C643	Change in Acoustical Absorption of Ceiling Materials Due to Repainting
D635	Rate of Burning and/or Extent and Time of Burning of Self-Supporting Plastics in a Horizontal Position
D2843	Measuring the Density of Smoke from the Burning or Decomposition of Plastics
E84	Surface Burning Characteristics of Building Materials
E119	Fire Tests of Building Construction and Materials
E477	Duct Linear Materials and Prefabricated Silencers for Acoustical and Airflow Performance
E492	Impact Sound Transmission Through Floor-Ceiling Assemblies Using the Tapping Machine
	Standard Recommended Practice for:
C636	Installation of Metal Ceiling Suspension Systems for Acoustical Tile and Lay-In Panels
E90	Laboratory Measurement of Airborne-Sound Transmission Loss of Building Partitions
E336	Airborne Sound Insulation in Buildings
	Classification for:
E413	Sound Transmission Class

CBD	**Candadian Building Digests**
10	Noise Transmission in Buildings
41	Sound and People
51	Sound Insulation in Office Buildings
92	Room Acoustics-Design for Listening
139	Acoustical Design of Open-Planned Offices

CISC	**Ceilings and Interior Systems Contractors Association**
	"Acoustical Ceilings Use and Practice"

CSI	**Construction Specifications Institute**
T 13070	Integrated Ceilings

	Federal Specification
SS-S-118A(3)	Sound Controlling Blocks and Board

INTERIOR EQUIPMENT

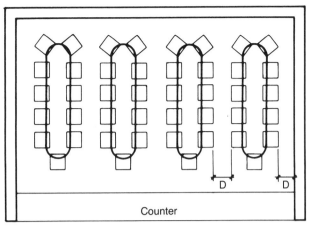

Plan of checkroom

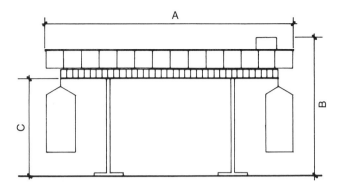

One-shelf conveyer

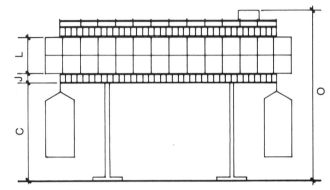

Two-shelf conveyer

Dimensions (not to scale):

	in.	cm		in.	cm		in.	cm
A =	54	137.16	F =	72	182.88	K =	40	101.60
B =	81	205.74	G =	42	106.63	L =	13½	34.29
C =	63	160.02	H =	51	129.54	M =	12	30.48
D =	6	156.24	I =	27	68.58	N =	95	241.30
E =	66	167.34	J =	4	10.16	O =	90	228.60

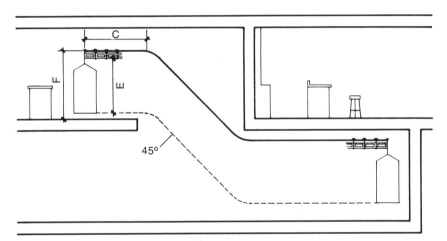

Section of checkroom with storage area at separate level

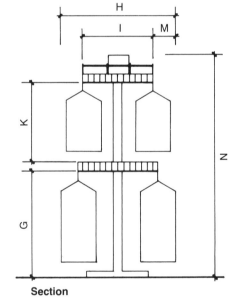

Section

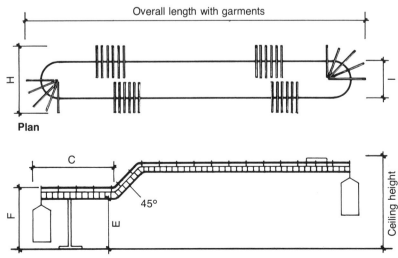

Plan

Elevation

Notes: Bins and shelves are not used when the conveyer is installed on a separate floor level.

In fast-retrieval installations such as theaters, where large numbers of people are entering or leaving at the same time, shorter conveyer distances are recommended. This allows for faster retrieval of more garments.

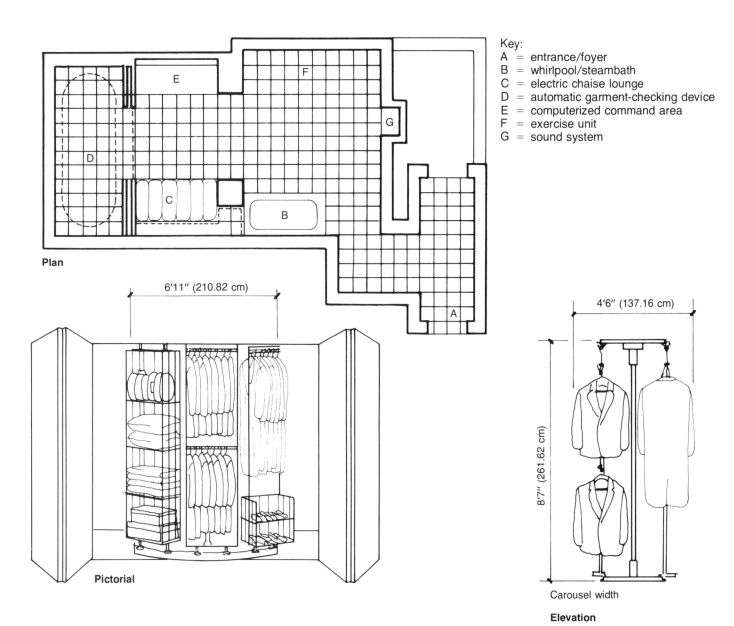

Plan

Key:
A = entrance/foyer
B = whirlpool/steambath
C = electric chaise lounge
D = automatic garment-checking device
E = computerized command area
F = exercise unit
G = sound system

6'11" (210.82 cm)

Pictorial

4'6" (137.16 cm)

8'7" (261.62 cm)

Carousel width

Elevation

Typical layouts

Almost any closet area that has a minimum dimension of 4'6" X 7'6" (137.16 X 228.60 cm) can accommodate this type of automated clothing carousel. The door or doors may be placed in several different locations in the closet design. A 3' (91.44 cm) clearance beyond the dimensions shown should be provided on all sides of the unit.

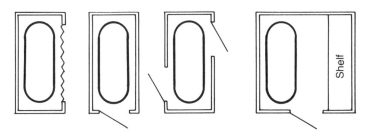

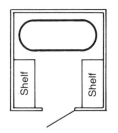

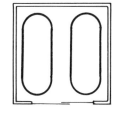

Standard sizes

Overall height	7'6" (228.60 cm). Minimum ceiling height of 7'8" (233.68 cm)	Storage sections	21" X 76" (53.34 X 193.04 cm)
		Garment rods	21" wide
Width with trays & garments	4'3" (129.54 cm)	Speed	40' (12.19 m) per minute
		Electrical	110/1/60 2-amp circuit protection
Lengths with trays & garments	Vary from 7' to 15' (2.13 to 4.57 m) in 1' (0.30 m) increments	Operation	One direction only
		Control	Contact hand switch

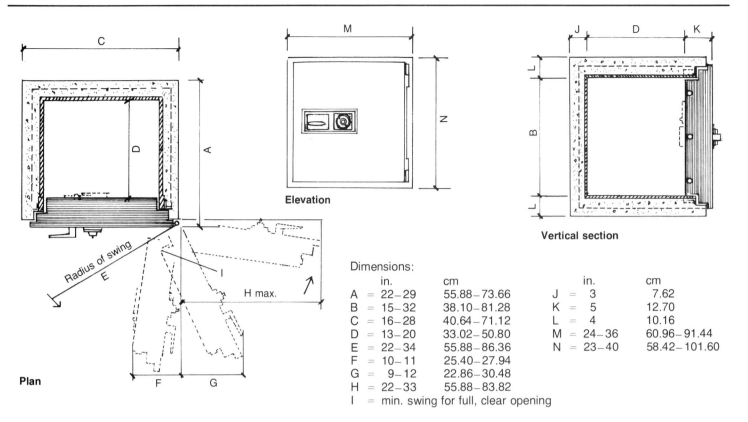

Elevation

Vertical section

Plan

Dimensions:

		in.	cm				in.	cm
A	=	22–29	55.88–73.66		J	=	3	7.62
B	=	15–32	38.10–81.28		K	=	5	12.70
C	=	16–28	40.64–71.12		L	=	4	10.16
D	=	13–20	33.02–50.80		M	=	24–36	60.96–91.44
E	=	22–34	55.88–86.36		N	=	23–40	58.42–101.60
F	=	10–11	25.40–27.94					
G	=	9–12	22.86–30.48					
H	=	22–33	55.88–83.82					
I	=	min. swing for full, clear opening						

Note: Any safe less than 750 lb (340.50 kg) must be secured in place to fully comply with UL-TL 15 requirements. Safe shall resist burglary tools for minimum 15 minutes.

Suggested installation methods

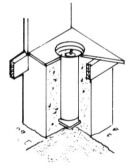

Under floor

On top of floor

Lift out of floor

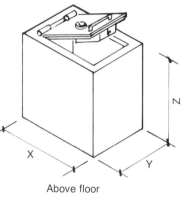

Above floor

Height (Q) = 16"–20" (40.64–50.80 cm)

Safe ratings for fire
Class A = 4-hr fire resistance
Class B = 2-hr fire resistance
Class C = 1-hr fire resistance

Dimensions:

		in.	cm
X	=	18–22	45.72–55.88
Y	=	14–16	35.56–40.64
Z	=	16–20	40.64–50.80

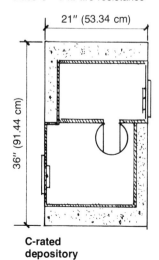

21" (53.34 cm)

36" (91.44 cm)

C-rated depository

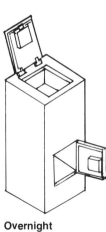

Overnight storage

Note: Fire classes also include a "drop test." If safe drops through a floor during a fire, it must resist damage to contents.

Safe ratings for security
Best   E rating: 1" (2.54 cm) steel body with 1½" (3.81 cm) steel over bolts
Better   C rating: ½" (1.27 cm) steel body with 1" steel over bolts; has relocking device
Good   B rating: key lock or combination ¼" (0.64 cm) steel walls and doors of ½" steel

Counter level

Safe

Counter storage in convenience store

ACCESSIBLE DESIGN REQUIREMENTS FOR VENDING MACHINES

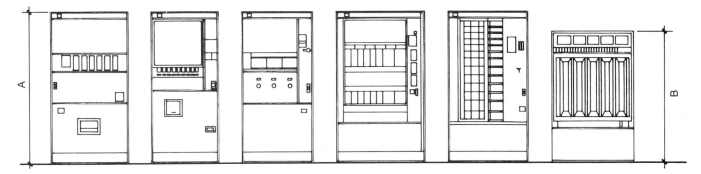

Machine widths vary from 36", 40", to 42" (91.44, 101.60, to 106.68 cm). All controls and operating mechanisms shall adjoin floor or ground space so that both forward and parallel approaches are allowed. Controls shall be operable with one hand and shall not require tight grasping, pinching, or twisting of the wrist. The force required to activate shall not exceed 5 lb (1.82 kg).

Dimensions:

	in.	cm
A	72	182.88
B	51	129.54
C	48	121.92
D	15	38.10
E	60	152.40
F	42	106.68

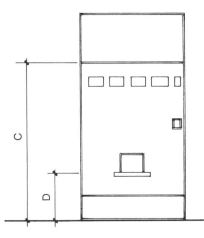

Wheelchair forward approach

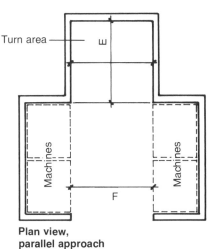

Plan view, parallel approach

Note: When vending machines are located in an alcove (see left), adequate space must be allowed for a turn-around area. Parallel approach measurements must be used with this plan.

ACCESSIBLE DESIGNS FOR PUBLIC TELEPHONES

Note: For a forward reach, J can be 48" (121.94 cm).

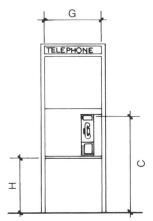

Diagonal reach from wheelchair

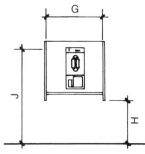

Plan for forward or side approach

In banks of telephones a minimum of one telephone per bank shall be provided with the operable control at 4' (121.92 cm).

Dimensions:

	in.	cm
G	30	76.20
H	27	68.58
I	19	48.26
J	54	137.16

Side reach from wheelchair

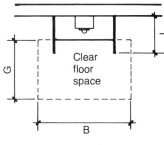

Plan of side reach

WALL-HUNG FOUNTAINS

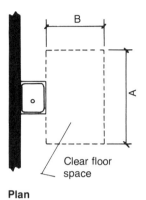

Plan

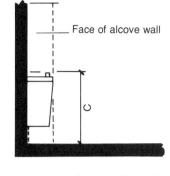

Face of alcove wall

Elevation of free-standing unit

ACCESSIBLE DESIGN REQUIREMENTS

Clearances

Drinking fountains and water coolers shall have clear floor or ground spaces that comply with the following:

Free-standing or built-in units shall have a clear space allowing for a parallel approach and not have knee space.

Spouts of drinking fountains shall be mounted no higher than 3'0" (91.44 cm) above the finished floor.

Spouts shall be at the front of the unit and shall direct the water trajectory parallel or nearly parallel to the front of the unit.

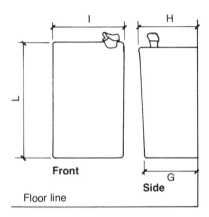

Front
Side
Floor line

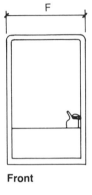

Front

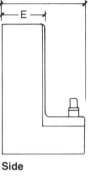

Side

Dimensions (not to scale):

A	=	48"	121.92 cm
B	=	2'6"	76.20 cm
C	=	36"	91.44 cm
D	=	18"	45.72 cm
E	=	9½"	24.13 cm
F	=	17"	43.18 cm
G	=	11"	27.94 cm
H	=	12"	30.48 cm
I	=	15"	38.10 cm
J	=	27"	68.58 cm
K	=	33"	83.82 cm
L	=	23"	58.42 cm

CANTILEVERED FOUNTAINS

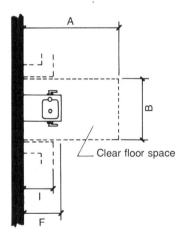

Plan

Face of alcove wall

Spout height

Knee space

Elevation

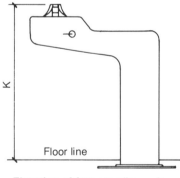

Floor line

Elevation of free-standing unit

Front
Side

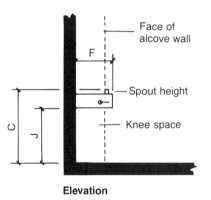

ACCESSIBLE DESIGN REQUIREMENTS

Cantilevered units shall have a clear space allowing for a forward approach and a knee space under the unit that is at least 2'6" (76.20 cm) wide and 1'5" (43.18 cm) deep.

Fully recessed fountain

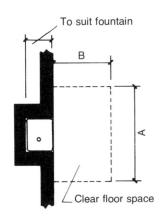

To suit fountain

Clear floor space

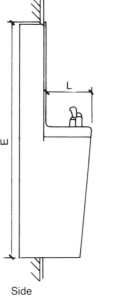

Front   Side

Dimensions (not to scale):

		in.	cm
A	=	48	121.92
B	=	30	76.20
C	=	38	96.52
D	=	40	101.60
E	=	36–44	91.44–111.76
F	=	61	154.94
G	=	21	53.34
H	=	17–18	43.18–45.72
I	=	15	38.10
J	=	11–12	27.94–30.48
K	=	14	35.56 deep
		17	43.18 wide
L	=	9	22.86
M	=	3	7.62

Semirecessed fountain

Front   Side

ACCESSIBLE DESIGN REQUIREMENTS

Drinking fountains and water coolers should be provided for all to use. Fifty percent of those provided on any floor of a building shall comply with federal and local codes regarding disabled accessibility. If only one water fountain is provided on any floor, it shall have two levels and the lower level shall comply with code requirements.

Controls
Water units shall have controls on the front or side near the front edge. Controls shall allow spouts to direct water flow at least 4" (10.16 cm) above the unit basin to facilitate cup or glass insertion.

Fully recessed fountain

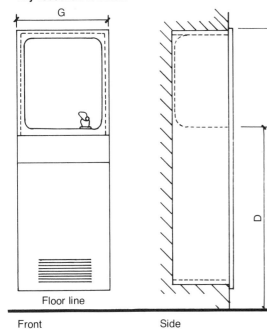

Floor line

Front   Side

Fountain flush to wall

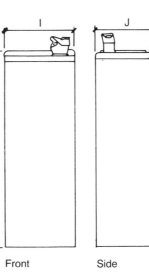

Front   Side

Bottle-type water cooler

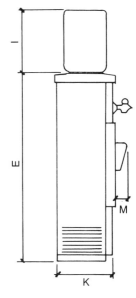

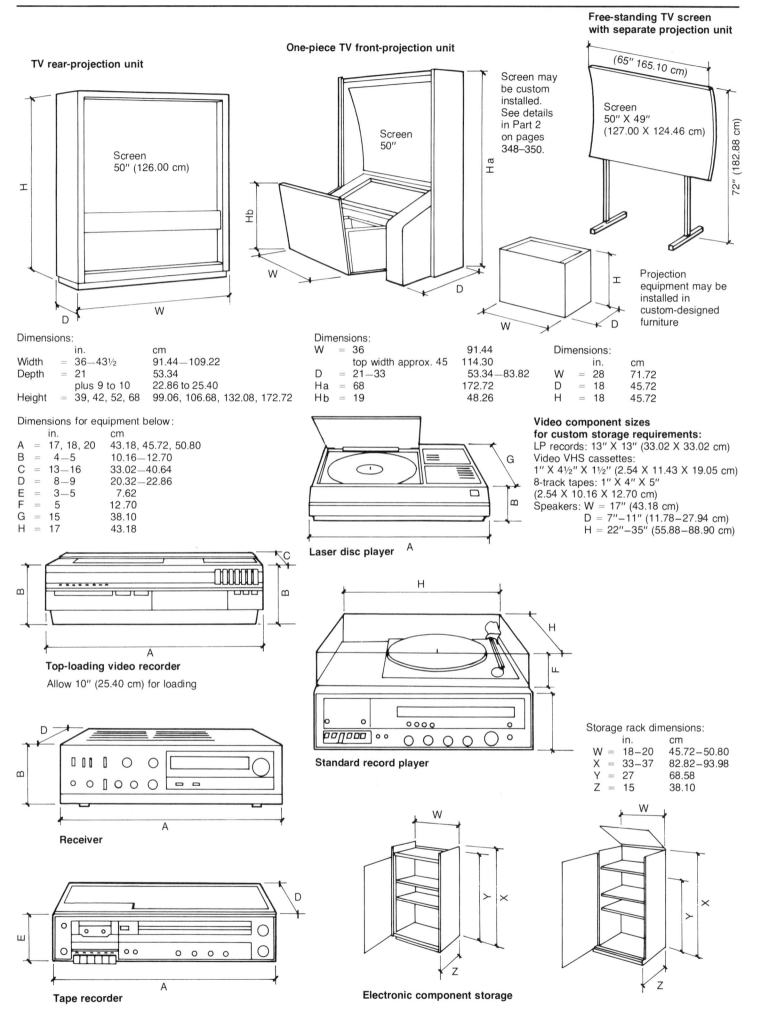

TV rear-projection unit

Screen
50" (126.00 cm)

One-piece TV front-projection unit

Screen
50"

Screen may
be custom
installed.
See details
in Part 2
on pages
348–350.

**Free-standing TV screen
with separate projection unit**

(65" 165.10 cm)

Screen
50" X 49"
(127.00 X 124.46 cm)

72" (182.88 cm)

Projection
equipment may be
installed in
custom-designed
furniture

Dimensions:

		in.	cm
Width	=	36—43½	91.44—109.22
Depth	=	21	53.34
		plus 9 to 10	22.86 to 25.40
Height	=	39, 42, 52, 68	99.06, 106.68, 132.08, 172.72

Dimensions for equipment below:

		in.	cm
A	=	17, 18, 20	43.18, 45.72, 50.80
B	=	4—5	10.16—12.70
C	=	13—16	33.02—40.64
D	=	8—9	20.32—22.86
E	=	3—5	7.62
F	=	5	12.70
G	=	15	38.10
H	=	17	43.18

Dimensions:

		in.	cm
W	=	36	91.44
		top width approx. 45	114.30
D	=	21—33	53.34—83.82
Ha	=	68	172.72
Hb	=	19	48.26

Dimensions:

		in.	cm
W	=	28	71.72
D	=	18	45.72
H	=	18	45.72

Laser disc player

**Video component sizes
for custom storage requirements:**
LP records: 13" X 13" (33.02 X 33.02 cm)
Video VHS cassettes:
1" X 4½" X 1½" (2.54 X 11.43 X 19.05 cm)
8-track tapes: 1" X 4" X 5"
(2.54 X 10.16 X 12.70 cm)
Speakers: W = 17" (43.18 cm)
          D = 7"—11" (11.78—27.94 cm)
          H = 22"—35" (55.88—88.90 cm)

Top-loading video recorder

Allow 10" (25.40 cm) for loading

Standard record player

Receiver

Storage rack dimensions:

		in.	cm
W	=	18—20	45.72—50.80
X	=	33—37	82.82—93.98
Y	=	27	68.58
Z	=	15	38.10

Tape recorder

Electronic component storage

Security furniture-top swivel for 19″ (48.26 cm) TV set

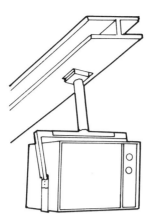

Security pedestals

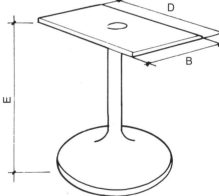

Hospital cart for TV
50″ (127.00 cm) tall will support 19″ TV set

Security ceiling mounts

Structural ceiling mount
Mounts directly to a beam or slab by bolting, welding, or lagging the ceiling box section in place. Yoke can be extended down with extension column. Rotation and tilting are unlimited. Supports any size set.

Note: Technological advances have produced 1″ (2.54 cm) thick TV screens that may be installed directly on or recessed into walls, thus providing built-in security.

Exposed grid-suspended ceiling mount
Large 25″ (63.50 cm) screen sets can be mounted below the true ceiling. Ceiling tiles are removed and the metal box section is mounted on tubular steel support bars 8″ (20.32 cm) in length. Extra support is provided by using tie wires to the metal box section.

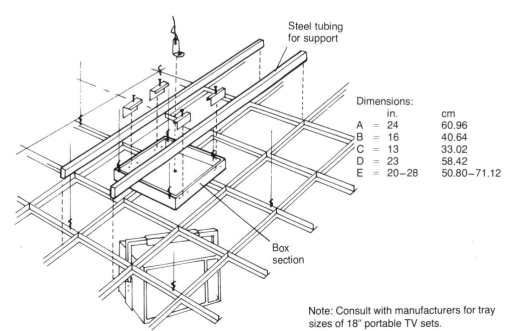

Steel tubing for support

Box section

Dimensions:		
	in.	cm
A =	24	60.96
B =	16	40.64
C =	13	33.02
D =	23	58.42
E =	20−28	50.80−71.12

Note: Consult with manufacturers for tray sizes of 18″ portable TV sets.

Security wall mountings

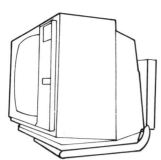

Bracket types
1. Swivel with no tilt
2. Swivel with fixed tilt
3. Swivel with adjustable tilt

Will hold 13″ to 25″ (33.02 to 63.60 cm) TV sets. Ideal for larger sets.

Yoke-style wall bracket

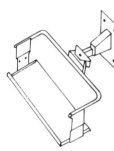

Provides maximum head clearance in small areas. Tray sizes vary.

Horizontal-yoke-style wall bracket

CEILING SPRINKLERS

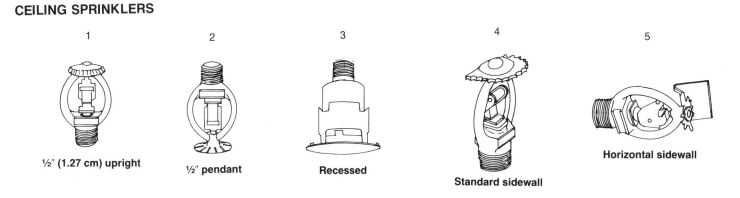

1 — ½″ (1.27 cm) upright

2 — ½″ pendant

3 — Recessed

4 — Standard sidewall

5 — Horizontal sidewall

Note: Basic sprinkler types are classified by temperature and deflector design. The deflector determines the water distribution. (1) A ½″ upright sprinkler is used where there are exposed plumbing and high, unfinished ceilings. (2) A ½″ pendant sprinkler is best for finished ceiling areas. (3) A recessed sprinkler, with a bottom plate that falls away and a head that lowers, can handle temperatures of 165° to 212° F (74° to 100° C). (4) The standard sidewall sprinkler is appropriate for halls and small rooms. (5) The horizontal sidewall sprinkler, which accommodates temperatures from 135° to 280° F (57° to 138° C), is excellent for hotels, nursing homes, and residential applications.

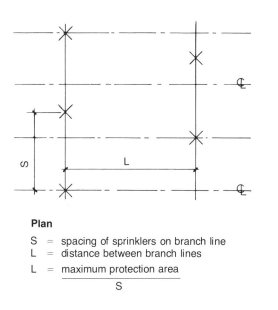

Plan

S = spacing of sprinklers on branch line
L = distance between branch lines
L = maximum protection area
$$\frac{L}{S} = \text{maximum protection area}$$

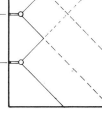

Elevation of recessed sprinkler

	in.	cm
A =	3	7.62
B =	2¼	5.72

Plan

If a room is more than 30′ (9.14 m) wide, the room will require ceiling sprinklers

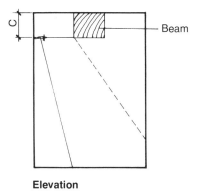

Elevation

C = 4″–6″ (10.16–15.24 cm) from ceiling

Beams or columns should not be allowed to interfere with water flow

Sprinkler activation is based on temperature levels. Sprinklers do not operate until a fire produces considerable heat. The number of sprinklers that might be expected to open in fast-developing fires can often be limited by the use of intermediate- or high-temperature-rated sprinklers, which may not operate at low enough temperatures to produce the cooling effect desired.

Sprinkler temperature classification

Maximum ceiling temperature °F	Temperature rating °F				Classification	Color code
100	135	150	160	165	Ordinary	Uncolored
150	175	212			Intermediate	White
225	250	280	286		High	Blue
300	325	340	350	360	Extra high	Red
375	400				Very extra high	Green
475	500				Ultra high	Orange

PORTABLE FIRE EXTINGUISHERS

Note: Check local codes for additional occupancy requirements.

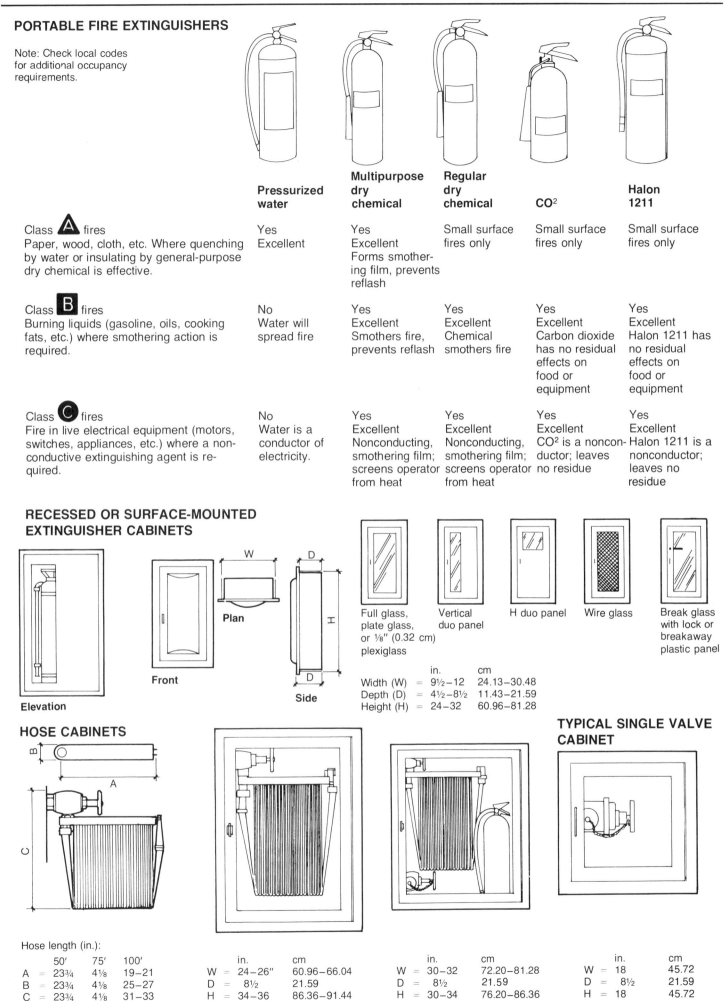

	Pressurized water	Multipurpose dry chemical	Regular dry chemical	CO$_2$	Halon 1211
Class A fires Paper, wood, cloth, etc. Where quenching by water or insulating by general-purpose dry chemical is effective.	Yes Excellent	Yes Excellent Forms smothering film, prevents reflash	Small surface fires only	Small surface fires only	Small surface fires only
Class B fires Burning liquids (gasoline, oils, cooking fats, etc.) where smothering action is required.	No Water will spread fire	Yes Excellent Smothers fire, prevents reflash	Yes Excellent Chemical smothers fire	Yes Excellent Carbon dioxide has no residual effects on food or equipment	Yes Excellent Halon 1211 has no residual effects on food or equipment
Class C fires Fire in live electrical equipment (motors, switches, appliances, etc.) where a non-conductive extinguishing agent is required.	No Water is a conductor of electricity.	Yes Excellent Nonconducting, smothering film; screens operator from heat	Yes Excellent Nonconducting, smothering film; screens operator from heat	Yes Excellent CO$_2$ is a nonconductor; leaves no residue	Yes Excellent Halon 1211 is a nonconductor; leaves no residue

RECESSED OR SURFACE-MOUNTED EXTINGUISHER CABINETS

Full glass, plate glass, or 1/8" (0.32 cm) plexiglass

Vertical duo panel

H duo panel

Wire glass

Break glass with lock or breakaway plastic panel

	in.	cm
Width (W) =	9½–12	24.13–30.48
Depth (D) =	4½–8½	11.43–21.59
Height (H) =	24–32	60.96–81.28

Elevation

Front

Plan

Side

HOSE CABINETS

Hose length (in.):

	50'	75'	100'
A =	23¾	4⅛	19–21
B =	23¾	4⅛	25–27
C =	23¾	4⅛	31–33

	in.	cm
W =	24–26"	60.96–66.04
D =	8½	21.59
H =	34–36	86.36–91.44

	in.	cm
W =	30–32	72.20–81.28
D =	8½	21.59
H =	30–34	76.20–86.36

TYPICAL SINGLE VALVE CABINET

	in.	cm
W =	18	45.72
D =	8½	21.59
H =	18	45.72

FOLDING PLATFORMS

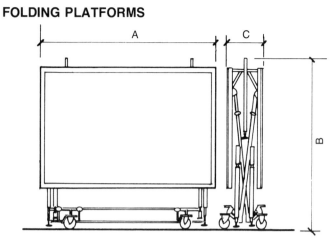

Elevation: platform closed for storage

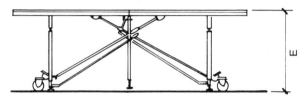

Elevation: open platform

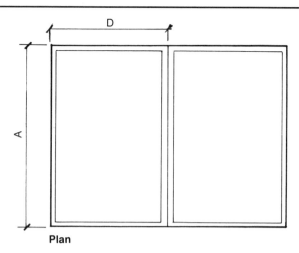

Plan

Dimensions:

		in.	cm
A	=	60–72	152.40–182.88
B	=	62–110	157.48–279.40
C	=	22½	57.15
D	=	48–72	212.92–182.88
E	=	three adjustable heights:	
		16–24	40.64–60.95
		24–32	60.96–81.28
		32–40	81.28–101.60

STAGES

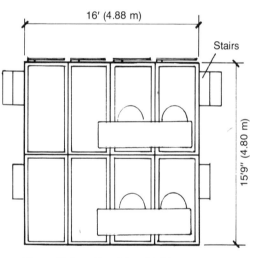

16′ (4.88 m)

Stairs

15′9″ (4.80 m)

Plan with two-tiered head table
[Four stages 4′ X 8′ (1.22 X 2.4 m)]

Notes:
1. Seated audience requires a 36″ (91.44 cm) platform; heights available in 8″ (20.32 cm) increments from 8″ to 32″ (81.28 cm)
2. Seated dining with head tables, which includes two-tier head table requiring 16′ (4.88 m) total depth
3. Seated dining with one single head table requiring 6′ (1.83 m) platform to allow 30″ (76.20 cm) for the table, 18″ (45.72 cm) for chairs, and 24″ (60.96 cm) for serving

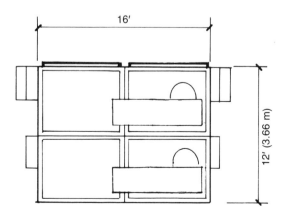

16′

12′ (3.66 m)

Plan with one head table
[Four 6′ X 8′ (1.83 X 2.4 m) stages]

LECTERNS

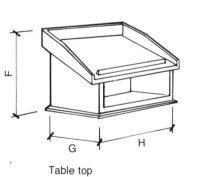

Table top

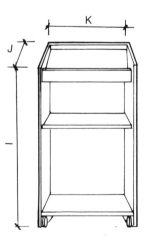

Dimensions:

		in.	cm				in.	cm
F	=	30	76.20		I	=	48	121.92
G	=	15–19	38.10–48.26		J	=	19	48.26
H	=	17–25	43.18–63.50		K	=	25	63.50

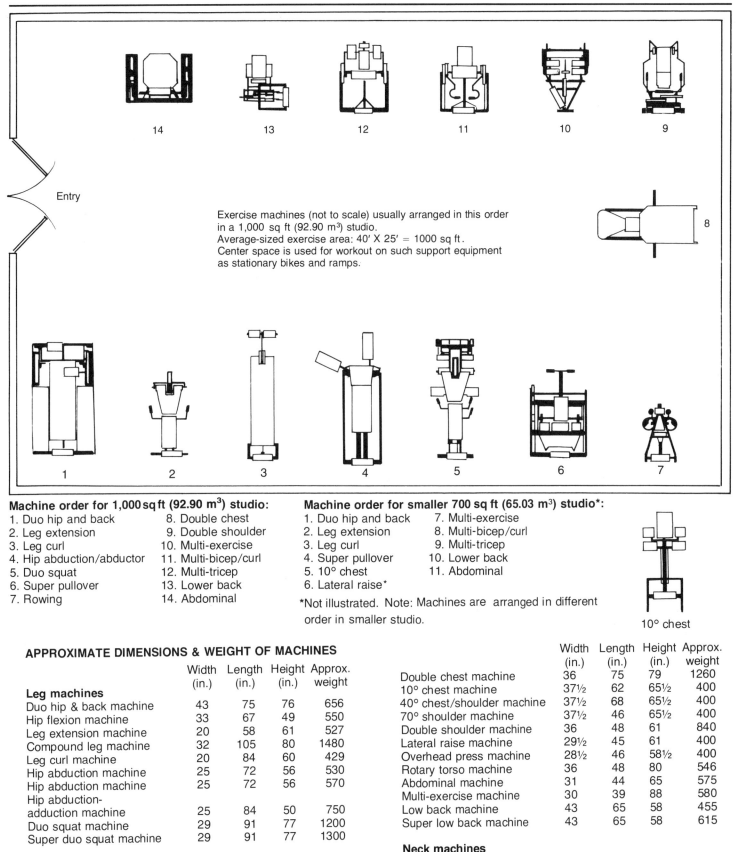

Exercise machines (not to scale) usually arranged in this order in a 1,000 sq ft (92.90 m³) studio.
Average-sized exercise area: 40' X 25' = 1000 sq ft.
Center space is used for workout on such support equipment as stationary bikes and ramps.

Entry

Machine order for 1,000 sq ft (92.90 m³) studio:

1. Duo hip and back	8. Double chest
2. Leg extension	9. Double shoulder
3. Leg curl	10. Multi-exercise
4. Hip abduction/abductor	11. Multi-bicep/curl
5. Duo squat	12. Multi-tricep
6. Super pullover	13. Lower back
7. Rowing	14. Abdominal

Machine order for smaller 700 sq ft (65.03 m³) studio*:

1. Duo hip and back	7. Multi-exercise
2. Leg extension	8. Multi-bicep/curl
3. Leg curl	9. Multi-tricep
4. Super pullover	10. Lower back
5. 10° chest	11. Abdominal
6. Lateral raise*	

*Not illustrated. Note: Machines are arranged in different order in smaller studio.

10° chest

APPROXIMATE DIMENSIONS & WEIGHT OF MACHINES

	Width (in.)	Length (in.)	Height (in.)	Approx. weight
Leg machines				
Duo hip & back machine	43	75	76	656
Hip flexion machine	33	67	49	550
Leg extension machine	20	58	61	527
Compound leg machine	32	105	80	1480
Leg curl machine	20	84	60	429
Hip abduction machine	25	72	56	530
Hip abduction machine	25	72	56	570
Hip abduction-adduction machine	25	84	50	750
Duo squat machine	29	91	77	1200
Super duo squat machine	29	91	77	1300
Torso machines				
Super pullover machine	40	42	69	889
Women's pullover machine	31	37	67	550
Pullover/torso-arm machine	40	77	80	1240
Pullover machine (plateloading)	36	36	62	350
Behind neck machine	29	35	77	425
Behind neck/torso-arm machine	40	40	90	685
Torso-arm machine	28	27	88	450
Rowing torso machine	30	35	72	337

	Width (in.)	Length (in.)	Height (in.)	Approx. weight
Double chest machine	36	75	79	1260
10° chest machine	37½	62	65½	400
40° chest/shoulder machine	37½	68	65½	400
70° shoulder machine	37½	46	65½	400
Double shoulder machine	36	48	61	840
Lateral raise machine	29½	45	61	400
Overhead press machine	28½	46	58½	400
Rotary torso machine	36	48	80	546
Abdominal machine	31	44	65	575
Multi-exercise machine	30	39	88	580
Low back machine	43	65	58	455
Super low back machine	43	65	58	615
Neck machines				
Neck & shoulder machine	23	58	69	304
4-way neck machine	41	36	63	396
Rotary neck machine	35	36	72	460
Arm machines				
Compound position biceps machine	42	31	69	480
Multi-biceps machine	38	37	54	385
Multi-triceps machine	38	46	54	405
Biceps/triceps machine (plateloading)	36	48	49	412

ENERGY CONSERVATION

Breakage of annealed glass can occur when the temperature differential within the glass is large. The design and location of hot air outlets should be carefully considered to direct heat away from the glass and prevent high temperature differences between the center and edge of the glass. When heating systems are initially activated during low-temperature periods, special care should be exercised to shield the glass.

Draperies, venetian blinds, or other interior shading devices must be hung away from the glass so that space is provided at the bottom and top, or bottom and one side, to provide natural air movement over the roomside face of the glass. For blinds in open or closed position, a 2″ (5.08 cm) minimum clearance between the frame and the shading device must be observed as shown in the drawing on this page. If these clearances cannot be provided in the case of venetian blinds, a positive stop or lock-out that limits the movements of the blinds should be used. For horizontal blinds, for instance, the lock-out should limit the rotation of the blinds so that they are in a position 60° off the horizontal in the most closed position. For vertical blinds, the lock-out should limit the movement of the blinds so that a ½″ (1.27 cm) spacing exists between the blinds in the most closed position.

Suspended ceiling soffits must be well to the roomside or should include vent slots to allow roomside air convection.

DRAPERY ESTIMATION

After the placement of the hardware has been determined, the designer may proceed to measure for the amount of drapery fabric required and specify the method of fabrication. Standard traverse drapery yardage (without pattern repeat) is calculated in the following manner:

1. **Finished length:** the distance from the top of the rod to the desired bottom of the drapery [allow 1″ (2.54 cm) clearance at the floor].

2. **Cut length:** the distance from the top of the rod to the desired bottom of the drapery *plus hems and top headings.* These measurements may vary depending on the type of fabric and fabrication. Many designers add 18″ (45.72 cm) for sheer drapery; 17″ (43.18 cm) for unlined drapery; 13″ (33.02 cm) for lined drapery. Example:

   Finished length = 84″ + 17″ = 101″ (256.54 cm) cut length

3. **Finished width:** the distance of the rod from bracket to bracket *plus* the number of inches the brackets extend from the wall. This distance is known as the "return." To this measurement add another 6″ (15.24 cm) for the center overlap. Example: If the rod is 120″ (304.80 cm) wide and the brackets extend 3″ (7.62 cm) from the wall, the total finished width would be 132″ (335.28 cm):

   120″ + 3″ + 3″ + 6″ = 132″

4. **Number of widths required:** the number of fabric panels needed to span this distance depends on the desired fullness. One hundred percent fullness is 2 times the width; 150 percent fullness is 2.5 times the width. Some sheers may require 200 percent fullness, or 3 times the width.

   Finished width × 2.5 fullness ÷ width of fabric = number of widths

   Example:
   Finished width 132″ × 2.5 = 330″ ÷ 48″ fabric (838.20 ÷ 121.92 cm) = 6.87, or 7 panels

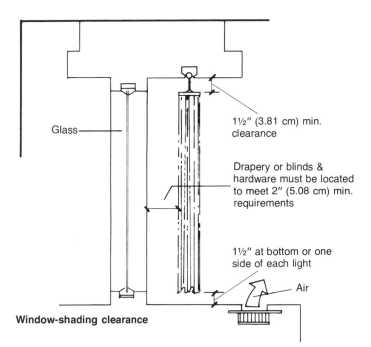

Window-shading clearance

1½″ (3.81 cm) min. clearance

Glass

Drapery or blinds & hardware must be located to meet 2″ (5.08 cm) min. requirements

1½″ at bottom or one side of each light

Air

FABRICATION SPECIFICATION CHECKLIST

Designers should provide the following information to drapery fabricators:

1. **Specified fabric**
   Name
   Number (mill number and purchase order number)
   Color
   Width
   Pattern repeat size
   Sample piece to verify correct shipment
   Total yardage required

2. **Drapery measurement**
   Width
   Stacking width
   Finished width
   Number of fabric widths
   Percentage of fullness
   Finished length
   Hems and headings
   Cutting length

3. **Hardware**
   Type
   Length of track
   Operational method
       One way
       Two way
       Multiple
       Cord operated
       Hand operated
       Motorized

4. **Hardware installation**
   Ceiling
   Wall
   Distance above casing
   Within casing
   Extension beyond window (inches on each side)

Hardware installation instructions should include a drawing of the window and wall with specific bracket locations clearly marked. Separate drawings should be made for each window and room.

SHADES FOR SKYLIGHTS OR GREENHOUSE WINDOWS

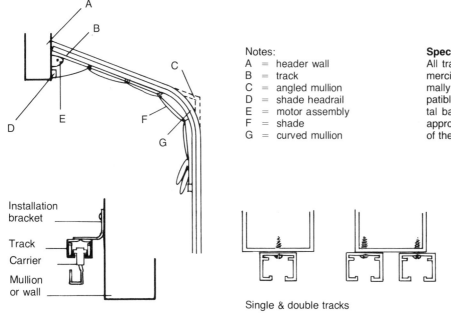

Notes:
A = header wall
B = track
C = angled mullion
D = shade headrail
E = motor assembly
F = shade
G = curved mullion

Specifications
All track members should be constructed of commercial-quality extruded aluminum. Tracks are normally .898" wide x .690" high. Carriers must be compatible with the track. They shall engage the horizontal batten sewn into pockets of the shade's cloth approximately every 8¾" (22.23 cm) along the face of the shade.

Installation bracket
Track
Carrier
Mullion or wall

Single & double tracks

VERTICAL BLINDS

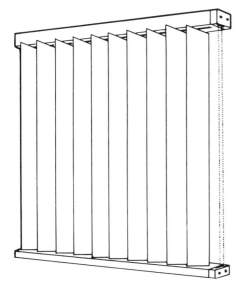

Inside mount with track clip

Free-hanging blinds

Specifications
Free-hanging blinds with fabric or plastic louvers are maintained by a pair of nickel-plated steel bead chains connecting and aligning each louver and attached with swivel action to plated metal ballasts. Each louver vane should be weighted in the hem to attain plum-line exactness.

Louver vane widths

in.	cm
3	7.62
3½	8.89
4⅜	11.11
5	12.70

Louver vane spacing
Spaced on centers ⅜'
(0.95 cm) less than louver width.

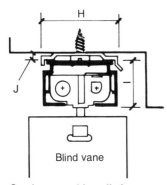

Semirecessed installation

Blind vane

Dimensions:

	in.	cm
H =	1⅞	4.76
I =	1¼	3.18
J =	⅛	0.32
K =	1¾	4.45
L =	3	7.62

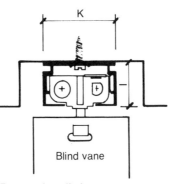

Blind vane

Reverse installation

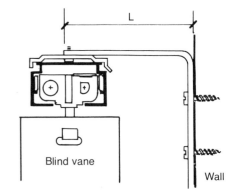

Blind vane

Wall

Surface mounting available top & bottom

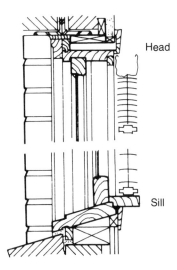

Outside installation, double-hung window, masonry wall with furred plaster

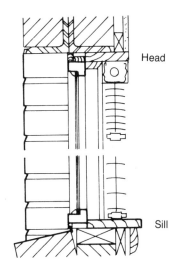

Inside window frame, awning metal window, masonry walls

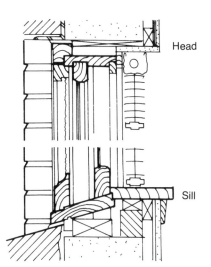

Inside existing construction, double-hung windows

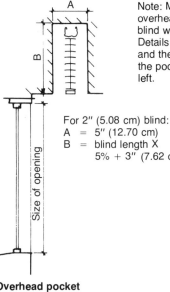

Note: Many installations require an overhead pocket to conceal the blind when in a raised position. Details of this type of installation and the formula for computing the pocket size are shown on the left.

For 2″ (5.08 cm) blind:
A = 5″ (12.70 cm)
B = blind length X
    5% + 3″ (7.62 cm)

Overhead pocket installation

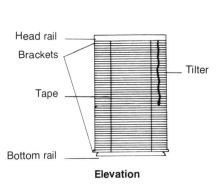

Head rail
Brackets
Tape
Tilter
Bottom rail

Elevation

Note: See page 124 for glass-encased blinds.

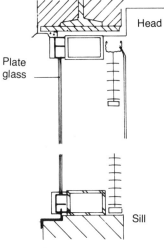

Plate glass

Store front window

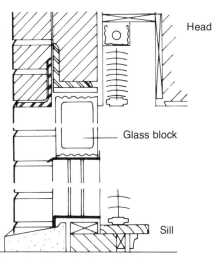

Glass block

Metal window in glass-block masonry wall

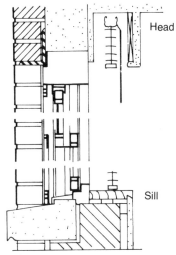

Metal double-hung window in masonry & concrete wall

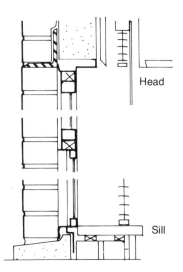

Awning window in masonry & concrete wall

X = divider rail

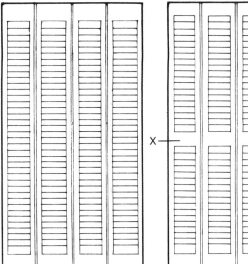

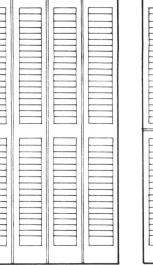

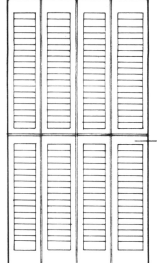

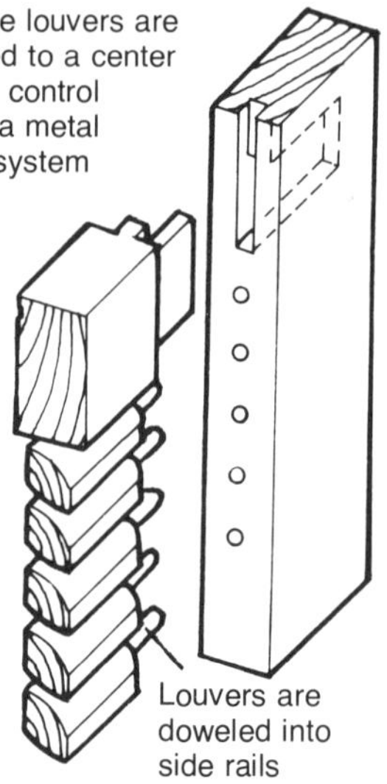

X —

Movable louvers are attached to a center vertical control bar by a metal staple system

Double hung-panels

Louvers are doweled into side rails

Shutter construction

Center rail location relates to panel height. Panels under 40″ (101.60 cm) high have no center rail. Panels from 40″ to 78″ (198.12 cm) have one center horizontal divider rail. Panels 78″ to 84″ (213.36 cm) have one divider rail located at door knob height [36″ (91.44 cm)]. Panels over 84″ high have two divider rails.

Fabric panels

Panels 60″ (152.40 cm) high and under have no divider rails. Panels 60″ to 78″ high have one centered divider rail. Panels 1⅛″ (2.86 cm) thick and 78″ to 84″ high have a divider rail centered 36″ from the floor.

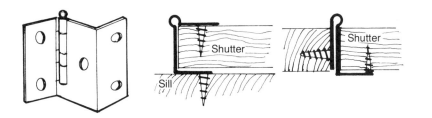

Shutter wrap-around hinge with loose pins

Louver selection chart (in.)

Louver size	Panel thickness	Protrusion*
1¼	¾	⅝
1¼	1⅛	9/16
1¼	1⅛	⅝
2½	¾	1
2½	1¼	¾
3½	1¼	1¼
4½	1¼	1¾

*Protrusion figures include ⅛″ (0.32 cm) for clearance.

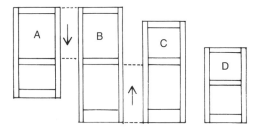

Shutter panels should be aligned from either the top or the bottom, and center rails should be aligned. A and B align from the top, B and C from the bottom, and C and D do not align.

SPECIFICATION CHECKLIST

Installation
1. _____ Number of openings
2. _____ Number of panels per opening
3. _____ Width of opening
4. _____ Height of opening
5. _____ Number of panels to fold: right or left
6. _____ Arch or fan tops (provide template)
7. _____ Mounting: within window frame or outside frame?

Design
1. _____ Panel thickness
2. _____ Louver blade size
3. _____ Special placement of divider rail
4. _____ Align panels: top or bottom?

5. _____ Panels: rabbeted or nonrabbeted?
6. _____ Track: top or bottom?
7. _____ Casters on bottom? (predrill required?)
8. _____ Hanging strips required?
   _____ Strip attached to panel
   _____ Predrilled, but not attached
   _____ Not predrilled or attached
9. _____ Hardware
   _____ Brass-plated hinges
   _____ Knobs
   _____ Magnetic catches
10. _____ Finish: paint, stain, or other?

BEYOND WINDOW FRAME INSTALLATION

1. Measure the height and width as shown on drawings. Measure at several points and record the largest dimension. On double-hung windows measure for top and bottom separately and show each measurement.

2. Standard panel trimming allowances should be considered. For panels with 1⅛" (2.86 cm) blades and the following thicknesses (in inches), trim the following amounts:

		Top	Side	Bottom
¾" thick	=	½	¼	1½
1⅛" thick	=	1	¼	3

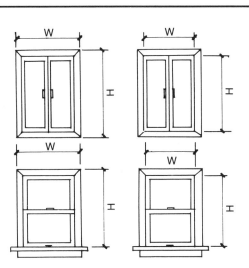

INSIDE WINDOW FRAME INSTALLATION

1. Measure the height and width as shown on the drawings.
2. If hanging strips are planned, indicate the type of installation as shown below.
3. Use the largest measurement, because shutters are made to this figure and custom trimmed at the job site.
4. Manufacturer usually provides calculated clearances for recommended hardware.
5. All hardware is usually mortised on these installations.

Note: Louver protrusion must be calculated on installations 1, 2, 4, 5, 6, 7.

See chart on page 236 for other factors affected by louver size.

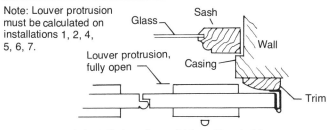

1. Installed on face of trim without strip

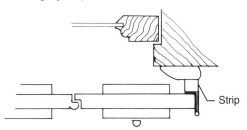

2. Hanging strip beside panels & on face

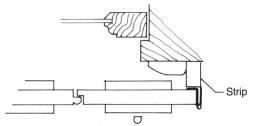

3. Hanging strip behind panel & on face of trim

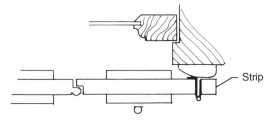

4. Strip on wall behind trim & panel

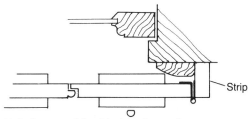

5. Strip on wall beside trim & panel

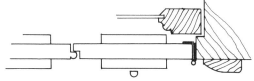

6. Panel installed on casing without strip

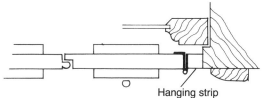

7. Hanging strip beside panel

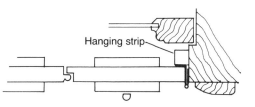

8. Hanging strip behind panel

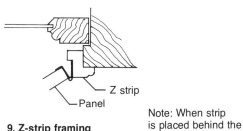

9. Z-strip framing

Note: When strip is placed behind the panel as in 3, 8, 9, 10, panel should be ¾" (1.91 cm) thick.

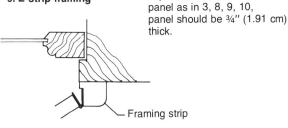

10. Framing for windows without trim

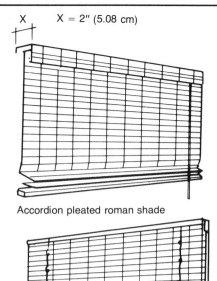

X   X = 2" (5.08 cm)

Accordion pleated roman shade

Spring roller

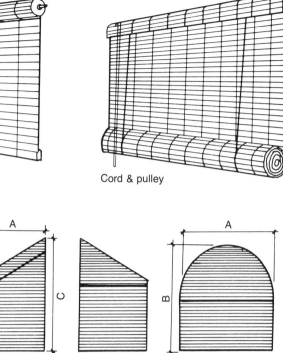

Cord & pulley

Back view

Note: Always specify in inches, *not* feet. Specify if cords are to be on left or right side.

Angle top, angled valance   Angle top, straight valance   Cathedral

Spring roller roll diameter★ (in.)

Drops to	Roll diameter	Drops to	Roll diameter
36	4	72	6
48	4½	84	6½
60	5¼	96	7½

*These dimensions are approximate and will be less for lighter material and slightly more for heavy material. To determine stacking area, add 4½" (11.43 cm) to roll diameter, which allows for headrail and hardware at top of shade. Adding a trimmed skirt will increase the stacking area by 4" (10.16 cm). Most shades wider than 60" (152.40 cm) use metal rollers adding ½" (1.27 cm) to diameters shown above.

Roman shade stacking area* (in.)

Drops to	Stacks to	Drops to	Stacks to
36	7½	96	15
48	9	108	16
60	11	120	17
72	13	132	18
84	14	144	19

*These stacking areas are approximate and will be less for lighter material and slightly more for heavy material. Adding a trimmed skirt will increase these stacking areas by 4".

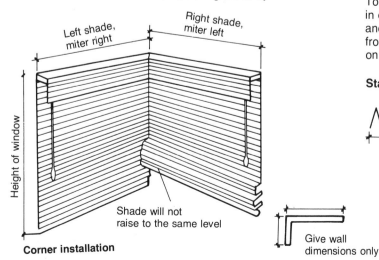

Left shade, miter right

Right shade, miter left

Height of window

Shade will not raise to the same level

Corner installation

Give wall dimensions only

Angle top with angled valance & straight valance

For use with slanted windows or for dramatic effect over regular windows, angled valances may be ordered for roman and cord and pulley shades. Two valance styles are available (see illustration): the angled valance is finished with gimp top and bottom; the straight valance is finished with gimp at the top only.

Technical tip: The shade can be drawn up only to where the pleated stack (or roll) meets the lowest point of the angle.

Measuring: Take measurements A (width), B (left-side height), and C (right-side height) as illustrated; the factory will determine the angle. Specify whether valance is to be "angle" or "straight"; provide all other specifications for a roman shade.

Technical tip: The shade can be drawn up only to the point where the pleated stack (or roll) meets the bottom of the valance.

Corner installation

To provide more complete opening coverage, shades installed in corners, bay windows, and alcoves may have a mitered valance. Shades are patterned in corner installations right and left from the miter and right and left from the center point of opening on bay windows.

Stacking area for 50% fullness (in.)

Widths to	Stacks to	Widths to	Stacks to
36	13	96	30
48	16	108	33½
60	19	120	37
72	23	132	41½
84	26	144	44

BUILT-IN INSTALLATIONS
WOOD FRAMING DETAILS

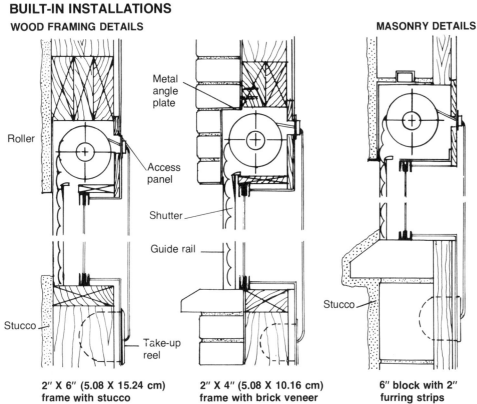

MASONRY DETAILS

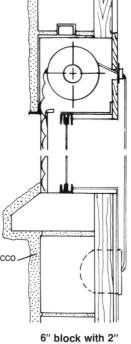

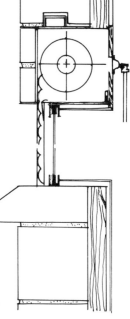

2″ X 6″ (5.08 X 15.24 cm) frame with stucco

2″ X 4″ (5.08 X 10.16 cm) frame with brick veneer

6″ block with 2″ furring strips

8″ (20.32 cm) block with ¾″ (1.91 cm) furring

Note: All the above installations are shown with manual operations.

Specification data: Energy conservation

Radiation transmittance
   White aluminum, closed = 0.02
   White PVC, closed = 0.01

Shading coefficient
   White PVC = 0.0436
   White aluminum = 0.0596

U-value
   Foam & aluminum (winter) = .51   R = 1.943
   PVC with air space (winter) = .45   R = 2.232

Noise reduction
   85% in closed position
   52% in vented position

Standard height & width

Maximum height					
Box size		Aluminum		PVC	
in.	cm	in.	cm	in.	cm
6	16.57	84	213.36	80	213.20
7	17.78	110	279.40	96	243.84
8	20.32	144	365.76	120	304.80

Maximum widths		
	in.	cm
Aluminum	144	365.76
Reinforced PVC	78	198.12
PVC only	60	152.40

Retrofit installation

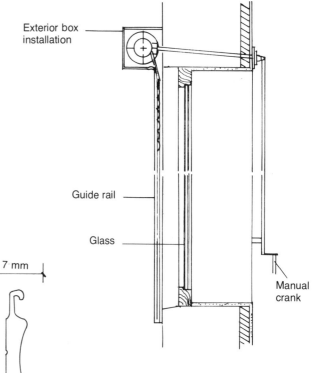

Notes: Shutters may be motorized or manually operated.

Extruded profiles made from PVC either have dead air space as insulation or are filled with polyurethane insulation.

7 mm

33 mm

Shutter

HARDWARE DETAILS

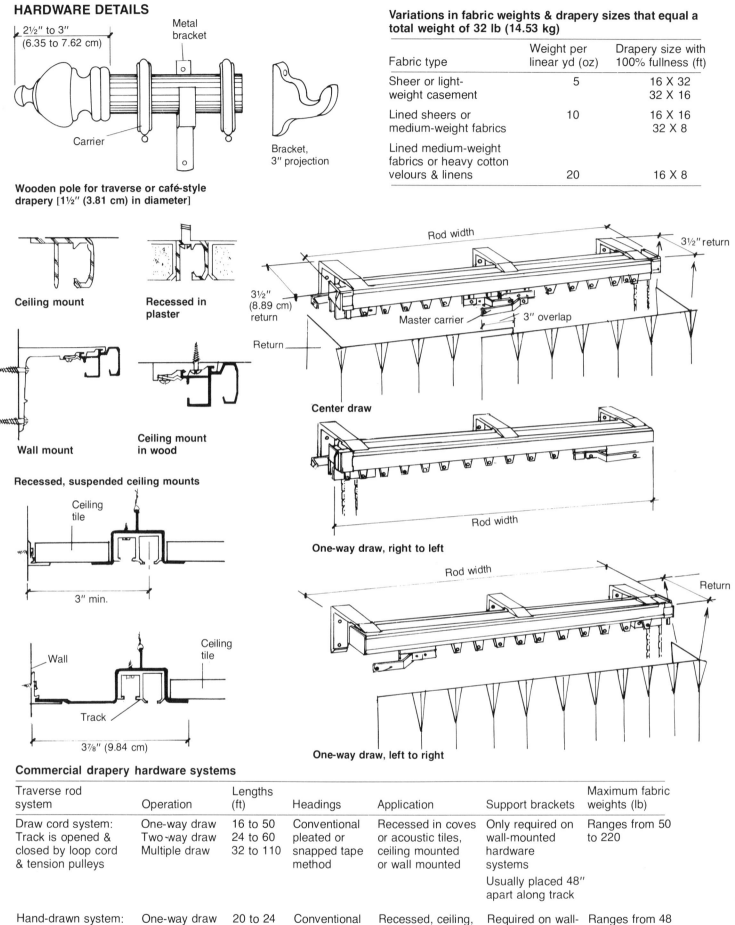

2½" to 3"
(6.35 to 7.62 cm)

Metal bracket

Carrier

Bracket, 3" projection

Wooden pole for traverse or café-style drapery [1½" (3.81 cm) in diameter]

Ceiling mount

Recessed in plaster

Wall mount

Ceiling mount in wood

Recessed, suspended ceiling mounts

Ceiling tile

3" min.

Wall

Ceiling tile

Track

3⅞" (9.84 cm)

Variations in fabric weights & drapery sizes that equal a total weight of 32 lb (14.53 kg)

Fabric type	Weight per linear yd (oz)	Drapery size with 100% fullness (ft)
Sheer or light-weight casement	5	16 X 32 32 X 16
Lined sheers or medium-weight fabrics	10	16 X 16 32 X 8
Lined medium-weight fabrics or heavy cotton velours & linens	20	16 X 8

Rod width

3½" return

3½" (8.89 cm) return

Return

Master carrier

3" overlap

Center draw

Rod width

One-way draw, right to left

Rod width

Return

One-way draw, left to right

Commercial drapery hardware systems

Traverse rod system	Operation	Lengths (ft)	Headings	Application	Support brackets	Maximum fabric weights (lb)
Draw cord system: Track is opened & closed by loop cord & tension pulleys	One-way draw Two-way draw Multiple draw	16 to 50 24 to 60 32 to 110	Conventional pleated or snapped tape method	Recessed in coves or acoustic tiles, ceiling mounted or wall mounted	Only required on wall-mounted hardware systems Usually placed 48" apart along track	Ranges from 50 to 220
Hand-drawn system: Track is opened & closed with hand batons that are attached to lead carrier; no pull cords used	One-way draw Two-way draw	20 to 24 Up to 48	Conventional pleated or snapped tape method	Recessed, ceiling, or wall installation	Required on wall-mounted systems	Ranges from 48 to 96

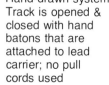

SNAP CARRIER PLACEMENT

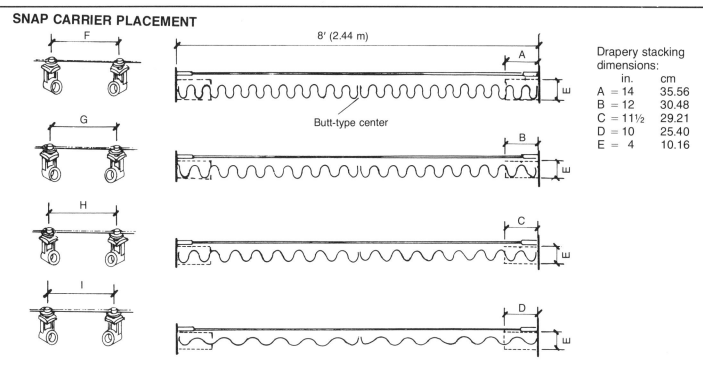

Butt-type center

Drapery stacking dimensions:

	in.	cm
A =	14	35.56
B =	12	30.48
C =	11½	29.21
D =	10	25.40
E =	4	10.16

Snap carriers provide a very pleasing appearance from both the interior and the exterior of the building. The snap tape is suspended below the track to prevent sagging. The advantages are that little stacking space is required and there is no flat area in the center of the drapery. (Compare with standard traverse rod.) The snap carriers shown above on the left can be spaced to vary the fullness and stack-back widths. When using the 4¼″ (10.80 cm) snap tape, the drapery fullness is shown in the chart to the right.

Fullness determined by carrier spacing

Carrier spacing		Percentage of fullness
in.	cm	
F = 1⅞	4.76	120
G = 2⅛	5.39	100
H = 2⅜	6.03	80
I = 2⅝	6.67	60

Calculate drapery rod placement to allow drapery to stack clear of the glass area:

1. Add 12″ (30.48 cm) to the total width of the window.
   Example: 100″ + 12 = 112″

2. Divide this total by 6.
   112″ ÷ 6 = 18⅔″
   Round off to 19″.

3. Extend drapery bracket placement 19″ on each side of the window, and the fully opened drapery will clear the glass area.

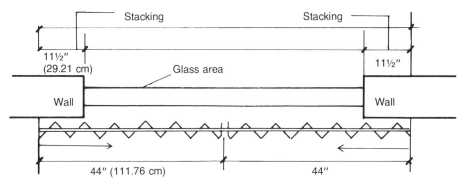

Center draw drapery with stacking on each side

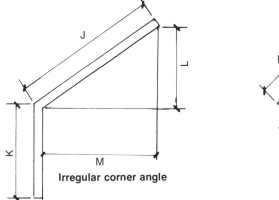

Irregular corner angle

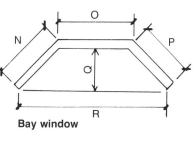

Bay window

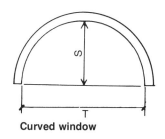

Curved window

Note: Letters designate dimensions that must be given to drapery fabricator.

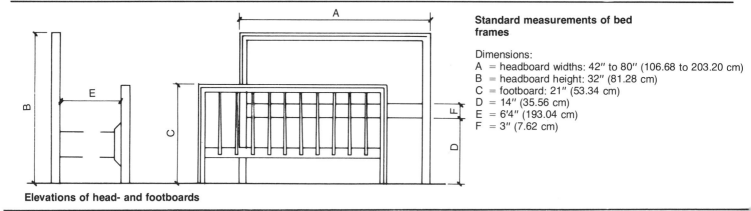

Standard measurements of bed frames

Dimensions:
A = headboard widths: 42" to 80" (106.68 to 203.20 cm)
B = headboard height: 32" (81.28 cm)
C = footboard: 21" (53.34 cm)
D = 14" (35.56 cm)
E = 6'4" (193.04 cm)
F = 3" (7.62 cm)

Elevations of head- and footboards

SPACE STANDARDS FOR BEDROOM CONVENIENCE & MAINTENANCE

Dimensions (not to scale):
G = 15'8" (4.77 m)
H = 11'2" (3.60 m)
I = 9'11" to 10'4"
      (3.01 to 3.14 m)

J = cleaning space: 48" (121.92 cm)
K = 42" (106.68 cm)
L = space to use dresser: 40" (101.60 cm)
M = 8'2" (2.48 m)

N = 6'10" (2.07 m)
O = 36" (91.44 cm)
P = bed-making space: 22" (55.88 cm)
Q = opening space: 16" (40.64 cm)

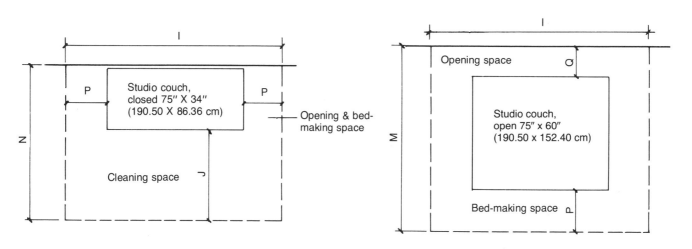

Studio couch, closed 75" X 34" (190.50 X 86.36 cm)

Opening & bed-making space

Cleaning space

Studio couch, open 75" x 60" (190.50 x 152.40 cm)

Opening space

Bed-making space

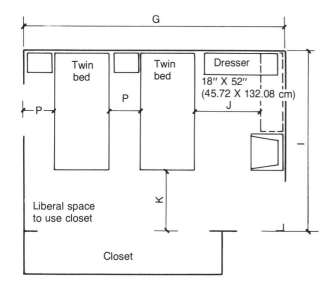

Twin bed

Twin bed

Dresser 18" X 52" (45.72 X 132.08 cm)

Liberal space to use closet

Closet

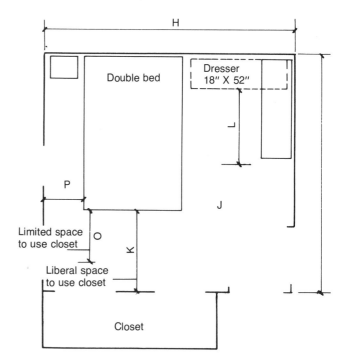

Double bed

Dresser 18" X 52"

Limited space to use closet

Liberal space to use closet

Closet

Note: In these drawings "limited space" refers to minimum space needed to remove clothes from the closet. "Liberal space" allows a person room to remove and put on clothing.

TYPES OF CONVERTIBLE BEDDING

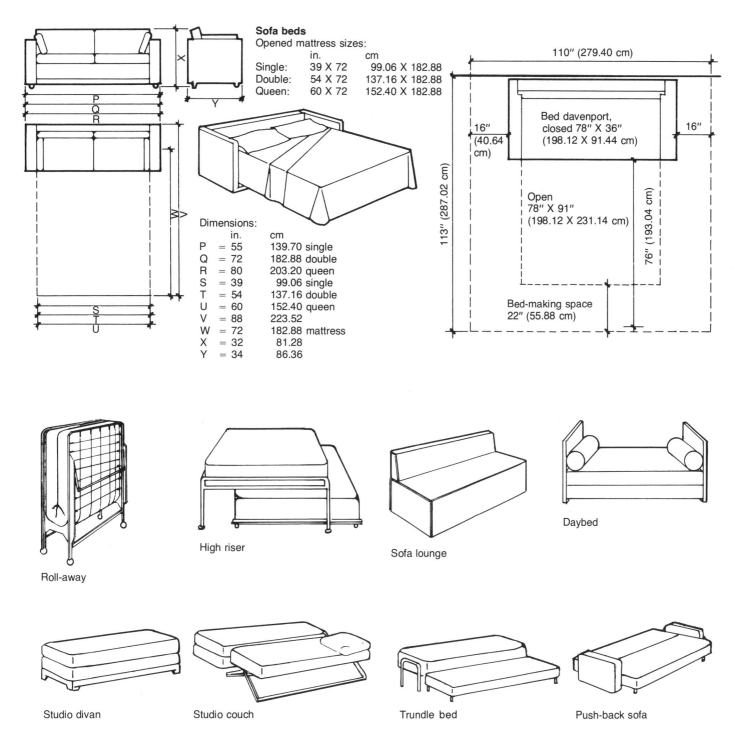

Sofa beds
Opened mattress sizes:

	in.	cm
Single:	39 X 72	99.06 X 182.88
Double:	54 X 72	137.16 X 182.88
Queen:	60 X 72	152.40 X 182.88

Dimensions:

		in.	cm	
P	=	55	139.70	single
Q	=	72	182.88	double
R	=	80	203.20	queen
S	=	39	99.06	single
T	=	54	137.16	double
U	=	60	152.40	queen
V	=	88	223.52	
W	=	72	182.88	mattress
X	=	32	81.28	
Y	=	34	86.36	

110" (279.40 cm)

Bed davenport, closed 78" X 36" (198.12 X 91.44 cm)

16" (40.64 cm)

16"

113" (287.02 cm)

Open 78" X 91" (198.12 X 231.14 cm)

76" (193.04 cm)

Bed-making space 22" (55.88 cm)

Roll-away

High riser

Sofa lounge

Daybed

Studio divan

Studio couch

Trundle bed

Push-back sofa

Selected types of convertible bedding as defined in the Federal Standard for Flammability of Mattresses and Mattress pads (FF 4-72):

Roll-away: Portable bed with mattress and frame that folds in half for compact storage.

High riser: One frame of seating height has a mattress without a backrest. Another frame slides out below it with an equal-size mattress and rises to form a double bed or two single beds.

Studio couch: Upholstered seating section on an upholstered foundation may convert to twin beds.

Trundle bed: A low bed rolls under a larger bed and springs up to form a double bed or two single beds as in a high riser.

Push-back sofa: When back is pushed, it lowers to form portion of bed.

WATER BED COMPONENTS

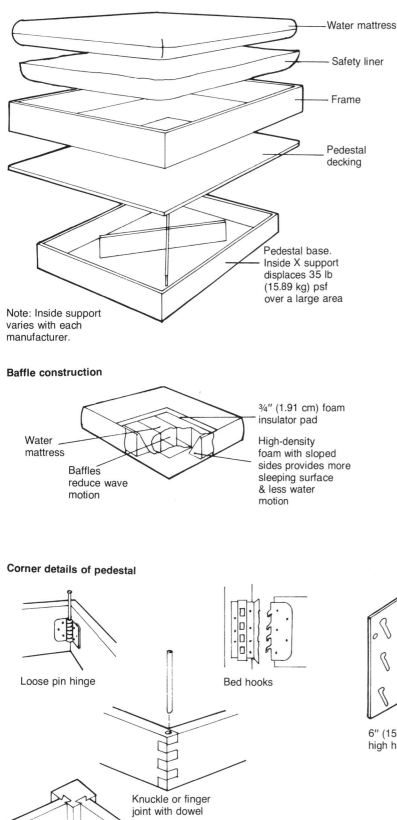

Water mattress

Safety liner

Frame

Pedestal decking

Pedestal base. Inside X support displaces 35 lb (15.89 kg) psf over a large area

Note: Inside support varies with each manufacturer.

Baffle construction

¾″ (1.91 cm) foam insulator pad

High-density foam with sloped sides provides more sleeping surface & less water motion

Water mattress

Baffles reduce wave motion

Lap seam

Butt seam

Seams
Butt and lap seams are welded together by a microwave method that joins vinyl.
1. **Butt seams:** Two pieces of vinyl are cut exactly the same size and placed together with the valve in one corner and then welded. This is the least expensive method of production.
2. **Lap seams:** Two pieces of vinyl are cut exactly the same size and one overlaps the other. The valve is welded into the corner. This method is more expensive and complex to produce.

Heaters
Recommended for keeping the water 80° F. Heater uses about 3 kw per day.

Sizes & weights*

Size	Standard dimensions (in.)	All-water mattress	
		Gallons	Weight (lb)
King	72 X 84	235	2028
Queen	60 X 84	196	1690
Double	54 X 84	176	1520
Single	48 X 84	152	1301
Twin	39 X 84	128	1101
Round	96 dia.	282	2428

*Caution: Water beds and all flotation furnishings must be carefully placed in multistoried buildings because of their weight.

Corner details of pedestal

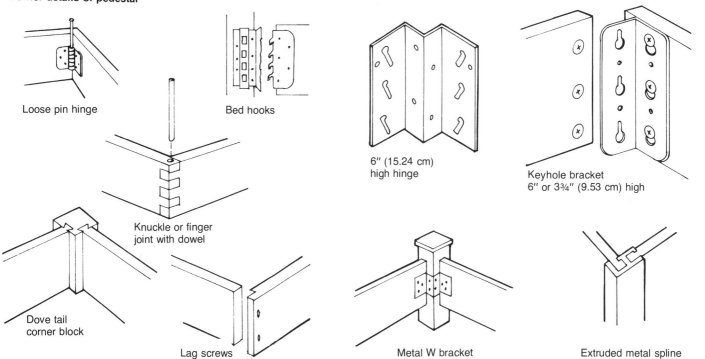

Loose pin hinge

Bed hooks

6″ (15.24 cm) high hinge

Keyhole bracket 6″ or 3¾″ (9.53 cm) high

Knuckle or finger joint with dowel

Dove tail corner block

Lag screws

Metal W bracket

Extruded metal spline

WALL BEDS

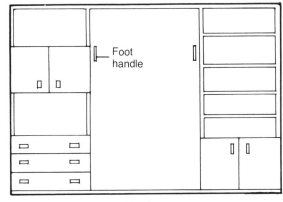

Elevation of closed wall bed

Finished dimensions of recessed openings:

		Single		Double		Queen	
		in.	cm	in.	cm	in.	cm
A	= depth	18 to 24	45.72 to 60.96	24		24	
B	= width	41	104.14	56	142.24	63	160.02
C	= height	88¾	225.43	88	223.52	92½	252.73
D	= opened bed	78	198.12	78	198.12	84	213.36
	length	30	76.20	30		30	
E	= side cabinet						

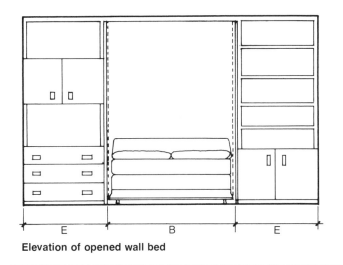

Elevation of opened wall bed

Foot handle [elevates bed 1½″ (3.81 cm) off floor]

Elevation and section of bed closed

MATTRESS PEDESTALS

Note: Specify for hotel use where maintenance is critical.

Headboard & box base
Base = 7½″ (19.05 cm) high finished on three sides

Typical widths:

ft	in.			in.	cm
3	3	twin	=	29½ to 31½	74.93 to 80.01
4	6	double	=	44½ to 47	113.03 to 119.38
5	0	queen	=	47 to 51½	119.38 to 130.81
6	6	king	=	67½ to 71	171.45 to 180.34

All boxes 71″ (180.34 cm) long

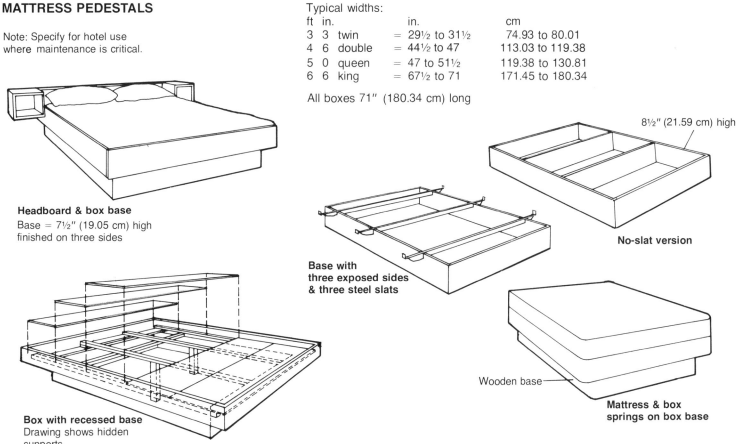

8½″ (21.59 cm) high

No-slat version

Base with three exposed sides & three steel slats

Wooden base

Mattress & box springs on box base

Box with recessed base
Drawing shows hidden supports

Fabric width	36" (yd + repeats†)	48" (yd + repeats†)	54" (yd + repeats†)
Spreads			
Twin	11¾ + 2	11¾ + 2	8 + 1
Full	15¾ + 3	11¾ + 2	11¾ + 2
Queen	16¼ + 3	12¼ + 2	12¼ + 2
King	16¾ + 3	12¾ + 2	12¾ + 2
Dual twin	16 + 3	16 + 3	12 + 2
Dual king	16¼ + 3	16¼ + 3	12¼ + 2
Coverlets			
Twin	11 + 2	7½ + 1	7½ + 1
Full	11 + 2	7½ + 1	7½ + 1
Queen	11½ + 2	11½ + 2	7½ + 1
King	15¾ + 3	11¾ + 2	11¾ + 2
Dual twin	15 + 3	11 + 2	11 + 2
Dual king	15¼ + 3	11½ + 2	11½ + 2
Comforters: reversible	For each side	For each side	For each side
Twin	9 + 2	6 + 1	6 + 1
Full	9 + 2	6 + 1	6 + 1
Queen	9½ + 2	9½ + 2	6½ + 1
King	13¼ + 3	10 + 2	10 + 2
Dual twin	12 + 3	9 + 2	9 + 2
Dual king	12¾ + 3	9½ + 2	9½ + 2
Dust ruffles: shirred			
Twin	7	5¼	4¾
Full	7½	6¼	5¼
Queen	8	6½	5¾
King	9	7¼	6¼
Dual twin	9	7	6¼
Dual king	9½	7½	6¾
Dust ruffles: box pleated			
Twin	8¾	6¾	6
Full	9	7	6½
Queen	10	7½	7
King	10¾	8	7½
Dual twin	10¾	8	7½
Dual king	11	8½	8
Dust ruffles: tailored	Whichever is greater:	Whichever is greater:	Whichever is greater:
Twin	4 or 8	3¼ or 7	3 or 6
Full	4 or 8	3¼ or 7	3 or 6
Queen	4¾ or 10	3½ or 7	3 or 6
King	5 or 10	3¾ or 8	3¾ or 7
Dual twin	5 or 10	3¾ or 8	3¾ or 7
Dual king	5½ or 10	3¾ or 8	3¾ or 7
Bolsters: finished sizes (in.)			
30	1½	1½	1
36	1½	1½	1
39	2	1½	1
60	2	2	2
72	2½	2	2

*One yard is *linear* 36".
†Repeat is defined on page 253.

Standard drops‡(in.)

Bedspreads	21
Comforters & coverlets	12
Dust ruffles (box pleated)	14
Fitted caps§	10

‡Drop is the distance from the top of the mattress to the floor.
§Fitted caps fit around mattress the same way fitted sheets function.

SIZES OF MATTRESSES & COMFORTERS

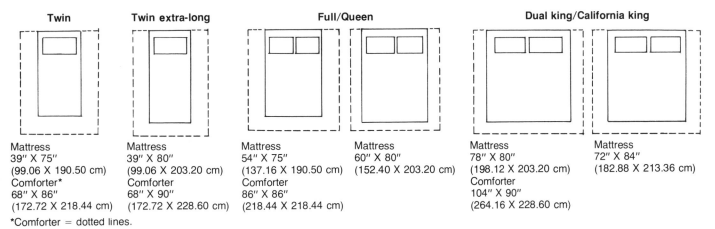

Twin
Mattress
39″ X 75″
(99.06 X 190.50 cm)
Comforter*
68″ X 86″
(172.72 X 218.44 cm)

Twin extra-long
Mattress
39″ X 80″
(99.06 X 203.20 cm)
Comforter
68″ X 90″
(172.72 X 228.60 cm)

Full/Queen
Mattress
54″ X 75″
(137.16 X 190.50 cm)
Comforter
86″ X 86″
(218.44 X 218.44 cm)

Mattress
60″ X 80″
(152.40 X 203.20 cm)

Dual king/California king
Mattress
78″ X 80″
(198.12 X 203.20 cm)
Comforter
104″ X 90″
(264.16 X 228.60 cm)

Mattress
72″ X 84″
(182.88 X 213.36 cm)

*Comforter = dotted lines.

Specification checklist for mattresses
1. Surface measurements _____
2. Mattress surface
   deep-quilted _____
   multi-needle _____
   quilt surface _____
   smooth _____
   tufted _____
3. Ticking
   method of attachment
      topper pad _____
      secondary cushioning _____
      crown* _____
4. Primary insulator (provide the following information)
   material _____
   method of attachment _____
   measurement (length & width) _____
   weight _____
5. Springs
   wire guage _____
   border wire _____
   full _____
   end _____
   gauge _____
   method of joining ends _____
6. Edge support
   style _____
   side _____
   end _____
   corners _____
7. Frame
   material _____
   slats (width & thickness) _____
   side rails (width & thickness) _____
   end rails (width & thickness) _____
   center rails (width & thickness) _____

*See page 250 for definition of crown.

Specification checklist for boxsprings
1. Surface measurements _____
2. Ticking (provide the following information)
   material _____
   thickness _____
   measurement (length & width) _____
   method of attachment
      primary cushioning _____
      secondary cushioning _____
      primary insulator _____
      secondary insulator _____
3. Springs
   unit type _____
   coil type _____
   border wire _____
      gauge _____
   style _____
   method of joining ends _____
   edge support _____
   side _____
   end _____
   corner _____
4. Foamcore
   material _____
   compression rating (Cornell testing procedure) _____
   dimensions _____

Sizes for conventional mattresses
(dimensions: width & length)

Conventional bedding	Finished mattress [± ½″ (1.27 cm)]				Inner unit or core											
					Innerspring unit construction for mattress [± ¼″ (0.68 cm)]				Molded foamcore for mattress				Urethane core for mattress (+ ½″-0)			
	W		L		W		L		W		L		W		L	
	in.	cm	in.	cm	in.	cm	in.	cm	in.	cm	in.	cm	in.	cm	in.	cm
Twin or bunk	38	96.52	74	189.96	36	91.44	73	185.42	38	96.52	76	193.04	38	96.52	75	190.50
Extra long twin	39	99.06	80	203.20	36	91.44	78	198.12	38	96.52	81	205.74	38	96.52	80	203.20
Double	53	134.62	74	189.96	51	129.54	73	185.42	53	134.62	76	193.04	53	134.62	75	190.50
Extra long double	53	134.62	80	203.20	51	129.54	78	198.12	53	134.62	81	205.74	53	134.62	80	203.20
Queen	60	151.20	79	200.66	58	147.32	78	198.12	60	152.40	81	205.74	60	152.40	80	203.20
Dual king	78	198.12	80	203.20	74	187.96	78	198.12	76	193.04	81	205.74	76	193.04	80	203.20
California king	72	182.88	84	213.36	70	177.80	82	208.28	72	182.88	85	215.90	72	182.88	84	213.36

Carpet casters

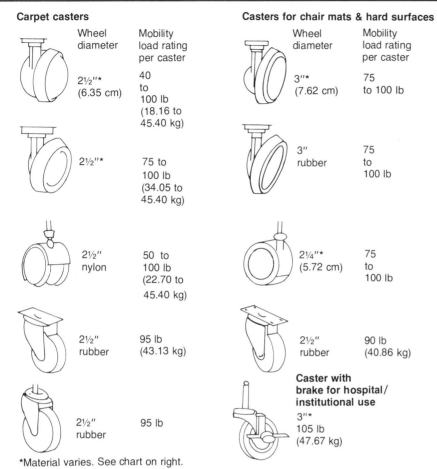

Wheel diameter	Mobility load rating per caster
2½"* (6.35 cm)	40 to 100 lb (18.16 to 45.40 kg)
2½"*	75 to 100 lb (34.05 to 45.40 kg)
2½" nylon	50 to 100 lb (22.70 to 45.40 kg)
2½" rubber	95 lb (43.13 kg)
2½" rubber	95 lb

*Material varies. See chart on right.

Casters for chair mats & hard surfaces

Wheel diameter	Mobility load rating per caster
3"* (7.62 cm)	75 to 100 lb
3" rubber	75 to 100 lb
2¼"* (5.72 cm)	75 to 100 lb
2½" rubber	90 lb (40.86 kg)

Caster with brake for hospital/institutional use

3"*
105 lb (47.67 kg)

Notes: Casters are not recommended for use on rubber or foam-backed carpeting. Hospital casters and casters used around sensitive computers should have conductive treads. Carbon coatings are also used to control static electricity.

SPECIFICATION CRITERIA

Caster size
Compare the caster size to the furniture size.

Caster mobility load rating
The mobility load rating shown for each caster indicates the load that can be moved easily. A large diameter caster allows greater mobility.

Caster selection
Carpet construction and installation method must be considered in caster selection.
1. Direct glue down installation of a low level loop construction requires casters in the moderate, heavy, and severe traffic classes.
2. Cut pile that is direct glue down will require chair pads in heavy and severe traffic class areas.
3. Tackless strip carpet installation with pad (level loop and cut pile) requires chair pads.

Caster material selection chart

Floor surfaces	Wheel material
Carpet	Metal, phenolic styrene, acetal, nylon, plastic, hard rubber
Wood, tile, chair pads, terrazzo	Soft rubber, urethane
Concrete	Semisteel, rubber, urethane

Square plate   Grip neck   Grip neck

Casegood casters

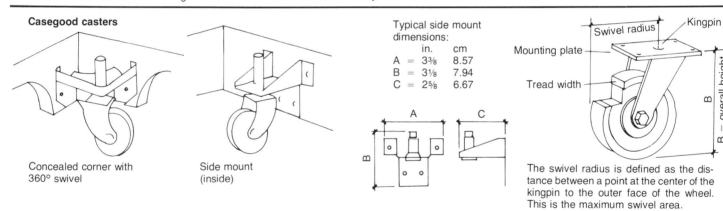

Concealed corner with 360° swivel

Side mount (inside)

Typical side mount dimensions:

	in.	cm
A =	3⅜	8.57
B =	3⅛	7.94
C =	2⅝	6.67

Swivel radius   Kingpin

Mounting plate

Tread width

B = overall height

The swivel radius is defined as the distance between a point at the center of the kingpin to the outer face of the wheel. This is the maximum swivel area.

Caster traffic frequency
Every installation is subject to different caster traffic frequencies. These can be categorized into three basic classes:

Moderate (M)	Slight to moderate caster abrasion.
Heavy (H)	Heavy abrasion in areas subjected to frequent caster movement consistently following the same directional pattern.
Severe (S)	Severe abrasion in areas subjected to exceptionally high levels of frequent and concentrated caster movement following the same directional pattern.

For example, listed here are some typical commercial and institutional installations and the caster traffic class suggested for each.

Apartments, hotels, & motels	Caster traffic class
Lobby: lounge furniture	M
Guest rooms: chairs/beds	M
Office area: secretarial chairs	S
Dining room: chairs	H
Lounge (public areas): chairs	S
Meeting rooms: chairs	H
Banks	
Executive office	H
Reception (waiting)	M
Bank teller chairs	S
General equipment areas	H
Health care facilities*	
Executive offices	H
Patient rooms	M
Lounge	H
Nurse stations	S
Corridor (equipment)	H
Lobby	M

	Caster traffic class
Office buildings	
Executive	H
Clerical	S
Cafeteria	H
Lobby	M
Board room	H
Restaurants	
Dining room	H
Lounge (bar)	S
Schools & colleges	
Executive offices	H
Administration	H
Class room	S
Dormitory	H
Cafeteria	S
Library	H

*See Chapter 21 for health care facilities.

SWIVEL ARM CHAIR

Construction details shown here are typical of office chairs

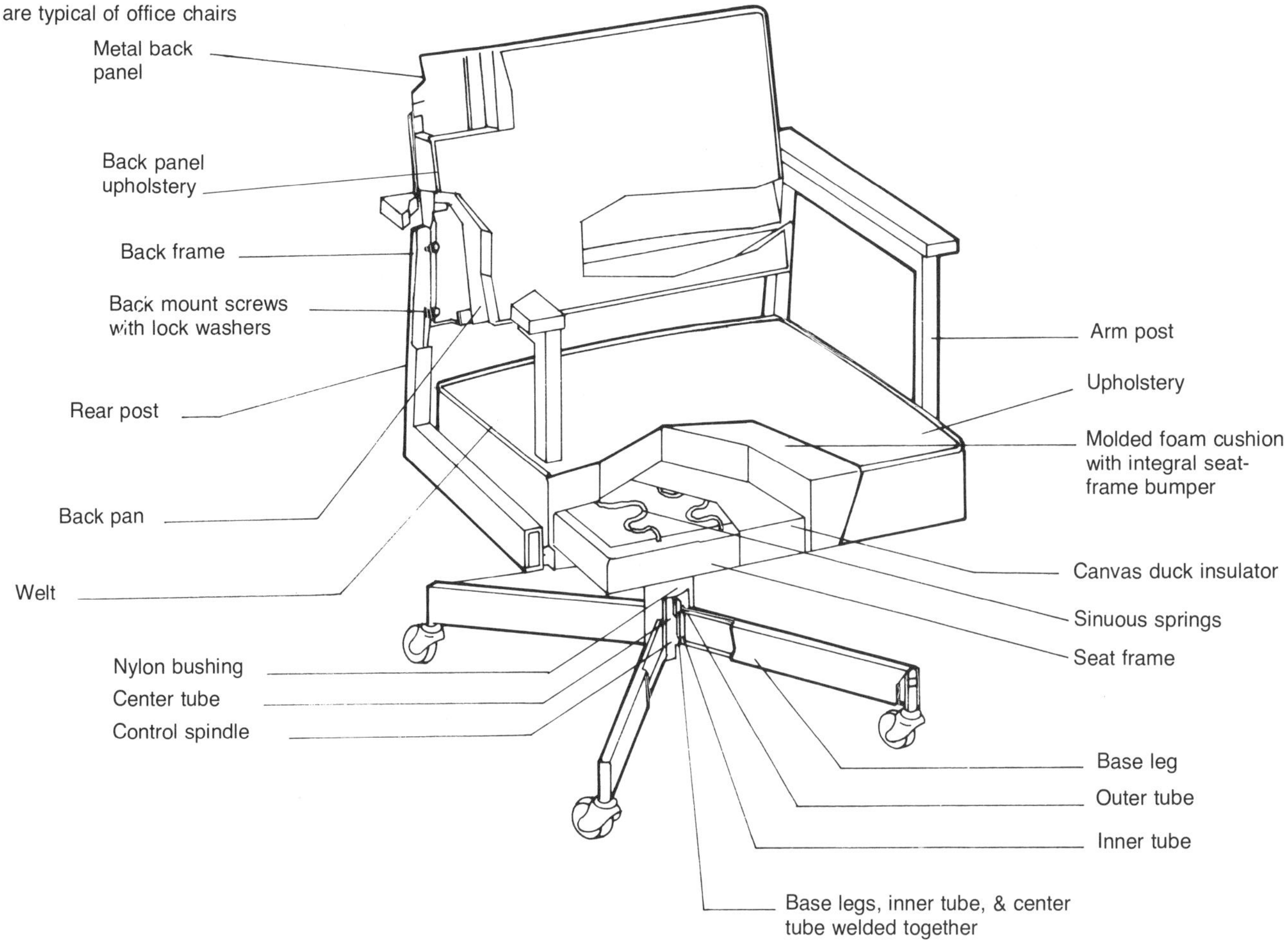

Metal back panel

Back panel upholstery

Back frame

Back mount screws with lock washers

Rear post

Back pan

Welt

Nylon bushing
Center tube
Control spindle

Arm post

Upholstery

Molded foam cushion with integral seat-frame bumper

Canvas duck insulator

Sinuous springs

Seat frame

Base leg

Outer tube

Inner tube

Base legs, inner tube, & center tube welded together

POSTURE CHAIR

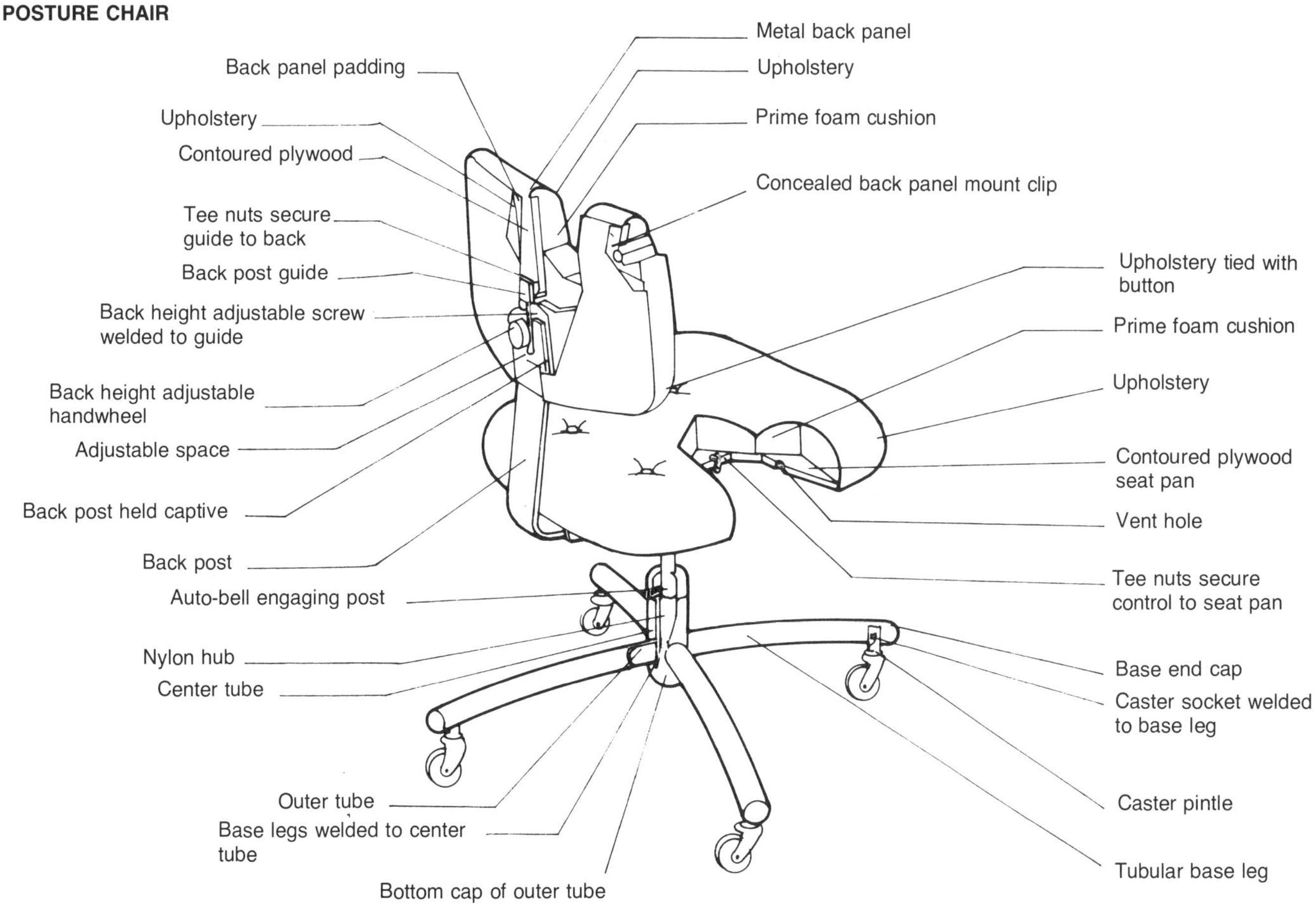

Back panel padding

Upholstery

Contoured plywood

Tee nuts secure guide to back

Back post guide

Back height adjustable screw welded to guide

Back height adjustable handwheel

Adjustable space

Back post held captive

Back post

Auto-bell engaging post

Nylon hub

Center tube

Metal back panel

Upholstery

Prime foam cushion

Concealed back panel mount clip

Upholstery tied with button

Prime foam cushion

Upholstery

Contoured plywood seat pan

Vent hole

Tee nuts secure control to seat pan

Base end cap

Caster socket welded to base leg

Caster pintle

Tubular base leg

Outer tube

Base legs welded to center tube

Bottom cap of outer tube

FRAME REQUIREMENTS

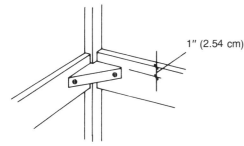

1″ (2.54 cm)

When legs do not brace rail corners, corner blocks should be placed as shown

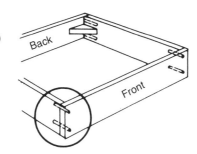

Back

Front

Dowels placed in front & back rails near the top & bottom prevent rails from turning

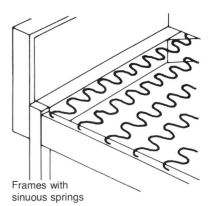

Frames with sinuous springs

1. Concave stretchers

2. Flat stretcher supports

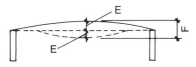

3. Deflection range

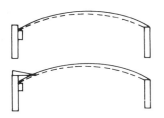

4 & 5. Sinuous springs on rails

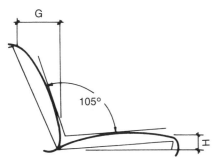

105°

6. Frame pitch

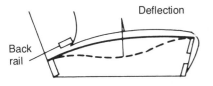

Deflection

Back rail

7. Frame pitch

Dimensions:

	in.	cm
A =	5	12.70
B =	3½	8.89
C =	3	7.62
D =	6	15.24
E =	2	5.08
F =	4	10.16
G =	6 to 8	20.32
H =	2 to 4	

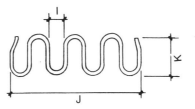

Typical sinuous spring dimensions:

	in.	cm
I =	¾ to ⅞	1.91 to 2.22
J =	1⅞	4.76
K =	± ⅛ to 20	0.32 to 50.80
	length tolerance	

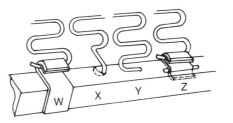

Attachment methods

W = surface-mounted clip
X = clip inserted in frame
Y = clip inserted in frame
Z = clip inserted in frame

SPECIFICATION INFORMATION

Frame requirements

In order to withstand the live pull of the sinuous springs, front and rear rails should extend over the ends of the side rails when possible to prevent separation of joints.

The longer frames of sofas and love seats should have two equally spaced stretchers. These stretchers should be edge-sawed with at least a 3″ (7.62 cm) concave dip (1). A stretcher may also be a flat board braced with corner blocks at front and rear. The blocks should have a 6″ (15.24 cm) base (2). These blocks should also be securely doweled and glued.

Pitch of frame

It is recommended that the rear rail be placed lower than the front rail to provide more comfort. Increased pitch should be accompanied with a higher crown that provides deeper spring action and promotes more restful posture. When the pitch of the seat is increased, the back should be angled proportionately (6 & 7).

Crowns

Crowning may be required on tight seats, that is, those without loose cushions. Crowning or stuffing the center higher than the edge areas prevents tightly stretched fabrics from pressing all the stuffing toward the side rail. Standard spring specifications provide a crown of 1¼″ to 2″ (3.18 to 5.08 cm) depending on the gauge and length of the spring. The amount of crown above the rails will permit approximately the same amount of deflection below the rails when under load and properly cross tied. Total deflection will be about double the amount of the crown. Each ½″ (1.27 cm) increase or decrease in spring length will increase or decrease crowning approximately ¼″ (0.64 cm). The length of back springs can be longer than the inside dimension between the rails because back springs support body weight and can be crowned up to 3½″ (8.89 cm) when properly cross-tied.

Caution

Any significant deviation from these guidelines can create problems. For example, crowns exceeding 2″ may produce "pocketing," which is the industry term for sagging (as shown in drawing 3).

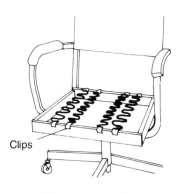

Clips

Springs clipped to frame

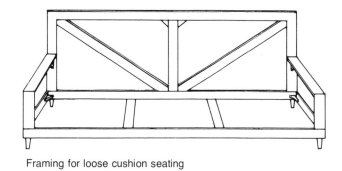

Framing for loose cushion seating

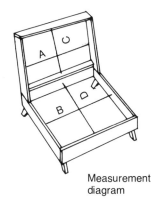

Measurement diagram

Sinuous springs are installed front to rear on seats and top to bottom on backs. These springs are spaced on the furniture frame by first positioning the two outside strands. Spacing is calculated from center to center of each clip. To determine the required gauge, length, number of springs, and spacing, measure the inside furniture rail openings (dimensions A–D, shown on the drawing above). The table below left gives standard spring use. Crown height can be determined by using the two tables on the right.

Standard spring application

Distance between arms along front seat rail (in.)	Number of strands	Center-to-center spacing of clips (in.)	Center spacing of two outside clips from inside arm posts (in.)	Size of connecting links (in.)
21 chair	5	4¼	2	2⅝
22 chair	5	4½	2	2⅞
23 chair	5	4¾	2	3⅛
24 chair	5	5	2	3⅜
25 chair	6	4¼	1⅞	2⅝
40 sectional	9	4½	2	2⅞
50 love seat	11	4½	2½	2⅞
52 love seat	11	4¾	2¼	3⅛
58 sofa	12	5	1½	3⅜
59 sofa	12	5	2	3⅜
60 sofa	13	4¾	1½	3⅛
61 sofa	13	4¾	2	3⅛
62 sofa	13	4¾	2½	3⅛
63 sofa	14	4½	2¼	2⅞
64 sofa	14	4½	2¾	2⅞
65 sofa	14	4¾	1⅝	3⅛
66 sofa	14	4¾	2⅛	3⅛

Determining seat crowns

Inside-to-inside measure	Seats crowns		
I-I rails (in.)	Spring length (in.)	Recommended gauge	Crown height (in.)
12	11¾	11	1¼
13	12¾	10½	1¼
14	13¾	10	1⅜
15	14¾	10	1½
16	15¾	10	1⅝
17	16¾	9½	1⅝
18	17¾	9	1¾
19	18¾	9	1¾
20	19¾	9	1⅞
21	20¾	9	1⅞
22	21¾	8½	1⅞
23	22¾	8½	2
24	23¾	8½	2
25	24¾	8	2
26	25¾	8	2
27	26¾	8	2

Determining back crowns

Inside-to-inside-measure	Back crowns		
I-I rails (in.)	Spring length (in.)	Recommended gauge	Crown height (in.)
16	16	12 or 13	1½
17	17	12 or 13	1⅝
18	18¼	12 or 13	1¾
19	19¼	12	1⅞
20	20¼	12	2
21	21¼	12	2
22	22¼	12	2
23	23½	11½ or 12	2¼
24	24½	11½	2¼
25	25½	11	2½
26	26½	11	2½

The following information must be supplied on upholstery orders to manufacturers and upholstery workshops:

1. A small sample of the fabric should be stapled to the order. This is also necessary when supplying the client's own material (COM) with the order.

2. Indicate which side of the fabric is to be exposed on the furniture.

3. Specify the fabric supplier's name, the fabric color, and its stock number as well as a description of the fabric.

Yardage requirements shown in most manufacturers' catalogs are usually based on 54" (137.16 cm) wide fabric without a pattern or a nap. The following tables provide information on the quantity of additional fabric required for fabrics less than 54" wide or fabrics that have a pattern repeat.

4. If the fabric is a stripe or pattern, specify vertical or horizontal upholstery application. If desired, fabric may be railroaded (selvaged used parallel to the floor as illustrated on page 253).

Fabric width (less than 54")		Additional fabric (%)
in.	cm	
50	127.00	10
48	121.92	15
45	114.30	20
36	91.44	50

Fabric repeat (54" wide)		Additional fabric* (%)
in.	cm	
8 to 14	20.32 to 35.56	10
15 to 19	38.10 to 48.26	15
20 to 27	50.80 to 68.58	20
28 to 36	71.12 to 91.44	25

*Fabric 54" wide.

Specification of client's own material requires that the designer increase the standard COM fabric order by the following quantities:

	Fabric widths (%)				
	54"	53–48"	47–42"	41–36"	35–30"
Railroadable up to 13" repeat	0	10	25	45	75
Not railroadable up to 13" repeat	35	45	60	80	110
Railroadable 14" to 27" repeat	10	20	35	55	85
Not railroadable 14" to 27" repeat	45	55	70	90	120
Railroadable 28" to 36" repeat	25	35	50	70	100
Not railroadable 28" to 36" repeat	55	65	80	100	130
Railroadable 37" to 48" repeat	40	50	65	85	115
Not railroadable 37" to 48" repeat	65	75	90	110	140

Notes: Fabrics with repeats moving in both directions (see page 253) will require 20 percent increase in quantity.

If a furniture platform or deck area is to be covered in COM, add 1¼ yd (114.30 cm) for chairs, 2¼ yd (205.74 cm) for sofa or love seat up to 60" (152.40 cm) wide, and 3⅞ yd (354.33 cm) for sofa over 60" (152.40 cm) wide.

LEATHER & SUEDE

The COM requirements for leather are equal to 18 sq ft (1.67 m²) per COM yard required. Example: If a style requires 10 yd (9.14 m) COM, 180 sq ft (16.72 m²) of leather will be required. Therefore, multiply the COM yardage specified for any item by 18 sq ft. If suede is required, increase leather square footage by 10 percent.

Yardage conversion chart

Fabric width	32"	35"–36"	39"	41"	44"–45"	50"	52"–54"	58"–60"
Yardage	1⅞	1¾	1½	1½	1⅜	1¼	1⅛	1
	2¼	2	1¾	1¾	1⅝	1½	1⅜	1¼
	2½	2¼	2	2	1¾	1⅝	1½	1⅜
	2¾	2½	2¼	2¼	2⅛	1¾	1¾	1⅝
	3⅛	2⅞	2½	2½	2¼	2	1⅞	1¾
	3⅜	3⅛	2¾	2¾	2½	2¼	2	1⅞
	3¾	3⅜	3	2⅞	2¾	2⅜	2¼	2
	4	3¾	3¼	3⅛	2⅞	2⅝	2⅜	2¼
	4⅜	4¼	3½	3⅜	3⅛	2¾	2⅝	2⅜
	4⅝	4½	3¾	3⅝	3	3	2¾	2⅝
	5	4¾	4	3⅞	3⅝	3¼	2⅞	2¾
	5¼	5	4¼	4⅛	3⅞	3⅜	3⅛	2⅞

Specification guidelines

Fabric yardage listed on pages 254–255 may vary depending on fabric width, pattern repeat size, and type of pattern.

Yardage fraction chart

Yardage	in.	cm	Yardage	in.	cm
⁹⁄₁₆	2¼	5.72	½	18	45.72
⅛	4½	11.43	⅝	22½	57.15
¼	9	22.86	⅔	24	60.96
⅓	12	30.48	¾	27	68.58
⅜	13½	34.29	⅞	31½	80.01

Example of chart usage:
If upholstery yardage requirements are listed as three yards of 54" fabric and the customer's material (COM) is 60" wide, the yardage requirement would be reduced to 1⅞ yards.

Pattern types

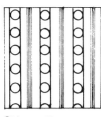

Stripe pattern

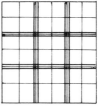

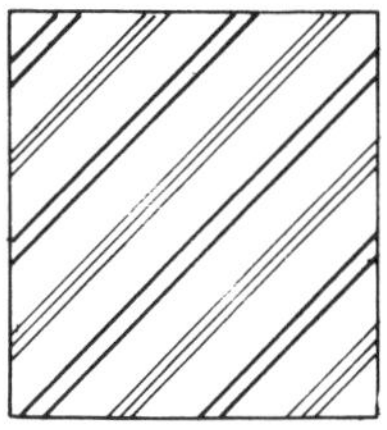

Diagonal stripe

Plaid pattern*

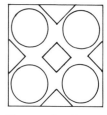

Diagonal plaid

Diaper pattern*

*Repeat moves in both directions. See other examples of diaper patterns on page 18.

Set match pattern

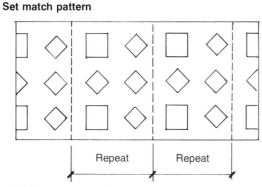

| Repeat | Repeat |

Motifs are positioned or set side by side on the same level to form a straight line across the width of the fabric

Drop match pattern

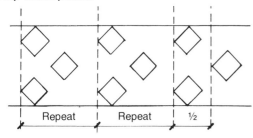

| Repeat | Repeat | ½ |

Half the length of every other repeat is dropped to produce a diagonal match of patterns

Note: Some fabric patterns will not be suitable for some furniture frames. Example: A small-framed French side chair would require a smaller pattern than a large wing chair.

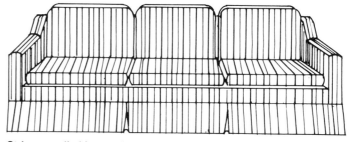

Stripes applied in standard manner
Velvets and other fabrics with nap usually cannot be applied horizontally (selvage parallel to floor).

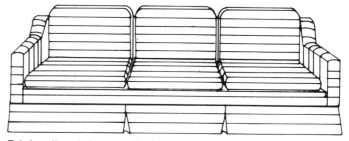

Fabric railroaded across the furniture (selvage runs parallel to the floor)

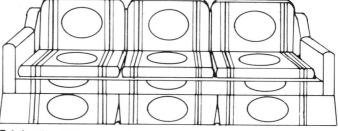

Fabric with obvious repeat
Major pattern motif should be placed so it falls on flat vertical and horizontal surfaces

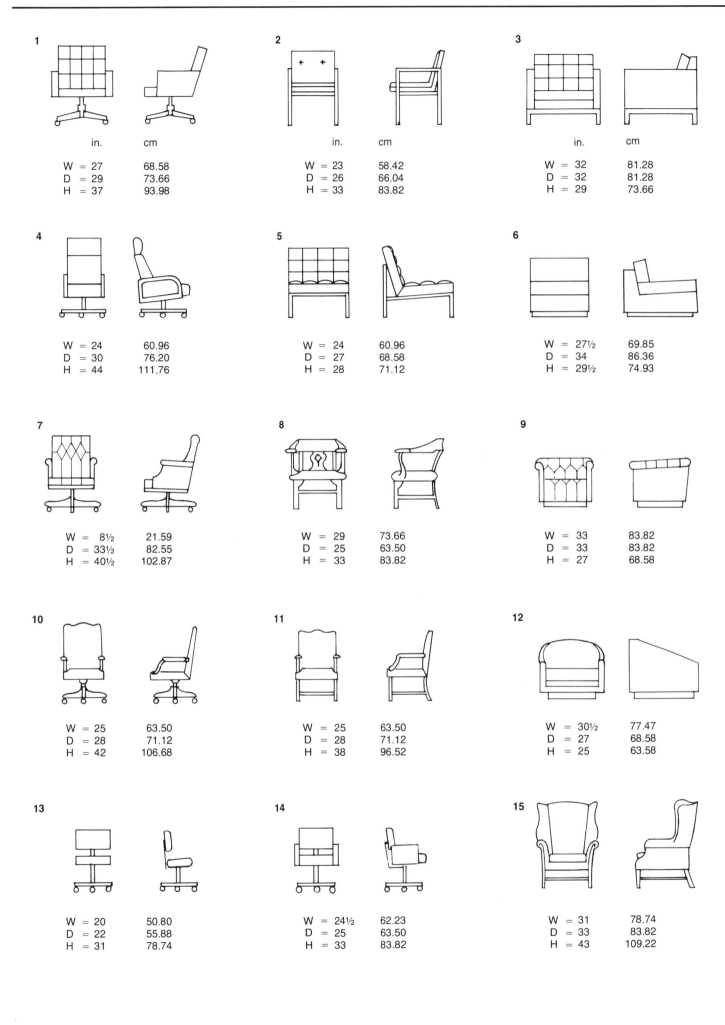

1

	in.	cm
W = 27	68.58
D = 29	73.66
H = 37	93.98

2

	in.	cm
W = 23	58.42
D = 26	66.04
H = 33	83.82

3

	in.	cm
W = 32	81.28
D = 32	81.28
H = 29	73.66

4

W = 24	60.96
D = 30	76.20
H = 44	111.76

5

W = 24	60.96
D = 27	68.58
H = 28	71.12

6

W = 27½	69.85
D = 34	86.36
H = 29½	74.93

7

W = 8½	21.59
D = 33½	82.55
H = 40½	102.87

8

W = 29	73.66
D = 25	63.50
H = 33	83.82

9

W = 33	83.82
D = 33	83.82
H = 27	68.58

10

W = 25	63.50
D = 28	71.12
H = 42	106.68

11

W = 25	63.50
D = 28	71.12
H = 38	96.52

12

W = 30½	77.47
D = 27	68.58
H = 25	63.58

13

W = 20	50.80
D = 22	55.88
H = 31	78.74

14

W = 24½	62.23
D = 25	63.50
H = 33	83.82

15

W = 31	78.74
D = 33	83.82
H = 43	109.22

16

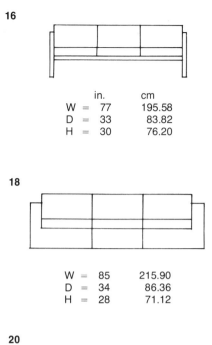

	in.	cm
W =	77	195.58
D =	33	83.82
H =	30	76.20

17

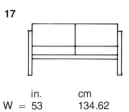

	in.	cm
W =	53	134.62
D =	33	83.82
H =	30	76.20

18

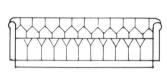

W =	85	215.90
D =	34	86.36
H =	28	71.12

19

W =	61	154.94
D =	34	86.36
H =	28	71.12

20

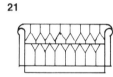

W =	90	228.60
D =	33	83.82
H =	27	68.58

21

W =	57	144.78
D =	33	83.82
H =	27	68.58

22

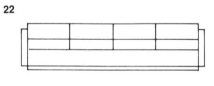

W =	108	274.32
D =	34	86.36
H =	29½	74.93

23

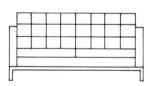

W =	64	162.56
D =	34	86.36
H =	29½	74.93

24

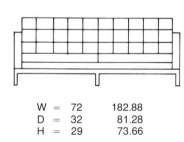

W =	72	182.88
D =	32	81.28
H =	29	73.66

25

W =	60	152.40
D =	32	81.28
H =	29	73.66

26

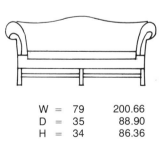

W =	79	200.66
D =	35	88.90
H =	34	86.36

27

W =	60	152.40
D =	35	88.90
H =	34	86.36

Upholstery required

	Fabric		Leather	
	yd	m	ft²	m²
1	3¼	2.97	55	5.11
2	2	1.83	36	3.34
3	4	3.66	72	6.69
4	4⅞	4.46	90	8.36
5	2¼	2.06	45	4.18
6	6	5.49	108	10.03
7	4⅓	3.93	77⅖	7.19
8	1¼	1.14	23	2.14
9	7⅝	6.97	135	12.54
10	2½	2.29	45	4.18
11	2	1.83	36	3.34
12	4	3.66	72	6.69
13	1	0.91	18	1.67
14	3½	3.20	63	5.85
15	5½	5.03	99	9.20
16	9½	8.69	171	15.89
17	6⅜	5.83	117	10.87
18	15	13.72	270	25.08
19	13¾	12.57	252	23.41
20	12⅝	11.54	234	21.74
21	9⅝	8.80	180	16.72
22	22⅛	20.23	396	36.79
23	12¼	11.20	216	20.07
24	8	7.32	144	13.38
25	7	6.40	112	10.41
26	9	8.23	162	15.05
27	7½	6.86	135	12.54

Notes: All yardage is based on 54″ (137.16 cm) wide plain fabric.

When furniture platform is to be covered in matching fabric, add the following yardage:

Chair	1¼ (114.30 cm)
Sofa or love seat to 60″ (152.40 cm) wide	2¼ (205.74 cm)
Sofa over 60″ wide	3⅞ (354.33 cm)

TYPICAL UPHOLSTERED SECTIONALS

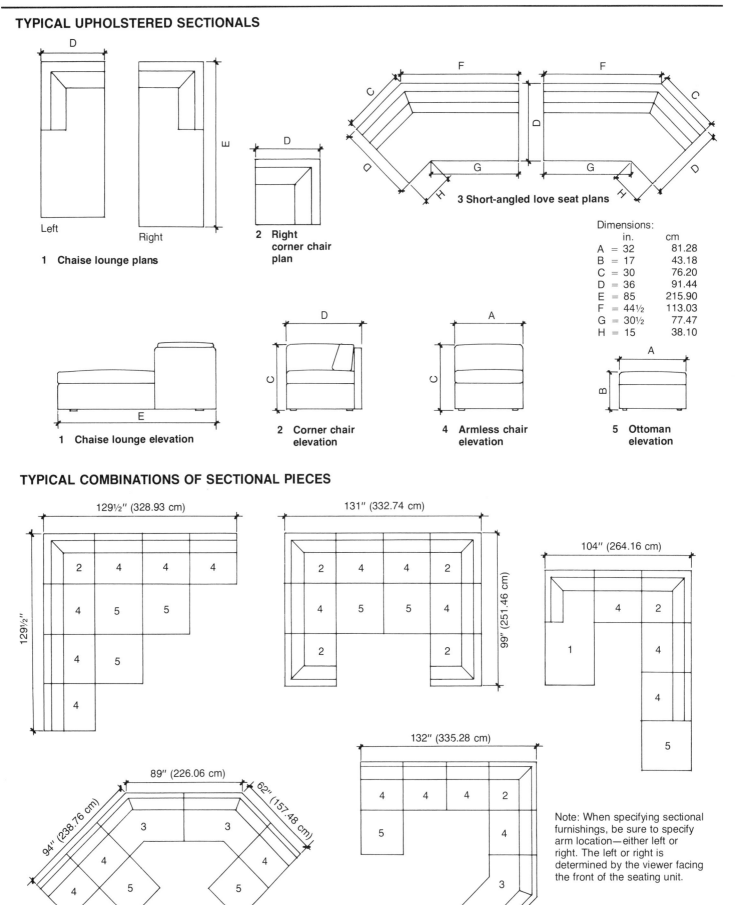

Left

Right

1 Chaise lounge plans

2 Right corner chair plan

3 Short-angled love seat plans

Dimensions:

	in.	cm
A =	32	81.28
B =	17	43.18
C =	30	76.20
D =	36	91.44
E =	85	215.90
F =	44½	113.03
G =	30½	77.47
H =	15	38.10

1 Chaise lounge elevation

2 Corner chair elevation

4 Armless chair elevation

5 Ottoman elevation

TYPICAL COMBINATIONS OF SECTIONAL PIECES

129½″ (328.93 cm)

129½″

131″ (332.74 cm)

99″ (251.46 cm)

104″ (264.16 cm)

89″ (226.06 cm)

62″ (157.48 cm)

94″ (238.76 cm)

132″ (335.28 cm)

Note: When specifying sectional furnishings, be sure to specify arm location—either left or right. The left or right is determined by the viewer facing the front of the seating unit.

Barathea
A rib weave usually done in a minute brick fashion, giving a pebbly appearance.

Batik
A method of resist dyeing, which employs wax as the resist. The pattern is covered with wax, and the fabric is then dyed, producing a white design on a dyed ground. The waxed patterns will not take the dye, and the wax is removed after dyeing. The process is repeated to obtain multicolored designs. The effect is sometimes imitated in machine prints.

Boucle
Plain weave using plied or uneven yarns with looped surfaces, giving a rough appearance to the face of the cloth.

Bourette
A twill or plain weave that originated in France. The yarns are interspersed with nubs, giving the material a dull, nubbed surface effect.

Brocade
Multicolored jacquard woven fabric with floral or figured pattern emphasized by contrasting colors. The color is introduced through the filler yarns. The background may be either satin or twill weave.

Brocatelle
A tightly woven jacquard fabric with a warp effect in the figure, which is raised to give a puffed appearance. The puff effect is created by several kinds of fillings, tension weaving of a linen, or nylon that shrinks after a heat process.

Chenille fabric
A fabric woven with chenille yarns, which produce a pile effect similar to velvet and, when woven through various warps, can create a pile like velvet or, if woven on a jacquard loom, can look similar to a cut velvet.

Chevron
Broken twill or herringbone weave giving a chevron effect, creating a design of wide Vs across the width of the fabric. See Herringbone.

Chintz
A plain, tightly woven cotton fabric with fine yarns and processed with a glazed finish. Used as a plain dyed fabric or a printed fabric. The term is sometimes used for unglazed fine-count cottons.

Color flag
The series of clippings attached to a purchase sample to show the color line.

Color line
Refers to the complete color range of a given series.

Colorway
An individual color of a particular style or pattern.

Crewel
Chainstitch embroidery made with a fine, loosely twisted, two-ply worsted yarn on a plain weave fabric. Done by hand, for the most part, in the Kashmir Province of India and in England.

Crocking
Rubbing off of color from woven or printed fabrics.

Damask
A jacquard woven fabric with floral or geometric patterns created with different weaves. Can be self-tone or with one color warp and a different filling.

Dobby
A type of weave.

Double cloth
Two separate cloths combined in weaving through use of binding threads. Face and back may contrast in weave and color.

Faille
A flat, ribbed fabric woven in a plain weave with fine yarns in the warp and heavier yarns in the filling. The ribbed effect is flatter than grosgrain and smaller than a repp. The fabric is the base cloth used for moire.

Fiber content
The make-up of the yarn content of any given fabric (that is, 60 percent cotton and 40 percent rayon). By regulation of the Federal Trade Commission, this information must be provided in all price lists.

Fiberglass
Fibers and yarns produced from glass and woven into flexible fabrics noted for their fireproof qualities. Beta fiberglass is a trademarked glass fiber.

Fibers
Natural:

Cotton	Linen	Wool
Hemp	Silk	

Manufactured (generic classification):

Acetate	Nylon	Saran
Acrylic	Olefin	Spandex
Glass	Polyester	Vinyl
Modacrylic	Rayon	

Fill or filling
The threads running widthwise across a piece of fabric.

Finished goods
Fabric that has been processed by dyeing, printing, applying of special resins and finishes.

Finishing
The process of dyeing and printing of greige goods.

Frieze
A very strong, plain fabric with a fine low-loop surface woven on a wire loom to maintain even loop size. Usually made with wool warp, cotton filling, but can be of other fibers.

Gauze
A thin, sheer fabric constructed with plain, leno, or dobby weave. Specifically used for curtains next to glass windows to diffuse light.

Greige goods
The raw or unfinished goods that have been woven but are otherwise unprocessed (dyed, printed, and so on).

Haircloth
A very stiff, wiry cloth made with a single horsehair filling, usually on a cotton warp. A plain, satin, leno or dobby weave. The width of the fabric is determined by the length of the horsehair in the filling; no more than 26″ (66.04 cm) wide (width is determined by length of horse's tail).

Herringbone
A broken twill weave composed of vertical sections that are alternately right hand and left hand in direction. Also called chevron weave, especially when arranged in wide stripes.

Houndstooth
Broken twill weave forming four-pointed star.

Jacquard design
A woven design made with the aid of a jacquard head (this constitutes a jacquard loom) and may vary from simple, self-colored spot effects to elaborate, multicolored, all-over effects.

Lampas
A jacquard fabric made with two or more warps and two or more fillings, usually in different colors. Similar to a brocade.

Leather
The skin of an animal tanned or otherwise dressed for use. Full Top Grain indicates the very best hides available on the world market today. Only the finest hides, those that do not require sanding or buffing to remove defects or imperfections, can be classified as Full Top Grain. These premium hides in their natural, unadulterated state retain the superior characteristics of suppleness and tuftability found only in genuine Full Top Grain leather.

Leno
Pairs of warp yarns are wound around each other resulting in a net effect.

Lisere
A jacquard fabric usually made with a taffeta or faille ground. The design is created by colored warp threads brought up on the face of the fabric, leaving loose yarns on the back. These threads are sometimes clipped.

Marquisette
A transparent, open-mesh leno weave for sheer draperies.

Matelassé
A jacquard fabric woven with heavy "stuffer" filling yarns to create a puffed, quilted effect.

Mill
The place where fabric is woven.

Moiré
Base cloth must be a faille. A finish achieved with engraved rollers that press the design into the fabric, causing the crushed and uncrushed parts to reflect light differently (called "watermarked"). Sometimes it is done with the fabric folded the length of the goods, leaving a center crease, but more often it is folded with a crease on the width of the goods and the fabric is cut at this fold.

Natural fibers
Those fibers that come from cotton, wool, silk, and flax (linen).

Ninon
A smooth, light-weight fabric made in a plain weave, giving a fine mesh effect.

Plissé
A fabric with a crinkled or puckered effect, generally in the direction of the warp, which is created either by tension weaving or through the application of a caustic soda solution that shrinks part of the yarns on the back.

Plush
Warp pile fabric of silk or wool. Pile is longer than that of standard velvet. Often heat-set to lay in one direction to resemble animal fur.

Pocket weave
A jacquard double-layered fabric with several warps. The design is created with both warps and fillings.

Polished cotton
A plain weave cotton cloth characterized by a sheen ranging from dull to bright. Polish can be achieved either through the weave or the addition of a resin finish. Can be a solid color, usually piece dyed or printed.

Rep
Plain weave fabric with narrow ribs running the width of the fabric. Usually a fine warp and heavier filling yarns.

Sateen
A highly lustrous fabric, usually made of mercerized cotton with a satin weave.

Seersucker
Light-weight cotton fabric with crinkley stripes made by weaving some warp yarns slack and others tight. Woven seersucker is more expensive and longer wearing than chemically achieved plisses.

Selvage
Narrow edge of woven fabric (warp direction), usually of stronger yarns or denser construction than body of cloth.

Strike off
The term used to refer to the first run of a new pattern or series.

Suede
A tanned animal skin, with the flesh side rubbed into a nap.

Swatch
A small sample of a piece of fabric.

Taffeta
This is the simplest weave—one thread up and one thread down. Warp and filling yarns are usually the same size.
Antique taffeta: Uses a plain warp with a thick and thin filling (such as douppioni silk).

Tapestry
A heavy jacquard fabric usually multicolored. Warps and filling very tightly woven. The designs vary from traditional to contemporary. Used for upholstery only.

Toile de Jouy
A floral or scenic design usually printed on cotton or linen. Originally printed in Jouy, France, the fabrics were printed in single colors from engraved copper plates. The designs were characterized by classic motifs, beautifully engraved and finely colored.

Tussah
The product of the undomesticated silk worm—more uneven, coarser, and stronger than true or cultivated silk. Tussah is woven in its natural colors, which range from ecru to dark brown. Considerable color variance within each length is not unusual and is considered an intrinsic characteristic of the fabric.

Velour
A term loosely applied to all types of fabrics with a nap or cut pile on one side. Specifically, it is a cut pile fabric similar to regular velvet but with a higher pile.

Velvet
A closely woven pile fabric, it can be made of many fibers: silk, cotton, rayon, dralon, olefin.
Crushed velvet: Most often the fabric is pulled through a narrow cylinder to create the crush. Sometimes, as with linen velvet, a roller is used to give a repeat to the design.
Cut velvet: A jacquard design, usually cut and uncut pile on a plain ground. Sometimes the design is a solid color and sometimes multicolor.

Vinyl upholstery
A polyvinyl chloride film with a fabric backing.

Warp
The yarn running through the length of a piece of cloth.

Yarn dyed
Goods made from yarns that are dyed before they are woven or knitted into a fabric.

Period	Italian	French	English	American
Gothic	1226–1400	1140-1500	1189–1377	
Renaissance	1407–1540	Louis XII 1498–1515 Francis I 1515–1544 Henry II 1547–1559 Henry IV 1589–1610	Tudor 1500–1588 Elizabethan 1558–1603 Jacobean 1603–1649 Cromwellian 1649–1660	Colonial 1608–1720 Early influences: Jacobean William & Mary
Baroque	1600–1670	Louis XIV 1643–1715	Stuart 1660–1689 William & Mary 1689–1702 Queen Anne 1702–1714	
Rococo Age of Mahogany	1700–1748 Venetian	Regency 1715–1730 Louis XV 1715–1774	Georgian 1714–1750 Chippendale 1718–1779	Georgian 1720–1790 Queen Anne, Chippendale, Hepplewhite, Sheraton
18th century	Neoclassicism 1748–1796	Neoclassicism Louis XVI 1774–1789 Directoire 1789–1804	Robert & James Adam 1730–1794 Hepplewhite 1765–1786 Sheraton 1751–1806	
19th century	1796–1830	Empire 1804–1820	Regency 1810–1820 Greek Revival 1820–1830	Federal 1790–1820 Adam, Hepplewhite, Sheraton Duncan Phyfe 1768–1854
	Emanuelian	Restoration 1830–1870 Louis Philippe 1830–1848 Second Empire	Victorian 1830–1900 Early: 1830–1860 Mid: 1860–1880 Late: 1880–1900	Greek Revival 1820–1860 Victorian 1840–1860

Note: Dates and periods are not precise and are subject to interpretations.

Typical wall elevation
Area (A) over doors or windows, known as *trumeau,* was filled with mirrors or paintings

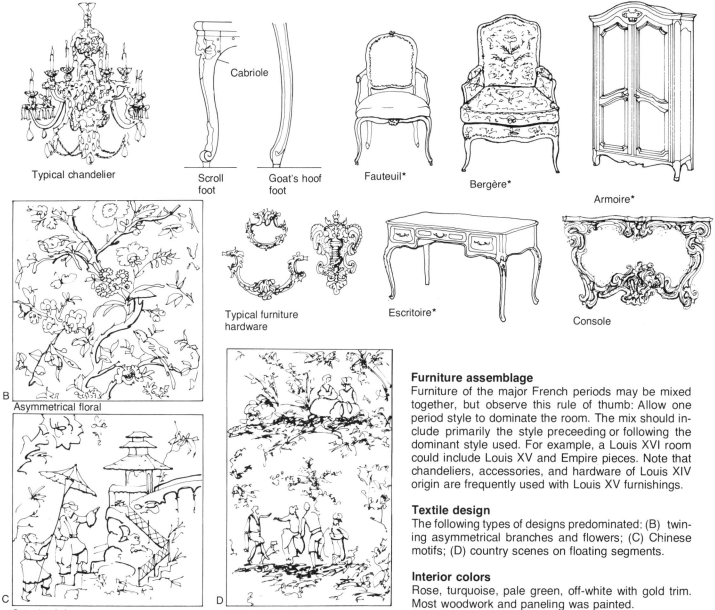

Typical chandelier

Cabriole

Scroll foot

Goat's hoof foot

Fauteuil*

Bergère*

Armoire*

B
Asymmetrical floral

Typical furniture hardware

Escritoire*

Console

C
Chinoiserie*

D
Toile de Jouy fabric

Furniture assemblage
Furniture of the major French periods may be mixed together, but observe this rule of thumb: Allow one period style to dominate the room. The mix should include primarily the style preceeding or following the dominant style used. For example, a Louis XVI room could include Louis XV and Empire pieces. Note that chandeliers, accessories, and hardware of Louis XIV origin are frequently used with Louis XV furnishings.

Textile design
The following types of designs predominated: (B) twining asymmetrical branches and flowers; (C) Chinese motifs; (D) country scenes on floating segments.

Interior colors
Rose, turquoise, pale green, off-white with gold trim. Most woodwork and paneling was painted.

*See French Decorative Terms, page 263.

Neoclassic rooms and walls were carefully planned to appear symmetrical. Walls were designed with rectangular panels, often painted and otherwise void of decorative motifs. Man-tels were straight, and the molding around the fireplace opening repeated motifs found in furnishings.

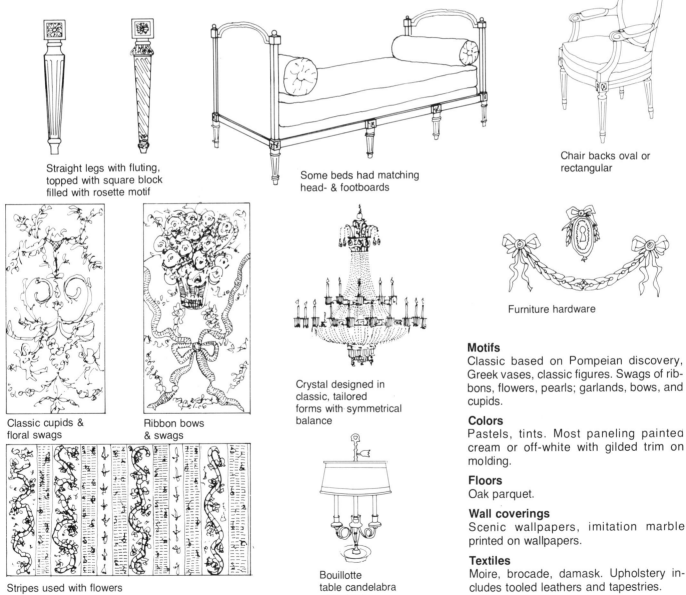

Straight legs with fluting, topped with square block filled with rosette motif

Some beds had matching head- & footboards

Chair backs oval or rectangular

Classic cupids & floral swags

Ribbon bows & swags

Crystal designed in classic, tailored forms with symmetrical balance

Furniture hardware

Stripes used with flowers

Bouillotte table candelabra with shade

Motifs
Classic based on Pompeian discovery, Greek vases, classic figures. Swags of ribbons, flowers, pearls; garlands, bows, and cupids.

Colors
Pastels, tints. Most paneling painted cream or off-white with gilded trim on molding.

Floors
Oak parquet.

Wall coverings
Scenic wallpapers, imitation marble printed on wallpapers.

Textiles
Moire, brocade, damask. Upholstery includes tooled leathers and tapestries.

Walls in both periods were often covered in fabric that was shirred or draped; in fact some rooms were designed to resemble tents. Woodwork, doors, and mantels were designed with classic details. Classic figures and vases were also popular.

Empire swan motif

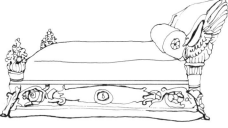

Empire state bed

Empire sphinx motif

Empire tripod table, Roman influence

Draped fabric pattern

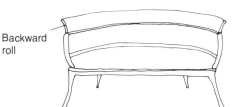

Backward roll

Directoire sofa

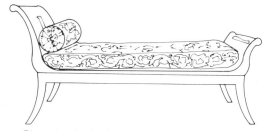

Directoire day bed

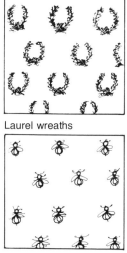

Laurel wreaths

Bumblebee motif

Bronze chandelier

DIRECTOIRE

Furniture design displayed strong influences of Greek furniture, such as the backward roll and the gracefully curved legs of the Greek klismos chair. Carving and ornate gold ormolu were not heavily used. Tripod wrought-iron tables were popular. Striped wallpapers and fabrics were common.

Motifs

Drums, spears, sheaves of wheat represented the war and rise of the working class.

EMPIRE

A short-lived style reflecting the power and pomp of the Napoleonic era.

Motifs

Egyptian and Roman inspired. Sphinxes, winged figures, eagles, laurel wreaths.

Colors

Deep, rich reds, yellows, emerald greens, and cerulean blues. Much gold ormolu on carved furniture.

Armoire (ar-muar)
A large cabinet, which was originally used to store armor.

Aubusson (o-bu-son)
The location of the French factory where rugs of a destinctive style by that name were made.

Bergère (bear-jher)
An easy chair with closed arms.

Bombé (bomb-bay)
A swelling or bulging front curve on a commode.

Bouillotte (bull-yauth)
A small-scale lamp with narrow shade, which had an arrow motif on the center shaft above the shade. Tray effect formed by base.

Cabriole (kab-ree-ol)
Literally "a goat's leap," used to describe legs curving outward from the seat and inward toward the foot.

Canape (ka-na-pay)
A sofa.

Chaise-longue (shez-long)
Literally "a long chair"; a bergère or armchair with the seat extended to form a couch.

Chinoiserie (sheen-wa-zree)
French interpretation of Chinese decorative ornament.

Credence (kred-ons)
Small sideboard or table.

Escritoire (a-kree-twar)
Writing desk.

Ètagere (a-ta-jher)
Hanging or standing shelves that are open on all sides.

Fauteuil (faux-toy)
Upholstered armchair. Area below arm is open and un-upholstered.

Jardiniere (jar-din-yair)
Plant container.

Lit canape (lit)
A sofa bed.

Ormolu (or-mo-lou)
A rich, golden metal for decorative embellishment, composed of copper and zinc and covered with gold leaf.

Panetiere (pan-e-tyair)
A cabinet to store bread.

Poudreuse (poo-druz)
Small dressing table.

Psyche (si-ke)
A large, full-length mirror made of Cheval glass (Empire) that swings from vertical posts.

Ratchet (raash-a)
A sofa with movable arms that let down for sleeping.

Salon (sa-lon)
A French parlor or drawing room.

Sconce (skons)
A lighting bracket on the wall.

Semainier (sa-man-yair)
Tall bedroom chest with seven drawers.

Singerie (san-zree)
Motif using the monkey as subject.

Tabouret (ta-boo-ret)
A foot stool.

Tole (toll)
Painted sheet metal or tin.

Trompe l'oeil (tromp-loy)
A painting of real objects that creates an illusion of depth that fools the eye.

Trumeau (tru-mo)
Decorative treatment over mantel, door, window, or mirror. Used very often in Louis XV and Louis XVI periods.

Typical English walls in both periods were paneled in waxed oak or walnut. Doorways, windows, niches, and mantels were treated with classical moldings and complete entablatures.

Queen Anne

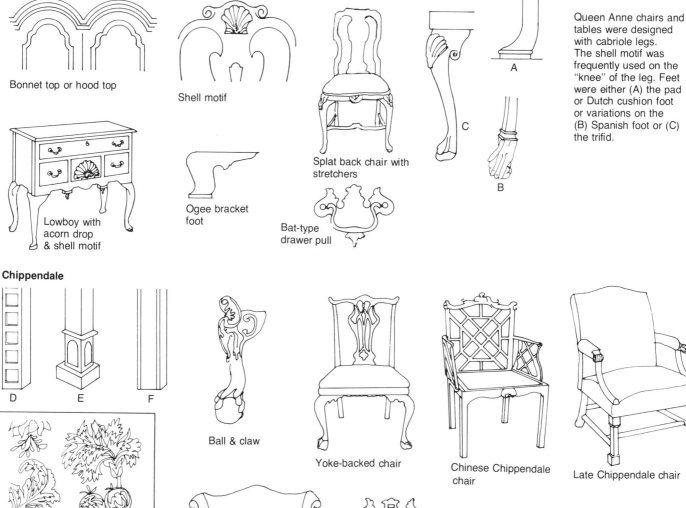

Bonnet top or hood top

Shell motif

Splat back chair with stretchers

Queen Anne chairs and tables were designed with cabriole legs. The shell motif was frequently used on the "knee" of the leg. Feet were either (A) the pad or Dutch cushion foot or variations on the (B) Spanish foot or (C) the trifid.

A

C

B

Lowboy with acorn drop & shell motif

Ogee bracket foot

Bat-type drawer pull

Chippendale

D E F

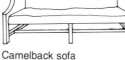

Typical crewel embroidery pattern

Ball & claw

Yoke-backed chair

Chinese Chippendale chair

Late Chippendale chair

Camelback sofa with Marlborough legs

Drawer pull with cut work

Chippendale furniture was a product of the Georgian era in England and was popular from ca. 1740–1770. It was a highly eclectic style. Typical Chippendale legs included the ball and claw as well as three varieties of straight legs: (D) the Chinese leg with fretwork, (E) the Marlborough block foot, and (F) the Marlborough leg.

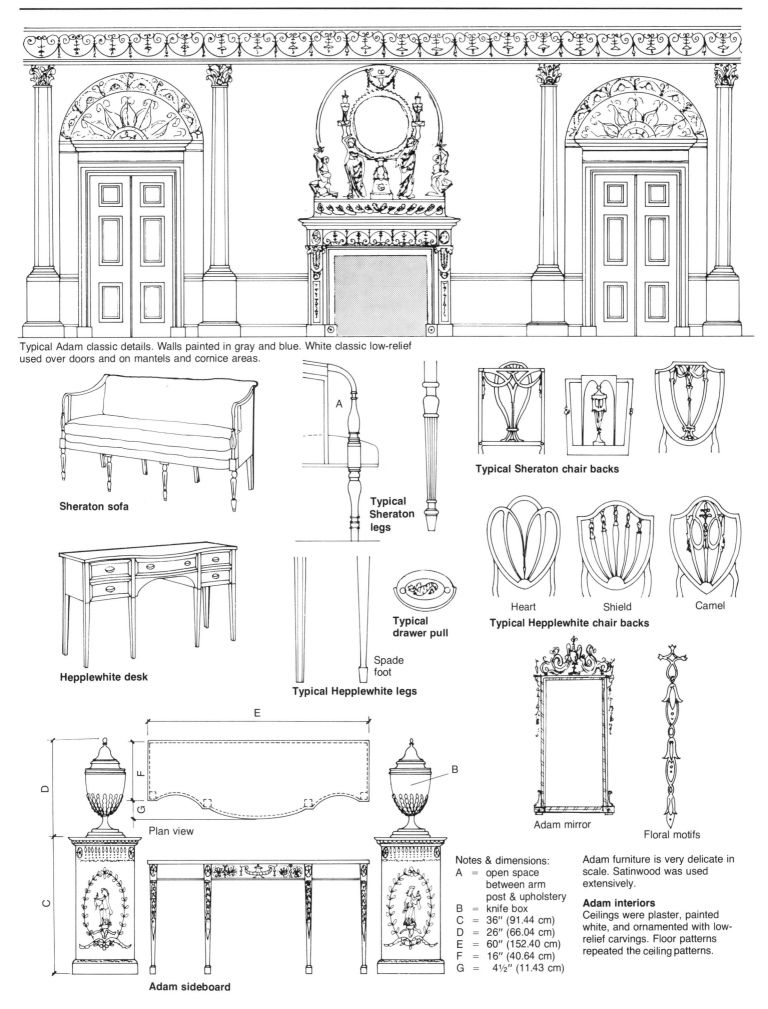

Typical Adam classic details. Walls painted in gray and blue. White classic low-relief used over doors and on mantels and cornice areas.

Sheraton sofa

Hepplewhite desk

A

Typical Sheraton legs

Typical drawer pull

Spade foot

Typical Hepplewhite legs

Typical Sheraton chair backs

Heart   Shield   Camel

Typical Hepplewhite chair backs

Adam mirror

Floral motifs

E

F

G

B

Plan view

D

C

Adam sideboard

Notes & dimensions:
A = open space between arm post & upholstery
B = knife box
C = 36″ (91.44 cm)
D = 26″ (66.04 cm)
E = 60″ (152.40 cm)
F = 16″ (40.64 cm)
G = 4½″ (11.43 cm)

Adam furniture is very delicate in scale. Satinwood was used extensively.

Adam interiors
Ceilings were plaster, painted white, and ornamented with low-relief carvings. Floor patterns repeated the ceiling patterns.

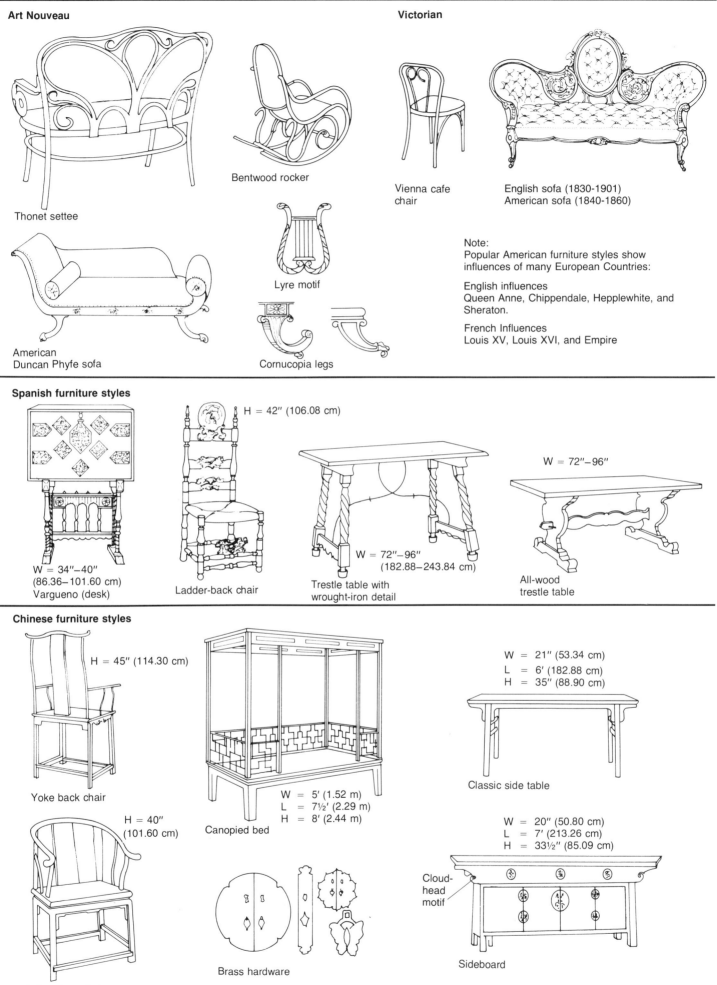

Art Nouveau

Thonet settee

Bentwood rocker

Lyre motif

American
Duncan Phyfe sofa

Cornucopia legs

Victorian

Vienna cafe
chair

English sofa (1830-1901)
American sofa (1840-1860)

Note:
Popular American furniture styles show
influences of many European Countries:

English influences
Queen Anne, Chippendale, Hepplewhite, and
Sheraton.

French Influences
Louis XV, Louis XVI, and Empire

Spanish furniture styles

W = 34″–40″
(86.36–101.60 cm)
Vargueno (desk)

H = 42″ (106.08 cm)

Ladder-back chair

W = 72″–96″
(182.88–243.84 cm)
Trestle table with
wrought-iron detail

W = 72″–96″

All-wood
trestle table

Chinese furniture styles

H = 45″ (114.30 cm)

Yoke back chair

H = 40″
(101.60 cm)

Lohan-type chair

W = 5′ (1.52 m)
L = 7½′ (2.29 m)
H = 8′ (2.44 m)
Canopied bed

Brass hardware

W = 21″ (53.34 cm)
L = 6′ (182.88 cm)
H = 35″ (88.90 cm)

Classic side table

W = 20″ (50.80 cm)
L = 7′ (213.26 cm)
H = 33½″ (85.09 cm)

Cloud-
head
motif

Sideboard

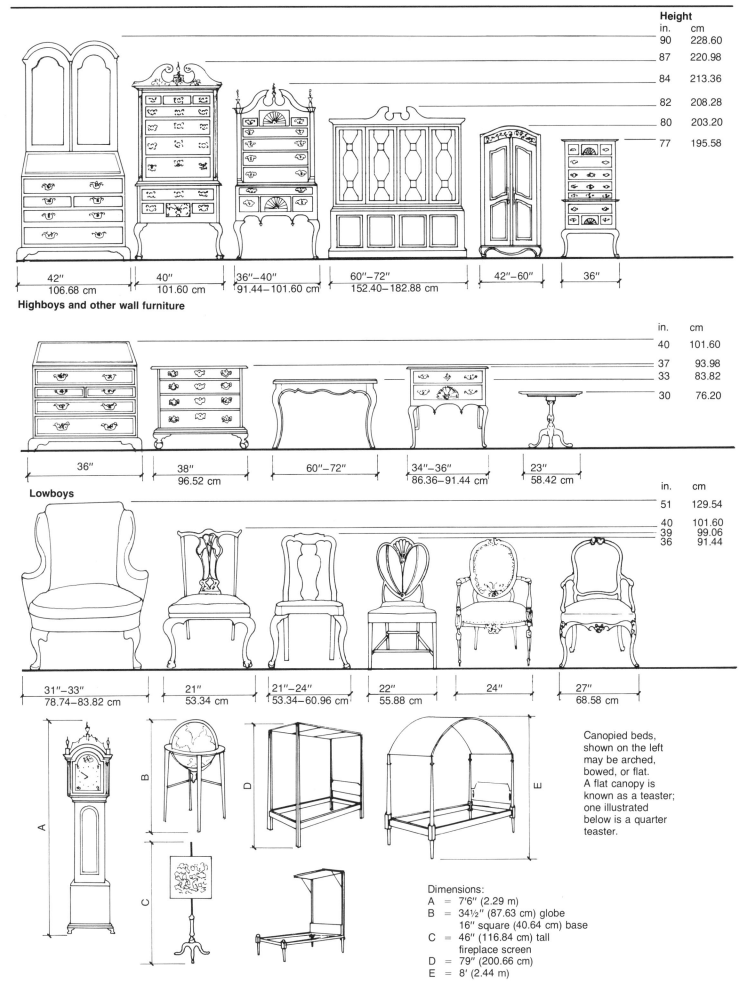

Height

in.	cm
90	228.60
87	220.98
84	213.36
82	208.28
80	203.20
77	195.58

42"
106.68 cm

40"
101.60 cm

36"–40"
91.44–101.60 cm

60"–72"
152.40–182.88 cm

42"–60"

36"

Highboys and other wall furniture

in.	cm
40	101.60
37	93.98
33	83.82
30	76.20

36"

38"
96.52 cm

60"–72"

34"–36"
86.36–91.44 cm

23"
58.42 cm

Lowboys

in.	cm
51	129.54
40	101.60
39	99.06
36	91.44

31"–33"
78.74–83.82 cm

21"
53.34 cm

21"–24"
53.34–60.96 cm

22"
55.88 cm

24"

27"
68.58 cm

Canopied beds,
shown on the left
may be arched,
bowed, or flat.
A flat canopy is
known as a teaster;
one illustrated
below is a quarter
teaster.

Dimensions:
A = 7'6" (2.29 m)
B = 34½" (87.63 cm) globe
      16" square (40.64 cm) base
C = 46" (116.84 cm) tall
      fireplace screen
D = 79" (200.66 cm)
E = 8' (2.44 m)

CONTEMPORARY DESKS

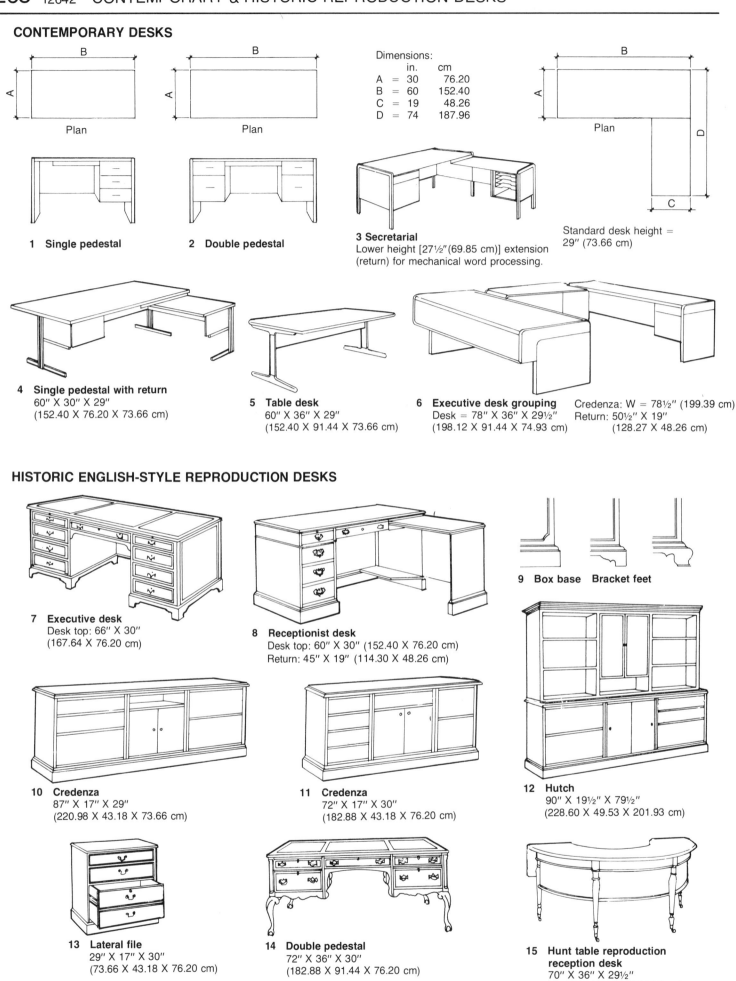

Dimensions:

	in.	cm
A =	30	76.20
B =	60	152.40
C =	19	48.26
D =	74	187.96

Standard desk height = 29" (73.66 cm)

1 Single pedestal

2 Double pedestal

3 Secretarial
Lower height [27½"(69.85 cm)] extension (return) for mechanical word processing.

4 Single pedestal with return
60" X 30" X 29"
(152.40 X 76.20 X 73.66 cm)

5 Table desk
60" X 36" X 29"
(152.40 X 91.44 X 73.66 cm)

6 Executive desk grouping
Desk = 78" X 36" X 29½"
(198.12 X 91.44 X 74.93 cm)

Credenza: W = 78½" (199.39 cm)
Return: 50½" X 19"
(128.27 X 48.26 cm)

HISTORIC ENGLISH-STYLE REPRODUCTION DESKS

7 Executive desk
Desk top: 66" X 30"
(167.64 X 76.20 cm)

8 Receptionist desk
Desk top: 60" X 30" (152.40 X 76.20 cm)
Return: 45" X 19" (114.30 X 48.26 cm)

9 Box base   Bracket feet

10 Credenza
87" X 17" X 29"
(220.98 X 43.18 X 73.66 cm)

11 Credenza
72" X 17" X 30"
(182.88 X 43.18 X 76.20 cm)

12 Hutch
90" X 19½" X 79½"
(228.60 X 49.53 X 201.93 cm)

13 Lateral file
29" X 17" X 30"
(73.66 X 43.18 X 76.20 cm)

14 Double pedestal
72" X 36" X 30"
(182.88 X 91.44 X 76.20 cm)

**15 Hunt table reproduction
reception desk**
70" X 36" X 29½"
(177.80 X 91.44 X 74.93 cm)

Numbers refer to manufacturers. See Data Sources in the Appendix.

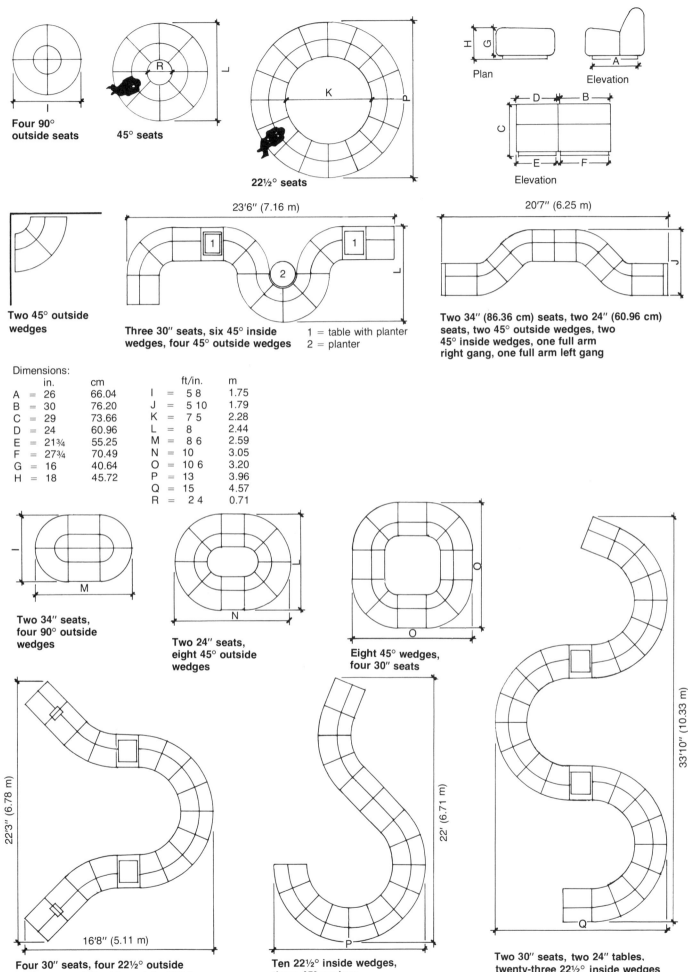

**Four 90°
outside seats**

45° seats

22½° seats

Plan

Elevation

Elevation

**Two 45° outside
wedges**

**Three 30″ seats, six 45° inside
wedges, four 45° outside wedges**

1 = table with planter
2 = planter

23′6″ (7.16 m)

**Two 34″ (86.36 cm) seats, two 24″ (60.96 cm)
seats, two 45° outside wedges, two
45° inside wedges, one full arm
right gang, one full arm left gang**

20′7″ (6.25 m)

Dimensions:

	in.	cm			ft/in.	m
A	= 26	66.04	I	=	5 8	1.75
B	= 30	76.20	J	=	5 10	1.79
C	= 29	73.66	K	=	7 5	2.28
D	= 24	60.96	L	=	8	2.44
E	= 21¾	55.25	M	=	8 6	2.59
F	= 27¾	70.49	N	=	10	3.05
G	= 16	40.64	O	=	10 6	3.20
H	= 18	45.72	P	=	13	3.96
			Q	=	15	4.57
			R	=	2 4	0.71

**Two 34″ seats,
four 90° outside
wedges**

**Two 24″ seats,
eight 45° outside
wedges**

**Eight 45° wedges,
four 30″ seats**

**Four 30″ seats, four 22½° outside
wedges, two 24″ tables, eight 22½°
outside wedges**

16′8″ (5.11 m)

22′3″ (6.78 m)

**Ten 22½° inside wedges,
three 45° wedges,
three 30″ seats**

22′ (6.71 m)

**Two 30″ seats, two 24″ tables,
twenty-three 22½° inside wedges**

33′10″ (10.33 m)

Note: Consult local codes for the required riser/run relationship to determine dimensions.

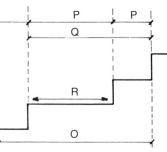

Auditorium treads

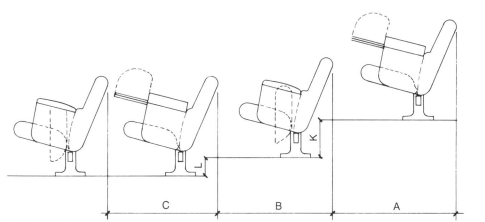

Elevations of writing arm chairs

Rows shall be spaced not less than 33″ (83.82 cm) measured from the back of one chair to back of the next

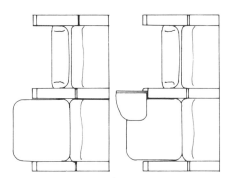

Plan view of writing armchairs

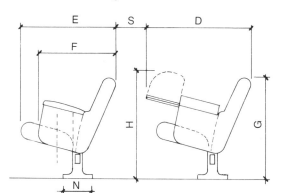

Dimensions:

		in.	cm
A	=	40	101.60
B	=	38	96.52
C	=	36	91.44
D	=	33¾	85.73
E	=	29	73.66
F	=	24	60.96
G	=	31½	80.01
H	=	33¼	84.46
I	=	19⅞	50.48
J	=	3⅜	8.57
K	=	not to exceed 8″ (20.32 cm) unless aisle gradient exceeds 8″ in rise and 11″ (27.94 cm) in run. In this case the riser should not exceed 11″ (consult local codes)
L	=	6	15.24
		4	10.16 min.
M	=	22⅞	58.10
N	=	9⅝	24.45
O	=	on aisle
P	=	tread
Q	=	platform in seating area
R	=	tread greater than other treads; min. 11″
S	=	12	30.48 min.

Writing arm in down & up positions

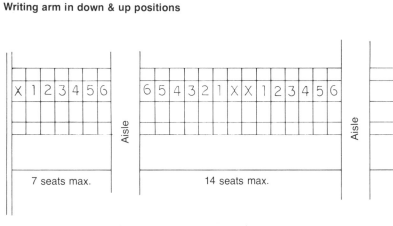

7 seats max.

14 seats max.

Aisle

Aisle

Recommended travel distance from seating locations to aisles

To determine spacing of rows, horizontal measurements shall be made between vertical planes. When all chairs in a row have automatic or self-rising seats, the measurements can be made with seats in the seat-up position.

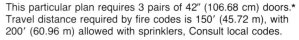

Main doors*

Lobby 12′6″ (3.81 m) wide

14 seats | 14 seats | 14 seats

6′ (1.83 m) cross aisle

3′6″ (1.07 m)

14 rows 4′ (1.22 m) | 14 rows 4′ | 14 rows 3′6″

6′ cross aisle

Plan   Stage or screen area

This particular plan requires 3 pairs of 42″ (106.68 cm) doors.* Travel distance required by fire codes is 150′ (45.72 m), with 200′ (60.96 m) allowed with sprinklers, Consult local codes.

Chair/arm combinations

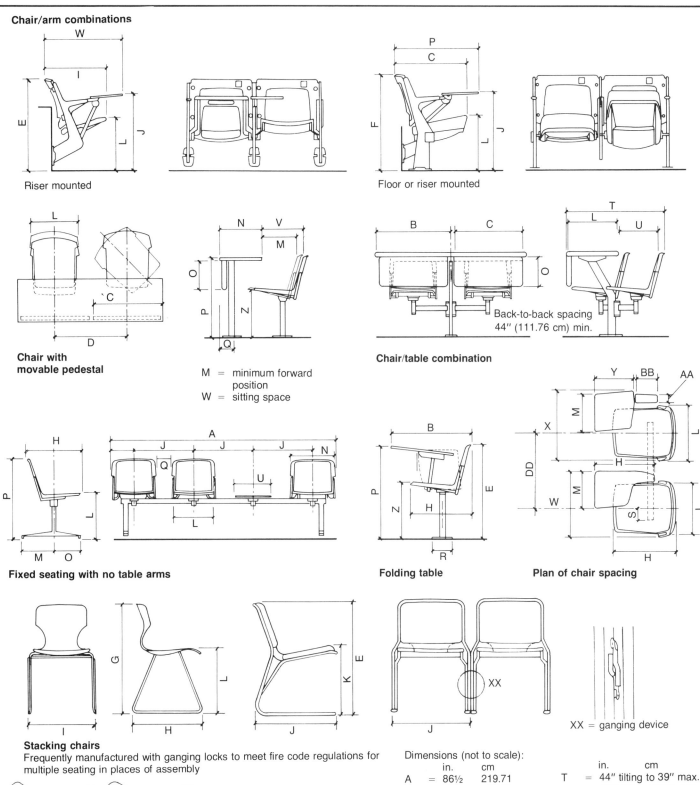

Riser mounted

Floor or riser mounted

Chair with movable pedestal

M = minimum forward position
W = sitting space

Chair/table combination

Back-to-back spacing 44" (111.76 cm) min.

Fixed seating with no table arms

Folding table

Plan of chair spacing

XX = ganging device

Stacking chairs
Frequently manufactured with ganging locks to meet fire code regulations for multiple seating in places of assembly

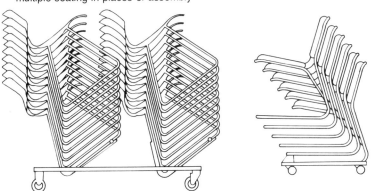

Stacking dolly
Some accommodate two stacks of 20 unupholstered chairs. Chairs can also be stacked on the floor with 10 per stack. Consult manufacturer.

Dimensions (not to scale):

	in.	cm
A =	86½	219.71
B =	27	68.58
C =	24½	62.33
D =	26	66.04 min.
E =	30	76.20
F =	30½	77.47
G =	30¾	78.11
H =	20	50.80
I =	19	48.26
J =	23	58.42
K =	18¾	47.63
L =	17½	44.45
M =	12	30.48
N =	16	40.64
O =	10	25.40
P =	29	73.66
Q =	5	12.70
R =	8	20.32
S =	4	10.16

	in.	cm
T =	44" tilting to 39" max. (111.76 to 99.06 cm)	
U =	14	35.56
V =	15	38.10
W =	21½	54.61
X =	22¼	56.52
Y =	13¼	33.66
Z =	18	45.72
AA =	2½	6.35
BB =	7¼	18.42
CC =	8¾	22.23
DD =	24	60.96
	side-to-side spacing recommended for folding table	
or =	26	66.04
	recommended for fixed table	

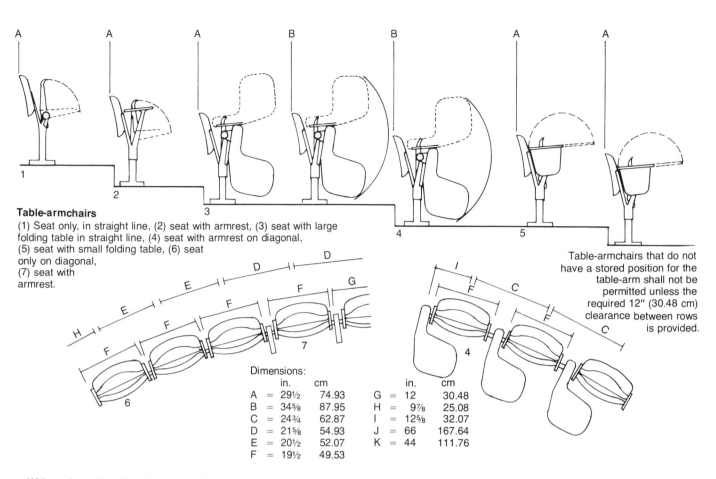

Table-armchairs

(1) Seat only, in straight line, (2) seat with armrest, (3) seat with large folding table in straight line, (4) seat with armrest on diagonal, (5) seat with small folding table, (6) seat only on diagonal, (7) seat with armrest.

Table-armchairs that do not have a stored position for the table-arm shall not be permitted unless the required 12″ (30.48 cm) clearance between rows is provided.

Dimensions:

		in.	cm				in.	cm
A	=	29½	74.93		G	=	12	30.48
B	=	34⅝	87.95		H	=	9⅞	25.08
C	=	24¾	62.87		I	=	12⅝	32.07
D	=	21⅝	54.93		J	=	66	167.64
E	=	20½	52.07		K	=	44	111.76
F	=	19½	49.53					

With continental seating, the spacing of rows of unoccupied chairs shall provide a clear width between rows measured horizontally as follows (automatic or self-rising seats shall be measured in the seat-up position; other seats shall be measured in the seat-down position):18″ (45.72 cm) clear width between rows of 18 chairs or less; 20″ (50.80 cm) clear width between rows of 35 chairs or less; 21″ (53.34 cm) clear width between rows of 45 chairs or less; 22″ (55.88 cm) clear width between rows of 46 chairs or more.

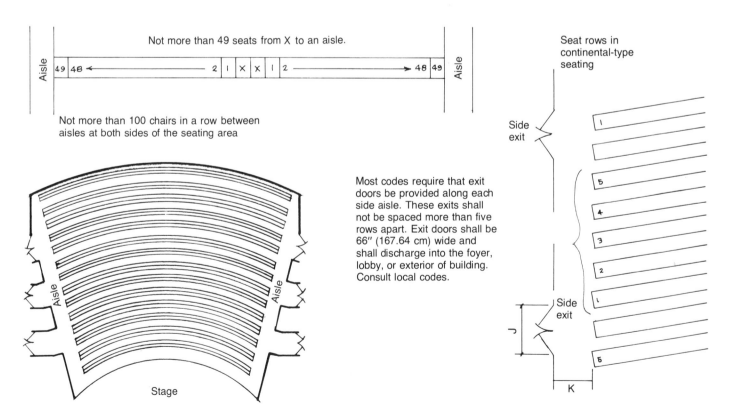

Not more than 49 seats from X to an aisle.

Not more than 100 chairs in a row between aisles at both sides of the seating area

Most codes require that exit doors be provided along each side aisle. These exits shall not be spaced more than five rows apart. Exit doors shall be 66″ (167.64 cm) wide and shall discharge into the foyer, lobby, or exterior of building. Consult local codes.

Seat rows in continental-type seating

TWO-LEVEL SEATING

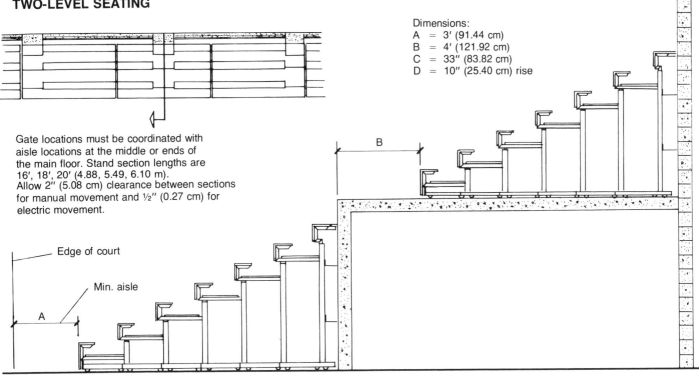

Dimensions:
A = 3' (91.44 cm)
B = 4' (121.92 cm)
C = 33" (83.82 cm)
D = 10" (25.40 cm) rise

Gate locations must be coordinated with aisle locations at the middle or ends of the main floor. Stand section lengths are 16', 18', 20' (4.88, 5.49, 6.10 m). Allow 2" (5.08 cm) clearance between sections for manual movement and ½" (0.27 cm) for electric movement.

Edge of court

Min. aisle

BLEACHERS

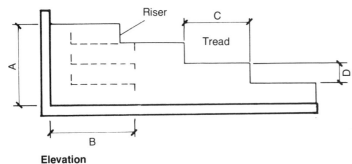

Riser

C

Tread

D

A

B

Elevation

Seating capacity*

Rows	12' (3.66 m) section	16' (4.88 m) section	20' (6.10 m) section
3	24	30	39
4	32	40	52
5	40	50	65
6	48	60	78
7	56	70	91
8	64	80	104
9	72	90	117
10	80	100	130
11	88	110	143
12	96	120	156
13	104	130	169
14	112	140	182
15	120	150	195
20	NA	250	325
30	NA	300	390

*18" (45.72 cm) linear width per person

Recessed seating

This type of seating is used to recover floor space normally covered by closed seating units. The seating has the same open and closed dimensions as wall-attached seating. Recessed size should include 3" (7.63 cm) clearance in height and depth dimensions.

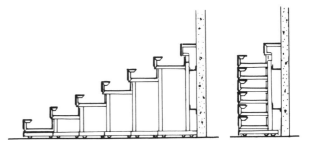

Wall-attached seating

These units are available in lengths up to 20' (6.10 m) wide. For economy, designers should specify long sections. Aisles may be located either at the ends or in the center of each section.

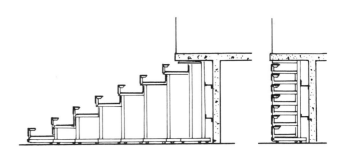

DESIGN, INSTALLATION, & MAINTENANCE PROCESS CHECKLIST

1. Involve the services of an interior plantscaping expert.

2. Consider plant functions: acoustics, screening, and aesthetics.

3. Consult lighting specifications for lamp locations and types.

4. Calculate natural lighting planned for the space.

5. Develop an interior planting plan.

6. Select the types of tropical plants to be used.

7. Select container sizes.

8. Determine weight of planters and consult with structural engineers or the architect.

9. Calculate the time required for plants to acclimatize.

10. Evaluate pros and cons of plant leasing with maintenance versus purchasing.

PLANT MATERIAL CATEGORIES

A = multistem tree

This is a woody plant that produces three or more main trunks above the soil line. This type of plant produces a rather distinct and elevated foliage crown.

B = standard tree

This woody plant produces one main trunk with a distinct and elevated foliage crown.

C = plant clump

This plant is formed by the massing of major and minor stems above the soil mass. It is typically installed in a planter scaled to sit on the floor.

D = hanging plant

This plant can form a vine or can climb with rootlets. It is contained in a hanging basket suspended by rope, wire, or chains.

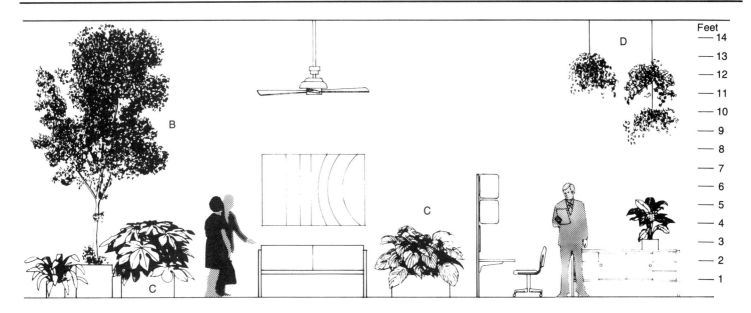

TYPICAL INTERIOR PLANTS

Common name	Botanical name
Areca Palm	Chrysalidocarpus lutescens
Bamboo Palm	Chamaedorea erumpens
Bausei Dieffenbachia	Dieffenbachia x "Bausei"
Butterfly Palm	Chrysalidocarpus lutescens
Chinese Aralia	Polyscias fruiticosa
• Cleveland Peace Lily	Spathiphyllum x "Clevelandii"
• Corn Plant Dracaena	Dracaena fragrans "Massangeana"
Decorative India Rubbertree	Ficus elastica "Decora"
Dumbcane	Dieffenbachia picta
Exotic Dumbcane	Dieffenbachia x "Exotica"
Exotic Perfection Dumbcane	Dieffenbachia x "Exotica Perfection"
• Franscher Evergreen	Aglaonema x "Fransher"
Giant Dumbcane	Dieffenbachia amoena
• Golden Evergreen	Aglaonema "Pseudobracteatum"
Golden Snow Dumbcane	Dieffenbachia picta "Golden Snow"
Indian Laurel Fig	Ficus retusa nitida
• Janet Craig Dracaena	Dracaena deremensis "Janet Craig"
Madagascar Dragon Tree	Dracaena marginata
• Malay Beauty Aglaonema	Aglaonema "Malay Beauty"
Massange's Dracaena	Dracaena fragrans "Massangeana"
• Mauna Loa Peace Lily	Spathiphyllum x "Mauna Loa"
"Memoria Corsii" Dieffenbachia	Dieffenbachia x "Memoria Corsii"
Ming Aralia	Polyscias fruticosa
Ming Tree	Polyscias fruiticosa
• Neanthe Bella Palm	Chamaedorea elegans "Bella"
• Parrot Jungle Evergreen	Aglaonema "Parrot Jungle"
Parsley Aralia	Polyscias fruticosa
• Pewter Aglaonema	Aglaonema "Malay Beauty"
Queensland Umbrella Tree	Brassaia actinophylla
Red-band Dracaena	Dracaena marginata
Reed Palm	Chamaedorea seifrizii
Rudolph Roehrs Dumbcane	Dieffenbachia picta "Rudolph Roehrs"
Schefflera	Brassaia actinophylla
Silver Evergreen	Aglaonema commutatum
• Silver King Evergreen	Aglaonema x "Silver King"
• Silver Queen Evergreen	Aglaonema x "Silver Queen"
• Snow Queen Evergreen	Aglaonema x "Snow Queen" (Pat. No. 3399)
• Striped Dracaena	Dracaena deremensis "Warneckei"
Tropic Snow Dumbcane	Dieffenbachia x "Tropic Snow"
• Variegated Chinese Evergreen	Aglaonema commutatum
• Warneck Dracaena	Dracaena deremensis "Warneckei"
Weeping Fig	Ficus benjamina
• White Rajah	Aglaonema "Pseudobracteatum"

Note: • indicates plants that will tolerate low light. The remainder require medium to high lighting levels.
Minimum = 50 footcandles; low = 50 to 85 footcandles; medium = 85 to 91 footcandles; high = 92+ footcandles.

Artificial lighting \ Plant response	Foliage: green	Foliage: deep green	Foliage: pale green	Stems: elongate slowly	Stems: elongate fast	Stems: spindly brittle	Stems: extra thick	Flowering: long period	Flowering: rapid	Flowering: late	Side shoots: multiple	Side shoots: few	Growth: height only	Growth: parallel to lamp	Growth: toward lamp	Growth: rapid mature/decline	Notes
Fluorescent																	Notes: Minimum 25 footcandles. Daily light 12 to 16 hours. Day temperature 65° to 95°F; night temperature 50° to 65°F. Minimum humidity 25 to 50.
Cool White (CW)	X			X				X			X			X			
Warm White (WW)	X			X				X			X			X			
Grow Lux (GL)		X		X			X			X	X						
Vita Lite (VITA)			X	X					X			X			X	X	
Argo Lite (Argo)			X	X					X			X			X	X	
High-intensity discharge (HID)	X			X				X			X			X			
Mercury (phosphor coated)	X			X				X			X			X			
Metal halide (MH)				X	X				X				X			X	
Sodium																	
High pressure (HPS)		X		X			X				X	X					
Low pressure (LPS)		X		X			X				X	X					
Incandescent (INC)				X	X				X				X			X	
Mercury (INC HG)				X	X				X				X			X	Do not use with vines

Information from USDA Agriculture Research, Beltsville, MD.

Overall plant height

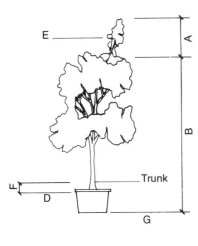

Notes:
A = not included
B = mean plant height
C = mean foliage width
D = soil line
E = outstanding branch
F = 6" (15.24 cm)
G = base of container
H = foliage origin
I = rooted canes
J = overall plant height
K = cane height (varies)

These living green plants are commercially grown in containers for their form, texture, and growth habits instead of their flowers or blooms. They are capable of living indoors for long periods at relatively constant temperatures and under low light intensities (that is, lower than they were used to in production).

Plant width & origin

GENERAL SPECIFICATIONS FOR FOLIAGE No. 1 QUALITY

Plant material of Foliage No. 1 quality shall have the following general characteristics:

Canes, trunks, stems, & branches

1. Must be visibly free of pests and pathogens that could, by their presence, induce (or contribute to) the decline of the plant.
2. Must be reasonably free of conspicuous scarring evidence: scars, conspicuous or not, must be substantially healed, providing no point of entry for deleterious pathogens or boring insects. There must be no splitting of canes or trunks at branching points.
3. Dead wood and branches must be removed. Major pruning points shall be painted with pruning paint.
4. All canes or trunks must be well formed, sturdy, and well rooted and therefore stable and self-supporting in the growing container.
5. Plant height: Overall plant height shall be measured from base of growing container to mean foliage top.
6. Cane heights: With some ppp/cane plant varieties*, quality is determined by the height of rooted canes. Cane heights shall always be measured from the base of the growing container. Overall height of the plant shall be from base of growing container to mean foliage top.

*PPP (plants per pot) indicates the number of individual rooted cuttings or rooted canes that have been planted together to form a single plant.

Cane plant

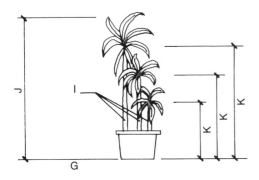

Information from Florida Foliage Association, Apoka, FL, and Interior Landscape Division of Associated Landscape Contractors of America

' Foliage

1. Must be visibly free of pests and pathogens that could, by their presence, induce (or contribute to) the decline of the plant.
2. Must be reasonably free of any chlorosis, yellowing, or poor chlorophyll formation, turgid and substantially erect, as well as substantially free of blemishes resulting from mechanical, chemical, pathological, or pest-induced damage.
3. Must be cleaned of all dust and water-borne pesticide and fertilizer residue at time of project acceptance.
4. Must be present in such quantity as may be required to produce an appearance representative of species.
5. Foliage width and origin: Measured across mean foliage width dimension, not including random outstanding branches. Foliage origin along a main trunk, cane, or stem shall be measured from soil line.
Note: Width of foliage to be specified as a percentage of total plant height for best proportion.

Root system & soil mass

1. The root system shall be well-developed and upon inspection shall be found to be visibly free of pests and/or pathogens. Development shall be adequate to:
   a. Be well distributed throughout the container, such that the roots visibly extend on all sides to the inside face of the growing container. Conversely, the root formation within the container shall not have developed to the point where it becomes excessive (that is, "potbound") and prohibits water from permeating to the fine water-absorbing root hairs.
   b. Afford firm support and ensure physical stability of the plant parts above the soil.
   c. Maintain life systems required to produce vigorous, healthy growth.
2. The growing medium shall be comprised of such constituents as may be necessary to provide:
   a. Thorough drainage and satisfactory aeration of the root zone. The soil mass should be as uniform as possible.
   b. Adequate moisture and nutrient retention as may be necessary to promote vigorous but controlled plant growth.
   c. Sufficient density in the growing container to ensure stability of the entire unit, that is, plant and container.
3. The growing medium shall be visibly free of pests, pathogens, and weeds.
4. The growing medium shall be free of chemical residues that could be harmful to consumers.

Standard sizes

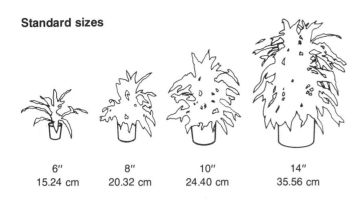

| 6″ | 8″ | 10″ | 14″ |
| 15.24 cm | 20.32 cm | 24.40 cm | 35.56 cm |

Note: The containers shown above represent current sizes used in the nursery industry.

The industry advises designers not to assume that a plant in a slightly larger container is a better quality plant. When the designer is specifying plant material to fit into specific decorative movable planters, the nursery must be informed of the interior diameter size of the decorative planter.

Hanging planters are defined as either a wire basket or a plastic self-watering container designed to be hung by wire, rope, or chain.

Pot sizes in relation to minimum plant height of multi-stem plants (OAW = overall width)

OAW pot size (in.)	Min. plant height (ft)	Approx. plant weights (lb)
10	3-5	
12	4-5	
14	5-7	
17	7-9	
21	10-14	3-stem, 18′ (medium) 435
26	14-16	3-stem, 20′ 630
30	16-18	multi, 13′ (medium) 615
36	18-24	multi, 18′ (medium) 975
48	20 plus	

Pot sizes in relation to minimum plant height of standard tree-type plants

OAW pot size (in.)	Min. plant height (ft)	Approx. plant weights (lb)
10	3-5	
12	4-5	
14	5-7	6′ (wet) 51
17	7-9	7-8′ (medium) 94
21	10-14	12′ (medium) 192
26	14-16	14′ (wet) 200
30	16-18	16′ (medium) 700
36	18-24	18′ (medium) 840
48	20 plus	18-20′ (medium) 1,755

Standard nursery pot designations

Pot size Nominal dimensions (in. diameter)	Actual dimensions OAW x OAH (in.)	Metric dimensions OAW x OAH (mm)	Trade designation (gallons)
6	6½ x 6	165.1 x 152.4	1 (standard)
6 tub	6½ x 5	165.1 x 127.0	6″ tub
8	8 x 7	203.2 x 177.8	2 (standard)
9	9 x 8	228.6 x 203.2	2
8 tub	8 x 5¾	203.2 x 146.1	8″ tub
10	10 x 9½	254.0 x 241.3	3
11 tub	11 x 8	279.4 x 203.2	3
12	12 x 11	304.8 x 279.4	4
11	11 x 10½	279.4 x 266.7	4
14	13½ x 12	342.9 x 304.8	7
16	15½ x 26	393.7 x 660.4	30
16	16 x 31	406.4 x 787.4	40
17	17 x 14	431.8 x 355.6	10
17	17 x 15	431.8 x 381.0	15
21	21 x 16	533.4 x 406.4	20
21	21 x 18	533.4 x 457.2	26
21	21 x 24	533.4 x 609.6	35
26	26 x 15½	660.4 x 393.7	30
26	26 x 24	660.4 x 609.6	45
30	29 x 17	736.6 x 431.8	35
30	29 x 20	736.6 x 508.0	45
31	31 x 16	787.4 x 406.4	40
32	32 x 22	812.8 x 558.8	65
36	36 x 24	914.4 x 609.6	95
48	48 x 30	1219.9 x 762.0	125

*Based on information from the Florida Foliage Association, Apopka, FL.

Information from Florida Foliage Association, Apoka, FL, and Interior Landscape Division of Associated Landscape Contractors of America

Movable decorative planter

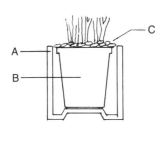

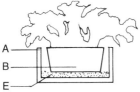

Double planting

2"–3"
(5.08–7.62 cm)

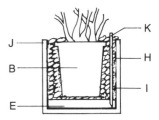

Direct planting

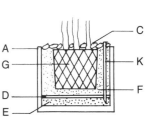

Notes:

A = planter
B = nursery pot
C = mulch
D = soil separator
E = drainage fill
F = soil mix

G = root ball
H = plastic liner
I = fill only if
      necessary
J = basket
K = syphon tube

Note: Movable planters may require either double or direct potting. Plants should be planted plumb and secure within the planter. Immediately after direct planting, plants shall be watered to settle the soil mix.

When planters have drainage holes and separate drainage trays, such as clay pots with saucers, soil separators or syphon tubes shall not be required.

Fixed planting beds

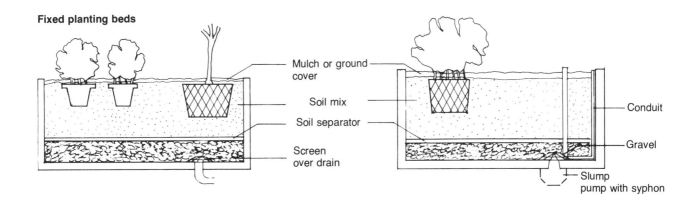

Mulch or ground cover

Soil mix

Soil separator

Screen over drain

Conduit

Gravel

Slump pump with syphon

Seasonal & other planting

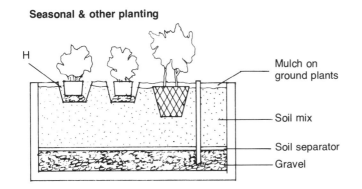

Mulch on ground plants

Soil mix

Soil separator

Gravel

Seasonal planting includes plants that are frequently rotated. They are often triple potted to facilitate moving and allow for various watering requirements.

Information from Florida Foliage Association, Apoka, FL, and Interior Landscape Division of Associated Landscape Contractors of America

Specification information for fixed beds

Generally, fixed beds shall be direct planted, with plants removed from nursery pots. A light, airy, well-draining soil mix of neutral pH shall be employed. Unless specific plant requirements dictate otherwise, a consistent mix shall be used throughout the entire project. The contractor shall use discretion regarding the composition of the mix.

All fixed planting beds should have an integral drainage system provided by the owner. The best type of system is where drain(s) are tied into the project's plumbing system. A sump pump linked to a syphon tube is acceptable; a syphon tube alone will suffice for smaller beds.

Depending upon the environmental conditions, however, it can be best to double pot all or some of the plants (especially if frequent plant rotations are expected or if plants within the same bed will require different soil moisture levels). The contractor should be consulted prior to specifying direct or double potting.

Musical furnishings

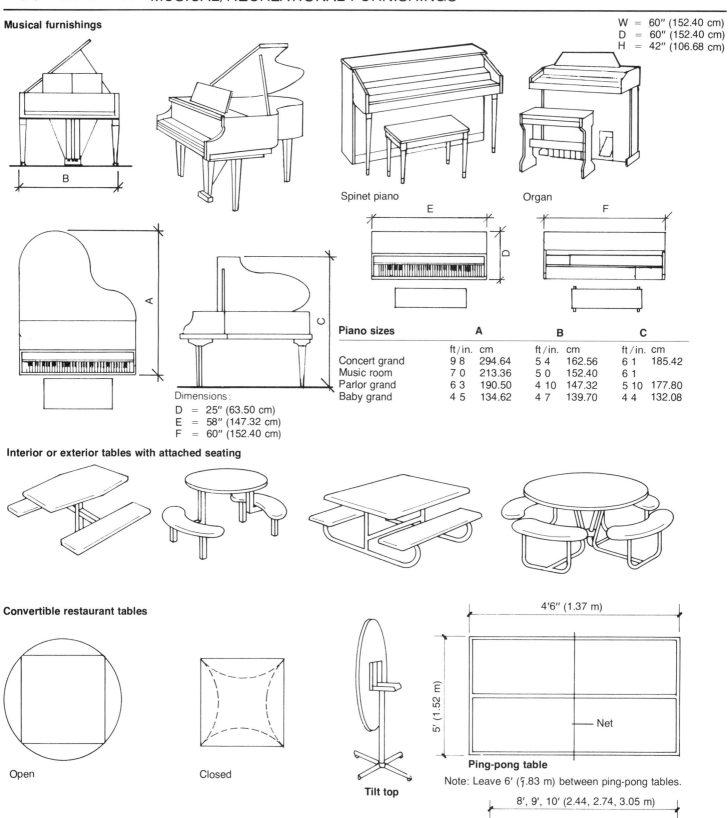

W = 60" (152.40 cm)
D = 60" (152.40 cm)
H = 42" (106.68 cm)

Spinet piano

Organ

Dimensions:
D = 25" (63.50 cm)
E = 58" (147.32 cm)
F = 60" (152.40 cm)

Piano sizes

	A		B		C	
	ft/in.	cm	ft/in.	cm	ft/in.	cm
Concert grand	9 8	294.64	5 4	162.56	6 1	185.42
Music room	7 0	213.36	5 0	152.40	6 1	
Parlor grand	6 3	190.50	4 10	147.32	5 10	177.80
Baby grand	4 5	134.62	4 7	139.70	4 4	132.08

Interior or exterior tables with attached seating

Convertible restaurant tables

Open

Closed

Tilt top

4'6" (1.37 m)

5' (1.52 m)

Net

Ping-pong table

Note: Leave 6' (1.83 m) between ping-pong tables.

Typical top sizes:
in.	cm		in.	cm	
32 square	81.28	opens to	45	114.30	diameter
34 square	83.36	opens to	48	121.92	diameter
36 square	91.44	opens to	51	129.54	diameter
42 square	106.68	opens to	60	152.40	diameter

8', 9', 10' (2.44, 2.74, 3.05 m)

4'9"–8'9" (1.45–2.67 m)

Pool table

Note: On both these game tables,
allow a minimum of 3' (0.91 m)
on all sides for players' use.

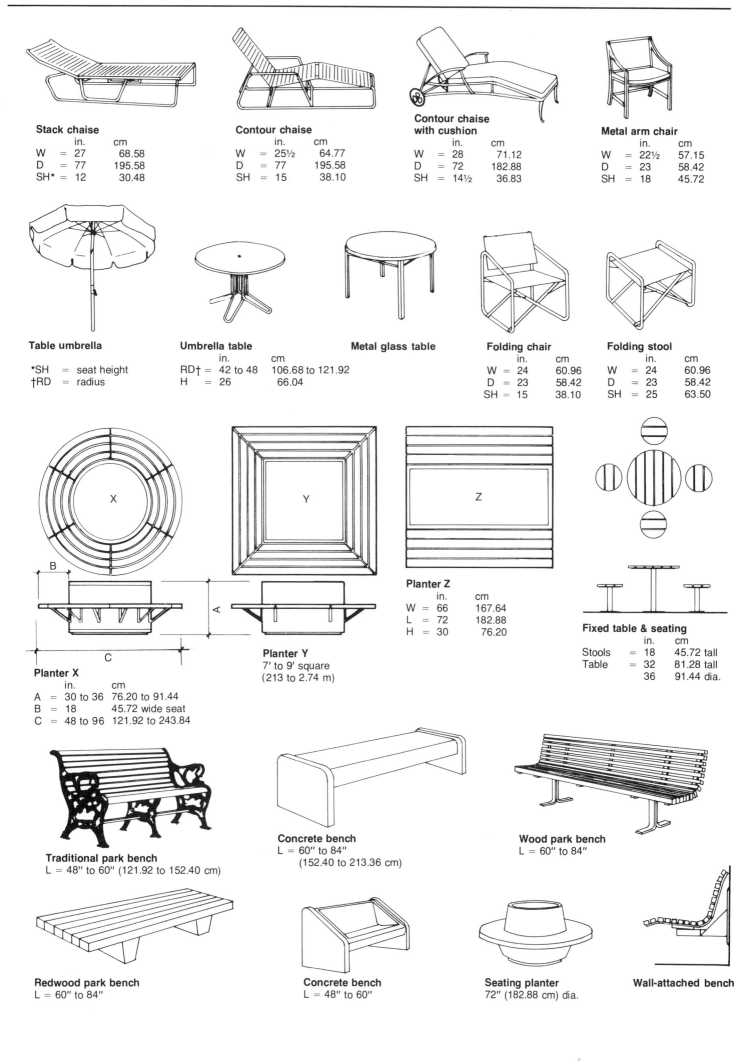

Stack chaise

	in.	cm
W =	27	68.58
D =	77	195.58
SH* =	12	30.48

Contour chaise

	in.	cm
W =	25½	64.77
D =	77	195.58
SH =	15	38.10

Contour chaise with cushion

	in.	cm
W =	28	71.12
D =	72	182.88
SH =	14½	36.83

Metal arm chair

	in.	cm
W =	22½	57.15
D =	23	58.42
SH =	18	45.72

Table umbrella

*SH = seat height
†RD = radius

Umbrella table

	in.	cm
RD† =	42 to 48	106.68 to 121.92
H =	26	66.04

Metal glass table

Folding chair

	in.	cm
W =	24	60.96
D =	23	58.42
SH =	15	38.10

Folding stool

	in.	cm
W =	24	60.96
D =	23	58.42
SH =	25	63.50

Planter X

	in.	cm
A =	30 to 36	76.20 to 91.44
B =	18	45.72 wide seat
C =	48 to 96	121.92 to 243.84

Planter Y
7′ to 9′ square
(213 to 2.74 m)

Planter Z

	in.	cm
W =	66	167.64
L =	72	182.88
H =	30	76.20

Fixed table & seating

	in.	cm
Stools =	18	45.72 tall
Table =	32	81.28 tall
	36	91.44 dia.

Traditional park bench
L = 48″ to 60″ (121.92 to 152.40 cm)

Concrete bench
L = 60″ to 84″
(152.40 to 213.36 cm)

Wood park bench
L = 60″ to 84″

Redwood park bench
L = 60″ to 84″

Concrete bench
L = 48″ to 60″

Seating planter
72″ (182.88 cm) dia.

Wall-attached bench

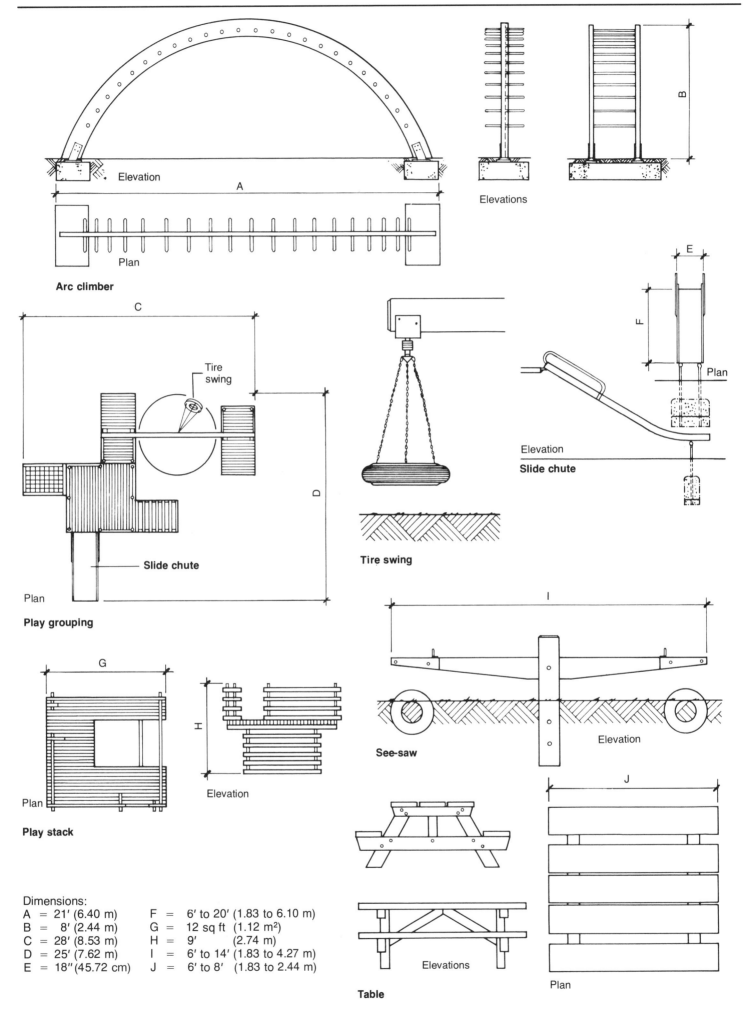

Arc climber

Elevation

Plan

A

Elevations

B

Play grouping

C

Tire swing

Slide chute

Plan

D

Tire swing

E

F

Plan

Elevation

Slide chute

Play stack

G

Plan

H

Elevation

See-saw

I

Elevation

Table

Elevations

J

Plan

Dimensions:
A = 21′ (6.40 m) F = 6′ to 20′ (1.83 to 6.10 m)
B = 8′ (2.44 m) G = 12 sq ft (1.12 m²)
C = 28′ (8.53 m) H = 9′   (2.74 m)
D = 25′ (7.62 m) I = 6′ to 14′ (1.83 to 4.27 m)
E = 18″ (45.72 cm) J = 6′ to 8′ (1.83 to 2.44 m)

AA	Aluminum Association 818 Connecticut Ave., N.W. Washington, DC 20006		FFA	Florida Foliage Association P.O. Box Y Apopka, FL 32704
AAMA	Architectural Aluminum Manufacturers Association 117 E. Palatine Rd. Palatine, IL 60067		ICBO	International Conference of Building Officials 5360 So. Workman Mill Rd. Whittier, CA 90601
AH&MA	American Hotel and Motel Association 888 Seventh Ave. New York, NY 10019		NAAMM	National Association of Architectural Metal Manufacturers 221 N. LaSalle Chicago, IL 60601
ALCA	Associated Landscape Contractors of America 1750 Old Meadow Rd. McLean, VA 22101		NFPA	National Fire Protection Association Batterymarch Park Quincy, MA 02269
ASTM	American Society for Testing and Materials 1916 Race St. Philadelphia, PA 19103		SBCCI	Southern Building Code Congress International, Inc. 900 Montclair Rd. Birmingham, AL 35213
BIFMA	Business and Institutional Manufacturers Association 2335 Burton Street S.E. Grand Rapids, MI 49506		UL	Underwriters Laboratories, Inc. 333 Pfingsten Rd. Northbrook, IL 60062
BO&CAI	Building Officials & Code Administrators International, Inc. Country Club Hills, IL 60477		USVBA	U.S. Venetian Blind Association 355 Lexington Ave. New York, NY 10016

VERTICAL & HORIZONTAL LOUVER BLINDS

STANDARDS

ASTM   **American Society for Testing and Materials**

B 221   Specification for Aluminum and Aluminum-Alloy Extruded Bar, Rod, Wire, Shape and Tube. (ANSI/ASTM B221)

D 568   Test Method for Rate of Burning and/or Extent and Time of Burning of Flexible Plastics in a Vertical Position. (ANSI/ASTM D568)

1784   Specification for Rigid Poly (Vinyl Chloride) (PVC) Compounds and Chlorinated Poly (Vinyl Chloride) (CPVC) Compounds.

E 84   Test Method for Surface Burning Characteristics of Building Materials.

E 162   Test Method for Surface Flammability of Materials Using a Radiant Heat Energy Source.

FS   **FEDERAL SPECIFICATIONS**

AA-V-200   Venetian Blinds. Federal Supply Classification (FSC) 7230

AA-V-00200   Venetian Blinds. (FSC) 7230

QQ-A-200   Aluminum Alloy, Bar, Rod, Shapes, Tube, and Wire, Extruded, and Structural Shapes, General Specification for (FSC) 9530

REGULATIONS

BO&CAI   **Building Officials & Code Administrators International, Inc.**
Basic Building Code (1981).

Sec. 1421.0   Interior Finish and Trim

ICBO   **International Conference of Building Officials**
Uniform Building Code (1979)

Chap. 42   Interior Wall and Ceiling Finish

NFPA   **National Fire Protection Association**

101   Code for Safety to Life from Fire in Buildings and Structures

255   Method of Test of Surface Burning Characteristics of Building Materials

SBCCI   **Southern Building Code Congress International, Inc.**
Standard Building Code (1979):

Sec. 404.6   Assembly Occupancy—(A): Interior Finish.

Sec. 704   Restrictions on Interior Use of Combustible Materials

UL   **Underwriters Laboratories, Inc.**

723   Test for Surface Burning Characteristics of Building Materials

SPECIFICATION AIDS

Department of the Army
U.S. Army Corps of Engineers
Guide Specifications for Military Construction:

CEGS-12501   Venetian Blinds, Draw Curtains, and Window Shades
Guide Specifications for Military Family Housing:

12.1   Venetian Blinds

FCC   **Federal Construction Council**
Federal Construction Guide Specifications:

FCGS-12510   Blinds, Venetian (and Audio Visual)

GSA   **General Services Administration**
Design Management Div.
Public Buildings Service Guide Specifications:

4-1224   Vertical Blinds

12503   Blinds, Venetian (and Audio Visual)

NASA   **National Aeronautics & Space Administration**
SPECSINTACT:

12511   Venetian Blinds (Vertical Louvers)

12512   Venetian Blinds (Horizontal Louvers)

NIHGS   **National Institutes of Health Guide Specifications:**

12510   Venetian Blinds

The AIA Service Corp.; Professional Systems Div.
MASTERSPEC:

12500   Window Treatment

SHADES

STANDARDS

ASTM   **American Society for Testing and Materials**

D 568   Test Method for Rate of Burning and/or Extent and Time of Burning of Flexible Plastics in a Vertical Position. (ANSI/ASTM D568)

E 84   Test Method for Surface Burning Characteristics of Building Materials.

E 162   Test Method for Surface Flammability of Materials Using a Radiant Heat Energy Source.

FS   **Federal Specifications**

L-S-001787   Shade, Window, (Vinyl), with Roller, Slat, Ring Pull and Accessories and Vinyl Film (in Piece Goods). Federal Supply Classification (FSC) 7230

CCC-C-521   Cloth, Coated, Window Shade. (FSC) 8305

DDD-S-251   Shade, Roller, Window, Roller, Slat, Cord, and Accessories. (FSC) 7230

REGULATIONS

BO&CAI   **Building Officials & Code Administrators International, Inc.**
Basic Building Code (1981):

Sec. 1424.0   Decorative Material Restrictions

ICBO   **International Conference of Building Officials**
Uniform Building Code (1979):

Chap. 42   Fire-Resistive Standards for Fire Protection

NFPA   **National Fire Protection Association**

101   Code for Safety to Life from Fire in Buildings and Structures:

255   Method of Test of Surface Burning Characteristics of Building Materials

701   Methods of Fire Tests for Flame-Resistant Textiles and Films

SBCCI   **Southern Building Code Congress International, Inc.**
Standard Building Code (1979):

704.2   Restrictions on Interior Use of Combustible Materials: Classification.

UL   **Underwriters Laboratories, Inc.**

723   Test for Surface Burning Characteristics of Building Materials.

SPECIFICATION AIDS

Department of the Army
U.S. Army Corps of Engineers
Guide Specifications for Military Construction:

CEGS-12501   Venetian Blinds, Draw Curtains, and Window Shades

CEGS-12503   Audiovisual Blinds and Curtains and Lightproof Shades.
Guide Specifications for Military Family Housing:

12-2a   Shades and Draw Curtains
Short-Form Guide Specifications for Army Reserve Centers:

CE-R-12.1   Roller Shades

NASA   **National Aeronautics & Space Administration**
SPECSINTACT:

12514   Lightproof Shades

NIHGS   **National Institutes of Health Guide Specifications**

12520   Lightproof Shades
Veterans Administration Guide Specifications:

12513   Window Shades.

12514   Lightproof Shades.

The AIA Service Corp.; Professional Systems Div.— MASTERSPEC:

12513   Window Shades.

DRAPERY AND CURTAIN HARDWARE

STANDARDS

ASTM — **American Society for Testing and Materials**

A 424 — Specification for Steel Sheet for Porcelain Enameling. (ANSI/ASTM A424)

B 221 — Specification for Aluminum and Aluminum-Alloy Extruded Bar Rod, Wire, Shape and Tube. (ANSI/ASTM B221)

C 313 — Test Method for Adherence of Porcelain Enamel and Ceramic Coatings to Sheet Metal. (ANSI/ASTM C313)

MS — **Military Specifications**

DOD-C 24556 — Curtain, Track and Suspension System, Bert (Shipboard Use) (Metric). Federal Supply Classification (FSC) 7230

REGULATIONS

UL — **Underwriters Laboratories, Inc.**

325 — Door, Drapery, Gate, Louver, and Window Operators and Systems. (ANSI/UL 325)

CONSTRUCTION AIDS

CSRF — **Construction Sciences Research Foundation**—SPECTEXT:

12531 — Drapery Track

Department of the Army
U.S. Army Corps of Engineers
Guide Specifications for Military Construction:

CEGS-12501 — Venetian Blinds, Draw Curtains, and Window Shades.

CEGS-12503 — Audiovisual Blinds and Curtains and Lightproof Shades.

Guide Specifications for Military Family Housing:

12.2a — Shades and Draw Curtains

Department of the Navy
Naval Facilities Engineering Command (NAV-FAC) Guide Specifications:

NFGS-12502 — Draperies

FCC — **Federal Construction Council**
Federal Construction Guide Specifications:

FCGS-12502 — Draperies

NASA — **National Aeronautics & Space Administration**—SPECSINTACT:

12526 — Audio-Visual Draw Curtains

The AIA Service Corp.; Professional Systems Div.—MASTERSPEC:

12500 — Window Treatment

VA — **Veterans Administration**
Guide Specifications:

12501 — Drapery and Curtain Hardware

ACCESSORIES

STANDARDS

ASTM — **American Society for Testing and Materials**

A 256 — Test for Impact Resistance of Plastics and Electrical Insulating Materials. (ANSI/ASTM D256)

D 635 — Test for Rate of Burning and/or Extent and Time of Burning of Self Supporting Plastics in a Horizontal Position. (ANSI/ASTM D635)

D 638 — Test for Tensile Properties of Plastics. (ANSI/ASTM D638)

D 792 — Test for Specific Gravity and Density of Plastics by Displacement (ANSI/ASTM D792)

D 1338 — Test for Working Life of Liquid or Paste Adhesives by Consistency and Bond Strength. (ANSI/ASTM D1338)

D 1525 — Test for Vicat Softening Temperature of Plastics. (ANSI/ASTM D1525)

E 84 — Test for Surface Burning Characteristics of Building Materials. (ANSI/ASTM E84)

FS — **Federal Specifications**

GG-C-001072 (4) — Clocks, Wall (Battery Operated).

GG-C-00466E1 — Clocks, Wall, Synchronous Motor.

MATTRESSES AND MATTRESS PADS

STANDARDS

FF 4-72 — Standard for the Flammability of Mattresses and Mattress Pads

TESTING

AH&MA/NABM Cornell Testing Procedure Support Firmness, Cumulated Dimple, Load Deflection Curve

SPECIFICATION AIDS

AH&MA — **American Hotel and Motel Association**
"Guidelines for Quality in Contract Mattresses and Box Springs"

AUDITORIUM & THEATER SEATING

STANDARDS

ASTM — **American Society for Testing and Materials**

D635 — Test for Rate of Burning and/or Extent and Time of Burning Self-Supporting Plastics in a Horizontal Position (ANSI/ASTM D635)

D1175 — Test for Abrasion Resistance of Textile Fabrics (ANSI/ASTM D1175)

E 162 — Test for Surface Flammability of Materials Using a Radiant Heat Energy Source.

FS — **Federal Specifications**

L-P-508H — Plastic Sheet, Laminated, Decorative and Non-Decorative.

TT-E-491B (1) — Enamel; Gloss Synthetic (For Metal and Wood Hospital Furniture).

TT-L-57C (a) — Lacquer; Rubbing, Clear (For Wood Furniture).

TT-L-58D — Lacquer; Spraying, Clear, and Pigmented (General Interior Use).

TT-P-659C — Primer Coating and Surfacer, Synthetic, Tints and White (For Metal and Wood Surfaces).

TT-S-300A — Shellac, Cut.

TT-S-711B (2) — Stain; Oil Type, Wood, Interior.

TT-S-720A (1) — Stain; Wood, Non-Grain Raising, Solvent-Dye Type.

CCC-A-680A INT AMD 1 — Artificial Leather (Cloth Coated) Vinyl Re-Expanded Layer (Upholstery).

CCC-C-700G (1) — Cloth, Coated, Vinyl, Coated (Artificial Leather).

PS — **Product Standards**

PS 1-74 — Construction and Industrial Plywood.

PS 51-71 — Hardwood and Decorative Plywood.

SPECIFICATION AIDS

Corps of Engineers
Guide Specifications:

CE-236.03 — Theater Chairs July, 1975

Department of the Navy
Naval Facilities Engineering Command (NAVFAC)-Type Specifications:

TS-12711 — Theater Chairs May, 1974

FCGS — **Federal Construction Guide Specification**
U.S. Army Construction Engineering Research Laboratory

Theater Chairs, April, 1975

VA — **Veterans Administration**
Office of Construction, Master Construction (Guide) Specifications:

VA 57 — Theater Chairs

STADIUM & ARENA SEATING

REGULATIONS

BO&CAI — **Building Officials & Code Administrators International, Inc.**
Basic Building Code (1981):

Sec. 302.0 — Use Group A, Assembly Buildings

Sec. 619.0 — Stadiums and Grandstands.

ICBO — **International Conference of Building Officials**
Uniform Building Code (1979):

Sec. 601 — Group A Occupancies Defined.

Sec. 3321 — Reviewing Stands, Grandstands and Bleachers.

Sec. 3322 — Folding and Telescoping Seating.

NFPA — **National Fire Protection Association**

NFPA 101 — Code for Safety to Life from Fire in Buildings and Structures.

NFPA 102 — Assembly Seating, Tens, and Air-Supported Structure

SBCCI — **Southern Building Code Congress International, Inc.**
Standard Building Code (1979):

Sec. 404 — Assembly Occupancy—(A).

Sec. 502 — Reviewing Stands, Grandstands and Bleachers.

SPECIFICATION AIDS

Department of the Army
U.S. Army Corps of Engineers
Guide Specifications for Military Construction:

CEGS-12710 — Theater Chairs

Department of the Navy
Naval Facilities Engineering Command (NAVFAC) Guide Specifications:

TS-12711 — Theater Seating

VERTICAL EXITS: STAIRS, RAMPS, AND ESCALATORS

Calculation of stair height and number of treads is achieved by the following method:
1. Measure distance (X = total rise) from the finished floor to the finished ceiling.
2. This measurement is then divided by 7, which is the recommended maximum riser height in inches. The answer is the number of risers needed.

The table below illustrates how the ceiling height affects the total run and well hole dimensions. Most codes regulate the headroom or ceiling height above the stairs; the minimum should not be lower than 7'6" (228.60 cm).

Stair dimension table

Height floor to floor H	No. of risers	Height of risers (in.) R	Width of treads (in.) T	Total run L	Well width W
8'0"	12	8	9	8'3"	8'1"
	13	7⅜ +	9½	9'6"	9'2½"
	13	7⅜ +	10	10'0"	9'8½"
8'6"	13	7⅞	9	9'0"	8'3"
	14	7⁵⁄₁₆ −	9½	10'3½"	9'4"
	14	7⁵⁄₁₆ −	10	10'10"	9'10"
9'0"	14	7¹¹⁄₁₆ +	9	9'9"	8'5"
	15	7³⁄₁₆ +	9½	11'1"	9'6½"
	15	7³⁄₁₆ +	10	11'8"	9'11½"
9'6"	15	7⅝ −	9	10'6"	8'6½"
	16	7⅛	9½	11'10½"	9'7"
	16	7⅛	10	12'6"	10'1"

Note: Dimensions under W are based on 78" (198.12 cm) minimum headroom. As the headroom increases, so does the well opening.

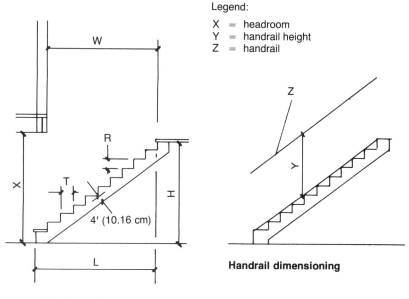

Legend:
X = headroom
Y = handrail height
Z = handrail

Handrail dimensioning

Stair dimensioning

Note: See safety recommendations on pages 288, 289, 290.

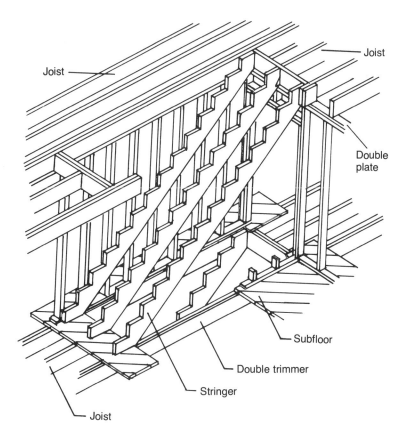

Standard stair framing

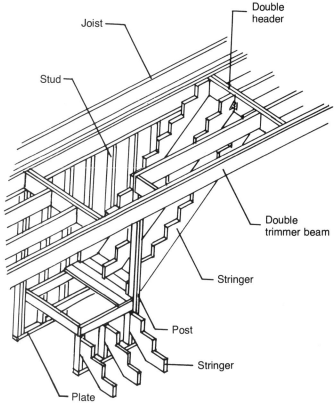

Framing for right-angle stairs

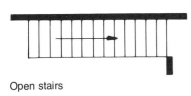

Open stairs

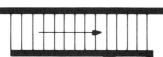

Closed stairs,
walls on each side

Straight run, partially
open & closed

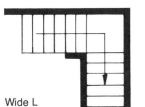

Wide L

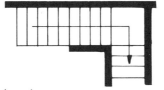

Long L

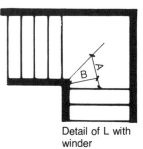

Double L

Note: Most
fire codes
that permit
exit stairs
with "winders"
(steps wider
at one end
than at the
other) require
a minimum
depth of (C)
6" (15.24 cm) and
a minimun depth of tread
(A) 9" (22.86 cm) at a point
(B) 12" (30.48 cm) from the
narrowest edge.

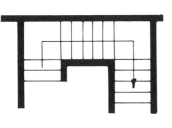

Wide U

Narrow U

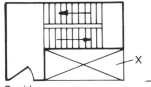

Detail of L with
winder

Wide U

Narrow U

**Fire-resistant
construction**
Smoke-proof tower X
opens at top to vent smoke

**Fire stairs with
smoke-proof tower
that opens to outside
atmosphere**

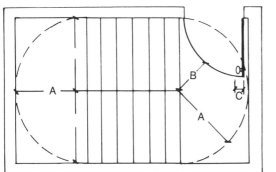

Corridor   Corridor

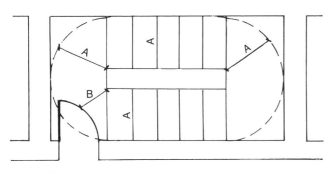

Existing building

New building

FIRE-PROTECTED STAIRS

Existing buildings
Stair widths and landing radii A are equal. Clearance B between the opening door and the stair newel post must be at least 22" (55.88 cm), that is, one unit of exit width.

New buildings
If the stair is to be 66" (167.64 cm) wide, dimension B must be at least 33" (83.82 cm).

Protected stairwells
Doors opening into stairs should not block stair landings or the stairs.

Access to pressurized stairs
The force required to open any door in a means or egress shall not exceed 50 lb (22.70 kg) applied to the latch side. Panic hardware is an important requirement on doors opening into pressurized stairs, and it may increase the force required to open the door. Relief dampers can correct this problem. Designers should check barrier-free codes and with local fire authorities for the minimum pressure required for exits to protected stairs. Check local codes for requirements.

Dimensions:
A = required width
B = at least one-half of A
C = 3½" (8.89 cm) max.

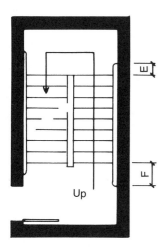

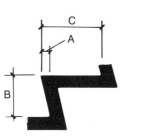

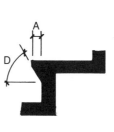

Dimensions:
A = 1½″ (3.81 cm)
B = 7″ (17.78 cm) max.
C = to suit stair formula
D = 60° radius min.
E = 12″ (30.48 cm) min.
F = 12″ plus the depth of one tread beyond bottom riser
G = 2′8″ to 2′10″ (81.28 to 86.36 cm)
H = one tread depth

Stair risers & nosings
Open risers are not permitted in barrier-free codes. Nosings shall have a leading edge with a maximum radius of ½″ (1.27 cm).

Stairwell with handrail extensions

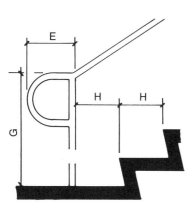

Stair bottom extension

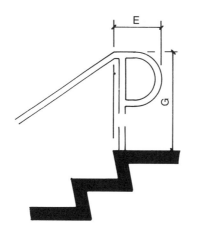

Stair top extension

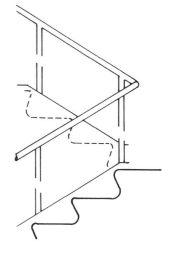

Elevation of center handrail

HANDRAILS

Handrails shall be provided on both sides of the stairway.

Mounting heights
Accessible stairs and ramps shall have rails of 2′8″ to 2′10″ (81.28 to 86.36 cm) above the stair nosing.

Structural strength
Handrails shall support minimum momentary concentrated load applied at the top edge of 200 lb (90.80 kg) horizontally and 30 percent of the load downward vertically. When the railing system is installed in public assembly occupancies, this load shall increase 50 percent. The handrails shall not rotate within their fittings. All handrail materials shall meet the same requirements.

Hazards
Ends of free-standing handrails shall be either rounded or returned smoothly to floor or post.

Projections
If outside handrails are not continuous, then:

At a ramp landing, handrails shall project parallel with ramp or landing surface for a length of 1′ (30.48 cm) beyond the top and bottom of ramp surfaces.

At a stair landing, handrails shall project at least 1′ beyond the top riser plus the depth of one tread beyond the bottom riser. The 1′ projection shall in each instance be parallel with the floor.

Exception: Full extension of handrails shall not be required in alterations where such extensions would be hazardous or impossible due to plan configurations.

Gripping surfaces shall not be interrupted with newel posts, balusters, or other obstructions.

Elevation

Treads

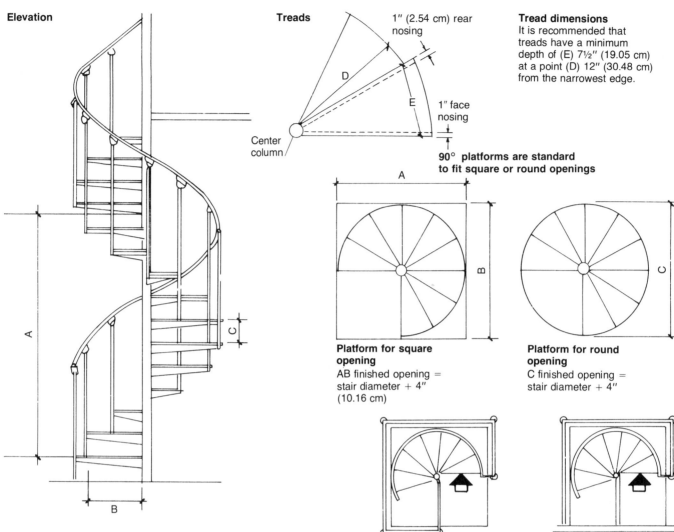

1" (2.54 cm) rear nosing

D

E

1" face nosing

Center column

Tread dimensions
It is recommended that treads have a minimum depth of (E) 7½" (19.05 cm) at a point (D) 12" (30.48 cm) from the narrowest edge.

90° platforms are standard to fit square or round openings

A

B

C

Platform for square opening
AB finished opening = stair diameter + 4" (10.16 cm)

Platform for round opening
C finished opening = stair diameter + 4"

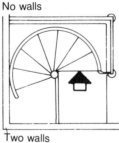

No walls

Two walls

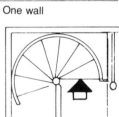

One wall

Three walls

Minimum & maximum dimensions required for some code agencies

A = 6'6" (1.98 m) min. headroom
B = 26" (66.04 cm) min. clear width of treads
C = 9½" (24.13 cm) maximum height of riser

In some occupany classifications spiral stairs may serve as means of egress from areas with an occupancy load limited to five people. Consult local codes.

Most fire codes require that all treads be identical.

Note: In the design of the method of transition from the top of the spiral stair to the building floor, the depth of the platform must be subtracted from the height between the upper finished floor and the surface of this tread in order to create the clear minimum headroom.

Finish
The platform may be finished in a subfloor configuration and mounting height adjusted to receive the extension of the interior floor finish. Most landings and stair treads are finished in the same surface material.

Note: Stairs may be constructed for either left hand (ascending clockwise) or right hand (ascending counter-clockwise).

*Standard stair diameters are 3'6', 4'0', 4'6', 5'0', 5'6', and 6'0' (1.07, 1.22, 1.37, 1.52, 1.68, 1.83 m).

†These figures are for standard layouts using standard platforms.

Riser/tread calculations*

Number of risers	30° treads, 12 treads per circle, 8½" to 9½" riser height†	Stair circle (degrees)
8	5'8" to 6'4"	210
9	6'4½" to 7'1½"	240
10	7'1" to 7'11"	270
11	7'9½" to 8'8½"	300
12	8'6" to 9'6"	330
13	9'2½" to 10'3½"	360
14	9'11" to 11'1"	390
15	10'7½" to 11'10½"	420
16	11'4" to 12'8"	450
17	12'0½" to 13'5½"	480
18	12'9" to 14'3"	510
19	13'5½" to 15'0½"	540
20	14'2" to 15'10"	570

NEWEL POSTS

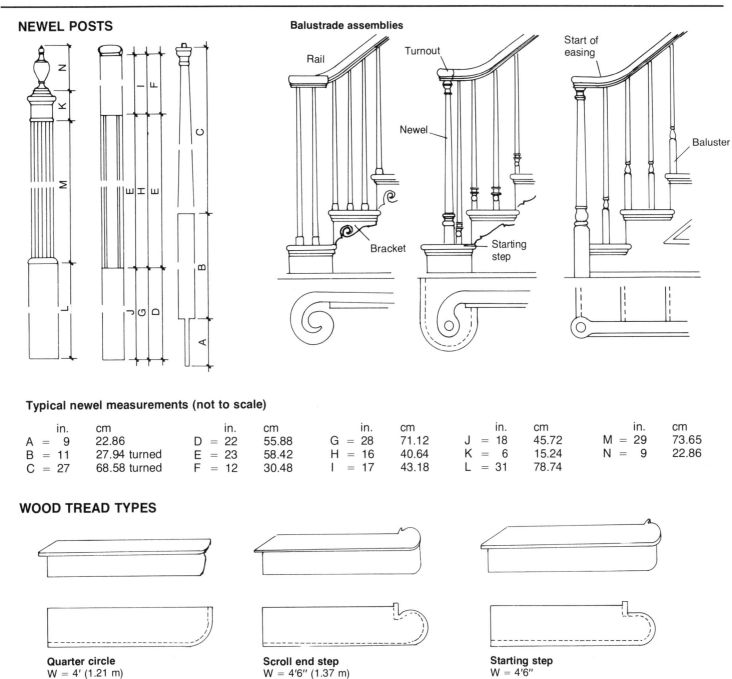

Balustrade assemblies

Rail

Bracket

Turnout

Newel

Starting step

Start of easing

Baluster

Typical newel measurements (not to scale)

	in.	cm		in.	cm		in.	cm		in.	cm		in.	cm
A =	9	22.86	D =	22	55.88	G =	28	71.12	J =	18	45.72	M =	29	73.65
B =	11	27.94 turned	E =	23	58.42	H =	16	40.64	K =	6	15.24	N =	9	22.86
C =	27	68.58 turned	F =	12	30.48	I =	17	43.18	L =	31	78.74			

WOOD TREAD TYPES

Quarter circle
W = 4′ (1.21 m)

Scroll end step
W = 4′6″ (1.37 m)

Starting step
W = 4′6″

CURVED STAIRS

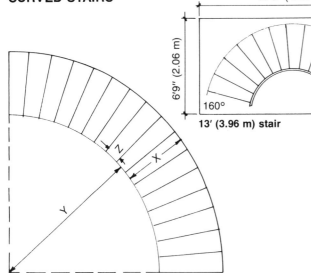

13′6″ (4.12 m)

6′9″ (2.06 m)

160°

13′ (3.96 m) stair

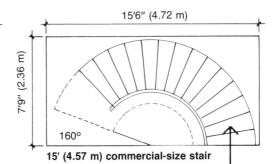

15′6″ (4.72 m)

7′9″ (2.36 m)

160°

15′ (4.57 m) commercial-size stair

Most codes allow curved stairs as means of egress if minimum depth of tread is 10″ (25.40 cm) and the radius is not less than twice the stair width.

Curved stair tread width should be at least 44″ (111.76 cm) as shown by dimension line X. Dimension Y should be at least twice dimension X.

Note: Marble stair treads should be specified with a minimum abrasive hardness (HA) of 10.0.

Dimensions:
A = 10 treads at 11″ (27.94 cm) = 110″ (279.40 cm)
B = 56″ (142.24 cm)
C = 52″ (132.08 cm)
D = 24″ (60.96 cm)
E = 12″ (30.48 cm)
F = 4½″ (11.43 cm)
G = 39″ (99.06 cm)
H = 33″ (83.82 cm)
I = varies, but 10″ (25.40 cm) min.
J = 21 risers (varies)
K = 11 risers at 7″ (17.78 cm) = 77″ (195.58 cm)
L = 54″ (137.16 cm)
M = 9″ (22.86 cm)

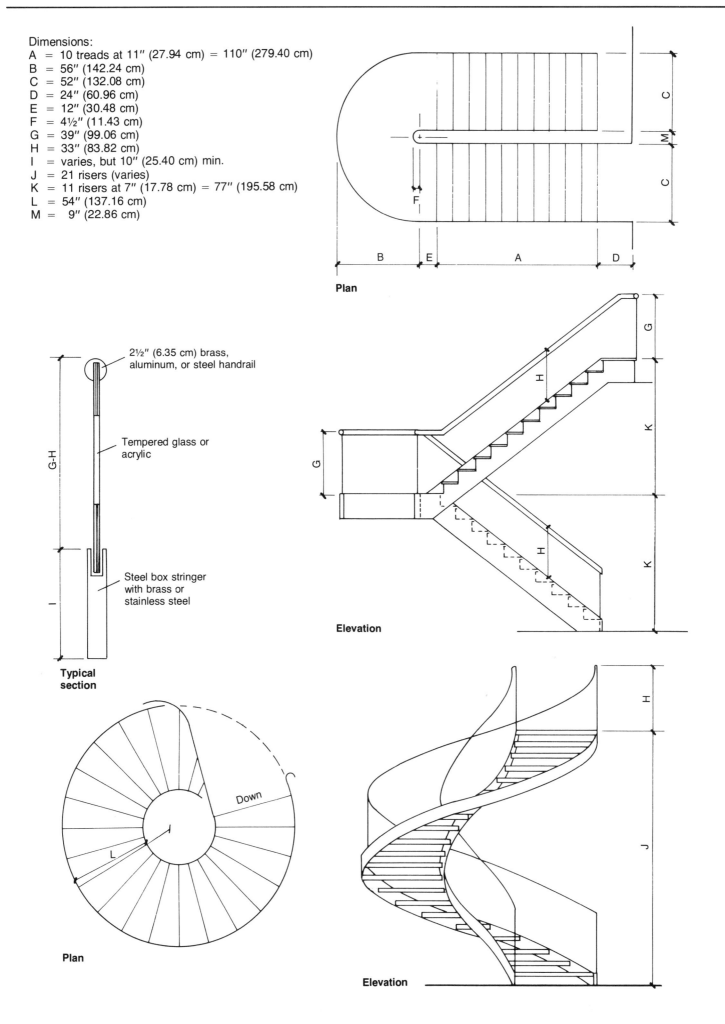

Plan

2½″ (6.35 cm) brass, aluminum, or steel handrail

Tempered glass or acrylic

Steel box stringer with brass or stainless steel

Typical section

Elevation

Down

Plan

Elevation

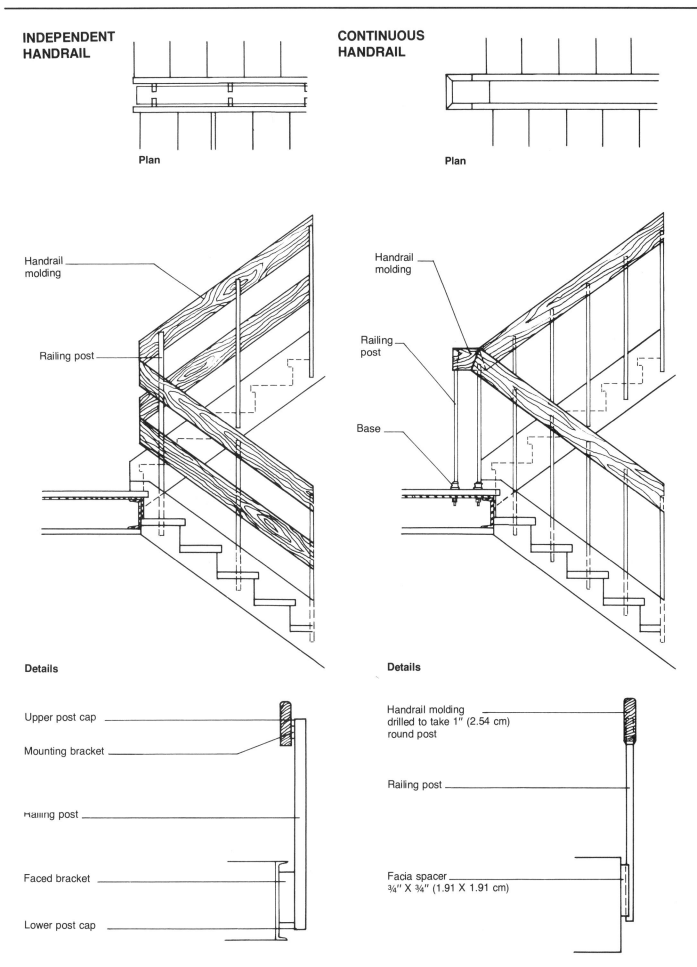

INDEPENDENT HANDRAIL

Plan

Handrail molding

Railing post

Details

Upper post cap

Mounting bracket

Railing post

Faced bracket

Lower post cap

CONTINUOUS HANDRAIL

Plan

Handrail molding

Railing post

Base

Details

Handrail molding drilled to take 1″ (2.54 cm) round post

Railing post

Facia spacer ¾″ X ¾″ (1.91 X 1.91 cm)

Folding stairs

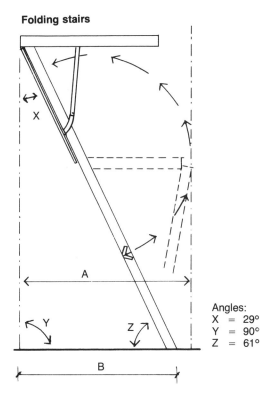

Angles:
X = 29°
Y = 90°
Z = 61°

Folding and disappearing stairs are built with high-grade door panels that may also be available with a 90-minute fire rating.

Typical dimensions for folding stairs

Rough opening (in.)	Ceiling height*	Projection A (in.)	Landing space B (in.)
22 X 54	8'9"	66	65
22 X 54	10'	79	73
25½ X 54	8'9"	66	65
25½ X 54	10'	79	73
30 X 54	8'9"	66	65
30 X 54	10'	79	73

*Folding stairs require floor-to-ceiling measurement.

Note: the drawing below illustrates (1) the rough opening, (2) the finished opening, and (3) the panel opening area.

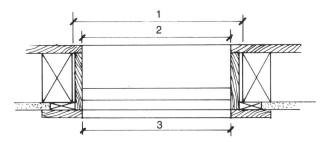

Attic opening

Disappearing stairs

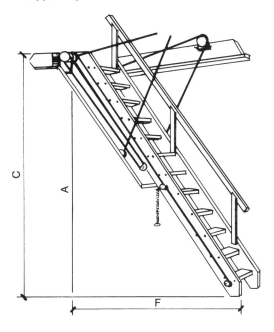

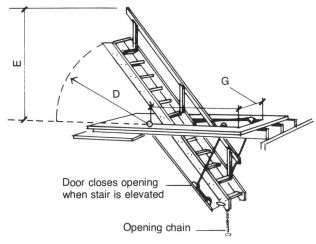

Door closes opening when stair is elevated

Opening chain

Ladder

Note: Typical ladder width is 18"–19" (45.72–48.26 cm). Full-length handrail is usually standard.

Disappearing stair dimensions

Floor to floor (C)	Radius above (D)	Plumb height (E)	Run below (F)	Panel opening (G)
7'7" to 7'10"	4'4"	3'2"	6'5"	2'6" X 5'10"
7'11" to 8'4"	4'11"	3'8"	6'10"	2'6" X 5'10"
8'5" to 8'10"	5'7"	4'1"	7'3"	2'6" X 5'10"
8'11" to 9'4"	6'2"	4'6"	7'7"	2'6" X 6'0"
9'5" to 9'10"	6'4"	4'9"	8'0"	2'6" X 6'4"
9'11" to 10'4"	6'8"	5'0"	8'4"	2'6" X 6'8"
10'5" to 10'10"	7'0"	5'3"	8'9"	2'6" X 7'0"

TYPICAL LIFT INSTALLATION

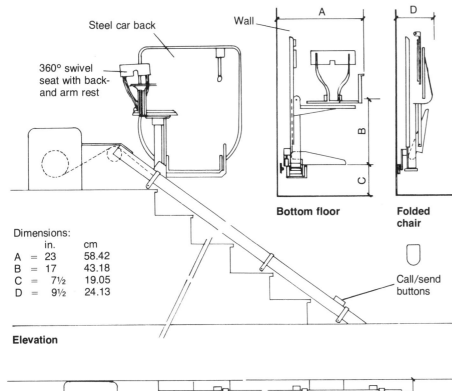

Steel car back

360° swivel
seat with back-
and arm rest

Wall

A

D

Bottom floor

Folded chair

Call/send buttons

Dimensions:

	in.	cm
A =	23	58.42
B =	17	43.18
C =	7½	19.05
D =	9½	24.13

Elevation

Plan

AA BB

Rail to be placed on wall side

ST

H

R

L

CC

W

SB

DD

HB

EE

Basement

Note: AA–EE indicate optional power unit locations.

Specification checklist

1. ST = blank wall space at the top of the stairs on the wall side
2. SB = space at the bottom of the steps on the wall side
3. H = height of top floor
4. HB = height of the basement
5. L = length of travel (State if rail can be placed in one length.)
6. List the number of steps, including the one to landing
7. W = width of tread less nosing
8. R = rise of steps and width of stair

WHEELCHAIR LIFT

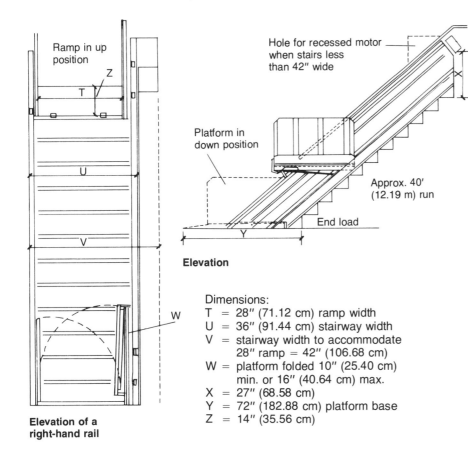

Ramp in up position

Z

T

U

V

W

Elevation of a right-hand rail

Hole for recessed motor when stairs less than 42" wide

Platform in down position

X

Approx. 40' (12.19 m) run

End load

Y

Elevation

Dimensions:

T = 28" (71.12 cm) ramp width
U = 36" (91.44 cm) stairway width
V = stairway width to accommodate 28" ramp = 42" (106.68 cm)
W = platform folded 10" (25.40 cm) min. or 16" (40.64 cm) max.
X = 27" (68.58 cm)
Y = 72" (182.88 cm) platform base
Z = 14" (35.56 cm)

Specification guidelines

Platforms are usually 45" to 48" (114.30 to 121.92 cm) long.

Side-loading platforms: The overall length is the measured length plus 18" (45.72 cm) from the bottom step.

End-loading platforms: Minimum overall length requires an 8' (2.44 m) distance to the stairway wall.

The stairwell track requires a minimum of 3½" (8.89 cm). The maximum width required is 9½" (24.13 cm).

A ¾ horsepower motor will serve a load capacity of 350 to 450 lb (158.90 to 204.30 kg).

Section AA

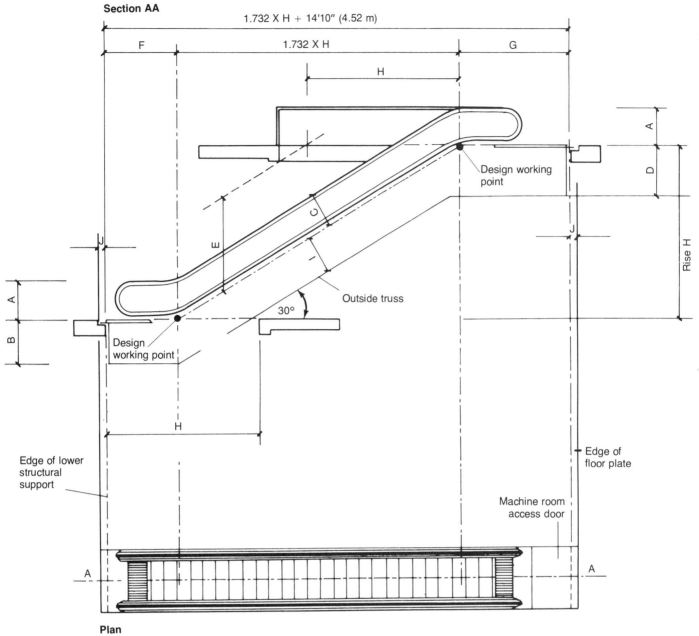

Plan

Plan & section dimensions:

		ft	in.	m
A	=	3	3	0.99
B	=	3	7	1.09
C	=	2	8	0.84
D	=	4	2	1.27
E	=	7	0	2.13
F	=	5	10	1.78
G	=	9	0	2.74
H	=	12	0	3.66 min.
I	=	3	2	0.96
J	=		6	0.15

Note: Measurements are rounded off.

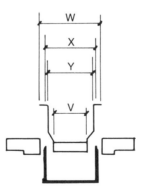

Section through incline

Widths

Unit (in.)	V (in.)	W	X	Y (in.)
32	24	4'1¼"	3'1¼"	32
48	40	5'4¼"	4'4¼"	48

Fire safety factors

Interior spaces serviced by escalators and moving walks, such as hotels, shopping malls, and other public areas, may require that designers use caution in specifying interior finishes in those areas.

Most codes require that escalators and moving walks serving as required exits shall be protected or enclosed in the same manner as exit stairways. This requirement can include fire-rated enclosures and finishes, as well as entrances and discharge doors.

Code variance

When used in hotel atriums and enclosed shopping malls, enclosures may not be required in a fully sprinklered building when one of the following or a combination of the following is used:

1. Sprinkler-vent method: This is a combination of automatic fire and smoke detection systems, an automatic exhaust system, and an automatic water curtain.

2. Spray nozzle method: This combines automatic fire or smoke detection with a high-velocity water spray discharge closely in line with the slope of the escalator.

3. Rolling shutter method: Used only above street level, the shutter closes off the wellway opening.

4. Partial enclosure method: Doors are used to prevent the spread of smoke and fire between floors.

Designers should not obstruct any entry or exit with plants, directional signage, counters, or displays.

Moving walks

Note: Moving walks may be used inside as well as outside.

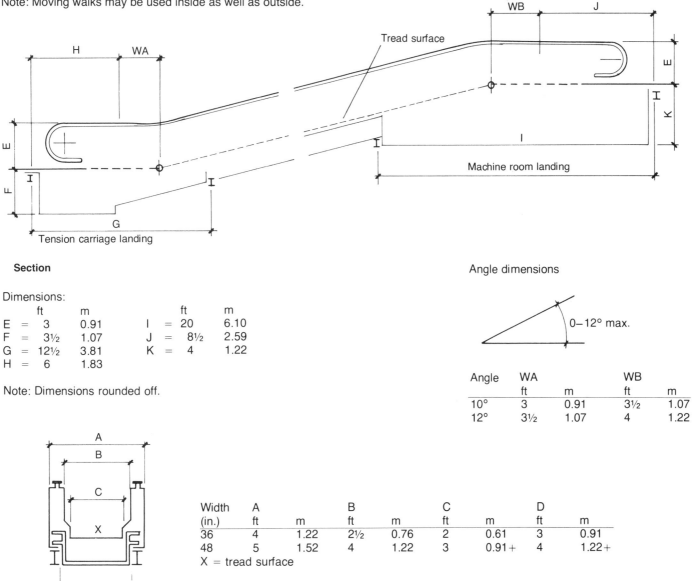

Section

Dimensions:

		ft	m			ft	m
E	=	3	0.91	I	=	20	6.10
F	=	3½	1.07	J	=	8½	2.59
G	=	12½	3.81	K	=	4	1.22
H	=	6	1.83				

Note: Dimensions rounded off.

Angle dimensions

0–12° max.

Angle	WA		WB	
	ft	m	ft	m
10°	3	0.91	3½	1.07
12°	3½	1.07	4	1.22

Section through incline

Width	A		B		C		D	
(in.)	ft	m	ft	m	ft	m	ft	m
36	4	1.22	2½	0.76	2	0.61	3	0.91
48	5	1.52	4	1.22	3	0.91+	4	1.22+

X = tread surface

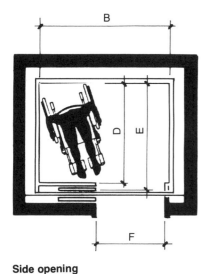

Side opening

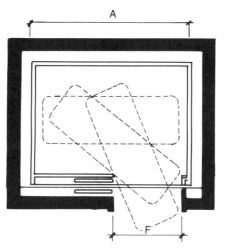

Side opening for stretchers

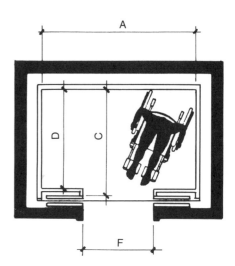

Center opening

General

1. Elevators shall comply with ANSI A117.1-1961, Subpart C—Scope. For additional information see the *American National Standard Safety Code for Elevators, Dumbwaiters, Escalators and Moving Walks, A17.1,* and see also National Elevator Industry, Inc. (NEII) *Suggested Minimum Elevator Requirements for the Handicapped.*
2. Freight elevators shall not be considered as meeting the requirements of this section.

Operation & leveling

Elevators shall be automatic and shall be provided with a self-leveling feature that will automatically bring the car to the floor landing within a tolerance of ½″ (12.70 mm) under normal loading and unloading conditions. The self-leveling feature shall, within its zone, be entirely automatic and independent of the operating device and shall correct for overtravel or undertravel and shall maintain the car approximately level irrespective of loading conditions.

Elevator door operation

Elevator doors shall be a minimum of 3′ (91.44 cm) wide, and automatic door controls shall comply with the following requirements:

1. The minimum acceptable time from notification that a car is answering a hall call until the doors of that car start to close shall be as shown in the accompanying table. The travel distance shall be established from a point in the center of the corridor or lobby [maximum of 5′ (1.52 m)] directly opposite the farthest hall button to the centerline of the farthest hoistway entrance.
2. Doors shall remain fully open for a minimum of 5 seconds.
3. Provide doors with a reopening device that will function to stop and reopen the car door and adjacent hoistway door in case the car door is obstructed while the door is closing. This reopening device shall also be capable of sensing an object or person in the path of a closing door without requiring contact for activation at a nominal height of 5″ and 2′5″ (12.70 and 73.66 cm) above finish floor. Such devices shall remain effective for a period of not less than 20 seconds. For additional information, see ANSI A17.1.

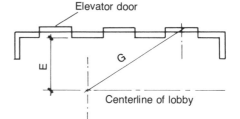

Travel distance to elevator doors

Door timing

Distance		Time
ft	m	sec
0–5	1.52	4
10	3.05	7
15	4.57	10
20	6.10	13

Dimensions (not to scale):

		ft/in.	m
A	=	6 8	2.06
B	=	5 8	1.75
C	=	4 6	1.37
D	=	4 3	1.29
E	=	5 0	1.52
F	=	3 0	0.91
G	=	travel distance	

Elevator cars

1. The minimum floor areas of elevator cars shall comply with the dimensions illustrated above.
   Exception. Where existing shaft or structural elements prohibit strict compliance in alteration work, these dimensions may be reduced by the minimum amount necessary, but in no case shall they be less than 4′ square (1.22 m) clear.
2. Car floors shall comply with §1190.50. Walks, Floors and Accessible Routes. The clearance between the car platform sill and the edges of any hoistway landing shall be no greater than 1¼″ (3.18 cm).

Car controls shall be readily accessible from a wheelchair

1. Buttons, exclusive of border, shall have a minimum dimension of ¾″ (1.91 cm) and shall be raised or flush with the operating panel.
2. Provide a visual signal indicating when each call is registered and answered.
3. Mount the highest floor buttons to a maximum of 4′ (1.22 m) above the floor and the lowest buttons at a minimum of 2′11″ (0.89 m) above the floor. *Exception:* If there is a substantial increase in cost as a result of the 4′ requirement, the highest floor buttons may be mounted at a maximum of 4′6″ (1.37 m).
4. Group emergency buttons at the bottom of the panel with their centerlines no lower than 2′11″.
5. Designate all control buttons by raised standard alphabet characters for letters, arabic characters for numerals, or standard symbols shown on right. For additional information see ANSI A17.1 and see also *NEII Suggested Minimum Elevator Requirements for the Handicapped.* Place raised designations to the immediate left of the button which they apply. Permanently attached, applied plates are acceptable. Locate the call button for the main entry floor in the left-most column and designate it with a raised star.
6. Locate control panels as shown in the illustrations at the right.

Door jamb markings

Provide floor designation markings at each hoistway entrance on both jambs that comply with the following:

1. The center lines of characters shall be located 5′ (1.52 m) above finish floor.
2. Characters shall be a minimum of 2″ (5.08 cm) high and shall comply with §1190.200, Signage.
3. Permanently applied plates are acceptable.

Lobby call buttons

1. Call buttons shall:
   a. Be mounted with centerlines at 3′6″ (1.07 m) above finish floor.
   b. Be a minimum of ¾″ (1.91 cm) in diameter.
   c. Have visual signals indicating when a call is registered and answered.
   d. Be raised or flush.
   e. Have the button designating "up" mounted on top.
2. Objects mounted beneath lobby call buttons shall not project into the elevator lobby more than 4″ (10.16 cm).

Hall lanterns

Provide an audible and visual signal at each hoistway entrance to indicate car arrival and its travel direction.

1. Audible signals shall sound once for the up direction and twice for the down direction or shall annunciate the words "up" or "down."
2. Visual signals shall:
   a. Be mounted with their centerline a minimum of 6′ (1.83 m) above finish floor.
   b. Have a minimum dimension of 2½″ (6.35 cm).

c. Distinguish between up and down travel directions.
d. Be visible from the vicinity of call buttons.
3. In-car lanterns mounted on car door jambs that comply with paragraph 1190.100(e)(2) are acceptable.

Car position indicator and signal

Provide audible and visual car position indicators within each elevator car as follows:

1. Audible indicators shall:
   a. Signal as the car passes or stops at each landing. Signal shall exceed the ambient noise level by at least 20 decibels with a frequency below 1,500 Hz.
   b. Provide an automatic verbal announcement.
2. Visual indicators shall:
   a. Be located above the car operating panel or over the car door.
   b. Visually display the floor number as the car passes or stops at a landing.
   c. Have characters that are a minimum of ½″ (1.27 cm) high and that comply with §1190.200, Signage, except for paragraph 1190.200(c) (2).

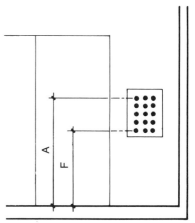

Control panel location

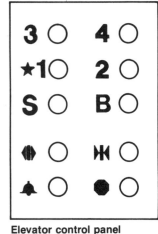

Elevator control panel

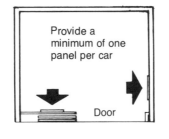

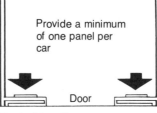

Control locations

Illumination levels

Illuminate car controls, platform, car threshold, and landing sill to a minimum of 5 footcandles.

Intercommunication systems

If provided, emergency intercommunication systems shall comply with the following:

1. Locate the highest operable part of the system no higher than 4′ (1.22 m) above car floor.
2. Identify the system with raised lettering or symbols complying with §1190.200, Signage.
3. If system employs a handset, provide a 2′5″ (0.76 mm) cord length.
4. If system is located in a closed compartment, compartment door hardware shall conform to §1190.170, Controls and Operating Mechanisms.
5. Provide a momentary contact button to allow hearing-impaired individuals to summon assistance.

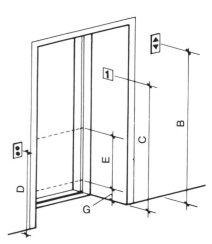

Elevator entrance

Dimensions:

	ft/ in.	m
A =	4 0	1.22
B =	6 0	1.83
C =	5 0	1.52
D =	3 6	1.07
E =	2 0	0.61
F =	2 11	0.89
G =	3 5	12.70 cm

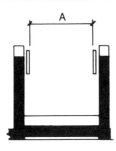

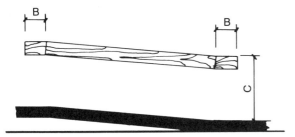

Ramp with walls

A walkway that slopes 1:20 or greater is considered an accessible ramp and should comply with handicapped requirements. Cross-slopes on accessible routes shall not exceed 1:48 or ¼" (0.64 cm) per foot.

Landings

Ramps must be provided with landings at the top and bottom and wherever the ramp changes direction. Landings must have a minimum area of 5' X 5' (1.52 X 1.52 m) at directional changes or should be at least as wide as the widest ramp run approaching it. Landings must also have a minimum length of 5'.

Handrails

Any ramp exceeding a 6" (15.24 cm) rise or a 6' (1.83 m) horizontal projection shall be required to have handrails. Note: ANSI does not specify handrail height.

Edge treatments

Some changes in level or grade in accessible routes require an edge treatment. However, any slope up to ½" vertical does not require an edge treatment. A slope ¼" to ½" (0.64 to 1.27 cm) requires a beveled edge with its slope not exceeding 1:2.

Ramps and landings that end abruptly or drop off must provide curbs, walls, vertical guards, or projected edges. The minimum curb height shall be 2" (5.08 cm).

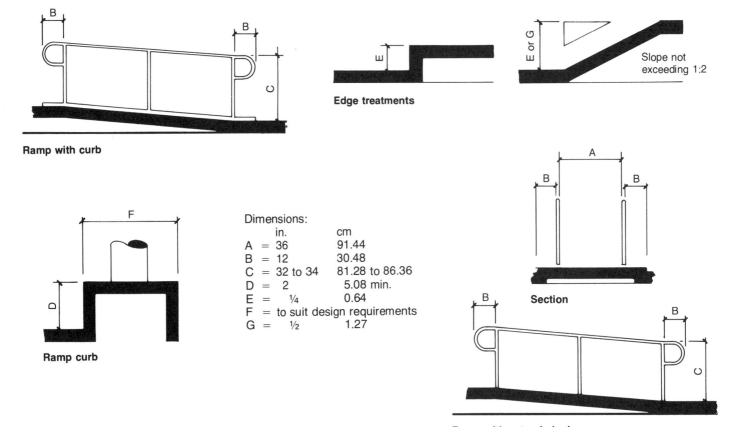

Ramp with curb

Edge treatments

Slope not exceeding 1:2

Ramp curb

Dimensions:

		in.	cm
A	=	36	91.44
B	=	12	30.48
C	=	32 to 34	81.28 to 86.36
D	=	2	5.08 min.
E	=	¼	0.64
F	=	to suit design requirements	
G	=	½	1.27

Section

Ramp with extended edge

STANDARDS

ANSI	**American National Standards Institute**

Specification for Making Buildings and Facilities Accessible to and Usable by Physically Handicapped People.

4. Accessible Elements and Spaces

4.8	Ramps
4.9	Stairs
4.10	Elevators

ATBCB	**Architectural and Transportation Barriers Compliance Board**

36 CFR Part 1190

1190.70	Ramps and curbs
1190.80	Stairs
1190.90	Handrails
1190.100	Elevators

NFPA	**National Fire Protection Association**

101-1985	Life Safety Code
5-2.5.2	Class A Ramps
5-2.2.2	Class A Stairs
5-2.5.2	Class B Ramps
5-2.2.2	Class B Stairs
	Elevators: 7-4; 12-6; 13-6; 14-5; 15-5; 16-5; 17-5; 18-2; 19-2; 20-2

5-2	Enclosures for ramps
5-2	Escalators
6-2	Handrails
5-2	Moving walks
5-10	
5-2	Outside ramps
8-2	Railings
9-2	
5-2	Swing stairs
3-2	Vertical openings

TESTS

NFPA	220 "Standard Type Building Construction Types I and II."

REGULATIONS

Building Officials & Code Administrators International, Inc.
Basic Building Code (1981)

International Conference of Building Officials
Uniform Building Code (1979)

Southern Building Code Congress International, Inc.
Standard Building Code (1979)

National Fire Protection Association

INTERIOR LIGHTING SPECIFICATIONS

The following factors should be considered when specifying uniform and nonuniform lighting systems (see page references for general guidelines):

A. Space function
1. Geometry of the space (page 309)
2. Activity in the space (pages 306, 336–339)
3. Who performs this activity? (pages 336–339)
4. Level of task accuracy required (page 336)
5. Color accuracy desired (pages 306–307)

B. Type of light distribution (page 308)
1. Direct
2. Indirect
3. Semidirect
4. Semi-indirect
5. Diffused, general
6. Direct-indirect

C. Lamp & luminaire selection (pages 310–311)
1. General lighting system (page 312)
2. Local lighting system (page 314)
3. Task-ambient systems (page 314)

D. Quality & quantity calculations
1. Lamp selections (pages 305–307)
2. Footcandle levels (page 336)
3. Zonal cavity/room cavity ratio (page 313)
4. Reflectance levels (page 309)
5. Visual comfort probability (pages 318–319)
6. Veiling reflections/glare (pages 318–319)

E. Installation requirements
1. Number of fixtures: spacing (pages 314–315)
2. Energy conservation
3. Emergency and safety lighting (page 327)

F. Economic considerations
1. LLD—lamp lumen depreciation
2. LDD—luminaire dirt depreciation
3. CU—coefficient of utilization

Summary

____ Room length

____ Room width

____ Room area

____ Required footcandles

____ Light distribution

____ Activity in the space

____ Occupants of the space

____ Lamp

____ Fixture

____ Spacing & mounting height ratio

____ Surface reflectance

____ Color requirements

____ LLD

____ CU photo data

____ Initial lumens per lamp

LIGHTING COST STUDY CHECKLIST

____ Lamp type

____ Fixture type

____ Lamp number

____ Fixture number

____ Number of fixtures

____ Footcandles maintained

Basic data

____ Room length

____ Room width

____ Room square area

____ Initial lumens per lamp

____ Lamp life

____ Lamp list price, each

____ Lamp cost: list less percent

____ Number of lamps per fixture

____ Lamp cost per fixture

____ Fixture cost, each

____ Accessory cost per fixture

____ Number of fixture rows

____ Number of fixtures per row

____ Total number of fixtures

____ Wiring & installation cost per fixture

____ Voltage

____ Watts per fixture, input

____ Energy rate: $/kWH

____ Burning hours per year

____ Labor to replace one lamp

____ Labor to clean one fixture

____ Years per cleaning

____ LLD

____ LDD

____ CU

Economic summary

____ Total initial cost

____ Annual fixed charges

____ Annual lamp replacement cost

____ Annual cleaning costs

____ Watts per square foot

____ Annual kWH

____ Annual energy cost

____ Annual operating cost

____ Total annual cost

____ Annual cost per footcandle

____ Relative annual cost

____ Number of years required for system to pay for itself

For more information on the cycle costing for lighting open office facilities, see S.C. Reznikoff, *Specifications for Commercial Interiors.* (Whitney Library of Design, 1979) pp. 173-174.

BULB DESIGNATION

A letter is used to indicate the bulb shape, and a number gives the approximate diameter in eighths of an inch. Thus, an R-40 bulb is of the R shape and 40 eighths (40/8) or 5″ (12.70 cm) in diameter.

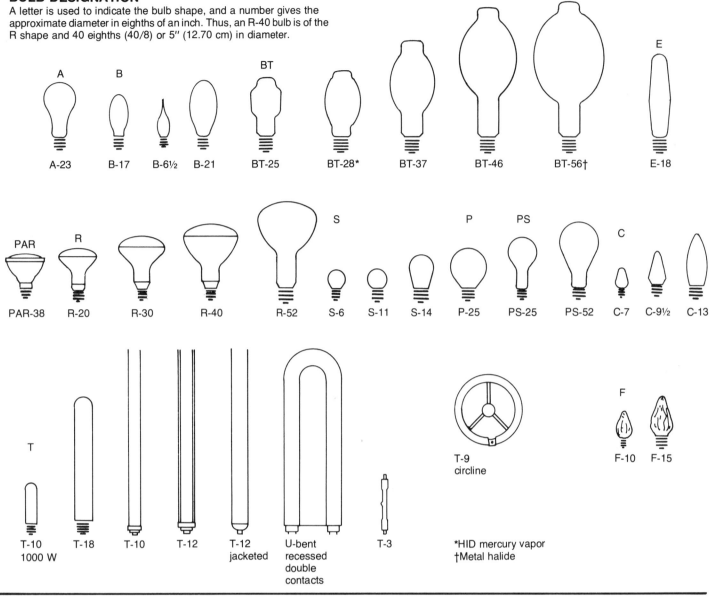

A-23   B-17   B-6½   B-21   BT-25   BT-28*   BT-37   BT-46   BT-56†   E-18

PAR-38   R-20   R-30   R-40   R-52   S-6   S-11   S-14   P-25   PS-25   PS-52   C-7   C-9½   C-13

T-10 1000 W   T-18   T-10   T-12   T-12 jacketed   U-bent recessed double contacts   T-3   T-9 circline   F-10   F-15

*HID mercury vapor
†Metal halide

LAMP BASES & PRONG

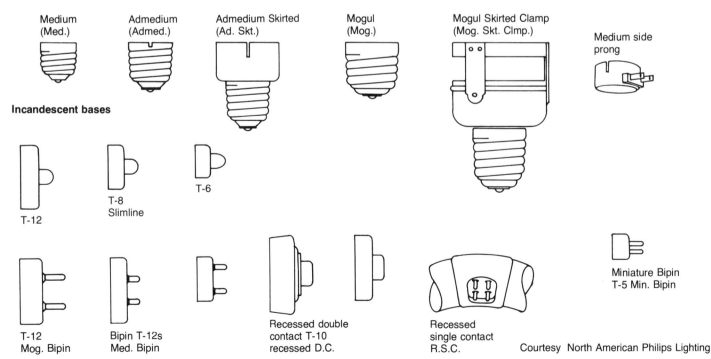

Medium (Med.)   Admedium (Admed.)   Admedium Skirted (Ad. Skt.)   Mogul (Mog.)   Mogul Skirted Clamp (Mog. Skt. Clmp.)   Medium side prong

Incandescent bases

T-12   T-8 Slimline   T-6

T-12 Mog. Bipin   Bipin T-12s Med. Bipin   Recessed double contact T-10 recessed D.C.   Recessed single contact R.S.C.   Miniature Bipin T-5 Min. Bipin

Fluorescent bases

Courtesy North American Philips Lighting

Incandescent lamp data

Watts	Bulb/base	Rated lumens* (initial)	Rated life (hr)
General service (A-PS) lamps			
40	A-19/Med.	455	1500
60	A-19/Med.	870	1000
75	A-19/Med.	1190	750
100	A-19/Med.	1750	750
	A-21/Med.	1690	750
150	A-21/Med.	2880	750
	A-23/Med.	2780	750
200	A-23/Med.	4010	750
	PS-30/Med.	3710	750
300	PS-25/Med.	6360	750
	PS-30/Med.	6110	750
Projector (PAR) lamps			
25	PAR-36/Scr. Term. (12V)	200	2000
35	PAR-36/Scr. Term. (12V)	200	2000
50	PAR-36/Scr. Term. (12V)	400	2000
75	PAR-38/Med.	765	2000
120	PAR-56/Scr. Term. (12V)	1250	2000
150	PAR-38/Med.	1740	2000
	PAR-38/Med. (Krypton)	1660	4000
240	PAR-56/Scr. Term. (12V)	2750	2000
250	PAR-38/Med. (Tung.—Hal.)	3220	6000
	PAR-38/Med. (Krypton)	3100	4000
Reflector (R) lamps			
30	R-20/Med.	210	2000
50	R-20/Med.	440	2000
75	R-30/Med.	900	2000
150	R-40/Med.	1900	2000
300	R-40/Med.	3650	2000
Elliptical reflector (ER) lamps			
75	ER-30/Med.	850	2000
120	ER-40/Med.	1475	2000
Tungsten-Halogen (T) lamps			
100	T-4/Min. Can.	1800	1000
250	T-4/Min. Can.	4700	2000
400	T-4/Min. Can.	7850	2000
500	T-4/Min. Can.	9500	2000

*Lumens per watt is one of several ways to measure a lamp. The relationship is called "lamp efficacy." This is similar to efficiency, but, unlike it, efficacy is a relationship of unlike terms (lumens and watts).

Bulb designations

A & PS	A is an arbitrary bulb shape; PS stands for *pear-shape*. These are the most common shapes for general lighting.
PAR & R	These are bulbs with built-in reflectors. The PAR, or *parabolic aluminized reflector*, offers good beam control, is relatively expensive, may be heavy, and can be used outdoors. The R lamp uses a *reflector* that is less accurate in its beam control, less expensive, lightweight, and generally restricted to interior use unless constructed of special glass.
ER	*Ellipsoidal reflector* lamps cross light rays at a point slightly in front of the bulb's lens, thereby producing an efficient light distribution when these lamps are used in luminaires with small aperture openings or deep baffles.
T	*Tubular.*
C	*Conical.*
B	Flame-shaped (one of the few codes that does not relate to its meaning). B bulbs have smooth exteriors.
F	*Flame-shaped.*
S	*Straight-sided.*
P	*Pear-shaped.*
G	*Globe* (round).
GT	*Globe-tubular* (also called "chimney shape").

Color or beam shape code chart

Code	Meaning
/A	*Amber* color
/B	*Blue* color
/BW	*Blue-white* color
/C	*Clear*
/CL	*Clear*
/DC	*Double contact* base
/FL	*Flood* (beam shape)
/G	*Green* color
/GO	*Golden* color
/IF	*Inside frosted* diffuser
/N+	*Natural glass* color when followed by a color code
/NSP	*Narrow spot* (beam shape)
/O	*Orange* color
/PK	*Pink* color
/R	*Red* color
/R2	*Rose* color
/RS	*Rough service*
/RFL	*Reflector* (not a PAR- or R-shaped bulb)
/SB	*Silver-bowl* reflector
/SC	*Single-contact* base
/SP	*Spot* (beam shape)
/T	*Transparent* when followed by a color code
/VNSP	*Very narrow spot* (beam shape)
/VS	*Vibration service*
/VWFL	*Very wide flood* (beam shape)
/W	*White* (a painted finish)
/WFL	*Wide flood* (beam shape)
/Y	*Yellow* color
/1Y	*Bug light (yellow* color)
/2	Low heat output with a dichroic filter
/99	Long life

Applications	HID* /R Mercury Vapor	/4 Metal Halide Clear	/C Metal Halide Phosphor	Fluorescent /N Natural Soft White	/SMW Supermarket White	/3000U Ultralume	/4100U Ultralume	/5000U Ultralume	/WW Warm White	/W White	/CW Cool White	/D Daylight	/CWX Deluxe Cool White	/WWX Deluxe Warm White	/LW Living White	/MWX Merchandising White
Banks	X			X										X		X
Beauty salons														X	X	
Boutiques						X										
Color-matching areas								X								
Computer rooms											X					
Conference rooms													X		X	
Corridors											X					
Department stores						X										
Factories										X	X	X				
Jewelry stores								X								
Libraries	X								X		X				X	
Lobbies	X			X											X	
Meat showcases				X	X											
Museums								X								
Offices	X					X			X	X	X		X		X	
Restaurants	X			X					X				X	X	X	
Schools											X		X		X	
Stores	X	X	X	X		X	X	X			X	X	X		X	X
Supermarkets	X			X									X			

*HID = high intensity discharge.

EFFECT OF LAMP COLORS ON OBJECT COLORS (COLOR RENDITION)

Color	Incandescent	Cool White Fluorescent	Warm White Fluorescent	Deluxe White Mercury Vapor	Ceramalux High Pressure Sodium	Metal Halide
Red	Red	Grayish red	Red	Grayish red	Rust Red orange	Dull red
Orange	Orange	Grayish orange	Slightly yellow orange	Yellow orange	Dark yellow	Grayish orange
Yellow	Yellow	Light greenish yellow	Yellow	Light yellow	Yellow	Yellow
Green	Green	Green	Green	Grayish green	Blue green	Green
Blue	Blue	Blue	Blue violet	Dark blue	Dark blue Violet	Blue
Violet	Violet	Violet	Violet	Light blue Violet	Brownish violet	Violet
Brown	Brown	Brown	Gray brown	Brown	Golden yellow Brown	Brown
White	White	White	Pinkish white	White	Pinkish white	White
Skin (whites) complexion	Ruddy	Pale	Natural	Pale tan	Suntan look	Pale
Skin (blacks) complexion	Natural	Grayish brown	Yellowish brown	Grayish brown	Yellowish brown	Pale

RECOMMENDED HID LAMP COLORS TO BLEND WITH FLUORESCENT (CHROMATICITY)

Lamp color now in use	HID choice to blend with present lamp in appearance	Notes*
Cool White Fluorescent or Supermarket White	Beauty Lite	Close enough. Beauty Lite is more violet. Cool White is more green.
	Metal Halide (Clear)	Similar to Beauty Lite.
	Deluxe White	Close enough. Deluxe White is warmer. Cool White is more blue.
Cool White Deluxe	Beauty Lite	Close.
Natural	Beauty Lite	Fairly close. Beauty Lite is less violet.
Warm White	Metal Halide/C (phosphor coated)	Close.
	Deluxe White	Close enough. Deluxe White is slightly more green. Warm White is slightly more yellow.
	Style-Tone	Close enough. Style-Tone is more yellow.
Warm White Deluxe	Deluxe White	Fairly close. Deluxe White is slightly more yellow-green.
	Style-Tone	Close enough. Style-Tone is more yellow.
Merchandising White	Deluxe White	Fairly close. Deluxe White is more yellow-green.
	Style-Tone	Close enough. Style-Tone is more yellow.
Incandescent	Style-Tone	Close enough. Style-Tone is more yellow and green; incandescent is more orange.

*Remarks concern source as per original color appearance and have nothing to do with color rendition.

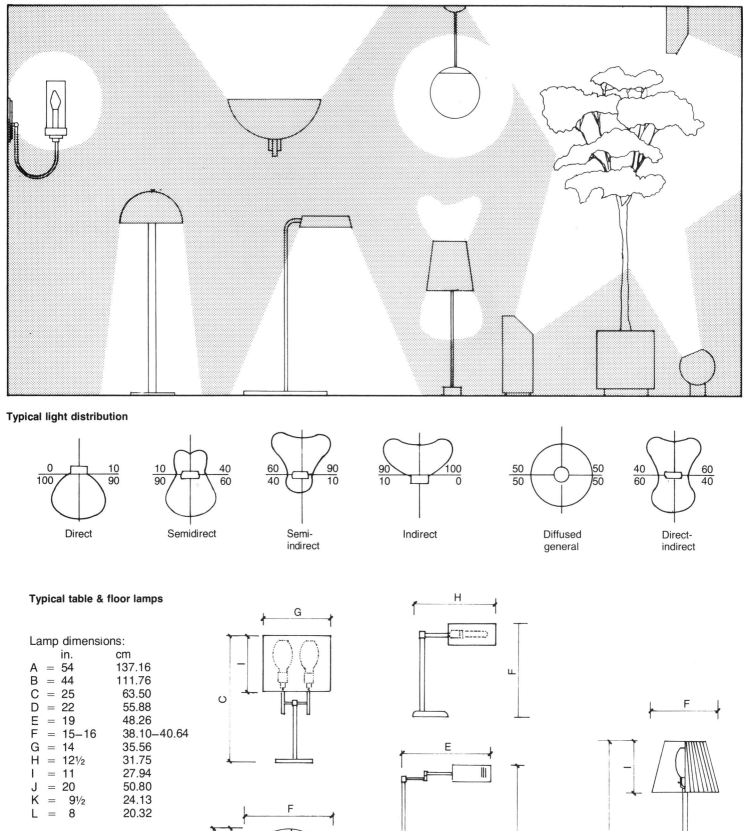

Typical light distribution

Direct	Semidirect	Semi-indirect	Indirect	Diffused general	Direct-indirect

Typical table & floor lamps

Lamp dimensions:

	in.	cm
A =	54	137.16
B =	44	111.76
C =	25	63.50
D =	22	55.88
E =	19	48.26
F =	15–16	38.10–40.64
G =	14	35.56
H =	12½	31.75
I =	11	27.94
J =	20	50.80
K =	9½	24.13
L =	8	20.32

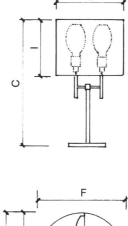
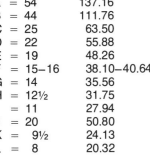
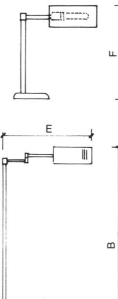
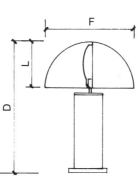

Typical reflectance percentages

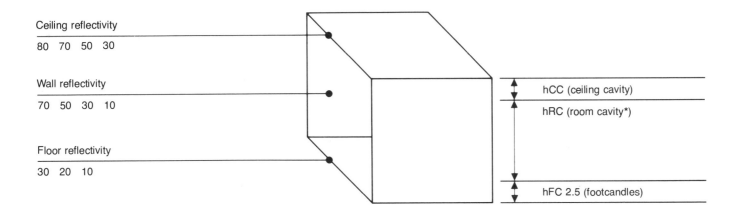

Ceiling reflectivity

80 70 50 30

Wall reflectivity

70 50 30 10

Floor reflectivity

30 20 10

hCC (ceiling cavity)

hRC (room cavity*)

hFC 2.5 (footcandles)

Most precalculated fixture quantity charts assume the following reflectance percentages:

Commercial reflectances:
  80% ceiling
  50% wall
  20% floor

Industrial reflectances:
  50% ceiling
  50% wall
  20% floor

School classrooms:
  70–90% ceiling
  40–60% wall
  30–50% floor
  35–50% desk top
  20% blackboard

Percent of light reflected from typical walls & ceilings*

Class	Surface	Color	Percentage of light reflected
Light	Paint	White	81
	Paint	Ivory	79
	Paint	Cream	74
	Stone	Cream	69
Medium	Paint	Buff	63
	Paint	Light green	63
	Paint	Light gray	58
	Stone	Gray	56
Dark	Paint	Tan	48
	Paint	Dark gray	26
	Paint	Olive green	17
	Paint	Light oak	32
	Paint	Dark oak	13
	Paint	Mahogany	8
	Cement	Natural	25
	Brick	Red	13

*Each paint manufacturer's reflection values differ for similar colors; the above table gives some idea of the colors and their average reflecting qualities.

Note: See manufacturers' specification information for
reflectance percentages on all interior finishes.

Cross sections	Lamps*	Typical data*							
		For 9′ ceiling				For 12′ ceiling			
		Distance to wall (in.)	C to C distance (in.)	Fc at 5′6″ above floor	Evenness rating†	Distance to wall (in.)	C to C distance (in.)	Fc at 5′6″ above floor	Evenness rating†
	200W PAR-46/3NSP	12	12	85	E	12	12	70	E
	150W PAR-38/3SP	12	12	67	E	12	12	39	VG
	150W R-40/SP	10½	12	102	G	10½	12	45	F
	75W R-30/SP	5	10	25	G				
	75W A-19	9	24	23	F				
	50W R-20/FL	8	12	21	F				
	150W PAR-38/3FL	36	36	42	VG	48	48	25	G
	150W A-21	36	36	35	E	36	36	25	VG
	100W A-19	24	24	34	VG	36	36	15	VG
	300W R-40/SP	36	36	36	E	36	36	39	E
	150W R-40/SP	24	24	31	E	36	36	19	E
	300W R-40/FL	36	36	56	E	36	36	42	VG
	150W R-40/FL	30	30	24	VG	36	36	10	F
	100W A-19	18	18	18	F				
	150W R-40/FL	36	36	43	VG	36	36	19	VG
	1 Lt.—40W T-12 (fluorescent)	Flush to wall	Continuous run (overlap)	16	VG				

*Typical data are for multiple unit installations and for lamps listed. Footcandles are measured in the vertical plane. All values are average and rounded off.
†Evenness rating is ratio of maximum to minimum footcandles. E (excellent) = 2:1; VG (very good) = 4:1; G (good) = 6:1; and F (fair) = 8:1. Values are rounded off to nearest ratio.

Courtesy Lightolier

Cross sections	Lamps*	For 9' ceiling				For 12' ceiling			
		Distance to wall (in.)	Fc at 5'6" above floor	Vertical beam spread†	Horizontal beam spread†	Distance to wall (in.)	Fc at 5'6" above floor	Vertical beam spread†	Horizontal beam spread†
A	100W T-4 (tungsten-halogen)	24	25	62 max.	24 max.	48	6	127 max.	49 max.
	100W T-4 (tungsten-halogen)	24	22	65 max.	25 max.	48	6	131 max.	50 max.
	150W PAR-38/SP	24	344	38	22	46	94	74	41
	150W R-40/SP	24	219	42	23	46	60	81	44
	75W R-30/SP	24	54	48	28	46	15	92	54
	75W R-30/FL	24	13	66	54	46	4	127	104
	150W PAR-38/SP	24	344	38	22	46	94	74	41
	150W PAR-38/FL	24	219	42	23	46	60	81	44
	75W R-30/SP	24	54	48	28	46	15	92	54
	75W R-30/FL	24	13	66	54	46	4	127	104
	300W T-3 (tungsten-halogen)	24	98	86	125	46	27	166	239
B	3 Lt. 40W T-10	7	30	28	48	7	30	28	48
	2 Lt. 40W T-10	7	30	24	40	7	30	24	40
C	1 Lt. 40W T-12 (fluorescent)	18	19	48	62	18	19	48	62

Typical data*

*Typical data are for single-unit installations (except undershelf flood lights) for lamps listed. Footcandles are measured on the vertical plane. All values are averaged and rounded off.

†Beam spread is where illumination drops to approximately 10 percent of maximum or where illumination becomes insignificant.

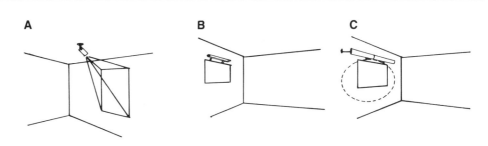

These examples are keyed to luminaires shown above.

Courtesy Lightolier

BEAM SPREAD

The downward distribution of light varies from concentrated to very widespread. The spread is controlled by the reflector design, the shielding, and the light source. The ratio of the mounting height to the spacing of the fixtures must be included in design decisions.

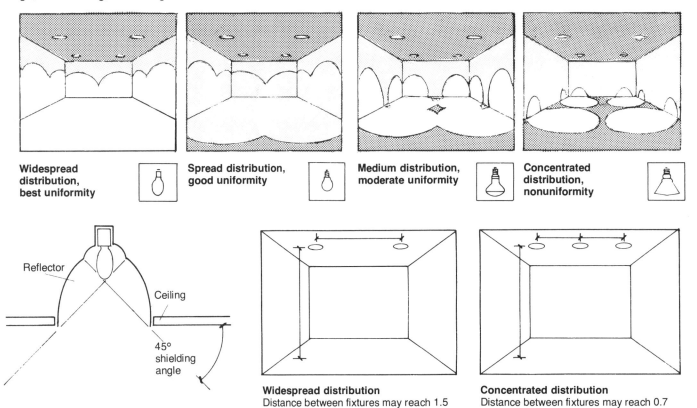

Widespread distribution, best uniformity

Spread distribution, good uniformity

Medium distribution, moderate uniformity

Concentrated distribution, nonuniformity

Reflector

Ceiling

45° shielding angle

Widespread distribution
Distance between fixtures may reach 1.5 times the room height

Concentrated distribution
Distance between fixtures may reach 0.7 times the room height

Shielding angle
Glare can be controlled by the shielding angle. Usually a 45° angle corrects most glare problems. The angle is formed by the ceiling line and the connecting line between the reflector edge and the lamp. Special applications may require other angles. (See page 318.)

Spacing to mounting height (S/MH) ratio
Mounting distances between luminaires are expressed by a ratio of spacing to mounting height (S/MH) that is related to beam spread. For uniform illumination, concentrated beam spread types should be located at comparatively close intervals while widespread beams can be spaced farther apart.

PARTIAL ROOM ILLUMINATION

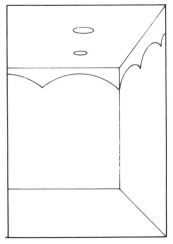

Complete illumination for a narrow space or single wall produces uniformity of illumination

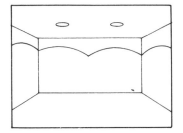

Light "scalloped" on walls can be created by the degree of shielding angle in relation to the distance of the luminaire from the wall

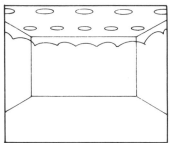

To clearly define the space and create a transparent room impression, do not exceed the S/MH ratio. Use of a wide beam spread will provide better overlapping and avoid harsh shadows

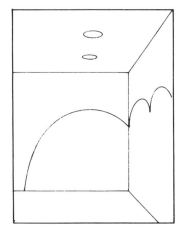

Hallways or foyers are best with narrow beams and wide fixture spacing

COEFFICIENT OF UTILIZATION (CU)

The coefficient of utilization (CU) is the percentage of light from a fixture that reaches the seeing task. It is a function of the fixture, each having its own CUs depending on a wide range of the following factors: fixture efficiency, distribution, and mounting height; room proportions; room surface reflectancies. It is calculated through the use of a CU table provided by lighting manufacturers. The table below provides the reflectance percentages of ceilings and walls. Each column contains CUs, and each row identifies the RCR (room cavity ratio). Where the two cross lies the CU. Each lamp-fixture combination requires its own CU table.

CU table
Lamp: 150W A-21
% effective ceiling cavity reflectance

		80			50			10		
		% wall reflectance								
		50	30	10	50	30	10	50	30	10
Room cavity ratio	1	.82	.80	.79	.77	.76	.75	.72	.72	.71
	2	.77	.74	.72	.73	.72	.70	.69	.68	.67
	3	.72	.69	.66	.69	.67	.65	.67	.64	.63
	4	.68	.65	.62	.66	.63	.61	.63	.61	.59
	5	.64	.60	.57	.62	.59	.57	.60	.58	.55
	6	.60	.56	.53	.58	.55	.53	.57	.54	.52
	7	.56	.52	.50	.55	.51	.49	.53	.50	.48
	8	.53	.49	.46	.52	.48	.46	.50	.47	.46
	9	.49	.45	.42	.48	.45	.42	.47	.44	.42
	10	.46	.42	.39	.45	.42	.39	.44	.41	.39

Conversion factors:
100W A-19 (Clear): CU x 1.0.
100W A-19/150W A-21 (Gold): CU x 0.9.

To find number of luminaires, use formula A

$$\mathbf{A} \quad N = \frac{A \times fc}{L/L \times CU \times LDD}$$

To find footcandles, use formula B

$$\mathbf{B} \quad fc = \frac{L/L \times N \times CU \times LDD}{A}$$

fc (footcandles) = average *maintained* illumination at work plane, normally 30″ (76.20 cm) above floor.

L/L (Lumens per Luminaire) = number of lamps per luminaire X initial lumens per lamp (see lamp data provided by manufacturers).

CU (Coefficient of Utilization) = the percentage of lamp lumens that falls on work plane. To obtain the CU, first find the RCR (Room Cavity Ratio) for the room (see below). Then enter CU table at the RCR and at the effective ceiling cavity reflectance and wall reflectance column. Use 80% ceiling, 50% walls, and 20% floor when room surface reflectances are unknown but room has white ceiling and light walls. Note: CU table in catalogs are for typical 20% effective floor cavity reflectance.

LDD (Luminaire Dirt Depreciation = light loss due to the accumulation of dirt on luminaire.

A (Area) = room length x room width, in feet.

N = number of luminaires.

Example

Given	Luminaires: lamp: 150W A-21 Room: 20′ x 60′ x 8½′, clean area with white ceiling and light walls	
Find	**A** No. of luminaires required for 50 fc, avg. maint.	**B** Avg. maint. fc with luminaires on 5′ x 5′ centers
Solution	RCR for 20′ x 60′ x 6′ = 2.0. Assume room refl. = 80%, 50%, 20%. CU = .77. L/L = 1 x 2880 = 2880. LDD = .75	

$$\mathbf{A} \text{ No. of luminaires} = \frac{20 \times 60 \times 50}{2880 \times .77 \times .75} = 36$$

$$\text{No. of luminaires} = \frac{area}{area/lum.} = \frac{20 \times 60}{5 \times 5} = 48$$

$$\mathbf{B} \text{ fc} = \frac{2880 \times 48 \times .77 \times .75}{20 \times 60} = 67$$

FINDING THE ROOM CAVITY RATIO (RCR)

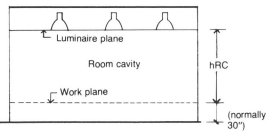

Find RCR from table below or determine as follows:

$$RCR = \frac{5hrc (L + W)}{LW}$$

Cavity depth data

Room dim., ft		Cavity depth (hRC), ft								
W	L	5	6	7	8	9	11	14	20	30
10	10	5.0	6.0	7.0	8.0	9.0	11.0			
	14	4.3	5.1	6.0	6.9	7.8	9.5	12.0		
	20	3.7	4.5	5.3	6.0	6.8	8.3	10.5		
	30	3.3	.0	4.7	5.3	6.0	7.3	9.4		
	40	3.1	3.7	4.4	5.0	5.6	6.9	8.7	12.5	
12	12	4.2	5.0	5.8	6.7	7.5	9.2	11.7		
	16	3.6	4.4	5.1	5.8	6.5	8.0	10.2		
	24	3.1	3.7	4.4	5.0	5.6	6.9	8.7	12.5	
	36	2.8	3.3	3.9	4.4	5.0	6.0	7.8	11.0	
	50	2.6	3.1	3.6	4.1	4.6	5.6	7.2	10.2	
14	14	3.6	4.3	5.0	5.7	6.4	7.8	10.0		
	20	3.0	3.6	4.2	4.9	5.5	6.7	8.6	12.3	
	30	2.6	3.1	3.7	4.2	4.7	5.8	7.3	10.5	
	42	2.4	2.9	3.3	3.8	4.3	5.2	6.7	9.5	
	60	2.2	2.6	3.1	3.5	3.9	4.8	6.1	8.8	
17	17	2.9	3.5	4.1	4.7	5.3	6.5	8.2	11.7	
	25	2.5	3.0	3.5	4.0	4.5	5.5	7.0	10.0	
	35	2.2	2.6	3.1	3.5	3.9	4.8	6.1	8.7	
	50	2.0	2.4	2.8	3.1	3.5	4.3	5.4	7.7	11.6
	80	1.8	2.1	2.5	2.9	3.3	4.0	5.1	7.2	10.9
20	20	2.5	3.0	3.5	4.0	4.5	5.5	7.0	10.0	
	30	2.1	2.5	2.9	3.3	3.7	4.5	5.8	8.2	12.4
	45	1.8	2.2	2.5	2.9	3.3	4.0	5.1	7.2	10.9
	60	1.7	2.0	2.3	2.7	3.0	3.7	4.7	6.7	10.1
	90	1.5	1.8	2.1	2.4	2.7	3.3	4.2	6.0	9.0

Room dim., ft		Cavity depth (hRC), ft								
W	L	5	6	7	8	9	11	14	20	30
24	24	2.1	2.5	2.9	3.3	3.7	4.5	5.8	8.2	12.4
	32	1.8	2.2	2.6	2.9	3.3	4.0	5.1	7.2	11.0
	50	1.5	1.8	2.2	2.5	2.8	3.4	4.4	6.2	9.4
	70	1.4	1.7	2.0	2.2	2.5	3.0	3.8	5.5	8.2
	100	1.3	1.6	1.8	2.1	2.4	2.9	3.7	5.2	7.9
30	30	1.7	2.0	2.3	2.7	3.0	3.7	4.7	6.7	10.0
	45	1.4	1.7	1.9	2.2	2.5	3.0	3.8	5.5	8.2
	60	1.2	1.5	1.7	2.0	2.2	2.7	3.5	5.0	7.4
	90	1.1	1.3	1.6	1.8	2.0	2.5	3.1	4.5	6.7
	150	1.0	1.2	1.4	1.6	1.8	2.2	2.8	4.0	5.9
42	42	1.2	1.4	1.6	1.9	2.1	2.6	3.3	4.7	7.1
	60	1.0	1.2	1.4	1.6	1.8	2.2	2.8	4.0	6.0
	90	0.9	1.0	1.2	1.4	1.6	1.9	2.4	3.5	5.2
	140	0.8	0.9	1.1	1.2	1.4	1.7	2.2	3.1	4.6
	200	0.7	0.9	1.0	1.1	1.3	1.6	2.0	2.9	4.3
60	60	0.8	1.0	1.2	1.3	1.5	1.8	2.3	3.3	5.0
	100	0.7	0.8	0.9	1.1	1.2	1.5	1.9	2.7	4.0
	150	0.6	0.7	0.8	0.9	1.0	1.3	1.6	2.3	3.5
100	100	0.5	0.6	0.7	0.8	0.9	1.1	1.4	2.0	3.0
	200	0.4	0.4	0.5	0.6	0.7	0.8	1.0	1.5	2.2
	300	0.3	0.4	0.5	0.6	0.6	0.7	0.9	1.3	2.0

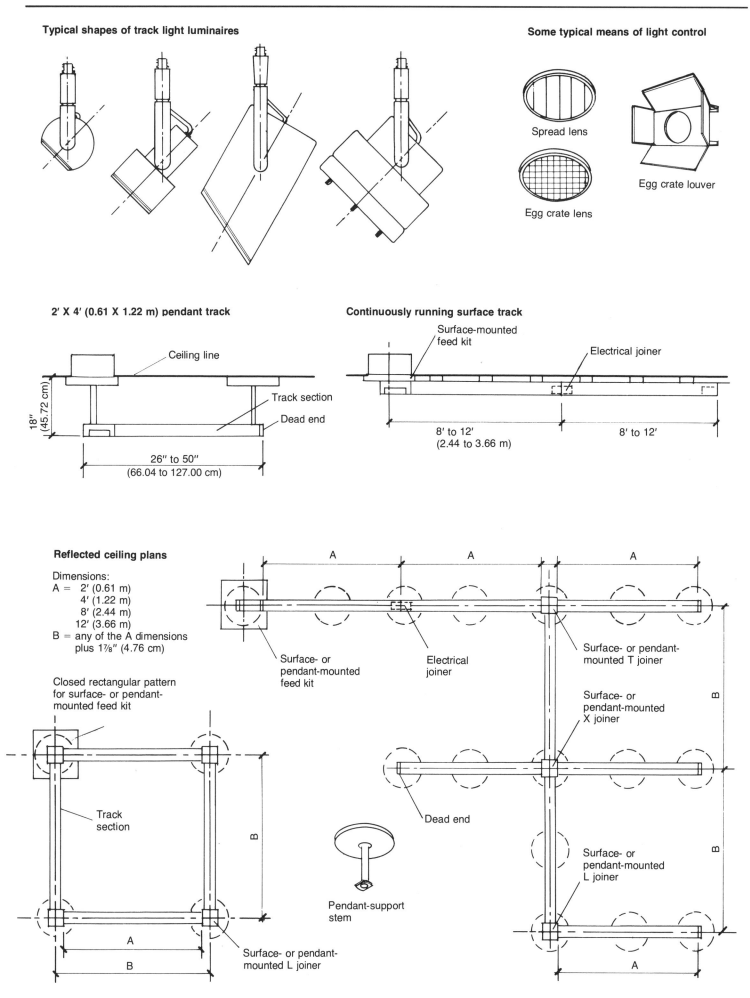

Typical shapes of track light luminaires

Some typical means of light control

Spread lens

Egg crate lens

Egg crate louver

2' X 4' (0.61 X 1.22 m) pendant track

Ceiling line

Track section

Dead end

18" (45.72 cm)

26" to 50"
(66.04 to 127.00 cm)

Continuously running surface track

Surface-mounted feed kit

Electrical joiner

8' to 12'
(2.44 to 3.66 m)

8' to 12'

Reflected ceiling plans

Dimensions:
A = 2' (0.61 m)
    4' (1.22 m)
    8' (2.44 m)
    12' (3.66 m)
B = any of the A dimensions plus 1⅞" (4.76 cm)

Closed rectangular pattern for surface- or pendant-mounted feed kit

Track section

Surface- or pendant-mounted L joiner

Pendant-support stem

A   A   A

Surface- or pendant-mounted feed kit

Electrical joiner

Surface- or pendant-mounted T joiner

Surface- or pendant-mounted X joiner

Dead end

Surface- or pendant-mounted L joiner

A

B

B

A

B

TRACK LIGHTING APPLICATIONS

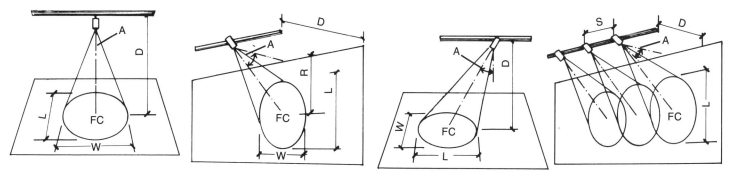

A = aiming angle
D = distance
FC = initial footcandles at the center of the beam
L & W for narrow and medium beam lamps = point that the candlepower drops to 10 percent of maximum
L & W for wide beam lamps = the point that the candlepower drops to 50 percent of maximum
R = beam center location
S = maximum spacing of spots for even illumination

TO DETERMINE BEAM LOCATION, FOOTCANDLES, BEAM SIZE, & SPACING

Known: track location, lamp, & aiming angle*

Given: Track located 5' (1.52 m) from the wall. 150W PAR-38 Spot Lamp aimed at 45°

Find	Solution
Beam center location (R)	Using the 45° aiming angle chart, the beam center location (R) is 5' from the ceiling
Footcandles (FC) at beam center	The data show footcandles (FC) at beam center = 156 FC
Length (L) and width (W) of beam	Length (L) of beam = 5.8' (1.75 m) Width (W) = 3.8' (1.14 m)
Spacing (S) for even illumination on a large area	Spacing (S) for even illumination = 2.5' (0.76 m)

*See typical lighting performance data provided by manufacturers.

Performance data example

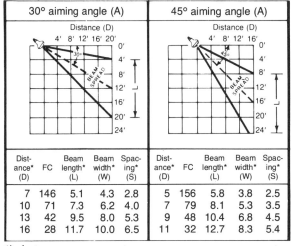

30° aiming angle (A)					45° aiming angle (A)				
Dist-ance* (D)	FC	Beam length* (L)	Beam width* (W)	Spac-ing* (S)	Dist-ance* (D)	FC	Beam length* (L)	Beam width* (W)	Spac-ing* (S)
7	146	5.1	4.3	2.8	5	156	5.8	3.8	2.5
10	71	7.3	6.2	4.0	7	79	8.1	5.3	3.5
13	42	9.5	8.0	5.3	9	48	10.4	6.8	4.5
16	28	11.7	10.0	6.5	11	32	12.7	8.3	5.4

*In feet.

TO DETERMINE TRACK PLACEMENT & LAMP (FOR A GIVEN AIMING ANGLE)

Known: object to be lighted, footcandles required, & ceiling height*

Given	Lamp aiming at 60° from horizontal; painting 6' long and 2' wide (1.83 and 0.61 m) to be lighted to 150 footcandles; ceiling height 11' (3.35 m)	
Find	Track placement	Lamp
Solution	Enter the chart at 11' ceiling height, move to the right to the 60° line, and proceed vertically to read approximately 3' (0.91 m) from the wall.	Scanning the lighting performance data shown for the 60' aiming angle shows that a narrow distribution is required. The 150W PAR-38 Spot Lamp is selected. This lamp provides 153 footcandles and lights an area 8.2' long by 2.1' wide (2.50 X 0.64 m), which is more than enough to cover the painting.

*See typical lighting performance data provided by manufacturers.

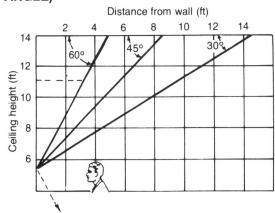

The preferred aiming angle to minimize reflected glare from paintings and other shiny objects is 60° from the horizontal. This chart shows where to place the track for various ceiling heights. Track locations are also shown for other aiming angles.

Medical office

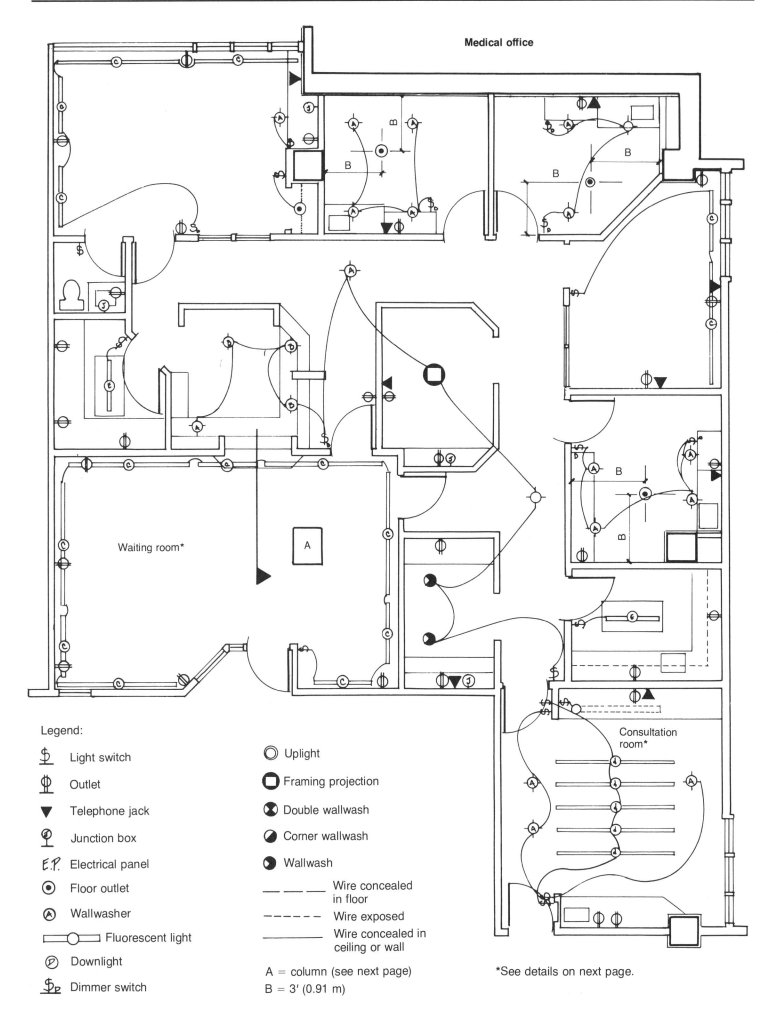

Waiting room*

A

Consultation room*

Legend:

$ Light switch

⚎ Outlet

▼ Telephone jack

⚲ Junction box

E.P. Electrical panel

⊙ Floor outlet

Ⓐ Wallwasher

⬭⊸ Fluorescent light

Ⓓ Downlight

$_D Dimmer switch

◯ Uplight

⬛ Framing projection

⊗ Double wallwash

◐ Corner wallwash

◖ Wallwash

— — — Wire concealed in floor

- - - - - Wire exposed

——— Wire concealed in ceiling or wall

A = column (see next page)

B = 3' (0.91 m)

*See details on next page.

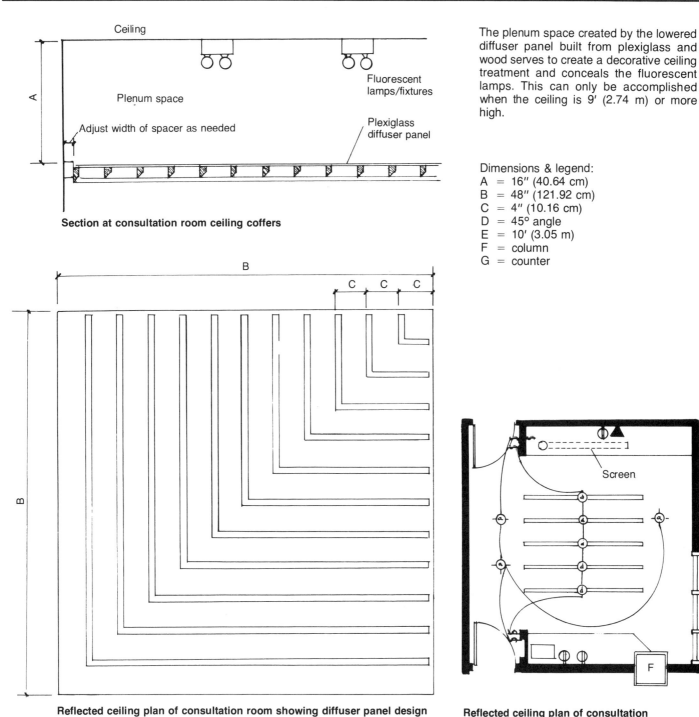

Section at consultation room ceiling coffers

The plenum space created by the lowered diffuser panel built from plexiglass and wood serves to create a decorative ceiling treatment and conceals the fluorescent lamps. This can only be accomplished when the ceiling is 9' (2.74 m) or more high.

Dimensions & legend:
A = 16" (40.64 cm)
B = 48" (121.92 cm)
C = 4" (10.16 cm)
D = 45° angle
E = 10' (3.05 m)
F = column
G = counter

Reflected ceiling plan of consultation room showing diffuser panel design

Reflected ceiling plan of consultation room showing concealed ceiling lighting & electrical outlets in wall

Waiting room elevation

*Shown in plan on page 316.

Planes of intensity distributions

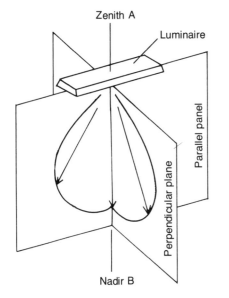

Zenith A

Luminaire

Parallel panel

Perpendicular plane

Nadir B

CP curve

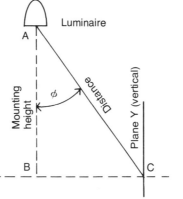

Candlepower direction

The nadir B is the point directly below the light source or luminaire. In the drawings immediately below, the nadir is any point along line AB, and the direction of the candlepower is measured by angle ϕ.

In the CP curve (candlepower curve) diagram below left, the curve is that of a 400-watt mercury vapor, 2' (0.61 m) round, recessed luminaire. The curve illustrates that the candlepower at 40° is about 6250 CP. At 60° it is almost 3000 CP, while at 0° (nadir), it is slightly under 5000 CP.

Note: The readings obtained from the candlepower curve represent the initial CP and not maintained values. Visual comfort is usually attained with values of 70 or more VCP (visual comfort probability).

Direct glare is minimized if luminaire luminance values and the ratio:

$$\frac{\text{Maximum luminaire luminance}}{\text{Average luminaire luminance}}$$

is less than 5 (3 is preferred), all in accordance with the following table:

ϕ Angle from nadir	Maximum allowable luminance
45°	2250
55°	1605
65°	1125
75°	750
85°	495

Calculations of vertical & horizontal footcandles

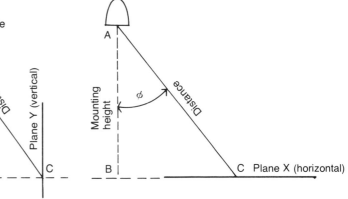

Applications of controlled CP direction

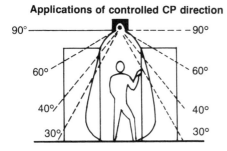

Narrow or stack lens

Parabolic lens controls light distribution for even lighting of vertical surfaces in high, narrow areas such as library stacks.

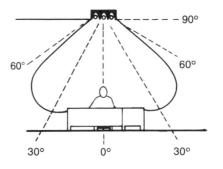

Wide parabolic lens

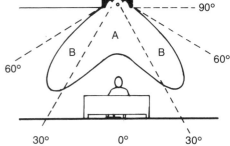

Batwing light control
A = veiling reflection zone
B = energy-efficient zone

Parabolic units

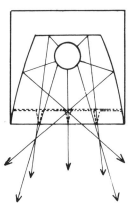

Wide light distribution with
high degree of glare control

2 lamps

1' X 4'
(0.31 X 1.22 m)

3 lamps

2' X 4'
(0.61 X 1.22 m)

4 lamps

2' X 4'

Lensed units

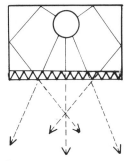

Prismatic reflectors offer good control
of glare by restricting light distribution.
Recommended for use in areas
where demanding tasks are
performed. Also use where an
extensive area of the ceiling is in
peripheral vision.

Prismatic reflectors are pyramidal
or conical and are referred to as
either a male lens (raised) or a female
lens (recessed).

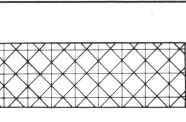

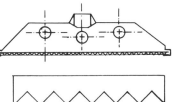

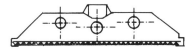

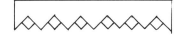

Diffusers

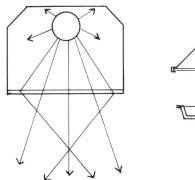

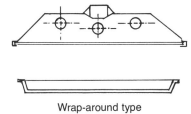

Wrap-around type

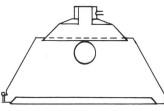

Batwing reflector

Diffusers provide very broad light distribution, but do not normally control glare-producing light rays. The batwing type of
diffuser controls veiling reflections by concentrating most of the
light output in the 30° to 60° zone. This leaves a small portion of
light directed in the 0° to 30° veiling reflection zone and in the
60° to 90° glare zone.

Modular exposed grid

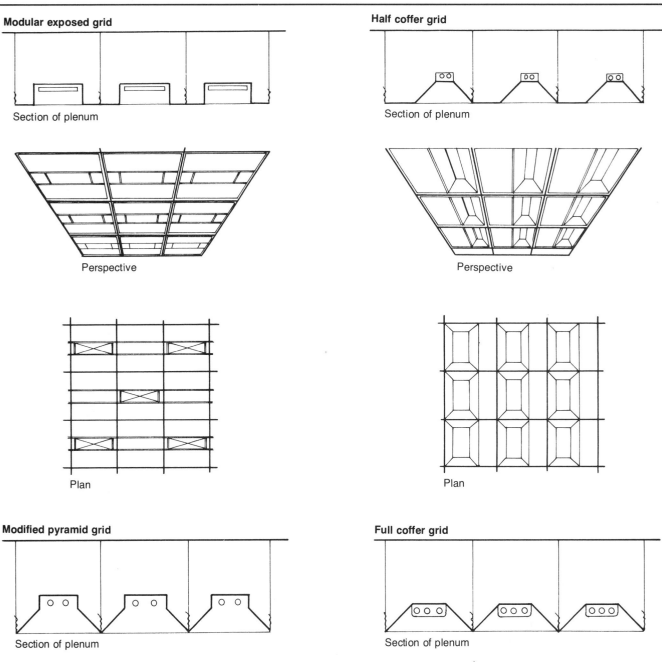

Section of plenum

Perspective

Plan

Half coffer grid

Section of plenum

Perspective

Plan

Modified pyramid grid

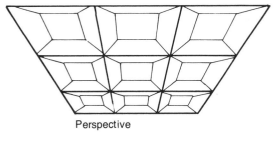

Section of plenum

Perspective

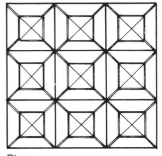

Plan

Full coffer grid

Section of plenum

Perspective

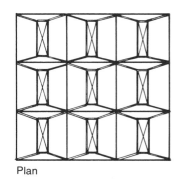

Plan

Pyramidal grid

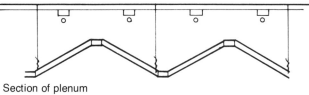

Section of plenum

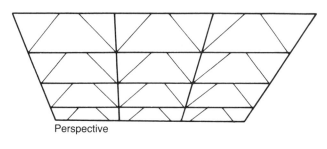

Perspective

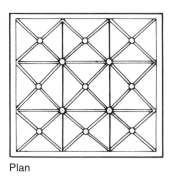

Plan

Concave radial grid

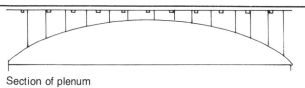

Section of plenum

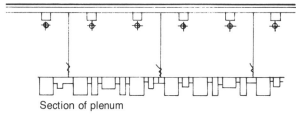

Perspective

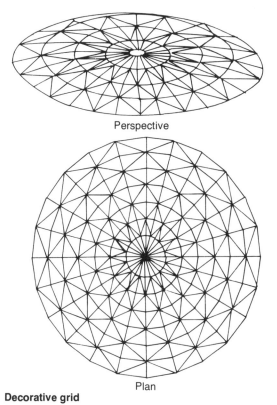

Plan

Modular square grid

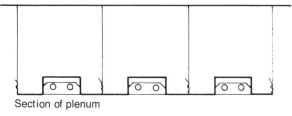

Section of plenum

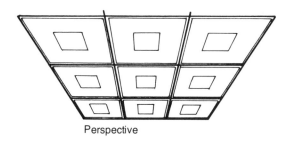

Perspective

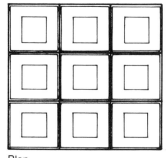

Plan

Decorative grid

Section of plenum

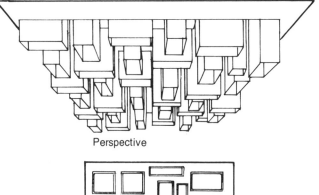

Perspective

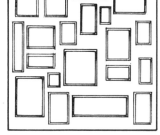

Plan

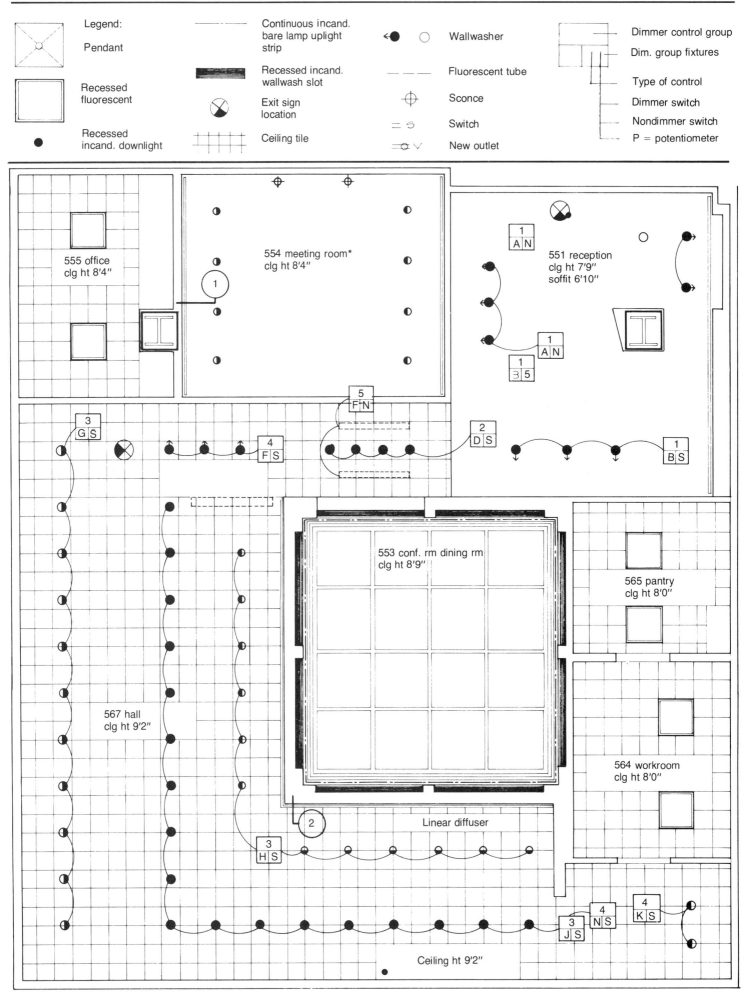

Legend:

Pendant

Recessed fluorescent

Recessed incand. downlight

Continuous incand. bare lamp uplight strip

Recessed incand. wallwash slot

Exit sign location

Ceiling tile

Wallwasher

Fluorescent tube

Sconce

Switch

New outlet

Dimmer control group

Dim. group fixtures

Type of control

Dimmer switch

Nondimmer switch

P = potentiometer

555 office
clg ht 8′4″

554 meeting room*
clg ht 8′4″

551 reception
clg ht 7′9″
soffit 6′10″

553 conf. rm dining rm
clg ht 8′9″

565 pantry
clg ht 8′0″

564 workroom
clg ht 8′0″

567 hall
clg ht 9′2″

Linear diffuser

Ceiling ht 9′2″

*Plan for meeting room shown on next page.

ELECTRICAL & TELEPHONE PLAN FOR MEETING ROOM

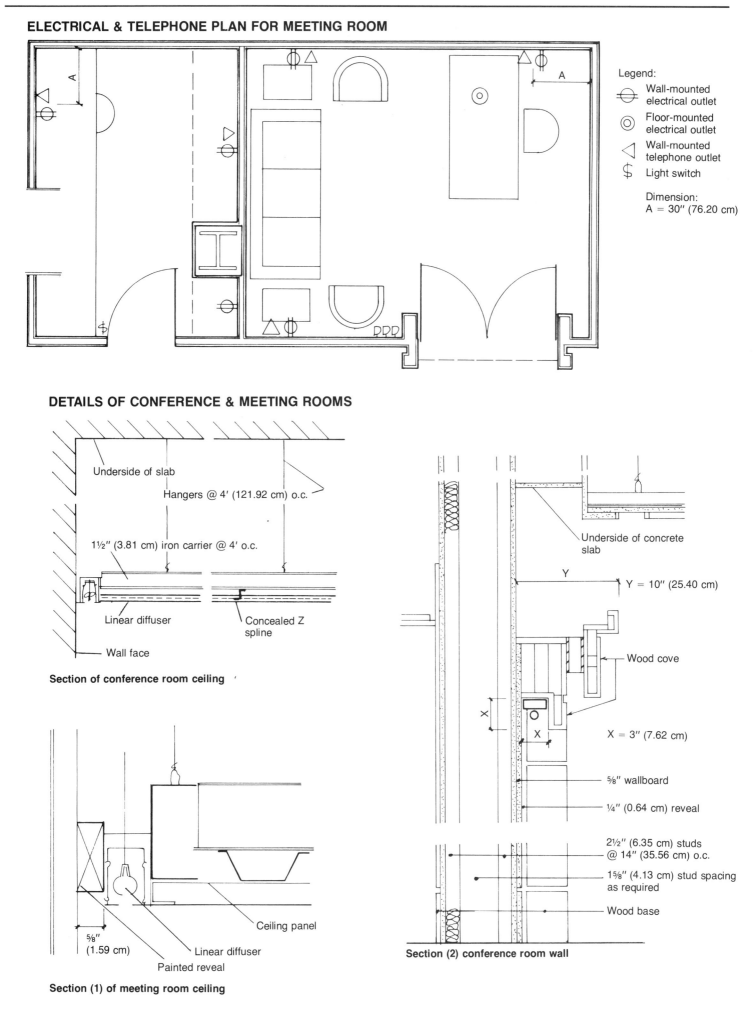

Legend:

⊖ Wall-mounted electrical outlet

◎ Floor-mounted electrical outlet

◁ Wall-mounted telephone outlet

$ Light switch

Dimension:
A = 30″ (76.20 cm)

DETAILS OF CONFERENCE & MEETING ROOMS

Underside of slab

Hangers @ 4′ (121.92 cm) o.c.

1½″ (3.81 cm) iron carrier @ 4′ o.c.

Linear diffuser

Concealed Z spline

Wall face

Section of conference room ceiling

Underside of concrete slab

Y = 10″ (25.40 cm)

Wood cove

X = 3″ (7.62 cm)

⅝″ wallboard

¼″ (0.64 cm) reveal

2½″ (6.35 cm) studs @ 14″ (35.56 cm) o.c.

1⅝″ (4.13 cm) stud spacing as required

Wood base

Section (2) conference room wall

Ceiling panel

⅝″ (1.59 cm)

Linear diffuser

Painted reveal

Section (1) of meeting room ceiling

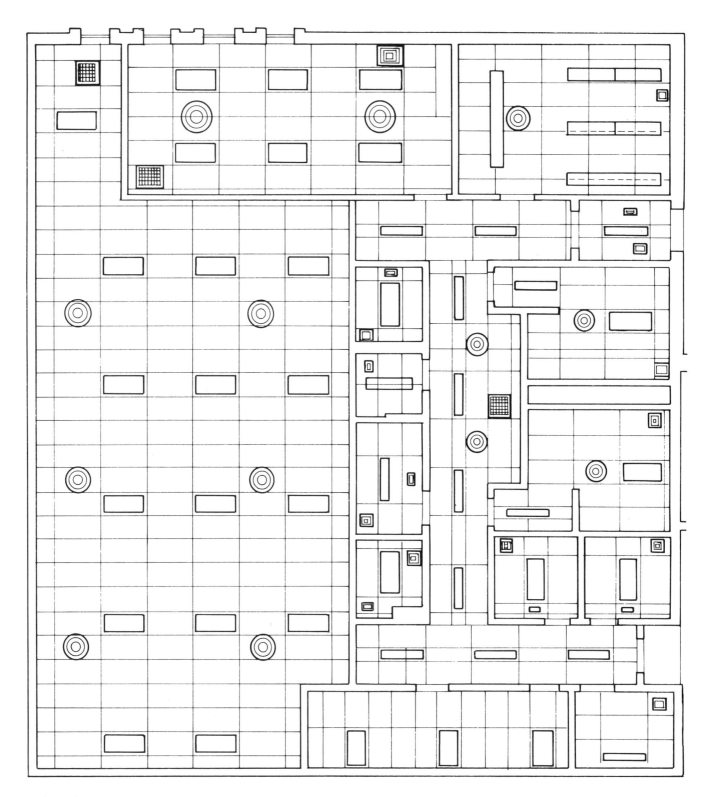

Legend:

□ 2′ X 4′ (60.96 X 121.92 cm) recessed light fixture

▭ 1′ X 4′ (30.48 X 121.92 cm) recessed light

▭ 1′ X 4′ surface-mounted or suspended light

▢ Diffuser

▦ Return air register

▭ Exhaust fan grille

◎ Diffuser

Notes:
1. Suspended ceiling system noncombustion ⅝″ X 2′ X 4′ (1.59 X 60.96 X 121.92 cm) lay-in panels with metal 1″ (2.54 cm) suspension system.

2. This drawing was designed to show the placement of electrical and mechanical equipment.

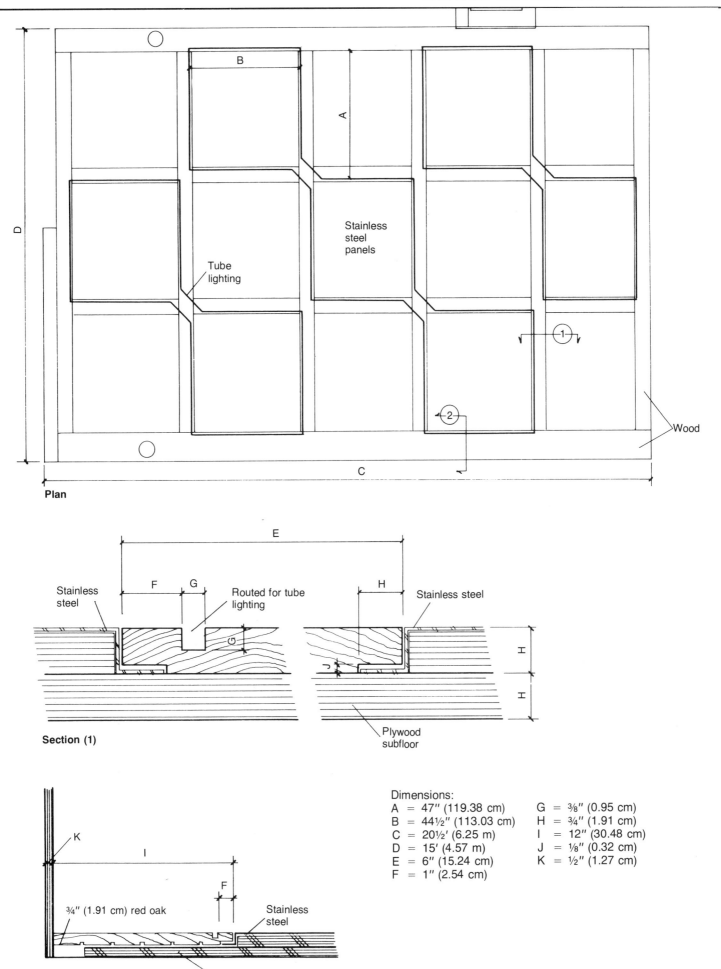

Plan

B

A

Stainless
steel
panels

Tube
lighting

Wood

D

C

①

②

Section (1)

E

F   G   Routed for tube
lighting

Stainless
steel

H

Stainless steel

G

J

H

H

Plywood
subfloor

Section (2)

K

I

F

¾″ (1.91 cm) red oak

Stainless
steel

Plywood subfloor

Dimensions:
A = 47″ (119.38 cm)   G = ⅜″ (0.95 cm)
B = 44½″ (113.03 cm)   H = ¾″ (1.91 cm)
C = 20½′ (6.25 m)   I = 12″ (30.48 cm)
D = 15′ (4.57 m)   J = ⅛″ (0.32 cm)
E = 6″ (15.24 cm)   K = ½″ (1.27 cm)
F = 1″ (2.54 cm)

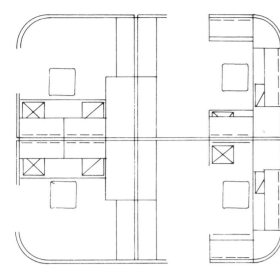

Work-surface plan

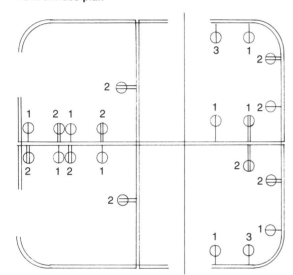

Circuit plan
Circuit no. 1 = task lights
Circuit no. 2 = general convenience
                      outlets, duplex
Circuit no. 3 = CRT

—⊖— Single receptacle

⊖ Duplex receptacle

▯B Base feed module

▯T Top feed module

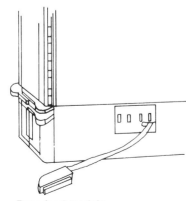

Base feed module
Verify that panel units with base
outlets are UL approved.

Amperage* of common electrical devices

	AMPS based on 120V supply
Adding machine	0.5
Answering machine	0.08
Calculator (large) electronic	0.2
Calculator (small) and charger	0.07
Clock	0.05
Computer equipment	
Desk-top plotter	1.5
Draft/letter quality printers	3.0
Modems	0.15
Personal computers	2.0-4.0
Processor/disk drive unit	1.2
Video display terminal	0.8
Copiers	
Desk-top	7.0-10.0
Floor model	14.0-18.0
Dictating machine	0.25
Electric eraser	0.5
Electric typewriter	1.2
Lights	
Counter cap light	0.55
Critical task light	0.35
General task light/display light [4' (1.22 m)]	0.67
General task light/display light [2' (0.61 m)]	0.35
100 watt	0.8
Mail processing machines	
Letter opener	1.9
Postage meter	2.7
UPS stamp machine	3.0
Microfiche reader	1.0
Miscellaneous	
Coffee brewer	4.0-10.0
Microwave	8.0-12.0
Space heater	10.0-14.0
Warmer	1.5
Paper shredder	4.5-13.0
Pencil sharpener	1.2
Radio	0.05
Slide projector	2.0-6.0
Tape recorder	0.1
Telecopier	0.5
Telex	5.0
Word processer	1.5

*Amperage is also found by dividing the wattage by the voltage.

Note: When planning electrical power requirements for open office systems, it is important not to overload the circuits. The National Electrical Codes recommend that a maximum of 80 percent, or 16 amps per circuit, not be exceeded.

Circuit planning
After the designer has planned the position of all work surfaces and related power requirements, then plans like those shown above left can be drawn up. Locate all feed modules and receptacles. If the office system specified has outlets rated 120-volt, 20-amp branch circuits, this provides a 2400-watt maximum capacity (120 X 20 = 2400). Therefore, to find the allowable number of receptacles divide 2400 by 180 (2400 ÷ 180 = 13.33 receptacles).

By checking the above list of typical office equipment and corresponding power requirements, a designer can begin to determine the amperes allowed. By adding up items in this list, it is possible to develop an accurate summary of the office's electrical power requirements.

This list illustrates that one piece of equipment can use the maximum recommended amperage on one 20-amp circuit. Therefore, some manufacturers recommend that their product be placed on a separate circuit. The drawings above left illustrate the use of three circuits. Some codes also require that lighting be on a separate circuit. It is also possible to have as many as 39 receptacles from one connection to the building wiring. Individual circuit limits and local electrical codes should be consulted.

Typical installation layout for emergency lighting

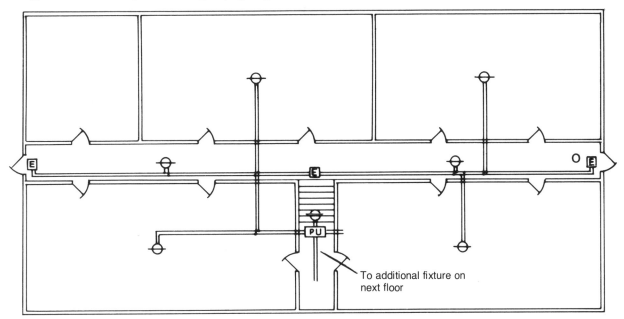

To additional fixture on next floor

Legend:

| PU | Power unit/battery |

Emergency fixture

| E | Emergency light |

O Fire sign. See exit signage on page 211. Typical spacing recommended is 50′ (15.24 m) in uninterrupted space.

Typical emergency fixtures

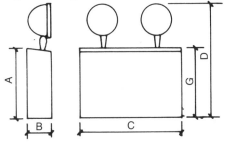

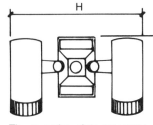

The mounting plate measures 3″ X 5″ (7.62 X 12.70 cm). The depth with lamps in the vertical position is 4½″ (11.43 cm).

The light may be placed on either the top or the sides. The lamp adds 5⅞″ (14.92 cm) to the top or side.

Dimensions:

	in.	cm		in.	cm
A =	7	17.78	F =	9	22.86
B =	2½	6.35	G =	6	15.24
C =	10	25.40	H =	11	27.94
D =	13½	34.29	I =	5¾	14.61
E =	15	38.10	J =	8	20.32

Aisle or stair lighting

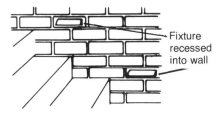

Fixture recessed into wall

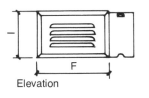

Elevation

4″ (10.16 cm) deep

Section

Code requirements

Most codes require that emergency lighting systems which must change from one energy source to another do so with little or no interruption in the lighting. A minimum level of 1 footcandle illumination should be provided for 1½ hours in all exit access areas, which include corridors, ramps, escalators, stairs, aisles, and passageways leading to an exit.

Emergency lighting is usually required in all public facilities, apartment buildings with more than 12 units and more than three stories; and places of business occupying buildings with more than two stories and with occupancy of 100 people using space above or below the level of exit discharge. Emergency lighting is also required when occupancy reaches 1000 or more.

Hotels with more than 25 rooms are normally required to provide emergency lighting, except if all guest rooms open directly to the outside on the garden level. Consult local codes.

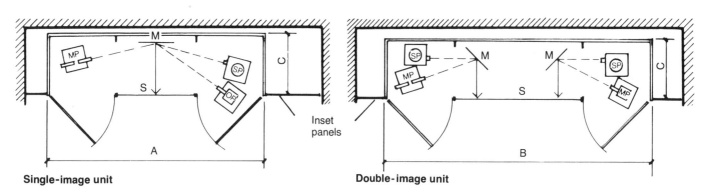

Single-image unit   **Double-image unit**

Legend:

M   = mirror
MP = movie projector
OP = overhead projector
S   = rear projection screen
SP = slide projector

**Elevation of typical wall
for rear projection**

Legibility standards

Farthest viewing image (ft)	Image size (S) (in.)	Height (E)	Width Single (A)	Width Dual (B)	Depth: Allow 1″ (2.54 cm) if recessed (C)	Recommended base cabinet height (D)
22	36	5′6″	8′8″	11′8″	2′9″	2′6″
28	45	5′10″	9′5″	13′2″	3′6″	2′2″
34	54	6′0″	10′2″	14′8″	4′1″	2′0″

Note: The screen image is large enough to accommodate viewers seated up to the maximum distance when correct legibility standards are applied in preparing the visuals. For satisfactory legibility within the above listed viewing distances, the smallest alphanumeric symbol used to prepare original copy for overhead transparencies in 6¾″ X 9″ (17.15 X 22.86 cm) copy area, or 35mm slides in 6″ X 9″ (15.24 X 22.86 cm) copy area [on 12″ X 12″ (30.48 X 30.48 cm) art board] should be 3/16″ (0.48 cm).

Equipment checklist

1. Preset optical system that includes a 94 percent reflective front surface mirror on selected ¼″ (0.64 cm) float glass with optical alignment positions controlled manually/automatically from the front of the cabinet.
2. A nonglare ¼″ (0.64 cm) thick acrylic rear projection screen. Specify height and width.
3. Control panel layout for approved installation. Voltages at the control panel shall not exceed 24 volts DC. Relay circuitry shall utilize relays and be of binary design to permit possible additional future control locations.
4. Self-threading 16mm sound motion picture projector with necessary wide angle lens and 2000′ (609.60 m) reel film capacity.
5. Autofocusing 35mm slide projector(s) with remote focus override, special wide angle lenses, and wide light distribution condensing system. Picture illumination measured 5″ (12.70 cm) in from each side of horizontal image shall not be less than 70 percent of center illumination.
6. Overhead projector on alignment shelf so can be pulled out for use.

Specification checklist

1. Specify self-contained audiovisual systems.
2. Specify equipment that will allow single or dual images of slides, sound motion pictures, or overhead transparencies.
3. Order projectors with preset alignment positions and low-voltage relay control circuits.
4. Place all equipment in positions that allow loading and operation without leaving the meeting room.
5. Specify equipment that will allow operation in lighted rooms.
6. Require that all equipment be pretested and operational within two working days.
7. Paint interior of projection room black.

TYPICAL INSTALLATIONS

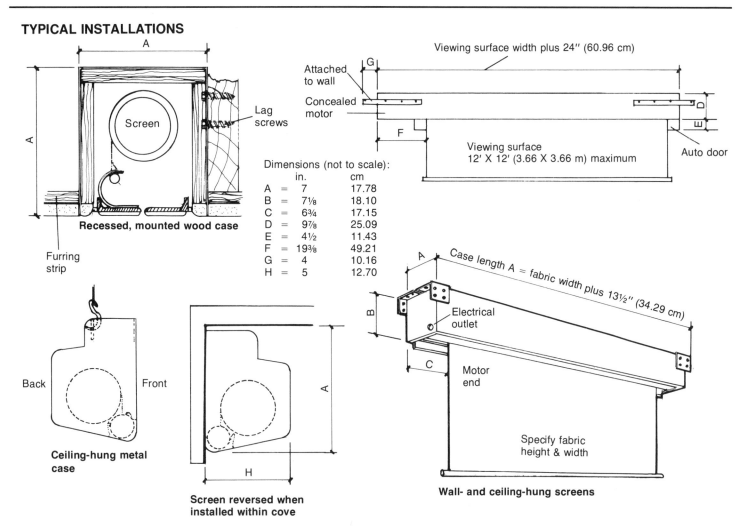

Recessed, mounted wood case

Furring strip

Screen

Lag screws

Dimensions (not to scale):

	in.	cm
A =	7	17.78
B =	7⅛	18.10
C =	6¾	17.15
D =	9⅞	25.09
E =	4½	11.43
F =	19⅜	49.21
G =	4	10.16
H =	5	12.70

Viewing surface width plus 24″ (60.96 cm)

Attached to wall

Concealed motor

Viewing surface 12′ X 12′ (3.66 X 3.66 m) maximum

Auto door

Ceiling-hung metal case

Back   Front

Screen reversed when installed within cove

Case length A = fabric width plus 13½″ (34.29 cm)

Electrical outlet

Motor end

Specify fabric height & width

Wall- and ceiling-hung screens

Specification of screen size required by room size

Room ratio length: width	1:1		4:3		3:2	
Minimum screen size (in./ft.)	Room size (ft)	Seating capacity	Room size (ft)	Seating capacity	Room size (ft)	Seating capacity (ft)
40	20 X 20	21	20 X 15	16	20 X 13	10
50	24 X 24	33	24 X 18	26	24 X 16	23
60	30 X 30	57	30 X 22	47	30 X 20	41
70	36 X 35	82	35 X 26	69	35 X 23	48
84	42 X 42	124	42 X 33	118	42 X 28	90
6 X 8	48 X 48	167	48 X 36	141	48 X 32	128
7 X 9	56 X 56	234	56 X 42	200	56 X 37	182
8 X 10	60 X 60	272	60 X 45	223	60 X 40	208
9 X 12	72 X 72	402	72 X 54	347	72 X 48	318

To determine screen size required by projection equipment, use the following formula (all dimensions in inches):

$$\text{Screen width} = \frac{\text{aperture width X projection distance}}{\text{lens focal length}}$$

Standard formats

	Aperture width (in.)	Lens focal length (in.)
8mm movie	0.172	1
Super 8mm movie	0.210	1
16mm movie	0.380	2
35mm slide	1.35	4-5
Filmstrip	0.885	3

Viewing distance calculations

The 2 and 6 rule prescribed by the Society of Motion Picture and Television Engineers is calculated as follows:
1. One-half the distance from the screen to the first row of seats should equal the screen width.
2. One-sixth the distance from the screen to the last row of seats should equal the screen width.
If the two resulting figures are not identical, a compromise may be made.

This rule fits the screen to the audience, not to the projector. The projector lens must also be adjusted. Rear projection has the same criteria.

No row of seats should be any wider than its distance from the screen.

Wide screen ratio

Find the proper size screen using the above formula; then keep the same height, but double the width. For example, a 9′ X 12′ (2.74 X 3.66 m) screen would be increased to one 9′ X 24′ (2.74 X 7.32 m) wide. The minimum height should be 4′ (1.22 m).

Screen surface

A beaded surface is recommended.

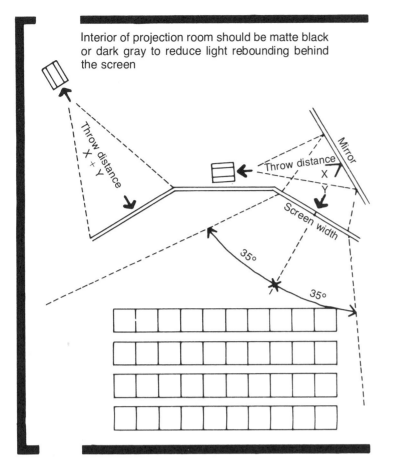

Interior of projection room should be matte black or dark gray to reduce light rebounding behind the screen

Rear screen projection space requirements

Rear screen projection

Screen size & angle in relation to seating arrangement in seminar or lecture facilities

Screen width*	T.6	Lenses	
		2X adapter†	½ X adapter†
4'	12'3"	5'9"	24'7"
8'	24'2"	11'9"	50'0"
12'	36'3"	18'0"	75'0"
16'	48'3"	24'4"	99'0"
20'	60'4"	30'7"	122'8"

*Projected from a 1.10" rasterwidth.
†Measured from front rim of adapter lens.
Note: Consult codes for aisle widths.

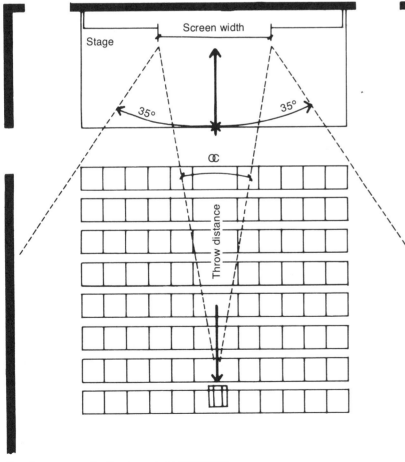

Front screen projection space requirements

Front screen projection

Specify projector placement in relation to seating depth & width

Screen width*	T.6	Lenses	
		2X adapter†	½ X adapter†
4'	12'3"	5'9"	24'7"
8'	24'2"	11'9"	50'0"
12'	36'3"	18'0"	75'0"
16'	48'3"	24'4"	99'0"
20'	60'4"	30'7"	122'8"

*Projected from a 1.10" rasterwidth.
†Measured from front rim of adapter lens.

∝ = is proportional to.

Basic procenium stage

For use in concert and recital halls, dinner theaters, schools, and drama departments

Notes & legend:
A = cyclorama
B = 3rd border
C = 2nd border
D = 1st border
E = stage apron
F = beam
G = control booth

6″ X 9″ (15.24 X 22.86 cm) ellipsoidal spotlight

6″ fresnel spotlight

Borderlight

14″ (35.56 cm) scoop/floodlight

Floor pocket light

Plugging box

Control console receptacle

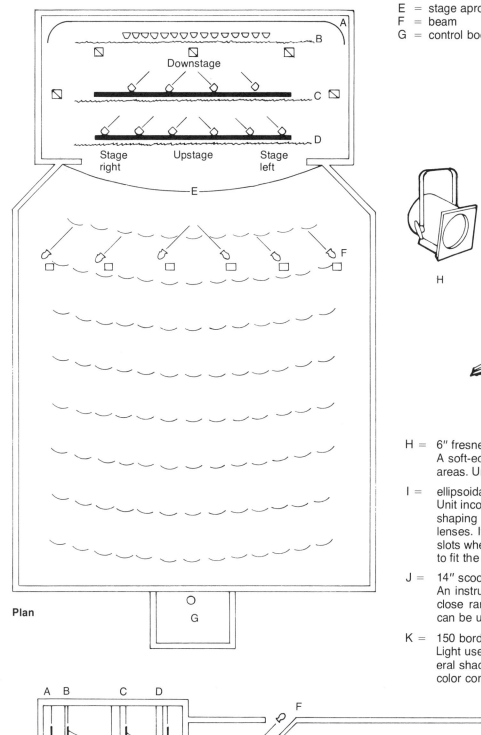

Plan

Downstage

Stage right   Upstage   Stage left

A

B

C

D

E

F

G

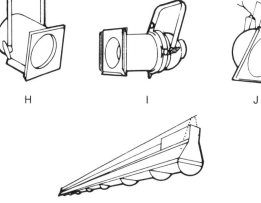

H   I   J

K

H = 6″ fresnel spotlight
A soft-edge spotlight used for blending and toning areas. Unit has adjustable focus from spot to flood.

I = ellipsoidal spotlight
Unit incorporating an ellipsoidal reflector beam with shaping shutters and two 6″ X 9″ piano convex lenses. It is typically used in ceiling covers or side slots where the beam of light must be cut or shaped to fit the proscenium opening.

J = 14″ scoop/floodlight
An instrument used to illuminate large surfaces at close range. Banks or rows of these instruments can be used effectively to light a large cyclorama.

K = 150 borderlight
Light used to tone acting areas and provide a general shadowless illumination over a large area with color control.

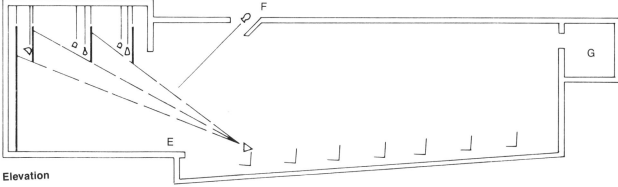

A B   C   D

F

G

E

Elevation

Specification requirements

Two-way teleconferencing is frequently designed to accommodate communication between sites within the same company. Prior to equipment selection, the designer must first determine the communication requirements. Equipment could include full-motion or free-frame video with or without audio. After those primary decisions, the following selections can be made: (1) conference table shape, (2) conference room size, and (3) placement of major video equipment.

Teleconference rooms require detailed drawings and specifications of the following:
1. Distance limitations of camera lens
2. Precise locations of all equipment
3. Table and seating details
4. Control panel layouts
5. Information about the ventilation systems
6. Information on acoustical treatments
7. Room finishes

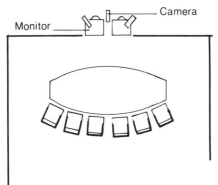

(1) Semicircular table

The semicircular table (1) provides two important optical parameters: (1) It allows each participant to be equidistant from the video cameras and monitors, which facilitates the use of full-motion video systems. (2) The table shape gives the illusion of a continuous conference room.

Disadvantages: The table design creates a formal setting that is not conducive to open discussion.

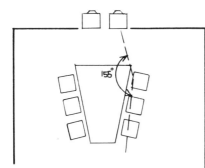

(2) Wedge-shaped table

The wedge-shaped table (2) provides a setting conducive to discussion and allows better overview pictures than standard monitor systems. Fewer cameras are therefore required and the total system cost is less than that used with the semicircular table system.

Disadvantages: The chairperson would normally be seated at the table apex and would appear in a dominant position on the monitor screen. The table shape requires participants to make a 180° head movement in order to look from an adjacent participant to the image on the monitor.

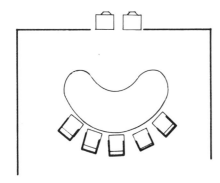

(3) Kidney-shaped table

The kidney-shaped table (3) also has the two outstanding features of the previous table, while the participants are seated at an equidistance from the monitors and each can see the faces around the table without leaning forward.

Disadvantage: The greatest is that none of the participants is able to move closer to the monitor to read graphic displays.

*The discussion of teleconferencing rooms continues on pages 333–335.

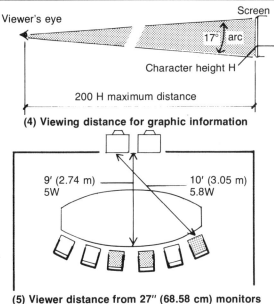

(4) Viewing distance for graphic information

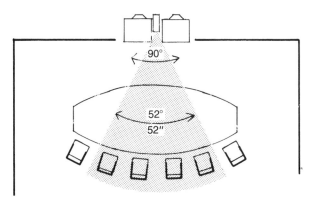

(5) Viewer distance from 27" (68.58 cm) monitors at semicircular table

The visual information transmitted during a video conference tends to be heavily oriented to graphics rather than views of participants. Legibility of graphs, charts, and written information that must be read by the participants should govern the selection of electronic equipment, table shapes, and seating arrangements.

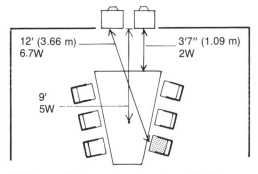

(6) Viewer distance at wedge-shaped table

Video graphic display

Three factors limit a person's ability to read graphic displays:

1. The capabilities of the human eye: Video experts suggest that good readability of monitor screens requires that letter or number height should subtend no less than 17° minimum of arc at viewer's eye level. This may also be explained using the character 8; that is, the number 8 should be no less than 1/200 of the viewer distance as shown in drawing 4.

2. Legibility requirements: The density of written information should be no more than 15 lines per page, with no line exceeding 40 characters across. This is based on the use of a video system with 525 scanning lines.

3. Size of available monitors: The calculations discussed above are based on the use of monitors with diagonal measurements of 25", 27", and 30" (63.50, 68.58, and 76.20 cm).

The 5W Rule

Drawing 4 illustrates how viewer distance is calculated using the 15 lines of text per page and the 1/200 distance criteria. The viewer should be no further from the monitor screen than 5 times the screen width. This is referred to as the 5W rule. As a rule of thumb the width of a television image is approximately 0.8 times the diagonal measurement. Therefore a 27" monitor with an image width of 21½" (54.61 cm) would require that the viewer be seated 9' (2.74 m) from the monitor. Example: 21½" X 5 = 108" or 9'.

At the semicircular table shown in 5, the person seated at the end would be 10' (3.05 m) from the monitor, that is, beyond optimum range.

Drawing 6 illustrates the 2W and 5W rules applied to a wedge-shaped table. The nearest viewer sits almost at 2W, while the person farthest away (6.7W) sits beyond the optimum distance.

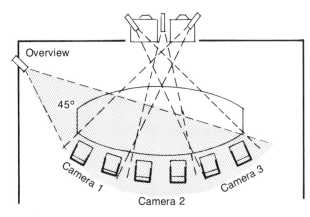

(7) Center lens viewing angle at semicircular table

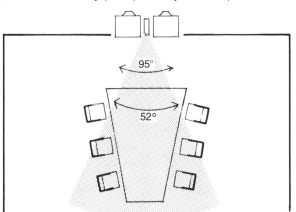

(8) Single lens viewing angle at wedge-shaped table

(10) Camera placement above monitors

Good viewing, seating, and camera lens selection must be carefully coordinated. Semicircular (7) and wedge-shaped tables (8) both require wide-angle lenses for overview shots. The shaded triangles shown in 7 and 8 illustrate the 52° viewing angle provided by the single center lens. Any center lens that would provide a larger 95° viewing angle would result in perspective distortion.

When semicircular and wedge-shaped tables are used, most video experts specify three cameras plus an additional overview lens (9). These cameras are placed above the monitors, which are located at eye level (10).

(9) Multiple-camera use at semicircular table

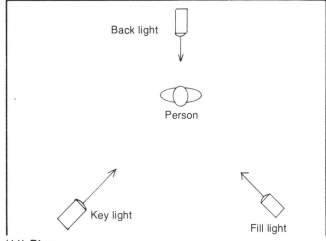

(11) Plan

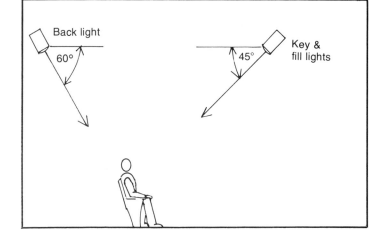

(12) Elevation

Simple light plot for a fixed single person. The key light provides the main apparent source of illumination for the picture. In a studio environment, it is typically a Fresnel lens instrument, which causes sharp shadows. The fill light is normally a soft-light instrument, such as a scoop, that partially fills in the dark shadows caused by the key light. The back light provides the all-essential rim lighting on heads and shoulders to give a three-dimensional illusion to the two-dimensional picture.

More specifically for video conference room lighting, there are several main criteria:
1. The intensity of the lighting should meet the technical requirements of the color cameras with the selected lenses set at the desired f-stop. For typical designs, 50 to 100 fc incident is usually adequate.
2. Illumination should preferably be specular in nature rather than diffuse in order to delineate form and substance.
3. Illumination should be as unobtrusive as possible. Lighting angles should be outside the glint angle of the subjects' eyes. Room surfaces should not produce spectral reflections. Do not specify shiny table tops or chrome chairs.
4. Backlighting should be provided to accent the third dimension of the picture.
5. Participants should not feel that they are in a studio.
6. Ambient light falling on the monitor screens must be reduced to as low a level as possible to maintain a good picture contrast ratio on the monitors.
7. If lighting is provided by mixed types of luminaires, they should be corrected so that each has the same color temperature.
8. In addition to lighting for the participants at the table, proper lighting must also be provided for graphics, wall pin-up surfaces, and participants not seated at the table.

9. The lighting design must be coordinated with other functions shared by the ceiling system, such as document cameras mounted overhead and HVAC.

Desired vertical lighting angles. Front lighting should be angled at about 45° below the horizontal to prevent squinting and deep facial shadows. Back lighting angled at 60° provides necessary contrast between the subject and the background.

One approach to lighting video conferencing rooms—a very simplistic one—is to provide standard, flush-mounted ceiling fluorescent fixtures in sufficient quantities to achieve the required intensity of illumination. This approach may provide adequate illumination, but little else. Lighting will be diffuse, ambient spill light will be difficult to control, and most of the illumination will be top light. Therefore, it is not recommended.

It is important to use relatively neutral colors for walls, carpet, and upholstery to avoid problems with colorimetry. Highly saturated colors can produce a pall on the participants and conflict with clothing colors.

Another lighting type that is not recommended is flush-mounted down lighting because it prevents necessary directional control. Although dimmers may control light levels, they should not be specified unless they are specially constructed to prevent interference with video and audio systems. Track lighting should also be avoided unless it can be placed in ceiling coves.

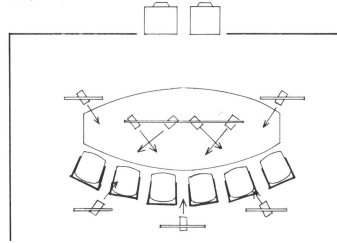

(13) Plan

Semicircular table with incandescent track lighting adjusted to serve as key, fill, and backlighting

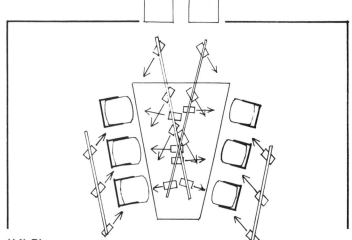

(14) Plan

Because participants at the wedge-shaped table face each other obliquely across the table, lighting becomes complex

Video conference rooms should be located within a quiet area of the facility. Noise originating outside the room, either from areas above or below or from surrounding rooms, must be considered.

Ambient noise inside the room should not exceed NC-30 levels (NC = noise criterion). NC-25 would be superior, but may involve too many additional expenses. Total ambient noise includes noise from the heating and air conditioning systems and fluorescent lighting ballasts. Table tops may need cushioning to prevent impact and surface noise.

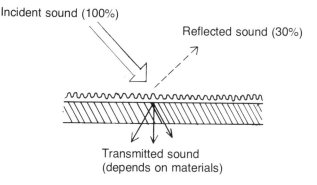

Incident sound (100%)

Reflected sound (30%)

Transmitted sound
(depends on materials)

Sound absorption NRC 0.7

(15) Control of interior reverberation

Reverberation is the multiple reflection of sounds off of surfaces within a room. Although acceptable in nominal amounts, excessive reverberation can cause severe problems in video conferencing rooms where speech intelligibility is of major importance. Too much reverberation at high frequencies will cause echoes or acoustic feedback.

Room reverberations are controlled by the kinds of materials applied to the interior surfaces. All materials have different sound absorption characteristics at different frequencies. Sound barriers and sound-absorbing materials perform better at high frequencies. The application of carpet to the floor of the video conference room is a relatively ineffective sound absorber at lower frequencies.

The carpet shown in drawing 15, with a sound absorption coefficient of 0.7 at the low frequency of 123 Hz, would reflect 30 percent sound.

(16) Sound absorption coefficients for typical materials

Materials/Frequencies	125 Hz	250 Hz	500 Hz	1000 Hz	2000 Hz	4000 Hz
Gypsum board, ½″ (1.27 cm) on studs	0.29	0.10	0.05	0.04	0.07	0.09
Plate glass	0.18	0.06	0.04	0.03	0.02	0.02
Heavy carpet on concrete	0.02	0.06	0.14	0.37	0.60	0.65
Velour drape, medium weight	0.07	0.31	0.49	0.75	0.70	0.60
Ceiling tile on hard surface	0.10	0.30	0.56	0.70	0.68	0.50
Suspended ceiling tile with 16″ (40.64 cm) air space	0.45	0.48	0.65	0.75	0.72	0.55
Mineral wool, 2″ (5.08 cm) with 1″ (2.54 cm) air space	0.30	0.70	0.85	0.86	0.87	0.87
Fiberglass, 4″ (10.16 cm) on hard surface	0.40	0.92	0.98	0.97	0.93	0.88

Note: Multiply coefficients by 100 for absorption percentage.

The sound absorption coefficient, or Noise Reduction Coefficient (NRC), has a value from 0 to 1. When multipled by 100, the coefficient indicates the percentage of sound absorbed. For instance, the carpet at 0.7 would absorb 70 percent of the sound energy.

The table (16) provides the sound absorption qualities of several interior materials. NRC is the average of the sound-absorption coefficients for only four frequencies—250, 500, 1,000 and 2,000 Hz. For rooms with critical acoustical considerations, NRC is inadequate because it does not include very low- or high-frequency absorption. The numbers can also be misleading since two materials with the same NRC values can have considerably different sound-absorption characteristics. One must be careful not to confuse NRC with reduction of intrusive noises. NRC relates *only* to absorption.

The answer to the question of how much absorption does a teleconferencing room need is usually simple: as much as can be achieved using practical materials. Some newer microphones designed specifically for teleconferencing seem to perform better in a slightly reverberant environment. It is important that the absorption be flat over the entire speech-frequency range of 125 to 4,000 Hz. The designer should remember that a teleconferencing room and its equipment must be considered an integrated system. The safest approach when designing a teleconferencing facility is to specify the desired end result, not the method of achieving it, and to leave the details of execution to a competent acoustician.

CURRENTLY RECOMMENDED ILLUMINANCE CATEGORIES & ILLUMINANCE VALUES FOR LIGHTING DESIGN: TARGET MAINTAINED LEVELS

The tabulations that follow are a consolidated listing of the current illuminance recommendations of the Illuminating Engineering Society of North America (IESNA). This listing is intended to guide the lighting designer in selecting an appropriate illuminance for design and evaluation of lighting systems.

Guidance is provided in Parts I and II as an *illuminance category,* representing a range of illuminances by letter designations A through I. Illuminance values are given in *lux,* with an approximate equivalence in *footcandles* and as such are intended as

target (nominal) values with deviations expected. These target values also represent *maintained* values.

Part I provides a listing of both illuminance categories and illuminance values for generic types of interior activities and normally is to be used when illuminance categories for a specific area/activity cannot be found in Part II.

In all cases the recommendations in this table are based on the assumption that the lighting will be properly designed to take into account the visual characteristics of the task.

PART I. ILLUMINANCE CATEGORIES & ILLUMINANCE VALUES FOR GENERIC TYPES OF ACTIVITIES IN INTERIORS

Type of activity	Illuminance category	Ranges of illuminances		Reference work plane
		Lux	Footcandles	
Public spaces with dark surroundings	A	20–30–50	2–3–5	
Simple orientation for short, temporary visits	B	50–75–100	5–7.5–10	General lighting throughout spaces
Working spaces where visual tasks are only occasionally performed	C	100–150–200	10–15–20	
Performance of visual tasks of high contrast or large size	D	200–300–500	20–30–50	
Performance of visual tasks of medium contrast or small size	E	500–750–1000	50–75–100	Illuminance on task
Performance of visual tasks of low contrast or very small size	F	1000–1500–2000	100–150–200	
Performance of visual tasks of low contrast and very small size over a prolonged period	G	2000–3000–5000	200–300–500	Illuminance on task, obtained by a combination of general and local (supplementary lighting)
Performance of very prolonged and exacting visual tasks	H	5000–7500–10000	500–750–1000	
Performance of very special visual tasks of extremely low contrast and small size	I	10000–15000–20000	1000–1500–2000	

Material on pages 336 through 339, used with the permission of IESNA, is from the *IES Lighting Handbook, 1981 Application Volume.* © 1981, Illuminating Engineering Society of North America, 345 East 47th Street, New York, NY 10017

PART II. COMMERCIAL, INSTITUTIONAL, RESIDENTIAL, & PUBLIC ASSEMBLY INTERIORS

Area/Activity	Illuminance category
Air terminals (see Transportation terminals)	
Armories	C[1]
Art galleries (see Museums)	
Auditoriums	
Assembly	C[1]
Social activity	B
Banks (also see Reading)	
Lobby	
General	C
Writing area	D
Tellers' stations	E[2]
Barber shops and beauty parlors	E
Club and lodge rooms	
Lounge and reading	D
Conference rooms	
Conferring	D
Critical seeing (Refer to individual task described above)	D
Courtrooms	
Court activity area	E[2]
Seating area	C
Dance halls and discotheques	B
Depots, terminals, and stations (see Transportation terminals)	
Drafting	
Prints	
Blue line	E
Blueprints	E
Sepia prints	F
Tracing paper	
High contrast	E[2]
Low contrast	F[2]
Vellum	
High contrast	E[2]
Low contrast	F[2]
Educational facilities	
Cafeterias (see Food service facilities)	
Classrooms	
Drafting (see Drafting)	
General (see Reading)	
Home economics (see Residences)	

Area/Activity	Illuminance category
Lecture rooms	
Audience (see Reading)	
Demonstration	F
Music rooms (see Reading)	
Science laboratories	E
Sight saving rooms	F
Study halls (see Reading)	
Typing (see Reading)	
Dormitories (see Residences)	
Elevators, freight and passenger	C
Exhibition halls	C[1]
Fire halls (see Municipal buildings)	
Food service facilities	
Dining areas	
Cashier	D
Cleaning	C
Dining	B[4]
Food displays (see Merchandising spaces)	
Kitchen	E
Graphic design and material	
Charting and mapping	F
Color selection	F[6]
Graphs	E
Keylining	F
Layout and artwork	F
Photographs, moderate detail	E[8]
Health care facilities	
Nursing stations[9]	
Corridors, day	C
Corridors, night	A
Desk	E
General	D
Medication station	E
Patients' rooms[9]	
Critical examination	E
General[10]	B
Observation	A
Reading	D
Waiting areas[9]	
General	C
Local for reading	D

For footnotes, see page 339. For illuminance ranges for each illuminance category, see page 336.

Area/Activity	Illuminance category
Homes (see Residences)	
Hospitals (see Health care facilities)	
Hotels	
Bathrooms, for grooming	D
Bedrooms, for reading	D
Corridors, elevators, and stairs	C
Front desk	E[2]
Lobby	
General lighting	C
Reading and working areas	D
Kitchens (see Food service facilities or Residences)	
Libraries	
Book stacks [vertical 30″ (76.20 cm) above floor]	
Active stacks	D
Inactive stacks	B
Card files	E
Carrels, individual study areas (see Reading)	
Cataloging	D[2]
Circulation desks	D
Locker rooms	C
Merchandising spaces	
Feature display	F-G[5]
Fitting room	
Dressing areas	D
Fitting areas	F
Merchandise	D-E[5]
Sales transaction area	E
Show windows	D-H[5]
Motels (see Hotels)	

Area/Activity	Illuminance category
Museums	
Displays or nonsensitive materials	D
Lobbies, general gallery areas, corridors	C
Restoration or conservation shops and laboratories	E
Nursing homes (see Health care facilities)	
Offices	
Accounting (see Reading)	
Conference areas (see Conference rooms)	
Drafting (see Drafting)	
General and private offices (see Reading)	
Libraries (see Libraries)	
Lobbies, lounges, and reception areas	C
Mail sorting	E
Offset printing and duplicating area	D
Post offices (see Offices)	
Reading	
Copied tasks	
Ditto copy	E[2]
Microfiche reader	B[7][8]
Mimeograph	D
Photographs, moderate detail	E[8]
Thermal copy, poor copy	F[2]
Xerograph	D
Xerography, 3rd generation and greater	E
Electronic data processing tasks	
CRT screens	B[7][8]
Impact printer	
Good ribbon	D
Poor ribbon	E
2nd carbon and greater	E
Ink jet printer	D
Keyboard reading	D

For footnotes, see page 339.

Area/Activity	Illuminance category
Residences	
General lighting	
Conversation, relaxation, and entertainment	B
Kitchen duties	
Kitchen counter	
Critical seeing	E
Noncritical	D
Kitchen range	
Difficult seeing	E
Noncritical	D
Reading	
Desk	
Primary task plane, casual	D
Primary task plane, study	E
In bed	
Normal	D
Prolonged serious or critical	E
In a chair	
Books, magazines, and newspapers	D
Handwriting, reproductions, and poor copies	E

Area/Activity	Illuminance category
Sewing	
Machine sewing	
Dark fabrics, low contrast	F
Light to medium fabrics	E
Occasional, high contrast	D
Toilets and washrooms	C
Transportation terminals	
Concourse	B
Ticket counters	E
Waiting room and lounge	C

[1]Include provisions for higher levels for exhibitions.

[2]Task subject to veiling reflections. Illuminance listed is not an equivalence sphere illumination (ESI) value. Currently, insufficient experience in the use of ESI target values precludes the direct use of ESI in the present consensus approach to recommend illuminance values. Equivalent sphere illumination may be used as a tool in determining the effectiveness of controlling veiling reflections and as a part of the evaluation of lighting systems.

[3]Degradation factors: Overlays—add 1 weighing factor for each overlay; used material—estimate additional.

[4]Provide higher level over food service or selection areas.

[5]Illuminance values developed for various degrees of store area activity.

[6]For color matching, the spectral quality of the color of the light source is important.

[7]Veiling reflections may be produced on glass surfaces. It may be necessary to treat plus weighting factors as minus in order to obtain proper illuminance.

[8]Especially subject to veiling reflections. It may be necessary to shield the task or to reorient it.

[9]Good to high color-rendering capability should be considered in these areas. As lamps of higher luminous efficacy and higher color rendering capability become available and economically feasible, they should be applied in all areas of health care facilities.

[10]Variable (dimming or switching).

[11]General lighting should not be less than one-third of visual task illuminance nor less than 200 lux (20 footcandles).

acrylic
The generic term for a family of quality light-stabilized plastics used in making fixture diffusers and lenses.

air-handling
A term applied to a recessed fixture that supplies or returns air to or from a room. This is usually accomplished through slots along the sides/ends of the fixture.

ambient
The surrounding environment of a device such as a fixture or ballast. It usually refers to temperature or sound conditions.

ballast
An auxiliary device used with fluorescent, mercury vapor, metal halide, and high-pressure sodium lamps. In addition to acting as a current limiting device, it provides the starting voltage that the lamp(s) require. This is a must in the electrical circuit.

beam lumens
The lumens contained within the beam spread of a floodlight.

beam spread
The angle between the two directions in which the candlepower of a floodlight is 10 percent of its maximum candlepower.

candela (cd)
A term used to express candlepower.

candlepower (cp)
The intensity of light given off by a light source in a particular direction. Also *candela.*

cavity
An upper, lower, or intermediate zone or region of a room designated as ceiling, floor, or room cavity.

cavity ratio (CR)
Geometric proportions of the ceiling, floor, and room cavities.

$$\text{Room cavity ratio} = \frac{5H\ (\text{room length} + \text{room width})}{\text{room length} = \text{room width}}$$

coefficient of beam utilization (CBU)
The percentage of light from a floodlight that reaches the seeing task relative to beam lumens.

coefficient of utilization (CU)
The percentage of light from a fixture that reaches the seeing task. It is a function of the fixture, each having its own set of CUs for a wide range of the following factors:

Fixture efficiency, distribution, and mounting height

Room proportions

Room-surface reflectances

diffuser
See *lens.*

efficacy
A lamp term indicating the relationship of lamp lumens to watts required to generate the lumens and expressed as lumens per watt.

efficiency
See *luminaire efficiency.*

equivalent sphere illumination (ESI)
The amount of light in footcandles produced by a luminous sphere on a seeing task in the center of the sphere that will render the same "seeability" as the raw footcandles render the same task in the specific seeing environment under consideration.

fixture
The device that holds, protects, and provides an optical system and power connections for the lamp(s). Fixture usually refers to interior lighting. See *luminaire.*

flux (luminous flux)
See *lumen.*

footcandle (fc)
The *amount* of light falling on a surface. The most widely used term in light applications.

$$\text{fc} = \frac{\text{lumens}}{\text{square feet}}$$

The quantitative target for all lighting design. See *metercandle* for metric equivalent of footcandle.

footlambert (fl)
A unit of brightness as detected by the eye, either directly from the source or reflected.

glare
Excessive brightness either direct or indirect.

grid (lay-in)
A type of ceiling construction where the supporting members (inverted Ts) are exposed and the ceiling tiles and lighting fixtures are laid-in on the flanges of the Ts.

heat extraction
A type of recessed fixture with provisions for the return of room air through the fixture's lamp cavity, thus removing some of the heat generated by the lamps and ballasts.

high bay
Generally refers to industrial lighting where high mounting heights may be encountered. Many industrial HID-type fixtures are called high bays.

high intensity discharge (HID)
The term that applies to a family of light sources consisting of mercury vapor, metal halide, and high-pressure sodium lamps.

isolux
A line that is plotted on a graph or diagram to show all points on a surface where the illumination is the same.

lamp
The accepted term for all commercial artificial light sources.

lamp lumen depreciation (LLD)
A factor used in lighting calculations to account for the light loss that takes place in a lamp due to the gradual decay in lumen output over a designated period of burning time. The LLD is contingent upon relamping schedules and the specific lamp involved.

lens
The shielding or diffuser portion of a fixture, made of plastic or glass, through which the light passes on its way to the seeing task. Note: Plastic lenses may be manufactured by the extrusion process or the injection molded process. Injection molded lenses are more expensive.

lighting system
The packaged combination of fixtures, ballasts, lamps, and sometimes ceilings.

louver
A series of baffles used in place of a lens to shield the lamp(s) in a fixture from view at certain angles or to block unwanted light. The battles are usually arranged in a geometric pattern.

lumen (lm)
Used to indicate the total amount of light given off by a light source. The most widely used term in the rating of lamps. The quantitative light measure for all lamps. Also, a unit of luminous flux.

luminaire
A more sophisticated term for fixture. Most outdoor units are called luminaires.

luminaire dirt depreciation (LDD)
A factor used in lighting calculations to account for the light loss due to the accumulation of dirt on the luminaire. The LDD is contingent upon environment, cleaning schedules, and the type of luminaire involved.

luminaire efficiency
The lumens emitted by a luminaire divided by the lumens generated by the luminaire's lamps.

luminance
Photometric brightness. See *footlambert*.

lux (lx)
See *metercandle*.

maintenance factor (MF)
Percentage allowance for the decline in the effectiveness of a lighting fixture. It takes into account the loss of light due to lamp depreciation as well as light loss due to such things as accumulation of dirt on all reflecting and transmitting surfaces of the fixture, lamp(s), and room.

metercandle (lux, lx)
The metric equivalent of *footcandle*.

lx	= lumens/square meters
1 footcandle	= 10.76 lux
1 lux	= 0.0929 footcandles

optical system
The lamp cavity or environment (including diffusing media) designed as part of the fixture for the purpose of controlling the light output.

parabolic
The term applied to certain low brightness louver and reflector shapes as derived from the geometric shape (curve) called a parabola where, if a light source is placed at its focal point, the resultant emitted light will be redirected parallel to the parabola's geometric axis.

plenum
That space between the structural ceiling slab and the finished ceiling. This space may contain air ducts, electrical wiring, and so on. It's the area that conceals the housing part of a recessed fixture.

polychlorinated biphenyl (PCB)
A dielectric substance used in ballast capacitors.

recessed
The term for a fixture mounted in a ceiling opening so that the housing of the fixture is hidden from view. The fixture's lens/door assembly may be slightly protruding, flush, or slightly regressed relative to the ceiling surface.

reflector
A device used to redirect light from a source by the process of reflection.

refractor
A device used to redirect light from a source by the process of refraction. The glass or plastic lenses in roadway luminaires are called refractors.

shielding
See *lens* or *louver*.

static
A fixture with no air-handling provisions.

styrene (polystyrene)
The generic term for a family of plastics used in the making of fixture diffusers and lenses. Tends to yellow in time due to the effect of ultraviolet radiation from fluorescent and HID lamps.

surface mounted
Any fixture mounted directly on a ceiling is surface mounted.

suspension or pendant mounted
Any fixture hung from a ceiling by supports (such as chains, hangers, or stems) is suspension or pendant mounted.

troffer
A recessed lighting fixture.

visual comfort probability (VCP)
An empirical comfort rating system for fixtures as measured in various proportioned rooms at different mounting heights. The VCP number represents the number of people, out of a hundred, who would be comfortable in the specified situation when seated in the most undesirable location.

work plane
The plane at which level work is usually performed and at which the illumination is specified and measured. Unless it is otherwise specified, this plane is assumed to be a horizontal plane 2½' (76.20 cm) above the floor.

wraparound (wrap)
A surface- or suspension-mounted fixture with a one-piece plastic lens that encloses the lamp compartment on both sides and across the bottom, literally wrapping the lamps.

zonal cavity
The lastest and most advanced method used by the lighting industry in the determination of coefficients of utilization for various fixtures.

ABBREVIATIONS

AC	alternating current	HID	high intensity discharge	MH	metal halide
CBS	Certified Ballast Manufacturers	HO	high output	MV	mercury vapor
CBU	coefficient of beam utilization	HPS	high power factor	NPF	normal power factor
CC	ceiling cavity	HPS	high pressure sodium	PCB	polychlorinated biphenyl
cd	candela	I	ampere	pf	power factor
cp	candlepower	ITL	Independent Testing	R	ohm
CR	cavity ratio		Laboratories	RC	room cavity
CU	coefficient of utilization	KW	kilowatt	RCR	room cavity ratio
DC	direct current	kWH	kilowatthour	SHO	super high output
E	volt	LDD	luminaire dirt depreciation	Sp/MH	spacing to mounting height ratio
ESI	equivalent sphere illumination	LLD	lamp lumen depreciation	UL	Underwriters' Laboratories
ETL	Electrical Testing Laboratories	lm	lumen	V	volt
fc	footcandle	LPS	low pressure sodium	VCP	visual comfort probability
FC	floor cavity	lx	lux		
fl	footlambert	MF	maintenance factor		

QUANTITY FORMULAS

General lighting

$$\text{Footcandles} = \frac{\text{effective lumens}}{\text{square feet}}$$

$$\text{Footcandles} = \frac{(\text{initial lumens per lamp}) (\text{number of lamps per luminaire}) (\text{number of luminaires}) (CU)(LLD)(LDD)}{\text{square feet}}$$

$$\text{Number of luminaires} = \frac{(fc) (\text{square feet})}{(\text{initial lumens per lamp}) (\text{number of lamps per luminaire}) (CU) (LLD) (LDD)}$$

Point-by-point lighting

$$\text{Footcandles} = \frac{\text{effective candlepower}}{\text{distance}^2}$$

$$\text{Vertical fc} = \frac{(\text{initial cp}) (\sin \theta)(LLD)(LDD)}{\text{distance}^2}$$

$$\text{Horizontal fc} = \frac{(\text{initial cp}) (\cos \theta) (LLD) (LDD)}{\text{distance}^2}$$

$$\text{Vertical fc} = \frac{(\text{initial cp})(\cos^2 \theta)(\sin \theta)(LLD)(LDD)}{(\text{mounting height})^2}$$

$$\text{Horizontal fc} = \frac{(\text{initial cp}) (\cos^3 \theta)(LLD)(LDD)}{(\text{mounting height})^2}$$

Lighting for irregularly shaped rooms

$$RCR = \frac{2.5 (\text{cavity height}) (\text{cavity perimeter})}{\text{Area of cavity base}}$$

The effective ceiling cavity ratio for nonhorizontal ceilings* can be determined by:

$$pCC = \frac{pAo}{As - pAs + pAo}$$

where
Ao = area of ceiling opening
As = area of ceiling surface
p = reflectance of ceiling surface

*If distance from luminaire to ceiling exceeds 3' (91.44 cm), add additional distance to ceiling height.

Conversion chart

Multiply	By	To obtain
BTU	252	calories (gram) (15°C)
	777.50	foot pounds
	0.0003927	horsepower hours
	1054	joules
	0.0002928	kilowatthours
BTU per minute	12.96	foot pounds per second
	0.02356	horsepower
	17.57	watts
Calories	0.003968	BTU
Degrees	0.01745	radians
Foot pounds per second	0.07717	BTU per minute
	0.001818	horsepower
	0.001356	kilowatts
Footcandle	10.765	lux

Multiply	By	To obtain
Horsepower	42.44	BTU per minute
	33.000	foot pounds per minute
	550	foot pounds per second
	0.7457	kilowatts
Hours	0.04167	days
1 day = 86,400 seconds		
1 year = 8,760 hours (approx.)		
kWH	3415	BTU per minute
Lux	0.0929	footcandles
Radians	57.30	degrees
Watts	0.05692	BTU per minute
	44.62	foot pounds per minute
	0.00134	horsepower

PART TWO

RESIDENTIAL GRAPHIC AND DESIGN STANDARDS

Chapter 11

SINGLE-FAMILY AND MULTIPLE-FAMILY DWELLINGS

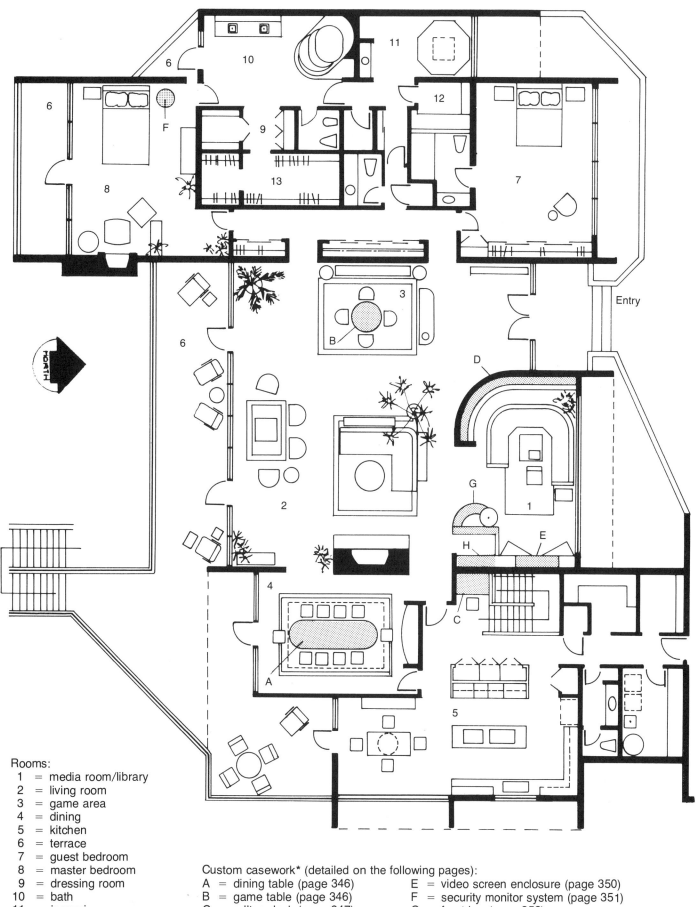

Rooms:
1 = media room/library
2 = living room
3 = game area
4 = dining
5 = kitchen
6 = terrace
7 = guest bedroom
8 = master bedroom
9 = dressing room
10 = bath
11 = jacuzzi
12 = steam room
13 = closet

Custom casework* (detailed on the following pages):
A = dining table (page 346)
B = game table (page 346)
C = rolltop desk (page 347)
D = library shelves/media storage
    (pages 348–349)
E = video screen enclosure (page 350)
F = security monitor system (page 351)
G = front bar (page 352)
H = back bar (page 353)

*Custom casework denoted by shaded areas.

DINING TABLE (A)

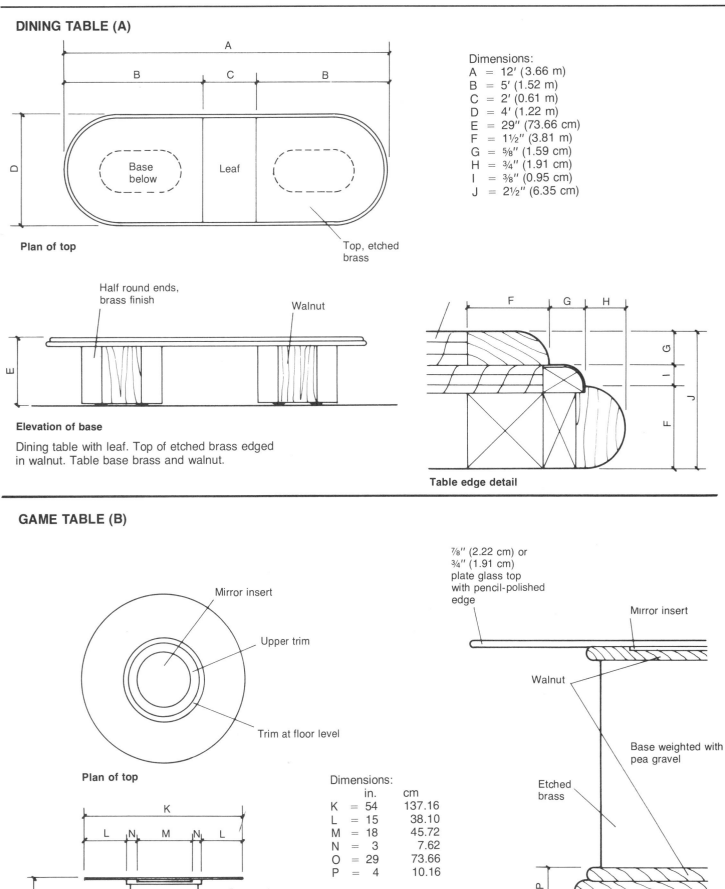

Plan of top

Top, etched brass

Dimensions:
A = 12′ (3.66 m)
B = 5′ (1.52 m)
C = 2′ (0.61 m)
D = 4′ (1.22 m)
E = 29″ (73.66 cm)
F = 1½″ (3.81 m)
G = ⅝″ (1.59 cm)
H = ¾″ (1.91 cm)
I = ⅜″ (0.95 cm)
J = 2½″ (6.35 cm)

Half round ends, brass finish

Walnut

Elevation of base

Dining table with leaf. Top of etched brass edged in walnut. Table base brass and walnut.

Table edge detail

GAME TABLE (B)

Mirror insert
Upper trim
Trim at floor level

Plan of top

Dimensions:
	in.	cm
K =	54	137.16
L =	15	38.10
M =	18	45.72
N =	3	7.62
O =	29	73.66
P =	4	10.16

Pedestal base

Elevation of base

*Shown in plan on page 345.

⅞″ (2.22 cm) or ¾″ (1.91 cm) plate glass top with pencil-polished edge

Mirror insert

Walnut

Base weighted with pea gravel

Etched brass

Elevation detail of base

Four 2″* (5.08 cm) diameter glides

BUILT-IN DESK IN KITCHEN AREA (C)

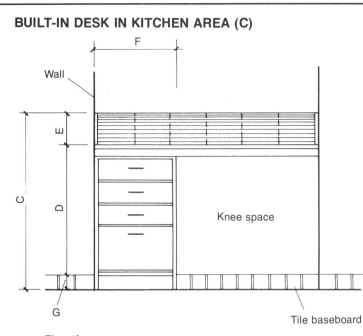

Wall

F

E

C

D

Knee space

G

Tile baseboard

Elevation

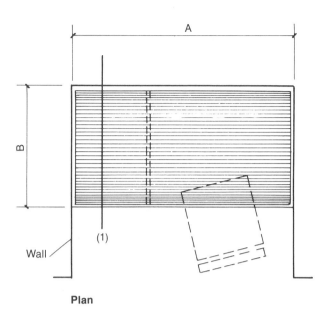

A

B

Wall

(1)

Plan

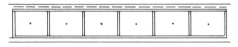

X = six drawers at back top of desk

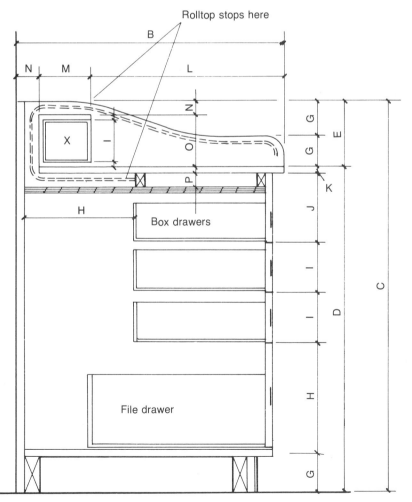

Rolltop stops here

B

N M L

N

O

X

I

P

H

Box drawers

J

I

I

H

File drawer

G

G G

E

K

C

D

Dimensions (not to scale):

	in.	cm
A =	57	144.78
B =	30	76.20
C =	44	111.76
D =	36	91.44
E =	8	20.32
F =	18	45.72
G =	4	10.16
H =	11½	29.21
I =	5½	13.97
J =	7½	19.05
K =	1	2.54
L =	21½	54.61
M =	6	15.24
N =	1½	3.81
O =	6½	16.51
P =	2	5.08

Section (1)

*Shown in plan on page 345.

MEDIA AREA (D)

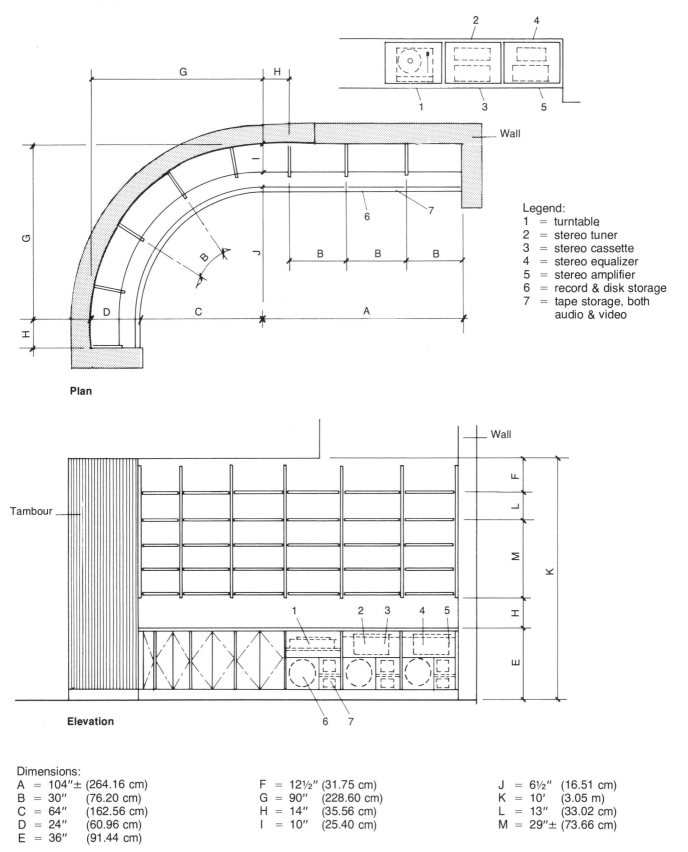

Plan

Elevation

Tambour

Legend:
1 = turntable
2 = stereo tuner
3 = stereo cassette
4 = stereo equalizer
5 = stereo amplifier
6 = record & disk storage
7 = tape storage, both audio & video

Dimensions:
A = 104"± (264.16 cm)
B = 30" (76.20 cm)
C = 64" (162.56 cm)
D = 24" (60.96 cm)
E = 36" (91.44 cm)

F = 12½" (31.75 cm)
G = 90" (228.60 cm)
H = 14" (35.56 cm)
I = 10" (25.40 cm)

J = 6½" (16.51 cm)
K = 10' (3.05 m)
L = 13" (33.02 cm)
M = 29"± (73.66 cm)

Note: Casework shop to field-verify dimensions prior to installation.

*Shown in plan on page 345.

STEREO CABINET (D)

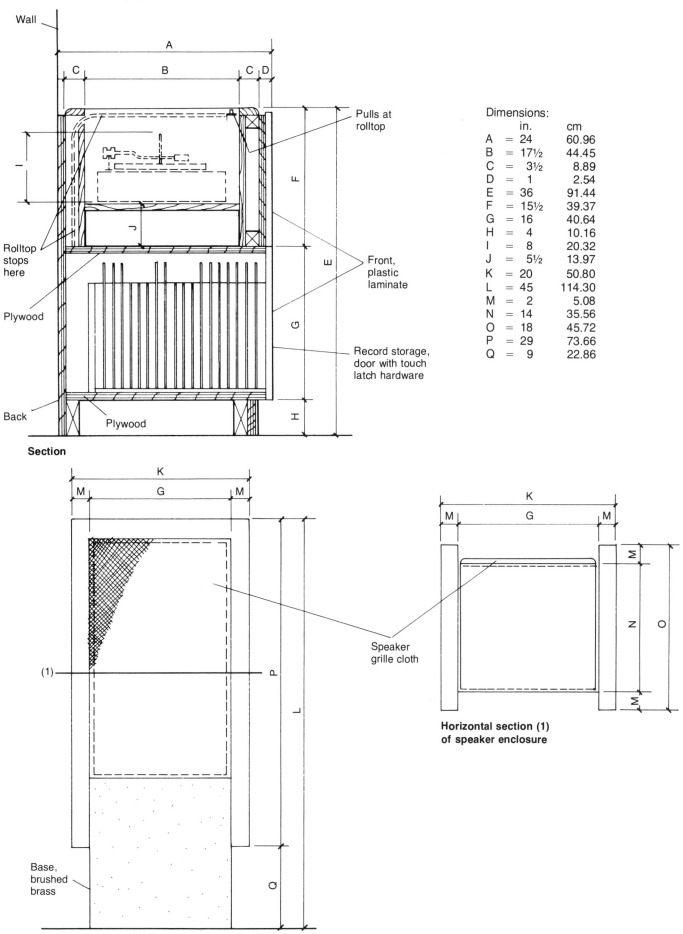

Wall

Pulls at rolltop

Rolltop stops here

Plywood

Back

Plywood

Front, plastic laminate

Record storage, door with touch latch hardware

Section

Dimensions:

		in.	cm
A	=	24	60.96
B	=	17½	44.45
C	=	3½	8.89
D	=	1	2.54
E	=	36	91.44
F	=	15½	39.37
G	=	16	40.64
H	=	4	10.16
I	=	8	20.32
J	=	5½	13.97
K	=	20	50.80
L	=	45	114.30
M	=	2	5.08
N	=	14	35.56
O	=	18	45.72
P	=	29	73.66
Q	=	9	22.86

(1)

Speaker grille cloth

Base, brushed brass

Elevation of speaker enclosure

Horizontal section (1) of speaker enclosure

*Shown in plan on page 345.

CUSTOM-BUILT VIDEO SCREEN ENCLOSURE (E)

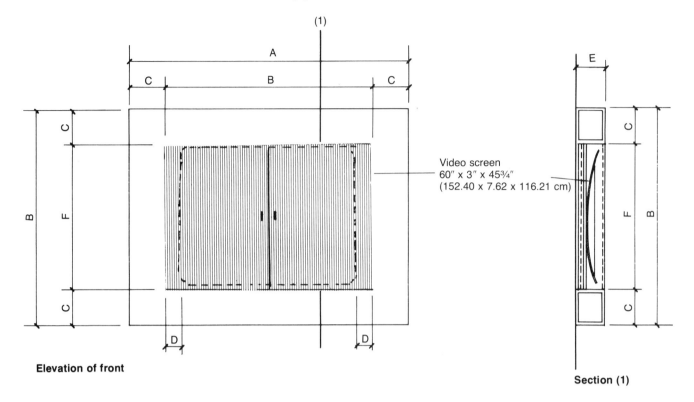

Elevation of front

Video screen
60″ x 3″ x 45¾″
(152.40 x 7.62 x 116.21 cm)

Section (1)

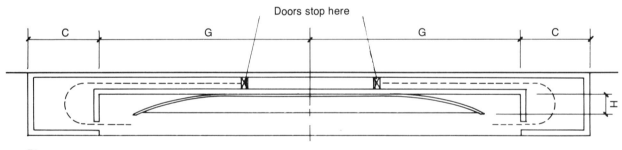

Plan

Front projection type of video. (See page 226 for more details on various types of large screens.) These details correspond to the media area marked E on page 345. Other video systems have screen 3″ (7.62 cm) in thickness.

Dimensions (not to scale):

	in.	cm
A =	96	243.84
B =	72	182.88
C =	12	30.48
D =	6	15.24
E =	10	25.40
F =	48±	121.92
G =	36	91.44
H =	3	7.62

*Shown in plan on page 345.

MOBILE SECURITY INTERCOM CONSOLE (F)

Legend:
1 = monitor screen
2 = pan-tilt unit
3 = intercom
4 = four single gang switches
5 = speaker
6 = two 6-station master control panels
7 = void space for additional components when needed
8 = tambour in satin bronze finish
9 = recessed carpet casters

Dimensions:

	in.	cm
A =	30	76.20 diameter
B =	13	33.02
C =	9	22.86
D =	4	10.16
E =	2	5.08
F =	18	45.72
G =	21	53.34
H =	42	106.68
I =	1	2.54

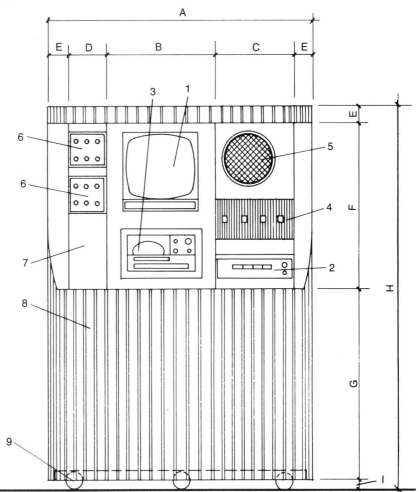

Elevation of front

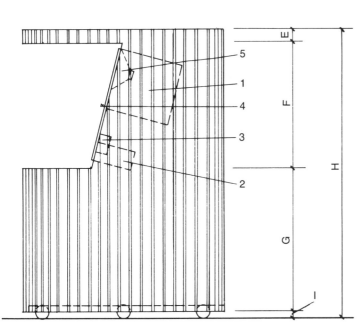

Elevation of side

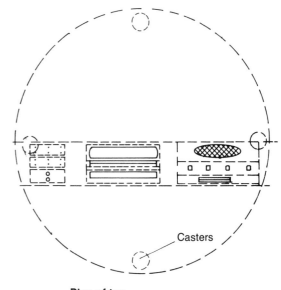

Casters

Plan of top
Top covered in metal laminate

Note: Console unit may be moved around home as needed.

*Shown in plan on page 345.

CUSTOM-BUILT BAR AREAS (G & H)

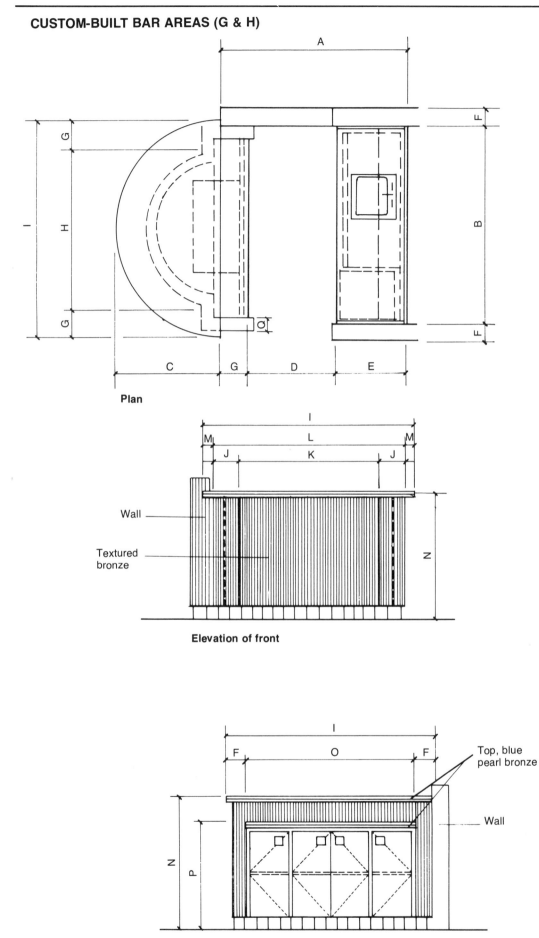

Plan

Elevation of front

Wall

Textured
bronze

Elevation of back

Top, blue
pearl bronze

Wall

Dimensions (not to scale):

		in.	cm
A	=	77	195.58
B	=	65	165.10
C	=	36	91.44
D	=	32	81.28
E	=	24	60.96
F	=	6	15.24
G	=	10	25.40
H	=	52	132.08
I	=	72	182.88
J	=	9	22.86
K	=	50	127.00
L	=	68	172.72
M	=	2	5.08
N	=	43	109.22
O	=	60	152.40
P	=	34½	87.63
Q	=	4	10.16

Note: Millwork shop to field-
verify dimensions prior to
completion and installation.

*Shown in plan on page 345.

CUSTOM-BUILT BACK BAR (H)

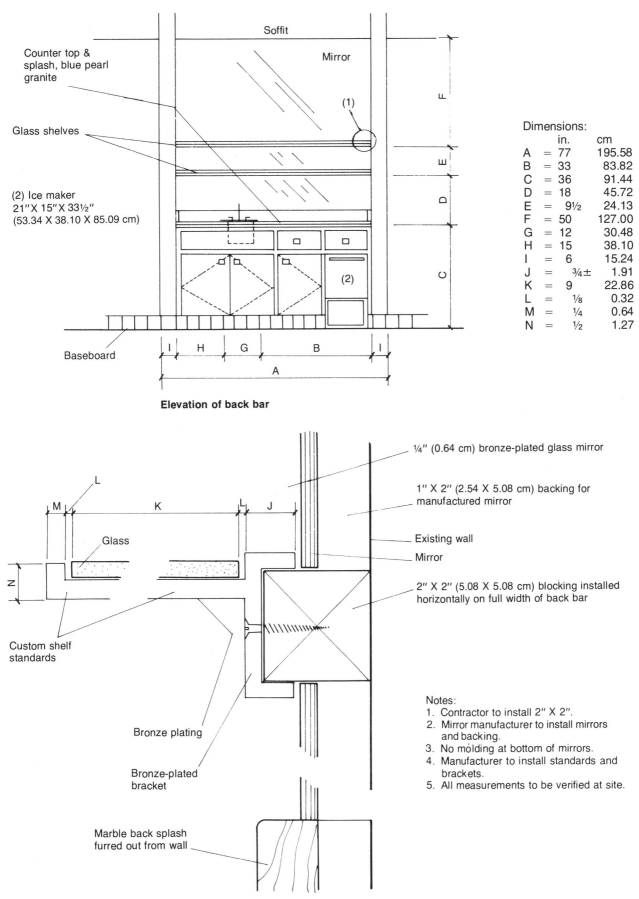

Elevation of back bar

Soffit

Mirror

Counter top & splash, blue pearl granite

Glass shelves

(2) Ice maker
21" X 15" X 33½"
(53.34 X 38.10 X 85.09 cm)

(1)

(2)

Baseboard

Dimensions:			
		in.	cm
A	=	77	195.58
B	=	33	83.82
C	=	36	91.44
D	=	18	45.72
E	=	9½	24.13
F	=	50	127.00
G	=	12	30.48
H	=	15	38.10
I	=	6	15.24
J	=	¾±	1.91
K	=	9	22.86
L	=	⅛	0.32
M	=	¼	0.64
N	=	½	1.27

¼" (0.64 cm) bronze-plated glass mirror

1" X 2" (2.54 X 5.08 cm) backing for manufactured mirror

Existing wall

Mirror

2" X 2" (5.08 X 5.08 cm) blocking installed horizontally on full width of back bar

Glass

Custom shelf standards

Bronze plating

Bronze-plated bracket

Marble back splash furred out from wall

Notes:
1. Contractor to install 2" X 2".
2. Mirror manufacturer to install mirrors and backing.
3. No molding at bottom of mirrors.
4. Manufacturer to install standards and brackets.
5. All measurements to be verified at site.

Section (1)

*Shown in plan on page 345.

Greek style atrium home

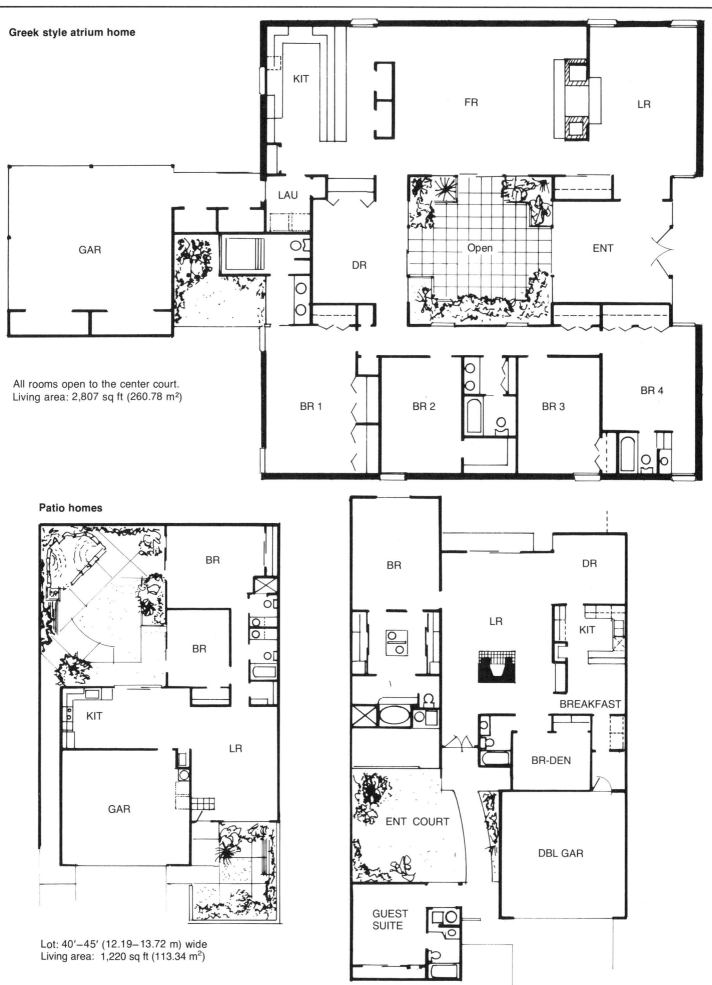

All rooms open to the center court.
Living area: 2,807 sq ft (260.78 m²)

Patio homes

Lot: 40'–45' (12.19–13.72 m) wide
Living area: 1,220 sq ft (113.34 m²)

Narrow lot

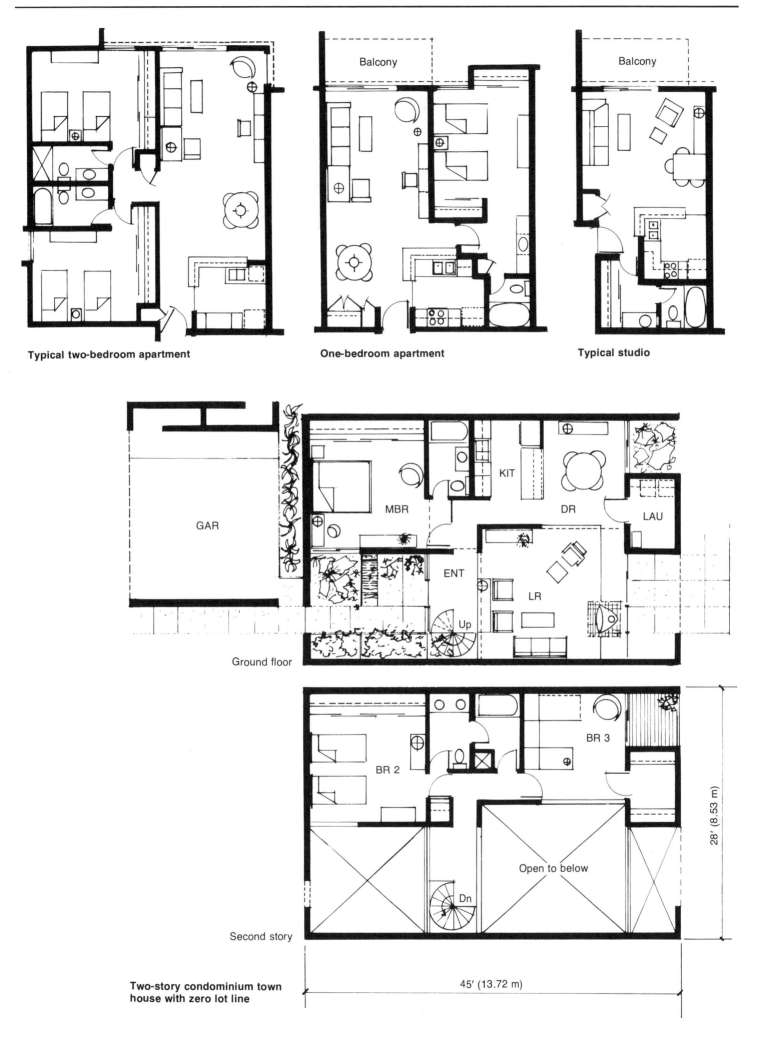

Typical two-bedroom apartment

One-bedroom apartment

Typical studio

Ground floor

Second story

Two-story condominium town house with zero lot line

45' (13.72 m)

28' (8.53 m)

COMBINED SPACES

Living unit with screened sleeping & kitchen areas

Notes:
A = bed should be accessible from two sides and end
B = not too great a walking distance to bath and closet; 36" (91.44 cm) max
C = 32" (81.28 cm) for chair plus access
D = 48" (121.92 cm) from table to base cabinet
E = 21" (53.34 cm) mixing counter
F = 15" (38.10 cm) min. counter

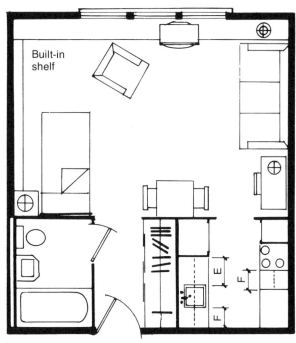

Living unit with sleeping alcove

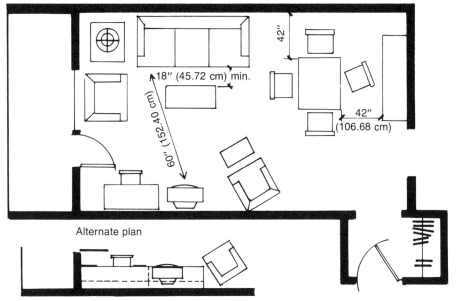

Critical distances in living areas

Note: Where possible, built-in desks, shelves, or wall units can save space and provide ease of maintenance. To save space, avoid coffee tables where possible.

Furnishings

A typical living unit should include the following minimum amount of furniture:

One-bedroom unit:
  Two easy chairs
  One couch or sofa*
  Television
  Dining table & two chairs

Two-bedroom unit:
In addition to furniture listed above:
  One desk 20" X 42" (50.80 X 106.68 cm) min.

Spaces along the walls should be provided to allow for alternate furniture arrangements. Doors and window should be arranged to allow easy access.

Elderly people who move into apartments from homes have many small pieces of furniture, accessories, and other items that require wall space and storage.

Maximum distance between seating and the television screen is 60".

*Use of a 60" (152.40 cm) love seat makes it possible to fit service tables at either end.

EXAMPLES OF DINING AREAS COMBINED WITH KITCHENS

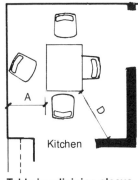

Kitchen

Table in adjoining alcove

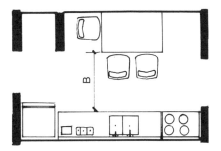

Table parallel to wall

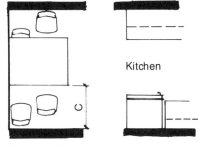

Kitchen

Table at right angle to wall

Although these spaces may be small, seating for four should be made available.

Critical measurements
A = 36" (91.44 cm) between table and wall
B = 48" (121.92 cm) between table and adjoining base cabinet
C = 42" (106.68 cm) between table and wall when table is used at a right angle to the wall; this allows for access behind an occupied chair
D = 30" (76.20 cm) should be allowed for access between seating unit and other areas

Tables
Minimum width of 36" and 24" (60.96 cm) length for each person. Square tables: minimum 3' X 3' (0.91 X 0.91 m). Round tables: minimum of 42" diameter.

BEDROOMS

When a two-bedroom unit is shared by two unrelated people the following furnishings should be specified for both bedrooms:

Two night stands: 18" X 18" (45.72 X 45.72 cm) min.
Portable television
One table for hobbies: 18" X 30" min.

Always try to provide enough space for twin beds, although the space may be designed for single occupancy.

It is recommended that closets be placed on the same wall as the entry door. This makes it possible to reserve at least two walls for furnishings.

The following clearances should be considered in furniture specification and placement:

30" clearance between furnishings in the path of traffic, such as between bed and closet or between front door and major seating
24" between twin beds
36" in front of storage units that require drawer use
18" (45.72 cm) between bed and wall for maintenance

Note: See Residential Kitchens and Baths on pages 368–369 and 403–407 for more information on designs for the disabled and the elderly.

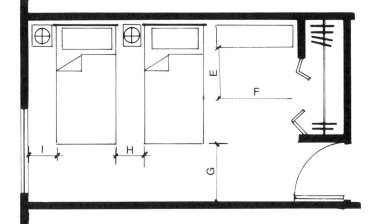

Typical bedroom with twin beds

Dimensions:
E = 36" clearance to open dresser drawers
F = 42" for dressing
G = 30" for major walk spaces
H = 24" min. between twin beds
I = 18" min. between bed and wall

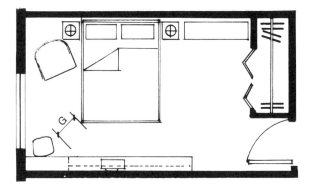

Typical bedroom with double bed and built-in storage on one wall

Chapter 12

KITCHENS

GENERAL CHECKLIST & SPATIAL DESIGN CONSIDERATIONS

1. Space dimensions between work centers
_____ a. Refrigerator/mix center
_____ b. Sink/clean-up center
_____ c. Range/cooking center
Kitchen shape
_____ a. One wall
_____ b. L-shaped
_____ c. U-shaped
_____ d. Corridor

2. Adjacent areas
_____ a. Laundry room
_____ b. Pantry
_____ c. Hobby room

3. Storage requirements
_____ a. Accessible cabinet frontage (linear inches)
_____ b. Total linear feet of base cabinets
_____ c. Total linear feet of wall-hung cabinets
_____ d. Total linear feet of counter surface
_____ e. Total square feet of shelf space
_____ f. Total square feet of drawer space

4. Major appliances: Electrical & gas requirements
_____ a. Ovens
_____ b. Range
_____ c. Dishwashers
_____ d. Disposals
_____ e. Refrigerators

5. Electrical & venting requirements
_____ a. Range/cook tops
_____ b. Ovens
_____ c. Microwave ovens

6. Lighting
_____ a. General
_____ Reflected ceiling
_____ Recessed
_____ Surface-mounted track
_____ b. Task lighting
_____ Cabinet mounted
_____ Range mounted
_____ Appliance mounted

7. Finish requirements
_____ a. Walls and soffit
_____ b. Ceiling
_____ c. Floor
_____ d. Cabinet
_____ e. Counter tops

8. Cabinet hardware
_____ a. Drawer & door pulls
_____ b. Drawer slides (see page 49)
_____ c. Door hinges (see pages 42, 44–47)
_____ d. Door latch/catches

9. Manufactured compact kitchens
_____ Unit kitchens

10. Special consideration
_____ a. Elderly requirements
_____ b. Disabled requirements

RESIDENTIAL KITCHEN APPLIANCES CHECKLIST

This list includes important data about major appliances that normally must be considered in the initial phase of kitchen design.

1. **Back-splash built-in convenience appliances**
   _____ a. Placement of wall supports (studs)
   _____ b. Location of obstructions such as vents, ducts, pipes, and pocket doors
   _____ c. List of convenience appliances:
   _____ 1. Mixer
   _____ 2. Blender
   _____ 3. Coffee maker
   _____ 4. Ice maker

2. **Cooktops & hoods**
   _____ a. Electrical or gas requirements
   _____ b. Duct path to building exterior
   _____ c. Cooktop thickness
   _____ d. Cut-out and overall dimensions listed on plan
   _____ e. Design of shallow drawers below cooktop (if desired)
   _____ f. Finish on back-splash behind or below hood

3. **Dishwasher & compactors**
   _____ a. Electrical or gas requirements
   _____ b. Trim kit* & extra panel requirements
   _____ c. Height clearances required from finished floor to counter top
   _____ d. Overall depth including handles
   _____ e. Clearance for loading appliances (door opening requirements)

4. **Disposals**
   _____ a. Electrical requirements
   _____ b. Waste line height & length

5. **Ovens**
   _____ a. Built-in
   _____ 1. Electrical & gas requirements
   _____ 2. Venting requirements
   _____ 3. Overall depth including handles
   _____ 4. Cut-out and overall dimensions
   _____ b. Microwave oven
   _____ 1. Electrical requirements
   _____ 2. Required trim kits*
   _____ 3. Clearances required from adjoining heat-generating appliance
   _____ 4. Appliance overall depth
   _____ 5. Appliance height & width dimensions

6. **Ranges (drop-in or free standing)**
   _____ a. Electrical or gas requirements
   _____ b. Counter cut-out dimensions for drop-in range
   _____ c. Method of support required for drop-in range
   _____ d. Required side clearances for drop-in range with flange overlapping adjacent cabinets
   _____ e. Actual depth of free-standing range including handles
   _____ f. Distance from floor to top of drop-in range

7. **Refrigerators**
   _____ a. Electrical or gas requirements
   _____ b. Required trim kits*
   _____ c. Required waterline (locate) for ice makers
   _____ d. Required depth & air space requirements
   _____ e. Handle projections
   _____ f. Finished height including air space from floor
   _____ g. Required width, including air circulation space

*Trim kit supplies additional material needed to fill pre-cut spaces that are too large for the appliance.

METHODS OF CALCULATING STORAGE SPACE (IN SQUARE FEET)

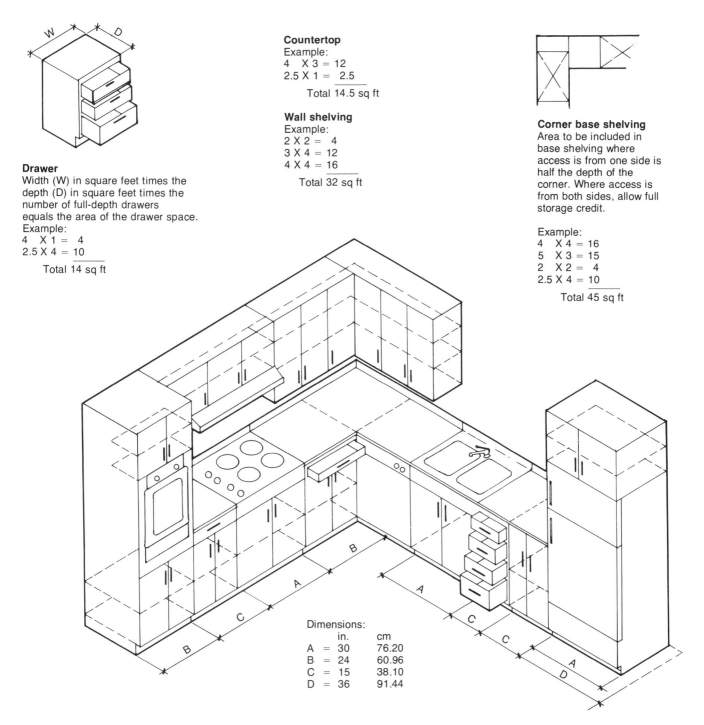

Drawer
Width (W) in square feet times the depth (D) in square feet times the number of full-depth drawers equals the area of the drawer space.
Example:
4 X 1 = 4
2.5 X 4 = 10

Total 14 sq ft

Countertop
Example:
4 X 3 = 12
2.5 X 1 = 2.5

Total 14.5 sq ft

Wall shelving
Example:
2 X 2 = 4
3 X 4 = 12
4 X 4 = 16

Total 32 sq ft

Corner base shelving
Area to be included in base shelving where access is from one side is half the depth of the corner. Where access is from both sides, allow full storage credit.

Example:
4 X 4 = 16
5 X 3 = 15
2 X 2 = 4
2.5 X 4 = 10

Total 45 sq ft

Dimensions:

	in.	cm
A =	30	76.20
B =	24	60.96
C =	15	38.10
D =	36	91.44

Minimum federal kitchen storage requirements
(Based on the number of bedrooms in the residential structure)

	Number of bedrooms				
Storage location	0	1	2	3	4
Min. sq ft shelf area (1, 2, 3, 4)	24	30	38	44	50
Min. sq ft drawer area (5)	4	6	8	10	12

Notes:
1. A dishwasher may be counted as 4 sq ft (0.31 m²) of base cabinet storage.
2. Wall cabinets over refrigerators shall not be counted as required shelf area.
3. Shelf area above 74″ (187.96 cm) shall not be counted as required area.
4. Inside corner cabinets shall be counted as 50 percent of the shelf area. Except where revolving shelves are used, the actual shelf area may be counted.
5. Drawer area in excess of the required area may be counted as shelf area if drawers are at least 6″ (15.24 cm) in depth.

In housing for the elderly, at least half of the 10 percent of the living units with bathrooms designed for wheelchair users shall have kitchen equipment, work space, and storage space that is accessible to and usable by wheelchair occupants.

For seasonal homes, the following kitchen requirements may be used in lieu of the preceding criteria:
1. 5 lin ft (1.52 m) of base cabinet.
2. 5 lin ft of wall cabinet.
3. 6 sq ft (0.56 m²) of countertop
4. Separate kitchens shall have a minimum area of 50 sq ft (4.65 m²).

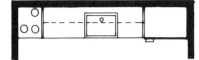

One-wall assembly

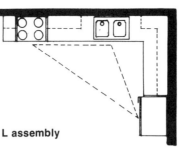

L assembly

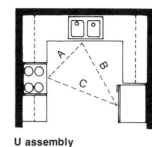

U assembly

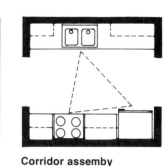

Corridor assemby

Countertops & fixtures

Work center	Number of bedrooms				
	0	1	2	3	4
	Minimum frontages in linear inches				
Sink	18	24	24	32	32
Countertop, each side	15	18	21	24	30
Range or cooktop space	21	21	24	30	30
Countertop, one side	15	18	21	24	30
Refrigerator space	30	30	36	36	36
Countertop, one side	15	15	15	15	18
Mixing countertop	21	30	36	36	42

Note: Total distance between the three major work centers: A plus B plus C. Maximum distance: 22' (6.71 m); minimum distance: 12' (3.66 m).

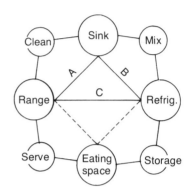

NET ACCESSIBILITY FRONTAGE (linear inches required for work centers)

Counter frontage

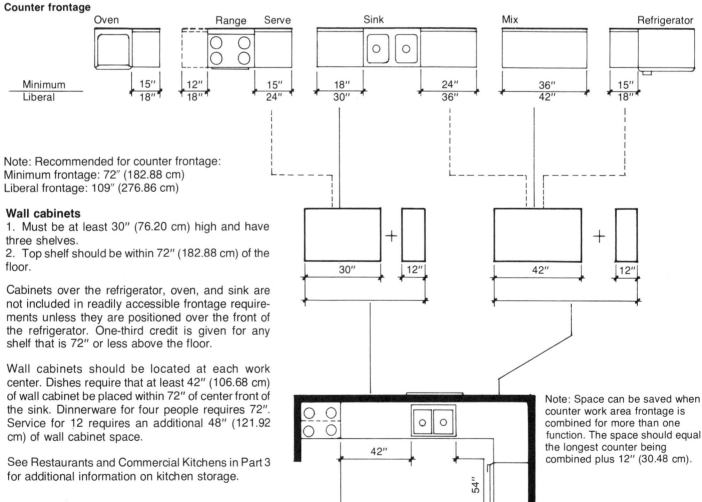

	Oven	Range	Serve	Sink		Mix	Refrigerator
Minimum	15"	12"	15"	18"	24"	36"	15"
Liberal	18"	18"	24"	30"	36"	42"	18"

Note: Recommended for counter frontage:
Minimum frontage: 72" (182.88 cm)
Liberal frontage: 109" (276.86 cm)

Wall cabinets
1. Must be at least 30" (76.20 cm) high and have three shelves.
2. Top shelf should be within 72" (182.88 cm) of the floor.

Cabinets over the refrigerator, oven, and sink are not included in readily accessible frontage requirements unless they are positioned over the front of the refrigerator. One-third credit is given for any shelf that is 72" or less above the floor.

Wall cabinets should be located at each work center. Dishes require that at least 42" (106.68 cm) of wall cabinet be placed within 72" of center front of the sink. Dinnerware for four people requires 72". Service for 12 requires an additional 48" (121.92 cm) of wall cabinet space.

See Restaurants and Commercial Kitchens in Part 3 for additional information on kitchen storage.

Note: Space can be saved when counter work area frontage is combined for more than one function. The space should equal the longest counter being combined plus 12" (30.48 cm).

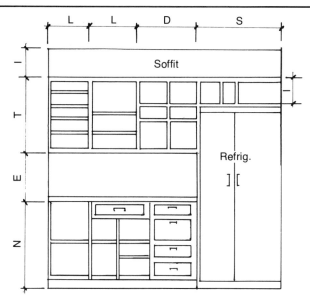

REFRIGERATOR/MIX CENTER

The mix center provides equipment and supplies for assembling and mixing foods. The refrigerator is included to provide storage of perishable items.

Utensils, supplies, & appliances

Mixing bowls	Pitchers, tumblers
Blending forks, spoons	Trays
Measuring cups, spoons	Storage containers
Knives, cutting board	Refrigerator containers
Baking tools, pans	Food wrappers, sandwich bags
Can & bottle openers	Food blender, processor, food center
Scale	Electric cooker
Baskets, bowls	

Food*

Flour, sugar	Baking condiments
Leavening agents	Salad condiments
Extracts	Prepared mixes, beverages
Shortenings	Snack foods
Spices, herbs	

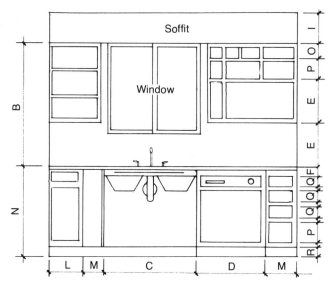

SINK/CLEAN-UP CENTER

Utensils & supplies

Dish drainboard tray	Measuring cups & spoons
Brushes, scrapers, sponges	Towels: paper, fabric
Cutlery, peelers	Plastic & paper bag containers
Chopping board	Storage containers
Colander & strainers	Cleaning supplies
Bottle & can openers	

Appliances

Sink	Hot water dispenser
Dishwasher	Juicer
Trash compactor	Serving pitchers
Disposer	Carafes

Food

Dried vegetables	Dried & condensed foods
Potatoes, onions	Instant beverages
Dried fruits	

Dimensions:

	in.	cm		in.	cm		in.	cm		in.	cm
A	= 56	142.24	F	= 16½	41.91	K	= 10	25.40	P	= 8	20.32
B	= 30	76.20	G	= 14	35.56	L	= 15	38.10	Q	= 5	12.70
C	= 36	91.44	H	= 13	33.02	M	= 9	22.86	R	= 4	10.16
D	= 24	60.96	I	= 12	30.48	N	= 34½	87.63	S	= 33	83.82
E	= 18	45.72	J	= 19½	49.53	O	= 3	7.62	T	= 28½	72.39

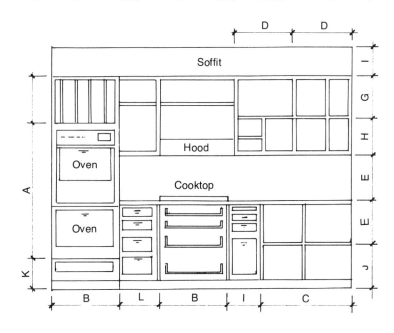

RANGE/COOKING CENTER

The range center provides heat for preparation of food. If the cooktop and oven(s) are separated, centers may be divided into two distinct areas.

Utensils, supplies, & appliances

Mixing spoons, whisks	Casseroles
Turning forks, tongs	Roasting pans
Measuring cups & spoons	Baking pans
Spatulas, shears	Cooling racks
Thermometers	Serving bowls, platters
Miscellaneous gadgets	Serving trays
Microwave paper products	Tea kettle
Microwave cookware	Tea pots
Skillets & covers	Coffee maker
Griddles, wok	Thermo bottles
Saucepans & covers	Small electric appliances

Food

Spices, herbs	Uncooked cereal products
Cooking oils, wines	Soups
Cooking condiments	

*A countertop of wood or marble is desirable for foods requiring special preparation surfaces. It may either be built into the counter or drawer or be a portable unit.

Storage requirements

Item	Number stored		Storage space per item* (in.)		
	Limited	Liberal	Side to side	Front to back	Height
Equipment					
Electric mixer	1	1	7½–12	10–14	10–17
Flour sifter	1	1	6½	9	7
Mixing bowl, 3½ qt	1	1	12½	12½	6
Mixing bowl, 2 qt	1	2	9½	9½	5½
Mixing bowl, 1 qt	1	1	7½	7½	5
Pint measure	1	1	4½	6½	5½
Cup measure, set	1	1	4	5	5
Baking dish, 10½″ dia.	0	1	11	12½	4½
Baking dish, 9½″ dia.	1	1	10	11½	4½
Loaf pan	1	2	6	10½	3½
Biscuit pan	1	1	10	13½	3
Pie pans	1	3	10	10	2½
Cake pans	2	2	12	12	2½
Muffin pan	1	2	11	14	2½
Cookie (baking) sheet	1	2	12½	16	2
Egg beater	1	1	4	12½	4
Cookie cutter	1	1	3	3	3½
Rolling pin	1	1	3	19	3½
Mixing & blending forks	2	6	3	12½	2½
Measuring spoons, 4 sets	1	2	3	6	2½
Egg whisk	0	1	4	12½	2½
Knives & spatulas	2	6	3	14	2
Food supplies					
Cornmeal, 5 lb	1	1	8	8	9
Flour, 5 lb	1	1	8	8	9
Sugar, 5 lb	1	1	8	8	9
Pancake flour, 2-lb pkg.	0	1	2½	6½	10½
Cake flour, 2¾-lb pkg.	1	1	3	7	10½
Vinegar, 1-qt bottle	1	1	4	4	10
Powdered sugar, 1-lb pkg.	1	1	2½	4	8½
Brown sugar, 1-lb pkg.	1	1	2	4	8
Coconut, 7-oz pkg.	1	1	2	4	8
Shortening, 3-lb can	1	1	5½	5½	8
Cornstarch, 1-lb pkg.	1	1	2½	4	7½
Cocoa, 1-lb pkg.	1	1	3	4	7½
Raisins, 15-oz pkg.	1	1	2½	4½	7½
Flavorings, 6″ tall bottle	3	5	1½	2½	7
Salt, 1-lb, 10-oz pkg.	1	2	4	4	7
Baking powder, 1-lb pkg.	1	1	3½	3½	6½
Baking soda, 1-lb pkg.	1	1	2½	4	6½
Package desserts, ⅝-oz pkg.	1	3	2	4	6½
Spices, 4½″ tall can	2	3	2½	3½	5½
Spices, 3″ tall can	4	6	1½	2½	4

*Dimensions of the item (including lid, if any) plus clearance for handling.

Food can sizes	oz	Diameter	Height
#3	46	7	8
#2½	29	4	4¾
#303	16	3¼	4½
#300	14½	3	4½
#2	12	¾	5
#1	10½	2½	3¾
	8	3	2½
	6	2	2¾
	4	2	2½

Coffee cans	lb	Diameter	Height
	3	6	7
	2	5⅛	5½
	1	4	5

Storage requirements

Item	Number stored*		Storage space per item† (in.)		
	Limited	Liberal	Side to side	Front to back	Height
Equipment					
Paper napkins, box	1	2	8	8	3½
Tablecloth, luncheon	0	1	10	14	2
Tablecloth, dinner	1	2	10	19	3
Cups	8(4)	12(6)	4½	5½	6
Cereal dishes	6(2)	8(2)	7½	7½	5
Dinner plates	8(1)	12(1)	11	11	4½
Salad or pie plates	8(1)	12(1)	9	9	4½
Fruit dishes	6(1)	12(1)	5½	5½	6
Saucers	8(1)	12(1)	7½	7½	4½
Juice glasses‡	6	8	3	3	5
Pitchers, large	1	2	7½	10½	10
Pitchers, medium	1	1	7	8	10
Water glasses‡	8	12	3½	3½	6
Bowls, oval	2(1)	3(2)	13½	9½	9½
Bowls, round	2(1)	4(2)	9½	9½	7½
Platter, large	1(1)	1(1)	16½	13	2½
Platter, medium	1(1)	2(1 or 2)	14	11	2½
Platter, small	0	1(1)	12	9	2½
Serving plates	0	2(1 or 2)	11	11	4½
Tray, medium	0	1(1)	15½	11½	3
Creamer	1(1)	1(1)	5	7	5
Sugar	1(1)	1(1)	5½	6½	5½
Gravy boat	0	1(1)	6	10½	5½
Jelly-relish dishes	2(1)	2(1)	7½	7½	2
Refrigerator dishes, set of 4	1(1)	1(1)	8	8½	7
Toaster	1	1	6–7	9–12	7–8
Food supplies					
Prepared cereals, 11″ (27.94 cm) tall box	2	4	3	8	14
Cookies, 1-lb pkg.	1	2	3	6½	11½
Crackers, 1-lb pkg.	1	2	4½	10½	6½
Peanut butter, 1-lb 4-oz jar	1	1	3	3	6½
Mayonnaise, 1-pt jar	1	1	3½	3½	6
Jam and pickles, 1-pt jar	1	3	3½	3½	2
Bread	1	2	5½	12	6
Cake	1	1	9½	9½	2½
Potatoes, lb	10	10	9	11	8
Onions, lb	3	3	9	7	8
Fruit, lb	3	3	9	7½	5
Lentils and peas, 2-lb pkg.	1	1	3½	5	9½
Dry beans, 2-lb pkg.	1	1	3½	5	8½
Prunes, 1-lb pkg.	1	1	3	5	8

*Dimensions include clearance for handling.

†Number in parentheses refers to number of items in stack for which storage space dimension is given.

‡For stemware storage, see Restaurants on pages 489 and 519.

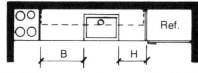

Sink & range counters combined to form a mixing counter (B)
Frontage 72 lin ft (21.95 m)

Minimum counter frontage is based on number of bedrooms in a residential dwelling. The three kitchens shown above are recommended for a one-bedroom home or apartment. The drawings show minimum storage and counter space between fixtures.

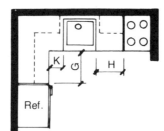

Sink & range counters combined (H)
Frontage: 72 lin ft

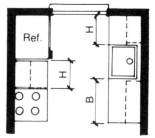

Sink counter combined with mixing counter (B)

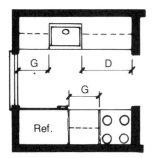

Sink & range counters combined (G); sink & refrigerator counters combined (E)
Total frontage: 81 lin ft (24.69 m)

Note: See regulations for combination of counter functions on page 362.

Minimum kitchens recommended for two- and three-bedroom homes and apartments.

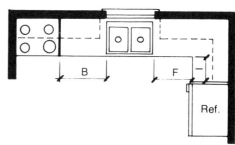

Range & sink counters combined (B); sink & mixing counters combined (F)
Total frontage: 96 lin ft (29.26 m)

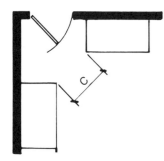

Range counter combined with refrigerator counter (G); mixing counter (D)
Total frontage: 81 lin ft

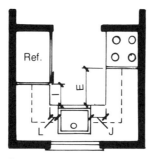

Sink & refrigerator counter combined (L); range & sink counter combined (E)
Total frontage: 81 lin ft

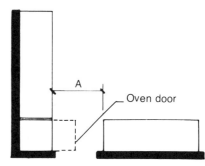

Minimum distance for oven use

Minimum distance through door access area

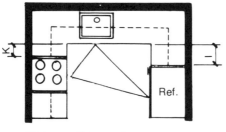

Minimum distance from any appliance to the inside cabinet corner (I & K)

Dimensions:

	in.	cm
A	= 38	96.52 min.
B	= 30	76.20
C	= 34	86.36
D	= 36	91.44
E	= 24	60.96
F	= 27	68.58
G	= 21	53.34
H	= 18	45.72
I	= 15	38.10
J	= 12	30.48
K	= 9	22.86
L	= 6	15.24

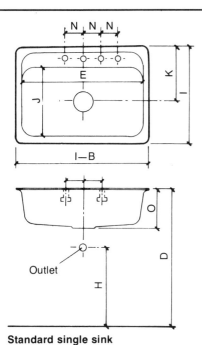

Standard single sink

Outlet

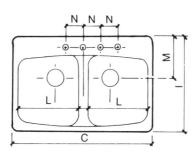

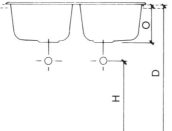

Double sink

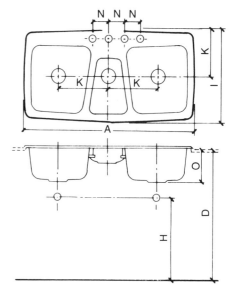

Double sink with center disposal area

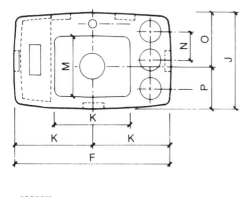

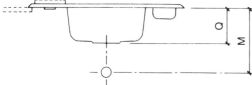

Sink for beverage center
Cutting board (left)
Condiment containers (right)

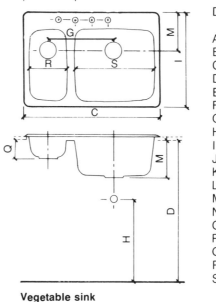

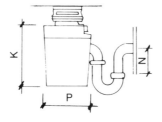

Vegetable sink

Dimensions:

	in.	cm
A =	43	109.22
B =	30	76.20
C =	33	83.82
D =	36	91.44
E =	13–27½	33.02–69.85
F =	25	63.50
G =	21½	54.61
H =	23	58.42
I =	22	55.88
J =	15	38.10
K =	12	30.48
L =	13	33.02
M =	10	25.40
N =	4	10.16
O =	8½	21.59
P =	6½	16.51
Q =	5½	13.97
R =	9	22.86
S =	20	50.80

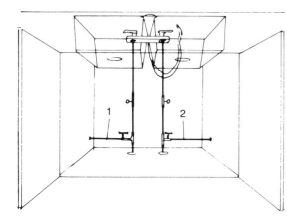

Sink installation
1 = hot water to dishwasher
2 = cold water to ice maker

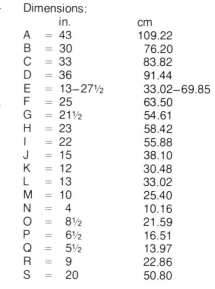

Typical size garbage disposal

Special design considerations
Installations involving sinks and related equipment such as garbage disposals and water softeners require special treatment when accommodating the disabled. Space must be provided for wheelchair approach to the sink. Allow 30″ (76.20 cm) width space under the sink.

Sink faucets and faucet controls should be specified for side use; that is, the entire control unit should be installed on either the right or the left side. Consult plumbing codes in your local area as needed.

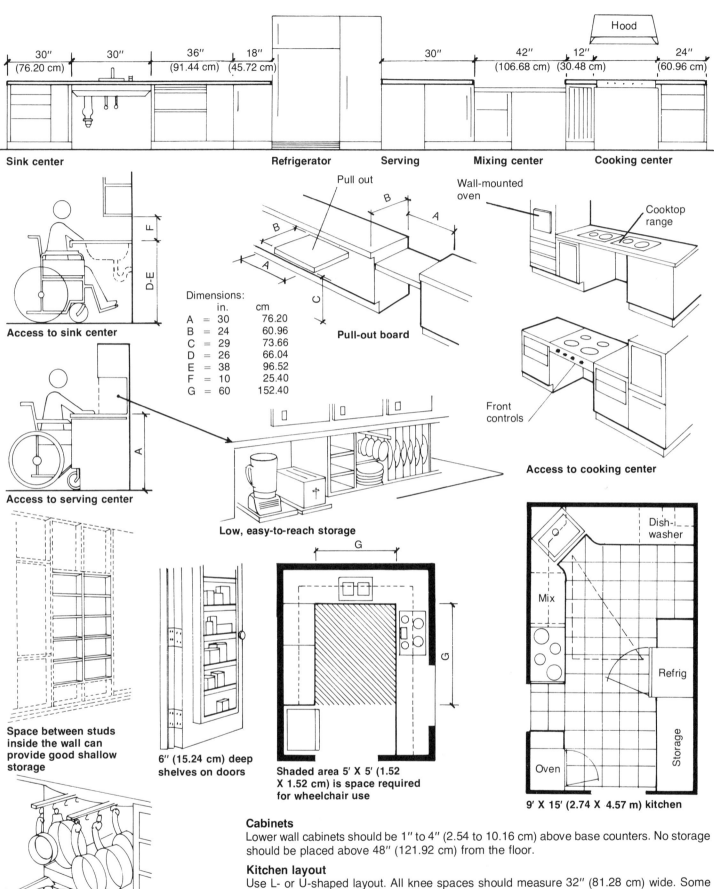

Sink center   Refrigerator   Serving   Mixing center   Cooking center

Access to sink center

Access to serving center

Dimensions:

		in.	cm
A	=	30	76.20
B	=	24	60.96
C	=	29	73.66
D	=	26	66.04
E	=	38	96.52
F	=	10	25.40
G	=	60	152.40

Pull-out board

Low, easy-to-reach storage

Access to cooking center

Space between studs inside the wall can provide good shallow storage

6″ (15.24 cm) deep shelves on doors

Shaded area 5′ X 5′ (1.52 X 1.52 cm) is space required for wheelchair use

9′ X 15′ (2.74 X 4.57 m) kitchen

Pantry storage with glide-out shelves; minimum 40 cu ft (1.13 cu m)

Cabinets

Lower wall cabinets should be 1″ to 4″ (2.54 to 10.16 cm) above base counters. No storage should be placed above 48″ (121.92 cm) from the floor.

Kitchen layout

Use L- or U-shaped layout. All knee spaces should measure 32″ (81.28 cm) wide. Some counter heights should be adjustble from 2′4″ to 3′6″ (0.71 X 1.07 m).

Appliances

Use (1) side-by-side refrigerator, (2) dishwasher, (3) cooktop with controls on front or side, (4) ovens on countertops or wall mounted with side opening door. Allow 30″ under counter for "pull-in" wheelchair space next to oven to allow reach into rear of oven. A pull-out board should be located under an open oven door as a resting place for heavy items removed from the oven.

This checklist highlights the various applications that are possible to make residential kitchens more usable for the disabled person.

1. Appliance considerations

    ____ a. Provide platforms for front-opening appliances to allow reach into the appliance by the wheelchair user.
    (1) Clothes dryer
    (2) Compact upright freezer
    (3) Dishwasher

    ____ b. Refrigerator and freezer doors are equipped with magnetic gaskets to create a firm seal, maintain even temperatures, and conserve energy. The strong suction may make opening these doors very difficult for people with reduced strength in their arms and hands.
    (1) Specify a vacuum break that can be placed along the gasket to reduce the suction.
    (2) If vacuum break is unavailable, apply electrical tape across the lower door gasket in one or two places.

    ____ c. Cooktops, built-in ovens, and microwave ovens should be installed at a height most convenient for the individual using the space. These appliances should be usable from a seated or standing position. Microwaves may be built-in or placed on a movable table.

    ____ d. Counter and floor space surrounding appliances should provide adequate hand grip to support and balance a person on crutches or using a walker. This space should be provided in addition to the space needed to remove cooking pans and dishes.

    ____ e. Provide visual control of cooking pots by installing an adjustable mirror over the range or cooktop that permits the cook to see into the pots on the back burners. The mirror may be tilted by use of a chain and hook.

    ____ f. Exhaust hood controls must be installed at counter level for use by those in wheelchairs.

2. a. Counters and base cabinets
    ____ (1) Depth not to exceed 24″ (60.96 cm).
    ____ (2) Height ranging from 2′4″ to 3′6″ (71.12 to 106.68 cm).

    b. Wall-hung cabinets
    ____ (1) Height above counter top 1″ to 4″ (2.54 to 10.16 cm).
    ____ (2) Maximum storage height not to exceed 48″ (121.92 cm) above the floor.

3. Organizers
    a. Specify and design organizers that allow items to be stored near the front or back of cabinets.
    ____ (1) Pull-out baskets or shelves [minimum 40 cu ft (1.13 cu m)]
    ____ (2) Plate racks
    ____ (3) Suction-held turntables
    ____ (4) Hanging baskets
    ____ (5) Dispensers for cans and bottles

4. Operating information
    ____ a. Provide appliance operational information in braille on the front of the appliance at the control center.

    ____ b. Provide ridges or other tactile cues for those with loss of feeling in fingertips.

    ____ c. Care and use of appliances may also be tape recorded.

5. Reaching aids
    People who have limitations in reaching, bending, or stooping may need a reaching tool to operate high controls, turn faucets, or remove items from shelves.

    ____ a. Knob turners: may be 12″ to 18″ (30.48 to 45.72 cm) long with an attachment that fits over the knob on one end.

    ____ b. "Push-pullers" allow users to push oven racks in and pull racks out when laden with hot pots and pans.

    ____ c. Tongs allow reaching into refrigerators and to high shelves.

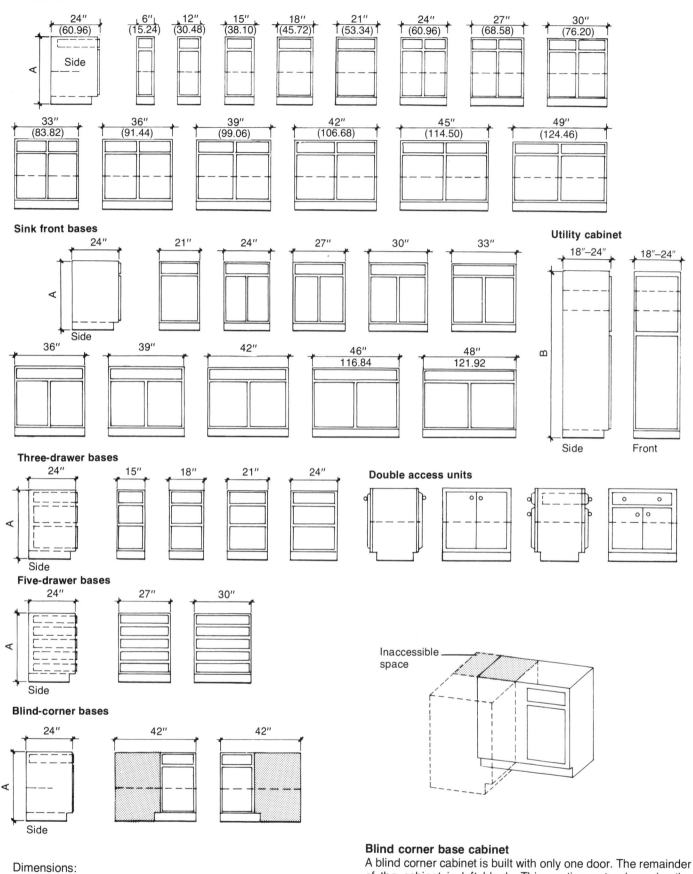

Standard bases

Sink front bases

Utility cabinet

Three-drawer bases

Double access units

Five-drawer bases

Blind-corner bases

Inaccessible space

Dimensions:

	in.	cm
A =	34½	87.63
B =	84	213.36

Blind corner base cabinet

A blind corner cabinet is built with only one door. The remainder of the cabinet is left blank. This section extends under the counter into the corner, and the blind face is covered by the adjoining assembly. Some corner base cabinets can be pulled out from the wall as much as 9" (22.86 cm). Check cabinet specifications for correct pull-out dimensions and use of filler strips.

12″ (30.48 cm) high wall units

Wall cabinets: 12½″ (31.75 cm) deep
Kitchen cabinets are designed in 3″ (7.62 cm) units of measurement.

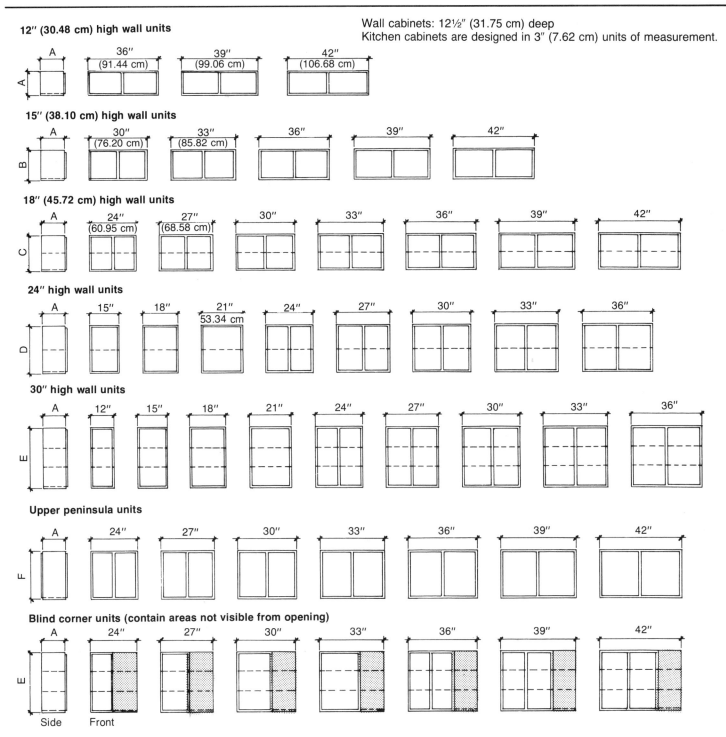

15″ (38.10 cm) high wall units

18″ (45.72 cm) high wall units

24″ high wall units

30″ high wall units

Upper peninsula units

Blind corner units (contain areas not visible from opening)

Side   Front

Dimensions:

	in.	cm
A =	12	30.48
B =	15	38.10
C =	18	45.72
D =	24	60.96
E =	30	76.20
F =	24	60.96

Note: For special hardware applications and details on countertop applications, see Custom Casework on pages 38–53. Also see Chapter 18, Restaurants, in Part 3 for custom storage of stemware, wine bottles, and calculations on storage of larger quantities of dinnerware.

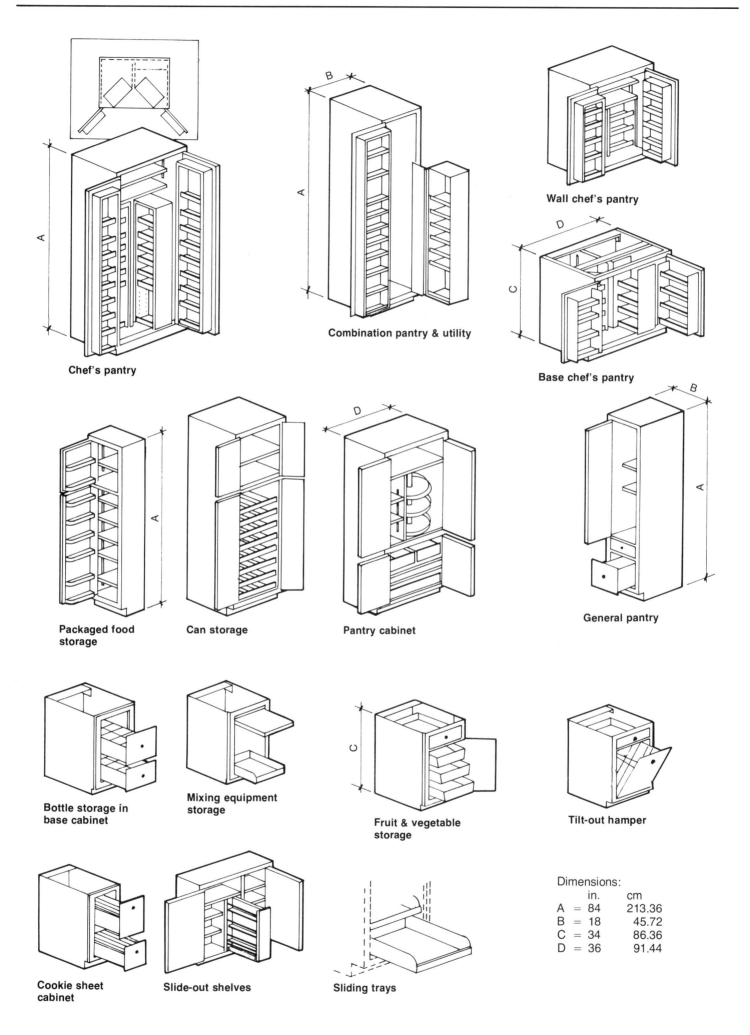

Chef's pantry

Combination pantry & utility

Wall chef's pantry

Base chef's pantry

Packaged food storage

Can storage

Pantry cabinet

General pantry

Bottle storage in base cabinet

Mixing equipment storage

Fruit & vegetable storage

Tilt-out hamper

Cookie sheet cabinet

Slide-out shelves

Sliding trays

Dimensions:

	in.	cm
A =	84	213.36
B =	18	45.72
C =	34	86.36
D =	36	91.44

Corner shelves & carousels

Base units 24″ (60.96 cm) deep

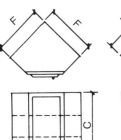
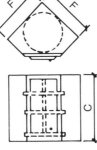
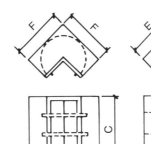
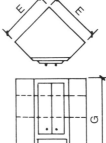
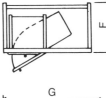

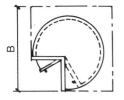

Shelves   Carousel   Carousel   Shelves

Dead corner turnout
(half carousel)

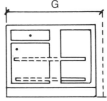

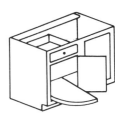

Drum carousel

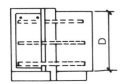

Merry-go-round

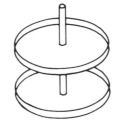

Revolving shelf unit for full-depth cabinets

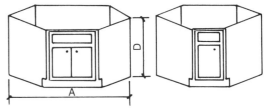

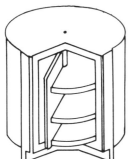

Revolving shelves

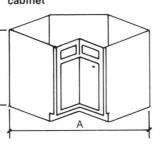

Note: The cabinets shown on this page are designed to provide added storage spaces in corner cabinets.

Dimensions:

	in.	cm
A =	36 to 42	91.44 to 106.68
B =	33, 36, 39	83.82, 91.44, 99.06
C =	33	83.82
D =	34	86.36
E =	30	76.20
F =	24	60.96
G =	48	121.92
H =	29	73.66

Recessed corner sink front compartment

Right-angled sink cabinet

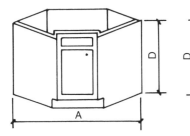

Flared corner sink cabinets

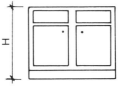
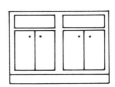

One-piece under-sink units

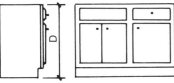

Sink cabinets

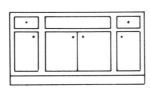

Specify left or right installation

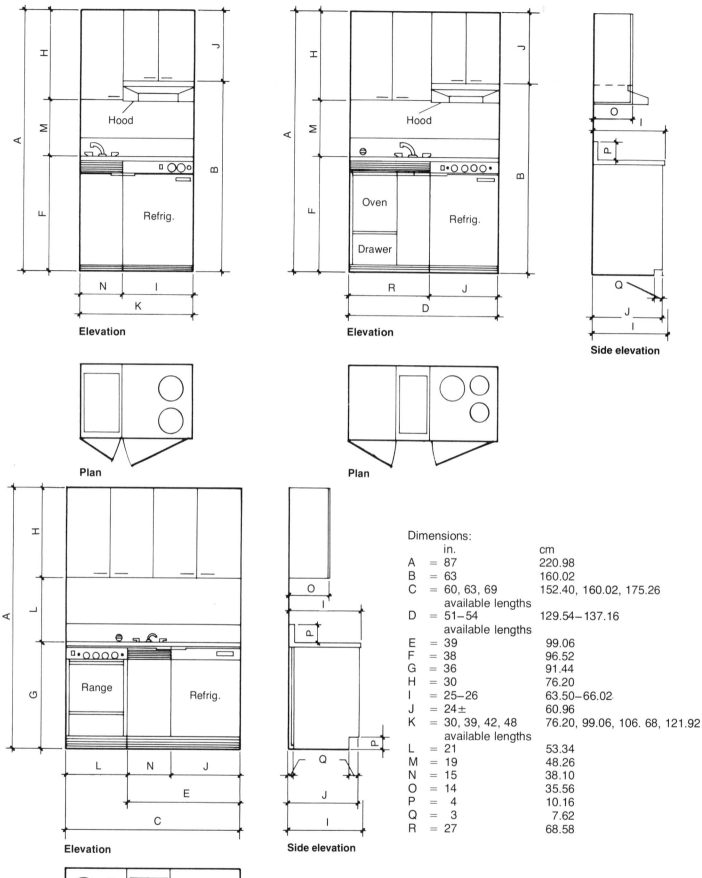

Elevation

Plan

Elevation

Plan

Side elevation

Elevation

Side elevation

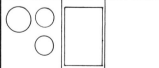

Plan

Dimensions:

		in.	cm
A	=	87	220.98
B	=	63	160.02
C	=	60, 63, 69	152.40, 160.02, 175.26
		available lengths	
D	=	51–54	129.54–137.16
		available lengths	
E	=	39	99.06
F	=	38	96.52
G	=	36	91.44
H	=	30	76.20
I	=	25–26	63.50–66.02
J	=	24±	60.96
K	=	30, 39, 42, 48	76.20, 99.06, 106. 68, 121.92
		available lengths	
L	=	21	53.34
M	=	19	48.26
N	=	15	38.10
O	=	14	35.56
P	=	4	10.16
Q	=	3	7.62
R	=	27	68.58

UNIT KITCHEN
Available in the following lengths: 72″, 84″, 87″ (182.88, 213.36, 220.98 cm)

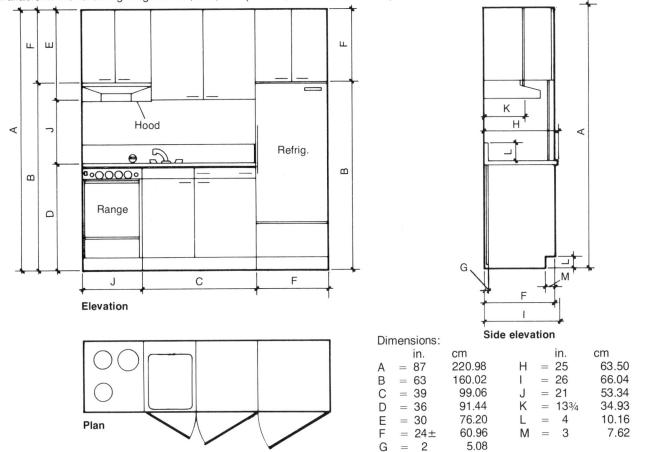

Elevation

Plan

Side elevation

Dimensions:

	in.	cm			in.	cm
A	= 87	220.98	H	= 25		63.50
B	= 63	160.02	I	= 26		66.04
C	= 39	99.06	J	= 21		53.34
D	= 36	91.44	K	= 13¾		34.93
E	= 30	76.20	L	= 4		10.16
F	= 24±	60.96	M	= 3		7.62
G	= 2	5.08				

MICROWAVE & GAS COOKTOP INSTALLATIONS

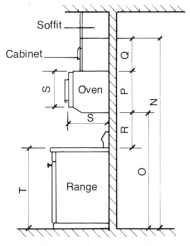

Installation above conventional range

Dimensions:

	in.	cm
N	= 84	213.36
O	= 48 to 51	121.92 to 129.54
	or shoulder height of shortest user	
P	= 17⅜	44.13
Q	= 15 to 18	38.10 to 45.72
R	= 12 to 15	30.48 to 38.10
S	= 15	38.10
T	= 36	91.44

Standard microwave

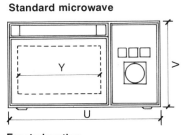

Front elevation

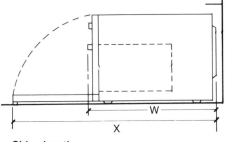

Side elevation

Dimensions:

	in.	cm
U	= 22	55.88
V	= 15½	39.37
W	= 18	45.72
X	= 29¼	74.30
Y	= 13	33.02

Gas cooktop
Electric cooktops vary in
size from gas cooktops

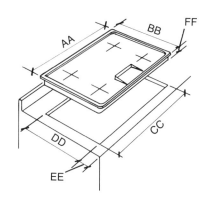

Dimensions:

	in.	cm
AA	= 21 to 36	53.34 to 91.44
BB	= 16 to 21	40.64 to 53.34
CC	= 20 to 35	50.80 to 88.90
DD	= 15 to 20¾	38.10 to 54.71
EE	= 1¾ to 3	4.45 to 7.62
FF	= 3 & 5	7.62 & 12.70

GAS RANGES & APPLIANCES

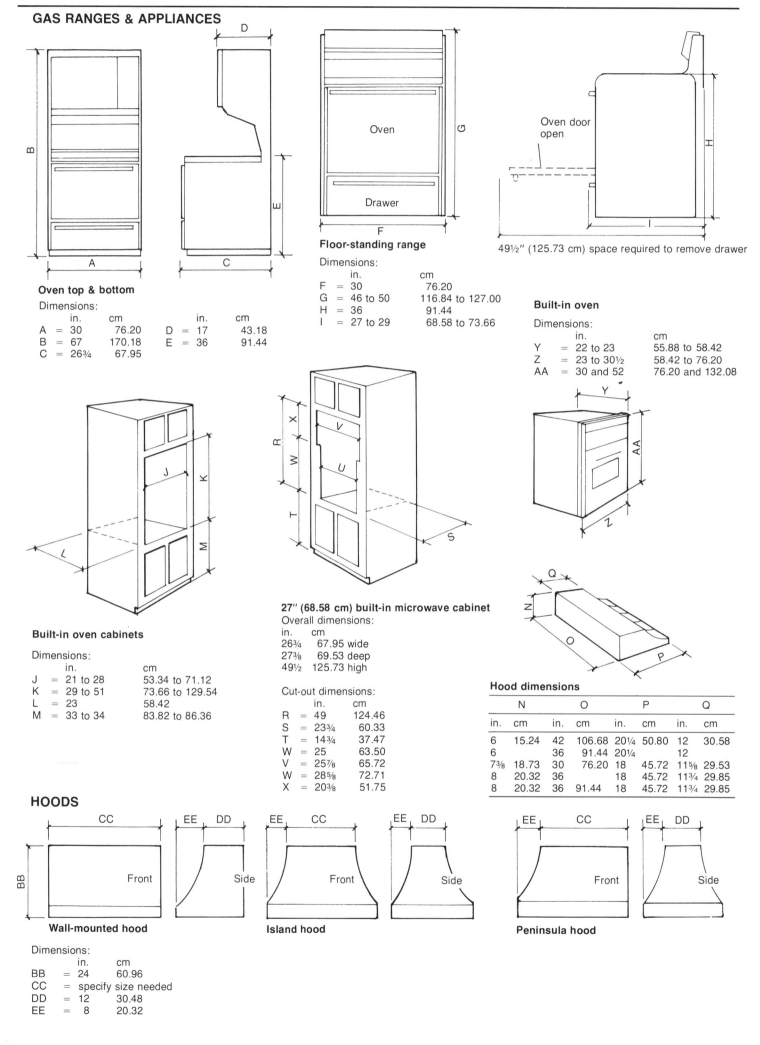

Oven top & bottom

Dimensions:

	in.	cm		in.	cm
A	= 30	76.20	D	= 17	43.18
B	= 67	170.18	E	= 36	91.44
C	= 26¾	67.95			

Floor-standing range

Dimensions:

	in.	cm
F	= 30	76.20
G	= 46 to 50	116.84 to 127.00
H	= 36	91.44
I	= 27 to 29	68.58 to 73.66

49½" (125.73 cm) space required to remove drawer

Built-in oven

Dimensions:

	in.	cm
Y	= 22 to 23	55.88 to 58.42
Z	= 23 to 30½	58.42 to 76.20
AA	= 30 and 52	76.20 and 132.08

Built-in oven cabinets

Dimensions:

	in.	cm
J	= 21 to 28	53.34 to 71.12
K	= 29 to 51	73.66 to 129.54
L	= 23	58.42
M	= 33 to 34	83.82 to 86.36

27″ (68.58 cm) built-in microwave cabinet

Overall dimensions:

in.	cm	
26¾	67.95	wide
27⅜	69.53	deep
49½	125.73	high

Cut-out dimensions:

	in.	cm
R	= 49	124.46
S	= 23¾	60.33
T	= 14¾	37.47
W	= 25	63.50
V	= 25⅞	65.72
W	= 28⅝	72.71
X	= 20⅜	51.75

Hood dimensions

N		O		P		Q	
in.	cm	in.	cm	in.	cm	in.	cm
6	15.24	42	106.68	20¼	50.80	12	30.58
6		36	91.44	20¼		12	
7⅜	18.73	30	76.20	18	45.72	11⅝	29.53
8	20.32	36		18	45.72	11¾	29.85
8	20.32	36	91.44	18	45.72	11¾	29.85

HOODS

Wall-mounted hood

Island hood

Peninsula hood

Dimensions:

	in.	cm
BB	= 24	60.96
CC	= specify size needed	
DD	= 12	30.48
EE	= 8	20.32

RANGE EXHAUST HOODS

Parallel wall installation

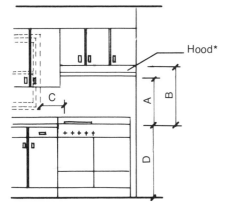

Hood*

*Hoods should extend the entire length of the range surface and be at least 17″ (43.18 cm) wide.

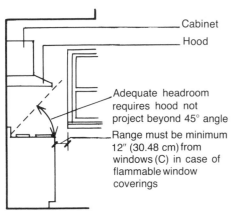

Cabinet

Hood

Adequate headroom requires hood not project beyond 45° angle

Range must be minimum 12″ (30.48 cm) from windows (C) in case of flammable window coverings

Section

Hood installation requirements

The parallel positioned hood should be placed 30″ (76.20 cm) above the counter. This distance (A) can be reduced to (B) 24″ (60.96 cm) when the underside of the wall cabinet is protected with ¼″ (0.64 cm) flameproof millboard covered in not less than 28 gauge sheet metal such as stainless steel, aluminum, or copper. The hood should not be placed less than 56″ to 60″ (142.24 to 152.40 cm) from the floor (D).

Federal requirements regarding hood fan capacity

Minimum CFM per linear foot of hood length

Parallel to wall installation	= 40 CFM
Peninsula or island installation	= 50 CFM

Recommended industry standards

Parallel to wall installation	= 100 CFM
Peninsula or island	= 120 CFM

Sample calculation

Hood required for 48″ (117.60 cm) range installed parallel to the wall:

Fan capacity = length of hood in feet X 100 CFM per foot
4 X 100 = 400 CFM

Note that fan capacity for hoods is not based on room size.

Hood fans should be vented or exhausted to the outside, but if this is impossible, nonducted hoods may be used. Nonducted hoods do not remove heat or moisture.

Ovens

Hoods should also be installed over recessed ovens for broiling foods.

Note: CFM = cubic feet per minute
Fans should be capable of exhausting air in a given space 15 times per hour. This is the equivalent of one air change every 4 minutes.

GENERAL VENTILATION

Most codes require that kitchens and baths which do not have natural ventilation such as a window must have some form of mechanical air change.

There are four types of fans generally available for kitchens and baths. (1) In centrifugal fans (or blowers), a revolving wheel makes air flow radially through the impeller within a scroll-shaped housing. (2) In propeller fans, a stamped disc with three or more blades moves the air. (3) In axial flow fans (improved propeller type) the air flows straight through an impeller that is mounted within a close-fitting tube. (4) The mixed flow impeller is like a propeller at intake and like a blower at discharge.

The following information is needed in order to properly select an exhaust fan:
1. The amount of air (CFM) that must be handled.
2. The resistance of the system (whether there is ductwork or not).
3. Noise level that can be tolerated.

When there is little or no resistance in the system (no ductwork involved) a propeller-type fan can be used. When *long* ductwork is involved, a centrifugal *may be* in order.

To calculate the fan capacity for ventilating a kitchen, the following problem should prove useful: If a kitchen is 10′ (3.05 m) wide and 15′ (4.57 m) long with an 8′ (2.44 m) ceiling height, what should the capacity of a wall exhaust fan be?

$$\text{Fan capacity:} \quad \frac{\text{Volume (cubic feet in kitchen)}}{\text{No. of minutes for each air change}}$$

$$= \frac{10' \times 15' \times 8'}{4 \text{ minutes}} = \frac{1200 \text{ cubic feet}}{4 \text{ minutes}}$$

$$= 300 \text{ CFM}$$

Typical household loads

Load	Voltage	Power or rating	115/230 v service current
General lighting	115	3 watts/sq ft	1.3 A/100 sq ft
Range top	115/230	7.7 kw*	33 A
Oven	115/230	4.5 kw	20 A
Water heater	115/230	9.0 kw	40 A
Clothes dryer	115/230	6.0 kw	26 A
Central air conditioner	230		0.75 A/1000 BTU
Electric heating	115 or 230		4.35 A/kw
Washer	115	½ hp	4.9 A
Garbage disposer	115	¼ hp	3.0 A
		½ hp	4.9 A
Dishwasher	115	1.0 kw	4.5 A
Color TV	115	0.35 kw	1.5 A
Freezer	115	⅙ hp	2.2 A
Refrigerator	115	⅙ hp	2.2 A
Iron	115	1.2 kw	5.2 A
Gas furnace blower	115	⅓ hp	3.6 A
Motors	115 or 230	⅙ hp	2.2 A
(Shop tools)		¼ hp	2.9 A
		⅓ hp	3.6 A
		½ hp	4.9 A
		¾ hp	6.9 A
		1 hp	8.0 A
20A small appliance			
Branch circuit	115	1.9 kw	

*kw = 1000 watts

Note: Standard amperes usually required in the following interior living spaces:
1. 1500 sq ft (139.35 m²) = 150 amps
2. 3500 to 4000 sq ft (325.16 to 371.61 m²) = 200 amps
3. Up to 12,000 sq ft (1114.84 m²) = 400 amps

Receptacles

The most common outlet is the duplex receptacle, which accepts two plugs. Single, triplex, and quad receptacles are also available.

If many outlets are needed in a small area it may be convenient to use a multi-outlet assembly that has prewired receptacles spaced from 6" to 36" (15.24 to 91.44 cm) apart along its length. The units are usually mounted on the surface of the wall just above the baseboard or above a counter.

Grounding receptacles are outlets designed to receive a 3-prong plug. The third prong is connected to a wire that leads to the frame or housing of the appliance. The third slot in the receptacle is connected to the conduit system or to a grounding wire (bare or coded green) that extends to the ground at the meter or to a separate ground, such as a nearby cold water pipe. Grounding receptacles are outlets designed to receive a 3-prong plug. The third prong is connected to a wire that leads to the frame or

housing of the appliance. The third slot in the receptacle is connected to the conduit system or to a grounding wire (bare or coded green) that extends to the ground at the meter or to a separate ground, such as a nearby cold water pipe. Grounding receptacles are especially desirable for damp areas or places that may have wet floors.

Consult with local electrical codes about required grounding receptacles that may be required on all 15- and 20-amp circuits.

Locking receptacles and plugs are available for overhead outlets and other places where it is desirable to engage the plug securely. They are operated by inserting the plug in the receptacle and twisting a quarter-turn. Locking receptacles are especially useful in preventing accidental disconnection of freezers.

Other special forms of outlets include receptacle and switch combinations, clock receptacles, safety receptacles, dual-voltage units that supply both 120 and 240 volts.

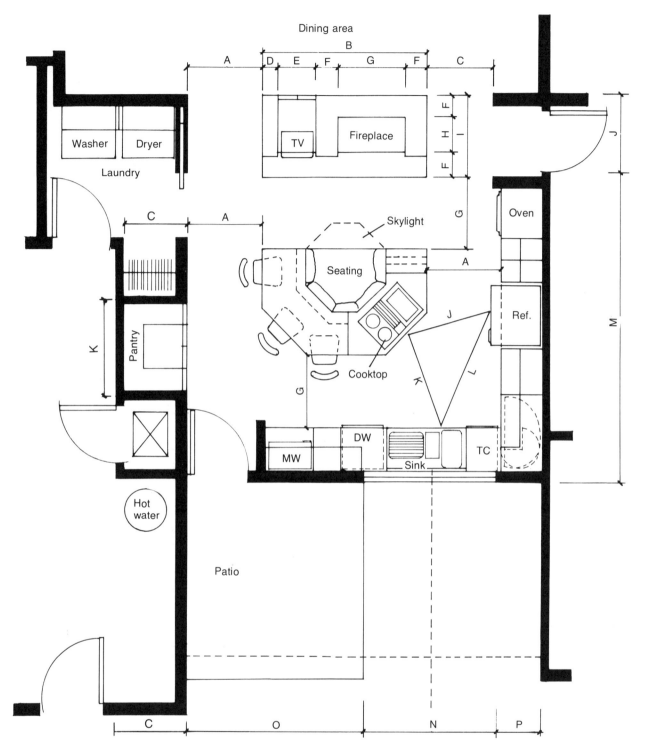

Kitchen with built-in breakfast bar & banquette lounging area

Dimensions & notes:
A = 42″ (106.68 cm)
B = 94″ (238.76 cm)
C = 39″ (99.06 cm)
D = 8″ (20.32 cm)
E = 22″ (55.88 cm)
F = 12″ (30.48 cm)
G = 40″ (101.60 cm)
H = 20″ (50.80 cm)
I = 46″ (116.84 cm)
J = 48″ (121.94 cm)

K = 54″ (137.26 cm)
L = 72″ (182.88 cm)
M = 13′ (3.96 m)
N = 6′4″ (1.93 m)
O = 8′4″ (2.54 m)
P = 26″ (66.04 cm)
TC = trash compactor
DW = dishwasher
MW = microwave oven

REFRIGERATORS & FREEZERS

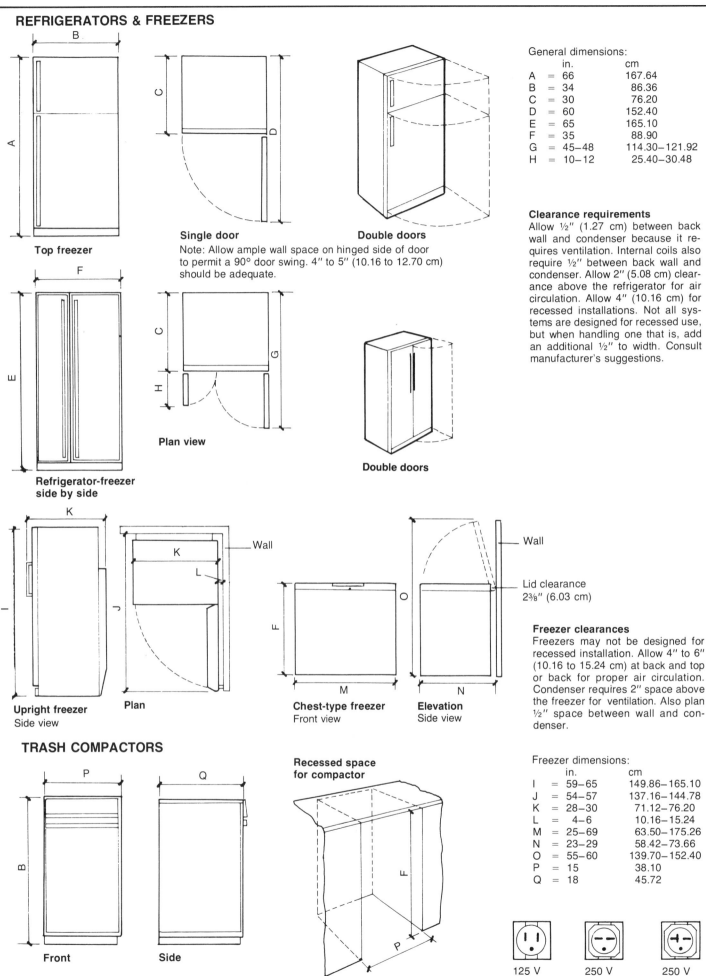

Top freezer

Single door

Note: Allow ample wall space on hinged side of door to permit a 90° door swing. 4″ to 5″ (10.16 to 12.70 cm) should be adequate.

Double doors

Plan view

Refrigerator-freezer side by side

Double doors

Upright freezer
Side view

Plan

Wall

Chest-type freezer
Front view

Elevation
Side view

Wall

Lid clearance
2⅜″ (6.03 cm)

General dimensions:

		in.	cm
A	=	66	167.64
B	=	34	86.36
C	=	30	76.20
D	=	60	152.40
E	=	65	165.10
F	=	35	88.90
G	=	45–48	114.30–121.92
H	=	10–12	25.40–30.48

Clearance requirements

Allow ½″ (1.27 cm) between back wall and condenser because it requires ventilation. Internal coils also require ½″ between back wall and condenser. Allow 2″ (5.08 cm) clearance above the refrigerator for air circulation. Allow 4″ (10.16 cm) for recessed installations. Not all systems are designed for recessed use, but when handling one that is, add an additional ½″ to width. Consult manufacturer's suggestions.

Freezer clearances

Freezers may not be designed for recessed installation. Allow 4″ to 6″ (10.16 to 15.24 cm) at back and top or back for proper air circulation. Condenser requires 2″ space above the freezer for ventilation. Also plan ½″ space between wall and condenser.

Freezer dimensions:

		in.	cm
I	=	59–65	149.86–165.10
J	=	54–57	137.16–144.78
K	=	28–30	71.12–76.20
L	=	4–6	10.16–15.24
M	=	25–69	63.50–175.26
N	=	23–29	58.42–73.66
O	=	55–60	139.70–152.40
P	=	15	38.10
Q	=	18	45.72

TRASH COMPACTORS

Front

Side

Recessed space for compactor

125 V
15 amps

250 V
15 amps

250 V
20 amps

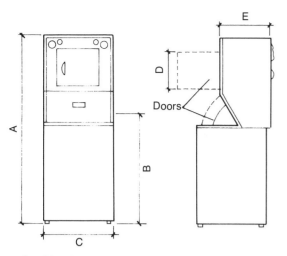

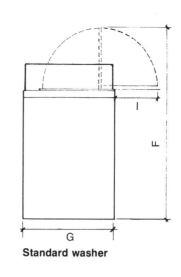

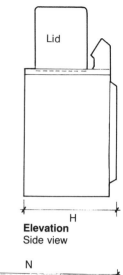

Combination washer/dryer, stack unit

Standard washer

Elevation
Side view

Dimensions:

	in.	cm
A =	65	165.10
B =	38	96.52
C =	24	60.96
D =	13	33.02
E =	18	45.72

Standard washer dimensions:

	in.	cm
F =	53½	135.89
G =	27	68.58
H =	28¼	71.76
I =	12½±	31.75

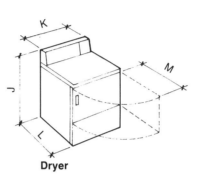

Dryer

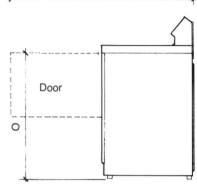

Elevation
Side view

Standard dryer dimensions:

	in.	cm
J =	42½–43½	107.95–110.49
K =	27–31	68.58–78.74
L =	25–31	63.50–78.74
M =	26–27½	66.04–69.85
N =	53±	134.62
O =	34¾±	88.27

Note: Rear clearance for venting dryer is 4″ (10.16 cm). Consult manufacturer's specifications.

Recessed ironing surface

*Opening between studs 14¼″ X 4″ X 59½″ (36.20 X 10.16 X 151.13 cm). Start opening 20″ (50.80 cm) above the floor for ironing surface height of 34″ (86.36 cm) when ironing in standing position. For ironing in seated position place ironing surface at 28″–29″ (68.58–73.66 cm) above the floor.

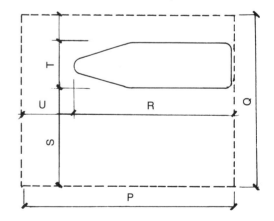

Dimensions (extension into room):

	in.	cm
P =	72	182.88
Q =	55	139.70
R =	54	137.16
S =	32	81.28
T =	15	38.10
U =	18	45.72
V =	8	20.32

Start opening 14″–15″ (35.56–38.10 cm) above the floor.

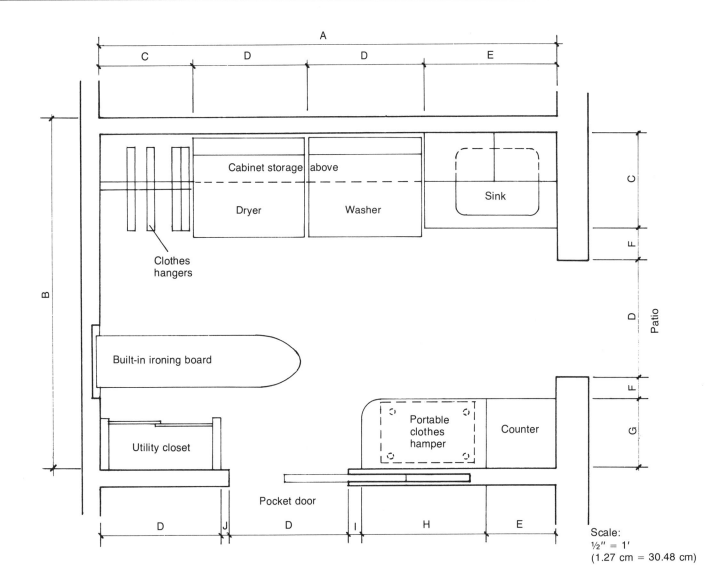

Scale:
½" = 1'
(1.27 cm = 30.48 cm)

Laundry room design checklist

1. Dimensions vary depending on anticipated activities
2. Activities
   a. Sorting
   b. Spot cleaning & treatment
   c. Washing
   d. Hanging clothing
   e. Folding clothing
   f. Sewing & mending
   g. Pressing
3. Appliances: electrical or gas requirements & venting
   a. Washing machine
   b. Dryer
   c. Sewing machine
   d. Iron
4. Storage requirements
   a. Detergents/spot removers
   b. Filters
   c. Hamper(s)
   d. Clothes racks
   e. Hanging space
   f. Ironing board
   g. Stool

5. Design considerations based on spatial relationships to the following areas:
   a. Kitchen
   b. Outside
   c. Bedooms
   d. Linen storage
   e. Bedding & bath linen storage

Dimensions:
A = 10' (3.05 m)
B = 7' (2.13 m)
C = 24" (60.96 cm)
D = 30" (76.20 cm)
E = 36" (91.44 cm)
F = 6" (15.24 cm)
G = 18" (45.72 cm)
H = 33" (83.82 cm)
I = 3" (7.62 cm)
J = 2" (5.08 cm)

BATHROOMS

POWDER ROOMS

5' X 5'
(1.52 X 1.52 m)

4' X 6'
(1.22 X 1.83 m)

4' X 4'
(1.22 X 1.22 m)

4' X 4'6"
(1.22 X 1.37 m)

3' X 6'
(0.91 X 1.83 m)

4'6" X 5'
(1.37 X 1.52 m)

Dimensions:

	in.	cm
A =	30	76.20
B =	15	38.10
C =	1	2.54
D =	16	40.64
E =	20–24	50.80–60.96

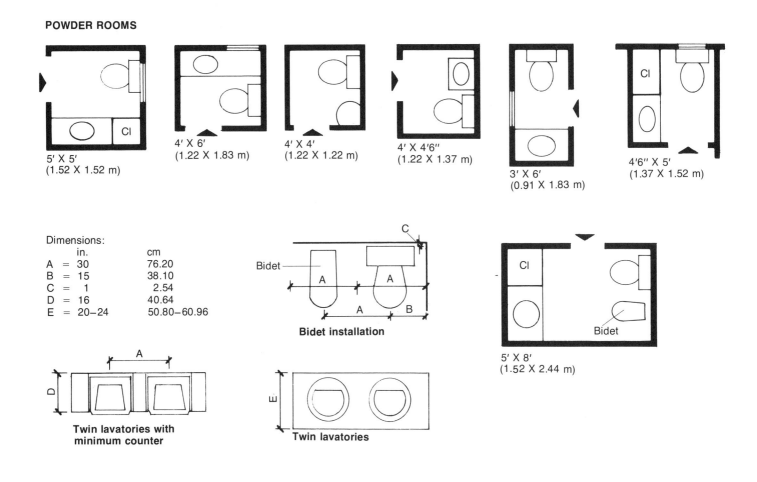

Bidet installation

5' X 8'
(1.52 X 2.44 m)

Bidet

Twin lavatories with minimum counter

Twin lavatories

SMALL FAMILY BATHROOMS

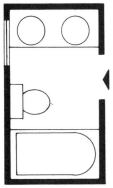

5' X 9'
(1.52 X 2.74 cm)

5' X 9'

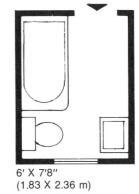

6' X 7'8"
(1.83 X 2.36 m)

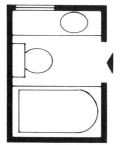

5' X 6'
(1.52 X 1.83 m)

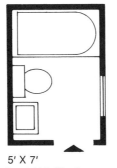

5' X 7'
(1.52 X 2.13 m)

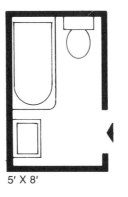

5' X 8'

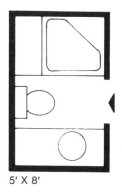

5' X 8'

FAMILY BATHROOMS

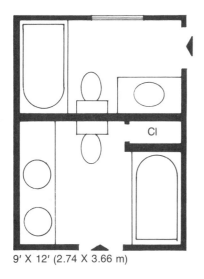

9' X 12' (2.74 X 3.66 m)

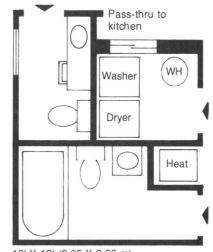

Pass-thru to kitchen

Washer

WH

Dryer

Heat

10' X 12' (3.05 X 3.66 m)

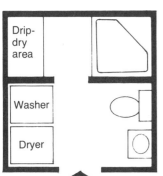

Drip-dry area

Washer

Dryer

8' X 8' (2.44 X 2.44 m)

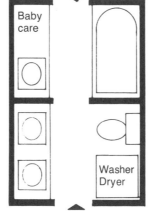

Baby care

Washer Dryer

8' X 10' (2.44 X 3.05 m)

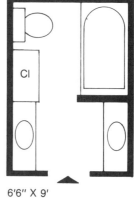

Cl

6'6" X 9'
(1.98 X 2.74 m)

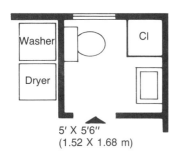

Washer

Dryer

Cl

5' X 5'6"
(1.52 X 1.68 m)

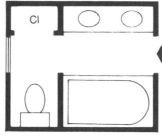

Cl

8' X 6'6" (2.44 X 1.98 m)

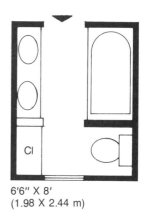

Cl

Cl

6'6" X 8'
(1.98 X 2.44 m)

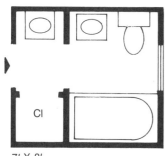

Cl

7' X 8'
(2.13 X 2.44 m)

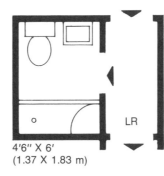

LR

4'6" X 6'
(1.37 X 1.83 m)

Note: For barrier-free baths, see public washrooms, pages 404–407.

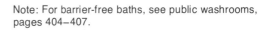

LARGE SIZE BATHROOMS

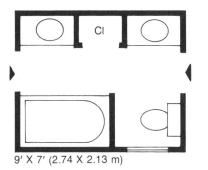

9' X 7' (2.74 X 2.13 m)

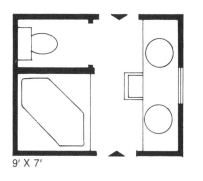

9' X 7'

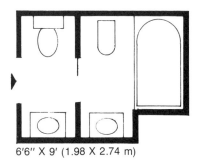

10' X 7'6" (3.05 X 2.29 m)

MEDIUM SIZE BATHROOMS

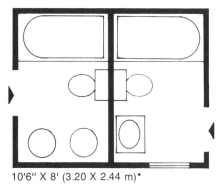

10'6" X 8' (3.20 X 2.44 m)*

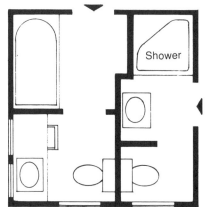

10' X 10' (3.05 X 3.05 m)*

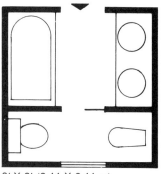

6'6" X 9' (1.98 X 2.74 m)

*Dimensions are for total area of adjoining baths.

BATHROOMS WITH DRESSING AREAS

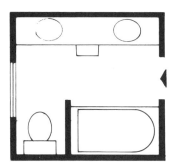

7'6" X 8' (2.29 X 2.44 m)

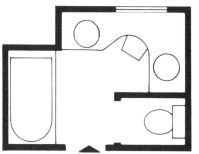

7' X 10' (2.13 X 3.05 m)

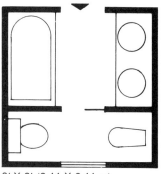

8' X 8' (2.44 X 2.44 m)

BATHS CONNECTING TWO ROOMS

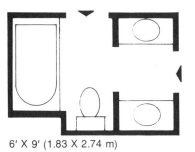

6' X 9' (1.83 X 2.74 m)

6' X 10' (1.83 X 3.05 m)

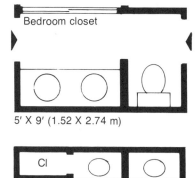

5' X 9' (1.52 X 2.74 m)

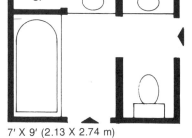

7' X 9' (2.13 X 2.74 m)

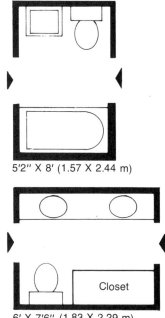

5'2" X 8' (1.57 X 2.44 m)

6' X 7'6" (1.83 X 2.29 m)

Drawer base combinations

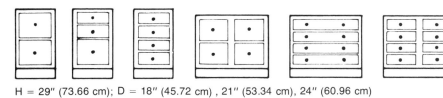

H = 29″ (73.66 cm); D = 18″ (45.72 cm) , 21″ (53.34 cm), 24″ (60.96 cm)

All storage cabinets on
this page are designed in
three heights: 29″ (73.66 cm),
34½″ (87.63 cm), and 84″ (213.36 cm).

Base cabinets for sink installations (H = 34½″)

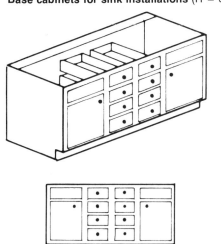

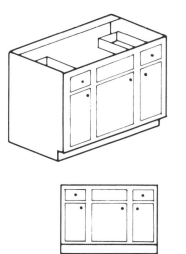

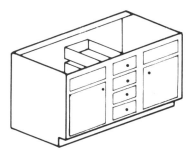

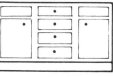

W = 72″ (182.88 cm)

W = 48″ (121.92 cm)

W = 60″ (152.50 cm)

Note: For other vanity-sink counters for handicapped use,
see Public Washrooms on pages 403, 404, 406.

Wardrobe units

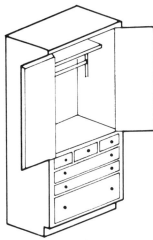

Tall storage cabinets

1   2   3   4

W = (1) 12″ (30.48 cm), (2) = 18″, (3) = 36″, (4) = 48″
D = 12″, 18″, 21″, or 24″

H = 84″; adjustble shelves: W = 36″ (91.44 cm)

Drawers

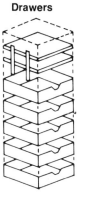

D = 21″ or 24″

Shelves

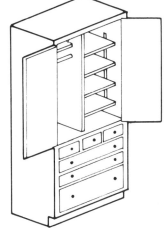

D = 12″–24″

Shoe storage

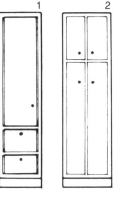

D = 12½″ (31.75 cm)

Tilt-out hamper

Swing-out hamper

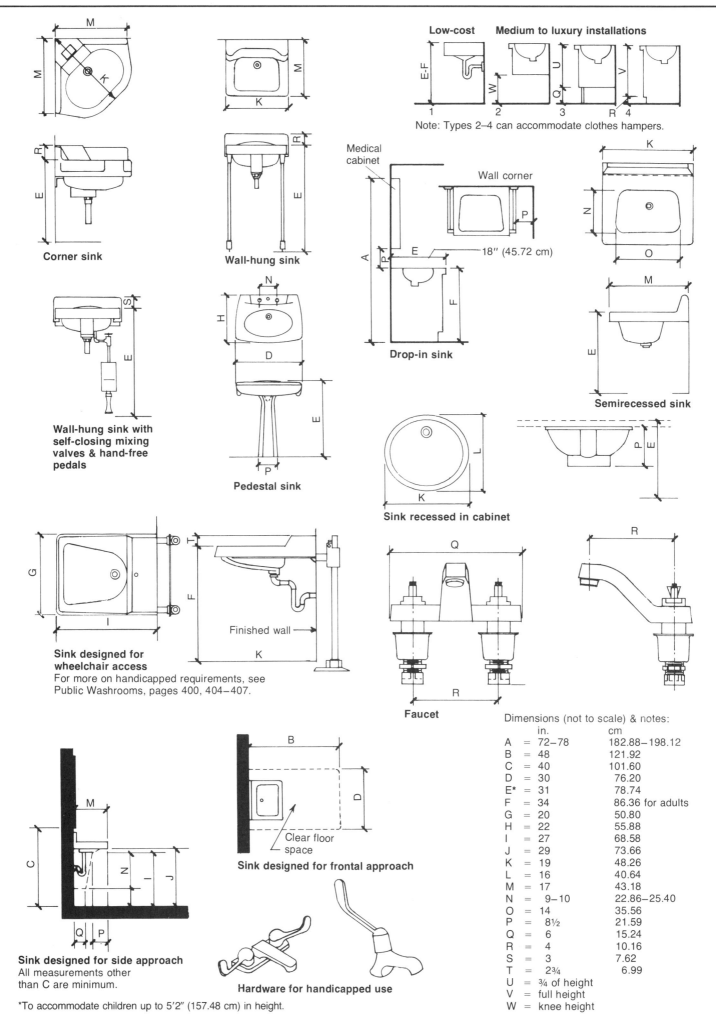

Corner sink

Wall-hung sink

Wall-hung sink with self-closing mixing valves & hand-free pedals

Pedestal sink

Low-cost

Medium to luxury installations

Note: Types 2–4 can accommodate clothes hampers.

Medical cabinet

Wall corner

18″ (45.72 cm)

Drop-in sink

Semirecessed sink

Sink recessed in cabinet

Sink designed for wheelchair access
For more on handicapped requirements, see Public Washrooms, pages 400, 404–407.

Finished wall

Faucet

Sink designed for side approach
All measurements other than C are minimum.

*To accommodate children up to 5′2″ (157.48 cm) in height.

Sink designed for frontal approach

Clear floor space

Hardware for handicapped use

Dimensions (not to scale) & notes:

	in.	cm
A =	72–78	182.88–198.12
B =	48	121.92
C =	40	101.60
D =	30	76.20
E* =	31	78.74
F =	34	86.36 for adults
G =	20	50.80
H =	22	55.88
I =	27	68.58
J =	29	73.66
K =	19	48.26
L =	16	40.64
M =	17	43.18
N =	9–10	22.86–25.40
O =	14	35.56
P =	8½	21.59
Q =	6	15.24
R =	4	10.16
S =	3	7.62
T =	2¾	6.99
U =	¾ of height	
V =	full height	
W =	knee height	

Water closet bowl parts:
A = water surface
B = water seal (depth)
C = trapway
D = jet
E = rim flush

Specification guidelines
It is recommended that water closets have (1) a large water surface and (2) federally approved minimum trapway dimensions. A large water surface indicates the following: (1) the closet has positive siphon-jet action; (2) a strong flushing action; (3) a deep water seal to ensure against obnoxious gases.

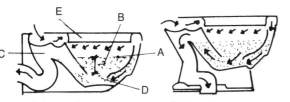

Wall-hung siphon jet 3″ (7.62 cm) seal **Siphon jet** 3″ seal **Washdown** **Reverse trap** 2½″ (6.35 cm) seal **Low-profile siphon action (one piece)**

FOUR TYPES OF FLUSHING ACTIONS

Washdown
The washdown is the least expensive, the least efficient, and the noisiest. It is flushed by a simple wash-out action through a trapway in front of the bowl and because of its small, irregular passageway may clog more easily than the other types. Most of the inside bowl area is not covered by water and is subject to fouling, staining, and contamination.

Reverse trap
The reverse trap is the least expensive of the siphon-action closets. It is flushed by creating a siphon action in the trapway, assisted by a water jet located at the inlet to the trapway. This siphon pulls the waste from the bowl. It is moderately noisy, but efficient. The trapway must pass a 1½″ (3.81 cm) ball, and the siphon makes this closet less likely to clog. More of the interior bowl surface is covered with water than in the washdown model. Therefore, it is less subject to fouling.

Siphon jet
Siphon jet bowls are improved versions of the reverse trap bowls. They have a larger water surface, with most of the interior surface of the bowl covered with water. The trapway is larger and must pass a 2⅛″ (5.40 cm) ball; thus, the flushing action is quieter and less subject to clogging. Siphon jet closets are usually more expensive than reverse trap closets.

Siphon action
The siphon action is a term applied by most manufacturers to the flushing action of a low-profile, one-piece closet. Since the bowl and tank are one piece, they are naturally more difficult and expensive to manufacture. However, they have an almost silent flushing action and almost no dry surfaces on the bowl interior and are extremely attractive-looking closets.

TYPICAL WATER CLOSETS & BIDET

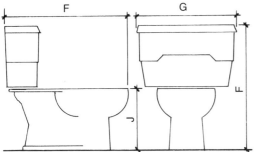

Shelf-top with elongated bowl

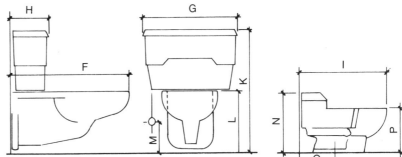

Wall-hanging water closet

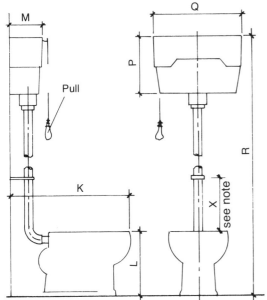

Water closet with overhead tank

Bidet

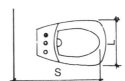

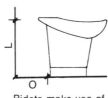

Bidets make use of hot, cold, or tempered water to flush the rim or spray-rinse

Dimensions:

	in.	cm
F =	29	73.66
G =	23¾	60.33
H =	9¼	23.50
I =	28½	72.39
J =	14½	36.83
K =	29½	74.93
L =	15	38.10
M =	7½	19.05
N =	18¾	47.63
O =	12	30.48
P =	14	35.56
Q =	21	53.34
R =	80½	204.47
S =	27¾	70.49

Note (X): Supply may be installed at 2¼″ (5.72 cm) minimum height to 60″ (152.40 cm) maximum height above the finished floor.

TUBS

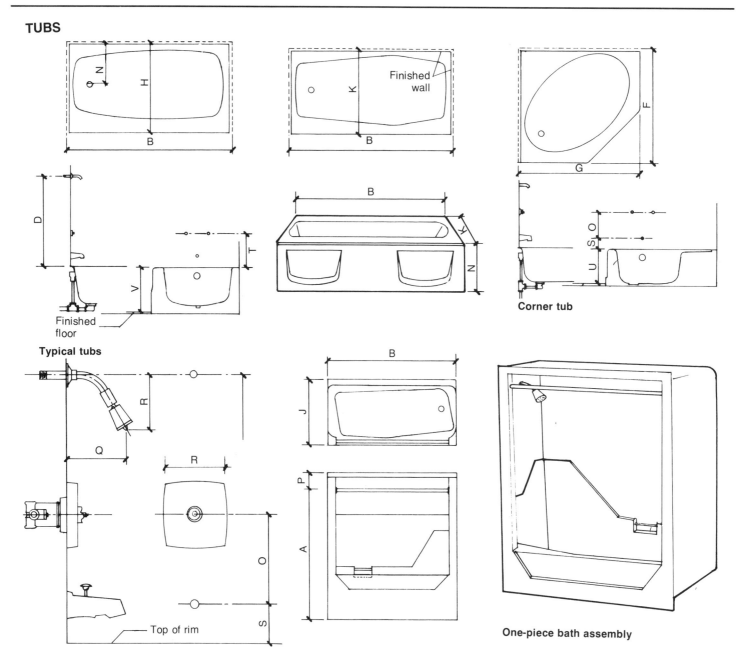

Finished wall

Corner tub

Typical tubs

Finished floor

Top of rim

One-piece bath assembly

WHIRLPOOL TUBS

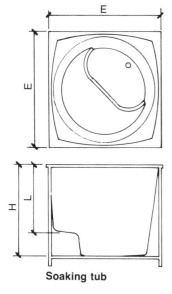

Soaking tub

Jets set for swirl

Jets set for turbulence

Standard tubs with whirlpool jets

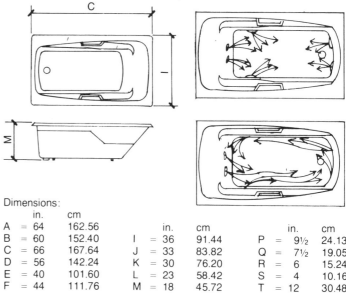

Dimensions:

	in.	cm		in.	cm		in.	cm
A =	64	162.56				P =	9½	24.13
B =	60	152.40	I = 36	91.44		Q =	7½	19.05
C =	66	167.64	J = 33	83.82		R =	6	15.24
D =	56	142.24	K = 30	76.20		S =	4	10.16
E =	40	101.60	L = 23	58.42		T =	12	30.48
F =	44	111.76	M = 18	45.72		U =	14	35.56
G =	48	121.92	N = 15	38.10		V =	16	40.64
H =	32	81.28	O = 10	25.40				

TILE & GYPSUM INSTALLATIONS

Water-resistant gypsum backing board should be attached with nails or screws spaced not more than 8″ (20.32 cm) o.c. When ceramic tile more than 3/8″ (0.95 cm) thick is to be applied, the nail or screw spacing should not exceed 4″ (10.16 cm) o.c. When it is necessary that joints between adjoining pieces of gypsum board (including those at all angle intersections) and nail heads under areas to receive tile or wall panels be treated with joint compound and tape, use either waterproof, nonhardening caulking compound or seal-treated joints and nail heads with a compatible sealer prior to tile installation. (Note: The caulking compound or the sealer must be compatible for use with the adhesive to be used for tile application.)

Interior angles should be reinforced with supports to provide rigid corners. The cut edges and openings around pipes and fixtures should be caulked flush with waterproof, nonhardening caulking compound or adhesive complying with American National Standard for Organic Adhesives for Installation of Ceramic Tile, Type I (ANSI A 136.1). Directions of the manufacturer of the tile, wall panel, or other surfacing material should be followed.

The surfacing material should be applied down to the top surface or edge of the finished shower floor, return, or tub and installed to overlap the top lip of receptor, sub-pan, or tub and should completely cover the areas shown in the perspective drawings on the right.

Corner showers

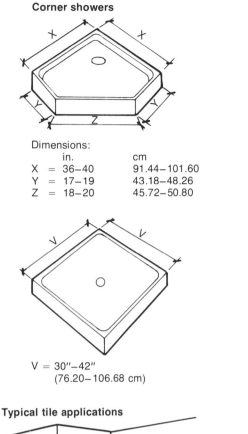

Dimensions:

	in.	cm
X	= 36–40	91.44–101.60
Y	= 17–19	43.18–48.26
Z	= 18–20	45.72–50.80

Height = 6′8″ (2.03 m)

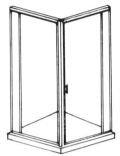

V = 30″–42″
(76.20–106.68 cm)

Height = 6′3″–6′8″
(1.90–1.98 m)

Typical tile applications

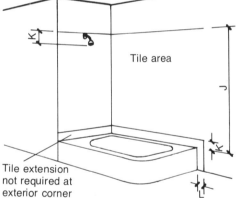

Tile area

Tile area

Tile extension not required at exterior corner

Note: Tile in baths and showers should be installed to the heights shown here.

Dimensions:
I = 6′ (1.83 m)
J = 5′ (1.52 m)
height to be used with shower in tub
K = 6″ (15.24 cm) min. with no shower
L = 4″ (10.16 cm) min.

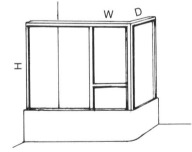

Corner tub with shower door enclosure

Dimensions:

	in.	cm
W	= 57½	146.05
D	= 28	71.12
H	= 58	147.32

Details of tile over gypsum board

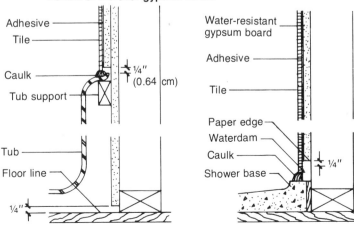

Adhesive
Tile
Caulk
Tub support
¼″ (0.64 cm)
Tub
Floor line
¼″

Water-resistant gypsum board
Adhesive
Tile
Paper edge
Waterdam
Caulk
Shower base
¼″

GYPSUM BOARD WITH ORGANIC ADHESIVE

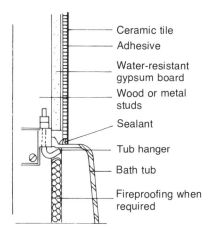

- Ceramic tile
- Adhesive
- Water-resistant gypsum board
- Wood or metal studs
- Sealant
- Tub hanger
- Bath tub
- Fireproofing when required

CEMENT MORTAR

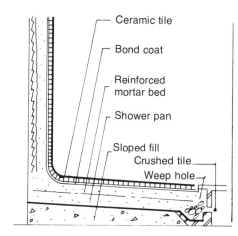

- Ceramic tile
- Bond coat
- Reinforced mortar bed
- Shower pan
- Sloped fill
- Crushed tile
- Weep hole

GYPSUM BOARD WITH WOOD & METAL STUDS & ORGANIC ADHESIVE

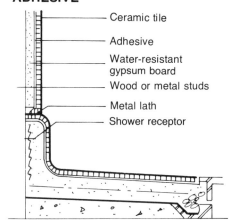

- Ceramic tile
- Adhesive
- Water-resistant gypsum board
- Wood or metal studs
- Metal lath
- Shower receptor

RECOMMENDED USES
In tub enclosures and tub-showers over water-resistant gypsum backing board on wood or metal studs.

Requirements
To be used in conjunction with Methods W223 or W242.*

Water-resistant gypsum backing board single-layer thickness shall be minimum ½" (1.27 cm) thick over studs spaced at maximum 16" (40.64 cm) o.c.

Water-resistant gypsum backing board shall be applied horizontally with the factory paperbound edge spaced a minimum of ¼" (0.64 cm) above the lip of the tub.

Materials
See Methods W223 or W242.*

Preparation by other trades
All openings cut in backing board for plumbing and all cut joints between adjoining pieces shall be sealed with adhesive or other materials recommended by manufacturer of backing board.

All gypsum backing board joints shall be taped and finished.

Preparation by tile trade
Seal surface of taped joints in water-resistant gypsum backing board installations to prevent water damage.

Prime surface before applying adhesive when recommended by adhesive manufacturer.

Allow minimum of 24 hr after tile is set for solvent evaporation before grouting.

Installation specifications
See Methods W223 or W242.*

RECOMMENDED USES
Over wood or concrete subfloors.

Requirements
Slope required in pan or membrane ¼" per foot to weep holes in drain.

Membrane or pan to turn up wall at least 5" (12.70 cm) above high point of shower floor.

Materials
Portlant cement: ASTM C-150 Type 1.
Sand: ASTM C-144.
Mortar: 1 part portland cement, 4 parts damp sand by volume. (Use an admixture to make mortar bed water resistant.)
Reinforcing: 2" X 2" (5.08 X 5.08 cm) X 16/16 gauge wire mesh or equivalent.
Grout: specify type.

Preparation by other trades
Shower floor membrane as required by local Administrative Authority.

Form slope for membrane with cement mortar or preformed liners.

Preparation by tile trade
Surround drain with broken pieces of tile or crushed stone to prevent mortar from blocking weep holes.

Installation specifications
ANSI A108.1

RECOMMENDED USES
In showers over water-resistant gypsum backing board on wood or metal studs.

Requirements
To be used in conjunction with Methods W223 or W242.*

Water-resistant gypsum backing board single-layer thickness shall be minimum ½" thick over studs spaced at maximum 16" o.c.

Water-resistant gypsum backing board shall be applied horizontally with the factory paperbound edge spaced a minimum of ¼" above the lip of the receptor or subpan.

Materials
See Methods W223 or W242.*

Preparation by other trades
All openings cut in backing board for plumbing and all cut joints between adjoining pieces shall be sealed with adhesive or other materials recommended by manufacturer of backing board.

All gypsum backing board joints shall be taped and finished.

See Methods W223 or W242* for additional preparations.

Preparation by tile trade
Seal surface of taped joints in water-resistant gypsum backing board installations to prevent water damage.

Prime surface before applying adhesive when recommended by adhesive manufacturer.

Allow minimum of 24 hr after tile is set for solvent evaporation before grouting.

Installation specifications
See Methods W223 or W242.*

*See pages 154–155.

WATERPROOF MEMBRANE WITH CEMENT MORTAR

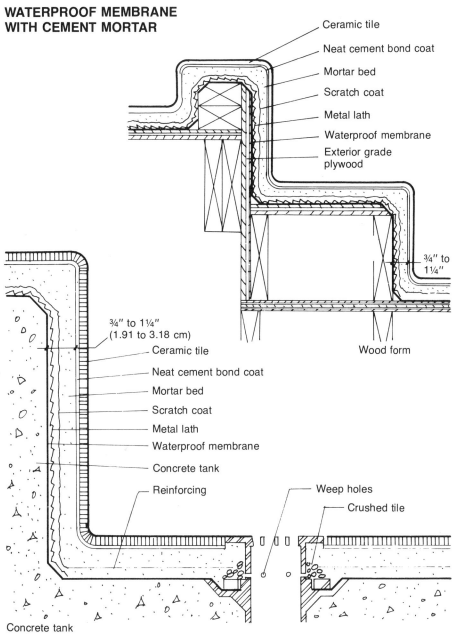

Ceramic tile
Neat cement bond coat
Mortar bed
Scratch coat
Metal lath
Waterproof membrane
Exterior grade plywood

¾" to 1¼"

Wood form

¾" to 1¼"
(1.91 to 3.18 cm)

Ceramic tile
Neat cement bond coat
Mortar bed
Scratch coat
Metal lath
Waterproof membrane
Concrete tank
Reinforcing

Weep holes
Crushed tile

Concrete tank
(preferred)

Requirements

Waterproof membrane required except in slab-on-grade installatons where membrane may be omitted.

Slope tank so that membrane will slope to the drain.

Flange drain with weep holes required.

Wood framing, if used, should be pressure treated and designed to resist deflection and movement.

Preparation by other trades

Test tank, membrane, and drainage fittings for leaks before starting tile work.

Installation methods

Attach metal lath only above water line.

*See page 154.
†See page 156.

WOOD & METAL STUDS

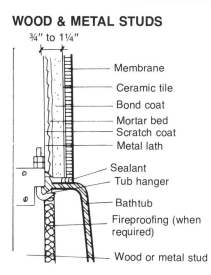

¾" to 1¼"

Membrane
Ceramic tile
Bond coat
Mortar bed
Scratch coat
Metal lath
Sealant
Tub hanger
Bathtub
Fireproofing (when required)
Wood or metal stud

RECOMMENDED USES

Over dry, well-braced wood studs, furring, or metal studs.

Preferred method of istallation over wood studs for bathtubs.

Requirements

Wood studs or furring must be protected from moisture by roofing felt or polyethylene film.

Over metal studs, see Method W241.*

Apply membrane, metal lath, and scratch coat.

Require a leveling coat if variations in scratch coat exceeds ¼" (0.64 cm) in 8' (2.44 m) from the required plane or if thickness of mortar bed would exceed ¾".

Materials

Membrane: 15 lb (1.81 kg) roofing felt or 4 mil polyethelene film.

Portland cement: ASTM C-150 type 1.

Lime: ASTM C-206 Type S or ASTM C-207 Type S.

Sand: ASTM C-144.

Water: Portable.

Scratch coat: 1 part portland cement, ½ part lime, and 4 parts dry sand or 5 parts damp sand; or 1 part portland cement, 3 parts dry sand, or 4 parts damp sand.

Mortar bed: 1 part portland cement, ½ part lime, and 5 parts damp sand to 1 part portland cement, 1 part lime, and 7 parts damp sand, by volume.

Bond coat: portland cement paste. For dry-set or latex portland cement mortar on concrete glass fiber reinforced backer board, follow Method W213.† Dry-set or latex portlant cement mortar.

Grout: Specify type.

Elastometric caulking: After tile work and grout is dry.

Metal studs: ASTM C-645.

Preparation by other trades

Over metal studs, see Method W241.*

Stud spacing not to exceed 16"(40.64 cm)o.c.

Studs square and plumb, opening for recessed bathtubs not to exceed ½" (1.27 cm) more than total length of tub.

Bathtub installed level and supported with metal hangers or on-end grain wood blocks. Fireproofing behind tub when required.

INTERIOR WALLS & FLOORS

Ceramic tile may be considered as a surfacing material over existing wall finishes such as paint, wood paneling, cold glazes (sprayed on plastic), plastic laminates and steel plate, or existing floor surfacing such as epoxy coatings, paint, vinyl or asphalt tile, seamless flooring, exposed concrete, hardwood flooring, and steel plate. Ideally, existing finishes should be completely removed so that the tile work can be placed on the substructure (consult manufacturer's recommendations). However, this is not always practical. The following, therefore, is intended as a general guide for renovation with ceramic tile. In all cases consult the setting material manufacturer or the literature before starting the work. Consideration should be given to covering the existing surface with a more suitable base. For example, badly cracked or irregular walls should be overlaid with firmly attached gypsum board, concrete glass fiber reinforced backer board, or plywood to provide a sound tile-setting base.

Warning: Special installation precautions are necessary when installing thin-set tile over old concrete floors in bakeries, kitchens, and meat processing areas. Fats and greases penetrate into concrete floors and cannot be completely neutralized. Note preparation sections below.

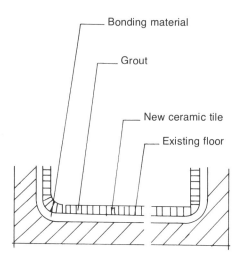

Bonding material

Grout

New ceramic tile

Existing floor

ORGANIC ADHESIVE
Suitable backings
Smooth walls of all types including plaster, gypsum board, plywood, and masonry.

Smooth floors of all types including wood, concrete, and terrazzo in residences or areas of equivalent light performance requirements. Deflection not to exceed 1/360 of span.

New gypsum board nailed or glued over existing walls.

Plastic laminate counter tops and walls.

Requirements
The backing surface must be sound, clean, and dry.

Maximum variation in backing surface shall not exceed ⅛" (0.32 cm) in 8' (2.44 m) from the required plane.

Abrupt irregularities such as trowel marks, ridges, and grains shall be less than 1/32" (0.79 mm) above adjacent area.

Preparation
Roughen surfaces that are glossy or painted or that have loose surface material by sanding or scarifying.

Surface material must be removed if non-compatible with adhesive.

Use primer when recommended by the adhesive manufacturer as proper for the particular backing.

Clean thoroughly to remove all oil, dirt, and dust.

Apply underlayment as needed according to manufacturer's directions.

Tile installation
Follow ANSI A108.4.

DRY-SET OR LATEX-PORTLAND CEMENT MORTAR
Suitable backings
Prepared portland cement plaster, concrete, concrete masonry, structural clay tile, brick or concrete glass fiber reinforced backer bond nailed over existing walls.

New gypsum board nailed or glued over properly furred existing wall in dry areas.

Use water-resistant gypsum backer board in wet areas.

Requirements
The backing surface must be sound, clean, and dry.

Maximum permissible variation in floor surfaces: ⅛" in 10' (3.05 m); in wall surfaces ⅛" in 8' from the required plane.

Preparation
Roughen concrete or masonry walls and floors that are glossy, painted, or effloresced or that have loose surface material. This should be accomplished by sand-blasting, chipping, or scarifying.

Clean thoroughly to remove all sealers, coatings, oil, dirt, and dust to expose masonry surface.

Tile installation
Follow ANSI A108.5 for dry-set mortar and latex-portlant cement mortar.

TILE-SETTING EPOXY & EPOXY ADHESIVE
Suitable backings
Generally all sound wall and floor finishes.

Especially valuable for setting tile floors over nonmasonry surfaces where moderate performance level is required.

Suitable for speedy installation where downtime must be kept to a minimum.

Requirements
Backing surface must be sound, clean, and dry.

Maximum permissible variation in floor surfaces: ⅛" in 10'; in wall surfaces, ⅛" in 8' from the required plane.

Preparation
Roughen surfaces that are glossy, painted, or effloresced or that have loose surface material by sanding or scarifying.

Clean thoroughly to remove all waxes, oil, dirt, and dust.

With epoxy adhesives, use primer when recommended by the manufacturer as proper for the particular backing.

Tile installation
Follow ANSI A108.6 for tile-setting epoxy and manufacturer's specifications for epoxy adhesive.

Epoxy formulations vary with respect to chemical resistance and use on vertical surfaces. Consult manufacturer's specifications.

RECOMMENDED USES
For alteration of ceramic-tiled areas where modernization or a change of design is desired in residences, motels and hotels, restaurants, public rest rooms, and so on.

Also applicable to smooth floors of terrazzo, stone, slate, and so forth.

Requirements
Existing installation must be sound, well bonded, and without structural cracks.

When possible, floor-mounted plumbing and heating fixtures should be removed before beginning work.

Threshold required to adjust between adjacent floors.

Preparation
Remove soap scum, wax, coatings, oil and so on from existing tile surfaces. Mechanical abrasion with a carborundum disk followed by a clear water wash is recommended. Other cleaning methods involve use of soapless detergents, commercial tile cleaners, and, in special cases, solvents or acid. Solvents and acids should be used with care and only when necessary because of their hazardous nature.

Installation must be thoroughly rinsed and dry before setting the new tile.

Materials, grouting, expansion joints, installation specifications
For epoxy mortar or latex-portland cement mortar installation, refer to ANSI A108.6.

For dry-set mortar or latex-portland cement mortar installation, see Method F113.*

For organic adhesive installation refer to ANSI A108.4 and follow manufacturer's directions.

Require current certification that adhesive conforms with ANSI A136.1 from adhesive manufacturer.

Notes: Use Ceramic Tile Floor Performance-Level Requirement Guide. Select adequate installation method.

If installation is not sound, Methods F111* and F141† may be applicable.

*See page 152.
†See page 148.

INTERIOR WALLS

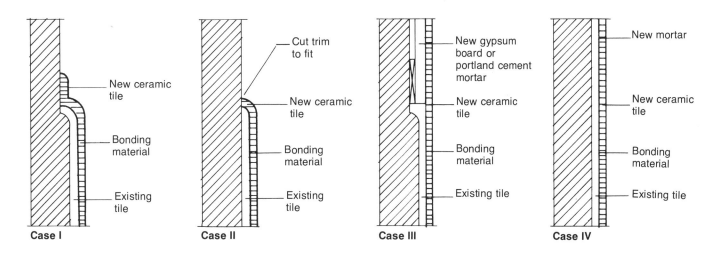

New ceramic tile

Bonding material

Existing tile

Case I

Cut trim to fit

New ceramic tile

Bonding material

Existing tile

Case II

New gypsum board or portland cement mortar

New ceramic tile

Bonding material

Existing tile

Case III

New mortar

New ceramic tile

Bonding material

Existing tile

Case IV

RECOMMENDED USES

For alteration of ceramic-tiled areas where modernization or a change of design is desired in residences, motels and hotels, restaurants, public rest rooms, and so on.

Also applicable to smooth walls of marble, stone, slate, and so forth.

Requirements

Existing installation must be sound, well bonded, and without major structural cracks.

Note: If installation is not sound, Methods W221 and W222* may be applicable.

Materials, grouting, expansion joints, installation specifications

For organic adhesive installation, see Method W223.*

For dry-set or latex-portland cement mortar installation, see Method W213.†

For epoxy mortar installation, refer to ANSI A108.6.

For epoxy adhesive installation, refer to manufacturer's literature.

Preparation

Remove soap scum, wax, coatings, oil, and so on from existing tile surfaces. Mechanical abrasion with a carborundum disk followed by a clear water wash is recommended. Other cleaning methods involve use of soapless detergents, commercial tile cleaners, and, in special cases, solvents or acid. Solvents and acids should be used with care and only when necessary because of their hazardous nature.

Installation must be thoroughly rinsed and dry before setting the new tile.

Case I: Prepare wall above tile to receive trim tile as shown.

Case II: Cut trim tile to fit over existing trim.

Cases III & IV: Apply new gypsum board above existing wainscot tile to prepare for full wall tiling.

Use portland cement mortar, water-resistant gypsum backing board, or concrete glass fiber reinforced backer board in tub enclosures and shower stalls.

In wet areas the application of water-resistant gypsum backer board over any base that causes a vapor barrier to exist, such as old tile or paint shown in Cases III and IV, will lead to failure unless such barrier is vented.

RENOVATION OF SHOWER RECEPTOR USING CEMENT MORTAR

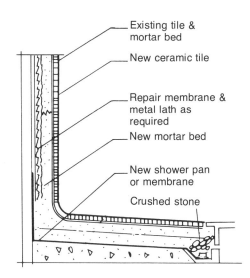

Existing tile & mortar bed

New ceramic tile

Repair membrane & metal lath as required

New mortar bed

New shower pan or membrane

Crushed stone

RECOMMENDED USES

Over wood or concrete subfloors; where old shower pan has failed.

Requirements

Remove existing shower receptor, waterproof pan, and wall tile as required to install new pan.

Replace any damaged wall or floor substrate materials.

Slope required in new pan or membrane ¼" (0.64 cm) per foot to weep holes in drain.

New membrane or pan to turn up wall at least 5" (12.70 cm) above high point of shower floor.

Materials & installation

For gypsum board walls, see Methods W223* or W242 (see page 154).

For mortar bed walls, see Methods W222, W231, or W241 (see pages 154–155).

For concrete glass fiber mesh reinforced backer board walls, see Method W213.†

*See page 155.
†See page 156.

CERAMIC COUNTERTOPS OVER WOOD BASE & CEMENT MORTAR

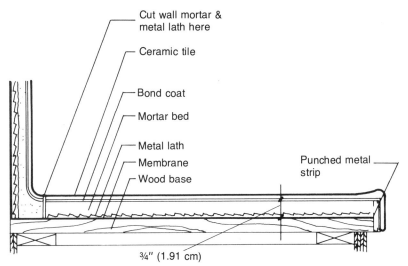

Cut wall mortar & metal lath here

Ceramic tile

Bond coat

Mortar bed

Metal lath

Membrane

Wood base

Punched metal strip

¾" (1.91 cm)

STEAM ROOM WITH MEMBRANE

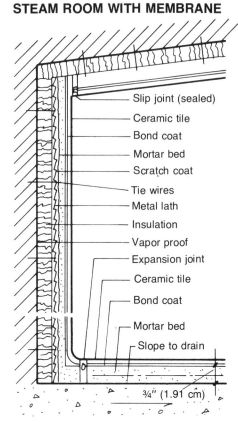

Slip joint (sealed)

Ceramic tile

Bond coat

Mortar bed

Scratch coat

Tie wires

Metal lath

Insulation

Vapor proof

Expansion joint

Ceramic tile

Bond coat

Mortar bed

Slope to drain

¾" (1.91 cm)

RECOMMENDED USES
On countertops, drainboards, lavatory tops, and so on.
Preferred method where sink or lavatory is to be recessed.

Requirements
The bottom edge of the countertop trim must be set the proper distance above the finish floor material to allow clearance for dishwashers, compactors, and so forth.
Cut lath off at corner as shown.
Use extra-duty glazed tile or unglazed tile.

Materials
Membrane: 15 lb (6.81 kg) roofing felt or 4 mil polyethylene film or duplex type reinforced asphalt paper.
Portland cement: ASTM C-150 Type 1.
Sand: ASTM C-144.
Water: Potable.

Mortar: 1 part portland cement. 6 parts damp sand by volume.
Reinforcing: 3.4 lb (1.54 kg) metal lath, 2" X 2" (5.08 X 5.08 cm) welded wire mesh or other approved wire mesh.
Grout: Specify type.

Preparation by other trades
Base to be 1" X 6" (2.54 X 15.24 cm) boards with ¼" (0.64 cm) gap between boards or ¾" (1.91 cm) exterior plywood with dot and dash saw cuts 6" X 8" (15.24 to 20.32 cm) o.c. through the length of the plywood board to prevent warping.
Where overhangs or cantilever counters are used, adequate support must be provided to prevent movement.

Preparation by tile trade
A punched metal strip attached to the front

edge of the cabinet is used in some geographical areas as a screed and support for the countertop trim. It is filled with wall mortar.

Installation specifications
ANSI A108.1.

THIN-SET MORTAR

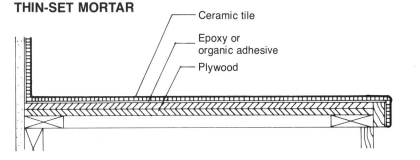

Ceramic tile

Epoxy or organic adhesive

Plywood

RECOMMENDED USES
On countertops where thin-set method is desired.

Requirements
¾" exterior plywood base required.
The bottom edge of the countertop trim must be set the proper distance above the finish floor material to allow clearance for dishwashers, compactors, and so on.

Materials
Epoxy mortar: ANSI A118.3.
Organic adhesive: ANSI A136.1. Type I.
Dry-set or latex-portland cement mortar over glass mesh mortar units.
Modified epoxy emulsion mortar.
Grout: Specify type.

Preparation by other trades
When tile is set with epoxy, leave ¼" gap

between sheets of plywood. Apply batten to under side of sheets to cover gap.
Where overhangs or cantilever counters are used, adequate support must be provided to prevent movement.

Preparation by tile trade
When tile is set with epoxy, completely fill gap between sheets of plywood with epoxy.
Protect plywood from exposure to water and high humidity.

Installation specifications
Adhesive: ANSI A108.4.
Epoxy: ANSI A108.6.
Dry-set or latex portland mortar: ANSI A108.5.

Requirements
Steam rooms require a continuous waterproof membrane on all surfaces to prevent moisture from penetrating adjoining spaces.
Most membranes will require insulation on walls and ceilings to protect them from excessive heat. Insulation must be capable of withstanding 240° F.
Install open slip joints in all corners between walls and ceilings and to divide areas that exceed 16" (4.88 m) in length.
Anchor galvanized metal lath to walls and ceilings with monel or stainless steel wire extending through insulation to supporting members.
Slope ceilings (2" per foot minimum) to avoid condensation from dripping onto occupants (sometimes sloped to center to minimize run-down on walls).

Tile installation
Floors: Follow Method F121 (see page 149).
Walls and ceiling: Follow Method W221 with waterproof membrane (see page 155).

PART THREE

COMMERCIAL GRAPHIC AND DESIGN STANDARDS

Chapter 14

PUBLIC WASHROOMS

INDUSTRIAL WASHROOM WITH SHOWERS

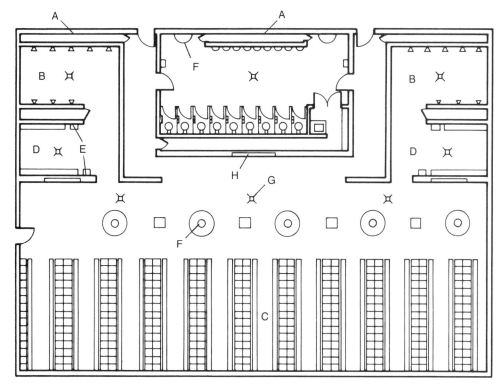

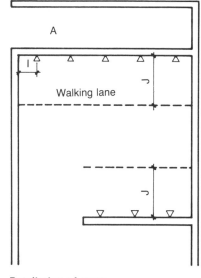

Detail plan of gang shower placement

Scale: 3/32″ = 2′ (0.24 cm = 60.96 cm)
Note: 315 lockers provided in this space.

Legend & dimensions (not to scale):
A = plumbing space
B = shower rooms
C = lockers/benches
D = dressing rooms
E = waste disposals
F = wash fountains
G = floor drains
H = recessed mirror
I = 24″ (60.96 cm)
J = 50″ (127.00 cm)

Recommended fixture ratio

Toilets		Urinals	
People	No.	People	No.
	1	1-20	1
	2	21-60	2
	3	61-100	3
	4		
75-100	5		
Over 100	*		

*One for each additional 30 people.

DESIGN CRITERIA

Floors, walls, & drains
Waterproof materials such as terrazzo or ceramic tile are essential for maintenance. Drains must be installed to permit quick hosing and mopping. Wall surfaces should be moisture-proof and nonporous for easy cleaning.

Coved floors eliminate dirt-catching corners. Splashboards can be placed behind wash basins, or the entire washroom can be wainscoted as desired.

Heating & ventilation
Mechanical ventilation should allow 20 air changes an hour to remove objectionable odors. Outside air intake should be located at points where the air is unpolluted. Air temperature should be maintained at approximately 70° F.

Lighting
Bright light in washrooms tends to be associated with sanitation and has a positive psychological effect on employees and users of public restrooms. Lighting fixtures should be located over facilities and recessed for better reflection and easier cleaning. Fluorescent lights of 30 footcandles or more are recommended.

WASHROOM INSTALLATION CHECKLIST
The following items are frequently specified for washrooms:
____ Couch
____ Courtesy areas
____ Facial tissue dispensers
____ Floor drains
____ Foot flush valves
____ Grab bars
____ Hair blow dryer
____ Hand blow dryers
____ Lockers
____ Mirrors: standard or tilted
____ Mixing faucets
____ Napkin receptacle
____ Package shelves
____ Paper cup dispenser
____ Paper towel dispensers
____ Powder bars
____ Sanitary napkin fixtures
____ Soap dispensers
____ Supply closets
____ Toilet seat cover dispensers
____ Toilet stall shelf
____ Toilet tissue dispensers
____ Towel cabinets
____ Vanity cabinets
____ Wall-hung partitions
____ Wall-hung urns
____ Wash fountains
____ Waste receptacles

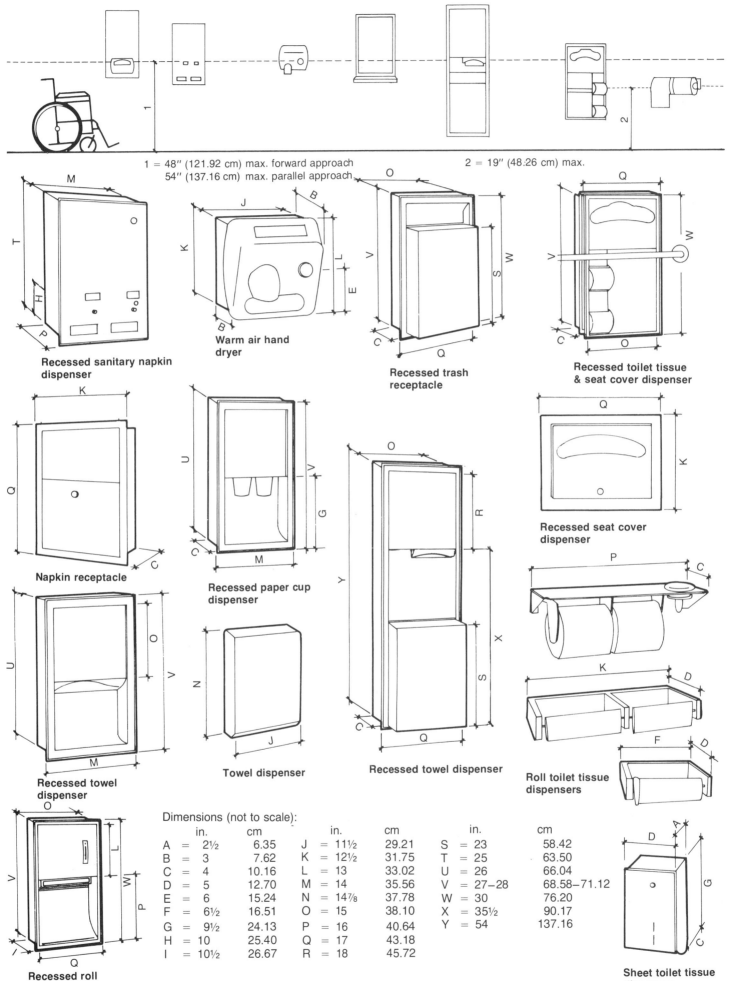

1 = 48″ (121.92 cm) max. forward approach
54″ (137.16 cm) max. parallel approach

2 = 19″ (48.26 cm) max.

Recessed sanitary napkin dispenser

Warm air hand dryer

Recessed trash receptacle

Recessed toilet tissue & seat cover dispenser

Napkin receptacle

Recessed paper cup dispenser

Recessed seat cover dispenser

Recessed towel dispenser

Towel dispenser

Recessed towel dispenser

Roll toilet tissue dispensers

Recessed roll paper dispenser

Sheet toilet tissue dispenser

Dimensions (not to scale):

	in.	cm		in.	cm		in.	cm
A =	2½	6.35	J =	11½	29.21	S =	23	58.42
B =	3	7.62	K =	12½	31.75	T =	25	63.50
C =	4	10.16	L =	13	33.02	U =	26	66.04
D =	5	12.70	M =	14	35.56	V =	27–28	68.58–71.12
E =	6	15.24	N =	14⅞	37.78	W =	30	76.20
F =	6½	16.51	O =	15	38.10	X =	35½	90.17
G =	9½	24.13	P =	16	40.64	Y =	54	137.16
H =	10	25.40	Q =	17	43.18			
I =	10½	26.67	R =	18	45.72			

SOAP DISPENSERS

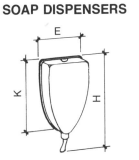

Powder

Liquid

Liquid

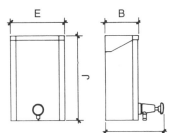

Powder

Liquid

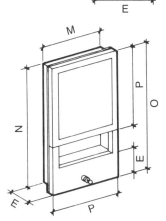

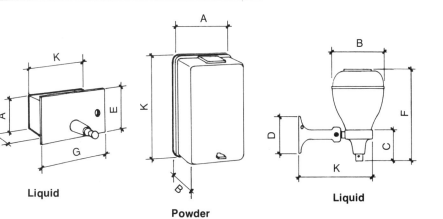

Tank at center   Tank at end

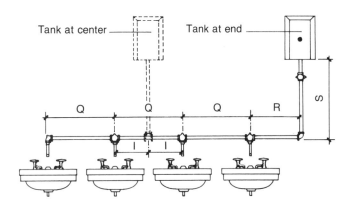

Soap tank installation

When specifying soap tanks, it is recommended that the tank's capacity be directly related to estimated traffic rather than the number of soap valves used or lavatories serviced.

For example, a conservative figure would be one hand-washing with soap and water per day per person. An office building with 3,000 employees on a normal 8-hr day, using liquid soap in a lather-dispensing system, would consume approximately 1 gallon of soap. A straight liquid system would provide approximately 30% less.

Recessed liquid dispenser with shelf, mirror, & towel holder

CIGARETTE URNS

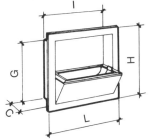

Semirecessed

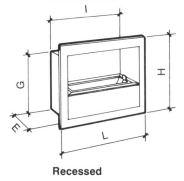

Recessed

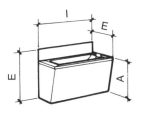

Surface mounted

URINAL ASH TRAYS

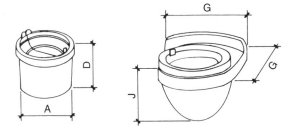

Dimensions (not to scale):

	in.	cm		in.	cm
A =	4	10.16	K =	8½	21.59
B =	3½	8.89	L =	14	35.56
C =	2	5.08	M =	15	38.10
D =	2½	6.35	N =	28±	71.12
E =	5½±	13.97	O =	30±	76.20
F =	6±	15.24	P =	19±	48.26
G =	9½	24.13	Q =	24	60.96
H =	11½	29.21	R =	18	45.72
I =	12	30.48	S =	36	91.44
J =	7½	19.05			

HOTEL BATH ACCESSORIES

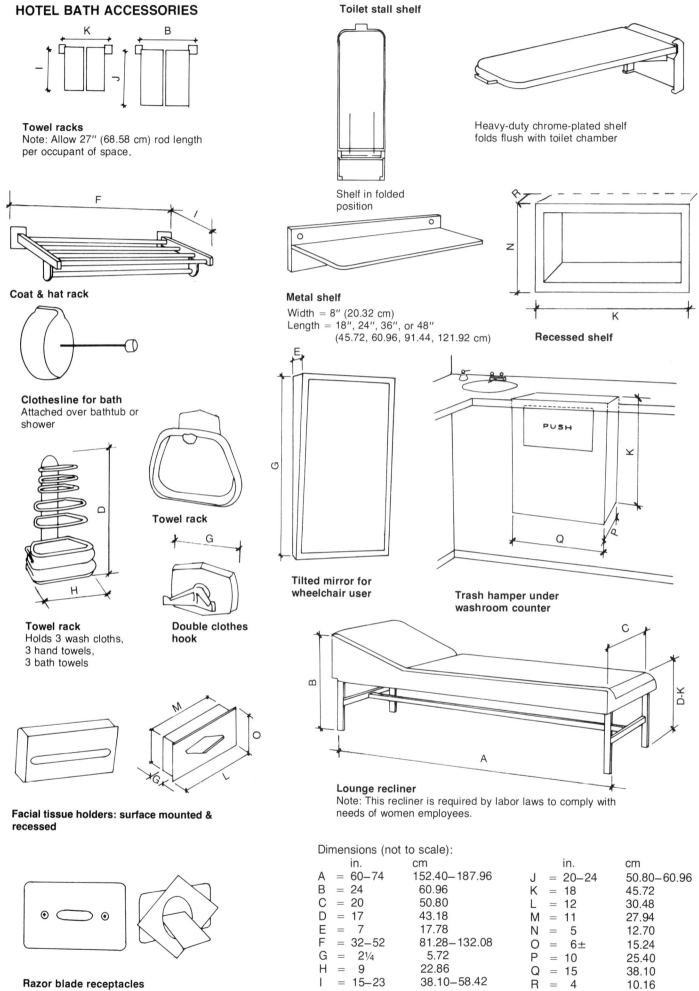

Towel racks
Note: Allow 27″ (68.58 cm) rod length per occupant of space.

Coat & hat rack

Clothesline for bath
Attached over bathtub or shower

Towel rack
Holds 3 wash cloths, 3 hand towels, 3 bath towels

Towel rack

Double clothes hook

Facial tissue holders: surface mounted & recessed

Razor blade receptacles

Toilet stall shelf

Shelf in folded position

Metal shelf
Width = 8″ (20.32 cm)
Length = 18″, 24″, 36″, or 48″
    (45.72, 60.96, 91.44, 121.92 cm)

Heavy-duty chrome-plated shelf folds flush with toilet chamber

Recessed shelf

Tilted mirror for wheelchair user

Trash hamper under washroom counter

PUSH

Lounge recliner
Note: This recliner is required by labor laws to comply with needs of women employees.

Dimensions (not to scale):

	in.	cm		in.	cm
A =	60–74	152.40–187.96	J =	20–24	50.80–60.96
B =	24	60.96	K =	18	45.72
C =	20	50.80	L =	12	30.48
D =	17	43.18	M =	11	27.94
E =	7	17.78	N =	5	12.70
F =	32–52	81.28–132.08	O =	6±	15.24
G =	2¼	5.72	P =	10	25.40
H =	9	22.86	Q =	15	38.10
I =	15–23	38.10–58.42	R =	4	10.16

SINGLE BOWL CABINET

Dimensions:

	in.	cm
A =	34	86.36
B =	29	73.66
C =	22	55.88
D =	26	66.04
E =	24	60.96
F =	12	30.48
G =	39–102	99.06–259.08
H =	5	12.70
I =	4	10.16
J =	8	20.32

Special construction is frequently required for lavatory cabinets in public washrooms.
Accessories: Towel dispenser, waste receptacle, and soap dispenser.

2" X 8"
(5.08 X 20.32 cm)
wood block,
full length of
cabinet

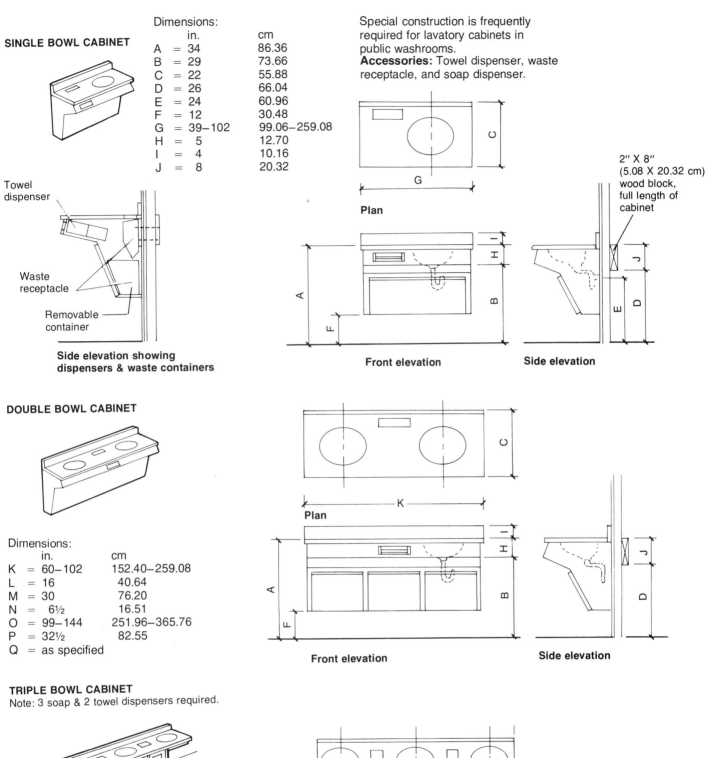

Towel dispenser

Waste receptacle

Removable container

Side elevation showing dispensers & waste containers

Plan

Front elevation

Side elevation

DOUBLE BOWL CABINET

Dimensions:

	in.	cm
K =	60–102	152.40–259.08
L =	16	40.64
M =	30	76.20
N =	6½	16.51
O =	99–144	251.96–365.76
P =	32½	82.55
Q =	as specified	

Plan

Front elevation

Side elevation

TRIPLE BOWL CABINET
Note: 3 soap & 2 towel dispensers required.

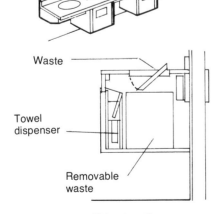

Waste

Towel dispenser

Removable waste

Side elevation

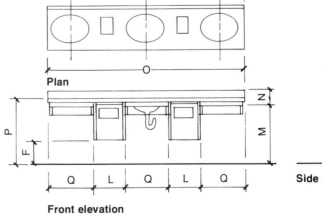

Plan

Front elevation

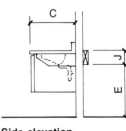

Side elevation

In multiple-stall restrooms, be sure (1) the entry is properly laid out; (2) all passageways are 3'8" (111.76 cm) wide minimum; and (3) there is a 5' X 5' (152.40 X 152.40 cm) wheelchair turn-around space. Space under the lavatory may be used as part of this space, but only that portion which is clear to a height of 27" (68.58 cm). (4) The working parts of at least one of each type of dispenser, receptacle, and vendor (coin slots, pushbuttons, dispenser openings) are no more than 40" (101.60 cm) above the floor. (5) Waste receptacles are recessed into the wall, out of everyone's way. Free-standing, movable receptacles may block the corridor and become a barrier for the disabled.

Usually the end toilet compartment is designed to accommodate

the handicapped. The door is out-swinging and hinged on the wall side to avoid interference with other compartments.

Toilet compartments for the disabled should be at least 38" (96.52 cm) wide for front entry and 42" (106.68 cm) wide for side entry compartments and have 4' (121.92 cm) of clear space in front of the toilet to allow the wheelchair to enter and the door to close.

Toilet compartments with side entry require a wider door than those having front entry to provide additional turning space for wheelchairs. Side-entry compartments may occupy the entire end of the room when room width does not permit sufficient depth for a front-entry toilet compartment for the disabled.

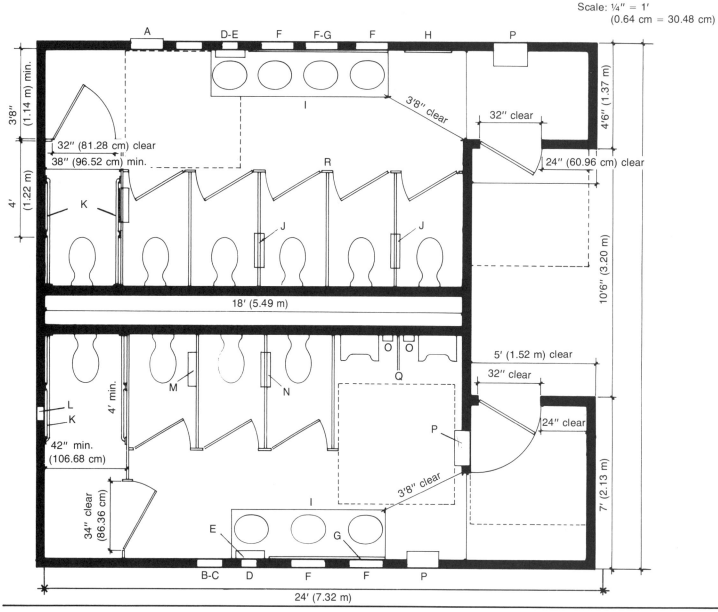

Scale: ¼" = 1'
(0.64 cm = 30.48 cm)

Legend:
A = recessed feminine napkin dispenser
B = recessed waste receptacle
C = recessed paper towel dispenser
D = recessed soap dispenser
E = fixed tilt mirror 16" X 30" (40.64 X 76.20 cm)
F = multipurpose unit with paper towel dispenser and soap dispenser
G = mirror
H = full length mirror 24" X 60" (60.96 X 152.40 cm)
I = laminated plastic countertop

mounting height 34" (86.36 cm) from countertop to floor; 30" (76.20 cm) clear from bottom of 4" apron to floor
J = partition-mounted toilet seat cover dispenser, feminine napkin disposal, toilet tissue dispenser
K = wheelchair toilet compartment grab bar, 1½" (3.81 cm) diameter, 1½" clearance from wall
L = recessed multiroll toilet tissue dispenser (below bar)

M = surface-mounted toilet seat cover dispenser, roll toilet tissue dispenser
N = partition-mounted toilet seat cover dispenser, roll toilet tissue dispenser
O = stainless steel wall-mounted ash-tray
P = recessed waste receptacle
Q = laminated plastic wall-hung urinal screen
R = ceiling-hung laminated plastic toilet compartments

GRAB BARS

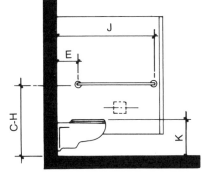

Grab bars shall support
250 lb (113.50 kg)
Note: Towel bars cannot
serve as grab bars.

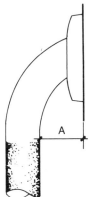

The textured portions
of grab bars serve as
cues to the blind

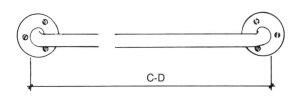

Projecting accessories must be located so
they will not interfere with the use of grab bars.
Where possible, accessories within a toilet
compartment should be located below the grab
bars. Placing them on the panels or side walls
just back of the front edge of the toilet bowl will
keep the wheelchair area free of hazardous
projections.

TOILET FACILITIES

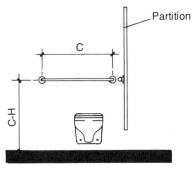

BATHING FACILITIES: TUBS

See page 407 for shower stall design for the handicapped.

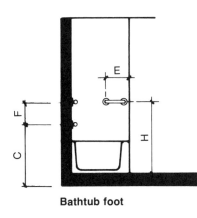

Bathtub foot

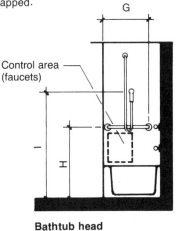

Bathtub head

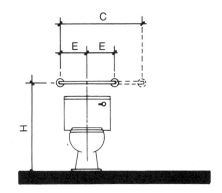

Bathtub side

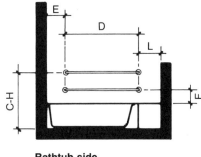

Alternate bathtub side

Dimensions:

	in.	cm		in.	cm
A =	1½	3.81	G =	24	60.96
B =	1¼	3.18	H =	33	83.82
C =	36	91.44	I =	54	137.16
D =	48	121.92	J =	52	132.08
E =	12	50.80	K =	17–19	43.18–48.26
F =	9	22.86	L =	15	38.10

Note: Pages 405–407 are based on ANSI A117.1.

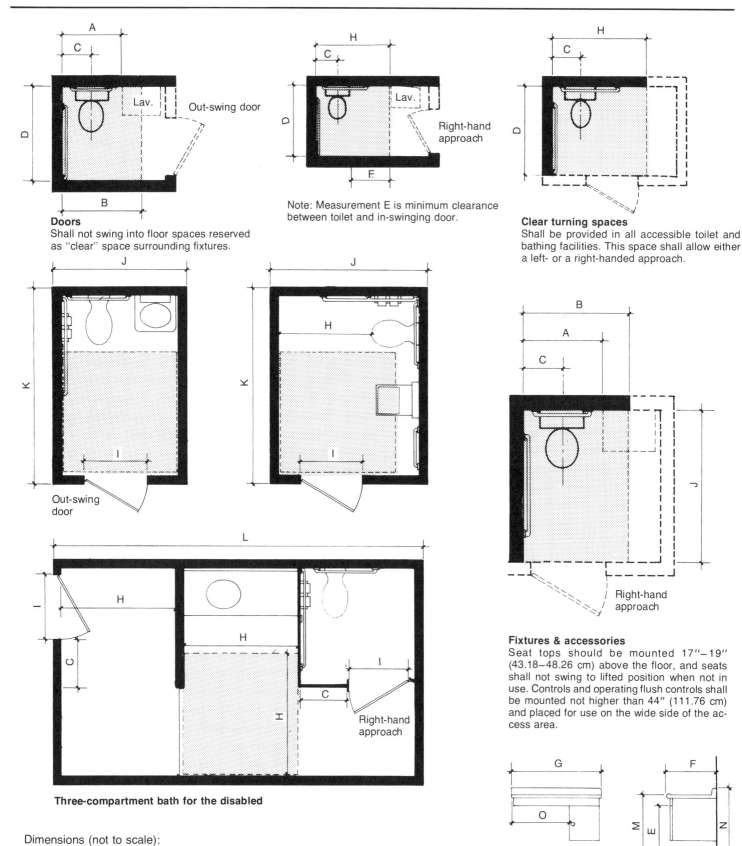

Doors
Shall not swing into floor spaces reserved as "clear" space surrounding fixtures.

Note: Measurement E is minimum clearance between toilet and in-swinging door.

Out-swing door

Clear turning spaces
Shall be provided in all accessible toilet and bathing facilities. This space shall allow either a left- or a right-handed approach.

Right-hand approach

Fixtures & accessories
Seat tops should be mounted 17"–19" (43.18–48.26 cm) above the floor, and seats shall not swing to lifted position when not in use. Controls and operating flush controls shall be mounted not higher than 44" (111.76 cm) and placed for use on the wide side of the access area.

Three-compartment bath for the disabled

Washbasin cabinets
Designed for use by the disabled, cabinets should not exceed 34" (86.36 cm) in height

Dimensions (not to scale):
A = 36" (91.44 cm)   F = 24" (60.96 cm)   K = 8'5" (2.59 m)
B = 48" (121.92 cm)   G = 44" (111.76 cm)   L = 14" (35.56 cm)
C = 18" (45.72 cm)   H = 60"–66" (152.40–167.64 cm)   M = 34" (86.36 cm)
D = 56" (142.24 cm)   I = 32" (81.28 cm)   N = 38" (96.52 cm)
E = 30" (76.20 cm)   J = 5'5" (1.67 m)   O = 31" (78.74 cm)

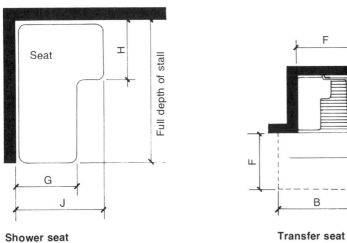

Shower seat

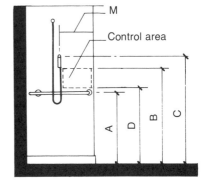

Transfer seat

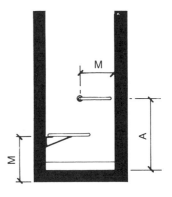

Elevation of shower back wall with seat

Note: Seats shall safely support a 250 lb (113.50 kg) continuous load without deflecting. Seats shall not move during use.

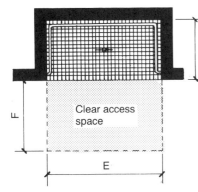

Shower for wheelchair entry

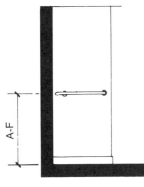

Grabrail height

Elevation of roll-in shower
Note: Shower curbs shall be no higher than ½" (1.27 cm) beveled.

Clear access space

Control area

Elevation of control wall
Note: The shower spray unit must have a flexible hose 5' (1.52 m) long (min.).

Dimensions:

	in.	cm		in.	cm
A	= 33	83.82	H	= 15	38.10
B	= 48	121.92	I	= 30	76.20
C	= 54	137.16	J	= 22	55.88
D	= 38	96.52	K	= 75	190.50
E	= 60	152.40	L	= 27	68.58
F	= 36	91.44	M	= 18	45.72
G	= 16	40.64			

Note: For more information consult the *U.S. Architectural and Transportation Barriers Compliance Requirements*; see Part 1190.150.

Note: In-tub seats shall be portable

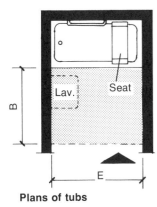

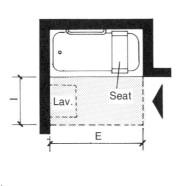

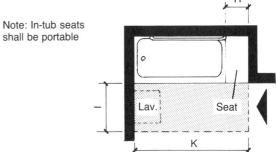

Plans of tubs

Notes: Areas within dotted lines indicate clear floor space for wheelchair use.
*These dimensions are based on ANSI A117.1, which apply to any facilities that provide care for the disabled or the elderly.

STANDARD & STOCK HEIGHT TOILET SCREENS

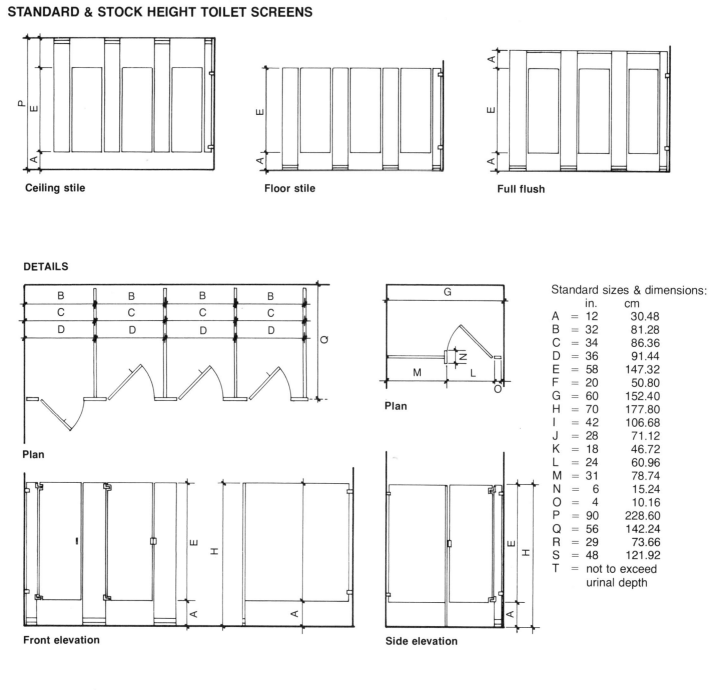

Ceiling stile

Floor stile

Full flush

DETAILS

Plan

Plan

Front elevation

Side elevation

Standard sizes & dimensions:

		in.	cm
A	=	12	30.48
B	=	32	81.28
C	=	34	86.36
D	=	36	91.44
E	=	58	147.32
F	=	20	50.80
G	=	60	152.40
H	=	70	177.80
I	=	42	106.68
J	=	28	71.12
K	=	18	46.72
L	=	24	60.96
M	=	31	78.74
N	=	6	15.24
O	=	4	10.16
P	=	90	228.60
Q	=	56	142.24
R	=	29	73.66
S	=	48	121.92
T	=	not to exceed urinal depth	

URINAL SCREENS

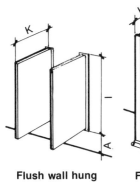

Flush wall hung

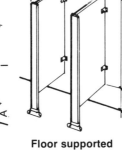

Floor supported

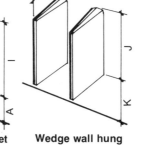

Wall hung, bracket supported

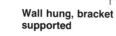

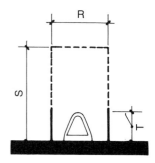

Wedge wall hung

Note: Handicapped use requires that urinal shields not extend beyond the front edge of the urinal rim (T).

Disabled requirements

URINALS

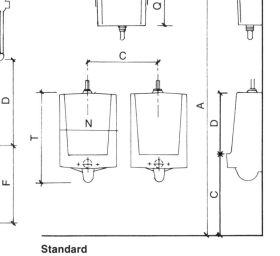

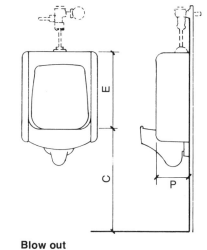

Siphon jet

Standard

Blow out

Note: Standard placement
is 24″ (60.96 cm) o.c.

Dimensions (not to scale):
A = 99″ (251.46 cm)
B = 48″± (121.92 cm)
C = 24″ (60.96 cm)
D = 19″± (48.26 cm)
E = 18″ (45.72 cm)
F = 17½″ (43.82 cm)
G = 16¼″ (41.28 cm)
H = 25¾″ (65.41 cm)
I = 10″ (25.40 cm)
J = 15″± (38.10 cm)
K = 14″± (35.56 cm)
L = 9″ (22.86 cm)

M = 29½″ (74.93 cm)
N = 8″ (20.32 cm)
O = 16″ (40.64 cm)
P = 8¼″ (20.96 cm)
Q = 12½″ (31.75 cm)
R = 38″ (96.52 cm)
S = 4′, 5′, 6′
 (1.22, 1.52, 1.83 cm)
T = 28″ (71.12 cm)
U = 27″ (68.58 cm)
V = 17″ (43.18 cm) max.
W = 35½″ (90.17 cm)

Trough
Finished floor

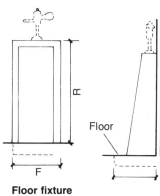

Barrier-free installation

WATER CLOSETS

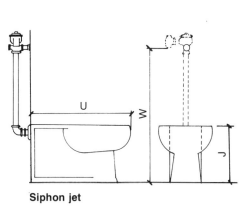

Siphon jet

Note: Finished floor should be sloped to
drain into the lip of the floor urinal.

Pit should be provided in the rough floor
deep enough to allow the lip of the urinal
to set flush with the edge of the sloped
finished floor.

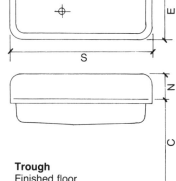

Floor fixture

BIDET

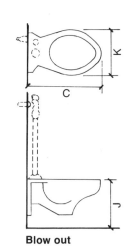

Blow out

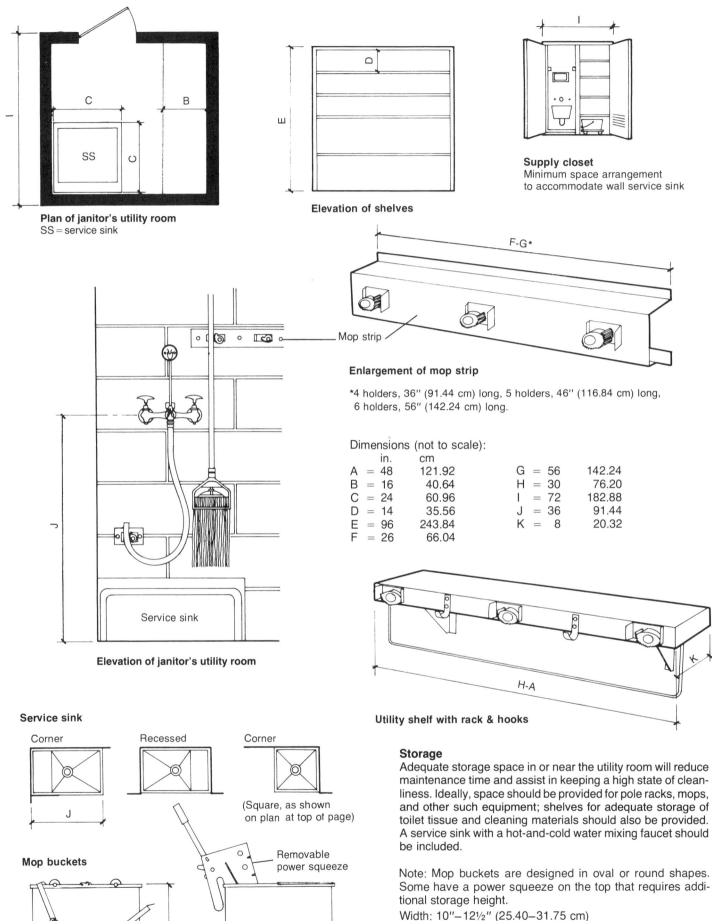

Plan of janitor's utility room
SS = service sink

Elevation of shelves

Supply closet
Minimum space arrangement
to accommodate wall service sink

Mop strip

Enlargement of mop strip

*4 holders, 36" (91.44 cm) long, 5 holders, 46" (116.84 cm) long,
6 holders, 56" (142.24 cm) long.

Dimensions (not to scale):

	in.	cm			in.	cm
A	= 48	121.92		G	= 56	142.24
B	= 16	40.64		H	= 30	76.20
C	= 24	60.96		I	= 72	182.88
D	= 14	35.56		J	= 36	91.44
E	= 96	243.84		K	= 8	20.32
F	= 26	66.04				

Service sink

Elevation of janitor's utility room

Utility shelf with rack & hooks

Service sink

Corner

Recessed

Corner

(Square, as shown
on plan at top of page)

J

Mop buckets

Removable
power squeeze

Storage

Adequate storage space in or near the utility room will reduce
maintenance time and assist in keeping a high state of cleanliness. Ideally, space should be provided for pole racks, mops,
and other such equipment; shelves for adequate storage of
toilet tissue and cleaning materials should also be provided.
A service sink with a hot-and-cold water mixing faucet should
be included.

Note: Mop buckets are designed in oval or round shapes.
Some have a power squeeze on the top that requires additional storage height.
Width: 10"–12½" (25.40–31.75 cm)
Length: oval = 13¼"–15¾ (33.66–40.01 cm); round =
15"–17" (38.10–43.18 cm) dia.
Height: 10"–15" (25.40–38.10 cm)

Designation Description

Washroom Equipment & Accessories
Federal Specification. WW-P-541/8A (GSA-FSS), October 12, 1971, & Amendment-1, June 17, 1974, Plumbing Fixtures (Accessories, Land Use).

Designation	Description
Type I, Class 1	**Toilet Tissue Dispensers**
Mounting S	Surface Mounted
Style A	Roller mounted on 2 support brackets
Style B	Roller mounted on single continuous bracket
Kind a	Household
Kind b	Medium duty, retarded action
Kind c	Heavy duty, anti-pilfer
Style C	Oval roller on single continuous bracket
Style D	Two rollers, side by side on single continuous bracket
Style G	Cabinet, 2 vertical rolls
Style J	Cabinet, folded tissue
Mounting R	Recessed
Style G	Cabinet, 2 vertical rolls
Style K	Single roller mounted
Mounting P	Partition mounted
Type I, Class 2	**Toilet Seat Cover Dispensers**
Mounting S	Surface mounted
Style L	Seat cover only
Style M	With sanitary napkin disposal
Style M	With sanitary napkin disposal & toilet tissue dispenser
Mounting R	Recessed
Style L	Seat cover only
Style M	With sanitary napkin disposal & toilet tissue dispenser
Mounting P	Partition mounted
Style M	With sanitary napkin disposal
Style M	With sanitary napkin disposal & toilet tissue dispenser
Type I, Class 3	**Paper Towel Dispensers**
Mounting S	Surface mounted
Style N	Folded towels, C & M fold Single fold
Kind a-Household	Folded towels
Kind b-Heavy duty, anti-pilfer	Folded towels, C & M fold Single fold
Style O	Rolled paper towel dispenser
Mounting R	Recessed
Style P	Without waste receptacle
Kind a	Towel compartment, mirror door, soap dispenser, cup dispenser, with or without light & convenience outlet
Kind b	Towel compartment, utility shelf, mirror door, soap dispenser and recessed shelf
Kind d	Towel compartment, stainless steel door, soap dispenser, with or without cup dispenser

Designation	Description
Kind e	Towel compartment, stainless steel door
Kind f	Towel compartment concealed behind wall or mirror, soap dispenser and recessed shelf
Style Q	Folded paper towel dispenser with semirecessed waste receptacle
Style T	Folded paper towel dispenser with waste receptacle
Type I, Class 4	**Facial tissue dispensers**
Mounting S	Surface mounted
Mounting R	Recessed
Type I, Class 5	**Sanitary napkin dispensers**
Mounting S	Surface mounted sanitary napkin or tampon dispensers
Mounting R	Recessed sanitary napkin or tampon dispensers
Mounting S and R Capacities	
a	22 napkins only
c	15 napkins or 20 tampons
d	15 napkins and 22 tampons
f	20 napkins and 20 tampons
Type II	**Waste Receptacles**
Mounting S	Surface and floor mounted
Mounting R	Recessed mounted, .3 to 1.6 cu ft cap.
Mounting SR	Semirecessed, open top or covered
1.6 cu ft cap.	5-7/16" ext. from wall, 2¾" recess 4½" ext. from wall, 3¾" recess
2.4 cu ft cap.	8½" ext. from wall, 3¾" recess 4" ext. from wall, 8" recess 8" ext. from wall, 4" recess Semirecessed, with push door
Mounting P	Partition mounted
Type III, Class 1	**Slide Door Medicine Cabinets**
Mounting S	Surface mounted
Mounting R	Recessed
Type III, Class 2	**Swing Door Medicine Cabinets**
Mounting S	Surface mounted
Mounting R	Recessed
Type IV, Class 1	**Towel Bars**
Mounting S	Surface mounted Square bar
	Round bar
Type IV, Class 2	**Corrosion Resistant Grab Bars**
	Surface mounted

Designation Description

Type IV, Class 3	**Soap & Bar**
Type V, Class 2 Surface mounted	**Shelves** Single metal shelf with or without ashtray
Type VI, Class 1 Mounting S	**Soap Holders** Surface mounted With or without drain holes For shower
Type VI, Class 2 Mounting R	**Soap Holders** Recessed
Type VI, Class 3 Mounting S	**Toothbrush & tumbler** **Holder** Surface mounted

Soap Dispensers

Federal specification, FF-D-00396G (GSA-FSS), February 11, 1972, Soap Dispensers.

Type I	Liquid
Type III	Power
Type IV	Lather

Mirrors

Federal Specification, DD-M-0041b (GSA-FSS), April 5, 1968 & Amendment-1, April 7, 1970, Mirrors.

Class 2, Style E	**Metal Frame, Stainless Steel**
Grade 1	Type 302 stainless steel
Grade 2	Type 430 stainless steel

Designation Description

Federal Specification, WW-P-541b, Interim Amendment-6, November 5, 1963, Plumbing Fixtures, Land Use.

Type 447	Toilet Paper Cabinet, Surface Mounted
Type 448	Toilet Paper Cabinet, Recessed
Type 449	Cabinet for Folded Paper Towels
Type 450	Soap Holder
Type 451	Tumbler & Toothbrush Holder
Type 452	Double Robe Hook
Type 454	Metal Shelf
Type 455	Towel Bar
Type 456	Toilet Paper Holder, Surface Mounted
Type 457	Toilet Paper Holder, Recessed
Type 458	Grab Bars, Vertical
Type 459	Soap & Bar, Recessed
Type 460	Soap & Bar, Surface Mounted
Type 461	Medicine Cabinet, Recessed

Federal Specification, WW-P-541b, Amendment-4, March 22, 1962, Plumbing Fixtures, Land Use.

Federal Specifications, WW-P-541b, September 20, 1954, Plumbing Fixtures, Land Use

Type 416	Tumbler & Toothbrush Holder
Type 421	Double Robe Hook
Type 426M & 428	Metal Shelf
Type 431 & 431M	Metal Towel Bar
Type 433	Toilet Paper Holder
Type 437	Toilet Paper Holder
Type 438	Toilet Paper Holder
Type 445	Cabinet for Folded Paper Towels

COMMERCIAL OFFICES

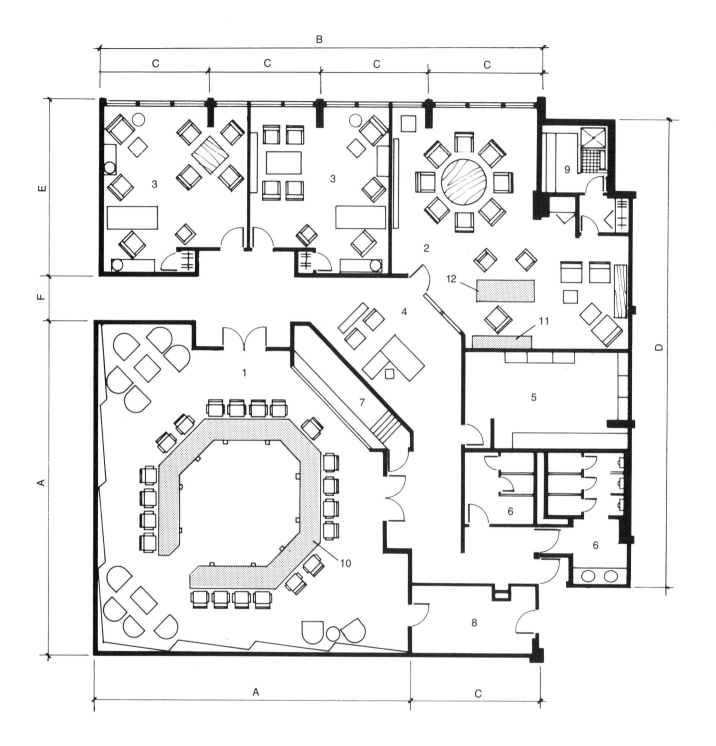

Legend:

1 = conference room
2 = president's office
3 = director's offices
4 = reception area
5 = storage, with copy equipment
6 = washrooms
7 = projection area
8 = entry
9 = president's private bath
10 = custom conference table*
11 = custom console*
12 = custom desk*

*See details and sections of shaded furnishings on pages 415–417.

Dimensions:

	ft/in.	m
A =	46 6	14.17
B =	62	18.90
C =	15 6	4.72
D =	69±	21.03
E =	24±	7.32
F =	6±	1.83

DETAILS OF (10)

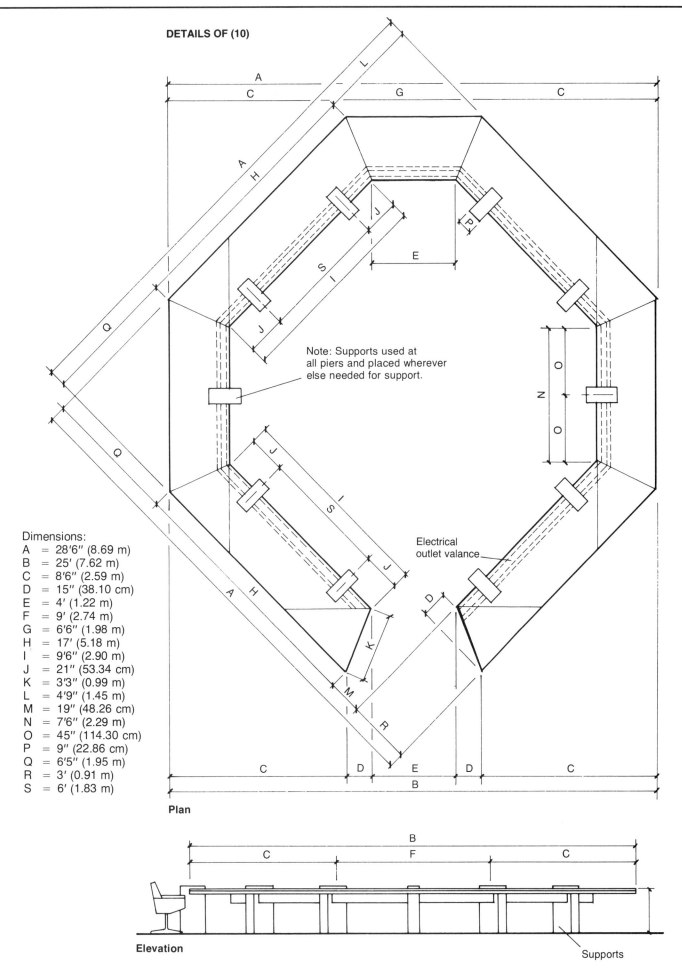

Note: Supports used at all piers and placed wherever else needed for support.

Electrical outlet valance

Dimensions:
A = 28'6" (8.69 m)
B = 25' (7.62 m)
C = 8'6" (2.59 m)
D = 15" (38.10 cm)
E = 4' (1.22 m)
F = 9' (2.74 m)
G = 6'6" (1.98 m)
H = 17' (5.18 m)
I = 9'6" (2.90 m)
J = 21" (53.34 cm)
K = 3'3" (0.99 m)
L = 4'9" (1.45 m)
M = 19" (48.26 cm)
N = 7'6" (2.29 m)
O = 45" (114.30 cm)
P = 9" (22.86 cm)
Q = 6'5" (1.95 m)
R = 3' (0.91 m)
S = 6' (1.83 m)

Plan

Elevation

Supports

*Shown in plan on page 414.

DETAILS OF (11)

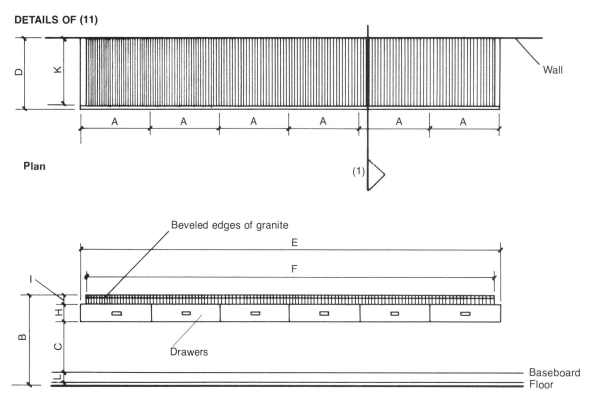

Plan

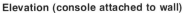

Elevation (console attached to wall)

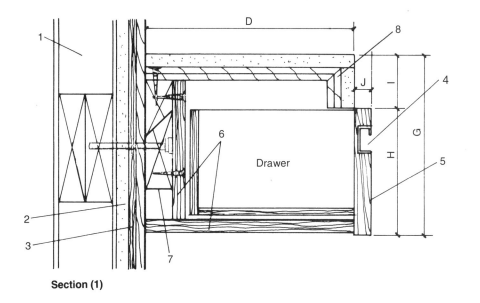

Section (1)

Legend:
1 = 3⅝″ (9.21 cm) metal studs
2 = ⅝″ (1.59 cm) gypsum board
3 = ¾″ (1.91 cm) wood paneling
4 = drawer pulls, copper recessed
5 = drawer to have concealed slides
6 = rift-cut red oak
7 = cleat-mounted wood anchor
    with bolts & screws
8 = plywood under granite

Dimensions (not to scale):
A = 24″ (60.96 cm)
B = 30″ (76.20 cm)
C = 17″ (43.18 cm)
D = 13″ (33.02 cm)
E = 12′ (3.66 m)
F = 11′8″ (3.58 m)
G = 9″ (22.86 cm)
H = 6″ (15.24 cm)
I = 3″ (7.62 cm)
J = 1″ (2.54 cm)
K = 12″ (30.48 cm)
L = 4″ (10.16 cm)

*Shown in plan on page 414.

DETAILS OF (12)

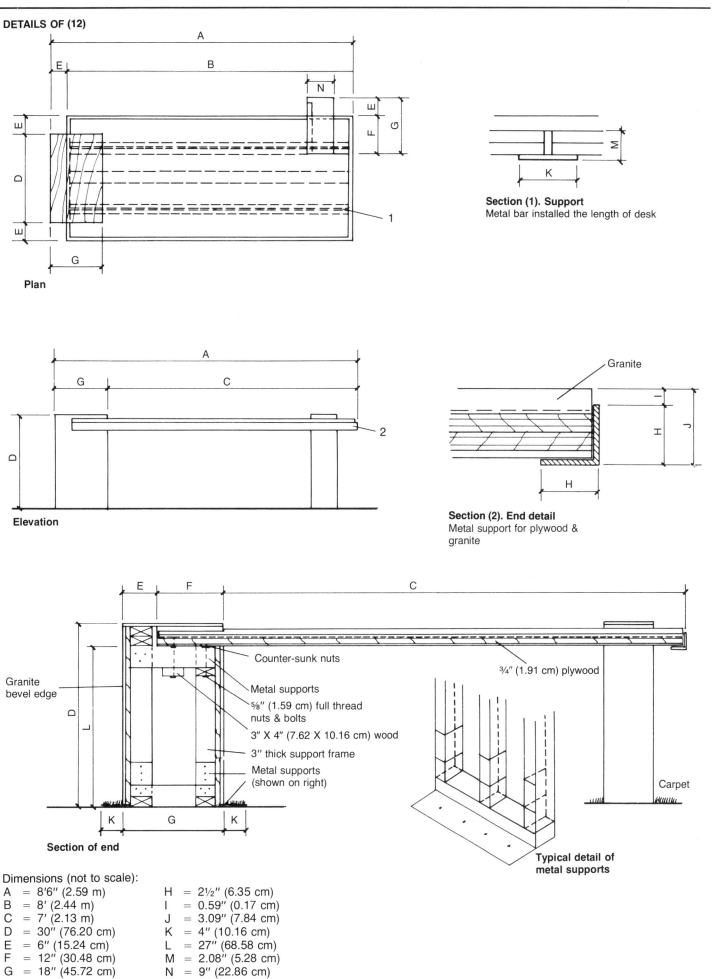

Plan

Elevation

Section (1). Support
Metal bar installed the length of desk

Granite

Section (2). End detail
Metal support for plywood & granite

Counter-sunk nuts

Metal supports

⅝″ (1.59 cm) full thread nuts & bolts

3″ X 4″ (7.62 X 10.16 cm) wood

3″ thick support frame

Metal supports (shown on right)

Granite bevel edge

Section of end

¾″ (1.91 cm) plywood

Carpet

Typical detail of metal supports

Dimensions (not to scale):

A = 8′6″ (2.59 m)   H = 2½″ (6.35 cm)
B = 8′ (2.44 m)   I = 0.59″ (0.17 cm)
C = 7′ (2.13 m)   J = 3.09″ (7.84 cm)
D = 30″ (76.20 cm)   K = 4″ (10.16 cm)
E = 6″ (15.24 cm)   L = 27″ (68.58 cm)
F = 12″ (30.48 cm)   M = 2.08″ (5.28 cm)
G = 18″ (45.72 cm)   N = 9″ (22.86 cm)

*Shown in plan on page 414.

ELEVATIONS OF PANEL-HUNG SYSTEMS

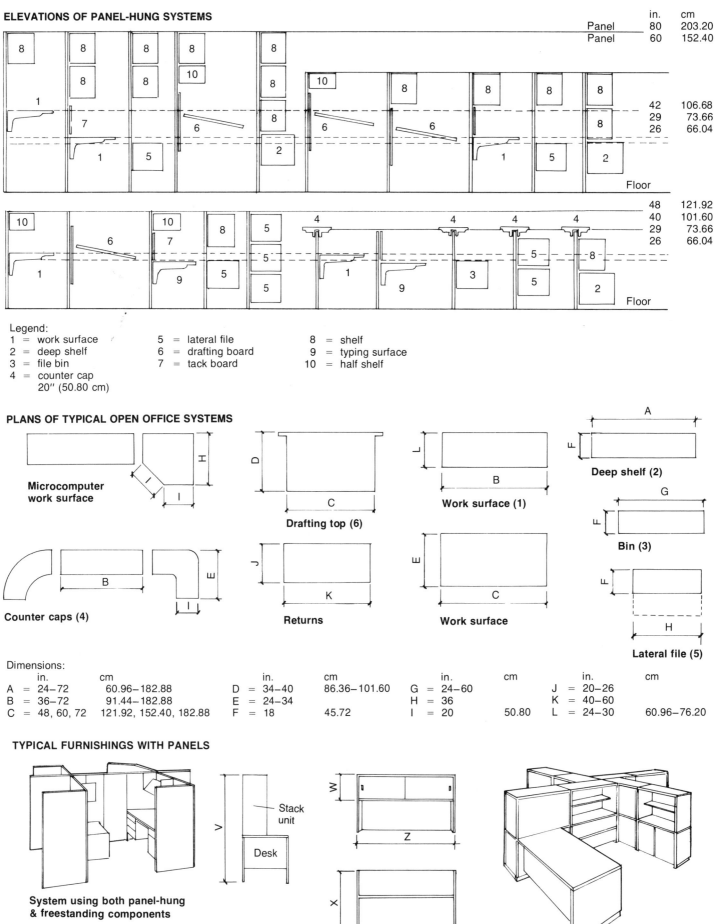

	in.	cm
Panel	80	203.20
Panel	60	152.40
	42	106.68
	29	73.66
	26	66.04
	48	121.92
	40	101.60
	29	73.66
	26	66.04

Legend:
1 = work surface
2 = deep shelf
3 = file bin
4 = counter cap
    20″ (50.80 cm)
5 = lateral file
6 = drafting board
7 = tack board
8 = shelf
9 = typing surface
10 = half shelf

PLANS OF TYPICAL OPEN OFFICE SYSTEMS

Microcomputer work surface

Drafting top (6)

Work surface (1)

Deep shelf (2)

Bin (3)

Counter caps (4)

Returns

Work surface

Lateral file (5)

Dimensions:

	in.	cm		in.	cm		in.	cm		in.	cm
A =	24–72	60.96–182.88	D =	34–40	86.36–101.60	G =	24–60		J =	20–26	
B =	36–72	91.44–182.88	E =	24–34		H =	36		K =	40–60	
C =	48, 60, 72	121.92, 152.40, 182.88	F =	18	45.72	I =	20	50.80	L =	24–30	60.96–76.20

TYPICAL FURNISHINGS WITH PANELS

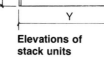

System using both panel-hung & freestanding components

Dimensions:

	in.	cm
V =	48–64	121.92–162.56
W =	18	45.72
X =	48	121.92
Y =	72	182.88
Z =	60	152.40

Stack unit

Desk

Elevations of stack units

Freestanding desks with stacking files & storage forming privacy barriers

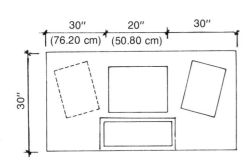

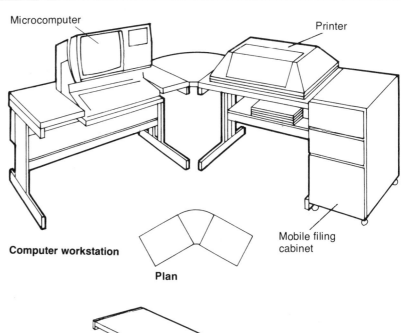

Microcomputer

Printer

Computer workstation

Mobile filing cabinet

Plan

Work surface requirements

Minimum space on each side of terminal is 30″ (76.20 cm). This space may be provided for the use of a right- or left-hand return. Keyboard height should not exceed 27″ (68.58 cm). Keyboard cable should allow the rear of the keyboard to extend at least 14″ (35.56 cm) in front of terminal base. Depth of work surface should be a maximum of 30″. Knee wall should be 16″ (40.64 cm) deep.

Storage

Storage should accommodate an operational manual 2″ X 25″ (5.08 X 63.50 cm). Computer disks and print-out sheets should be considered in planning storage needs. Storage above the work surface should not exceed 21″ to 22″ (53.34 to 55.88 cm) in height.

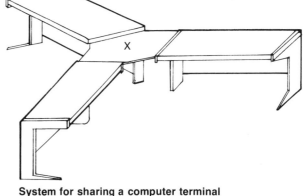

System for sharing a computer terminal
Terminal located at center (X) on a rotating base

Terminal desk

Mobile, adjustable terminal table

Dimensions & notes:

	in.	cm
A =	48	121.92
B =	40	101.60
C =	29½	74.93
D =	28	71.12
E =	26½	67.31
F =	20	50.80
G =	left hand	
H =	right hand	

Terminal station

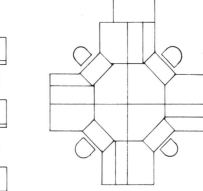

Furniture systems based on the cluster concept

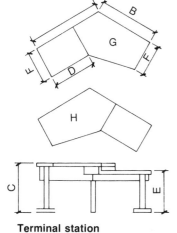

Permanent printer stand

Dimensions:

	in.	cm
U =	30–48	76.20–121.92
V =	24–30	60.96–76.20
W =	14	35.56
X =	36	91.44
Y =	24	60.96
Z =	26	66.04

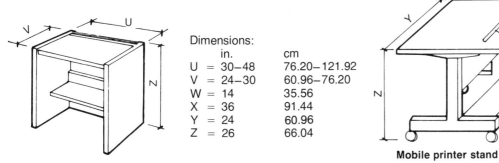

Paper

Paper feed

Mobile printer stand

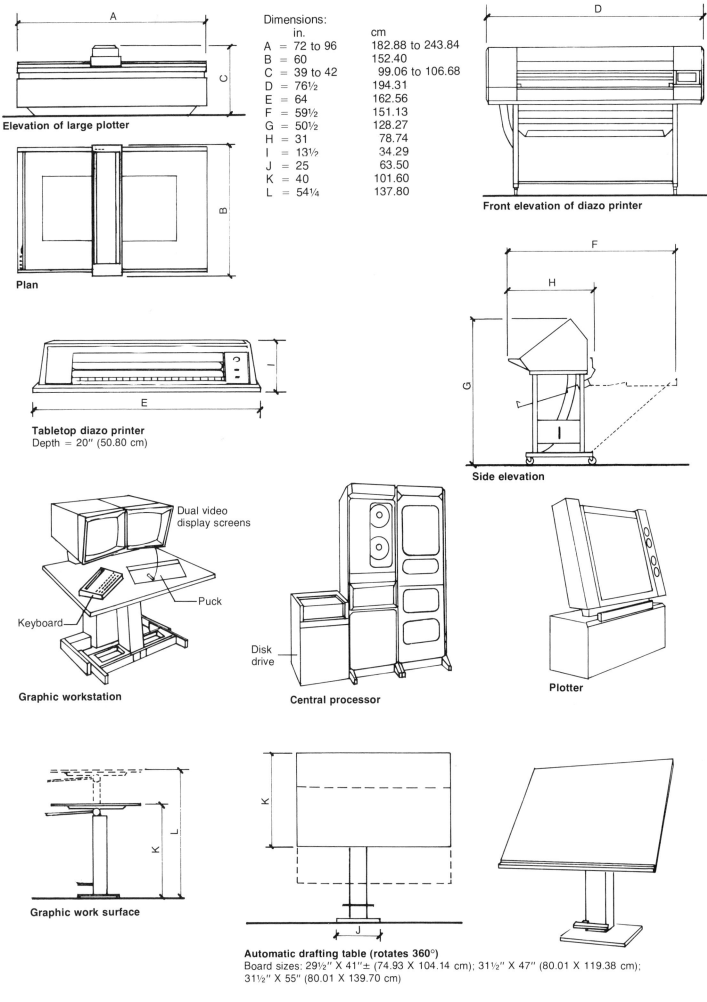

Elevation of large plotter

Plan

Dimensions:

	in.	cm
A =	72 to 96	182.88 to 243.84
B =	60	152.40
C =	39 to 42	99.06 to 106.68
D =	76½	194.31
E =	64	162.56
F =	59½	151.13
G =	50½	128.27
H =	31	78.74
I =	13½	34.29
J =	25	63.50
K =	40	101.60
L =	54¼	137.80

Front elevation of diazo printer

Tabletop diazo printer
Depth = 20″ (50.80 cm)

Side elevation

Graphic workstation

Dual video
display screens

Puck

Keyboard

Central processor

Disk
drive

Plotter

Graphic work surface

Automatic drafting table (rotates 360°)
Board sizes: 29½″ X 41″± (74.93 X 104.14 cm); 31½″ X 47″ (80.01 X 119.38 cm);
31½″ X 55″ (80.01 X 139.70 cm)

RECTANGULAR TOPS

Dimensions (in.)

l	w	Approximate seating
60	24	4
72	24	4
36	30	4
48	30	4
60	30	6
72	30	6

Dimensions (in.)

l	w	Approximate seating
48	36	4
60	36	6
72	36	6
84	36	8
96	36	8

Dimensions (in.)

l	w	Approximate seating
72	42	6
84	42	8
96	42	8
108	42	10
120	42	10

Dimensions (in.)

l	w	Approximate seating
72	48	6
84	48	8
96	48	8
108	48	10
120	48	10
144	48	12

BOAT TOPS

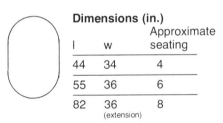

Dimensions

Length (ft)	Center (in.)	End (in.)	Approximate seating
6	36	30	6
7	38	31	6
8	40	32	8
10	44	33	10
12	48	34	12
14	52	35	14
16	56	36	16
18	60	37	18
20	60	38	18
22	60	39	20
24	60	40	22

RACETRACK TOPS

Dimensions

l (ft)	w (in.)	Approximate seating
8	48	8
10	48	10
12	48	12
10	60	12
10	60	12
12	60	12
15	60	16

All seating calculations on this page are based on the use of a 23″ (58.42 cm) wide chair. Allow an additional 4″ (10.16 cm) between chairs. If specifying a wider chair, adjust accordingly.

BLUNT END OVAL TOPS

Dimensions (in.)

l	w	Approximate seating
44	34	4
55	36	6
82	36	8
(extension)		

ROUND TOPS

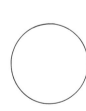

Diameter (in.)

	Approximate seating
42	4
48	5
54	6
60	7
66	7
72	8
84	9
96	11
108	12
120	14

ELLIPTICAL TOPS*

Dimensions (in.)

l	w	Approximate seating
60	30	4
72	34	4
8	42	6
96	48	6
108	48	8
120	48	8
144	48	10

*For conference use, no seating at end.

SQUARE TOPS

Dimensions (in.)

l	w	Approximate seating
36	36	4
42	42	4
48	48	4

OVAL CONFERENCE TOPS

Dimensions (in.)

l	w	Approximate seating
70	36	4
78	48	6
96	48	8
108	52	9
120	55	10
144	60	12

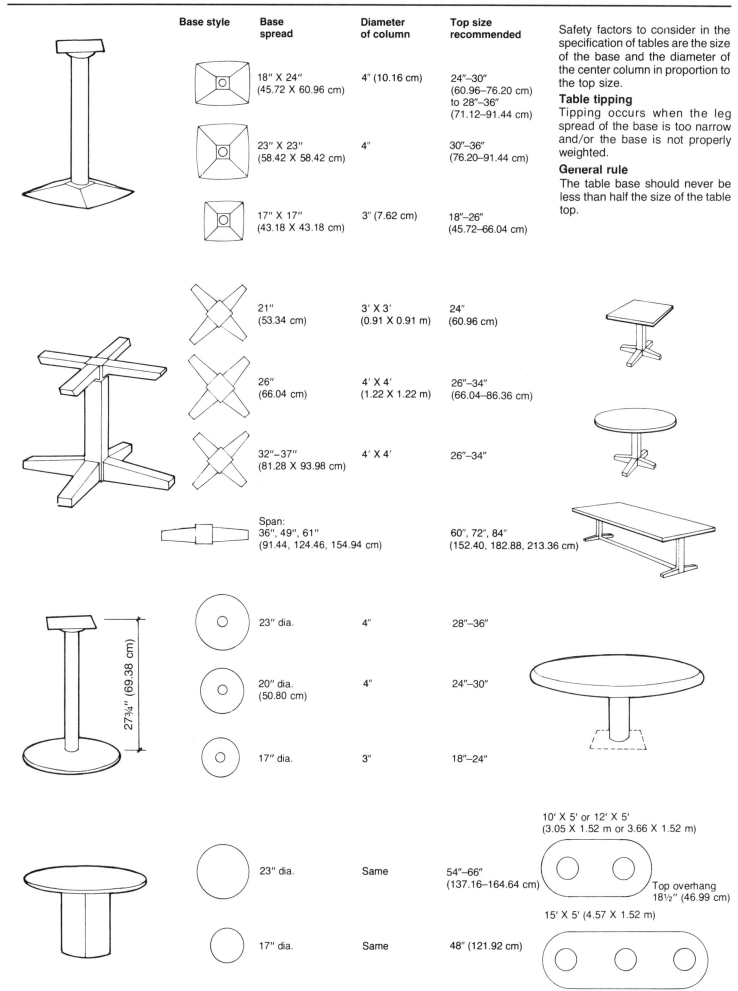

Base style	Base spread	Diameter of column	Top size recommended
	18" X 24" (45.72 X 60.96 cm)	4" (10.16 cm)	24"–30" (60.96–76.20 cm) to 28"–36" (71.12–91.44 cm)
	23" X 23" (58.42 X 58.42 cm)	4"	30"–36" (76.20–91.44 cm)
	17" X 17" (43.18 X 43.18 cm)	3" (7.62 cm)	18"–26" (45.72–66.04 cm)
	21" (53.34 cm)	3' X 3' (0.91 X 0.91 m)	24" (60.96 cm)
	26" (66.04 cm)	4' X 4' (1.22 X 1.22 m)	26"–34" (66.04–86.36 cm)
	32"–37" (81.28 X 93.98 cm)	4' X 4'	26"–34"
	Span: 36", 49", 61" (91.44, 124.46, 154.94 cm)		60", 72", 84" (152.40, 182.88, 213.36 cm)
	23" dia.	4"	28"–36"
	20" dia. (50.80 cm)	4"	24"–30"
	17" dia.	3"	18"–24"
	23" dia.	Same	54"–66" (137.16–164.64 cm)
	17" dia.	Same	48" (121.92 cm)

27¾" (69.38 cm)

Safety factors to consider in the specification of tables are the size of the base and the diameter of the center column in proportion to the top size.

Table tipping

Tipping occurs when the leg spread of the base is too narrow and/or the base is not properly weighted.

General rule

The table base should never be less than half the size of the table top.

10' X 5' or 12' X 5' (3.05 X 1.52 m or 3.66 X 1.52 m)

Top overhang 18½" (46.99 cm)

15' X 5' (4.57 X 1.52 m)

LATERAL FILES

Depth = 15″ to 18″ (38.10 to 45.72 cm)

	Height	
	in.	cm
	65	165.10
	53	134.62
	40	101.60
	28	71.12
	12*	30.48

Floor

Width | 42″ (106.68 cm) | 36″ (91.44 cm) | 30″ (76.20 cm) | 36″

Note: Safety factors are tested according to voluntary BIFMA Standard (LF 1-1978). This standard tests for structural quality, loading, and weight distribution.

Caution: Lateral files tend to tip forward unless properly installed according to instructions. Do not load more than 2 lb (0.91 kg) per linear foot.

*Drawer heights range from 6″, 9″, 12″ to 15″ (15.24, 22.86, 30.48, 38.10 cm).

UPRIGHT FILES

Capacity: One 4-drawer upright file provides 1000 linear in. (2540 cm) of filing space.

		Height	
		in.	cm
		60	152.40
		52	132.08
		41	104.14
Desk height		29	73.66
Pedestal height		27	68.58

Floor

SPECIAL CARD FILES

A   B   C   D

X = heights range from 42″, 52″, to 60″ (106.68, 132.08, to 152.40 cm)

Standard widths & depths

	Width		Depth	
Upright files	in.	cm	in.	cm
Letter size	15	38.10	18	
			25	63.50
			29	73.66
Legal size	18	45.72	29	
File A, 6″ X 9″ (15.24 X 22.86 cm)	22	55.88		
File B, 5″ X 8″ (12.70 X 20.32 cm)	19	48.26		
File C, 3″ X 5″ (7.62 X 12.70 cm)	18			
File D, 4″ X 6″ (10.16 X 15.24 cm)	15			

LATERAL FILES

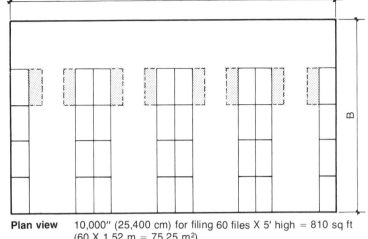

Plan view 10,000″ (25,400 cm) for filing 60 files X 5′ high = 810 sq ft
(60 X 1.52 m = 75.25 m²)

VERTICAL (UPRIGHT) 4-DRAWER FILES

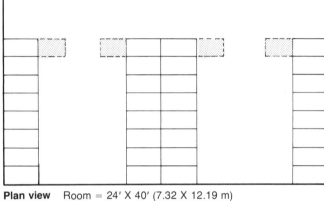

Plan view Room = 24′ X 40′ (7.32 X 12.19 m)

OPEN-SHELF FILE STORAGE

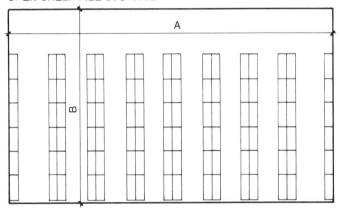

10,000″ for filing

MOBILE OPEN-SHELF FILES

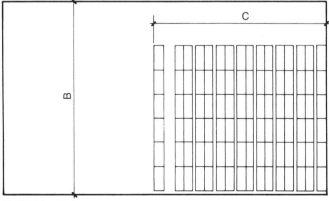

10,000″ for filing

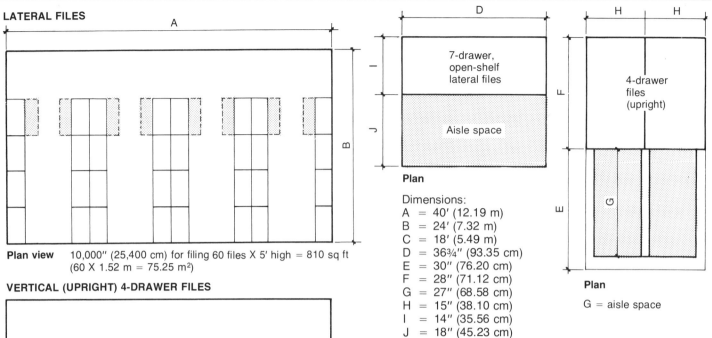

Plan

Dimensions:
A = 40′ (12.19 m)
B = 24′ (7.32 m)
C = 18′ (5.49 m)
D = 36¾″ (93.35 cm)
E = 30″ (76.20 cm)
F = 28″ (71.12 cm)
G = 27″ (68.58 cm)
H = 15″ (38.10 cm)
I = 14″ (35.56 cm)
J = 18″ (45.23 cm)

Plan

G = aisle space

Space comparisons

Filing type	Space sq ft	m²	Files required	Net filing sq ft	m²
Lateral 5-drawer	810	75.25	60	12.4	1.15
Vertical 4-drawer	728	67.63	104	13.7	1.27
Open shelf	250	23.23	37	40	3.72
Mobile open	141	13.10	37	70.9	6.59

Permanent placement open files

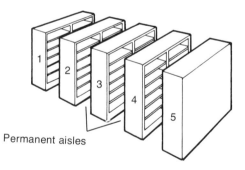

Permanent aisles

Mobile filing units
Units move on tracks, thus allowing installation
of required storage in less space

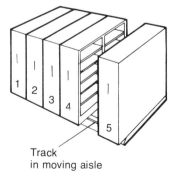

Track
in moving aisle

OPEN METAL SHELVING
See chart below for storage capacity

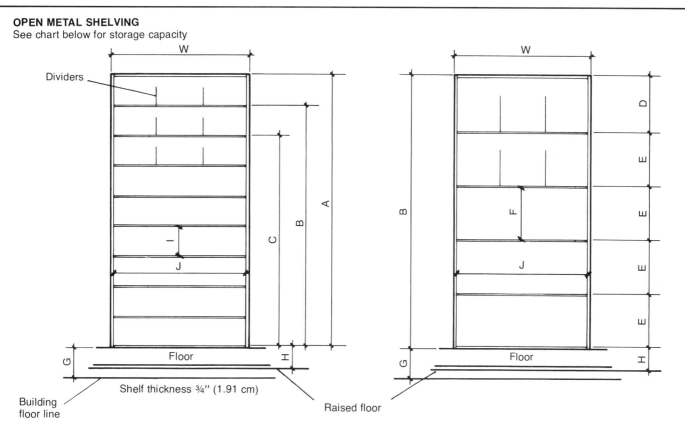

Dividers

W

A

B

C

J

Floor

G

H

Shelf thickness ¾″ (1.91 cm)

Building
floor line

Raised floor

W

D

E

E

F

E

J

E

B

G

Floor

H

Dimensions:

	in.	cm
D =	18	45.72
E =	16½	41.91
F =	15½	38.74
G =	9±	22.86
H =	6	15.24
I =	9¾	24.77
J =	34, 40, 46	86.36, 101.60, 116.84

Storage capacity

	Widths W		Heights					
			A		B		C	
Items	in.	cm	in.	cm	in.	cm	in.	cm
Letter	36	91.44	238	604.52	272	690.88	306	777.24
&	42	106.68	280	711.20	320	812.80	360	914.40
legal sizes	48	121.92	322	817.88	368	934.72	414	1051.56
X-ray film					170	431.80		
					200	508.00		
					230	584.20		

Shelf thickness (18 gauge steel)

Depth		¾″*	1¼″†	
in.	cm	(1.91 cm)	(3.18 cm)	Size
10	25.40	•		Single book
12	30.48	•		Single letter
15	38.10	•	•	Single level file
18	45.72		•	Single X-ray
20	50.80	•		Single book
24	60.96	•		Letter
30	76.20	•		Legal file

*500 lb (227.06 kg) per shelf
†700 lb (317.80 kg) per shelf

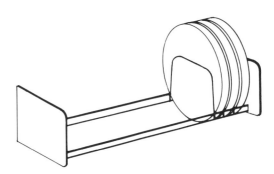

File & tape storage

Note: Films and tapes require special storage that is magnetic-, shock-, and drop-proof. Calculate storage of seven reels per linear foot. Use 10″ (25.40 cm) deep film rack shelf for 400′ (121.92 m) reels. Use 16″ (40.64 cm) deep film rack shelf for 800′, 1200′, or 1600′ (243.84, 365.76, 487.68 m) reels.

SPACE REQUIREMENTS

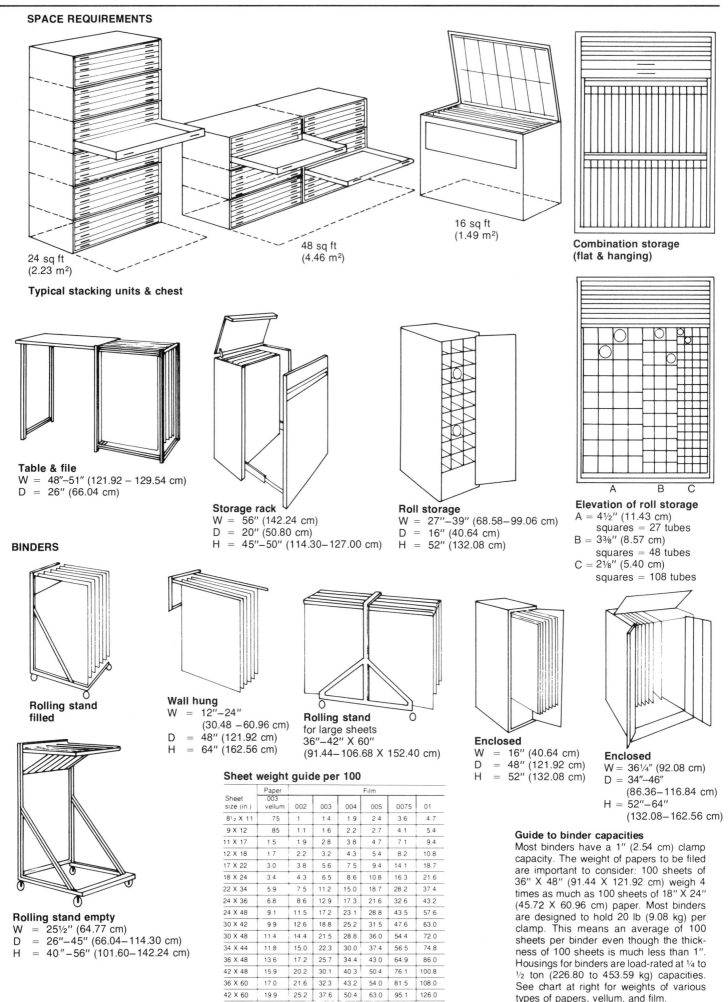

24 sq ft
(2.23 m²)

48 sq ft
(4.46 m²)

16 sq ft
(1.49 m²)

**Combination storage
(flat & hanging)**

Typical stacking units & chest

Table & file
W = 48″–51″ (121.92 – 129.54 cm)
D = 26″ (66.04 cm)

Storage rack
W = 56″ (142.24 cm)
D = 20″ (50.80 cm)
H = 45″–50″ (114.30–127.00 cm)

Roll storage
W = 27″–39″ (68.58–99.06 cm)
D = 16″ (40.64 cm)
H = 52″ (132.08 cm)

Elevation of roll storage
A = 4½″ (11.43 cm)
    squares = 27 tubes
B = 3⅜″ (8.57 cm)
    squares = 48 tubes
C = 2⅛″ (5.40 cm)
    squares = 108 tubes

BINDERS

**Rolling stand
filled**

Wall hung
W = 12″–24″
    (30.48 –60.96 cm)
D = 48″ (121.92 cm)
H = 64″ (162.56 cm)

Rolling stand
for large sheets
36″–42″ X 60″
(91.44–106.68 X 152.40 cm)

Enclosed
W = 16″ (40.64 cm)
D = 48″ (121.92 cm)
H = 52″ (132.08 cm)

Enclosed
W = 36¼″ (92.08 cm)
D = 34″–46″
    (86.36–116.84 cm)
H = 52″–64″
    (132.08–162.56 cm)

Rolling stand empty
W = 25½″ (64.77 cm)
D = 26″–45″ (66.04–114.30 cm)
H = 40″–56″ (101.60–142.24 cm)

Sheet weight guide per 100

Sheet size (in.)	Paper 003 vellum	Film					
		002	003	004	005	0075	01
8½ X 11	.75	1	1.4	1.9	2.4	3.6	4.7
9 X 12	.85	1.1	1.6	2.2	2.7	4.1	5.4
11 X 17	1.5	1.9	2.8	3.8	4.7	7.1	9.4
12 X 18	1.7	2.2	3.2	4.3	5.4	8.2	10.8
17 X 22	3.0	3.8	5.6	7.5	9.4	14.1	18.7
18 X 24	3.4	4.3	6.5	8.6	10.8	16.3	21.6
22 X 34	5.9	7.5	11.2	15.0	18.7	28.2	37.4
24 X 36	6.8	8.6	12.9	17.3	21.6	32.6	43.2
24 X 48	9.1	11.5	17.2	23.1	28.8	43.5	57.6
30 X 42	9.9	12.6	18.8	25.2	31.5	47.6	63.0
30 X 48	11.4	14.4	21.5	28.8	36.0	54.4	72.0
34 X 44	11.8	15.0	22.3	30.0	37.4	56.5	74.8
36 X 48	13.6	17.2	25.7	34.4	43.0	64.9	86.0
42 X 48	15.9	20.2	30.1	40.3	50.4	76.1	100.8
36 X 60	17.0	21.6	32.3	43.2	54.0	81.5	108.0
42 X 60	19.9	25.2	37.6	50.4	63.0	95.1	126.0

Guide to binder capacities
Most binders have a 1″ (2.54 cm) clamp capacity. The weight of papers to be filed are important to consider: 100 sheets of 36″ X 48″ (91.44 X 121.92 cm) weigh 4 times as much as 100 sheets of 18″ X 24″ (45.72 X 60.96 cm) paper. Most binders are designed to hold 20 lb (9.08 kg) per clamp. This means an average of 100 sheets per binder even though the thickness of 100 sheets is much less than 1″. Housings for binders are load-rated at ¼ to ½ ton (226.80 to 453.59 kg) capacities. See chart at right for weights of various types of papers, vellum, and film.

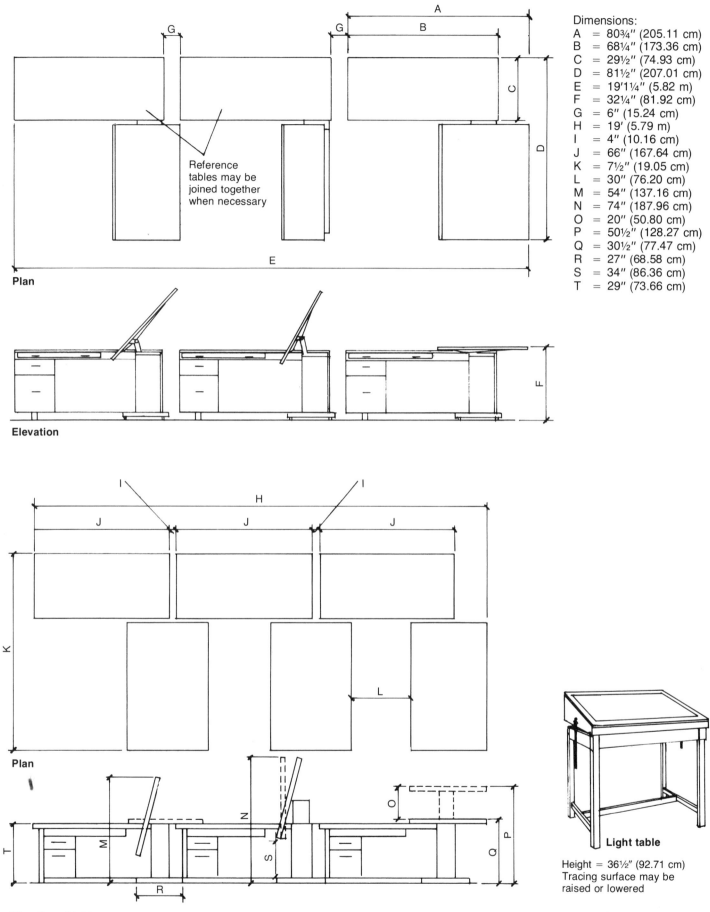

Plan

Reference tables may be joined together when necessary

Elevation

Plan

Elevation of tables

Dimensions:
A = 80¾" (205.11 cm)
B = 68¼" (173.36 cm)
C = 29½" (74.93 cm)
D = 81½" (207.01 cm)
E = 19'1¼" (5.82 m)
F = 32¼" (81.92 cm)
G = 6" (15.24 cm)
H = 19' (5.79 m)
I = 4" (10.16 cm)
J = 66" (167.64 cm)
K = 7½" (19.05 cm)
L = 30" (76.20 cm)
M = 54" (137.16 cm)
N = 74" (187.96 cm)
O = 20" (50.80 cm)
P = 50½" (128.27 cm)
Q = 30½" (77.47 cm)
R = 27" (68.58 cm)
S = 34" (86.36 cm)
T = 29" (73.66 cm)

Light table

Height = 36½" (92.71 cm)
Tracing surface may be raised or lowered

Light table dimensions (in.)

Glass size	Overall size	Tubes
20" x 25"	24" x 29"	2-20W
24" x 36"	28" x 40"	2-30W
36" x 48"	40" x 52"	4-40W

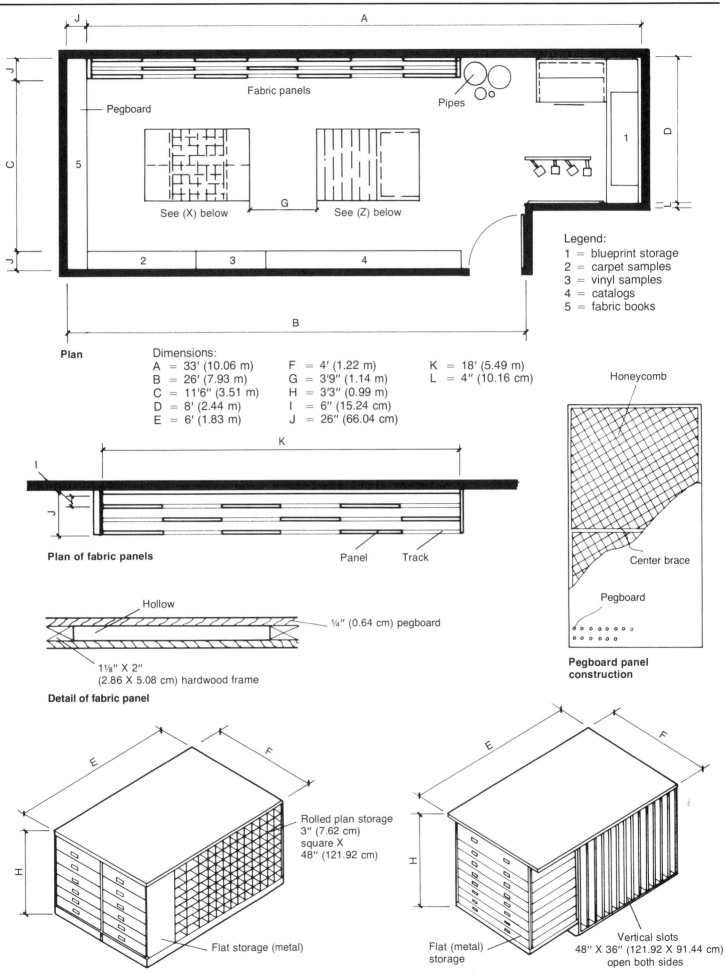

Plan

Dimensions:

A = 33′ (10.06 m)	F = 4′ (1.22 m)	K = 18′ (5.49 m)
B = 26′ (7.93 m)	G = 3′9″ (1.14 m)	L = 4″ (10.16 cm)
C = 11′6″ (3.51 m)	H = 3′3″ (0.99 m)	
D = 8′ (2.44 m)	I = 6″ (15.24 cm)	
E = 6′ (1.83 m)	J = 26″ (66.04 cm)	

Legend:
1 = blueprint storage
2 = carpet samples
3 = vinyl samples
4 = catalogs
5 = fabric books

Fabric panels

Pegboard

Pipes

Plan of fabric panels

Panel   Track

Detail of fabric panel

Hollow

¼″ (0.64 cm) pegboard

1⅛″ X 2″
(2.86 X 5.08 cm) hardwood frame

Honeycomb

Center brace

Pegboard

Pegboard panel construction

Rolled plan storage
3″ (7.62 cm)
square X
48″ (121.92 cm)

Flat storage (metal)

(X) Storage of plans & drawings

Vertical slots
48″ X 36″ (121.92 X 91.44 cm)
open both sides

Flat (metal)
storage

(Z) Storage of drawings & presentation boards

Typical mailroom layout

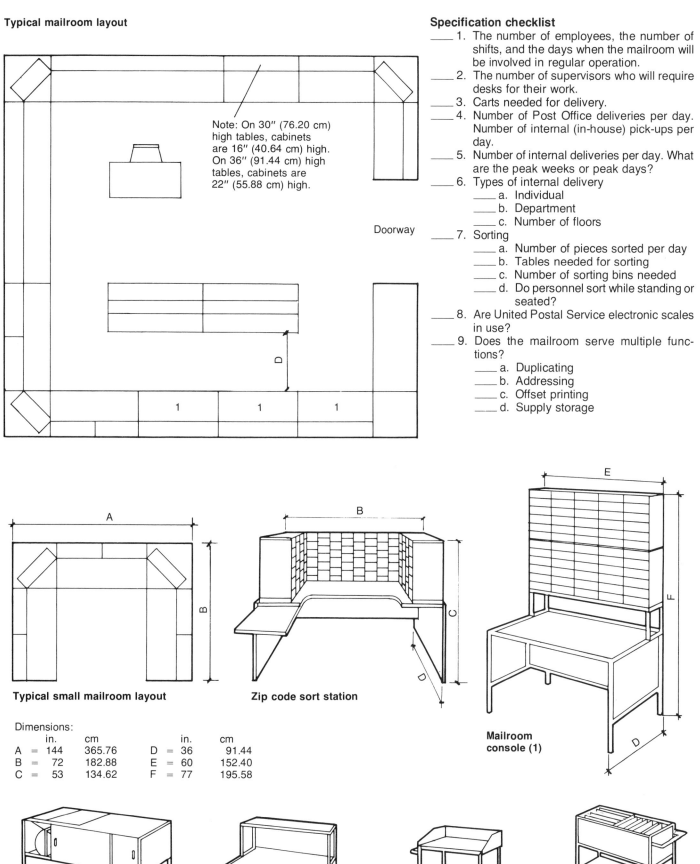

Note: On 30″ (76.20 cm) high tables, cabinets are 16″ (40.64 cm) high. On 36″ (91.44 cm) high tables, cabinets are 22″ (55.88 cm) high.

Doorway

Specification checklist

_____ 1. The number of employees, the number of shifts, and the days when the mailroom will be involved in regular operation.
_____ 2. The number of supervisors who will require desks for their work.
_____ 3. Carts needed for delivery.
_____ 4. Number of Post Office deliveries per day. Number of internal (in-house) pick-ups per day.
_____ 5. Number of internal deliveries per day. What are the peak weeks or peak days?
_____ 6. Types of internal delivery
  _____ a. Individual
  _____ b. Department
  _____ c. Number of floors
_____ 7. Sorting
  _____ a. Number of pieces sorted per day
  _____ b. Tables needed for sorting
  _____ c. Number of sorting bins needed
  _____ d. Do personnel sort while standing or seated?
_____ 8. Are United Postal Service electronic scales in use?
_____ 9. Does the mailroom serve multiple functions?
  _____ a. Duplicating
  _____ b. Addressing
  _____ c. Offset printing
  _____ d. Supply storage

Typical small mailroom layout

Zip code sort station

Mailroom console (1)

Dimensions:

	in.	cm		in.	cm
A =	144	365.76	D =	36	91.44
B =	72	182.88	E =	60	152.40
C =	53	134.62	F =	77	195.58

Wrapping table
W = 36″ (91.44 cm)
H = 30″ to 36″ (76.20 to 91.44 cm)

Meter table

Dump cart

Mail cart

Chapter 16

BANKS

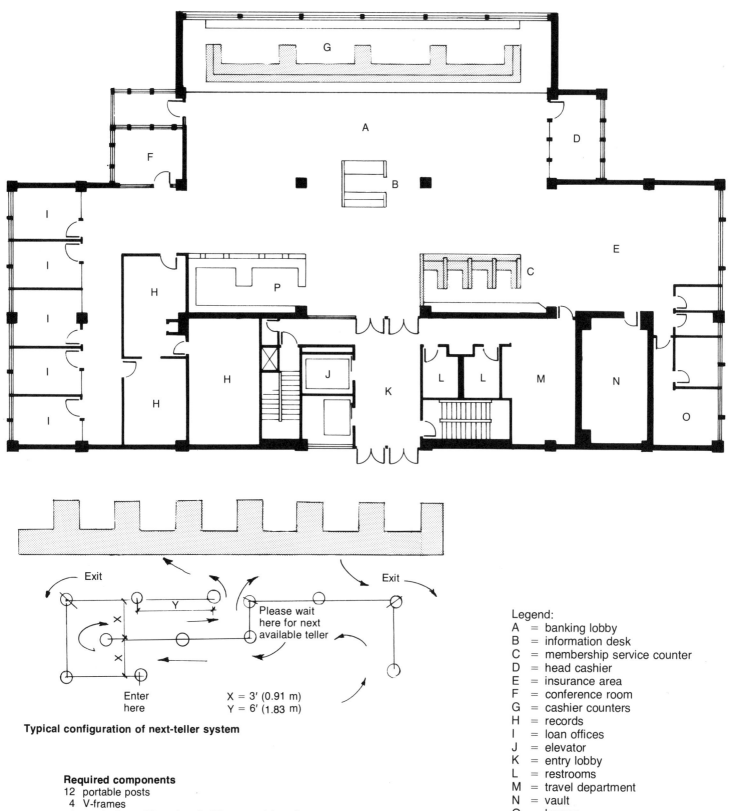

Typical configuration of next-teller system

Enter here
X = 3′ (0.91 m)
Y = 6′ (1.83 m)

Required components
12 portable posts
4 V-frames
4 stock signs: "Enter here"; "Please wait here"
"Exit" signs
10 velour-covered ropes: nine 6′ (1.83 m) long
and one 3′ (0.91 m) long
20 snap ends

Legend:
A = banking lobby
B = information desk
C = membership service counter
D = head cashier
E = insurance area
F = conference room
G = cashier counters
H = records
I = loan offices
J = elevator
K = entry lobby
L = restrooms
M = travel department
N = vault
O = lounge
P = customer service desk

*Shaded areas are shown in detail on pages 432-435.

DETAILS OF (C)

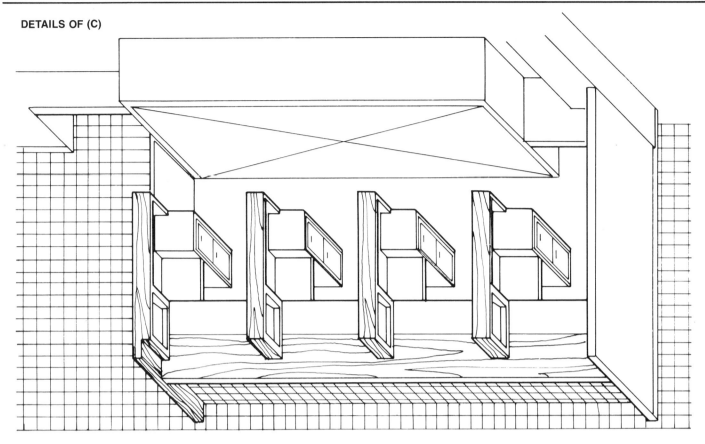

Axonometric

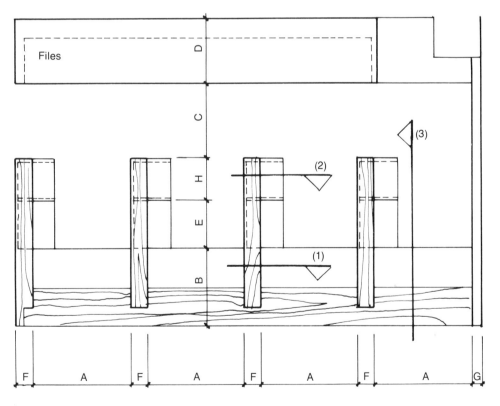

Files

Dimensions:

		in.	cm
A	=	50	127.00
B	=	39	99.06
C	=	37	93.98
D	=	32	81.28
E	=	24	60.96
F	=	9	22.86
G	=	4½	11.43
H	=	18	45.72

Note: See sections on facing page.

F   A   F   A   F   A   F   A   G

Plan

*Shown in plan on page 431.

DETAILS OF (C)

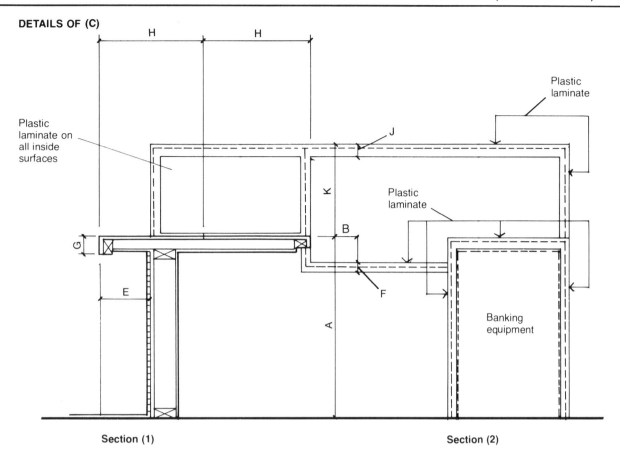

Plastic laminate

Plastic laminate on all inside surfaces

J

K

B

G

E

A

F

Banking equipment

Plastic laminate

Section (1)   Section (2)

Dimensions:

	in.	cm
A =	30	76.20
B =	9	22.86
C =	21	53.34
D =	12	30.48
E =	4	10.16
F =	1½	3.81
G =	3	7.62
H =	18	45.72
I =	70°	
J =	2	5.08
K =	15	38.10

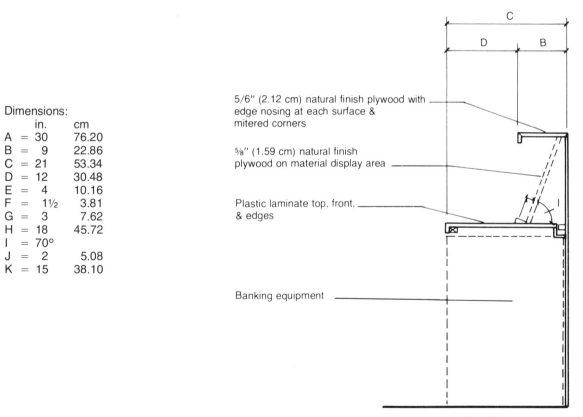

C

D   B

5/6″ (2.12 cm) natural finish plywood with edge nosing at each surface & mitered corners

⅝″ (1.59 cm) natural finish plywood on material display area

Plastic laminate top, front, & edges

I

Banking equipment

Section (3)

*Shown in plan on page 431.

DETAILS OF (G)

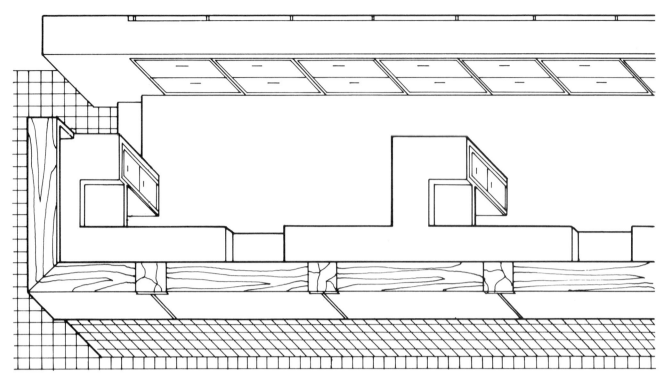

Axonometric

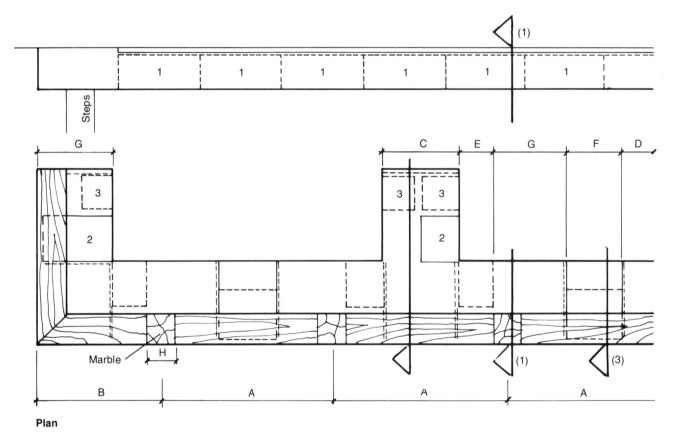

Plan

Dimensions:
A = 7'6" (2.29 m) E = 18" (45.72 cm)
B = 5'3" (1.60 m) F = 30" (76.20 cm)
C = 3'3" (0.99 m) G = 37½" (95.25 cm)
D = 3' (0.91 m) H = 16" (40.64 cm)

Equipment:
1 = lateral files
2 = micocomputer
3 = files

Shown in plan on page 431.

Note: See sections on facing page.

DETAILS OF (G)

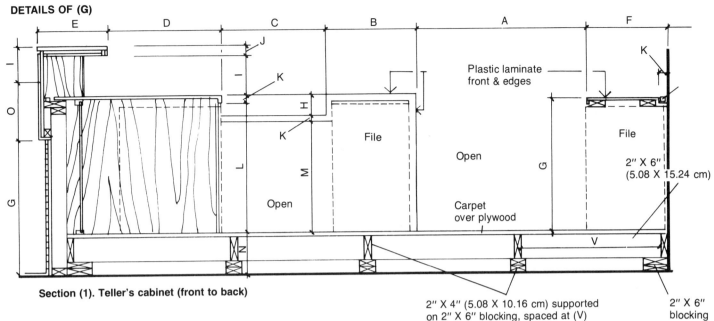

Plastic laminate front & edges

2" X 6"
(5.08 X 15.24 cm)

Carpet over plywood

Section (1). Teller's cabinet (front to back)

2" X 4" (5.08 X 10.16 cm) supported
on 2" X 6" blocking, spaced at (V)
maximum center to center

2" X 6"
blocking

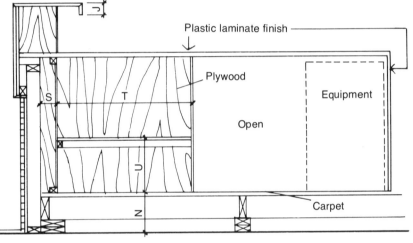

Plastic laminate finish

Plywood

Equipment

Open

Carpet

Section (2). Cashier counter

Dimensions (not to scale):

A = 3'3" (0.99 m)   N = 9¼" (23.50 cm)
B = 21" (53.34 cm)   O = 20" (50.80 cm)
C = 24" (60.96 cm)   P = 25" (63.50 cm)
D = 26" (66.04 cm)   Q = 8" (20.32 cm)
E = 16" (40.64 cm)   R = 14" (35.56 cm)
F = 18½" (46.99 cm)   S = 3" (7.62 cm)
G = 30" (76.20 cm)   T = 32" (81.28 cm)
H = 4" (10.16 cm)   U = 12" (30.48 cm)
I = 9" (22.86 cm)   V = 48" (121.92 cm)
J = 2" (5.08 cm)   W = 10⅛" (25.72 cm)
K = 1½" (3.81 cm)   X = 5 equal spaces
L = 28½" (72.39 cm)   Y = 9" (22.86 cm) deep
M = 24½" (62.23 cm)

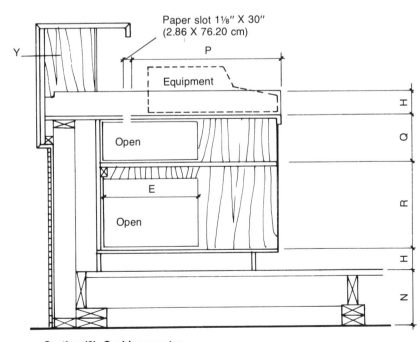

Paper slot 1⅛" X 30"
(2.86 X 76.20 cm)

Equipment

Open

Open

Masonite dividers

Section (3). Cashier counter

Elevations of cashier counters

*Shown in plan on page 431.

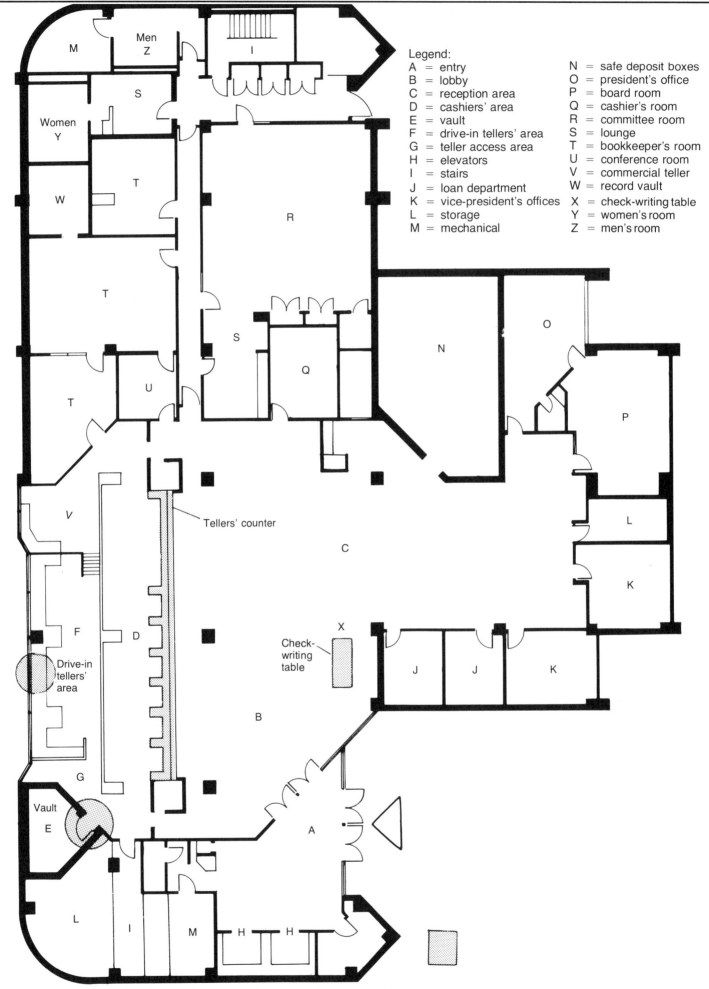

Tellers' counter

Check-writing table

Drive-in tellers' area

Vault

Legend:
A = entry
B = lobby
C = reception area
D = cashiers' area
E = vault
F = drive-in tellers' area
G = teller access area
H = elevators
I = stairs
J = loan department
K = vice-president's offices
L = storage
M = mechanical

N = safe deposit boxes
O = president's office
P = board room
Q = cashier's room
R = committee room
S = lounge
T = bookkeeper's room
U = conference room
V = commercial teller
W = record vault
X = check-writing table
Y = women's room
Z = men's room

*See details of custom millwork & prefabricated banking equipment on pages 437-441.

DETAILS OF (D)

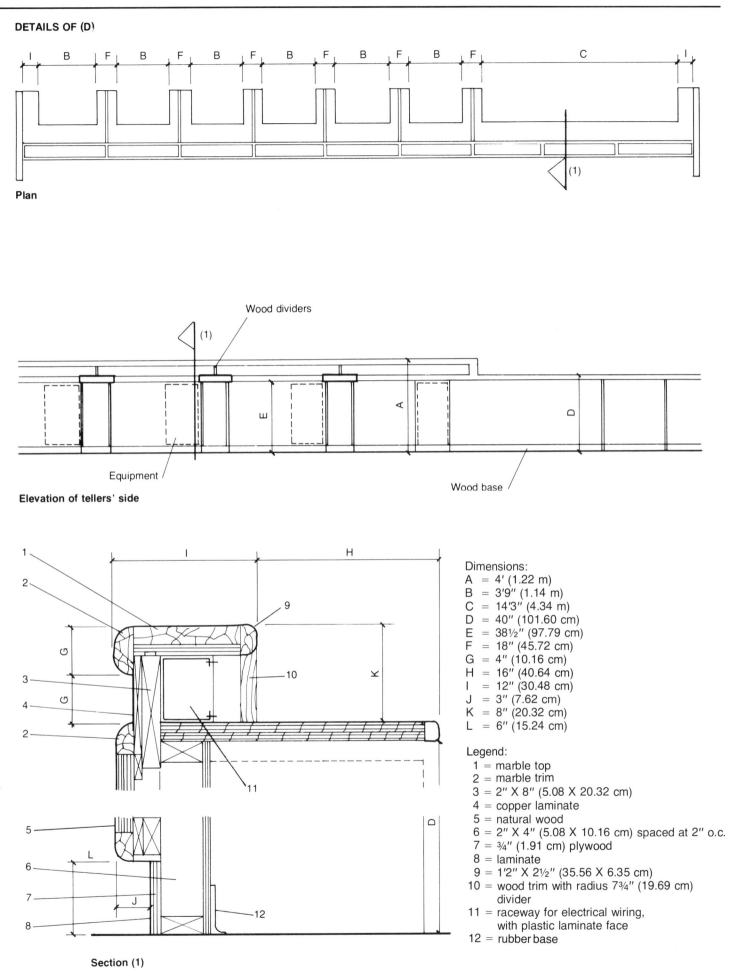

Plan

Wood dividers

Equipment

Wood base

Elevation of tellers' side

Dimensions:
A = 4' (1.22 m)
B = 3'9" (1.14 m)
C = 14'3" (4.34 m)
D = 40" (101.60 cm)
E = 38½" (97.79 cm)
F = 18" (45.72 cm)
G = 4" (10.16 cm)
H = 16" (40.64 cm)
I = 12" (30.48 cm)
J = 3" (7.62 cm)
K = 8" (20.32 cm)
L = 6" (15.24 cm)

Legend:
 1 = marble top
 2 = marble trim
 3 = 2" X 8" (5.08 X 20.32 cm)
 4 = copper laminate
 5 = natural wood
 6 = 2" X 4" (5.08 X 10.16 cm) spaced at 2" o.c.
 7 = ¾" (1.91 cm) plywood
 8 = laminate
 9 = 1'2" X 2½" (35.56 X 6.35 cm)
10 = wood trim with radius 7¾" (19.69 cm) divider
11 = raceway for electrical wiring, with plastic laminate face
12 = rubber base

Section (1)

*Shown in plan on page 436.

DETAILS OF (X)

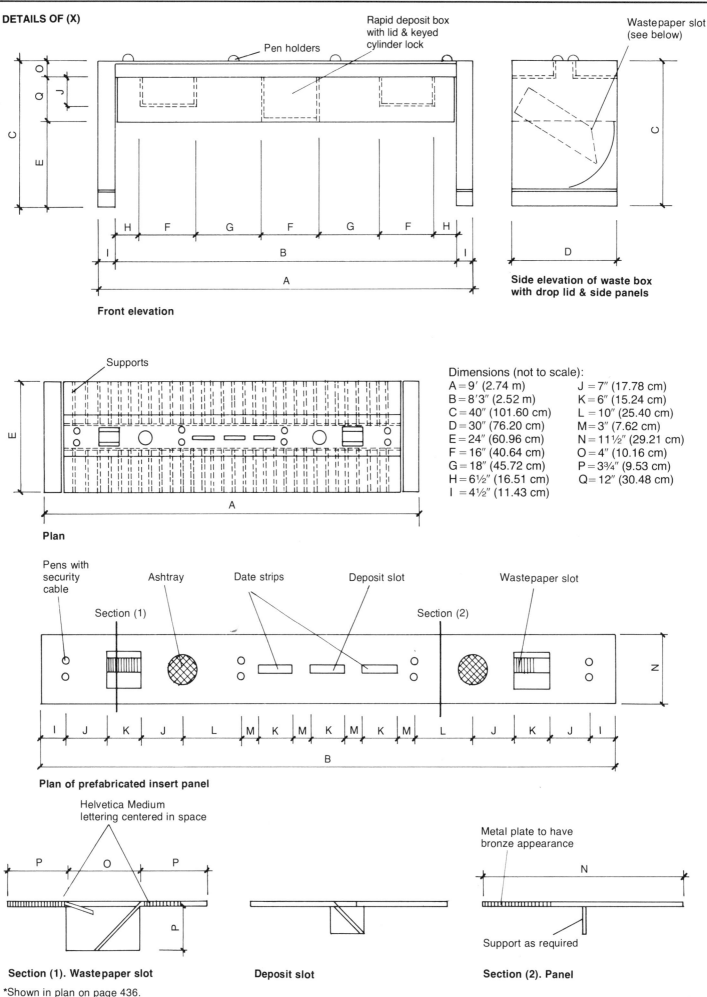

Pen holders

Rapid deposit box
with lid & keyed
cylinder lock

Wastepaper slot
(see below)

Front elevation

**Side elevation of waste box
with drop lid & side panels**

Supports

Plan

Dimensions (not to scale):

A = 9′ (2.74 m)	J = 7″ (17.78 cm)
B = 8′3″ (2.52 m)	K = 6″ (15.24 cm)
C = 40″ (101.60 cm)	L = 10″ (25.40 cm)
D = 30″ (76.20 cm)	M = 3″ (7.62 cm)
E = 24″ (60.96 cm)	N = 11½″ (29.21 cm)
F = 16″ (40.64 cm)	O = 4″ (10.16 cm)
G = 18″ (45.72 cm)	P = 3¾″ (9.53 cm)
H = 6½″ (16.51 cm)	Q = 12″ (30.48 cm)
I = 4½″ (11.43 cm)	

Pens with
security
cable

Section (1)

Ashtray

Date strips

Deposit slot

Section (2)

Wastepaper slot

Plan of prefabricated insert panel

Helvetica Medium
lettering centered in space

Metal plate to have
bronze appearance

Support as required

Section (1). Wastepaper slot

Deposit slot

Section (2). Panel

*Shown in plan on page 436.

CLASS II VAULT DOOR

Insurance classifications
Class II vault door currently provides 5R [12″ (30.48 cm) wall] or 9R [18″ (45.72 cm) wall] vault classifications. See current I.S.O. Vault Classification Chart in Burglary Insurance Manual.

Important dimensions
Clear opening: 78⅛″ X 36⅞″ (198.44 X 93.66 cm).
Door thickness: Door proper is 5½″ (13.97 cm) thick overall with ½″ (1.27 cm) steel backplate and 5″ (12.70 cm) of improved security material, forming a uniform, integrally designed monolithic security structure. It is more resistant than steel or reinforced concrete. Extensive laboratory testing has proven its effectiveness against all attack methods that must be prevented. These attack tests have included oxyacetylene cutting torch, abrasive wheels, rotating and jack hammers, carbide drills, hole saws, diamond core drills, and all commonly used hammers and tools.

Vestibule
All exposed portion of vestibule and frame clad with polished stainless steel clasps 12¾″ (32.39 cm) wall maximum standard for 5R insurance rating or 18¾″ (47.63 cm) wall maximum standard for 9R insurance rating.

Architrave
Standard: 85¾″ X 54⅝″ (217.81 X 137.76 cm).
Deluxe: 85¾″ X 84″ (217.81 X 213.36 cm).

Floor level
Minimum ramp, ½″ floor differential.

Swing
Right or left 180°.

Day gate (rod type)
Right-hand in-swing for right-hand doors; left-hand in-swing for left-hand doors. Self-closing, keylock outside, release latch inside.

Locks
a. Two counter-spy, 4 tumbler combination locks, UL listed group 1R with mechanical and thermal relock.
b. 3-movement, 120-hr shock-mounted timelock with emergency release.
c. Dayguard keylock.

Mechanism
Continuous full-height locking bars, interlock with frame both sides.

Ventilator
Emergency ventilator located in door frame, opposite hinge. Conduit and wiring (UL listed) supplied from vent to masonry opening power supply junction box. Alarm conduit, if required, furnished by others.

Foundations
Foundation below door masonry opening to support 3,500 lb (1589 kg) minimum, 8″ (20.32 cm) corbel to be full width of pit. Face of foundation and finish wall to be on same vertical plane.

Classification
The classification and the amount of protection are based upon the net working time to effect entry. The specific attack test passed by Class II consisted of the following:
1. An attempt to knock off the combination dial, punch or drill the spindle, and then release the lock mechanism by means of picking tools.
2. An attempt to penetrate through the door to the lock box, lug, carrying bar, or other parts of the mechanism and then release the boltwork by punching, prying, picking, or cutting.

VAULT DOORS USED WITH VARIOUS TYPES OF WALL MATERIALS

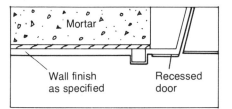

Paneling or sheetrock

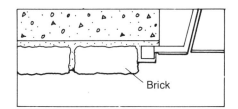

Brick or stone

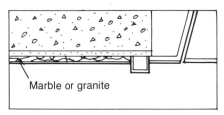

Marble or granite

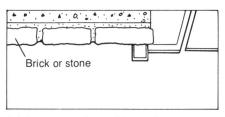

Brick or stone clasped by architrave

3. An attempt to cut a 96 sq in (0.74 m²) opening entirely through the door.
4. An attempt to cut all or sufficient bolts to allow the door to open.

UL marking
UL label to be attached to vault door plainly marked with the manufacturer's name or trademark with the specific earned classification rating—Class 1 (½ hr), Class II (1 hr) described above, Class III (2 hr). Each vault door shall be marked with its date of manufacture.

DETAILS OF (E)

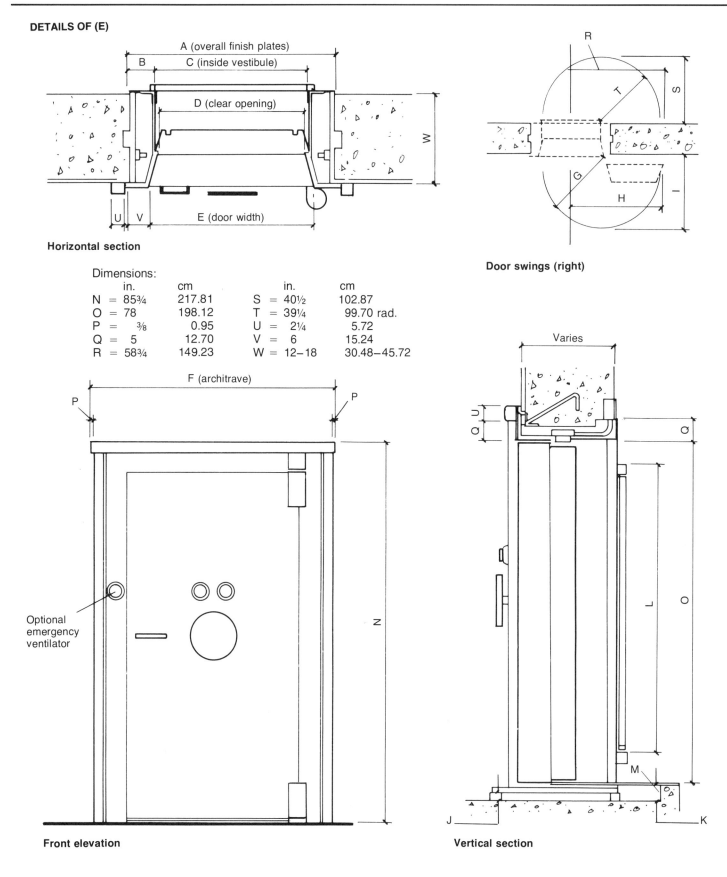

Horizontal section

Dimensions:

	in.	cm		in.	cm
N =	85¾	217.81	S =	40½	102.87
O =	78	198.12	T =	39¼	99.70 rad.
P =	⅜	0.95	U =	2¼	5.72
Q =	5	12.70	V =	6	15.24
R =	58¾	149.23	W =	12–18	30.48–45.72

Door swings (right)

Optional emergency ventilator

Front elevation

Vertical section

Dimensional variances in class II 3½", 7", & 10" doors

Models (in.)	A	B	C	D	E	F	G	H	I	J	K	L	M
American 3½"	51⅜	7	37⅜	36⅜	38¾	54⅝	39¼ rad.	59⅛	42⅜	2	2½	60	9¼
American 7"	51⅜	7	37⅜	36⅞	40½	56⅜	41 rad.	61⅛	44	3	3½	60	9¼
American 10"	53⅜	8	37⅜	37	42	58	42¾ rad.	64⅜	46⅝	3	3½	60	9¼

*Shown in plan on page 436.

DETAILS OF (F)

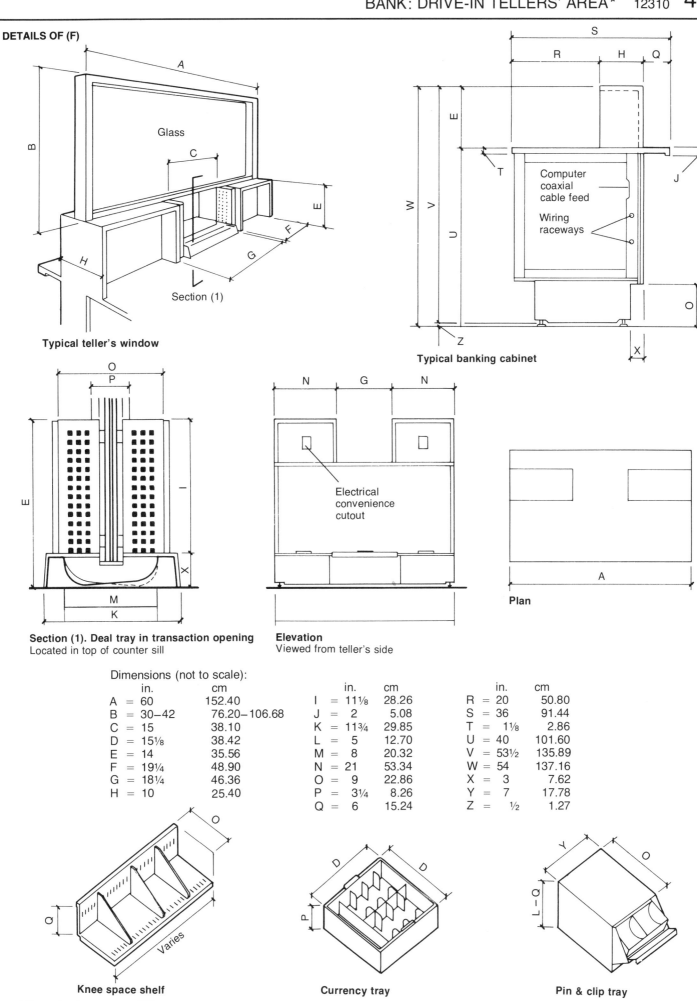

Glass

Section (1)

Typical teller's window

Computer coaxial cable feed

Wiring raceways

Typical banking cabinet

Electrical convenience cutout

Section (1). Deal tray in transaction opening
Located in top of counter sill

Elevation
Viewed from teller's side

Plan

Dimensions (not to scale):

	in.	cm		in.	cm		in.	cm
A =	60	152.40	I =	11⅛	28.26	R =	20	50.80
B =	30–42	76.20–106.68	J =	2	5.08	S =	36	91.44
C =	15	38.10	K =	11¾	29.85	T =	1⅛	2.86
D =	15⅛	38.42	L =	5	12.70	U =	40	101.60
E =	14	35.56	M =	8	20.32	V =	53½	135.89
F =	19¼	48.90	N =	21	53.34	W =	54	137.16
G =	18¼	46.36	O =	9	22.86	X =	3	7.62
H =	10	25.40	P =	3¼	8.26	Y =	7	17.78
			Q =	6	15.24	Z =	½	1.27

Knee space shelf

Currency tray

Pin & clip tray

*Shown in plan on page 436.

Chapter 17

RETAIL SPACES, BEAUTY SALONS, AND HEALTH STUDIOS

Planning merchandise locations

Retail spatial concepts are based on knowledge of merchandising psychology aimed at arousing and maintaining customer interest.

Merchandise is grouped into three major categories that determine department and subdepartment arrangements.
1. Impulse merchandise is the expensive luxury item placed in very obvious spots in the retail space:
   a. Near the front entry
   b. At junction of major aisles
   c. At the ends of counter islands
   d. In showcases in the cash/wrapping areas
2. Convenience items are not always high profit, but encourage customers to return. These are placed near the impulse items.
3. Demand items are staple merchanise for which customers frequently return. These items are placed in the center of islands or counters and along side walls.

Planning merchandise locations must be carefully coordinated with customer paths of travel (aisles) and the following service areas: (1) cashier and wrapping counters and (2) information counters. Customer convenience areas should include restrooms, dressing rooms, mirrors, sitting areas, and water fountains.*

*Conveniences vary depending on the size and type of store.

Typical retail store dimensions

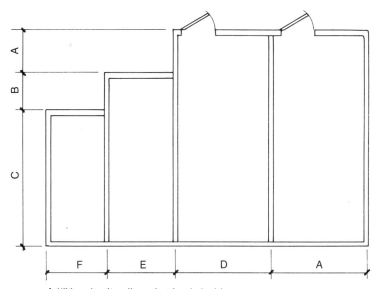

Additional exits allowed at back & sides

Typical aisle dimensions

	Min. length†		Width	
	ft/in.	m	ft/in.	m
Customer:				
Center aisles	13'	3.96	3'6"	1.07
Side aisles	5'6"–7'	1.68–2.13	4'6"	1.37
Employee aisles			2'–3'	0.61–0.91
Islands/showcases	10'	3.05	5'-10'	1.52–3.05
Floor tables	4'–7'	1.22–2.13	2'6"–3'	0.76–0.91

†Check local codes.

Dimensions:

		ft	m
A	=	80	24.38
B	=	60	18.29
C	=	50	15.24
D	=	40	12.19
E	=	20	6.10
F	=	15	4.57
G	=	8–10	2.44–3.05
H	=	5	1.52
I	=	7	2.13
J	=	6	1.83
K	=	2.5	0.76
L	=	4	1.22
M	=	3	0.91

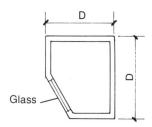

Glass

Typical corner retail space in a mall

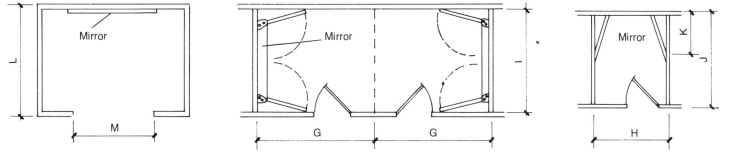

Typical dressing & fitting room dimensions

Dressing room sizes vary from large spaces for fitting wedding gowns to small-sized cubicles. Large fitting rooms are often equipped with chairs, a table, and a stool for fitting adjustments. Small dressing rooms in women's clothing stores normally have only essential clothes hooks, a small shelf, and a mirror. Some have drapery over the opening or a half door.

Small fitting rooms in men's clothing stores are not equipped with mirrors. The mirror is purposefully placed in the clothing display area so the customer must leave the fitting room to view the garment's fit. This allows the salesperson to encourage the customer to make the purchase.

Note: (X) Many retail stores are planned on a 4' (1.22 m) module to accommodate standard retail fixtures.

Legend:
A = storage
B = dressing rooms
C = comfort zone (seating)
D = cash/wrap counters
E = display, small items
MR = mirror
X = see note

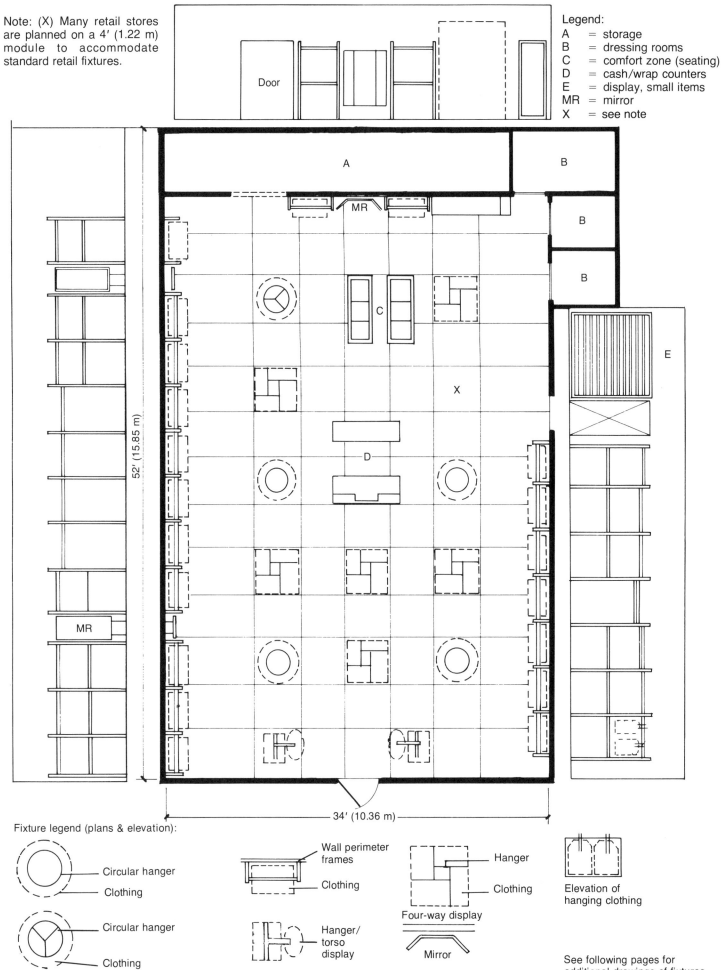

Door

A

B

MR

B

B

C

E

X

D

MR

52' (15.85 m)

34' (10.36 m)

Fixture legend (plans & elevation):

Circular hanger
Clothing

Circular hanger
Clothing

Wall perimeter frames
Clothing

Hanger/ torso display

Hanger
Clothing

Four-way display

Mirror

Elevation of hanging clothing

See following pages for additional drawings of fixtures.

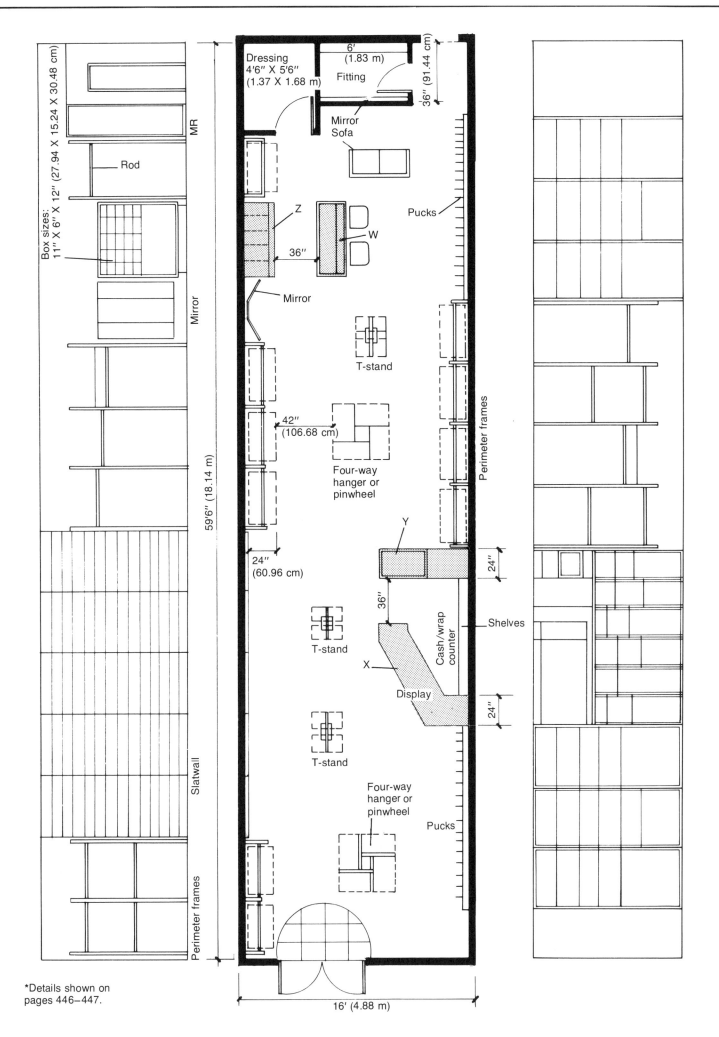

Box sizes:
11" X 6" X 12" (27.94 X 15.24 X 30.48 cm)

MR

Rod

Mirror

Slatwall

Perimeter frames

Dressing
4'6" X 5'6"
(1.37 X 1.68 m)

Fitting

6'
(1.83 m)

36" (91.44 cm)

Mirror
Sofa

Pucks

Z

W

36"

Mirror

T-stand

42"
(106.68 cm)

Four-way
hanger or
pinwheel

59'6" (18.14 m)

Perimeter frames

Y

24"

36"

X

Display

Cash/wrap
counter

Shelves

24"

24"
(60.96 cm)

T-stand

T-stand

Four-way
hanger or
pinwheel

Pucks

16' (4.88 m)

*Details shown on
pages 446–447.

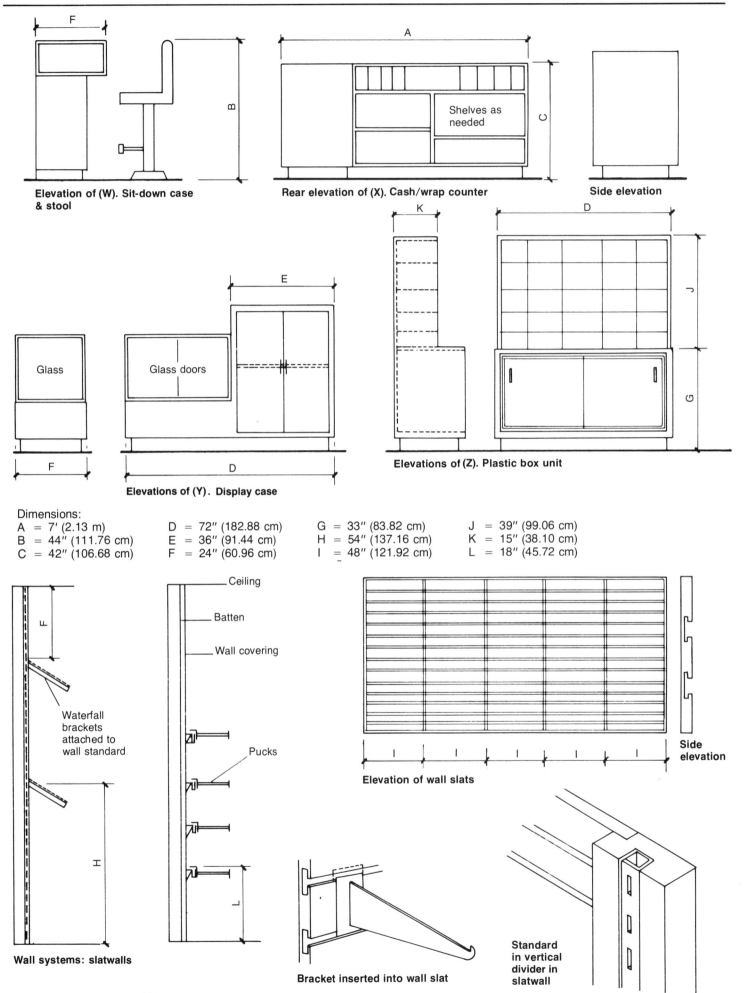

Elevation of (W). Sit-down case & stool

Rear elevation of (X). Cash/wrap counter

Shelves as needed

Side elevation

Glass

Glass doors

Elevations of (Y). Display case

Elevations of (Z). Plastic box unit

Dimensions:
A = 7' (2.13 m) D = 72" (182.88 cm) G = 33" (83.82 cm) J = 39" (99.06 cm)
B = 44" (111.76 cm) E = 36" (91.44 cm) H = 54" (137.16 cm) K = 15" (38.10 cm)
C = 42" (106.68 cm) F = 24" (60.96 cm) I = 48" (121.92 cm) L = 18" (45.72 cm)

Ceiling

Batten

Wall covering

Waterfall brackets attached to wall standard

Pucks

Elevation of wall slats

Side elevation

Wall systems: slatwalls

Bracket inserted into wall slat

Standard in vertical divider in slatwall

*Shown in plan on page 445.

MODULAR PERIMETER FRAMES

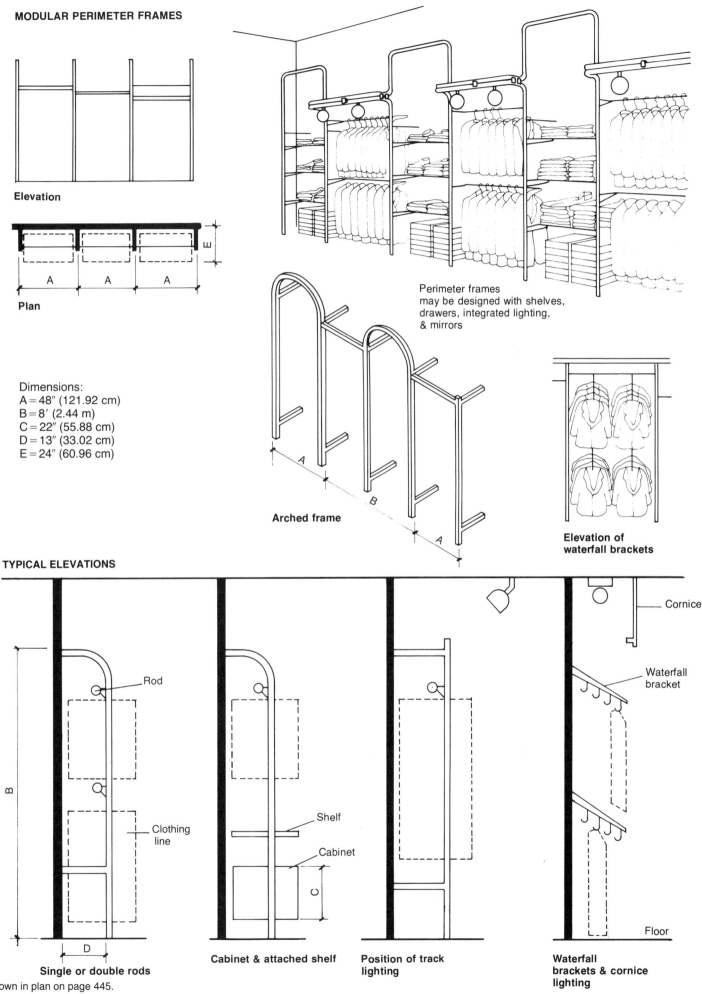

Elevation

Plan

Dimensions:
A = 48″ (121.92 cm)
B = 8′ (2.44 m)
C = 22″ (55.88 cm)
D = 13″ (33.02 cm)
E = 24″ (60.96 cm)

Arched frame

Perimeter frames
may be designed with shelves,
drawers, integrated lighting,
& mirrors

**Elevation of
waterfall brackets**

TYPICAL ELEVATIONS

Rod

Clothing
line

Single or double rods

Shelf

Cabinet

Cabinet & attached shelf

**Position of track
lighting**

Cornice

Waterfall
bracket

Floor

**Waterfall
brackets & cornice
lighting**

*Shown in plan on page 445.

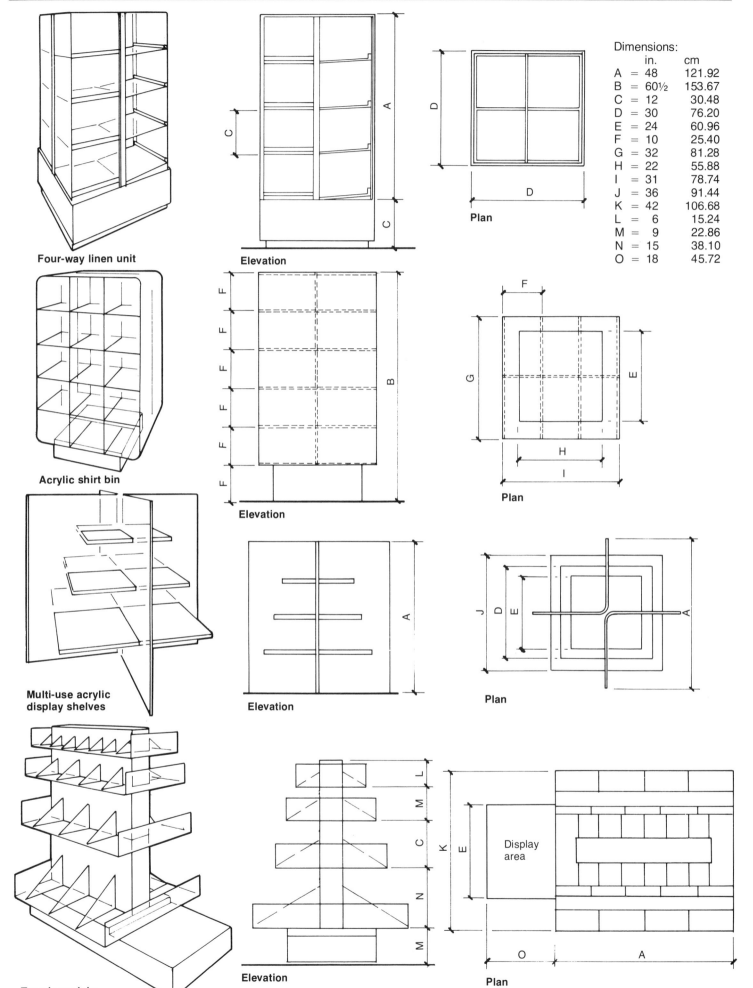

Four-way linen unit

Elevation

Plan

Dimensions:

		in.	cm
A	=	48	121.92
B	=	60½	153.67
C	=	12	30.48
D	=	30	76.20
E	=	24	60.96
F	=	10	25.40
G	=	32	81.28
H	=	22	55.88
I	=	31	78.74
J	=	36	91.44
K	=	42	106.68
L	=	6	15.24
M	=	9	22.86
N	=	15	38.10
O	=	18	45.72

Acrylic shirt bin

Elevation

Plan

Multi-use acrylic display shelves

Elevation

Plan

Towel gondola

Elevation

Plan

Display area

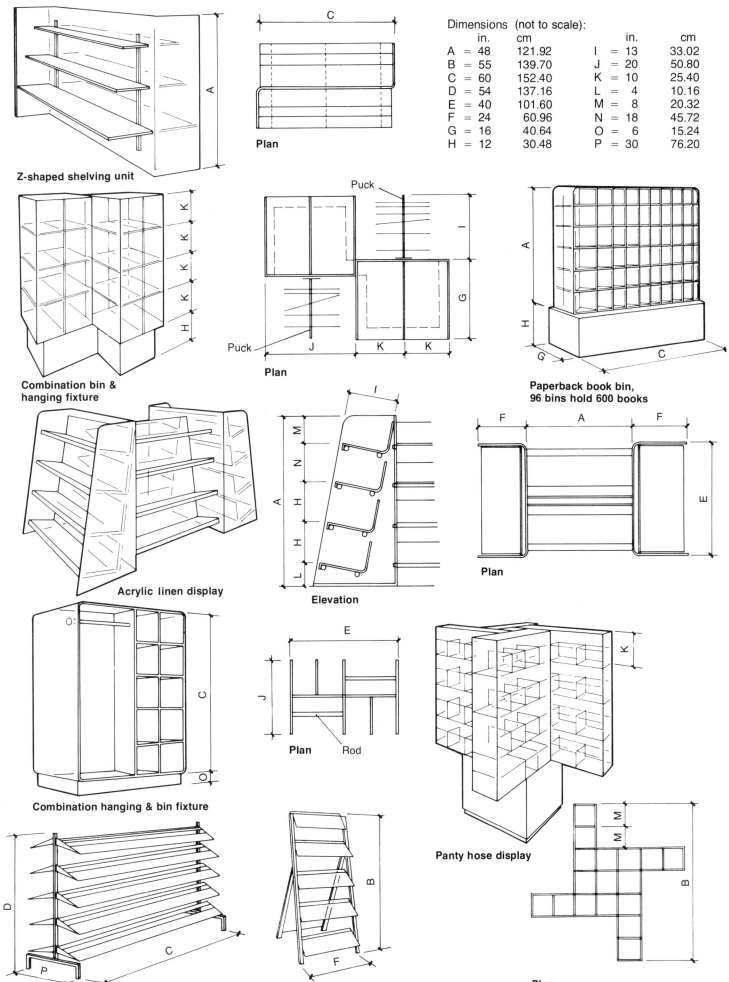

Plan

Dimensions (not to scale):

	in.	cm			in.	cm
A	= 48	121.92	I	=	13	33.02
B	= 55	139.70	J	=	20	50.80
C	= 60	152.40	K	=	10	25.40
D	= 54	137.16	L	=	4	10.16
E	= 40	101.60	M	=	8	20.32
F	= 24	60.96	N	=	18	45.72
G	= 16	40.64	O	=	6	15.24
H	= 12	30.48	P	=	30	76.20

Z-shaped shelving unit

Combination bin & hanging fixture

Puck

Plan

Paperback book bin, 96 bins hold 600 books

Acrylic linen display

Elevation

Plan

Combination hanging & bin fixture

Plan   Rod

Panty hose display

Shoe display

Acrylic racks 9″, (22.86 cm) wide shelves

Plan

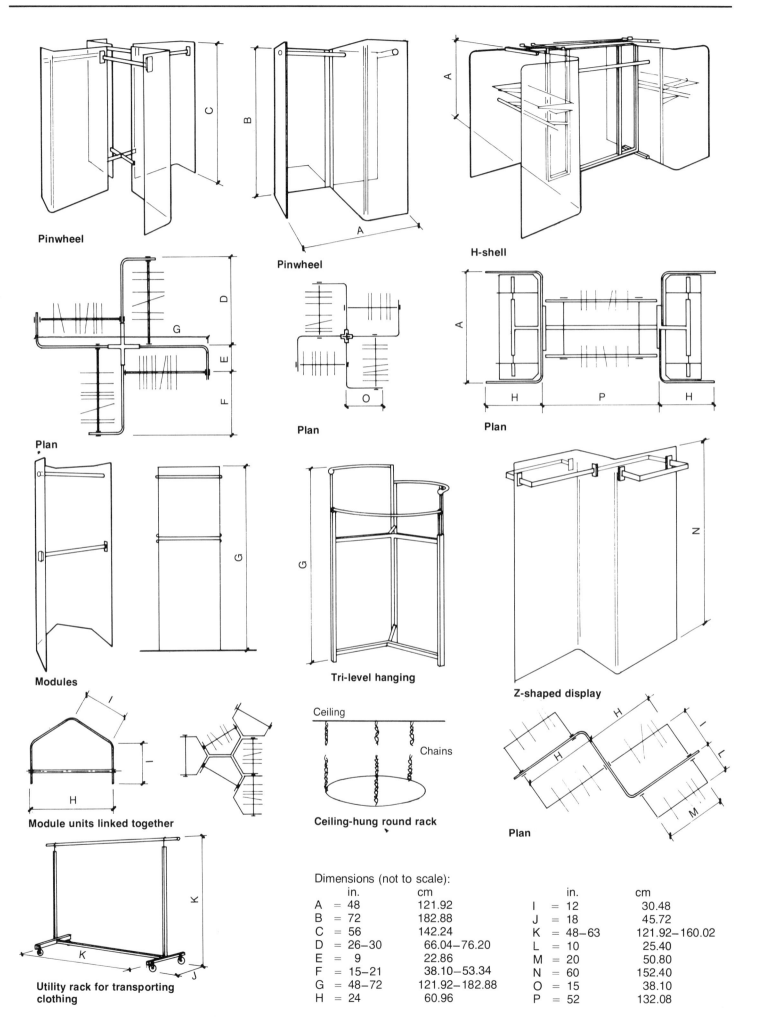

Pinwheel

Pinwheel

H-shell

Plan

Pinwheel

Plan

Plan

Plan

Modules

Tri-level hanging

Z-shaped display

Module units linked together

Ceiling

Chains

Ceiling-hung round rack

Plan

Utility rack for transporting clothing

Dimensions (not to scale):

	in.	cm			in.	cm
A =	48	121.92		I =	12	30.48
B =	72	182.88		J =	18	45.72
C =	56	142.24		K =	48–63	121.92–160.02
D =	26–30	66.04–76.20		L =	10	25.40
E =	9	22.86		M =	20	50.80
F =	15–21	38.10–53.34		N =	60	152.40
G =	48–72	121.92–182.88		O =	15	38.10
H =	24	60.96		P =	52	132.08

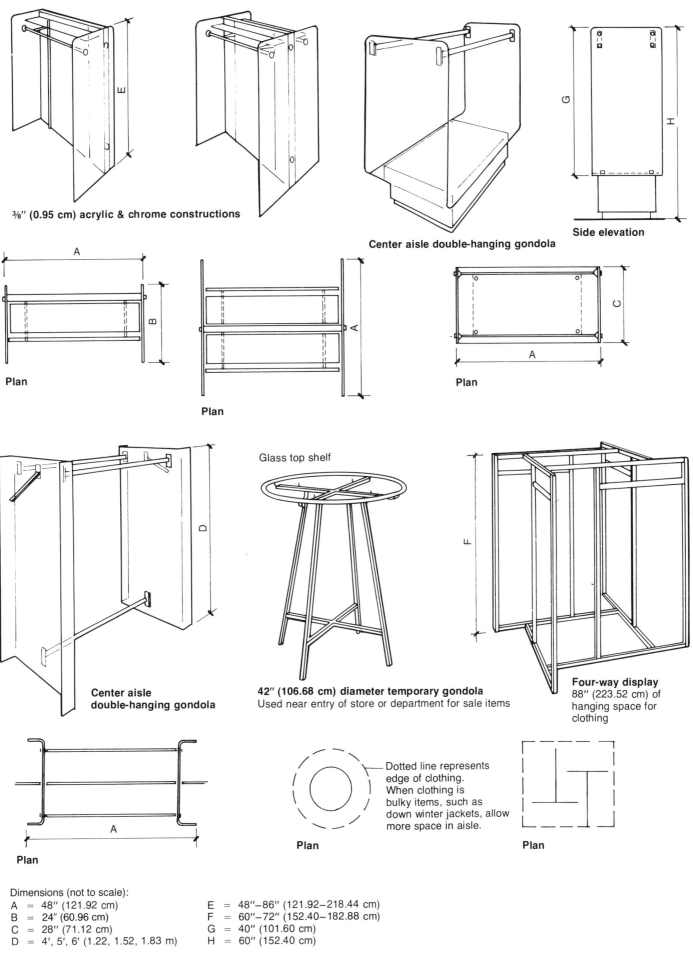

⅜″ (0.95 cm) acrylic & chrome constructions

Center aisle double-hanging gondola

Side elevation

Plan

Plan

Plan

**Center aisle
double-hanging gondola**

Glass top shelf

42″ (106.68 cm) diameter temporary gondola
Used near entry of store or department for sale items

Four-way display
88″ (223.52 cm) of
hanging space for
clothing

Plan

Dotted line represents
edge of clothing.
When clothing is
bulky items, such as
down winter jackets, allow
more space in aisle.

Plan

Plan

Dimensions (not to scale):
A = 48″ (121.92 cm)
B = 24″ (60.96 cm)
C = 28″ (71.12 cm)
D = 4′, 5′, 6′ (1.22, 1.52, 1.83 m)

E = 48″–86″ (121.92–218.44 cm)
F = 60″–72″ (152.40–182.88 cm)
G = 40″ (101.60 cm)
H = 60″ (152.40 cm)

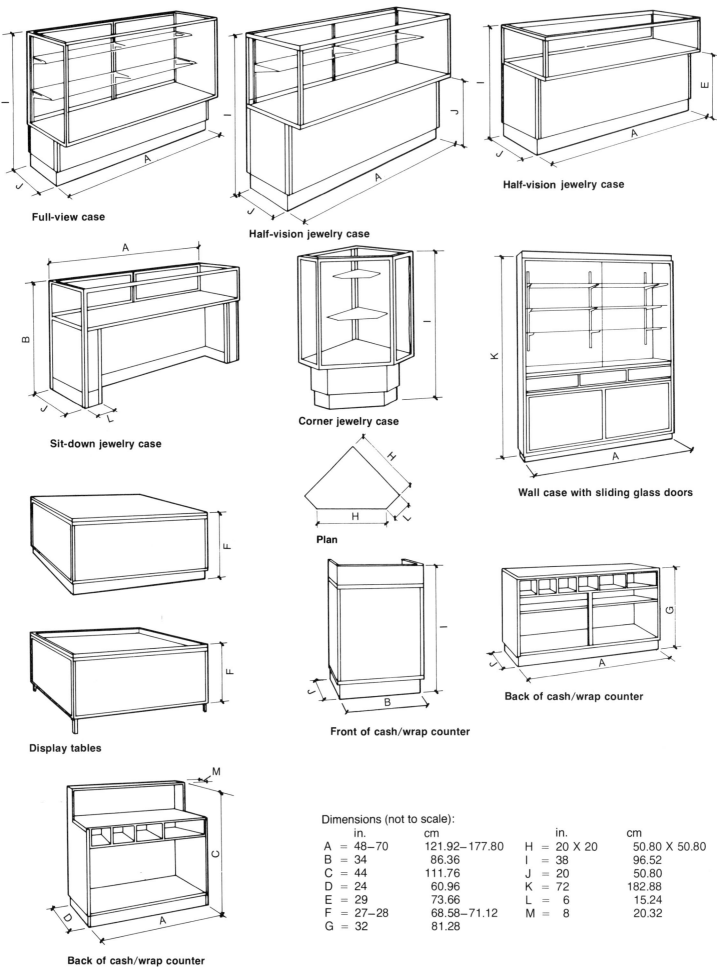

Full-view case

Half-vision jewelry case

Half-vision jewelry case

Sit-down jewelry case

Corner jewelry case

Plan

Wall case with sliding glass doors

Display tables

Front of cash/wrap counter

Back of cash/wrap counter

Back of cash/wrap counter

Dimensions (not to scale):

	in.	cm		in.	cm
A =	48–70	121.92–177.80	H =	20 X 20	50.80 X 50.80
B =	34	86.36	I =	38	96.52
C =	44	111.76	J =	20	50.80
D =	24	60.96	K =	72	182.88
E =	29	73.66	L =	6	15.24
F =	27–28	68.58–71.12	M =	8	20.32
G =	32	81.28			

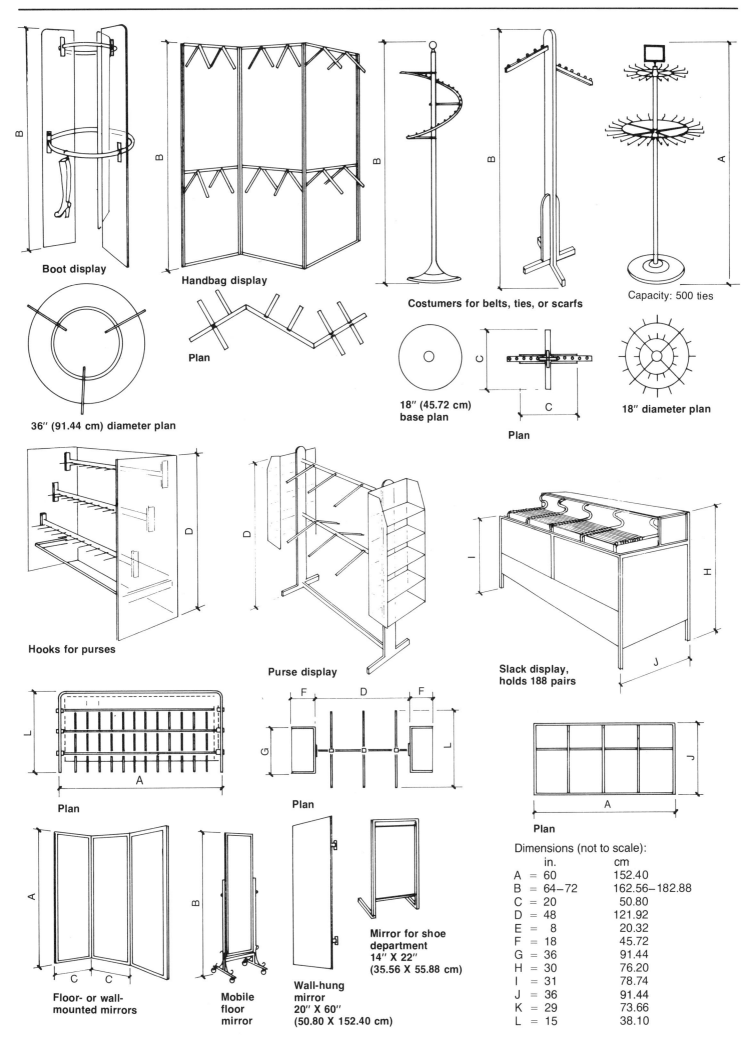

Boot display

36" (91.44 cm) diameter plan

Handbag display

Plan

Costumers for belts, ties, or scarfs

18" (45.72 cm)
base plan

Plan

18" diameter plan

Capacity: 500 ties

Hooks for purses

Purse display

**Slack display,
holds 188 pairs**

Plan

Plan

Plan

Plan

**Floor- or wall-
mounted mirrors**

**Mobile
floor
mirror**

**Wall-hung
mirror
20" X 60"
(50.80 X 152.40 cm)**

**Mirror for shoe
department
14" X 22"
(35.56 X 55.88 cm)**

Dimensions (not to scale):

	in.	cm
A =	60	152.40
B =	64–72	162.56–182.88
C =	20	50.80
D =	48	121.92
E =	8	20.32
F =	18	45.72
G =	36	91.44
H =	30	76.20
I =	31	78.74
J =	36	91.44
K =	29	73.66
L =	15	38.10

WRAPPING DISPENSERS

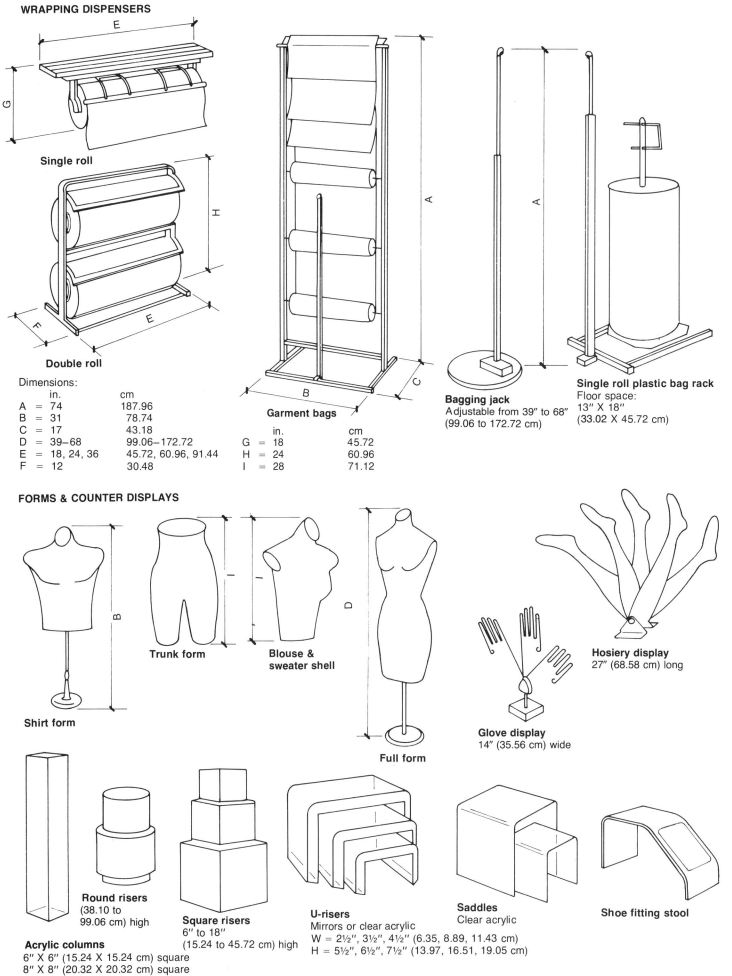

Single roll

Double roll

Dimensions:

	in.	cm
A	= 74	187.96
B	= 31	78.74
C	= 17	43.18
D	= 39–68	99.06–172.72
E	= 18, 24, 36	45.72, 60.96, 91.44
F	= 12	30.48

Garment bags

	in.	cm
G	= 18	45.72
H	= 24	60.96
I	= 28	71.12

Bagging jack
Adjustable from 39″ to 68″
(99.06 to 172.72 cm)

Single roll plastic bag rack
Floor space:
13″ X 18″
(33.02 X 45.72 cm)

FORMS & COUNTER DISPLAYS

Shirt form

Trunk form

**Blouse &
sweater shell**

Full form

Glove display
14″ (35.56 cm) wide

Hosiery display
27″ (68.58 cm) long

Acrylic columns
6″ X 6″ (15.24 X 15.24 cm) square
8″ X 8″ (20.32 X 20.32 cm) square
12″–30″ (30.48–76.20 cm) high

Round risers
(38.10 to
99.06 cm) high

Square risers
6″ to 18″
(15.24 to 45.72 cm) high

U-risers
Mirrors or clear acrylic
W = 2½″, 3½″, 4½″ (6.35, 8.89, 11.43 cm)
H = 5½″, 6½″, 7½″ (13.97, 16.51, 19.05 cm)

Saddles
Clear acrylic

Shoe fitting stool

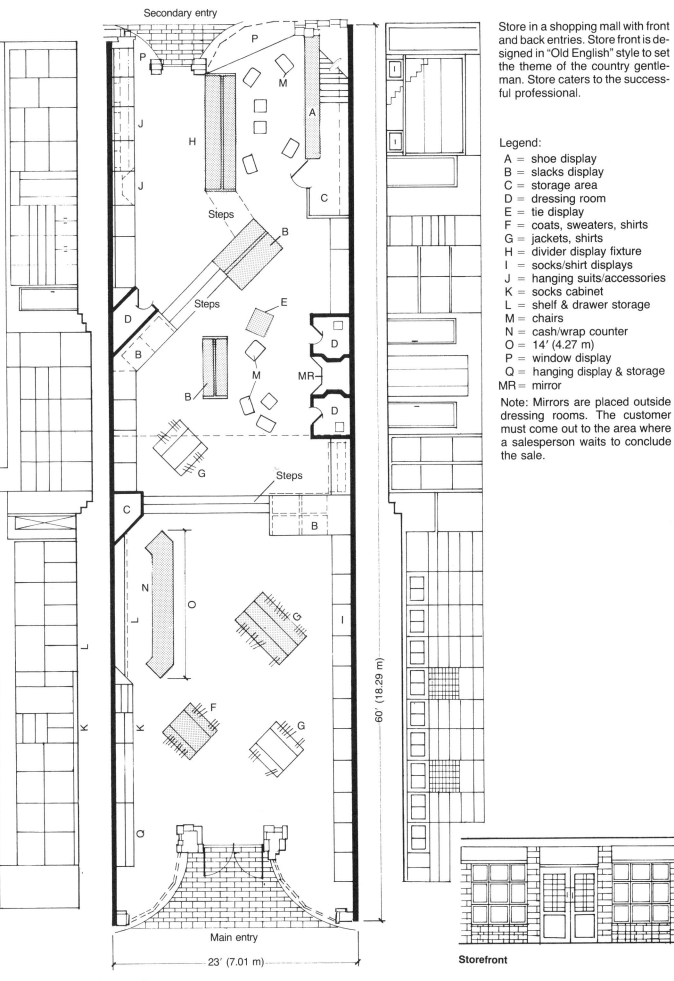

Secondary entry

Steps

Steps

Steps

Steps

D

B

B

B

E

M

MR

D

D

C

A

P

P

M

H

J

J

G

C

N

L

O

L

K

K

K

F

G

G

I

Q

Main entry

60' (18.29 m)

23' (7.01 m)

Store in a shopping mall with front and back entries. Store front is designed in "Old English" style to set the theme of the country gentleman. Store caters to the successful professional.

Legend:
A = shoe display
B = slacks display
C = storage area
D = dressing room
E = tie display
F = coats, sweaters, shirts
G = jackets, shirts
H = divider display fixture
I = socks/shirt displays
J = hanging suits/accessories
K = socks cabinet
L = shelf & drawer storage
M = chairs
N = cash/wrap counter
O = 14' (4.27 m)
P = window display
Q = hanging display & storage
MR = mirror

Note: Mirrors are placed outside dressing rooms. The customer must come out to the area where a salesperson waits to conclude the sale.

Storefront

*See details on pages 456–459.

DETAILS OF (F) & (G)

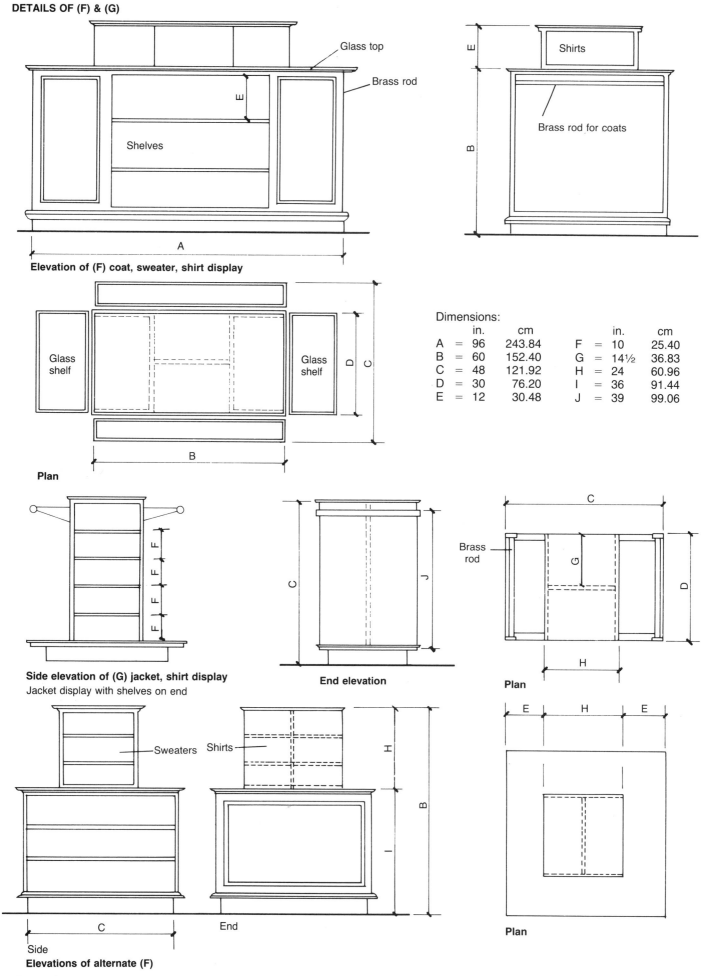

Glass top

Brass rod

Shelves

Elevation of (F) coat, sweater, shirt display

Shirts

Brass rod for coats

Glass shelf

Glass shelf

Plan

Dimensions:

		in.	cm			in.	cm
A	=	96	243.84	F	=	10	25.40
B	=	60	152.40	G	=	14½	36.83
C	=	48	121.92	H	=	24	60.96
D	=	30	76.20	I	=	36	91.44
E	=	12	30.48	J	=	39	99.06

Side elevation of (G) jacket, shirt display
Jacket display with shelves on end

End elevation

Brass rod

Plan

Sweaters

Shirts

Plan

Side

End

Elevations of alternate (F)

*Shown in plan on page 455.

DETAILS OF (A), (B), (E), (H), & (N)

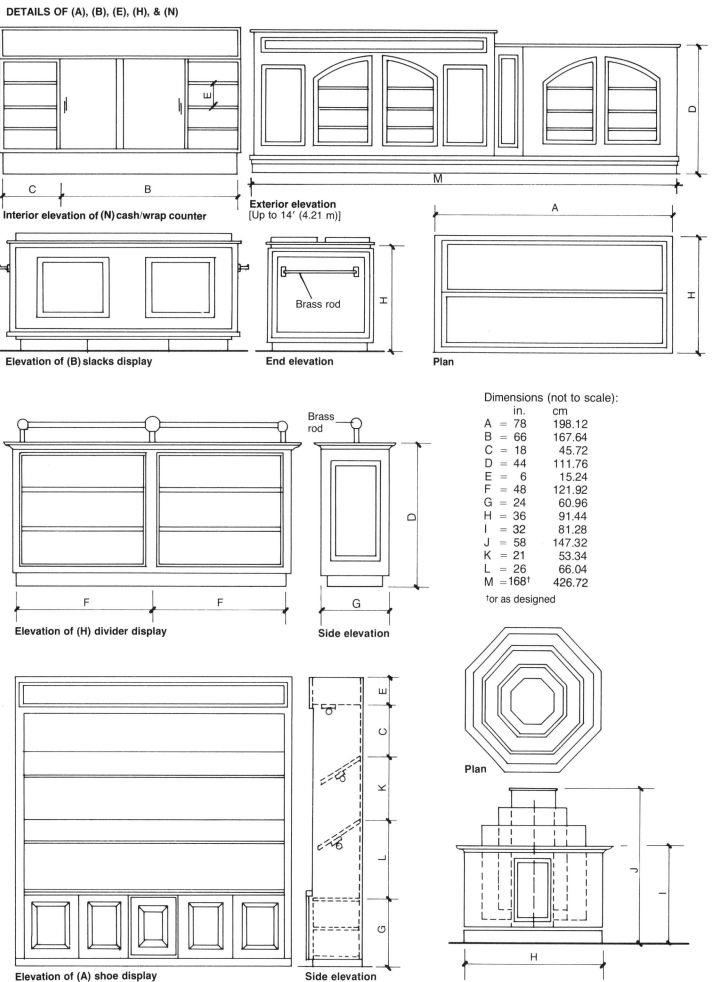

Interior elevation of (N) cash/wrap counter

Exterior elevation
[Up to 14′ (4.21 m)]

Elevation of (B) slacks display

Brass rod

End elevation

Plan

Elevation of (H) divider display

Brass rod

Side elevation

Dimensions (not to scale):

		in.	cm
A	=	78	198.12
B	=	66	167.64
C	=	18	45.72
D	=	44	111.76
E	=	6	15.24
F	=	48	121.92
G	=	24	60.96
H	=	36	91.44
I	=	32	81.28
J	=	58	147.32
K	=	21	53.34
L	=	26	66.04
M	=	168†	426.72

†or as designed

Plan

Elevation of (A) shoe display

Side elevation

Section of (E) tie display

*Shown in plan on page 455.

DETAILS OF (H) & (Q)

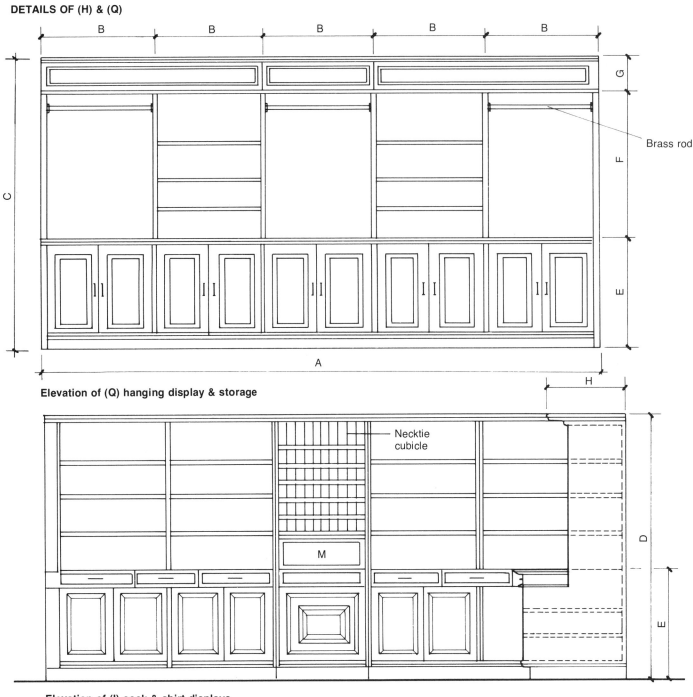

Brass rod

Elevation of (Q) hanging display & storage

Necktie cubicle

M

Elevation of (I) sock & shirt displays

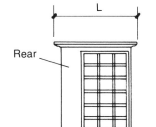

Rear

Elevations of (I) necktie cubicle

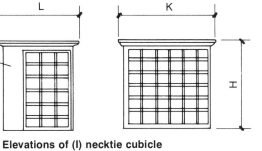

Back

*Shown in plan on page 455.   **Plan**

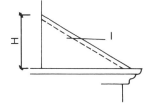

Elevation of (M) slant presentation

Dimensions (not to scale):
A = 16' (4.88 m)
B = 36" (91.44 cm)
C = 96" (243.84 cm)
D = 84" (213.36 cm)
E = 38" (96.52 cm)
F = 48" (121.92 cm)
G = 12" (30.48 cm)
H = 16" (40.64 cm)
I = 30°
J = 3" (7.62 cm)
K = 30" (76.20 cm)
L = 24" (60.96 cm)
M = slanted glass display for shirts & ties (called "slant presentation")

Note: Cubicles can be designed for ties or socks: 6" X 6" (15.24 X 15.24 cm) [ties are stored rolled]; 3" X 3" (7.62 X 7.62 cm).

DETAILS OF (J), (K), & (L)

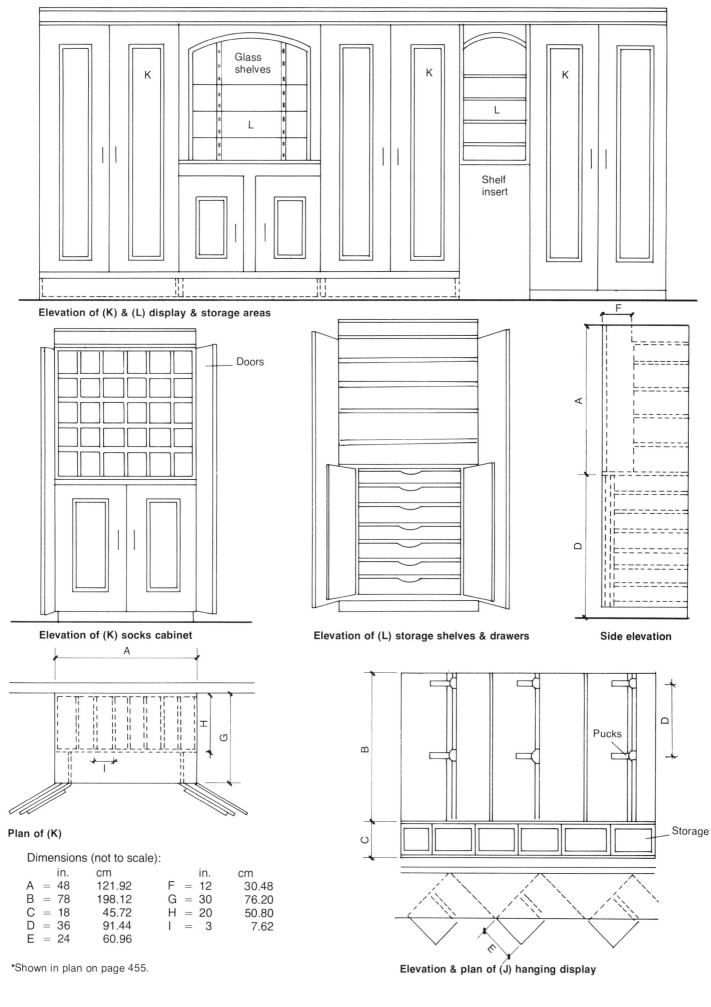

Elevation of (K) & (L) display & storage areas

Elevation of (K) socks cabinet

Elevation of (L) storage shelves & drawers

Side elevation

Plan of (K)

Dimensions (not to scale):

	in.	cm		in.	cm
A =	48	121.92	F =	12	30.48
B =	78	198.12	G =	30	76.20
C =	18	45.72	H =	20	50.80
D =	36	91.44	I =	3	7.62
E =	24	60.96			

*Shown in plan on page 455.

Elevation & plan of (J) hanging display

Location: mall
Square footage: 3,618 (336.12 m²)

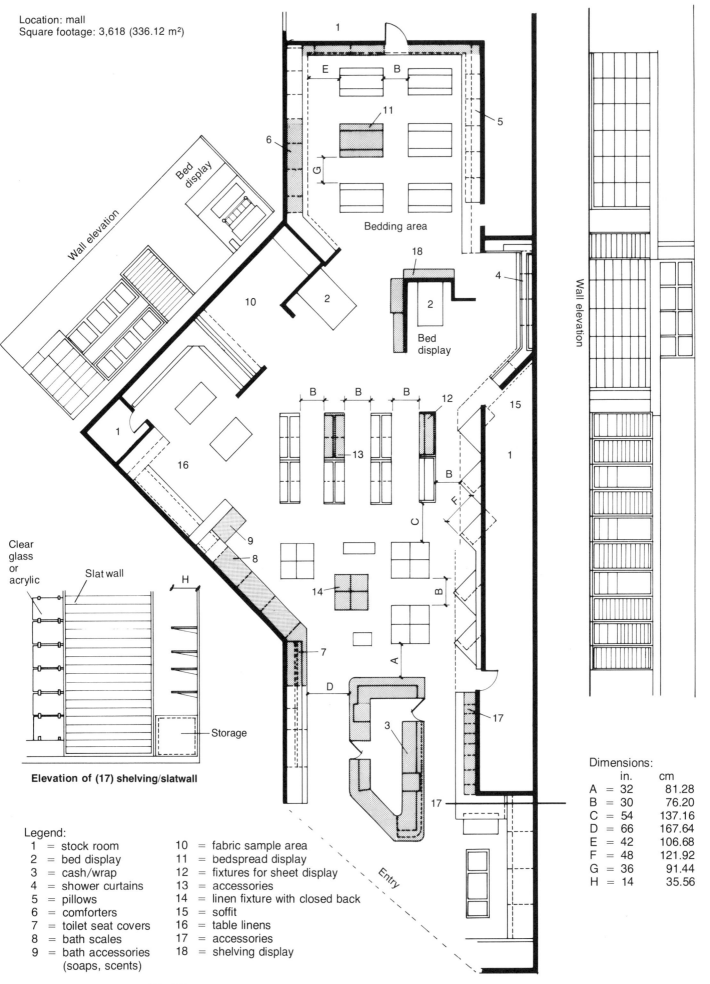

Wall elevation

Bed display

Wall elevation

1

E   B

6

5

11

G

Bedding area

10

2

18

2

Bed display

4

B   B   B

12

15

13

1

16

1

B

9

F

8

C

Clear
glass
or
acrylic

Slat wall

H

14

B

Storage

A

Elevation of (17) shelving/slatwall

7

D

3

17

17

Entry

Legend:
1 = stock room
2 = bed display
3 = cash/wrap
4 = shower curtains
5 = pillows
6 = comforters
7 = toilet seat covers
8 = bath scales
9 = bath accessories
    (soaps, scents)
10 = fabric sample area
11 = bedspread display
12 = fixtures for sheet display
13 = accessories
14 = linen fixture with closed back
15 = soffit
16 = table linens
17 = accessories
18 = shelving display

Dimensions:
	in.	cm
A =	32	81.28
B =	30	76.20
C =	54	137.16
D =	66	167.64
E =	42	106.68
F =	48	121.92
G =	36	91.44
H =	14	35.56

*Details shown on pages 461–463.

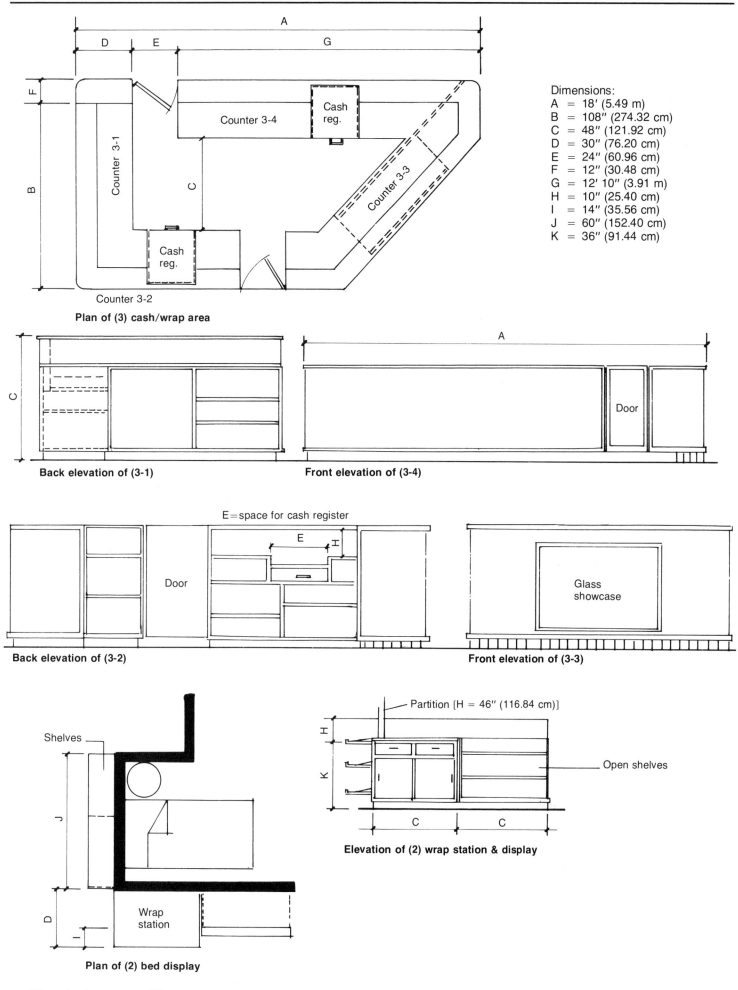

Plan of (3) cash/wrap area

Counter 3-1
Counter 3-2
Counter 3-3
Counter 3-4
Cash reg.
Cash reg.

Dimensions:
A = 18' (5.49 m)
B = 108" (274.32 cm)
C = 48" (121.92 cm)
D = 30" (76.20 cm)
E = 24" (60.96 cm)
F = 12" (30.48 cm)
G = 12' 10" (3.91 m)
H = 10" (25.40 cm)
I = 14" (35.56 cm)
J = 60" (152.40 cm)
K = 36" (91.44 cm)

Back elevation of (3-1)

Door

Front elevation of (3-4)

E = space for cash register

Door

Back elevation of (3-2)

Glass showcase

Front elevation of (3-3)

Shelves

Wrap station

Plan of (2) bed display

Partition [H = 46" (116.84 cm)]

Open shelves

Elevation of (2) wrap station & display

*Shown in plan on page 460.

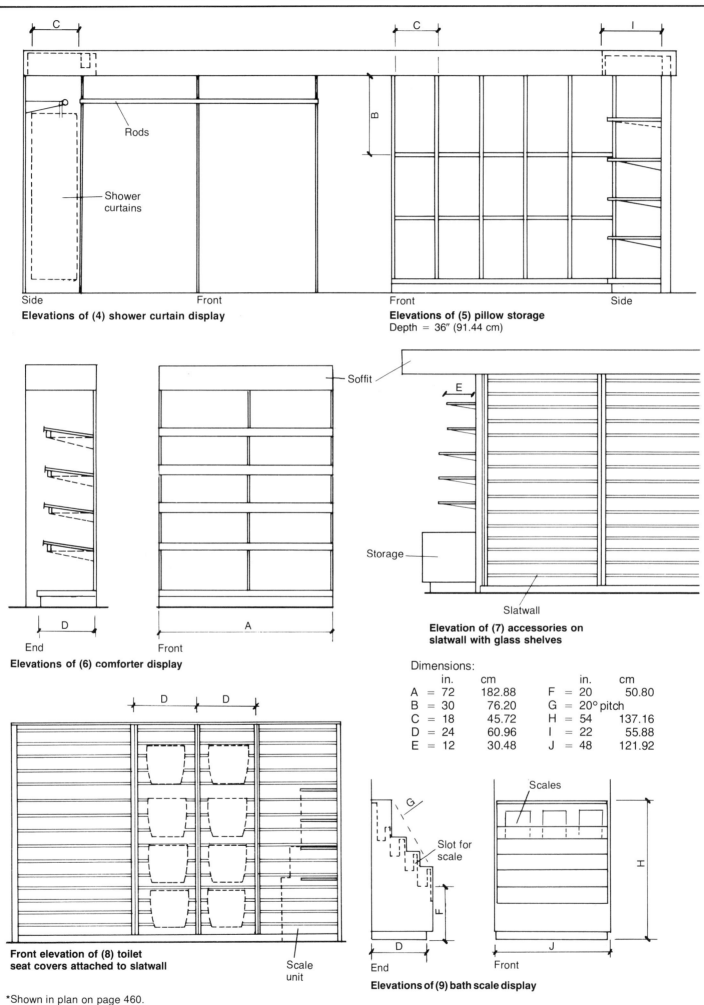

Rods

Shower
curtains

Side
Front
Elevations of (4) shower curtain display

Front
Side
Elevations of (5) pillow storage
Depth = 36″ (91.44 cm)

End
Elevations of (6) comforter display

Front

Soffit

Storage

Slatwall

**Elevation of (7) accessories on
slatwall with glass shelves**

Dimensions:

	in.	cm		in.	cm
A =	72	182.88	F =	20	50.80
B =	30	76.20	G =	20° pitch	
C =	18	45.72	H =	54	137.16
D =	24	60.96	I =	22	55.88
E =	12	30.48	J =	48	121.92

**Front elevation of (8) toilet
seat covers attached to slatwall**

Scale
unit

Scales

Slot for
scale

End
Front
Elevations of (9) bath scale display

*Shown in plan on page 460.

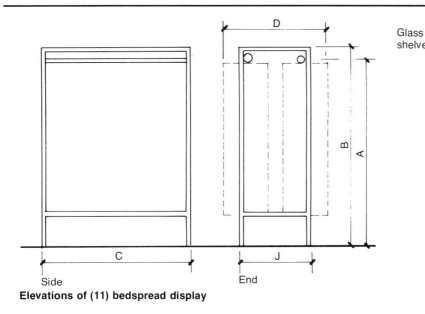

Side

End

Elevations of (11) bedspread display

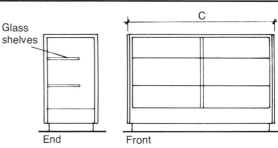

Glass shelves

End   Front

Elevations of (12) glass full-vision fixture

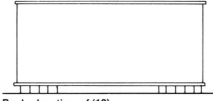

Back elevation of (12)

Dimensions:

	in.	cm		in.	cm
A =	72	182.88	F =	58	147.32
B =	76	193.04	G =	28	71.12
C =	60	152.40	H =	12	30.48
D =	42	106.68	I =	14	35.56
E =	64	162.56	J =	30	76.20

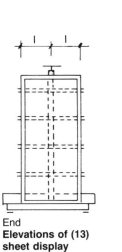

End

Elevations of (13) sheet display

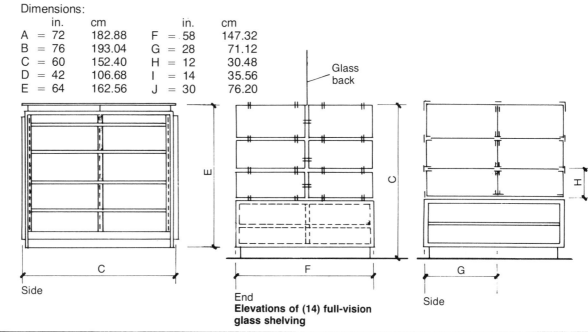

Side

Glass back

End

Elevations of (14) full-vision glass shelving

Side

Folded linen sizes† (in.)

	W	D	H
Flat sheets:			
Twin	8¼	13	1½
Double ‡	10⅛	13	2
Queen	11¼	13¾	2
King	13½	13¾	2
Fitted sheets:			
Twin	9	13	1½
Double	9	13	2
Queen	9	13	2
King	9	13	2
Pillowcases:			
Standard ‡	8	12	1
King	8	12	1½
Pillows ‡	20	26	6
King pillows	20	36	6

	W	D	H
Blankets ‡:			
Twin	16½	22½	8
Double	20	22½	8½
Queen/king	27	22½	9½
Towels:			
Hand	5½	9	1
Face	7½	13	1
Bath	11	11	2
	12	12	2
	13	12½	2
	14	13	2
Bath sheet	12	17	2½
Washcloth	6	12	1
Bath mat	10	8½	2½
	10	9	2½

‡For storage of linen and fixed shelves.
For storage in drawers deduct 1″ to 2″ (2.54 to 5.08 cm) [height].

6 double sheets	12	14	12
5 pillowcases	12	8	8
4 blankets	23	19	26
3 pillows	18	26	17

*Shown in plan on page 460.

†Folded linen sizes can be used to make decisions on the number and size of storage and display shelves required.

This store is located in a shopping mall. The back portion of the store contains a small, exclusive clothing area.

Dimensions:
A = 5'0"   (1.52 m)
B = 4'0"   (1.22 m)
C = 6'0"   (1.83 m)

Legend:
W = jewelry display
X = cash/wrap desk
Y = clothing display
Z = jewelry showcases

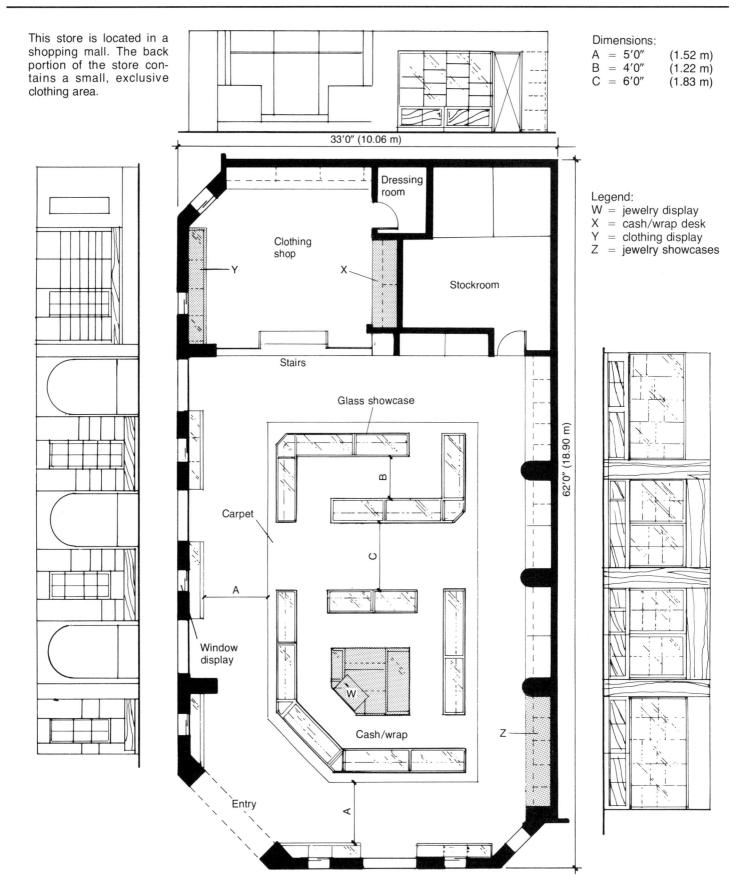

33'0" (10.06 m)

62'0" (18.90 m)

Dressing room

Clothing shop

Y

X

Stockroom

Stairs

Glass showcase

B

Carpet

C

A

Window display

W

Cash/wrap

Z

Entry

A

*Details shown on page 465.

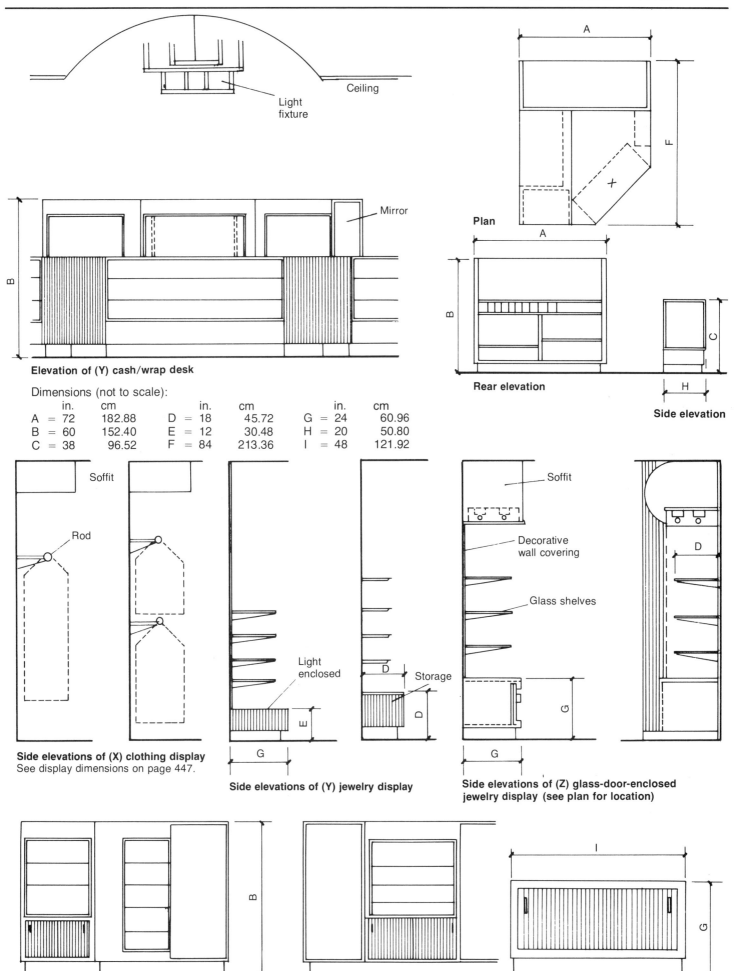

Ceiling

Light fixture

Mirror

Plan

Rear elevation

Side elevation

Elevation of (Y) cash/wrap desk

Dimensions (not to scale):

	in.	cm			in.	cm			in.	cm
A =	72	182.88	D =	18		45.72	G =	24		60.96
B =	60	152.40	E =	12		30.48	H =	20		50.80
C =	38	96.52	F =	84		213.36	I =	48		121.92

Soffit

Rod

Side elevations of (X) clothing display
See display dimensions on page 447.

Light enclosed

Side elevations of (Y) jewelry display

Storage

Soffit

Decorative wall covering

Glass shelves

Side elevations of (Z) glass-door-enclosed jewelry display (see plan for location)

Elevations of jewelry showcases in cash/wrap area

*Shown in plan on page 464.

Customer service area of large department store requires careful planning of the following functions:

Credit
Gift wrapping
Workroom & storage for gift boxes & paper
Lay-away
Waiting

Other stores often combine other functions, such as shipping, mailroom, and various management business offices, in this area.

Dimensions:
A = 44'6" (13.56 m)
B = 24'0" (7.32 m)
C = 18'6" (5.64 m)
D = 19'0"± (5.79 m)
E = 10'0" (3.05 m)
F = 8'7" (2.61 m)
G = 6'0" (1.83 m)
H = 16'0"± (4.88 m)
I = 42" (106.68 cm)

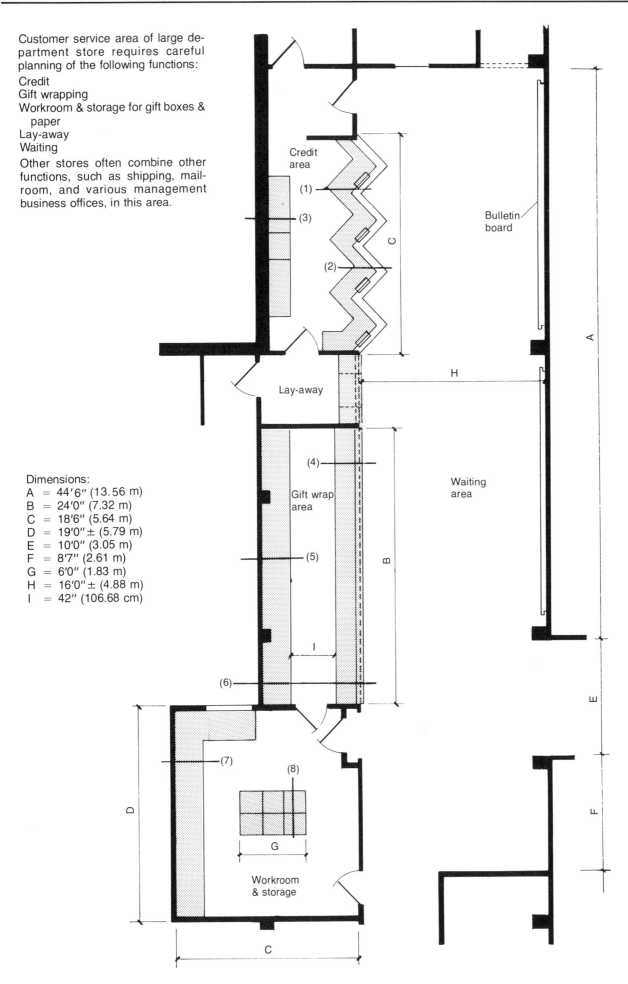

*Details shown on pages 467–473.

Plan of counters

Dimensions:

	in.	cm		in.	cm		in.	cm		in.	cm
A	= 43½	110.49	D	= 23½	59.69	G	= 9	22.86	J	= 22	55.88
B	= 20	50.80	E	= 12	30.48	H	= 18	45.72	K	= 31	78.74
C	= 24	60.96	F	= 4	10.16	I	= 21	53.34	L	= 2	5.08
									M	= 19	48.26

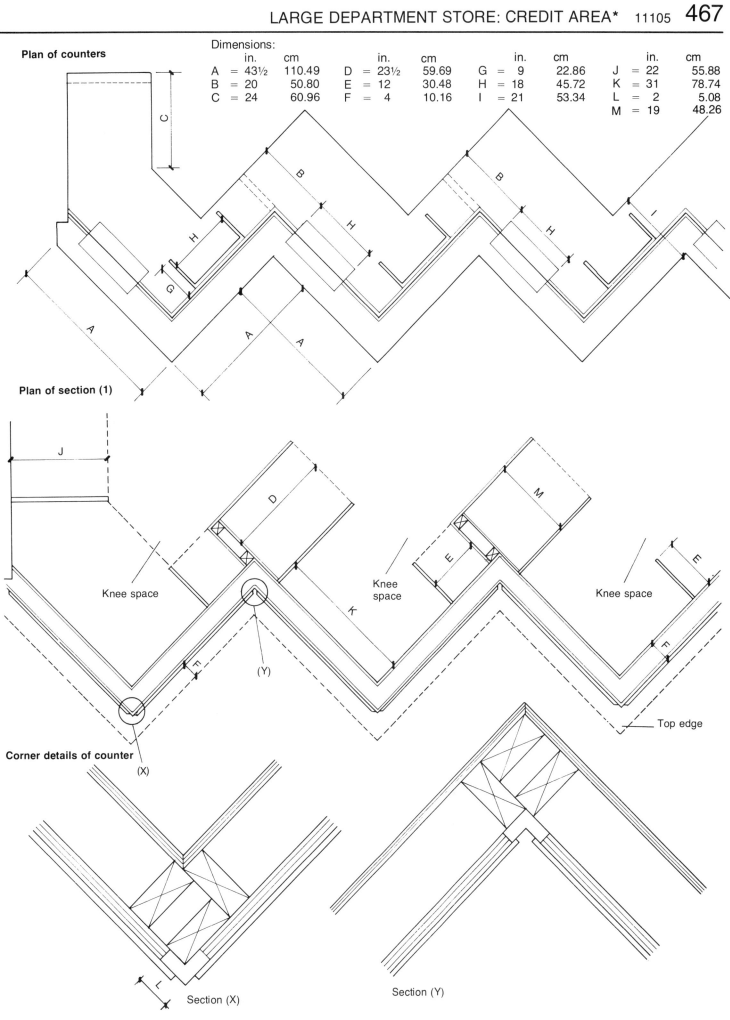

Plan of section (1)

Knee space

Knee space

Knee space

Top edge

(Y)

(X)

Corner details of counter

Section (X)

Section (Y)

*Shown in plan on page 466.

Elevation of (2) back of front counter

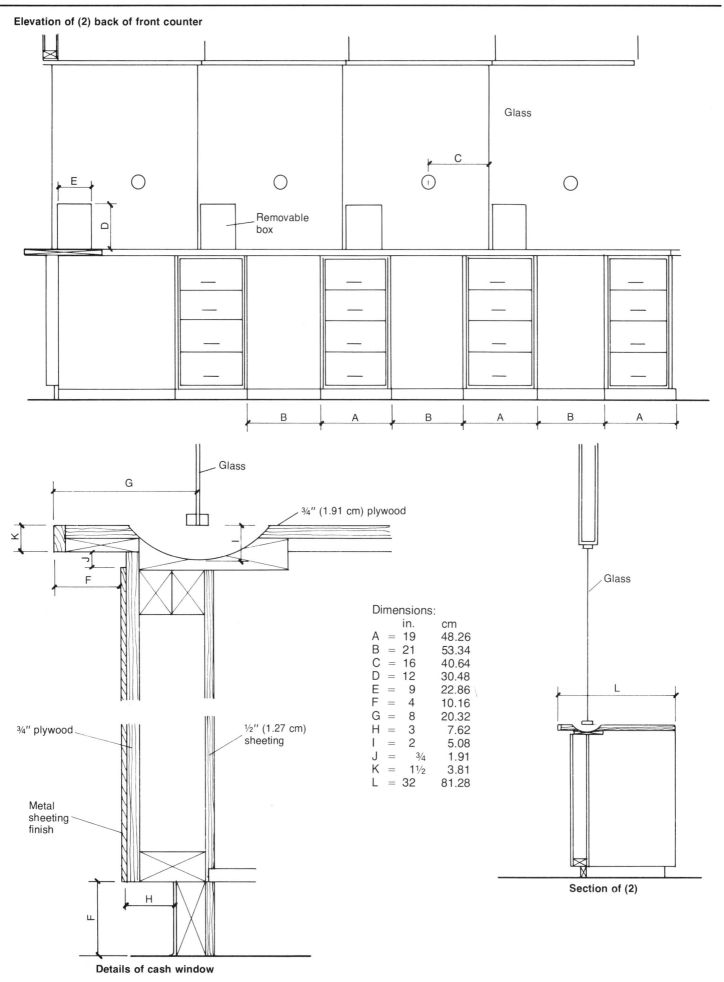

Glass

C

E

D

Removable box

B · A · B · A · B · A

Glass

G

¾″ (1.91 cm) plywood

K

J

F

I

H

¾″ plywood

½″ (1.27 cm) sheeting

Metal sheeting finish

F

Details of cash window

Dimensions:

	in.	cm
A =	19	48.26
B =	21	53.34
C =	16	40.64
D =	12	30.48
E =	9	22.86
F =	4	10.16
G =	8	20.32
H =	3	7.62
I =	2	5.08
J =	¾	1.91
K =	1½	3.81
L =	32	81.28

Glass

L

Section of (2)

*Shown in plan on page 466.

Note: See page 441 for more details of cashier windows.

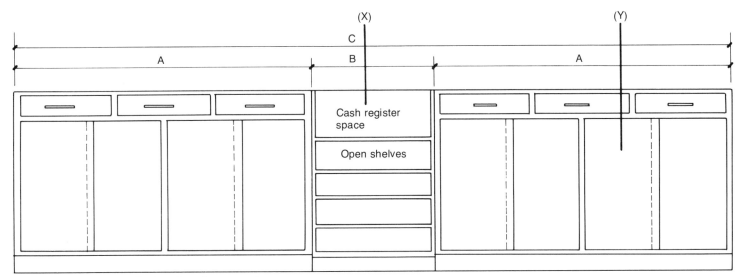

Cash register space

Open shelves

Elevation of (3) back wall of cash register counter

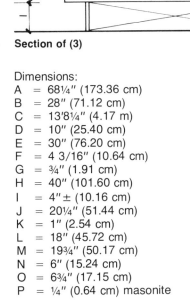

Drawer

Shelf standards

Sliding doors

Section of (3)

Dimensions:
A = 68¼" (173.36 cm)
B = 28" (71.12 cm)
C = 13'8¼" (4.17 m)
D = 10" (25.40 cm)
E = 30" (76.20 cm)
F = 4 3/16" (10.64 cm)
G = ¾" (1.91 cm)
H = 40" (101.60 cm)
I = 4"± (10.16 cm)
J = 20¼" (51.44 cm)
K = 1" (2.54 cm)
L = 18" (45.72 cm)
M = 19¾" (50.17 cm)
N = 6" (15.24 cm)
O = 6¾" (17.15 cm)
P = ¼" (0.64 cm) masonite

*Shown in plan on page 466.

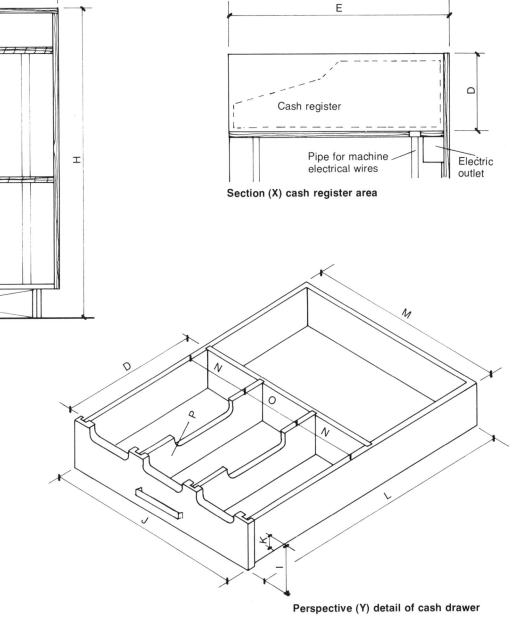

Cash register

Pipe for machine electrical wires

Electric outlet

Section (X) cash register area

Perspective (Y) detail of cash drawer

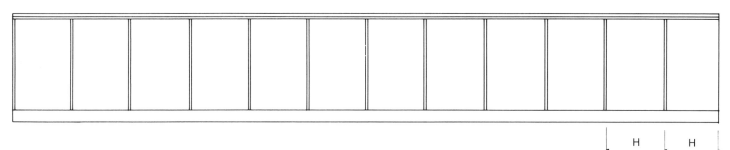

Elevation of (4) front of front counter

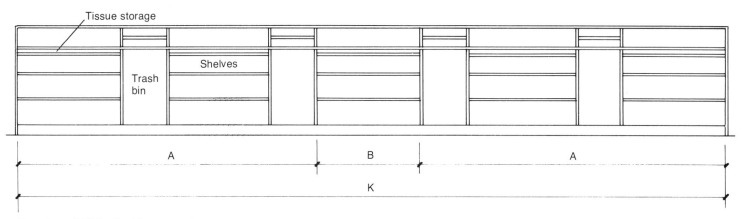

Elevation of (4) back of front counter

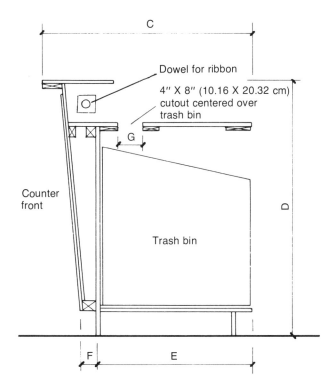

Section of (4) trash bin

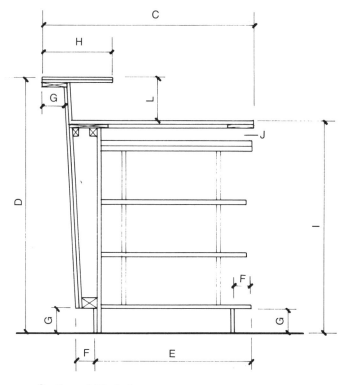

Section of (4) shelves

Dimensions:

A = 10'0" (3.05 m)   G = 4" (10.16 cm)
B = 54½" (138.43 cm)   H = 12" (30.48 cm)
C = 36" (91.44 cm)   I = 35" (88.90 cm)
D = 42" (106.68 cm)   J = 2¼" (5.72 cm)
E = 27" (68.58 cm)   K = 24'0" (7.32 m)
F = 3" (7.62 cm)   L = 7" (17.78 cm)

*Shown in plan on page 466.

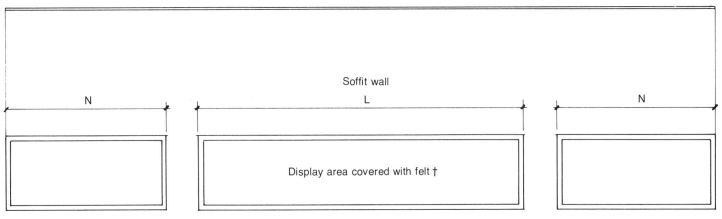

Soffit wall

N   L   N

Display area covered with felt †

Elevation of (5)

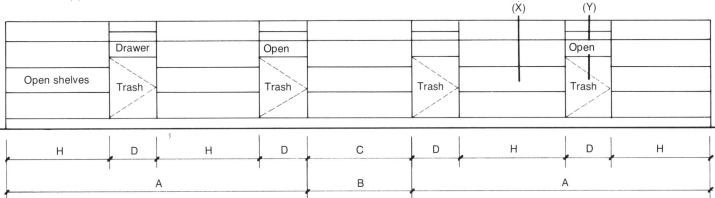

| Drawer | | Open | | | Open |
| Open shelves | Trash | | Trash | | Trash | | Trash |

(X)   (Y)

H   D   H   D   C   D   H   D   H

A   B   A

Elevation of (5) back wall

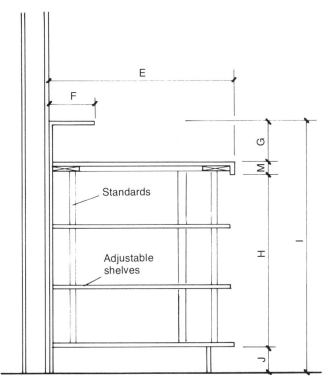

E

F

G

M

Standards

Adjustable shelves

H

I

J

Section (X)

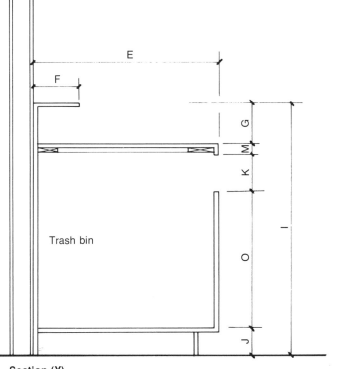

E

F

G

K   M

Trash bin

I

O

J

Section (Y)

Dimensions:
A = 10′ (3.05 m)   I = 42″ (106.68 cm)
B = 44½′ (13.56 m)   J = 4″ (10.16 cm)
C = 43″ (109.22 cm)   K = 6″ (15.24 cm)
D = 18″ (45.72 cm)   L = 10′8″ (3.25 m)
E = 32″ (81.28 cm)   M = 2″ (5.08 cm)
F = 8″ (20.32 cm)   N = 60″ (152.40 cm)
G = 7″ (17.78 cm)   O = 23″ (58.42 cm)
H = 29″ (73.66 cm)

*Shown in plan on page 466.   †To display different types of gift wrapping.

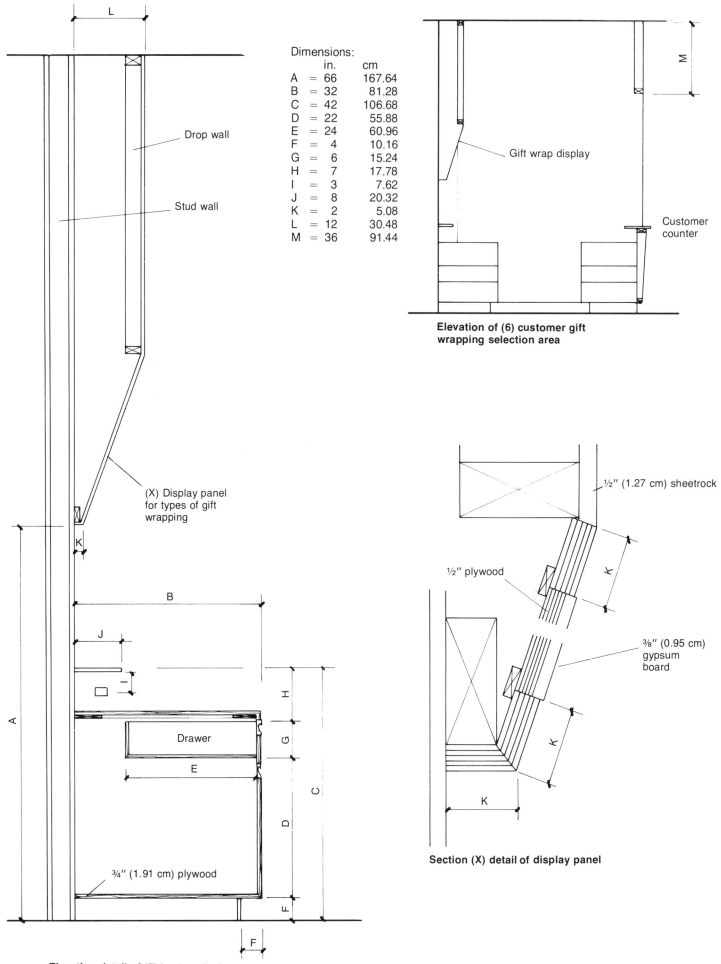

Dimensions:

	in.	cm
A =	66	167.64
B =	32	81.28
C =	42	106.68
D =	22	55.88
E =	24	60.96
F =	4	10.16
G =	6	15.24
H =	7	17.78
I =	3	7.62
J =	8	20.32
K =	2	5.08
L =	12	30.48
M =	36	91.44

Drop wall

Stud wall

(X) Display panel for types of gift wrapping

Drawer

¾" (1.91 cm) plywood

Elevation detail of (5) back wall of customer gift wrapping selection area

Gift wrap display

Customer counter

Elevation of (6) customer gift wrapping selection area

½" (1.27 cm) sheetrock

½" plywood

⅜" (0.95 cm) gypsum board

Section (X) detail of display panel

*Shown in plan on page 466.

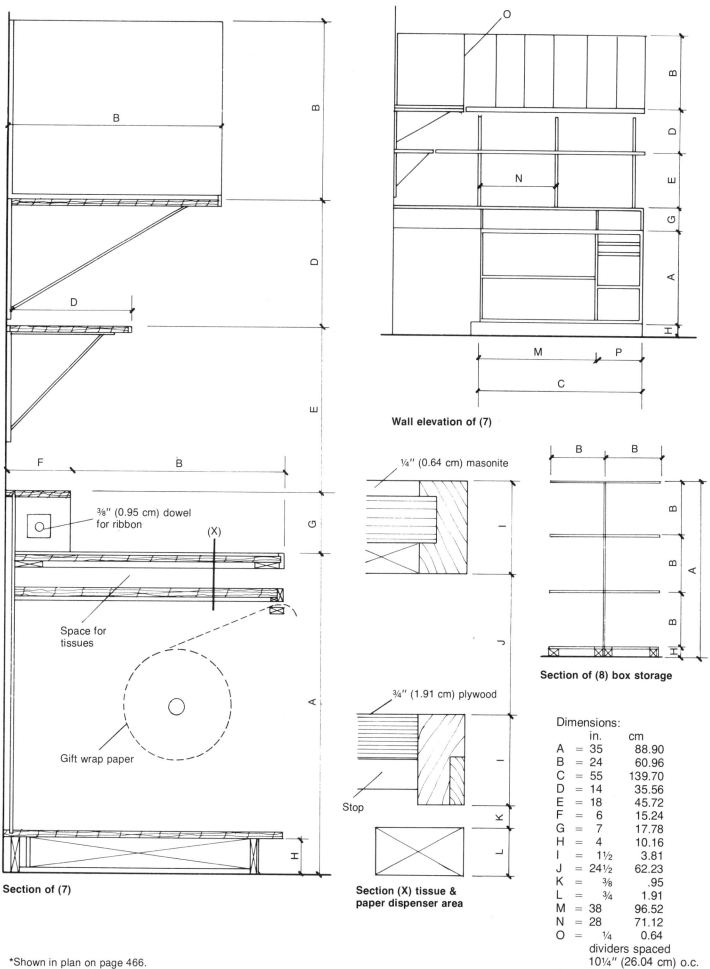

Section of (7)

³⁄₈″ (0.95 cm) dowel for ribbon

(X)

Space for tissues

Gift wrap paper

Wall elevation of (7)

¼″ (0.64 cm) masonite

¾″ (1.91 cm) plywood

Stop

Section (X) tissue & paper dispenser area

Section of (8) box storage

Dimensions:

		in.	cm
A	=	35	88.90
B	=	24	60.96
C	=	55	139.70
D	=	14	35.56
E	=	18	45.72
F	=	6	15.24
G	=	7	17.78
H	=	4	10.16
I	=	1½	3.81
J	=	24½	62.23
K	=	³⁄₈	.95
L	=	¾	1.91
M	=	38	96.52
N	=	28	71.12
O	=	¼	0.64
		dividers spaced	
		10¼″ (26.04 cm) o.c.	
P	=	17	43.18

*Shown in plan on page 466.

Designers may use the following charts of box and bag sizes to estimate required shelf and drawer dimensions to store merchandise as well as boxes and bags in the wrapping area.

Merchandise & bag size dimensions

Paper (l x w x h*)	Plastic (l x w x h*)	Merchandise
5 x 2 x 10½		Hobby kits
6 x 9	6½ x 9½	Art supplies, notions, cosmetics
7 x 10½	7 x 10½	Greeting cards, candy, books
8 x 3⅝ x 21		Shoes, cameras, gifts, sporting goods
8½ x 11	9 x 11	Notions, accessories, jewelry, records
9⅝ x 13	10 x 13	Underwear, gloves, accessories, office supplies
11⅝ x 15	12 x 15	Blouses, shoes, lingerie, office supplies

Paper (l x w x h*)	Plastic (l x w x h*)	Merchandise
11½ x 3 x 18	12 x 3 x 18	Shirts, dresses, sportswear, gifts, office supplies
11½ x 3 x 21		Handbags
14 x 3 x 21	14 x 3 x 21	Sportswear, slacks, sweaters, dresses, hats, fabrics, office supplies
17 x 4 x 24	17 x 4 x 24	Sportswear, coats, hats, sporting goods
	20 x 5 x 30	Bedspreads, blankets, multiple purchases, boxed goods
17 x 21	15 x 18	Dresses, slacks, skirts, sweaters, handbags, hats

Storage and/or box sizes for china, silver, & flatware

Size (l x w x h*)	Suggested uses
3 x 3 x 3	Salt & peppers, baby cups
3½ x 3½ x 2	Miscellaneous
4 x 4 x 4	Cups, glass figures
5 x 5 x 3	Salt & peppers, cups, demitasse, ashtrays, coaster sets
6 x 4 x 4	Novelties, figurines, china
6 x 6 x 4	Cup-saucer, ashtray
6 x 6 x 6	Clocks, compotes
6 x 6 x 18	Tall vases, bottles, bar B-Q sets Extends to over 30″ (76.20 cm)
6½ x 6½ x 1¾	Bread & butter plates, small trays, ashtrays, bon-bon dishes
7 x 7 x 7	Large compotes, 2 goblets, cream & sugars
8 x 1¾ x 1 (no cotton)	Teaspoons, salad forks
8 x 8 x 2	Relish dishes, bread trays
8 x 8 x 4	Sherbets, plates
8 x 8 x 6	Toasters, juice sets, compotes
8½ x 8½ x ¾	Salad plates
9 x 5 x 4	Cream & sugars, vases
9 x 9 x 4½	China, glassware, teapots, salad bowls, vegetable dishes
9 x 9 x 9	Large silver bowls, small ice buckets, extra large compotes
10 x 2 x 1	Knife & fork, dinner knives

Size (l x w x h*)	Suggested uses
10 x 6 x 6	Vases, glasses
10 x 10 x 6	Stemware, bowls
10 x 10 x 8	1 dozen sherbets, 1 dozen plates
10½ x 10½ x 2	Plates
11 x 2½ x 1¾	Place settings, serving spoons, ½ dozen forks or ½ dozen knives, pastry server
11 x 4 x 4	Bud vases, figures
11 x 11 x ⅞	Single plates
11 x 11 x 7	China, water sets
12 x 6 x 6	Glassware, figurines, vases, stemware
12 x 9 x 4	Purses, glassware
12 x 12 x 1½	Dinner plates, silver platters
12 x 12 x 2½	Platters
12 x 12 x 3	Cake plates, serving trays
12 x 12 x 4	Place settings, cocktail sets, serving dishes
12 x 12 x 6	Flower bowls, salad bowls
12 x 12 x 8	Pottery, glassware
14 x 4½ x 4½	Large figurines, vases
14 x 7¾ x 2¼	Relish dishes, bread trays
14 x 14 x 1½	Pictures, sandwich trays, large plates
14 x 14 x 3	Cake plates, bread trays
14 x 14 x 5	Salad bowls, tea sets
14 x 14 x 10	Punch bowls, lamps, ice buckets, cake stands
15 x 9 x 7½	Pottery, glassware
15 x 15 x 3	Round mirrors, lazy susans
16 x 16 x 2½	Lazy susans, trays
18 x 18 x 3	Round platter, tray, plaques

Jewelry & silver boxes

Size (l x w x h*)	Suggested uses
2½ x 1½ x 1	Earrings, scatter pins
3 x 2 x 1	Pins, brooches, etc.
3½ x 3½ x 1	Compacts, large jewelry
3½ x 3½ x 2	Wide bracelets
5¼ x 3¾ x ⅞	Chokers, billfolds
6¼ x 1½ x 1¹⁵⁄₁₆	Teaspoons, butter knives
6 x 6 x ¾	Compacts, bracelets, cases
7½ x 1¾ x 1	Necklaces, chokers, pens
8 x 8 x 1	3-piece jewelry sets
8½ x 3 x 2½	Gravy ladles, forks
9¼ x 2⅛ x 1⅝	Tablespoons, knives
9¾ x 3 x 1½	Silverware place settings

Clothing boxes

Size (l x w x h*)	Suggested uses
10 x 7 x 1½	Small lingerie
11 x 10 x 2	Square shirt
12½ x 4½ x 1½	Socks, gloves, men's hose
12 x 8 x 1½	Blouses, lingerie
13½ x 9 x 2	Shirts, sweaters
15 x 9½ x 2	Longfold shirts, towels
16 x 9½ x 2¼	New longer fold shirts
17 x 11 x 2½	Double dress, linens
19 x 12 x 3	Robes, stoles, jackets
22 x 18 x 5	Large blankets, pile jackets, furs
23 x 12 x 3	Suits, jackets, coats, spreads
24 x 14 x 4	Coats, robes, large linens

*Height not provided in some cases.

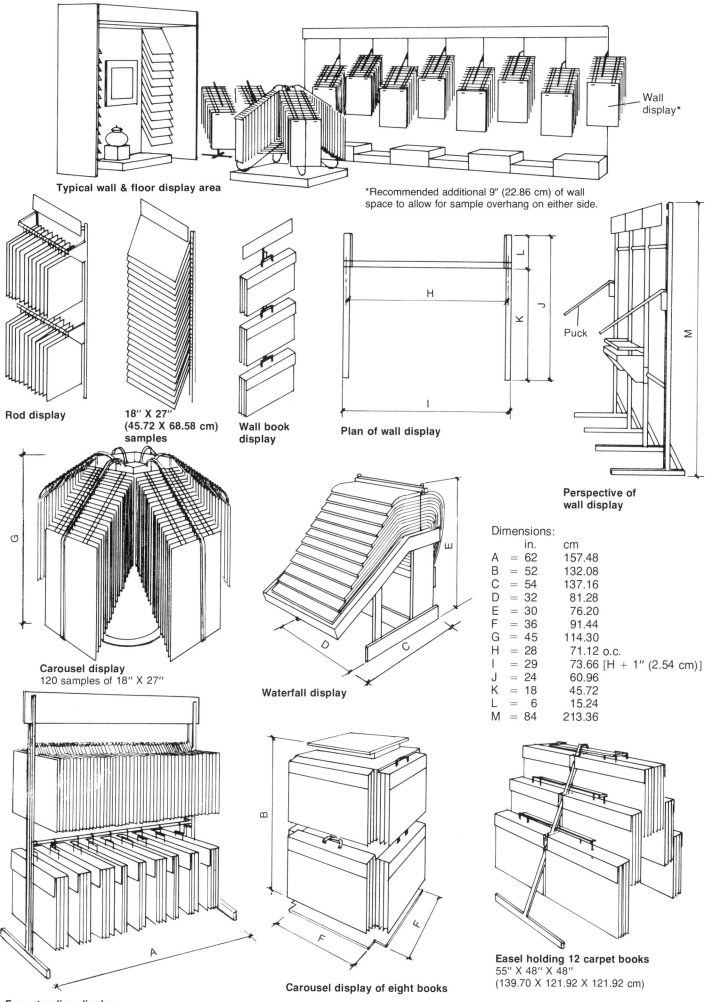

Typical wall & floor display area

*Recommended additional 9″ (22.86 cm) of wall space to allow for sample overhang on either side.

Rod display

18″ X 27″ (45.72 X 68.58 cm) samples

Wall book display

Plan of wall display

Puck

Perspective of wall display

Carousel display
120 samples of 18″ X 27″

Waterfall display

Dimensions:

	in.	cm
A	= 62	157.48
B	= 52	132.08
C	= 54	137.16
D	= 32	81.28
E	= 30	76.20
F	= 36	91.44
G	= 45	114.30
H	= 28	71.12 o.c.
I	= 29	73.66 [H + 1″ (2.54 cm)]
J	= 24	60.96
K	= 18	45.72
L	= 6	15.24
M	= 84	213.36

Wall display*

Free-standing display
20 books or 120 individual samples

Carousel display of eight books

Easel holding 12 carpet books
55″ X 48″ X 48″
(139.70 X 121.92 X 121.92 cm)

Twenty samples per unit
Samples 18″ X 13″ (45.72 X 33.02 cm) and
18″ X 27″ (45.72 X 68.58 cm) installed
on 18″ single hanger bars. Allow
22″ (55.88 cm) extra wall space
from end of wall unit to allow for
removal of samples.

Double rows of unit shown at left

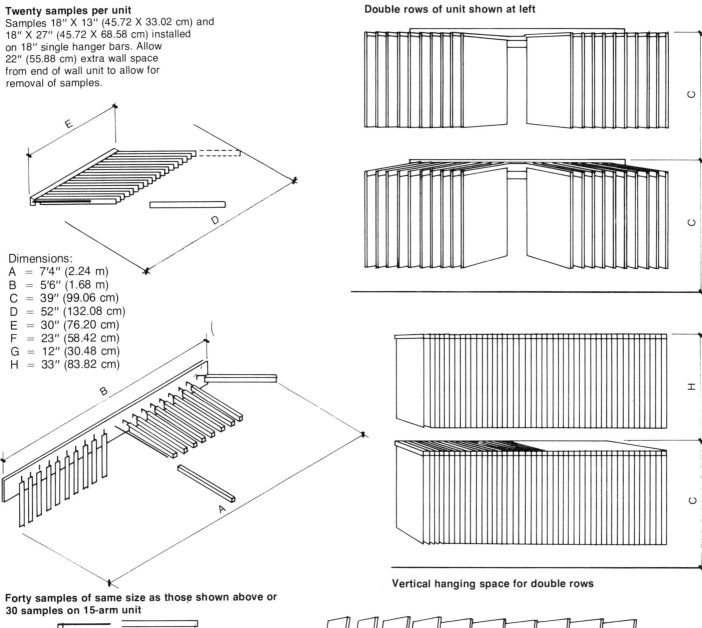

Dimensions:
A = 7′4″ (2.24 m)
B = 5′6″ (1.68 m)
C = 39″ (99.06 cm)
D = 52″ (132.08 cm)
E = 30″ (76.20 cm)
F = 23″ (58.42 cm)
G = 12″ (30.48 cm)
H = 33″ (83.82 cm)

Vertical hanging space for double rows

**Forty samples of same size as those shown above or
30 samples on 15-arm unit**

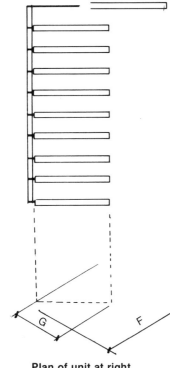

Plan of unit at right

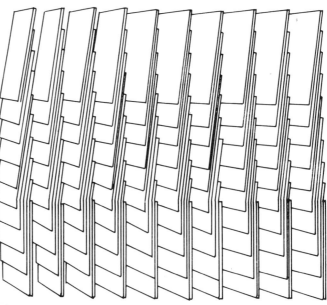

Wall carpet sample assembly
Ten samples per unit. Samples are displayed at a
45° angle. Samples sized 18″ X 13″ and 18″ X 27″ are
hung on ½″ (1.27 cm) rods welded to vertical steel frames.

Fifty-arm wall display with 9′ (2.74 m) arms

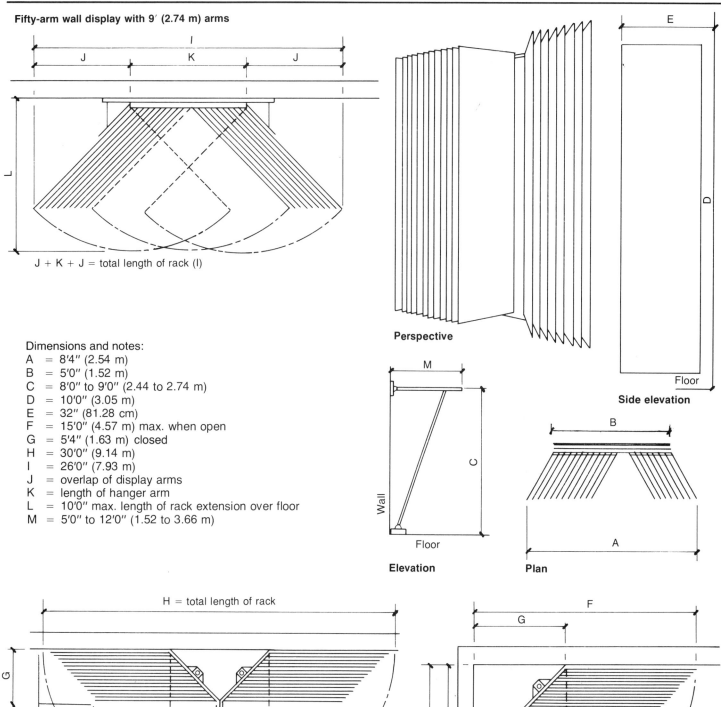

J + K + J = total length of rack (I)

Dimensions and notes:
A = 8′4″ (2.54 m)
B = 5′0″ (1.52 m)
C = 8′0″ to 9′0″ (2.44 to 2.74 m)
D = 10′0″ (3.05 m)
E = 32″ (81.28 cm)
F = 15′0″ (4.57 m) max. when open
G = 5′4″ (1.63 m) closed
H = 30′0″ (9.14 m)
I = 26′0″ (7.93 m)
J = overlap of display arms
K = length of hanger arm
L = 10′0″ max. length of rack extension over floor
M = 5′0″ to 12′0″ (1.52 to 3.66 m)

Perspective

Side elevation

Elevation

Plan

H = total length of rack

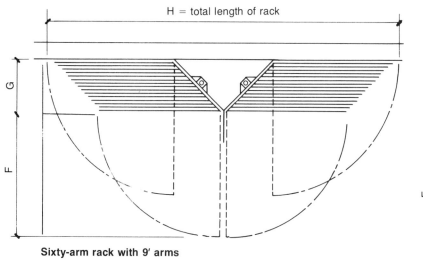

Sixty-arm rack with 9′ arms

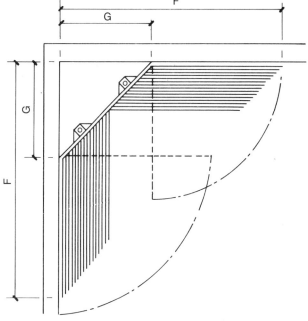

Wall display used in corner

*The displays on this page are used for rugs and
carpet cuts. Wall coverings and fabric may
also be displayed on similar units.

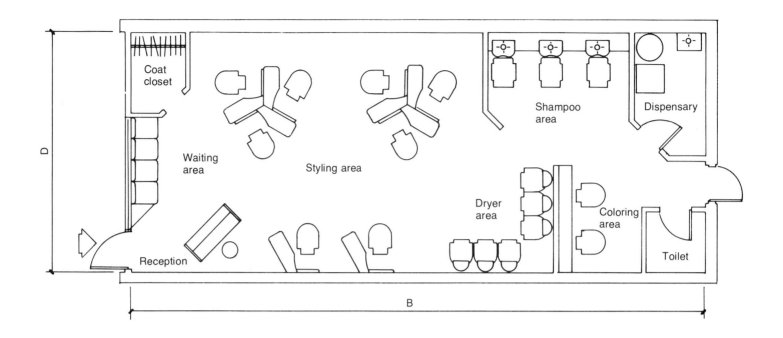

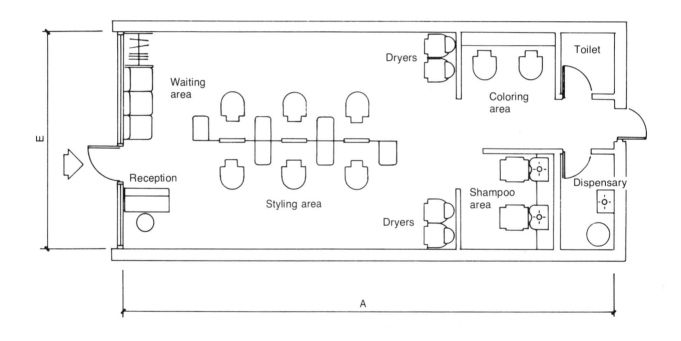

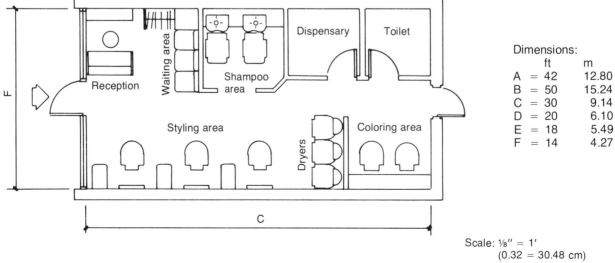

Dimensions:

		ft	m
A	=	42	12.80
B	=	50	15.24
C	=	30	9.14
D	=	20	6.10
E	=	18	5.49
F	=	14	4.27

Scale: 1/8″ = 1′
(0.32 = 30.48 cm)

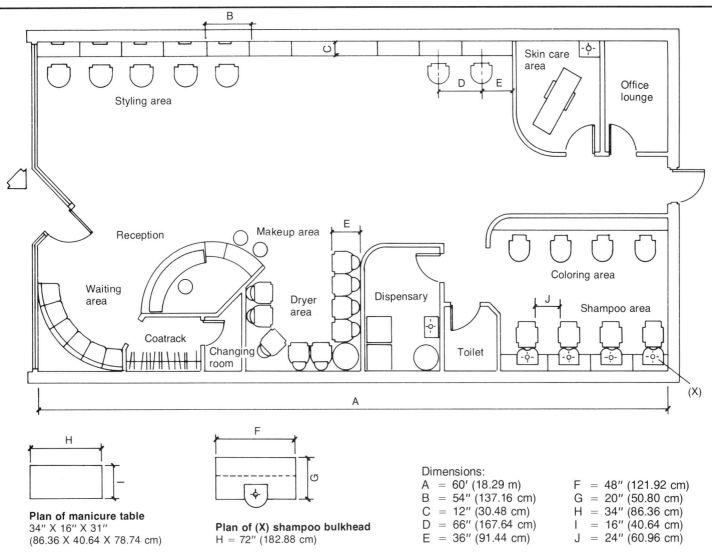

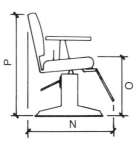

Plan of manicure table
34″ X 16″ X 31″
(86.36 X 40.64 X 78.74 cm)

Plan of (X) shampoo bulkhead
H = 72″ (182.88 cm)

Dimensions:

A = 60′ (18.29 m)		F = 48″ (121.92 cm)	
B = 54″ (137.16 cm)		G = 20″ (50.80 cm)	
C = 12″ (30.48 cm)		H = 34″ (86.36 cm)	
D = 66″ (167.64 cm)		I = 16″ (40.64 cm)	
E = 36″ (91.44 cm)		J = 24″ (60.96 cm)	

CHAIR DIMENSIONS

Styling chair

Hydraulic chair

Shampoo chair

Dryer chair

All-purpose & styling hydraulic chairs (in.)

L	M	N	O	P	Q
21¼	19	32	22	36½	
24	20	32½	22	35	
24	18¼	31½	20¾	32½	46
29½	18½	33	21	33¼	41½
23¾	18	28½	21¼	34	43
26	19½	32	21½	34	44
25¼	18½	30¾	20¼	32½	

Dryer chairs (in.)

L	M	N	O	P
21¼	19	33	15	33
24	19	33	17	30½
25	17½	31	15½	29
29½	18½	32¼	17½	31
29	17½	32	17	30
25	19	32	16	31
26	19½	33½	17½	32
25	19	33½	17	31¼

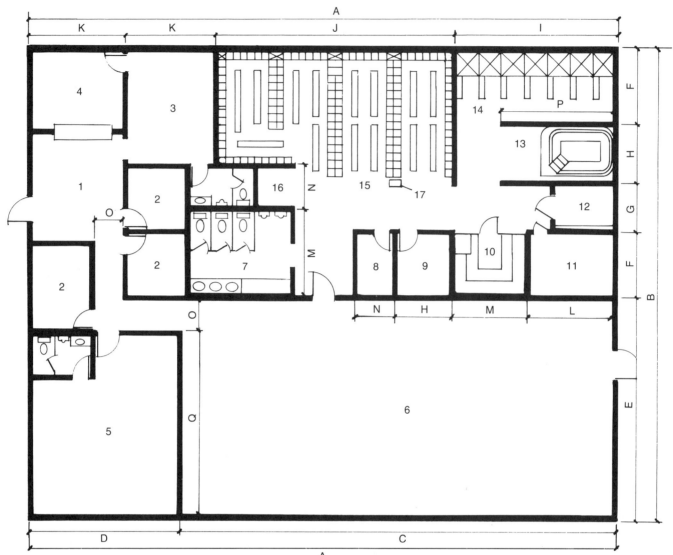

Legend:
1 = entrance
2 = office
3 = lounge
4 = reception
5 = nursery
6 = main exercise area
7 = restroom
8 = inhalation room
9 = massage/sun room
10 = sauna
11 = steam room
12 = whirlpool equipment
13 = whirlpool
14 = showers
15 = lockers
16 = hair dryers
17 = scale

Dimensions:

	ft/in	m			ft/in	m
A	= 80 0	24.38		J	= 32 0	9.75
B	= 61 0	18.59		K	= 13 0	3.96
C	= 59 0	17.98		L	= 11 4	3.45
D	= 21 0	6.40		M	= 10 2	3.10
E	= 28 0	8.53		N	= 5 0	1.52
F	= 9 0	2.74		O	= 4 0	1.22
G	= 7 0	2.13		P	= 15 6	4.72
H	= 8 0	2.44		Q	= 23 0	7.01
I	= 22 0	6.71				

Design considerations
The interior space arrangement should reflect the sequence of use: (1) reception area, (2) lockers, (3) toilets, (4) lavatories, (5) sauna, (6) exercise room, (7) showers, (8) hair dryers, and so forth. The sequence varies according to the conveniences offered.

Additional space requirements
Track running areas: 80' X 40' (24.38 X 12.19 m)
Medium-size aerobic exercise area with mats: 50' X 40' (15.24 X 12.19 m).
Small exercise machine area: 34' X 24' (10.36 X 7.32 m).

Lockers
Calculating the number needed is based on the size of membership; 20 percent of the membership or a minimum of 100 lockers is usually specified.

Locker benches should range from 3' to 12' (0.91 to 3.66 m) long and should be positioned to allow 2½' or 3' (0.76 or 0.91 m) on each side for ease of movement.

Steam rooms
Ceiling requires 1½ pitch to allow water condensation to run to one wall. The tilt should be toward the longest wall opposite the entry. Consult local codes.

Whirlpool areas
These usually require about 4' (1.22 m) walking width around the edges.

Chapter 18

RESTAURANTS AND BARS

Small neighborhood bar

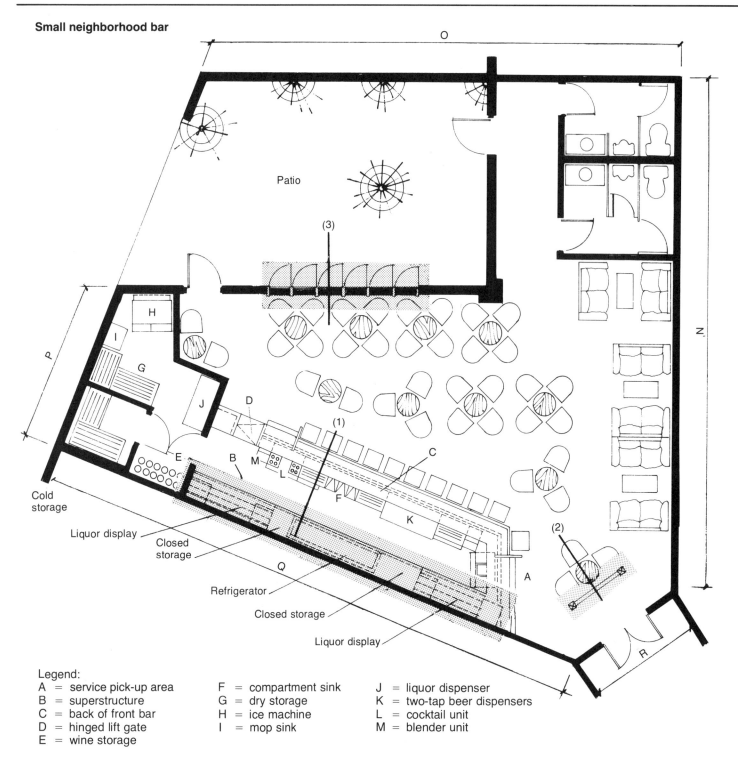

Patio

Cold
storage

Liquor display

Closed
storage

Refrigerator

Closed storage

Liquor display

Legend:
A = service pick-up area
B = superstructure
C = back of front bar
D = hinged lift gate
E = wine storage
F = compartment sink
G = dry storage
H = ice machine
I = mop sink
J = liquor dispenser
K = two-tap beer dispensers
L = cocktail unit
M = blender unit

Bar designed to resemble an English pub in a small "after-work" meeting place

Furnishings	Seating	Occupants
11 bar stools	11	11
9 tables†	4	36
3 tables	3	9
2 tables	2	4
	Capacity	60

†Includes tables at sofas.

Note: Designers should balance occupancy figure with that allowed by code and square footage. Assume periods of overcrowding that will exceed safe exit capacity.

Dimensions:

		ft	m
N	=	44	13.41
O	=	41	12.50
P	=	14	4.27
Q	=	49	14.96
R	=	10	3.05

*Details shown on pages 483–488: Section (1) pages 483–485; Section (2) pages 486–487; Section (3) page 488.

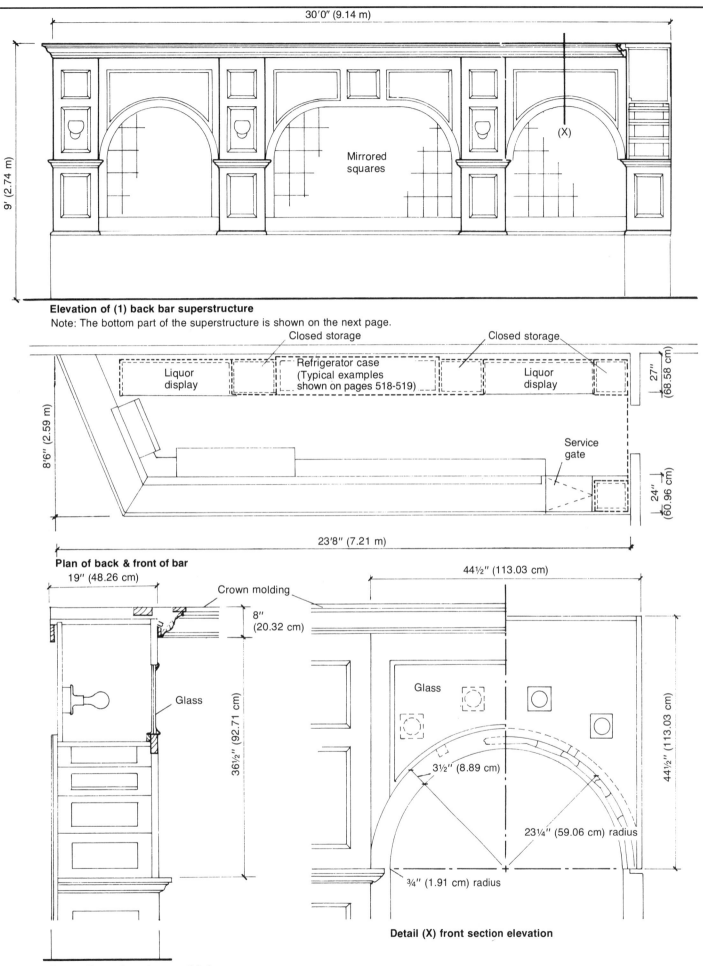

30'0" (9.14 m)

9' (2.74 m)

Mirrored squares

(X)

Elevation of (1) back bar superstructure
Note: The bottom part of the superstructure is shown on the next page.

Closed storage

Closed storage

Liquor display

Refrigerator case
(Typical examples
shown on pages 518-519)

Liquor display

27" (68.58 cm)

8'6" (2.59 m)

Service gate

24" (60.96 cm)

23'8" (7.21 m)

Plan of back & front of bar

19" (48.26 cm)

Crown molding

8"
(20.32 cm)

44½" (113.03 cm)

Glass

Glass

36½" (92.71 cm)

44½" (113.03 cm)

3½" (8.89 cm)

23¼" (59.06 cm) radius

¾" (1.91 cm) radius

Detail (X) front section elevation

Detail (X) section of upper third
Note: Front superstructure constructed in three parts & assembled on the job site.

*Shown in plan on page 482.

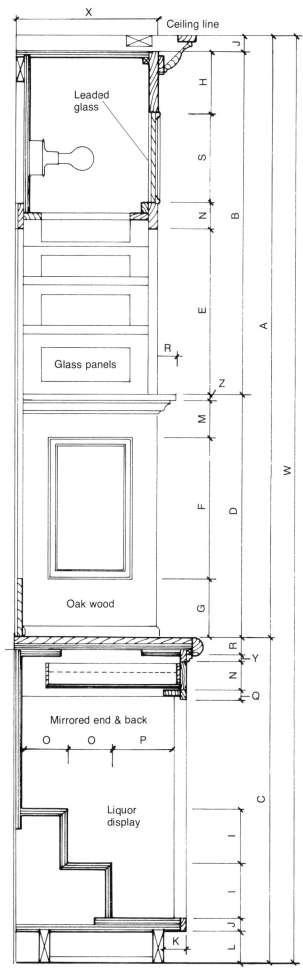

Side elevation of (1) back bar superstructure

*Shown in plan on page 482.

Dimensions & note:

		in.	cm			in.	cm
A	=	78	198.12	N	=	3½	8.89
B	=	44½	113.03	O	=	6	15.24
C	=	42	106.68	P	=	10¼	26.04
D	=	31½	80.01	Q	=	1¼	3.18
E	=	21¼	53.98	R	=	2¼	5.72
F	=	18¼	46.35	S	=	15	38.10
G	=	7½	19.05	T	=	12	30.48
H	=	8	20.32	U	=	24	60.96
I	=	7	17.78	V	=	39¾	100.97
J	=	1½	3.81	W	=	108	274.32
K	=	3	7.62	X	=	19	48.26
L	=	4	10.16	Y	=	¾	1.91
M	=	5	12.70	Z	=	spliced to bottom	

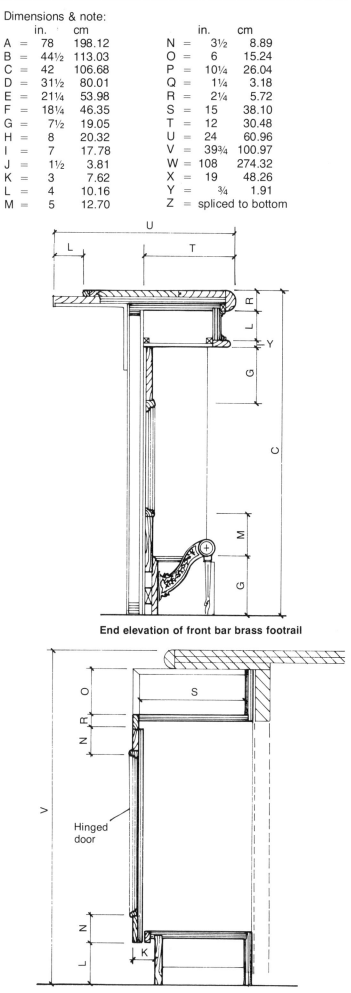

End elevation of front bar brass footrail

Side elevation of back of front bar

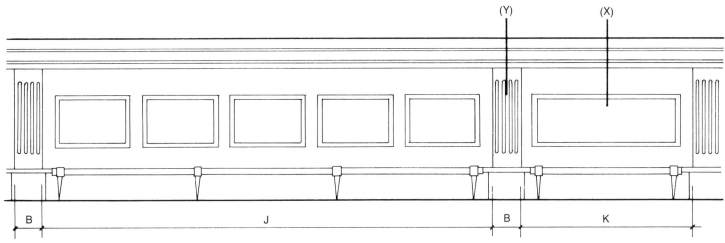

Elevation of (1) front bar
Oak panel with brass footrail

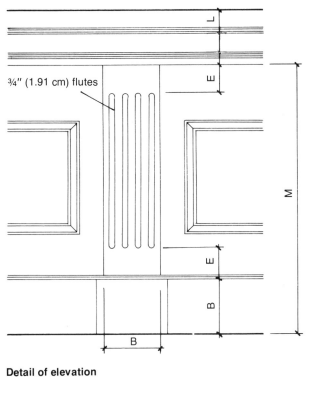

¾" (1.91 cm) flutes

Detail of elevation

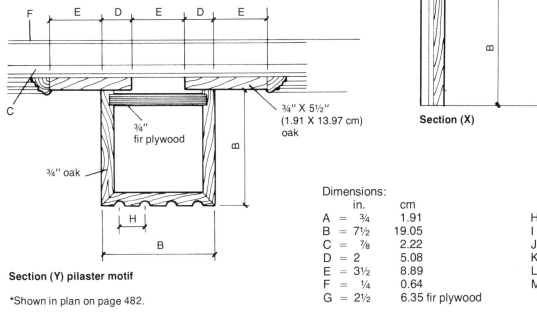

Section (Y) pilaster motif

*Shown in plan on page 482.

¾"
fir plywood

¾" oak

¾" X 5½"
(1.91 X 13.97 cm)
oak

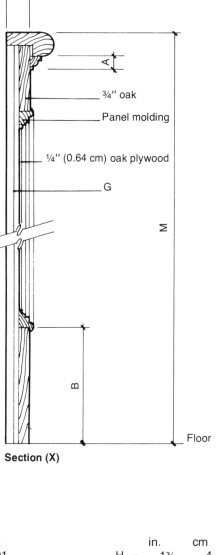

¾" oak
Panel molding
¼" (0.64 cm) oak plywood

Floor

Section (X)

Dimensions:

	in.	cm			in.	cm
A =	¾	1.91	H =		1¾	4.45
B =	7½	19.05	I =		1½	3.81
C =	⅞	2.22	J =		120	304.80
D =	2	5.08	K =		46	116.84
E =	3½	8.89	L =		7	17.78
F =	¼	0.64	M =		35¾	90.81
G =	2½	6.35 fir plywood				

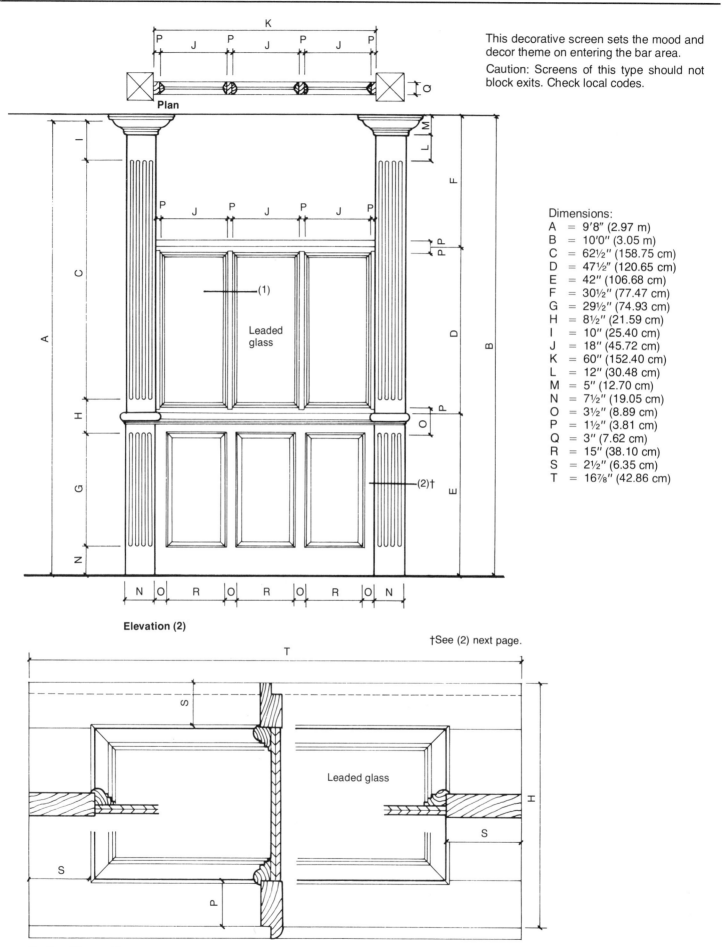

This decorative screen sets the mood and decor theme on entering the bar area.

Caution: Screens of this type should not block exits. Check local codes.

Plan

Elevation (2)

†See (2) next page.

Dimensions:
A = 9'8" (2.97 m)
B = 10'0" (3.05 m)
C = 62½" (158.75 cm)
D = 47½" (120.65 cm)
E = 42" (106.68 cm)
F = 30½" (77.47 cm)
G = 29½" (74.93 cm)
H = 8½" (21.59 cm)
I = 10" (25.40 cm)
J = 18" (45.72 cm)
K = 60" (152.40 cm)
L = 12" (30.48 cm)
M = 5" (12.70 cm)
N = 7½" (19.05 cm)
O = 3½" (8.89 cm)
P = 1½" (3.81 cm)
Q = 3" (7.62 cm)
R = 15" (38.10 cm)
S = 2½" (6.35 cm)
T = 16⅞" (42.86 cm)

Leaded glass

Leaded glass

Section (1) panel from entry screen

*Shown in plan on page 482.

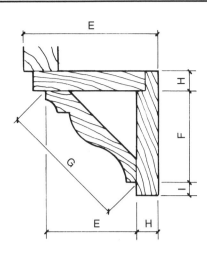

Detail of crown molding

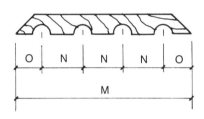

Detail of post flutes

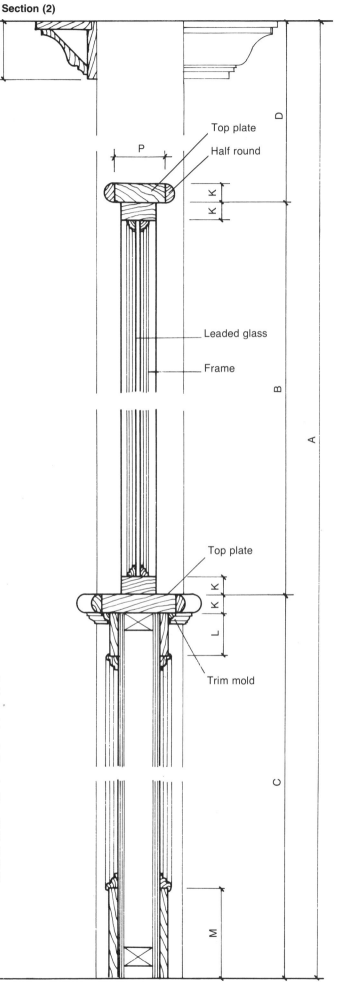

Section (2)

Top plate

Half round

Leaded glass

Frame

Top plate

Trim mold

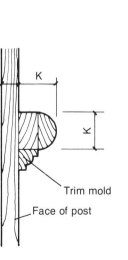

Trim mold

Face of post

Detail of trim mold
Scale: 3″ = 1′
(7.62 = 30.48 cm)

Dimensions:

		in.	cm
A	=	120	304.80
B	=	43	109.22
C	=	42	106.68
D	=	34½	87.63
E	=	5½	13.97
F	=	3¾	9.53
G	=	5¼	13.33
H	=	¾	1.91
I	=	½	1.27
J	=	5	12.70
K	=	1½	3.81
L	=	3½	8.89
M	=	7½	19.05
N	=	1¾	4.45
O	=	1⅛	2.86
P	=	3	7.62

Scale: 1½″ = 1′ (3.81 = 30.48 cm)

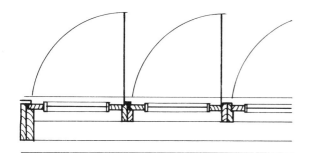

Plan of (3)

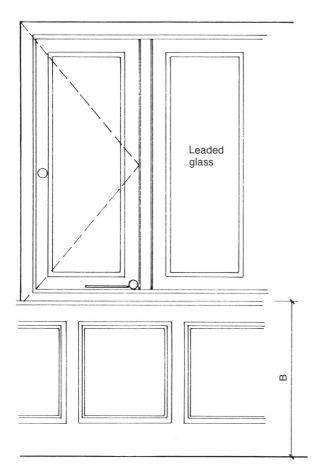

Elevation of window wall with wainscot

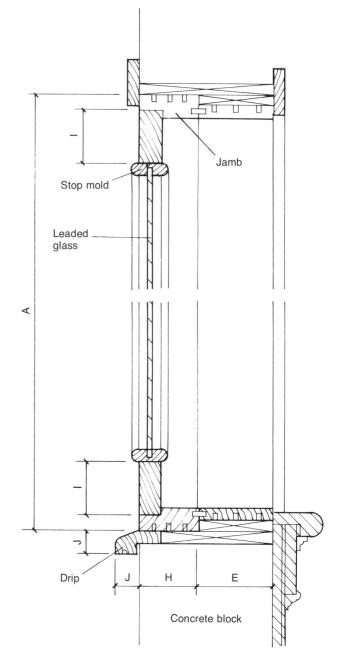

Section of (3) leaded casement windows
Open to patio

Jamb

Stop mold

Leaded
glass

Drip

Concrete block

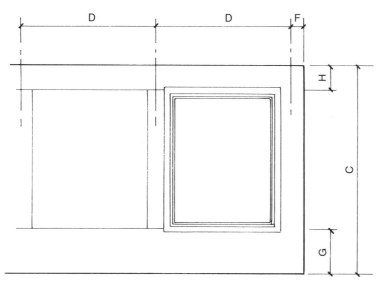

Elevation of wainscot detail

*Shown in plan on page 482.

Dimensions:

		in.	cm
A	=	59	149.86
B	=	36	91.44
C	=	35	88.90
D	=	23	58.42
E	=	5⅛	13.02
F	=	2¾	6.99
G	=	7½	19.05
H	=	4½	11.43
I	=	3½	8.89
J	=	1½	3.81

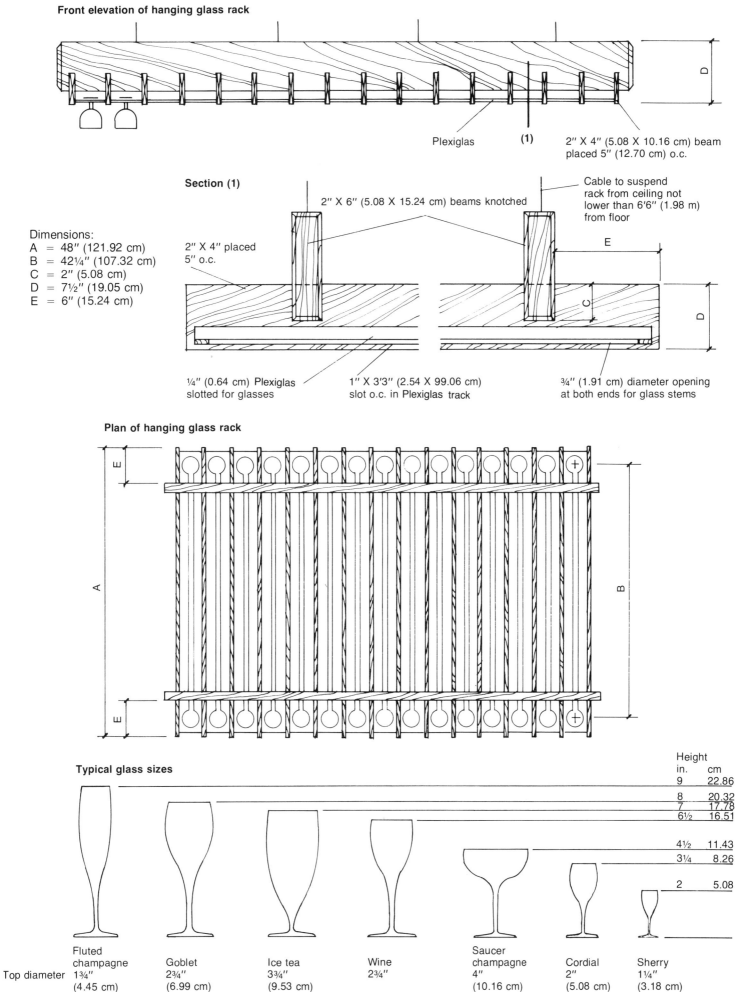

Front elevation of hanging glass rack

Plexiglas

(1)

2" X 4" (5.08 X 10.16 cm) beam placed 5" (12.70 cm) o.c.

Section (1)

2" X 6" (5.08 X 15.24 cm) beams knotched

Cable to suspend rack from ceiling not lower than 6'6" (1.98 m) from floor

2" X 4" placed 5" o.c.

Dimensions:
A = 48" (121.92 cm)
B = 42¼" (107.32 cm)
C = 2" (5.08 cm)
D = 7½" (19.05 cm)
E = 6" (15.24 cm)

¼" (0.64 cm) Plexiglas slotted for glasses

1" X 3'3" (2.54 X 99.06 cm) slot o.c. in Plexiglas track

¾" (1.91 cm) diameter opening at both ends for glass stems

Plan of hanging glass rack

Typical glass sizes

	Height	
	in.	cm
	9	22.86
	8	20.32
	7	17.78
	6½	16.51
	4½	11.43
	3¼	8.26
	2	5.08

Fluted champagne	Goblet	Ice tea	Wine	Saucer champagne	Cordial	Sherry
1¾"	2¾"	3¾"	2¾"	4"	2"	1¼"
(4.45 cm)	(6.99 cm)	(9.53 cm)	(10.16 cm)	(5.08 cm)	(3.18 cm)

Top diameter

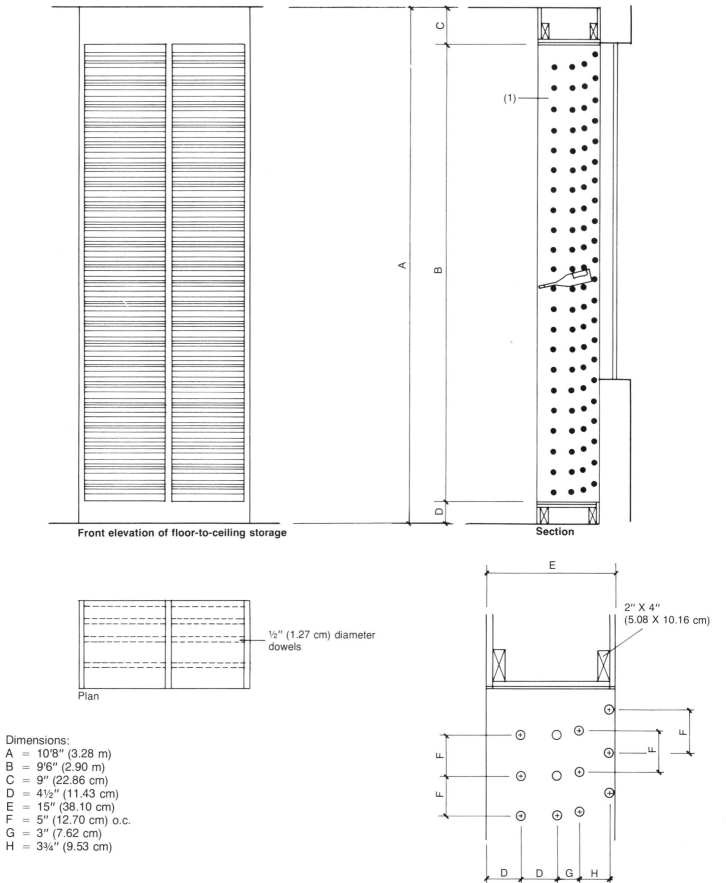

Front elevation of floor-to-ceiling storage

Section

Plan

½" (1.27 cm) diameter dowels

2" X 4" (5.08 X 10.16 cm)

Detail (1)

Dimensions:
A = 10'8" (3.28 m)
B = 9'6" (2.90 m)
C = 9" (22.86 cm)
D = 4½" (11.43 cm)
E = 15" (38.10 cm)
F = 5" (12.70 cm) o.c.
G = 3" (7.62 cm)
H = 3¾" (9.53 cm)

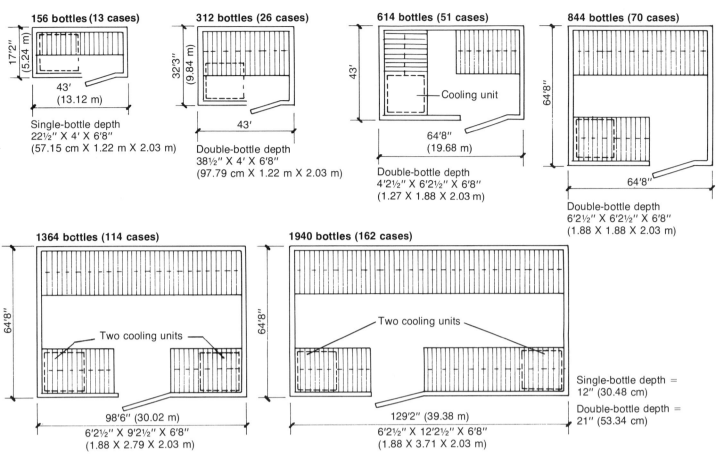

156 bottles (13 cases)
17'2" (5.24 m)
43' (13.12 m)
Single-bottle depth
22½" X 4' X 6'8"
(57.15 cm X 1.22 m X 2.03 m)

312 bottles (26 cases)
32'3" (9.84 m)
43'
Double-bottle depth
38½" X 4' X 6'8"
(97.79 cm X 1.22 m X 2.03 m)

614 bottles (51 cases)
43'
Cooling unit
64'8" (19.68 m)
Double-bottle depth
4'2½" X 6'2½" X 6'8"
(1.27 X 1.88 X 2.03 m)

844 bottles (70 cases)
64'8"
64'8"
Double-bottle depth
6'2½" X 6'2½" X 6'8"
(1.88 X 1.88 X 2.03 m)

1364 bottles (114 cases)
64'8"
Two cooling units
98'6" (30.02 m)
6'2½" X 9'2½" X 6'8"
(1.88 X 2.79 X 2.03 m)

1940 bottles (162 cases)
64'8"
Two cooling units
129'2" (39.38 m)
6'2½" X 12'2½" X 6'8"
(1.88 X 3.71 X 2.03 m)

Single-bottle depth =
12" (30.48 cm)
Double-bottle depth =
21" (53.34 cm)

Note: 24" X 24" X 10" (60.96 X 60.96 X 25.40 cm) = 42 bottles; 24" X 43" X 12" (60.96 X 109.22 X 30.48 cm) = 77 bottles;
24" X 24" X 21" (60.96 X 60.96 X 53.34 cm) = 84 bottles.

WINE STORAGE

Designers should be concerned with the following factors:

1. Ideal temperature
Keep wines between 52° and 56° F (10° and 14° C). If stored at lower degrees, wine development slows down. Storing above 60° F (16° C) speeds development, and wine ages prematurely. Most home basements lack insulation and depth that would allow them to serve as a wine cellar.

2. Desirable humidity levels
Lack of humidity causes corks to dry out, which in turn results in evaporation of the wine. Excess humidity encourages the growth of fungus.

3. Light control
Darkness is essential for proper aging.

4. Odor absorption
Because wine breathes through the cork, any odors, such as fuel, paint, or foods, are to be avoided.

5. Protection against vibrations
All vibrations should be kept to a minimum to prevent wines from throwing off their sediment too soon.

6. Aeration
Controlled air supply is essential.

Basic wine collection
204 bottles (17 cases)

BORDEAUX
Red Bordeaux:
12 Graves
Château de Chantegrive
12 St. Emilion
Château Figeac
12 Pomerol
Château La Conseillante
White Bordeaux:
12 Sauternes
Château La Tour Blanche

BURGUNDY
Red Burgundy:
12 Santenay
12 Nuits-St.-Georges
12 Beaujolais Village
12 Brouilly
White Burgundy:
12 Chablis

CHAMPAGNE
12 Brut

CALIFORNIA
36 bottles of red:
12 Cabernet Sauvignon
12 Zinfandel
12 Pinot Noir
24 bottles of white:
12 Chardonnay
12 Chenin Blanc

ITALY
24 red:
12 Barbera
12 Barolo

Expanded wine collection
432 bottles (36 cases)

BORDEAUX
24 Château Lafite Rothschild
24 Château Margaux
24 Château Petrus
24 Château Latour
12 Château Haut-Brion
12 Château Cheval Blanc
12 Château Talbot
12 Château d'Yquem

BURGUNDY
24 Romanée Conti
12 La Tache
12 Chambertin
12 Musigny
12 Pommard
12 Nuits-St-Georges
12 Santenay
12 Brouilly
12 Beaujolais Village
12 Meursault
12 Chablis
12 Montrachet

COTES-DU-RHONE
12 Châteauneuf du Pape
12 Tavel

LOIRE
12 Sancerre

CHAMPAGNE
12 Brut

CALIFORNIA
24 Cabernet Sauvignon
24 Pinot Noir
12 Pinot Chardonnay
12 Chardonnay

GERMANY
12 Schloss Johannisberg Riesling

**Plan of bar
with automated liquor
dispensers at each end**

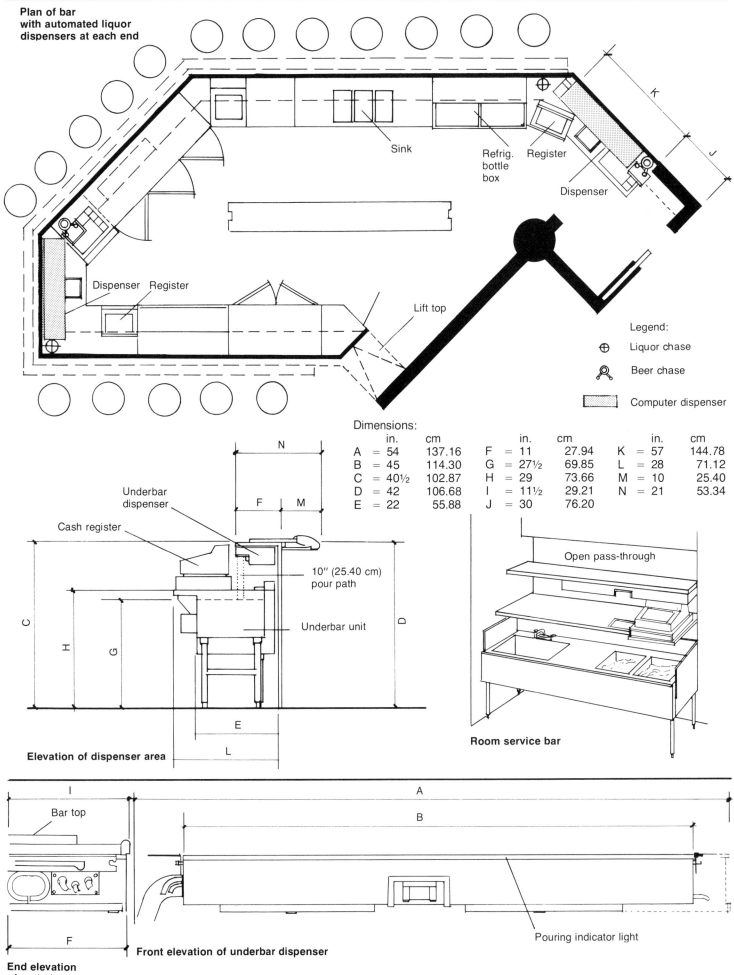

Sink

Refrig.
bottle
box

Register

Dispenser

Dispenser   Register

Lift top

Legend:

⊕   Liquor chase

Beer chase

Computer dispenser

Dimensions:

	in.	cm		in.	cm		in.	cm
A	= 54	137.16	F	= 11	27.94	K	= 57	144.78
B	= 45	114.30	G	= 27½	69.85	L	= 28	71.12
C	= 40½	102.87	H	= 29	73.66	M	= 10	25.40
D	= 42	106.68	I	= 11½	29.21	N	= 21	53.34
E	= 22	55.88	J	= 30	76.20			

Underbar
dispenser

Cash register

10″ (25.40 cm)
pour path

Underbar unit

Elevation of dispenser area

Open pass-through

Room service bar

Bar top

Pouring indicator light

Front elevation of underbar dispenser

**End elevation
of underbar
dispenser**

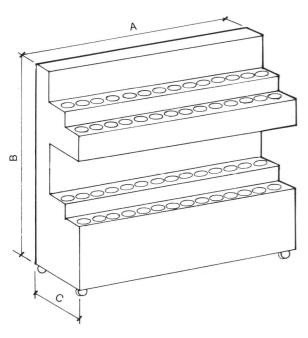

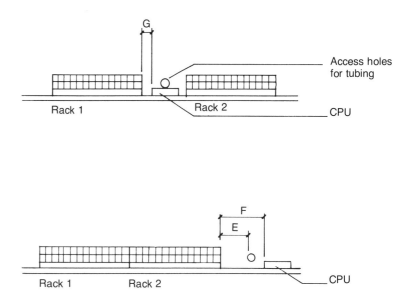

Various storage rack arrangements
CPU = central processing unit

Access holes for tubing

Split rack
Capacity: 112 fifths &
half gallons; 50 different
brands may be stored
Weight = 320 lb (145.28 kg)

Dimensions:

	in.	cm			
A	= 73	185.42	F	= 36	91.44
B	= 70	177.80	G	= 72	182.88
C	= 16½	41.91	H	= 40	101.60
D	= 96	243.84	I	= 48	121.92
E	= 12	30.48			

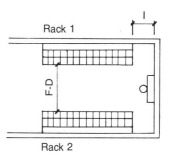

STORAGE REQUIREMENTS FOR THE COMPUTERIZED LIQUOR BAR

Electrical requirements
1. A wall-mounted 120V/12 amp dedicated computer grade circuit with isolated ground to supply power to the CPU.
2. A separate wall-mounted 120V/15 amp standard electrical outlet with breaker switch to supply power to the air compressor.

Spacing requirements between liquor racks
1. Provide a passageway and door to the storage area that will allow the racks to be delivered into the storage area; that is, do not design right-angle corners and narrow doors.
2. When specifying split racks as shown above, specify a piece of ¾" (1.91 cm) plywood cut at 26" X 48" (66.04 X 121.92 cm). This should be mounted with top 6' (1.83 m) above the floor level. This will provide a mounting base for the CPU and the air compressor.
3. Overall storage room dimensions should be a minimum of 8' X 10' (2.44 X 3.05 m).
4. All holes in floors, walls, and ceilings should be 6" (15.24 cm) in diameter, and all tubing chases must meet local building codes.
5. Separate chases will be required for soft drink lines or wines if they are not located in the rack room.
6. Separate chases are required for each pouring station as shown in the floor plan on the preceding page.

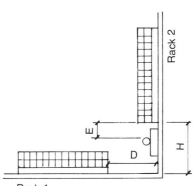

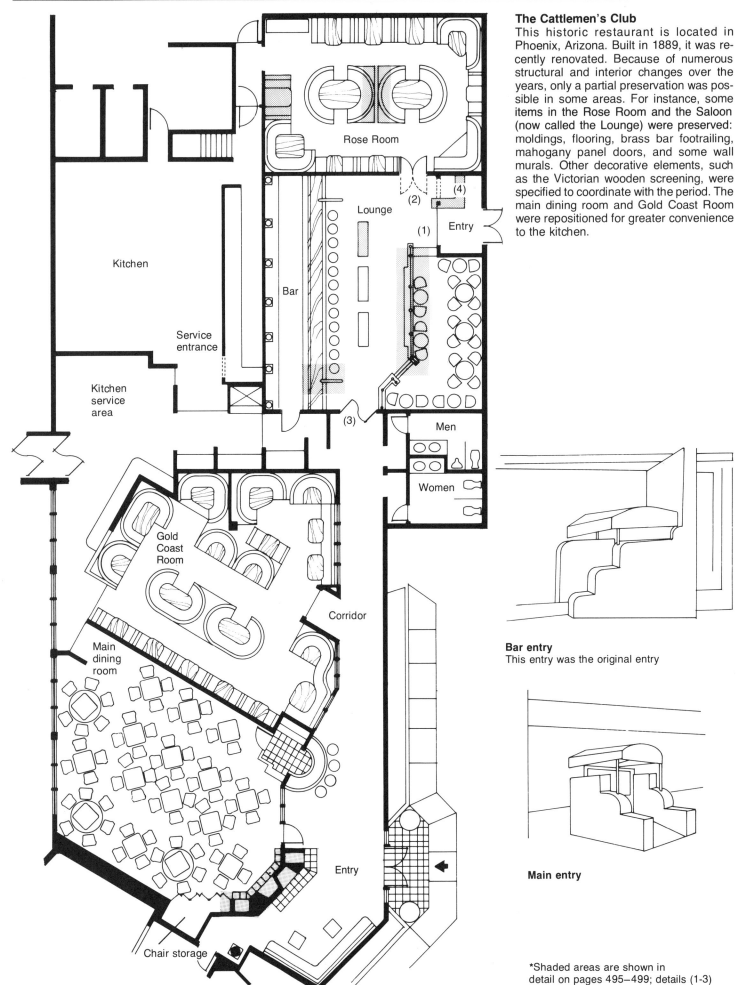

The Cattlemen's Club

This historic restaurant is located in Phoenix, Arizona. Built in 1889, it was recently renovated. Because of numerous structural and interior changes over the years, only a partial preservation was possible in some areas. For instance, some items in the Rose Room and the Saloon (now called the Lounge) were preserved: moldings, flooring, brass bar footrailing, mahogany panel doors, and some wall murals. Other decorative elements, such as the Victorian wooden screening, were specified to coordinate with the period. The main dining room and Gold Coast Room were repositioned for greater convenience to the kitchen.

Bar entry
This entry was the original entry

Main entry

*Shaded areas are shown in detail on pages 495–499; details (1-3) page 495; detail (4) page 499.

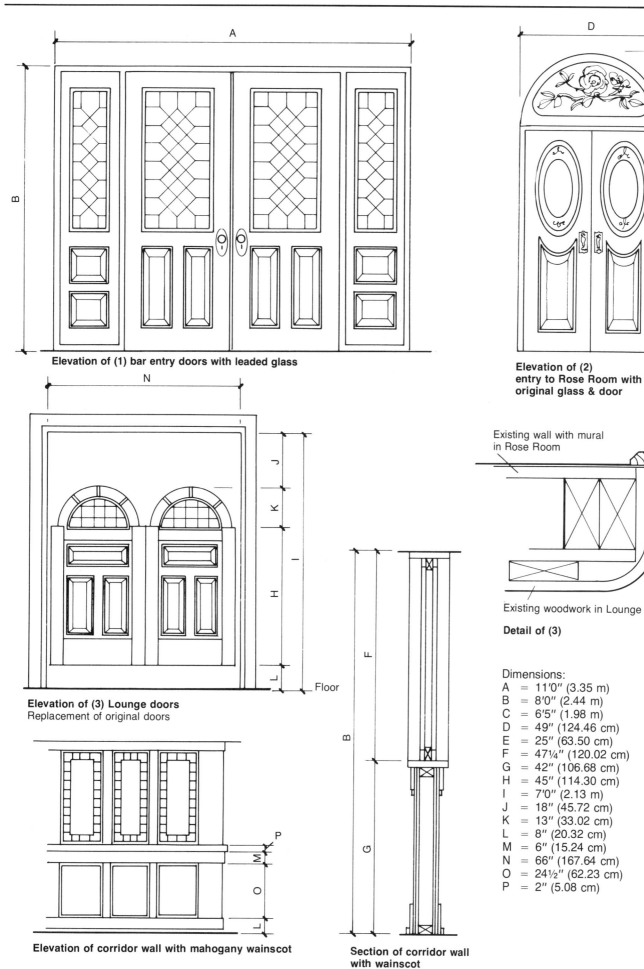

Elevation of (1) bar entry doors with leaded glass

**Elevation of (2)
entry to Rose Room with
original glass & door**

Elevation of (3) Lounge doors
Replacement of original doors

Existing wall with mural
in Rose Room

New door

New
door
trim

Existing woodwork in Lounge

Detail of (3)

Elevation of corridor wall with mahogany wainscot

**Section of corridor wall
with wainscot**

Floor

Dimensions:
A = 11′0″ (3.35 m)
B = 8′0″ (2.44 m)
C = 6′5″ (1.98 m)
D = 49″ (124.46 cm)
E = 25″ (63.50 cm)
F = 47¼″ (120.02 cm)
G = 42″ (106.68 cm)
H = 45″ (114.30 cm)
I = 7′0″ (2.13 m)
J = 18″ (45.72 cm)
K = 13″ (33.02 cm)
L = 8″ (20.32 cm)
M = 6″ (15.24 cm)
N = 66″ (167.64 cm)
O = 24½″ (62.23 cm)
P = 2″ (5.08 cm)

*Shown in plan on page 494.

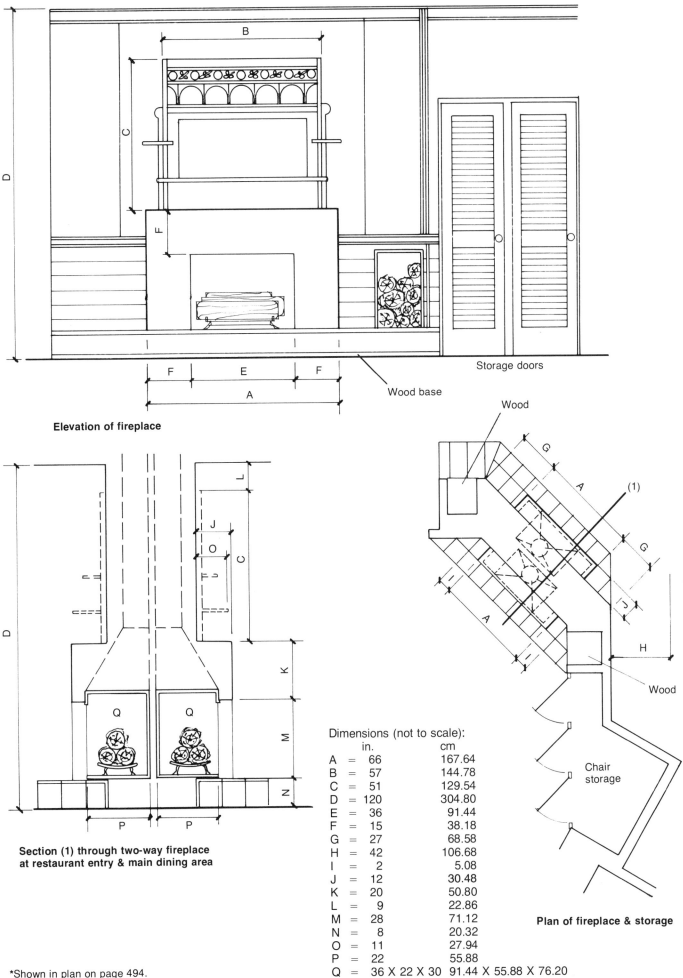

Elevation of fireplace

Storage doors

Wood base

**Section (1) through two-way fireplace
at restaurant entry & main dining area**

Wood

Wood

Chair
storage

Plan of fireplace & storage

*Shown in plan on page 494.

Dimensions (not to scale):

		in.	cm
A	=	66	167.64
B	=	57	144.78
C	=	51	129.54
D	=	120	304.80
E	=	36	91.44
F	=	15	38.18
G	=	27	68.58
H	=	42	106.68
I	=	2	5.08
J	=	12	30.48
K	=	20	50.80
L	=	9	22.86
M	=	28	71.12
N	=	8	20.32
O	=	11	27.94
P	=	22	55.88
Q	=	36 X 22 X 30	91.44 X 55.88 X 76.20

Plan of Rose Room

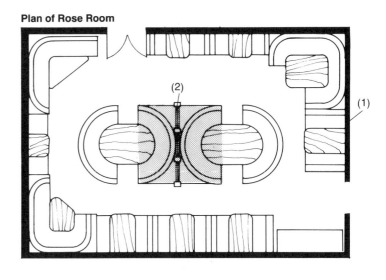

(2)

(1)

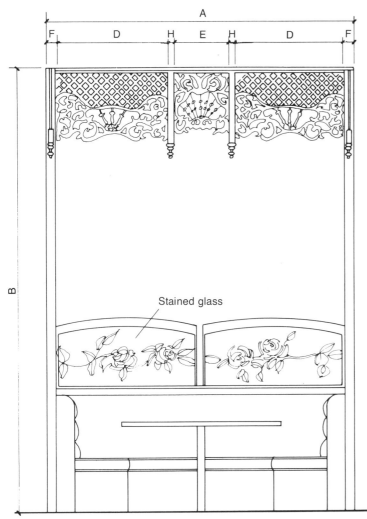

Stained glass

Elevation of (2) center booth area

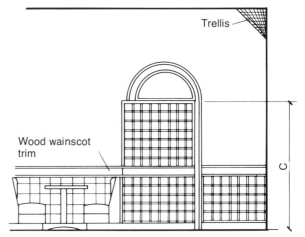

Trellis

Wood wainscot trim

Elevation of (1) trellis wall

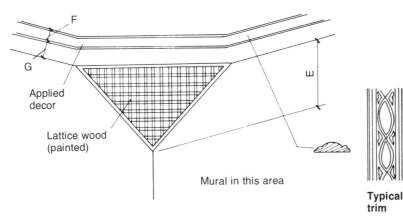

F

G

Applied decor

Lattice wood (painted)

E

Mural in this area

Trellis detail used in corners of room

Typical trim

Dimensions:
A = 8'6" (2.59 m)
B = 12'0" (3.66 m)
C = 7'0" (2.13 m)
D = 3'0" (0.91 m)
E = 18" (45.72 cm)
F = 3" to 4" (7.62 to 10.16 cm)
G = 6" to 8" (15.24 to 20.32 cm)
H = 2" (5.08 cm)

*Shown in plan on page 494.

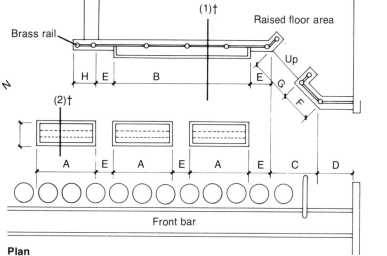

Plan

Lounge area was part of the original building design. The raised floor area and carpet were added. The remainder of the floor is reconditioned original terrazo. Other than the original brass footrail on the front bar, all other brass rails and fixtures were designed to match the original.

Dimensions:
A = 5'0" (1.52 m)
B = 11'6" (3.51 m)
C = 52" (132.08 cm)
D = 36" (91.44 cm)
E = 18" (45.72 cm)
F = 30" (76.20 cm)
G = 42" (106.68 cm)
H = 21" (53.34 cm)
I = 13" (33.02 cm)
J = 2" (7.62 cm)
K = 3" (7.62 cm)
L = 12" (30.48 cm)
M = 9" (22.86 cm)
N = 24" (60.96 cm)
O = 9¼" (23.54 cm)

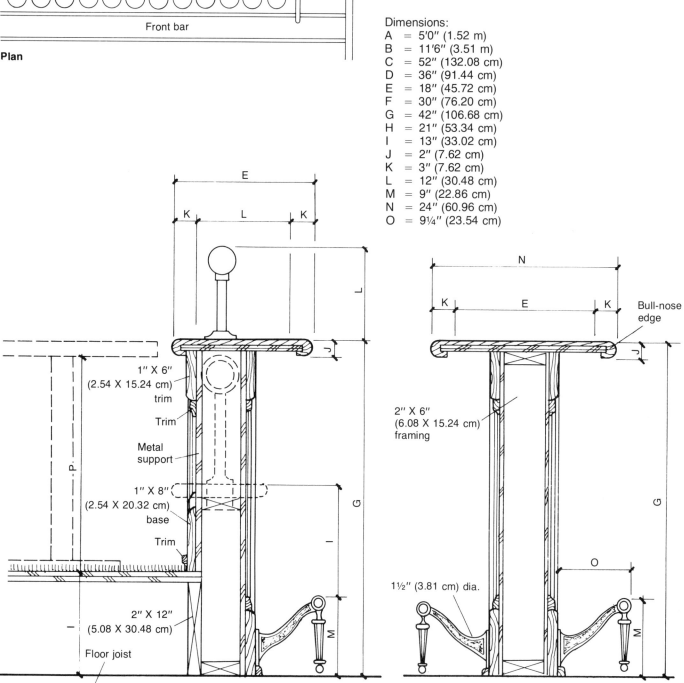

Section (1) through raised area

Section (2) through stand-up bar area

Note: The brass footrail on the main bar was the original. Other rails were made to match.

*Shown in plan on page 494.
†Shown above and on next page.

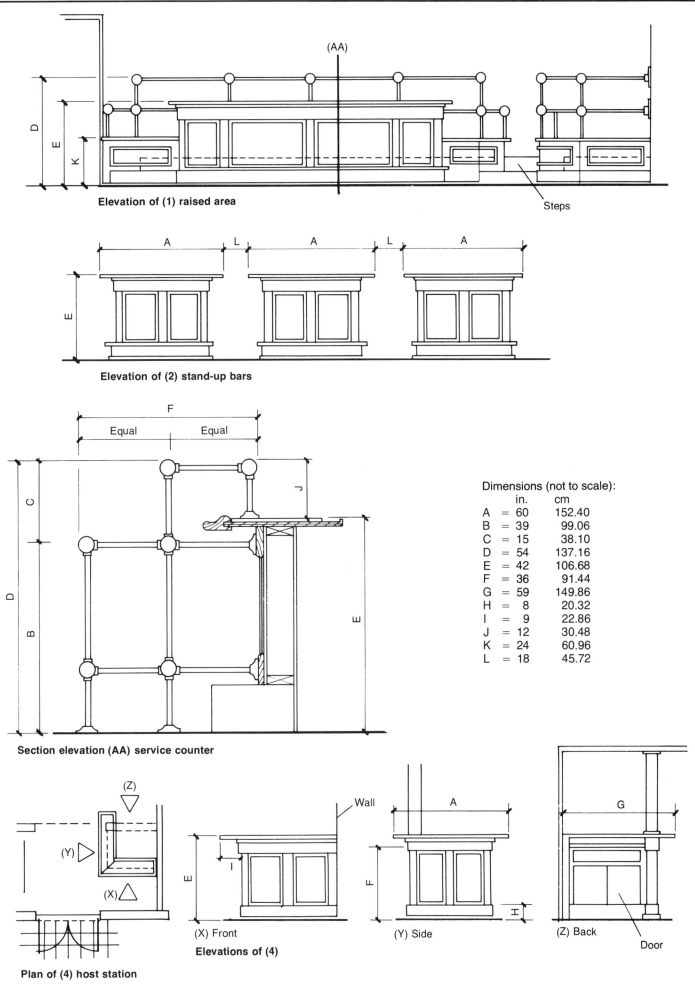

Elevation of (1) raised area

Steps

Elevation of (2) stand-up bars

F

Equal   Equal

Section elevation (AA) service counter

Dimensions (not to scale):

		in.	cm
A	=	60	152.40
B	=	39	99.06
C	=	15	38.10
D	=	54	137.16
E	=	42	106.68
F	=	36	91.44
G	=	59	149.86
H	=	8	20.32
I	=	9	22.86
J	=	12	30.48
K	=	24	60.96
L	=	18	45.72

Plan of (4) host station

Wall

(X) Front

Elevations of (4)

(Y) Side

(Z) Back

Door

*Shown in plan on page 494.

This restaurant was designed with a theme based on school surroundings such as gym, locker room, and classrooms. Wall elevations (A) through (E) illustrate the theme motifs. Custom casework details (F) are shown on pages 502-503.

Legend:

1 = entry
2 = main dining room
3 = coffee shop
4 = coffee shop service area
5 = women's restroom entry lounge
6 = women's restroom
7 = men's restroom
8 = lounge area
9 = bar area
10 = dancing area

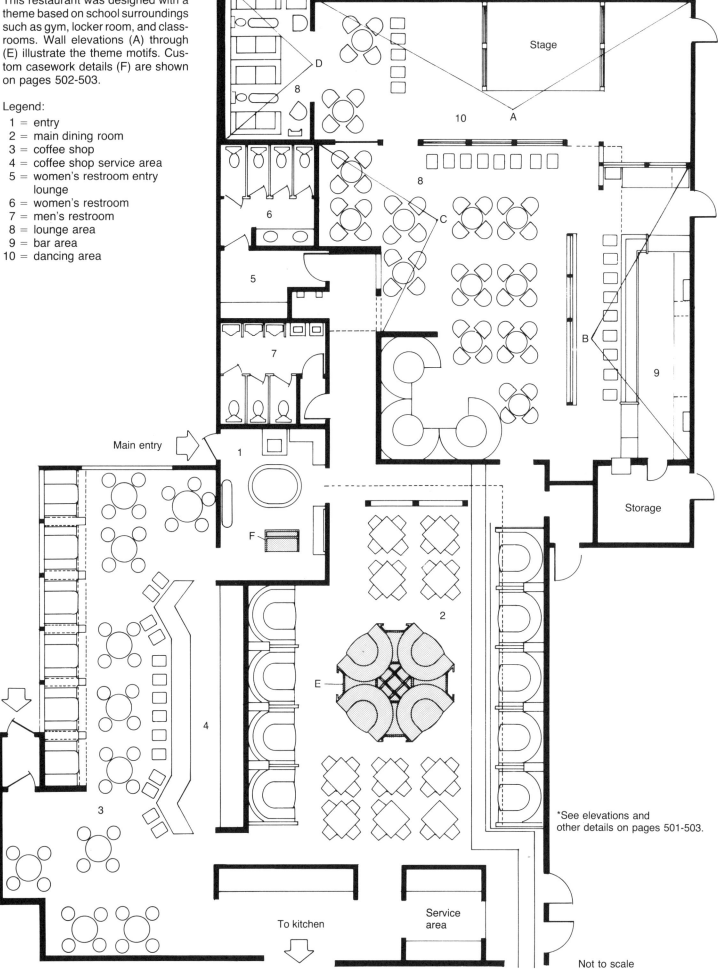

Stage

Main entry

Storage

*See elevations and other details on pages 501-503.

To kitchen

Service area

Not to scale

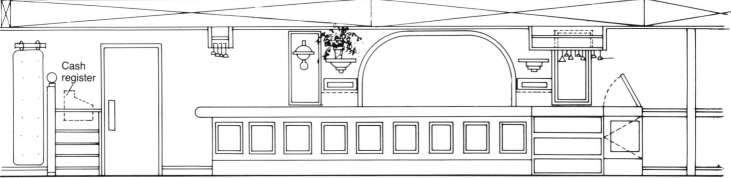

Elevation of (A) wall showing front bar & back superstructure

Cash register

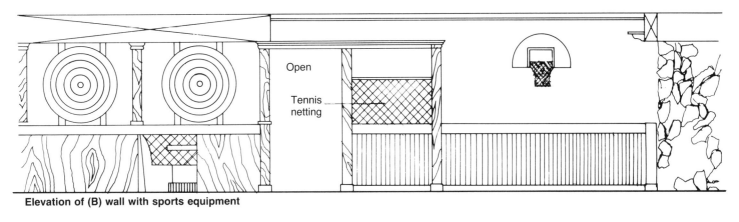

Elevation of (B) wall with sports equipment

Open

Tennis netting

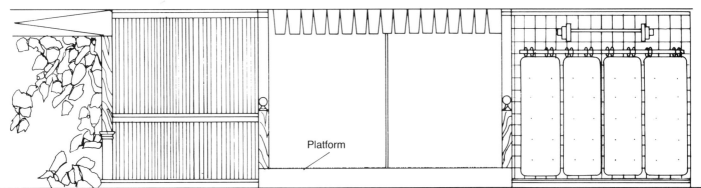

Elevation of (C) wall with raised orchestra platform
Dancing in surrounding area

Platform

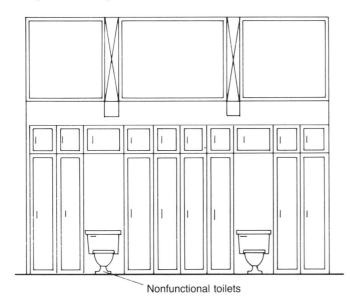

Nonfunctional toilets

Elevation of (D) wall showing locker room

Shelf

Table

Booth

Table

Booth

Elevation of (E) center booths with decorative library elements.
Note: Bookshelves, plants, and paintings built around the booths.

*Shown in plan on page 500.

DETAILS OF (F)

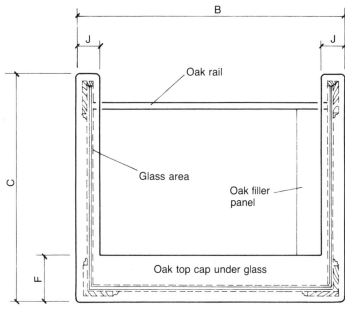

Plan

Oak rail

Glass area

Oak filler panel

Oak top cap under glass

Dimensions:

		in.	cm
A	=	50	127.00
B	=	36	91.44
C	=	30	76.20
D	=	15¾	40.01
E	=	4	10.16
F	=	6	15.24
G	=	6¾	17.15
H	=	12	30.48
I	=	5	12.70
J	=	3	7.62
K	=	¾	1.91
L	=	4½	11.43
M	=	3½	8.89
N	=	7	17.78
O	=	6¼	15.88
P	=	1½	3.81

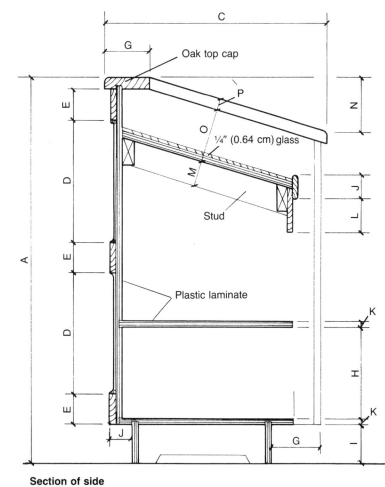

Oak top cap

P

¼" (0.64 cm) glass

O

M

Stud

Plastic laminate

Section of side

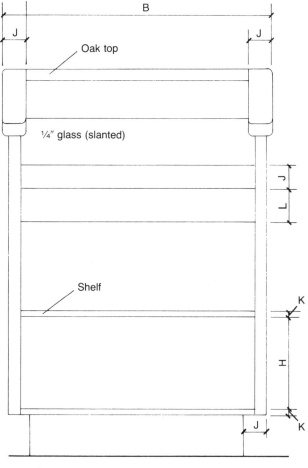

Oak top

¼" glass (slanted)

Shelf

Section of back

*Shown in plan on page 500.

DETAILS OF (F)

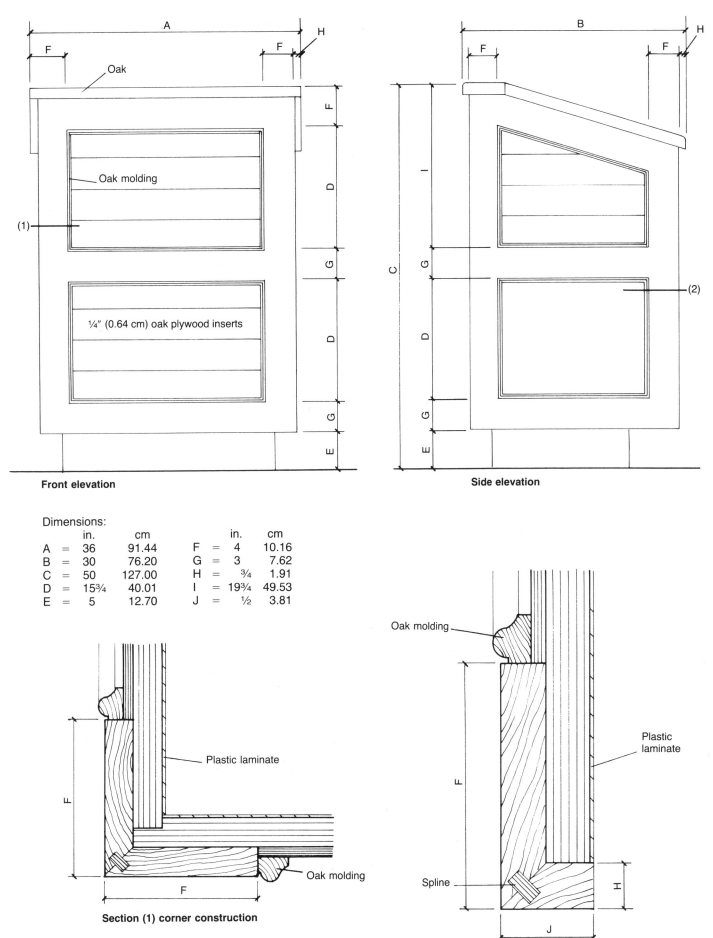

Oak

Oak molding

(1)

¼″ (0.64 cm) oak plywood inserts

Front elevation

Side elevation

(2)

Dimensions:

		in.	cm				in.	cm
A	=	36	91.44		F	=	4	10.16
B	=	30	76.20		G	=	3	7.62
C	=	50	127.00		H	=	¾	1.91
D	=	15¾	40.01		I	=	19¾	49.53
E	=	5	12.70		J	=	½	3.81

Plastic laminate

Oak molding

Section (1) corner construction

Oak molding

Plastic laminate

Spline

Section (2) panel

*Shown in plan on page 500.

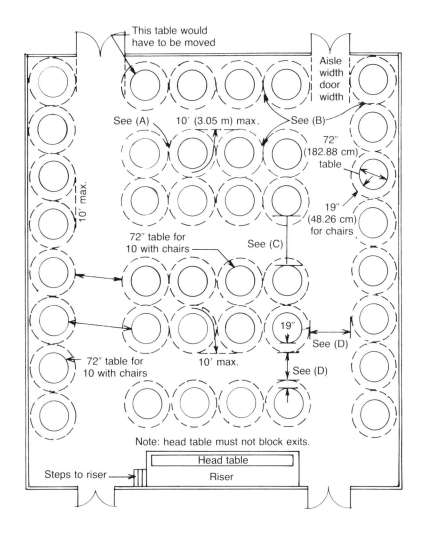

This table would have to be moved

Aisle width door width

See (A) 10' (3.05 m) max. See (B)

72" (182.88 cm) table

19" (48.26 cm) for chairs

10' max.

72" table for 10 with chairs See (C)

72" table for 10 with chairs 10' max.

19" See (D)

See (D)

Note: head table must not block exits.

Steps to riser

Head table

Riser

Aisle requirements

Aisle requirements for banquet-type arrangement require that the path of travel should not exceed 10' from any point to an aisle or an exit.

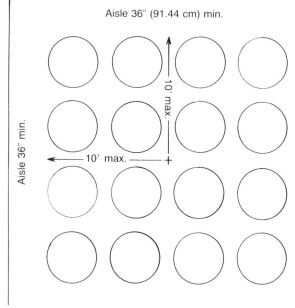

Aisle 36" (91.44 cm) min.

Aisle 36" min.

10' max.

10' max.

This drawing provides design guidelines for banquet seating aisle requirements when movable tables and chairs are to be used on both sides of an aisle. This arrangement of tables cannot be used to increase occupancy load or serve as an approved layout for code officials because no space has been provided for the service areas.

(A) A small aisle would normally be provided for waiter/waitress access.
(B) No aisle requirement with travel is less than 10'.
(C) Distance between tables must be greater than required aisle width plus 19" (48.26 cm) for chairs on one or 38" (96.52 cm) for chairs on both sides.
(D) Aisle must be sized not less than 36".

Banquet seating with cross aisles

The drawings shown below illustrate the necessary space between tables in a banquet room where it is assumed that an even number of people will use the means of egress paths provided. Designers should note the additional space allocated between tables where two chairs are back to back. Tables marked A illustrate the arrangement that would permit two people in chairs B to both push chairs back simultaneously and not block passage.

Rectangular-type banquet seating

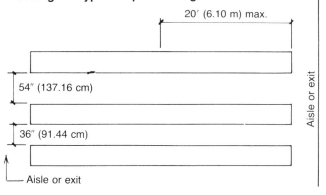

20' (6.10 m) max.

54" (137.16 cm)

36" (91.44 cm)

Aisle or exit

Aisle or exit

Note: When travel distance to aisles exceeds 10', tables and chairs should not exceed the distances shown above.

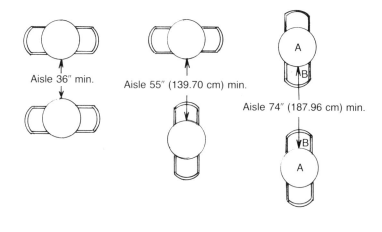

Aisle 36" min.

Aisle 55" (139.70 cm) min.

A

B

Aisle 74" (187.96 cm) min.

B

A

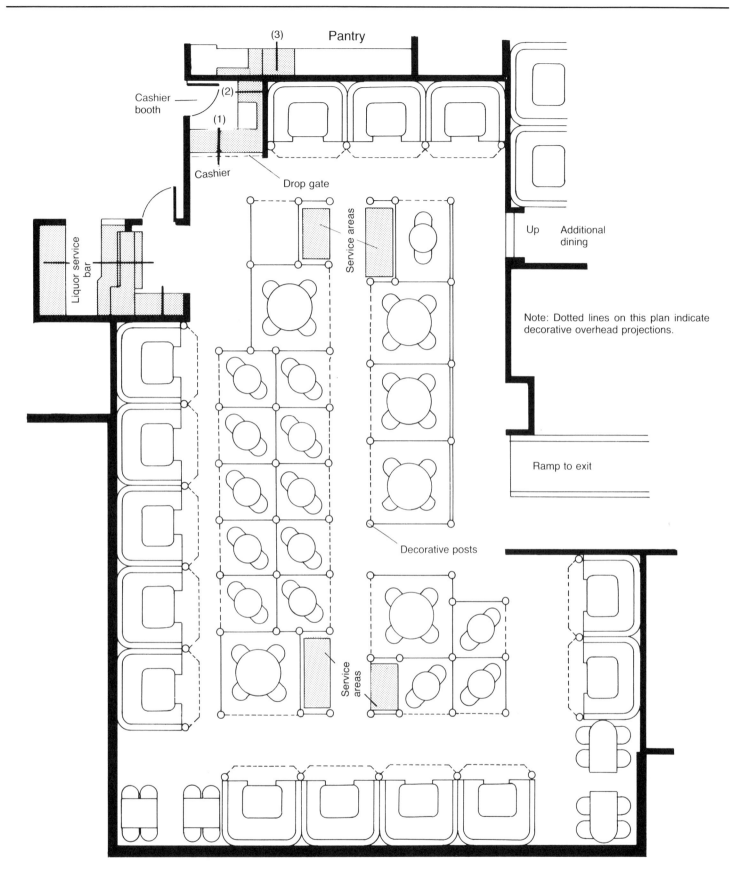

Pantry

(3)

Cashier booth

(2)

(1)

Cashier

Drop gate

Liquor service bar

Service areas

Up   Additional dining

Note: Dotted lines on this plan indicate decorative overhead projections.

Ramp to exit

Decorative posts

Service areas

Capacity:

Furnishings	Seating	Occupants
9 tables	4	36
14 tables	2	28
14 booths †	4	56
	Total	120

*Shaded areas are shown in detail on pages 506–513: Detail (1) page 506; detail (2) page 507; detail (3) page 508.

†Booths may seat 5 when necessary.

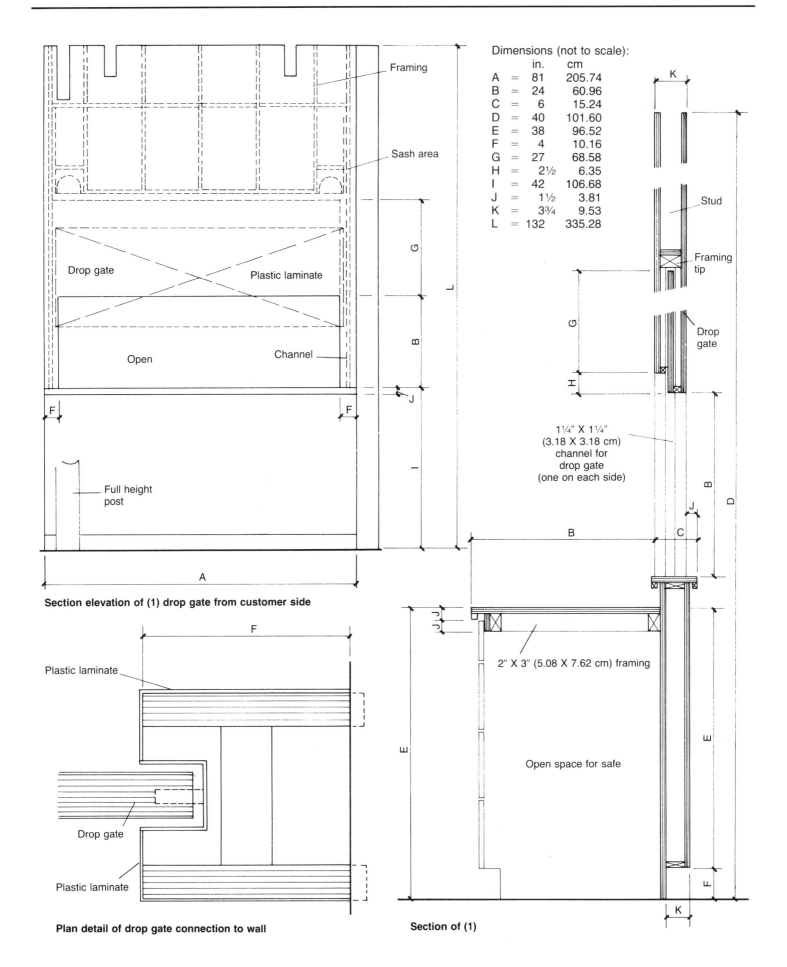

Dimensions (not to scale):

	in.	cm
A =	81	205.74
B =	24	60.96
C =	6	15.24
D =	40	101.60
E =	38	96.52
F =	4	10.16
G =	27	68.58
H =	2½	6.35
I =	42	106.68
J =	1½	3.81
K =	3¾	9.53
L =	132	335.28

Framing

Sash area

Drop gate

Plastic laminate

Open

Channel

Full height post

Section elevation of (1) drop gate from customer side

Stud

Framing tip

Drop gate

1¼" X 1¼" (3.18 X 3.18 cm) channel for drop gate (one on each side)

Plastic laminate

Drop gate

Plastic laminate

Plan detail of drop gate connection to wall

2" X 3" (5.08 X 7.62 cm) framing

Open space for safe

Section of (1)

* Shown in plan on page 505.

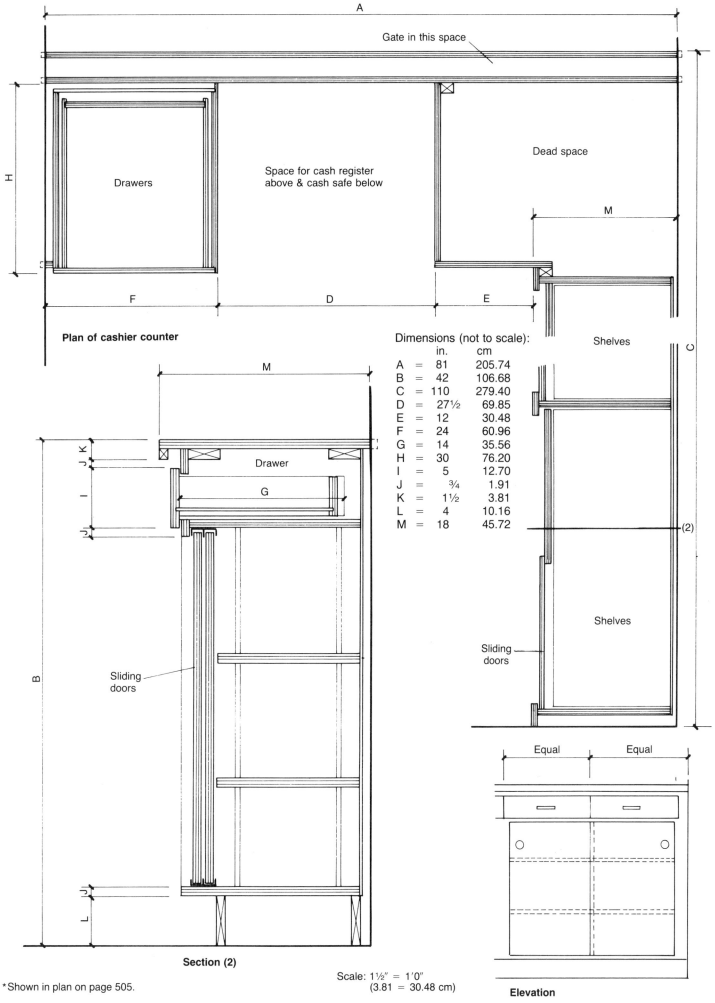

Gate in this space

Drawers

Space for cash register
above & cash safe below

Dead space

M

Plan of cashier counter

M

Drawer

G

Sliding
doors

Shelves

Shelves

Sliding
doors

(2)

Dimensions (not to scale):

		in.	cm
A	=	81	205.74
B	=	42	106.68
C	=	110	279.40
D	=	27½	69.85
E	=	12	30.48
F	=	24	60.96
G	=	14	35.56
H	=	30	76.20
I	=	5	12.70
J	=	¾	1.91
K	=	1½	3.81
L	=	4	10.16
M	=	18	45.72

Section (2)

Scale: 1½″ = 1′0″
(3.81 = 30.48 cm)

Equal   Equal

Elevation

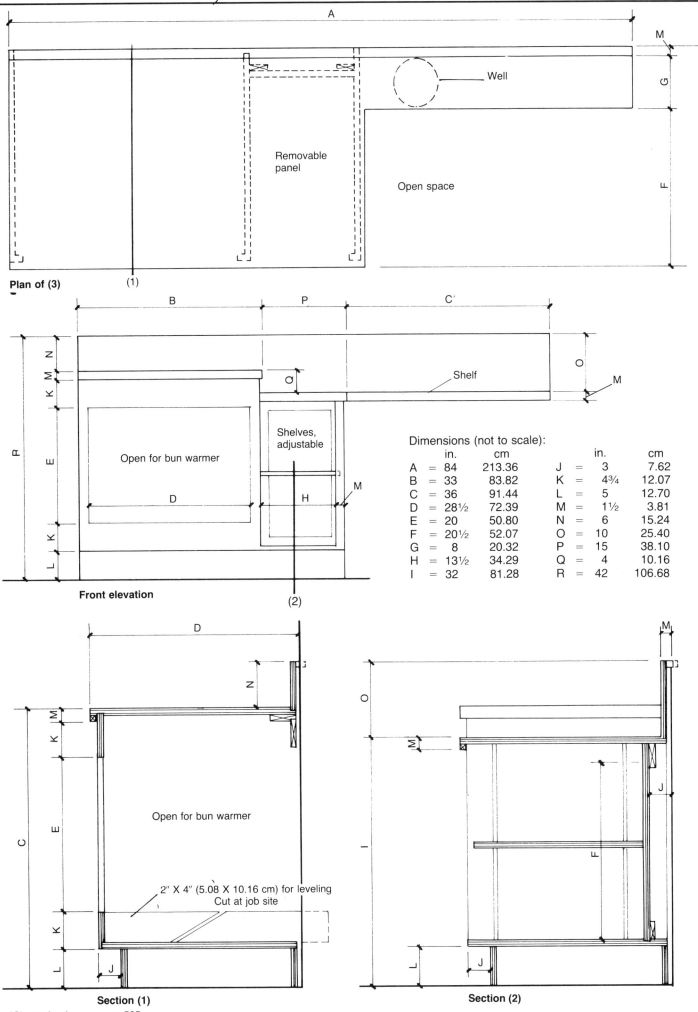

A

M

G

Well

Open space

F

Removable
panel

Plan of (3)

(1)

B   P   C

N

K   M

K

Q

Shelf

O

M

R

E

Open for bun warmer

Shelves,
adjustable

D

H

M

K

L

Front elevation

(2)

Dimensions (not to scale):

	in.	cm			in.	cm
A =	84	213.36	J =		3	7.62
B =	33	83.82	K =		4¾	12.07
C =	36	91.44	L =		5	12.70
D =	28½	72.39	M =		1½	3.81
E =	20	50.80	N =		6	15.24
F =	20½	52.07	O =		10	25.40
G =	8	20.32	P =		15	38.10
H =	13½	34.29	Q =		4	10.16
I =	32	81.28	R =		42	106.68

D

N

M

K

C

E

Open for bun warmer

2" X 4" (5.08 X 10.16 cm) for leveling
Cut at job site

K

L

J

Section (1)

M

O

M

I

J

F

L

J

Section (2)

*Shown in plan on page 505.

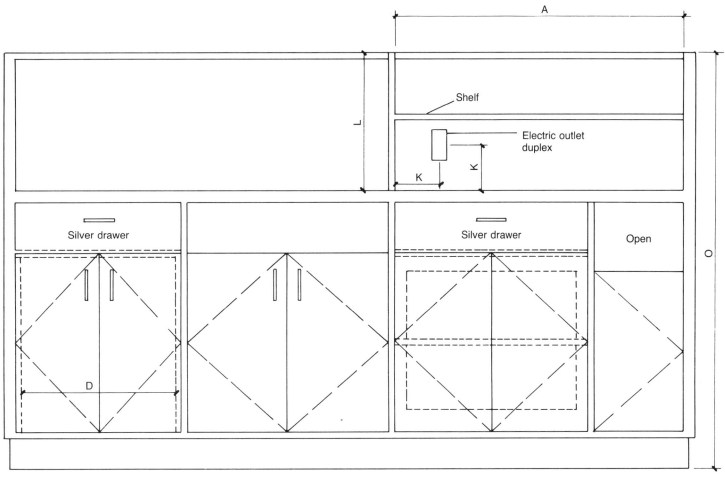

Elevation of service area
All exterior surfaces covered with plastic laminate

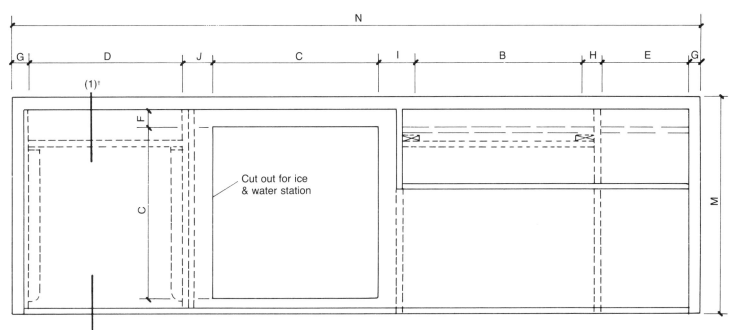

Plan of service area

*Shown in plan on page 505.
†Shown on next page.

Dimensions (not to scale):

	in.	cm			in.	cm			in.	cm
A	= 39¼	99.70	F	=	2¼	5.72	K	=	6	15.24
B	= 23½	59.69	G	=	1½	3.81	L	=	18	45.72
C	= 22¼	56.52	H	=	2	5.08	M	=	28	71.12
D	= 20	50.80	I	=	5	12.70	N	=	93	236.22
E	= 12	30.48	J	=	4	10.16	O	=	54	137.16

ICE & WATER STATIONS

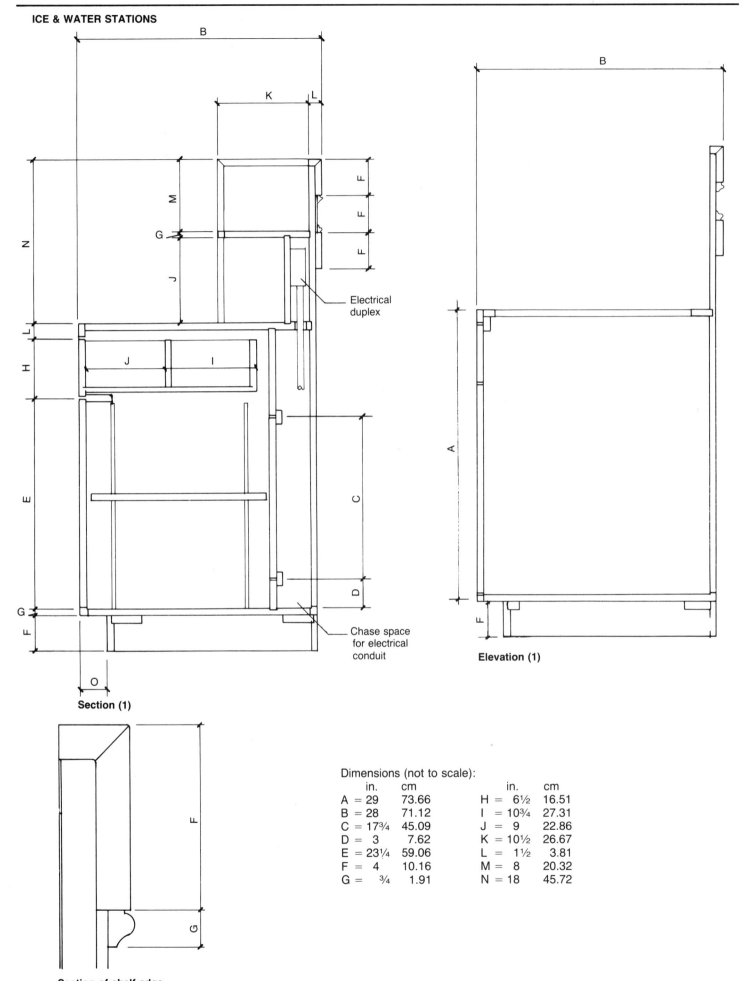

Electrical
duplex

Chase space
for electrical
conduit

Section (1)

Elevation (1)

Section of shelf edge
*Shown in plan on page 505.

Dimensions (not to scale):

	in.	cm		in.	cm
A	= 29	73.66	H	= 6½	16.51
B	= 28	71.12	I	= 10¾	27.31
C	= 17¾	45.09	J	= 9	22.86
D	= 3	7.62	K	= 10½	26.67
E	= 23¼	59.06	L	= 1½	3.81
F	= 4	10.16	M	= 8	20.32
G	= ¾	1.91	N	= 18	45.72

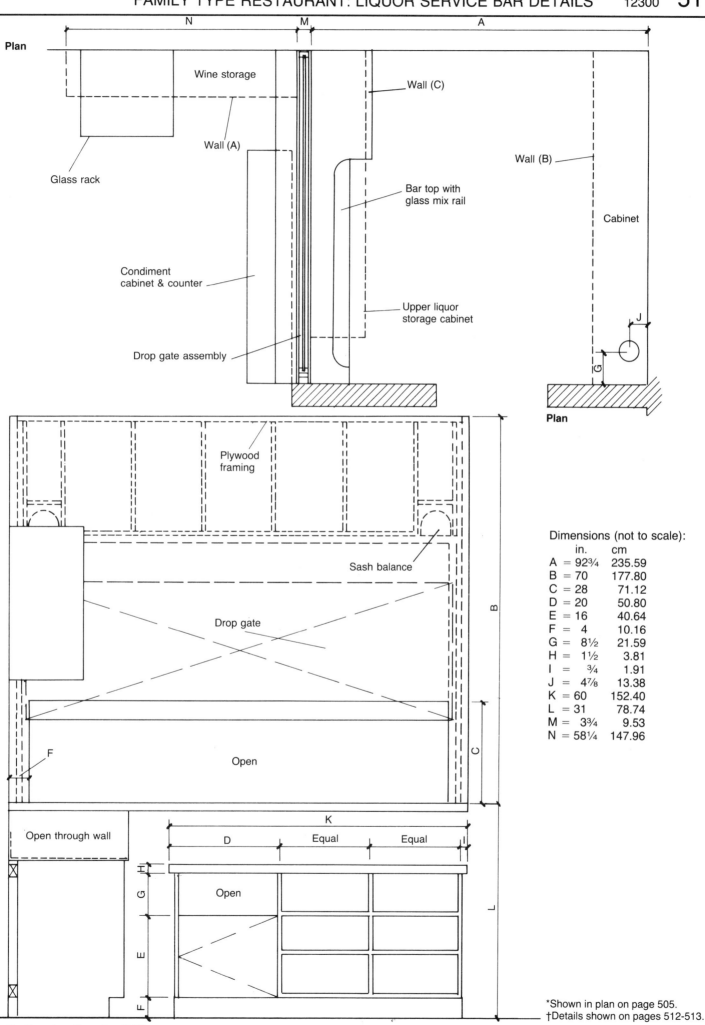

Plan

Wine storage

Wall (C)

Wall (A)

Glass rack

Bar top with
glass mix rail

Wall (B)

Condiment
cabinet & counter

Cabinet

Upper liquor
storage cabinet

Drop gate assembly

J

G

Plan

Plywood
framing

Sash balance

Drop gate

Open

Dimensions (not to scale):

	in.	cm
A =	92¾	235.59
B =	70	177.80
C =	28	71.12
D =	20	50.80
E =	16	40.64
F =	4	10.16
G =	8½	21.59
H =	1½	3.81
I =	¾	1.91
J =	4⅞	13.38
K =	60	152.40
L =	31	78.74
M =	3¾	9.53
N =	58¼	147.96

Open through wall

K

D   Equal   Equal

Open

Open

*Shown in plan on page 505.
†Details shown on pages 512-513.

Section elevation of wall (C)

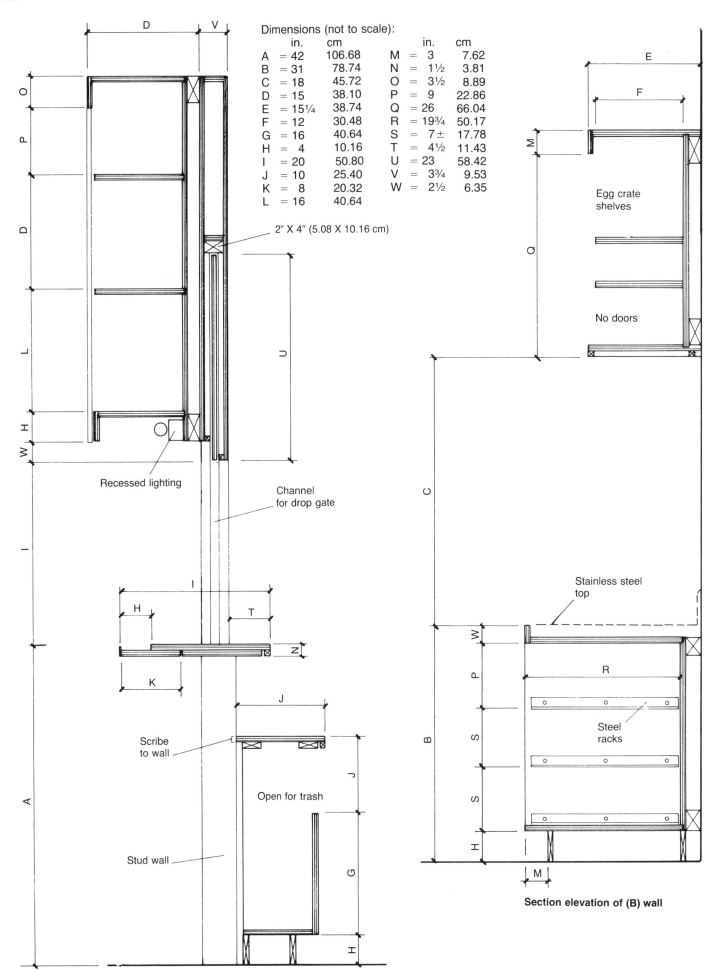

Dimensions (not to scale):

	in.	cm			in.	cm
A	= 42	106.68	M	=	3	7.62
B	= 31	78.74	N	=	1½	3.81
C	= 18	45.72	O	=	3½	8.89
D	= 15	38.10	P	=	9	22.86
E	= 15¼	38.74	Q	=	26	66.04
F	= 12	30.48	R	=	19¾	50.17
G	= 16	40.64	S	=	7 ±	17.78
H	= 4	10.16	T	=	4½	11.43
I	= 20	50.80	U	=	23	58.42
J	= 10	25.40	V	=	3¾	9.53
K	= 8	20.32	W	=	2½	6.35
L	= 16	40.64				

2″ X 4″ (5.08 X 10.16 cm)

Recessed lighting

Channel for drop gate

Scribe to wall

Open for trash

Stud wall

Section of (C) wall

*Shown in plan on page 505.

Egg crate shelves

No doors

Stainless steel top

Steel racks

Section elevation of (B) wall

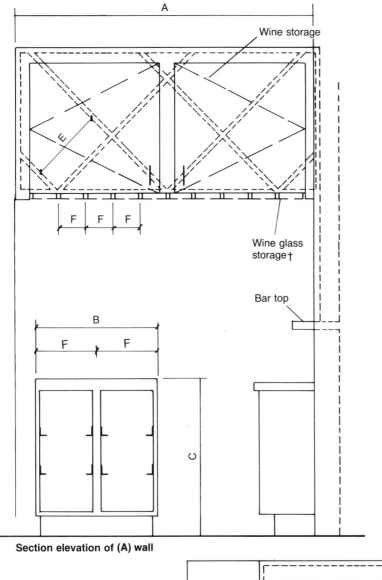

Wine storage

Wine glass storage†

Bar top

F F F

B

F F

C

Section elevation of (A) wall

Dimensions (not to scale):

	in.	cm
A	= 58¼	147.96
B	= 24½	62.23
C	= 31	78.74
D	= 10¾	27.31
E	= 15	38.10
F	= equal	

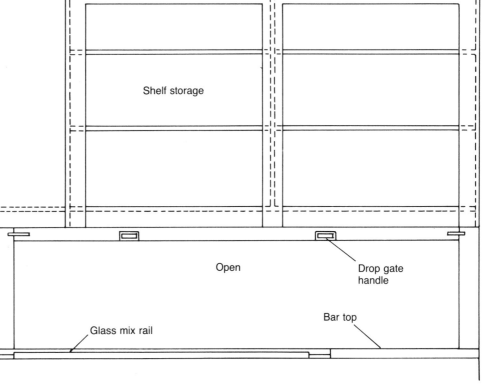

Shelf storage

Open

Drop gate handle

Bar top

Glass mix rail

Elevation of (C) wall from bar top to ceiling

*Shown in plan on page 505.
†See details on wine glass storage
  on page 489.

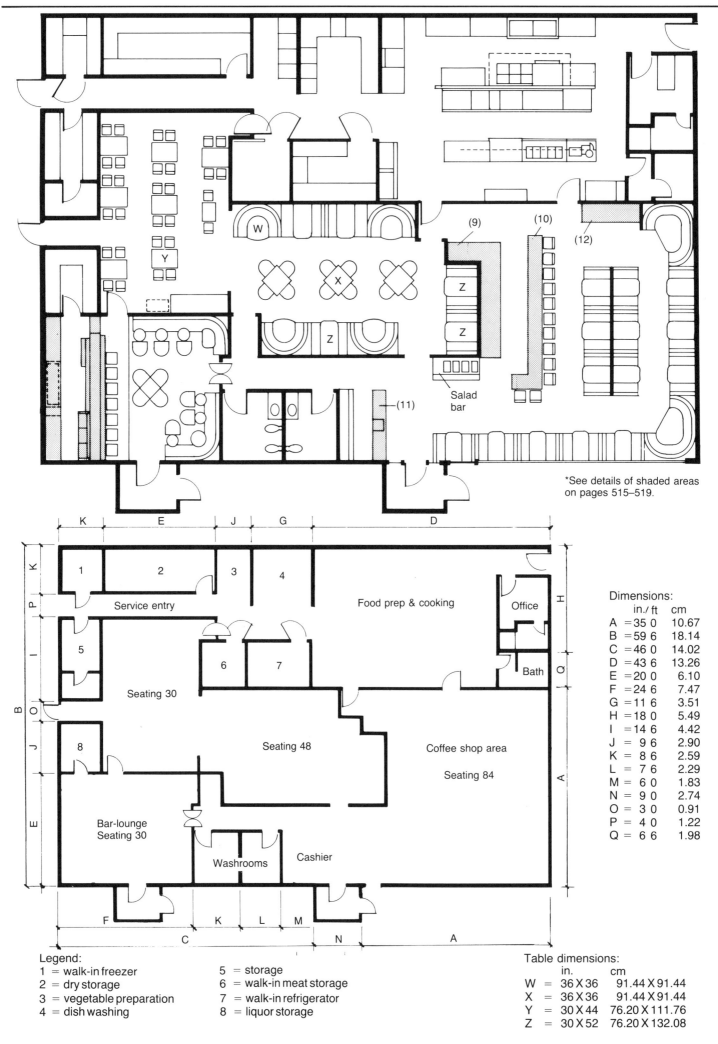

*See details of shaded areas on pages 515–519.

Dimensions:

	in./ft	cm
A =	35 0	10.67
B =	59 6	18.14
C =	46 0	14.02
D =	43 6	13.26
E =	20 0	6.10
F =	24 6	7.47
G =	11 6	3.51
H =	18 0	5.49
I =	14 6	4.42
J =	9 6	2.90
K =	8 6	2.59
L =	7 6	2.29
M =	6 0	1.83
N =	9 0	2.74
O =	3 0	0.91
P =	4 0	1.22
Q =	6 6	1.98

Legend:
1 = walk-in freezer
2 = dry storage
3 = vegetable preparation
4 = dish washing
5 = storage
6 = walk-in meat storage
7 = walk-in refrigerator
8 = liquor storage

Table dimensions:

	in.	cm
W =	36 X 36	91.44 X 91.44
X =	36 X 36	91.44 X 91.44
Y =	30 X 44	76.20 X 111.76
Z =	30 X 52	76.20 X 132.08

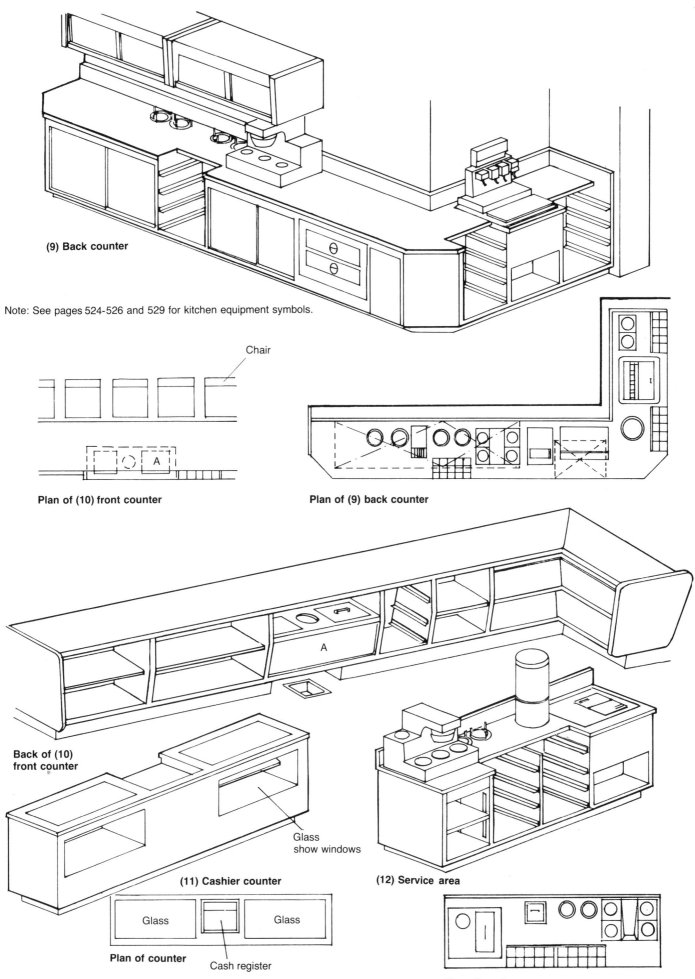

(9) Back counter

Note: See pages 524-526 and 529 for kitchen equipment symbols.

Chair

Plan of (10) front counter

Plan of (9) back counter

Back of (10) front counter

Glass show windows

(11) Cashier counter

(12) Service area

Glass

Glass

Plan of counter

Cash register

Plan of service area

*Shown in plan on page 514.

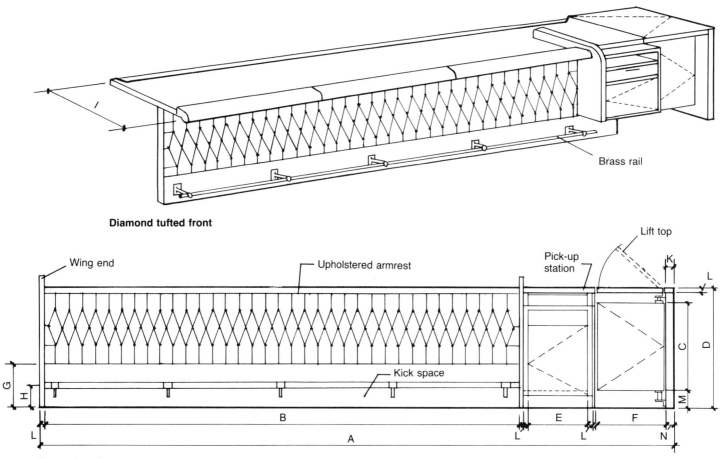

Diamond tufted front

Front elevation

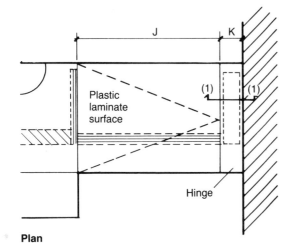

Plan

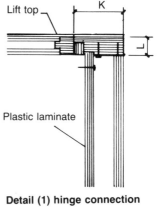

Detail (1) hinge connection of lift-up top

Dimensions (not to scale):

A	= 19′	(5.79 m)	H	= 7½″	(19.05 cm)
B	= 14′4″	(4.37 m)	I	= 25″	(63.50 cm)
C	= 30″	(76.20 cm)	J	= 24″	(60.96 cm)
D	= 42″	(106.68 cm)	K	= 4″	(10.16 cm)
E	= 21½″	(54.61 cm)	L	= 1½″	(3.81 cm)
F	= 28½″	(72.39 cm)	M	= 6″	(15.24 cm)
G	= 15″	(38.10 cm)	N	= 3″	(7.62 cm)

*Shown in plan on page 514.

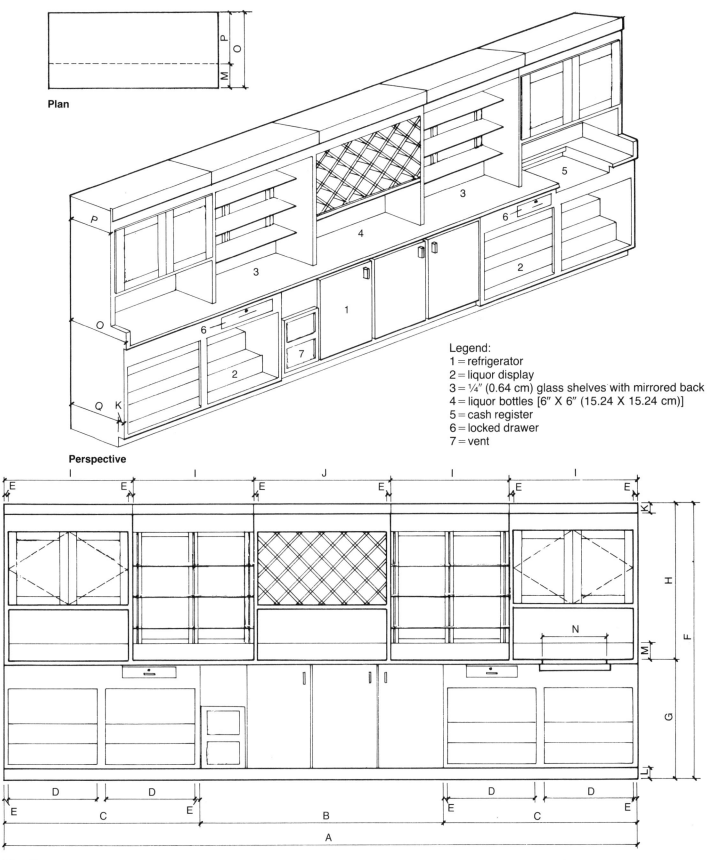

Plan

Perspective

Legend:
1 = refrigerator
2 = liquor display
3 = ¼″ (0.64 cm) glass shelves with mirrored back
4 = liquor bottles [6″ X 6″ (15.24 X 15.24 cm)]
5 = cash register
6 = locked drawer
7 = vent

Elevation

Dimensions:

A =	19′0″	(5.79 m)	G =	42″	(106.68 cm)	M =	6″	(15.24 cm)
B =	7′4″	(2.24 m)	H =	57½″	(146.05 cm)	N =	24″	(60.96 cm)
C =	70½″	(179.07 cm)	I =	45″	(114.30 cm)	O =	28″	(71.12 cm)
D =	32″	(81.28 cm)	J =	49″	(124.46 cm)	P =	22″	(55.88 cm)
E =	1½″	(3.81 cm)	K =	3½″±	(8.89 cm)	Q =	25″	(63.50 cm)
F =	8′0″	(2.44 m)	L =	4″	(10.16 cm)			

*Shown in plan on page 514.

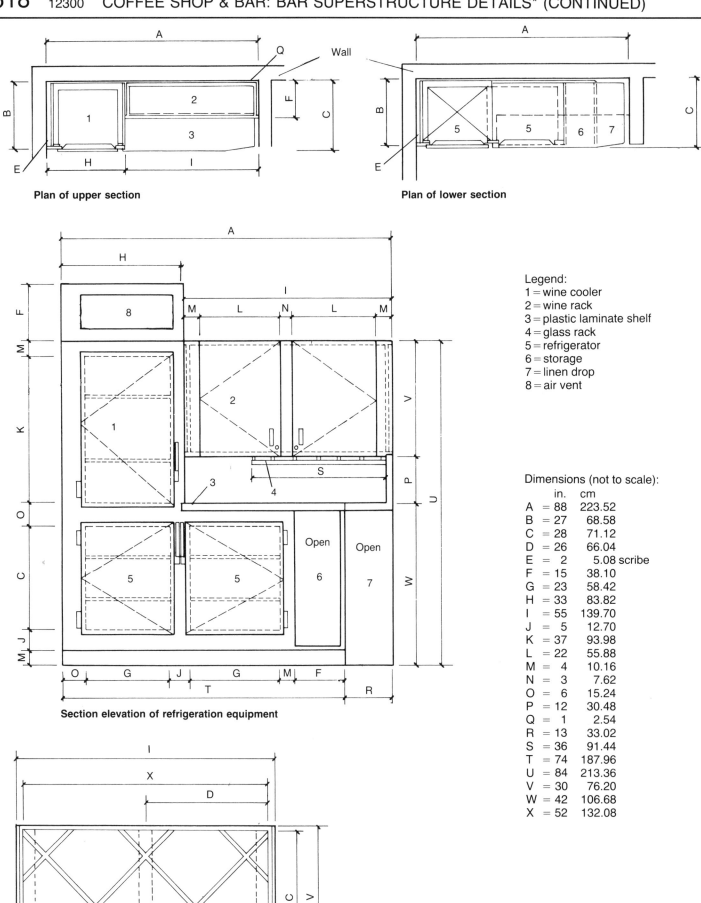

Plan of upper section

Plan of lower section

Section elevation of refrigeration equipment

Elevation of (2) wine rack

Legend:
1 = wine cooler
2 = wine rack
3 = plastic laminate shelf
4 = glass rack
5 = refrigerator
6 = storage
7 = linen drop
8 = air vent

Dimensions (not to scale):

	in.	cm
A	= 88	223.52
B	= 27	68.58
C	= 28	71.12
D	= 26	66.04
E	= 2	5.08 scribe
F	= 15	38.10
G	= 23	58.42
H	= 33	83.82
I	= 55	139.70
J	= 5	12.70
K	= 37	93.98
L	= 22	55.88
M	= 4	10.16
N	= 3	7.62
O	= 6	15.24
P	= 12	30.48
Q	= 1	2.54
R	= 13	33.02
S	= 36	91.44
T	= 74	187.96
U	= 84	213.36
V	= 30	76.20
W	= 42	106.68
X	= 52	132.08

Note: Do not install cabinet doors until wine rack is installed.

*Shown in plan on page 514.

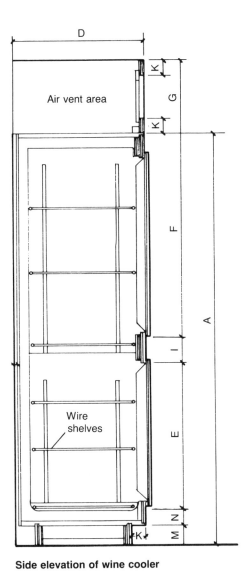

Side elevation of wine cooler

Dimensions (not to scale):

	in.	cm
A	= 84	2.13
B	= 42	106.68
C	= 30	76.20
D	= 27	68.58
E	= 28	71.12
F	= 41½	105.41
G	= 15	38.10
H	= 12	30.48
I	= 6	15.24
J	= 36	91.44
K	= 3	7.62
L	= 11⅜	28.89
M	= 4	10.16
N	= 4¼	10.80
O	= 5¾	14.61
P	= ¾	1.91
Q	= 2	5.08
R	= 1¾	4.45
S	= 1	2.54

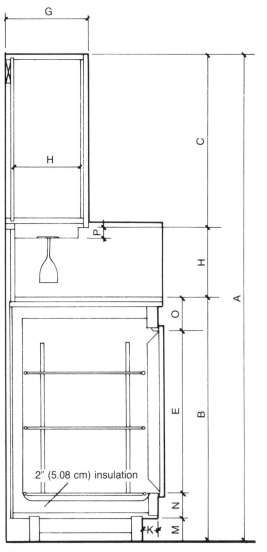

Side elevation of refrigerator with wine bottle storage & glass storage rack above

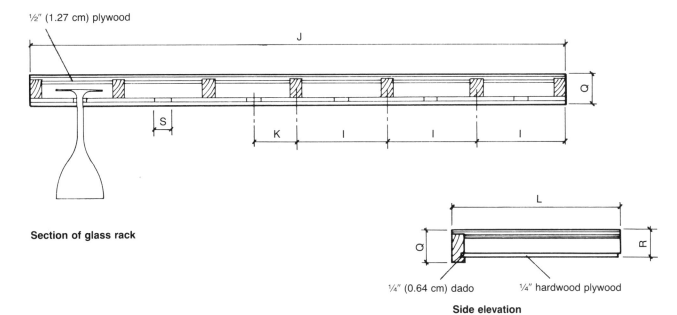

Section of glass rack

Side elevation

¼″ (0.64 cm) dado   ¼″ hardwood plywood

*Shown in plan on page 514.

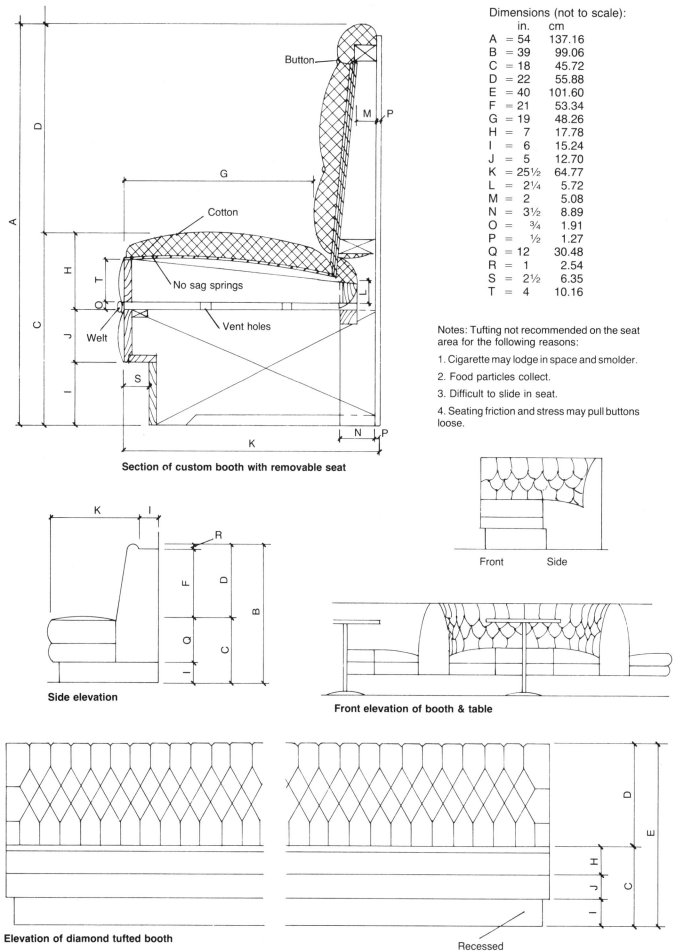

Dimensions (not to scale):

	in.	cm
A	= 54	137.16
B	= 39	99.06
C	= 18	45.72
D	= 22	55.88
E	= 40	101.60
F	= 21	53.34
G	= 19	48.26
H	= 7	17.78
I	= 6	15.24
J	= 5	12.70
K	= 25½	64.77
L	= 2¼	5.72
M	= 2	5.08
N	= 3½	8.89
O	= ¾	1.91
P	= ½	1.27
Q	= 12	30.48
R	= 1	2.54
S	= 2½	6.35
T	= 4	10.16

Notes: Tufting not recommended on the seat area for the following reasons:

1. Cigarette may lodge in space and smolder.

2. Food particles collect.

3. Difficult to slide in seat.

4. Seating friction and stress may pull buttons loose.

Section of custom booth with removable seat

Front   Side

Side elevation

Front elevation of booth & table

Elevation of diamond tufted booth

Recessed

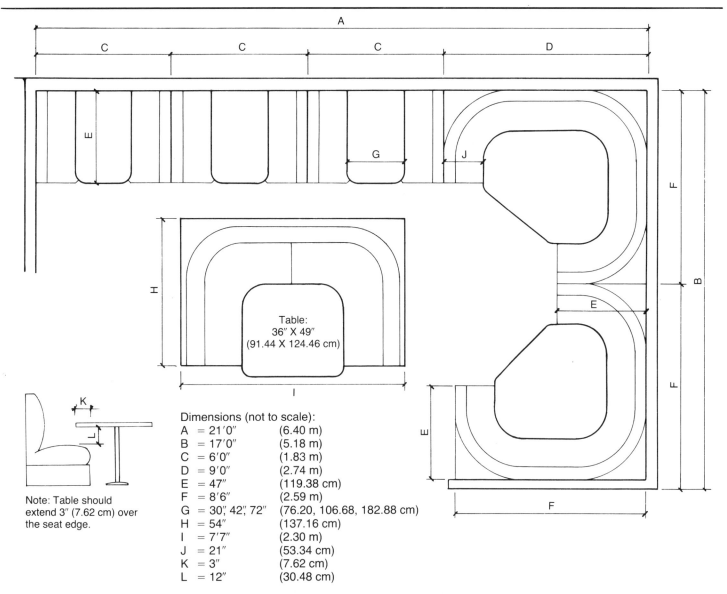

Note: Table should extend 3″ (7.62 cm) over the seat edge.

Dimensions (not to scale):
A = 21′0″   (6.40 m)
B = 17′0″   (5.18 m)
C = 6′0″   (1.83 m)
D = 9′0″   (2.74 m)
E = 47″   (119.38 cm)
F = 8′6″   (2.59 m)
G = 30″, 42″, 72″ (76.20, 106.68, 182.88 cm)
H = 54″   (137.16 cm)
I = 7′7″   (2.30 m)
J = 21″   (53.34 cm)
K = 3″   (7.62 cm)
L = 12″   (30.48 cm)

Table:
36″ X 49″
(91.44 X 124.46 cm)

SPECIFICATION OF RIGID COIL SPRING BOOTHS

Note: Dimensions to be provided according to custom design.

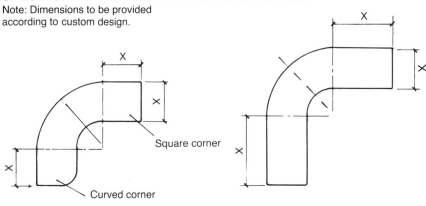

Square corner

Curved corner

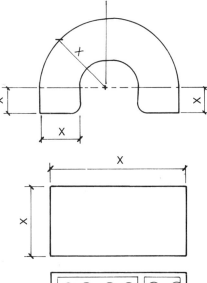

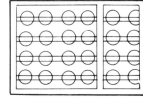

One-spring seat unit

Drop-in rigid springs

Coil springs are mounted to rigid steel channel bars, and the booth frame is made more solid by stapling or nailing these spring units into place. Strong back-to-front support is provided.

The designer should provide drawings like the ones shown here. The drawings should not be scaled, but should show the measurements of (X) areas. Drawings should illustrate either rounded or square corners, and the radius of curve in round booths should also be provided. The manufacturer will determine the number of coils necessary for the proper support.

A typical, large, quick-order coffee shop and snack bar requires extensive seating and excellent circulation to allow efficient service during peak hours.(See other circulation layouts in Chaper 19, Commercial Kitchens, pages 531–545.)

Dimensions (not to scale):

A = 18'0" (5.49 m)	H = 51"	(129.54 cm)
B = 13'0" (3.96 m)	I = 8'4"	(2.54 m)
C = 48" (121.92 cm)	J = 6'6"	(1.98 m)
D = 53" (134.62 cm)	K = 6'4"	(1.93 m)
E = 5'6" (1.68 m)	L = 44"	(111.76 cm)
F = 49" (124.46 cm)	M = 42"	(106.68 cm)
G = 12'0" (3.66 m)		

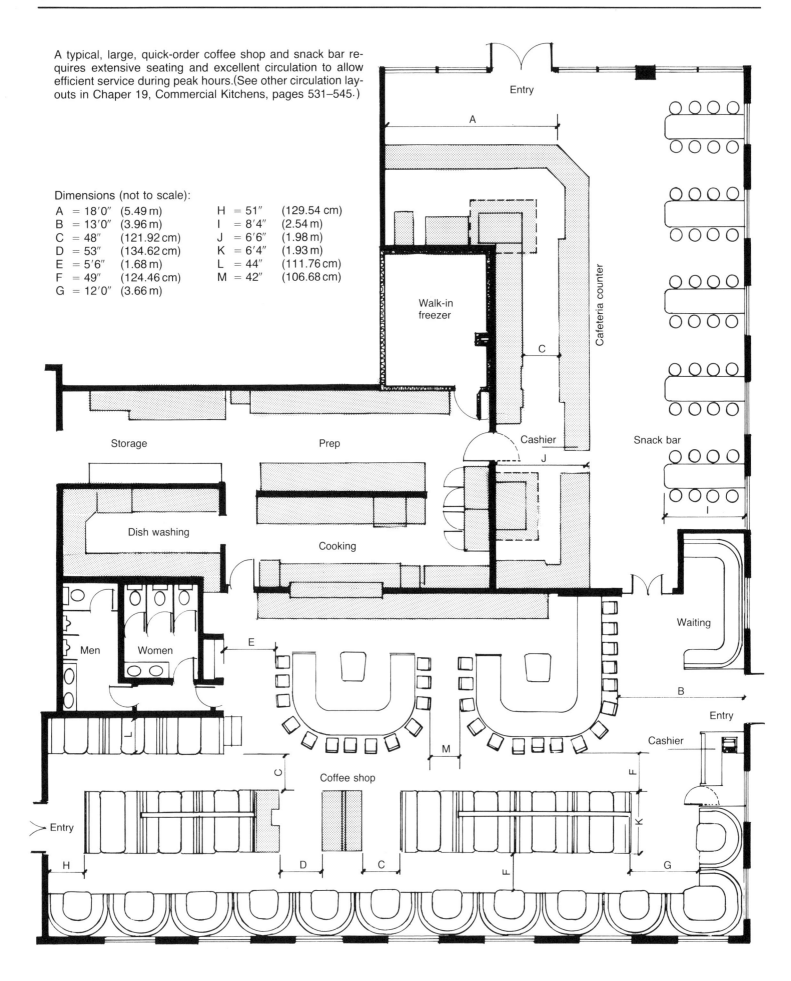

*The shaded areas are drawn to scale on pages 523–526.

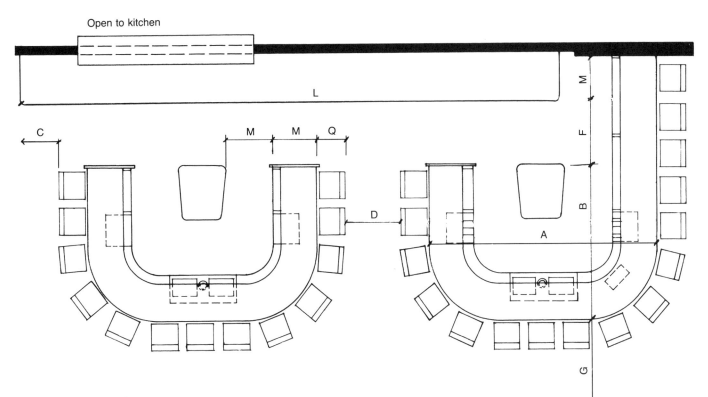

Open to kitchen

Plan of counter seating

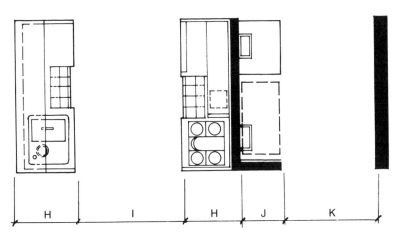

Plan of service areas

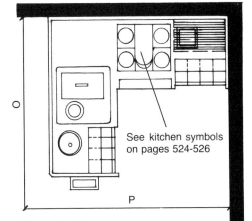

See kitchen symbols
on pages 524-526

**Example of corner
service area**

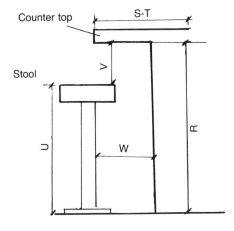

Counter top

Stool

Counter height
From floor: 2′6″ (0.76 m)
Over 2′6″ will require a
footrail 9″ (22.86 cm) from
floor.
Countertop width
Lunch: 18″–32″ (45.72–81.28 cm)
Dining: 24″–32″ (60.91–81.28 cm)
Seat height (top)
From floor: 18″ (45.72 cm)
From underside of counter
top: 12″ (30.48 cm)
Distance from stool pedestal to counter
Knee space: 18″

*Shown in plan on page 522.

A = 13′0″	(3.96 m)
B = 8′6″	(2.59 m)
C = 5′6″	(1.68 m)
D = 3′6″	(8.89 cm)
E = 33″	(83.82 cm)
F = 41″	(104.14 cm)
G = 49″	(124.46 cm)
H = 2½″	(6.35 cm)
I = 4′6″	(1.37 m)
J = 21″	(53.34 cm)
K = 48″	(121.92 cm)
L = 23′0″	(7.01 m)
M = 24″	(60.96 cm)
N = 20″	(50.80 cm)
O = 8′0″	(2.44 m)
P = 9′0″	(2.74 m)
Q = 18″	(45.72 cm)
R = 2′6″	(76.20 cm)
S = 18″–32″	(45.72–81.28 cm)
T = 24″–32″	(60.96–81.28 cm)
U = 18″	(45.72 cm)
V = 12″	(30.48 cm)
W = 18″	(45.72 cm)

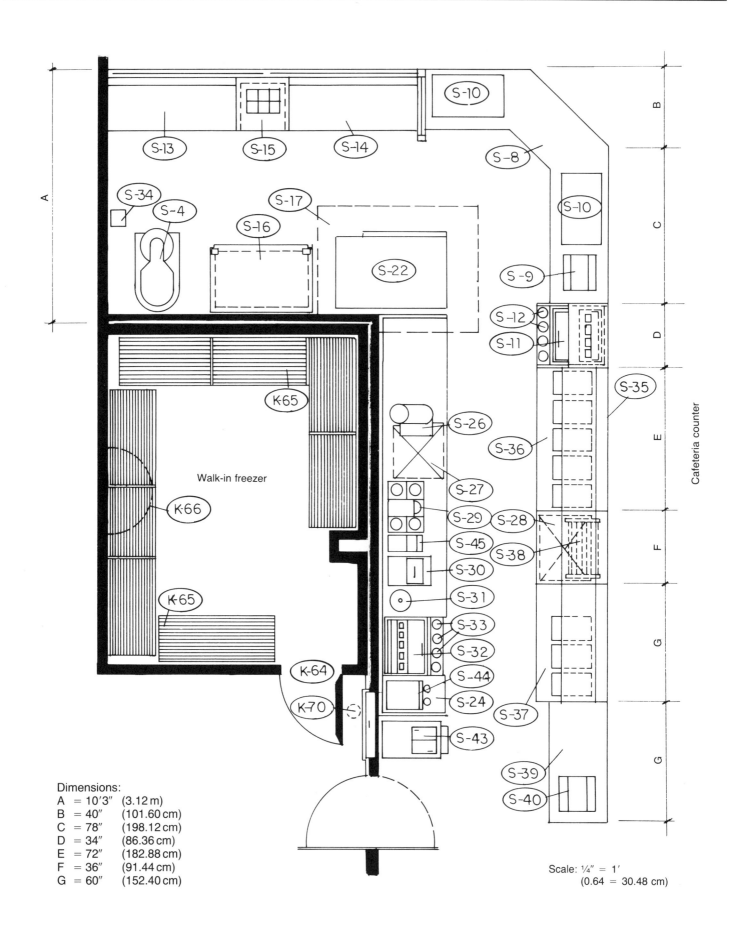

Dimensions:
A = 10'3" (3.12 m)
B = 40"   (101.60 cm)
C = 78"   (198.12 cm)
D = 34"   (86.36 cm)
E = 72"   (182.88 cm)
F = 36"   (91.44 cm)
G = 60"   (152.40 cm)

Scale: ¼" = 1'
(0.64 = 30.48 cm)

*Shown in plan on page 522 and keyed to Equipment Schedule on pages 527–529.

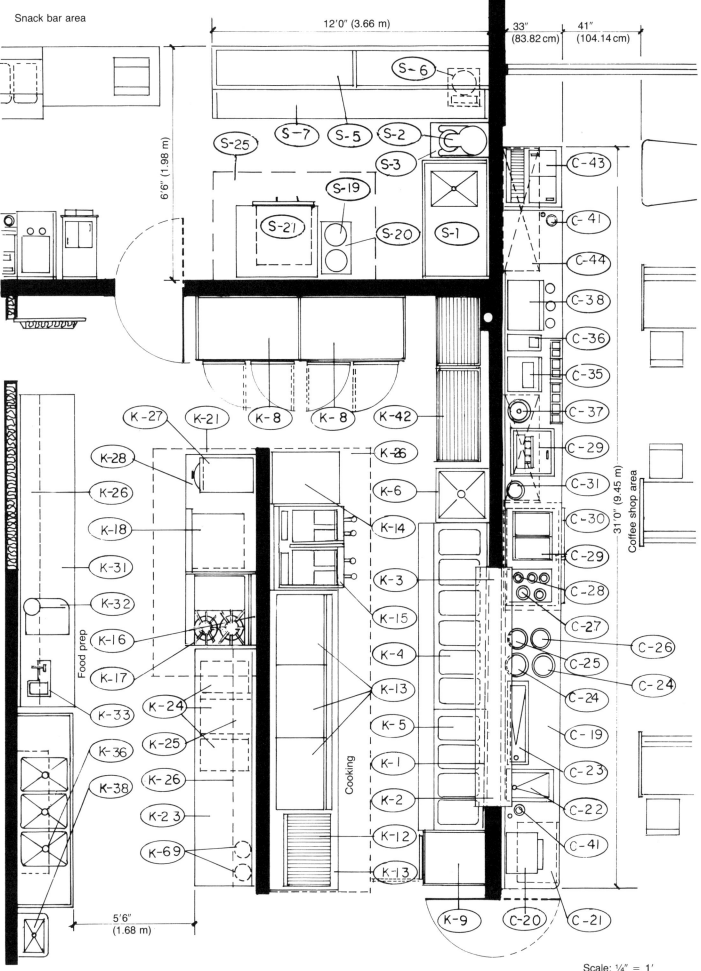

Snack bar area

12'0" (3.66 m)

33" (83.82 cm)

41" (104.14 cm)

6'6" (1.98 m)

S-6

S-7 S-5 S-2

S-25

S-3

S-19

S-21 S-20 S-1

C-43

C-41

C-44

C-38

C-36

C-35

C-37

C-29

C-31

C-30

C-29

C-28

C-27

C-26

C-25

C-24

C-24

C-19

C-23

C-22

C-41

31'0" (9.45 m)

Coffee shop area

K-27 K-21 K-8 K-8 K-42

K-26

K-28

K-26

K-18

K-31

K-32

Food prep

K-16

K-17

K-33

K-36

K-38

K-24

K-25

K-26

K-23

K-69

K-6

K-14

K-3

K-15

K-4

K-13

K-5

K-1

Cooking

K-2

K-12

K-13

K-9

C-20

C-21

5'6" (1.68 m)

Scale: ¼" = 1'
(0.64 = 30.48 cm)

*Shown in plan on page 522 and keyed to Equipment Schedule on pages 527–529.

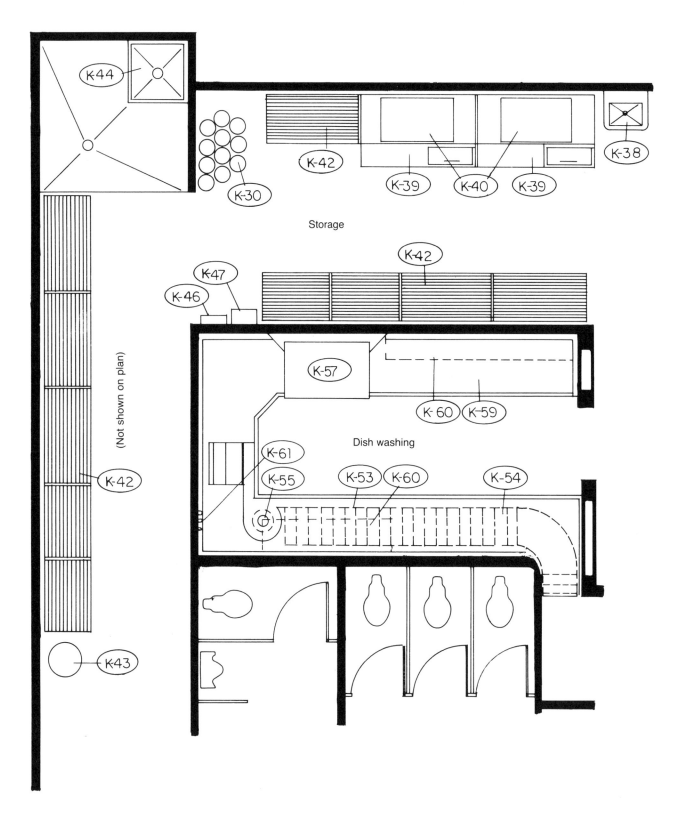

Storage

(Not shown on plan)

Dish washing

COFFEE SHOP   **ELECTRICAL**

Item	Quant.	Description	Volt	Phɸ	Load
C-1	1 lot	Booth seating			
C-2	1	Waiting settee			
C-3	1 lot	Tabletops & bases			
C-4	2	Planter dividers			
C-5					
C-6	1	Pastry cart			
C-7	1	Service area			
C-8	1	Ice & water station			
C-9	1	Service area	208	1	4580 watt
C-10	1	Coffee maker			
C-11	2	Bus cart			
C-12	1	Coffee portioner			
C-13	2	Lunch counter			
C-14	29	Counter stools & bases			
C-15	2	Ice & water station with hand sink	115	1	180 watt
C-16	2	Coffee warmers			
C-17	2	Display cabinets			
C-18					
C-19	1	Back counter with refrigerator base	208	1	6.5 kw
C-20	1	Toaster	115	1	1.0 kw
C-21	1	Roll warmer			
C-22	1	Cold pan			
C-23	1	Cold pan	115	1	450 watt/ea
C-24	2	Soup wells without drain			
C-25	1	Lowerator (underliner)	115	1	250 watt
C-26	1	Soup bowl lowerator (heated)			
C-27	2	Salad bowl lowerator (perforated)			
C-28	3	Dressing pans			
C-29	1	Salad pan	115	1	100 watt
C-30	1	Refrigerator base (included in C-19)			
C-31	1	Fruit & vegetable bowl lowerator	115	1	6 amp
C-32	1	Refrigerator display case			
C-33			115	1	¼ hp
C-34	1	Drink dispenser	115	1	1800 watt
C-35	1	Juice dispenser	115	1	1.7 amp
C-36	1	Hot chocolate			
C-37	1	Iced tea dispenser	115	1	1.7 amp
C-38	1	Milk dispenser with mixer			
C-39					
C-40					
C-41	2	Dipper wells			
C-42			115	1	4.5 amp
C-43	1	Ice cream cabinet	115	1	800 watt
C-44	1	Dry display case			
C-45	2	Telephone	115	1	800 watt
C-46	1	Cashier stand with display	115	1	800 watt
C-47	1	Cash register			
C-48			115	1	800 watt
C-49	1	Cigarette machine			
C-50					
C-51					
C-52					
C-53					
C-54					
C-55					
C-56	1 lot	Menu boxes			

Legend:
volt = voltage   kw   = kilowatt
phɸ = phase   amp = ampere
watt = wattage   hp   = horsepower

SNACK BAR			ELECTRICAL		
Item	Quant.	Description	Volt	Ph⌀	Load
S-1	1	Worktable with sink			
S-2	1	Mixer	115	1	⅓ hp
S-3	1	Mixer stand			
S-4	1	Mixer	208	3	1½ hp
S-5	1	Bakers' wrap around with display above	115	1	800 watt
S-6	1	Compressor (included in S-5)	115	1	⅓ hp
S-7	1	Bakers' table (included in S-5)			
S-8	1	Cashier counter			
S-9	1	Cash register	115	1	800 watt
S-10	2	Pizza display	115	1	1075 watt
S-11	1	Drink dispenser	115	1	½ hp
S-12	4	Cup dispenser			
S-13	1	Makeup counter			
S-14	1	Slice and box counter			
S-15	1	Salad top refrigerator	115	1	4 amp
S-16	1	2-door refrigerator	115	1	11.2 amp
S-17	1	Exhaust hood	See local code requirements		
S-18	1	Portable rack (not shown)			
S-19	1	Hot plate	208	1	5.4 kw
S-20	1	Hot plate stand			
S-21	1	Convection oven (bakers')	115	1	16.3 amp
S-22	1	Pizza oven			
S-23					
S-24	1	Beverage counter			
S-25	1	Exhaust hood	See local code requirements		
S-26	1	Slicer	115	1	¼ hp
S-27	1	Undercounter refrigerator	115	1	4 amp
S-28	1	Roll warmer	115	1	1.0 kw
S-29	1	Coffee maker	208	1	4580 watt
S-30	1	Juice dispenser	115	1	1800 watt
S-31	1	Iced tea dispenser			
S-32	1	Drink dispenser	115	1	¼ hp
S-33	4	Cup dispenser			
S-34	1	Water meter	115	1	5.0 amp
S-35	1	Plastic laminate die			
S-36	1	Hot food display case	208	1	7200 watt
S-37	1	Cold food display case	115	1	1000 watt
S-38	1	Hot dog grill	115	1	1760 watt
S-39	1	Cashier counter			
S-40	1	Cash register	115	1	800 watt
S-41					
S-42					
S-43	1	Soft ice cream	208	1	14 amp
S-44	1	Milk dispenser with mixer	115	1	1.7 amp
S-45	1	Hot chocolate	115	1	1800 watt
S-46					
S-47					
S-48					
S-49					
S-50					
S-51					
S-52					
S-53	5	Tabletops with cantilever bases			
S-54	40	Stool seats			
S-55					
S-56					

	KITCHEN		ELECTRICAL		
Item	**Quant.**	**Description**	**Volt**	**Ph∅**	**Load**
K-1	1	Pass shelf			
K-2	6	Heat lamp	115	1	225 watt
K-3	1	Service call light system	115	1	800 watt
K-4	1	Hot food table	208	1	4.0 kw
K-5	1	Cold food table	115	1	6 watt
K-6	1	Utility sink			
K-7					
K-8	2	Two-door freezer	115/208	1/1	10/5.7 amp
K-9	1	Reach-in refrigerator	115	1	3.7 amp
K-10					
K-11	1	Equipment stand with dish storage			
K-12	1	Broiler			
K-13	3	Griddle			
K-14	1	Holding cabinet			
K-15	2	French fryers			
K-16	1	Pot filler			
K-17	1	Hot top range with oven			
K-18	1	Convection oven	115/230	1/1	¾ hp
K-19	1 lot	Stainless steel wall flashing			
K-20	1	Exhaust hood	See local code requirements		
K-21	1	Exhaust hood	See local code requirements		
K-22					
K-23	1	Prep table with sink			
K-24	3	Portable ingredient bins			
K-25	1	Food chopper	115	1	⅓ hp
K-26	2	Stainless steel overshelves			
K-27	1	Steamer	208	3	12
K-28	1	Steamer stand			
K-29					
K-30	1 lot	Syrup tank storage			
K-31	1	Worktable			
K-32	1	Slicer	115	1	¼ hp
K-33	1	Tenderizer	115	1	½ hp
K-34					
K-35	1	Pot sink with 2 faucets			
K-36	1	Pot rack			
K-37					
K-38	1	Hand sink			
K-39	2	Ice bin			
K-40	4	Ice machine (2 future)	208	3	1½ hp
K-41	1	Condenser (remote on roof)			
K-42	1 lot	Shelving			
K-43	1	Central vacuum system	115	1	22 amp
K-44	1	Utility sink			
K-45					
K-46	2	Time card holders			
K-47	1	Time clock	115	1	800 watt
K-48					
K-49					
K-50					
K-51					
K-52					
K-53	1	Soiled dishtable			
K-54	1	Dirty dish conveyor			
K-55	1	Waste disposal	208	3	1½ hp
K-56					
K-57	1	Dishwasher	208	3	1 hp
K-58					
K-59	1	Clean dishtable			
K-60	2	Overshelves			
K-61	1	Spray rinse			
K-62					
K-63					
K-64	1	Walk-in refrigerator	115	1	800 watt
K-65	1	Walk-in shelving			
K-66	1	Blower coil	Verify		
K-67	1	Compressor (remote on roof)	See local code requirements		
K-68					
K-69	2	Fire protection system (coffee shop)	115	1∅	10 amp
K-70	1	Fire protection system (snack bar)	115	1	10 amp

Chapter 19

COMMERCIAL KITCHENS

AREA ALLOCATION FLOWCHART

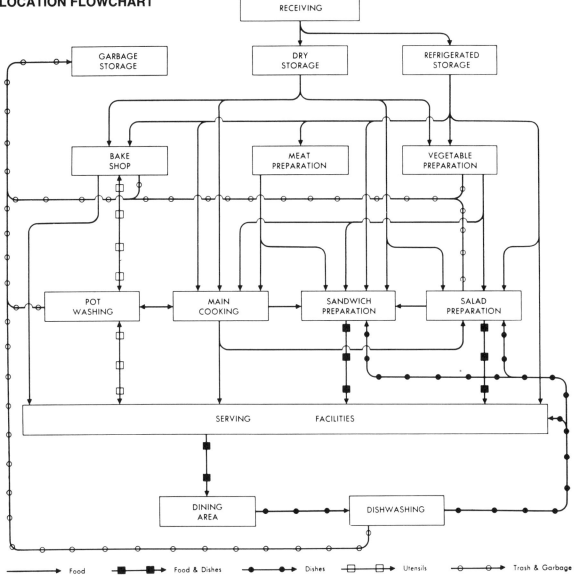

Work center allocation by approximate percentage of total space (includes aisles prorated to work centers)

Area	Hospital	Restaurant	Cafeteria
Receiving	3	3	3
Refrigeration (shelf)	11	12	12
Freezer	5	7	6
Unrefrigerated storeroom	9	14	12
Meat preparation	2	3	4
Vegetable & salad preparation	7	8	8
Production cooking	12	14	14
Pot washing	4	5	4
Bakery	5	6	5
Offices	5	5	5
Tray service	11		
Serving line (area)	11	12	14
Dishwashing	12	11	13
Tray cart storage	3		

Suggested minimum quantities for specific operations

Items per seat or bed	Fine dining	Family dining	Theme dining	Cafeteria	Banquet	Institutional dining
Dinner plates	2½	3	3	2	1¼	2
Salad/dessert plates	2½	3	3	3	2	
Bread & butter plates	2½	3	3	4	2	3
Cups	2½	3	3	2	1¼	1½
Saucers/underliners	2½	3½	3½	2½	1¼	1½
Fruits	2½	3	3	5	2½	3
Grapefruit/cereal	2	3	2	2½		1½

Note: It is possible to get a rough estimate of the amount of china you need by using this chart. It outlines the recommended minimum number of items per seat for several different types of operations.

Aisle dimensions

	Width	
	in.	cm
Work aisle guide		
For 1 person working	36	91.44
For 2 people working back to back	42	106.68
Traffic aisle guide		
For 2 people to pass	30	76.20
For 1 truck to pass one person	24+ truck width	60.96
Multi-usage aisle guide (These are not recommended but must sometimes be employed)		
For personnel passing 1 worker at his/her station	42	106.68
For personnel passing 2 workers back to back at their stations	48	121.92
For trucks passing 2 workers, back to back at their stations	60+ truck width	152.40

Note: It is definitely not recommended to move traffic through aisles where workers must constantly cross between two stations. The width of the aisle becomes excessive and there are potential dangers to personnel.

SERVING FACILITIES LOCATED WITHIN LARGER COMMERCIAL KITCHENS

The flow diagrams shown below indicate the typical locations and recommended layout of food service areas. These areas are best located where adequate staff control can be maintained, yet near the people to be served. In restaurants with table service, use the range battery and pantry as service areas. Current restaurant management trends combine pantry and cold service items in service areas. Banquet service areas outside the main kitchen are often necessary because of the location of the banquet areas. Dishes may be washed in this area and some food preparation that requires little or no cooking may also take place here.

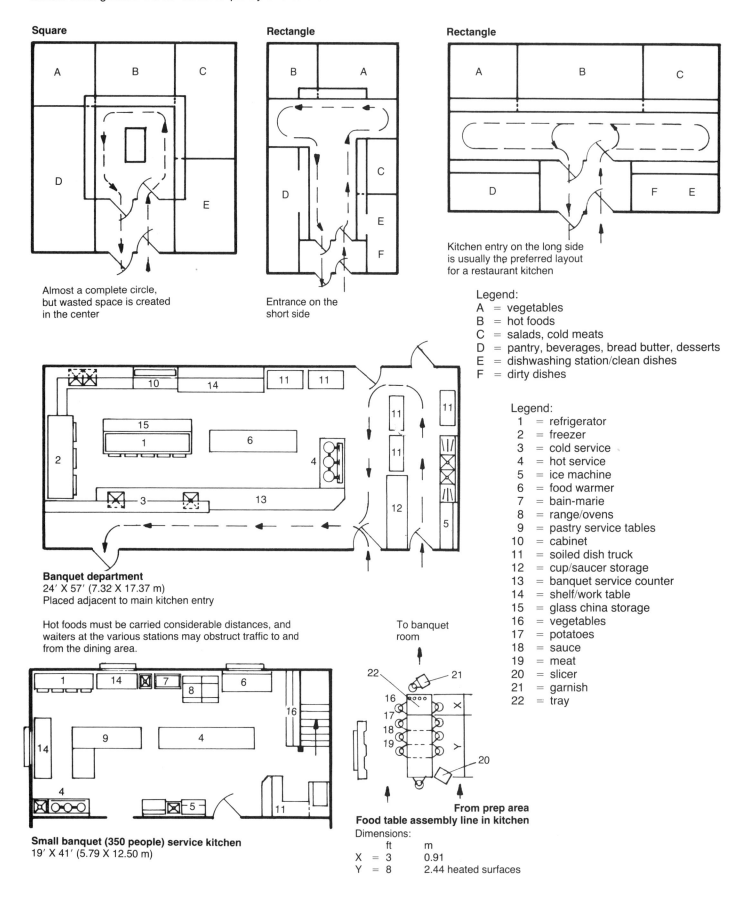

Square

Almost a complete circle, but wasted space is created in the center

Rectangle

Entrance on the short side

Rectangle

Kitchen entry on the long side is usually the preferred layout for a restaurant kitchen

Legend:
A = vegetables
B = hot foods
C = salads, cold meats
D = pantry, beverages, bread butter, desserts
E = dishwashing station/clean dishes
F = dirty dishes

Legend:
1 = refrigerator
2 = freezer
3 = cold service
4 = hot service
5 = ice machine
6 = food warmer
7 = bain-marie
8 = range/ovens
9 = pastry service tables
10 = cabinet
11 = soiled dish truck
12 = cup/saucer storage
13 = banquet service counter
14 = shelf/work table
15 = glass china storage
16 = vegetables
17 = potatoes
18 = sauce
19 = meat
20 = slicer
21 = garnish
22 = tray

Banquet department
24' X 57' (7.32 X 17.37 m)
Placed adjacent to main kitchen entry

Hot foods must be carried considerable distances, and waiters at the various stations may obstruct traffic to and from the dining area.

Small banquet (350 people) service kitchen
19' X 41' (5.79 X 12.50 m)

To banquet room

From prep area
Food table assembly line in kitchen
Dimensions:

	ft	m
X =	3	0.91
Y =	8	2.44 heated surfaces

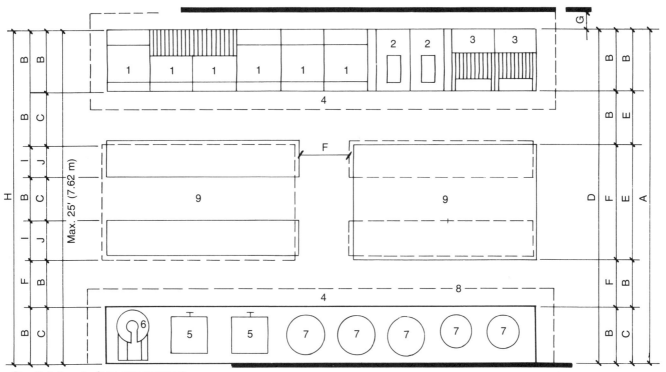

Parallel, face-to-face arrangement

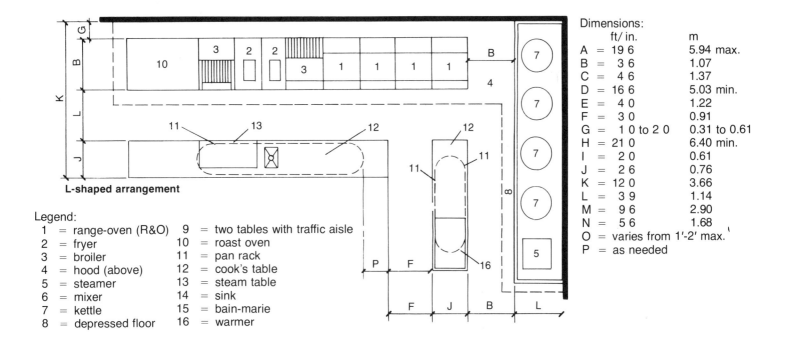

L-shaped arrangement

Legend:
1 = range-oven (R&O)
2 = fryer
3 = broiler
4 = hood (above)
5 = steamer
6 = mixer
7 = kettle
8 = depressed floor
9 = two tables with traffic aisle
10 = roast oven
11 = pan rack
12 = cook's table
13 = steam table
14 = sink
15 = bain-marie
16 = warmer

Dimensions:

	ft/ in.	m
A =	19 6	5.94 max.
B =	3 6	1.07
C =	4 6	1.37
D =	16 6	5.03 min.
E =	4 0	1.22
F =	3 0	0.91
G =	1 0 to 2 0	0.31 to 0.61
H =	21 0	6.40 min.
I =	2 0	0.61
J =	2 6	0.76
K =	12 0	3.66
L =	3 9	1.14
M =	9 6	2.90
N =	5 6	1.68
O =	varies from 1'-2' max.	
P =	as needed	

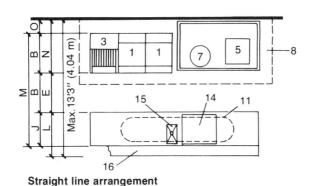

Straight line arrangement

Meat preparation space design flowchart

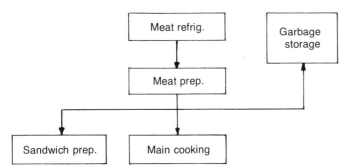

The American Gas Association defines a meat preparation center as the area that receives the meat in the state in which it is delivered and where it is converted into products suitable for further processing by the main cooking staff.

Current cooking practices often bypass the meat preparation process by getting ready-to-cook meat. This has proven more economical in time saved and in the amount of floor space required. Often a 40 percent space savings can be realized.

TYPICAL LAYOUTS

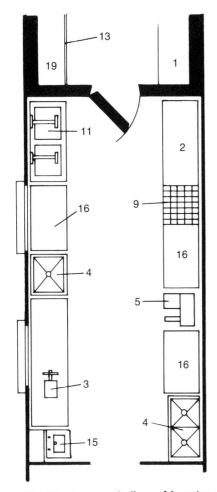

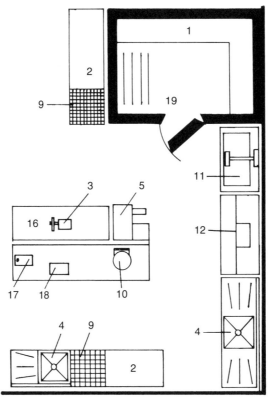

Corridor type, excluding refrigerator
11'0" X 22'6" (3.35 X 6.86 m)

Square arrangement, including refrigerator
16' X 24' (4.88 X 7.32 m)

Legend:
1 = shelves
2 = bench
3 = slicer
4 = sink
5 = saw
6 = refrigerator
7 = oyster bar
8 = cold pan
9 = block
10 = scale
11 = fish box
12 = fish preparation unit
13 = meat rail
14 = cold plate
15 = lavatory
16 = table
17 = blender
18 = tenderizer
19 = walk-in meat refrigerator

Cold storage areas

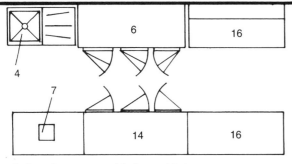

Awkward arrangement to be avoided

Alternate arrangement

Salad preparation centers should be located near service areas. The work methods to be followed in the preparation of salads determine the layout of the department. Items already prepared by the vegetable and fruit staff and stored in the vegetable refrigerator, as well as some meat and dairy products, are used in this area. Breakfast rolls are also heated and served from here.

Such areas are usually designed for large hotels or restaurants that serve large banquets.

Dimensions:
A = 3'-4' (0.91-1.22 m)
B = 10'3" (3.12 m)
C = 27" (68.58 cm)
D = 30" (76.20 cm)
E = 13'9" (4.19 m)
F = 4'0" (1.22 m)
G = 8'0" (2.44 m)
H = 7'6"-9'6" (2.29-2.90 m)
I = 30"-36" (76.20-91.44 cm)
J = 24"-30" (60.96-76.20 cm)
K = 10'0" (3.05 m)
L = 7'9" (2.36 m)

Legend:
1 = table
2 = vegetable bins
3 = vegetable preparation
4 = root storage rack
5 = peeler
6 = pass-through refrigerator
7 = vegetable chopper

SALAD PREPARATION AREAS

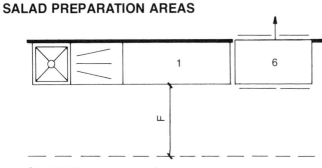

Straight line arrangement

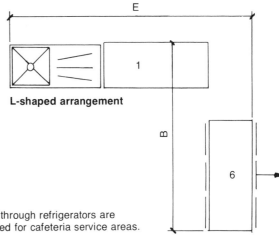

Parallel arrangement

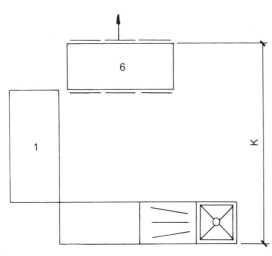

U-shaped arrangement

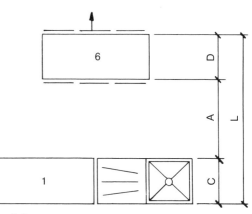

L-shaped arrangement

Note: Pass-through refrigerators are recommended for cafeteria service areas.

VEGETABLE PREPARATION AREAS

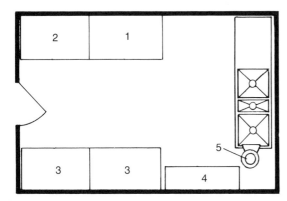

Separate vegetable preparation room
12' X 18' (3.66 X 5.49 m)

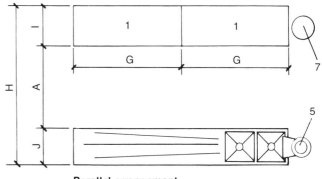

Parallel arrangement

TYPICAL BAKE SHOP LAYOUTS

The layout within the bake shop should follow typical processing steps as much as possible. The oven should be near the exit landing table. There should be sufficient space in front of the oven to remove baked goods with a peel that reaches to the innermost corners of the oven. In general, as much clear space should be provided in front of a bake oven as the bake oven is deep (from front to back). The proof box should be near the oven, as should the baker's table. The mixer, pastry stove, or hot plate and steam-jacketed kettle, if used, should be near the baker's table.

Bake shop flowchart

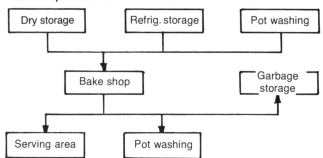

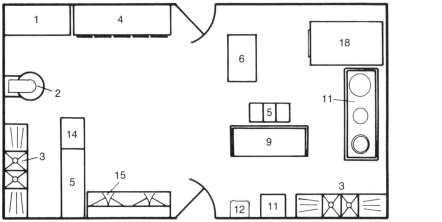

Large capacity
22' X 40' (6.71 X 12.19 m)

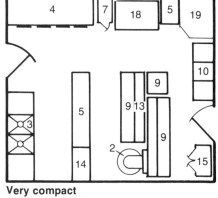

Very compact
18' X 22' (5.49 X 6.71 m)

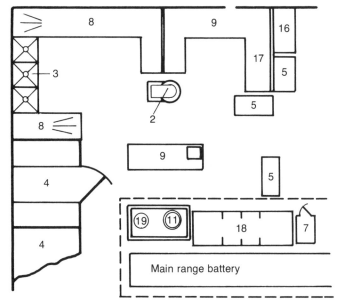

Placement in corner of kitchen
24' X 32' (7.32 X 9.75 m)

Small & complete
18' X 25' (5.49 X 7.62 m)

Legend:
1 = shelves	6 = exit landing table	11 = stove	16 = cake box
2 = mixer	7 = proof box	12 = lavatory	17 = pastry table
3 = pan sink	8 = pan storage	13 = shelves	18 = oven
4 = refrigerator	9 = table	14 = attendant	19 = kettle
5 = pan racks	10 = dough trough	15 = cabinet	

ROOM SERVICE AREAS

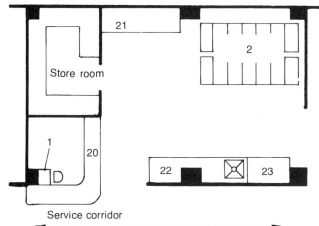

Room service areas are placed near or in the main kitchen and near the elevators. Storage of room service carts and tables is a major concern when designing this space. The total square footage and equipment needs are based on the number of hotel rooms to be served.

Legend:

1 = desk for checker	13 = egg boiler
2 = room service tables	14 = ice cream
3 = butter	15 = urns
4 = garnish	16 = refrigerator
5 = ice cubes	17 = cold pan
6 = ice water sink	18 = service counter
7 = dishes	19 = shelf above counter
8 = trucks	20 = counter
9 = heater	21 = plate warmer
10 = cabinet	22 = set-up table
11 = griddle	23 = cracked ice bin
12 = toaster	

Service area for 800-room hotel
600 sq ft (55.74 m²)

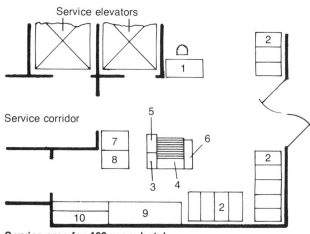

Service area for 400-room hotel
400 sq ft (37.16 m²)

PANTRY AREAS

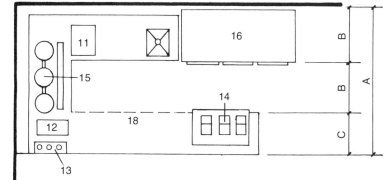

The pantry is the most important area in the kitchen. Usually breakfast orders are prepared and served from here. Items of food include:

Beverages	Toasted sandwiches
Cereals	Fruits
Eggs	Jams
Waffles	Soda fountain drinks

The following equipment is needed:

Griddle	Short-order range
Toasters	Roll warmer
Waffle iron	Plate & cup warmer
Coffee urns	Egg boiler
Salamander	

Pantry for a small kitchen

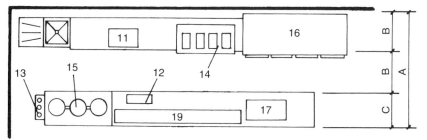

Dimensions:

	ft/ in.	m
A =	8 6	2.59
B =	3 0	0.91
C =	2 6	0.76

Pantry for a large kitchen

DISHWASHING EQUIPMENT

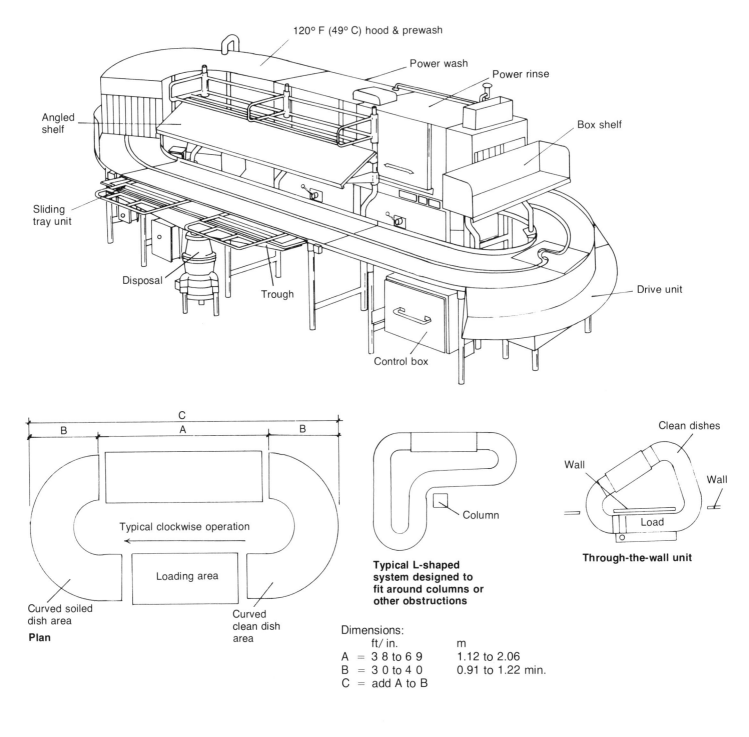

120° F (49° C) hood & prewash

Power wash

Power rinse

Angled shelf

Box shelf

Sliding tray unit

Disposal

Trough

Drive unit

Control box

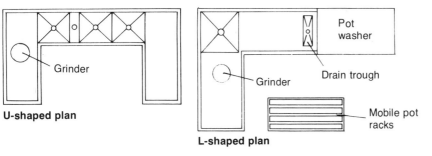

C

B A B

Typical clockwise operation

Loading area

Curved soiled dish area

Plan

Curved clean dish area

Column

Typical L-shaped system designed to fit around columns or other obstructions

Dimensions:
	ft/ in.	m
A =	3 8 to 6 9	1.12 to 2.06
B =	3 0 to 4 0	0.91 to 1.22 min.
C =	add A to B	

Clean dishes

Wall

Wall

Load

Through-the-wall unit

POT WASHING LAYOUTS

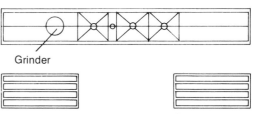

Grinder

U-shaped plan

Pot washer

Grinder

Drain trough

Mobile pot racks

L-shaped plan

Grinder

Straight line with portable pot racks

AUTOMATED DISHWASHING AREAS

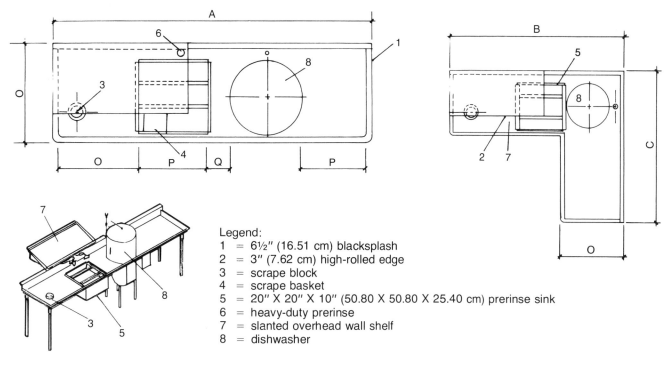

Legend:
1 = 6½" (16.51 cm) blacksplash
2 = 3" (7.62 cm) high-rolled edge
3 = scrape block
4 = scrape basket
5 = 20" X 20" X 10" (50.80 X 50.80 X 25.40 cm) prerinse sink
6 = heavy-duty prerinse
7 = slanted overhead wall shelf
8 = dishwasher

DISHROOM INTERIOR MATERIALS SPECIFICATION

Dishrooms are usually very damp and should have hoods and steam-removal ducts placed above entrance and exit doors. Also forced-air inlets should be installed to bring in cool, dry air.

Floors

Avoid floors that create hard-to-clean crevices. Terrazzo or quarry tile with a moderate coating of abrasive material to prevent slipping should be used. Floor should also be pitched ¼" (0.64 cm) to a foot toward several floor drains so that the floor can be washed down with a hose.

Walls

Consult with the local health department about requirements. Most require glazed or easy-to-clean tile or cement up to 5' (1.52 m) above the floor. Due to noise, walls and ceilings above 5' should be coated with some sound-absorbing material allowed by the codes. The underside of the dish table should also be coated with special mastic to reduce noise.

Lighting

For general lighting, 30 to 50 footcandles are needed. To make transparent dish films visible, 70 to 100 footcandles are needed for the clean end of the dishwasher area.

MANUAL DISHWASHING

Dimensions:
A = 99" (251.46 cm)
B = 75" (190.50 cm)
C = 63" (160.02 cm)
D = 3'0" (0.91 m)
E = 5'0" (1.52 m)
F = 6'0" (1.83 m)
G = 10'0" (3.05 m)
H = 32½" (82.55 cm)
I = 29" (73.66 cm)
J = 3½" (8.89 cm)
K = 16½" (41.91 cm)
L = 18½" (46.99 cm)
M = 10" (25.40 cm)
N = 19" (48.26 cm)
O = 27" (68.58 cm)
P = 20" (50.80 cm)
Q = 11" (27.94 cm)
R = 12" (30.48 cm)
S = 25" (63.50 cm)

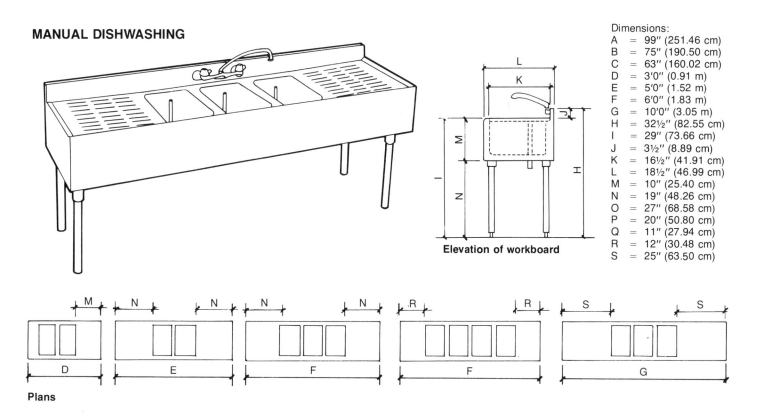

Elevation of workboard

Plans

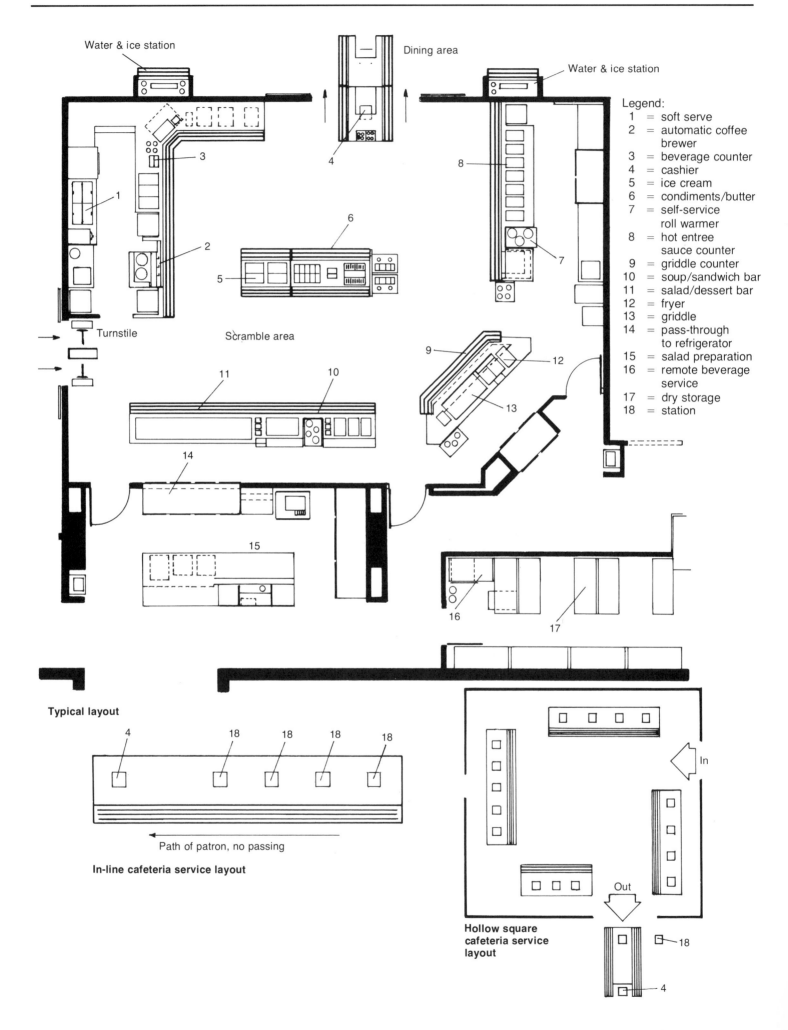

Water & ice station

Dining area

Water & ice station

3

4

8

1

2

6

7

5

Turnstile

Scramble area

11

10

9

12

13

14

15

16

17

Legend:
1 = soft serve
2 = automatic coffee brewer
3 = beverage counter
4 = cashier
5 = ice cream
6 = condiments/butter
7 = self-service roll warmer
8 = hot entree sauce counter
9 = griddle counter
10 = soup/sandwich bar
11 = salad/dessert bar
12 = fryer
13 = griddle
14 = pass-through to refrigerator
15 = salad preparation
16 = remote beverage service
17 = dry storage
18 = station

Typical layout

4   18   18   18   18

Path of patron, no passing

In-line cafeteria service layout

In

Out

18

4

Hollow square cafeteria service layout

SALAD BAR CAROUSEL PLAN

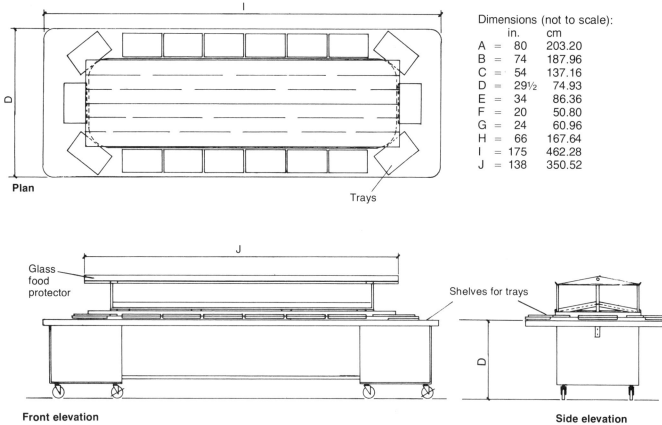

Plan

Trays

Dimensions (not to scale):

		in.	cm
A	=	80	203.20
B	=	74	187.96
C	=	54	137.16
D	=	29½	74.93
E	=	34	86.36
F	=	20	50.80
G	=	24	60.96
H	=	66	167.64
I	=	175	462.28
J	=	138	350.52

Glass
food
protector

Shelves for trays

Front elevation

Side elevation

STAND-BY MEAL CART

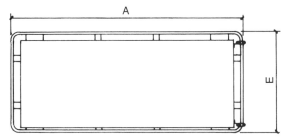

Plan

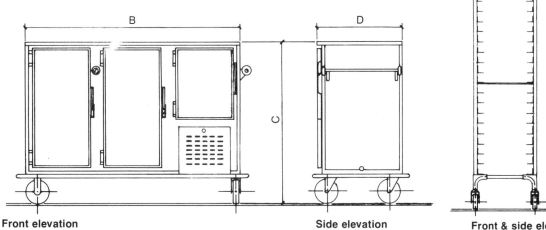

Front elevation

Side elevation

CART FOR SERVING TRAYS

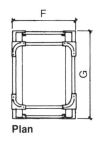

Plan

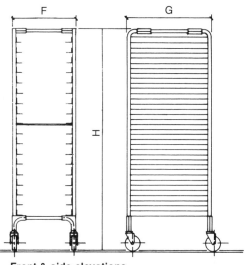

Front & side elevations

SALAD BAR

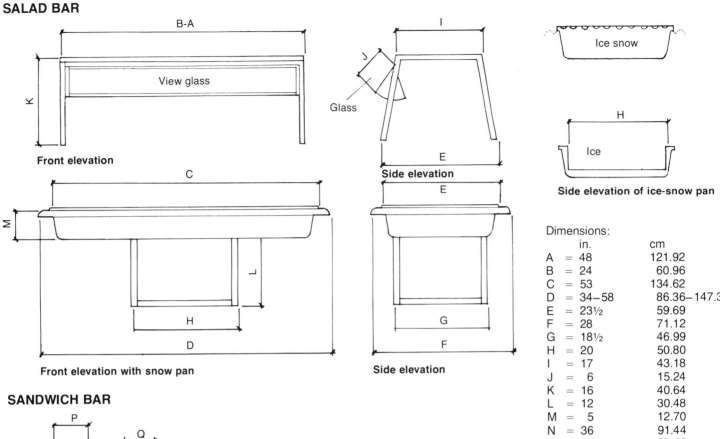

Front elevation

Side elevation

Ice snow

Front elevation with snow pan

Side elevation

Side elevation of ice-snow pan

Ice

Dimensions:

	in.	cm
A =	48	121.92
B =	24	60.96
C =	53	134.62
D =	34–58	86.36–147.32
E =	23½	59.69
F =	28	71.12
G =	18½	46.99
H =	20	50.80
I =	17	43.18
J =	6	15.24
K =	16	40.64
L =	12	30.48
M =	5	12.70
N =	36	91.44
O =	27	68.58
P =	8	20.32
Q =	7	17.78
R =	78	198.12
S =	34	86.36
T =	9½	24.13
U =	30½	77.47
V =	83	210.82
W =	14	35.56

SANDWICH BAR

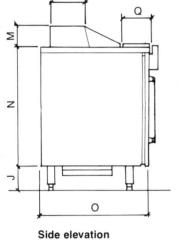

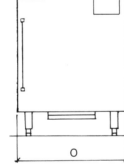

Sandwich ingredients

Side elevation

Front elevation

Plan

PORTABLE REFRIGERATOR/FREEZER COMBINATIONS

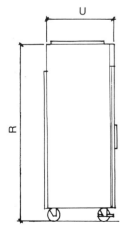

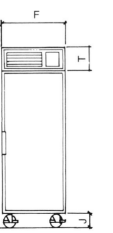

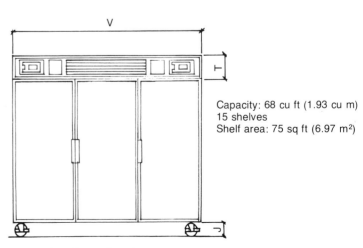

Capacity: 68 cu ft (1.93 cu m)
15 shelves
Shelf area: 75 sq ft (6.97 m²)

Side elevation

Single-door front elevation

Door/two drawer front elevation

Three-door front elevation

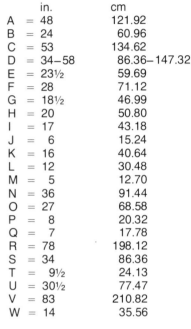
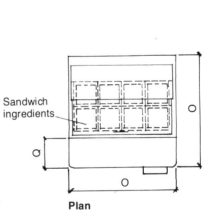

REFRIGERATED CASES

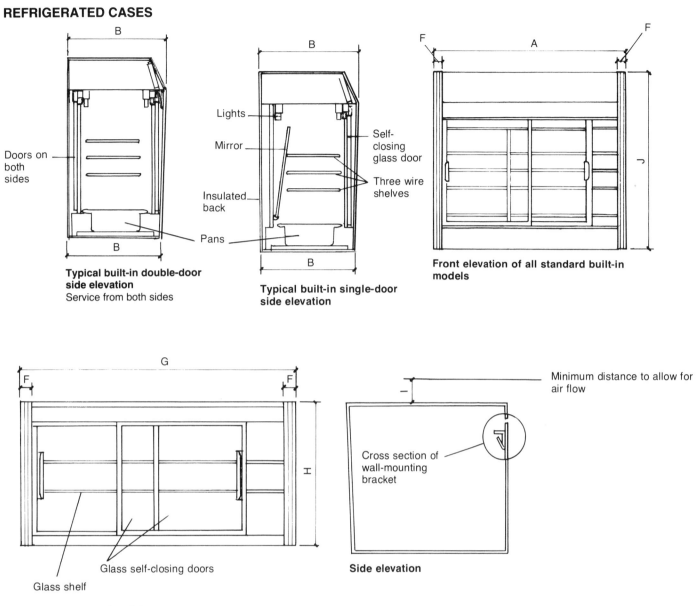

Typical built-in double-door side elevation
Service from both sides

Doors on both sides

Lights

Mirror

Insulated back

Pans

Typical built-in single-door side elevation

Self-closing glass door

Three wire shelves

Front elevation of all standard built-in models

Glass shelf

Glass self-closing doors

Front elevation of wall-hung case

Minimum distance to allow for air flow

Cross section of wall-mounting bracket

Side elevation

NONREFRIGERATED CASES

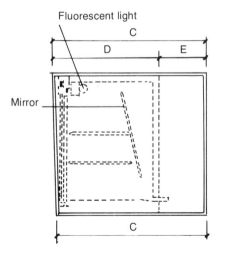

Fluorescent light

Mirror

Side elevation of nonrefrigerated case

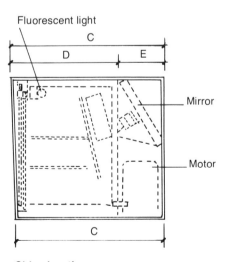

Fluorescent light

Mirror

Motor

Side elevation

Dimensions:

	in.	cm
A =	48	121.92
B =	23	58.42
C =	21½	54.61
D =	15¼	38.74
E =	6½	16.51
F =	2	5.08
G =	36 to 72	91.44 to 182.88
H =	19½	49.53
I =	3	7.62
J =	42½	107.95

MOBILE BARS

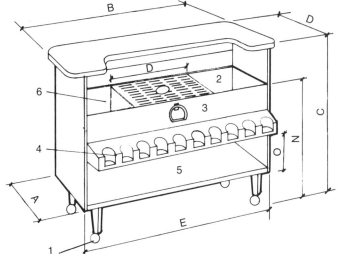

Small mobile bar for small parties

Dimensions (not to scale):
A = 8'8" (2.64 m)
B = 57" (144.78 cm)
C = 39" (99.06 cm)
D = 22" (55.88 cm)
E = 50" (127.00 cm)
F = 45" (114.30 cm)
G = 31" (76.74 cm)
H = 38" (96.52 cm)
I = 60" (152.40 cm)
J = 72" (182.88 cm)
K = 9'0" (2.74 m)
L = 13" (33.02 cm)
M = 25" (63.50 cm)
N = 29" (73.66 cm)
O = 10" (25.40 cm)
P = 26½" (67.31 cm)
Q = 9" (22.86 cm)
R = 18" (45.72 cm)
S = 48" (121.92 cm)
T = 24" (60.96 cm)
U = 19" (48.26 cm)

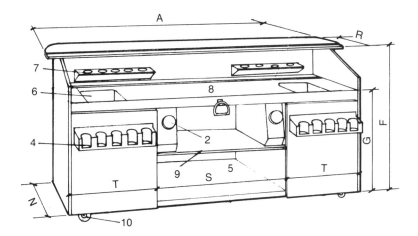

Large mobile bar for large banquets
Space provided for soda system if required

UNDERBAR WORKBOARD

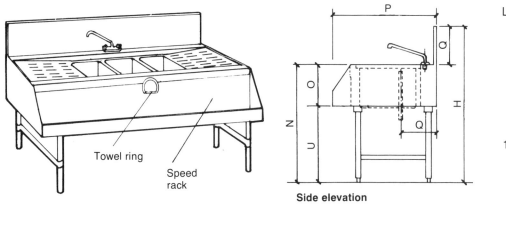

Towel ring

Speed rack

Side elevation

Legend:
1 = ball casters
2 = waste chute
3 = towel ring
4 = bottle trough
5 = open storage
6 = ice compartment
7 = condiment racks
8 = stainless steel counter
9 = removable shelf
10 = 5" (12.70 cm) swivel caster

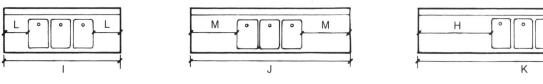

Typical dimensions for larger installations

ICE MACHINES

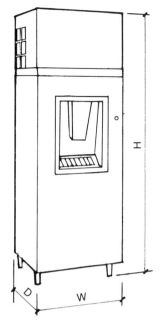

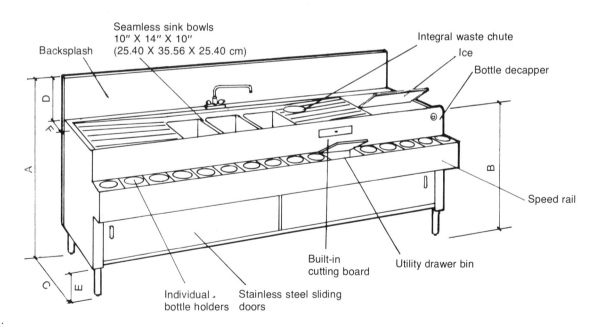

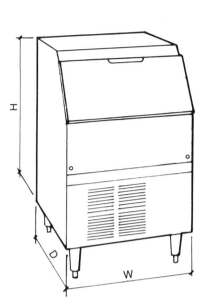

400-cube, 280-lb (127.12-kg) storage capacity
This unit is designed for filling buckets. Used in hotels and restaurants. Amps required are 5.8

	in.	cm
W =	30	76.20
D =	25	63.50
H =	86	218.44

1100-cube/½ ton per hour, 1040-lb (472.16-kg) storage capacity
Used in areas that require a large daily volume such as fast food and cafeteria facilities, institutions, resorts, supermarkets, and convenience stores

	in.	cm
W =	48	121.92
D =	30	76.20
H =	79	200.66

100-cube, 40-lb (18.16-kg) storage capacity
Restaurant & bar use under counter as backup ice maker. Requires minimum 8 to 8.6 amps

	in.	cm
W =	24	60.96
D =	24	60.96
H =	39	99.06

BAR SERVICE EQUIPMENT

Seamless sink bowls
10″ X 14″ X 10″
(25.40 X 35.56 X 25.40 cm)
Backsplash
Integral waste chute
Ice
Bottle decapper
Speed rail
Built-in cutting board
Utility drawer bin
Individual bottle holders
Stainless steel sliding doors

Dimensions:

	in.	cm
A =	39	99.06
B =	30	76.20
C =	27½	69.85
D =	9	22.86
E =	6	15.24
F =	4	10.16

Chapter 20

HOTELS
AND MOTELS

TYPICAL 300 SQ FT (27.87 m²) HOTEL LAYOUTS

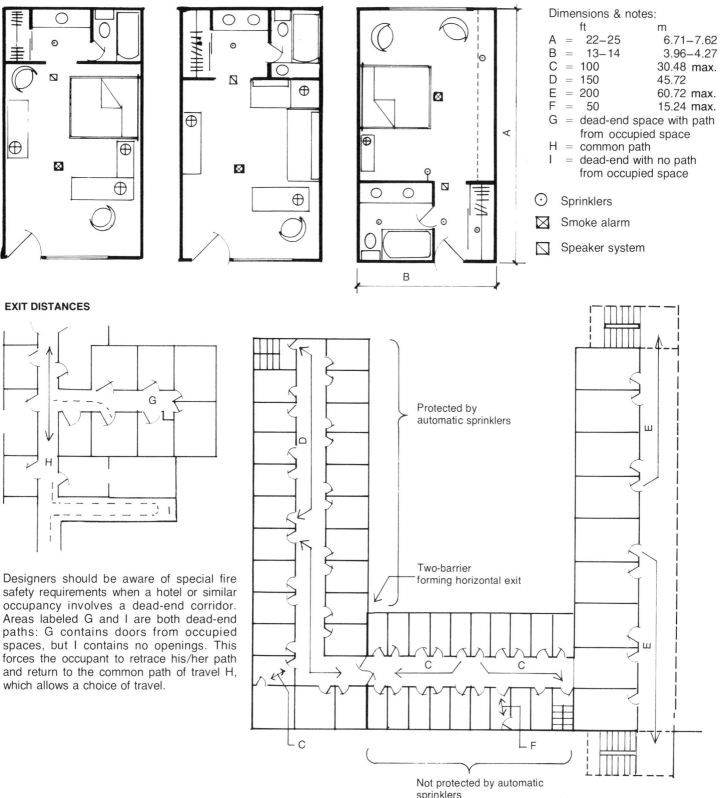

Dimensions & notes:

	ft	m
A =	22–25	6.71–7.62
B =	13–14	3.96–4.27
C =	100	30.48 max.
D =	150	45.72
E =	200	60.72 max.
F =	50	15.24 max.
G =	dead-end space with path from occupied space	
H =	common path	
I =	dead-end with no path from occupied space	

⊙ Sprinklers

⊠ Smoke alarm

▱ Speaker system

EXIT DISTANCES

Protected by automatic sprinklers

Two-barrier forming horizontal exit

Not protected by automatic sprinklers

Designers should be aware of special fire safety requirements when a hotel or similar occupancy involves a dead-end corridor. Areas labeled G and I are both dead-end paths: G contains doors from occupied spaces, but I contains no openings. This forces the occupant to retrace his/her path and return to the common path of travel H, which allows a choice of travel.

Maximum travel distances

Travel distance requirements are based on the types of occupancies and the level of fire protection provided. Travel distances may be increased by 100 percent, that is, from 100′ to 150′ (30.48 to 45.72 m) with the addition of automatic sprinklers. Travel distance from the most remote door in a suite (F) to the corridor is also regulated by most local codes.

Note: Hotel room doors should have automatic door closures. Consult your local codes.

Storage

Legend:
A = living room
B = bar
C = kitchen
D = dressing room
E = bedroom
F = bar-TV

This space was designed as a time-sharing resort suite. It also serves as an executive suite. Each bedroom suite is self-contained. A third person or guest can be accommodated in the living room area. Note that the couch opens into a double bed and an additional bath is located near the kitchen.

*Details shown on pages 549–551.

DETAILS OF CUSTOM FURNISHINGS IN (A)

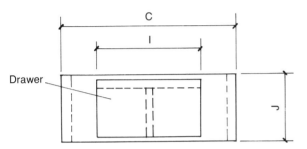

Elevation of (1) desk

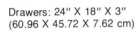

Plan

Drawers: 24″ X 18″ X 3″
(60.96 X 45.72 X 7.62 cm)

Drawer

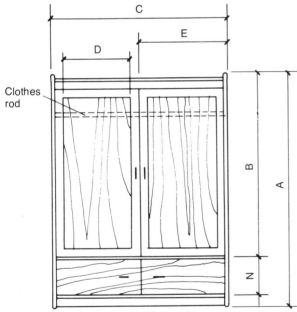

Clothes rod

Front elevation of (2) armoire

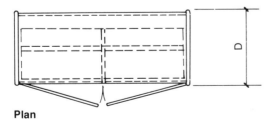

Plan

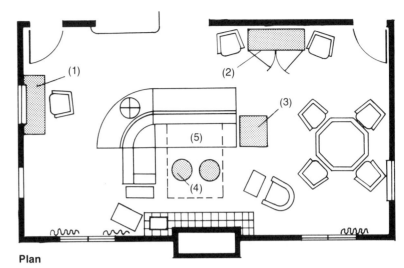

Plan

Note: Sofa opens into a double bed for extra guest (5).

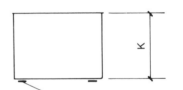

Elevation & plan of (3) end table

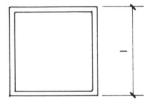

Elevation & plan of (4) cocktail table

Dimensions:

	in.	cm
A =	80	203.20
B =	50	127.00
C =	60	152.40
D =	24	60.96
E =	29¾	75.57
F =	29	73.66
G =	20	50.80
H =	16	40.64
I =	36	91.44
J =	21	53.34
K =	22	55.88
L =	3	7.62
M =	2	5.08
N =	12	30.48

*Shown in plan on page 548.

DETAILS OF CUSTOM FURNISHINGS IN (A)

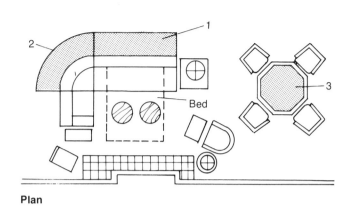

Plan

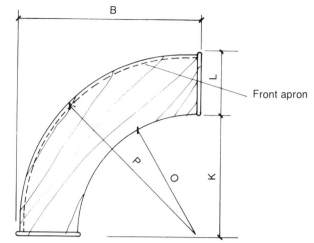

Plan of (2) curved section of sofa table

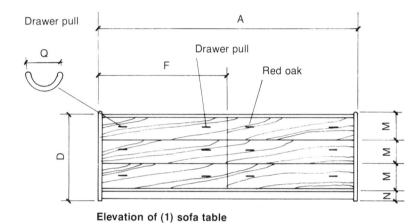

Elevation of (1) sofa table

Plan

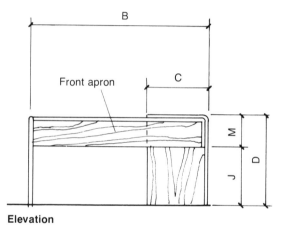

Elevation

Dimensions:
A = 7'9" (2.36 m)
B = 5'0" (1.52 m)
C = 31" (78.74 cm)
D = 29" (73.66 cm)
E = 21" (53.34 cm)
F = 46½" (118.11 cm)
G = 36" (91.44 cm)
H = 4'6" (1.37 m)
I = 10½" (26.67 cm)
J = 18¼" (46.36 cm)
K = 39" (99.06 cm)
L = 24" (60.96 cm)
M = 8" (20.32 cm)
N = 3" (7.62 cm)
O = 3'3" (0.99 m) radius
P = 5'0" (1.52 m) radius
Q = 2½" (6.35 cm)

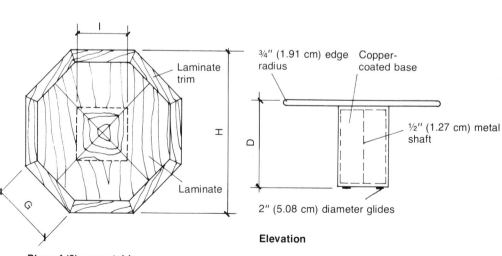

Plan of (3) game table

Elevation

*Shown in plan on page 548.

DETAILS OF CUSTOM FURNISHINGS IN (E)

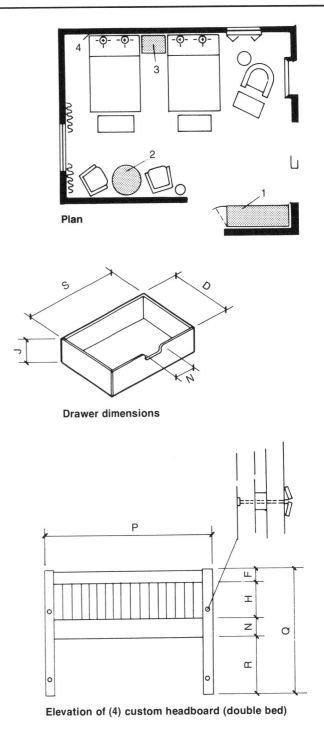

Plan

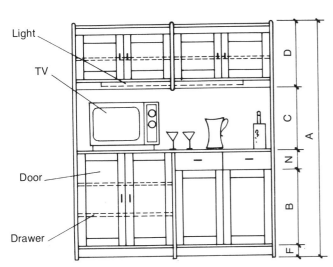

Front elevation of (1) bar

Light
TV
Door
Drawer

Drawer dimensions

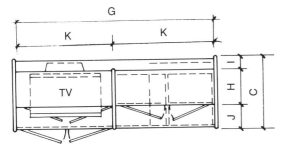

Plan

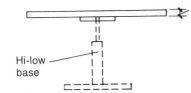

Hi-low base

Elevation of (2) table
Lifts to dining height

Elevation of (4) custom headboard (double bed)

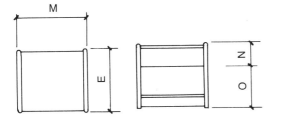

Plan & elevation of (3) night stand

Dimensions:

	in.	cm			in.	cm
A	= 88	203.20	K	=	33	83.82
B	= 27	68.58	L	=	1½	3.81
C	= 24	60.96	M	=	22½	57.15
D	= 20	50.80	N	=	6	15.24
E	= 21	53.34	O	=	15	38.10
F	= 3	7.62	P	=	58	147.32
G	= 68	172.72	Q	=	42	106.68
H	= 12	30.48	R	=	20½	52.07
I	= 4	10.16	S	=	30	76.20
J	= 8	20.32				

*Shown in plan on page 548.

UTILITY CARTS, TRUCKS, & OTHER EQUIPMENT

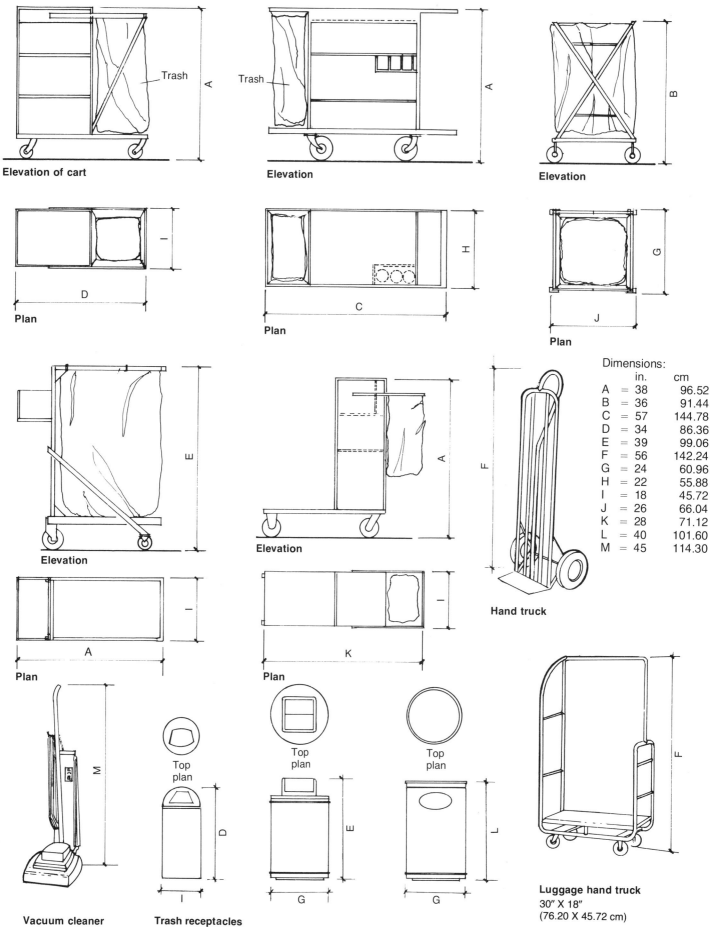

Elevation of cart

Trash

Elevation

Trash

Elevation

Plan

Plan

Plan

Elevation

Elevation

Plan

Plan

Hand truck

Dimensions:

		in.	cm
A	=	38	96.52
B	=	36	91.44
C	=	57	144.78
D	=	34	86.36
E	=	39	99.06
F	=	56	142.24
G	=	24	60.96
H	=	22	55.88
I	=	18	45.72
J	=	26	66.04
K	=	28	71.12
L	=	40	101.60
M	=	45	114.30

Vacuum cleaner
12" X 19"
(30.48 X 48.26 cm)

Top plan

Trash receptacles

Top plan

Top plan

Luggage hand truck
30" X 18"
(76.20 X 45.72 cm)

Chapter 21

MEDICAL AND DENTAL OFFICES, SURGICAL SUITES, AND TREATMENT FACILITIES

Square footage: 1650 (153.29 m²)

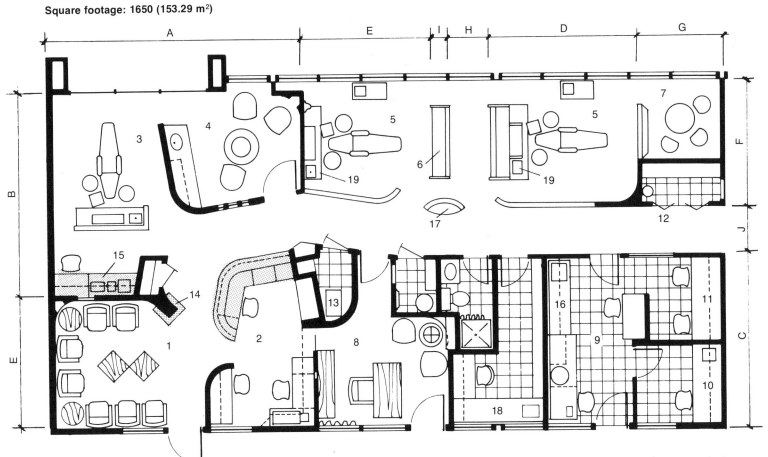

This general dentistry office has two operating areas that are surrounded on the hall side by low partitions. Both stations in this area are served by (19) rear delivery systems. The delivery system contains the necessary dental tools. It can be located on the side or on a tray above the patient chair. Other requirements for operating rooms include a dental light, sinks, and outlets for nitrous oxide and oxygen.

Dimensions (not to scale):

A = 22'0" (6.71 m)
B = 17'0" (5.18 m)
C = 15'0" (4.57 m)
D = 13'0" (3.96 m)
E = 11'6" (3.51 m)
F = 11'0" (3.35 m)
G = 10'0" (3.05 m)
H = 3'6" (1.07 m)
I = 1'6" (0.46 m)
J = 4'0" (1.22 m)
K = 3'0" (0.91 m)
L = 30" (76.20 cm)
M = 24" (60.96 cm)
N = 54" (137.16 cm)
O = 1½" (3.81 cm)
P = 2½" (6.35 cm)
Q = 4" (10.16 cm)
R = 5" (12.70 cm)
S = 12" (30.48 cm) depth

Legend:

1 = reception area
2 = business office
3 = hygienist's area
4 = learning center
5 = operating room
6 = make-ready counter
7 = patient rest area
8 = private office
9 = laboratory
10 = porcelain room
11 = gold room
12 = storage
13 = darkroom
14 = aquarium
15 = hygienist's workcounter
16 = plaster area
17 = water fountain
18 = model storage
19 = delivery system

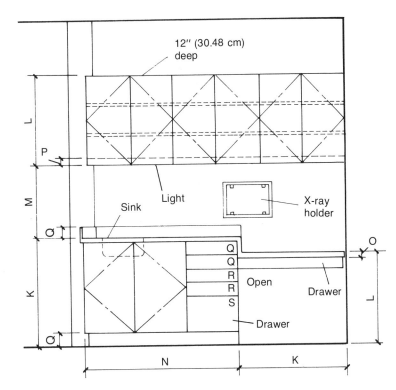

Elevation of (15) hygienist's workcounter
Base cabinets are 24" (60.96 cm) deep

*Shown in detail on pages 555–557.

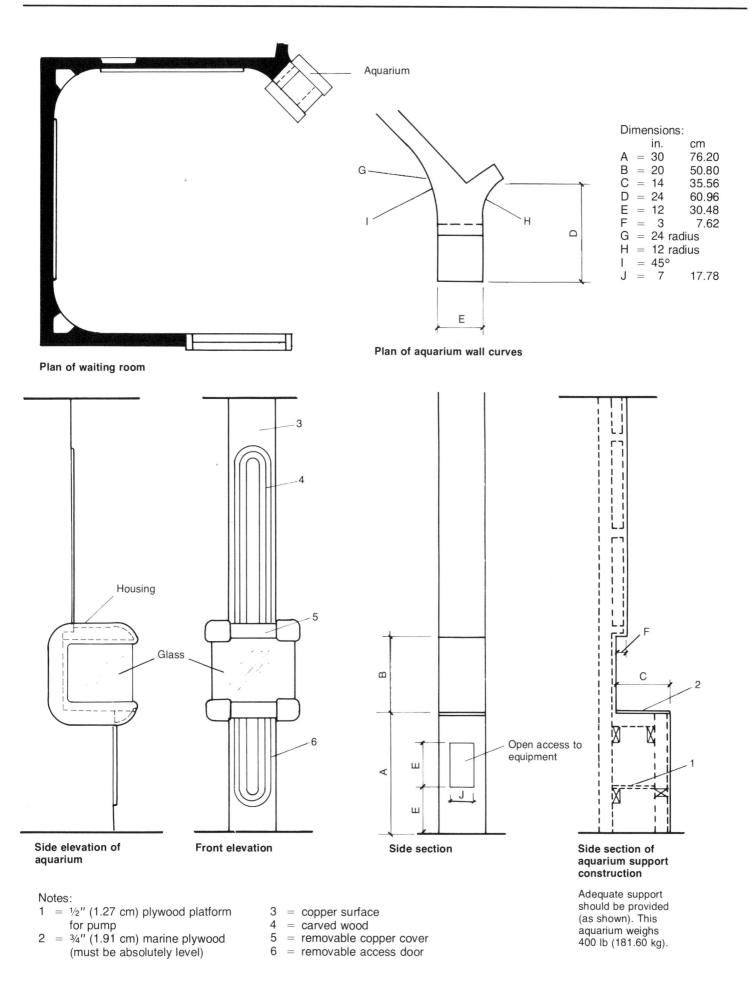

Plan of waiting room

Aquarium

Plan of aquarium wall curves

Dimensions:

	in.	cm
A =	30	76.20
B =	20	50.80
C =	14	35.56
D =	24	60.96
E =	12	30.48
F =	3	7.62
G =	24 radius	
H =	12 radius	
I =	45°	
J =	7	17.78

Housing

Glass

Side elevation of aquarium

Front elevation

Open access to equipment

Side section

Side section of aquarium support construction

Adequate support should be provided (as shown). This aquarium weighs 400 lb (181.60 kg).

Notes:
1 = ½" (1.27 cm) plywood platform for pump
2 = ¾" (1.91 cm) marine plywood (must be absolutely level)

3 = copper surface
4 = carved wood
5 = removable copper cover
6 = removable access door

*Shown in plan on page 554.

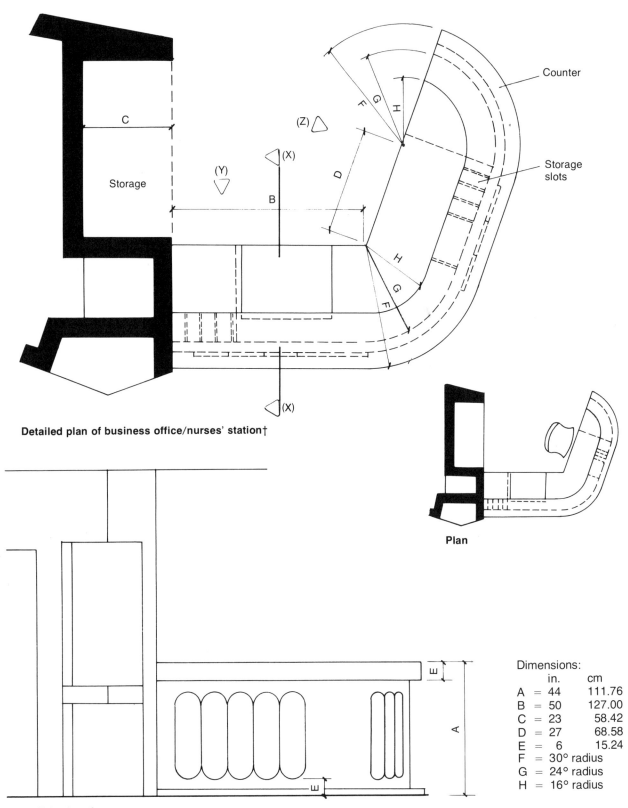

Detailed plan of business office/nurses' station†

Plan

Side elevation

Dimensions:

	in.	cm
A =	44	111.76
B =	50	127.00
C =	23	58.42
D =	27	68.58
E =	6	15.24
F =	30° radius	
G =	24° radius	
H =	16° radius	

*Shown in plan on page 554.
†Sections (XX), (Y), (Z) shown on next page.

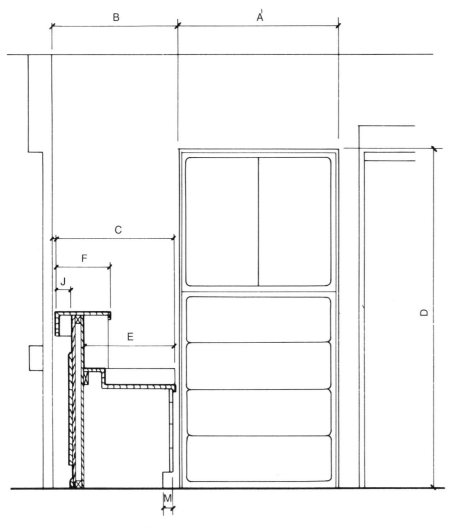

Dimensions:

		in.	cm
A	=	44	111.76
B	=	33	83.82
C	=	30	76.20
D	=	84	213.36
E	=	24	60.96
F	=	14	35.56
G	=	15	38.10
H	=	28	71.12
I	=	26	66.04
J	=	4	10.16
K	=	16	40.64
L	=	1½	3.81
M	=	3	7.62
N	=	12	30.48
O	=	6	15.24

Section (XX) reception desk

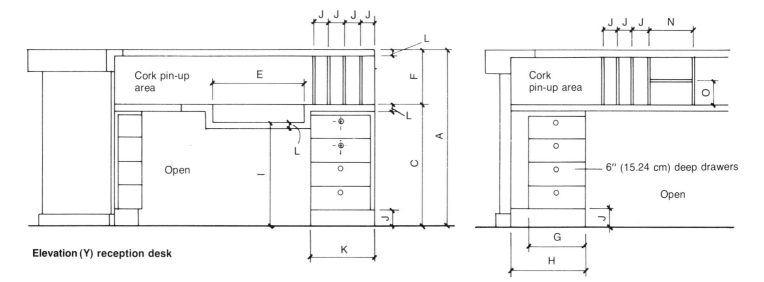

Cork pin-up area

Open

Elevation (Y) reception desk

*Shown in plan on page 554.

Cork pin-up area

6″ (15.24 cm) deep drawers

Open

Elevation (Z) reception desk

Square footage: 1721 (159.89 m²)

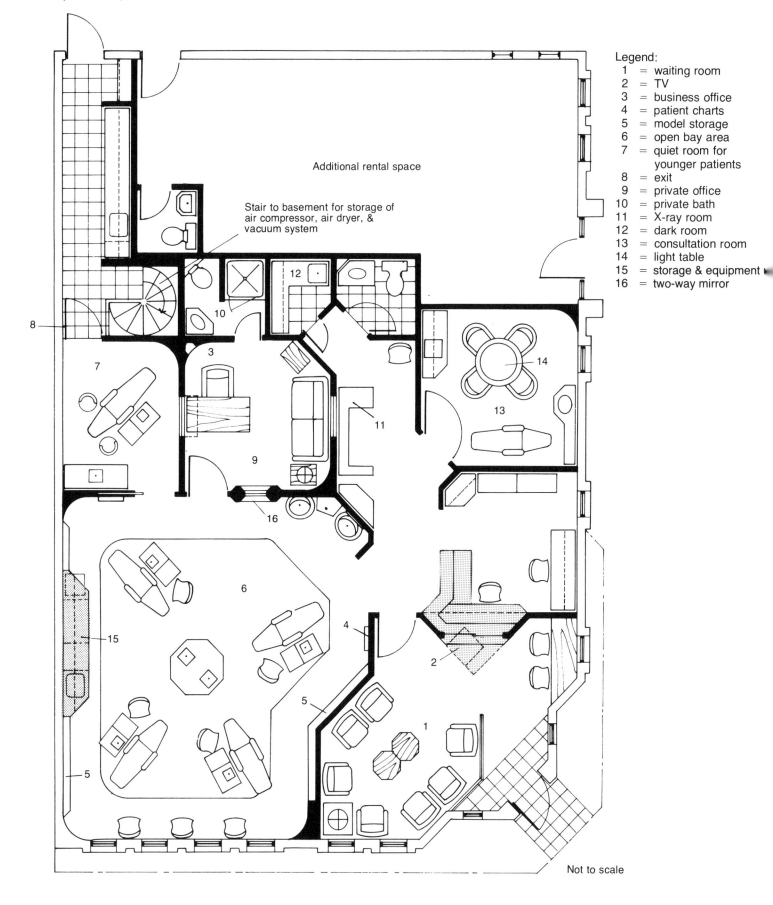

Additional rental space

Stair to basement for storage of
air compressor, air dryer, &
vacuum system

Not to scale

Legend:
 1 = waiting room
 2 = TV
 3 = business office
 4 = patient charts
 5 = model storage
 6 = open bay area
 7 = quiet room for
      younger patients
 8 = exit
 9 = private office
10 = private bath
11 = X-ray room
12 = dark room
13 = consultation room
14 = light table
15 = storage & equipment
16 = two-way mirror

Note: Exit (8) may not meet code requirements for an official exit because it must be
reached through a work space. Check local codes.

*Details shown on pages 559–564.

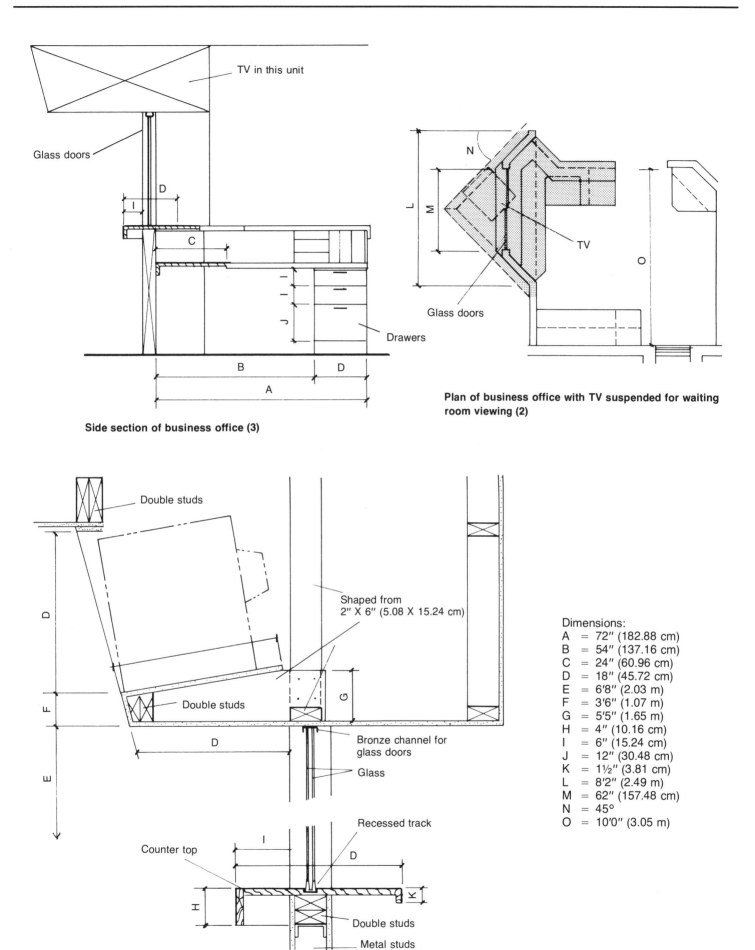

TV in this unit

Glass doors

D

I

C

J

B

D

A

Side section of business office (3)

N

L

M

TV

Glass doors

O

Plan of business office with TV suspended for waiting room viewing (2)

Double studs

D

Shaped from
2″ X 6″ (5.08 X 15.24 cm)

F

Double studs

G

D

Bronze channel for
glass doors

Glass

E

Recessed track

I

D

Counter top

H

K

Double studs

Metal studs

Dimensions:
A = 72″ (182.88 cm)
B = 54″ (137.16 cm)
C = 24″ (60.96 cm)
D = 18″ (45.72 cm)
E = 6′8″ (2.03 m)
F = 3′6″ (1.07 m)
G = 5′5″ (1.65 m)
H = 4″ (10.16 cm)
I = 6″ (15.24 cm)
J = 12″ (30.48 cm)
K = 1½″ (3.81 cm)
L = 8′2″ (2.49 m)
M = 62″ (157.48 cm)
N = 45°
O = 10′0″ (3.05 m)

Side section of TV support & window details

*Shown in plan on page 558.

26' (7.93 m)

20' (6.10 m)

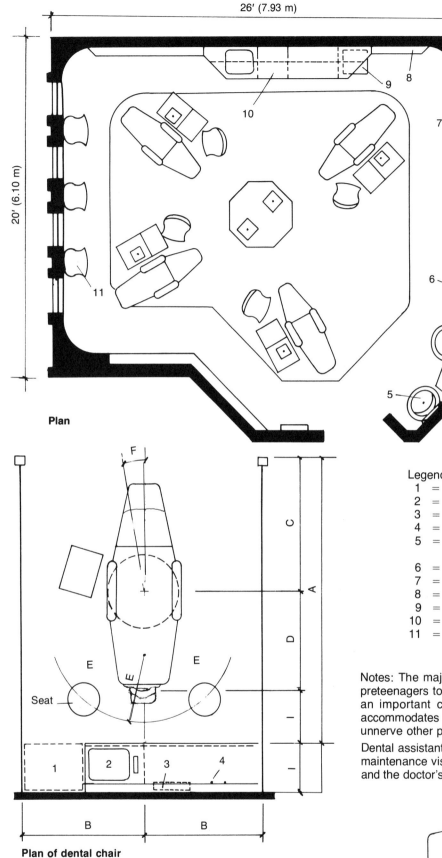

Plan

Open bay design concept (6)

The open bay was developed to encourage children to cooperate while having braces fitted in the orthodontic office. The placement of other young patients in the same area at the same time offers psychological peer support during frequent brace adjustments.

Plan of dental chair

Dimensions:

A = 9'2" (2.79 m)   F = 12" (30.48 cm)
B = 3'6" (1.07 m)   G = 6'0" (1.83 m)
C = 3'8" (1.12 m)   H = 21" to 28" (53.34 to 71.12 cm)
D = 2'8" (0.81 m)   I = 16" to 24" (40.64 to 60.96 cm)
E = 2'8" radius

*Shown in plan on page 558.

Legend:
1 = mobile tray
2 = sink
3 = X-ray
4 = nitrous oxide
5 = brush area (patients brush before
    seeing dentist)
6 = two-way mirror
7 = mirror in which patients attach dental work
8 = model storage
9 = mobile cart
10 = refrigerator
11 = "on-deck" chairs (patients wait their turn here)

Notes: The majority of orthodontic patients range in age from preteenagers to young adults. Therefore the open bay area is an important concept. The quiet room near the open bay accommodates younger children whose noisy responses may unnerve other patients.

Dental assistants frequently work with patients during standard maintenance visits. The two-way mirror between the open bay and the doctor's office permits medical supervision at all times.

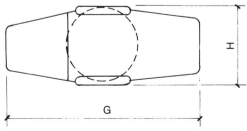

Chair length varies according to manufacturer

Plan

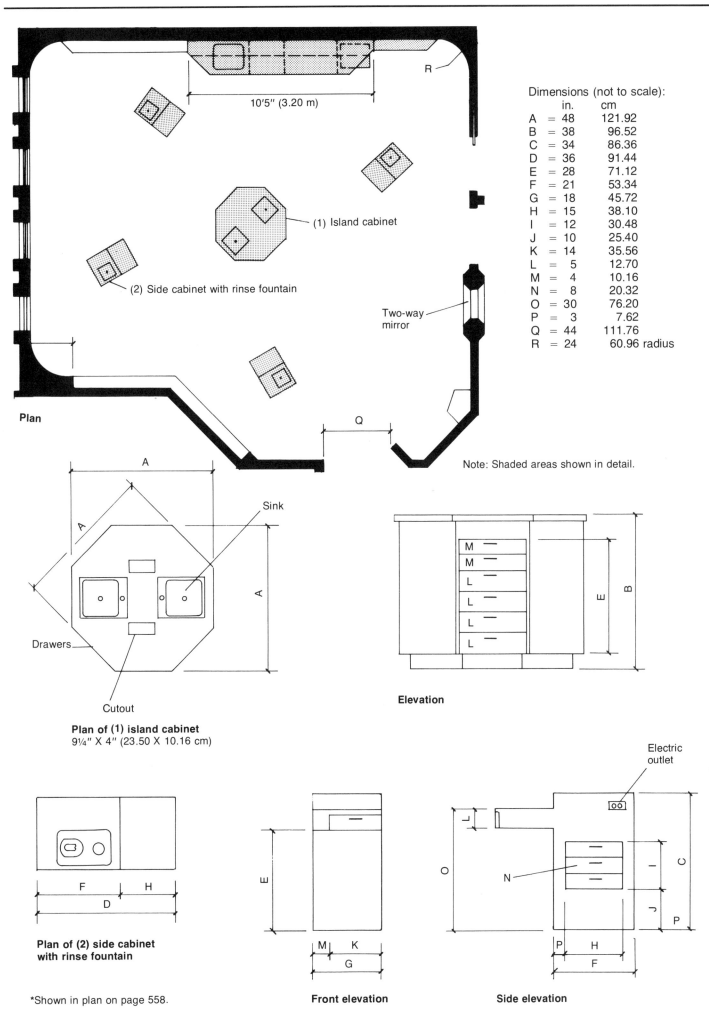

Plan

10'5" (3.20 m)

R

(1) Island cabinet

(2) Side cabinet with rinse fountain

Two-way mirror

Q

Dimensions (not to scale):

		in.	cm
A	=	48	121.92
B	=	38	96.52
C	=	34	86.36
D	=	36	91.44
E	=	28	71.12
F	=	21	53.34
G	=	18	45.72
H	=	15	38.10
I	=	12	30.48
J	=	10	25.40
K	=	14	35.56
L	=	5	12.70
M	=	4	10.16
N	=	8	20.32
O	=	30	76.20
P	=	3	7.62
Q	=	44	111.76
R	=	24	60.96 radius

Note: Shaded areas shown in detail.

A

A

A

Sink

Drawers

Cutout

Plan of (1) island cabinet
9¼" X 4" (23.50 X 10.16 cm)

M
M
L
L
L
L

E

B

Elevation

F   H

D

Plan of (2) side cabinet with rinse fountain

E

M   K

G

Front elevation

Electric outlet

L

O

N

I

C

J

P

P   H

F

Side elevation

*Shown in plan on page 558.

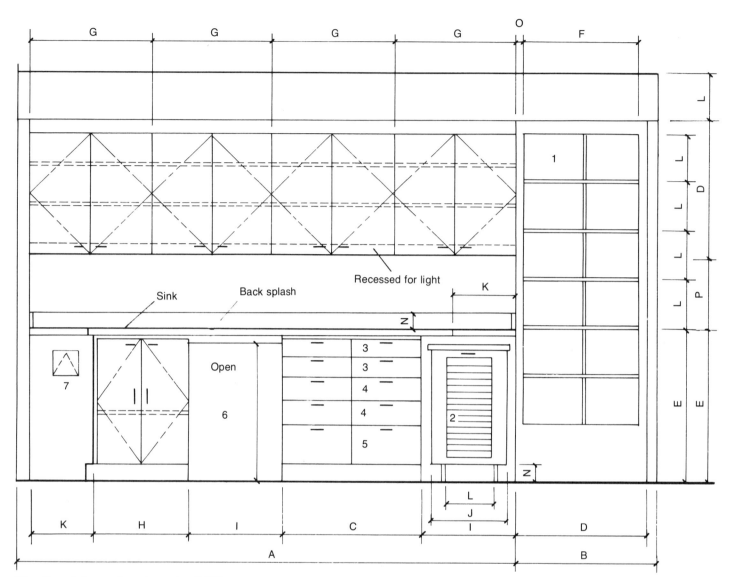

Elevation of storage & equipment unit (15)

Section elevation

Dimensions:

		in.	cm
A	=	125	317.50
B	=	42	106.68
C	=	36	91.44
D	=	34	86.36
E	=	38	96.52
F	=	30	76.20
G	=	31½	80.01
H	=	26	66.04
I	=	24	60.96
J	=	20	50.80
K	=	16	40.64
L	=	12	30.48
M	=	90	228.60
N	=	4	10.16
O	=	2	5.08
P	=	18	45.72
Q	=	2½	6.35

Legend:
1 = model storage*
2 = cart on casters
   20″ X 18″ X 34″
   (50.80 X 45.72 X 86.36 cm).
   This cart contains 13 shelves
   spaced 1½″ (3.81 cm) apart.
   Cart is open on both sides
3 = drawers 5″ (12.70 cm) deep
4 = drawers 6″ (15.24 cm) deep
5 = drawer 10″ (25.40 cm) deep
6 = open for refrigerator
7 = trash

*Shown in plan on page 558.

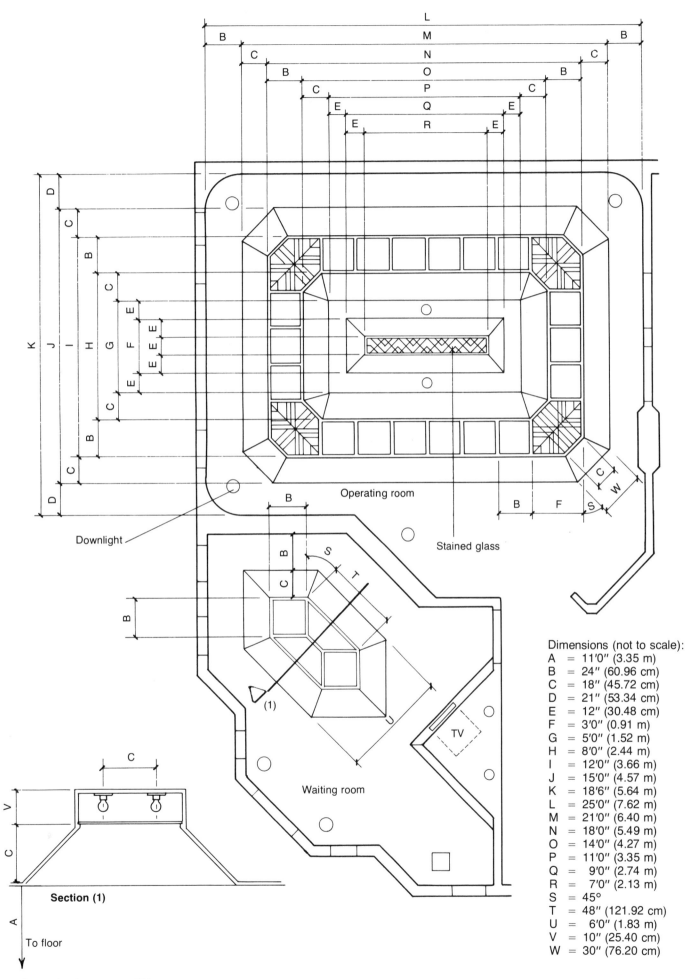

Operating room

Downlight

Stained glass

Waiting room

TV

(1)

Section (1)

To floor

C

V

C

A

*Shown in plan on page 558.

Dimensions (not to scale):
A = 11′0″ (3.35 m)
B = 24″ (60.96 cm)
C = 18″ (45.72 cm)
D = 21″ (53.34 cm)
E = 12″ (30.48 cm)
F = 3′0″ (0.91 m)
G = 5′0″ (1.52 m)
H = 8′0″ (2.44 m)
I = 12′0″ (3.66 m)
J = 15′0″ (4.57 m)
K = 18′6″ (5.64 m)
L = 25′0″ (7.62 m)
M = 21′0″ (6.40 m)
N = 18′0″ (5.49 m)
O = 14′0″ (4.27 m)
P = 11′0″ (3.35 m)
Q = 9′0″ (2.74 m)
R = 7′0″ (2.13 m)
S = 45°
T = 48″ (121.92 cm)
U = 6′0″ (1.83 m)
V = 10″ (25.40 cm)
W = 30″ (76.20 cm)

Plan of reflected ceiling over surgery area

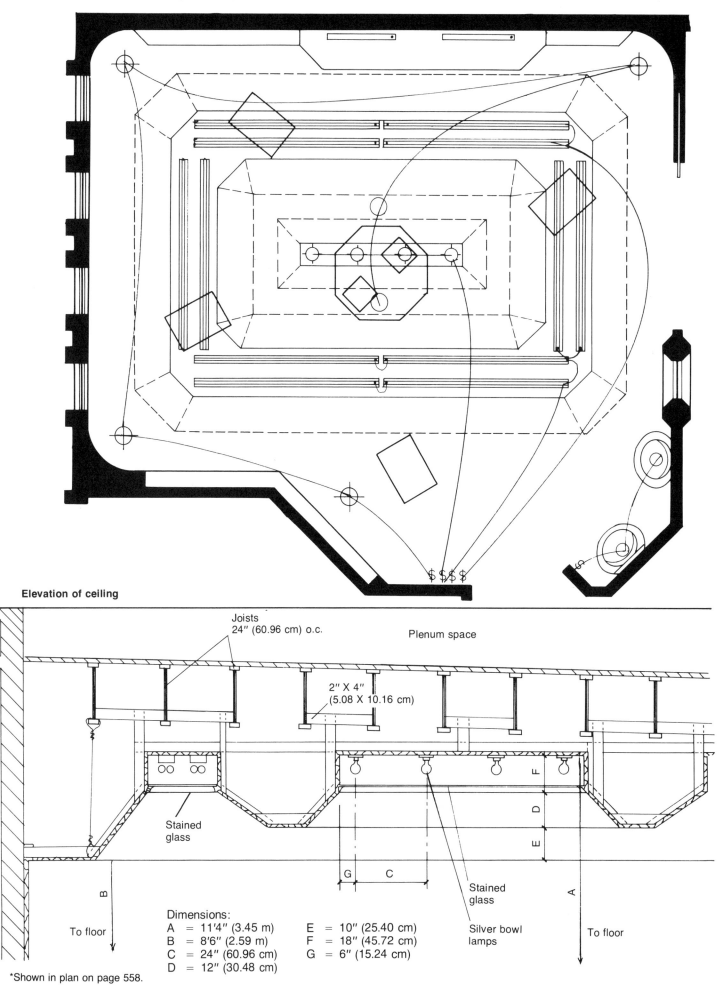

Elevation of ceiling

Joists
24" (60.96 cm) o.c.

Plenum space

2" X 4"
(5.08 X 10.16 cm)

Stained
glass

Stained
glass

Silver bowl
lamps

To floor

To floor

Dimensions:
A = 11'4" (3.45 m)   E = 10" (25.40 cm)
B = 8'6" (2.59 m)   F = 18" (45.72 cm)
C = 24" (60.96 cm)   G = 6" (15.24 cm)
D = 12" (30.48 cm)

*Shown in plan on page 558.

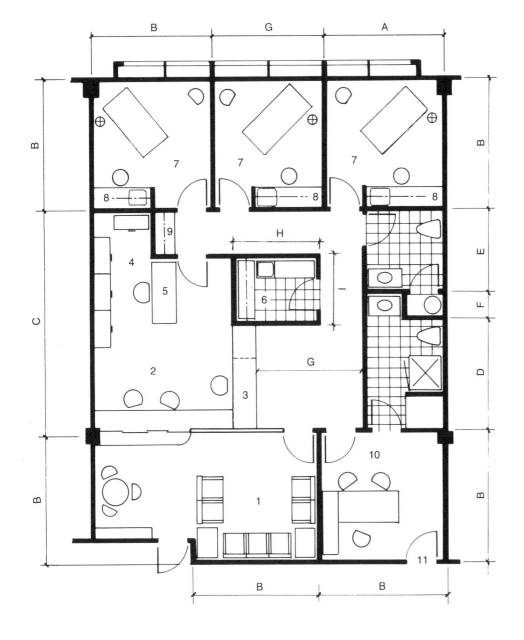

Dimensions:

		ft	m
A	=	13	3.96
B	=	12	3.66
C	=	21	6.40
D	=	10	3.05
E	=	9	2.74
F	=	2	0.61
G	=	11	3.35
H	=	8	2.44
I	=	6	1.83

Legend:
1 = waiting room
2 = admitting room
3 = cashier
4 = files
5 = nurses' station
6 = laboratory
7 = exam room
8 = counters
9 = storage
10 = doctor's office
11 = private entry

TYPICAL SMALL OFFICE FOR ONE MEDICAL DOCTOR

Approximate square footage: 1,645 (152.83 m²)

Exam rooms
Vary from 8' X 10' (2.44 X 3.05 m) to 10' X 10' (3.05 X 3.05 m). Exam tables measure 3' X 6'6" (0.91 X 1.98 m).

Waiting rooms
The size varies depending on the type of practice involved. Generally patient's prefer to sit in single chair rather than on a sofa. Chairs should have arms and straight backs to provide comfort for all age groups. The number of chairs for patients should be multiplied by 1½ to accommodate people who accompany patients to the office.

Carpet should be a low-level loop pile to provide accessibility for disabled people. Designers should provide adequate lighting for reading.

Business office
Storage for patient files usually involves a major portion of the space. Designers should provide for expansion of filing areas. Most offices also need space for microcomputers, printers, and copy machines.

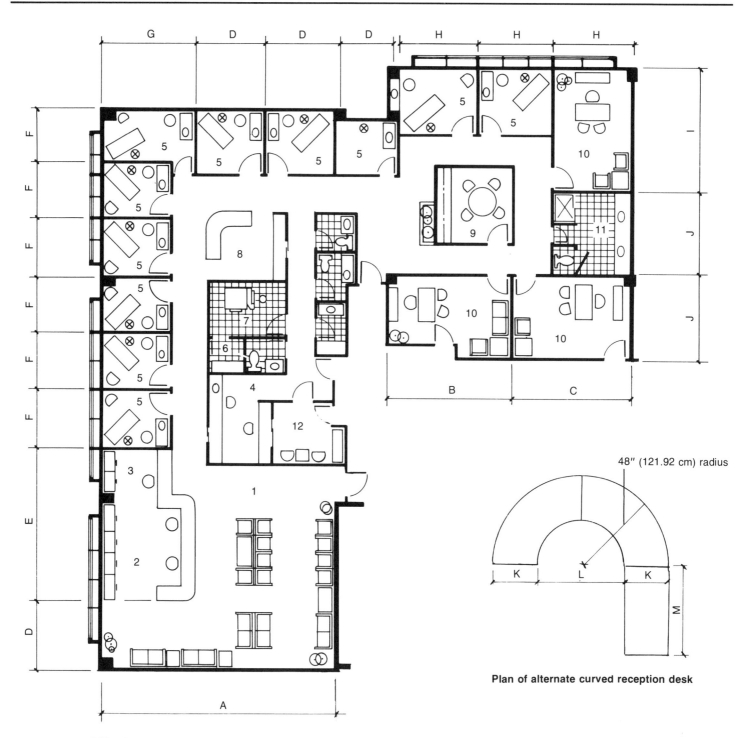

Office for small group practice (three doctors)

48″ (121.92 cm) radius

Plan of alternate curved reception desk

Dimensions:

	ft/in.	m
A =	37 0	11.28
B =	19 0	5.79
C =	18 0	5.49
D =	10 0	3.05
E =	22 0	6.71
F =	8 0	2.44
G =	13 6	4.12
H =	11 0	3.35
I =	17 0	5.18
J =	12 0	3.66
K =	2 0	0.61
L =	4 8	1.22
M =	3 6	1.07

Legend:
1 = waiting room
2 = reception room
3 = cashier
4 = lab
5 = exam rooms
  [typical sizes:
  8′ X 10′ (2.44 X 3.05 m);
  10′ X 10′ (3.05 X 3.05 m)]
6 = darkroom
7 = X-ray room
8 = nurses' station
9 = conference/consultation room
10 = doctor's office
11 = bath
12 = critical care/treatment room

Square footage: 1927 (179.02 m²)
This office space is 41′ X 47′ (12.50 X 14.33 m)

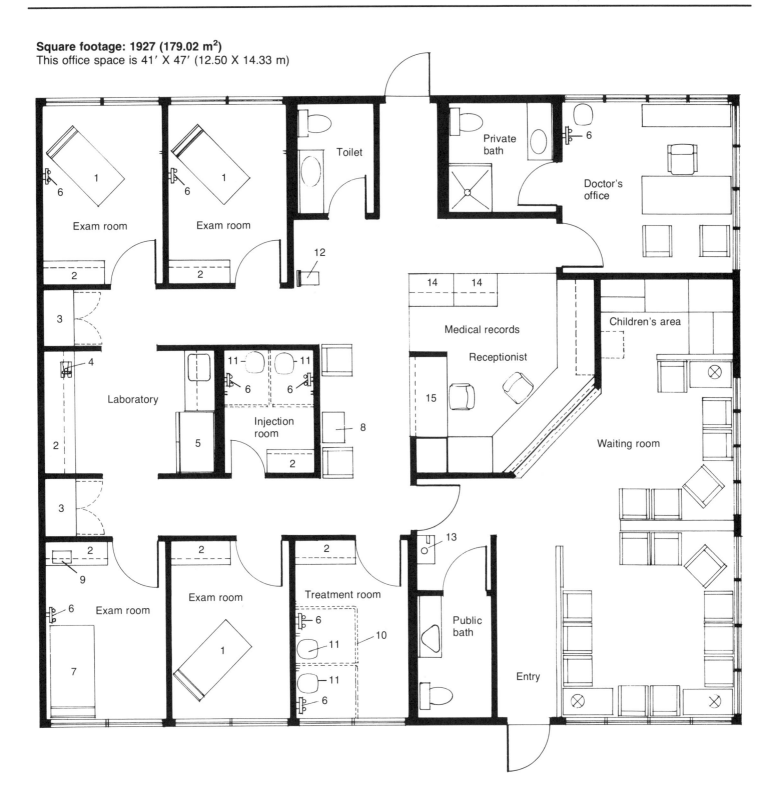

Legend:
1 = exam table
2 = cabinet
3 = storage
4 = microscope
5 = refrigerator
6 = monitoring device
7 = skin test table
8 = sparometer

9 = skin test kit
10 = curtained cubicle
11 = stool
12 = scale
13 = drinking fountain
14 = files
15 = cashier

The design of this office must provide for patients who return for frequent (weekly) treatments and injections. The additional traffic must be considered in the design of the waiting room and the layout of the inner office. Therefore, note that the treatment rooms are located close to the waiting area.

An important factor in designing this type of office is providing easy access between the refrigerator and the injection room. A large refrigerator with doors on back and front is ideal.

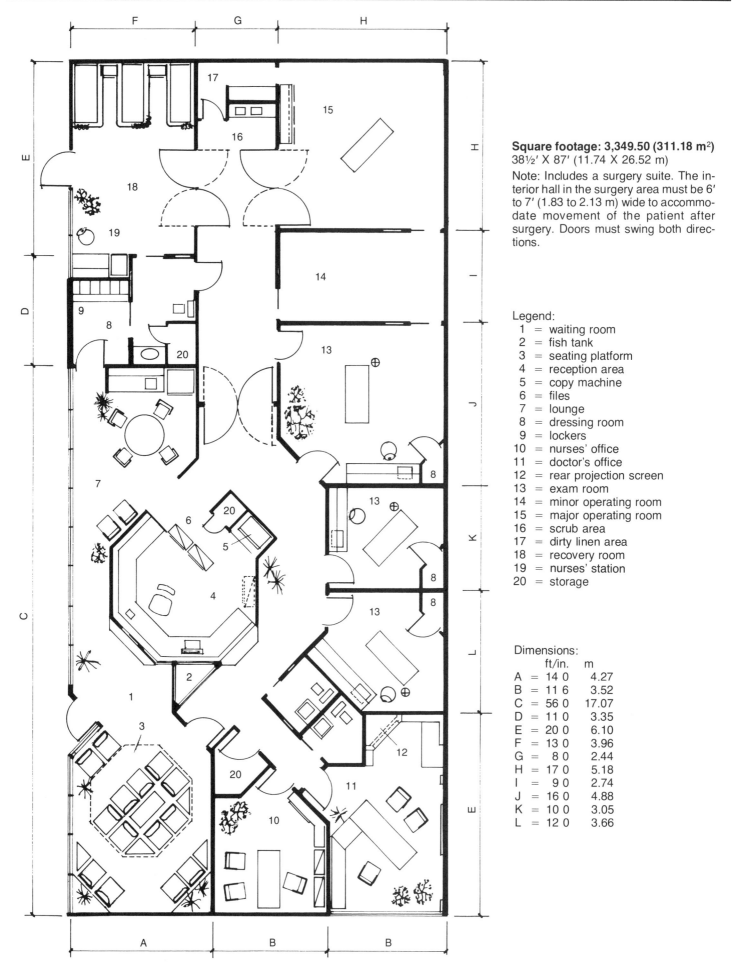

Square footage: 3,349.50 (311.18 m²)
38½′ X 87′ (11.74 X 26.52 m)

Note: Includes a surgery suite. The interior hall in the surgery area must be 6′ to 7′ (1.83 to 2.13 m) wide to accommodate movement of the patient after surgery. Doors must swing both directions.

Legend:
1 = waiting room
2 = fish tank
3 = seating platform
4 = reception area
5 = copy machine
6 = files
7 = lounge
8 = dressing room
9 = lockers
10 = nurses' office
11 = doctor's office
12 = rear projection screen
13 = exam room
14 = minor operating room
15 = major operating room
16 = scrub area
17 = dirty linen area
18 = recovery room
19 = nurses' station
20 = storage

Dimensions:
	ft/in.	m
A =	14 0	4.27
B =	11 6	3.52
C =	56 0	17.07
D =	11 0	3.35
E =	20 0	6.10
F =	13 0	3.96
G =	8 0	2.44
H =	17 0	5.18
I =	9 0	2.74
J =	16 0	4.88
K =	10 0	3.05
L =	12 0	3.66

TYPICAL CONSOLES

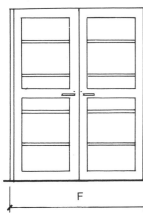

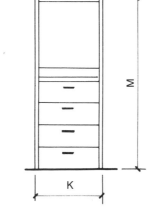

Plans of storage consoles

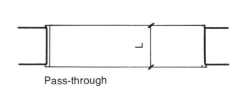

Recessed

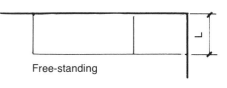

Pass-through

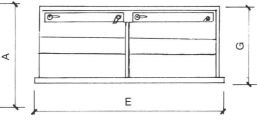

Free-standing

Dimensions (not to scale):

	in.	cm		in.	cm		in.	cm
A =	52	132.08	E =	64	162.56	J =	20	50.80
B =	76	193.04	F =	48	121.92	K =	24	60.96
C =	83	210.82	G =	28	71.12	L =	18	45.72
D =	72	182.88	H =	36	91.44	M =	60	152.40
			I =	22	55.88			

SURGICAL LIGHTS

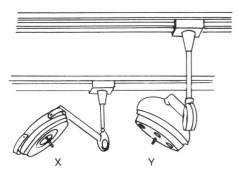

X   Y

Lights can be used with ceilings ranging from 8'2" to 12'0" (2.49 to 3.66 m). Mounting arrangements vary.

Space requirements

Light type	in.	Length X width cm	Weight of fixture lb	kg
Single light (X)				
Track: 54" (137.16 cm) rotating	87 X 87	220.98 X 220.98	175	79.45
54" L fixed	136 X 99	345.44 X 251.46	150	68.10
Double lights (Y)				
Track: 54" L fixed	136 X 167	345.44 X 424.18	300	136.20
108" (274.32 cm) L fixed	190 X 167	482.60 X 424.18	350	158.90
Three lights (Y)				
24" (60.96 cm) arm	148 X 148	375.92 X 375.92	140	63.56
36" (91.44 cm) arm	172 X 172	436.88 X 436.88	140	63.56

SCRUB STATIONS

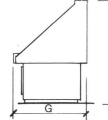

Side elevation

Plan of double scrub station

Note: Wall-mounted scrub stations have automatic digital water timing, temperature control, knee control of soap and water. Specify up to three bays.

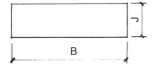

Plan of X-Y coordinate table
Cardiovascular surgery requires pivot mount. Height adjustable from 33" to 48" (83.82 to 121.92 cm).

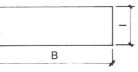

Plan of seven-section major surgical table
Requires a pivot mount. Height adjustable from 30" to 45" (76.20 to 114.30 cm).

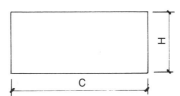

Plan of urology table
Height adjustable from 33" to 45"; 120 volt/ 10 amp electric service required.

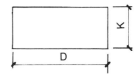

Plan of major surgical table
Pivot mount with electrical cords required. Height adjustable from 29" to 47" (73.66 to 119.38 cm).

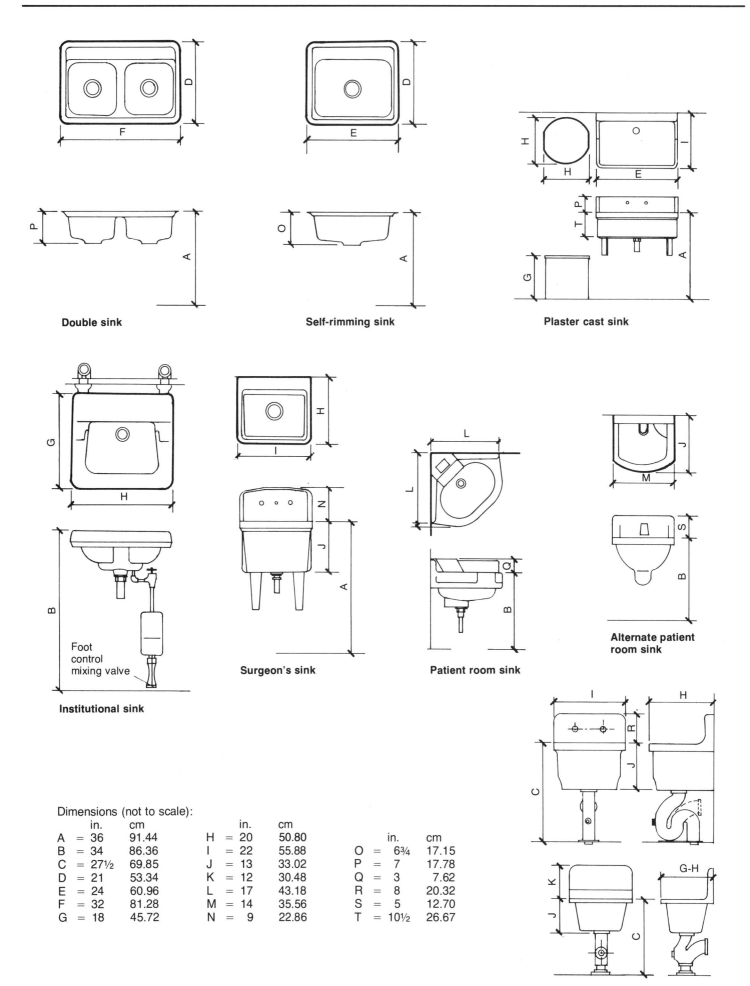

Double sink

Self-rimming sink

Plaster cast sink

Institutional sink

Foot control mixing valve

Surgeon's sink

Patient room sink

Alternate patient room sink

Service sinks

Dimensions (not to scale):

	in.	cm		in.	cm			in.	cm
A =	36	91.44	H =	20	50.80				
B =	34	86.36	I =	22	55.88	O =		6¾	17.15
C =	27½	69.85	J =	13	33.02	P =		7	17.78
D =	21	53.34	K =	12	30.48	Q =		3	7.62
E =	24	60.96	L =	17	43.18	R =		8	20.32
F =	32	81.28	M =	14	35.56	S =		5	12.70
G =	18	45.72	N =	9	22.86	T =		10½	26.67

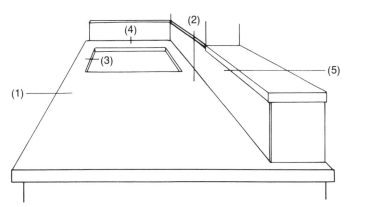

Acid-resistant, laminated top

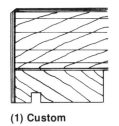

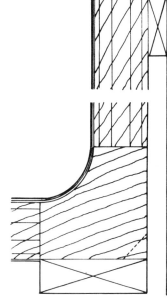

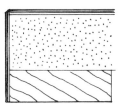

Laminate

(1) Economy

Acid-resistant sealer

(1) Premium

(1) Premium

(1) Custom

(2) All grades

(3) Economy

Premium
⅛" (0.32 cm) extended edge

(3) Custom & premium

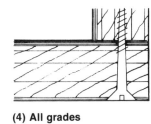

(4) All grades

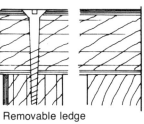

Removable ledge

(5) All grades

ACID-RESISTANT LAMINATED PLASTIC FOR LABORATORY TOPS & SPLASHES

Specifications

Tops shall meet the requirements of the National Electrical Manufacturers Association (NEMA) LD 3-75 or latest standard revision. Tests should require that chemicals be left in contact with surfaces for a minimum of 16 hours. Resistance should be provided against the following acids, alkalies, solvents, salts, and other reagents.

Acids	**%**
Acetic acid	98
Citric acid	10
Formic acid	90
Hydrochloric acid	37
Nitric acid	30
Perchloric acid	60
Phenol	85
Phosphoric acid	85
Sulfuric acid	77

Alkalies	
Ammonium hydroxide	28

Solvents
Acetone
Amyl alcohol
Benzene
Carbon tetrachloride
Chloroform
Dioxane
Ethyl acetate
Ethyl alcohol
Ethyl ether
Ethylacetoacetate
Formaldehyde
Furfural

Gasoline
Kerosene
Naptha
Toluene
Trichlorethylene
Xylene

Salts
Calcium hypochlorite, saturated
Potassium permanganate
Silver nitrate 1%
Sodium bisulfite
Sodium bisulfate

Sodium chloride
Zinc chloride 1%

Other reagents
Chlorobenzene
Cresol
Detergent (dreit)
Hydrogen peroxide
Iodine, 1% in alcohol
Mercurochrome
Mineral oil
Urea 6.6%

Laboratory sinks

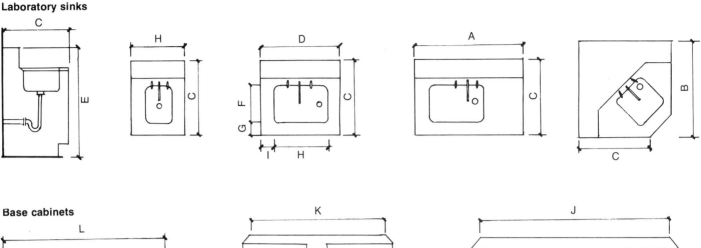

Base cabinets

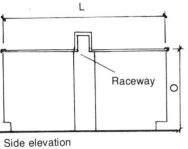

Side elevation

Square peninsula base

Hexagonal peninsula base

Note: The raceway space between the cabinet and wall provides a service area for wires and drains. Provide 8" (20.32 cm) for repair access

Refrigerator

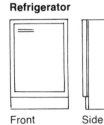

Front   Side

6 cu ft (0.17 cu m)
23" X 21"
(58.42 X 53.34 cm)

Incubator

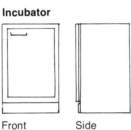

Front   Side

23" X 21"

Blood bank

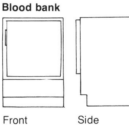

Front   Side

24" X 24"
(60.96 X 60.96 cm)

Washer

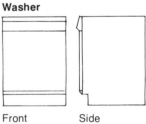

Front   Side

24" X 20"
(60.96 X 50.80 cm)

Floor case with glass doors

W = 35" to 47"
    (88.90 X 119.38 cm)
D = 16" (40.64 cm)
H = 84" (213.36 cm)

Unit designed to vent chemical fumes from labs

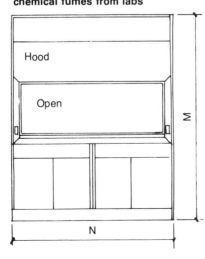

Hood

Open

Dimensions:

	in.	cm			in.	cm
A =	47	119.38		I =	6	15.24
B =	39	99.06		J =	72	182.88
C =	31	77.74		K =	57	144.78
D =	35	88.90		L =	55	139.70
E =	41	104.41		M =	96	243.84
F =	16	50.64		N =	94	238.76
G =	4	10.16		O =	28	71.12
H =	24	60.96				

Glass pass-through case
Depth = 12" (30.48 cm)

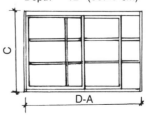

Note: This open shelving is ideal for island-type situations and for linking labs and treatment rooms.

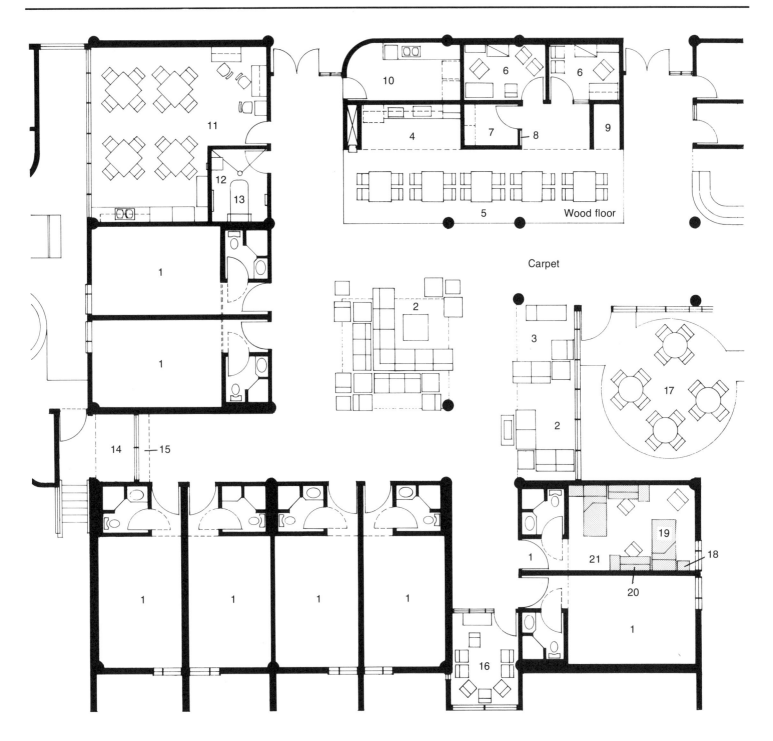

Note: The unit is designed as a self-contained area. Patients may move about, visit with other patients, have group therapy, and receive visitors without leaving the unit.

Legend:
1 = semiprivate or private room
2 = group seating
3 = television viewing
4 = kitchen/snack area
5 = snack-eating area
6 = office
7 = medication in locked cabinets

8 = tackboard with breakproof glass
9 = wheelchair alcove
10 = laundry area
11 = dining area
12 = bath
13 = bathtub
14 = planter

15 = seating
16 = group therapy room
17 = gameroom
18 = bedside table*
19 = bed*
20 = desk*
21 = clothing storage*

*See detailed drawings on pages 574-575.

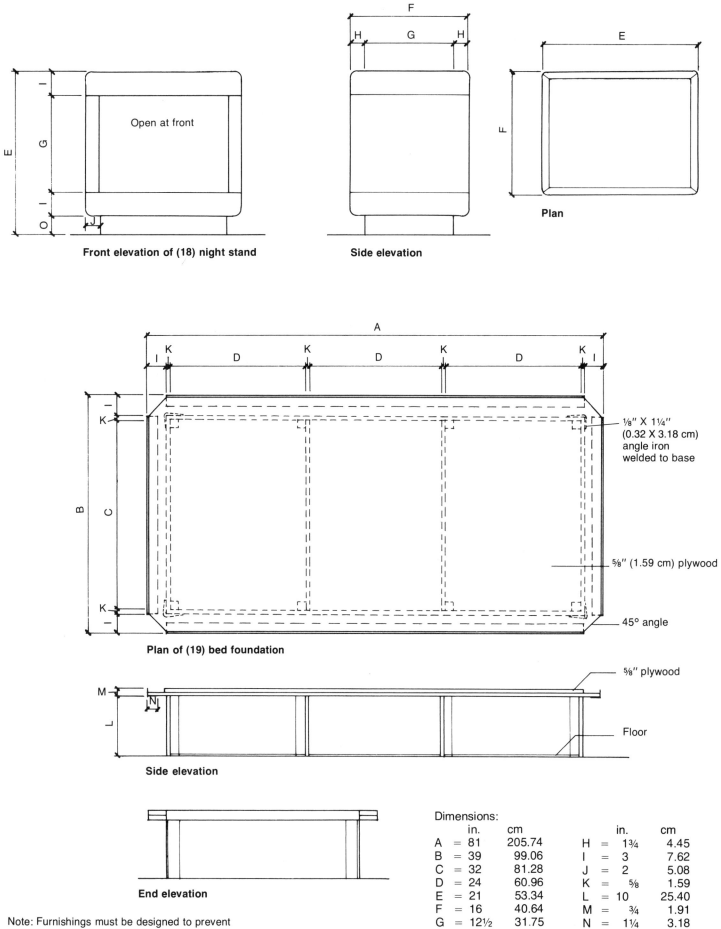

Front elevation of (18) night stand

Open at front

Side elevation

Plan

Plan of (19) bed foundation

⅛" X 1¼"
(0.32 X 3.18 cm)
angle iron
welded to base

⅝" (1.59 cm) plywood

45° angle

⅝" plywood

Floor

Side elevation

End elevation

Dimensions:

		in.	cm			in.	cm
A	=	81	205.74	H	=	1¾	4.45
B	=	39	99.06	I	=	3	7.62
C	=	32	81.28	J	=	2	5.08
D	=	24	60.96	K	=	⅝	1.59
E	=	21	53.34	L	=	10	25.40
F	=	16	40.64	M	=	¾	1.91
G	=	12½	31.75	N	=	1¼	3.18
				O	=	2½	6.35

Note: Furnishings must be designed to prevent
patients from hurting themselves or others with
sharp points and angles. Avoid loose components
that can be used as weapons.

*Shown in plan on page 573.

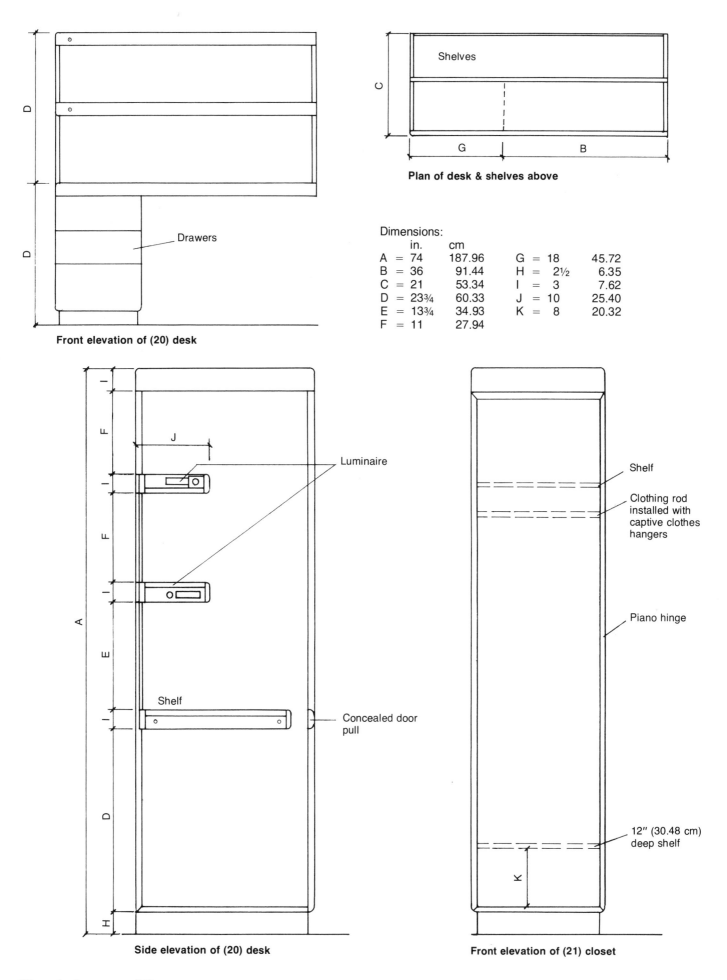

Plan of desk & shelves above

Drawers

Dimensions:

	in.	cm				
A	= 74	187.96	G	= 18	45.72
B	= 36	91.44	H	= 2½	6.35
C	= 21	53.34	I	= 3	7.62
D	= 23¾	60.33	J	= 10	25.40
E	= 13¾	34.93	K	= 8	20.32
F	= 11	27.94			

Front elevation of (20) desk

Luminaire

Shelf

Concealed door pull

Side elevation of (20) desk

Shelf

Clothing rod installed with captive clothes hangers

Piano hinge

12″ (30.48 cm) deep shelf

Front elevation of (21) closet

*Shown in plan on page 573.

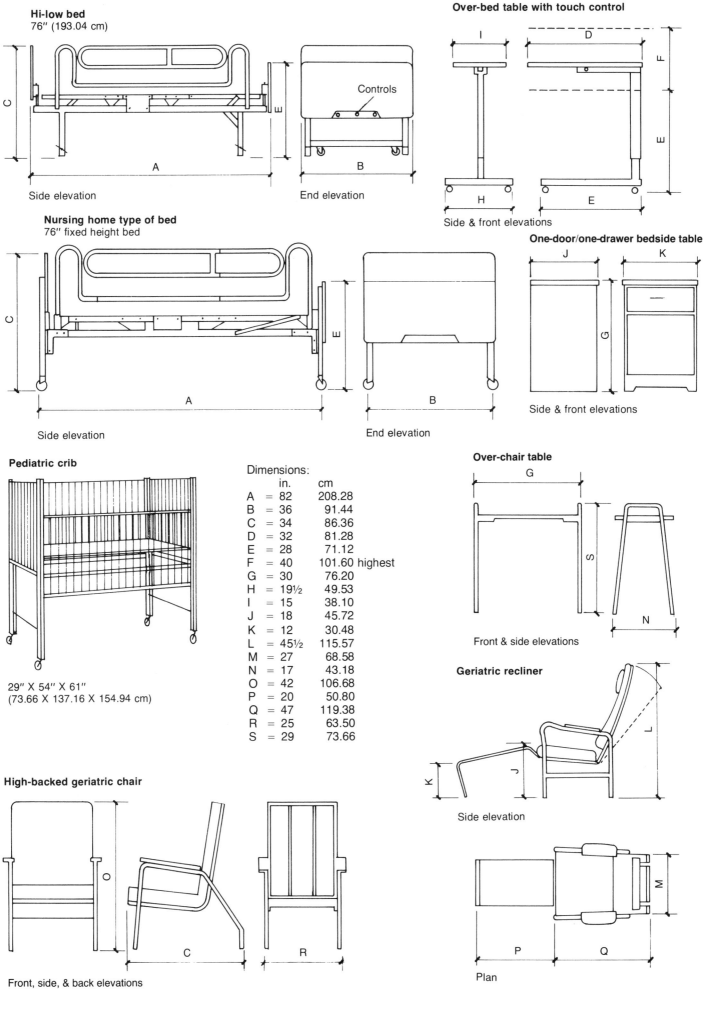

Hi-low bed
76″ (193.04 cm)

Side elevation

End elevation

Controls

Over-bed table with touch control

Side & front elevations

Nursing home type of bed
76″ fixed height bed

Side elevation

End elevation

One-door/one-drawer bedside table

Side & front elevations

Pediatric crib

29″ X 54″ X 61″
(73.66 X 137.16 X 154.94 cm)

Dimensions:

		in.	cm
A	=	82	208.28
B	=	36	91.44
C	=	34	86.36
D	=	32	81.28
E	=	28	71.12
F	=	40	101.60 highest
G	=	30	76.20
H	=	19½	49.53
I	=	15	38.10
J	=	18	45.72
K	=	12	30.48
L	=	45½	115.57
M	=	27	68.58
N	=	17	43.18
O	=	42	106.68
P	=	20	50.80
Q	=	47	119.38
R	=	25	63.50
S	=	29	73.66

Over-chair table

Front & side elevations

Geriatric recliner

Side elevation

High-backed geriatric chair

Front, side, & back elevations

Plan

Plans of typical cubicle layouts

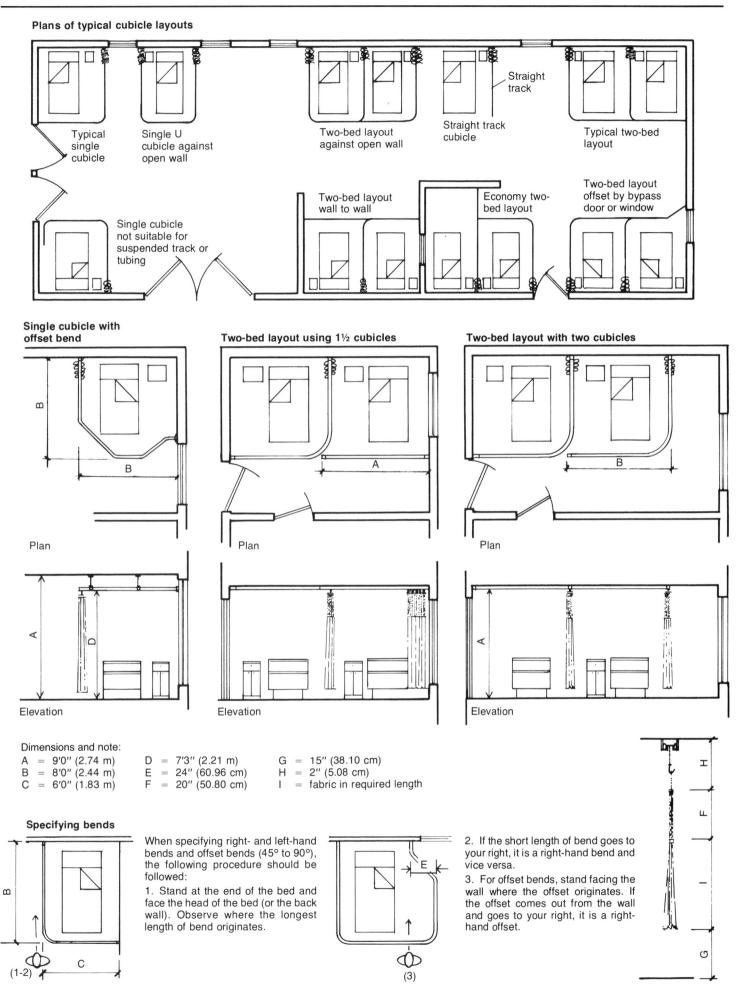

Typical single cubicle

Single U cubicle against open wall

Two-bed layout against open wall

Straight track

Straight track cubicle

Typical two-bed layout

Single cubicle not suitable for suspended track or tubing

Two-bed layout wall to wall

Economy two-bed layout

Two-bed layout offset by bypass door or window

Single cubicle with offset bend

Plan

Elevation

Two-bed layout using 1½ cubicles

Plan

Elevation

Two-bed layout with two cubicles

Plan

Elevation

Dimensions and note:

A	= 9'0" (2.74 m)	D	= 7'3" (2.21 m)	G	= 15" (38.10 cm)
B	= 8'0" (2.44 m)	E	= 24" (60.96 cm)	H	= 2" (5.08 cm)
C	= 6'0" (1.83 m)	F	= 20" (50.80 cm)	I	= fabric in required length

Specifying bends

(1-2)

When specifying right- and left-hand bends and offset bends (45° to 90°), the following procedure should be followed:

1. Stand at the end of the bed and face the head of the bed (or the back wall). Observe where the longest length of bend originates.

(3)

2. If the short length of bend goes to your right, it is a right-hand bend and vice versa.

3. For offset bends, stand facing the wall where the offset originates. If the offset comes out from the wall and goes to your right, it is a right-hand offset.

Elevations of core module

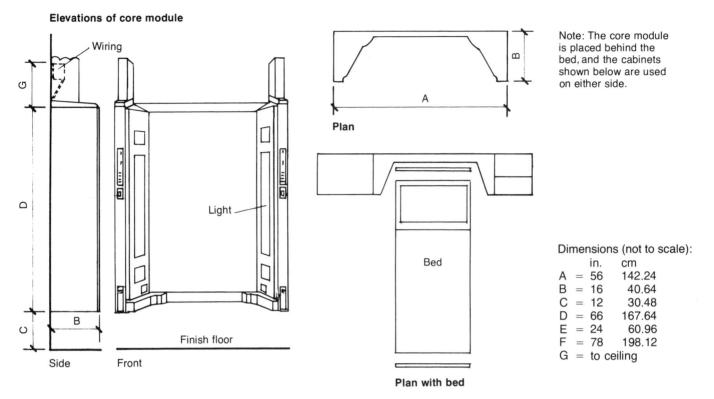

Wiring

Light

Finish floor

Side   Front

Plan

Note: The core module is placed behind the bed, and the cabinets shown below are used on either side.

Bed

Plan with bed

Dimensions (not to scale):

		in.	cm
A	=	56	142.24
B	=	16	40.64
C	=	12	30.48
D	=	66	167.64
E	=	24	60.96
F	=	78	198.12
G	=	to ceiling	

Typical patient room modules

The units below contain spaces for the patient's personal items, sinks, and medical equipment.

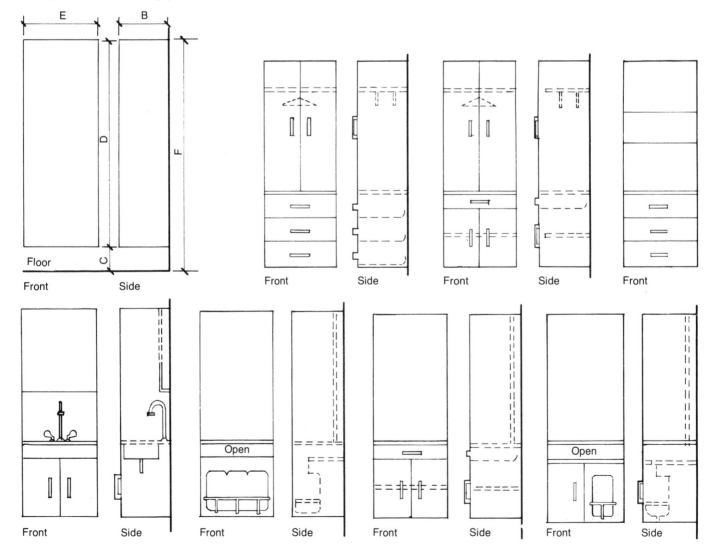

Floor

Front   Side

Front   Side   Front   Side   Front

Open

Open

Front   Side   Front   Side   Front   Side   Front   Side

Elevation of intensive care unit

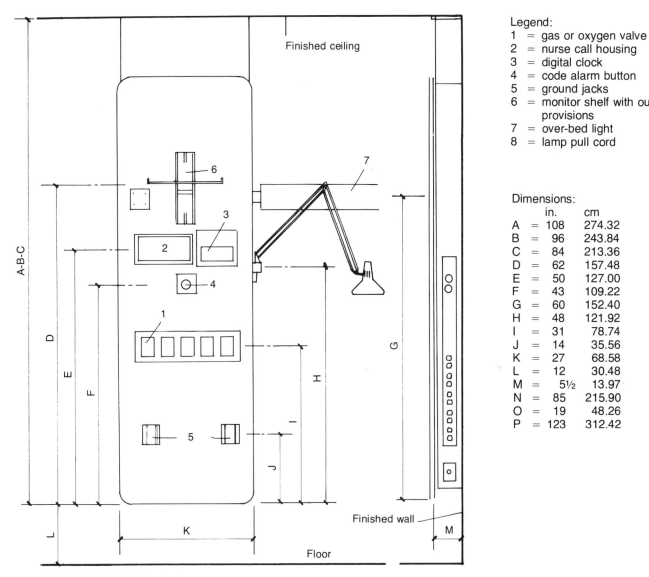

Legend:
1 = gas or oxygen valve
2 = nurse call housing
3 = digital clock
4 = code alarm button
5 = ground jacks
6 = monitor shelf with outlet provisions
7 = over-bed light
8 = lamp pull cord

Dimensions:

		in.	cm
A	=	108	274.32
B	=	96	243.84
C	=	84	213.36
D	=	62	157.48
E	=	50	127.00
F	=	43	109.22
G	=	60	152.40
H	=	48	121.92
I	=	31	78.74
J	=	14	35.56
K	=	27	68.58
L	=	12	30.48
M	=	5½	13.97
N	=	85	215.90
O	=	19	48.26
P	=	123	312.42

General care units for semiprivate room with two beds

This wall system is the same as the intensive care unit except that it has the addition of an electrical console, overbed light, and vacuum and oxygen outlets. Units such as these are surface mounted. Check with local fire codes regarding installation requirements.

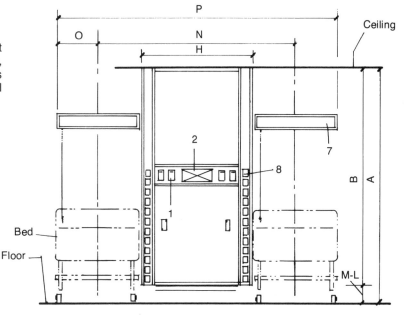

Elevation of general care unit

X-RAY ILLUMINATORS, RECESSED OR SURFACE MOUNTED

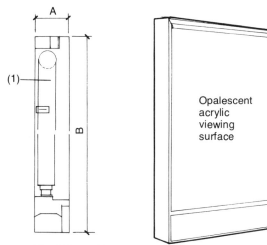

(1) = 240-watt U-type
fluorescent lamps

Opalescent
acrylic
viewing
surface

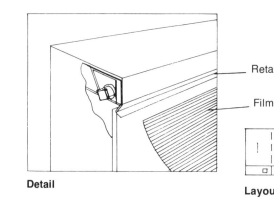

Retainer clip

Film

Detail

Layouts for mounting versatility

Dimensions:

	in.	cm
A =	3⅜	8.57
B =	27 X 14	68.58 X 35.56
C =	22½	57.15
D =	13⅝ X 14¾	34.60 X 37.47
E =	12⅞	32.70
F =	6	15.24

X-RAY PROCESSING ROOM LIGHTING

Lighting must provide both filtered & high-intensity task lighting

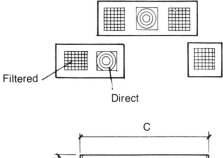

Filtered

Direct

Wall-mounted luminaire designed to provide high-task illumination & filtered downlight for darkroom film processing

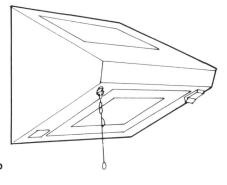

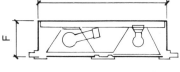

Recessed ceiling luminaire providing dual lighting needs

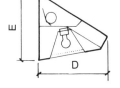

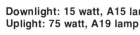

Downlight: 15 watt, A15 lamp
Uplight: 75 watt, A19 lamp

SURGICAL LIGHTING SYSTEMS

Anti-RFI (radio frequency interference) luminaires
Specify: MILSTD-461A, 462, and 463 (standards for RFI)

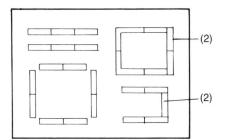

Typical ceiling layout

This layout illustrates concentrated perimeter and operating area lighting plus general lighting. Special diffuser lenses provide a 50-50 asymmetrical and symmetrical light distribution to reduce extreme contrast between intense surgical light and surrounding surfaces. Diffuser shielding grids intercept RFI from power supply and line feedback.

(2) Typical luminaire for surgical areas

Lamp

Symmetrical

Asymmetrical

Ceiling

(2) = supplemental surgical lighting placement (recessed)

Lens for general lighting

Luminaire for intense lighting

Alternate supplemental lighting

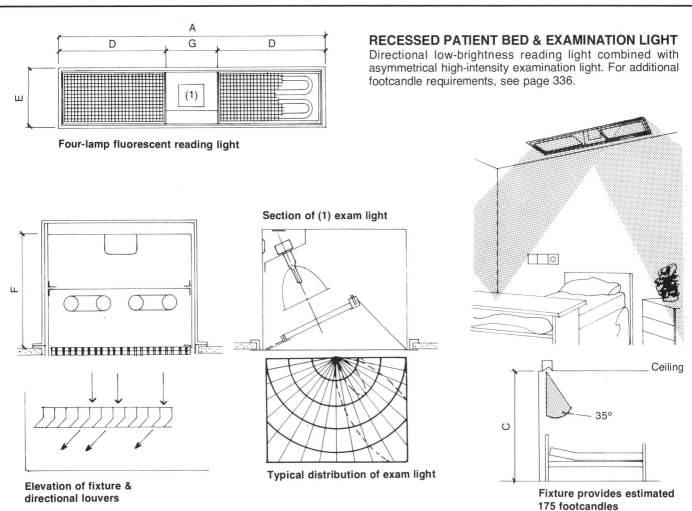

Four-lamp fluorescent reading light

RECESSED PATIENT BED & EXAMINATION LIGHT

Directional low-brightness reading light combined with asymmetrical high-intensity examination light. For additional footcandle requirements, see page 336.

Section of (1) exam light

Elevation of fixture & directional louvers

Typical distribution of exam light

Fixture provides estimated 175 footcandles

35°

BIDIRECTIONAL PATIENT BED LIGHTING

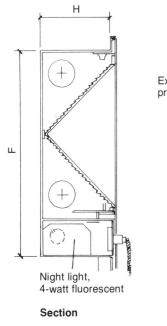

Extrusion prismatic lens

Bidirectional lens

Night light, 4-watt fluorescent

Section

Indirect

Direct

Direct & indirect patient lighting

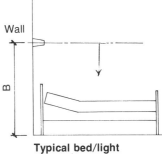

Wall

Typical bed/light installation

Note:

Reflectance	%
Wall	50
Ceiling	80
Floor	10

Dimensions:
A = 62" (157.48 cm)
B = 6'8" (2.03 m)
C = 9'0" (2.74 m)
D = 25" (63.50 cm)
E = 13½" (34.29 cm)
F = 9½" (24.13 cm)
G = 12" (30.48 cm)
H = 4" (10.16 cm)

APPLICABLE STANDARDS

ASTM — **American Society for Testing and Materials**

A 167	Specification for Stainless and Heat-Resisting Chromium-Nickel Steel Plate, Sheet, and Strip.
A 263	Specification for Corrosion-Resisting Chromium Steel-Clad Plate, Sheet and Strip. (ANSI/ASTM A 263)
A 264	Specification for Stainless Chromium-Nickel Steel Clad Plate, Sheet, and Strip. (ANSI/ASTM A264)
A 446	Specification for Steel Sheet, Zinc-Coated (Galvanized) by the Hot-Dip Process, Structural (Physical) Quality. (ANSI/ASTM A446)
A 611	Specification for Steel, Cold-Rolled Sheet, Carbon, Structural. (ANSI/ASTM A611)

FS — **Federal Specifications**

L-P-508	Plastic Sheet, Laminated, Decorative, and Nondecorative Federal Supply Classification. (FSC) 9330
QQ-S-698	Steel, Sheet and Strip, Low Carbon. (FSC) 9515
TT-S-00227	Sealing Compound, Elastomeric Type, Multi-component (For Calking, Sealing, and Glazing in Buildings and Other Structures). (FSC) 8030
TT-S-00230	Sealing Compound, Elastomeric Type, Single Component (For Calking, Sealing, and Glazing in Buildings and Other Structures). (FSC) 8030

MIL — **Military Specifications**

MIL-C-20709	Casework, Metal and Wood (Medical and Dental). (FSC) 6530

MILSTD — **Military Standards**

MIL-STD-1691	Construction and Material Schedule for Military Medical and Dental Facilities. (FSC) 6530

AVAILABLE SPECIFICATION AIDS

CSRF — **Construction Sciences Research Foundation**

SPECTEXT:

12301	Metal Casework

Department of the Army

U.S. Army Corps of Engineers
Guide Specifications for Military Construction:

CEGS-11701	Casework, Metal and Wood (For Medical and Dental Facilities).

GSA — **General Services Administration**

Public Buildings Service Construction Guide Specifications:

4-1160	Laboratory Furniture (and Equipment).
244-1	Hospital Casework.

NASA — **National Aeronautics & Space Administration**

SPECSINTACT:

12304	Cabinets, Steel and Wood

NIH — **National Institutes of Health**

NIH Guide Specifications:

11610	Laboratory Furniture

Department of the Navy

Naval Facilities Engineering Command (NAVFAC) Guide Specifications:

NFGS-11701	Casework, Metal and Wood (Medical and Dental)

VA — **Veterans Administration**

VA Master Guide Specifications:

12301	Metal Casework

The AIA Service Corp., PSAE Div.

MASTERSPEC:

12345	Laboratory Casework and Fixtures

LIBRARIES

1. Project location _____

2. Submit a blueprint showing accurate
   measurements and location of all
   building elements that could affect
   equipment placement

   a. Placement of all doors and windows
   b. Position of electrical outlets,
      vents, and switches

3. Desired location of the following:

   Charging desk
   Lounge area
   Reference and general desks
   Reserve area

4. Specify furniture style

5. Shelving capacity: ____ Volumes ____ Catalog cards
   a. Wall shelving desired
      ____ sections 42 X 8 ____ 10 ____ 12 ____ 16 ____
      ____ sections 60 x 8 ____ 10 ____ 12 ____ 16 ____
      ____ sections 82 X 8 ____ 10 ____ 12 ____ 16 ____
   b. Peninsula shelving desired
      ____ sections 42 X 16 ____ 20 ____ 24 ____
      ____ sections 60 X 16 ____ 20 ____ 24 ____
      ____ sections 82 X 16 ____ 20 ____ 24 ____
   c. Double-faced free-standing shelving sections
      ____ sections 42 X 16 ____ 20 ____ 24 ____
      ____ sections 60 X 16 ____ 20 ____ 24 ____
      ____ sections 82 X 16 ____ 20 ____ 24 ____
   d. Magazine capacity ____ sections of ____ X ____ size
   e. Newspaper capacity ____ sections of ____ X ____ size
   f. Record shelving ____ sections of ____ X ____ size
   g. Picture book capacity ____ sections of ____ X ____ size

6. Seating capacity total
   a. Standard seat height 18" ____ Secondary 16" ____ Juvenile
      14" ____
   b. Reading tables ____ Units: 4 student ____ 6 student ____
      (1) Round ____
      (2) Rectangular ____
   c. Study tables ____ units
   d. Individual carrels ____ units
      (1) Single face ____
      (2) Double face ____
      (3) Modular ____

   e. Audiovisual carrels ____ units
      (1) Single face ____
      (2) Double face ____
      (3) Electrified ____
   f. Index tables ____ units
      (1) Single face ____
      (2) Double face ____
   g. Sofa for casual reading area ____ units
      (1) 1-seater ____
      (2) 2-seater ____
      (3) 3-seater ____
      (4) lounge tables ____ size ____
   h. Sloped top tables
      (1) Double face ____
      (2) Single face ____
      (3) Type of seating: Benches ____ Stools ____

7. Charging desk requirements (supply layout sketch)
   a. Sitting height   ____
   b. Standing height
      (1) Book return   ____
      (2) Knee space   ____
      (3) Charge machine   ____
      (4) Discharge   ____
      (5) Cupboard   ____
      (6) Shelf   ____
      (7) Corner unit   ____
      (8) Gate   ____

8. Additional furnishings
   a. Attendants' desks ____ Office desks ____
   b. Atlas cases ____
   c. Card catalogs ____ Reference tables ____
   d. Dictionary stands: Cupboard type ____ Revolving ____
   e. Book displays: A-frame ____ Shelf type ____
   f. Magazine racks: 20-capacity ____ 35-capacity ____
   g. Newspaper rack tables ____
   h. Exhibit cases: Upright ____ Table type ____
   i. File cabinets: 2-drawer horizontal ____ 3-drawer upright ____
      4-drawer ____
   j. Extra book trucks ____
   k. Stepstools ____

Typical table placement

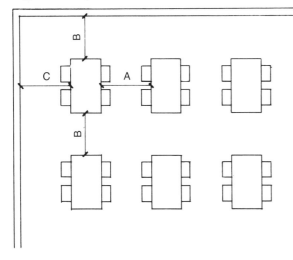

Dimensions:

	ft	m
A =	5	1.52
B =	4	1.22
C =	9	2.74

SCHOOL LIBRARIES

The library should be large enough to seat from 10 to 15 percent of the school's enrollment. An area of 30 to 35 sq ft (2.79 to 3.25 m²) per reader is considered a requisite for adequate service. In elementary schools, the seating capacity may be estimated roughly by the maximum class or platoon enrollment. In the larger elementary schools, this number must be multiplied by the number of classes expected to occupy the room at any one period.

DETERMINATION OF SEATING & ROOM SIZE

As a shortcut to approximate the size of the room, allow 30 sq ft per reader for the gross area sufficient for both reading tables and technical equipment. For example, in a school with an enrollment of 480, provide for 72 readers (15 percent of enrollment) and allow 2160 sq ft (200.67 m³) for the room. A more accurate method for determining the size and best proportions for the room is to make a rough sketch.

Assume that the ideal table size is 3' X 5' (0.91 X 1.52 m) with four readers, two on each long side. Calculate the number of tables required. Allow 5' between them where chairs are back to back or where there is bookshelving behind chairs. Allow 4' (1.22 m) for all other aisles.

BOOK CAPACITY

No definite formula can be established to determine the number of books that can be accommodated per square foot, per cubic foot, or per gross stack area. The size and type of books, the number and width of the main and side aisles, stairways, elevators, and book lifts are only a few of the factors that can influence the book capacity. The Library Bureau has tested plans of many kinds of stack rooms and has found the capacity

ranges from 13½ to 19 books per square foot. Therefore, for the convenience of those who prefer a rough rule of thumb, 16 books per square foot of the gross area would represent an average figure.

COMPUTING BOOK CAPACITY

-For example, 16 books per square foot: books counted in hundreds — 14,400.*

Width	Length of room (ft)						
(ft)	30	35	40	45	50	55	60
30	144*	168	192	216	240	264	288
35	168	196	224	252	280	308	336
40	192	224	256	288	320	352	384
45	216	252	288	324	360	396	432
50	240	280	320	360	400	440	480
55	264	308	352	396	440	484	528
60	288	336	384	432	480	528	576

Ranges

These consist of one or more 3' wall or double-faced sections or units. These ranges may be added to or shortened because of the unit-type design. Each range will have an initial unit that has two end uprights. Additional units will require only one intermediate upright assembly.

Aisle widths

Ranges of 4'6" (1.37 m) center to center will yield an aisle of 3' using the 8" (20.32 cm) shelf size. Additional aisle space may be desirable for the open stack concept and for more freedom of movement in the stack area.

These specifications are intended for general basic information.

WEIGHT ESTIMATES

These calculations can be used to determine whether the floor of a room in an existing library will safely sustain the weight of double-faced bookstack ranges. If the ranges are spaced 4'6" apart on center, with 3' wide cross aisles, the weight per square foot of the gross area of the room is 63½ lb (28.83 kg) for 12,907 stacks (8" deep shelving). This figure also includes the dead load of books computed at 25 lb (11.35 kg) per cubic foot. If 12,909 stacks [10" (25.40 cm) deep shelves] are used, the weight per square foot is 66½ lb (30.19 kg). The live load for people in stack aisles is 40 lb (18.16 kg) per square foot for the gross area. Note: Weights for welded frame stacks are very slightly higher.

When loaded with books, single-tier, double-faced bookstacks have a concentrated load of 900 lb (408.60 kg) at the base of an intermediate stack column and 450 lb (204.30 kg) at the base of an end stack column.

PICTURE BOOK SHELVING

This refers to shelves that hold oversized books 12" to 24⅛" (30.48 to 61.28 cm) deep. Phonograph records are stored on high-wall 16" (40.68 cm) wide shelves with seven adjustable dividers per shelf.

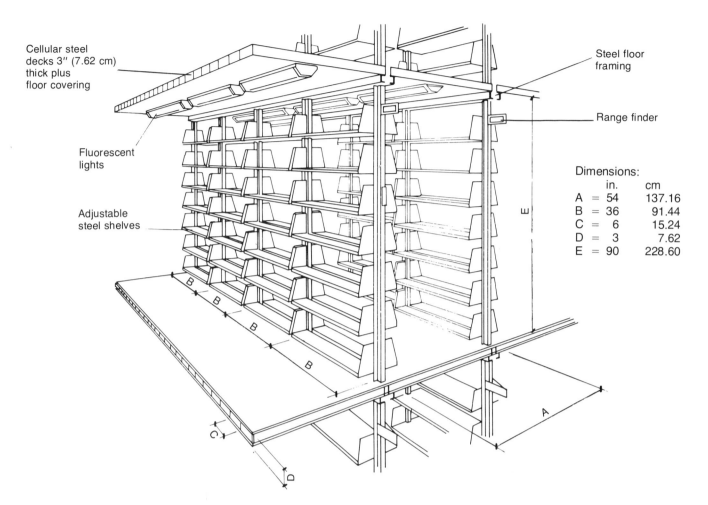

Cellular steel
decks 3″ (7.62 cm)
thick plus
floor covering

Fluorescent
lights

Adjustable
steel shelves

Steel floor
framing

Range finder

Dimensions:
		in.	cm
A	=	54	137.16
B	=	36	91.44
C	=	6	15.24
D	=	3	7.62
E	=	90	228.60

DIMENSIONAL DATA

Height
Standard stack tiers measure 7′6″ (2.29 m) from deck floor top to deck floor top. A greater height is sometimes required to meet special building conditions.

Stack widths
The shelf load for multitier bookstacks, including books, shelves, brackets, and uprights, averages 30 lb (13.62 kg) per cubic foot.

Ventilation
Each level of stack should be ventilated independently; do not rely on air from any other level. Wall ducts similar to those of other rooms in the building should be provided for each stack level.

Ranges
Wherever possible, range lengths should be in multiples of 3′ (0.91 m) from center of uprights. Allow 9¼″, 11¼″, and 13¼″ (23.50, 28.58, 33.66 cm) for depths of ranges across ends of wall stacks, and 16½″, 20½″, and 24½″ (41.91, 52.07, 62.23 cm) for double-faced stacks to accommodate 8″, 10″, and 12″ (20.32, 25.40, 30.48 cm) deep shelves respectively (nominal depth).

Accessories
Shelf label holder, 5″ X ¾″ (12.79 X 1.91 cm); range finders for cards 5″ X 3″ (12.70 X 7.62 cm); wire book supports; lockers; and newspaper sticks.

Fire codes
Consult local codes for stack height hazard classification.

Loads
Cellular steel floors are engineered to carry 12 lb (5.45 kg) per square foot of gross area. For column loads, assume 60 lb (27.24 kg) per square foot of aisle area for live load, and reduce the figure 5 percent for each deck below the top deck.

The table of loads below applies to the Library Bureau 8″ double-faced bracket stacks, spaced 4′6″ (1.37 m) apart o.c. Figures signify total loads at upright bases for stacks [7′6″ from floor to floor]. Weights include bookstacks, books, floors (dead load), and live load.

	Uprights at 3′6″ (1.07 m) aisles	Intermediate uprights	Upright at wall
No. of tiers	Cellular steel floor	Cellular steel floor	Cellular steel floor
1	450	900	450
2	1900	2600	1300
3	3200	4200	2100
4	4300	5600	2800
5	5300	7000	3500
6	6100	8200	4100
7	7000	9400	4700
8	7800	10700	5350
9	8900	12100	6050
10	9900	13400	6700
11	11000	14800	7400
12	12000	16200	8100

Note: Data based on 8″ deep shelves and 7′6″ height to floors.

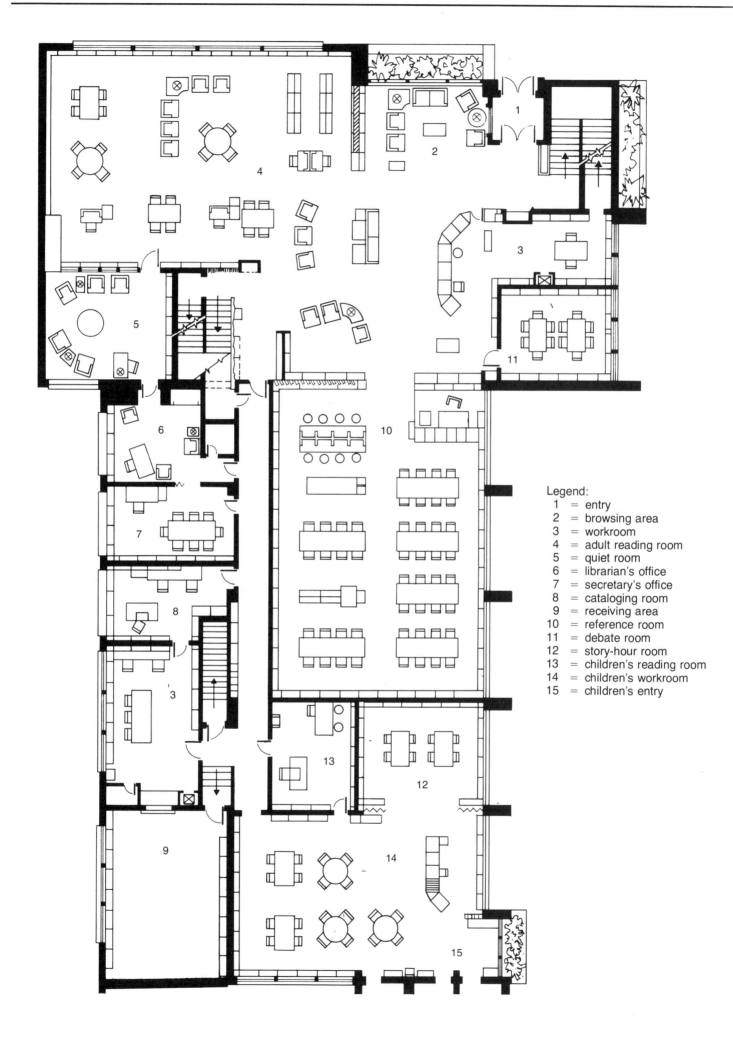

Legend:
1 = entry
2 = browsing area
3 = workroom
4 = adult reading room
5 = quiet room
6 = librarian's office
7 = secretary's office
8 = cataloging room
9 = receiving area
10 = reference room
11 = debate room
12 = story-hour room
13 = children's reading room
14 = children's workroom
15 = children's entry

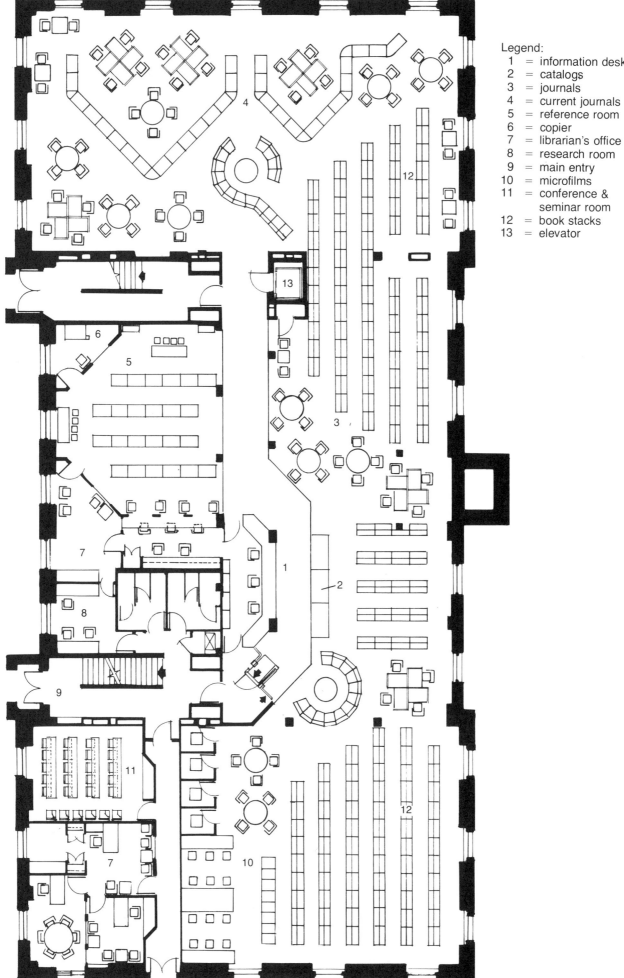

Legend:
1 = information desk
2 = catalogs
3 = journals
4 = current journals
5 = reference room
6 = copier
7 = librarian's office
8 = research room
9 = main entry
10 = microfilms
11 = conference &
     seminar room
12 = book stacks
13 = elevator

MODULAR CHARGING DESK EQUIPMENT

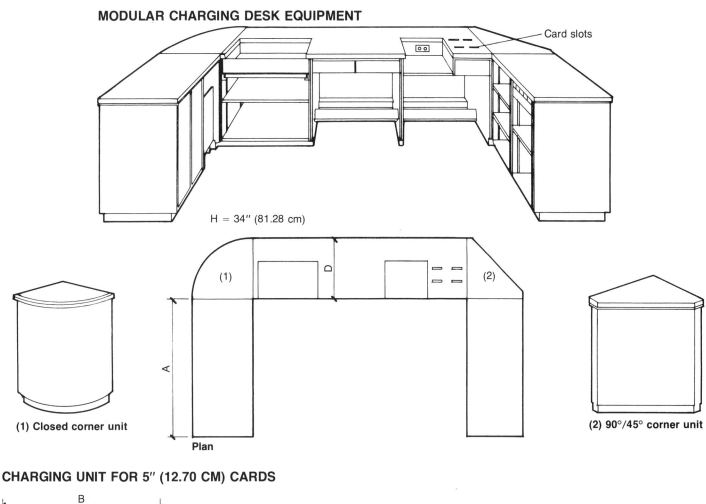

Card slots

H = 34″ (81.28 cm)

(1) Closed corner unit

Plan

(2) 90°/45° corner unit

CHARGING UNIT FOR 5″ (12.70 CM) CARDS

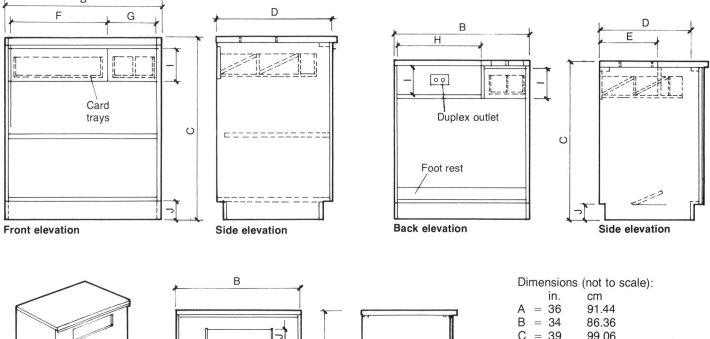

Card trays

Front elevation

Side elevation

Duplex outlet

Foot rest

Back elevation

Side elevation

SMALL BOOK RETURN UNIT

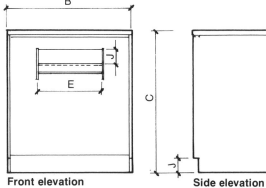

Front elevation

Side elevation

Dimensions (not to scale):

		in.	cm
A	=	36	91.44
B	=	34	86.36
C	=	39	99.06
D	=	26	66.04
E	=	18	45.72
F	=	22	55.88
G	=	11	27.94
H	=	21	53.34
I	=	7	17.78
J	=	4	10.16

CARD CATALOGS

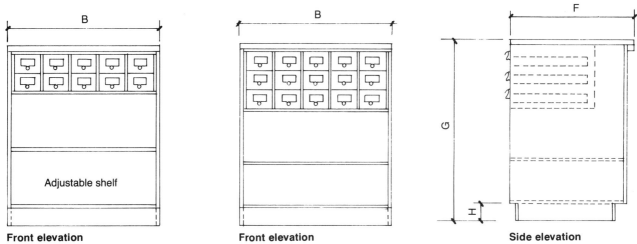

Front elevation   Front elevation   Side elevation

Modular card catalog components

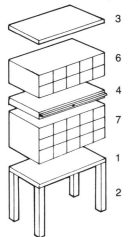

Legend:
1 = low base unit 17" (43.18 cm) high
2 = high base unit 25½" (64.77 cm) high
3 = top unit
4 = reference shelf
5 = five-tray unit
6 = ten-tray unit
7 = fifteen-tray unit

Note: Units may be stacked and arranged as needed.

Dimensions:

	in.	cm
A =	65	165.10
B =	34	86.36
C =	46	116.84
D =	25	63.50
E =	14	35.56
F =	26	66.04
G =	39	99.06
H =	4	10.16
I =	36	91.44
J =	17	43.18
K =	40	101.60

CARD CATALOGS CAN RANGE FROM 30 TO 120 TRAYS

Perspective of 30-tray unit

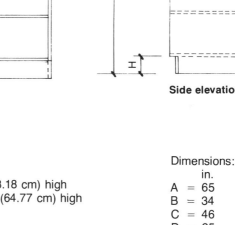

Front elevation   Side elevation

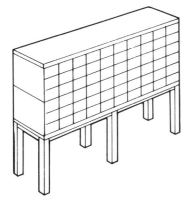

Perspective of 60-tray unit

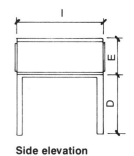

Front elevation   Side elevation

BOOK TRUCKS

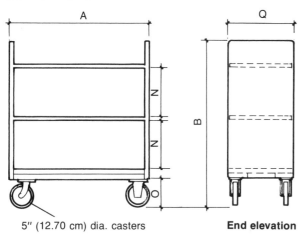

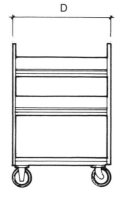

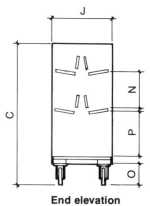

5″ (12.70 cm) dia. casters

Side elevation

End elevation

Side elevation

End elevation

REVOLVING DICTIONARY STAND

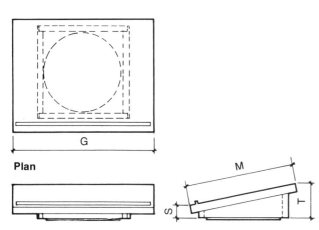

Plan

Front & side elevations

DICTIONARY STAND

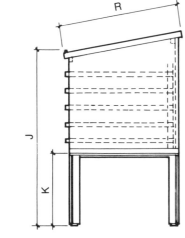

Front & side elevations

ATLAS CASE WITH PULL-OUT RACKS

Front & side elevations

BOOK DISPLAY CABINET

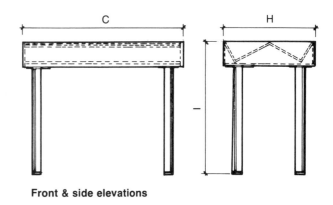

Front & side elevations

	in.	cm		in.	cm		in.	cm		in.	cm
A =	30 to 39	76.20 to 99.06	F =	41	104.14	K =	15	38.10	P =	13	33.02
B =	35	88.90	G =	22	55.88	L =	45	114.30	Q =	14	35.56
C =	42	106.68	H =	24	60.96	M =	16	40.64	R =	27	68.58
D =	30	76.20	I =	33	83.82	N =	10	25.40	S =	2	5.08
E =	43	109.22	J =	40	101.60	O =	6	15.24	T =	5	12.70

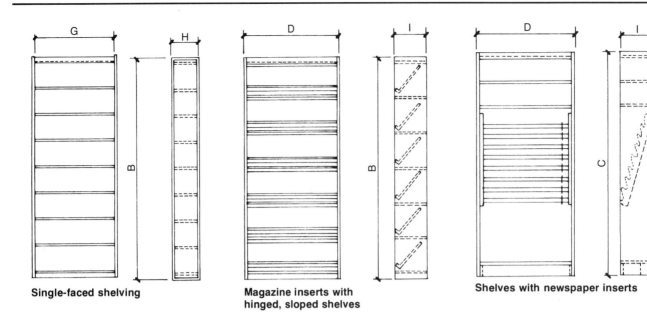

Single-faced shelving

Magazine inserts with hinged, sloped shelves

Shelves with newspaper inserts

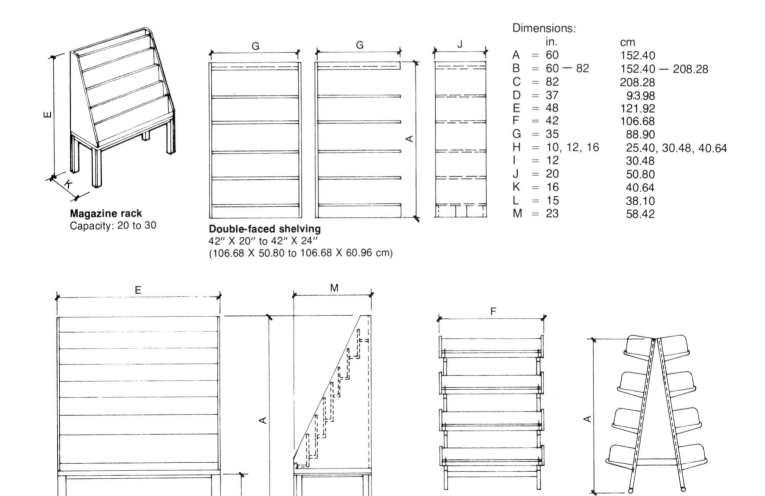

Magazine rack
Capacity: 20 to 30

Double-faced shelving
42" X 20" to 42" X 24"
(106.68 X 50.80 to 106.68 X 60.96 cm)

Dimensions:

	in.	cm
A	= 60	152.40
B	= 60 — 82	152.40 — 208.28
C	= 82	208.28
D	= 37	93.98
E	= 48	121.92
F	= 42	106.68
G	= 35	88.90
H	= 10, 12, 16	25.40, 30.48, 40.64
I	= 12	30.48
J	= 20	50.80
K	= 16	40.64
L	= 15	38.10
M	= 23	58.42

Magazine rack
Capacity: 35

A frame with shelving on both sides

CARREL TABLES

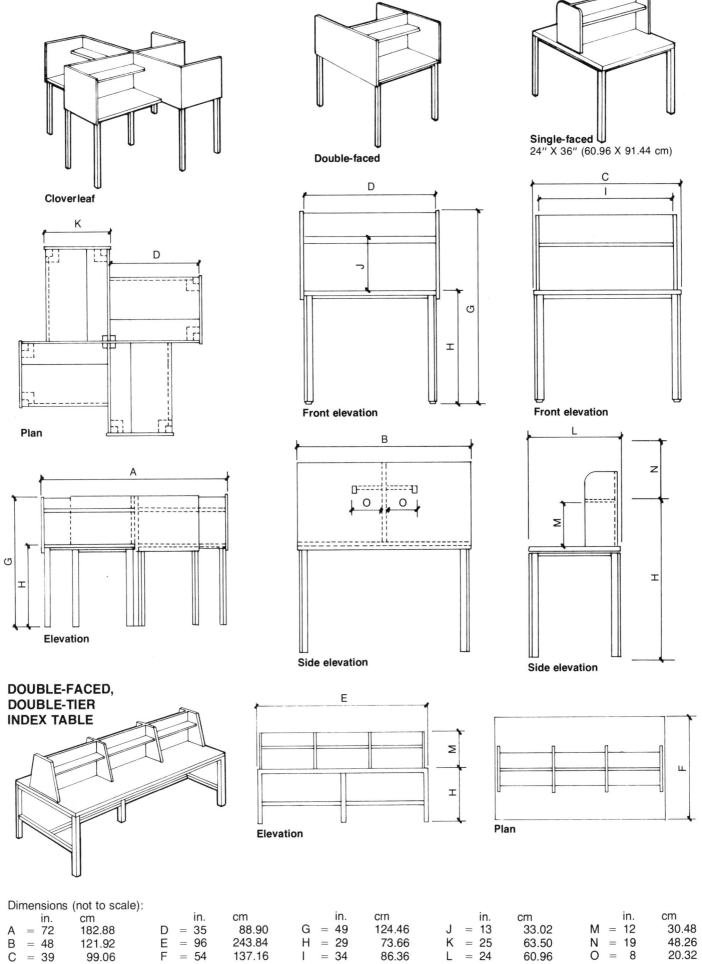

Cloverleaf

Plan

Elevation

Double-faced

Single-faced
24″ X 36″ (60.96 X 91.44 cm)

Front elevation

Side elevation

Front elevation

Side elevation

DOUBLE-FACED, DOUBLE-TIER INDEX TABLE

Elevation

Plan

Dimensions (not to scale):

	in.	cm		in.	cm		in.	cm		in.	cm		in.	cm
A =	72	182.88	D =	35	88.90	G =	49	124.46	J =	13	33.02	M =	12	30.48
B =	48	121.92	E =	96	243.84	H =	29	73.66	K =	25	63.50	N =	19	48.26
C =	39	99.06	F =	54	137.16	I =	34	86.36	L =	24	60.96	O =	8	20.32

Chapter 23

RELIGIOUS SPACES

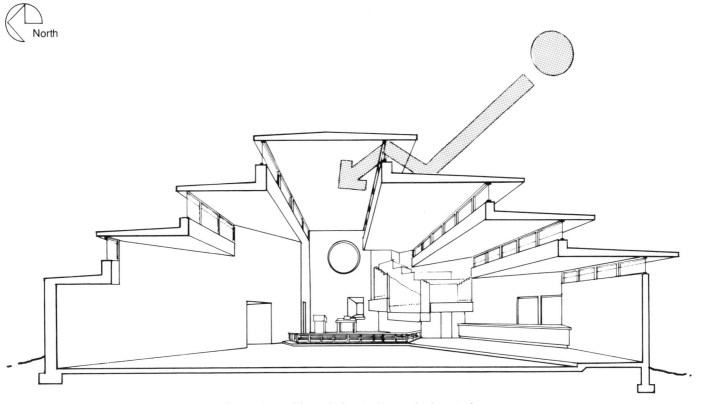

North

Section illustrates daylighting concepts & the sun's position relative to the south clerestories

Case study

The sanctuary of the St. Mark's Episcopal Church in Mesa, Arizona, was designed to take advantage of natural lighting during all daylight hours. The plan has a diagonal orientation to the central aisle, which focuses on a rose window behind the chancel. The stepped arrangement of roof planes creates a continuous clerestory on the south and north orientations. The south orientation has properly designed overhangs to exclude direct sunlight during all times of the year. The stepped clerestory was designed with ceiling heights ranging from 13' to 28' (3.96 to 8.53 m) in 5' (1.52 m) intervals with 14' (4.27 m) wide ceiling planes.

The daylighting concept was developed through extensive model testing to ascertain the distribution, quantity, and quality of light in the sanctuary. Actual lighting conditions in the space are glare-free and meet the minimum illuminance requirements of 30 to 50 footcandles. No artificial illumination is required during daylight hours.

The design strategy follows many basic daylighting guidelines. It brings light in from up high and from more than one direction; direct sunlight is excluded from the space; high-reflectance, matte interior materials are used; light is bounced off surrounding surfaces (the roof plane at each clerestory); and ceiling heights are maximized to ensure better light distribution. The project was designed with the clear sky as the dominant daylight condition since the geographic region has clear skies 85 percent of the year.

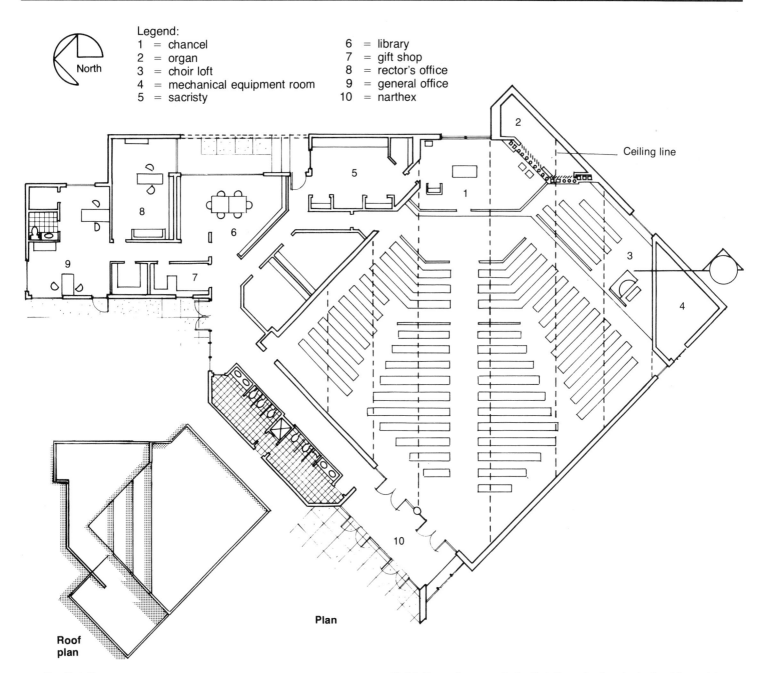

Legend:
1 = chancel
2 = organ
3 = choir loft
4 = mechanical equipment room
5 = sacristy
6 = library
7 = gift shop
8 = rector's office
9 = general office
10 = narthex

North

Ceiling line

Plan

Roof plan

Daylighting

Daylighting has always been a factor in architecture and has played a significant role in providing for people's biological needs. Proper utilization of daylight provides the architect and designer with one of the most effective means of lighting interior spaces, achieving aesthetic expression, and conserving energy.

Goals for good daylighting design include the need to get as much daylight as possible deep into a building's interior without creating excessive brightness for the occupants. Controlling the brightness of surfaces that fall within the occupant's field of view and reducing the potential for veiling reflections are essential. An effective daylighting solution should also provide adequate lighting for the visual tasks being performed. The more daylight is controlled and properly distributed across an interior space, the less artificial light will be needed and the less energy consumed.

To use daylight advantageously, several issues must be considered: (1) daylight sources and availability; (2) sky conditions; (3) effects of climatic and geographic variations; (4) impacts of site conditions and nearby buildings; (5) the geometry and characteristics of the room; (6) placement, size, and height of windows; (7) methods of daylight control (internal versus external and static versus dynamic); and (8) interior space planning and furniture layout.

Guidelines for good daylighting design include: (1) avoid direct skylight and sunlight on critical visual tasks; (2) bounce daylight off surfaces into the room; (3) bring daylight in from up high for better distribution and visual comfort; (4) filter daylight to avoid the harshness of direct skylight and sunlight; (5) mass and configure building forms so that the maximum number and areas of rooms are near perimeter daylight sources; (6) locate activities requiring high lighting levels closest to the daylight; (7) maximize ceiling heights to ensure better light distribution; (8) use medium- to high-reflectance matte finishes on interior surfaces; (9) integrate daylighting with other environmental concerns; (10) evaluate thermal implications of the design strategy; (11) use design strategies that separate view glass from lighting glass to achieve better visual comfort for the occupant; (12) admit light from more than one direction to achieve better distribution and brightness control; and (13) integrate daylighting with artificial lighting and control strategies to allow reduction of peak electricity demand periods.

Typical strategies are illustrated on page 595. These include unilateral, or single-sided, lighting; bilateral; roof monitor; clerestory; sawtooth; and skylight. Other variations of these concepts and additional design strategies allow the architect and designer extensive flexibility in using daylight for primary or supplementary lighting for interior spaces.

This church worship area seats 80 people. The total building occupancy is 290 people

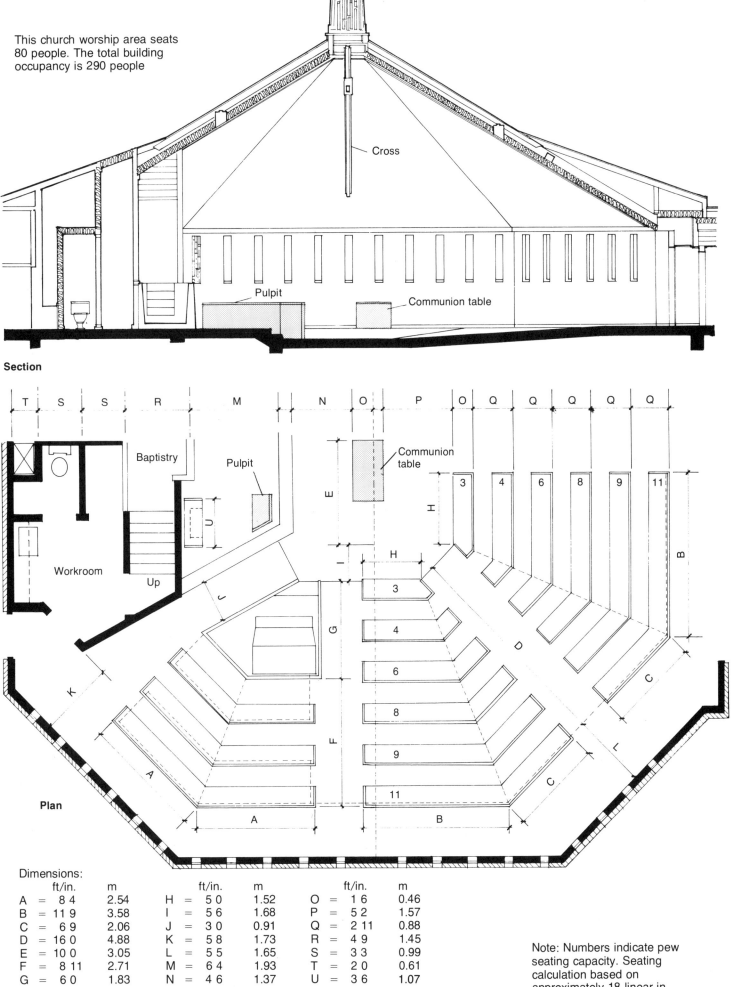

Cross

Pulpit

Communion table

Section

T S S R M N O P O Q Q Q Q Q

Baptistry

Pulpit

Communion table

3 4 6 8 9 11

Workroom

Up

3

4

6

8

9

11

Plan

A

B

Dimensions:

	ft/in.	m		ft/in.	m		ft/in.	m
A =	8 4	2.54	H =	5 0	1.52	O =	1 6	0.46
B =	11 9	3.58	I =	5 6	1.68	P =	5 2	1.57
C =	6 9	2.06	J =	3 0	0.91	Q =	2 11	0.88
D =	16 0	4.88	K =	5 8	1.73	R =	4 9	1.45
E =	10 0	3.05	L =	5 5	1.65	S =	3 3	0.99
F =	8 11	2.71	M =	6 4	1.93	T =	2 0	0.61
G =	6 0	1.83	N =	4 6	1.37	U =	3 6	1.07

*Shaded areas are shown in detail on pages 598–599.

Note: Numbers indicate pew seating capacity. Seating calculation based on approximately 18 linear in. (45.72 cm) per person.

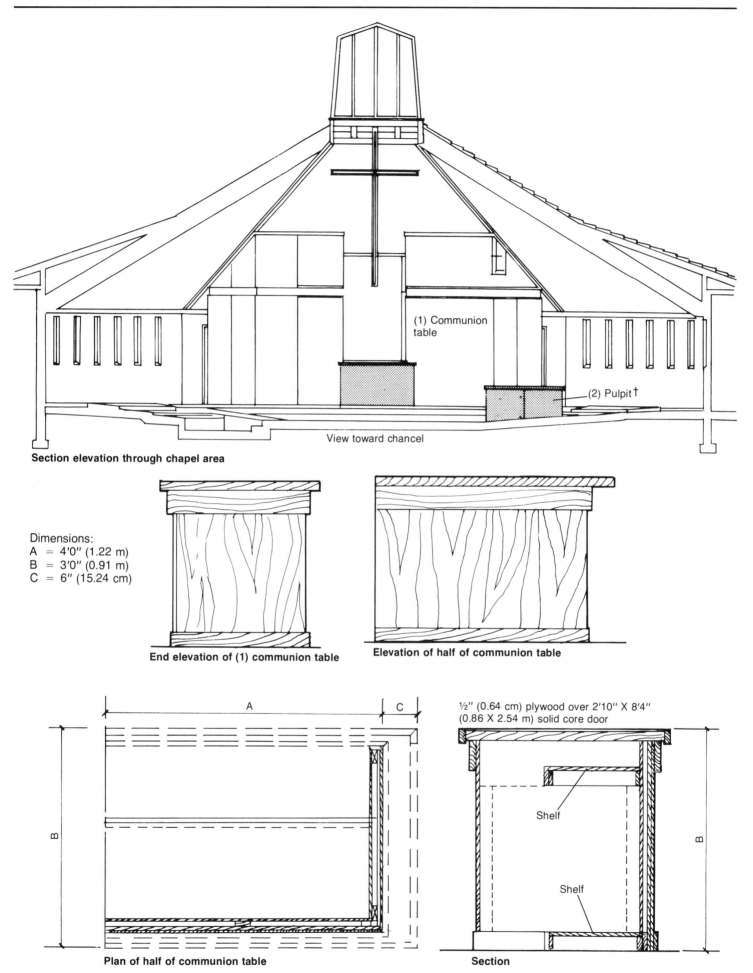

Section elevation through chapel area

(1) Communion table

(2) Pulpit †

View toward chancel

Dimensions:
A = 4′0″ (1.22 m)
B = 3′0″ (0.91 m)
C = 6″ (15.24 cm)

End elevation of (1) communion table

Elevation of half of communion table

½″ (0.64 cm) plywood over 2′10″ X 8′4″ (0.86 X 2.54 m) solid core door

Shelf

Shelf

Plan of half of communion table

Section

*Shown in plan on page 597.
†Shown on page 599.

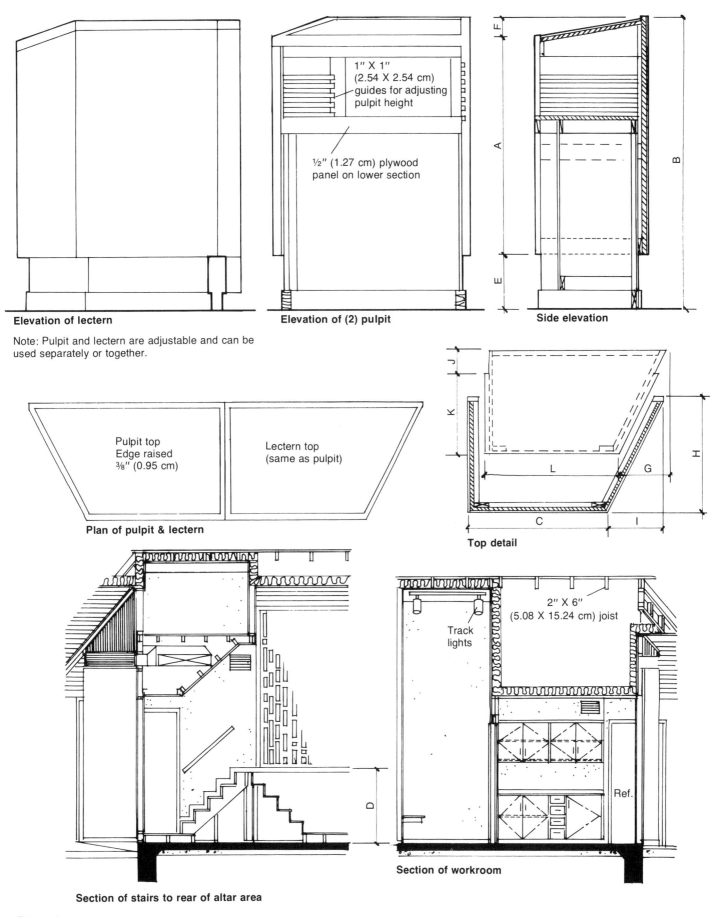

Elevation of lectern

Note: Pulpit and lectern are adjustable and can be used separately or together.

1" X 1"
(2.54 X 2.54 cm)
guides for adjusting
pulpit height

½" (1.27 cm) plywood
panel on lower section

Elevation of (2) pulpit

Side elevation

Pulpit top
Edge raised
⅜" (0.95 cm)

Lectern top
(same as pulpit)

Plan of pulpit & lectern

Top detail

2" X 6"
(5.08 X 15.24 cm) joist

Track
lights

Ref.

Section of workroom

Section of stairs to rear of altar area

Dimensions:
A = 3'0" (0.91 m)
B = 3'6" to 4'0" (1.07 to 1.22 m)
C = 2'0" (0.61 m)

D = 4'0" (1.22 m)
E = 3" to 9" (7.62 to 22.86 cm)
F = 3" (7.62 cm)

G = 8" (20.32 cm)
H = 19" (48.26 cm)
I = 9½" (24.13 cm)

J = 4" (10.16 cm)
K = 13½" (34.29 cm)
L = 21" (53.34 cm)

*Shown in plan on page 597.

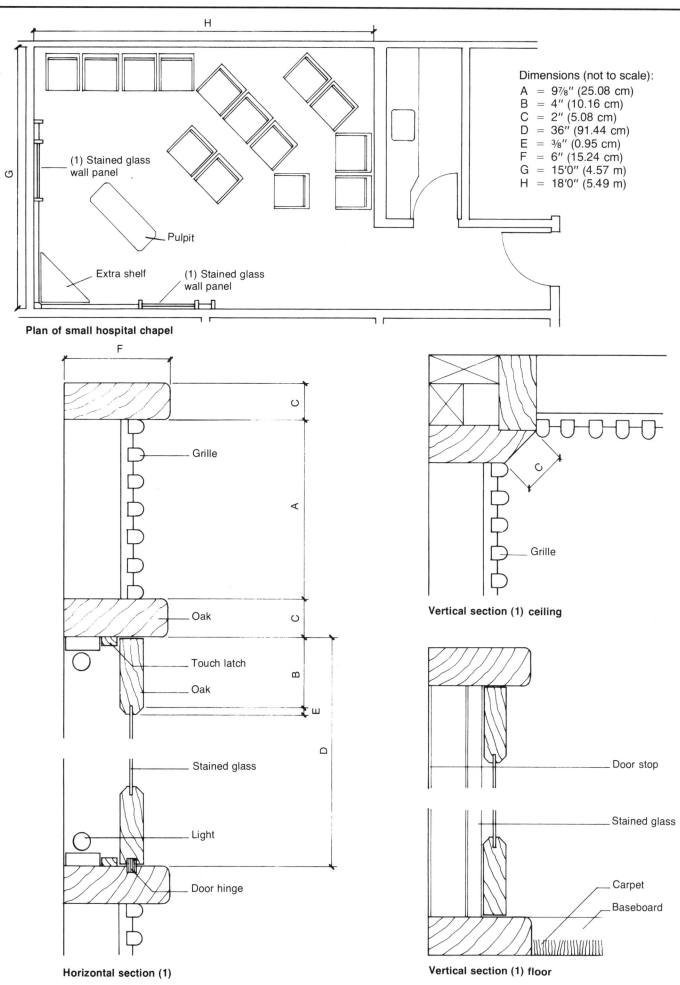

Plan of small hospital chapel

Dimensions (not to scale):
A = 9⅞″ (25.08 cm)
B = 4″ (10.16 cm)
C = 2″ (5.08 cm)
D = 36″ (91.44 cm)
E = ⅜″ (0.95 cm)
F = 6″ (15.24 cm)
G = 15′0″ (4.57 m)
H = 18′0″ (5.49 m)

(1) Stained glass wall panel

Pulpit

Extra shelf

(1) Stained glass wall panel

Grille

Oak

Touch latch

Oak

Stained glass

Light

Door hinge

Horizontal section (1)

Grille

Vertical section (1) ceiling

Door stop

Stained glass

Carpet

Baseboard

Vertical section (1) floor

ALTAR

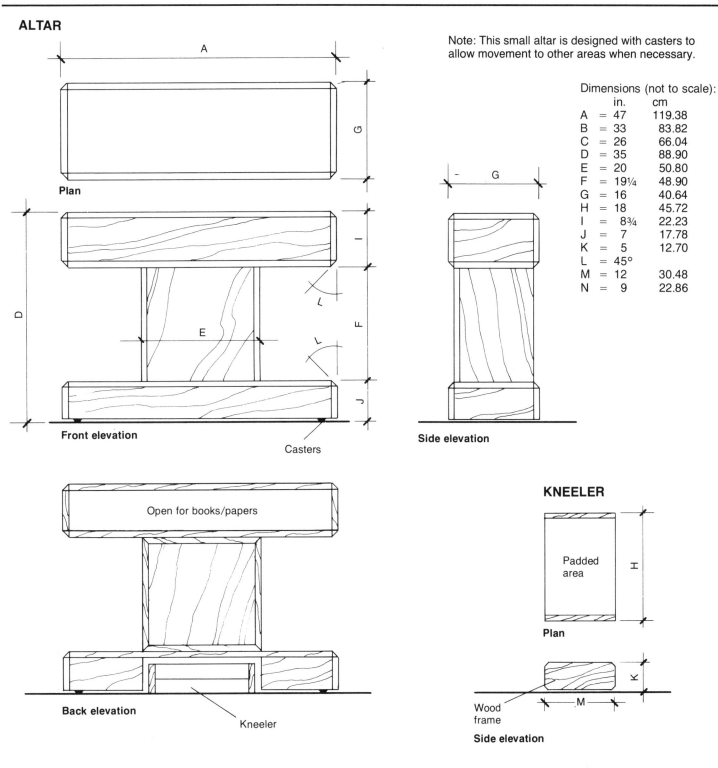

Note: This small altar is designed with casters to allow movement to other areas when necessary.

Dimensions (not to scale):

		in.	cm
A	=	47	119.38
B	=	33	83.82
C	=	26	66.04
D	=	35	88.90
E	=	20	50.80
F	=	19¼	48.90
G	=	16	40.64
H	=	18	45.72
I	=	8¾	22.23
J	=	7	17.78
K	=	5	12.70
L	=	45°	
M	=	12	30.48
N	=	9	22.86

Plan

Front elevation

Casters

Side elevation

Open for books/papers

Back elevation

Kneeler

KNEELER

Padded area

Plan

Wood frame

Side elevation

WALL-HUNG SHELF FOR CORNER STORAGE BEHIND ALTAR

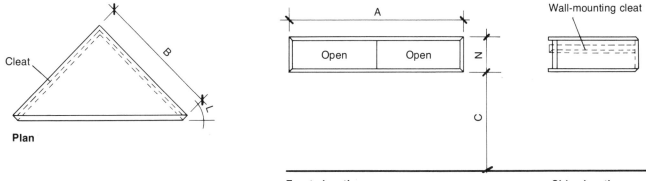

Cleat

Plan

Wall-mounting cleat

Open   Open

Front elevation

Side elevation

DATA SOURCES

CSI MASTERFORMAT
Broadscope Section Titles and Numbers

DIVISION 1—GENERAL REQUIREMENTS
01010 SUMMARY OF WORK
01020 ALLOWANCES
01025 MEASUREMENT AND PAYMENT
01030 ALTERNATES/ALTERNATIVES
01040 COORDINATION
01050 FIELD ENGINEERING
01060 REGULATORY REQUIREMENTS
01070 ABBREVIATIONS AND SYMBOLS
01080 IDENTIFICATION SYSTEMS
01090 REFERENCE STANDARDS
01100 SPECIAL PROJECT PROCEDURES
01200 PROJECT MEETINGS
01300 SUBMITTALS
01400 QUALITY CONTROL
01500 CONSTRUCTION FACILITIES AND TEMPORARY
       CONTROLS
01600 MATERIAL AND EQUIPMENT
01650 STARTING OF SYSTEMS/COMMISSIONING
01700 CONTRACT CLOSEOUT
01800 MAINTENANCE

DIVISION 2—SITE WORK
02010 SUBSURFACE INVESTIGATION
02050 DEMOLITION
02100 SITE PREPARATION
02140 DEWATERING
02150 SHORING AND UNDERPINNING
02160 EXCAVATION SUPPORT SYSTEMS
02170 COFFERDAMS
02200 EARTHWORK
02300 TUNNELING
02350 PILES AND CAISSONS
02450 RAILROAD WORK
02480 MARINE WORK
02500 PAVING AND SURFACING
02600 PIPED UTILITY MATERIALS
02660 WATER DISTRIBUTION
02680 FUEL DISTRIBUTION
02700 SEWERAGE AND DRAINAGE
02760 RESTORATION OF UNDERGROUND PIPELINES
02770 PONDS AND RESERVOIRS
02780 POWER AND COMMUNICATIONS
02800 SITE IMROVEMENTS
02900 LANDSCAPING

DIVISION 3—CONCRETE
03100 CONCRETE FORMWORK
03200 CONCRETE REINFORCEMENT
03250 CONCRETE ACCESSORIES
03300 CAST-IN-PLACE CONCRETE
03370 CONCRETE CURING
03400 PRECAST CONCRETE
03500 CEMENTITIOUS DECKS
03600 GROUT
03700 CONCRETE RESTORATION AND CLEANING
03800 MASS CONCRETE

DIVISION 4—MASONRY
04100 MORTAR
04150 MASONRY ACCESSORIES
04200 UNIT MASONRY
04400 STONE
04500 MASONRY RESTORATION AND CLEANING
04550 REFRACTORIES
04600 CORROSION RESISTANT MASONRY

DIVISION 5—METALS
05005 METAL FORMING
05010 METAL MATERIALS
05030 METAL FINISHES
05050 METAL FASTENING
05100 STRUCTURAL METAL FRAMING
05200 METAL JOISTS
05300 METAL DECKING
05400 COLD-FORMED METAL FRAMING
05500 METAL FABRICATIONS
05580 SHEET METAL FABRICATIONS
05700 ORNAMENTAL METAL
05800 EXPANSION CONTROL
05900 HYDRAULIC STRUCTURES

DIVISION 6—WOOD & PLASTICS
06050 FASTENERS AND ADHESIVES
06100 ROUGH CARPENTRY
06130 HEAVY TIMBER CONSTRUCTION
06150 WOOD-METAL SYSTEMS
06170 PREFABRICATED STRUCTURAL WOOD
06200 FINISH CARPENTRY
06300 WOOD TREATMENT
06400 ARCHITECTURAL WOODWORK
06500 PREFABRICATED STRUCTURAL PLASTICS
06600 PLASTIC FABRICATIONS

DIVISION 7—THERMAL AND MOISTURE PROTECTION
07100 WATERPROOFING
07150 DAMPPROOFING
07190 VAPOR AND AIR RETARDERS
07200 INSULATION
07250 FIREPROOFING
07300 SHINGLES AND ROOFING TILES
07400 PREFORMED ROOFING AND CLADDING/SIDING
07500 MEMBRANE ROOFING
07570 TRAFFIC TOPPING
07600 FLASHING AND SHEET METAL
07700 ROOF SPECIALTIES AND ACCESSORIES
07800 SKYLIGHTS
07900 JOINT SEALERS

DIVISION 8—DOORS & WINDOWS
08100 METAL DOORS AND FRAMES
08200 WOOD AND PLASTIC DOORS
08250 DOOR OPENING ASSEMBLIES
08300 SPECIAL DOORS
08400 ENTRANCE AND STOREFRONTS
08500 METAL WINDOWS

08600 WOOD AND PLASTIC WINDOWS
08650 SPECIAL WINDOWS
08700 HARDWARE
08800 GLAZING
08900 GLAZED CURTAIN WALLS

DIVISION 9—FINISHES
09100 METAL SUPPORT SYSTEMS
09200 LATH AND PLASTER
09230 AGGREGATE COATINGS
09250 GYPSUM BOARD
09300 TILE
09400 TERRAZZO
09500 ACOUSTICAL TREATMENT
09540 SPECIAL SURFACES
09550 WOOD FLOORING
09600 STONE FLOORING
09630 UNIT MASONRY FLOORING
09650 RESILIENT FLOORING
09680 CARPET
09700 SPECIAL FLOORING
09780 FLOOR TREATMENT
09800 SPECIAL COATINGS
09900 PAINTING
09950 WALL COVERINGS

DIVISION 10—SPECIALTIES
10100 CHALKBOARDS AND TACKBOARDS
10150 COMPARTMENTS AND CUBICLES
10200 LOUVERS AND VENTS
10240 GRILLES AND SCREENS
10250 SERVICE WALL SYSTEMS
10260 WALL AND CORNER GUARDS
10270 ACCESS FLOORING
10280 SPECIALTY MODULES
10290 PEST CONTROL
10300 FIREPLACES AND STOVES
10340 PREFABRICATED EXTERIOR SPECIALTIES
10350 FLAGPOLES
10400 IDENTIFYING DEVICES
10450 PEDESTRIAN CONTROL DEVICES
10500 LOCKERS
10520 FIRE PROTECTION SPECIALTIES
10530 PROTECTIVE COVERS
10550 POSTAL SPECIALTIES
10600 PARTITIONS
10650 OPERABLE PARTITIONS
10670 STORAGE SHELVING
10700 EXTERIOR SUN CONTROL DEVICES
10750 TELEPHONE SPECIALTIES
10800 TOILET AND BATH ACCESSORIES
10880 SCALES
10900 WARDROBE AND CLOSET SPECIALTIES

DIVISION 11—EQUIPMENT
11010 MAINTENANCE EQUIPMENT
11020 SECURITY AND VAULT EQUIPMENT
11030 TELLER AND SERVICE EQUIPMENT
11040 ECCLESIASTICAL EQUIPMENT
11050 LIBRARY EQUIPMENT
11060 THEATER AND STAGE EQUIPMENT
11070 INSTRUMENTAL EQUIPMENT
11080 REGISTRATION EQUIPMENT
11090 CHECKROOM EQUIPMENT
11100 MERCANTILE EQUIPMENT
11110 COMMERCIAL LAUNDRY AND DRY CLEANING
      EQUIPMENT
11120 VENDING EQUIPMENT
11130 AUDIO-VISUAL EQUIPMENT
11140 SERVICE STATION EQUIPMENT
11150 PARKING CONTROL EQUIPMENT
11160 LOADING DOCK EQUIPMENT
11170 SOLID WASTE HANDLING EQUIPMENT
11190 DETENTION EQUIPMENT
11200 WATER SUPPLY AND TREATMENT EQUIPMENT
11280 HYDRAULIC GATES AND VALVES
11300 FLUID WASTE TREATMENT AND DISPOSAL EQUIPMENT
11400 FOOD SERVICE EQUIPMENT
11450 RESIDENTIAL EQUIPMENT
11460 UNIT KITCHENS
11470 DARKROOM EQUIPMENT
11480 ATHLETIC, RECREATIONAL, AND THERAPEUTIC
      EQUIPMENT
11500 INDUSTRIAL AND PROCESS EQUIPMENT
11600 LABORATORY EQUIPMENT
11650 PLANETARIUM EQUIPMENT
11660 OBSERVATORY EQUIPMENT
11700 MEDICAL EQUIPMENT
11780 MORTUARY EQUIPMENT
11850 NAVIGATION EQUIPMENT

DIVISION 12—FURNISHINGS
12050 FABRICS
12100 ARTWORK
12300 MANUFACTURED CASEWORK
12500 WINDOW TREATMENT
12600 FURNITURE AND ACCESSORIES
12670 RUGS AND MATS
12700 MULTIPLE SEATING
12800 INTERIOR PLANTS AND PLANTERS

DIVISION 13—SPECIAL CONSTRUCTION
13010 AIR SUPPORTED STRUCTURES
13020 INTEGRATED ASSEMBLIES
13030 SPECIAL PURPOSE ROOMS
13080 SOUND, VIBRATION, AND SEISMIC CONTROL
13090 RADIATION PROTECTION
13100 NUCLEAR REACTORS
13120 PRE-ENGINEERED STRUCTURES
13150 POOLS
13160 ICE RINKS
13170 KENNELS AND ANIMAL SHELTERS
13180 SITE CONSTRUCTED INCINERATORS
13200 LIQUID AND GAS STORAGE TANKS
13220 FILTER UNDERDRAINS AND MEDIA
13230 DIGESTION TANK COVERS AND APPURTENANCES

13240 OXYGENATION SYSTEMS
13260 SLUDGE CONDITIONING SYSTEMS
13300 UTILITY CONTROL SYSTEMS
13400 INDUSTRIAL AND PROCESS CONTROL SYSTEMS
13500 RECORDING INSTRUMENTATION
13550 TRANSPORTATION CONTROL INSTRUMENTATION
13600 SOLAR ENERGY SYSTEMS
13700 WIND ENERGY SYSTEMS
13800 BUILDING AUTOMATION SYSTEMS
13900 FIRE SUPPRESSION AND SUPERVISORY SYSTEMS

DIVISION 14—CONVEYING SYSTEMS
14100 DUMBWAITERS
14200 ELEVATORS
14300 MOVING STAIRS AND WALKS
14400 LIFTS
14500 MATERIAL HANDLING SYSTEMS
14600 HOISTS AND CRANES
14700 TURNTABLES
14800 SCAFFOLDING
14900 TRANSPORTATION SYSTEMS

DIVISION 15—MECHANICAL
15050 BASIC MECHANICAL MATERIALS AND METHODS
15250 MECHANICAL INSULATION
15300 FIRE PROTECTION
15400 PLUMBING
15500 HEATING, VENTILATING, AND AIR CONDITIONING
      (HVAC)
15550 HEAT GENERATION
15650 REFRIGERATION
15750 HEAT TRANSFER
15850 AIR HANDLING
15880 AIR DISTRIBUTION
15950 CONTROLS
15990 TESTING, ADJUSTING, AND BALANCING

DIVISION 16—ELECTRICAL
16050 BASIC ELECTRICAL MATERIALS AND METHODS
16200 POWER GENERATION
16300 HIGH VOLTAGE DISTRIBUTION (ABOVE 600-VOLT)
16400 SERVICE AND DISTRIBUTION (600-VOLT AND BELOW)
16500 LIGHTING
16600 SPECIAL SYSTEMS
16700 COMMUNICATIONS
16850 ELECTRIC RESISTANCE HEATING
16900 CONTROLS
16950 TESTING

MASTERFORMAT
Its Application

Keyword Index
An alphabetical subject list is provided to assist the user in locating a particular product, material, system, or unit of work. Each full entry is cross-referenced to one or more 5-digit Broadscope number.

The data filing procedure under Masterformat is primarily concerned with the needs of users for rapid retrieval of technical product data relating to the specifying of products or systems in a design or construction project.

Subordinate levels of classification are left to the discretion of users and their specific office practices—alphabetical by product or manufacturer, or an internally assigned numeric or alphanumeric system.

Division 1 Broadscope titles are applicable. It is recommended that they be incorporated into the system with the same number as contained in Masterformat, e.g., 01070—Abbreviations and Symbols, 01090—Reference Standards.

Examples of Flexible Usage
For a contemporary four-post bed, Mediumscope numbers offer the following options:
   12620—Furniture
   12632—Historic furnishings and accessories
   12633—Beds and bedding
Because this bed is not an authentic antique or reproduction of a historic bed, it may be filed under 12633 or 12620.

Note: Used with permission of Construction Specifications Institute (CSI)

DIVISION 12—FURNISHINGS (CSI MASTERFORMAT)

Broadscope Explanation

12050—FABRICS
Drapery and upholstery materials.
Note: *This section is used for data filing of information on fabrics. The application of these materials is usually specified in the section where used.*

12100—ARTWORK
Art objects, such as paintings, murals, sculpture, and stained glass.
Related Work:
Ornamental Metal: Section 05700.
Prefabricated chancel fittings: Section 11040.

12300—MANUFACTURED CASEWORK
Stock design, prefabricated cabinets and other specialized casework and units. Laboratory countertops, sinks, countertop-mounted service fixtures, and accessories.
Related Work:
Custom built casework: Sections 06200 and 06400.
Specialized equipment: Division 11.
Unit Kitchens: Section 11460.
Specialized movable furniture: Section 12600.
Note: *Sections 12301 and 12302 may be used as titles for FILING or for specifying casework for multiple use. This section may include equipment integral with casework.*

12500—WINDOW TREATMENT
Interior window coverings and controls, such as blinds, shades, shutters, draperies and curtains. Includes hardware.
Related Work:
Exterior Sun Control Devices: Section 10700

12600—FURNITURE AND ACCESSORIES
Items of movable furniture and furnishings.
Related Work:
Chairs for public assembly: Section 12800.

12670—RUGS AND MATS
Includes loose rugs and pads, foot grilles, entrance mats, and frames, and runner mats.
Related Work:
Carpet: Section 09680.

12700—MULTIPLE SEATING
Movable, fixed, and telescoping seating for use in auditoriums, churches, gymnasiums, stadiums, waiting areas, and wherever group seating of a similar type is required.
Related Work:
Individual seating: Section 12600.
Grandstands and fixed bleachers: Section 13120.

12800—INTERIOR PLANTS AND PLANTERS
Interior plants and planters, including soil and fertilizer.
Related Work:
Exterior planting: Section 02900.

Mediumscope Section Titles and Numbers

Section Number	Title
12050	**FABRICS**
12100	**ARTWORK**
−110	Murals
	Photo Murals
−120	Wall Hangings
−130	Paintings
−140	Carved or Cast Statuary
−150	Carved or Cast Relief Work
−160	Custom Chancel Fittings
−170	Stained Glass Work
12300	**MANUFACTURED CASEWORK**
−301	Metal Casework
−302	Wood Casework
−304	Plastic Laminate-faced Casework
−310	Bank Fixtures and Casework
−315	Library Casework
−320	Restaurant and Cafeteria Casework
−325	Educational Casework
−330	Dormitory Casework
−335	Medical and Laboratory Casework
	Nurse Server Cabinets
−340	Pharmacy Casework
−345	Laboratory Casework
	Metal Laboratory Casework
	Wood Laboratory Casework
	Laboratory Tops, Sinks and Accessories
−350	Hospital Casework
−355	Dental Casework
−360	Optical Casework
−365	Veterinary Casework
−370	Hotel and Motel Casework
−375	Ecclesiastical Casework
−380	Display Casework
−390	Residential Casework
	Kitchen and Bath Cabinets
12500	**WINDOW TREATMENT**
−510	Blinds
	Horizontal Louver Blinds
	Vertical Louver Blinds
−520	Shades
	Insulating Shades
	Lightproof Shades
	Woven Wood Shades
−525	Solar Control Film
−530	Drapery and Curtain Hardware
−540	Draperies and Curtains
	Curtains
	Fabric Draperies
	Lightproof Draperies
	Vertical Louver Draperies
	Woven Wood Draperies
12600	**FURNITURE AND ACCESSORIES**
−610	Landscape Partitions and Components
	Room Dividers and Screens
−620	Furniture
	Classroom Furniture
	Dormitory Furniture
	Ecclesiastical Furniture
	Hospital Furniture
	Hotel and Motel Furniture
	Laboratory Furniture
	Library Furniture
	Lounge Furniture
	Residential Furniture
	Restaurant and Cafeteria Furniture
	Specialized Furniture
−640	Furniture Systems
	Integrated Work Units
−650	Furniture Accessories
	Ash Receptacles
	Desk Accessories
	Lamps
	Wall Clocks
	Waste Receptacles
12670	**RUGS AND MATS**
−675	Rugs
−680	Foot Grilles
−690	Floor Mats and Frames
	Floor Mats
	Floor Runners
	Matting
	Mat Frames
12700	**MULTIPLE SEATING**
−705	Chairs
	Interlocking
	Portable Folding
	Stacking
−710	Auditorium and Theater Seating
−730	Stadium and Arena Seating
−740	Booths and Tables
−750	Multiple-Use Fixed Seating
	Pedestal Table Armchairs
−760	Telescoping Stands
	Telescoping Bleachers
	Telescoping Chair Platforms
−770	Pews and Benches
12800	**INTERIOR PLANTS AND PLANTERS**
−810	Interior Plants
−815	Planters
−820	Interior Plants Maintenance

Section Titles and Numbers Used in *Interior Graphic and Design Standards*

Section Number	Title
12050	**FABRICS**
−051	*Upholstery Components, Springs, Foundation, Foam, Welt Cording*
−052	*Terms, Standards*
−060	*Upholstery Fabrics, Testing, Backings*
−070	*Drapery Fabrics*
−080	*Wall Fabrics*
12550	*Shutters*
−632	*Historic Furnishings and Accessories**
−632.1	*Italian*Furnishings include textiles and wall coverings*
−632.2	*Spanish*
.3	*French*
.3a	*[further subdivisions]*
.4	*English*
.5	*American*
.6	*Chinese*
.7	*Japanese*
.8	*Near Eastern*
.9	*Russian*
−633	*Beds and Bedding*
.1	*Residential*
.2	*Hospital*
.3	*Hotel*
.4	*Flotation (Water)*
−634	*Upholstered Furniture*
−635	*Custom Residential Casework*
−636	*Custom Electronic Media Casework*
−640	*Furniture Systems*
−641	*Integrated Work Units*
−642	*Specialized Office Furniture*
.1	*Custom Office Furnishings*
.2	*Computer Work Surface*
.3	*Seating*

Note: Section numbers and section titles shown in italics have been designed for *Interior Graphic and Design Standards* to extend the usefulness of the Masterformat system for interiors work. These numbers and titles are used with the approval of Construction Specifications Institute (CSI).

Note: Used with permission of Construction Specifications Institute (CSI)

INDEX